The
Debonairs

The Debonairs

**JAMES ROBERT PARISH
AND DON E. STANKE**

Editor
T. Allan Taylor
Research Associates
John Robert Cocchi, Michael R. Pitts, Florence Solomon
Introduction by
Earl Anderson

ARLINGTON HOUSE·PUBLISHERS
NEW ROCHELLE, NEW YORK

MANUFACTURED IN THE UNITED STATES OF AMERICA

Library of Congress Cataloging in Publication Data

Parish, James Robert.
  The debonairs.

  Includes index.
  1. Moving-picture actors and actresses—Biography. I. Stanke, Don E., joint author. II. Title.
PN1998.A2P388   791.43'028'0922   [B]
ISBN 0–87000–293–7   75–29375

For
HERBERT MARSHALL
(1890 - 1966)
and
ADOLPHE MENJOU
(1890 - 1963)
Who Were
Debonair Gentlemen on and off the screen

TABLE OF CONTENTS

KEY TO THE FILM STUDIOS

AA   Allied Artists Picture Corporation

AVCO/ Avco Embassy Pictures Corporation

  EMB

CIN   Cinerama Releasing Corporation

COL   Columbia Pictures Industries, Inc.

EMB   Embassy Pictures Corporation

FN   First National Pictures, Inc. (later part of Warner Bros.)

FOX   Fox Film Corporation

LIP   Lippert Pictures, Inc.

MGM   Metro-Goldwyn-Mayer, Inc.

MON   Monogram Pictures Corporation

PAR   Paramount Pictures Corporation

RKO   RKO Radio Pictures, Inc.

REP   Republic Pictures Corporation

20th   Twentieth Century-Fox Film Corporation

UA   United Artists Corporation

UNIV   Universal Pictures, Inc.

WB   Warner Bros. Inc.

Acknowledgements

Research Consultant: Doug McClelland
Manuscript Verifier: Earl Anderson

Jack Barnich
George Brent
Bruco Enterprises
Loraine Burdick
Kingsley Canham
Cinemabilia Book Shop (Ernest Burns)
Lois Cole
Olivier Eyquem
Film Fan Monthly
Filmfact
Films and Filming
Films in Review
Connie Gilchrist
Pierre Guinle
George Habit
Mrs. R. F. Hastings
Richard Hudson
Martha Hyer
Ken D. Jones
Miles Kreuger

Albert B. Manski
Alvin H. Marill
David McGillivray
Mrs. Earl Meisinger
Jim Meyer
Peter Miglierini
Movie Poster Service (Bob Smith)
Movie Star News (Paula Klaw)
Pat Nix
Vera Ralston
Hal Richardson
Lizabeth Scott
Screen Facts (Alan G. Barbour)
Charles Smith
Mrs. Peter Smith
Charles K. Stumpf
Theatre 80 St. Marks (Howard Otway)
Views and Reviews

And special thanks to Paul Myers, curator of the Theatre Collection at the Lincoln Center Library for the Performing Arts (New York City) and his staff: Monty Arnold, David Bartholomew, Rod Bladel, Donald Fowle, Maxwell Silverman, Dorothy Swerdlove, Betty Wharton, and Don Madison of Photographic Services.

INTRODUCTION

by Earl Anderson

Picture Play and *Photoplay,* the names of two of the leading magazines chronicling motion pictures, attest to the link between the stage and the movies. A movie is a story, a play, told not on the printed page, or live on a stage, but photographed and presented on a screen.

The techniques of acting in the theatre, where emotion must be projected so that it can reach and affect equally spectators sitting a few feet away as well as those at a considerable distance, and on the screen where everyone has the equivalent of the best seat in the house, are somewhat different. A number of the most successful actors in motion pictures have come from the stage, and their careers have alternated between the two media.

Before the movies made international exposure an immediate possibility, a number of great actors in the nineteenth century enjoyed, on both sides of the Atlantic, perhaps even greater fame than our present-day film stars. They were a rarer commodity. People remembered for a lifetime the perhaps unique opportunity they had to see Kean or Booth or Irving perform. The great stars were obliging. They undertook arduous international tours so that a wide public could see them. Such a public did see them, providing many of them with considerable fortunes, with which they passed into immortality.

This introduction offers a brief survey of some of the trends in the nineteenth-century English-speaking theatre, of some of the great actors who made an imprint on that theatre, and explanation of how the debonair style of acting, the primary subject of this book, grew logically in the late nineteenth century from what had gone before.

According to Harriet Beecher Stowe, Topsy just grew. Everything else in life, however, is a product of natural evolution. Choosing Kean's debut at Drury Lane as an arbitrary beginning, let us consider to what this propitious event led.

Watching him was like having Shakespeare revealed by "flashes of lightning," the nineteenth-century critic Samuel Taylor Coleridge wrote of the performances of Edmund Kean. On the night of January 26, 1814, at Drury Lane, with Kean's performance as Shylock in *The Merchant of Venice,* the naturalistic style of acting was born. Unlike his great rival of the period, John Philip Kemble, who played in a cold, formal, declamatory style, Kean seemed not to be acting the part of Shylock, but to actually *be* Shylock.

His triumph was repeated during the season when he played Richard III, Hamlet, Othello, and Iago. His new approach to this familiar material found an eager public and saved the new theatre from bankruptcy. Six years earlier he had played opposite the statuesque Mrs. Siddons, Kemble's sister, and the most famous actress of her time, who called him a "horrid little man." Later she grudgingly admitted that while he played very well, unfortunately "there was too little of him to make a great actor."

11

Kean (1787–1833) was a small, slender man, five feet, five inches tall, with dark, burning eyes and black, curly hair. Drury Lane, which is still in active use, is an exceptionally large theatre, and Kean's triumph occurred three-quarters of a century before the use of electric lights to illuminate the players. It was the custom at the end of a season that a performer have a benefit. The benefit at the end of Kean's first season brought him £1,150.

He played roles other than Shakespearean, notably Sir Giles Overreach in Philip Massinger's *A New Way to Pay Old Debts.* Lord Byron wrote that he was frightened out of his life at Kean's performance. The leading lady, Mrs. Glover, fainted on the stage. At the end of the performance Kean received a standing ovation.

In 1817 gas was installed in the theatres of London as an illuminant. It provided a better view of the performers but, at first, the public was doubtful of its merits. *The Times* commented, "... after having sat through a whole evening in the theatre, playgoers felt a burning and prickling sensation in their eyes, a soreness in the throat, and a headache which lasted for several days afterwards."

When he played *Hamlet,* a very old lady nearing ninety was in front to see the only man who had challenged her husband's memory as the greatest actor. It was the widow of David Garrick, and she invited Kean to come see her. She permitted him to sit in Garrick's favorite chair and gave him some of Garrick's stage jewels.

Kean's success brought rivals willing to contest him. One of them was a young American, Junius Brutus Booth (1796–1852), who had founded his style on that of Kean. He had even deputized for Kean once in Brighton when the older actor was "indisposed." Booth was presented at the rival theatre, Covent Garden, a block away from Drury Lane, and enjoyed great success as Richard III. By genuine public demand, and in an atmosphere similar to a modern prizefight, the champion and the challenger appeared together on February 20, 1817, at Drury Lane in *Othello* with Kean in the title role and Booth as Iago. Kean was the victor.

Perhaps this success tempted Kean to come to America. In November 1820 he arrived in the United States to appear in New York, Philadelphia, Boston, and Baltimore in his greatest successes. He was the second star of the London theatre to play in this country. The first had been George Frederick Cooke (1756–1811), who had spent the last year of his life, 1809–10, in America, rapidly becoming the idol of the new country. Like Kean, Cooke was a dipsomaniac. At his best he was capable of great performances, but too many performances had been canceled in London when he was drunk to make him welcome any longer there. When he died in 1811, all the leading public figures in New York followed Cooke's funeral procession to St. Paul's Church, where he was buried in the "stranger's vault." Kean erected a monument to Cooke in the churchyard, the first monument to be erected to an actor in the United States.

Kean safely back in England, Booth made his American debut on October 5, 1821, with the same kind of success that Kean had experienced in England a few years earlier. With the profits from his benefit he purchased a farm near Bel Air, Maryland, which became his permanent home and the birthplace of his three sons, one of whom, Edwin, was to become famous, and another, John Wilkes, infamous. During the balance of his career the elder Booth continued to play, accompanied by his sons, when they were old enough, as members of his company, on endless tours of the United States.

The 1820s found another actor rising in England to challenge Kean's power, William Macready (1793–1873). Kean returned for a second American tour in 1825, which proved to be his last, but he succeeded this time only in alienating the press. Macready made the long and difficult trip (at least twenty-five days by boat) the following year. In 1832 Macready and Kean were paired in eight performances of *Othello.* Macready was tall and Kean short. Though wracked with gout, Kean played and won again.

The following year, Kean played Othello again, this time to the Iago of his son, Charles. On March 25, 1833, he struggled feebly through the first two acts. In the third act, after the lines "Othello's occupation's gone," he collapsed and told his son: "O God, I am dying. Speak to them for me." This was the point in the play at which he had dwarfed such younger rivals as Booth and Macready. He died on May 15, 1833.

Meanwhile, in America, Edwin Forrest (1806–1872) was establishing himself as America's foremost actor. Kean had seen and praised him in 1825. Three years after Kean's death Forrest went to England, where he encountered biased criticism. The English press wondered how an American dared to come to Shakespeare's own country and set himself up for comparison? Macready proffered to the actor an air of friendship on the surface, while never missing an opportunity to undermine the American upstart.

Forrest encouraged American dramatists to write new plays for him in an attempt to enlarge his repertoire. His greatest success along these lines was the role of Spartacus in George Bird's *The Gladiator,* a role which remained in his repertoire long after age and increasing portliness should have indicated that he give it up.

Macready made an American tour in 1843, and an acrimonious debate began in the American press concerning the respective merits of Macready and Forrest as actors. Macready was preferred by the intellectuals and fashionable society, while Forrest's more impassioned style was more popular with the great public. Why there could not have been room for both is not clear at this point in time. The best solution would seem to have been for each to have remained supreme on his own side of the Atlantic.

Forrest, however, returned to England in 1845, accompanied by Charlotte Cushman, who had emerged as the first great American tragedienne, to play *Macbeth.* On the opening night he was greeted with a storm of hisses, while Miss Cushman was as equally loudly applauded. Faced with a fierce attack on his performance in the press, he abandoned the engagement a few nights later, attributing the violence of his reception to Macready. He continued to tour the provinces, eventually appearing in Edinburgh, where Macready was also playing. During Macready's performance of *Hamlet,* Forrest from his box hissed him loudly. Again the press took it up, and the rivalry between the two actors began to assume the proportions of an international incident.

In the autumn of 1848, Macready returned to the United States for a third tour. During most of his tour, fanned by the patriotic American press, he met with a hostile reception. Forrest wished to be known as the greatest living actor, but his British rival, thirteen years older, was regarded as the more "polished" of the two. On the evening of May 10, 1849, tragedy was the result of the rivalry.

On that evening, while Forrest was playing *The Gladiator* at the Broadway Theatre, Macready played *Macbeth* at the Astor Place Opera House. A riot broke out in the streets outside. Paving stones were hurled. A detachment of the Seventh Regiment arrived on the scene. The mob attacked the soldiers, who fired on them. The next morning the toll was taken. Twenty-two rioters had been killed, and the wounded on both sides numbered several hundred. The performance of *Macbeth* continued to the end, while the noise of breaking windows, the shouts of the mob, and the sound of gunfire were heard inside the theatre. At the end, Macready was smuggled out of the theatre, and the next day he was bundled onto a train for Boston, where he sailed for home.

Although Forrest had not personally engineered the riot, he gained nothing in popularity from it. Many years later Lawrence Barrett, who had become one of the leading actors of the next generation of American players, described Forrest's style of playing: "His obtrusive personality often destroyed the harmony of the portrait he was painting, but in his inspired moments, which were many, his touches were sublime. He passed over quiet scenes with little elaboration, and dealt strongly upon the grand features of the characters he represented. His Lear, in the great scenes, rose to majestic heights, but fell in other moments almost to mediocrity. His art was unequal to his natural gifts."

Until mid-century, the staples of the repertory on both sides of the Atlantic had been essentially the same, with a heavy emphasis on Shakespeare and the dramatists who followed him. New plays in the repertoire, like Bulwer-Lytton's *A Lady of Lyons* and *Richelieu* or Bird's *The Gladiator,* were what we would call today "spectaculars." Generally written in verse which today is almost unreadable, they dealt with episodes of the past in the grand manner. Before a truly natural, debonair style of acting could evolve, there had to be plays that dealt with situations that could happen in everyday life, with dialogue appropriate to the situation.

During the fifties and sixties in London, two British playwrights began to supply this new kind of drama and comedy, Tom Taylor (1817–1880) and Tom Robertson (1829–1871). Tay-

13

lor's first great hit was *Masks and Faces* (1852), which was filmed in England in 1917 with the greatest all-star cast ever assembled for any motion picture. His *Ticket of Leave Man* (1863) introduced the character of Hawkshaw, the detective. Between the two plays, he wrote a comedy in 1858 which is his best remembered play. President Lincoln went to Ford's Theatre in Washington on April 14, 1865, to see a performance of Taylor's *Our American Cousin* during which he was shot by the actor John Wilkes Booth.

Robertson's plays, most of them with one-word titles, carried realism even further. They were played in London in smaller theatres, it being believed that realistic playing was impossible in larger houses. Lacking most of the romantic characteristics of the plays that had gone before, his play scripts reported life as he saw it. Predating Ibsen he gave drama naturalistic settings, and his speeches sounded like natural dialogue. The plays included *Society* (1865), *Ours* (1866), *Caste* (1867), *Play* (1868), *School* (1869), and *M.P.* (1870). The players in them, Squire Bancroft (1841–1926), his wife, Marie Wilton (1839–1921), and John Hare (1844–1921), established not only their reputations but a whole new school of acting.

A different kind of contemporary play, with broad melodramatic effects, became popular in America with the arrival in 1853 of the Irish playwright-actor Dion Boucicault (1822–1890). He had achieved his first great success in London before he was twenty with the production of *London Assurance* (1841), which was stylistically not unlike the comedies of Sheridan a half-century earlier. Boucicault's *The Sidewalks of New York* (1857) started with realistic scenes depicting the financial panic of 1857, and included a fire scene. *The Octoroon* (1859) concerned the problems and tragedy of slavery. Several of his most successful plays, *The Colleen Bawn* (1860), *Arrah-na-Pogue* (1864), and *The Shaughraun* (1874), dealt with contemporary Irish settings.

His *Rip Van Winkle* (1865) held the stage for the next forty years and provided Joseph Jefferson (1829–1905) with the most celebrated role of his career. Jefferson continued to play this famous title role until his death.

Boucicault is also remembered today for two important changes he instituted in theatrical procedure. In 1856 he secured the passage of a copyright law which gave the playwright "along with the sole right to print and publish the said composition, the sole right also to act, perform, or represent the same." To protect his plays from pirating, he staged road-company versions and sent them across the country. Until that time one or two actors would tour in a famous vehicle supported in various cities by the actors of the local stock company.

In the classic drama, two new exponents of realism were emerging: Edwin Booth (1833–1893) in America, and Henry Irving (1838–1905) in England. Booth had made his debut in 1850 as a member of his father's company. On the eastern seaboard of the United States, Junius Brutus Booth was no longer regarded as a star of the first magnitude. In the spring of 1852 he and Edwin took a ship to California, where the elder Booth was the second established star to appear in San Francisco. Junius Brutus returned to the East, dying en route, but Edwin remained in California to tour the mining camps, where he played every kind of role from blackface singer in farce to Shakespeare.

Edwin came to New York as a star in 1857 where, at twenty-four, he was viewed as a daring innovator. Unlike Forrest and the great actors of the past, he did not stand and declaim the great speeches. The passion of his characters seemed spontaneous. His handsome face, coupled with a flexible, sonorous voice, aided him in presenting what seemed to be a vigorous truthfulness.

On November 25, 1864, he appeared as Brutus in a production of *Julius Caesar* to raise funds for the erection of a statue of Shakespeare in Central Park. His brothers, Junius Brutus, Jr. as Cassius and John Wilkes as Mark Antony, appeared with him for the only time in their careers. The following night Edwin began a revival of *Hamlet,* which ran for one hundred nights, establishing a New York record which was not broken for almost fifty years. He was playing *Hamlet* in Boston when his brother shot President Lincoln. His return to the New York stage was in the same role in January 1866, when a contemporary critic recorded that he never acted better than he did on that memorable occasion.

Three years later he built an expensive theatre bearing his name where he was determined that every element of the productions be part of a whole regardless of cost. It was so costly that he played very little in it after offering unprecedentedly sumptuous productions of some of the great plays in his repertory. He plunged into bankruptcy and his magnificent theatre was pulled down in 1883 to make room for a department store.

Perhaps with his personal genius as an actor he didn't need the elaborate trappings of his theatre. Once, on tour with his company for a single performance in Waterbury, Connecticut, he arrived with the company to find that the train carrying the costumes and scenery had not yet arrived. He announced the circumstances to the audience and played the first three acts of *Hamlet* on a bare stage with the actors wearing their street clothes. The scenery and costumes finally arrived in time for the last two acts, but as one of the company wrote: "It was one of the greatest triumphs an actor ever had, for Mr. Booth to compel the vast audience to forget the ludicrous surroundings and think only of the character he was portraying."

When Booth made his first professional visit to England, in 1861, he appeared at the Theatre Royal, Manchester, where Irving was a member of the stock company. Booth's "intellectual approach to his art, his poetic imagination, his flexible technique and his extraordinary naturalness deeply impressed Irving," Lloyd Morris wrote in his invaluable book *Curtain Time*. Between 1861 and 1880 Irving had become the foremost actor in England, playing at the Lyceum. Irving's co-star was the beautiful Ellen Terry. The Lyceum productions, faultlessly cast and impeccably mounted, were a perfect showcase for Irving. He had achieved and made workable Booth's dream.

Booth's return to London in 1880 found him playing in a second-class company with stock scenery. Irving invited him to the Lyceum where, for twenty-one performances, the two foremost actors of the English-speaking stage alternated as Othello and Iago, with Ellen Terry as Desdemona.

The difference between the two was great. Irving had an arrogant, hawklike face and pronounced personal mannerisms of both movement and speech. Booth became the character. Irving adapted the character to his own unique personality, which cast a nevertheless powerful spell over his audiences. With Miss Terry he appeared on six tours in the United States, beginning in 1883, bringing with him the full scenery and company of the Lyceum productions.

In 1874, in his brilliant and unconventional manner, Irving had appeared at the Lyceum as Hamlet in two hundred consecutive performances. In 1895 he became the first actor to receive a knighthood, a worthy tribute to his services in drama and, furthermore, a recognition that actors were no longer classed as "rogues and vagabonds."

Three years later a disastrous fire in a South London warehouse destroyed the scenery and properties for forty-four of the Lyceum productions. Valued at £30,000, the scenery and properties had been insured for only £6,000. The loss was a blow from which Irving never recovered, although he continued to play. In the meantime, at a more centrally located theatre, Her Majesty's, Herbert Beerbohm Tree had begun to attract the London public with a series of sumptuous Shakespearean revivals, which became as fashionable as Irving's had been in the eighties.

While Booth and Irving were building their reputations as the foremost tragic actors of the late nineteenth century, the modern theatre was being created by an actor-manager, Lester Wallack (1820–1888), and an author-manager, Augustin Daly (1838–1899), in New York theatres bearing their names. Although Daly created a number of stars, he was opposed to the star system and his most celebrated achievements were created with four players, John Drew (1853–1927), Ada Rehan, and two character actors, Mrs. Anne Gilbert and James Lewis. Playing for Daly and from 1892–1915 for manager Charles Frohman, John Drew, uncle of the Barrymores, John, Ethel, and Lionel, was the creator of one important aspect of the debonair style in America, as we know it from some of the films of John Barrymore and from those of William Powell. In private life Drew was a sophisticated man of the world—suave, witty, debonair, and a model of sartorial elegance. With Daly, Drew had appeared occasionally in Shakespeare, most notably in a production of *The Taming of the Shrew* with Ada Rehan. These American stars were the first to perform that play in the Memorial Theatre at Stratford-on-

15

Avon. As for Frohman, he was generally confined to dress-suit roles in drawing-room comedies to which he brought his unique style, and which were generally considered unworthy vehicles for him. He was called "the first gentleman of the stage."

Frohman's second star, William Gillette (1855–1937), was one of the first exponents in this country of the modern school of underacting. In a book he wrote about acting, he described the importance of creating the illusion of "the first time." What seemed to be natural and spontaneous was the result of calculated, deliberate artifice. Appearing both in comedy and melodrama, he combined urbanity, poise, restraint, and unruffled self-control. His two greatest successes occurred in plays he had written for himself in order to exploit his personal gifts: a Civil War drama, *Secret Service* (1896), which featured a strong, silent man in the leading role (played by Richard Dix in a 1931 film), and *Sherlock Holmes.* The latter play opened in New York in November 1899 for a run of 256 performances, whereupon Gillette took it to London to Irving's Lyceum for an equally successful engagement. He appeared in a film version in 1916 and continued to revive *Sherlock Holmes* in both countries, last playing it in America in 1931, at the age of seventy-six.

Trained in the old style, a member of the companies of Booth, Jefferson, and Daly, Otis Skinner (1858–1942) represented the perfect blending of the grandeur of the old style and the more naturalistic style of the new drama. He played the classics but seemed even more admirable when he made inferior plays seem important to those who were watching him play them. Perhaps his greatest success in the theatre was as Hajj in *Kismet,* which he recreated in films, both as a silent (1920) and as a talkie (1930).

In the early years of the twentieth century, one of the most popular actors in elaborate costume plays like *The Prisoner of Zenda,* with their share of swordplay, was James K. Hackett (1869–1926), who had become a popular matinee idol. Effective in swashbuckling melodrama, he was less appropriate in contemporary realistic drama. His career seemed finished when he became the unexpected heir of more than a million dollars from a relative who neither liked nor approved of him. With the money, he mounted productions of *Othello* and *Macbeth,* which he played in London and Paris, where he was acclaimed for restoring the grand style of Shakespearean acting. Hackett, retaining his sense of humor, told his friend, playwright George Middleton: "Isn't it odd, George! They always called me a ham actor in the States. I seldom got a good notice. And now I come to London and Paris and they call me a great actor. I don't feel I am any different."

The Governor's Son (1901) brought George M. Cohan (1878–1942) to New York as the star of a musical which he had written. His was a new style, born of vaudeville, where effects had to be made quickly. Brash, breezy, and flippant in character and style, he wrote a series of plays and musicals, in many of which he created the leading roles. It was like seeing life as it (ideally) really was in the world of Broadway. His opposite number in the London theatre, the multitalented Seymour Hicks (1871–1949), was creating a similar image in London. (In 1914 Hicks played Cohan's *Broadway Jones* in London.)

Charles Hawtrey (1858–1923), wearing a mustache when most of his contemporaries were clean-shaven, was playing in London many of the same plays that his contemporary, John Drew, played in New York. At the height of his fame in 1907, he shaved off his mustache to appear in a costume play, *Mr. George,* with the twenty-two-year-old Billie Burke as his leading lady. The play ended after two months, and Hawtrey grew his mustache again. For the balance of his career, he played in his own naturalistic manner the type of roles with which his public associated him. He was a profound influence upon a whole generation of actors who came after him.

While giving Hawtrey his proper credit as the originator of a certain kind of naturalistic acting, the great chronicler of the British theatre, W. MacQueen-Pope, credits Gerald Du Maurier (1873–1934) as the creator of the "debonair" style of acting as we know it today. After having created the role of John Shand in *What Every Woman Knows,* as well as Mr. Darling and Captain Hook in the original *Peter Pan,* Du Maurier had won a large public in the title role of *Raffles, the Amateur Cracksman* and later of *Arsene Lupin* and *Bulldog Drummond.* MacQueen-Pope writes: "On the stage, apparently, Gerald Du Maurier exploited his own personality. . . . He moved swiftly and with a curious effect of being blown along; when he crossed the stage, his shoulders seemed to go before his feet, as if compelled by a wind. . . . He had not a voice of great range, but he used it expertly, shooting out the sentences, in speedy jerks. . . . He always had a cigarette case handy. . . . He spoke quietly and naturally, he played up stage, behind furniture and he turned his back on the audience. He was not being himself at all, in reality. He was seeming to be himself. . . . But his 'naturalness' was acting."

Younger actors were misled by his seeming effortlessness. It did require more than just getting up and being yourself. Toward the end of his career he appeared in several talking films, including Galsworthy's *Escape* (1930), which he had not played in its original West End engagement, but which had served as the first starring vehicle for the much younger Leslie Howard (1893–1943) in New York. (It was remade as a film with Rex Harrison in the leading role in 1948.) Du Maurier's last film appearance was in a completely uncharacteristic role in Paul Czinner's *Catherine the Great* starring Elisabeth Bergner. A sense of Du Maurier's style can be gathered from Herbert Marshall's performance as an actor-manager in Hitchcock's 1930 film, *Murder*. Marshall had played with Du Maurier, and the film character was loosely modeled on that English actor's personality.

For almost forty years, Alfred Lunt, in company with his gifted wife, Lynn Fontanne, brought the debonair style at its apogee to theatregoers on both sides of the Atlantic. They could be seen in New York early in the run of a comedy like *O Mistress Mine* (which they had already played in England with the title *Love in Idleness*), and so skillful was their ability to conceal art that the audiences were convinced it was all happening spontaneously. Almost two years later, at the end of a long tour in the same play, they conveyed the same effect in San Francisco. Fortunately their artistry is preserved in the 1931 film version of one of their greatest stage hits, *The Guardsman*.

The Lunts' good friend Noël Coward (1899–1973), the most protean figure of the modern theatre, once wrote a play to star himself and them, *Design for Living* (1933). In the winter of 1973, *Design for Living* was enjoying a successful revival in London. At another theatre the revival of *Private Lives* (1929), which Coward wrote for himself and Gertrude Lawrence, was in its second year. At a third, a revival of his *Relative Values* (1951) was enjoying similar success.

Coward's gifts as an actor out of the Du Maurier school are perhaps overshadowed by his talents as a playwright and songwriter, but they should never be underestimated.

Toward the end of the nineteenth century, the motion picture began to be a viable new form of entertainment. For more than a decade it was no more than a novelty which some segments of the population watched in converted stores called nickelodeons. As early as 1896, May Irwin and John C. Rice could be seen in the "peep-shows" re-enacting the famous kiss scene from their play *The Widow Jones*. It is difficult for us today to conceive how this could ever have been considered shocking. The frankly middle-aged Mr. Rice kisses the fully clothed, well-corseted Miss Irwin. It seems as erotic as a home movie of our grandparents greeting each other at the end of a day's work.

It is equally impossible today to capture any idea of the sensation that *The Great Train Robbery* (1903) was for its contemporary audiences. By 1908 the film as an art form had blossomed and captured the imagination of a mass audience. The one- and two-reelers featured unbilled players. Ultimately public interest demanded a change in this practice. The "Biograph Girl" was Florence Lawrence (1886–1938), the first screen star to receive billing.

The twentieth century, in this country at least, is dominated by the ladies. There had been important actresses in the nineteenth century who had created their own legends: Rachel, Sarah Bernhardt (both of whom played in the United States), Charlotte Cushman, the first great American actress, who was at her best either as Lady Macbeth or playing Romeo to a paler female personality cast as Juliet. Actresses like Clara Morris and Ada Rehan, the latter being the usual leading lady to John Drew, and Helena Modjeska, Polish-born but a potent figure in the late-nineteenth-century American drama, had developed their own following, and had acquired a celebrity equal to that of Booth. Ellen Terry had been a full partner to Irving in their productions, and had been judged generally a better actress than he was an actor. Nevertheless, it took the twentieth century and the movies, in America, to redress the basic imbalance between male and female stars.

The major figures in the American theatre during the last half-century have all been women, with the singular exception of Alfred Lunt. The heralded performances have been those of Ethel Barrymore, Katharine Cornell, Helen Hayes, Ina Claire, Ruth Gordon, Gertrude Lawrence, Lynn Fontanne, and, in our own time, Julie Harris, among others. None of the vis-à-vis of these talented stars is remembered today, although the achievements of the distaff side loom high in the history of the twentieth-century American theatre.

In England the male star has retained his importance. Laurence Olivier, John Gielgud, Michael Redgrave, Alec Guinness, Robert Morley, and Paul Scofield, among others, are still potent stars, as well known internationally in films as they are in the theatre. The British actor or actress has always had a distinct advantage over his American counterpart, if the pure acquisition of money is not regarded as the guiding principle in life. The film studios are in the suburbs of London, and a performer can practice his craft simultaneously in the studio by day and the theatre at night.

The large provincial cities in England have long maintained repertory companies where the young actor has an opportunity to learn his craft thoroughly before he tries for the West End.

For sixty years the centers of film production and live theatre in the United States have been three thousand miles apart, which meant that one became a performer in New York *or* Hollywood. This dichotomy became permanent.

In the theatre Ethel Merman played *Gypsy,* Julie Andrews *My Fair Lady,* Carol Channing *Hello, Dolly,* and Angela Lansbury *Mame.* Although their performances became theatrical legends, immortalized on best-selling record albums, and played with great success in cities other than New York, they were not considered sufficient box-office names to be cast in the film versions of their hit shows.

Florence Lawrence was the first screen personality whose name became known to the public. The following year, 1909, Mary Pickford, aged sixteen, began a long and successful career which made her the reigning queen of the screen for twenty years until the advent of sound. The year 1909 also saw the rise of the first screen matinee idol, Maurice Costello, but his career was soon eclipsed by that of Francis X. Bushman.

In 1912 a four-reel French film, *Queen Elizabeth,* which starred Sarah Bernhardt, the greatest and most celebrated actress of her time, was imported to the United States with great acclaim. Mme. Bernhardt enthused about her performance "this is my claim to immortality." It is nothing of the sort. A great deal of Bernhardt's success was based on her golden voice, which couldn't be heard. Her presence on film, however, had two far-reaching effects, one of which did not become apparent for some time. It lent respectability to the new medium. People who had never seen a film went to see Bernhardt. Following her lead, major figures from the American and British theatre, and even from opera, consented to appear at enormous salaries in film versions of their stage vehicles.

Rose Coghlan, at sixty-two and decidedly plump, recreated her famed role in *As You Like It* for the camera. James K. Hackett appeared in *The Prisoner of Zenda* in 1912. Minnie Maddern Fiske played the title roles in *Becky Sharp* and *Tess of the d'Urbervilles* the same year. In 1915 Mrs. Leslie Carter came and went. Sir Johnston Forbes-Robertson (1853–1919), noted for his flawless elocution and regarded as the finest Hamlet since Booth or Irving, appeared in a film version of the play in 1913, but audiences only saw a thin old man who hardly suggested the melancholy prince. James O'Neill's *Count of Monte Cristo* saw an equally aging star discovering the treasure against a patently false painted backdrop of the cave. William Gillette's 1916 film of *Sherlock Holmes* found the master detective markedly older, but of course the character was never meant to be a juvenile. Character actor Wilton Lackaye, at least, modestly played a character role for his film debut.

With considerable fanfare, the leading figure of the English theatrical profession, Sir Herbert Beerbohm Tree (1853–1917), was brought to Hollywood to make a film of *Macbeth* (with Constance Collier as Lady Macbeth). He was greeted warmly with banners reading "Welcome Sir Tree." Sir Herbert's idea of his assignment was to play Macbeth before the camera as he had played it at His Majesty's Theatre, although he cannot have been unaware that there was no means of recording his voice. In order to complete the film another actor doubled all the action shots.

Even the opera house was raided for film performers. The singers chosen were more than willing to appear on film at lucrative salaries. It saved their voices. Whatever magic Mary Garden could create on the operatic stage was dissipated in her silent film, *Thaïs*. Lina Cavalieri and Lucien Muratore appeared in *Manon Lescaut*. Geraldine Farrar, the reigning glamour girl at the Metropolitan Opera, had better success in films because at the beginning she was directed by Cecil B. DeMille, who already understood the new medium thoroughly. More important, Miss Farrar was only thirty-three and still young enough to learn and master the film medium. Enrico Caruso (1873–1921), the foremost tenor of his time, was signed for two films. The first had such a poor response that the second was never released.

Some actors from the stage, William Farnum (1876–1953), Douglas Fairbanks (1883–1939), and William S. Hart (1870–1946) most notably, came to Hollywood without important stage reputations and remained to become major stars in the new medium. A music-hall comedian, Charlie Chaplin, became the foremost motion-picture star of all time. Ethel Barrymore and her brother John followed Lionel into silent films, and such rising young theatrical stars as Jane Cowl, Florence Reed, and Pauline Frederick made impressions on film. All four of the ladies had rich musical voices. Three of them preferred to return to the stage, where their voices could be heard. Miss Frederick stayed to become the foremost dramatic actress on the early silent screen.

The lesson had been learned. The silent screen demanded a whole new technique of playing for the camera. It was not something a stage performer could easily "pick up." The nature of the silent screen demanded broad stereotypes. Behind the footlights and with the help of their voices, skillful stage actors or actresses, especially the actresses, could convincingly play characters years younger than their actual ages. On film, especially with the primitive film stock in use at the time, it was preferable that the performer be somewhere near the age of the character. Mary Pickford, possibly the finest actress of the silent screen, ultimately became a victim of this truism. After playing a wide variety of characters all within the ingenue mold, at twenty-four she played a young child in *The Poor Little Rich Girl* with such success that the public wanted only to see "Our Mary" in similar roles. She gave the public what it demanded as long as she could. Her last adolescent role, in *Sparrows* (1926), required careful lighting to disguise the fact that the heroine was really thirty-three and not thirteen, although her playing was as brilliant as ever.

William Farnum was the man of action; William S. Hart, the strong silent man from the West; Douglas Fairbanks, the athletic go-getter; Charles Ray (1891–1943), the country boy. The comedians established their individual images. The film public knew what to expect when they saw Charlie Chaplin, Roscoe "Fatty" Arbuckle, and, somewhat later, Buster Keaton.

Among the first to establish the debonair image in films were Max Linder (1883–1925), who is considered one of the major influences on Chaplin, and John Barrymore (1882–1942). Beginning in 1914 Barrymore appeared in eleven silent film comedies for Famous Players. They were film versions of stage comedies which had starred Nat C. Goodwin, Leo Ditrichstein, and William Collier. In 1917 Barrymore was the first screen Raffles. The films were extremely successful, and captured well his debonair charm and youthful good looks. They are largely forgotten today. All but one of them, *The Incorrigible Dukane,* are lost, and that is in the Eastman House archives where it has been seen by relatively few. While he was appearing in the comedies by day he was appearing on the stage at night in *Justice, Peter Ibbetson, Redemption,* and other heavy dramas which built his reputation as the foremost actor of his generation, and eventually led to his highly praised revivals of *Richard III* and *Hamlet.* His *Hamlet* was so well-regarded that he took it to London where it enjoyed a similar success with everyone but George Bernard Shaw.

The films of the twenties were for the most part costume dramas in which Barrymore cut a highly romantic figure. The advent of sound, however, brought his screen career to its highest point. The first sound film under his MGM contract, *Arsene Lupin* (1932), co-starring his brother, Lionel, showed him at his brilliant debonair best. A whole series of superb performances during the next five years demonstrated Barrymore's wide range as an actor. Although most of his last films are completely unworthy of him, in *Midnight* (1939) he had a role which suited him, a director, Mitchell Leisen, who could bring out his best, and a superb cast headed by Claudette Colbert, probably the best of the group of fine comediennes of the period. It is unfortunate that *Midnight* could not have been his last professional engagement.

Rudolph Valentino (1895–1926) introduced a new type of lover in Rex Ingram's *The Four Horseman of the Apocalypse* and *The Conquering Power*. His performances are still effective more than fifty years later. If Valentino had remained with Ingram he might be credited with introducing the debonair lover to the screen. Instead, he next appeared in *The Sheik,* which offered a much broader and steamier kind of sex appeal. In that picture, cast as the other man, was Adolphe Menjou, who, throughout the twenties, became the foremost exponent of the debonair style. Menjou (1890–1963) had been in films since 1912 without creating any over-whelming impression. Impeccably groomed, he played with a disarming casualness. With an eyebrow lifted slightly, a cigarette ash casually flicked by one hand, and manifesting an easy air of worldly experience, he was neither pure villain nor pure hero. Others, like Lew Cody, had appeared in bigger parts doing the same kind of thing, but it was Menjou's good fortune to be seen in a blockbuster where the contrast of his apparently easygoing style contrasted favorably with that of the eye-popping style urged on Valentino by director George Melford.

Two years later Menjou had his big opportunity in Chaplin's *A Woman of Paris* (1923). This is one of those legendary pictures that no one has seen since its original release. Until the unfortunate *The Countess from Hong Kong* it was the only film directed by Chaplin in which he did not play the leading role. Modern fans have to be content with reading reports of the subtle innovations Chaplin brought to his well-tried theme. For example, to establish the fact that Menjou was familiar with the apartment of his mistress, played by Edna Purviance, Chaplin had him enter her bedroom and withdraw a man's pocket handkerchief from the top drawer.

Ernst Lubitsch, who in Europe had already used many of the same types of subtle effects, arrived in Hollywood to direct Mary Pickford in *Rosita*. Menjou was in the cast of Lubitsch's next two Hollywood films, *Forbidden Paradise,* as the worldly-wise, all-knowing chamberlain of Catherine the Great, and *The Marriage Circle.* During the balance of the twenties he became a major Paramount star playing variations on the same themes. *The King on Main Street, The Grand Duchess and the Waiter,* and *Service for the Ladies* are still interesting to watch because of his debonair playing of the leading roles. His great skill as an actor of highly varied roles was only truly revealed with the advent of the talking film.

During the twenties, two other actors who figured prominently in the early advent of bring-ing the debonair character alive on screen were Clive Brook and William Powell. Trained in the English theatre, Brook had numerous credits during the twenties as a leading man without ever becoming a star. Powell had appeared in a number of films as the villain, but a villain with a sense of humor, not the mustache-twirling one-dimensional character of the early silent films.

In 1928 Brook and Powell were cast in the roles created the year before in the London theatre by Gerald Du Maurier and Herbert Marshall in a film version of *Interference.* Fortu-nately for the careers of both Brook and Powell, it was determined that this would be the first Paramount all-talking film. Dialogue was dubbed after the film had been completed as a silent.

Clive Brook found himself with a new career in talking-film versions of well-known London plays, often as leading man to Ruth Chatterton. For more than five years during the early talking-film period he was a major star conveying the Du Maurier influence (possibly without Du Maurier's personal magic) to a world audience. He would appear in film versions of two other Du Maurier plays, *If I Were Free* (1933) (called on the stage *Behold, We Live*), and *The Ware Case* (1939).

Other roles that Du Maurier had played with enormous success in the theatre found their way to the talking screen, played in the manner he had established. Ronald Colman found success in *Bulldog Drummond* (1929), and in a sequel filmed in 1934, and then in *Raffles* (1930) and *Cynara* (1932). The Du Maurier role in *The Last of Mrs. Cheyney* was played in the first two film versions by Basil Rathbone and Robert Montgomery.

Eighty-seven years after the Astor Place riot, a less bloody but equally dramatic contest between two actors in the same role took place in New York when John Gielgud opened his

Hamlet on October 8, 1936, for a run of 132 performances. A month later Leslie Howard opened his *Hamlet* on November 10, 1936. That production lasted only thirty-nine performances.

During the twenties Howard had built an enviable reputation on the New York stage as one of the leading romantic, debonair actors, a reputation which he duplicated in films where he recreated three of his theatre successes: *The Animal Kingdom* (1932), *Berkeley Square* (1933), and *The Petrified Forest* (1936). At the same time Gielgud in England was playing the classics as well as modern roles. Howard's only classical role had been in MGM's 1936 film version of *Romeo and Juliet.* John Mason Brown, one of New York's leading critics, called Howard's production "Hamlet with the Hamlet left out," and informed Gielgud that he was at liberty to drop to the first part of his name and call his "the Gud Hamlet."

Howard had backed his production with his own money and found he could only recoup some of the loss by taking his *Hamlet* on a national tour where his movie name brought receptive audiences. The war of the Hamlets offered the final proof that there were two different, equally valid styles of acting, the classic and the debonair. The practitioner of each was best advised to stick to his own method.

The Debonairs traces in detail the careers of eight of the principal exemplars of the sophisticated style in film, a style which hit a particularly responsive chord in the audiences of the 1930s and 1940s. In the 1930s in particular, during the Great Depression, many in the audience were out of work or feared that they might be. It was eminently reassuring to see on film the impeccably groomed debonair actor who seemed not to have a care in the world and had a perfect wardrobe for every situation. He was the possessor of a ready wit and a nimble brain, namely a man whose purpose was to have a good time in opulent settings beyond the reach of most of the audience. Often he was larcenous, and this aspect too had a kind of vicarious appeal for the have-nots of the period. What appealed most was his courage and *style* in meeting and conquering the seemingly insuperable obstacles placed before him in what appeared to be an easygoing manner. It is a style that wears well. Audiences in the 1970s can obtain the same pleasure watching these old films with these impeccably stylish actors. Fashions run in cycles. The debonair style appears to be ripe for revival.

With Barbara Stanwyck in MY REPUTATION (WB '46)

Chapter One

George Brent

6′1/2″
180 pounds
Black hair
Hazel eyes
Pisces

In her autobiography, *The Lonely Life* (1962), Bette Davis graciously suggests that one of the prime reasons even-keeled George Brent remained such a favorite with Hollywood leading ladies was that he did not hog the limelight while on camera. (His detractors insist this happened because he was generally asleep in front of the Kleig lights.)

For a clean-cut performer who specialized in passive performances, Brent still managed to create a vivid impression with audiences. Whether they liked or hated him, they were most definitely aware of his presence.

The bulk of George's screen work occurred at Warner Bros. between 1932 and 1942. First as leading man to his wife-to-be, Ruth Chatterton, then to Kay Francis, and later to Bette Davis, Brent specialized in offering sterling characterizations of blandly conceived "hero" roles. He might be a detective in *Miss Pinkerton* (1932), a love-sick medical student enamored of a foreign spy in *Stamboul Quest* (MGM, 1934), a disillusioned society pilot in *Living on Velvet,* (1935) or a spectacular brain surgeon in *Dark Victory* (1939), but his screen presence was always as well modulated as his Irish-accented voice and as trim as his famed mustache.

He could be solid and stolid instead of wiry and facile and thus not excellent material for a grand farceur, as proven in *The Goose and the Gander* (1935) and *Twin Beds* (United Artists, 1942). However, few leading men were as dependable as George Brent. Whether he was in the lumber camps of *God's Country and the Woman* (1936), low decks in *Submarine D-1* (1937), or in the Old South of *Jezebel* (1938), audiences could be sure he would give them a refined, professional, orderly performance. His quiet, unflashy, gentlemanly charms were qualities to envy, not dismiss. Moviegoers, if not the critics, appreciated this fact, thus insuring George's lengthy screen tenure, not as a second-best William Powell or a superior Don Ameche, but as his own style of leading man. He has always been one heck of a nice guy, and would have done even better professionally had he had a little more oomph or more background.

George Brendan Nolan was born on Tuesday, March 15, 1904,* on the outskirts of the city of Galway, on the middle west coast of Ireland. His father, John Nolan, was a writer for the Galway newspaper, and his mother was a housewife. Two years later, a girl was born to the Nolans, and they named her Christen Kathleen.

One of young George Nolan's favorite pastimes was horses. He admired, talked to, and was awed by them, regardless of their antecedents. The sway-backed work nag received as much adulation as the proud racer. Both his grandfathers had been British Army cavalrymen, and after hearing of their wild adventures, he decided that that was what he, too, wanted to be when he grew up. Another of his enchantments was hiking the short distance from the Nolan house to Galway Bay. There, he often sat for hours, staring at the rippling water and wondering who, or what, existed on the far side of the Atlantic Ocean.

When George was seven his father died suddenly. Four years later his mother passed away. George and his sister then went to live with their mother's parents in Dublin. Two years later, at the outbreak of World War I, the children were put aboard a New York–bound freighter and sent to live with an aunt in Manhattan. George attended public schools in New York City until he was eighteen, when he returned to Dublin via freighter. On board he met a man known as Father Dan, an Irish patriot en route to Ireland to aid the Irish Republican Army in the coming revolt against British domination. George's sister remained in New York City.

George enrolled at the National University in Dublin with full intentions of later joining the Irish Army, but, instead, he became interested in dramatics. He performed in a few plays at the university and also joined the Abbey Theatre Players. With that group, Brent explained to Don Stanke, the co-author of *The Debonairs,* he "did numerous walk-on parts and studied the other performers." In the same interview he said: "In those days we didn't have instant actors. It wasn't like it is now where someone becomes famous overnight. One needed more than a guitar and a horse. It often took years and years to become an actor." Reminiscing, he said: "It was the theatre at its best. And how we loved it, the good thing, the artistic. We were all a bit mad with the intensity of our endeavor, I guess. We believed in the splendor and the integrity of the Irish drama."

One of the rebel leaders, Michael Collins, re-

*Some sources indicate 1899 as the correct birth year.

quired a fresh dispatch rider, and Father Dan suggested George, who had earlier revealed his ability to ride and had expressed a desire to help the Cause whenever possible. Collins put him to work immediately, carrying messages between outlying command posts, which, George now admits, was the most adventurous part of his life. It was also the most dangerous. He soon became an expert at eluding bullets and soldiers. After Collins was killed in ambush, the persistent British offered sizable rewards for the capture of his renegade followers. Now a hunted man, George fled to Glasgow, but as the British net closed in, he escaped to the English Port of Plymouth with Father Dan's timely help. It was reasoned that the British would be less likely to look for the wanted man in their own country. From Plymouth, George was smuggled aboard a freighter bound for Canada.

The next few months were spent roaming eastern Canada doing odd jobs but with his goal set at finding stage work. He had a lot more to learn about acting and he was eager to begin. Members of the Abbey Theatre troupe had encouraged him to continue in the profession because of his good looks and his masculine six-foot, one-inch-plus frame. He joined a Canadian stock company and changed his surname to Brent, an adaptation of his middle name, Brendan. After almost two years of touring Canada in assorted theatricals, he ventured into the state of New York, where he first obtained stock work with a company in the Bronx. "I was a strapping young fellow," he says, "and had a slight brogue. It happened they needed somebody just like that at the moment."

In 1925 George was given the role of Abie—an offbeat bit of casting—in a national touring company of the ultrasuccessful *Abie's Irish Rose.* After twenty-two months on the road with the comedy, he left the show while in Denver and remained in that city to appear in productions at the famed Elitch's Gardens Theatre. He played in seventeen successive productions. He possessed the gift of near-instant memory. "I could learn twenty-five pages in an hour of fast scrutiny."

With the money earned in Denver, Brent then chose the coastal town of Pawtucket, Rhode Island, as the site of his very own summer-stock company. In three months, he staged and acted in twelve plays. However, the theatre venture was not a success. The good people of Pawtucket were not ready for such a steady stream of theatrics. Next, he went to Florida, where he formed a second stock company. This one fared better, but he sold out his interest in the troupe when he was offered the lead in a Broadway play, *The K-Guy.* Unfortunately, the play folded during pre-Broadway tryouts. Brent then rented a theatre in Massachusetts for his third attempt at owning his own stock company.

During this hectic period of his acting life, George estimates, he worked in more than three hundred plays. He also recalls that there were various actresses whom he met during his early stock years who made it quite clear they would like to marry him. His customarily flip reply was: "The first rainy Thursday I'll marry you." But one girl, prettier than the others, and more persistent, actually maneuvered him before a justice of the peace. "And it was raining, too," he chuckles in remembering. Her name was Helen Campbell, and they were married in 1922. The union was unhappy, however, and they divorced in 1929. Today, Brent has only scant memories of his first wife.

George finally gravitated to Broadway in the late 1920s and earned minuscule roles in several productions. One was *Golden Dawn,* a musical comedy starring Louise Hunter and Paul Gregory in which he hoofed it as a chorus boy on the stage of the Hammerstein Theatre. The show opened on Wednesday, November 30, 1927, and closed 184 performances later. Also in the cast, as the singing juvenile lead, was Archie Leach, later to become known to the world as Cary Grant.

George then landed the role of the chauffeur in the 1930 Broadway production, *Love, Honor and Betray* (Eltinge Theatre: March 2, 1930, 45 performances). Also in the cast were Alice Brady, the show's star, and Glenda Farrell and Clark Gable. Brent and Gable were both tall, dark, wide-eyed, and slow-moving. They dressed well, and each moved his mouth a good deal when he talked onstage. Because of the similarities, they were often mistaken for one another, and it was said that Gable resembled Brent (not the other way around). The comedy by Andre-Paul Antoine, as translated from the French by Frederic and Fanny Hatton, was not even mildly received. The *New York World* termed the production as filled with "cheap and soggy callousness." One of the few reviewers even to comment on Brent's performance was Arthur Pollock (*Brooklyn Daily Eagle*), who approved of both him and Farrell, who "stood out by virtue of their moderation." The show closed after a little more than a month of performances. Later, Brent confided to Charles Grayson of *Motion Picture* magazine that Alice Brady "was grand to work with, if she likes you," and she apparently liked him.

George thought he had several possible jobs in Hollywood, so he took a chance and traveled westward. Erich Von Stroheim had been engaged by Universal to prepare a talkie remake of his 1918 hit, *Blind Husbands,* and Brent was selected for the lead in this project. However, the production was abandoned. Then a scout from Fox Studios suggested to Brent that he might obtain the hero's part in that studio's remake of its 1924 George O'Brien–starring vehicle, *The Man Who Came Back.* But once again, Brent lost out. The picture was transformed into a Janet Gaynor–Charles Farrell production, and there was no role for him. His disappointment, understandably, was deeper because this was his second failure in such short order.

He told Fox executives that he would be willing to accept any type of role. "It was a tough thing, being an unknown actor," Brent recalls. "But we don't know you," was the common response to his requests for work. "Give me a chance to show you what I can do," Brent pleaded, and they did. He received bit parts in two programmers, *Under Suspicion* (1931), a mystery, and *Fair Warning* (1931), a Western based on a Max Brand novel and starring George O'Brien as Whistlin' Dan Barry.

Over at Mascot Productions, George was assured of a few weeks work in *The Lightning Warrior* (1931), a twelve-chapter serial starring Rin-Tin-Tin, Frankie Darro, and Georgia Hale, the latter being Charles Chaplin's leading lady in *The Gold Rush* (1925). Early in this cliffhanging account of the pioneers of the Kern River Valley, who are menaced both by Indians and by the mysterious Wolf Man, Brent's Alan Scott is killed. His dog, Rin-Tin-Tin, passes into the keeping of Darro, and together the animal and the boy eventually uncover Brent's killer and solve the plot to stir up the Indians against the settlers.

Thereafter, Fox placed him in two low-budget films, *Once a Sinner* (1931), starring Dorothy Mackaill as a girl trying to make amends for a moral false step in her past, and *Charlie Chan Carries On* (1931), the first Warner Oland-Fox Oriental detective film. In both, Brent had nominal roles. With a studio roster consisting of Will Rogers, James Dunn, Charles Farrell, George O'-Brien, Warner Baxter, Victor McLaglen, John Boles, Ralph Bellamy, Alexander Kirkland, El Brendel, and Spencer Tracy, Fox had little need for the likes of George Brent. Therefore, when he went over to Universal for the part of Jimmy in *Homicide Squad* (1931), they unconcernedly dropped him from their payroll. He received fifth billing as the son of the police chief (Noah Beery) who is later murdered by Leo Carrillo's gang. His next role, also at Universal, and also small, was an interesting departure. In *Ex-Bad Boy* (1931) Robert Armstrong starred as the different paint salesman who, in order to impress his local sweetheart (Jean Arthur), insists that he knows movie star Letta Lardo (Lola Lane) quite well. When the temperamental actress *does* arrive in town, Armstrong must follow through with his ruse, which leads him into a fight with Lane's fiancé (Brent). Boastful Brent is soundly beaten(!) by Armstrong.

In mid-1931, George developed a severe case of conjunctivitis, an inflammation of the mucous membrane that lines the inner surface of the eyelids. Consequently, the eyelids extend uncontrollably down over the eyes. Because he was an avid reader, it was ascertained that his condition was derived from overuse of his eyes. Looking back, he described the situation as "a hell of a mess," and since he was getting nowhere in Hollywood with mediocre roles in mediocre films, he went to live with his sister in New York City. Adhering to medical instructions, he bathed his eyes with cotton soaked with an Epsom salts mixture in hour-long sessions, as well as applying oxide of mercury around the eye lashes. Weeks later, after the infection was cured, he took stock of his life.

Thus far, at the age of twenty-seven, he was broke, with no prospects of employment. He was despondent, and for the first time in his life he did not much care what happened to him. No longer willing to be dependent on his sister, he spent his last few dollars on a bus ticket to California. He figured that he would rather be depressed where the climate was more to his liking.

His first move on returning to Hollywood, almost before he unpacked his single suitcase, was to obtain an agent. The agent promptly lined him up to assist in a screentest at Warner Bros. for the male lead in *The Rich Are Always with Us* (1932). George described the event to Fred Watkins of *Film Fan Monthly* magazine: "I was supposed to help out another guy who was making the test. In those days you went out for every job that came your way. Screen tests are cold potatoes, so I downed a shot of whiskey before I left the apartment. I didn't care, it wasn't my test. Just before we shot it, I started to get a glow on. I stopped shaking. It was the steadiest performance I ever gave."

Ruth Chatterton, whom Warners had lured away from Paramount via her agent, Myron Selznick, was the star of *The Rich Are Always with Us*, and when she saw Brent in the test, she perked up with immediate interest. "Where has *he* been all my life?" she asked.*

The Brothers Warner wanted to know the same thing and decided that this big Irish fellow might be able to compete with MGM's "flapper-flutterer," Clark Gable, already far up the popularity ladder. George was offered a seven-year contract at $250 weekly. He signed immediately. "I was flat broke; it was a heaven-sent deal."

Put to work in two films simultaneously, he had little difficulty in learning both scripts, nor did he become confused from playing two roles. *So Big* (Warner Bros.) was released first, on April 30, 1932. An adaptation of Edna Ferber's novel and directed by William Wellman, it is the chronicle of farm woman Selina Peake (Barbara Stanwyck), who lives only for her son Dirk, nicknamed "So Big" (Dickie Moore). When the boy grows up (Hardie Albright), he fails to understand, let alone implement, the ideals his mother has so carefully set. Mother and son become alienated, while Albright's childhood friend, Rolf (George), who has become a successful sculptor, returns to the farm to tell Stanwyck that she has always been his inspiration. Stanwyck is secure in knowing that George and Albright's girlfriend (Bette Davis) will give her son the direction he needs. Brent's name appeared in second billing, after Stanwyck's.†

Later that same month, *The Rich Are Always*

*Born on December 24, 1893, in New York City, she obtained her first theatre job when she was fourteen, as a chorus girl in a musical show in Washington. She performed in stock and made her New York stage bow in *The Great Name* (1911), but it was her performance in *The Rainbow* the following year that earned her exceptional notices and won her a contract with actor-producer Henry Miller. Over the next thirteen years she starred in New York and on the road in such plays as *Daddy Long Legs, A Bit o' Love, Perkins, A Marriage of Convenience, Mary Rose, The Changelings, La Tendresse,* and *Come out of the Kitchen.*

During the run of the musical *The Magnolia Lady* (1924), she wed her leading man, British actor Ralph Forbes, he being eight years her junior. When Paramount signed him for a role in *Beau Geste* (1926), she followed, and while he was making movies, she produced and starred in two stage vehicles, *The Green Hat* (1926) and *The Devil's Plum Tree* (1927).

She had rejected a Selznick Pictures Corp. movie offer in 1918 because it did not contain story approval; in the 1920s the film companies did not want to pay her her asking price. However, she did play Emil Jannings's second wife in *Sins of the Fathers* (Paramount, 1928) and the next year made her talkie feature debut in *The Doctor's Secret* (Paramount). It was her loan-out picture to MGM, *Madame X* (1929), which insured her sound-movie career as a star. Her thirteenth and final Paramount picture was *Tomorrow and Tomorrow* (1932), a "poor man's *Strange Interlude*" which teamed her for a fourth time with Paul Lukas. It was yet again another soggy woman's picture, the formula movie that had become her cinema stock-in-trade.

†In First National's 1925 silent film version of *So Big*, the character of Rolf was eliminated. In the 1953 Warner Bros.' remake, Sterling Hayden portrayed Rolf.

With Ruth Chatterton in THE RICH ARE ALWAYS WITH US (FN '32)

with Us was released. Herein, George is a novelist and famous newspaper correspondent who has a difficult time persuading Ruth Chatterton to wed him because of her loyalty to her ex-husband (John Miljan), presently beset by troubles. Bette Davis is in this film, too, as the blonde who loves Brent but finally loses him to Chatterton. The critics wondered why Miss Chatterton had chosen so "bromidic" a tale for her Warner Bros.–First National debut. Mordaunt Hall wrote in the *New York Times*: "George Brent, who impersonates Julian, does capitally." Miss Chatterton, a cool veteran of films and stage, stated: "I have never had a leading man who pleased me more." And for the record it was in this film, a full decade before Paul Henreid performed the famous catchy business in *Now, Voyager* (Warner Bros., 1942), that Brent lit two cigarettes, one for his beloved (Chatterton) and one for himself.

His third assignment was in support of Loretta Young and Norman Foster in *Week-end Marriage* (First National, 1932). He is a business associate of Loretta's and one of the causes for the near breakup of her marriage to Foster.

Miss Pinkerton (First National, 1932) came next. Based on a story by Mary Roberts Rinehart, the film is a flippant comedy-drama with Brent as a detective sergeant who solves a murder case with the timely help of private nurse Joan Blondell. In *The Detective in Film* (1972), William K. Everson suggests that it was this Lloyd Bacon-directed feature which set the pattern of a police detective being the foil for a much smarter female amateur sleuth in so many films to follow. As for the quality of this gloomy mansion whodunit, Everson feels that it packs "a surprising amount of traditional 'old house' chills (including a black-cloaked killer, clutching hands, and the inevitable storm) into a more up to-date mystery about the murder that everybody (except the heroine) wants to dismiss as a suicide. . . Joan Blondell . . . and George Brent . . . made a good team, Brent's suppressed frustration making for a better contrast than when her cohort was James Cagney, whose pepper and wisecracks matched her own." *Miss Pinkerton* would be remade as *The Nurse's Secret* (Warner Bros., 1941) with Lee Patrick and Regis Toomey in the leads.

In a fan-magazine interview of June 1932, George upheld the worthiness of the motion-picture industry by saying: "It's creative work, in its way. Of course, it is not on the plane of painting great pictures, or writing fine books, or other more personal methods of self-expression—but it does have a manner of satisfying to some degree the artistic itch of people ungifted in other arts." In

With Joan Blondell in MISS PINKERTON (FN '32)

reponse to certain remarks by other stage actors belittling the industry, he said: "this talk about movie-acting being dull work, a job and a tiresome one at that, seems silly to me. Because I do not believe that any of us ever stay for long in a pursuit that does not interest us."

His response to a blanket statement that Irishmen are irresponsible was: "I do not fear responsibilities. I simply have never seen anything I consider worth being tied to." Ironically, a few weeks after Brent made that admission, he and Ruth Chatterton announced to the press that they would be married as soon as she obtained her divorce from Ralph Forbes. That divorce was decreed on August 12, 1932.* The next day, to the shock of conventional Americans, Chatterton and Brent, who were on the East Coast making public appearances in connection with their films, were married in Harrison, New York, by Justice of the Peace Winfred C. Allen. The witnesses were Frances Starr and Virginia Hammond. Miss Chatterton was thirty-nine, and George was twenty-eight. Her weekly salary was $9,375 compared to his paltry $250, the latter still no light sum considering that America was deep into the depression.

Meanwhile, in July 1932, George was seen onscreen in *The Purchase Price* (Warner Bros.), again teamed with Barbara Stanwyck. This time he is a North Dakota farmer whose want ad seeking applicants as his wife and cook is answered by Stanwyck, a Manhattan nightclub girl wanting to get away from the big city. The course of their marriage is obstructed by mortgages and wheatfield fires, but they discover that they love each other in spite of it all. Director William Wellman captured the various turns of their relationship within a fast-paced seventy minutes. *Time* magazine relayed to its readers that "the viewpoint of *The Purchase Price* is simple and masculine. It advertises the virtue of hard work and loyalty."

A month after their marriage, Mr. and Mrs. Brent were seen in *The Crash* (First National). *Time* unnecessarily observed: "When George Brent kisses Ruth Chatterton now, he kisses his wife." *The Crash* is a sordid tale, based on Larry Barratto's novel *Children of Pleasure*, in which Geoffrey Gault (Brent) is an opportunist who plays the stock market based on tips given to his attractive wife, Linda (Chatterton), by wiser Wall Street manipulators. A banker who has unwittingly aided their previous financial earnings fails to

*From Minden, Nevada, where the Chatterton-Forbes marriage was dissolved, Forbes responded to his spouse's charge of mental cruelty and "divergence of taste," with the statement that, like most people, he functioned best during the daytime, but that Miss Chatterton "wanted to remain in bed all day and live at night."

deliver a second time and, not wishing to tell her demanding husband that she was unsuccessful in obtaining the needed information, Chatterton lies and gives him her own advice, which results in his losing heavily on the market. George played his thankless role efficiently. Already a trend was being set that would haunt him throughout the remainder of his film career, namely, that he would be taken for granted by the reviewers. In Mordaunt Hall's *New York Times* analysis of *The Crash,* which he thought "scarcely a stimulating piece of work," there are appraisals of Chatterton and four other cast members, but no mention of Brent's performance.

Nevertheless, George's studio bosses continued to utilize his services on a full-scale, if hardly consequential, basis. He was rushed into *They Call It Sin* (First National, 1932) in his first doctor role. As young Dr. Tony Travers, he turns Loretta Young's demure head after she discovers that her fiancé (David Manners) is a married man. This time around, Hall of the *Times* evaluated that George "does quite well as Tony." But such praise was not enough to compensate for the stinging review from the *Los Angeles Times:* "The only trace of novelty in *They Call It Sin* . . . is supplied by George Brent, who, though his performance is dull, manages to project electrifying surprises in his pronounciation of a common word. He accents the second syllable in 'difficulty' instead of the first."

In one year with Warner Bros.–First National, George had appeared in seven features, in several as the pivotal but undistinguished leading man. Although his wife was undeniably Queen of the Warner Bros.–First National lots, the executives, including Darryl F. Zanuck, did not succumb to the temptations of nepotism and elevate George to star status. That Warners considered him still a utility mannequin, much in the manner of David Manners, was clearly indicated in studio advertisements, which blazoned: "And here are The 16 Most Important Pictures of 1933. . . ." Thereafter, in the ads, were photographs (in ranking order) of James Cagney, Chatterton, George Arliss, Edward G. Robinson, Paul Muni, Joe E. Brown, William Powell, Richard Barthelmess, Barbara Stanwyck, Loretta Young, Kay Francis, Douglas Fairbanks, Jr., Warren William, Bebe Daniels, Bette Davis, and Joan Blondell.

If industry observers assumed, however, that George was as placid offcamera as on, they were mistaken, for he had definite plans of promoting his career. Obviously, if he remained at Warners, he would have to counter such debonair competition as that supplied by William Powell and Fairbanks. In his own way he accepted the challenge, and began acting like the "star" he thought he was fast becoming. He urged the studio to raise his salary. They complied, especially when he stopped being cooperative with the press. A little item in the December 1932 issue of *Photoplay* magazine is a good indicator of the change: ". . . George Brent, that erstwhile nice Irish lad who's married to Ruth Chatterton, constantly ignores the publicity department's requests. Has his marriage gone to his head? And if so, we wonder why. And isn't it a pity?"

Brent's first loan-out from Warners was to Paramount for *Luxury Liner* (1933), again in the role of a doctor, but this time aboard a German ocean-liner bound for New York from Bremerhaven. An early-day *Ship of Fools* (Warner Bros., 1965), the film script shuttled between events in the third-class section of the ship and those going on between events in the first class, etc. It was designed, although not successfully, to appeal to all audiences, and was not just "a women's picture." The lady of the piece was Zita Johann, an actress then married to John Houseman, and she was a personality better suited to the stage than to the silver screen.

Then came *42nd Street* (Warner Bros., 1933), a big, splashy "lose those depression blues" musical, which was launched at New York's Strand Theatre on March 9, 1933. It had everything: thirty-seven-year-old Busby Berkeley staged the opulent song and dance numbers;* Warner Baxter played a tired, worn-out director of stage musicals; Bebe Daniels was cast as the prima donna star who breaks an ankle while drunk, thus giving Mrs. Al Jolson (Ruby Keeler) the chance to make it big as her replacement; Dick Powell was the pretty juvenile crooner; Ginger Rogers was Anytime Annie, the gin-soaked dancer who parades in a monocle and a phony British accent; and Brent walked through his role as Miss Daniels's true love. In retrospect, he says: "I felt lost in that film. It was no place for me, but they told me I had to do it, and 'they' were boss."

The role of Pat Denning was one of Brent's most passive, nebulous parts in the 1930s, and because *42nd Street* is such a frequently revived, well-remembered picture, new generations of movie watchers tend to think his performance here was typical of his usual screen roles. Not

---

*"42nd Street," "Shuffle off to Buffalo," "Young and Healthy," and "You're Getting to Be a Habit with Me," all composed by Al Dubin and Harry Warren.

only is this a false impression, but it is also a great shame, since his performance in *42nd Street* is hardly either his best or worst performance of that decade. To begin, the part of Pat Denning is an embarrassing script device. He is the catchall sounding board for both Daniels and Keeler, and, as such, has little personality of his own. What character there is to his performance is neither positive nor virile. Within the story, Daniels's Dorothy Brock had met Brent's Pat Denning in vaudeville and they formed a partnership, he teaching her all the rudiments of stagecraft. She had gone on to Broadway musicals, while he stagnated in the hinterland, obviously lacking sufficient talent to break into the big leagues. To his moral discredit, he has broken his vow to himself to stay out of her life. Now he is hanging around the Manhattan rehearsal hall, hoping to have a few minutes time with Daniels when she is not catering to her sugar daddy (Guy Kibbee), who is backing the new show.

Brent suffers two particularly embarrassing moments in the generally brisk picture. The first episode occurs when he is waiting at the stage door for Daniels, only to see her come out of the theatre with Kibbee. While he stands aside looking foolish, she give him the high sign to get lost, since Kibbee has first demands on her attentions. Later in the picture, after he has been beaten up by Warner Baxter's pals as a hint to leave Daniels alone for the duration, he is befriended by Keeler. When she is thrown out of her boarding house for having a man in her rooms (the bruised Brent), he invites her to stay at his apartment. She elects to snooze on the living-room couch, but cannot rest peacefully until he double-locks the door between their rooms. The mere thought of this parasitic, bland man making a pass at the naive chorine has always sent theatregoers into laughter. George and Daniels are nearly dropped from the plotline during the Philadelphia sequences. After she hurts her ankle and is forced out of the show, she admits to Keeler that she plans to marry Brent and return to the vaudeville circuit, adding that even though her starring days are over, she will find personal happiness with him. All these problems make it very difficult to understand how *Liberty* magazine could ever state in its 1933 review of *42nd Street* that George did "much to inject pleasure into the fast-moving and kaleidoscopic film."

Along with filmmaking, public relations occupied a large segment of a contractee's attention and time under the studio system. Jack L. Warner, a staunch Republican up until 1932, vigorously supported Franklin D. Roosevelt in that year's Presidential election. Consequently, Warner was one of the top Hollywood personages invited to attend the Democrat's inauguration in Washington, D.C. He coupled business with pleasure by running a special train to the nation's capital, carrying such studio players as Warner Baxter, Bette Davis, Glenda Farrell, Bebe Daniels, Loretta Young, James Cagney, Joe E. Brown, Warren William, Lyle Talbot, Douglas Fairbanks, Jr., and Brent. En route, the train stopped at thirty-two cities in as many days, where the stars plugged *42nd Street* from the train platforms. In addition they visited local department stores to demonstrate General Electric kitchens, a special arrangement Warner had made with G.E. On their arrival in New York, the stars marched in parade through Manhattan, handing advertising flyers to surprised citizens informing them of the Strand's newest picture show.

The Keyhole (Warner Bros.) was in general release beginning with March 31, 1933. It was the first of six films in which George played court to Warners' elegant queen of the melodrama, dark-haired Kay Francis. Originally they had been scheduled to team in *42nd Street,* but she was tied up with the lensing of *Trouble in Paradise* (1933) at Paramount, and her part went to Bebe Daniels.

In the Michael Curtiz–directed *The Keyhole,* George was saddled with another negative-type "hero" role. In this enterprise, he is a snooping private detective commissioned by Francis's husband (Henry Kolker) to follow her every move, since he is suspicious of her questionable past and her unreliable present activities while on holiday in Havana. Although surrounded by lush sets and high style costumes, the two stars, aided by Allen Jenkins and Glenda Farrell, fail to make it a film worth remembering. *Liberty* magazine's observation was: "When a beautiful fellow like George Brent and a ravishing creature like Kay Francis are cast in the same picture, what's the answer? You're right; they've gotta fall in love."

Lilly Turner (First National, 1933) was Brent's third celluloid production with his wife. It was based on the Philip Dunning–George Abbott play (Morosco Theatre: September 13, 1932, 24 performances) starring Dorothy Hall, which had languished on Broadway. George is cast as an engineer fallen on tough depression times. For these reasons he is forced to join a traveling circus as the strong man to replace the one who was sent to an asylum. In the circus he meets Lilly (Chatterton) and falls in love with her, although she is wed to alcoholic barker Frank McHugh, a union of convenience when her first husband and the father of her child turned out to be a bigamist. If it was difficult to conceive of genteel George lumbering about in the tights outfit of his new big-top trade, it was even more impossible to accept mature, sophisticated Chatterton as a cooch dancer in the Mae West tradition.

George was reunited with Barbara Stanwyck for his next film, in which he is no more than a supporting actor, and one without a first name at that. He is cast as Mr. Trenholm, a smart banker in *Baby Face* (Warner Bros., 1933), who eventually weds the tarnished lady (Stanwyck) with the misleading nickname of the film's title. Changes in the film were demanded by the censorship office of Will Hays before it could be released, and this problem was supposedly one of the reasons Darryl F. Zanuck quit as production head at Warners.

Thus concluded the first twelve months of Brent's Warners' contract. During that time, he had averaged a film a month. As he has stated: "On the first day of any picture it was a diplomatic tour. We stood around for a while making small talk or telling jokes to break the tension. What we needed was a court jester. That getting-to-know-each–other period before the start of a picture helped tremendously." There were a number of films he would prefer not to have made, but "we had to do them whether we liked them or not because of that contract. It was very much like being in bondage." It was a six-day-a-week schedule, often beginning at sunrise and not ending until midnight. "I would be given a script on Thursday, let's say, which gave me three days to learn; rehearsals were held Monday, and we'd begin shooting on Tuesday. The bigger productions consumed between twelve and fourteen weeks, but the cheapies were done in much less time."

Film viewers had to look closely to spot George Brent wandering through a club scene in *Private Detective 62* (Warner Bros., 1933), another example of Hollywood folk enjoying their own "in" jokes. Michael Curtiz had directed that William Powell entry, and in Curtiz's next picture *Female* (First National, 1933), Brent again had the co-starring role with his wife, Ruth Chatterton. She appeared as a serious-by-day, flirt-by-candlelight businesswoman who finds herself succumbing to the romantic powers of engineer Brent. The picture was aimed at titillating the viewer with its modern Catherine-the-Great theme, and, with Miss Chatterton's flair to guide the production, it succeeded admirably. Brent recalls the prolific, totalitarian Curtiz as "a nice guy, but difficult to work with. He was a screamer and a shouter."

In contrast, George recalls William Dieterle, the unbilled co-director of *Female,* who helmed the actor's next film, *From Headquarters* (Warner Bros., 1933), as "a good man and easy to work with." The picture was interesting to some audiences for its use and explication of police department methods employed in crime detecting. Or, as the *London Times* explained it: "There is nothing like strict attention to detail for giving an air of verisimilitude to an otherwise bald and unconvincing narrative. . . ." It was particularly unfortunate that *From Headquarters* was released only a few months after the similar *Bureau of Missing Persons* (First National, 1933); the latter film benefited not only from Roy Del Ruth's better pacing and plot focusing, but also from the breezy performance of Pat O'Brien. Long before *From Headquarters's* sixty-three minutes had unreeled, the plot action aimed at exploring the basic question of who really killed Gordon Bates becomes repetitious and boring. In a role that would have better suited William Powell, a miscast George Brent exuded gentility as the police official whose low-keyed detecting methods differ so markedly from those of gruff Sergeant Boggs (Eugene Pallette).

In June 1933, the Brents returned from Europe where, in Spain, they had visited the Duke of Tover and made several well-publicized excursions to the Madrid bullfights. While abroad, both Brents seemed to have had their rebellious natures. Ruth Chatterton blithely announced she preferred going on suspension to performing in a half-baked affair entitled *Mandalay* (First National, 1934), which Michael Curtiz was scheduled to direct from a Charles Kenyon screenplay. To the Warner hierarchy this was an upsetting, but predictable, move. With some shifting of schedules, the studio gamely substituted Kay Francis as the unscrupulous heroine who rids herself of an undesirable lover (Ricardo Cortez). George Brent was still cast as the amiable doctor who falls in love with the immoral Tanya. Or so the studio thought. On October 26, 1933, he announced he would not appear in the picture, but insisted his decision had nothing to do with the casting of Miss Francis in the Oriental-set production. He also refused the lead opposite Ann Dvorak and Aline MacMahon in *Heat Lightning* (Warner Bros., 1934). Concerning the latter film, the *Hollywood Reporter* stated: "[he] rejected the role on the ground that he would not accept the part of a villainous gangster, a rat character who is shot and killed at the end of the story."

At the heart of George's display of independence was a desire for contract improvements, not only in salary, but also in preferential treatment by the studio. For the time being, Warner Bros. cast Lyle Talbot in Brent's *Mandalay* part and Preston Foster in the *Heat Lightning* assignment. The studio then put Brent on a ninety-day suspension, but by mid-December employer and employee had patched up their differences. Brent was now scheduled to receive $1,000 a week in salary plus other considerations. It was thought that he might be loaned to RKO for Katharine Hepburn's *Spitfire* (1934), joining Joel McCrea as the second of that picture's leading men. However, when the John Cromwell–directed feature went into production, it was Robert Young and Ralph Bellamy who were Hepburn's co-players. Instead, George was sent over to MGM for *Stamboul Quest* (1934) in which Myrna Loy was being given her first solo leading role by that studio. This assignment pleased him because he admired the quality of production at the Culver City lot and also because he openly envied the actors at that studio, whose salaries were higher than his. "At MGM," Brent remembers wistfully, "they didn't make pictures, they *re-made* them. They took more time and if there was something about the picture that wasn't liked, that portion would

be re-done as many times as necessary until it was considered perfect. MGM had style!"

In *Stamboul Quest*, George is an American medical student in Germany of 1915 who accidentally encounters and falls in love with Germany's most successful spy, Fraulein Doktor (Loy). Frank S. Nugent said in the *New York Times* that he was "thoroughly natural in his part, treating it with the desirable lightness and sincerity."

Housewife (Warner Bros. 1934) was a triangle affair with Brent happily wed to Ann Dvorak until his old flame (Bette Davis) appears on the scene. Obviously, the inevitable happens, but the young marrieds are reconciled before the judge can pronounce them divorced. It was Dvorak who gave George the label of "Warner's favorite leading man." Such a description seemed justified now that William Powell had defected to MGM and rival Warren William was experiencing a career decline.

In his next film, *Desirable* (Warner Bros., 1934), pretty blonde Jean Muir was a femme fatale with eager George in panting pursuit.

In 1934, the editors of *Vanity Fair* magazine formed a composite facial photograph of the "ideal male star" by superimposing one or another of the features of nine of Hollywood's better-

With Myrna Loy and Lionel Atwill in STAMBOUL QUEST (MGM '34)

32

A publicity pose, c. 1934

vyn Douglas. In Greta Garbo's *The Painted Veil* (1934), he is Jack Townsend,† a diplomatic attaché in China who has an affair with Garbo, who, at the same time, is married to a much-absent physician (Herbert Marshall). When faced with the decision of making an honest woman of her, George turns coward, ostensibly for career reasons, and allows her to depart for the Chinese interior where she and her husband fight a cholera epidemic.

It was Brent's only film with the famed Garbo, but they became close friends offscreen. They got along famously since both were recluses by nature (he was often referred to as the "male Greta Garbo" by Hollywood columnists). Miss Garbo frequently visited him and, on several occasions, they donned boxing gloves and engaged in a few rounds in the privacy of his fenced-in backyard. As a gift of friendship, Miss Garbo presented him with a marine-motif painting which he displayed above the fireplace mantel in his living room.

For the greater part of the next two years, through the inducement of periodic salary raises, George obediently acted the role of the well-dressed male prop for the "sob sisters" of Warner Bros. In *The Right to Live* (1935) he was starred with Josephine Hutchinson, as her lover. They discovered each other's charms during the height of a thunderstorm while her invalid husband (Colin Clive), who is also George's brother, dies in his bedroom. The nurse (Peggy Wood) dramatically states that her patient did not die a natural death, and the finger of accusation is pointed at Hutchinson. George's Colin Trent remarks that "life doesn't always fit the copybook maxims," but his mother (Henrietta Crosman) proves that the bedridden son's death was in no way unnatural. William Keighley directed this adaptation of W. Somerset Maugham's play *The Sacred Flame*, which had had a short Broadway run (Henry Miller Theatre: November 19, 1928, 24 performances) and had been filmed previously by Warners in 1930 with Lila Lee (wife), Pauline Frederick (mother), Dale Fuller (nurse), Conrad Nagel (lover), and Walter Byron (husband).

In *Living on Velvet* (Warner Bros., 1935), a well-mounted drama with Kay Francis, Brent is a happy-go-lucky aviator whose parents and sister are killed when the plane he is piloting crashes. Because his life was spared, he feels his existence is unreal, as though he is living on a velvet cloud. "I'm on the wrong side of the road, outside look-

known actors. Brent was one of the group, along with Gary Cooper, Fredric March, Franchot Tone, Richard Arlen, Robert Montgomery, Johnny Weissmuller, Dick Powell, and George Raft.

On October 4, 1934, after little more than two years of marriage, Ruth Chatterton obtained a divorce from the leading man who had once pleased her so much.* They had separated in March, 1934, with Miss Chatterton stating that Brent was "surly, moody, unreasonable and disagreeable." In September 1934, when her attorneys filed for divorce in Los Angeles (she was not present, as she was resting at a ranch in the Coachella Valley desert of Southern California), it was reported that Brent objected to her friends and was sulky and unsociable in their presence. It was further alleged that he refused to speak to her for a week or more at a time, that he was constantly critical of her and was domineering. Brent did not contest the suit, but hinted that he was tired of having Chatterton's previous husband, Ralph Forbes, around the house "even at breakfast."

Brent was loaned to MGM a second time, as a replacement for the previously considered Mel-

---

*Ruth Chatterton's film career, at this point, was in eclipse. She retired from the screen in 1938, performed onstage throughout the 1940s, wrote novels, and performed in early-day live TV. She died on November 21, 1961.

†In the 1957 remake of the story, entitled *The Seventh Sin* (MGM), Jean Pierre Aumont inherited the Brent role, now called Paul Duvelle.

With Kay Francis in LIVING ON VELVET (WB '35)

ing in." His one faithful friend (Warren William) takes him to a party where he meets William's sophisticated girlfriend (Francis). She leaves the party, of which she is the hostess, to be alone with him. They marry and honeymoon at a cottage provided for them by William, who also makes $8,000 available for Brent to finance a one-plane commuter service from Patchogue, Long Island, to Manhattan. When Brent survives a near-fatal auto accident,* he is made to realize the value of life and becomes the good husband he should have been from the start. *Variety*'s conclusion on Brent's performance was that "he gives just the right impulsiveness to his aberration, and purely as acting, it is commendable." This film represented Brent's best performance up to that time.

Stranded (Warner Bros., 1935), again teamed him with Miss Francis, her name appearing above the title and George's beneath the title. Again, the film was directed by Frank Borzage, who had helmed *Living on Velvet.*† In the poorly blended comedy-drama, Brent is a San Francisco bridge-construction supervisor with union problems who calls on the Travelers Aid Society for

information concerning a troublesome worker. A well-dressed lady social worker (Francis) provides him with help and later manages to talk the steelworkers out of striking until Brent can reappraise the situation. Barton MacLane is the racketeer who hopes to prevent the bridge from being constructed, and is eventually repaid for a beating he gives Brent earlier in the proceedings. Generous amounts of the film's footage are devoted to actual shots of bridge construction (the San Francisco–Oakland Bay Bridge), which become monotonous after a while. The *New York Herald-Tribune*'s Marguerite Tazelaar found that Brent "displays a delightful drollery in his lighter scenes," while *Variety* complained that he "is forceful, but is weakened by plot limitations." Frank S. Nugent in *New York Times* stated that "Mr. Brent's engaging comedy is an excellent antidote for Miss Francis's penchant for heavy tragedy and keeps her from taking her art too seriously."

For the first time in their joint appearances on the screen, Bette Davis received star billing over George in *Front Page Woman* (Warner Bros., 1935), a happy comedy directed by Michael Curtiz, which concerns two reporters on rival newspapers who also happen to be engaged to each other. To disprove her fiancé's belief that women make "bum newspapermen," Davis sets out to scoop him on a big story. She succeeds in one phase of the situation, but he hands her incorrect information, which, later, results in her losing her job. When Brent goes to jail on contempt of court charges, she persists in tracking down the answers and, upon learning the truth, hands in a sensational story to her editor, who reinstates her as a full-fledged reporter. Brent has to admit, finally, that maybe women do sometimes make "good newspapermen." *Film Daily* said that "this newspaper story makes satisfying entertainment," and lauded Brent and Davis for their "good work."

The Goose and the Gander (Warner Bros., 1935) came next, a thin, madcap comedy with Miss Francis, George as her leading man, and another ex-spouse of Ruth Chatterton, Ralph Forbes, in a supporting role. This proved to be the very weakest of the Francis-Brent offerings. George returned to Bette Davis for *Special Agent* (Warner Bros., 1935). He is cast in the title role as a newspaperman appointed by the Internal Revenue Ser-

---

*Before script alterations, the scenario provided for George's character to die and for Warren William to make claim to Francis.
†Astute moviegoers noted that the same bathroom shower set-up used for George in *Living on Velvet* was readapted with little alteration for Miss Francis in *Stranded*, revealing one of the more obvious economies in these two back-to-back productions, which also had overlapping of technical and cast talent.

With Patricia Ellis and Kay Francis in STRANDED (WB '35)

vice to gather evidence against a racketeer (Ricardo Cortez) for income tax evasion. The racketeer's bookkeeper is Miss Davis, who soon succumbs to Brent's charms and is persuaded, for patriotic reasons, to aid him in gathering the necessary facts. When Cortez is arrested, he discovers that Davis was instrumental in implicating him and orders his gang to kidnap her. Brent races to her rescue and, after the racketeer is sent to Alcatraz, asks Davis to give up her books in favor of a wedding band.

For his seventh and final release of 1935, George was loaned to RKO for the role of Emory Muir, a handsome gent who befriends a film star, Carol Corliss (Ginger Rogers). She suffers from a morbid fear of being recognized by her public, and dons disguises so as not to be mauled by her legions of fans when they spot her *In Person* (1935). The film, which opened at New York's Radio City Music Hall on December 11, 1935, was labeled by Andre Sennwald of that city's *Times* as a "Pre-Christmas Turkey." Sennwald wrote that "Mr. Brent is gracious and prodigal in contributing his personal magnetism to the photoplay, but his efforts get neither him nor *In Person* very far."

George's initial film of 1936 was low-budgeted and devised as his very own vehicle without the distraction of a big-name female star. Unfortu-nately, because of its uninspired script by F. Hugh Herbert and Brown Holmes, *Snowed Under* (First National) was nothing more than sixty-three minutes of tedium. Brent is a playwright who isolates himself at his rural lodge where he hopes to complete the troublesome third act of his play. All goes well until his first wife (Genevieve Tobin) shows up at the lodge during a heavy snowstorm. Next, his second wife (Glenda Farrell) appears with a demand for past alimony payments, being accompanied by her lawyer (John Eldredge) and a sheriff (Frank McHugh). As the storm quickens, a third lady (Patricia Ellis), who wants to marry him, enters the picture. Within the snowbound lodge, a series of complex events occur, but despite, or maybe because of, it all, Brent manages to finish his vital third act and achieve reconciliation with his first wife.

In *The Golden Arrow* (First National, 1936), derived from a Michael Arlen play, George was co-starred with Bette Davis in another comedy. He is a New York reporter itching to write a meaningful novel. His bosses send him to Florida to interview a well-known cosmetic heiress (Davis) who is about to marry an impoverished nobleman (Ivan Lebedeff). In reality, the heiress is a phony. She is actually a cafeteria cashier hired by the cosmetic company to keep the family business

With Ginger Rogers on the set of IN PERSON (RKO '35), being interviewed

name alive. She does not want the titled foreigner for a spouse, and, instead, proposes to Brent, who calls her bluff by accepting. Troubles ensue when he considers himself nothing more than a paid escort, but then he learns her true identity, decides he loves her, and all ends happily. *Motion Picture Herald* politely pointed out that "the story is actionful and swift-moving and at no point approaches the serious."

Next, Brent was loaned to Walter Wanger for *The Case against Mrs. Ames* (Paramount, 1936) in which he was cast as the assistant district attorney who is convinced that Mrs. Ames (Madeleine Carroll) has murdered her husband. The dead man's mother (Beulah Bondi) viciously turns the defendant's child (Scotty Beckett) against his accused mother. However, her evil is rectified when Carroll is proved guiltless, by which time Brent appropriately has fallen in love with her. As directed by William A. Seiter, *The Case against Mrs. Ames* proved to be one of the most listless productions of the year.

Give Me Your Heart (Warner Bros., 1936)* reunited George with Kay Francis. In this tasteful woman's picture, Francis sacrifices her baby boy,

born out of wedlock, to the child's British father (Patric Knowles) and his invalid wife (Frieda Inescort). She receives assurances from the grandfather, Lord Farrington (Henry Stephenson), and her friend, Tubbs Barrow (Roland Young), that the child will benefit far more in his new environment than from anything she could offer. Francis goes to America, where she marries a wealthy man (Brent). Although she has all she wants or needs, including a spectacular wardrobe (a requisite necessity for any self-respecting Kay Francis movie), she cannot stop worrying about her lost baby. When Knowles and Inescort pay her a visit in New York, she learns that the child is happy and well cared for, which alleviates her fears. Frank S. Nugent, in the *New York Times*, stated that "George Brent gives to the role of [the] baffled husband a blunt, masculine incomprehension of his wife's turmoil, which is precisely what the part required." The picture demonstrated once again what a malleable leading man Brent actually was, able to accommodate both the requirements of his leading-lady-of-the-moment and the particular twists of the script at hand. If George were a passive, untalented player, as

---

*Jay Mallory (Joyce Carey) authored the play original, *Sweet Aloes*, which ran for 476 performances at London's Wyndham's Theatre (October 31, 1934), but only lasted for 24 showings at the Booth Theatre (March 2, 1936) in New York.

many critics would contend over the years, he never could have handled with such adeptness roles like that of Jim Baker in *Give Me Your Heart.*

At Columbia, Brent was the vegetarian publisher of *Body and Brain* magazine in *More Than a Secretary* (1936)—an onscreen madcap who had made his office "a shrine to health," devoutly believing in calisthenics and lunching on buttermilk and a bran muffin. Unfortunately, it was a tepid comedy that did not live up to its initial funny sequences. Jean Arthur was cast as the head of a secretarial agency who drops by Brent's office to find out why he is having trouble keeping a secretary. She stays to take his dictation and to further the plot by falling in love with him.

No one held too much enthusiasm for the success of *God's Country and the Woman* (Warner Bros., 1936), based on a James Oliver Curwood novel and directed by William Keighley. It was, after all, to be strictly a "B" production. Bette Davis refused the part, and relative newcomer Beverly Roberts was substituted as the heroine. Then studio producer Hal Wallis decided to film the outdoor picture in color (on location at Longview, Washington), reasoning that perhaps nature could be its own reward in this production. The Technicolor gimmick worked and the picture became the surprise success of the year, despite adverse reviews on the story itself: ". . . an undistinguished tale of love and work in the lumber camps. . . . This is the kind of film where the parts are definitely marked off, not by their characters, but by their rank as hero, heroine, villain and the followers of each group" (Eileen Creelman, *New York Sun*). Brent was thrust into the foray as the disinterested junior partner of a lumber company. In the great North Woods, he discovers Roberts as the owner of a small, rival logging outfit. Under an assumed name, he joins Robert's company, eventually arranging a merger between his outfit and hers.

In *The Go Getter* (Warner Bros., 1937) a comedy directed by Busby Berkeley, George is a sailor who loses a leg in the crash of a U.S. Navy dirigible, but he is determined that the loss of a limb will not prevent him from becoming a success. He takes on a job as a salesman for Ricks Lumber and Navigation Company owned by Charles Winninger. He marries the boss's daughter, Anita Louise, and, later, becomes the hero of the hour by settling a labor strike and taking over

With Jean Arthur in MORE THAN A SECRETARY (Col '36)

the management of the company. Besides being an interesting but minor entry in the Busby Berkeley film canon, *The Go Getter* holds some mild historical interest as one more feature to focus on the adventures of rascally, lovable Cappy Ricks.*

In *Mountain Justice* (Warner Bros., 1937), George is again opposite Josephine Hutchinson, who is now on trial in the hinterland of Tennessee for the murder of her father (Robert Barrat). Barrat had attempted to beat her when she opposed his decision to give away her very young sister (Marcia Mae Jones) in marriage. George is the lawyer who is summoned to defend her.

Warners then scheduled George for yet another Kay Francis tearjerker. "It was a lousy script," he says of the film, the title of which he has forgotten. "I simply did not want to do it. I was suspended for four months and tried to find work in English films. No way! Warners blocked my every move. I went to court in an attempt to break the contract but there wasn't a chance." During the period of suspension, he moved into a house near the Warners' Burbank studios formerly

---

*Among the Cappy Ricks screen adventures were *Cappy Ricks* (Paramount, 1921) with Charles Abbe, and *Cappy Ricks Returns* (Republic, 1935) with Robert McWade.

owned by Charles Farrell. He took up flying (a hobby undertaken a few years prior by Miss Chatterton), along with perfecting his polo game.

On May 10, 1937, in Tijuana, Mexico, he married Constance Worth, an Australian-born blonde actress who had hopes of making it big in American movies.† The marriage was ill-fated and they separated on June 14. In August, Brent sought a court annulment on the grounds that he had married her "because of pressure." He insisted that the marriage was illegal because they had not supplied the Mexican authorities with proper certificates of health, nor were they attended by the correct number of people who had known them prior to the ceremony. Miss Worth countersued.

Brent told the press: "I hope we can limit this trial to the legal points on which I have based my suit for annulment. However, if she wants to make this a mud-slinging contest, I can give her all the dirt she wants."

For her part, Miss Worth told reporters: "If Brent is a gentleman, he will explain what he meant by 'pressure.' When a man repeatedly proposes marriage, as he did to me, I do not see where the pressure comes in. I have no idea what he meant by using that word." In court she testified that, among other things, Brent had returned to their home on June 1 after a five-day absence

and when she queried him where he had been, he allegedly snapped: "It's none of your business."

Although she legally blocked his bid for an annulment, the couple later instituted divorce proceedings, which was granted on December 7, 1937. George has only one comment today on those faraway times: "It was a real mess." That was an understatement if an entry in the Australian legislative record in late 1937 is taken into account. One Mr. Kilpatrick (U.C.P., Wagga) asked in the New South Wales legislative assembly at Sydney whether, "in view of the universal disgust at the treatment of a beautiful Australian girl named Howarth in America by a man named Brent, the Chief Secretary (Mr. Chaffey) would take steps to prevent the exhibition in this State of any picture in which this despicable man takes part." Mr. Chaffey duly agreed to take the matter under consideration, but no further action was taken.

Prior to the finalization of the divorce, George had no professional recourse but to "eat crow" and give in to the demands of his powerful employers. On his return to the studio, he was surprised with a pay hike of $500 weekly, which he thought was only "a drop in the bucket." He was then cast in a man's picture, *Submarine D-1* (Warner Bros., 1937), as Lieutenant Commander

†Her real name was Jocelyn Howarth. She was signed by RKO on her arrival in Hollywood, but made only six films between 1937 and 1946.

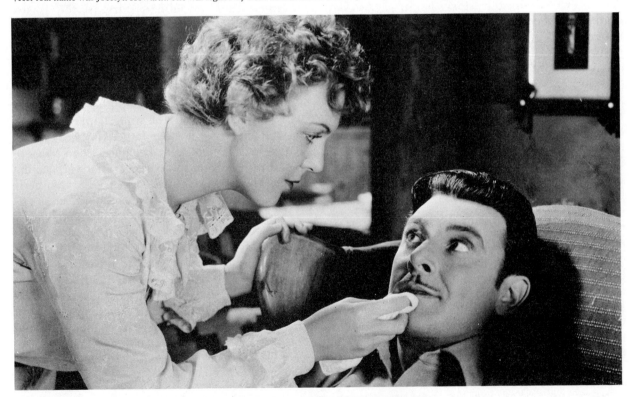

With Beverly Roberts in GOD'S COUNTRY AND THE WOMAN (WB '36)

Matthews aboard an experimental submarine.

His initial introduction to Olivia de Havilland occurred with *Gold Is Where You Find It* (Warner Bros., 1938). It was a Technicolor successor to the earlier success, *God's Country and the Woman,* this time given a solid "A" mounting. Although the storyline was trite ("might seem sombre . . . were it not dipped in a Tiffany glare of Technicolor" said the *New Yorker* magazine), the film provided some interesting insights into the mining of gold in early California. Regarding Miss de Havilland, George recalls: "At the time she was a bit shy and not yet the actress she would later become, but she was beautiful to look at."

Bette Davis wanted, but lost, the role of Scarlett O'Hara in *Gone with the Wind* (MGM, 1939). However, she did have the consolation of playing another strong-willed, self-centered southern beauty who mistreats her true love. The film was William Wyler's *Jezebel* (Warner Bros., 1938), based on the Owen Davis play (Ethel Barrymore Theatre: December 19, 1933, 32 performances), which had starred Miriam Hopkins, a last-minute replacement for an ailing Tallulah Bankhead. In the film George was given the third-billing role of Miss Davis's polite suitor, Buck Cantrell, a gentleman of 1850s New Orleans. He is killed in a duel instigated by Davis, who has been made jealous when the man she hoped to marry (Henry Fonda) returns south with a Yankee wife (Margaret Lindsay).

With a screenplay by Clements Ripley, Abem Finkel, and John Huston, *Jezebel* went into production on October 21, 1937, and was completed on January 18, 1938. At an elaborate press preview held in Hollywood on March 7, 1938, it was "revealed" by the Warners publicity department that all props and furnishings on the picture were authentic antiques. Four coal-oil lamps used in one key scene were reputedly worth $1,000, while Miss Davis had loaned the studio her heirloom candlesticks with hurricane chimneys. Orry-Kelly's period costumes for the distaff members of the cast cost over $30,000.

George's next film, *Racket Busters* (Warner Bros., 1938), was lifted—ripped, according to studio publicity releases—from New York headline accounts of District Attorney Thomas E. Dewey's campaign to rid the city of organized crime. As an honest truck-driver, Brent acted a full gamut of emotions from humility to self-sacrifice to anger in his dealings with a notorious gang leader (Humphrey Bogart) who is out to control the trucking business.

By the time of *Secrets of an Actress* (Warner Bros., 1938), the studio and Kay Francis were

In GOLD IS WHERE YOU FIND IT (WB '38)

With Bette Davis in JEZEBEL (WB '38)

reaching an end to their partnership. As George succinctly put it later: "*They* [had] moved Kay Francis down to the 'B' lot. That was the ploy *They* used when trying to get rid of someone. *They* tried the same tactic with Stanwyck, but she was stronger and overcame it."

Secrets of an Actress was the sixth and final Francis-Brent screen teaming and it was a sorry affair, being threadbare in nearly every creative facet. Under William Keighley's direction, the film employed the eternal love-triangle theme. Francis is the actress and Ian Hunter is her lover and the backer of the show. George, as his partner, completes the trio and eventually steals Kay away from Hunter. On realizing their feelings for one another, Francis becomes talkative while kissing Brent. "And I thought I hated you. It's ridiculous. This is so sudden," she murmurs. His reply between pecks: "Lightning never struck faster." With increased fervor, she pleads: "Don't talk. I want to think about us."

In addition to his film work, Brent became a regular and popular guest on Cecil B. DeMille's "Lux Radio Theatre," beginning with May 1938, when he did *The Girl from Tenth Avenue.* His

was the part taken by Ian Hunter in the 1935 Warners film. "The Girl" was played for the radio broadcast by Loretta Young. "I really enjoyed working with radio," Brent admits. "The Lux Show was a delight and I was glad to do three or four shows a year."

Wings of the Navy ushered in 1939 with George, John Payne, and Frank McHugh, plus other men from the Warners supporting roster. Most were cast as Navy pilots exploiting the marvels of peacetime aviation. This film was barely in the can when Brent was handed his next script, which turned out to be one of his favorite outings.

In *Dark Victory* (Warner Bros., 1939) he is Dr. Frederick Steele,[*] the patient, understanding, compassionate physician who diagnoses as a brain tumor the headaches and dizziness experienced by Judith Traherne (Bette Davis), the latter the hedonistic leader of the local "station wagon set." He persuades her to undergo immediate surgery, which temporarily delays the ultimate outcome. During this time she marries him, and then, upon discovering her actual condition, learns to accept her fate. As he prepares to leave their picturesque New England home (where they had

[*]Played by Earle Larimore in the 1934 Broadway play (Plymouth) Theatre: November 7, 1934, 55 performances) opposite Tallulah Bankhead, and by Michael Craig in *Stolen Hours,* the 1963 remake by United Artists, with Susan Hayward in the Traherne role. In the 1975 telefeature version, Elizabeth Montgomery has the lead.

With John Ridgely and Frank McHugh in WINGS OF THE NAVY (WB '38)

moved for purposes of his medical researches) to attend a convention, she realizes that blindness and death are fast approaching. However, she keeps the fact from her husband. After he has gone, she bravely sends her best friend (Geraldine Fitzgerald) away, and she retires to her bedroom to die quietly and peacefully on her own.

It was the best acting job of George's entire screen career, but the histrionic honors went (and continue to go) to Miss Davis, who was Oscar-nominated.* *Dark Victory* represented his eighth film with Miss Davis, of whom he says: "I worked well with her and had no difficulties. I liked her because she was *Good.* I don't mind temperament if an actress has talent and can deliver." At the time of the film's release, he said, it was "the greatest performance of her life." Edmund Goulding directed Casey Robinson's screenplay based on the play by George Emerson Brewer, Jr. and Bertram Block. "Ah, Goulding," Brent says with reverence. "I enjoyed working with him the most; an extremely sensitive man." The success of the film, together with his very convincing portrayal, gained a raise to $3,000 a week for Brent, the most salary he was to earn while at Warners.

There is only one screen role that Brent would liked to have had—one for which he was not even considered—in the years he spent in Hollywood: Rhett Butler! "It was Gable's role from the start, but I have often wished that I'd been allowed to take a stab at it. Of course, Warners didn't want any of us to get too big because they were afraid we might ask for more dough."†

Goulding also directed *The Old Maid* (Warner Bros., 1939), a period melodrama which remains an all-time favorite women's picture. George's role was almost that of a guest star. He was Clem Spender,‡ who fathers Bette Davis's child before he goes to battle, never to return. The child grows up (Jane Bryan) without knowing that Davis is her mother; instead, Miriam Hopkins, a cousin, is accepted as "mother." Zöe Akins's play of the same title won a Pulitzer Prize in 1935 and was adapted from the novel by Edith Wharton. Casey Robinson did the screenplay. Tony Gaudio's cinematography was described as being of "high standard," as was Max Steiner's lush music score. The *Los Angeles Times*'s critic noted that Brent, "in support, is okay as the original lover." Few reviewers were indelicate enough to say outright

---

*Miss Davis lost to Vivien Leigh for *Gone with the Wind*.
†When it was rumored that Warner Bros. might package *Gone with the Wind*, Bette Davis and Errol Flynn were mentioned for the leads.
‡In the Broadway production (Empire Theatre: January 7, 1935, 305 performances), the character of Clem Spender is mentioned but never seen onstage; Judith Anderson was Delia; Helen Menken was Charlotte.

that George's part in the mother-love tale was no more than that of a scenario stud, needed to get Davis's character pregnant and then disappearing from the storyline.

George's cinematic year was concluded with a loan-out as Tom Ransome‡ in Twentieth Century –Fox's $55,000 property, *The Rains Came* (1939), taken from Louis Bromfield's best-selling novel of 1937. Ronald Colman had been the original choice for the part, but he demanded too high a salary. George's Ransome (and he almost makes one forget any disappointment about not having Colman in the role) is a cognac-swigging wastrel meandering through Ranchipur with no particular purpose to his useless life. In the mythical Indian state he encounters his old flame, Lady Edwina Esketh (Myrna Loy). He soon becomes the love object of a missionary's daughter§ whom he later saves from the floods that engulf Ranchipur. *Newsweek* magazine stated that George was "persuasive and sincere" in his characterization. Kate Cameron (*New York Daily News*) was even more enthusiastic about Brent's interpretation in her four-star reviews: "[he] plays with great artistry, an English artist, living indolently and plea-surably on his patrimony in Ranchipur." Many Hollywood observers were surprised that Fox mogul Darryl F. Zanuck allowed borrowed stars Brent and Loy to outshine his fair-haired contract lead, Tyrone Power, in this expensive vehicle. Filmgoers who had been following Brent's career throughout the 1930s were intrigued to rediscover the fact that given a role of substance, he could provide more than adequate support within the dramatic situations. Detractors of the star were forced to admit that he was much more than a handsome prop for a dress shirt, cummerbund, and tuxedo, his usual film costume.

In re-examining his film years at Warners, George has complained that other than the four-month suspension, he was not permitted a vacation of more than a day or two throughout his studio association. "They'd tell me to go ahead and take a week off in Mexico or wherever I wanted. But, by the time I was in my car on the highway headed south, there would be a radio announcement or a highway patrolman on my tail saying that I was wanted back in Burbank at once!" Naturally, this was a frustrating situation, and, as George Brent of today recalls: "One time,

‡To be played by Fred MacMurray in the 1955 CinemaScope-color version by Twentieth Century–Fox, *The Rains of Ranchipur.*
§Enacted by Brenda Joyce in her screen debut.

With Maria Ouspenskaya and Myrna Loy in THE RAINS CAME (20th '39)

I didn't tell anyone where I was going, but within forty-eight hours, someone from the studio found me, handed me a script, and ordered me to report for work the next day. *They* owed me."

Yet late in 1939, on the expiration of his original contract, he re-signed with Warners, on a short-term, four-year basis, basically he says, "because I wanted to work. I needed the dough, and no one offered anything better."

In September 1939, Warners purchased for $55,000 the screen rights to S. N. Behrman's Broadway success *No Time for Comedy* (Ethel Barrymore Theatre: April 17, 1939, 185 performances) as a vehicle for Bette Davis, with George scheduled to portray Gaylord Esterbrook. These plans did not materialize, and when the picture was filmed for 1940 release, Rosalind Russell and James Stewart had the leads.

Instead, George was cast in *The Fighting 69th* (Warner Bros., 1940) for marquee dressing. He very nearly did not appear in this picture, because during production he contracted influenza and, for a time, the studio considered replacing him in the action film with William Gargan. *The Fighting 69th* was primarily a James Cagney vehicle, with that rugged actor cast as a tough, nonmilitary rebel, Jerry Plunkett, who redeems himself as part of an all-Irish regiment during World War I. The film was voted by the Boys Clubs of America as a favorite. Brent appeared as Colonel "Wild Bill" Donovan, who leads the group to victory and immortality.* When the eighty-nine-minute feature was screened for Donovan, then a New York corporation lawyer, he commented: "I think Brent makes me more than I was. . . . It was like seeing a picture about someone else. Through most of it, I was unconscious of being a character."

After this atypical role for the Irishman, he was loaned to Paramount for *Adventure in Diamonds* (1940), as a Britisher in South Africa who befriends and falls in love with a somewhat dishonest Isa Miranda. She is a lady seeking the diamonds that exist in the mines. As recorded by B. R. Crisler in the *New York Times,* "from this point forward, the plot becomes too delightfully complicated to be followed by any one save a professional screen writer or a melodrama fancier who simply dotes on being fooled."

Next came *'Til We Meet Again* (Warner Bros., 1940),† directed by Edmund Goulding, and considered by George to be his second-favorite movie. Originally Marlene Dietrich was scheduled for

With Isa Miranda in ADVENTURE IN DIAMONDS (Par '40)

the female lead, but she backed out of the venture and Merle Oberon, newly signed with Warners, assumed the part. The bittersweet love tale concerns a man and a woman (Brent and Oberon) destined for untimely death, his by a prison electric chair, hers by heart failure. They meet aboard a luxury ship bound for San Francisco, fall in love, and promise to meet on New Year's eve at the Palace Bar in Mexico City, each knowing full well that it will be an impossibility. However, they toast the idea with Paradise cocktails and break the stems off their drinking glasses to indicate their eternal fidelity. The final scene occurs in Mexico at the appointed meeting place, crowded with holiday revelers. The bartender is astounded when the stems of two cocktail glasses on top of the bar suddenly break at midnight. "It is a lovely, romantic story," Brent fondly recalls. Unfortunately, at the time the film suffered unfavorable comparisons to the original and was passed off by the press and public alike as just another love movie. One of the most debilitating aspects of the film was the combination of Brent and Oberon. Each was meticulously outfitted and performed with the utmost discretion, but neither

*Donovan went on to become a major general in World War II and established the Office of Strategic Services (O.S.S.). *13 Rue Madeleine* (Twentieth Century–Fox, 1946), starring James Cagney, is ostensibly a tribute to Donovan's tactical-espionage outfit.
†Originally called *One Way Passage,* it was a film of 1932 which had starred William Powell and Kay Francis.

With Binnie Barnes and Frank McHugh in 'TIL WE MEET AGAIN (WB '40)

was more than a straight person for the other. Thus, neither one dominated their joint scenes, providing only a very bland ambiance to the proceedings.

In 1940, Brent informed columnist Sidney Skolsky that, if he ever married again, it would be to a film actress because a woman outside the profession would bore him. "I'd rather have a screwball around my house any day than a solid something from Pasadena." At this point, he was rumored to be romantically inclined toward his agent, Minna Wallis, the sister of Warners producer Hal Wallis. Skolsky further revealed to his readers that Brent loved steak and strawberry shortcake and that he slept in pajamas, both tops and bottoms, with his head atop two pillows and with the windows wide open. He didn't like to sleep in the dark, however, and always kept lit the adjoining bathroom light with that door open. His at-home preferences were chess and playing the piano. What Skolsky did not mention was that the thirty-six-year-old Brent was suffering from premature grayness, and, at the studio's insistence, was dying his salt-and-pepper hair dark.

Virginia Bruce was George's leading lady in *The Man Who Talked Too Much* (Warner Bros., 1940), first made by the studio in 1932 as *The Mouthpiece*, which starred Warren William in one of his best oncamera performances. Brent had the title role, with Bruce as his secretary who is in love with him. Brent is harried and sullen throughout the assembly-line proceedings in which he is pitted against a gangland mob headed by Richard Barthelmess (!) on whom he gets the "goods" when a fellow mobster (George Tobias) is forced into talking. Even the kindest of reviewers could only call this programmer efficient and Brent's performance competent. It was the type of role that Pat O'Brien would have handled much better.

When studio tough guy George Raft refused *South of Suez* (Warner Bros., 1940), Brent accepted the part. It was a lackluster affair shown on the top half of a double bill (with *Michael Shayne, Private Detective*, Twentieth Century–Fox, 1940) at most first-run theatres. This time Brent is in a more carefree mood as an adventurer in love with Brenda Marshall. Two murders take place, one of which finds Brent as the accused (wrongfully, of course). The action takes place in South Africa and London. A pose from this film, with George in a white dinner jacket, was used as a formal-wear advertisement, and could be found decorating the walls of neighborhood tailor shops around the country for years to come.

Two projects Warners planned for Brent in

44

1941 never came to pass. One was to be entitled *Captain of the Ship* and dealt with the life of Captain Giles Stedman of the S.S. *America.* The other was to team Brent with James Cagney, Ronald Reagan, and Alan Hale in *The Iron Cavalry* about the Army Tank Corps and was to be directed by William Keighley from a Norman Reilly Raine script.

Honeymoon for Three (Warner Bros., 1941)* began as just another film bordering on comedy, involving a novelist (Brent) on tour in Cleveland who is saved by his secretary (Ann Sheridan)† from the unworthy clutches of an old flame (Osa Massen). The film's only chance of box-office success was to trade on the marquee lure of "oomph girl" Sheridan. However, reported William Boehnel (*New York World-Telegram*), "it takes more than oomph—even the 14-carat variety—to keep a comedy, especially one as porous-knit as this, bubbling on its merry way. . . . It takes invention, wit and humor, and *Honeymoon for Three* is lacking in all three."

But for George, the picture was the start of an offscreen romance with Miss Sheridan that included vodka, rum, yachts, and nightclub-hopping. The latter was unusual for Brent, who had not even been to Ciro's, Hollywood's popular nightspot, when he first met Miss Sheridan. He had been rather notorious for spurning such places and disliked Hollywood parties to the point of rudeness in his refusal of invitations. Mrs. Basil Rathbone, then the number-one filmland hostess, announced that she would trade Stokowski, Rubinstein, and Rachmaninoff for just one appearance at a party by Brent. Interviews were another of his "hates," and he simply ignored requests from fan-magazine writers. "It's all publicity junk," he said. In 1940 he attended a weekly class in marine navigation, and, in July, bought a new eighty-five-foot yawl.

*A remake of *Goodbye Again* (Warner Bros., 1933), which had starred Warren William, in turn based on the Broadway play (Masque Theatre: December 23, 1932, 212 performances), which had Osgood Perkins in the lead role.
†Born Clara Lou Sheridan on February 21, 1915, in Denton, Texas, she came to Hollywood in 1933 and was signed to a contract with Paramount, where she had mostly bit parts during her stay. *Sing Me a Love Song* (Warner Bros., 1936) was her first picture under her new studio contract, but it was not until co-starring with James Cagney in *Angels with Dirty Faces* (1938) that she attracted good acting reviews and began a meteoric climb to stardom based more on her luscious looks and sharp oncamera wit and elan than on her very solid emoting talents. She had been married to actor Edward Norris (1936–39). By 1941 her "oomph girl" publicity had made her the reigning sex goddess at Warner Bros., obscuring the innate versatility of a performer who could simultaneously emote in two such pictures as *Kings Row* and *The Man Who Came to Dinner*, both Warner Bros. releases of 1941–42.

With Ann Sheridan in HONEYMOON FOR THREE (WB '41)

With Thurston Hall and Mary Astor in THE GREAT LIE (WB '41)

In *The Great Lie* (Warner Bros., 1941) he is an irresponsible playboy flyer loved by both Bette Davis and concert pianist Mary Astor. As in the earlier *The Old Maid* he makes one of the ladies pregnant and then leaves while the girls figure out who is to keep the baby. This time he comes back, however, to find Davis in possession of the child borne by Astor. Astor then wants the child back, thinking that Brent, as the father, will want her too. However, her hope is forlorn. Since career woman Astor cannot be tied down with an illegitimate offspring, she leaves the baby with them. The histrionics of Brent and Miss Astor,* the underplaying of Davis, and Max Steiner's score, make the fluffy film worthwhile.

Two more loan-outs were arranged by Minna Wallis, who thought her client George needed diversity of celluloid exposure. He went to Columbia for *They Dare Not Love* (1941), which boasted a first-rate cast which was unable to elevate the film above the level of passable mediocrity. As a dethroned Austrian prince, George battles Gestapo agents in his country. While the Nazis engulf Austria, the prince falls for a maiden (Martha Scott) of nonroyal parentage. They escape to America, where they are still pursued by

the Germans, and the prince sacrifices his freedom by returning to Germany in exchange for the Nazis' sparing the lives of seven of his countrymen.

At United Artists, in *International Lady* (1941), he is an FBI man who takes Axis agent Ilona Massey from London to America, where he falls in love with her. She transmits information from U.S.-based saboteurs via song to cohorts in the Fatherland. Naturally she is caught, and in the final scene Brent informs her: "One day, when this is all over, we'll just be you and I." Bosley Crowther (*New York Times*) cited this picture as "one prolonged cliche," and wrote, "the incredibly routine manner in which Miss Massey falls for Brent and he for her are positively in the tradition of spy pictures, circa 1922."

Brent's dating of Sheridan culminated in marriage on January 5, 1942, when they were wed in Palm Beach, Florida, at the home of Brent's sister, the widowed Mrs. Sam H. Harris. Judge Richard P. Robbins performed the ceremony, with William Q. Cain, a local attorney, giving away the bride, and George's nephew, Pat, serving as best man. The only other witness was Mrs. Walter Giblin, better known as the former actress Constance Talmadge. For the record, Miss Sheridan wore a champagne-colored tulle dinner gown adorned

*The winner of that year's Best Supporting Actress Oscar.

46

With Paul Lukas in THEY DARE NOT LOVE (Col '41)

with white orchids, and a white mantilla. George was thirty-seven and she was twenty-six. Her pet name for him was revealed to be "Brenty."

Joan Bennett was Brent's next screen playmate in the comic *Twin Beds* (1942) at United Artists. It was a somewhat dated screen situation,* which had Brent as the husband who wants to spend an evening quietly at home with his bride without her eccentric chums. Eccentricity enters in full force in the persons of Mischa Auer, Una Merkel, Glenda Farrell, et al., to make the couple's bedroom a place for madcap escapades.

In This Our Life (Warner Bros., 1942), directed by John Huston,† was based on Ellen Glasgow's sensible novel about a family of Richmond, Virginia, with two daughters bearing male names. George received third billing, above the title, as Craig Fleming, attorney-at-law, who is engaged to Stanley (Bette Davis). Impetuous, willful, and thrill-seeking Davis runs off with the husband (Dennis Morgan) of sister Roy (Olivia de Havilland). While the runaways try to find modest happiness in Baltimore, de Havilland encounters downcast Brent in a park. "I don't believe in any-

thing," he tells her. "If we could only get free of ourselves." They become engaged and when de Havilland tells him, "I'd like to marry you just as soon as we can," he replies simply, "Golly!" Morgan kills himself, however, and Davis returns home to complicate matters, first by killing a little girl in a hit-and-run auto incident and then by denying her involvement in the accident. George defends the accused black boy (Ernest Anderson) and Davis, after her rich uncle (Charles Coburn) hints at an incestuous arrangement, flees from his estate, and is killed when her car goes out of control on a curve. It is presumed that de Havilland and Brent will continue in the marital life. The best acting of the picture was performed by Brent, de Havilland, and Coburn, while the Kewpie-doll makeup of Miss Davis failed to convince nearly everyone of her extraordinary seductive powers. This film marked George's eleventh and final screen appearance with Miss Davis.

In *The Gay Sisters* (Warner Bros., 1942) George is an enterprising millionaire who has designs on the mansion owned by the dour Gaylor Sisters (Barbara Stanwyck, Geraldine Fitzgerald, Nancy

*Based on the Broadway play (Fulton Theatre: August 14, 1914, 411 performances) which had starred Madge Kennedy and John Westley. It had been filmed twice already by First National, in 1920 and 1929, the latter starring Jack Mulaall and Patsy Ruth Miller.
†Walter Huston, the director's father, appeared in the unbilled, unheralded part of the bartender at the South Side Tavern, who mixes a drink for Miss Davis and complains that her jukebox playing interferes with his listening to a baseball game on the radio.

47

Coleman) as the site for his proposed Barclay Square, a Radio City Music Hall type of edifice.

Insisting on remaking previous hits, Warners then tossed together a revised but hardly improved edition of the 1934 feature, *Hi, Nellie,* which had starred Paul Muni and Glenda Farrell. Now called *You Can't Escape Forever* (1942) this purported comedy has George and Brenda Marshall as a newspaper editor and his star reporter who get a hot tip on a crime ring. The tip is ignored until the tipster (Erville Anderson) is murdered, which opens up a whole new scandal. The trail leads Brent and Marshall to such offbeat locations as a graveyard and a friendship club. The criminals are eventually uncovered and the principals return to more routine newspaper chores.

After 263 days of marriage, George and Ann Sheridan discontinued living together and she obtained a divorce in Cuernavaca, Mexico, on January 5, 1943. They had been married for one year to the day. Today, Brent either refuses to remember his ex-wives or has simply chosen to forget who was whom, but of fire-haired Miss Sheridan, he sadly shakes his head and murmurs: "What a waste of what could have been a good life."*

He then quietly announced that he was quitting the acting business for the duration of World War II and went to work as a civilian flying instructor at a temporary wartime Army Air Force base set up in Oxnard, California. This occurred simultaneously with the finish of his Warners contract.

Through the war years, George took time out from flying to make one film a year. In 1943, it was *Silver Queen,* a Paramount production that was released through United Artists. His co-star was Priscilla Lane, another evacuee from the Warners lot. The film was a period melodrama and Western which relied on emotions rather than gunplay. Brent was a chivalrous gambler who rescues Miss Lane from the wiles of Bruce Cabot.

In his 1944 release, George was Dr. Huntington Bailey in the attempted psychological thriller, *Experiment Perilous* (RKO). The picture begins on a train during a rainstorm in the spring of 1903. The doctor narrates his encounter with a frightened, somewhat mysterious, elderly woman. "This chance meeting," explains narrator Brent, "became for me the strangest days of my life." Quite naturally viewers look forward to what might be an interesting thriller, as Brent becomes entangled innocently with Hedy Lamarr and her

*Sheridan died of cancer on January 21, 1967, at the age of fifty-two. She was then wed to her third husband, actor Scott McKay.

With Brenda Marshall and Frank Richards in YOU CAN'T ESCAPE FOREVER (WB '42)

With Priscilla Lane in SILVER QUEEN (UA '42)

husband (Paul Lukas), the latter a madman who is keeping his son a virtual prisoner. However, the public did not cotton to this half-baked chiller, which fell to pieces when the plotline focused on inept actress Lamarr. In fact, Brent has few pleasant memories of the production. "Hedy was a lovely woman," Brent says, "but her memory for remembering lines or set-ups was god-awful. The delays and cuts and re-takes caused by this woman were unbearably exasperating."

In May 1944, Hedda Hopper conjectured that George was contemplating another marriage, this time to Janet Michael, a onetime San Francisco model and dress designer who was best remembered in her native city for her creation of the Glass Raincoat. Miss Michael, red-haired and pretty, was in Hollywood in pursuit of a career in designing.

With Joan Fontaine, George starred in Paramount's *The Affairs of Susan* (1945), a satiny comedy built on the premise that a woman can be, and often is, many things to many men. The names of the two stars were billed above the title, and, prior to unreeling the remainder of the credits, the picture showed Brent, Dennis O'Keefe, Don DeFore, and Walter Abel singing "If You Knew Susan." In the William A. Seiter–directed movie, Brent is Roger Burton, Broadway producer and ex-husband

of actress Susan Darrow (Fontaine), who, it is learned via flashback, he first met in a New England cottage wearing a checkered shirt and levis. He believes that every woman is after him for a stage role and tells the "unaffected" country girl: "That Peter Pan outfit doesn't fool me one bit, I know what you're after." When she convinces him that she neither knows nor cares who he is, he informs her that, "I'm kind of important," and proceeds to show her the reviews of his latest play, which he just happens to be carrying in his wallet. Shortly after this meeting he casts her in a Broadway show and she becomes a star, starting her romantic chronicle on its merry way. Of Miss Fontaine, Brent reflects: "She was great; a girl who has been wasted a great deal. She should have done better in films. She was capable of doing beautiful things."

Near the end of the war, in 1944, Brent returned to Warners to make what was to be his last film with Barbara Stanwyck. In *My Reputation* (released abroad in mid-1945 and distributed in the United States in early 1946), he is an Army major in love with the widow Stanwyck, mother of two teenage sons who complicate their mom's love life because they do not want her to remarry. Bosley Crowther (*New York Times*), long an anti-Brent critic, wrote that the actor "is about as ur-

With Joan Fontaine in a publicity pose for THE AFFAIRS OF SUSAN (Par '45)

ads and lobby cards proclaimed that the film contained "Suspense that takes your breath—conflicts that freeze your emotions—in this, the fascinating story all Hollywood called 'Impossible to Make.'" Hiding behind the cloak of respectability, Brent, as Professor Warren, is the mad slayer who is suspected by no one but his mother (Ethel Barrymore), who shoots him as he pursues his next victim, a mute (Dorothy McGuire). Although his reviews were generally favorable ("plays a difficult role well" reported *Variety*), Brent feels that "I was not very convincing. I don't think I'm very good at being the heavy. Actually, the film should have been a hell of a lot better, too."

His second film in the RKO package was *Tomorrow Is Forever* (1946), where he was put into the third slot as Claudette Colbert's second husband. It was yet another of the passive, good-natured leading-men assignments that were the bane of his 1930s filmmaking. Within the well-remembered tale, Colbert's first husband (Orson Welles), thought dead in the war, returns. He is much marked by the intervening years and battle wounds. Contrary to what the moviegoer might expect, Welles does not disrupt the current household. Particularly for its focus on traumatized war orphan Natalie Wood, the film is of the weepy variety, and it persistently gives Brent little to do but stand about in dapper support of the rest of the cast. *Tomorrow Is Forever* grossed $3.25 million in U.S.-Canadian rentals, an improvement over *The Spiral Staircase,* which had a $2.78 million domestic-gross-rentals tally.

Another freelance period followed, with Universal's *Lover, Come Back* (1946), a mild, polite comedy dealing with matrimonial differences with Lucille Ball. Six months later, Brent was seen in the costume drama *Temptation* (Universal, 1946), yet another screen version of the novel *Bella Donna,* which had been dramatized on Broadway (Empire Theatre: November 11, 1912, 72 performances) starring Alla Nazimova.[†] In this expensively mounted edition, George comes dangerously close to drinking the poison served by Merle Oberon until she decides to withdraw the "special" drink and serve it, instead, to her lover, Charles Korvin. Another six months later and encased in another costume epic, he was a skirt-chasing American who is sent to Tripoli to ran-

bane as a high school sophomore." On the other hand, Brent was enthusiastic about Stanwyck and claims that "she was marvelous to work with. She was always a joy, along with being a real professional."

Although Hollywood was emerging with new ideas and tastes in production, and a fresh crop of players were appearing, 1945 was still a transitional period and moviemakers were still relying on the big-box-office names of the 1930s and early 1940s for marquee insurance. George, at age forty-one, though considered passé by the new breed of filmmaker, was still able to make a good industry deal. He signed a two-picture contract with RKO at $17,500 a week. *The Spiral Staircase* (1946)[*] came first. Directed by Robert Siodmak, adapted for the screen from Ethel Lina White's novel *Some Must Watch,* it told the story of a town in 1906 New England which is terrorized by a psychopathic killer of young girls. Until the film's taut finale, only the killer's eyes are revealed by Nicholas Musuraca's camera. Magazine

[*] 1975 film remake of *The Spiral Staircase* directed by Peter Collinson starred Jacqueline Bisset in the deaf-and-dumb girl (originally played by Dorothy McGuire) with Christopher Plummer interpreting Brent's old role. Others in the cast were Gayle Hunnicutt, Mildred Dunnock, Sam Wanamaker, John Phillip Law, and Elaine Stritch. It was filmed in England.

[†] The 1915 screen version starred Pauline Frederick, the 1923 edition featured Pola Negri in her American movie debut, and Mary Ellis headed the 1935 British version.

Advertisement for TOMORROW IS FOREVER (RKO '46)

With Wallace Ford in LOVER COME BACK (Univ '46)

With Merle Oberon in TEMPTATION (Univ '46)

som a group of sailors but gets romantically involved with a *Slave Girl* (Universal, 1947), played by Yvonne De Carlo. The multihued settings and the pulchritudinous Miss De Carlo were the chief attractions of this mock swashbuckling yarn that could not, and should not, be taken seriously. By the point of *Experiment Perilous*, filmgoers were noticing that Brent's countenance had taken on a permanently tired and distracted look; by the time of *Slave Girl*, his waistline was losing its once firm shape.

Although George's salary was $10,000 a week, his career was slipping into a slow fade-out with a "B" production at Columbia called *The Corpse Came C.O.D.* (1947) with Joan Blondell, and a not-much-better Eagle Lion release, *Out of the Blue*. This latter film was a feckless comedy set in Greenwich Village. Next, George was a playboy with dishonest leanings in *Christmas Eve* (United Artists, 1947) as one of the three wards of elderly Ann Harding.

On December 17, 1947, George fulfilled Hedda Hopper's prognostication of three years previous by marrying Janet Michael, who in 1946 had been picked by the New York International Artists' Committee as one of the ten most glamorous women in the United States. They were wed by Superior Court Judge Henry C. Kelly in Yuma,

Arizona, with Hollywood physician Lee Seigel as best man. Brent was forty-three, and his bride was twenty-seven. They purchased a ranch in Ventura, California, where he began in earnest to raise and train thoroughbred horses.

George likes his next film for MGM, *Luxury Liner* (1948).* (One suspects that George was still impressed by the glamour and prestige of that studio.) "That film was gorgeous," he says. "It took three months to make and the whole thing was a lot of fun. Richard Whorf was a love to work with as a director." Brent was the captain of the ship and father to teenaged songbird Jane Powell ("Boy, she could sing)."

A brief, nonexclusive contract with Republic was negotiated in 1948, and George permitted himself to be cast in *Angel on the Amazon*. An inane script by Lawrence Kimble has him and Constance Bennett bobbing along the shores of the Amazon River trying to discover the mystery surrounding heroine Vera Ralston. It is later revealed that the latter's aging processes had been reversed after she was scared by a panther and, although she is actually seventy years of age, she looks (or tries to look) twenty-five. Vera Ralston, now Mrs. Charles de Alva of Santa Barbara, California, says: "I think George was one of the nicest people I ever worked with. I was quite new [*sic*]

*Not to be confused with Brent's 1933 Paramount film of the same title.

With Lois Collier in SLAVE GIRL (Univ '47)

With Wilton Graff, Jim Bannon, William Forrest, and Joan Blondell in THE CORPSE CAME C.O.D. (Col '47)

at the game, and he helped me a lot. He was very considerate." Despite their efforts, *Angel on the Amazon* proved to be one of the bigger celluloid embarrassments of that year.

Brent's next two films, for Universal, were *Red Canyon* (1949), a Zane Grey Western shot in color in the sagebrush of Utah with Ann Blyth and Howard Duff in the leads, and *Illegal Entry* (1949), concerned with the smuggling of aliens into the United States from Mexico. Then back at Republic, he was a sports announcer upstaged by

juvenile actor Rusty Tamblyn in *The Kid from Cleveland* (1949), the script of which was all about baseball and the Cleveland Indians.

RKO then claimed him as Robert Young's friend in *Bride for Sale* (1949) for which he pretends to be wealthy in order to confuse Young's girlfriend, Claudette Colbert, who is intent on snaring a rich husband. It was very professional job but overtaxed by the extremely thin and outdated material.

The Brents' first child, a girl named Suzanne,

With Richard Lane, Virginia Mayo, Carole Landis, and Turhan Bey in OUT OF THE BLUE (Eagle Lion '47)

With Molly Lamont and Joan Blondell in CHRISTMAS EVE (UA '47)

With Marina Koshetz and Lauritz Melchior in LUXURY LINER (MGM '48)

54

was born at Santa Monica Hospital on August 3, 1950. Brent was then forty-six years old.

The training and racing of horses at his Ventura ranch occupied all of Brent's attention in 1950, along with being a new father. His stables were frequently represented in races throughout the Southern California area. Character player Connie Gilchrist and her writer husband Edwin O'Hanlon were among those in Hollywood who often bet on his horses because, as Connie says, "George was a sterling character, but that didn't help us to win any money on his beauties."

None of George's next three films was memorable, leading to a possible conclusion that he did them only for the financial rewards. *FBI Girl* (Lippert, 1951) has him halfheartedly lumbering through a cops 'n' robbers tale in his attempt to capture crime lord Raymond Burr. *The Last Page* (a.k.a. *Man Bait*) (Exclusive, 1952) finds him sandwiched between Diana Dors and Marguerite Chapman in a British-made entry. Finally, the third entry was not even good camp, just a bad film. In this film, entitled *Montana Belle*, completed in November 1948, but not released by Howard Hughes's RKO until 1952, George was Tom Bradfield, the smooth, well-spoken owner of the Bird Cage Saloon in the old West. Belle Starr (Jane Russell) comes off the trail with the pseudonym of Mrs. Lucy Winters. "I find the name Mrs. Winters very formal," he tells the well-proportioned miss. "Okay, call me Montana," she replies in a very frisky manner. He takes her on as his partner and protects her from the law. Of the entire cast, only Brent displays any element of cinema professionalism.

On March 16, 1952, *Variety* reported that George had signed a five-year agreement with producer Lindsley Parsons to appear in two pictures a year to be released by Monogram–Allied Artists. In the deal, negotiated by Brent's agents, the William B. White Agency, his financial arrangement was $250,000 cash, plus a percentage of the ten pictures to be realized. Only two films came to pass, however. In *Tangier Incident* (1953) ("A routine round of espionage melodramatics, put together in stock fashion," printed *Variety*), he was a U.S. agent in North Africa in search of a spy ring that was selling atomic secrets to the Russians. Then he helped to solve an old crime in *Mexican Manhunt* (1953), which found Hillary Brooke on the wrong side of the law.

After a mutual dissolution of the Lindsley Par-

With Walter Reed and Gus Schilling in ANGEL ON THE AMAZON (Rep '48)

sons pact, Brent relaxed from his show-business interests. On December 14, 1954, a son, Barry, was born to the Brents in Santa Monica, California.

It seemed almost inevitable that the still well remembered George Brent would be lured into a television-series deal. "Wire Service," a thirty-nine-episode, sixty-minute show, which premiered on ABC-TV on October 4, 1956, provided that George alternate as program star with Dane Clark and Mercedes McCambridge. This show, organized by Official Films, dealt with experienced reporters on global assignments. Brent did just one episode and made a speedy exit. "I didn't like any of it," he says. "The entire script was never revealed, which was a completely frustrating matter to me." In this video appearance, audiences discovered that George now had a full head of white hair.

George continued to make occasional appearances on television anthology shows,* his most recent being on "Rawhide" (CBS-TV, April 3, 1959) and "Mystery Show" (NBC-TV, July 24, 1960). He also made one more bid to return to theatrical films. He came out of his screen retirement for a supporting role in *Death of a Scoundrel* (RKO, 1956) starring George Sanders and Yvonne De Carlo. However, a severe case of lar-

---

*Brent made his TV debut in 1953 on such shows as "Ford Theatre" (episode *Double Exposure*—NBC, March 26, 1953), "Schlitz Playhouse of Stars" (episode *Medicine Woman*—CBS, May 1, 1953), and "Mirror Theatre" (episode *Key in the Lock*—CBS, November 14, 1953). He was a frequent guest star on Fireside Theatre" (NBC, 1955) and "Crossroads" (ABC, 1956).

With Howard Duff in RED CANYON (Univ '49)

yngitis kept him from completing the job and he was replaced by John Hoyt. A scene showing white-haired Brent in the background does appear in the finished product, with *no* credit tag for the once famous star. "That was the very first time I was unable to finish a film," he now recalls with a sad shake of his head. "One of those things, I guess."

During these years, Brent mostly tended to his horse breeding, seemingly realistic about his retirement from show business. "I'm not bitter because things slowed up," he said a few years ago. "I saved my money. You can't play Shirley Temple all your life."

By 1965, George sold his Ventura property and bought a ranch at Rancho Santa Fe, California, near San Diego. Daughter Suzanne was enrolled at a school in Switzerland, while son Barry was at a military academy. Hedda Hopper cornered Brent at Rancho Santa Fe and asked what he had been doing since his retirement. His reply was: "I was restless for about three years, but my ranch keeps me busy. Horses are more interesting than people and there's a new crop each year. Training is worse than picture-making. Up at 4:30 a.m., work seven days a week. Horses don't have a union."

On May 31, 1966, Mike Connolly reported in his *Hollywood Reporter* column: "George Brent

is blowing the Rancho Santa Fe scene to reside permanently in Ireland." With Janet, George rented an older house near Dublin, where they lived for one year. "It was the wettest and coldest winter I have ever endured. I couldn't take it. It was different when I was young; then, I'd bounce back every day." As Brent told Fred Watkins of *Film Fan Monthly,* "I shipped my Rolls-Royce over and they scratched the doors; they thought it belonged to a British official. I had a hell of a time getting it repaired."

When the Brents returned to Rancho Santa Fe, George was contacted by George Raft, his *Christmas Eve* co-star, who talked him into doing a television commercial for Pontiac automobiles. They appeared together in what Raft predicted would be an easy day's work. "It was the hardest *two* days I've ever worked in my life. Never—*Never* again."

At this point, Janet took ill, and the specialists diagnosed the problem as cancer. She was given two years to live. Brent sold his horses and devoted all his time to being with his wife, except for occasional and expensive trips to the races. "There's a guy here [San Diego] who's won a million bucks from me, but that's the way things are sometimes." Brent, who was accustomed to reaching for a cigarette the first thing each morning, and who smoked between three and four

56

With Harry Cheshire, Eula Guy, Stephen Chase, and Claudette Colbert in BRIDE FOR SALE (RKO '49)

packs a day, suddenly gave it up. For six months he sat reading, watching television movies, and eating cakes and cookies. He gained forty pounds.

He then picked up the cigar habit. "Anthony and Cleopatras were my favorite. I smoked those like there was no tomorrow." In the spring of 1973 he quit those, too, and kept his weight down by pool swimming and knocking off the sweets. He has no hobbies to fill in his many vacant hours. "I can't paint and I hate gardening. I've never been any good with my hands. But, I love California—its mountains and the ocean. It's the only place to live. Not in Los Angeles, but down here [Rancho Santa Fe] where the air is clear."

In the summer of 1973, Barry Brent, at nineteen, stood six feet, four inches tall and was on active duty with the U.S. Army. Suzanne Brent was a designer for the J. C. Penney Company in its San Diego office. Neither Brent offspring showed any desire to go into acting. During that

With Gene Roth and Glenn Strange in MONTANA BELLE (RKO '52)

With Karen Sharpe and Morris Ankrum in MEXICAN MANHUNT (AA '53)

summer, Janet Brent was still confined to the house and a regimen of rest and medication. Brent says that her condition is much the same as the day in 1968 when the doctors gave her only two years to live.

In looking back on his extensive screen career, George has no regrets about any of it. He does not want to return to film acting, but he *would* be interested in filling some technical capacity. "I'm afraid most people think I'm dead or not interested. Also, there are a great many now in the industry who have never heard of me. But, I'll tell you one thing. I may have been around since Christ was a corporal, but most of us in those days were professionals. We didn't get by on looks alone, like so many of them do nowadays."

George Brent of the 1960s

58

George Brent

UNDER SUSPICION (FOX, 1931) 66 M.

Director, A. F. Erickson; story-screenplay, Tom Barry; camera, George Schneiderman; editor, J. Edwin Robbins.

Lois Moran (Alice Freel); J. Harold Murray (Johnny Smith); J. M. Kerrigan (Doyle); Edwin Connelly (Dassy); Lumsden Hare (Frey); George Brent (Inspector Turner); Marie Saxon (Suzanne); Rhoda Cross (Marie); Herbert Bunston (Major Manners); Vera Gerald (Ellen).

FAIR WARNING (FOX, 1931) 74 M.

Director, Alfred L. Werker; based on the novel The Untamed by Max Brand; screenplay, Ernest L. Pascal; sound, Bernard Freericks; camera, Ross Fisher; editor, Ralph Dietrich.

George O'Brien (Whistlin' Dan Barry); Louise Huntington (Kate Cumberland); Mitchell Harris (Jim Silent); George Brent (Les Haines); Nat Pendleton (Purvis); John Sheehan (Kelduff); Erwin Connelly (Morgan); Willard Robertson (Tex Calder); Alphonz Ethier (Mr. Cumberland); Ernest Adams (Jordan).

THE LIGHTNING WARRIOR (Mascot serial, 1931) 12 chapters

Directors, Armand Schaefer, Ben Kline; screenplay, Wyndham Gittens, Ford Beebe, Helmar Bergman.

Rin Tin Tin (Rinty); Frankie Darro (Jimmy Carter); Georgia Hale (Dianne); George Brent (Alan Scott); Pat O'Malley (Sheriff); Theodore Lorch (Pierre La Farge); Lafe McKee (John Hayden); Bob Kortman (Wells); George Magrill (Man); Frank Lanning (Indian George); Frank Brownlee (McDonald); Hayden Stevenson (Carter); Dick Dickinson (Adams); Kermit Maynard (Townsman/Deputy); Yakima Canutt (Ken Davis/Deputy); George Morrell (Debtor/Townsman); Bertee Beaumont (Pioneer); Helen Gibson (Woman).

ONCE A SINNER (FOX, 1931) 76 M.

Director, Guthrie McClintic; story-screenplay, George Middleton; sound, Al Von Kirbach; camera, Arthur L. Todd; editor, Ralph Dietrich.

Dorothy Mackaill (Diana Barry); Joel McCrea (Tommy Mason); C. Henry Gordon (Serge Ratoff); Ilka Chase (Kitty Kelly); Clara Blandick (Mrs. Mason); Myra Hampton (Mary Nolan); George Brent (James Brent); Sally Blane (Hope Patterson); Nanette Faro (Marie the Maid); Theodore Lodi (Bit).

CHARLIE CHAN CARRIES ON (FOX, 1931) 76 M.

Director, Hamilton MacFadden; based on a story by Earl Derr Biggers; screenplay, Philip Klein, Barry Connors; sound, George P. Costello; camera, George Schneiderman; editor, Al Degaetano.

Warner Oland (Charlie Chan); John Garrick (Mark Kennaway); Marguerite Churchill (Pamela Potter); Warren Hymer (Max Minchin); Marjorie White (Sadie Minchin); C. Henry Gordon (John Ross); William Holden (Patrick Tait); George Brent (Captain Ronald Keane); Peter Gawthorne (Inspector Duff); John T. Murray (Dr. Lofton); John Swor (Elmer Benbow); Goodee Montgomery (Mrs. Benbow); Jason Robards (Walter Honywood); Lumsden Hare (Inspector Hanley); Zeffie Tilbury (Mrs. Luce); Betty Francisco (Sybil Conway); Harry Beresford (Kent); John Rogers (Martin); J. G. Davis (Eben).

HOMICIDE SQUAD (UNIV, 1931) 69 M.

Director, George Melford; story, Henry LaCossitt; screenplay, John Thomas Neville; sound, C. Roy Hunter; camera, George Robinson; editors, Maurice Pivar, Harry Lieb.

Leo Carrillo (Louie); Noah Beery (Captain Buckley); Mary Brian (Millie); Russell Gleason (Joe Riley); George Brent (Jimmy); Walter C. Percival (Proctor); J. Carroll Naish (Hugo).

EX-BAD BOY (UNIV, 1931) 66 M.

Director, Vin Moore; based on the play The Whole Town's Talking by Anita Loos, John Emerson; screenplay, Dale Van Every; dialog, Fred Niblo, Jr.; sound, C. Roy Hunter; camera, Jerome Ash.

Robert Armstrong (Chester Binney); Jean Arthur (Ethel Simmons); Jason Robards (Roger Shields); Spencer Charters (Henry Simmons); Grayce Hampton (Mrs. Simmons); Lola Lane (Letta Lardo); George Brent (Donald Swift); Mary Doran (Sadie Bloom); Tony Stakenau (Trainer); Eddie Kane (Theatre Manager); Eddie Hearn (Assistant Manager).

SO BIG (WB, 1932) 82 M.

Producer, Jack L. Warner; director, William A. Wellman; based on the novel by Edna Ferber; screenplay, J. Grubb Alexander, Robert Lord; music, W. Franke Harling; costumes, Orry-Kelly; camera, Sid Hickox; editor, William Holmes.

Barbara Stanwyck (Selina Peake); George Brent (Roelf); Dickie Moore (Dirk as a Boy); Guy Kibbee (August Hemple); Bette Davis (Dallas O'Mara); Mae Madison (Julie Hemple); Hardie Albright (Dirk as an Adult); Robert Warwick (Simson Peake); Arthur Stone (Jan Steen); Earle Foxe (Pervus Dejong); Alan Hale (Klaas Pool); Dorothy Peterson (Maartje); Anne Shirley (Selina as a Little Girl); Dick Winslow (Roelf as a Boy); Harry Beresford (Adam Ooms); Eulalie Jensen (Mrs. Hemple); Elizabeth Patterson (Mrs. Tebbits); Rita LaRoy (Paula); Blanche Frederici (Widow Parrlenburg); Willard Robertson (The Doctor); Harry Holman (Country Doctor); Lionel Belmore (Reverend Dekker).

THE RICH ARE ALWAYS WITH US (FN, 1932) 73 M.

Producer, Samuel Bischoff; director, Alfred E. Green; based on the novel by E. Pettit (Mrs. Arthur Somers Roche); screenplay, Austin Parker; music, W. Franke Harling; gowns, Orry-Kelly; camera, Ernest Haller; editor, George Marks.

Ruth Chatterton (Caroline Grannard); George Brent (Julian Tierney); Adrienne Dore (Allison Adair); Bette Davis (Malbro); John Miljan (Gregory Grannard); John Wray (Davis); Robert Warwick (The Doctor); Virginia Hammond (Flo); Walter Walker (Dante); Eula Guy (Mrs. Drake); Berton Churchill (The Judge); Edith Allen, Ethel Kenyon, Ruth Lee (Girls); Ruth Hall (Gossip in 1930); Georges Renavent (Headwaiter); Bill Elliott (Gambling Extra); Sam McDaniel (Max, the Butler); Lee Phelps (Messenger); Cecil Cunningham (Admirer).

WEEK-END MARRIAGE (FN, 1932) 66 M.

Director, Thornton Freeland; based on the novel Part-Time Wives by Faith Baldwin; screenplay, Sheridan Gibney; camera, Barney McGill; editor, Herbert Levy.

Loretta Young (Lola Davis); Norman Foster (Ken Hays); George Brent (Peter Acton); Aline MacMahon (Agnes); Vivienne Osborne (Shirley); Sheila Terry (Shirley); J. Farrell MacDonald (Davis); Louise Carter (Mrs. Davis); Grant Mitchell (The Doctor); Harry Holman (The Judge); Luis Alberni (Louis); J. Carroll Naish (Joe); Richard Tucker (Jameson).

MISS PINKERTON (FN, 1932) 66 M.

Director, Lloyd Bacon; based on the story by Mary Roberts Rinehart; screenplay, Lillian Hayward, Niven Busch; camera, Barney McGill; editor, Ray Curtis.

Joan Blondell [Miss Adams (Miss Pinkerton)]; George Brent (Inspector Patten); Mae Madison (Second Nurse); John Wray (Hugo); Ruth Hall (Paula Brent); Allan Lane (Herbert Wynne); C. Henry Gordon (Dr. Stewart); Donald Dillaway (Charles Elliott); Elizabeth Patterson (Aunt Juliet); Blanche Friderici (Mary); Mary Doran (Florence Lenz); Holmes Herbert (Arthur Glenn); Eulalie Jensen (Miss Gibbons); Treva

Lawler, Luana Walter (Nurses); Lucien Littlefield (Henderson); Nigel de Brulier (Coroner); Walter Brennan (Police Broadcaster); Lyle Talbot (Editor).

THE PURCHASE PRICE (WB, 1932) 70 M.

Director, William A. Wellman; based on the story "The Mud Lark" by Arthur Stringer; screenplay, Robert Lord; art director, Jack Okey; camera, Sid Hickox; editor, Bill Holmes.

Barbara Stanwyck (Joan Gordon); George Brent (Jim Gilson); Lyle Talbot (Ed Fields); Hardie Albright (Don Leslie); David Landau (Bull McDowell); Murray Kinnell (Spike Forgan); Leila Bennett (Emily); Matt McHugh (Waco); Clarence Wilson (Justice of the Peace); Lucille Ward (His Wife); Craufurd Kent (Peters); Anne Shirley (A Farmer's Daughter); Victor Potel (Clyde); Adele Watson (Mrs. Tipton); Snub Pollard (Joe).

THE CRASH (FN, 1932) 58 M.

Director, William Dieterle; based on the novel Children of Pleasure *by Larry Barretto; screenplay, Earl Baldwin, Barretto; camera, Ernest Haller.*

Ruth Chatterton (Linda Gault); George Brent (Geoffrey Gault); Paul Cavanagh (Ronald Sanderson); Barbara Leonard (Celeste); Henry Kolker (John Fair); Lois Wilson (Marcia Peterson); Ivan Simpson (Hodge); Helen Vinson (Esther Parish); Hardie Albright (Arthur); Edith Kingdon (Landlady); Richard Tucker (Frank Parrish); Virginia Hammond (Nadine).

THEY CALL IT SIN (FN, 1932) 75 M.

Director, Thornton Freeland; based on the novel by Alberta Stedman Eagan; screenplay, Lillian Hayward, Howard J. Green; camera, James Van Trees; editor, James Gibbons.

Loretta Young (Marion Cullen); George Brent (Dr. Tony Travers); David Manners (James Decker); Louis Calhern (Ford Humphries); Una Merkel (Dixie); Joseph Cawthorn (Mr. Hollister); Helen Vinson (Enid Hollister); Nella Walker (Mrs. Hollister); Miki Morita (Mato); Erville Alderson (Timothy Cullen); Elizabeth Patterson (Mrs. Cullen).

LUXURY LINER (PAR, 1933) 72 M.

Director, Lothar Mendes; based on the novel by Gina Kaus; screenplay, Gene Markey, Kathryn Scola; camera, Victor Milner.

George Brent (Dr. Thomas Bernhard); Zita Johann (Miss Morgan); Vivienne Osborne (Sybil Bernhard); Alice White (Milli Stern); Verree Teasdale (Luise Marheim); C. Aubrey Smith (Edward Thorndyke); Frank Morgan (Alex Stevanson); Henry Wadsworth (Fritz); Wallis Clark (Dr. Veith); Billy Bevan (Schultz); Theodor Von Eltz (Exl).

42nd STREET (WB, 1933) 89 M.

Producer, Darryl F. Zanuck; director, Lloyd Bacon; story, Bradford Ropes; screenplay, Rian James, James Seymour; songs, Al Dubin and Harry Warren; dances staged-directed by Busby Berkeley; camera, Sol Polito.

Warner Baxter (Julian Marsh); Bebe Daniels (Dorothy Brock); George Brent (Pat Denning); Una Merkel (Lorraine Fleming); Ruby Keeler (Peggy Sawyer); Guy Kibbee (Abner Dillon); Ned Sparks (Barry); Dick Powell (Billy Lawler); Ginger Rogers (Anytime Annie); Allen Jenkins (MacElroy); Henry B. Walthall (The Actor); Edward J. Nugent (Terry); Harry Akst (Jerry); Clarence Nordstrom (Leading Man); Al Dubin, Harry Warren (The Songwriters); George Irving (House Doctor); Robert McWade (Jones); George E. Stone (Andy Lee); Jack LaRue (Mug); Charles Lane (Author); Milton Kibbee (News Spreader); Harry Seymour (Aide); Kermit Maynard (42nd Street Dancer); Lyle Talbot (One of Dorothy's Friends); Rolfe Sedan (Stage Aide); June Glory, Jayne Shadduck, Adele Lacy, Dorothy Coonan, Loretta Andrews, Margaret La Marr, Mary Jane Halsey, Ruthie Eddings, Edna Callaghan, Patsy Farnum, Maxine Cantway, Lynn Browning, Donna Mae Roberts, Ann Hovey, Barbara Rogers, Renee Whitney, Lorena Layson, Geraine Grear (later Joan Barclay), Alice Jans, Gertrude Keeler, Helen Keeler, Pat Wing (Chorus Girls).

THE KEYHOLE (WB, 1933) 69 M.

Director, Michael Curtiz; based on the story "Adventuress" by Alice D. G. Miller; screenplay, Robert Presnell; dialog director, Arthur Greville Collins; art director, Anton Grot; gowns, Orry-Kelly; music director, Leo F. Forbstein; camera, Barney McGill; editor, Ray Curtiss.

Kay Francis (Anne Brooks); George Brent (Neil Davis); Glenda Farrell (Dot); Allen Jenkins (Hank Wales); Monroe Owsley (Maurice Le Brun); Helen Ware (Portia Brooks); Henry Kolker (Schuyler Brooks); Ferdinand Gottschalk (Brooks' Lawyer); Irving Bacon (Grover, the Chauffeur); Clarence Wilson (Weems, the Head of the Detective Agency); George Chandler (Joe, the Desk Clerk); Heinie Conklin (Departing Guest); Renee Whitney (Cheating Wife); John Sheehan (Bartender); Bill Elliott (Dancing Extra); George Humbert, Gino Corrado (Waiters); Maurice Black (Salesman); Leo White (Porter).

LILLY TURNER (FN, 1933) 63 M.

Director, William A. Wellman; based on the play by Philip Dunning, George Abbott; screenplay, Gene Markey, Kathryn Scola; camera, Sid Hickox; editor, Jim Morley.

Ruth Chatterton (Lilly Turner); George Brent (Bob Chandler); Frank McHugh (Dave Dixon); Ruth Donnelly (Edna); Guy Kibbee (Doc McGill); Gordon Westcott (Rex Durkee); Marjorie Gateson (Mrs. McGill); Arthur Vinton (Sam); Robert Barrat (Fritz); Grant Mitchell (Dr. Hawley); Margaret Seddon (Mrs. Turner); Hobart Cavanaugh (Earle); Mayo Methot (Mrs. Durkee); Katherine Clare Ward (Mrs. Flint); Lucille Ward (Mother); Mae Busch (Hazel).

BABY FACE (WB, 1933) 70 M.

Director, Alfred E. Green; story, Mark Canfield; screenplay, Gene Markey, Kathryn Scola; art director, Anton Grot; costumes, Orry-Kelly; camera, James Van Trees; editor, Howard Bretherton.

Barbara Stanwyck (Lily Powers); George Brent (Mr. Trenholm); Donald Cook (Mr. Stevens); Arthur Hohl (Ed Sipple); John Wayne (Jimmy McCoy); Henry Kolker (Mr. Carter); James Murray (Brakeman); Robert Barrat (Nick Powers); Margaret Lindsay (Ann Carter); Douglass Dumbrille (Mr. Brody); Theresa Harris (Chico); Renee Whitney (The Girl); Nat Pendleton (Stovich); Alphonze Ethier (Cragg); Harry Gribbon (Doorman); Arthur De Kuh (Lutza).

PRIVATE DETECTIVE 62 (WB, 1933) 67 M.

Director, Michael Curtiz; based on the short story by Raoul Whitfield; screenplay, Rian James; art director, Jack Okey; camera, Tony Gaudio.

William Powell (Donald Free); Margaret Lindsay (Janet Reynolds); Ruth Donnelly (Amy Moran); Gordon Westcott (Tony Bandor); James Bell (Whitey); Arthur Byron (Tracey); Natalie Moorhead (Helen Burns); Sheila Terry (Mrs. Wright); Arthur Hohl (Dan Hogan); Hobart Cavanaugh (Harcourt S. Burns); Theresa Harris (Maid); Renee Whitney (Alice); Ann Hovey (Rose); Irving Bacon (Cab Driver); Georges Renavent (Captain La Farge); Eddie Phillips (Lover); Toby Wing (Girl Friend); Pat Wing (Secretary); Eddie Dunn (Doorman); George Brent (Club Extra); Bill Elliott (Gambling Kibitzer); Rolfe Sedan (Casino Man); Harry Seymour (Gambler); Charles Wilson, Heinie Conklin (Bartenders); Charles Lane (Process Server).

Television title: MAN KILLER.

FEMALE (FN, 1933) 60 M.

Directors, Michael Curtiz, William Dieterle; based on the novel by Donald Henderson Clark; screenplay, Gene Markey, Kathryn Scola; art director, Jack Okey; camera, Sid Hickox; editor, Jack Killifer.

Ruth Chatterton (Alison Drake); George Brent (Jim Thorne); Johnny Mack Brown (Cooper); Ruth Donnelly (Miss Frothingham); Lois Wilson (Harriet Brown); Ferdinand Gottschalk (Pettigrew); Phillip Reed (Claybourne); Rafaela Ottiano (Della); Gavin Gordon (Briggs); Kenneth Thomson (Red); Huey White (Puggy); Douglass Dumbrille (Mumford); Walter Walker (Jarratt); Charles Wilson (Falihee); Edward Cooper (Butler); Spencer Charters (Tom).

FROM HEADQUARTERS (WB, 1933) 63 M.

Director, William Dieterle; story, Robert N. Lee; screenplay, Robert N. Lee, Peter Milne; dialog director, A. G. Collins; camera, William Reese.

George Brent (Lieutenant J. Stevens); Margaret Lindsay (Lou Ann Winton); Eugene Pallette (Sergeant Boggs); Hugh Herbert (Manny); Dorothy Burgess (Dolly White); Theodore Newton (Jack Winton); Hobart Cavanaugh (Muggs Manton); Robert Barrat (Anderzian); Henry O'Neill (Inspector Donnelly); Edward Ellis (Dr. Van de Water); Ken Murray (Mac); Kenneth Thomson (Gordon Bates); Robert Homans (Sergeant-Orderly); Frank Darien (Manly).

STAMBOUL QUEST (MGM, 1934) 88 M.

Director, Sam M. Wood; story, Leo Birinski; screenplay, Herman J. Mankiewicz; camera, James Wong Howe; editor, Hugh Wynn.

Myrna Loy (Annemarie); George Brent (Beall); Lionel Atwill (Von Strum); C. Henry Gordon (Ali Bey); Douglass Dumbrille (General); Rudolf Amendt (Anders) (Earl); Mischa Auer (Roberts); Robert Gleckler (Naval Officer); Reginald Barlow, Joseph Sawyer (German Officers); Christian Rub (Dentist); Judith Vosselli (Mata Hari); Belle Mitchell (Maid); Harry Schultz (Doorman); Edward Keane (Companion); Barlow Borland, Adrian Rosley (Waiters); Theodore Lodi (Officer); Otto H. Fries, Anders Von Haden (Conductors); Perry Ivins (Steward); Georges Renavent (Manager); Lal Chand Mehra (Turkish Officer); Tito H. Davison (Bellhop); Russ Powell (Fat German); Hans Joby, Frank Puglia (German Aides); Ralph Fitzsimmons (General); Hooper Atchley (German Colonel); Helen Freeman (Nun); Max Barwyn, Jamiel Hasson (Aides).

HOUSEWIFE (WB, 1934) 69 M.

Executive producer, Jack L. Warner; director, Alfred E. Green; story, Robert Lord, Lillie Hayward; screenplay, Manuel Seff, Hayward; songs, Mort Dixon and Allie Wrubel; music director, Leo F. Forbstein; art director, Robert Haas; gowns, Orry-Kelly; camera, William Rees; editor, James Gibbon.

George Brent (William Reynolds); Bette Davis (Patricia Berekeley); Ann Dvorak (Nan Reynolds); John Halliday (Paul Duprey); Ruth Donnelly (Dora); Hobart Cavanaugh (George); Robert Barrat (Sam Blake); Joseph Cawthorne (Kruger); Phil Regan (Radio Singer); Willard Robertson (Judge); Ronnie Cosbey (Buddy Reynolds); Leila Bennett (Jennie); Harry Tyler (Mr. Simmons); Charles Coleman (Bolton); Bill Elliott (Clerk); Pauline True (Typist); Leo White (Waiter); Eula Guy (Miss Finch); John T. Murray (Salesman); John Hale (Doctor); William B. Davidson (Bill's Lawyer); Lee Phelps (Court Clerk); Charles Coleman (Bolton); Johnny Murray (A Bouncer).

DESIRABLE (WB, 1934) 68M.

Director, Archie Mayo; based on a story by Mary McCall, Jr.; screenplay, McCall, Jr.; camera, Ernest Haller; editor, Thomas Pratt.

Jean Muir (Lois Johnson); George Brent (Stuart McAllister); Verree Teasdale (Helen Walbridge); John Halliday (Austin Stevens); Charles Starrett (Russell Gray); Russell Hopton (Chet); Virginia Hammond (Mrs. Gray); Joan Wheeler (Barbara); Catherine Sheldon (Volunteer Worker); Harry Tyler (Boxoffice Man); Gladys Gale (Large Woman); Edward Keane (Playgoer); Arthur Treacher (Butler); George Humbert (Mario, the Maitre d'); Johnny Skins Miller (Elevator Man); Pauline True

(Secretary); Jane Darwell, Maude Turner Gordon (Dowagers); Bill Elliott, Dennis O'Keefe (Party Guests); Cornelius Keefe (Eager Young Man); Helene Millard (Blonde); Georgia Cooper (Jennie); Theresa Harris (Maid).

THE PAINTED VEIL (MGM, 1934) 84 M.

Director, Richard Boleslawski; based on the novel by W. Somerset Maugham; screenplay, John Meehan, Salka Viertel, Edith Fitzgerald; Chinese production number, Chester Hale; camera, William Daniels; editor, Hugh Wynn.

Greta Garbo (Katherine Koerber Fane); Herbert Marshall (Dr. Walter Fane); George Brent (Jack Townsend); Warner Oland (General Yu); Jean Hersholt (Professor Koerber); Bodil Rosing (Frau Koerber); Katharine Alexander (Mrs. Townsend); Cecilia Parker (Olga); Soo Yong (Amah); John Billy Bevan (Bridegroom); Forrester Harvey (Waddington); Alice Cook (Curious Woman); Jane Kerr (Cruel Woman); Vernon Dent (Chief of Police); Gus Leonard (Major-Domo); Dorothea Wolbert (Stuttering Woman); Delmar Watson (Crying Boy); Lillian Lawrence (Spinster); Keye Luke (Shay Kee Seng, the Clerk); Olaf Hytten (Dr. Somerset); Herbert Farjean (Dr. Simons); James Wang (Proprietor of Curio Shop); Ethel Griffies (Lady Coldchester); Margaret Mann (Mother Superior); Leonard Mudie (Secretary); Lawrence Grant (English Governor); Colin Kenny (Bit).

THE RIGHT TO LIVE (WB, 1935) 75 M.

Director, William Keighley; based on the play The Sacred Flame by W. Somerset Maugham; screenplay, Ralph Block; camera, Sid Hickox; editor, Jack Killifer.

Josephine Hutchinson (Stella Houghton); George Brent (Colin Trent); Colin Clive (Maurice Trent); Peggy Wood (Nurse Wayland); Henrietta Crosman (Mrs. Trent); C. Aubrey Smith (Major Liconda); Leo G. Carroll (Dr. Harvester); Claude King (Mr. Pride); Nella Walker (Mrs. Pride); Halliwell Hobbes (Sir Stephen Barr); Phillis Coghlan (Maid); Gunnis Davis (Gardener); Jack H. Richardson (Chauffeur); Vesey O'Davoren (Waiter); Forrester Harvey (English Bobbie).

LIVING ON VELVET (WB, 1935) 77 M.

Supervisor, Edward Chodorov; director, Frank Borzage; story-screenplay, Jerry Wald, Julius Epstein; art director, Robert M. Haas; gowns, Orry-Kelly; music director, Leo F. Forbstein; camera, Sid Hickox; editor, William Holmes.

Kay Francis (Amy Prentiss); Warren William (Walter "Gibraltar" Pritcham); George Brent (Terrence Clarence Parker); Helen Lowell (Aunt Martha Prentiss); Henry O'Neill (Thornton); Samuel S. Hinds (Henry L. Parker); Russell Hicks (Major); Maude Turner Gordon (Mrs. Parker); Martha Merrill (Cynthia Parker); Edgar Kennedy (Counterman); Austa (Max, the Dachshund Dog); Sam Hayes (Announcer); Lee Shumway (Officer); Walter Miller (Leader); Emmett Vogan (Officer); Stanley King (Private); Niles Welch (Major's Aide); Selmer Jackson (Captain); May Beatty, Mrs. Wilfrid North (Dowagers); Harry Bradley (Party Guest); Grace Hayle (Woman); Harry Holman (Bartender); Wade Boteler (Desk Sergeant); Eric Wilton (Travis, Pritcham's Butler); Harold Nelson (Sexton); Frank Dodd (Minister); William Norton Bailey (Drew); David Newell (Smalley); John Cooper (Messenger Boy); Jack Richardson (Taxi Driver); Jay Eaton, Lloyd Whitlock (Men); Eddy Chandler (Policeman); Paul Fix (Interne); Frank Fanning (Doorman); Bud Geary (Aunt Martha's Chauffeur); Eddie Phillips (Eddie at Party); William Wayne (Butler); Bill Elliott (Commuter).

STRANDED (WB, 1935) 76 M.

Supervisor, Sam Bischoff; director, Frank Borzage; based on the story "Lady with a Badge" by Frank Wead. Ferdinand Reyher; screenplay, Delmer Daves; additional dialog, Carl Erickson; assistant director, Lew Borzage; art directors, Anton Grot, Hugh Reticker; gowns, Orry-Kelly; music director, Leo F. Forbstein; camera, Sid Hickox; editor, William Holmes.

Kay Francis (Lynn Palmer); George Brent (Mack Hale); Patricia Ellis (Velma Tuthill); Donald Woods (John Wesley); Barton MacLane (Sharkey); Robert Barrat (Stanislaus Januaschek); June Travis [Jennie Holden (Mary Rand)]; Henry O'Neill (Mr. Tuthill); Ann Shoemaker (Mrs. Tuthill); Frankie Darro (Jimmy Rivers); William Harrigan (Updyke); Joseph Crehan (Johnny Quinn); John Wray (Mike Gibbons); Edward McWade (Tim Powers); Gavin Gordon (Jack); Mary Forbes (Grace Dean); Emmett Vogan (Officer on Ferry); Sam McDaniel (Porter); Joan Gay (Diane Nichols); Edwin Mordant (Surgeon); Wilfred Lucas (Pat, a Worker); Mia Liu (Japanese Girl); Rita Rozelle (Polish Girl); Louise Seidel (Danish Girl); Frank LaRue (Doctor); Tom Wilson (Immigrant); Philo McCullough (Immigration Officer); Adrian Rosley (Headwaiter); Junior Coghlan (Page); Edwin Stanley (Police Surgeon); Milton Kibbee (Pat, the Timekeeper); Adrian Morris (Rivet Boss); Claudia Coleman (Madame); Sarah Padden (Workman's Wife); Richard Loo (A Groom); Frank Marlowe (Rollins, an Agitator); Leo White (Haines, a Drunken Worker); Vesey O'Davoren (Butler).

FRONT PAGE WOMAN (WB, 1935) 80 M.

Producer, Samuel Bischoff; director, Michael Curtiz; based on the story "Women Are Bum Newspapermen" by Richard Macaulay; screenplay, Roy Chanslor, Lillie Hayward, Laird Doyle; music, Heinz Roemheld; art director, John Hughes; camera, Tony Gaudio; editor, Terry Morse.

Bette Davis (Ellen Garfield); George Brent (Curt Devlin); Roscoe Karns (Toots); Winifred Shaw (Inez Cordova); Joseph Crehan (Spike Kiley); Joseph King (Hartnett); J. Farrell Macdonald (Hallohan); Addison Richards (District Attorney); Dorothy Dare, June Martel (Show Girls); Selmer Jackson (Joe Davis); Gordon Westcott (Maitland Colter); J. Carroll Naish (Mr. Roberts); Walter Walker (Judge Rickard); DeWitt C. Jennings (Lieutenant); Huntley Gordon (Marvin Q. Stone); Adrian Rosley (Tailor); Georges Renevant (Chinard); Miki Morita (Fuji); Adrian Morris, Eddie Shubert (Guards); George Guhl, James Burtis (Motor Cops); Frank Glendon, Edward Keane, Jack Norton, Charles E. Delaney, Harry Seymour (Reporters); Mary Treen (Nurse); Mary Foy (Landlady); Dick Winslow (Copy Boy); Leo White, Ben F. Hendricks (Taxi Drivers); James Farley (Bailiff); Wade Boteler (Cop).

THE GOOSE AND THE GANDER (WB, 1935) 65 M.

Director, Alfred E. Green; story-screenplay, Charles Kenyon; art director, Robert M. Haas; gowns, Orry-Kelly; music director, Leo F. Forbstein; camera, Sid Hickox; editor, Howard Leonard.

Kay Francis (Georgiana); George Brent (Bob McNear); Genevieve Tobin (Betty Summers); John Eldredge (Lawrence); Claire Dodd (Connie Thurston); Helen Lowell (Aunt Julia); Ralph Forbes (Ralph Summers); William Austin (Arthur Summers); Spencer Charters (Winklesteinbergher); Eddie Shubert (Sweeney); John Sheehan (Murphy); Charles Coleman (Jones); Wade Boteler, Davison Clark, Nick Copeland, Cliff Saum, Glen Cavender (Detectives); Al Woods (Bellboy); Milton Kibbee (Garageman); Jack Richardson (Baggage Man); David Newell (Hotel Clerk); Eddy Chandler (Policeman); Guy Usher (Sergeant); Edward McWade (Justice of Peace); Helen Woods (Violet); Bill Elliott (Teddy); Jan Buckingham (Mrs. Burns); Carlyle Blackwell, Jr. (Barkley); Olive Jones (Miss Brent).

SPECIAL AGENT (WB, 1935) 76 M.

Producer, Martin Mooney; director, William Keighley; idea, Mooney; screenplay, Laird Doyle, Abem Finkel; art director, Esdras Hartley; music director, Leo F. Forbstein; camera, Sid Hickox; editor, Clarence Kolster.

Bette Davis (Julie Carston); George Brent (Bill Bradford); Ricardo Cortez (Nick Carston); Joseph Sawyer (Rich); Joseph Crehan (Chief of Police); Henry O'Neill (District Attorney); Irving Pichel (U.S. District Attorney); Jack La Rue (Andrews); Robert Strange (Armitage); Joseph King (Wilson); William B.

Davidson (Young); J. Carroll Naish (Durrell); Paul Guilfoyle (Secretary to D.A.); Robert Barrat (Head of Internal Revenue Department); Charles Middleton, Thomas Jackson, Jack Mower (Cops); Jack McHugh, Billy Naylor (Newsboys); Garry Owen, John Dilson (Men); Milton Kibbee (Player); Edwin Argus (Looker-on); John Alexander (Manager); Jerry Fletcher (Young Man); Lucille Ward (Matron); Herbert Skinner (Henry); Allan Cavaen (Starter); Bob Montgomery, Huey White, Dutch Hendrian (Gangsters); Louis Natheaux (Clerk); John Kelly (Capper); Emmett Vogan (Police Announcer); Frank G. Fanning (Driver); Douglas Wood (Judge).

IN PERSON (RKO, 1935) 85 M.

Producer, Pandro S. Berman; director, William A. Seiter; based on the novel by Samuel Hopkins Adams; screenplay, Allan Scott; songs, Dorothy Fields and Oscar Levant; choreography Hermes Pan; camera, Edward Cronjager; editor, Arthur Schmidt.

Ginger Rogers (Carol Corliss); George Brent (Emory Muir); Alan Mowbray (Jay Holmes); Grant Mitchell (Judge Thaddeus Parks); Samuel S. Hinds (Dr. Aaron Sylvester); Joan Breslau (Minna); Louis Mason (Sheriff Twing); Spencer Charters ("Parson" Lunk); Bob McKenzie (Theatre Manager); Lee Shumway (Studio Representative); Lew Kelly (Man Giving Directions); William B. Davidson (Bill Sumner, the Director).

SNOWED UNDER (FN, 1936) 63 M.

Director, Raymond Enright; story, Lawrence Saunders; screenplay, F. Hugh Herbert, Brown Holmes; camera, Arthur Todd; editor, Harold McLernon.

George Brent (Alan Tanner); Genevieve Tobin (Alice Merritt); Glenda Farrell (Daisy Lowell); Patricia Ellis (Pat Quinn); Frank McHugh (Orlando Rowe); John Eldredge (Robert McBride); Porter Hall (Arthur Layton); Helen Lowell (Mrs. Canterbury); Olin Howland (Sheriff); Joseph King (Jean); John Elliott, Stuart Holmes (Actors); Richard Purcell (Bert); Kay Hughes (Dumb Stenographer); George Sorel (Milkeimer); Eddie Shubert (Taxi Driver); Iris March, Naomi Judge (Girls); Shirley Lloyd (Blonde); Mary Treen, Alma Lloyd (Secretaries); George Andre Beranger (Maza); Lester Dorr, Edward Peil, Sr. (Men in Producer's Office).

THE GOLDEN ARROW (FN, 1936) 68 M.

Producer, Samuel Bischoff; director, Alfred E. Green; based on the play by Michael Arlen; screenplay, Charles Kenyon; music, W. Franke Harling, Heinz Roemheld; music director, Leo F. Forbstein; gowns, Orry-Kelly; camera, Arthur Edeson; editor, Thomas Pratt.

Bette Davis (Daisy Appleby); George Brent (Johnny Jones); Carol Hughes (Hortense Burke-Meyers); Eugene Pallette (Mr. Meyers); Dick Foran (Tommy Blake); Catharine Doucet (Mrs. Pommesby); Craig Reynolds (Jorgenson); Hobart Cavanaugh (De Wolfe); Henry O'Neill (Mr. Appleby); Ivan Lebedeff (Count Giggi Guilliano); G. P. Huntley, Jr. (Aubrey Rutherford); Rafael Storm (Prince Peter); E. E. Clive (Walker); Eddie Acuff (Davis); Earle A. Foxe (Parker); Carlyle Moore, Jr. (Mr. Rogers); Naomi Judge (Mrs. Clarke); Colleen Coleman (Miss Jones); Shirley Lloyd (Miss French); Larry Kent (Mr. Smith); George Andre Beranger (Florist); Billy Arnold (Officer); Ed Hart (Steward); Rudolf Amendt (Anders) (Max); Jose Rubic (Renaldo); Bess Flowers (Miss Hackett); Eddie Shubert (Swing Operator); Mary Treen (Secretary); Bill Elliott, Don Brodie, Eddie Fetherston, Frank Faylen (Reporters); Richard Powell (Motor Cop); Alma Lloyd (Telephone Girl); John T. Murray (City Editor).

THE CASE AGAINST MRS. AMES (PAR, 1936) 85 M.

Producer, Walter Wanger; director, William A. Seiter; based on the story by Arthur Somers Roche; screenplay, Gene Towne, Graham Baker; camera, Lucien Andriot; editor, Dorothy Spencer.

Madeleine Carroll (Hope Ames); George Brent (Matt Logan); Arthur Treacher (Griggsby); Alan Baxter (Lou); Beulah Bondi (Mrs. Livingston Ames); Alan Mowbray (Lawrence Waterson); Brenda Fowler (Mrs. Shumway); Esther Dale (Matilda); Edward Brophy (Sid); Richard Carle (Uncle Gordon); Scotty Beckett (Bobbie Ames); Mayo Methot (Cora); Guy Bates Post (Judge Davis); June Brewster (Laurette); Elvira Curci (Jeanette); Jonathan Hale (Judge); Margaret Bloodgood (Police Matron); Edward Earle (Maitland Harris); Ed LeSaint (Dr. Caswell); Max Wagner (Soupy); Richard Powell (Ferry Boat Porter); Otto Hoffman (Jury Foreman); Tom Ricketts, Bobby Bolder, Phil Dunham, Frank Hammond (Jurymen); Albert Conti (Headwaiter); Bruce Mitchell (Druggist).

GIVE ME YOUR HEART (WB, 1936) 87 M.

Supervisor, Robert Lord; director, Archie Mayo; based on the play Sweet Aloes *by Jay Mallory (Joyce Carey); screenplay, Casey Robinson; camera, Sidney Hickox; editor, James Gibbon.*

Kay Francis (Linda Warren); George Brent (Jim Baker); Roland Young (Tubbs Barrow); Patric Knowles (Robert Melford); Henry Stephenson (Edward, Lord Farrington); Frieda Inescort (Rosamond Melford); Helen Flint (Dr. Florence Cudahy); Halliwell Hobbes (Oliver); Zeffie Tilbury (Esther Warren); Elspeth Dudgeon (Alice Dodd); Russ Powell (Cab Driver); Edgar Norton (Servant); Dick French, Ethel Sykes (Guests); Bruce Warren (Young Man); Elsa Petersen (Young Woman); Louise Bates (Hostess); Carlyle Moore, Jr. (Elevator Man); Mitchell Ingraham (Bartender); Alphonse Martel (Dining Room Captain); Toekie Trigg (Edward, the Baby); Helena Grant (Nurse); Wayne and Teske (Dance Team).

MORE THAN A SECRETARY (Col, 1936) 77 M.

Producer, Everett Riskin; director, Alfred E. Green; based on a story by Ethel Hill, Aben Kandel, based on the story "Safari in Manhattan" by Matt Taylor; screenplay, Dale Van Every, Lyn Starling; camera, Henry Freulich; editor, Al Clark.

Jean Arthur (Carol Baldwin); George Brent (Fred Gilbert); Lionel Stander (Ernest); Ruth Donnelly (Helen Davis); Reginald Denny (Bill Houston); Dorothea Kent (Maizie West); Charles Halton (Mr. Crosby); Geraldine Hall (Enid); Charles Irwin (Mounted Policeman); Myra Marsh (Sour-Faced Woman); Ann Meril (Betty); William Bartlett (Contortionist); Tom Ricketts (Henry); Josephine McKim (Gladys); Dorothy Short (Ann); Francis Sayles (Waiter); Nick Copeland, C. L. Sherwood (Window Washers); Frances Morris (Clerk); George Hickman (Office Boy); Joy Kendell (Telephone Girl); Cyril Ring, Ralph McCullough (Department Heads); Lily Stewart (Woman); William Wagner (Man).

GOD'S COUNTRY AND THE WOMAN (WB, 1936) C—80 M.

Producer, Hal B. Wallis; associate producer, Lou Edelman; director, William Keighley; based on the novel by James Oliver Curwood; adaptors, Peter Milne, Charles Balden; screenplay, Norman Reilly Raine; Technicolor advisor, William V. Skall; camera, Tony Gaudio; editor, Jack Killifer.

George Brent (Steve Russett); Beverly Roberts (Jo Barton); Barton MacLane (Bullhead Fradette); Robert Barrat (Jeff Russett); Alan Hale (Big Bjorn Skalka); Addison Richards (Harry Gaskett); El Brendel (Ole Olson); Roscoe Ates (Gander); Billy Bevan (Plug Hat); Bert Roach (Kewpie); Joseph Crehan (Jordan); Mary Treen (Miss Flint); Joseph King (Alex Monroe); Vic Potel (Turpentine); Harry Hayden (Barnes); Pat Moriarity (Tim); Susan Fleming (Grace Moran); Eily Malyon (Mrs. Higginbottom); Shirley Lloyd (Secretary); Andre Cheron (Monsieur Gagnon); Georgette Rhodes (French Teletype Operator); Robert Bell (French Messenger); Joan Woodbury (French Woman); Minerva Urecal (Maisie); Herbert Rawlinson (Doyle); Hal Craig (Motorcycle Cop); Saul Gorss, Max Wagner (Loggers); Mathilde Comont (Mary); Bob Stevenson (Lars); George Chandler (Flunky).

THE GO-GETTER (WB, 1937) 90 M.

Producer, Hal B. Wallis; associate producer, Sam Bischoff; director, Busby Berkeley; story, Peter B. Kyne; screenplay, Delmer Daves; dialog director, Irving Rapper; music director, Leo F. Forbstein; song, Jack Scholl and M. K. Jerome; art director, Hugh Relicker; gowns, Orry-Kelly; camera, Arthur Edeson; editor, William Holmes.

George Brent (Bill Peck); Anita Louise (Margaret); Charles Winninger (Cappy Ricks); John Eldredge (Skinner); Henry O'Neill (Commander Tisdale); Willard Robertson (Matt Peasley); Eddie Acuff (Bob); Mary Treen (Bride); Craig Reynols, Carlyle Moore, Jr. (Macon Survivors); Gordon Oliver (Mr. Luce); James Robbins (Information Clerk); Joseph Crehan (Stone); Herbert Rawlinson (Lester Brent); Edward Gargan (Policeman); Helen Lowell (Mr. Luce's Mother); Harry Beresford (Mr. Barker); Helen Valkis (Skinner's Secretary); Minerva Urecal (Cappy Ricks' Secretary); Edward Price (Radio Operator); Max Hoffman, Jr. (Navigating Officer); Lane Chandler (Radio Officer); Myrtle Stedman (Nurse); George Chandler (Card Printer); Ann Doran (Maizie, the Maid); Charles Coleman (Butler); Ward Bond, Ben Hendricks, Alan Bridge, Pat Flaherty (Loggers); Sam McDaniel (Black Man); Etta McDaniel (Black Woman); Harrison Greene, Harry Depp (Men); Mathilde Comont (Marie).

MOUNTAIN JUSTICE (WB, 1937)

Director, Michael Curtiz; story-screenplay, Norman Reilly Raine, Luci Ward; art director, Max Parker; camera, Ernest Haller; editor, George Amy.

Josephine Hutchinson (Ruth Harkins); George Brent (Paul Cameron); Guy Kibbee (Dr. Barnard); Robert Barrat (Jeff Harkins); Mona Barrie (Evelyn Wayne); Elisabeth Risdon (Meg Harkins); Margaret Hamilton (Phoebe); Edward Pawley (Tod Miller); Marcia Mae Jones (Bethy Harkins); Fuzzy Knight (Clem Biggers); Robert McWade (Horace Bamber); Granville Bates (Judge Crawley); Russell Simpson (Turnbull); Sibyl Harris (Mrs. Turnbull); Guy Wilkerson (Asaph Anderson); Claire DuBrey (Young Woman); Gertrude Hoffman (Granny Burnside); Alice Lyndon (Charity Topping); Henry Hall (Henniger); Harry Davenport (Printer); Jim Toney (Makeup Man); Earle Hodgins (Vendor); Minerva Urecal (Ella Crippen); Herbert Heywood (Jury Foreman); Carl Stockdale (Stout); Walter Soderling (Sheriff Willis); Arthur Aylesworth (Justice of the Peace); Virginia Brissac (Miss Hughes); Heinie Conklin (Jury Foreman); Dennis Moore (Airplane Pilot)

SUBMARINE D-1 (WB, 1937) 98 M.

Director, Lloyd Bacon; story, Frank Wead; screenplay, Wead, Warren Duff, Lawrence Kimble; camera, Arthur Edeson; editor, William Holmes.

Pat O'Brien (Butch Rogers); George Brent (Lieutenant Commander Matthews); Wayne Morris (Sock McGillis); Doris Weston (Ann Callam); Frank McHugh (Lucky); Henry O'Neill (Admiral Thomas); Dennie Moore (Arabella); Veda Ann Borg (Dolly); Regis Toomey (Tom Callam); John Ridgely (Lieutenant Junior Grade); Owen King (Lieutenant Senior Grade); Wally Maher (Listener); Jerry Fletcher (Lieutenant Mason); Dick Wessel, Ralph Dunn, Jeffrey Sayre, Don DeFore, Dick French, Allan Kenward, Sol Gorss, Don Turner, John Shea, Mike Lally, Billy Vincent, Eric Pettit, Gordon Clifford (Sailors); Don Briggs (Instructor); Eddie Fetherston (Bluejacket); Pat Flaherty (Disagreeable Sailor); Walter Miller (Salvage Officer); John Elliott (Father); Walter Clyde (Orderly); Lee Phelps (Marine Orderly); Allan Cavan (Skipper).

GOLD IS WHERE YOU FIND IT (WB, 1938) C—90 M.

Producer, Hal B. Wallis; associate producer, Sam Bischoff; director, Michael Curtiz; story, Clements Ripley; screenplay, Warren Duff, Robert Buckner; music, Max Steiner; music director, Leo F. Forbstein; special effects, Byron Haskin; camera, Sol Polito; editor, Clarence Kolster.

George Brent (Jared Whitney); Olivia de Havilland (Serena Ferris); Claude Rains (Colonel Ferris); Margaret Lindsay

(Roseanne Ferris); John Litel (Ralph Ferris); Tim Holt (Lanceford Ferris); Barton MacLane (Slag Minton); Henry O'Neill (Judge); Marcia Ralston (Molly Featherstone); George F. Hayes (Enoch Hewitt); Sidney Toler (Harrison McCoy); Robert McWade (Crouch); Clarence Kolb (Senator Walsh); Harry Davenport (Dr. Parsons); Russell Simpson (McKenzie); Willie Best (Helper); Moroni Olsen (Senator Hearst); Granville Bates (Nixon); Charles Halton (Turner); Erville Alderson (Cryder); Cy Kendall (Kingan); Robert Homans (Grogan); Eddy Chandler (Deputy); Richard Botiller (Ramon); Cliff Saum (Medicine Man); Arthur Aylesworth (Rancher); Wilfred Lucas, Thomas Mills, John Harron (Men at Stock Exchange); Walter Rogers (General Grant); Daisy Lee (Chinese Maid); Eric Wilton (Butler); Edmund Cobb, James Farley (Miners); Alan Davis (Clerk).

JEZEBEL (WB, 1938) 104 M.

Executive producer, Hal B. Wallis; associate producer, Henry Blanke; director, William Wyler; based on the play by Owen Davis, Sr.; screenplay, Clement Ripley, Abem Finkel, John Huston; script contributor, Robert Buckner; costumes, Orry-Kelly; music, Max Steiner; music director, Leo F. Forbstein; song, Harry Warren and Johnny Mercer; art director, Robert Haas; camera, Ernest Haller; editor, Warren Low.

Bette Davis (Julie Morrison); Henry Fonda (Preston Dillard); George Brent (Buck Cantrell); Margaret Lindsay (Amy Bradford Dillard); Fay Bainter (Aunt Belle Massey); Richard Cromwell (Ted Dillard); Donald Crisp (Dr. Livingstone); Henry O'Neill (General Theopholus Bogardus); John Litel (Jean Le Cour); Gordon Oliver (Dick Allen); Janet Shaw (Molly Allen); Spring Byington (Mrs. Kendrick); Margaret Early (Stephanie Kendrick); Georgia Caine (Mrs. Petion); Irving Pichel (Huger); Georges Renavent (De Lautrec); Fred Lawrence (Bel); Ann Codee (Madame Poulard, the Dressmaker); Lew Payton (Uncle Cato); Eddie Anderson (Gros Bat); Theresa Harris (Zette); Stymie Beard (Ti Bat); Sam McDaniel (Driver); Charles Wagenheim (Customer); Jacques Vanaire (Duretta); Daisy Bufford (Flower Girl); Trevor Bardette (Sheriff at Plantation); Jack Norton (Drunk); Alan Bridge (New Orleans Sheriff)

RACKET BUSTERS (WB, 1938) 71 M.

Associate producer, Samuel Bischoff; director, Lloyd Bacon; story-screenplay, Robert Rossen, Leonardo Bercovici; music, Adolph Deutsch; orchestrator, Hugo Friedhofer; assistant director, Dick Mayberry; art director, Esdras Hartley; gowns, Howard Shoup; sound, Robert B. Lee; camera, Arthur Edeson; editor, James Gibbon.

George Brent (Denny Jordan); Humphrey Bogart (John "Czar" Martin); Gloria Dickson (Nora Jordan); Allen Jenkins (Skeets Wilson); Walter Abel (Hugh Allison); Penny Singleton (Gladys Christie); Henry O'Neill (Governor); Oscar O'Shea (Pop); Elliott Sullivan (Charlie Smith); Fay Helm (Mrs. Smith); Joe Downing (Joe); Norman Willis (Gus); Don Rowan (Cliff Kimball); Anthony Averill (Dave Crane); Mary Currier (Mrs. Allison); Wedgwood Nowell (Business Man); Egon Brecher (Peters); Herbert Heywood (Gas Station Owner); Irving Bacon (Counterman); Dale Van Sickel (Special Officer); Georgie Cooper (Woman); Gordon Hart (Minister); Harry Tenbrook (Hood); William B. Davidson (Union Chairman); Charles Trowbridge (Judge); Monte Vandergrift (Detective).

SECRETS OF AN ACTRESS (WB, 1938) 70 M.

Producer, David Lewis; director, William Keighley; based on the story "Lovely Lady"; ada tators, Milton Krims, Rowland Leigh, Julius J. Epstein; camera, Sid Hickox; editor, Owen Marks.

Kay Francis (Fay Carter); George Brent (Dick Orr); Ian Hunter (Peter Snowden); Gloria Dickson (Carla Orr); Isabel Jeans (Marian Plantagenet); Penny Singleton (Miss Reid); Dennie Moore (Miss Blackstone); Selmer Jackson (Thompson); Herbert Rawlinson (Harrison); Emmett Vogan (Spencer); James B. Carson (Carstairs).

WINGS OF THE NAVY (WB, 1939) 89 M.

Producers, Jack L. Warner, Hal B. Wallis; associate producer, Lou Edelman; director, Lloyd Bacon; story-screenplay, Michael Fessier; camera, Arthur Edeson, Elmer Dyer; editor, William Holmes.

George Brent (Cass Harrington); Olivia de Havilland (Irene Dale); John Payne (Jerry Harrington); Frank McHugh (Scat Allen); John Litel (Commander Clark); Victor Jory (Lieutenant Parsons); Henry O'Neill (Prologue Speaker); John Ridgely (Dan Morrison); John Gallaudet (Lieutenant Harry White); Don Briggs, Regis Toomey (Instructors); Edgar Edwards (Ted Parsons); Alberto Morin (Armando Costa); Pierre Watkin (Captain March); Don Douglas (Officer of the Day); Max Hoffman (Officer); Alan Davis (Check Pilot); Renie Riano (Woman); Lee Phelps (Conductor); Selmer Jackson (Doctor); Walter Miller (Henry); Max Wagner (Boss Mechanic); Carlyle Moore, Jr., Larry Williams, Ed Parker (Navy Men); Mary Gordon (Housekeeper); Joseph Crehan (Doctor); William Davidson (Brown); Howard Hickman (Captain Dreen); Jack Gardner (Mechanic).

DARK VICTORY (WB, 1939) 105 M.

Producer, Hal B. Wallis, in association with David Lewis; director, Edmund Goulding; based on the play by George Emerson Brewer, Jr., Bertram Block; screenplay, Casey Robinson; music, Max Steiner; music director, Leo F. Forbstein; costumes, Orry-Kelly; song, Goulding and Elsie Janis; art director, Robert Haas; camera, Ernest Haller; editor, William Holmes.

Bette Davis (Judith Traherne); George Brent (Dr. Frederick Steele); Humphrey Bogart (Michael O'Leary); Geraldine Fitzgerald (Ann King); Ronald Reagan (Alec Hamin); Henry Travers (Dr. Parsons); Cora Witherspoon (Carrie Spottswood); Virginia Brissac (Martha); Dorothy Peterson (Miss Wainwright); Charles Richman (Colonel Mantle); Herbert Rawlinson (Dr. Carter); Leonard Mudie (Dr. Driscoll); Fay Helm (Miss Dodd); Lottie Williams (Lucy); Diane Bernard (Agatha); Jack Mower (Veterinarian); William Worthington, Alexander Leftwich (Specialists); Ila Rhodes (Secretary); Jeffrey Sayre, Will Morgan, Wedgwood Nowell, Nat Carr, Ed Graham, Jack Goodrich (Doctors); Edgar Edwards (Trainer); Rosella Towne (Girl in Box); Sidney Bracy (Bartender); John Ridgely, John Harron (Men); Frank Darien (Anxious Little Man); Speirs Buskell (Dr. Steele's Assistant).

THE OLD MAID (WB, 1939) 95 M.

Producer, Hal B. Wallis, in association with Henry Blanke; director, Edmund Goulding; based on the play by Zöe Atkins as adapted from Edith Wharton's novel; screenplay, Casey Robinson; music, Max Steiner; music director, Leo F. Forbstein; costumes, Orry-Kelly; art director, Robert Haas; camera, Tony Gaudio; editor, George Amy.

Bette Davis (Charlotte Lovell); Miriam Hopkins (Delia Lovell); George Brent (Clem Spender); Jane Bryan (Tina); Donald Crisp (Dr. Lanskell); Louise Fazenda (Dora); James Stephenson (Jim Ralston); Jerome Cowan (Joe Ralston); William Lundigan (Lanning Halsey); Cecilia Loftus (Henrietta Lovell); Rand Brooks (Jim); Janet Shaw (Dee Ralston); William Hopper (John Ward); Marlene Burnett (Tina as a Child); Doris Lloyd (Aristocratic Maid); Frederick Burton (Mr. Halsey).

THE RAINS CAME (20th, 1939) 103 M.°

Producer, Darryl F. Zanuck; associate producer, Harry Joe Brown; based on the novel by Louis Bromfield; screenplay, Philip Dunne, Julien Josephson; music, Alfred Newman; songs, Mack Gordon and Harry Revel; Lal Chand Mehra; costumes, Gwen Wakeling; set designer, Thomas Little; sound, Alfred Bruzlin, Roger Heman; special camera effects, Fred Sersen; camera, Arthur Miller; editor, Barbara McLean.

Myrna Loy (Lady Edwina Esketh); Tyrone Power (Major Rama Safti); George Brent (Tom Ransome); Brenda Joyce (Fern Simon); Nigel Bruce (Albert, Lord Esketh); Maria Ous-

penskaya (Maharani); Joseph Schildkraut (Mr. Bannerjee); Mary Nash (Miss MacDaid); Jane Darwell (Aunt Phoebe Smiley); Marjorie Rambeau (Mrs. Simon); Henry Travers (Reverend Homer Smiley); H. B. Warner (Maharajah); Laura Hope Crews (Lily Hoggett-Egbury); William Royle (Raschild Ali Khan); Montague Shaw (General Keith); Harry Hayden (Reverend Elmer Simon); Herbert Evans (Bates); Abner Biberman (John the Baptist); Mara Alexander (Mrs. Bannerjee); William Edmunds (Mr. Das); Adele Labanset, Sonie Charsky (Princesses); Rita Page (Maid); Connie Leon, Rosina Galli (Nurses); Pedro Regas (Official); Frank Lackteen (Engineer); George Regas (Rajput); Leyland Hodgson (Doctor); Eddie Abdo (Soldier); Fern Emmett (Hindu Woman); Dominie Duval (Girl); Guy D'Ennery (Mr. Durga).
°Filmed in sepia.

THE FIGHTING 69th (WB, 1940) 89 M.

Executive producer, Hal B. Wallis; producer, Jack L. Warner; director, William Keighley; screenplay, Norman Reilly Raine, Fred Niblo, Jr., Dean Franklin; art director, Ted Smith, assistant director, Frank Heath; technical advisers, Captain John T. Prout, Mark White; music, Adolph Deutsch; orchestrator, Hugo Friedhofer; music director, Leo F. Forbstein; make-up, Perc Westmore; sound, Charles Lang; special effects, Byron Haskin, Rex Wimpy; camera, Tony Gaudio; editor, Owen Marks.

James Cagney (Jerry Plunkett); Pat O'Brien (Father Duffy); George Brent (Wild Bill Donovan); Jeffrey Lynn (Joyce Kilmer); Alan Hale (Sergeant Big Mike Wynn); Frank McHugh ("Crepe Hanger" Burke); Dennis Morgan (Lieutenant Ames); William Lundigan (Timmy Wynn); Dick Foran (John Wynn); Guinn "Big Boy" Williams (Paddy Dolan); Henry O'Neill (The Colonel); John Litel (Captain Mangan); Sammy Cohen (Mike Murphy); Harvey Stephens (Major Anderson); William Hopper (Private Turner); Tom Dugan (Private McManus); George Reeves (Jack O'Keefe); Charles Trowbridge (Chaplain Holmes); Frank Wilcox (Lieutenant Norman); Herbert Anderson (Casey); J. Anthony Hughes (Healey); Frank Mayo (Captain Bootz); John Harron (Carroll); George Kilgen (Ryan); Richard Clayton (Tierney); Edward Dew (Regan); Wilfred Lucas, Joseph Crehan, Emmett Vogan (Doctors); Frank Sully (Sergeant); James Flavin (Supply Sergeant); George O'Hanlon (Eddie); Jack Perrin (Major); Trevor Bardette, John Arledge, Frank Melton, Edmund Glover (Alabama Men); Edgar Edwards (Engineer Officer); Ralph Dunn (Medical Captain); Arno Frey, Roland Varno (German Officers); Layne Ireland (Hefferman); Elmo Murray (O'Brien); Jacques Lory (Waiter); Frank Coghlan, Jr. (Jimmy); Frank Faylen (Engineer Sergeant); Jerry Fletcher (Telephonist); Byron Nelson, Sol Gorss (Soldiers).

ADVENTURE IN DIAMONDS (PAR, 1940) 76 M.

Director, George Fitzmaurice; based on a story by Frank O'Connor; screenplay, Leonard Lee, Franz Schulz; camera, Charles Lang; editor, LeRoy Stone.

George Brent (Captain Stephen Bennett); Isa Miranda (Felice Falcon); John Loder (Michael Barclay); Nigel Bruce (Colonel J. W. Lansfield); Elizabeth Patterson (Nellie); Matthew Boulton (Lloyd); Rex Evans (Jimmy); Cecil Kellaway (Emerson); Walter Kingsford (Wakefield); Ernest Truex (Toutasche); Ralph Forbes (Mr. Ferrins); Nikolayeva (Mrs. Perrins); E. E. Clive (Mr. Macpherson); Vera Lewis (Mrs. Macpherson); Edward Gargan (Lou); Charles Irwin (Nelson); David Clyde (Bartender); Rex Downing ("Buttons," the Page Boy); Guy Bellis, Norman Ainsley (Immigration Officers); Hi Roberts (Bellhop); Major Sam Harris (Bill); Roger Gray (Sergeant at Airport); Wilfred Roberts (Man); Carleton Young (American Sailor); Ambrose Barker (Customs Official).

'TIL WE MEET AGAIN (WB, 1940) 99 M.

Producers, Jack L. Warner, Hal B. Wallis; associate producer, David Lewis; director, Edmund Goulding; story, Robert Lord; screenplay, Warren Duff; camera, Tony Gaudio; editor, Ralph Dawson.

Merle Oberon (Joan Ames); George Brent (Dan Hardesty); Pat O'Brien (Steve Burke); Geraldine Fitzgerald (Bonnie Coburn); Binnie Barnes (Countess de Vaubert); Frank McHugh (Achilles Peddicord); Eric Blore (Sir Harold Landamuir); George Reeves (Jimmy Coburn); Henry O'Neill (Dr. Cameron); Frank Wilcox (Assistant Purser); Doris Lloyd (Louise, the Maid); John Ridgely (Junior Officer); Marjorie Gateson (Mrs. Hestor); Regis Toomey (Freddy); William Halligan (Barman); Victor Kilian (McGillis); Wade Boteler (Stoddard); Charles Sherlock (Master-at-Arms); Frank Orth (Bartender); Maris Wrixon, Jane Gilbert, Mary Anderson (Girls); Frank Mayo, William Hopper (Men); Chester Gan (Hong Kong Policeman); Sol Gorss (Sailor); Jeffrey Sayre, Jack Mower (Stewards); Lynn Merrick (Daughter of Fussy Woman); Grace Hayle (Fussy Woman Passenger); William Gould (Chief of Police); Robert Elliott, Edwin Parker (Detectives); Walter Miller (American Bartender); Frank Puglia, George Regas (Mexican Bartenders).

THE MAN WHO TALKED TOO MUCH (WB, 1940) 75 M.

Associate producer, Edmund Grainger; director, Vincent Sherman; based on the play The Mouthpiece by Frank J. Collins; screenplay, Walter DeLeon, Tom Reed; camera, Sid Hickox; editor, Thomas Pratt.

George Brent (Stephen Forbes); Virginia Bruce (Joan Reed); Brenda Marshall (Celia Farraday); Richard Barthelmess (J. B. Roscoe); William Lundigan (Johnny Forbes); John Litel (D.A. Dixon); George Tobias (McNutt); Henry Armetta (Spirella); Alan Baxter (Garland); Marc Lawrence (Lofty Kyler); Clarence Kolb (Mr. Smith); John Ridgely (Assistant District Attorney Brooks); David Bruce (Wilson); Louis Jean Heydt (Barton); Ed Stanley (D.A. Nelson); Paul Phillips (Trigger); Elliott Sullivan (Bill); Dick Rich (Butch); William Forrest (Federal D.A. Greene); William Gould (Chief Kendall); Kay Sutton (Mrs. Knight); William Hopper, George Haywood, Creighton Hale (Reporters); Lottie Williams (Wilson's Mother); Frank Mayo (Keeper); Cliff Saum, Glen Cavender, Jack Richardson (Prisoners); Rosina Galli (Mrs. Spirella); Maris Wrixon, Phyllis Hamilton (Secretaries); Harry Seymour (Painter); Vera Lewis (Woman); Susan Peters (Girl); George Reeves (Hotel Clerk); Sam McDaniel (Porter); James Blaine (Guard).

SOUTH OF SUEZ (WB, 1940) 86 M.

Director, Lewis Seiler; story, Sheridan Gibney; screenplay, Barry Trivers; camera, Arthur Todd; editor, Clarence Kolster.

George Brent [John Gamble (Bradley)]; Brenda Marshall (Katherine Sheffield); George Tobias (Eli Snedeker); Lee Patrick (Delia Snedeker); James Stephenson (Inspector Thornton); Eric Blore (Limey); Miles Mander (Roger Smythe); Cecil Kellaway (Henry Putnam); Mary Forbes (Mrs. Putnam); Stanley Logan (Prosecutor); Frederic Worlock (Defense Counsel); Edward Fielding (Judge); Leonard Mudie (Registrar); Gilbert Emery (Manders); Charles Irwin (Gervia); Holmes Herbert (Simpson); Craufurd Kent (Sedley); Alec Harford (Pidgeon); James Robinson (Boy); Hassan Said (Mechanic); James Levis (Mako); Nathan Curry, Frank Baker (Guards); Frank Hagney (Miner); Ernie Stanton (Private Detective); Leyland Hodgson (Man); Sidney Bracy (Butler); Fern Emmett (Mrs. Wemsley).

HONEYMOON FOR THREE (WB, 1941) 77 M.

Director, Lloyd Bacon; based on the play Goodbye Again by Alan Scott, George Haight; screenplay, Earl Baldwin; camera, Ernest Haller; editor, Rudi Fehr.

Ann Sheridan (Anne Rogers); George Brent (Kenneth Bixby); Charles Ruggles (Harvey Wilson); Osa Massen (Julie Wilson); Jane Wyman (Elizabeth Clochessy); William T. Orr (Arthur Westlake); Lee Patrick (Mrs. Pettjohn); Walter Catlett (Waiter); Herbert Anderson (Floyd T. Ingram); Johnny Downs (Chester T. Farrington III).

THE GREAT LIE (WB, 1941) 102 M.

Producer, Hal B. Wallis, in association with Henry Blanke; director, Edmund Goulding; based on the novel January Heights *by Polan Banks; screenplay, Lenore Coffee; music, Max Steiner; music director, Leo F. Forbstein; gowns, Orry-Kelly; art director, Carl Jules Weyl; camera, Tony Gaudio; editor, Ralph Dawson.*

Bette Davis (Maggie Patterson); George Brent (Pete Van Allen); Mary Astor (Sandra Kovak); Lucile Watson (Aunt Ada); Hattie McDaniel (Violet); Grant Mitchell (Joshua Mason); Jerome Cowan (Jock Thomson); Sam McDaniel (Jefferson); Thurston Hall (Worthington James); Charles Trowbridge (Senator Greenfield); Russell Hicks (Colonel Harriston); Virginia Brissac (Sadie); Olin Howland (Ed); J. Farrell MacDonald (Dr. Ferguson); Doris Lloyd (Bertha); Alphonse Martell (Waiter); Georgia Caine (Mrs. Pine); Charlotte Wynters (Mrs. Anderson); Cyril Ring (Harry Anderson); George Kirby (Minister); Addison Richards (Mr. Talbot); Georges Renavent (Maitre d'Hotel); Richard Clayton (Page Boy); George Reed (Butler); Napoleon Simpson (Parker).

THEY DARE NOT LOVE (COL, 1941) 76 M.

Producer, Samuel Bischoff; director, James Whale; story, James Earl Grant; screenplay, Charles Bennett, Ernest Vajda; music director, Morris W. Stoloff; camera, Franz F. Planer; editor, Al Clark.

George Brent (Prince Kurt von Rotenburg); Martha Scott (Marta Keller); Paul Lukas (Baron von Helsing); Egon Brecher (Professor Keller); Roman Bohnen (Baron Shafter); Edgar Barrier (Captain Wilhelm Ekhardt); Kay Linaker (Barbara Murdock); Frank Reicher (Captain).

INTERNATIONAL LADY (UA, 1941) 102 M.

Producer, Edward Small; associate producer, Stanley Logan; director, Tim Whelan; story, E. Lloyd Sheldon, Jack De Witt; screenplay, Howard Estabrook; music director, Lud Gluskin; music, Lucien Moraweck; gowns, Gwen Wakeling; assistant director, Sam Nelson; sound, Earl Sitar; camera, Hal Mohr; supervising editor, Grant Whytock.

George Brent (Tim Hanley); Ilona Massey (Carla Nilson); Basil Rathbone (Reggie Oliver); Gene Lockhart (Sidney Grenner); George Zucco (Webster); Francis Pierlot (Dr. Rowan); Martin Kosleck (Brunner); Charles D. Brown (Tetlow); Marjorie Gateson (Mrs. Grenner); Leyland Hodgson (Moulton); Clayton Moore (Sewell); Gordon DeMain (Denby); Frederic Worlock (Sir Henry); Jack Mulhall (Desk Clerk); Ralph Dunn (Don); Robert Fiske (Headwaiter); Selmer Jackson (Colonel); John Dilson (Decoding Expert); William Forrest (Frank Cromwell, the American Consul); Martin Garralaga (Lisbon Cab Man); Charles McAvoy (New York Airport Guard); Marten Lamont (Lieutenant Fenwick); Trevor Bardette (Krell, the Chemist); Otto Reichow (German Radio Operator); Harold Goodwin (Decoder on Piano).

TWIN BEDS (UA, 1942) 85 M.

Producer, Edward Small; associate producer, Stanley Logan; director, Tim Whelan; based on the play by Margaret Mayo, Salisbury Field; screenplay, Curtis Kenyon, Kenneth Earl, E. Edwin Moran; art director, John DuCasse Schulze; music, Dimitri Tiomkin; camera, Hal Mohr; editor, Francis Lyons.

George Brent (Mike Abbott); Joan Bennett (Julie Abbott); Mischa Auer (Nicholai Cherupin); Una Merkel (Lydia); Glenda Farrell (Sonya); Ernest Truex (Lark); Margaret Hamilton (Maid); Charles Coleman (Butler); Charles Arnt (Butler); Cecil Cunningham (Secretary).

IN THIS OUR LIFE (WB, 1942) 97 M.

Producer, Hal B. Wallis, in association with David Lewis; director, John Huston; based on the novel by Ellen Glasgow; screenplay, Howard Koch; music, Max Steiner; music director, Leo F. Forbstein; gowns, Orry-Kelly; art director, Robert Haas; camera, Ernest Haller; editor, William Holmes.

Bette Davis (Stanley Timberlake); Olivia de Havilland (Roy Timberlake); George Brent (Craig Fleming); Dennis Morgan (Peter Kingsmill); Charles Coburn (William Fitzroy); Frank Craven (Asa Timberlake); Billie Burke (Lavinia Timberlake); Hattie McDaniel (Minerva Clay); Lee Patrick (Betty Wilmoth); Mary Servoss (Charlotte Fitzroy); Ernest Anderson (Parry Clay); William Davidson (Jim Purdy); Edward Fielding (Dr. Buchanan); John Hamilton (Inspector); William Forrest (Ranger); Elliott Sullivan, Eddie Acuff, Walter Baldwin, Herbert Heywood, Alan Bridge (Workers); Pat McVey (Man); George Reed (Waiter); Walter Huston (Bartender); Humphrey Bogart, Mary Astor, Peter Lorre, Sydney Greenstreet, Ward Bond, Barton MacLane, Elisha Cook, Jr. (Roadhouse Customers); Reid Kilpatrick (Announcer); Lee Phelps (Policeman); Sunshine Sammy Morrison, Napoleon Simpson, Billy Mitchell, Sam McDaniel, Ira Buck Wood (Blacks).

THE GAY SISTERS (WB, 1942) 110 M.

Producer, Henry Blanke; director, Irving Rapper; based on the novel by Stephen Longstreet; screenplay, Lenore Coffee; art director, Robert Haas; Ms. Stanwyck's costumes, Edith Head; music, Max Steiner; music director, Leo F. Forbstein; orchestrator, Hugo Friedhofer; camera, Sol Polito; editor, Warren Low.

Barbara Stanwyck (Fiona Gaylord); George Brent (Charles Barclay); Geraldine Fitzgerald (Evelyn Gaylord); Donald Crisp (Ralph Pedloch); Gig Young (Gig Young); Nancy Coleman (Susanna Gaylord); Gene Lockhart (Herschell Gibbon); Larry Simms (Austin); Donald Woods (Penn Sutherland Gaylord); Grant Mitchell (Gilbert Wheeler); William T. Orr (Dick Tone); Anne Revere (Ida Orner); Helene Thimig (Saskia); George Lessey (Judge Barrows); Charles D. Waldron (Mr. Van Rennsseler); Frank Reicher (Dr. Bigelow); David Clyde (Benson); Mary Thomas (Fiona at Age Eight).

YOU CAN'T ESCAPE FOREVER (WB, 1942) 77 M.

Producer, Mark Hellinger; director, Jo Graham; story, Roy Chanslor; screenplay, Fred Niblo, Jr., Hector Chevigny; art director, Stanley Fleischer; camera, Tony Gaudio; editor, Frank McGee.

George Brent (Steve Mitchell); Brenda Marshall (Laurie Abbott); Paul Harvey (Major Turner); Roscoe Karns ("Mac" McTurk); Gene Lockhart (Carl Robelink); Charles Halton (Charles Gates); Eduardo Ciannelli (Boss Greer); George Meeker (Cummings); Joseph Downing (Varney); Don De Fore (Reporter Davis); Erville Alderson (Crowder); Fay Helm (Kirsty); Ed McWade (Jimmy); John Dilson (Pop).

SILVER QUEEN (UA, 1942) 80 M.

Producer, Harry Sherman; director, Lloyd Bacon; screenplay, Bernard Schubert, Cecile Kramer; art director, Ralph Berger; camera, Russell Harlan; editor, Sherman A. Rose.

George Brent (James Kincaid); Priscilla Lane (Coralie Adams); Bruce Cabot (Gerald Forsythe); Lynne Overman (Hector Bailey); Eugene Pallette (Steve Adams); Janet Beecher (Mrs. Forsythe); Guinn "Big Boy" Williams (Blackie); Roy Barcroft (Dan Carson); Eleanor Stewart (Millicent Bailey); Arthur Hunnicutt (Brett); Sam McDaniel (Toby); Spencer Charters (Doc Stonebraker); Cy Kendall (Sheriff); Georges Renavent (Andre); Francis X. Bushman, Franklyn Farnum (Creditors); Marietta Canty (Ruby); Herbert Rawlinson (Judge); George Eldredge (Admirer); Earle Hodgins (Desk Clerk); Fred "Snowflake" Toones (Butler); Frederick Burton (Dr. Hartley); Ed Cassidy (Colonel); Jason Robards (Bank Teller).

EXPERIMENT PERILOUS (RKO, 1944) 91 M.

Executive producer, Robert Fellows; producer, Warren Duff; director, Jacques Tourneur; based on the novel by Margaret Carpenter; screenplay, Duff; art directors, Albert S. D'Agostino, Jack Okey; set decorators, Darrell Silvera, Claude Carpenter; music, Roy Webb; music director, C. Bakaleinikoff; assistant director, Dewey Starkey; sound, John E. Tribby; special effects, Vernon L. Walker; camera, Tony Gaudio; editor, Ralph Dawson.

Hedy Lamarr (Allida Bedereaux); George Brent (Dr. Huntington Bailey); Paul Lukas (Nick Bedereaux); Albert Dekker (Claghorne); Carl Esmond (John Maitland); Olive Blakeney (Cissie Bedereaux); George Neise (Alec Gregory); Margaret Wycherly (Maggie); Stephanie Bachelor (Elaine); Mary Servoss (Miss Wilson); Julia Dean (Deria); William Post, Jr. (D.A. MacDonald); Billy Ward (Alec at Age Five); Alan Ward (Shoes); Nolan Leary (Bellhop); Larry Wheat (Caterer); Sam McDaniel (Porter); Edward Clark (Train Steward); Joel Friedkin (Brakeman); Broderick O'Farrell (Frank); Jack Deery (Doorman); Almeda Fowler (Clerk); John Elliott (Telephone Operator); Charles McMurphy (Cop); Michael Orr (Nick at Age Three); Peggy Miller (Cissie at Age Eight); Evelyn Falke (Cissie at Age Five); Janet Clark (Deria as a Girl); Georges Renavent, Adrienne D'Ambricourt (Voice Instructors); John Mylong (Nick, Sr.); Michael Visaroff (Ballet Master); Perc Launders (Ambulance Man).

THE AFFAIRS OF SUSAN (PAR, 1945) 110 M.

Producer, Hal B. Wallis; director, William A. Seiter; story, Thomas Monroe, Laszlo Gorog; screenplay, Monroe, Gorog, Richard Flournoy; art directors, Hans Dreier, Franz Bachelin; set decorator, Kenneth Swartz; music, Frederick Hollander; assistant director, Dink Templeton; sound, Earl S. Hayman; process camera, Farciot Edouart; camera, David Abel; editor, Eda Warren.

Joan Fontaine (Susan Darell); George Brent (Roger Berton); Dennis O'Keefe (Bill Anthony); Walter Abel (Richard Aiken); Don De Fore (Mike Ward); Rita Johnson (Mona Kent); Mary Field (Nancy); Byron Barr (Chick); Francis Pierlot (Uncle Jemmy); Lewis Russell (Mr. Cusp); Vera Marshe (Brooklyn Girl); James Millican (Major); Crane Whitley (Colonel); Warren Hymer (Waiter); Alice Fleming (Dowager); Milton Kibbee (Whortle); Ruth Roman (Girl at "Bright Dollar"); Mira McKinney (Actress at First Party); Wallace Earl, Brooke Evans, June Harris, Lucy Knoch, Mavis Murray, Adelaide Norris, Marjorie Silk, Jane Starr (Chorus Girls).

MY REPUTATION (WB, 1946) 96 M.

Producer, Henry Blanke; director, Curtis Bernhardt; based on the novel Instruct My Sorrows *by Clare Jaynes; screenplay, Catherine Turney; art director, Anton Grot; set decorator, George James Hopkins; assistant director, Jesse Hibbs; music, Max Steiner; music director, Leo F. Forbstein; sound, Everett A. Brown; special effects, Roy Davidson; camera, James Wong Howe; editor, David Weisbart.*

Barbara Stanwyck (Jessica Drummond); George Brent (Major Scott Landis); Warner Anderson (Frank Everett); Lucile Watson (Mrs. Kimball); John Ridgely (Cary Abbott); Eve Arden (Ginna Abbott); Esther Dale (Anna); Jerome Cowan (George Van Ormand); Leona Maricle (Rietta Van Ormand); Scotty Beckett (Kim Drummond); Bobby Cooper (Keith Drummond); Ann Todd (Gretchen Van Ormand).

THE SPIRAL STAIRCASE (RKO, 1946) 83 M.

Producer, Dore Schary; director, Robert Siodmak; based on the novel Some Must Watch *by Ethel Lina White; screenplay, Mel Dinelli; art directors, Albert S. D'Agostino, Jack Okey; set decorator, Darrell Silvera; assistant director, Harry Scott; music, Roy Webb; music director, C. Bakaleinikoff; sound, John L. Cass; special effects, Vernon L. Walker; camera, Nicholas Musuraca; editors, Harry Marker, Harry Gerstad.*

Dorothy McGuire (Helen Capel); George Brent (Professor Warren); Ethel Barrymore (Mrs. Warren); Kent Smith (Dr. Parry); Rhonda Fleming (Blanche); Gordon Oliver (Steve Warren); Elsa Lanchester (Mrs. Oates); Sara Allgood (Nurse Barker); Rhys Williams (Mr. Oates); James Bell (Constable); Charles Wagenheim (Desk Clerk); Ellen Corby (Neighbor); Richard Tyler (Freddie); Erville Alderson (Dr. Harvey).

TOMORROW IS FOREVER (RKO, 1946) 105 M.

Producer, David Lewis; director, Irving Pichel; based on the novel by Gwen Bristow; screenplay, Lenore Coffee; assistant

director, John Sherwood; music, Max Steiner; associate music director, Lou Forbes; production designer, Wiard B. Ihnen; sound, Corson Jowett, Arthur Johns; camera, Joseph Valentine; editor, Ernest Nims.

Claudette Colbert (Elizabeth MacDonald Hamilton); Orson Welles [John (MacDonald) Kessler]; George Brent (Larry Hamilton); Lucile Watson (Aunt Jessie); Richard Long (Drew); Natalie Wood (Margaret); Sonny Howe (Brian); John Wengraf (Dr. Ludwig); Ian Wolfe (Norton); Douglas Wood (Charles Hamilton); Joyce MacKenzie (Cherry); Tom Wirick (Pudge); Henry Hastings (Butler); Lane Watson (Hamilton's Secretary); Michael Ward (Baby Drew); Jesse Graves (Servant); Lois Austin (Receptionist); Anne Loos (Freckled-Faced Nurse); Irving Pichel (Commentator's Voice); Thomas Louden (Englishman on Ship); Charles D. Brown (Immigration Officer); Milton Kibbee (Postman); Ann Howard, Marguerite Campbell, Betty Greco, Bobby Brooks, Barbara Bletcher (Girl Friends); Libby Taylor (Maid); Lane Chandler (Technician); Boyd Irwin (Dr. Callan).

LOVER COME BACK (UNIV, 1946) 90 M.

Executive producer, Howard Benedict; producers, Michael Fessier, Ernest Pagano; director, William A. Seiter; screenplay, Fessier, Pagano; art directors, Jack Otterson, Martin Obzina; set decorators, Russell A. Gausman, Ted Offenbecker; music, Hans J. Salter; sound, Bernard B. Brown; assistant director, Fred Frank; camera, Joseph Valentine; editor, Ray Snyder.

George Brent (Bill Williams); Lucille Ball (Kay); Vera Zorina (Madeline Laslo); Charles Winninger (Pa); Carl Esmond (Paul); Raymond Walburn (J. P. Winthrop); Elisabeth Risdon (Ma); Louise Beavers (Martha); Wallace Ford (Tubbs); Franklin Pangborn (Hotel Clerk); William Wright (Jimmy Hennessey); George Chandler (Waiter); Joan Shawlee (Janie); Pat Alphin, Dorothy Christy (Receptionists); Lane Chandler (Reporter); Ellen Corby (Rita); Lloyd Ingraham (Partner); Mary Moore, Joan Graham, Gwen Donovan (Show Girls).

TEMPTATION (UNIV, 1946) 92 M.

Producer, Edward Small; director, Irving Pichel; based on the novel Bella Donna *by Robert Hichens and the play by James Bernard Fagan; screenplay, Robert Thoeren; art director, Bernard Herzbrun; set decorator, Hugh Hunt; music, Daniele Amfitheatrof; assistant director, Frank Shaw; sound, Glenn Anderson; camera, Lucien Ballard; editor, Ernest Nims.*

Merle Oberon (Ruby); George Brent (Nigel); Charles Korvin (Bareudi); Paul Lukas (Isaacson); Lenore Ulric (Marie); Arnold Moss (Ahmed); Ludwig Stossel (Dr. Mueller); Gavin Muir (Smith-Harrington); Ilka Gruning (Frau Meuller); Robert Capa (Hamza); John Eldredge (Don Gibbs); Andre Charlot (Professor Dupont); Suzanne Cloutier (Yvonne Dupont); Gloria Lloyd (Jean McCormick); Mary Young (Mrs. McCormick); Aubrey Mather (Dr. Harding); Samir Rizkallah (Abdullah); Egon Brecher (Ibrahim); Reginald Sheffield (Wickersham); Eddie Abdo (Egyptian Policeman); Lane Watson (Guest); Nick Thompson (Native Waiter); Bobby Hale (Coachman); Jean Ransome (Receptionist).

SLAVE GIRL (UNIV, 1947) C—79 M.

Producers, Michael Fessier, Ernest Pagano; director, Charles Lamont; screenplay, Fessier, Pagano; art director, Abraham Grossman; set decorators, Russell A. Gausman, Edward R. Robinson; music, Milton Rosen; music arranger-orchestrator, David Tamkin; choreography, Si-Lan Chen; assistant director, Ralph Stosser; sound, Charles Felstead, Glenn E. Anderson; camera, George Robinson, W. Howard Greene; editor, Frank Gross.

Yvonne De Carlo (Francesca); George Brent (Matt Claibourne); Broderick Crawford (Chips Jackson); Albert Dekker (Pasha); Lois Collier (Aleta); Andy Devine (Ben); Carl Esmond (El Hamid); Arthur Treacher (Liverpool); Philip Van Zandt (Yusef); Dan Seymour (Telek Taurog); Trevor Bardette (Proprietor of "Sign of the Grapes"); Eddie Dunn (Captain);

Mickey Simpson (Head Guard); Rex Lease, George J. Lewis, Jack Ingram, Harold Goodwin, Don Turner, Phil Schumacher, Jack Shutta, Paul Bratti, Joseph Haworth (Americans); Toni Raimando (Slave Girl); June Marlowe (Mildred); Shimen Ruskin (Rug Merchant); Nancy Brinckman (Maid); Roseanne Murray (Sally); Harry Cording (Guard Captain); Noble Johnson (Native Guard); Jack Reitzen (Auctioneer); Rudolph Medina, Harry Lamont, Tony Del Rio (Natives in Torture Chamber); Bert Richman, Eddie Abdo, Michael Gaddis (Natives); Lloyd Ingraham (Locksmith).

THE CORPSE CAME C.O.D. (COL, 1947) 87 M.

Producer, Samuel Bischoff; director, Henry Levin; based on the novel by Jimmy Starr; screenplay, George Bricker, Dwight Babcock; art directors, Stephen Goosson, George Brooks; set decorators, Wilbur Menefee, James Crowe; music, George Duning; music director, Morris Stoloff; songs, Allan Roberts and Doris Fisher; assistant director, Carl Hiecke; sound, Jack Haynes; montage, Donald W. Starling; camera, Lucien Andriot; editor, Jerome Thoms.

George Brent (Joe Medford); Joan Blondell (Rosemary Durant); Adele Jergens (Mona Harrison); Jim Bannon (Detective Mark Wilson); Leslie Brooks (Peggy Holmes); John Berkes (Larry Massey); Fred Sears (Detective Dave Short); William Trenk (Fields); Grant Mitchell (Mitchell Edwards); Una O'Connor (Nora); Marvin Miller (Rudy Frasso); William Forrest (Lance Fowler); Mary Field (Felice); Cliff Clark (Emmett Willard); Wilton Graff (Maxwell Kenyon); Cosmo Sardo (Hector Rose); Judy Stevens (Specialty Singer); Wally Rose (Assistant Director); Robert Winkler (Copy Boy); Richard Abbott (Doctor); Alvin Hammer (Patient Man); Gregory Gay (Director); Lane Chandler (Prison Guard); Robert Kellard, Myron Healey, Paul Bryar, Michael Towne (Reporters); Martha West (Cigarette Girl); Leon Lenoir (Waiter).

OUT OF THE BLUE (Eagle Lion, 1947) 86 M.

Producer, Bryan Foy; director, Leigh Jason; story, Vera Caspary; screenplay, Caspary, Walter Bullock, Edward Eliscu; assistant director, Howard W. Koch; art director, Edward Jewell; set decorator, Armor Marlowe; music, Carmen Dragon; song, Will Jason and Henry Nemo; music director, Irving Friedman; sound, Leon Becker, William H. Lynch; special camera effects, George J. Teague; camera, Jackson Rose; editor, Norman Colbert.

George Brent (Arthur Earthleigh); Virginia Mayo (Deborah Tyler); Turhan Bey (David Gelleo); Ann Dvorak (Olive Jensen); Carole Landis (Mae Earthleigh); Elizabeth Patterson (Miss Spring); Julia Dean (Miss Ritchie); Richard Lane (Detective Noonan); Charles Smith (Elevator Boy); Paul Harvey (Holliston); Alton E. Horton (Detective Dombry); Hadda Brooks (Black Singer); Flame the Dog (Rabelais); Robert Bilder (Milkman); Dorothy Douglas (Hatcheck Girl); Billy Newell (Danny, the Bartender); Lee Phelps (Motorcycle Cop); Jerry Marlowe (Cop); Marcia Ralston (Patricia); Ralph Sanford (Desk Sergeant).

CHRISTMAS EVE (UA, 1947) 90 M.

Producer, Benedict Bogeaus; director, Edwin L. Marin; story, Laurence Stallings, Richard H. Landau; screenplay, Stallings; art director, Ernst Fegte; set decorator, Eugene Redd; music, Heinz Roemheld; music director, David Chudnow; assistant director, Joseph Depew; sound, William Lynch; camera, Gordon Avil; editor, James Smith.

George Raft (Mario Torio); George Brent (Michael Brooks); Randolph Scott (Jonathan); Joan Blondell (Ann Nelson); Virginia Field (Claire); Dolores Moran (Jean); Ann Harding (Matilda Reid); Reginald Denny (Phillip Hastings); Carl Harbord (Dr. Doremus); Clarence Kolb (Judge Alston); John Litel (F.B.I. Agent); Joe Sawyer (Gimlet); Douglass Dumbrille (Dr. Bunyan); Dennis Hoey (Williams); Molly Lamont (Harriett); Walter Sande (Hood); Konstantin Shayne (Reichman); Marie Blake (Girl Reporter); Soledad Jimenez (Rosita); Holly Bane (Mike Regan, Page Boy).
A.k.a.: SINNER'S HOLIDAY.

LUXURY LINER (MGM, 1948) C—98 M.

Producer, Joe Pasternak; director, Richard Whorf; screenplay, Gladys Lehman, Richard Connell; additional dialog, Karl Lamb; art directors, Cedric Gibbons, Paul Groesse; set decorators, Edwin B. Willis, Arthur Krams; music director, Georgie Stoll; song, Janice Torre, Fred Spielman, and Fritz Rotter; assistant director, Joseph Depew; choreography, Nick Castle; costumes, Jean Louis; sound, Frank McWhorter; camera, Ernest Laszlo; editor, James Smith.

George Brent (Captain Jeremy Bradford); Jane Powell (Polly Bradford); Lauritz Melchior (Olaf Ericksen); Frances Gifford (Laura Dene); Marina Koshetz (Zita Romaka); Xavier Cugat (Himself); Thomas E. Breen (Denis Mulvy); Richard Derr (Charles Morton); John Ridgely (Chief Officer Carver); Chuck Lowry, Harold Hopper, Clark Yocum, June Hutton (The Pied Pipers); Connie Gilchrist (Bertha); Lee Tung Foo (Fu Dong); Georgette Windsor (Perdita); Romo Vincent (Pierre); Michael Dugan (Officer); Kay Norton (Ship's Hostess); Shirley Johns (Count Karper); Betty Blythe (Miss Fenmoor); Juanita Quigley (Jean); Roger Moore, Wes Hopper (Waiters); May McAvoy (Woman).

ANGEL ON THE AMAZON (REP, 1948) 86 M.

Associate producer-director, John H. Auer; story, Earl Felton; screenplay, Lawrence Kimble; art director, James Sullivan; set decorators, John McCarthy, Jr., George Milo; music, Nathan Scott; music director, Morton Scott; makeup, Bob Mark; assistant director, Lee Lukather; sound, Victor B. Appel, Howard Wilson; special effects, Howard and Theodore Lydecker; camera, Reggie Lanning; editor, Richard L. Van Enger.

George Brent (Jim Warburton); Vera Ralston (Christine Ridgeway); Brian Aherne (Anthony Ridgeway); Constance Bennett (Dr. Karen Lawrence); Fortunio Bonanova (Sebastian Ortega); Alfonso Bedoya (Paulo); Gus Schilling (Dean Hartley); Richard Crane (Johnny MacMahon); Walter Reed (Jerry Adams); Ross Elliott (Frank Lane); Konstantin Shayne (Dr. Jungmeyer); Charles LaTorre (Waiter); Manuel Paris (Night Desk Clerk); Dick Jones (George); Alberto Morin (Radio Operator); Elizabeth Dunne (housekeeper); Geraldo Sei Groves (Bellhop).

RED CANYON (UNIV, 1949) C—84 M.

Producer, Leonard Goldstein; associate producer, Aaron Rosenberg; director, George Sherman; based on the novel Wildfire by Zane Grey; screenplay, Maurice Geraghty; art directors, Bernard Herzbrun, Frank A. Richards; set decorators, Russell A. Gausman, Joseph Kish; assistant director, John Sherwood; music, Walter Scharf; makeup, Bud Westmore, John Holden; costumes, Rosemary Odell; sound, Leslie I. Carey, Vernon W. Kramer; camera, Irving Glassberg; editor, Otto Ludwig.

Ann Blyth (Lucy Bostel); Howard Duff [Lin Slone (Cordt)]; George Brent (Mathew Bostel); Edgar Buchanan (Jonah Johnson); John McIntire (Floyd Cordt); Chill Wills (Brackton); Jane Darwell (Aunt Jane); Lloyd Bridges (Virgil Cordt); James Seay (Joel Creech); Edmund MacDonald (Farlane); Denver Pyle (Hutch); Willard Willingham (Van); Hank Patterson (Osborne); Ray Bennett (Pronto); Hank Worden (Charley); Sonny Chorres (Indian); Edmund Cobb, John Carpenter (Men).

ILLEGAL ENTRY (UNIV, 1949) 84 M.

Producer, Jules Shermer; director, Frederick de Cordova; based on a story by Ben Bengal, Herbert Kline, Dan Moore; adaptor, Art Cohn; screenplay, Joel Malone; art directors, Bernard Herzbrun, Richard A. Riedel; set decorators, Russell A. Gausman, John Austin; music director-orchestrator, Milton Schwarzwald; assistant director, Fred Frank; makeup, Bud Westmore; costumes, Yvonne Wood; sound, Leslie I. Carey, Joe Lapis; special effects, David S. Horsley; camera, William Daniels; editor, Edward Curtiss.

Howard Duff (Bert Powers); Marta Toren (Anna Duvak);

George Brent (Dan Collins); Gar Moore (Lee Sloan); Tom Tully (Nick Gruber); Paul Stewart (Zack Richards); Richard Rober (Dutch Lempo); Joseph Vitale (Joe Bottsy); James Nolan (Benson); Clifton Young (Bill Rafferty); David Clarke (Carl); Robert Osterloh (Crowthers); Anthony Caruso (Teague); Donna Martell (Maria); Kenneth Tobey (Dave); Curt Conway (Thin-Faced Man); Waldon Boyle (Payson); Pierce Lyden (Gunman); Vito Scotti (Mexican Youth); Ray Flynn (Bartender); Jack Chefe (Man); Slim Crow (Immigration Officer); Alex Akimoff, Betty Chay (Aliens).

THE KID FROM CLEVELAND (REP, 1949) 89 M.
Producer, Walter Colmes; associate producer, K. Elmo Lowe; director, Herbert Kline; story, Kline, John Bright; screenplay, Bright; music, Nathan Scott; orchestrator, Stanley Wilson; assistant director, Richard Moder; makeup, Bob Mark, Louis Hipple; sound, T. A. Carman, Howard Wilson; camera, Jack Marta; editor, Jason H. Bernie.

George Brent (Mike Jackson); Lynn Bari (Katherine Jackson); Rusty Tamblyn (Johnny Barrows); Tommy Cook (Dan Hudson); Ann Doran (Emily Novak); Louis Jean Heydt (Carl Novak); K. Elmo Lowe (Dave Joyce); John Berardino (Mac); Bill Veeck, Lou Boudreau, Tris Speaker, Hank Greenberg, Bob Feller, Gene Bearden, Satchell Paige, Bob Lemon, Steve Gromek, Joe Gordon, Mickey Vernon, Ken Keltner, Ray Boone, Dale Mitchell, Larry Doby, Bob Kennedy, Jim Hegan (Cleveland Indians Baseball Team).

BRIDE FOR SALE (RKO, 1949) 87 M.
Producer, Jack H. Skirball; director, William D. Russell; story, Joseph Fields, Frederick Kohner; screenplay, Bruce Manning, Islin Auster; art directors, Albert S. D'Agostino, Carroll Clark; set decorators, Darrell Silvera, William Stevens; music, Frederick Hollander; music director, C. Bakaleinikoff; assistant director, Fred Fleck; costumes, Sophie; makeup, Gordon Bau; sound, Frank Sarver, Clem Portman; camera, Joseph Valentine; editor, Frederic Knudtson.

Claudette Colbert (Nora Shelly); Robert Young (Steve Adams); George Brent (Paul Martin); Max Baer (Litka); Gus Schilling (Timothy); Charles Arnt (Dobbs); Mary Bear (Miss Stone); Ann Tyrrell (Miss Swanson); Paul Maxey (Gentry); Burk Symon (Sitley); Stephen Chase (Drake); Anne O'Neal (Miss Jennings); Eula Guy (Miss Clarendon); John Michaels (Terry); Georgia Caine (Mrs. Willis); William Vedder (Brooks); Thurston Hall (Mr. Trisby); Florence Auer (Eloise Jonathan); Grace Hampton (Harriet Jonathan); Archie Twitchell (Officer White); Harry Tyler (Wrestling Announcer); John Indrisano (Mug); Harry Cheshire (Haskins); Hans Conried (Jewelry Salesman); Ann Cameron (Girl); Frank Orth (Police Sergeant); Bokhara (Egyptian Dancer).

FBI GIRL (Lippert, 1951) 71 M.
Producer-director, William Berke; story, Rupert Hughes; screenplay, Richard Landau, Dwight Babcock; art director, F. Paul Sylos; music, Darrell Calker; camera, Jack Greenhaigh; editor, Phil Cahn.

Cesar Romero (Glen Stedman); George Brent (Jeff Donley); Audrey Totter (Shirley Wayne); Tom Drake (Carl Chercourt); Raymond Burr (Blake); Raymond Greenleaf (Governor Grisby); Tom Noonan, Pete Marshall (Television Act); Margia Dean (Natalie Craig); Alexander Pope (George Denton); Richard Monohan (Donald); Don Garner (Paul Craig); Jan Kayne (Doris); Walter Coy (Priest); Byron Foulger (Morgue Attendant); Joel Marston (Hotel Clerk); Marie Blake (Landlady).

THE LAST PAGE (Exclusive, 1952) 84 M.
Producer, Anthony Hinds; director, Terence Fisher; story,

James Hadley Chase; screenplay, Frederick Knott; camera, Walter Harvey; editor, Maurice Rootes.

George Brent (John Harman); Marguerite Chapman (Stella); Raymond Huntley (Clive); Peter Reynolds (Jeff); Diane Dors (Ruby); Eleanor Summerfield (Vi); Meredith Edwards (Dale); Harry Fowler (Joe); Conrad Phillips (Todd); Isabel Dean (May).

U.S. release title: MAN BAIT (Lippert, 1952) 80 M.

MONTANA BELLE (RKO, 1952) C—81 M.
Producer, Howard Welsch; associate producer, Robert Peters; director, Allan Dwan; story, M. Coates Webster, Welsch; screenplay, Horace McCoy, Norman S. Hall; art director, Frank Arrigo; set decorator, John McCarthy, Jr.; music, Nathan Scott; orchestrator, Stanley Wilson; sound, Earl Crain, Sr.; camera, Jack Marta; editor, Arthur Roberts.

Jane Russell (Belle Starr); George Brent (Tom Bradfield); Scott Brady (Bob Dalton); Forrest Tucker (Mac); Andy Devine (Pete Bivins); Jack Lambert (Ringo); John Litel (Matt Towner); Ray Teal (Emmett Dalton); Rory Mallinson (Grat Dalton); Roy Barcroft (Jim Clark); Holly Bane (Mike Regan) (Ben Dalton); Eugene Roth (Marshal Ripple); Gregg Barton (Deputy Stewart); Glenn Strange, Cactus Mack (Deputies); Dennis Moore (Messenger); Stanley Andrews (Marshal Combs); Dick Elliott (Jeptha Rideout, the Banker); Kenneth MacDonald (Sheriff Irving); Iron Eyes Cody (Cherokee); Rex Lease (Barfly); Franklyn Farnum (Man in Audience); Frank Ellis (Kibitzer); Hank Bell (Bartender).

TANGIER INCIDENT (AA, 1953) 77 M.
Producer, Lindsley Parsons; associate producer, Ace Herman; director, Lew Landers; story-screenplay, George Bricker; art director, David Milton; camera, William Sickner; editor, Leonard W. Herman.

George Brent (Steve); Mari Aldon (Millicent); Dorothy Patrick (Nadine); Bert Freed (Kozad); Dan Seymour (Rabat); Dayton Lummis (Henry Morrison); Alix Talton (Olga); John Harmon (Tony); Richard Karlan (Rosnev); Shepard Menken (Kravich); Benny Rubin (Blalu); Mike Ross (Ivan).

MEXICAN MANHUNT (AA, 1953) 71 M.
Producer, Lindsley Parsons; associate producer, Ace Herman; director, Rex Bailey; screenplay, George Bricker; assistant director, Art Lucker; music director, Edward J. Kay; art director, Dave Milton; set decorator, Ben Bone; sound, Jack Lilly; makeup, Ted Larsen; camera, William Sickner; editor, Leonard W. Harman.

George Brent (Dave Brady); Hillary Brooke (Eve Carter); Morris Ankrum (Tip Morgan); Karen Sharpe (Linda Morgan); Marjorie Lord (Sheila Barton); Douglas Kennedy (Dan McCracken); Alberto Morin (Pablo); Carleton Young (Caruthers); Stuart Randall (Lucky Gato); Marvin Press (Cookie).

DEATH OF A SCOUNDREL (RKO, 1956) 119 M.
Producer, Charles Martin; associate producer, J. Herbert Klein; director-screenplay, Martin; music, Max Steiner; camera, James Wong Howe; editor, Conrad Nervig.

George Sanders (Clementi Sabourin); Yvonne De Carlo (Bridget Kelly); Zsa Zsa Gabor (Mrs. Ryan); Victor Jory (Leonard Wilson); Nancy Gates (Stephanie North); Coleen Gray (Mrs. Van Renassalear); John Hoyt (Mr. O'Hara); Lisa Ferraday (Zina Monte); Tom Conway (Gerry Monte); Celia Lovsky (Mrs. Sabourin); Werner Klemperer (Herbert); Justice Watson (Butler); John Sutton (The Actor); Curtis Cooksey (Oswald Van Renassalear); Gabriel Curtis (Max Freundlich); Morris Ankrum (Captain Lafarge); George Brent (Man with Balloon).

With Claudette Colbert in I MET HIM IN PARIS (Par '37)

Chapter Two

Melvyn Douglas

6'2"
Brown hair
Hazel eyes
Aries

Had Melvyn Douglas devoted as much concentrated energy to his abiding interests and convictions in politics as to his acting craft, he undoubtedly would have gone into congress (like his ex-actress wife, Helen Gahagan Douglas) or become a governor. That he did not may be a pity for the country, but it certainly has been a boon for the entertainment world. For the onetime Melvyn Hesselberg of Macon, Georgia, the stage has always been *the* thing, and since the 1920s he has been determined to improve his histrionic talents by treading the Broadway boards.

Hollywood was always second best for Melvyn, and such feelings have been apparent both in his treatment of the movies and in the industry's controlled response to him. In his first year in the cinema he acted opposite three of the movies' most illustrious names: Gloria Swanson (*Tonight Or Never*, United Artists, 1931), Ann Harding (*Prestige*, RKO, 1932), and Greta Garbo (*As You Desire Me*, MGM, 1932). It is certainly true that none of these motion pictures had the dash of vitality or immortality often associated with these famed actresses, but one would hardly have expected Douglas to sink to the likes of *The Vampire Bat* (Majestic, 1933) or *Nagana* (Universal 1933) within such a short time. Obviously, neither did Douglas, and he fled back to New York to direct and co-star with his wife on the Broadway stage.

When Melvyn returned to picture-making, it was *She Married Her Boss* (Columbia, 1935) which proved the turning point and eventual damnation of his screen future. In this Claudette Colbert comedy, he displayed such an agile farceur quality that industry executives sat up in sheer delight. Here was a suave, polished, and seemingly effortless performer who might be, or possibly was already, "another William Powell." Columbia Pictures tied Douglas to a long-term contract, which, because of his rising salary, they soon shared with Metro-Goldwyn-Mayer.

Douglas was well aware of the special well-being he brought to any film in which he participated. He was also aware that Columbia did not have the facilities or initiative to showcase him in top-flight productions, and that at Metro he would always play second fiddle to Mr. Thin Man, William Powell. One suspects that a goodly portion of Melvyn's gluttonous work load (he made four to five features annually) was not for the sizable remuneration involved, but to blind himself to the stagnation of his talents. He could defrost Marlene

Dietrich in *Angel* (Paramount, 1937), put sweet Deanna Durbin back on the right romantic track in *That Certain Age* (Universal, 1938), make Garbo laugh in *Ninotchka* (MGM, 1939), and inject some dimension of feeling in mannequin Loretta Young (*He Stayed for Breakfast*, Columbia, 1940), but he was typecast into the rut of drawing-room comedies in which a sly grin, an arched brow, or a shaded vocal inflection was the limit of the histrionic capabilities demanded of him. And for Douglas this type of career soon became nothing.

World War II provided a legitimate escape into the relevancy of world problems. By the time of his military discharge, at age forty-four, Hollywood had passed the summit of its golden age and he was fast declining as a cinema leading man. There was a great deal of reality to his disillusioned newspaperman in the bizarre *The Guilt of Janet Ames* (Columbia, 1947). If moviegoers thanked heaven for his presence in the concoction known as *Mr. Blandings Builds His Dream House* (RKO, 1948), in which he shadow-boxed with box-office magnet Cary Grant and the ex–Mrs. Thin Man (Myrna Loy), it was a sad day to watch Douglas tinkling his way through *A Woman's Secret* (RKO, 1949) as an imitation Hoagy Carmichael.

As World War II had been his salvation in the 1940s, Broadway was Melvyn's redeeming influence in the 1950s, where he sparkled in less than superior comedies and dramas. By the time he returned to moviemaking with *Billy Budd* (Allied Artists, 1962) he was a character actor, and his performance as the salty old Texan in *Hud* (Paramount, 1963) confirmed his new status. For that film he won an Oscar as Best Supporting Player, a position he has consistently held in mediocre to excellent television and film fare over the past decade.

Some say that Oscar-Tony-Emmy winner Melvyn only gave a stock performance of his latter-day self in *I Never Sang for My Father* (Columbia, 1970), but beneath the facile surface was a deeply etched, very human characterization. It smacked of reality and, more important-ly, it demonstrated how much Douglas had grown as a player since dropping his comfortable mask as the mechanically perfect drawing-room dapper.

Melvyn Edouard Hesselberg was born on Friday, April 5, 1901, in Macon, Georgia, the son of concert pianist Edouard Hesselberg and the former Lana Schakleford, a southern girl from Kentucky of Scottish descent. Mr. Hesselberg, a Russian Jew, had come to America as a young concert-piano prodigy and found a job as a musician in Nashville, Tennessee. During the 1900s the family would move several times as Mr. Hesselberg changed jobs. In 1903 the Hesselbergs became the parents of a second son, George.

Melvyn's mother often enthralled Melvyn with romantic Scottish tales, frequently about the legendary Black Douglas, the swashbuckling Highlander. Years later Melvyn would adopt the gallant's surname as his own. When World War I broke out, the Hesselbergs were residing in Toronto, Canada, where the father was on the faculty of the Toronto Conservatory of Music. Adventure-seeking Melvyn attempted to enlist in the 48th Highland Regiment, but his protective father put a stop to this rash act. Mr. Hesselberg had ambitions for his son to become a concert pianist (Mrs. Hesselberg wanted Melvyn to be a lawyer), and, obviously, serving in the Army could do nothing for such a career. Later the family moved to Lincoln, Nebraska, where Melvyn was enrolled in the local high school. Thereafter, in his junior year, he was expelled from the public

institution for such combined misdemeanors as smoking, beer drinking, and being a member of a secret fraternity which practiced undisclosed initiation rites. For a spell the youth worked rather despondently at odd jobs about town, such as soda jerk, field hand, freelance writer, and newspaper reporter, and he even did a few walk-on parts for the local stock company.

Then Melvyn ran away to Omaha where he enlisted in the U.S. Army, and he served in the Medical Corps from 1917 to 1918, first at a Wyoming military post and then at Ft. Lewis, Washington. During his rather tame stay in the service, a new-found friend introduced him to the works of Spinoza, Schopenhauer, and Isaac Newton, thus beginning a lifelong romance with the arts and sciences.

After his service discharge, he returned to his family in Lincoln, which seemed far more staid than when he had left for the Army. One day he met William Owen, a popular midwestern stage figure of the time, whose effervescent personality and earnest love of the theatre convinced Melvyn to try his luck at acting. Later Melvyn moved to Chicago, believing he could not only find a means of livelihood more easily in such a wide-open city, but also would have a better opportunity to study the fundamentals of the acting craft under Owen's supervision. Years later, Melvyn would enjoy reminiscing about the "tottling" town of Chicago and its "yeasty" atmosphere with such other well-known former Chicagoans as Maxwell Bodenheim, Floyd Dell, Ben Hecht, and Charles MacArthur.

Among his jobs in Chicago, Melvyn worked as a hat salesman at Marshall Field's Department Store, an elevator operator (could it have been the same post that show-business hopeful Dorothy Lamour would undertake a decade later?), a gas meter reader, and a seller of pianos, sweaters, and encyclopaedias. One of his more responsible posts was as a reporter for the City News Bureau in Chicago. He was surviving the hazards of the helter-skelter job until, one seemingly dreary, uneventful night, a very big story broke while he was catnapping in the police-station press room. His irate boss informed him the next morning: "You can sleep as long as you like, you're fired." All during this time Melvyn had been hopeful of pursuing a career before the footlights, for, as he later recalled, "I thought acting meant sleeping late and being rich enough to buy silk shirts."

Now seemed as good a time as any to hazard his fortunes on an actual stage in order to see if his success as a Hindu character in a Lincoln high school version of *The Little Princess* was a fluke or an indication of aptitude for the field. William Owen agreed to let Melvyn join his repertory troupe, and he made his professional stage debut in the role of Bassanio in *The Merchant of Venice*. By this time he had adopted the stage name of Douglas.

In 1951, Melvyn would reminisce about those busy, apprentice years. "I started playing in stock and in road companies right after World War I [*sic*] and I have to this day a great curiosity to see the country. I toured all over America . . . with the Shakespearean actor, John E. Kellerd. Things were not too easy. Kellerd used to borrow from Catholic organizations to keep us going from town to town. In Bebit, Wisconsin, he went to the Mayor and told him that he'd either give us money or have 22 starving actors on his hands. We got enough to take us to Omaha. In Centralia, Washington—Kellerd had a repertoire of *Hamlet, Macbeth, Romeo and Juliet*—the word got around that we had no dough for Christmas dinner. Half the company was taken to one restaurant and the other half to another. We were finally stranded in Toronto. Those years were among the most stimulating I've ever had."

In Madison, Wisconsin, where Melvyn formed his own stock company, he met Rosalind Hitower and their brief marriage produced a son, Gregory.

(Douglas refuses to discuss this episode in his life.) After the unsuccessful marriage, which ended in divorce, he sailed to Europe for five months on money he had saved from his acting stints. He had planned to travel to Berlin and hopefully study his craft with Max Reinhardt, but he was waylaid in Paris by the cultural surroundings and remained there for many months. When he returned he spent two seasons in stock with the famed Jessie Bonstelle's company, acting in Detroit. Subsequent stock assignments took him to other midwestern cities.

By 1928 (some sources indicate 1926), Douglas had sufficient enough confidence in his theatrical experience to attempt a New York City showcase. He managed to obtain an introduction to energetic Broadway producer William A. Brady, who signed him to a three-year stage contract. His first assignment for this splashy showman was as Ace Wilfong in *A Free Soul* (Playhouse Theatre: January 12, 1928, 100 performances). The drama by Willard Mack was based on the sensational Adela Rogers St. John novel. Undoubtedly, Brady hoped this new play would equal the smash success of another courtroom melodrama, *The Trial of Mary Dugan*, a 1927 hit which then was reaching the midpoint of its eventual 437-performance run.

In *A Free Soul*, Kay Johnson was featured as a San Francisco society girl who finds more excitement with suave gangland figure Melvyn than she does with her respectable society friends. Lester Lonergran appeared as her drunken lawyer father. George Cukor, in his pre-Hollywood years, directed the production, which, unfortunately, did not earn the fabulous critical response or public endorsement that Brady had envisioned. "[It] is a fair-to-middling problem play that changes into a melodrama, thus proving that there can be too much freedom even in play writing!" (*New York Sun*). As for Douglas in his Broadway debut, Arthur Ruhl (*New York Herald-Tribune*) reported that he "made 'Ace' Wilfong attractive and possible—more possible as the man a comparatively sophisticated girl might fall in love with, than as what the lines suggested he was intended to be. . ."

The play would prove far more viable as a film vehicle for Norma Shearer (MGM, 1931). The film also would win an Oscar for Lionel Barrymore as her drunken criminal attorney father, and provide Clark Gable (in Douglas's part) an oncamera occasion to smack Shearer's face and thus insure his future career as MGM's virile leading man. (In 1953, Metro would casually remake the property under the disguised title of *The Girl Who Had Everything*, starring Elizabeth Taylor, a sadly too mature William Powell in a smallish role as her father, and, in the old Douglas part, Fernando Lamas.)

Brady next utilized Melvyn's services in *Back Here* (Klaw Theatre: November 26, 1928, 8 performances). Solidly in the tradition of the 1920s stark World War I drama, this Olga Prinzlau effort, staged by Victor Morley, was situated in a hospital for disabled war veterans. George Meeker played a careening evangelistic faith healer, and Douglas was Sergeant Terry O'Brien, a disillusioned top sergeant. "The performance of Melvyn Douglas, who acted the sergeant with ease and naturalness, was assuredly the best" (*New York Times*). For distaff interest, there were Peggy Shannon and Jean Dixon. However, in less than a week, this tearful war play with a superimposed gangland motif, folded.

When not engaged on Broadway, neither Douglas nor his employer Brady was averse to Melvyn's returning to the road. During 1928–29, he traveled with Fay Bainter in a hinterland version of her Broadway show *Jealousy*, in which she and Douglas comprised the entire cast. (John Halliday had done the male lead on Broadway.) Melvyn also barnstormed with Mary Nash in a touring company of *The Command to Love*.

Now-a-Days (Forrest Theatre: August 5, 1929, 8 performances) was certainly no commercial bonanza, but it did provide several interesting reunions for Douglas. William A. Brady, of course, produced the Arthur F. Brash drama, while Jessie Bonstelle, who had employed Melvyn back in Detroit, was the show's director. In addition, the cast reunited Douglas with Peggy Shannon. Picturing Melvyn as he looks today, it may be difficult for some modern viewers to conceive, but in *Now-a-Days* he was the dashing campus football hero(!) who is vamped by Mayo Methot. Critics of the day agreed that the role of Boyd Butler was poorly conceived, but that Melvyn did the best anyone might have with such a silly role. The reviewers were particularly scornful of the show's corny final line, in which a character says of the wild goings-on: "My God, what is America coming to nowadays?"

Preston Sturges, who would later gain fitting recognition for his wry Americana film comedies,

offered as his third playwriting effort, his first drama, *Recapture* (Etinge Theatre: January 29, 1930, 23 performances). Produced by the usually astute showman A. G. Woods, and staged by Don Mullally, the story concerned a divorced couple who try to recapture the joys of their onetime honeymoon in Vichy, only to find disappointment and disillusionment. J. Brooks Atkinson said in the *New York Times*: "Melvyn Douglas is positive and forthright as the divorced husband who still longs for the wife (Ann Andrews) of his youth." Others in the cast were Glenda Farrell, Hugh Sinclair, and Cecilia Loftus. This play was as much a failure as the optimism of the lead characters.

With the collapse of *Recapture*, Douglas was then cast in the final play to be produced on Broadway by David Belasco. *Tonight or Never* (Belasco Theater: November 18, 1930, 231 performances) proved to be a double "break" for the actor, who was paid $500 a week for his work. The play introduced him to his future wife, Helen Gahagan,* and it eventually took him to Hollywood.

From Lili Hatvany's Hungarian play, with adaptation by Frederic and Fanny Hatton, *Tonight or Never* was both staged and produced by Belasco. Miss Gahagan portrayed an Opera Prima Donna who is engaged to the Faithful Dog (Ferdinand Gottschalk) but becomes enamored of the Unknown Gentleman (Douglas). The latter romances her, but is really interested in obtaining her signature on an operatic contract.

This sophisticated idyll met with substantial popularity, with Stephen Rathbun (*New York Sun*) observing: "As a concert the play was a success." The gimmick of having Gahagan singing arias from *Tosca* and other operatic works did much to insure the production's success, for it gave the audience a novel bonus attraction with their night of theatre-going. Then, too, there was the titillating, though familiar, plot theme of "Will the prima donna spend the night with the handsome stranger?" The answer is, obviously, very much yes, and love does make her a better singer, which provides a "logical" opportunity for her to sing additional arias onstage. As the debonair leading man, Douglas received proper critical endorsement. "[He] makes a most acceptable hero . . . " (*New York American*). "Melvyn Douglas as the Unknown Gentleman who seems

*Born November 25, 1900, in Boonton, New Jersey, to contractor Walter Hamer and Lillian Rose (Mussen) Gahagan, she attended Berkeley School for Girls (Brooklyn, New York), Capen School for Girls (Northampton, Massachusetts), and Barnard College (New York City). In college she wrote and directed plays, making her first stage appearance in *Shoot!* (Macdowall Gallery: June 14, 1922) and her Broadway acting debut in *Manhattan* (Playhouse Theatre: August 14, 1922). After several stage shows, she decided upon a singing career and went on the concert stage, touring Europe as an opera singer (1928–30), appearing in *Tosca* (Prague, Czechoslovakia, 1929). As a David Belasco star she returned to the Broadway stage in her singing debut in *Tonight or Never*.

to be a gigolo but of course isn't, carries off his part with ease, and when he is called upon to bite the lady's neck—she *must live* or how is she to become a great singer with a *soul?*—bites it in an urbane and gentlemanly manner marvelous to behold" (Wilella Waldorf, *New York Evening Post*).

During the course of the lengthy run of *Tonight or Never,* Douglas paid serious court to Miss Gahagan. She remembers that "I was chaperoned practically all the time until I was married." He recalls that his most avid competitor for her attention during this crucial romance period was their boss, Belasco. At any rate, on Melvyn's thirtieth birthday, April 5, 1931, they were wed. Since the show contained one of the most extended, torrid love scenes on Broadway, the well-publicized marriage met with approval among elderly playgoers who had been somewhat shocked (excited?) by the curtain scene in which Melvyn carried Gahagan away to an offstage tryst. As one patron commented to the Douglases after the show one day, their legalized union was the only proper thing to do, given their heated romancing onstage.

At this juncture, the popular, vital Douglases might well have continued on Broadway as a team or solo performers (she would tour with *Tonight or Never*), but that extraordinary cinema figure, Gloria Swanson, entered the scene. The onetime grand star of Cecil B. DeMille extravaganzas and Paramount social dramas/comedies had turned independent producer at United Artists, attracting big box-office grosses with *The Love of Sunya* (1927), the offbeat theatrics of *Sadie Thompson* (1928), and her first all-talking film, *The Trespasser* (1929), for which she was Oscar-nominated and had the occasion to introduce the popular song "Love, Your Magic Spell Is Everywhere." The financial debacle of the incompleted Erich von Stroheim–directed *Queen Kelly* (1929) and the breakup of her financial liaison with producer Joseph P. Kennedy after *What a Widow!* (1930) led her in a determined search to restore her filmland status with a solid screen vehicle. *Indiscreet* (1931), directed by Leo McCarey and co-starring Ben Lyon, was not that elusive image-stabilizer. Thus she turned to United Artists' own Samuel Goldwyn, asking for his cooperation in creating her next movie project. Knowing her penchant for publicly exercising her vocal skills, he was impressed with the potential of *To-*

With Gloria Swanson in TONIGHT OR NEVER (UA '31)

night or Never as a celluloid venture. She agreed to the project.

Not only did mogul Goldwyn acquire the screen rights to the stage success, but he signed co-star Melvyn to a personal contract at a weekly salary of $900. (Other players from the Broadway show hired to repeat their assignments oncamera were Gottschalk, butler Robert Greig, maid Greta Meyer, and Warburton Gamble as the count.)

"When I started out on a stage career, it never occured to me to become a movie actor," Douglas later said. His official debut in that capacity, however, occurred very late in 1931 with the release of *Tonight or Never* (United Artists). It was politely received by the critics,* who found that "pictorially . . . [it] is an unusually striking production" (Mordaunt Hall, *New York Times*). The plotline followed that of the play in which prima donna Nella Vargo (Swanson) is intrigued by a Venetian gigolo (Douglas) who is seemingly being kept by a marchesa (Alison Skipworth). Douglas follows her back to Budapest, thereby consummating the romance, all of which transforms her into a opera singer with a depth of emotion. She learns that he

---

*The *London Times* review was quick to impolitely label the production "a film that might have been designed to make us despise art and artists. . . . neither Miss Swanson nor Mr. Melvin [*sic*] Douglas, for all her practised abandon and his cunning restraint, is able to dispel our nausea."

is actually an impresario who wishes to sign her for a Metropolitan Opera contract and that Skipworth is really his aunt. Those who had witnessed the stage production were prone to compare Gloria unfavorably to Gahagan, a fact no doubt aided by the film industry's penchant for diluting the bite of original stage farces, and by director Mervyn LeRoy's compliance with the removal of the operatic arias from the release print. (Movie executives reasoned that the film-musical cycle had saturated the market and was well on the wane). Many found this to be a most uncharacteristic Swanson appearance (despite her extravagant Chanel wardrobe and overtheatrical bearing), and felt that newcomer Douglas, billed low in the credits, outshone his vis-à-vis. An amusing rare comedy bit was provided by Boris Karloff as a waiter.

Quite justifiably, neither Goldwyn nor other Hollywood producers (nor the actor himself) was overly impressed by Douglas's screen debut. More importantly, Melvyn's home-lot employer, Goldwyn, was preoccupied with fostering the careers of dashing, dapper Ronald Colman and frenetic Ziegfeld comedian Eddie Cantor. Douglas was a minor adjunct to the Goldwyn actor stable and the executive felt no compulsion about loaning out his services to other film companies for whatever picture they would accept the newcomer.

RKO had already lined up urbane Adolphe Menjou as the dapper roué to play with delicate Ann Harding in *Prestige* (1932), but a genteel second male lead was required to complete the star complement. Harding, unnerved about the potential of this film (after it was finished she begged RKO to shelve the unworthy venture), agreed to the respectability of Douglas being used in the secondary role, and he came over to the RKO soundstages.

Miss Harding, then considered Hollywood's most ladylike actress, was correct in her estimation that *Prestige* would bring none of the title's virtue to anyone involved in the picture. Resilient director Tay Garnett attempted to instill realistic qualities in his study of Lao Bao, a desolate French penal colony in Indochina, but the consensus of critical opinion was that the film "is scarcely a successful entertainment. . . . the incidents are hopelessly illogical" (Mordaunt Hall, *New York Times*).

A brief rundown of the plotline is sufficient to indicate the melodramatic nature of the film. At the party celebrating his engagement to Harding, Lieutenant Andre Verlaine (Douglas) is advised

With Ann Harding in PRESTIGE (RKO '32)

he is to be stationed at the infamous Lao Bao penal colony, a hellhole of heat and monotony which drives most white men either to madness or to suicide. Douglas's worst fears are realized during his year's stay at the French outpost. He takes to drink, hoping to blot out the horrors of the unspeakable living conditions. Harding persuades her officer father (Ian MacLaren) to somehow arrange for her fiancé's transfer. In the meantime she treks to Indochina to be with her loved one. Douglas has turned into a rebellious lout, moody, half-crazed by drink and by his noxious responsibilities as the penal colony commandant. In despair, Harding accepts the succor of slick Menjou, almost agreeing to go off to Paris with him. However, Douglas's trusty servant (Clarence Muse) kills Menjou in an uprising, order is restored to the colony, and a regenerated Douglas begs the forgiveness of his lofty sweetheart.

Those who endured the embarrassments of *Prestige* (crude dialog, exploited living conditions and atrocities among the prisoners, etc.) were amazed that in the midst of a riot among the dour prisoners, all Melvyn had to do to quell the uprising was to swagger through their rank brandishing a rawhide whip, or that love of a noble woman and one's country (France) could redeem such a lost soul as Douglas. Hall of the *Times* acknowledged that Douglas played his subordinate role with "more tenacity and thoroughness than it deserves."

Meanwhile, Melvyn was loaned to Paramount to appear opposite Claudette Colbert in *The Wiser Sex* (1932), said to be based on Clyde Fitch's play *Her Confessions.* The critics were unable to find much resemblance between the Broadway play and the screenplay. Douglas was cast as a crusading young public prosecutor who claims he has no political ambitions but merely wishes to rid the city of its underworld elements. Having stirred up a hornet's nest among the local racketeers, he finds himself framed for the murder of his cousin (Franchot Tone), and only through the ingenious investigatory powers of his unorthodox blonde (!) fiancée (Claudette Colbert) is the idealistic young man saved from legal conviction. *Harrison's Reports,* a trade paper self-appointed to guard the exhibitors' and public's interests (commercial, moral, entertainment, and otherwise), rated the picture "dull and demoralizing" but did rank Melvyn as "the only one who arouses some sympathy." The *London Times* found Douglas "attractively simple." Any way this minor film was analyzed, it was an unmemorable, unconvincing first screen union for fumbling Douglas and the still unproven Colbert.

Fast on the heels of *The Wiser Sex* was *The Broken Wing* (Paramount, 1932), based on the Paul Dickey–Charles W. Goddard Broadway play.* Douglas was again out of his element, seemingly a last-minute replacement for a more athletic romantic player of the Ramon Novarro type. Lloyd Corrigan directed this potboiler featuring fiery Lupe Velez and flavorful Leo Carrillo, the latter in a role that would have been better handled by Wallace Beery on a much bigger MGM budget. Carrillo appeared as Captain Innocencio of El Suelo, Mexico, who is the town's mayor, chief of police, prosecuting attorney, judge, doctor, and lord high executioner. When señorita Velez, for whom he hankers, takes more than a motherly interest in Philip Marvin (Douglas), a handsome young American pilot whose plane has crashed nearby, Carrillo tries to have the intruder shot. Since Douglas has acquired a heavy case of amnesia (which evaporates at the proper moment), the proceedings, romantic and otherwise, are more lugubrious than need be. To his credit, Melvyn did quite well with his miscast assignment.

With such celluloid credentials so far, it would hardly seem that Douglas had made much of an impression on the Hollywood community. But it was obviously no fluke that two vastly important cinema leading ladies had chosen him to play opposite them, for none other than the illustrious Greta Garbo joined the ranks of Gloria Swanson and Ann Harding in requesting the services of Melvyn for her latest quality-film venture. Hollywood observers, well used to the bizarre casting peccadillos of temperamental celebrities, were vastly surprised that MGM's prestige symbol should have picked this fledgling screen player for her latest leading man.

On his part, Melvyn accepted the bid to appear in *As You Desire Me* (MGM, 1932) with alacrity. He undoubtedly cherished the notion that at last he would be receiving the respect due him as a stage performer of some reputation, and that for the first time his acting temperament would be in accord with the part given him. He was to be sadly disillusioned. It was well known that Robert Montgomery—and he was an MGM contract player at that—had received diffident treatment at the hands of Garbo and her creative entourage in *Inspiration* (MGM, 1931), but the reception accorded Douglas was icy by comparison. Arriving on the Culver City soundstage, Fitzmaurice took Melvyn aside and staidly advised him of his importance in this Garbo picture: "You're new to motion pictures, Mr. Douglas. You're from the stage? We . . . in motion pictures, we expect emotion from women, not from men." With this bald statement as a guide, Douglas knew that he was to be nothing more than an adroit stooge to the Swedish sphinx.

As You Desire Me was based on the Italian play by Luigi Pirandello,† which hardly provided a proper foundation for a Garbo film. She was Zara, the blonde cafe entertainer in Budapest who suffers from amnesia. Currently she is the mistress of a novelist (Erich von Stroheim) who has a hypnotic influence over her. A portrait painter (Owen Moore) identifies her as the wife of Count Bruno Varelli (Douglas), who believes she was killed when the Austrians invaded Italy during World War I. Wanting to escape von Stroheim, Garbo goes to Douglas, who accepts her, and they fall in love, despite von Stroheim's unnerving ploys to woo her back.

Once again, as occurred with both Swanson and Harding, Douglas overcame the impediment

---

*Opened at the 48th Street Theatre on November 29, 1920, for a run of 248 performances. The silent-film version (Preferred, 1923) starred Miriam Cooper and Kenneth Harlan.

†Seen on Broadway at the Maxine Elliott Theatre, as of January 28, 1931, for a 142-performance run.

With Greta Garbo in AS YOU DESIRE ME (MGM
'32)

of fighting for screen time in an essentially one-woman show and managed to make a favorable impression with the critics. "Douglas knows what a lover should be in such a case, and looks and acts the part . . ." (*New York World-Telegram*). "The love scenes between Douglas and Garbo are the high point of the film, and they are almost equal to the ones played so long ago by [John] Gilbert and Garbo. (*Photoplay* magazine). Undoubtedly, the tributes accorded to Douglas in this case were aided by the oversized performance of von Stroheim, who encased his performance with exaggerated, hissable villainy. Although she was not prone to speaking on the matter, Garbo must have been impressed by Douglas, who helped to make this film one of her sturdier properties in some time, for it was but the first of three features in which they would perform together.

Melvyn's last 1932 film found him top-billed for the first time in his screen career. The celluloid adventure also featured Boris Karloff, Charles Laughton, Gloria Stuart, Raymond Massey, Lilian Bond, and Ernest Thesiger. *The Old Dark House* (Universal, 1932) was directed by

James Whale, fresh from his *Frankenstein* (Universal, 1931) triumph.

The new picture had prestigious credits. Based on J. B. Priestley's novel, *Benighted,* the screenplay was by Benn W. Levy and R. C. Sherriff. Within the spooky proceedings, Melvyn was sensitive young Roger Penderel, one of a group of travelers forced to seek shelter in an isolated Wales mansion on a stormy night. The house is inhabited by the eccentric Femm family, and a series of weird happenings occurs as an unknown villain stalks the house. In horror thrillers the actor in the good-guy role (here Douglas) often receives little attention from the critics or the public, and this picture was no exception. In fact, Universal took special pains to give the bulk of the film's advertising attention to Karloff, who played the Femm family's lumbering mute butler. (When horror specialist William Castle remade the film in England in 1963 for Columbia release, it was reorganized into a mock thriller. Tom Poston played the arch hero, a variation of the part once handled by Douglas.)

Melvyn's screen career dipped into low gear in 1933. He was shunted off to poverty row to play in *The Vampire Bat* (Majestic, 1933), third-billed to Lionel Atwill and Fay Wray, who had worked together in *Dr. X* (First National, 1932) and would again be teamed in *Mystery of the Wax Museum* (Warner Bros., 1933). Douglas was cast here in a part which was much better suited to the likes of a David Manners. He played Karl Brettschneider, a skeptical detective who tries to prove to the natives of Kleinschloss that werewolves, not vampires, are the cause of the mysterious "blood killings" plaguing their small German village. Douglas apparently took none of the affair seriously, and his acting in this seventy-one-minute horror picture is embarrassing to watch. Director Frank L. Strayer obviously decided early on in the proceedings that he would have a "turkey" on his hands if the picture were played straight, so he transferred the limelight to the mad antics of Dwight Frye, who as Herman Gleib loved to pet "soft" bats, and to Maude Eburne, who impersonated the zany, hypochondriac aunt. Atwill, as the deranged, misunderstood doctor and the cause of the killings with his vampire bats, and screaming heroine Fay Wray (later to meet immortality with *King Kong* [RKO, 1933]) managed to stay above water in the affair, but Douglas sank in the morass of a poor part in an inane film.*

---

*Producers Releasing Corp. borrowed the plot of *The Vampire Bat* for its own *The Devil Bat* (1941) (a.k.a. *Killer Bats*) in which Bela Lugosi had the Atwell role and Dave O'Brien was in the Douglas part, this time a reporter.

Nagana (Universal, 1933) proved to be another downward step for Melvyn as well as a critical flop. The *New York Herald-Tribune* labeled it "[a] curious sort of farrago of educational picture and old-fashioned sawmill melodrama with a leitmotif of tom-tom music and ballets of skin-clad Ethiopians in ceremonial dances about as exciting as a newsreel shot of Sioux Indians inducting a Tammany brave into their mysteries." *Nagana* is a native African word for sleeping sickness, which this picture is all about and from which it obviously suffers. Among the scientific members of the Tropical Disease Institute of Western Africa are doctors Walter Radnor (Douglas) and Roy Stark (Onslow Stevens). When the latter becomes enchanted with countess Sandra Lubeska (Tala Birell) and deserts his post, the former goes in pursuit, only to fall prey himself to her magical charms. What follows "is feeble, trashy stuff and something you wouldn't believe either before or after seeing" (Thornton Delehanty, *New York Evening Post*). The film did little to boost the Hollywood stock of Viennese import Tala Birell or of Douglas.

At this juncture producer Samuel Goldwyn and actor Melvyn Douglas called a truce to their un-fruitful contract (Douglas would later call the film producer "marvelous" and an "un-typical mogul"). As a freelancer, Douglas accepted the "other man" role in the prestigious film version of Elmer Rice's *Counsellor-at-Law* (Universal, 1933).* In this "A" production, directed by William Wyler and scripted by its playwright, Elmer Rice, John Barrymore had the meaty role of Jewish lawyer George Simon, who has risen from an impoverished East Side childhood. A few hectic days in his life at the office comprise the picture's narrow, but flavorsome, range of view. Douglas functioned briefly as Roy Darwin of Park Avenue with whom Barrymore's wife (Doris Kenyon) carries on a flirtation. The *New York Times* noted that Douglas "appears to advantage," but he hardly had a chance to shine in the company of dominating Barrymore, ex-1920s light comedienne Bebe Daniels (as Barrymore's lovelorn secretary), Isabel Jewell as the chattering switchboard operator, Clara Langener as Barrymore's mother, and Elmer Brown as the culprit who hopes to have Barrymore disbarred.

At the end of this period of picture-making (nine films in less than a year), Melvyn was professionally unhappy. "I was tired, displeased

*Elmer Rice's drama, starring Paul Muni, opened at the Plymouth Theatre (November 6, 1931) for a 293-performance run, reestablishing its engagement at that theatre on September 12, 1932, for 104 additional performances. It was at the 46th Street Theatre on May 15, 1933, for 16 performances, and at the Royale Theatre (November 24, 1942) for a 258-performance revival.

With Tala Birell in NAGANA (Univ '32)

with some of the roles fed me." Probably if it had not been for the steady encouragement of his wife (she sustained her professional career by appearing as Shirley in a Los Angeles 1932 production of *The Cat and the Fiddle,* he might have left Hollywood long before he did. After *Nagana,* completed in mid-December 1932, the Douglases took a jaunt to Mexico City. After *Counsellor-at Law,* the couple were back in California, and on October 8, 1933, Mrs. Douglas gave birth to a son, Peter Gahagan. Douglas's son by his first marriage, Gregory, was a frequent member of the performers' household at this period.

Nevertheless, bred and matured in the Broadway theatre, Melvyn was anxious to return to stage work. Once back in New York he would explain about Hollywood: "For awhile it smacked of Paradise, then it began to pall, until finally boredom set in and the California sunshine took on a jaundiced haze. It wasn't that working conditions were not pleasant,* it was too little work. Once you learn your lines there, and the camera and sound tracks record your performance, it is all over.

"That is where the theatre offers greater interest than the movies. When you plan a play you first read the script to find out what sort of person you are to portray. You study him and at each rehearsal try to improve on the delineation of his character, and it gives quite a thrill on opening night to see if you have made the grade with the audience. It doesn't end there either. On subsequent performances you make him more realistic if possible.

"In motion pictures it is so different. The words just roll off your brain, usually, and the seasoned actor merely employs his craft to supply the realism momentarily required for the camera."

Douglas's return to Broadway was in a popular, if unedifying, vehicle. Lee Shubert was the presenter of A. E. Thomas's three-act comedy *No More Ladies* (Playhouse Theatre: January 23, 1934, 162 performances). As staged by Henry Wagstaff Gribble, the play was a meandering study of the smart East Side and Southampton set. "For no particular reason, except that it is produced with care and played with smiling ingenuity, *No More Ladies* . . . manages to tinkle a jauntily frivolous note" (Richard Lockridge, *New York Sun*). Melvyn was cast as bon vivant Sheridan Warren, a man who can scarcely tell the difference between monotony and monogamy. He

weds and, as the heroine's (Ruth Weston) grandmother (Lucile Watson) might have predicted, quickly runs astray. Of his performance, Bernard Sobel (*New York Mirror*) wrote: "[he] was likeable and effective even when his lines were a little unworthy." (When MGM picturized the play in 1935 as a Joan Crawford vehicle, Robert Montgomery and Edna May Oliver respectively played the Douglas and Watson parts.)

Scarcely had Melvyn concluded his acting tasks in *No More Ladies* than he turned to stage directing, supervising *Moor Born* (Playhouse Theatre: April 3, 1934, 63 performances), which starred his wife as Emily Brontë. Like the far more popular British play *Wild Decembers* by Clemence Dane, *Moor Born* was a chronicle of events in the emotional lives of the Brontë sisters. The critics rebuked Dan Totheroh for his theatrical effort: "the spectacle of the theatre making mud pies out of nourishing groceries is humiliating" (Brooks Atkinson, *New York Times*). A few aisle-sitters, such as Arthur Pollock (*Brooklyn Daily Eagle*), noted that "Melvyn Douglas staged the play with shrewd good taste."

After *Moor Born* closed, Helen Gahagan went on tour with *Mary of Scotland*, playing Mary Stuart, while Melvyn remained in New York City to stage Sean O'Casey's *Within the Gates* (National Theatre: October 22, 1934, 100 performances). Once again, as in *Moor Born*, his partners were producers John Tuerk and George Bushar. Lillian Gish † (The Young Whore) and Bramwell Fletcher (The Dreamer) starred in this fantasy of Hyde Park set in four parts *à la* the seasons. "Acted, the play is an unedited mixture of poetry and declamation, swooping from the something near the sublime to something precisely at the ridiculous with dizzying uncertainty. In much the same fashion, it darts from symbolism to realism and back again." As for Douglas's participation, John Mason Brown (*New York Evening Post*) reported: "To be sure, Melvyn Douglas' direction is wooden and awkward save in the final scene. He neither succeeds in creating a stylization that is appropriate to the text nor in keeping the majority of his players from performing in anything but the most literal manner of the workday theatre."

Undiscouraged, the team of Douglas, Tuerk, and Bushar created *Mother Lode* (Cort Theatre: December 22, 1934, 9 performances). This time Douglas not only directed but co-starred with his wife in this Dan Totheroh–George O'Neill paean

---

*When he first began making films Douglas noted that Gloria Swanson came onto the set of *Tonight or Never* very late and then left very early. She "would arrive late, serve tea from a silver service at 4:30 and go home. With that kind of beginning I got an erroneous impression how movies were made.

† At the April 15, 1971 Oscar telecast, Douglas would present "Miss Lillian" with the Irving Thalberg Memorial Award for her years of distinguished service to motion pictures.

to the Golden West of pioneer times. Gahagan (whom journalist Heywood Hale Broun had recently listed as one of the ten most beautiful women in America) was cast as a virgin songstress of the mining camps who meets New England visionary Douglas in Virginia City, Nevada. He holds true to his promise that he will become rich on gold and silver, and the next act finds them ensconced in an elaborate San Francisco mansion where Douglas has become the billionaire benefactor of the thriving city. Beulah Bondi appeared as Gahagan's mother. Douglas's appearance in the romantic lead was not greeted with any enthusiasm. "Mr. Douglas is dignity personified and magnified, given the good looks of one of those wooden figures in front of the tobacconists' shops of that period, and there his idea of both romance and realism seems to stop" (Gilbert Gabriel, *New York American*). As for his helming of the period piece: ". . . Mr. Douglas has not contributed much to the clarification, for the performance is unwielding in structure and undistinguished in its detail" (Brooks Atkinson, *New York Times*).

During 1934, which was largely devoted to Broadway efforts, Douglas did find time to make three pictures for RKO, the same studio that would sign Helen Gahagan to a contract in order that she might play the title figure in *She* (1935), the picturization of the H. Rider Haggard adventure classic. *Dangerous Corner* (RKO, 1934) found Douglas in the film version of the J. B. Priestley play* and a scantly reviewed picture at that. Said *Harrison's Report*: ". . . it will hardly please the masses. The absence of action and the continual talk may bore them. And the trick ending will puzzle them . . ." In *Dangerous Corner*, Melvyn joined an appealing cast, comprising Conrad Nagel, Virginia Bruce, Erin O'Brien Moore, Betty Furness, Ian Keith, and Henry Wadsworth. The play's argument finds a group of people gathered discussing the long-ago suicide of Nagel's brother. Someone suggests they all dance, but, just then, a radio tube blows out. The talking continues, but this time everyone speaks the *truth*. After this edifying parlay has run its gamut, the action turns to where the radio went dead. One of the party finds a new tube, the dancing continues, and the reality that might have been revealed (as in the fantasy) does not transpire.

Woman in the Dark (RKO, 1934), also directed by Phil Rosen, was a "B" production which rematched third-billed Douglas with his *The Vampire Bat* co-lead, Fay Wray, only this time around

Ralph Bellamy was the hero. In the course of this Dashiell Hammett tale ("It's a typical Hammett crook-cop yarn with enough different angles to make it fairly gripping" [*Variety*]), wealthy young Bellamy is paroled from prison, having served three years for assaulting a man who was abusing the sheriff's daughter (Nell O'Day). Bellamy harbors hopes of rekindling a romance with O'Day, but one nightgown-clad Wray arrives on his doorstep and begs him to protect her from a snarling Melvyn, fast on her heels. In the course of the film's seventy minutes, Douglas wangles himself into trouble with the law, leaving Bellamy and Wray free to pursue their romance. With its honest and realistic approach to the responsibilities of relationships, the picture was considered strong stuff for the dual-bill playbills.

Melvyn had much better luck with his third release for the studio, *The People's Enemy* (a.k.a. *Racketeers*) (RKO, 1935). This bottom-half-of-a-double-bill entry was unique in that it did not glorify the gangster image as so many films of the time did. Preston Foster had the lead in this Crane Wilbur–directed melodrama about a revengeful gangster, his long-suffering wife (Lila Lee), and his well-meaning, conniving lawyer (Douglas). The latter stays in the background until Foster's untimely death, and then promises devout Lee a much better future. Eileen Creelman (*New York Sun*) complimented Douglas here, for combining, "in a straightforward performance, a hard-boiled sense of honesty and loyalty."

Juxtaposed with this trio of RKO releases, which scarcely added to Douglas's reputation along the Broadway circuit, was his stage appearance in *De Luxe* (Booth Theatre: March 5, 1935, 15 performances). The Louis Bromfield–John Gearson play revolved around frustrated Americans in 1919 Paris who are liberally wasting their lives. Many contemporary reviewers thought this complex bit of interaction would have made a better novel. Melvyn, at age thirty-three, was (type) cast as a tired, dissipated gigolo who is fed up with accommodating his demanding mistress, Cora Witherspoon. Others involved in this vehicle, directed by Chester Erskine and Sidney Salkow, were Elsa Maxwell and Peggy DeAlbrew (social organizers), Blanche Ring (crude American widow), Violet Heming (busted society leader with a soul), Ann Andrews (radiant lass with a sharp tongue), and Claudia Morgan (ingenue with brains).

When Miss Gahagan traveled to Hollywood to

*The Priestley fantasy-drama opened at London's Lyric Theatre on May 17, 1932, for a 151-performance run. On Broadway, it was seen at the Empire Theatre (October 27, 1932) for a 210-performance engagement, reappearing at the Waldorf Theatre (July 17, 1933) for 93 performances.

fulfill her *She* contract, in which Randolph Scott was her co-star, Douglas accompanied her. He had no illusions about a further filmmaking career ("I'm only another leading man"), but his sparkling wife continued to encourage him to give the craft another try. (Her help led him to later say: "I challenge those who say an actor makes a mistake when he marries an actress.")

Douglas was not in the first rank of actors suggested to studio boss Harry Cohn when he was seeking a leading man for Claudette Colbert's *She Married Her Boss* (Columbia, 1935). However, as shooting time approached and no suitable lead could be found, Melvyn's name was submitted by a news-reporter pal of his, and Douglas was given the chance to prove himself.

Gregory La Cava directed *She Married Her Boss,* a merry thesis that marriage and the hearthside are better booty for a woman than a career in the competitive business world. Douglas, the stodgy widower head of Barclay's Department Store, is so impressed by the efficiency of his crisp executive assistant, Colbert, that it seems a good idea to wed her and see if she can bring order to his shambles of a household, which includes a spoiled brat daughter (Edith Fellows) and a dour sister-in-law (Katharine Alexander). Colbert, who gave up a fabulous Paris job offer just to be with Douglas, is aghast to discover that even as a bride

her groom considers her just an efficiency-expert fixture. When she goads Douglas into recognizing that she is no longer just a distaff businessman, he glumly responds: "You've changed. You're not the Julia Scott I know. I don't understand you anymore." As this escapade of *impolite* comedy continues, stuffed-shirt Melvyn believes that he has lost his wife's affection to Philadelphia department-store scion Lonnie Rogers (Michael Bartlett), and he promptly succumbs to a bout of self-pity, becoming drunk as a hatter with his tippling butler (Raymond Walburn). After a rousing harmony of "Home on the Range" with Walburn, Douglas abducts the amused-confused Colbert away from Bartlett, and the finally-in-love couple throw caution to the winds as they embark on a wild ride through town, climaxed by heaving bricks through the windows of Barclay's Department Store.

While this film helped to prove the pre–Women's Lib thesis ("A career leaves you empty. Do something really important. [Get Married]"), it also solidified and typecast Douglas into the very profitable Hollywood niche of a leading farceur. As the British *Daily Film Renter* would reflect: "Melvyn Douglas stands revealed a polished light comedian, bringing a wealth of humour to his part..."

As a result of his responsive performance in *She*

With Claudette Colbert in SHE MARRIED HER BOSS (Col '35)

Married Her Boss, Harry Cohn offered Melvyn a lucrative seven-year contract, with the usual options. Douglas's wife urged him to accept the stardom bid.

Meanwhile, before the Colbert picture was released and changed his professional future, Douglas made two other films and arranged to appear on Broadway in yet another play. *Mary Burns, Fugitive* (Paramount, 1935) found Sylvia Sidney in the tried and true part of a weepy society's pawn, who suffers the abuses of misfortune with the patience of a celluloid saint and earns regeneration with the easiness only provided by a contrived screenplay ("If the story were up to the performances and the direction it'd be sumpin'" [*Variety*]). In the course of this chronicle of an unfortunate rural maiden, Sidney is sent to jail on purely circumstantial evidence. She and her blonde chippie cellmate (Pert Kelton) are allowed to escape, for the police hope that Sidney will lead them to wanted criminal Alan Baxter. Along the path to freedom, Sidney takes a job as a hospital-kitchen dishwasher. One evening she is asked to bring a food tray to the room of Barton Powell (Douglas). The latter is a once jovial explorer who has turned into a terrible grouch as a result of suffering from snow blindness and has been confined to a hospital bed. He admits that sweet Sylvia has the only voice around there that "does not sound like morning in the barnyard." Soon, however, her past catches up with her and she must continue on the lam. In the finale, situated in Melvyn's well-appointed mountain retreat, Baxter is captured, and the Sidney-Douglas alliance can be legalized in marriage.

If Melvyn's role in *Mary Burns, Fugitive* can be delineated at all, it would be best described as comedy relief from the blubbery main story. He does have a startlingly effective sequence after his bandages have been removed in which he trepidaciously views Sylvia for the first time. John Reddington (*Brooklyn Daily Eagle*) wrote of Douglas: "[he] gives the most skillful comedy performance it has been my pleasure to observe in months."

Most people tend to recall the legendary Annie Oakley (1860–1926) as personified by Ethel Merman/Mary Martin/Betty Hutton in the Irving Berlin musical *Annie Get Your Gun* (1946), but in *Annie Oakley* (RKO, 1935), Barbara Stanwyck was a most credible backwoods sharpshooter ("If the picture misses as outstanding it's because the script and direction are not up to the star and title combination" [*Variety*]). Preston Foster appeared as Toby Walker, the World's Champion Shooter,

With Charles Laughton in a publicity pose for THE OLD DARK HOUSE (Univ '32)

who is miffed that dainty Stanwyck could have outshot him in a target competition if she had not found him just "too pretty." His consternation is even greater when Buffalo Bill (Moroni Olsen) signs Stanwyck to his traveling Wild West Show. Director George Stevens guided the action back and forth for ninety minutes between show events and the personal turmoil of Stanwyck's romance with Foster. Solid (not stolid) Douglas functioned as Jeff Hogarth, Olsen's general manager, who hankers for Stanwyck but realizes he does not stand a chance with Foster in the running. An engaging sidelight of the film was the misadventures of Sitting Bull (Chief Thunderbird) midst the white man's civilization, and his eventual return to native form when he chases an arch enemy through the city streets, dressed in full regalia and brandishing a tomahawk.

Three days after *Annie Oakley* opened at New York's Astor Theatre, Douglas was making his stage bow in *Tapestry in Gray* (Shubert Theatre: December 27, 1935, 24 performances). Marion Gering, who had directed many of Sylvia Sidney's Paramount outings, supervised this Martin Flavin tapestry of tableaux. Brooks Atkinson (*New York Times*) commented: "Seldom is such a commonplace little tale blown up into such a grandiose effigy." Melvyn and Minor Watson ap-

83

With Sylvia Sidney in a publicity pose for MARY BURNS, FUGITIVE (Par '35)

peared as medical students destined for greatness. During World War I, Douglas performs a brilliant piece of plastic surgery on the injured Watson. The operation is ruined when a nurse (Elissa Landi) accidentally removes the bandages to lessen Watson's pain. Years later Douglas weds Landi, only later discovering her relationship to his past. It destroys his life. The *New York Sun* recorded: "Mr. Douglas is rather boyish as the great surgeon, but this mattered comparatively little, since I never believed Mr. Flavin on that point anyway." The show, which closed in less than three weeks, would be Douglas's final Broadway foray for well over a decade. One cast member of *Tapestry in Gray* who received little publicity was George LaMarr, who functioned as Douglas's understudy and had his own small part in the play. He was Douglas's real-life younger brother.

In most anyone's recall of screen sleuths, such celluloid detectives as William Powell (Philo Vance, the Thin Man), Warren William (the Lone Wolf), Basil Rathbone (Sherlock Holmes), George Sanders (the Saint, the Falcon), Chester Morris (Boston Blackie), Warner Baxter (the Crime Doctor), and Margaret Rutherford (Miss Marple) are easily associated with particular series. Few remember how many screen gumshoes Melvyn Douglas would essay on film, largely because he seemed to accept whatever parts of momentary appeal he was offered, and it became nearly impossible for him to identify with any particular role due to the quantity of roles he essayed. One such example was *The Lone Wolf Returns* (1935).

Louis Joseph Vance created his fictional detective as Michael Lanyard, alias the Lone Wolf, a top-notch gentleman thief. He first appeared in American silent pictures in 1917 with Bert Lytell in the lead role, and in 1929 Lytell starred in *The Lone Wolf Returns* (Columbia), the last of the series' (semi) silent entries. The following year Lytell was in the first (and his last) talking series entry, *The Last of the Lone Wolf* (Columbia, 1930). In *Cheaters at Play* (Fox, 1932) Thomas Meighan assumed the part. Then, four years later, Columbia reactivated the detective property and made a wise decision in selecting urbane Douglas to play the aristocratic ex–jewel thief who is now very much on the side of the law (though the police can scarcely believe their good luck).

In the course of the film, Continental Douglas arrives in America, crashes Gail Patrick's masquerade party, and is about to snatch her impressive emerald necklace from the wall safe, when he spots her photograph on the dressing table, and takes that instead. As he later confides to the disbelieving law-enforcers: "The Lone Wolf prowls no more because he has at last met the girl of his dreams." Rounding out the facets of the urbane but formula picture were: Raymond Walburn (the comic butler), Douglass Dumbrille (the villain), Thurston Hall (a befuddled police inspector), and Tala Birell (the siren). For a so-so film which delved into a time-worn format, *The Lone Wolf Returns* garnered most satisfactory reviews as did Douglas. "It is first and foremost Melvyn Douglas' film, his portrayal possessing that lightness of touch and sense of poise which such a role as the Lone Wolf demands. He overdoes nothing—not altogether an easy accomplishment in a fictional part of this type—his whole performance being thoroughly acceptable throughout" (British *Daily Film Renter*). It is a shame that Douglas never had the occasion to play the character again.*

His busy schedule prevented Melvyn from

*Francis Lederer was the title character in *The Lone Wolf in Paris* (Columbia, 1938); the following year Warren William took over the part, until *The Notorious Lone Wolf* (Columbia, 1946), which featured Gerald Mohr. Ron Randell was the detective in *The Lone Wolf and His Lady* (Columbia, 1949), the final theatrical-film entry of the series to date. In 1954 Louis Hayward appeared as Michael Lanyard in a 39-episode half-hour television series entitled "Streets of Danger."

With Joan Crawford in THE GORGEOUS HUSSY (MGM '36)

joining Carole Lombard in *Love before Breakfast* (Universal, 1936), a part which went to Preston Foster, but he was available to receive top billing in *And So They Were Married* (Columbia, 1936), a seventy-four-minute comedy which was very closely related to *She Married Her Boss*. Elliott Nugent directed this pleasant farce about two widowed persons (Douglas, Mary Astor) who are in love and who are also conscientious parents. They are snowed in together at a resort, where they fall in love and decide to wed. Their children (Tommy Blake and Edith Fellows), however, hate one another and consort to break up the romance. The two succeed in their devilish plan but then find they like each other and plot to reunite their hapless parents. The predictable plot was re-worked some thirty years later for the Maureen O'Hara–Rossano Brazzi flop, *The Battle of the Villa Fiorita* (Warner Bros., 1965).

MGM then borrowed Douglas to play John Randolph in *The Gorgeous Hussy* (1936), an overly elaborate historical drama purporting to portray the Peggy O'Neill Eaton affair, one of the first major political scandals to hit Washington. Taking place during the administration of Andrew Jackson (Lionel Barrymore), former barmaid Peggy O'Neill (Crawford) loves gallant John Randolph (Douglas), later a senator, but she is

rejected by him. On the rebound she allows boyish naval lieutenant Bow Timberlake (Robert Taylor) to court her and they wed. But the marriage is short-lived, for he soon dies in action. Thereafter, she weds Jackson's Secretary of War, John Eaton (Franchot Tone), whose first wife had died mysteriously. Crawford is rejected by Washington society, led by Vice President John C. Calhoun's wife, Floride. Rather than cause further embarrassment to her "unofficial Presidential uncle," she leaves the nation's capitol, remembered by her friends and admirers with appreciation.

This expensive Clarence Brown–directed picture lost its potential public acceptance from the moment its apologetic foreword flashed on the screen: "This story of Peggy Eaton and her times is not presented as a precise account of either—rather as fiction founded upon historical fact. Except for historically important personages, the characters are fictional." The critics stumbled over themselves making snide jabs at this pretentious, phony claptrap: " . . . the film is not all political speeches, for the heroine's love affairs are remarkably complicated" (*London Times*). While the only bit of accurate Americana to be derived from the 105-minute proceedings was on the fine art of bundling, and while la Crawford and most of her company were sternly roasted for their flouncy performances, two cast members received almost universal praise: Beulah Bondi as the unjustly maligned rural wife of Barrymore, and Melvyn as the states'-rights member of Congress who is not afraid to protect his honor on the dueling field.

Melvyn was hardly impressed by the high-toned behavior of Crawford* or the other Metro talent aristocracy, but after the picture was released, he found that he was to be thrust in their midst more and more over the years. Louis B. Mayer and his executive staff were so impressed that Douglas had emerged artistically unscathed from the production that it was deemed wise to negotiate with Columbia and Harry Cohn for a possible share in Douglas's contract during the forthcoming years. Cohn reckoned that MGM screen assignments and publicity for Douglas could only strengthen the star's value on the home lot, and agreed to a pact which permitted Melvyn to jaunt over to Culver City for movie roles when he was not busy on the Columbia–Marathon Street soundstages. After all, reasoned Cohn, it would nicely cut down his overhead, when he had no films lined up for Douglas's services, if he were being paid by MGM and not by Columbia.

If *She Married Her Boss* did not clinch the fact that Douglas was, next to MGM's more highly touted William Powell and Robert Montgomery, Hollywood's most adept farceur (who else could maintain such a merry, captivating twinkle in his eyes?), *Theodora Goes Wild* (Columbia, 1936) settled the matter once and for all. As with another comedy classic, *It Happened One Night* (Columbia, 1934), it almost did not come to be, for the leading lady in question, Irene Dunne, initially balked at making such a contra type of picture. Since making her screen debut in 1930, she had safely alternated between tremendously popular women's sob stories (*Back Street* [Universal, 1932], *Magnificent Obsession* [Universal, 1935]) and tasteful musicals (*Roberta* [RKO, 1935] and *Showboat* [Universal, 1936]). Miss Dunne had even tried outdoor spectacle (*Cimarron* [RKO, 1931]) and a murder mystery involving a fake spiritualist (*Thirteen Women* [RKO, 1932]), but she saw no reason why she should risk her screen reputation by trying the unknown field of screw-

With Irene Dunne in THEODORA GOES WILD (Col '36)

ball comedy. Leave that to Carole Lombard and Claudette Colbert. Dunne arranged for herself and her doctor husband to embark on an European trek ostensibly to meet with the relatives of Mme. Curie, of whom Universal was preparing a screen biography to star Irene. The actress actually hoped that by the time she returned, Columbia, to whom she owed a picture, would have forgotten the silly notion. But Columbia, sensing that Dunne could master this genre as well as she had every other type of screen role, stood pat. When Dunne returned, *Theodora Goes Wild* awaited her. She then tried another ploy. Richard Boleslawski, who had been assigned to direct the picture, was a stranger to her. She was not sure how she could function in a strange metier with such an untested supervisor. Columbia skirted that issue. If she were not pleased with the immediate work of Boleslawski on *Theodora*, he would be replaced to her satisfaction.

As is cinema fact, the production then proceed-

*Years later, in a syndicated news-service interview with Rebecca Morehouse, Douglas would recall the type of behavior on the sets of *The Gorgeous Hussy*. He remembered that Crawford would arrive each day for the filming, followed by a procession of retainers. "I was very amused by it," Douglas said. "She would come out of her star dressing quarters with a retinue of 10 or 15 people, hairdressers, maids, her butler, her chauffeur, and so on, and they trailed along behind her to the set. . . . One day, I took my brother and the chauffeur and the cook and a couple of others and I walked on the set with my parade. Well, everybody froze. You would have thought I was a militant Black Panther. Nobody saw any humor in this. . . . At the lunch break, the assistant director came around and said the director, who was Clarence Brown, had asked him to tell me, 'That was not a very funny thing you did this morning.' As far as they were concerned, this was sacrilege."

ed with only a few problems, and the completed picture debuted at Radio City Music Hall on November 12, 1936. It was a true success and remains an effervescent example of full-bodied screen comedy. "Although it is an intensely artificial and lightweight affair, it is replete with sparkling wisecracks, literate light comedy writing and deft situations" (William Boehnel, *New York World-Telegram*). A good deal of the film's intrinsic success is due to the Douglas touch.

The Mary McCarthy story and the Sidney Buchman screenplay concern a small-town girl, here one Theodora Lynn (Dunne) from Lynnfield, Connecticut, who amazes even herself by writing a titillating best seller, *The Sinner*, which she has published under the pseudonym of Caroline Adams. A church organist since she was fifteen and a Sunday school teacher for the past decade, she is too embarrassed by her risque success to admit the truth, hardly daring to discuss the matter with her New York publisher (Thurston Hall). But matters soon change when she meets devil-may-care illustrator Michael Grant (Douglas), a married man (wed to Leona Maricle) who is immediately attracted by this repressed young miss. When he becomes inebriated and attempts to reconstruct the seduction scene from her novel in his apartment, all her rural inhibitions come to the fore and she holds him at bay, crying forth: "Don't you dare." He later follows her to Lynnfield, determined to liberate her. "I'm going to break you out of this jail and give you the world. . . . You're a strange, sad case, girlie. Desires being strangled to death. Break loose, be yourself." When he is later run out of town for having committed the shocking act of going fishing with Dunne on a Sunday, he leaves her a graduation note: "You're free, baby. Step out and be yourself. There are big things ahead and you'll travel faster alone." And that she does! But not for long. She returns to New York where she promptly goes wild, making speeches about women's liberation, and becoming involved in two scandals (one with Melvyn, another with her publisher). At the grand finale, love-smitten Douglas is waiting at the Lynnfield train station to greet the returning Dunne. She steps off the train with a baby in her arms. He jumps to an immediate conclusion, but she snaps at him: "It isn't mine, stupid." (It belongs to a friend of hers.)

Nearly everyone agreed that the new, frisky, hilarious, nifty Irene Dunne was a joy to watch. It launched her on a successful madcap-comedy career that would encompass her next decade of screen work. There were those who took the occasion to carp that *Theodora Goes Wild* fell down in its attempt to be the distaff *Mr. Deeds Goes To Town* (Columbia, 1936), a point still open to conjecture, but few disagreed over the virtues of Douglas as Dunne's straight man who has more than enough bounce on his own. "Melvyn Douglas is an excellent romantic partner for Miss Dunne. She, rather than he, gets the real acting chances but he is consistently intelligent" (*Variety*). The picture solidly established Douglas in what he later referred to as a "an international reputation for being one of the most debonair and witty farceurs in Hollywood . . . and a saleable commodity."

In the first of his five 1937 releases, Melvyn was cast as Richard Stark in *Women of Glamour* (Columbia), which Gordon Wiles directed. The impoverished production, a remake of Barbara Stanwyck's *Ladies of Leisure* (Columbia, 1930), met with scant approval. Marguerite Tazelaar (*New York Herald-Tribune*) panned it as being "full of phony glamour, stilted dialogue, and moth-eaten situations." Douglas played a wealthy artist who finds renewed inspiration for his craft when he encounters a pretty model (Virginia Bruce) as she is escaping from a dreary yacht party. Reginald Denny is the wealthy souse who attempts to lure Bruce on an around-the-world trip, while Leona Maricle is Douglas's fiancée, who attempts to point out that no matter how he changes Bruce from being cheap, frowsy, slangy, and ungrammatical, she will always remain true to form. However, Bruce does not, nor does Douglas, who eventually agrees to wed his discovery.

Melvyn's first chore under his new MGM contract was in many ways an unrewarding assignment. He was fifth fiddle to Freddie Bartholomew, Spencer Tracy, Lionel Barrymore, and Rudyard Kipling's tale in *Captains Courageous* (MGM, 1937). It was the box-office success that not only transformed Tracy into a major motion-picture star but earned him his first Academy Award. When the film debuted at New York's Astor Theatre on May 11, 1937, Howard Barnes (*New York Herald-Tribune*) properly acclaimed it a photoplay "with such eloquence, authority and beauty that it is certain to become a classic in its new medium."

Under Victor Fleming's direction, the feature soon catapults the viewer into the hectic life of Harvey Cheyne (Bartholomew), the rich, pampered, neglected son of a widowed business tycoon (Douglas). The youth maneuvers his way out of boarding school and the distraught Douglas accompanies him aboard a luxury liner to Europe. On the high seas, near the Grand Banks, Bartholomew, unnoticed, is swept overboard, but he is rescued by the salty crew of the Gloucester fishing schooner *We're Here*. Spoiled brat Bartholomew is at first ungrateful to Portuguese fisherman Manuel (Tracy), who saved him, and to crusty Captain Disko Troop (Barrymore), who allows him to remain aboard the vessel. However, the youth begins to mend his ways, and before long has established a rapport with the crew and discovered new values to his once meaningless young life. He and Tracy become great pals and dory mates. Just as the fish-full vessel is winning its race back to port against the rival *Jennie Cushman*, the topmast of the *We're Here* breaks under the strain, dumping the tangled rope, canvas, and a badly injured Tracy into the water. After a tearful farewell with Bartholomew, Tracy is cut loose and sinks beneath the water. Back in Gloucester, Bartholomew, with his father, attends funeral services for those who have died at sea. When Tracy's name is called, the boy throws a wreath into the water, as does grateful Melvyn. The two wreaths float off entwined, symbolizing the new fellowship between son and father. With his arm around his son, the two watch the wreaths drift off with the tide. It was a small enough part for capable Douglas, but he handled his cameo well.

Back in 1934, when MGM and Greta Garbo were casting for the second male lead opposite her in *The Painted Veil*, Douglas was considered as a possibility until it was decided that Warner Bros.' George Brent would better complement the star and be a better contrast to first male player, Herbert Marshall. Now, three years later, when Brent claimed he was overworked and needed a rest rather than more loan-out assignments, Melvyn was called upon to join with Metro's Robert Young in supporting Claudette Colbert in *I Met Him in Paris* (Paramount, 1938). With this engaging comedy, produced-directed by Wesley Ruggles, Douglas clinched the debate whether he or Fred MacMurray was the more advantageous helpmate to scintillating Colbert oncamera. In this delightful ode to winter sports, Douglas, of the star trio, was the best displayer of "a blithe sense of humor and a flair for the frolicsome" (Frank S. Nugent, *New York Times*).

Paramount spent over a million dollars and a good deal of creative talent to provide proper substitute backdrops for the Swiss resort scenes, transforming bits of Sun Valley and Lake Placid into a lookalike of the Alpines. The effort was worth it, for in the course of this "witty, worldly-wise and welcome" film, Colbert, who had become an avid skier and skater just a few years before, demonstrated that she, Douglas, and Young could handle farcical scenes on a St. Moritz ski slope, toboggan ride, or skating rink, as well as in the Ritz bar in Paris. Colbert appears as Kay Denham who, after five years of savings, abandons her department-store designer's job and her stuffy fiancé (Lee Bowman) for a three-week fling in Paris. Three days in the French capital and she is picked up at cocktail hour by cynical playwright Douglas and playboy novelist Young. Neither man is much on work, and when Young suggests that her European trip needs a fashionable Swiss lodge interlude to become memorable, she willingly agrees to the jaunt, with Douglas deciding to come along as chaperone. Should Colbert succumb to Young or to Douglas? Rebellious Colbert believes amusing Young could be the best man, but then she discovers he is already wed to Mona Barrie. Barrie agrees to divorce him, and Young hopes Colbert will now reconsider his proposal, but she tells him: "I want security. You're as irresponsible as a two-month-old kitten." So she decides to wed still-glum Melvyn. Is this the finish of Young's romantic interest in her? No! Ironically, *I Met Him in Paris* never maintained its sterling reputation as an impressive example of Hollywoodian comedy at its most talky peak. Ted Sennett, in his survey of the screwball movie comedies, *Lunatics and Lovers* (Arlington House, 1973), gives an explanation. "Claude Binyon's script was surprisingly devoid of solid humor and the result was a conventional and not especially amusing triangle comedy . . . there is not one memorable or truly comic sequence in the film, as it moves predictably from situation to situation."

Melvyn remained on loan-out to join Marlene Dietrich and Herbert Marshall in *Angel* (Paramount, 1937), the first of his three pictures with the renowned Continental wit and producer-director, Ernst Lubitsch. There are many reasons given for the financial and artistic disappointment created by *Angel*. It is well known that Paramount had at that time undergone another executive-regime change, and the new studio bosses were rather anxious to take Dietrich off their payroll. On a creative level, some critics suggest a stagnation on the part of Lubitsch. Frank S. Nugent (*New York Times*) analyzed: "It has little verve, faint traces of wit, a pretense to sophistication, a stage self-consciousness." *Variety* was a

With Herbert Marshall in ANGEL (Par '37)

little more indirect in its attack: "[it] is sophisticated, smart and provocative, perhaps too much so."

This book's authors suggest a more basic fault with *Angel*, the too similar acting styles of Dietrich's leading men. Both Marshall and Melvyn were dapper, debonair types, one British, one American, but each a performer who acted almost solely with his face and voice, rather than his body. Marshall had a valid reason for sticking to this visually inactive approach, for he had lost a leg in World War I. Despite a good artificial limb, he still limped noticeably, which embarrassed him beyond mention. Scripts were rewritten, action restaged, doubles used, to avoid his having to do much walking oncamera. But to combine these two polished drawing-room types, each more refined than dashing in manner, both ultrapolite rather than engagingly boisterous, with a leading lady noted for her immobile, masklike beauty, was a tragic entertainment error. It became a too elegant display of super-well-bred personalities involved in an audio drama. Dietrich's previous Josef von Sternberg–Paramount features had all relied on visuals for their luxurious, erotic appeal. In *Angel*, Dietrich looked more breathtakingly beautiful than ever before oncamera, but Lubi-

tsch failed to provide her or her co-players with an active chronicle.

The thesis of the dramatic (rather than comic) romance was that a woman can love two men at once. Sophisticated Dietrich is wed to prim Marshall, he being England's head delegate to the League of Nations. While he is away on one of his interminable diplomatic trips, she galavants to Paris where she arranges with a roguish Russian madam (Laura Hope Crews) to have the run of her whoring establishment. There she meets a fun-loving younger man (Douglas) who naturally mistakes her for one of Crews's "girls." Back in England, Melvyn becomes acquainted with Marshall, arrives at the man's Mayfair home, and there reencounters Dietrich. An accidental slip of her pet name ("Angel") signals disaster, for Marshall quickly surmises her indiscretion. The finale does have a hopeful note, for Marshall returns to Paris and meets with his estranged wife. He apologizes, and they embark on a second honeymoon to Vienna.

In the midst of this display of superior art direction and little actor supervision, Douglas had a few droll moments: his first meeting with "lady of the evening" Dietrich, his later encounter with Marshall in England, his tinkling of the title tune on the piano, his game recognition that his romance with Dietrich must give way to her basic love of stuffy Marshall. But it was not enough to carry the picture. As Nugent of the *New York Times* saw the situation: "Herbert Marshall plays the diplomatic Sir Frederick with a dignity uncommon to cuckolds, and Melvyn Douglas tries heroically, but forlornly, to invest a sophomoric role with maturity."

Melvyn returned to Columbia to rehash his *Tonight or Never* role in *I'll Take Romance* (1937). This time a proven Metropolitan opera singer was the prima donna, none other than Grace Moore, who had recouped her dismal early 1930s MGM operetta cycle with a liberated performance in *One Night of Love* (Columbia, 1934). In this Edward H. Griffith–directed musical, Moore was Metropolitan Opera diva Elsa Terry, who would much rather accept a tempting offer from the Paris Opera than fulfill her contract to open the opera season in Buenos Aires. Douglas is the American impresario who kidnaps her and takes her to South America. Love does win out, but not before Moore performs the title-song love ballad, arias from *La Traviata* and *Martha,* the love duet from *Madama Butterfly* (with Frank Forest), and offers the gavotte from *Manon.* A much-publicized musical interlude has classical-oriented Moore belting out a rendition of "Comin' Round the Mountain." Others in the cast included Helen Westley as Moore's aunt, an opera singer of the old school who has always insured that romance never interfered with Moore's career, bumbling Stuart Erwin as Douglas's pal, and Margaret Hamilton as Moore's companion. As Archer Winsten (*New York Post*) observed, the "picture is eminently satisfactory if you are willing to concede the inevitable opera star plot." No one could complain of Douglas's contribution to the film, for he was "suave and romantic, as usual" (*Brooklyn Daily Eagle*).

While Douglas had been busy with his filmmaking, Helen Gahagan had returned to Broadway in the short-lived *And Stars Remain* (Guild Theatre: October 12, 1936). Then, in 1937, she embarked on a concert tour of Europe, including an operatic engagement at the Salzburg Festival that year. It was in Austria that political events occurred which were to reshape both her and Douglas's future life. As he would later recall: "After her last concert, she was the guest of honor at a dinner of prominent musicians and composers. They began to tell her of the plans under way for setting up an Aryan race. They apparently hoped to convert her to their viewpoints, so that she would be one of their propagandists in America. Thoroughly revolted, and sick at heart, she couldn't get away soon enough.

"From that day to this, we have devoted every facility at our command to combating the Nazis. She gave up her career to do it. The next year, she was to be starred at the Vienna Opera House—the apex of achievement in the operatic world."

On August 14, 1938, the Douglases, who in fulfilling their anti-Fascist beliefs had become deeply committed to what many considered very left-wing causes, became the parents of a girl, Mary Helen, born in a Hollywood hospital. It was the actor's third and final child.

Melvyn then returned to Metro to take over John Barrymore's 1932 Arsene Lupin role, in *Arsene Lupin Returns* (MGM, 1938), yet another part rejected by the lot's prized William Powell. The plot has retired French thief Douglas returning to the cause of action by joining forces with an American detective (Warren William) to track down a master jewel thief. Virginia Bruce functioned as Douglas's pretty fiancée, Nat Pendleton and E. E. Clive were his henchmen, while the suspects included victimized John Halliday and ambiguous Monty Woolley. Douglas enhanced the proceedings (directed by his old Nemesis George Fitzmaurice) with assorted card and coin tricks, and demonstrated that his deductive powers were superior to William's. If Douglas's gentleman detective was a bit more English-Amerian than M. Le Blanc's original Lupin, most filmgoers on the action-theatre circuit were forgiving.

Melvyn worked for the first time with a soon-to-be favorite director, Alexander Hall, in *There's Always a Woman* (Columbia, 1938). Here he had three lovely leading ladies—Joan Blondell, Mary Astor, Frances Drake—in a mystery comedy in which an impoverished private detective returns to the district attorney's office while his goofy wife (Blondell) becomes involved with Astor's homicide case. Blondell is so eager to prove her detective abilities that she literally drags her unwilling husband into the caper, yanking him from swank setting to swank setting as the murders are solved. If one forgave the basic unpleasantness of Blondell's character (a no-holds-barred opportunist who has smartcracks rather than blood running through her pretty veins), and a badly handled drunk scene between Blondell and Douglas, the film was a rather pleasant, low-budget *Thin Man* take-off, snappy enough to engender enjoyment on its own.

Metro was having great difficulties in properly casting its petite Viennese beauty Luise Rainer in follow-up roles to her Oscar-winning performances in *The Great Ziegfeld* (MGM, 1936) and *The Good Earth* (MGM, 1937). Perhaps on paper *The Toy Wife* (MGM, 1938), based on a Zöe Akins screenplay* and to be directed by Richard Thorpe, seemed a good notion. After all, the publication of Margaret Mitchell's best-selling novel *Gone with the Wind,* which would be translated to the screen in 1939, had generated tremendous interest in Civil War southern tales; witness Bette Davis's *Jezebel* (Warner Bros., 1938). However, the expensively mounted *The Toy Wife* was a misfire, and just one more occasion where Douglas, cast as Rainer's leading man, was given a thankless role rejected by MGM's top-level actor aristocracy.

Perhaps Herbert Drake (*New York Herald-Tribune*) has best described *The Toy Wife:* "The picture falls into the category of tearjerker, a form of film apparently built upon the notion that nothing matters as long as the emotions get a thorough workout at regular intervals, leading up to the big death scene at the end." Set in the Louisiana country of the 1800s, it focuses on Gilberta Brigard (Rainer), an extravagant coquette who is called "Frou Frou" because she rustles her crinoline gowns so prettily. Dashing, refined attorney Melvyn once considered wedding Rainer's elder, more practical sister (Barber O'Neil), but flirtatious Rainer (she of the Continental accent) persuades him to wed her. Later, when he wishes to move permanently from New Orleans because of possible career gains, she pouts at the thought and runs off with gallant n'er-do-well Robert Young, her long-standing beau. In a subsequent duel, Young is killed; Douglas takes his child and leaves the bewildered Rainer, only to attempt a later reconciliation with her as she lays on her deathbed, coughing *à la Camille* from a bad dose of tuberculosis. To his credit, Douglas did not shirk his duty as the staunch bastion of respectability in *The Toy Wife,* but he could not cope with the role, his co-star, the treacly dramatics, or the sumptuous, attention-stealing sets. Even Wanda Hale (*New York Daily News*), a staunch Douglas supporter, admitted: "I will say of Melvyn Douglas—who, I think can do no wrong—that he is miscast."

*The play original, *Froufrou* by Meilhac and Halevy, was first performed by Aimee Desclee in Paris in 1859, with the U.S. premiere of the work in 1870, starring Agnes Ethel. One of the more famous revivals of *Froufrou* was by Sarah Bernhardt on tour in London and America in 1880. It became a standard part of La Bernhardt's repertory in future years, up until her "farewell American tour" in 1905–06.

With Virginia Bruce and Warren William in ARSENE LUPIN RETURNS (MGM '38)

With Luise Rainer in THE TOY WIFE (MGM '38)

A much more fortuitous, if far less costly, outing was Melvyn's *Fast Company* (MGM, 1938). Metro was not about to miss out on the profits to be gained in the programmer detective cycle, and decided to parody its own *Thin Man* series with a new sleuthing couple, Joel and Garda Sloane, who are in the rare book business and often, apparently, find themselves implicated in homicide. In this series' starter, the personable, irresponsible couple (Douglas, Florence Rice) are dragged into a murder case when rival book-dealer George Zucco is slain and the suspect initially seems to be his onetime employee, ex-convict Sheppard Strudwick, who happens to love Zucco's daughter (Mary Howard). Before long there is a trio of new suspects (Louis Calhern, Claire Dodd, Dwight Frye), leading up to seventy-five minutes of "swift and mystifying and thoroughly entertaining comedy-drama" (Irene Thirer, *New York Post*). An intriguing facet of this crime film was the viewer's education in the complex procedures of doctoring phony manuscripts to give them an "authentic" aged appearance. For a change, in *Fast Company,* Douglas was the first to portray a character in a new series, for when Metro made two additional Sloane capers, *Fast and Loose* (MGM, 1938) and *Fast and Furious* (MGM, 1939), Robert Montgomery and Franchot Tone,

respectively, took over the detective role.

As any filmgoer of the 1930s can attest, it seemed that Melvyn never took a vacation, simply hopping from one studio to another, to grind out one picture after another in a very competent manner. Maybe one in ten was a special product, but to his credit, very few of them were stinkers. Nor did audiences of the day seem to tire of his presence and his brand of performance. (Granted there was a contingent of male movie patrons then, and male late-show watchers today, who have wondered aloud just what mysterious romantic appeal super-smooth Douglas provided for distaff filmgoers.)

Melvyn would later recall, rather amused, that in the late 1930s, his wife would constantly berate him for his stamina-pounding pace: "Stand up and scream, Mel. Get yourself a vacation." But obviously he did not want one, perhaps thinking that elusive superb role might hit when he least expected it. *That Certain Age* (Universal, 1938) was an example of the Douglas acting theology. He had some free weeks away from Columbia or MGM commitments. He heard that Joe Pasternak, the Universal producer whom he much admired, was seeking a mature leading man for a new Deanna Durbin vehicle now that contractee Vincent Price had been vetoed for the part. Melvyn arranged to meet with Pasternak, approved the script and contract, and began work on the film. As simple as that!

In this, her fourth feature film, young Durbin was allowed to blossom into a woman, and to eschew the baby dresses of her previous films. Durbin appears as fifteen-year-old Alice Fullerton, the daughter of wealthy John Halliday and Irene Rich. Publisher Halliday brings roving foreign correspondent Douglas to his country estate, to convince him to prepare a series of articles. No sooner does adolescent Durbin spot the twenty- (at least)-year-older Douglas than she develops a mad crush on him, and tosses aside her contemporary (Jackie Cooper), who has a mad, puppy-dog crush on her. To throw Durbin and her most pesky younger sister (Juanita Quigley) off his scent, Douglas introduces Nancy Carroll as his wife. Melvyn was at the proper age, if not the right political persuasion, to play the world-weary reporter who has just returned from covering the tempestuous Spanish Civil War. It was child's play for him to adopt the bemused smirk of the man whom Durbin finds more stimulating than a fantasized Lord Byron. He had the intelligence not to be annoyed that the film was basically just a profitable excuse to display a more mature Dur-

With Deanna Durbin and Nancy Carroll in THAT CERTAIN AGE (Univ '38)

bin, and to allow her ample occasion to sing such songs as "Has Anyone Ever Told You Before?" and "You're as Pretty as a Picture." As B. R. Crisler (*New York Times*) reported of this very popular musical, a good deal of the film's success was owed to Douglas's "beautifully acted exposure of himself as a cad . . . [in] scenes of a gentle but highly effective comicality." (For the record, scenes in which Durbin carries out an elopement plot and indulges in some adult kissing were deleted upon the request of preview audiences.)

Melvyn's first good role in an "A" Metro production came in *The Shining Hour* (MGM, 1938), based on the play by Keith Winter.* The quartet of stars gracing this Frank Borzage film were Joan Crawford, Margaret Sullavan, Douglas, and amiable but ineffectual Robert Young. The film is "best described as a romantic conversation piece . . ." (*New York Journal American*). Taxi-dancer Olivia Riley (Crawford), formerly Maggie Riley of New York's unsavory Tenth Avenue, has risen from the ranks as a ritzy nightclub performer. She is about to wed Henry Linden (Douglas), the scion of a wealthy old Wisconsin family, when Douglas's younger brother (Young) comes to town, expresses his disapproval of the match, but

soon finds himself in love with her. All of which causes dire complications when the newly married couple (Douglas-Crawford) return to the midwestern manse, presided over by Young, his sweet wife (Sullavan), and the brothers' domineering sister (Fay Bainter). Only after embittered Bainter sets fire to the house do the couple's emotional entanglements untangle. Everyone involved in the film performed their standard oncamera tricks: Crawford (simpering beauty), Sullavan (righteous, teary, understanding), Melvyn (impeccably mannered, patient), Young (giddy, smiling), Bainter (restrained emotionchurning), Hattie McDaniel (jovial, simple domestic). Nevertheless as *Variety* dutifully explained, the picture "is a confused jungle of cross-purpose motivations and situations that fail entirely to arouse interest. Basic trouble with the production lies in confusing script." To show how little respect he had for *The Shining Hour*, Douglas gleefully participated in a burlesque of the story on Gulf's "Screen Guild Show" (February 26, 1939) with Shirley Ross, George Burns, and Gracie Allen as his co-spoofers.

Back at Columbia, Melvyn worked with Alexander Hall again in the sequel to *There's Always a*

*Booth Theatre: February 13, 1934, 120 performances, starring Gladys Cooper with Raymond Massey in the Douglas film role.

Woman entitled *There's That Woman Again* (1938). Virginia Bruce replaced Joan Blondell as Douglas's meddlesome spouse in this tale of a district attorney and his detective wife being hired to find jewel thieves and the murderer of a merchant. Beauteous Bruce tried too hard to fill Blondell's oversized shoes as the saucer-eyed wife who imperils her spouse's reputation and life in her attempt to prove she is a resourceful investigator. The highlight of this mild entertainment, which came so late in the screwball-comedy cycle, is a sequence in which Bruce is caught in a potential suspect's shower.

Former actor Leslie Fenton made a most successful directing debut in Melvyn's first 1939 release, the modestly budgeted *Tell No Tales* (MGM, 1939). William K. Everson, in *The Detective in Film* (1972), rates the picture "a beautiful minor classic . . . . the plotting and construction is pure Philip Marlowe." Here Douglas is the managing editor of the *Evening Guardian.* When the paper's big boss (Douglass Dumbrille) decides to suspend its publication, Melvyn sets out to solve a kidnap-murder case, reasoning that a big scoop may get the financial powers behind the newspaper to rescind their close-down order. He follows the clue of a $100 bill from the ransom money, and the trail leads through a maze of events. Aiding him in the case is pert schoolteacher Louise Platt, the only witness to the kidnapping crime in question. As predicted, Melvyn not only makes suckers out of the police, but ends by winning Platt's everlasting affection. An interesting sidelight of the film is Melvyn's pursuit of the case through unusual social worlds, such as when he attends the wake of a black fighter in order to question the deceased man's wife about a clue.

Melvyn was reunited with director Alexander Hall and actress Joan Blondell for the bubbly *Good Girls Go to Paris* (Columbia, 1939). (The censors thought the film's original title, *Good Girls Go to Paris, Too,* was too suggestive and demanded a name change.) The film met with an affectionate response from critics and filmgoers alike: "[It is] light, frothy, and just the thing to take your mind off your troubles . . ." (Kate Cameron, *New York Daily News*). Here Douglas is cast as an exchange professor from England teaching Greek mythology at Brand University in the Midwest. He finds himself becoming the confidant of Jenny Swanson (Blondell), a nice kid

from Maple Leaf, Minnesota, who has a notion that becoming a gold digger would be more profitable than being a coffeeshop waitress. Douglas urges her to return home, and even gives her the fare, but she boards a train for New York, and promptly becomes involved with the madcap Brand family (father Walter Connolly, mother Isabel Jeans, son Alan Curtis, daughter Joan Perry). After several beguiling, but silly, episodes, Douglas, who has come to Manhattan, realizes he loves Blondell, proposes, and the two set off on a Paris honeymoon, leaving the irresponsible Brands to tend to their own problems. The entire cast played their comedy scenes so broadly that the viewer scarcely had any opportunity to digest the possible subtleties lurking in the somewhat labored film script.

Ninotchka (MGM, 1939) proved to be the comedy smash of 1939 and the film for which Melvyn Douglas is best remembered.* Ernst Lubitsch, who had moved his production base from Paramount to Metro, was requested to prepare a film vehicle for Greta Garbo, one that would revitalize her sagging, but still very artistic, movie career. With the aid of a Melchior Lengyel story, and a screenplay by Charles Brackett, Billy Wilder, and Walter Reisch, he created this charming screen exercise which was yet another turning point in the Swedish actress's great cinema career. In *Anna Christie* (MGM, 1930) the ads had proclaimed: "Garbo Talks"; for *Ninotchka* the promotional banners heralded: "Garbo Laughs." And because Douglas was her leading man in this celluloid venture, he earned a spot in immortality.

Melvyn was very nearly not in the film. The role of Count Leon Dolga was first earmarked for William Powell, but he was recuperating from an ailment. Both Lubitsch and Garbo remembered Douglas, the director from *Angel,* she from *As You Desire Me,*† and he won the role over other likely contenders, such as Metro's own Robert Montgomery. Thanks to subsequent reuses of the plot,‡ the story of *Ninotchka* is quite familiar. Three Russians commissars (Sig Rumann, Felix Bressart, Alexander Granach) are sent to Paris to confiscate some Russian imperial jewels to allow the Soviets to purchase tractors. The gems were once owned by the Grand Duchess Swana (Ina Claire), a White Russian living in exile in the French capital. Her idle beau, Douglas, is put on the track of the Russians, his mission to halt the

---

*Scenes from *Ninotchka* appear in *Big Parade of Comedy* (MGM, 1964).
†She had considered him for *The Painted Veil* (MGM, 1934), but the role went to George Brent.
‡Elements of *Ninotchka* are found in *Comrade X* (MGM, 1940), Cole Porter's Broadway musical *Silk Stockings,* which became a 1957 MGM movie, and *The Iron Petticoat* (MGM, 1956).

sale of the precious stones. He is so successful that the Soviet leaders finally send Comrade Ninotchka (Garbo) to subdue the misguided trio. She and Melvyn meet, fall in love, but he thinks he has lost her when she returns to Moscow. But later the same three commissars are dispatched to Constantinople, again fall prey to capitalist ways, and once more, Garbo is sent to bail them out of trouble. When she arrives, whom does she find? Douglas!

In *Hollywood in the Thirties* (1968) John Baxter states: "*Ninotchka* (1939) is a film not especially typical of anybody associated with it. Garbo plays comedy with more enthusiasm than skill, Lubitsch directs a story that is unusually free of sexual innuendo and marked more by the wit of scenarists Billy Wilder and Charles Brackett than his own. The 'Lubitsch style' in which much was made of subtleties—glances, finger movements, raised eyebrows—has disappeared."

But even with the above in mind, few can dispute the joyousness of the picture, which documents the celluloid liberation of the Garbo spirit. It is also a field guide in the art of debonair screenfare, with Douglas oozing urbanity, gallantry, and *savoir faire*, all produced with a reckless devil-may-care jauntiness that makes his parasitic way of life and his conniving plot against Garbo delicious rather than offensive or tedious.

When the two lead players first meet somewhere in the film's third reel, it is on a safety island in the middle of a busy Paris street. As the traffic rushes by, she is busy examining a city map.

> *Garbo:* Correct me if I am wrong . . . we are facing north, aren't we? . . . I am looking for the Eiffel Tower.
> *Douglas:* Is that thing lost again.

A few minutes further into the conversation, Garbo asks, "Must you flirt?"

> *Douglas:* I don't have to but I find it natural.
> *Garbo:* Suppress it.
> *Douglas:* I'll try.

After a sightseeing trip to the top of the Eiffel Tower, Douglas persuades Garbo to examine his rooms. She agrees.

> *Douglas:* If there are any special aspects of the room you wish to study. I have nothing to conceal. . . . Where shall we begin?
> *Garbo:* I will start with you.
> *Douglas:* That's great. I'm thirty-five years old.

Just over six feet tall. I weigh a hundred and eighty-two pounds stripped.
> *Garbo:* And what is your profession?
> *Douglas:* Keeping my body fit, keeping my mind alert, keeping my landlord appeased. That's a full-time job.
> *Garbo:* And what do you do for mankind?
> *Douglas:* For mankind not a thing. For womankind the record is not quite so bleak.

A few minutes later, an aggressive Melvyn tires of persuasive talk; instead he kisses the surprised Garbo.

> *Douglas:* Was that talkative?
> *Garbo:* No that was restful. Again [He kisses her] Thank you.
> *Douglas:* Oh my barbaric Ninotchka. My impossible, unromantic, statistical . . . [The phone rings] Saved by the bell.

The film progresses animatedly toward the expected conclusion, including the famous cafe scene where Douglas breaks down Garbo's reserve through champagne and corny jokes, to the finale in Constantinople where he threatens to wreak havoc on Russian manpower unless she agrees to be with him for the rest of their lives.

Garbo concludes: "Well, when it is a choice between my personal interest and the good of my country, how can I waver? No one shall say Ninotchka was a bad Russian." They live (hopefully) happily ever after.

The picture, for most spectators at least, was one of those screen comedies where every ingredient seemed to mesh perfectly. For Garbo it meant renewed popularity and another Academy Award nomination. (She lost to Vivien Leigh of MGM's *Gone with the Wind*.) For Douglas it brought added prestige and more job offers in a cinema career already overburdened with work. Years later, when asked the inevitable question of what Garbo had been like, Douglas would recall: "She was already a legend then, kind of the first hippie. We were never very friendly, but I found her fascinating. If she was temperamental, it came out of a deep insecurity, but it was never because she was putting on a big actress stunt. I've seen her walk off the set frustrated because she couldn't get her zipper unstuck and the next day you'd read she was off walking in the rain naked."

When Melvyn was not busy with radio assignments, such as appearing with Virginia Bruce in *A Rose by Any Name* on the "Maxwell House Coffee's Good News" program (January 11,

1939), he managed to make more movies. His last assignment for 1939 was *The Amazing Mr. Williams* at Columbia, again matched with Joan Blondell and director Alexander Hall. In this outing he is the homicide-squad lieutenant and she is the mayor's secretary. They would like to marry, but something always comes up, such as the time Douglas remembers he has a date with Blondell and shows up at her apartment with a handcuffed hood, Edward Brophy. Douglas, knowing how much Blondell abhors his work interfering with their social life, tries to pass Brophy off as an old college chum. Jocular Melvyn suggests that perhaps Brophy could be the blind date of Blondell's roommate (Ruth Donnelly). At which the sentenced lawbreaker pipes up, "Nothin' doin'. I know me rights. I don't have to take no blind dates." The film may have been geared on a familiar pattern, but it was executed with much expert wisecracking and such an engaging rapport between Douglas and Blondell that few viewers minded the *déjà vu* qualities of the snappy production. Archer Winsten (*New York Post*) offered his own interpretation of the Douglas charm: "There is something about him, maybe his winter gray eyes, that makes you believe he will get his man while, at the same time, his charming smile absolves him of brutality."

Melvyn continued his screen career into the new decade with the same ferocity as before. MGM was so pleased with the utilization of his services that in the fall of 1940 they renegotiated his contract, which, in conjunction with his Columbia pact, loan-out privileges, and radio assignments, brought his yearly salary to the $150,000–$180,000 level.

As suggested before, both the Douglases had taken a tremendous interest in global situations since Mrs. Douglas's 1937 European trip. They were among the first members of the Hollywood colony to realize that America could not stay out of World War II forever, and that this country must prepare for that eventuality. This "revolutionary" concept, so heretical to the right-wing conservative Republican elements in California, made Douglas almost as loathsome to some of the industry's top-ranking executives as fellow MGM-er Robert Montgomery, who had led the Screen Actors Guild in its fights for craft recognition. One of Douglas's first civic-duty chores was to join with Russell Hicks and Lewis Stone in the formation of the California state guard. When in the following year it was necessary to appoint an official head of the state guard, Melvyn was suggested for the post. However, there was such an (instigated) outcry over the possible appointment

With Joan Blondell, Ruth Donnelly, and Ed Brophy in THE AMAZING MR. WILLIAMS (Col '39)

of Douglas—some quarters branded him a Communist sympathizer because of his association with the state welfare board—that he requested Governor Olsen to reject him as a candidate. Meanwhile, Mrs. Douglas was appointed an alternate delegate from California to the Democratic national convention in Chicago.

Although it had been suggested that Douglas would play Darcy in Norma Shearer's version of *Pride and Prejudice*, when MGM did finally make the picture in 1940, Laurence Olivier and Greer Garson had the leads in the screen rendition of Jane Austen's classic novel of manners. Instead the actor joined with Columbia's leading lady, Jean Arthur, in *Too Many Husbands* (1940), based on Somerset Maugham's play *Home and Beauty.*°

When director Wesley Ruggles and scenarist Claude Binyon, in their ninth collaboration, selected Maugham's play for their film's basis, they certainly realized that its Enoch Arden theme had been done many times before in the theatre and on film, but they certainly were not prepared to race another studio's similar venture to the box-office window. *Too Many Husbands* would beat RKO's *My Favorite Wife*† to the debut post by some five months, but the latter film, supervised by Leo McCarey, directed by Garson Kanin, and starring Irene Dunne, Cary Grant, Randolph Scott, and Gail Patrick, proved the more enduringly popular whenever any comparisons were made.

The basic plot promise of *Too Many Husbands* is that Arthur's husband (Fred MacMurray) is allegedly drowned while on a boat cruise. Even the Coast Guard agrees to this theory. A year later, after she has wed his publishing partner (Douglas), Arthur is greeted by a returned MacMurray, who relates that he has just been rescued from his base on a deserted isle. This bizarre turn of events first confuses, then delights Arthur, for neither man, until this competitive situation arose, had been particularly attentive to her. Now she wages her own battle of justice to be fair to each, but to teach both these male chauvinists a lesson in consideration. Both stymied "husbands" finally can take no more, and now being the best of friends again, they walk out on her. A judicial decision later determines that MacMurray is still her spouse, but Arthur learns that Melvyn cherishes the notion that she might yet find in his favor.

Noël Coward's *Design for Living*, which also

With Fred MacMurray in TOO MANY HUSBANDS (Col '40)

dealt with a *menage à trois*, was a far more felicitous in the handling of a two-men–one-woman triangle, for the scripting and direction of *Too Many Husbands* strained at the seams. The picture "tends to overdo its effects, squeezing its situations until the obvious screams like the eagle on the proverbial miser's dollar. In its less fortunate moments, it becomes extreme nonsense, almost the *reductio ad absurdum* of absurdity . . ." (B. R. Crisler, *New York Times*). Even more than the lead trio, Melville Cooper (as an imperious, snobbish butler) and Dorothy Peterson (as a love-lost secretary) were able to rise above director Wesley Ruggles's handling, which too often turned the characters into inanimate pawns, each striving to keep a straight face in the absurd situation. Columbia would later revamp the film into Betty Grable's musical *Three for the Show* (1955).

Ex-Twentieth Century–Fox screen heroine Loretta Young, who had learned career humility when she was forced to take a tremendous salary cut and sign a multifilm deal with Columbia, was the star of *He Stayed for Breakfast* (1940). Producer B. P. Schulberg, who had packaged Douglas's

°Maugham's play premiered on the London stage August 30, 1919, for a 235-performance run. In the United States it was called *Too Many Husbands* (Booth Theatre: October 8, 1919, 15 performances).
†Remade as *Move Over, Darling* (Twentieth Century–Fox, 1963) with Doris Day, James Garner, Chuck Connors, and Polly Bergen.

last Broadway fling, *Tapestry in Gray* (1935), produced this comedy directed by Alexander Hall. The movie's premise created the reverse situation of *Ninotchka* and *Comrade X*, for here the hero is Americanized by the leading lady. The film was based on Michael Duran's French play *Liberte Provisoire*, which had later been translated by Sidney Howard into the Broadway production *Ode to Liberty*.

Perhaps politically minded Douglas saw this film venture as an opportunity to express his allegiance to the American way of life, for, more than any other Hollywood picture to that date, *He Stayed for Breakfast* was geared to lambast and ridicule the Communist ideology. In Paris (where else could such a tale occur?) rabid Communist waiter Melvyn is so annoyed at obese baker Eugene Pallette, who sips coffee with his pinky finger extended, that he shoots the cup out of the capitalist's pudgy hand. Fleeing from the police, he hides in Young's apartment, soon discovering that priggish Pallette is her estranged husband and publishing editor Alan Marshal her current beau. By the finale, Young has also seen the light of day, taken her own potshot at Pallette, and agreed to go off to America with Douglas. What are Douglas's plans for the future in the United States? "I'm just going to be a plain member of the middle class. When I get to America I'm going to vote for Roosevelt."

If the belabored digs at the Communists (Pallette barks, "Scratch a Red and you'll find yellow") can be overlooked, *He Stayed for Breakfast* provides a capsule lesson in the adverse qualities of Douglas's screen persona. Whether smirking at Young's political naivete, storming around in Young's frilly dressing gown, refusing to appease his Red party bosses by denouncing Young, or taking her dancing one Parisian night, he was just too smug. Unlike the bulk of his other motion pictures, *He Stayed for Breakfast* offered neither the actor nor the viewer any alleviation from his droll smugness, his charmingly insulting behavior, or his arrogant obliviousness to anyone's ideologies and needs but his own. The unpleasant reality of the possibility of too much of Douglas in one picture was all too evident here.

Once again Melvyn filled in for recuperating William Powell in *Third Finger—Left Hand* (MGM, 1940) in which Powell and Myrna Loy were to have been rematched yet again. As the

With Myrna Loy in a publicity pose for THIRD FINGER-LEFT HAND (MGM '40)

Philadelphia Record decided: "The film works itself into a lather over an idea that isn't funny to begin with." Excessively competent ladies-fashion editor Loy fends off too persistent suitors and her boss's too jealous wife by telling them she is already married; but then she meets commercial artist Douglas. When he falls in love with her, he decides to teach her a lesson, and he poses as her alleged long-lost husband from South America. She really loves Douglas, but to keep the plot running (gasping?) for ninety-six minutes, she persists in avoiding his matrimonial bids and must contend with his assertions that he is her lawful spouse. Lawyer Lee Bowman is used by clever Loy to make persistent Douglas jealous.

Perhaps the most noteworthy element surrounding the production of *This Thing Called Love* (Columbia, 1941), based on the Edwin Burke play,* was that it was the first "A" picture to be unqualifiedly condemned by the Legion of Decency since that body was formed in 1934.† The Alexander Hall–directed comedy survived the ban to emerge on the nation's screens. "It is

---

*Opened at the Maxine Elliott Theatre on September 17, 1928, for a 138-performance run. The 1929 Pathe film version starred Constance Bennett and Edmund Lowe.
†The Legion's report stated: ". . . the treatment of the plot concentrates throughout a greater portion of the film upon a marriage situation which as screen material is highly suggestive and objectionable. The film, moreover, reflects ideas contrary to the Christian concept of marriage."

With Myrna Loy in a publicity pose for THIRD FINGER-LEFT HAND (MGM '40)

adult, it is amusing, it has sparkle, it has vim and —perhaps more to the point—it is cinch boxoffice" (*Variety*).

The thesis of *This Thing Called Love* raises the question: Can a new marriage survive on a purely platonic basis until the true qualities of mutual attraction are discerned? Rosalind Russell, once more a woman executive, is out to prove—with herself and Douglas as the guinea pigs—that marriage can be permanent, and the best way to insure this, she believes, is to have the couple start their wedded life together as *just* good friends. This is pretty tough for businessman Douglas to accept, for he has traveled six thousand miles from South America just to wed her, and the idea of a kissless honeymoon is horrendous. As predicted, persuasive Melvyn soon changes Russell's iron-clad philosophy. However, by this point he is suffering from an attack of poison oak. Now that she is primed for romantic action she cannot understand his present refusal to get cozy. She does a triple take, turns to the camera, and says: "I don't get it, do you?" Rounding out the pleasant cast ensemble were Binnie Barnes as an attractive secretary, and Allyn Joslyn as an attorney with a jealous wife (Gloria Dickson).

The second* of Douglas's five 1941 releases was United Artists' *That Uncertain Feeling,* which again teamed him with Ernst Lubitsch, and matched the dapper actor for the first time oncamera with exotic Merle Oberon. Lubitsch had transformed the same story† onscreen once before in *Kiss Me Again* (Warner Bros., 1925). The new results were less engaging: "call it middling fair entertainment," reported the *New York World-Telegram.* This touch-and-go comedy found seemingly happy-marrieds Douglas and Oberon discovering that her peculiar hiccoughs and restlessness are due to subconscious urges for a more stimulating marriage. To make the couple's adjustment more complicated (and hopefully more amusing), they are soon plagued by an iconoclastic concert pianist (Burgess Meredith) who not only moves into their abode, but begins to court Oberon.

Soap opera, espionage, and a love triangle made up the turgid ingredients for *A Woman's Face* (MGM, 1941), a remake of Ingrid Bergman's *En*

---

*Melvyn's busy schedule prevented him from co-starring with Claudette Colbert in *Skylark* (Paramount, 1941), and Ray Milland was substituted.
†Based on the 1880 play *Divorcons (Let Us Divorce)* by Victorien Sardou, first produced in New York at the Park Theatre (March 14, 1882) with Alice Dunning Lingard.

Kvinnas Ansikte (Svenskfilmindustri, 1938), which George Cukor directed with Melvyn appearing opposite Joan Crawford. The MGM actress, very anxious to restore her sagging box-office image, had recouped some of her fan appeal with *The Women* (MGM, 1939) and *Susan and God* (MGM, 1940), both also directed by Cukor, and here she delved into the aura of high dramatics. The first half of *A Woman's Face*, in which she is the lonely and embittered Anna Holm, works well. She has been badly scarred in a childhood accident, and her ravaged face leads her into a career of crime as the leader of a gang of blackmailers. One of her cohorts is impoverished aristocrat Conrad Veidt. However, once Crawford meets famed plastic surgeon Douglas and he operates on her disfigured face, the picture turns into more conventional fare, with Crawford becoming Crawford the move heroine. Will she or won't she follow Veidt's bidding to help kill his nephew so he can claim the inheritance, and will or will not Douglas divorce his wife and wed her, are the trite plot problems solved in an obvious manner.

From this overwrought women's picture, Douglas returned to Columbia for *Our Wife* (1941). In this screenplay he is the tippling composer, while Ruth Hussey is the inspiring lady scientist and Ellen Drew the shrewish ex-wife. With both Hussey and Drew angling to win the attentions of Douglas, the John M. Stahl–directed comedy might better have been titled *Our Husband.*

George Cukor was at the helm of *Two-Faced Woman* (MGM, 1941),* which attempted and failed dismally to make Greta Garbo into a contemporary farceuse *à la* Carole Lombard. Douglas struggled as hard as everyone else to buoy up this tale of a ski instructress (Garbo) who weds a New York publisher (Douglas). When she fears that his old flame, playwright Constance Bennett, might be winning him away from her, she poses as her own sexy twin sister. The original script had Douglas, true to the formula of *The Guardsman*, maintain his uncertainty whether this effervescent creature is actually his own wife. However, because the Legion of Decency raised such a howl over the film's immoral implications, a scene was inserted into the release print which has Douglas acknowledging his awareness that the new girl is actually his own wife.

This would-be comedy sensation of the year proved to be a fizzle. Of Melvyn, the *New York*

With Greta Garbo in three scenes from TWO-FACED WOMAN (MGM '41)

*Based on the Fulda play which had been previously filmed as *Her Sister from Paris* (First National, 1926) with Constance Talmadge and Ronald Colman, and then as *Moulin Rouge* (United Artists, 1933) with Constance Bennett and Franchot Tone.

es and bores into the sod" (*Richmond* (Va.) *News Leader*). Lee Bowman functioned here as the rejected groom-to-be, with Gail Patrick as the other woman with eyes for Douglas. In the abridged courtroom divorce sequences, rambunctious Marjorie Main presided over the proceedings as the curious judge, eager to learn details of high life among the idle rich.

During this hectic period of moviemaking, Melvyn's wife was engineering a political career for herself. She was first a committeewoman from her adopted state, then, with labor support, she became a candidate for the House of Representatives, and won on the Democratic ticket in 1944, 1946, and 1948. At the same time Douglas had been making his own political commitments. He had served as chairman of the Motion Picture Democratic Committee, and after the signing of the Hitler-Stalin Pact he presented a resolution to the committee which denounced both the Nazis and the Soviets. He was much maligned for his action; the resolution was unsuccessful and he resigned his post. In 1940 he became the first film actor to be a delegate to a national political convention when he represented California at the Democratic National Convention. In 1941, he accepted a nonpaying post as consultant for the arts division of the Office of Civilian Defense. Hardly had he settled down in Washington to his new tasks than a huge hullabaloo arose over the alleged $8,000 salary he was being paid for his volunteer work. It became a political football, with Eleanor Roosevelt being called to task for supposedly having approved the appointment. On his own Douglas clarified his position. He told the press later: "My trouble is that folks don't seem to think about me, the actor, but me the target. . . . If being a whipping boy for the Administration is my due then I guess it's okay by me."

Times printed: "Douglas, who probably spends more time in pyjamas than any other male in history, continues to look as though a brisk walk in the open air would refresh him. Apply that rule to the whole film." Nor was the superior supporting cast of much assistance. They were generally bland and tense: Roland Young as Douglas's twinkly partner, Ruth Gordon as a wise secretary, and even Bennett, who strained with the feckless dialog and situations to arouse a few laughs (as when she looks at her image in the powder room mirror and emits a nerve-shattering shriek, then immediately regains her composure).

Two-Faced Woman was to be Garbo's final motion picture, although no one was really aware of it at the time. However, it was common knowledge that Norma Shearer had tired of being Metro's queen of the screen (the feeling was nearly mutual) and *We Were Dancing* (MGM, 1942)* proved to be one of her last films. Directed by Robert Z. Leonard, its wispy plot had an underfinanced Polish princess (Shearer) running off with a Viennese gigolo (Douglas) at her engagement party. "Norma Shearer and Melvyn Douglas are good dancers, and the music is nice, but that hardly justifies a plot which limps on fallen arch-

Melvyn the champion would have happily remained in Washington, but Columbia Pictures demanded he return to the coast to fulfill his contractual obligations by appearing with Carole Lombard in *He Kissed the Bride*. Douglas reluctantly returned to California, only to have tragedy strike. Lombard was returning from an Indianapolis bond-selling trek, when, on January 16, 1942, the TWA plane in which she was a passenger crashed into Table Rock Mountain some thirty miles southwest of Las Vegas. Her tragic death stunned America and threw Columbia into confusion. Joan Crawford, long a friend of Clark Gable

*Allegedly based on one of the playlets from Noel Coward's *Tonight at 8:30,* which premiered in London at the Phoenix Theatre on January 9, 1936, for a 157-performance run. On Broadway, it was seen at the National Theatre (November 24, 1936) for 113 performances, and again at the National Theatre (February 20, 1948) for 26 performances.

Miss Eileen Lusby swearing in Melvyn Douglas as head of the Arts Council in the Office of Civilian Defense, February 6, 1942

and his wife Lombard, volunteered to substitute for the late star in the upcoming film, with her salary donated to charity. The Alexander Hall–directed film, retitled *They All Kissed the Bride* (Columbia, 1942) became a Crawford vehicle, instead of an evenly balanced vehicle of a woman executive who falls in love with the crusading writer (Douglas) who is out to expose the harshness of employee working conditions in her family-owned trucking company. Melvyn, looking quite bored with the proceedings, passed through the picture wearing one long smirk. The critics were well aware that he was not giving his all to this lightweight film. Eileen Creelman (*New York Sun*) labeled it "one of those smirking little comedies in which Melvyn Douglas runs about in a frenzy of passion. This is all getting pretty tiresome by now. Mr. Douglas wore out that joke a couple of years ago. Now his performance is simply a repetition of bad taste." As usual Douglas has a tipsy scene, and, again, he wakes up in a strange bed wearing a lady's nightgown (incidents such as this caused the Legion of Decency to give it a "B" rating, meaning the film was objectionable in part).

Melvyn found himself back on the Metro lot for *Three Hearts for Julia* (MGM, 1943) in which he and the long underrated and studio-ignored Ann

With Gail Patrick, Marjorie Main, and Lee Bowman in WE WERE DANCING (MGM '42)

With Joan Crawford in THEY ALL KISSED THE BRIDE (Col '42)

Sothern thumped through a routine, modest comedy. He is the budding musician who becomes a war correspondent and goes to the arena of battle, while his musically inclined wife joins an all-women orchestra. Lee Bowman is the orchestra conductor who nearly terminates the Douglas-Sothern marriage. For a minor-league effort, *Three Hearts for Julia* raised a lot of scorn. "Why any major studio, in these days and at this time, should have wasted time, talent and money on a picture like this is one of those things that continually brings Hollywood into public attention and investigation."

By the time *Three Hearts for Julia* was released (May 20, 1943), Melvyn had long since bid goodbye to Hollywood and joined the Army for the duration of World War II. Plans for Douglas to co-star in *Sahara* (Columbia, 1943), a World War II African desert feature, were scrapped. In December 1942, Douglas, who had resigned from the California social welfare board, reported to Camp Robinson, Arkansas, with the rank of Army private. The fact that a man of forty-two could endure the rigors of basic training would have made some headlines, but the celebrity requested that his wartime activities be unpublicized as much as possible. During the war years, he mainly organized troop entertainment units, serving in the China-Burma-India theatre of battle.

When he was discharged from the Army in November 1945, Melvyn was not anxious to return to filmmaking, particularly at MGM. When he enlisted, he recalled, "MGM thought I was a traitor, that I was deserting *them* just to go into the U.S. Army. My name was anathema." Like many of the other actors, including MGM's Clark Gable and Robert Montgomery, who had gone into the service, the strain of the combat had robbed them of their still youthful looks. Douglas, now nearing forty-five (and looking every bit his age), was anxious to break away from pictures. As he later explained: "I chose the time when the studios were breaking up to go back into the theatre. If I had stayed in Hollywood I'd have ended up typecast through life as a kind of drawing room playboy."

While Douglas and his attorneys were actively seeking ways of breaking his MGM-Columbia pacts, he found himself thrust into *Sea of Grass,* a Metro vehicle for Spencer Tracy and Katharine Hepburn that was made, then shelved, and finally released in February 1947. This overlong (123 minutes) frontier tale, directed by Elia Kazan from Conrad Richter's novel, had Douglas third-billed as Brice Chamberlain, a crusading lawyer who has an affair with the neglected wife (Hepburn) of a New Mexico Territory cattle baron (Tracy). From their illicit union, a son (Robert Walker) is born. The *New Yorker* commented

Helen Gahagan Douglas with the Douglases' children, Mary Helen and Peter, in their Washington home, June, 1945

With Spencer Tracy in THE SEA OF GRASS (MGM '47)

Douglas was "as gloomy as if *he* were the wronged husband, instead of being the worm in the domestic apple." Throughout the dirgeful prairie yarn, Douglas pontificates on the rights and duties of a woman. He tells Hepburn: "I'm told a good wife is only what a husband wants her to be." Later he asks her: "Why do women insist upon loving men for what they want them to be?" And at yet another juncture in the script he begs the unhappy heroine: "Just tell me you got what you want—even part of what you want." This certainly was not the gallant, spirited Douglas of old.

For Columbia he starred in *The Guilt of Janet Ames* (1947), which reunited him with Rosalind Russell, a great screen comedienne who had succumbed to the dramatic thespian syndrome. The Henry Levin–directed film was an embarrassing, unfathomable flight of fantasy as war-widowed Russell, imprisoned in a wheelchair because of hysterical paralysis, seeks to learn if the five soldiers who survived a grenade attack due to her husband's bravery were worth his sacrifice. Melvyn, one of the quintet, is the onetime newspaperman who is drowning his talent in drink. Through belabored basic psychotherapy, he and Russell redeem one another. Sid Caesar, another of the rescued soldiers, has a good skit as a stand-

With Cary Grant, Will Wright, Myrna Loy, Ian Wolfe, and Frank Darien in MR. BLANDINGS BUILDS HIS DREAM HOUSE (Selznick Releasing '48)

up comedian doing a burlesque of psychiatrists and psychoanalysis.

Having previously functioned on Broadway as both an actor and director, Douglas took a hand at producing with Herman Levin. The result was the successful *Call Me Mister* (National Theatre: April 18, 1946, 734 performances). Meanwhile, Melvyn and his legal advisors were able to find a loophole in his studio contracts under the California peonage law, and he was professionally a free man. He made four more pictures before returning to the Broadway stage, some of them concessions to close out past commitments interrupted by his war service. In *Mr. Blandings Builds His Dream House* (RKO, 1948), he was again typecast as the other man, but the film allowed him to play oncamera with his more successful genre competitor, Cary Grant. Today the benign antics of a city couple (Grant, Myrna Loy) attempting to survive the pitfalls of building a house in the country seem peculiarly trivial, but in its day it was considered chic comedy. Douglas, in a role that Rudy Vallee might have played better (and did in *The Bachelor and the Bobbysoxer* [RKO, 1947], which also starred Grant and Loy) was Loy's old flame,

who cast a joking eye on the harried proceedings.

My Own True Love (Paramount, 1948) was a "sincere but woebegone Hollywood attempt to produce a British speciality: the quiet little drama in which well-bred characters stiff-upperlip their way through an emotional crisis" (*Time* magazine). Douglas was the London widower who tries to cope with his embittered service-veteran son (Philip Friend) while romancing a sympathetic war-wearing A.T.S. lady (Phyllis Calvert). The only memorable ingredient of this film was its title song, which is still a standard today.

Back at RKO, Melvyn joined with Maureen O'Hara in *A Woman's Secret* (1949), directed by the now-cult figure Nicholas Ray. The jumbled flashback tale had O'Hara as a onetime vocalist who grooms tough-and-tumble Gloria Grahame as her protégée and lives to regret it. Douglas was cast as a second-rate Oscar Levant, the piano-playing confidant of O'Hara who ambles through the baffling plot mumbling kittenish dialog to the redheaded actress and cautiously observing the brazen actions of singer Grahame.

He ended this phase of his Hollywood career by appearing in a character assignment* in *The*

*Kirk Douglas had originally been cast for the part; it was rewritten for Melvyn.

With Gregory Peck and Ava Gardner in THE GREAT SINNER (MGM '49)

Great Sinner (MGM, 1949). Loosely based on Feodor Dostoevski's novel *The Gambler,* this ambitious production had cerebral, sartorially elegant Gregory Peck attempting to save sultry Ava Gardner from becoming the latest victim of gambling fever. Douglas was slick in the empty role of the suave, crass casino operator. The picture, and its illustrious cast, met with adverse public reaction: " . . . for all the romantic ostentation and the hovering tensely over clicking roulette wheels, *The Great Sinner* is a dreary picture" (Bosley Crowther, *New York Times*).

After this cinema flop, Melvyn relished the notion of returning to the Broadway stage where, hopefully, he could ply his craft in meatier fashion. Douglas was the first to admit that his stereotyped roles "were boring and I was soon fed up with them. It's true they gave me a world-wide reputation I could trade on, but they also typed me as a one-dimensional, non-serious actor." Like Robert Montgomery, another ex-MGMer who had headed eastward (for a career in television and national politics), Douglas realized that in post–World War II Hollywood there would be no backswing to the type of stories that required dapper boudoir gallants. They were a dying breed in reality and the neorealistic cinema (California style) insisted upon reflecting it. The result was that from the 1950s onward there would be fewer and fewer celluloid romantic comedies made, whether slapstick, madcap, or sophisticated. Raw-toned violence and message paeans were the order of the day, with gimmicky widescreen features, roadshow epic specials, and exploitation productions with daring sexuality the coming trend. Industrious William Powell and George Brent would learn these facts the hard way, forced into a retirement their vanity would not accept. Of the diminishing species (for no new debonair leading man emerged in the post-1950s), only Cary Grant, Ray Milland, the younger David Niven, and England's gift to America, Rex Harrison, would survive the transition into the 1950s as major film stars. And, more often than not, they lost out roles in the select number of bright, contemporary comedies to the likes of Rock Hudson, Tony Curtis, or Kirk Douglas.

In more recent years, Melvyn Douglas would expostulate on his continued love for the stage in contrast to filmmaking. "The theatre is the thing I know best and so I work at it. But something more than that—it is one of the few mediums left in which there is a certain freedom of expression, in which no club is held over one's head by sponsors, advertising agencies or pressure groups. In this age of conformity and mechanization, I feel more and more that anyone connected with any of the creative arts is a fortunate being."

For his return vehicle to the Broadway stage, Douglas picked a rather lightweight comedy, *Two Blind Mice* (Cort Theatre: March 2, 1949, 157 performances). It was staged by the show's author, Samuel Spewack, and concerned two nice old ladies (Laura Pierpont, Mabel Paige) who run the Office of Seeds and Standards, a government organization left over from the Hoover Administration. The outfit had long since been officially abolished, but, no one has bothered to tell the daffy women running it. Douglas was the newsman who decides to pull an impish experiment on Pierpont and Paige, one of whom is the aunt of Douglas's ex-wife (Jan Sterling). Melvyn gave the role of Tommy Thurston his amiable best. "[He] plays the part of the brash, unabashed and self-assured reporter as if he were having the time of his life. His spirit gets across the footlights and becomes infectious" (Thomas Dash, *Women's Wear Daily*).

He was not so fortunate with his next Broadway outing, *The Bird Cage* (Coronet Theatre: February 22, 1950, 21 performances). The Arthur Laurents melodrama, directed by Harold Clurman, presented Douglas as Wally Williams, a first-class heel, who does dirt to his two nightclub partners. In the finale, he sets fire to his establishment and seemingly dies in the blaze. *Variety's* reporter was on hand to record that "[he] is convincing and provides the proper drive for the part, but cannot overcome the lack of dimension and the repulsive quality of the character."

While Melvyn was emoting on Broadway, his wife was having great political difficulties in California. In 1950 she ran for the U.S. Senate on the Democratic ticket. Her Republican opponent was Richard M. Nixon. He won the senatorial contest by means which did not sit well with many observers of the race. Nixon's supporters had issued a flyer, printed on pink paper, which purported to link Helen Gahagan Douglas with Congressman Vito Marcantonio of New York, the latter being a well-known spokesman for the pro-Communist American Labor party. The 1930s political sentiments of Mrs. Douglas and her actor-husband were raked up *ad nauseam*. Six years later, when the retired politician was asked what she thought of Vice President Nixon, she publicly replied: "My impression of Dick Nixon is that of an opponent who was smart and adaptable, who dodged the real issues and who campaigned on character assassination. . . . I do not doubt that Nixon was much too wise in 1950 to have called me a Com-

munist in so many words. But at the time there was no question in my mind or in the minds of those working with me and supporting me that the entire Nixon campaign was deliberately designed to create the impression that I was a Communist or at least 'communistic.' "

With the demise of her political career, the Douglases sold their home near the Hollywood Bowl (it was purchased by Paul Douglas), and moved their permanent residence to upper Park Avenue in New York City.

Douglas was very active on the Broadway scene in 1951. In *The Little Blue Light* (ANTA Playhouse: April 29, 1951, 16 performances), an experimental production written by Edmund Wilson, Melvyn was a liberal magazine editor who resists all power groups and comes to grapple with a Greek immigrant (Burgess Meredith), now an important political figure. Said Brooks Atkinson (*New York Times*) of the short-lived drama: "[it] looks like a play and sounds like a play, it has no feet, hands or heart and no theatrical substance." The husband-and-wife team of Martin Gabel and Arlene Francis were also in the show.

For *Glad Tidings* (Lyceum Theatre: October 11, 1951, 100 performances), an Edward Mabley work and the type of smart-set romantic comedy that Hollywood no longer produced, Melvyn both directed and starred. Once again Douglas was a journalist, this time a man who returns home after nearly two decades to discover that his onetime lover (Signe Hasso) is the mother of their nineteen-year-old daughter (Patricia Benoit). Brooks Atkinson (*New York Times*) commended Douglas the performer: "[he] is not only a polished actor but a man of good instinct, and he makes something genuine out of the part." Atkinson, however, was less enthusiastic about Douglas's staging of the play, labeling it "purely mechanical."

While Melvyn had been back in Hollywood in 1950 assisting his wife in her futile bid for the Senate, he succumbed to offers of making more motion pictures. These were the last two films he was to make for more than a decade. *My Forbidden Past* (RKO, 1951) offered a very mature Douglas as a southern gentleman in love with his unscrupulous cousin (Ava Gardner), who is, in turn, in love with a married man. The belle comes into money, but she still cannot buy the man she truly loves, doctor Robert Mitchum. It was a forlorn melodrama, hinting "at hidden, spicy secrets which the film doesn't back up" (*Variety*). Douglas's secondary role was so overstated that he

With Ava Gardner in MY FORBIDDEN PAST (RKO '51)

emerged more as a ludicrous than a bearable screen figure. *On the Loose* (RKO, 1951), released at a time when television was the important medium, was a little "B" film that went virtually unnoticed. It concerned a set of overly indulgent parents (Douglas, Lynn Bari) and their wayward daughter (Joan Evans).

The play that solidified Douglas's reputation as a major force on Broadway was, ironically, a very silly, childish comedy, *Time out for Ginger* (Lyceum Theatre: November 26, 1952, 248 performances). The Ron Alexander comedy, staged by Shepperd Traube, was innocuously concerned with an adolescent girl (Nancy Malone) who craves to be a football player, and the repercussions this desire has on her all-American family. It was more a case of *Father Knows Best* coming to the New York stage, with the highlight of the show being Douglas's animated description of his tomboy daughter scoring the big touchdown. For all its inanity the show proved to be extremely popular, and Melvyn was lauded for giving "a thorough, understanding, wise and comical performance" (William Hawkins, *New York World-Telegram and Sun*). After its Broadway engagement, the hit show was taken on a national tour and to Australia, with Douglas recreating his popular role. (Hollywood would translate the comedy

into an insipid musical feature for Patty Duke, entitled *Billie* [United Artists, 1965].)

While Douglas was perpetuating his well-paying livelihood, Mrs. Douglas took occasion to return to theatre work herself, appearing in a short-term revival of *First Lady* at New York's City Center (May 1952). Three years later she would play with Basil Rathbone in a potpourri entertainment entitled *One Plus One* which was given at the Brooklyn Academy of Music (October 6, 1955). Plans for touring the presentation were dropped because her husband, who had staged the evening (having dropped out of the male lead due to other commitments), was unable to restage the vehicle.

Always a man anxious to expand the flexibility of his craft, Douglas thrived during the golden age of live television in New York. He appeared in a variety of roles on the assorted anthology series, such as "Celanese Theatre," "Lights Out," "Ford Theatre," "Kraft Theatre," and "Alcoa Hour." On June 12, 1952, he began starring in his only video series to date, "Hollywood Off Beat," telecast over ABC network.

Having completed his *Time out for Ginger* tour, Melvyn agreed to replace an ailing Paul Muni as Henry Drummond in *Inherit the Wind*, which had opened the previous April 21 at the

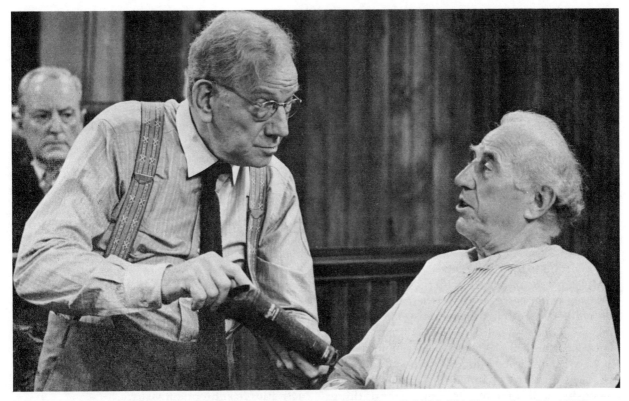

With Ed Begley in INHERIT THE WIND on "Hallmark Hall of Fame" (NBC-TV, November 18, 1965)

National Theatre. Critics usually tended to ignore replacements in Broadway shows, but Douglas's bow on September 17, 1955, was considered worthy of fresh reviews. Brooks Atkinson (*New York Times*) wrote: "Mr. Douglas is at the peak of his form" in the Clarence Darrow part in this historical drama about the infamous Scopes trial in 1920s Tennessee. Ed Begley continued in the role of Matthew Harrison Brady, a thinly disguised characterization of William Jennings Bryan. When the national touring company was organized, Melvyn headed the cast. The show opened at the Blackstone Theatre in Chicago (February 9, 1956) and concluded in Baltimore on January 19, 1957. Years later, when "Hallmark Hall of Fame" offered a television version of the Jerome Lawrence–Robert Lee drama (NBC, November 18, 1965), Melvyn recreated his stage role. (In the 1960 United Artists movie, Spencer Tracy was Drummond to Fredric March's Brady.)

Melvyn assumed another replacement chore (this time for the ailing Ralph Richardson) when he headed the touring version of *Waltz of the Toreadors,* a French sex farce by Jean Anouilh. The road company opened at the McCarter Theatre in Princeton, New Jersey, on September 26, 1957.

On March 9, 1958, he repeated the role in the second Broadway opening of the show at the Coronet Theatre,* which had a thirty-one-performance run. "If he lacks something of Mr. Richardson's bravura style and flourish, he nevertheless succeeds in combining the slightly ridiculous exterior of the grubby old romanticist with his inner wistfulness of spirit in a portrayal both touching and humorous" (Richard Watts, Jr., *New York Post*). (In the 1962 Continental film version, Peter Sellers had the lead.)

Along the way Douglas had been in a pre-Broadway casualty, *Maiden Voyage,* which opened and closed in Philadelphia. He played the part of Zeus.

On the little tube, Melvyn continued to offer a mixed bag of performances. He tried to recapture the debonair qualities of his old film roles by re-teaming with Myrna Loy on "G.E. Theatre" in *Love Came Late* (CBS, November 17, 1957), but the half-hour show was a trifle. Far more impressive was his appearance on the noteworthy David Karp drama, *The Plot to Kill Stalin,* televised by CBS on "Playhouse 90" on September 25, 1958. Fred Coe produced and Delbert Mann directed this controversial drama which drew protests

*The play's maiden Broadway engagement was at the Coronet Theatre (January 17, 1957) for 132 performances.

109

from the Soviets. Douglas appeared as Stalin with Eli Wallach as his aid, Oscar Homolka as Khrushchev, E. G. Marshall as Beria, Thomas Gomez as Malenkov, and Luther Adler as Molotov. In writing of this highly regarded television presentation, John Crosby (*New York Herald-Tribune*) observed: "Douglas, an inspired choice as Stalin, was a remarkably human dictator, very self-possessed and seemingly entirely in control even when surrounded by enemies." Later in the season, Douglas appeared again on "Playhouse 90" in *The Return of Ansel Gibbs* (CBS, November 27, 1958), which would typify his forthcoming video and stage appearances. It was a show dealing with politics, a favorite métier for Douglas. He portrayed a man of many posts asked to be a special assistant to the President.

Melvyn's second brush with the works of Sean O'Casey came early in 1959 when he co-starred with Shirley Booth in the musical version of *Juno and the Paycock,* entitled *Juno* (Winter Garden Theatre: March 9, 1959, 16 performances). The show, with music by Marc Blitzstein and directed by Jose Ferrer, was panned in all quarters. "It is expensive and pretentious, and certain things about it are wonderful, but the final tally is torpid" (John McClain, *New York Journal American*). As for Douglas, who had a few songs to talk-

With Jean Dixon on Broadway in THE GANG'S ALL HERE (1959)

sing and fewer dance steps to kick, Walter Kerr (*New York Herald-Tribune*) recorded: "Melvyn Douglas [as 'Captain' Jack Boyle] lifts his pint with a will and struts heartily; but he hasn't the slyness to steal a bit of sausage or a scene." Douglas was heard on the original cast album of the show (Columbia OL-5380/OS-2013), which, despite the production's short Broadway run, has become an LP collector's item. (In later years, Douglas would record an album for the Cademon label, #2016, called "Great American Speeches," in which he offers readings with Vincent Price, Ed Begley, and Carl Sandburg.)

Melvyn very nearly did not reach Broadway in *The Gang's All Here* (Ambassador Theatre: October 1, 1959, 132 performances). During the Philadelphia tryout engagement of the Jerome Lawrence–Robert E. Lee drama, in which he was Griffith P. Hastings, the *roman à clef* Warren Harding, he collapsed onstage at the Forrest Theatre. Paul McGrath stepped into the part. Melvyn recovered shortly from his bout of "overexhaustion," which really was heart trouble, a condition that would slow down his professional activities in subsequent years.

In *The Gang's All Here,* Douglas shone in the complex but nebulous role of a good but not too bright man who is catapulted into the American Presidency by his crooked friends. The actor received accolades for his performance. "In gesture, attitude, expression (and aided by highly effective makeup) Mr. Douglas epitomizes the politico whose veneer of splendor has succeeded in disguising an ex-small town editor as a senatorial worthy" (John Beaufort, *Christian Science Monitor*).

The apex of the actor's stage career came in 1960 when he received the Antoinette Perry (Tony) Award for his sterling performance as William Russell in Gore Vidal's *The Best Man* (Morosco Theatre: March 31, 1960, 520 performances). Co-starred with Lee Tracy and Frank Lovejoy, Melvyn offered a beautiful picture of a liberal political aspirant for the U.S. Presidency, one of several candidates seeking the endorsement of the incumbent chief executive. (In the 1964 United Artists picturization of *The Best Man,* Henry Fonda played the William Russell role.)

Added to the Look Television Award, which Douglas received in 1960 for his past year's performance in *The Plot to Kill Stalin,* Douglas was as far as he could be from his 1930s dapper Dan film career. And yet, in a very different vein, he was definitely at the head of the class.

After more than a decade away from filmmaking, partly by choice, partly because insurance companies would not provide the necessary coverage for Melvyn's participation due to his heart condition, the actor accepted the rather smallish but impressive part of Dansker in *Billy Budd* (Allied Artists, 1962). Based on the Herman Melville novel and the play by Louis O. Coxe and Robert H. Chapman,* Douglas offered a quiet, forthright performance as the knowing old sailmaker who crosses the path of a young British sailor (Terence Stamp) on the high seas of the eighteenth century. Peter Ustinov, produced–directed–co-scripted–co-starred in this adaptation which Bosley Crowther (*New York Times*) labeled "as forceful as the wind across the sea."

Because director Martin Ritt was so insistent on having Melvyn play Paul Newman's father in *Hud* (Paramount, 1963), the actor was given the job, despite the studio's inability to insure him. The film was a depressing, almost lonely study of the influence of a no-good son (Newman) on his decent younger brother (Brandon de Wilde) and their wise old cattleman father (Douglas). The latter detests his eldest son but cannot communicate with the younger boy. Complicating the story is the ranch's rough-skinned housekeeper (Patricia Neal) a lonely but distant woman, who is desired by Newman and deeply liked by de Wilde.

Even though Douglas was billed second in the credits, he found himself being Oscar-nominated in the Best Supporting Actor category, a fact which puzzled some, and annoyed others. His competition was Nick Adams (*Twilight of Honor*), Bobby Darin (*Captain Newman, M.D.*), Hugh Griffith (*Tom Jones*), and John Huston (*The Cardinal*). Douglas won the award, proving what a smooth transition he had made from leading man

*Opened at the Biltmore Theatre (February 10, 1951) for 105 performances. Later seen at the Masquers Theatre (May 2, 1955) for 23 performances.

With Thomas Heathcote, Terence Stamp (hidden), and Robert Brown in BILLY BUDD (AA '62)

111

On the set of HUD (Par '63) with Patricia Neal

With Paul Newman and Brandon de Wilde in HUD

With James Coburn in THE AMERICANIZATION OF EMILY (MGM '64)

With Patricia Gozzi in RAPTURE (International Classics '65)

to forceful character actor. There are many film fans who claim they prefer the saltier, new-style Douglas to the old slick model of the 1930s cinema.

The actor appeared in two more films the next year and in both he was liked by the critics, though they had mixed reactions to the pictures themselves. *Advance to the Rear* (MGM, 1964) reunited him with Joan Blondell, she as the bawdy lady, and he as hapless Colonel Brackenby who, in this slapdash Civil War comedy, must make something of his "raw" recruits. Glenn Ford was the star.

The other film was *The Americanization of Emily* (MGM, 1964), which received tremendous attention because it offered British-born, Broadway-comedy star Julie Andrews a mature characterization so different from her cotton-candy stage assignments. The dark comedy satire, scripted by Paddy Chayefsky from William Bradford Huie's novel, cast Melvyn as the eccentric Admiral William Jessup, who is certainly not adverse to expediency when his comfort is at stake. James Garner is the young American naval officer who cannot believe how the Allied chain of command is actually operating during the hectic days of World War II as the invasion of the Continent

is being structured. In the midst of his affair with widow Andrews, he learns that as punishment for his rebellious attitudes, he is to be made the first victim of the Omaha Beach campaign.

Melvyn's sole 1965 theatrical release, *Rapture* (International Classics), scarcely lived up to its title. The film focused on Agnes (Patricia Gozzi), a lonely, depressed young lass who fears she is on the verge of insanity. She is alienated from her stern father (Douglas) but achieves a new perspective on life through a tragic romance with a fugitive murderer (Dean Stockwell). Produced on an arty level, the film failed to find its market even in the specialty movie houses in the United States and abroad. That same year (September 12), Douglas appeared in a sixty-minute television film, *Once upon a Tractor*, telecast by ABC as part of the four video features produced by the United Nations. It was directed by Leopoldo Torre Nilsson and scripted by Arthur Ross. *Films in Review* labeled it "artistic rock bottom."

By 1966 Melvyn had reached an age where men in most any other profession would consider retiring. But except for catering to his heart condition, he continued as before, working steadily as the proper job offers permitted. His wife, who had made the LP record "300 Years of Great American Poetry" (Caedmon #2009) in 1962, and authored *The Eleanor Roosevelt We Remember* in 1963, continued her political interests. She was honorary chairman of the Women's International League for Peace and Freedom in 1964, and that same year headed the U.S. delegation at the Inaugural Ceremonies of President William V. S. Tubman of Liberia. She also continued her affiliations with the Jane Addams Peace Associations, Inc.

When he was interviewed in this period, one of the questions more frequently asked of Melvyn was whether he minded being a senior citizen (did he have a choice?). His sensible reply was: "Up until I was 45, the thought of old age never bothered me. However, when I began to get into the late 50s and 60s, I confess I felt awfully sad about the prospect. As horrible as the world may sometimes seem, there is a lot of ferment. There are many things I'd like to do and be around to see."

Melvyn could not resist the tempting offer to return to Hollywood for *Hotel* (Warner Bros., 1967). Based on the best-selling novel by Arthur Hailey and directed by Richard Quine, it was decked out to be a latter-day *Grand Hotel*. Douglas was cast as Warren Trent, the patriarchal figure who owns the St. Gregory Hotel in New Orleans. The old-time luxurious institution is beset by mounting debts, old age, and high-pressured competition from mass-market hotel chains. Intertwined in the widescreen color film were episodes from the lives of several of the hotel's guests, including a British peeress (Merle Oberon) and her noble husband (Michael Rennie), who accidentally killed a pedestrian, an ambitious but loyal chief hotel employee (Rod Taylor), the grasping representative of the hotel chain (Kevin McCarthy) and his unhappy mistress (Catherine Spaak), a hotel thief (Karl Malden), and the hotel's club singer (Carmen McRae), who vocalized the film's theme, "This Year."

In his *Hotel* characterization, Melvyn played a variation of his crochety old man, a person weak of limb (he uses a cane) but as tenacious as they come. Bigoted, steadfast to traditional ways, he fights a losing battle to resist the temptations of comfort and money in his declining years in order to keep everything his way. As the picture draws to its conclusion, Douglas's Trent snarls in perplexity: "I don't understand the whole damn world anymore." Although the film was conceived on a grand scale to encompass a commercially safe common denominator of public taste, it achieved nowhere the degree of mass endorsement that Hailey's later *Airport* (Universal, 1970) did.

The year 1967 also brought the actor two prestigious television assignments. On May 4, he appeared in Arthur Miller's *The Crucible*, a CBS special, and for the same network, on October 16 on the "CBS Playhouse," he was in *Do Not Go Gentle into That Good Night*. For his role in this ninety-minute drama, in which he and co-star Shirley Booth were members of an old-age home who wish to remain as functioning human beings instead of vegetables, he was awarded the Emmy for Best Male Performance of the Year. Rounding out the year, Melvyn gave in to his fond wish to return to Broadway, despite declining health and the difficult demands of the role, to appear in *Spofford* (ANTA Playhouse: December 14, 1967, 202 performances).* The Herman Shumlin comedy, based on Peter DeVries's novel *Reuben, Reuben*, featured Douglas as a retired chicken farmer out to culturally and emotionally enrich his life as a member of upper-middle-class suburbia. The reviewers were enthusiastic about Douglas's meticulous portrayal. "Looking like a wise, old tat-

With Helen Gahagan Douglas at the 43rd Annual Academy Awards telecast April 15, 1971)

tered terrier who has seen better days and still knows what it feels like to be a puppy . . . He makes Spofford into a real person before our eyes. . . . . underneath the conscious exaggeration, Mr. Douglas creates a flesh-and-blood rascality that defies grease paint." Featured in the cast was Pert Kelton, another cast member of RKO's *Annie Oakley* back in 1935.

When Robert Anderson's play *I Never Sang for My Father* was being prepared for Broadway (Longacre Theatre: January 25, 1968, 124 performances), Melvyn had been asked to play the role of the selfish eighty-year-old father of a successful playwright, an ex-mayor of a Long Island suburb and the pillar of wealthy, pseudo-society. He thought the stage run would be too strenuous for him (Alan Webb took the part instead), but when Columbia financed the picturization in 1970, he could not resist the bid to tackle the difficult part, especially since the movie would be made on location in New York with studio work at the old Biograph facilities in the Bronx.

The film rendition diluted the playwright's

*The star had had a bleeding-ulcer operation, been hospitalized for heart palpitation, and endured surgery for a malignancy on his foot. He told a reporter at the time of *Spofford:* "I didn't want to do anything strenuous, but I kept asking myself, 'Can I pull the Spofford assignment off?' It's pretty much a one-man show, and it's the longest part I've ever played."

concepts only slightly, but ran into more structural difficulties trying to create a proper balance of screen time between Melvyn, Gene Hackman (as the son), and Oscar-winner Estelle Parsons (the daughter banished to Detroit for having wed a Jew). In many respects a solid drama, the movie was not overly popular with audiences or critics, except for Melvyn's truthful performance. Even on this point some viewers felt his portrayal was too similar to his previous screen and stage work. Vincent Canby (*New York Times*) thought this depressing study of unwanted older folk and their alienation from the younger generation, was "without any sense of life's mystery . . . a wretched motion picture," but judged that Douglas gave the "professional sufficiency one expects." *Films in Review* lauded Douglas for projecting "the nuances as well as the blatancies

of such a tragedy, and his performance repays close attention . . . [but it cannot] by itself, carry a film as inconsistently written as this one." Douglas was nominated as Best Actor of the Year for *I Never Sang for My Father* but lost out to George C. Scott of *Patton*.

Douglas returned to the screen twice in 1972. *One Is a Lonely Number* (MGM) was an inconsistent soap opera about a young woman's (Trish Van Devere) acclimation to the single life after her husband leaves her for a nineteen-year-old. Douglas was cast in a cameo role as grocery-store-owner Joseph Provo, a lonely man after the death of his equally middle-aged wife.

If *One Is a Lonely Number* relegated Melvyn to an "unbearably sentimental" role, his equally small part in *The Candidate* (Warner Bros., 1972) was a role of a far different caliber. The motion

With Trish Van Devere in ONE IS A LONELY NUMBER (MGM '72)

With Myrna Loy and Yvette Mimieux in DEATH TAKES A HOLIDAY (ABC-TV, October 21, 1971)

picture, written by Jeremy Larne and directed by Michael Ritchie, explores a California Senate race between a young liberal (Robert Redford) and his incumbent conservative rival (Don Porter). The appeal of this political story to Melvyn was obvious. The elder actor portrayed John J. McKay, the father of the Robert F. Kennedy–style candidate, and himself a former governor and a power in the state. He is at first opposed to his son's candidacy and only openly supports him (he tells a political backer: "He's not going to get his ass kicked, he's cute") when the campaign is nearly over. After Redford wins the victory, the young man stands back from the hurrahs, bewildered,

disillusioned, and forced to ask those who ran his campaign: "What do we do now?" A nice added element in Melvyn's characterization was the presence of Leslie Allen as Mabel, the woman in his life now that he has publicly separated from Redford's mother. *The Candidate,* at the time of release, failed to garner much box-office respect, buried under the activities of the real-life presidential campaign between Richard M. Nixon and Senator George McGovern.

On April 10, 1974, Melvyn appeared in *Verdict: Murder or Mercy?,* an ABC "Wednesday Movie of the Week" entry. It was his fifth such telefeature appearance in recent years.* He had a small but

---

*In *Companions in Nightmare* (NBC, November 23, 1968) he was one of several patients undergoing group therapy and was a possible suspect for the killing of one of their number. In *Hunters Are for Killing* (CBS, March 12, 1970) he enacted the estranged, wealthy father of ex-convict Burt Reynolds, the latter falsely charged with manslaughter. *Death Takes a Holiday* (ABC, October 21, 1971) found him professionally reunited with Myrna Loy in a version of the Alberto Casella play in which they played the parents of Yvette Mimieux, the latter being beckoned by Death (Monte Markham). In *Death Squad* (ABC, January 8, 1974), he was a police captain dying of cancer, involved with stationhouse confederates who have taken it upon themselves to eliminate undesirable elements in the city via wholesale liquidation. The theme was very similar to the Clint Eastwood feature, *Magnum Force* (Warner Bros., 1973).

pivotal role as Dr. Paul Harelson, the doctor who cannot bear to see his wife (Mildred Dunnock) suffer any longer from her fatal case of cancer. He administers a lethal dose of morphine, an act which is observed by nurse Bettye Ackerman. Douglas is arraigned on a murder charge, and the case is handled by the father-son lawyer team of Denver Pyle–Bradford Dillman. Melvyn delivered his customary "polished performance" (*Daily Variety*).

In January, 1975, Melvyn was to be seen on CBS-TV in one of four ninety-minute drama specials based on the life of Benjamin Franklin. In other episodes, Eddie Albert, Lloyd Bridges, Beau Bridges, and Richard Widmark portrayed the famed American.

Although he is now well into his seventies, Melvyn still remains open for work in almost any medium *if* the part is right. He is still very politically oriented, describing himself as a "strongly anti-communist liberal." His political convictions, and those of his wife, have undoubtedly cost him many acting jobs over the years, and have also induced him to appear in such projects as Broadway's *The Little Blue Light* and later

films like *The Candidate*. But Douglas would change none of his life, always refusing to shy away from controversial issues and statements. "Why should I. I've always spoken out on what I considered important issues. I've never worried about the public's reaction. Over the years, I think I've gained their respect, if not their acceptance, of my views."

Today Melvyn and his wife live in an apartment on Manhattan's Riverside Drive and they have nine grandchildren. When interviewed, Douglas would just as soon talk about politics as his career. Like most liberals, he opposed the Vietnam action, which he labeled a "tragic, horrendous mistake." Like many older liberals, however, most of his political views are no longer considered leftist. Because of the still-remembered 1950 California Senate campaign, Helen Gahagan Douglas is still branded in many conservative circles as an anti-capitalist.

Inevitably reporters insist upon asking him about the good old days of Hollywood. He insists he doesn't wish to bring those allegedly halcyon cinema days back. "A lot of junk was made in the old days. Of course, a lot of junk is still being

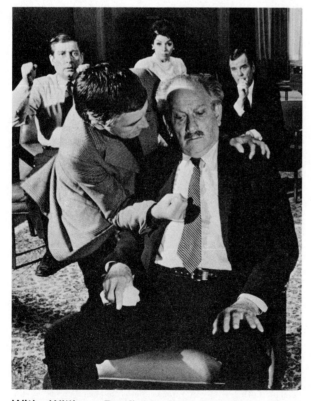

With William Redfield, Patrick O'Neal, Dana Wynter, and Gig Young in COMPANIONS IN NIGHTMARE (NBC-TV '68)

The Melvyn Douglas of the 1970s

made. But by and large, with the expansion of movie making to every corner of the world, the average of interesting films is better than it used to be." On another occasion he said: "We used to chew our nails and wonder when the industry would grow up. The pictures were pretty superficial, they were fun stuff or soap opera. There was little interest in anything serious."

As for the distinguished actor's array of acting prizes, he teasingly informed columnist Rex Reed not so long ago: "All those awards are in a closet. One hears that your price goes up if you win a prize, but that has never been my experience. One also hears about the conniving, the exploitation of soliciting votes, so that also puts you off in a way." Regarding Oscars, he said: "I really don't think there is any such thing as the *best* of everything. Actors can't be compared, roles can't be compared. It would make more sense if awards were set up like the honors list in school. Everyone could then be recognized for the contributions they've made."

As far as the new breed of actors goes, Melvyn charmingly warns: "Dustin Hoffman and Jack Nicholson had better step lively. I just might put a lot of these young chaps away before I'm through."

Melvyn Douglas

TONIGHT OR NEVER (UA, 1931) 80 M.
Producer, Samuel Goldwyn; director, Mervyn LeRoy; based on the play by Lily Hatvany; adaptors, Frederick Hatton, Fanny Hatton; screenplay, Ernest Vajda; music director, Alfred Newman; sound, Vinton Vernon; camera, Gregg Toland; editor, Grant Whytock.
Gloria Swanson (Nella Vargo); Ferdinand Gottschalk (Rudig); Robert Greig (Butler); Greta Meyer (Maid); Warburton Gamble (Count Albert Von Gronac); Melvyn Douglas (Fletcher the Unknown Gentleman); Alison Skipworth (Marchesa); Boris Karloff (Waiter).

PRESTIGE (RKO, 1932) 71 M.
Producer, Charles R. Rogers; director, Tay Garnett; based on the novel Lips of Steel by Harry Hervey; screenplay, Francis Edward Faragoh, Garnett, Rollo Lloyd; dialog, Garnett, Lloyd; sound, Earl Walcott; camera, Lucien Andriot; editor, Joe Kane.
Ann Harding (Therese Du Flos); Adolphe Menjou (Captain Remy Baudoin); Melvyn Douglas (Lieutenant Andre Verlaine); Ian MacLaren (Colonel Du Flos); Guy Bates Post (Major); Carmelita Geraghty (Felice); Rollo Lloyd (Emil de Fontenac); Clarence Muse (Nham).

THE WISER SEX (PAR, 1932) 76 M.
Director, Berthold Viertel; based on the play Her Confessions by Clyde Fitch; screenplay, Harry Hervey, Caroline Francke; camera, George Folsey.
Claudette Colbert (Margaret Hughes); Melvyn Douglas (David Rolfe); Lilyan Tashman (Claire Foster); William (Stage) Boyd (Harry Evans); Ross Alexander (Jimmie O'Neill); Franchot Tone (Phil Long); Effie Shannon (Mrs. Hughes); Granville Bates (City Editor); Paul Harvey (Blaney); Victor Kilian (Ed); Robert Fischer (Fritz); Douglass Dumbrille (Chauffeur).

THE BROKEN WING (PAR, 1932) 71 M.
Director, Lloyd Corrigan; based on the play by Paul Dickey, Charles W. Goddard; screenplay, Grover Jones, William Slavens McNutt; camera, Henry Sharp.
Lupe Velez (Lolita Farley); Leo Carrillo (Captain Innocencio); Melvyn Douglas (Philip Marvin); George Barbier (Luther Farley); Willard Robertson (Sylvester Cross); Claire Dodd (Cecelia Cross); Arthur Stone (Justin Bailey); Soledad Jiminez (Maria); Julian Rivero (Bassilio); Pietro Sosso (Pancho); Chris-Pin Martin (Mexican Husband); Charles Stevens (Chicken Thief); Joe Dominguez (Captain).

AS YOU DESIRE ME (MGM, 1932) 71 M.
Director, George Fitzmaurice; based on the play by Luigi Pirandello; adaptor, Gene Markey; camera, William Daniels; editor, George Hively.
Greta Garbo (Zara); Melvyn Douglas (Count Bruno Varelli); Erich Von Stroheim (Carl Salter); Owen Moore (Tony); Hedda Hopper (Madame Mantari); Rafaela Ottiano (Lena); Warburton Gamble (Baron); Albert Conti (Captain); William Ricciardi (Pietro); Roland Varno (Albert).

THE OLD DARK HOUSE (UNIV, 1932) 74 M.
Presenter, Carl Laemmle; producer, Carl Laemmle, Jr.; director, James Whale; based on the novel by J. B. Priestley; adaptor-screenplay, Benn W. Levy; added dialog, R. C. Sheriff; art director, Charles D. Hall; makeup, Jack P. Pierce; camera, Arthur Edeson; editor, Clarence Kolster.
Boris Karloff (Morgan); Melvyn Douglas (Roger Penderel); Charles Laughton (Sir William Porterhouse); Gloria Stuart (Margaret Waverton); Lilian Bond (Gladys DuCane); Ernest Thesiger (Horace Femm); Eva Moore (Rebecca Femm); Raymond Massey (Philip Waverton); Brember Wills (Saul Femm); John (Elspeth) Dudgeon (Sir Roderick).

THE VAMPIRE BAT (MAJ, 1933) 71 M.
Director, Frank Strayer; story-screenplay, Edward Lowe; camera, Ira Morgan; editor, Otis Garrett.
Lionel Atwill (Dr. Otto von Niemann); Fay Wray (Ruth Bertin); Melvyn Douglas (Karl Brettschneider); Maude Eburne (Gussie Schnappmann); George E. Stone (Kringen); Dwight Frye (Herman Gleib); Robert Frazer (Emil Borst); Rita Carlisle (Martha Mueller); Lionel Belmore (Burgomaster Gustave Schoen); William V. Mong (Sauer); Stella Adams (Georgiana); Paul Weigel (Holdstadt); Harrison Greene (Weingarten); William Humphrey (Dr. Haupt); Fern Emmett (Gertrude); Carl Stockdale (Morgue Keeper).

NAGANA (UNIV, 1933) 67 M.
Director, Ernst L. Frank; based on the story by Lester Cohen; adaptors, Dale Van Every, Don Ryan; camera, George Robinson.
Tala Birell (Countess Sandra Lubeska); Melvyn Douglas (Dr. Walter Radnor); Onslow Stevens (Dr. Roy Stark); Everett Brown (Nogu); Dr. Billie McClain (The King); William H. Dunn (Mukovo); Frank Lackteen (Ivory Trader); Noble Johnson (Head Boatman), Mike Morita (Doctor).

COUNSELLOR-AT-LAW (UNIV, 1933) 78 M.

Director, William Wyler; based on the play by Elmer Rice; adaptor, Rice; sound, Gilbert Kurland; camera, Norbert Brodine; editor, Daniel Mandell.

John Barrymore (George Simon); Bebe Daniels (Regina Gordon); Doris Kenyon (Cora Simon); Onslow Stevens (John P. Tedesco); Isabel Jewell (Bessie Green); Melvyn Douglas (Roy Darwin); Thelma Todd (Lillian LaRue); Mayo Methot (Zedorah Chapman); Marvin Kline (Herbert Howard Weinberg); Conway Washburn (Arthur Sandler); John Qualen (Breitstein); Bobby Gordon (Henry Susskind); John Hammond Dailey (McFadden); Malka Kornstein (Sarah Becker); Angela Jacobs (Goldie Rindskopf); Clara Langsner (Lena Simon); T. H. Manning (Peter J. Malone); Elmer Brown (Francis Clark Baird); Barbara Perry (Dorothy); Richard Quine (Richard); Victor Adams (David Simon); Frederick Burton (Crayfield); Vincent Sherman (Harry Becker).

DANGEROUS CORNER (RKO, 1934) 67 M.

Associate producer, Arthur Sibcom; director, Phil Rosen; based on the play by J. B. Priestley; screenplay, Anne Morrison Chapin, Madeleine Ruthven; camera, J. Roy Hunt; editor, Archie Marshek.

Melvyn Douglas (Charles); Conrad Nagel (Robert); Virginia Bruce (Olwen); Erin O'Brien Moore (Freda); Ian Keith (Martin); Betty Furness (Betty); Henry Wadsworth (Gordon).

WOMAN IN THE DARK (RKO, 1934) 70 M.

Director, Phil Rosen; based on the story by Dashiell Hammett; screenplay, Sada Cowan, Marcy Klauber, Charles Williams; camera, Joseph Ruttenberg.

Fay Wray (Louise Lorimer); Ralph Bellamy (Bradley); Melvyn Douglas (Robson); Roscoe Ates (Tommy Logan); Reed Brown, Jr. (Conroy); Ruth Gillette (Lil Grant); Nell O'Day (Helen Grant); Joe King (Detective); Granville Bates (Sheriff Grant); Frank Otto (Kraus); Clifford Dunstan (Doctor); Charlie Williams (Clerk).

THE PEOPLE'S ENEMY (RACKETEERS) (RKO, 1935) 66 M.

Producer, Burt Kelly; director, Crane Wilbur; story-screenplay, Edward Dean Sullivan, Gordon Kahn; camera, Joseph Ruttenberg.

Preston Foster (Vince); Lila Lee (Catherine); Melvyn Douglas (Traps); Shirley Grey (Ann); Roscoe Ates (Slip); William Collier, Jr. (Tony); Sybil Elaine (Mary); Herbert Rawlinson (Duke); Charles Coburn (Judge).

SHE MARRIED HER BOSS (COL, 1935) 85 M.

Producer, Everett Riskin; director, Gregory La Cava; story, Tyra Samter Winslow; screenplay, Sidney Buchman; camera, Leon Shamroy; editor, Richard Cahoon.

Claudette Colbert (Julia Scott); Michael Bartlett (Lonnie Rogers); Melvyn Douglas (Richard Barclay); Raymond Walburn (Franklin); Jean Dixon (Martha); Katharine Alexander (Gertrude); Edith Fellows (Annabel); Clara Kimball Young (Parsons); Grace Hayle (Agnes); Charles E. Arnt (Manager of Department Store); Schuyler Shaw (Chauffeur); Selmer Jackson (Andrews); John Hyams (Hoyt); Georgia Caine (Fitzpatrick); Edward Cooper (Russell); Geneva Mitchell (Saleswoman); Robert E. Homans, Christian J. Frank (Detectives); Arthur G. Wanzer, Sam Ash, David O'Brien, Louis Natheaux, Ernie Adams, John Ince, Oliver Eckhardt, Howard Chase, Harrison Greene (Men); William Jeffrey (Hayden); Grace Goodall, Arthur Stuart Hull, Dora Clement, Louis LaVoie, Corrinne William, Lillian Moore, Henry Sylvester, Billy Arnold (Department Heads); Adalyn Doyle, Lillian Rich (Telephone Operators); Lloyd Whitlock (Department Store Manager); Dewey Skipworth (Stunt Driver); Gladys Gale, Susan Lang, Ruth Clifford, Edna Lyall, Billie Van Every, Adda Gleason, Bess Flowers (Women); Edmund Burns, Jack Gardner (Assistant Window Dressers); Dorothy Short (Girl); Buddy Roosevelt (Chauffeur); Helen Woods, Ellen Clancy, Theo

Holly (Secretaries); Hal Greene (Office Boy); Isabelle LaMal, Marie Wells, Billie Lee, Pat Patrick (Saleswomen); Lynton Brent (News Photographer); Ruth MacAleese (Under Secretary); Rose Plummer (Cook).

MARY BURNS, FUGITIVE (PAR, 1935) 84 M.

Producer, Walter Wanger; director, William K. Howard; story, Gene Towne, Graham Baker; screenplay, Towne, Baker, Louis Stevens; camera, Leon Shamroy; editor, Pete Fritsch.

Sylvia Sidney (Mary Burns); Melvyn Douglas (Barton Powell); Alan Baxter ("Babe" Wilson); Pert Kelton (Goldie Gordon); Wallace Ford (Harper); Brian Donlevy (Spike); Esther Dale (Kate); Frank Sully (Steve); Boothe Howard (Red Martin); Norman Willis (Joe); Frances Gregg (Matron); Charles Waldron (District Attorney); William Ingersoll (Judge); Rita Stanwood Werner (Nurse Agens); Grace Hayle (Nurse Jennie); Daniel Haynes (Jeremiah); Joe Twerp (Willie); William Pawley (Mike); James Mack, Walter Downing (Farmers); Isabel Carlisle, Henry Hall (Tourists); Dorothy Vaughan (Irish Matron); Esther Howard (Landlady); Morgan Wallace (Managing Editor); Phil Tead (Reporter); Ann Doran (Newspaper Girl); Fuzzy Knight (Dance Hall Attendant); Max Wagner (Sailor); Gertrude Walker, Treva Lawler (Hostesses); Charles Wilson (G—Man in Dance Hall); George Chandler (Cashier); Sammy Finn (Dapper Mobster); Richard Pawley (Slim Fergus); Bert Hanlon (Hymie); Dan Merman (Man); Cora Sue Collins (Little Girl); Otto Fries (Clerk at Employment Agency); Earl Ebbe (Photographer); Gus Reed (Manager); Tom Ford (Orderly); Patricia Royale (Scullery Maid); Beverly King, Grace Haysell, Virginia George (Nurses); Bob Reeves, Bob Walker, Walter Shumway, Jack Mower, Ivan Miller, Kernan Cripps (G—Men).

ANNIE OAKLEY (RKO, 1935) 90 M.

Associate producer, Cliff Reid; director, George Stevens; based on the story by Joseph A. Fields, Ewart Adamson; screenplay, Joel Sayre, John Twist; art directors, Van Nest Polglase, Perry Ferguson; music director, Alberto Colombo; camera, J. Roy Hunt; editor, Jack Hively.

Barbara Stanwyck (Annie Oakley); Preston Foster (Toby Walker); Melvyn Douglas (Jeff Hogarth); Pert Kelton (Vera Delmar); Moroni Olsen (Buffalo Bill); Andy Clyde (MacIvor); Chief Thundercloud (Sitting Bull); Margaret Armstrong (Mrs. Oakley); Delmar Watson (Wesley Oakley).

THE LONE WOLF RETURNS (COL, 1935) 69 M.

Director, R. William Neill; based on the novel by Louis Joseph Vance; screenplay, Joseph Krumgold, Bruce Manning, Lionel Houser, Robert O'Connell; camera, Henry Freulich; editor, Viola Lawrence.

Melvyn Douglas (Michael Lanyard, the Lone Wolf); Gail Patrick (Marcia Stewart); Tala Birell (Liane); Henry Mollison (Mollison); Thurston Hall (Crane); Raymond Walburn (Jenkins); Douglass Dumbrille (Morphew); Nana Bryant (Aunt Julie); Robert Middlemass (McGowan); Robert Emmet O'Connor (Benson); Wyrley Birch (Mr. Cole); Eddy Chandler, John Thomas, William Howard Gould (Detectives); Arthur Rankin, Harry Depp (Men); George McKay (Maestro); Frank Reicher (Coleman); Harry Holman (Friar); Archie Robbins (Terry); Lois Lindsey (Baby); Fred Malatesta (French Official); Olaf Hytten (Bancroft Butler); Monte Vandergrift, Lew Kelly (Custom Officials); Maude Truanx (Fat Woman); Thomas Pogue (Old Man); Pat West (Mugg); Jack Clifford, Roger Gray, Hal Price, Jack Gray, Kernan Cripps, Lee Shumway (Cops); Gennaro Curci (Flute Player); John Piccori (Assistant to Official); Henry Roquemore, Ned Norton (Suburbanites); Arthur Loft (Oscar); Lloyd Whitlock (Drunk); Mort Greene (Crooner); Eddie Fetherston (Reporter); Harry Harvey (Photographer); Vesey O'Davoren (Stewart Butler); Dorothy Bay (Marjorie); Pat Somerset (Gladiator); Arthur Stuart Hull (Jackson); George Webb (Tarzan); David Horsley (Robin Hood); Ivan Christy, Tony Merlo, Arthur Raymond Hill

(Waiters); Harry Hollingsworth (Doorman); Helen Leyser (Young Girl); Earl Pingree (New York Traffic Cop).

AND SO THEY WERE MARRIED (COL, 1936) 74 M.

Producer, B. P. Schulberg; director, Elliott Nugent; story, Sarah Addington; screenplay, Doris Anderson, Joseph Anthony, A. Laurie Brazee; camera, Henry Freulich; editor, Gene Milford.

Melvyn Douglas (Stephen Blake); Mary Astor (Edith Farnham); Edith Fellows (Brenda Farnham); Jackie Moran (Tommy Blake); Donald Meek (Hotel Manager); Dorothy Stickney (Miss Peabody); Romaine Callender (Ralph P. Shirley); Douglas Scott (Horace); Margaret Armstrong (Horace's Butler); George McKay (Janitor); Wade Boteler (Police Captain); Charles Irwin (Tom Phillips, a Drunk); Gene Morgan, William Irving, (Drunks); Ernie Alexander, Dennis O'Keefe (Drunks in Car); Charles Arnt, Joseph Caits (Captains of Waiters); Phyllis Godfrey (Ellen, Edith's Maid); Olaf Hytten (Secretary); Jay Eaton (James, the Assistant Clerk); Hooper Atchley (Fred Cutler, the Hotel Clerk); Beatrice Curtis, Beatrice Blinn (Guests); Gennaro Curci (Greek); Alan Bridge (Motor Cop); Jessie Perry (Maid); Margaret Morgan (Stout Woman); Adolf Faylauer (Bald-Headed Man); Kernan Cripps (Turnkey); Anne Schaefer (Housekeeper); Gus Reed (Assistant Captain of Waiters).

THE GORGEOUS HUSSY (MGM, 1936) 105 M.

Producer, Joseph L. Mankiewicz; director, Clarence Brown; based on the novel by Samuel Hopkins Adams; art director, Cedric Gibbons; music, Herbert Stothart; costumes, Adrian; camera, George Folsey; editor, Blanche Sewell.

Joan Crawford (Peggy O'Neal); Robert Taylor (Bow Timberlake); Lionel Barrymore (Andrew Jackson); Franchot Tone (John Eaton); Melvyn Douglas (John Randolph); James Stewart (Rowdy Dow); Alison Skipworth (Mrs. Beall); Louis Calhern (Sunderland); Beulah Bondi (Rachel Jackson); Melville Cooper (Cuthbert); Sidney Toler (Daniel Webster); Gene Lockhart (Major O'Neal); Clara Blandick (Louisa Abbott); Frank Conroy (John C. Calhoun); Nydia Westman (Maybelle); Charles Trowbridge (Martin Van Buren); Willard Robertson (Secretary Ingham); Ruby de Remer (Mrs. Bellamy); Betty Blythe (Mrs. Wainwright); Zeffie Tilbury (Mrs. Daniel Beall); Edith Atwater (Lady Vaughn); Greta Meyer (Mrs. Orenrider); Phoebe Foster (Emily Donaldson); Fred "Snowflake" Toone (Horatius); Ward Bond (Officer); Bert Roach (Major Domo); William Orlamond (Herr Oxenrider); Tom Herbert (Bits); Lee Phelps (Bartender); George Reed (Braxton); Else Janssen (Dutch Minister's Wife); Oscar Apfel (Tompkins); Richard Powell (Doorman); Franklin Parker (Leader of Mob); Lew Harvey, Sid Saylor, Wade Boteler, Hooper Atchley (Agitators); Harry Holman (Auctioneer); Morgan Wallace (Slave Buyer); Parker (Leader of Mob); Harry C. Bradley (President's Secretary); Sam McDaniel (Butler); Samuel S. Hinds (Commander); Harry Strange (Navigator).

THEODORA GOES WILD (COL, 1936) 94 M.

Associate producer, Everett Riskin; director, Richard Boleslawski; story, Mary McCarthy; screenplay, Sidney Buchman; assistant director, William E. Mull; music-music director, Morris Stoloff; costumes, Bernard Newman; art director, Stephen Goosson; sound George Cooper; camera, Joseph Walker; editor, Otto Meyer.

Irene Dunne (Theodora Lynn); Melvyn Douglas (Michael Grant); Thomas Mitchell (Jed Waterbury); Thurston Hall (Arthur Stevenson); Rosalind Keith (Adelaide Perry); Spring Byington (Rebecca Perry); Margaret McWade (Aunt Elsie); Elisabeth Risdon (Aunt Mary); Nana Bryant (Ethel Stevenson); Henry Kolker (Jonathan Grant); Leona Maricle (Agnes Grant); Robert Greig (Uncle John); Frederick Burton (Governor Wyatt); Mary Forbes (Mrs. Wyatt); Grace Hayle (Mrs. Cobb); Sarah Edwards (Mrs. Moffat); Mary MacLaren (Mrs. Wilson); Wilfred Hari (Toki); Laura Treadwell (Mrs. Grant); Corbet Morris (Artist); Ben F. Hendricks (Taxi Driver); Frank

Sully (Clarence); James T. Mack (Minister); William Benedict (Henry); Carolyn Lee Bourland (Baby); Paul Barrett (Adelaide's Husband); Leora Thatcher (Miss Baldwin); Billy Wayne, Harold Goodwin, Jack Hatfield (Photographers); Harry Harvey, Don Brodie, Eddie Fetherston, Ed Hart, Lee Phelps, Sherry Hall, Ralph Malone, Beatrice Curtis (Reporters); Dennis O'Keefe (Man); Georgia Cooper, Jane Keckley, Jessie Perry, Noel Bates, Betty Farrington, Stella Adams, Isabelle LaMal, Georgia O'Dell, Dorothy Vernon (Women); Sven Borg (Bartender); Maurice Brierre (Waiter); Rex Moore (Newsboy).

WOMEN OF GLAMOUR (COL, 1937) 68 M.

Director, Gordon Wiles; story, Milton Herbert Gropper; screenplay, Lynn Starling, Mary McCall, Jr.; camera, Peverell Marley, Henry Freulich; editor, Otto Meyer.

Virginia Bruce (Gloria Hudson); Melvyn Douglas (Richard Stark); Reginald Denny (Frederick Eagan); Pert Kelton (Nan LaRoque); Leona Maricle (Carol Coulter); Thurston Hall (Mr. Stark); Mary Forbes (Mrs. Stark); John Spacey (Winkler); Maurice Cass (Caldwell); Miki Morita (Kito); Clarissa Selwynne, Bess Flowers, Addie McPhail, Mary Jane Temple, Leona Valde, Nadine Dore (Women); Thomas Pogue (Travis); Harvey Clark (Roger); Henry Roquemore (Travis' Friend); Virginia Carroll, Ann Roth (Girls); Paul Power, Bruce Sidney, Eric Alden, Richard Kipling (Men); Stanley Mack (Waiter); Douglas Gordon (Steward).

CAPTAINS COURAGEOUS (MGM, 1937) 116 M.

Producer, Louis D. Lighton; director, Victor Fleming; based on the novel by Rudyard Kipling; screenplay, John Lee Mahin, Marc Connelly, Dale Van Every; music, Franz Waxman; art directors, Cedric Gibbons, Arnold Gillespie, Edwin B. Willis; songs, Waxman and Gus Kahn; marine director, James Havens; sound, Douglas Shearer; camera, Harold Rosson; editor, Elmo Vernon.

Freddie Bartholomew (Harvey Cheyne); Spencer Tracy (Manuel); Lionel Barrymore (Captain Disko Troop); Melvyn Douglas (Mr. Cheyne); Mickey Rooney (Dan Troop); Charley Grapewin (Uncle Salters); Christian Rub (Old Clement); Walter Kingsford (Dr. Finley); Donald Briggs (Tyler); Sam McDaniel (Doc); Dave Thursby (Tom); John Carradine (Long Jack); William Stack (Elliott); Leo G. Carroll (Burns); Charles Trowbridge (Dr. Walsh); Richard Powell (Steward); Billie Burrud (Charles); Jay Ward (Pogey); Kenneth Wilson (Alvin); Roger Gray (Nate Rogers); Jack La Rue (Priest); Oscar O'Shea (Cushman); Gladden James (Secretary Cobb); Tommy Bupp, Wally Albright (Boys); Katherine Kenworthy (Mrs. Disko); Philo McCullough, James Kilgannon, Bill Fisher, Dick Howard, Larry Fisher, Gil Perkins, Jack Sterling, Stubby Kreuger (Crew); Dave Wengren (Lars); Murray Kinnell (Minister); Goldie Sloan (Black Woman); Myra McKinney, Lee Van Atta, Gene Reynolds, Sherry Hall, Jr., Henry Hanna, Betty Alden, Reggie Strester (Bits); Gertrude Sutton (Nate's Wife); Bobby Watson, Don Brodie, David Kernan, Billy Arnold (Reporters); Frank Sully (Taxi Driver); Billy Gilbert (Soda Steward); Lester Dorr (Corridor Steward); Jimmy Conlin (Thin Man); Lloyd Ingraham (Skipper of Ship); Art Berry, Sr., Captain Anderson, Edward Peil, Sr. (Fishermen); Jack Kennedy (Captain of Flying Swan); Monte Vandergrift (Sailor on Flying Swan); Charles Coleman (Butler); Wade Boteler (Skipper of Blue Gill); Norman Ainsley (Robbins); Myra Marsh (Chester's Wife).

I MET HIM IN PARIS (PAR, 1937) 86 M.

Producer-director, Wesley Ruggles; story, Helen Meinardi; screenplay, Claude Binyon; art directors, Hans Dreier, Ernst Fegte; music director, Boris Morros; song, Meinardi and Hoagy Carmichael; special camera effects, Farciot Edouart; camera, Leo Tover; editor, Otho Lovering.

Claudette Colbert (Kay Denham); Melvyn Douglas (George Potter); Robert Young (Gene Anders); Lee Bowman (Berk Sutter); Mona Barrie (Helen Anders); George Davis (Cutter Driver); Fritz Feld (Swiss Hotel Clerk); Rudolph Ament (Romantic Waiter); Alexander Cross (John Hadley); George Sorel, Arthur Burni (Hotel Clerks); Louis La Bey, Jacques Lory, Joe Ploski (Bartenders); Egon Brecher (Emile, the Upper Tower Man); Hans Joby (Lower Tower Man); Jacques Vanaire (Frenchman Flirt); Gennaro Curci (Double-Talk Waiter); Eugene Borden, Albert Morin (Headwaiters); Captain Fernando Garcia (Elevator Operator); Albert Pollet (Conductor); Francesco Maran, Yola d'Avril (French Couple in Apartment); Jean De Briac (Steward); Charles Haas, Otto Jehly, Paco Moreno, Roman Novins (Waiters); Alexander Schonberg (Porter); Gloria Williams, Priscilla Moran (Women); Joe Thoben (Assistant Bartender).

ANGEL (PAR, 1937) 98 M.

Producer-director, Ernst Lubitsch; based on the play by Melchior Lengyel; adaptors, Guy Bolton, Russell Medcraft; screenplay, Samson Raphaelson; music, Frederick Hollander; song, Hollander and Leo Robin; assistant director, Joseph Lefert; art directors, Hans Dreier, Robert Usher; special effects, Farciot Edouart; camera, Charles Lang; editor, William Shea.

Marlene Dietrich (Maria Barker); Herbert Marshall (Sir Frederick Barker); Melvyn Douglas (Anthony Halton); Edward Everett Horton (Graham); Ernest Cossart (Walton); Laura Hope Crews (Grand Duchess Anna Dmitrievna); Herbert Mundin (Greenwood); Ivan Lebedeff (Prince Vladimir Gregorovitch); Dennie Moore (Emma); Lionel Pape (Lord Davington); Phyllis Coghlan (Maid at Barker Home); Leonard Carey, Gerald Hamer, James Finlayson (Footmen); Eric Wilton (English Chauffeur); Michael S. Visaroff (Russian Butler); Olaf Hytten (Photographer); Gwendolen Logan (Woman with Maria); George Davis, Arthur Hurni (Taxi Drivers); Joseph Romantini (Headwaiter); Duci Kerekjarto (Prima Violinist); Suzanne Kaaren (Girl Who Gambles); Louise Carter (Flower Woman); Major Sam Harris (Extra at Club); Gino Corrado (Assistant Hotel Manager); Herbert Evans (Lord's Butler).

I'LL TAKE ROMANCE (COL, 1937) 85 M.

Producer, Everett Riskin; director, Edward H. Griffith; story, Stephen Morehouse Avery; screenplay, George Oppenheimer, Jane Murfin; songs, Oscar Hammerstein II and Ben Oakland, Milton Drake and Marie Costa; camera, Lucien Andriot; editors, Otto Meyer, William Lyon.

Grace Moore (Elsa Terry); Melvyn Douglas (James Guthrie); Helen Westley (Madame Della); Stuart Erwin ("Pancho" Brown); Margaret Hamilton (Margot); Walter Kingsford (William Kane); Ferdinand Gottschalk (Monsieur Girard); Esther Muir (Pamela); Frank Forest (Pinkerton); Walter O. Stahl (Johan); Barry Norton (Juan); Lucio Villegas (Señor Montez); Gennaro Curci (Bondini); Marek Windheim (Henri); Franklin Pangborn (Secretary); Greta Meyer (Opera Singer); Albert Conti (Lepino); Adia Kuznetzoff (Conductor); George Andre Beranger (Male Dressmaker); John Gallaudet (Photographer); Ernest Wood (Hotel Clerk); Mareo Vido, Al Hill (Taxi Drivers); Allan Garcia (Himself); Bruce Sidney (Stage Manager); Mildred Gover (Maid); Louis Mercier, Manuel Emanuel, Alex Palasthy, Genaro Spagneli, Manuel Paris (Men); Meeka Aldrich, Mariska Aldrich, Irene Crane (Women); Bruce Wyndham (Young German); Bud Wolfe (Bartender); Carrie Daumery (Dowager); Mary Emery (Girl); George Hickman (Page Boy); Len Davis (Sailor); Bill Lally (Steward).

ARSENE LUPIN RETURNS (MGM, 1938) 81 M.

Producer, John W. Considine, Jr.; director, George Fitzmaurice; story-screenplay, James Kevin McGuinness, Howard Emmett Rogers, George Harmon Coxe; music, Franz Waxman; art director, Cedric Gibbons; montage, John Hoffman; camera, George Folsey; editor, Ben Lewis.

Melvyn Douglas (Arsene Lupin/Rene Farrand); Virginia Bruce (Lorraine DeGrissac); Warren William (Steve Emerson); John Halliday (Count DeGrissac); Nat Pendleton (Joe Doyle); Monty Woolley (George Bouchet); George Zucco (Martell); E. E. Clive (Alf); Rollo Lloyd (Duval); Vladimir

Sokoloff (Ivan Pavloff); Tully Marshall (Monelli); Leonard Penn, Harry Tyler, Chester Clute (Reporters); Jonathan Hale (Chief of D.C.I.); Lillian Rich (Telephone Operator); Harvey Clark (Assistant Manager); Jack Norton (Hotel Manager); Robert Emmett Keane (Watkins); Pierre Watkin (Mr. Carter); Joseph King (Inspector Hennessey); Dell Henderson (Plainclothesman); George Davis (Guard at Dock); Frank Dawson (Franz); Stanley Fields (Groom); Mitchell Lewis, William Norton Bailey, Chris Frank (Detectives); Robert Middlemass (Sergeant); Perry Ivins (Fingerprint Man); Egon Brecher (Vasseur); Ian Wolfe (A. LeMarchand); Ruth Hart (Phone Girl); Otto Fries (Truck Driver); Priscilla Lawson (Switchboard Operator); Jacques Vanaire, Robert O'Connor (Gendarmes); Sid D'Albrook (Detective Alois); William H. Royle (Burly Detective); George Douglas, Jean Perry (Gendarmes); Frank Leigh (English Eddie).

THERE'S ALWAYS A WOMAN (COL, 1938) 82 M.

Producer, William Perlberg; director, Alexander Hall; story, Wilson Collison; (uncredited) screen treatment, Joel Sayre, Philip Rapp; screenplay, Gladys Lehman, (uncredited) Morrie Ryskind; art directors, Stephen Goosson, Lionel Banks; music director, Morris Stoloff; gowns, Kalloch; camera, Henry Freulich; editor, Viola Lawrence.

Joan Blondell (Sally Reardon); Melvyn Douglas (William Reardon); Mary Astor (Lola Fraser); Frances Drake (Anne Calhoun); Jerome Cowan (Nick Shane); Robert Paige (Jerry Marlowe); Thurston Hall (District Attorney); Pierre Watkin (Mr. Ketterling); Walter Kingsford (Grigson); Lester Matthews (Walter Fraser); Rita Hayworth (Ketterling's Secretary); Wade Boteler (Sam, the Radio Car Driver); Arthur Loft (Radio Patrolman); William H. Strauss (Rent Collector); Marek Windheim (Headwaiter); Bud Jamison (Jim, the Bartender); George Davis (Waiter); Robert Emmett Keane (*Dispatch* City Editor); John Gallaudet (Reporter); Eddie Fetherston (Photographer); Josef De Stefani (Cigar Stand Clerk); Ted Oliver (Cop); Gene Morgan (Officer Fogarty); Tom Dugan (Detective Flannigan); Bud Geary (D.A.'s Assistant); Billy Benedict (Bellhop); Lee Phelps (Police Broadcaster); Eddie Dunn, George McKay (Cops).

THE TOY WIFE (MGM, 1938) 95 M.

Producer, Merian C. Cooper; director, Eichard Thorpe; screenplay, Zöe Atkins; art director, Cedric Gibbons; music, Edward Ward; camera, Oliver T. Marsh; editor, Elmo Vernon.

Luise Rainer (Gilberta Brigard); Melvyn Douglas (Georges Sartoris); Robert Young (Andre Vallaire); Barbara O'Neil (Louise Brigard); H. B. Warner (Victor Brigard); Alma Kruger (Mme. Vallaire); Libby Taylor (Suzanne); Theresa Harris (Pick); Walter Kingsford (Judge Rondell); Clinton Rosemond (Pompey); Clarence Muse (Brutus); Leonard Penn (Gaston Vincent); Margaret Irving (Mdme. DeCambri); Alan Perl (Georgie); Rafaela Ottiano (Felicianne); Beulah Hall Jones (Sophie); George H. Reed (Gabriel); Madam Sul-te-wan (Eve); Hal Le Seuer, Douglas McPhail (Brothers); Tom Rutherfurd (Jacques); Alberto Morin (Emile); Edward Keane (Auctioneer); D'Arcy Corrigan (Actor); Natalie Garson (Woman in Spanish Costume); George Regas (Man in Court); Charles Albin (Priest); Esther Muir (Blonde Woman); Priscilla Lawson (Dark Woman); Brent Sargent (Young Man); Marguerite Whitten (Rose); Billy McClain (Black Orchestra Leader); George Humbert (Italian Organ Grinder); Henry Roquemore (Proprietor of Toy Shop); Robert Spindele (Italian Boy); Barbara Bedford (Woman in Doctor's Office); Ruby Elzy (Mulatto at Fruit Stand); Myrtle Anderson (Therese); Willa Curtis (Marguerite); Gertrude Saunders (Yellow Marie); Violet McDowell (Brown Marie); Cora Lang (Yvonne); Irene Allen (Agatha); Olive Ball, Geneva Williams, Mary Luster, Edna Franklin, Charles Andrews, Ernest Wilson, Henry Thomas, Louise Robinson, Fannie Washington (Servants).

FAST COMPANY (MGM, 1938) 75 M.

Producer, Frederick Stephani; director, Edward Buzzell;

story, Marco Page; screenplay, Page, Harold Tarshis; art director, Cedric Gibbons; music, Dr. William Axt; camera, Clyde DeVinna; editor, Frederick Y. Smith.

Melvyn Douglas (Joel Sloane); Florence Rice (Garda Sloane); Claire Dodd (Julia Thorne); Shepperd Strudwick (Ned Morgan); Louis Calhern (Elias Bannerman); Nat Pendleton (Paul Torison); Douglass Dumbrille (Arnold Stamper); Mary Howard (Leah Brockler); George Zucco (Otto Brockler); Minor Watson (Steve Langner); Donald Douglas (Lieutenant James Flanner); Dwight Frye (Sidney Wheeler); Thurston Hall (District Attorney MacMillan); Horace McMahon (Danny Scolado); Roger Converse (Assistant District Attorney Byers); Natalie Garson (Mildred); Henry Sylvester (Auctioneer); Edward Hearn (Policeman); James B. Carson (Safe Expert); Ronnie Rondell (Taxi Driver); Jack Foss (Attendant); Barbara Bedford (Secretary).

Television title: THE RARE BOOK MURDER.

THAT CERTAIN AGE (UNIV, 1938) 95 M.

Producer, Joseph Pasternak; director, Edward Ludwig; story, F. Hugh Herbert; screenplay, Bruce Manning; makeup, Bill Ely; art director, Jack Otterson; music director, Charles Previn; songs, Jimmy McHugh and Harold Adamson; vocal supervisor, Charles Henderson; billiards coach, Harold Baker; camera, Joseph Valentine; editor, Bernard W. Burton.

Deanna Durbin (Alice Fullerton); Melvyn Douglas (Vincent Bulitt); Jackie Cooper (Ken); Irene Rich (Mrs. Fullerton); Nancy Carroll (Grace); John Halliday (Mr. Fullerton); Juanita Quigley (The Pest); Jackie Searl (Tony); Charles Coleman (Stephens); Peggy Stewart (Mary Lee); Grant Mitchell (Jeweler); Claire DuBrey (Horsewoman); Helen Greco (Girl); Lon McCallister (Billy); Buddy Pepper, Vondell Darr (Friends); Leonard Sues (Orchestra Leader); Bess Flowers, Ed Mortimer (Guests); Ruth Weston (Admirer); David Oliver (Farmer); Russell Hicks (Scout Leader); Troop 536 Boy Scouts of Los Angeles (Themselves).

THE SHINING HOUR (MGM, 1938) 76 M.

Producer, Joseph L. Mankiewicz; director, Frank Borzage; based on the play by Keith Winter; screenplay, Jane Murfin, Ogden Nash; music, Franz Waxman; choreography, Tony De Marco; costumes, Adrian; art director, Cedric Gibbons; sound, Douglas Shearer; camera, George Folsey; editor, Frank E. Hull.

Joan Crawford (Olivia Riley); Margaret Sullavan (Judy Linden); Melvyn Douglas (Henry Linden); Robert Young (David Linden); Fay Bainter (Hannah Linden); Allyn Joslyn (Roger Franklin); Hattie McDaniel (Belvedere); Frank Albertson (Benny Collins); Oscar O'Shea (Charlie Collins); Harry Barris (Bertie); Tony De Marco (Olivia's Dance Partner); Claire Owen (Stewardess); Jim Conlin, Granville Bates (Men); Roger Converse (Clerk); Francis X. Bushman, Jr. (Doorman); Frank Puglia (Headwaiter); George Chandler (Press Agent); Sarah Edwards (Woman); Buddy Messinger (Elevator Boy); Charles C. Coleman (Butler); Edwin Stanley (Minister); E. Allyn Warren (Leonard); Grace Hayle (Mrs. Briggs); Jacques Vanaire (Waiter); Cyril Ring (Candid Cameraman); Bess Flowers (Nurse); Grace Goodall (Mrs. Smart); Jack Raymond (Farmer).

THERE'S THAT WOMAN AGAIN (COL, 1938) 70 M.

Associate producer, B. B. Kahane; director, Alexander Hall; based on the work by Gladys Lehman, Wilson Collison; screenplay, Philip G. Epstein, James Edward Grant, Ken Englund; art director, Lionel Banks; music director, Morris W. Stoloff; camera, Joseph Walker; editor, Viola Lawrence.

Melvyn Douglas (Bill Reardon); Virginia Bruce (Sally Reardon); Margaret Lindsay (Mrs. Nacelle); Stanley Ridges (Tony Croy); Gordon Oliver (Charles Crenshaw); Tom Dugan (Flannigan); Don Beddoe (Johnson); Jonathan Hale (Rolfe Davis); Pierre Watkin (Mr. Nacelle); Paul Harvey (Stone); Marc Lawrence (Stevens); Charles Wilson (Police Captain); Don Barry, Jack Hatfield (Bellboys); Harry Burns (Shoe Shop Proprietor); Helen Lynd (Pearl); Georgette Rhodes, Lillian

Yarbo (Attendants); Vivien Oakland (Large Woman); William Newell (Waiter); Gladys Blake (Fran); Pat Flaherty (Husky Gent); Dick Curtis (Subway Guard); June Gittelson (Fat Woman); Lucille Lund (Receptionist); John Dilson (Coroner's Deputy); Eric Mayne (Bearded Man); Maurice Costello, Russell Heustis (Headwaiters); Lola Jensen (Hat Check Girl); Frank Hall Crayne, Charles McMurphy (Detectives); Mantan Moreland (Porter); George Turner (Delivery Boy); Lee Shumway (Policeman); Nell Craig, Lillian West (Women); Allen Fox (Taxi Driver); Charles McMurphy (Detective); Larry Wheat (Clerk).

TELL NO TALES (MGM, 1939) 68 M.

Producer, Edward Chodorov; director, Leslie Fenton; story, Pauline London, Alfred Taylor; screenplay, Lionel Houser; art director, Cedric Gibbons; music, Dr. William Axt; montage, Peter Ballbusch; camera, Joseph Ruttenberg; editor, W. Donn Hayes.

Melvyn Douglas (Mike Cassidy); Louise Platt (Ellen Frazier); Gene Lockhart (Arne); Douglass Dumbrille (Matt Cooper); Florence George (Lorna Travers); Zeffie Tilbury (Miss Mary); Halliwell Hobbes (Dr. Lovelake); Harlan Briggs (Dave Bryant); Joseph Crehan (Chalmers); Addison Richards (Hollis); Jean Fenwick (Mrs. Lovell); Esther Dale (Mrs. Haskins); Gladys Blake (Myra Haskins); Hobart Cavanaugh (Charlie Daggett); Theresa Harris (Ruby); Ernest Whitman (Elab Giffin); Mary Gordon (Mrs. Bryant); Ray Walker (Dell); Ernie Alexander (Johnson); Jack Carlton (Wilson); Thomas Jackson (Eddie); Tom Collins (Phil Arno); Oscar O'Shea (Sam O'Neil); Frank Orth (Vic, the Bartender); Roger Imhof (Taxi Driver); Claire DuBrey (Miss Arnold); Chester Clute (Manders); Renie Riano (Swedish Maid); Charles D. Brown (Lieutenant Brandon); Norman Willis (Meves); Anthony Warde (Lewis); Ian Wolfe (Fritz); George Noisom (Office Boy); E. Alyn Warren (Janitor); Pat Flaherty (Printer); Fred Kelsey, James C. Morton, Jack Daley, Lee Phelps, Monte Vandergrift (Cops); Hilda Haywood, Bess Flowers (Teachers); Harry Depp (Robert E. More); James Flavin (Simmons); Gertrude Sutton (Gertrude); Harry Tyler (Man on Bus); Brandon Hurst (Butler); Everett Brown (Black Doorman); Mantan Moreland (Sporty Black); Mdme. Sul-te-wan (Alley Cat's Mother); Florence O'Brien (Belle); Rosalie Lincoln (Girl); Ruby Elsy (Woman in Chair); Thad Jones (Preacher); Ben Carter (Politician); Phil Tead (Marty); James G. Blaine (Captain Hendry); Gladden James (Male Secretary); Nick Copeland (Attendant); Claire Rochelle (Girl at Phone); Ward Wing (Kammy); George Magrill (Alex); Ben Taggart (Lieutenant); John Marlowe (Pianist); Heinie Conklin, Billy Engle (Tramp Comics); Joseph E. Bernard (Man).

GOOD GIRLS GO TO PARIS (COL, 1939) 75 M.

Producer, William Perlberg; director, Alexander Hall; story, Lenore Coffee, William Joyce Cowen; screenplay, Gladys Lehman, Ken Englund; art director, Lionel Banks; assistant director, William Mull; music director, Morris W. Stoloff; gowns, Kallock; sound, Jack Goodrich; camera, Henry Freulich; editor, Al Clark.

Melvyn Douglas (Ronald Brooke); Joan Blondell (Jenny Swanson); Walter Connolly (Olaf Brand); Alan Curtis (Tom Brand); Joan Perry (Sylvia Brand); Isabel Jeans (Caroline Brand); Stanley Brown (Ted Dayton); Alexander D'Arcy (Paul Kingston); Henry Hunter (Dennis); Clarence Kolb (Dayton, Sr.); Howard Hickman (Jeffers); Barlowe Borland (Chambers); Helen Jermone Eddy (Tearoom Hostess); Donald Dillaway, Forbes Murray, Johnny Tyrrell, James Craig (Men); Dave Willock, Richard Fiske, Robert Sterling, Dick Winslow, Jack Chapin, Robert Cherry, Tommy Seidel (Students); Dorothy Comingore, Beatrice Blinn (Girls); Ann Doran, Adrian Booth (Bridesmaids); Don Beddoe (Burton); Wright Kramer (Professor Guthrie); George Guhl (Constable); Sam McDaniel (Porter); George Douglas (Baxter); Leon Belasco (Violinist); George Lloyd (Schultz); William Newell (Waiter); Dora Clement, Jean Acker, Lillian Teneycke (Women); Harry Bailey

(Wedding Guest); Jane K. Loofbourrow, Catherine Courtney (Old Maids); Dorothy Fowler (Maid); Ray Turner (Red Cap); Leigh DeLacey (Cook); Bill Irving (Chef); Eleanor Counts, Beatrice Curtis (Waitresses); Mary Field (Ada); John Maurice Sullivan (Minister); Jack Daley (Train Conductor); Walter Sande, Walter Merrill (Ticket Agents).

NINOTCHKA (MGM, 1939) 110 M.

Producer-director, Ernst Lubitsch; based on story by Melchior Lengyel; screenplay, Charles Brackett, Billy Wilder, Walter Reisch; art directors, Cedric Gibbons, Randall Duell; music, Werner R. Heymann; makeup, Jack Dawn; assistant director, Horace Hough; sound, Douglas Shearer; camera, William Daniels; editor, Gene Ruggiero.

Greta Garbo [Ninotchka (Lena Yakushova)]; Melvyn Douglas (Count Leon Dolga); Ina Claire (Grand Duchess Swana); Sig Rumann (Michael Iranoff); Felix Bressart (Buljanoff); Alexander Granach (Kopalski); Bela Lugosi (Commissar Razinin); Gregory Gaye (Count Alexis Rakonin); Richard Carle (Vaston); Edwin Maxwell (Mercier); Rolfe Sedan (Hotel Manager); George Tobias (Russian Visa Official); Dorothy Adams (Jacqueline, Swana's Maid); Lawrence Grant (General Savitsky); Charles Judels (Pere Mathieu, the Cafe Owner); Frank Reicher, Edwin Stanley (Lawyers); Peggy Moran (French Maid); Marek Windheim (Manager); Mary Forbes (Lady Lavenham); Alexander Schonberg (Bearded Man); George Davis (Porter); Armand Kaliz (Louis, the Headwaiter); Wolfgang Zilzer (Taxi Driver); Tamara Shayne (Anna); William Irving (Bartender); Bess Flowers (Gossip); Elizabeth Williams (Indignant Woman); Paul Weigel (Vladimir); Harry Semels (Neighbor-Spy); Jody Gilbert (Streetcar Conductress); Florence Shirley (Marianne); Elinor Vandivere, Sandra Morgan, Bess Flowers, Emily Cabanne, Symona Boniface, Monya Andre (Gossips); Kay Stewart, Jenifer Gray (Cigarette Girls); Lucille Pinson (German Woman at Railroad Station).

THE AMAZING MR. WILLIAMS (COL, 1939) 80 M.

Producer, Everett Riskin; director, Alexander Hall; story, Sy Bartlett; screenplay, Dwight Taylor, Bartlett, Richard Maibaum; art director, Lionel Banks; music director, Morris W. Stoloff; camera, Arthur Todd; editor, Viola Lawrence.

Melvyn Douglas (Kenny Williams); Joan Blondell (Maxine Carroll); Clarence Kolb (Captain McGovern); Ruth Donnelly (Effie); Edward S. Brophy (Buck Moseby); Donald MacBride (Lieutenant Bixler); Don Beddoe (Deever); Jonathan Hale (Mayor); John Wray (Stanley); Robert Middlemass (Police Commissioner); Maurice Cass (Little Man); Barbara Pepper (Muriel); Luis Alberni (Rinaldo); Peggy Shannon (Kitty); Richard Lane (Reagan); Maude Eburne (Landlady); Ralph Peters (Tobacco Store Proprietor); Walter Miller (Browning); William Hall (Jamieson); William Forrest (Anderson); Sidney D'Albrook (Fat Pedestrian); John Locke (Shop Keeper); Tommy Mullins, Wyndham Standing, Frank Jaquet, Robert Dudley (Men); Adrian Booth (Nurse); Eddie Laughton (Mousey); Stanley Brown, Robert Sterling (Elevator Boys); William Newell, Herbert Clifton (Waiters); Billy Lally (Cop); Eleanor Wood, Eva McKenzie (Housewives); Jan Hopper, Cynthia Crane (Little Girls); William Tracy (Messenger Boy); James Conlin (Master of Ceremonies); Anthony Warde (Bouncer); Lela Bliss (Woman); Virginia Sale (Miss Mason); Sally Payne (Jean); Ada May Moore (Snake Charmer); Harrison Greene (Barker); Eddie Fetherston (Cab Driver); Dave Willock (Bell Boy); Hans Schumm (Pedestrian); Milton Kibbee (Liquor Store Proprietor); Walter Sande (Male Stenographer); Blanche Payson (Large Woman); Charles McAvoy (Turnkey); Fred Warren (Clerk); Jack Chefe (Headwaiter); Jane Barnes, Jenifer Gray, Rita Owin (Girls); James Crane (Johnny); Richard Scott (Boy).

TOO MANY HUSBANDS (COL, 1940) 84 M.

Producer-director, Wesley Ruggles; based on the play by W. Somerset Maugham; screenplay, Claude Binyon; camera, Joseph Walker; editors, Otto Meyer, William Lyon.

Jean Arthur (Vicky Lowndes); Fred MacMurray (Bill Cardew); Melvyn Douglas (Henry Lowndes); Harry Davenport (George); Dorothy Peterson (Gertrude Houlihan); Melville Cooper (Peter); Edgar Buchanan (McDermott); Tom Dugan (Sullivan); Garry Owen (Sign Painter); Lee White (Mailman); Mary Treen (Emma); William Brisbane (Lawyer); Sam McDaniel (Porter); Ralph Peters (Cab Driver); Walter Soderling (Customer); Jerry Fletcher (Man); Jacques Vanaire (Headwaiter).

HE STAYED FOR BREAKFAST (COL, 1940) 89 M.

Producer, B. P. Schulberg; director, Alexander Hall; based on the play Liberte Provisoire *by Michel Duran; screenplay, P. J. Wolfson, Michael Fessier, Ernest Vajda; camera, Joseph Walker; editor, Viola Lawrence.*

Loretta Young (Marianne Duval); Melvyn Douglas (Paul Boliet); Alan Marshal (Andre Derlay); Eugene Pallette (Maurice Duval); Una O'Connor (Doreta); Curt Bois (Comrade Tronavich); Leonid Kinskey (Nicky); Trevor Bardette (Police Lieutenant); Grady Sutton (Salesman); Frank Sully (Butcher); Evelyn Young, Ethelreda Leopold (Secretaries); William Castle (Policeman); Henry Hale (Police Lieutenant); Ernie Adams (Workman); Jack Rice (Marianne's Chauffeur); Harry Semels (Comrade); Jack Douglas, Nestor Paiva (Gendarmes); Ferdinand Munier (Cafe Proprietor); Guy Repp (Headwaiter); Charles Wagenheim (Timid Waiter); Vernon Dent (Chef); Frederic Worlock (Communist President); Leonard Mudie (Communist Secretary); George Burr McAnnan (Communist Vice President); Jack Lowe, Art Miles, Jack Raymond, Bob St. Angelo (Communists); George Andre Beranger (Maitre D'Hotel); Joseph Kamaryt, Bill Newell (Waiters); Eddie Colebrook (Bus Boy); Walter Merrill (Guard).

THIRD FINGER-LEFT HAND (MGM, 1940) 96 M.

Producer, John W. Considine, Jr.; director, Robert Z. Leonard; screenplay, Lionel Houser; music, David Snell; camera, George Folsey; editor, Elmo Vernon.

Myrna Loy (Margot Sherwood); Melvyn Douglas (Jeff Thompson); Lee Bowman (Phillip Booth); Bonita Granville (Vicki Sherwood); Raymond Walburn (Mark Sherwood); Felix Bressart (Mr. Flandarin); Sidney Blackmer (Hughie Wheeler); Ernest Whitman (Sam); Ann Morriss (Miss Hampshire); Edna Holland (Miss Lawton); Jean Fenwick (Miss Carruthers); William Halligan (Ralph Russell); Marjorie Gateson (Mrs. Russell); Halliwell Hobbes (Burton); Howard Lang (Reverend Johnson); Florence Shirley (Agnes); Olive Blakeney (Louise); Jeff Corey (Johann); Greta Grandstedt (Selma); Mira McKinney (Miss Dell); Marvin Stephens (Marton); Harry Tyler (Martin); Dick Paxton (Messenger Boy); Ray Cooke, Milton Kibbee (Stewards); Tim Ryan (Mate); Jimmy Conlin (Ernest); Jane Goude (Emma); Milton Parsons (Photographer); Joe Yule (Waiter); Philip Sleeman (Headwaiter); May McAvoy (Girl Operator); Forbes Murray (Wilbur); Lloyd Whitlock (Herbert); Jack Mulhall (Guide); Andrew Tombes (Mr. Kelland); Grace Hayle (Mrs. Kelland); Frank McGlynn (Reverend Holmes); Rita Quigley (Elvira Kelland); Frederick Burton (Mr. Thompson); Leila McIntyre (Mrs. Thompson); Ray Teal (Cameraman); John Butler (Telegrapher); Ken Christy (Pullman Conductor); Ed Cecil (Train Conductor); Ann Marsters, Barbara Bedford, Christina Teague, Dorothy Vernon, Alice Keating (Women at Railroad Station); Art Belasco, Frank O'Connor, John Webb Dillon, Ernie Alexander, Sid D'Albrook, Art Berry, Sr., Maurice Costello, Dick Rush, Cyril Ring, John Ince (Men at Railroad Station); Joe Whitehead (Barney); Helen Dickson, Gertrude Simpson (Women in Berths); Walter Soderling (Man in Berth).

THIS THING CALLED LOVE (COL, 1941) 98 M.

Producer, William Perlberg; director, Alexander Hall; based on the play by Edwin Burke; screenplay, George Seaton, Ken Englund, P. J. Wolfson; camera, Joseph Walker.

Rosalind Russell (Ann Winters); Melvyn Douglas (Tice Collins); Binnie Barnes (Charlotta Campbell); Allyn Joslyn

(Harry Bertrand); Gloria Dickson (Florence Bertrand); Lee J. Cobb (Julio Diestro); Gloria Holden (Genevieve Hooper); Paul McGrath (Gordon Daniels); Leona Maricle (Ruth Howland); Don Beddoe (Tom Howland); Rosina Galli (Mrs. Dietro); Sig Arno (Arno).

THAT UNCERTAIN FEELING (UA, 1941) 84 M.

Producer-director, Ernst Lubitsch; based on the play Divorcons *by Victorien Sardou, Emile de Najac; adaptor, Walter Reisch; screenplay, Donald Ogden Stewart; art director, Alexander Golitzen; music, Werner Heymann; gowns, Irene; camera, George Barnes; editor, William Shea.*

Merle Oberon (Jill Baker); Melvyn Douglas (Larry Baker); Burgess Meredith (Sebastian); Alan Mowbray (Dr. Vengard); Olive Blakeney (Margie Stallings); Harry Davenport (Attorney Jones); Eve Arden (Sally); Sig Rumann (Mr. Okfka); Richard Carle (Butler); Mary Currier (Maid); Jean Fenwick (Nurse).

A WOMAN'S FACE (MGM, 1941) 105 M.

Producer, Victor Saville; director, George Cukor; based on the play Il Etait Une Fois *by Francis de Croisset; screenplay, Donald Ogden Stewart; art director, Cedric Gibbons; music, Bronislau Kaper; costumes, Adrian; sound, Douglas Shearer; camera, Robert Planck; editor, Frank Sullivan.*

Joan Crawford (Anna Holm); Melvyn Douglas (Dr. Gustav Segert); Conrad Veidt (Torsten Barring); Reginald Owen (Bernard Dalvik); Albert Basserman (Consul Barring); Marjorie Main (Emma); Donald Meek (Herman); Connie Gilchrist (Christine Dalvik); Richard Nichols (Lars Erik); Osa Massen (Vera Segert); Charles Quigley (Eric); Henry Kolker (Judge); George Zucco (Defense Attorney); Henry Daniell (Public Prosecutor); Robert Warwick, Gilbert Emery (Associate Judges); William Farnum, Rex Evans (Notaries); Sarah Padden (Police Matron); Gwili Andre (Gusta); Manart Kippen (Olaf); Lionel Pape (Einer); Doris Day, Mary Ellen Popel (Party Girls); Clifford Brooke (Wickman); Cecil Stewart (Pianist); Veda Buckland, Lilian Kemble-Cooper (Nurses); Alexander Leftwich, George Pauncefort (Guests); Robert C. Flasher (Court Attendant); Catherine Proctor (Mrs. Segerblum).

OUR WIFE (COL, 1941) 95 M.

Producer, John M. Stahl; associate producer, Irving Starr; director, Stahl; based on the play by Lillian Day, Lyon Mearson; screenplay, P. J. Wolfson; art director, Lionel Banks; music, Leo Shuken; music director, Morris W. Stoloff; camera, Franz F. Planer; editor, Gene Havlick.

Melvyn Douglas (Jerry Marvin); Ruth Hussey (Susan Drake); Ellen Drew (Babe Marvin); Charles Coburn (Professor Drake); John Hubbard (Tom Drake); Harvey Stephens (Dr. Cassell); Theresa Harris (Hattie); Hobart Cavanaugh (Man); Barbara Brown (Passenger); Charles Hamilton (Sailor); Crauford Kent (Ship's Doctor); Addison Richards (Middle-Aged Man); Isabel Withers (Middle-Aged Woman); George McKay (Steward); Andre Beranger (Waiter); John Merton (Officer); Roland Varno, John Holland (Stewards); Juan Varro, Pedro Regas, Martin Garralaga, Thornton Edwards (Cuban Drivers); Paul Lopez (Cuban Official); Lloyd Bridges (Taxi Driver); Edward Fielding (Dr. Mandel); Irving Bacon (Doorman); Lloyd Whitlock (Customer); Hooper Atchley (Ticket Man); Paul McVey, Forbes Murray (Dress Bits); Grace Darmond, Betty Blythe (Dress Women); Frank Yaconelli (Hat Vender); Bob Benston Evans (Black Man); Lawrence Grant (Dr. Holgarth).

TWO-FACED WOMAN (MGM, 1941) 94 M.

Producer, Gottfried Reinhardt; director, George Cukor; based on the play by Ludwig Fulda; screenplay, S. N. Behrman, Salka Viertel, George Oppenheimer; music, Bronislau Kaper; art director, Cedric Gibbons; costumes, Adrian; sound, Dougas Shearer; camera, Joseph Ruttenberg; editor, George Boemler.

Greta Garbo (Karin Blake); Melvyn Douglas (Larry Blake); Constance Bennett (Griselda Vaughn); Roland Young (O. O.

Miller); Robert Sterling (Dick Williams); Ruth Gordon (Miss Ellis); George Cleveland (Sheriff); George P. Huntley, Jr. (Mr. Wilson); James Spencer (Carl); William Tannen (Ski Guide); Frances Carson (Miss Dunbar); John Marston (Graham); Olive Blakeney (Phyllis); Douglass Newland, Roy Gordon (Men); Mary Young (Wife); Hilda Plowright, Eula Guy (Women); Mark Daniels (Bellboy); Vinton Haworth (Guide); Connie Gilchrist, Bess Flowers (Receptionists); Cliff Danielson, Paul Leyssac (Clerks); Walter Anthony Merrill (Stage Manager); George Lollier (Cab Driver); Arno Frey (Waiter); Andre Cheron (Headwaiter); Lorin Raker, Tom Herbert, Grace Hayle, Emily Fitzroy (Rhumba Dancers); Robert Alton (Cecil); Gloria De Haven, Michaele Fallon (Debutantes); George Calligas (Hotel Clerk).

WE WERE DANCING (MGM, 1942) 93 M.

Producers, Robert Z. Leonard, Orville Dull; director, Leonard; based in part on the play Tonight at 8:30 *by Noel Coward; screenplay, Claudine West, Hans Rameau, George Froeschel; art director, Cedric Gibbons; costumes, Adrian; sound, Douglas Shearer; camera, Robert Planck; editor, George Boemler.*

Norma Shearer (Vicki Wilomirsky); Melvyn Douglas (Nicki Prax); Gail Patrick (Linda Wayne); Lee Bowman (Hubert Tyler); Marjorie Main (Judge Sidney Hawkes); Reginald Owen (Major Tyler-Blane); Alan Mowbray (Grand Duke Basil); Florence Bates (Mrs. Vanderlip); Sig Rumann (Baron Prax); Dennis Hoey (Prince Wilomirsky); Heather Thatcher (Mrs. Tyler-Blane); Connie Gilchrist (Olive Hansome); Florence Shirley (Mrs. Charteris); Paul Porcasi (Manager of Duquesne); John Piffle (Dutchman); Lionel Pape (Englishman); Philip Ahn (Chinaman); George H. Reed (Butler at Blane's House); Ottola Nesmith (Mrs. Quimby); Mary Forbes (Mrs. Sandys); Thurston Hall (Senator Quimby); Douglas Wood (Colonel Sandys); Alan Napier (Captain Blackstone); Martin Turner (Red Cap); Pierre Watkin (Mr. Bentley); Bryant Washburn, Sr. (Mr. Lambert); Nella Walker (Mrs. Bentley); Helene Millard (Mrs. Lambert); Florence Wix (Sporting Woman); Alfred Hall (Butler); Alex Callam (Clerk); Dick Elliott (Mr. Platt); Jessamine Newcombe (Mrs. Platt); Betty Hayward (Debutante); John Roche (Mr. Fox); Duncan Renaldo (Sam Estrella); Russell Hicks (Bryce-Carew); Norma Varden (Mrs. Bryce-Carew); Anthony Marsh (Tommy Brooke); Willy Castello (Felucci); Emmett Vogan (Bailiff); Harry Hayden (Clerk); Polly Bailey (Flower Woman); Tim Ryan (Traffic Cop); Jean Fenwick (Girl); Fred Santley (Clerk); Harold Minjir (Beverly); Ian Wolfe (Reggie); Barlowe Borland (McDonough); Dick Alexander (Moving Man); Alex Pollard (Ransome's Butler); Jacques Vanaire (Beverly's Assistant); Gino Corrado (Headwaiter in Inn); Esther Michelson (Headwaiter's Wife); Meeka Aldrich (Housemaid); Henry Roquemore (Mr. Ransome); Charles Sullivan (Train Announcer); Bill Fisher (Train Conductor); John "Buddy" Williams (Red Cap); John Holland, Herbert Rawlinson (Friends).

THEY ALL KISSED THE BRIDE (COL, 1942) 86 M.

Producer, Edward Kaufman; director, Alexander Hall; story, Gina Kaus, Andrew P. Solt; adaptors, Solt, Henry Altimus; screenplay, P. J. Wolfson; art directors, Lionel Banks, Cary Odell; music, Morris Stoloff; costumes, Irene; camera, Joseph Walker; editor, Viola Lawrence.

Joan Crawford (Margaret J. Drew); Melvyn Douglas (Michael Holmes); Roland Young (Marsh); Billie Burke (Mrs. Drew); Allen Jenkins (Johnny Johnson); Andrew Tombes (Crane); Helen Parrish (Vivian Drew); Emory Parnell (Mahony); Mary Treen (Susie Johnson); Nydia Westman (Secretary); Ivan Simpson (Dr. Cassell); Roger Clark (Stephen Pettingill); Gordon Jones (Taxi Driver); Larry Parks (Joe Krim); Tom Dugan (Callahan); John Dilson (Man); Charles Miller, George Pembroke, Wyndham Standing (Department Heads); Shirley Patterson (Receptionist); Douglas Wood (Hoover); Boyd Irwin (Endore); Frank Dawson (Nolan); Ann Doran (Maid); Alma Carroll (Bridesmaid); Charles Coleman (Butler); Father Neal Dodd (Minister); Ralph Sanford (Detective); Wheaton Chambers, Arthur Stuart Hull, Richard Kipling, Hal Cooke, John Merkyl (Board Members); Dale Van Sickel (Marine); Polly Bailey (Irish Woman); Walter Merrill, Terrance Ray, Harry Strang, Charles Sullivan, Frank Marlowe, Ernie Adams, Lyle Latell, Ralph Peters (Truck Drivers); Tom Lincir, Rosalie Miller (Dance Specialties); Kitty Kelly, Charles Lane (Spotters); George McKay (Announcer); Norman Willis (Cop); Charles Halton (Doctor).

THREE HEARTS FOR JULIA (MGM, 1943) 89 M.

Producer, John W. Considine, Jr.; director, Richard Thorpe; screenplay, Lionel Houser; music, Herbert Stothart; art directors, Cedric Gibbons, Howard Campbell; set decorators, Edwin Willis, Helen Conway; assistant director, Bert Spurling; sound, J. S. Burbridge; camera, George Folsey; editor, Irvine Warburton.

Ann Sothern (Julia Seabrook); Melvyn Douglas (Jeff Seabrook); Lee Bowman (David Terrance); Felix Bressart (Mr. Anton Ottaway); Reginald Owen (John Girard); Richard Ainley (Philip Barrows); Marta Linden (May Elton); Jacqueline White (Kay); Kay Medford (Thelma); Ann Richards (Clara); Elvia Allman (Miss Stickney); Marietta Canty (Mattie); Charles LaTorre (Bureau Clerk); Marek Windheim (Perfume Clerk); Bill Lally (Customs Man); William Tannen, Rudolph Cameron, Hooper Atchley, Art Belasco, George Lollier, Anthony Warde, Estelle Etterre (Reporters); Phyllis Cook (Western Union Girl); Oscar O'Shea (Doorman); Frank Faylen (Meek Gateman); Dick Rich (Mug Attendant); Joe Yule (Cab Driver); Fred Rapport, Bill Dill (Waiters); Dick Elliott (Smith); Ernie Alexander (Johnson); Russell Gleason (Jones); Max Willenz (Bartender); Robert Greig (Cairns); Nell Craig (Maid); Howard Hickman (Mr. Doran); James Warren (Program Vendor); Bert Hicks (Usher); Russell Hicks (Colonel Martin); Hans Von Morhart, John Van Eyck, Curt Furberg, Nicholas Vehr, Jack Deery (Nazis); Dick Wessel (Soldier); Mary Field, Eve Whitney, Marie Windsor, Mary Benoit, Natalie Draper (Musicians).

SEA OF GRASS (MGM, 1947) 123 M.

Producer, Pandro S. Berman; director, Elia Kazan; based on the novel by Conrad Richter; screenplay, Marguerite Roberts; art directors, Cedric Gibbons, Paul Groesse; set decorators, Edwin B. Willis, Mildred Griffiths; music, Herbert Stothart; assistant director, Sid Sidman; sound, Douglas Shearer; special effects, Arnold Gillespie, Warren Newcombe; camera, Harry Stradling; editor, Robert J. Kern.

Spencer Tracy (Colonel Jim Brewton); Katharine Hepburn (Lutie Cameron); Melvyn Douglas (Brice Chamberlain); Robert Walker (Brock Brewton); Phyllis Thaxter (Sarah Beth Brewton); Edgar Buchanan (Jeff); Harry Carey (Doc Reid); Ruth Nelson (Selina Hall); William "Bill" Phillips (Santy); Robert Armstrong (Floyd McCurtin); James Bell (Sam Hall); Robert Barrat (Judge White); Charles Trowbridge (George Cameron); Russell Hicks (Major Harney); Trevor Bardette (Andy Boggs); Morris Ankrum (Crane); Dan White (Ike Randall); Glenn Strange (Bill Roach); Douglas Fowley (Joe Horton); Guy Wilkerson (Wake); Buddy Roosevelt, Earle Hodgins, Robert Bice, John Rice, Hank Worden (Cowboys); Larry Lathrop (Messenger); George Reed (Uncle Nat); Dorothy Vaughan (Mrs. Hodges); Marietta Canty (Rachael); Vernon Dent (Conductor); Erville Alderson (Station Agent); Jack Davis (Foreman); Irving Smith (Black Servant); Jessie Graves (Luke); Bernice Pilot, Myrtle Anderson, Helen Dickson, Ruth Cherrington, Laura Treadwell, Leota Lorraine (Bits); Henry Adams, Wyndham Standing, William Holmes (Gamblers); Mickey Martin (Newsboy); Joseph Crehan (Senator Graw); John Hamilton (Forrest Cochran); John Vosper (Hotel Clerk); Bud Fine (Brakeman); Many Treaties (Indian); James O'Rear (Piano Tuner); Nora Cecil (Mrs. Ryan); Gertrude Chorre (Indian Nurse); Pat Henry (Brock at Age One); Ann Gowland (Sarah Beth at Age Two and One-Half); Polly Bailey, Vangie Beolby, Margaret Bert, Naomi Childers, Rose Langdon (Women); Sid D'Albrook, Franz Dorfler, Obed "Dad" Pickard,

Henry Sylvester, J. L. Palmer, Robert Malcolm, Jack Stoney, Fred Graham, Frank Hagney (Men); Frank Austin (Station Agent); Howard Mitchell (Conductor's Voice); Patty Smith (Sarah Beth at Age Four and One-Half); Duncan Richardson (Brock at Age Three); Frank Pharr, Bob Ingersoll (Station Loafers); Ray Teal, Eddie Acuff, Davison Clark, Joe Brockman, Rocky Wood, Fred Gilman, Dick Rush (Cattlemen); Charles Middleton (Charley); Carol Nugent (Sarah Beth at Age Seven); Jimmie Hawkins (Brock at Age Five and One-Half); Skeets Noyes (Beady-Eyed Man); Wheaton Chambers (Dean); George Magrill, Charles McAvoy, Nolan Leary, Eddy Waller, Forrest Taylor, Gene Stutenroth, Joe Bernard, Ralph Littlefield (Homesteaders); Frank Darien (Minister); William Challee (Deputy Sheriff); Stanley Andrews (Sheriff); Dick Baron (Newsboy); Mike Donovan, Bill Van Vleck (Nestors).

THE GUILT OF JANET AMES (COL, 1947) 83 M.

Director, Henry Levin; based on the story by Lenor Coffee; screenplay, Louella MacFarlane, Allen Rivkin, Devery Freeman; art directors, Stephen Goosson, Walter Holscher; set decorators, George Montgomery, Frank Tuttle; music, George Duning; music director, Morris W. Stoloff; songs, Allan Roberts and Doris Fisher; assistant director Milton Feldman; sound, Frank Goodwin; camera, Joseph Walker; editor, Charles Nelson.

Rosalind Russell (Janet Ames); Melvyn Douglas (Smithfield Cobb); Sid Caesar (Sammy Weaver); Betsy Blair (Katie); Nina Foch (Susie Pierson); Charles Cane (Walker); Harry Von Zell (Carter); Bruce Harper (Junior); Arthur Space (Nelson); Richard Benedict (Joe Burton); Frank Orth (Danny); Ray Walker (Sidney); Doreen McCann (Emmy Merino); Hugh Beaumont (Frank Merino); Thomas Jackson (Police Sergeant); Edwin Cooper (Surgeon); Emory Parnell (Susie's Father); Victoria Horne, Wanda Perry, Eve March, Kathleen O'Malley (Nurses); Pat Lane, Fred Howard (Doctors); Steve Benton (Ambulance Attendant); Doris Colleen (Student Nurse); William Trenk (Headwaiter); George Riley (Policeman); John Farrell (Janitor); Bill Wallace (Orderly); John Berkes (Customer); William Challee (Ambulance Surgeon); William Forrest (Dr. Morton); Isabel Withers (Marian); Denver Pyle (Masher).

MR. BLANDINGS BUILDS HIS DREAM HOUSE (RKO, 1948) 94 M.

Executive producer, Dore Schary; producers, Norman Panama, Melvin Frank; director, H.C. Potter; based on the novel by Eric Hodgins; screenplay, Panama, Frank; technical advisor, John Swope; art directors, Albert S. D'Agostino, Carroll Clark; set decorators, Darrell Silvera, Harley Miller; music, Leigh Harline; music director, C. Bakaleinikoff; assistant director, James Lane; makeup, Gordon Bau; costumes, Robert Kalloch; sound, Francis M. Sarver, Clem Portman; special effects, Russell A. Cully; camera, James Wong Howe; editor, Harry Marker.

Cary Grant (Jim Blandings); Myrna Loy (Muriel Blandings); Melvyn Douglas (Bill Cole); Reginald Denny (Simms); Sharyn Moffett (Joan Blandings); Connie Marshall (Betsy Blandings); Louise Beavers (Gussie); Ian Wolfe (Smith); Harry Shannon (Tesander); Tito Vuolo (Mr. Zucca); Nestor Paiva (Joe Appellenio); Jason Robards (John Retch); Lurene Tuttle (Mary); Lex Barker (Carpenter Foreman); Emory Parnell (Mr. PeDelford); Will Wright (Eph); Frank Darien (Judge Quarles); Stanley Andrews (Murphy); Cliff Clark (Jones); Franklin Parker (Simpson); Charles Middleton (Wrecker); Cy Slocum (Man); Jack Jahries (Elevator Operator); Robert Bray, Frederich Ledebur (Workmen); Don Brodie (Charlie); Hal K. Dawson (Mr. Selby); Kernan Cripps (Cop); Ralph Stein (Proprietor); Mike Lally, Bud Wiser (Customers); Gene Leslie (Taxi Driver).

MY OWN TRUE LOVE (PAR, 1948) 93 M.

Producer, Val Lewton; director, Compton Bennett; based on the novel Make You a Fine Wife *by Yolanda Foldes; adaptor,*

Arthur Kober; screenplay, Theodore Strauss, Josef Mischel; art directors, Hans Dreier, Henry Bumstead; set directors, Sam Comer, Ross Dowd; music, Robert Emmett Dolan; assistant director, Oscar Rudolph; costumes, Edith Head; sound, Harry Lindgren, John Cope; special effects, Gordon Jennings; process camera, Farciot Edouart; camera, Charles B. Lang, Jr.; editor, LeRoy Stone.

Phyllis Calvert (Joan Clews); Melvyn Douglas (Clive Heath); Wanda Hendrix (Sheila Heath); Philip Friend (Michael Heath); Binnie Barnes (Geraldine); Alan Napier (Kittredge); Arthur Shields (Iverson); Phyllis Morris (Mrs. Peach); Richard Webb (Corporal); Norma Varden (Red Cross Nurse); Peter Coe (Rene); Clifford Brooke (Coffee Stall Proprietor); Leyland Hodgson (Taxi Driver); David Thursby (Mechanic); Jean Fenwick (Corporal); Betty Fairfax, Mary MacLaren (Women—Nissen Hut); William Meader (Room Clerk); George Douglas (Cutter); Patrick Whyte (Flight Lieutenant); Wilson Benge (Waiter); Joseph Marr (Proprietor); Erno Verebes (Captain of Waiters); Paul Kreibich (Maitre D'); T. Arthur Hughes (Doorman); Marie Osborne (Woman Passenger); Leslie Denison (Man); Queenie Leonard (Woman); Robin Hughes (English Officer); Miriam Jordan (Miss Robinson).

A WOMAN'S SECRET (RKO, 1949) 85 M.

Executive producer, Dore Schary; producer, Herman J. Mankiewicz; director, Nicholas Ray; based on the novel Mortgage on Life by Vicki Baum; screenplay Mankiewicz; art directors, Albert S. D'Agostino, Carroll Clark; set decorators, Darrell Silvera, Harley Miller; music, Frederick Hollander; music director, C. Bakaleinikoff; assistant director, Doran Cox; makeup, Gordon Bau, James Barker, Jack Barron; costumes, Edward Stevenson; sound, Frank Sarver, Clem Portman; special effects, Russell A. Cully; camera, George Diskant; editor, Sherman Todd.

Maureen O'Hara (Marian Washburn); Melvyn Douglas (Luke Jordan); Gloria Grahame (Susan Caldwell); Bill Williams (Les); Victor Jory (Brook Matthews); Mary Phillips (Mrs. Fowler); Jay C. Flippen (Fowler); Robert Warwick (Roberts); Curt Conway (Doctor); Ann Shoemaker (Mrs. Matthews); Virginia Farmer (Millie); Ellen Corby (Nurse); Emory Parnell (Desk Sergeant); Dan Foster (Stage Manager); Alphonse Martel, Eddie Borden (Waiters); Charles Wagenheim (Piano Player); Marcelle De LaBrosse (Baker); Lynne Whitney (Actress); Rory Mallinson (Benson); George Douglas, Lee Phelps, Mickey Simpson, Guy Beach, Tom Coleman (Policemen); Raymond Bond (Dr. Ferris); Bill Purington (Interne); Bernice Young (Nurse); Loreli Vitek (Waitress); John Goldsworthy (Harold); Frederick Nay (Master of Ceremonies); Forbes Murray (Mr. Emory); Donna Gibson, Evelyn Underwood (Girls); John Parrish (Professor Camelli); Oliver Blake (Mr. Pierson); Paul Guilfoyle (Moderator); Jack Rourke, Norman Nesbitt (Announcers); Conrad Binyon (Messenger Boy); Ralph Stein (Mr. Harris); Robert Malcolm (Bit).

THE GREAT SINNER (MGM, 1949) 110 M.

Producer, Gottfried Reinhardt; director Robert Siodmak; suggested by the story "The Gambler" by Feodor Dostoevski; story, Ladislas Fodor, Rene Fulop-Miller; screenplay, Fodor, Christopher Isherwood; art directors, Cedric Gibbons, Hans Peters; set decorators, Edwin B. Willis, Henry W. Grace; music, Bronislau Kaper; music director, Andre Previn; assistant director, Marvin Stuart; makeup, Jack Dawn; costumes, Irene, Valles; technical advisor, Paul Elbogen; sound, Douglas Shearer, Conrad Kahn; special effects, Warren Newcombe; camera, George Folsey; editor, Harold F. Kress.

Gregory Peck (Feodor Dostoevski); Ava Gardner (Pauline Ostrovski); Melvyn Douglas (Armand Le Glasse); Walter Huston (General Ostrovski); Ethel Barrymore (Granny); Frank Morgan (Aristide Pitard); Agnes Moorehead (Emma Getzel); Ludwig Stossel (Hotel Manager); Ludwig Donath (Doctor); Erno Verebes (Hotel Valet); Curt Bois (Jeweler); Martin Garralaga (Maharajah); Antonio Filauri (Senor Pinto); Frederich Ledebur (De Classe's Secretary); Jean Del Val (Croupier); Vincent Renno (Casino Inspector); William H. Hawes (Nervous Englishman); Andre Charlot (Distinguished Man); Sam Scar (Turk); Elsa Heims (Woman with Cigar); Joan Miller (Cold Sexy Woman); John Piffle (Fat Man); Emil Rameau (Fearful Old Man); Elspeth Dudgeon (Fearful Old Woman); James Anderson (Nervous Young Man); Charles Wagenheim (Man with Ring); Gisella Werbisek (Greedy Woman); Hannelore Axmann (Staring Woman); Lorraine Crawford (Pretty Blonde); Ann Sturgis (Pretty Brunette); Leonid Kinskey (Band Leader); Ilka Gruning (Duenna); Fred Nurney (Porter); David McMahon (Station Master); Bob Stevenson, Daniel De Johghe, Michael Macey, Joe Ploski, Victor Denny (Hotel Valets); Sue Casey (Pretty Girl); Frank Elliott (Englishman); Lisa Golm (Elderly Lady); Sayre Deering, Perry Ivins, John Arnold (Croupiers); Bert Hanlon (Porter); Jeraldine Jordan (Maid); George Paris (Soldier); Tom Ingersoll, Wheaton Chambers (Priests); Peter Scott (Cabaret Waiter); Erica Strong (Girl in Flower Shop); Martha Bamattre (Woman Fountain Attendant); Everett Glass (Pince-nez Man); Frank Jacquet (Doorman); Neal Dowd (Young Man); Eloise Hardt (Young Girl); Dick Simmons (Voice); Irene Seidner (Woman Vendor); Fred Lorenz (Conductor); Hans Hopf (Hurdy-Gurdy Man); Marianne Budrow (Little Girl); Lotte Stein (Buxom Woman); Ken Tobey (Cabby); Walter Rode, June Booth (Couple in Room); Max Willenz (Policeman); Manfred Furst (Mr. Huber); Betty Jane Howarth (Girl at Baccarat Table); John Cortay (Inspector).

MY FORBIDDEN PAST (RKO, 1951) 81 M

Producers, Robert Sparks, Polan Banks; director, Robert Stevenson; based on the novel Carriage Entrance by Banks; adaptor, Leopold Atlas; screenplay, Marion Parsonnet; art directors, Albert D'Agostino, Alfred Herman; music director, C. Bakaleinikoff; camera, Harry J. Wild; editor, George Shrader.

Robert Mitchum (Mark); Ava Gardner (Barbara); Melvyn Douglas (Paul); Lucile Watson (Aunt Eula); Janis Carter (Corinne); Gordon Oliver (Clay Duchesne); Basil Ruysdael (Dean Cazzley); Clarence Muse (Pompey); Walter Kingsford (Coroner); Jack Briggs (Cousin Phillipe); Will Wright (Luther Toplady); Watson Downs (Hotel Clerk); Cliff Clark (Horse Vendor); John B. Williams (Fishmonger); Louis Payne (Man); Johnny Lee (Toy Vendor); George Douglas (Deputy); Ken MacDonald (Police Lieutenant); Everett Glass (Elderly Doctor); Barry Brooks (Policeman); Daniel DeLaurentis (Candle Boy).

ON THE LOOSE (RKO 1951) 74 M.

Producer, Collier Young; director, Charles Lederer; story, Malvin Wald, Young; screenplay, Dale Eunson, Katherine Albert; art directors, Albert D'Agostino, Walter E. Keller; music director, C. Bakaleinikoff; camera, Archie Stout; editor, Desmond Marquette.

Joan Evans (Jill Bradley); Melvyn Douglas (Frank Bradley); Lynn Bari (Alice Bradley); Robert Arthur (Larry Lindsay); Hugh O'Brien (Dr. Phillips); Constance Hilton (Susan Tanner); Michael Kuhn (Bob Vance); Susan Morrow (Catherine); Lillian Hamilton (Miss Druten); Elizabeth Flournoy (Mrs. Tanner); John Morgan (Mr. Tanner); Lawrence Dobkin (Ruegg); Tristram Coffin (Judge); Edwin Reimers (Prosecuting Attorney); Mark Tangner (Roy Marsh); Don Brodie (Bartender Grove); Jesse Kirkpatrick (Teacher at Fight); Don Megowan (Headwaiter); Jack Larson, Diane Ware (Charleston Bits); Leonard Penn (Dance Judge); Allen Harris (Dr. Wayne); Jerry Hausner (Gus); Lela Bliss (Nurse); Marc Rohm (Court Clerk).

BILLY BUDD (AA, 1962) 123 M.

Executive producer, A. Ronald Lubin; producer-director, Peter Ustinov; based on the novel Billy Budd, Foretopman by Herman Melville and the play by Louis O. Coxe, Robert H. Chapman; music-music conductor, Anthony Hopkins; production designer, Don Ashton; art director, Peter Morton; costumes, Anthony Mendelson; makeup, Bob Lawrence; assistant director, Michael Birkett; sound, Charles Crafford, Charles Foulton, Len Shilton; camera, Robert Krasker; editor, Jack Harris.

Terence Stamp (Billy Budd); Peter Ustinov (Captain Edward Vere); Robert Ryan (Master at Arms John Claggart); Melvyn Douglas (The Dansker); Ronald Lewis (Jenkins); David McCallum (Lieutenant Wyatt); John Neville (Lieutenant Ratcliffe); Paul Rogers (Lieutenant Seymour); Lee Montague (Squeak); Thomas Heathcote (Payne); Ray McAnally (O'Daniel); Robert Brown (Talbot); John Meillon (Kincaid); Cyril Luckham (Hallam); Niall MacGinnis (Captain Graveling).

HUD (PAR, 1963) 112 M.

Producers, Martin Ritt, Irving Ravetch; director Ritt; based on the novel Horseman, Pass By *by Larry McMurtry; screenplay, Ravetch, Harriet Frank, Jr.; art directors, Hal Pereira, Tambi Larsen; set decorators, Sam Comer, Robert Benton; costumes, Edith Head; makeup, Wally Westmore; assistant director, C. C. Coleman, Jr.; music, Elmer Bernstein, special camera effects, Paul K. Lerpae; process camera, Farciot Edouart; sound, John Carter, John Wilkinson; camera, James Wong Howe; second unit camera, Rex Wimpy; editor, Frank Bracht.*

Paul Newman (Hud Bannon); Melvyn Douglas (Homer Bannon); Patricia Neal (Alma Brown); Brandon de Wilde (Lon Brown); Whit Bissell (Burris); John Ashley (Hermy); Crahan Denton (Jesse); Val Avery (Jose); Sheldon Allman (Thompson); Pitt Herbert (Larker); Peter Brooks (George); Curt Conway (Truman Peters); Yvette Vickers (Lily Peters); George Petrie (Joe Scanton); David Kent (Donald); Frank Killmond (Dumb Billy); N. Candido (Patron); Monty Montana, John Indrisano, John M. Quijada (Cowboys); Sy Prescott (Man Greased in Pig Sequence); Carl Saxe (Proprietor); Robert Hinkle (Announcer); Sharyn Hillyer (Myra).

ADVANCE TO THE REAR (MGM, 1964) 97 M.

Producer, Ted Richmond; director, George Marshall; suggested by the book The Company of Cowards *by William Chamberlain; story, Jack Schaefer; screenplay, Samuel A. Peeples, William Bowers; music, Randy Sparks; music adaptor-conductor, Hugo Montenegro; art directors, George W. Davis, Eddie Imazu; set decorators, Henry Grace, Budd S. Friend; assistant director, William McGarry; makeup, William Tuttle; sound, Franklin Milton; special camera effects, J. McMillan Johnson; camera, Milton Krasner; editor, Archie Marshek.*

Glenn Ford (Jared Heath); Stella Stevens (Mary Lou Williams); Melvyn Douglas (Colonel Brackenby); Jim Backus (General Willoughby); Joan Blondell (Easy Jenny); Andrew Prine (Private Selous); Jesse Pearson (Corporal Geary); Alan Hale (Sergeant Davis); James Griffith (Hugo Zattig); Yvonne Craig (Ora); Whit Bissell (Captain Queeg); Michael Pate (Thin Elk); Chuck Roberson (Monk); Bill Troy (Fulton); Frank Mitchell (Belmont); J. Lewis Smith (Slasher O'Toole); Preston Foster (General Bateman); Harlan Warde (Major Hayward); Allen Pinson (Private Long); Sugar Geise (Mamie); Linda Jones (Junie); Britta Ekman (Greta); Paul Langton (Major Forsythe); Charles Horvath (Jones); Mary LeBow (Mary); Joe Brooks (Bannerman); Richard Adams (Courier); Eddie Quillan (Rebel Sergeant Smitty); Paul Smith (Lieutenant); Harvey Stephens (General Dunlap); Robert Carson (Colonel Holbert); Janos Prohaska (Flagg Pole Sitter); Clegg Hoyt, John Day (Loafers); Towyna Thomas (Law and Order League); Sailor Vincent (Deckhand); Barnaby Hale (Lieutenant); Bob Anderson (Steamer Captain); Gregg Palmer (Gambler); Kathryn Hart, Ann Blake (League Ladies); Peter Ford (Townsman); Ken Wales (Lieutenant Aide).

THE AMERICANIZATION OF EMILY (MGM, 1964) 115 M.

Producer, Martin Ransohoff; associate producer, John Calley; director, Arthur Hiller; based on the novel by William Bradford Huie; screenplay, Paddy Chayevsky; music, Johnny Mandel; song, Mandel and Johnny Mercer; art directors, George W. Davis, Hans Peters, Elliot Scott; set decorators, Henry Grace, Robert R. Benton; music conductor, Robert Armbruster; costumes, Bill Thomas; assistant director, Al Shenberg; makeup, William Tuttle; special camera effects, J. McMillan Johnston; sound, Franklin Milton; camera, Philip Lathrop; editor, Tom McAdoo.

James Garner (Lieutenant Commander Charles E. Madison); Julie Andrews (Emily Barham); Melvyn Douglas (Admiral William Jessup); James Coburn (Lieutenant Commander "Bus" Cummings); Joyce Grenfell (Mrs. Barham); Edward Binns (Admiral Thomas Healy); Liz Fraser (Sheila); Keenan Wynn (Old Sailor); William Windom (Captain Harry Spaulding); Douglas Henderson (Captain Marvin Ellender); John Crawford (Chief Petty Officer Paul Adams); Edmon Ryan (Admiral Hoyle); Steve Franken (Young Sailor); Paul Newlan (General William Hallerton); Gary Cockrell (Lieutenant Victor Wade); Alan Sues (Enright); Bill Fraser (Port Commander); Lou Byrne (Nurse Captain); Alan Howard (Port Ensign); Linda Marlowe (Pat); Janine Gray, Judy Carne, Kathy Kersh (Nameless Broads).

RAPTURE (International Classics, 1965) 104 M.

Producer, Christian Ferry; director, John Guillermin; based on the novel Rapture in My Rags *by Phyllis Hastings; screenplay, Stanley Mann; art director, Jean Andre; costumes, Jacques Fonteray; assistant directors, Louis Pitzele, Rik Wise; camera, Marcel Grignon; editors, Max Benedict, Francoise Diot.*

Melvyn Douglas (Larbaud); Dean Stockwell (Joseph); Patricia Gozzi (Agnes); Gunnel Lindblom (Karen); Leslie Sands (Elder Policeman); Murray Evans (Younger Policeman); Sylvia Kay (Genevieve); Peter Sallis (Armand).

HOTEL (WB, 1967) C—124 M.

Producer, Wendell Mayes; director, Richard Quine; based on the novel by Arthur Hailey; screenplay, Mayes; art director, Cary Odell; set decorator, George James Hopkins; gowns, Edith Head; costumes, Howard Shoup; makeup, Gordon Bau; assistant director, Mickey McCardle; music, Johnny Keating; sound, M. A. Merrick; camera, Charles Lang; editor, Sam O'Steen.

Rod Taylor (Peter McDermott); Catherine Spaak (Jeanne Rochfort); Karl Malden (Keycase); Melvyn Douglas (Warren Trent); Richard Conte (Dupere); Merle Oberon (The Duchess); Michael Rennie (Duke of Lanbourne); Kevin McCarthy (Curtis O'Keefe); Carmen McRae (Christine); Alfred Ryder (Captain Yolles); Roy Roberts (Bailey); Al Checco (Herbie); Sheila Bromley (Mrs. Grandin); Harry Hickox (Sam); William Lanteau (Mason); Ken Lynch (Laswell); Clinton Sundberg (Morgan); Tol Avery (Kilbrick); Davis Roberts (Dr. Adams); Jack Donner (Elliott); Lester Dorr (Elevator Operator); Dee Carroll (Mother); Judy Norton (Daughter).

COMPANIONS IN NIGHTMARE (NBC-TV, 1968) C— 90 M.

Producer-director, Norman Lloyd; teleplay, Robert L. Joseph; music, Bernard Herrmann; art director, Alexander A. Mayer; assistant director, Earl J. Bellamy, Jr.; camera, William Margulies; editor, Douglas Stewart.

Gig Young (Eric Nicholson); Anne Baxter (Carlotta Mauridge); Patrick O'Neal (Jeremy Siddack); Dana Wynter (Julia Klanton); Leslie Nielsen (Dr. Nessden); Melvyn Douglas (Dr. Lawrence Strelson); William Redfield (Richard Lyle); Bettye Ackerman (Sara Nicholson); Lou Gossett (Lieutenant Adam McKay); Stacy Harris (Phillip Rootes); and: Thomas Bellin, Gregory Mullavy, David Fresco, Connie Hunter, Syl Lamont.

HUNTERS ARE FOR KILLING (CBS-TV, 1970) C—90 M.

Producer, Hugh Benson; director, Bernard Girard; teleplay, Charles Kuenstle; music, Jerry Fielding; camera, Jerry Finnerman; editor, Edward Mann.

Burt Reynolds (L. G. Florin); Melvyn Douglas (Keller Florin); Suzanne Pleschette (Barbara Soline); Martin Balsam (Wade Hamilton); Larry Storch (Rudy Leroy); Jill Banner (Holly Fornell); Peter Brown (Raymond Pera); Angus Duncan (Richard Soline); A. Martinez (Jimmy Ramirez); Don Barry (Hank Phillips); Ivor Francis (Carl Fornell).

I NEVER SANG FOR MY FATHER (COL, 1970) C—92 M.

Producer-director, Gilbert Cates; based on the play by Robert Anderson; screenplay, Anderson; assistant directors, Stanley Panesoff, Allan Wertheim; art director, Hank Aldrich; costumes, Theoni V. Aldredge; titles, Bert Gold; music, Al Gorgoni, Barry Mann; song, Mann and Cynthia Weil; sound, Charles Federmack; camera, Morris Hartzband, George Stoetzel; editor, Angelo Ross.

Melvyn Douglas (Tom Garrison); Gene Hackman (Gene Garrison); Dorothy Stickney (Margaret Garrison); Estelle Parsons (Alice); Elizabeth Hubbard (Peggy); Lovelady Powell (Norma); Daniel Keyes (Dr. Mayberry); Conrad Bain (Reverend Pell); Jon Richards (Marvin Scott); Nikki Counselman (Waitress); Carol Peterson, Sloane Shelton (Nurses); James Karen (Old Age Home Director); Gene Williams (State Hospital Director).

DEATH TAKES A HOLIDAY (ABC-TV, 1971) C—90 M.

Producer, George Eckstein; director, Robert Butler; based on the play Le Morte in Vacanza written by Alberto Casella and adapted by Walter Ferris; screenplay, Rita Lakin; music, Laurindo Almeida; art director, Eugene Lourie; set decorator, Robert C. Bradfield; camera, Michael Margulies; editor, Michael Economou.

Melvyn Douglas (Judge Earl Chapman); Yvette Mimieux (Peggy Chapman); Monte Markham (David Smith); Myrna Loy (Selena Chapman); Bert Convy (John Cummings); Kerwin Mathews (Earl Chapman, Jr.); Priscilla Pointer (Marion Chapman); Austin Willis (Martin Herdon); Colby Chester (Tony Chapman); Maureen Reagan (Ellen Chapman); Regis Cordic, Mario Machado (TV Announcers).

ONE IS A LONELY NUMBER (MGM, 1972) C—97 M.

Executive producer, David L. Wolper; producer, Stan Margulies; director, Mel Stuart; based on the short story "The Good Humor Man" by Rebecca Morris; screenplay, David Seltzer; music-music conductor, Michel Legrand; art director, Walter M. Simonds; set decorator, George Gaines; assistant director, Donald C. Klune; camera, Michel Hugo; editor, David Saxon.

Trish Van Devere (Amy Brower); Monte Markham (Howard Carpenter); Janet Leigh (Gert Meredith); Melvyn Douglas (Joseph Provo); Jane Elliot (Madge Frazier); Jonathan Lippe (Sherman Cooke); Mark Bramhall (Morgue Attendant); Paul Jenkins (James Brower); A. Scott Beach (Frawley King); Henry Leff (Arnold Holzgang); Dudley Knight ("King Lear"); Maurice Argent (Pool Manager); Thomas McNallan (Hardware Clerk); Morgan Upton ("Earl of Gloucester"); Joseph Spano ("Earl of Kent"); Kim Allen (Ronnie Porter); Peter Fitzsimmons (Employment Office Clerk); Christopher Brooks (Marvin Friedlander).

a.k.a: TWO IS A HAPPY NUMBER.

THE CANDIDATE (WB, 1972) C—110 M.

Producer, Walter Coblenz; associate producer, Nelson Rising; director, Michael Ritchie; screenplay, Jeremy Larner; music, Jon Rubinstein; songs, Rubinstein and David Colloff; assistant directors, Michael Daves, Albert Shepard; production designer, Gene Callahan; set decorator, Patricia Von Brandenstein; costumes, Patricia Norris; makeup, Gary Liddiard; camera, Victor J. Kemper, John Korty; editors, Richard A. Harris, Robert Estrin.

Robert Redford (Biff McKay); Don Porter (Senator Crocker Jarmon); Melvyn Douglas (John J. McKay); Quinn Redeker (Rich Jenkin); Michael Lerner (Paul Corliss); Peter Boyle (Marvin Lucas); Allen Garfield (Howard Klein); Karen Carlson (Nancy McKay); Morgan Upton (Henderson); Kenneth Tobey (Starkey); Chris Prey (David); Joe Miksak (Neil Atkinson); Jenny Sullivan (Lynn); Tom Dahlgren (Pilot); Gerald Hiken (Station Master); Leslie Allen (Mabel); Susan Demott (Groupie); Jason Goodrow (Boy in Commercial); Robert De Anda (Jaime); Robert Goldsby (Fleischer); Michael Barnicle (Wilson); Lois Fraker (Large Girl); David Moody (Watts Heckler); George Meyer (Man in Urinal); Dudley Knight (Magazine Editor); Natalie Wood, Senator Hubert H. Humphrey, Senator George McGovern, Senator John V. Tunney, Mayor Sam Yorty, Howard K. Smith, Van Amberg, Jesse Bimbaum, Senator Alan Cranston, Maury Green, Lu Hurley, Assemblyman Walter Krabien, Assemblyman Robert Moretti, Rollin Post, Bill Stout, Dick Whittington, Richard Bergholtz, Assemblyman Ken Gory, Judy Hayward, Cedrick Hardman, Senator Fred Harris, Ken Jones, Grover Lewis, Terry McGovern, Harvey Orkin, Congressman Jerry Waldie, Jesse M. Unruh (Themselves); Barry Sullivan (*Voice of McKay* Narrator); Broderick Crawford (*Voice of Jarmon* Narrator); Pat Harrington, Jr. (Dinner M.C.).

DEATH SQUAD (ABC-TV, 1974) C—90 M.

Producers, Aaron Spelling, Leonard Goldberg; associate producer, Parke Perrine; director, Harry Falk; teleplay, James David Buchanan, Ronald Austin; music, David Grusin; camera, Tim Southcott; editor, Stefan Arnsten.

Robert Forster (Eric Benoit); Melvyn Douglas (Captain Earl Kreski); Michelle Phillips (Joyce Kreski); Claude Akins (Connie); Ken Tobey (Hartman); George Murdock (Vern Acker); Stephen Young (Andrece); Mark Goddard (Allen Duke); Dennis Patrick (Commissioner); Julie Cobb (Sharon); Bert Remsen (The Chief); Jesse Vint (Harmon).

VERDICT: MURDER OR MERCY? (ABC-TV, 1974) C—90 M.

Executive producer, Quinn Martin; producer, Adrian Samish; director, Harvey Hart; teleplay, Douglas Day Stewart; music, Pat Williams; camera, William W. Spencer.

Bradford Dillman (Sam Champion); Denver Pyle (Amos Champion); Melvyn Douglas (Dr. Paul Harelson); Mildred Dunnock (Lois Harelson); David Birney (Dr. Peter Peterson); Don Porter (Henry Balin); Robert Webber (Dr. Eric Stoneman); Kent Smith (Judge); Bettye Ackerman (Nurse Cantelli); Arthur Franz (Dr. Raymond Ecksorth); Bonnie Bartlett (Elana Champion); Regis J. Cordic (Arraignment Judge); Lindsay Workman (Bailiff); Warren Parker (Dr. Chadway); Stephen Coit (Coroner).

With Betta St. John and Deborah Kerr in a publicity pose for DREAM WIFE (MGM '53)

Chapter Three

Cary Grant

6'1"
172 pounds
Brown hair
Blue eyes
Capricorn

For years there has been a race to accurately define *the* Cary Grant charm, *the* Cary Grant look, *the* Cary Grant success formula. Tidbits from ex-wives, ex-loves, soured columnists, and even from the subject himself, have revealed a counter-side to this most enticing of living legends. Offcamera, he is full of self-doubts, contradictions, vanities, unfulfilled dreams, and regrets; in short, a bundle of frailties that play no part in the long-enduring public image known as Cary Grant. These seeming inconsistencies go to prove that he is much more of an actor than his supposedly effortless performances would indicate.

In exploring the formula of a typical Cary Grant film, *Life* magazine critic Richard Schickel once concluded that "the drama in a Cary Grant movie always lies in seeing if the star can be made to lose his wry, elegant and habitual aplomb. The joke lies in the fact that no matter what assaults and indignities the writer and director visit upon his apparently ageless person, he never does. His is surely the most ungettable goat in movie history and to watch this expert professional bob and weave his stylish way through one of his carefully stylized comedies is a pleasure that never dulls with familiarity."

As a Paramount contractee in the early 1930s, the former Archibald Leach of Bristol, England, made a slick transition from utility leading man (*Madame Butterfly,* 1932) to star (*Wedding Present,* 1936). The latter film, co-starring Joan Bennett, was not only his Paramount finale, but it was his first major screen effort in the screwball-comedy mold. He proved to be very resilient and capable in the genre, a judgment confirmed by *Topper* (MGM, 1937) with Constance Bennett, *The Awful Truth* (Columbia, 1937) with Irene Dunne, and *Bringing Up Baby* (RKO, 1938) with Katharine Hepburn. No matter who the leading lady was, it seemed, Cary could bring out the best oncamera facets she had to offer, without submerging his own very distinct screen presence.

Whatever Cary could do with a felicitous comedy, he could do equally well with a taut romantic thriller, as Alfred Hitchcock's *Suspicion* (RKO, 1941) and *Notorious* (RKO, 1946) ably demonstrated. Grant went dramatic as the Cockney in *None But the Lonely Heart* (RKO, 1944) and received an Oscar nomination for his efforts, but he was much more at ease playing relaxed, ebullient, vapid Cole Porter in *Night and Day* (Warner Bros., 1946).

There were creative lower points in Grant's career, as with *Room for One More* (Warner

Bros., 1952), made with his wife of the moment, Betsy Drake. It took Hitchcock to bring Grant out of a nearly two-year recess after this setback, and with *To Catch a Thief* (Paramount, 1955), the screen's Mr. Lucky was back on top. In fact, after his next ultrapopular Hitchcockian exercise, *North by Northwest* (MGM, 1959), genuine superstar Grant increased his creative control and salary intake by becoming his own producer, with five well-received Universal productions, including the Paris-set action yarn *Charade* (1963) with Audrey Hepburn.

Age has not seemed to wither Cary's box-office draw, but after *Walk, Don't Run* (Columbia, 1966), the sixty-two-year-old star balked at further screen ventures. He had taken on a new role as father, via his fourth wife, Dyan Cannon, and the once dashing Hollywood bachelor doted on his little daughter, Jennifer. He no longer needed the public's adulation.

With the recurrent popularity of the Cary Grant feature films making the rounds of television's late shows, it is unlikely that he would or could soon be forgotten by new generations of celebrity watchers. But just to make sure, and to keep himself "busy" in the 1970s, Cary took on a new guise as business executive for Faberge, Inc., where he has found a fresh peg to retain his glossy public image. He is as smiling, aloof, and charming as ever.

The clocks of Bristol, England, registered a few minutes past one A.M. on Monday, January 18, 1904, when a baby boy was born to Elsie and Elias Leach. The boy, baptized by an Anglican minister as Archibald Alexander, was to wear long baby clothes and curls much beyond the age when most mothers discard them for their growing children. Because Elsie Leach had given birth earlier to a boy who died after a few months, she was mortally afraid of revealing that her second-born was also a boy for fear of losing him too.

Elias Leach's weekly salary, earned by pressing suits for a local clothing manufacturer, was modest, but he did his best to provide the necessities for his dependents. They lived in a stone house, heated by coal fires in small fireplaces in each room. A year or two after Archie's birth, the Leaches moved to a larger house in Bristol which boasted a large garden with an old apple tree to which Elias attached a swing for his son. The exhilarating joy of swinging high, wide, and free was never fully appreciated by the boy, however, for he was afraid of the heights attained from his father's enthusiastic pushes.

Hardly satisfied with her husband's meager income, Elsie was constantly mindful of their having to "make do," and she conveyed to her observant son her desire for a better life. He was taught strict obedience to adults and to take good care of what possessions he had. He could not enter the family house without first wiping his shoes on a mat, nor was he allowed to make too much noise within the house. Since he had no playmates, Archie became intrigued with the solitary hobby of collecting foreign stamps. One Christmas he was given a set of tin soldiers in fancy uniforms, which he liked. Later, he received his own hussar's costume, consisting of gold braid, fringed epaulets, hat with insignia, and a toy sword. He considered himself dashing

and handsome, but no one paid too much attention to him.

Archie could see very little happiness shared by his parents, except when guests were in the house. His father, however, exhibited a more youthful, exuberant manner when he acquired a better-paying job in Southampton, eighty miles from Bristol. With Elias gone, Elsie moved into a more expensive house and two of her female cousins joined the household, contributing to the group's upkeep. The cousins lived in a separate section of the house which Archie was forbidden to enter. Not too long thereafter, Elias, unable to maintain his Bristol home along with lodgings in Southampton, quit his job and returned to Bristol, where he took up his former job.

When Archie entered public school at the age of four and one-half, he immediately enjoyed clay modeling, crayon drawing, and even the learning of the ABC's, but he hated the study of arithmetic. As he grew older, his parents, separately, took him to the cinema. Elsie had a preference for romantic films while Elias took his son to weekly serials. The latter did much to interfere with Archie's schoolwork since he spent the remainder of each week guessing what might occur in the ensuing episodes.

One day, at the age of nine, Archie came home from school as usual, but things were not as usual. His mother was not there. No explanation was given except that she was "away," nor was her return date indicated. It was not until some years later that he learned she had suffered a nervous breakdown and had been placed in an institution. He was not to see his mother again for more than twenty years.

When Archie was eleven, Elias and he moved in with his father's mother. It was at this time that Archie became a boy scout, which he enjoyed because of the uniform and the assigned task of extinguishing streetlamps in case of an air attack by the German Kaiser's forces. The attacks never came, although Archie always was prepared.

At the age of twelve, he won a scholarship to Fairfield secondary school in Bristol, where the students were required to buy special blazers, ties, and caps bearing the school's insignia. Archie's father could not possibly afford more than the requisite second-hand books, however, and the glamour of owning such a distinguished uniform was soon dismissed from the boy's mind. A year later, he experienced a wintery mishap by slipping on the ice, which resulted in the loss of an upper-middle tooth. He managed to conceal the gap from his father, and although the space soon filled in, he was to go through life with only one middle tooth.

When he was thirteen, Archie acquired as a friend an electrician employed at the newly constructed Hippodrome Theatre in Bristol. The friend permitted him to visit the theatre regularly. Archie's constant questioning about all aspects of stage work led to an introduction to the stage manager of another theatre, the Empire, who put him to work—at no pay—assisting the men who operated the powerful arc lights. The man who had been young Archie Leach described this adventure in the *Ladies Home Journal* of March 1963: "I was happy in the world of make-believe and that was all that mattered, and I dropped by that theatre as often as possible. I had a place to be. And people let me *be* there." But Archie's lighting-man's post came to an abrupt end one evening when he was told to operate the equipment for a time while the regular electrician took a break during a magician's act. So absorbed was Archie with the illusory routines that he forgot his duties and the spotlight drifted offstage to reveal the hidden mirrors utilized by the magician.

One day Archie learned of Bob Pender's troupe of thirty-five young knock-about comedians and of Pender's need for performers—boys of fourteen, the legal working age. Archie wrote Pender, enclosed a photograph, said he was fourteen, and signed his father's name. A short time later, a response arrived in the mail suggesting that Mr. Leach send his son to Norwich, where the troupe was performing. A railway ticket was enclosed in the envelope. Archie stole away from his grandmother's house one night and ventured to Norwich where he was accepted by Pender and put to work at ten shillings a week learning tumbling, acrobatic dances, and the art of makeup. Ten days later, at Ipswich, Elias claimed his son, who had yet to be given an opportunity to perform onstage. Elias returned him to Bristol and to school.

Whereas the formal routines of education had been only a mild source of disenchantment, Archie now devoted himself to flunking, along with committing brazen acts of mischief aimed at earning his dismissal. Expulsion was finally granted when he invaded the girls' lavatory wherein, at the time, he encountered a girls' physical-education teacher. Since he was then fourteen, he was allowed by Elias to rejoin Pender's acrobatic troupe. Three months later, Archie performed on the stage of the Empire Theatre while his former electrician buddies kept the arcs focused on him.

In the course of touring the English provinces, with occasional vaudeville appearances in London, Archie learned the importance of communicating to audiences through the means of pantomime, since no dialog was used in the act. "We learned not only dancing, tumbling and stilt-walking, but also how to convey a mood or meaning without words, using the minimum of movement and expression; how best immediately and precisely to effect an emotional response—a laugh or, sometimes, a tear."

The boys, under the Pender roof, led a happy though regimented sort of life, filled with rest, exercise, reading, and recitation. Meanwhile Archie's salary had been increased to a pound weekly ($5), and when Pender announced that he had booked an engagement for himself and eight of the boys in a Charles Dillingham production at New York City's Globe Theatre, Archie was one of those chosen. In July 1920, the group sailed on the S.S. *Olympic*. On arriving in New York harbor, eight boys, with eyes bleary from a sleepless night lest they miss a first glimpse of America, were lined up along the rail of the transatlantic ship. The highest building then in the city—the Woolworth—greeted sixteen-year-old Archie Leach as he peered anxiously at the impressive skyline.

On August 9, 1920, the Pender troupe opened at the Hippodrome Theatre in a musical, *Good Times*. During his offstage hours, Archie traveled all over New York City by bus and streetcar, attended movies on Sunday, and became a New York Giants baseball fan. When *Good Times* closed after an extensive 456-performance run, Pender signed his group for a six-month tour with the Keith vaudeville circuit, which took his troupe throughout the nation by bus and train. In Los Angeles, Archie especially fell in love with the climate and the palm trees.

By mid-summer of 1922, Bob Pender was preparing for his return to England, but Archie and several other of the boys decided to remain in New York on their own. With the money given him for return passage to England stashed away for emergencies, Archie set out to find work. With vaudeville on its annual summer vacation, he tried to obtain a short-term engagement as a regular actor, but his lack of experience in onstage speaking parts militated against him. Instead, he was forced to accept a job at Steeplechase Park, Coney Island, where he was a placard-carrying stiltwalker, earning $5 for each weekday, but hazard pay of $10 for Saturdays and Sundays since the children, on weekends, derived particular delight from attempting to de-stilt the tall man. This adventurous job came to a blessed end when, through other ex-members of Pender's group, Archie learned of the Hippodrome's planned sequel to *Good Times,* called *Better Times* (September 2, 1922, 408 performances). The boys gained employment as an act with that show.

From there, the gang perfected their act, which was performed on tour in 1924 with the Pantages Circuit of theatres. Although the tour was successful, the boys could not agree on their next allied course of action. Instead, they disbanded, with each going his own way.

Archie took up residence at the National Vaudeville Artists Club in Manhattan from whence he daily embarked in search of work. He managed to get an occasional weekend job on movie-theatre stages with a partner "comic" at $31.25 per diem. By this time, Archie, who had learned the fine art of talking onstage, played the straight-man parts and found proper timing to be of vital importance. He soon progressed to more entertaining routines and received regular bookings that took him to every small town in the United States. It was while playing "short but lucrative engagements in and around New York" that he met Reginald Hammerstein, a stage director and brother of Oscar Hammerstein II, who suggested that he switch from vaudeville to musical comedy. Archie considered it sound advice, since this genre of play was becoming popular in the Roaring Twenties. He took voice lessons for a few weeks prior to being introduced to Reginald's uncle, Arthur Hammerstein, who was preparing an operetta, *Golden Dawn,* which was to open his newly completed Hammerstein Theatre. Hammerstein signed Archie to a run-of-the-play contract and gave him the small part of an Australian named Anzac,* as well as designating him understudy to Paul Gregory, the production's juvenile lead. Archie's weekly salary was an astounding $350. With book and lyrics by Otto Harbach and Oscar

Hammerstein II, the show opened on November 30, 1927, and ran for 184 performances.

Arthur Hammerstein then decided to cast Archie as the lead in his next musical *Polly,†* which opened in Wilmington, Delaware, where a critic wrote: "Archie Leach has a strong masculine manner, but unfortunately fails to bring out the beauty of the score." Hammerstein was forced to admit the critic was right and replaced Archie in the show, which went on to play only fifteen Broadway performances.

Marilyn Miller, who was starring in Florenz Ziegfeld's *Rosalie,* then requested that Archie take over the male lead from comedian Jack Donahue, who was leaving the musical. Because Hammerstein was not on friendly terms with Ziegfeld, he refused to release Archie. Soon after the *Rosalie* vacancy was filled, however, Hammerstein sold Archie's contract to master showmen, J. J. and Lee Shubert, who, a week later, cast him in *Boom Boom* (Casino Theatre: January 28, 1929) with Jeanette MacDonald, Frank McIntyre, and Stanley Ridges. Before the show closed on its seventy-second performance at the Casino Theatre, Archie and Jeanette were tested for the screen by Paramount at their studio in Astoria, Long Island, but neither was immediately awarded with a contract. Archie was told: "You're bowlegged, and your neck is too thick."

Next, the Shuberts placed Archie opposite Gladys Baxter in Fanny Todd Mitchell's rewrite of *Die Fledermaus.* Using Johann Strauss's original music, the show was retagged *Wonderful Night;* it opened at the Majestic Theatre just two days after the stock-market collapse on October 31, 1929. This was obviously not a propitious period for theatre, unfortunately, but the show did eke out a 125-performance run. Archie was then given the assignment of acting and singing for J. J. Shubert's Municipal Opera Company of St. Louis, Missouri, during the summer of 1931. From May 29 through the month of August, he played a total of eighty-seven performances in twelve open-air productions. So successful was the summer festival that Archie was given an open invitation to return to St. Louis anytime he wanted. "In those years—1928, '29 and '30," he said, "I earned from $300 to $400 weekly with seasonable raises; more than many featured stage players earn today."

The Shuberts returned Archie to New York in late August for the male lead in their musical, *Nikki,* starring Fay Wray, the wife of the show's

---

*Also in the show, as a chorus boy, was young Irishman George Brent.
†A musical version of the 1917-produced play, *Polly with a Past.*

author, John Monk Saunders. The property was based on a magazine serial story and an already released film, *The Last Flight* (First National, 1931). The restructured play focused on a group of devil-may-care flyers who find time, after the First World War, to amuse themselves in Paris. Archie was seen as Cary Lockwood (played in the film version by Richard Barthelmess). The show opened on September 29, 1931, at the Longacre Theatre, where it proved unsuccessful. In an attempt to somehow improve attendance it was moved to the George M. Cohan Theatre, where it died after a total of thirty-nine performances.

Archie's next job almost but not quite, proved to be the fortuitous big break. He obtained the part of one of four sailors* who visit a bar operated by Anna Chang in a talking Paramount ten-minute one-reeler entitled *Singapore Sue*. Known as "fillers," these short films were used to complete movie-theatre programs. Casey Robinson, the writer and director of this particular short, was so impressed with Archie's good looks and ability that he wrote a special note to Paramount executives in Hollywood, urging them to take a good look at the film. His request was undoubtedly overlooked, because nothing came of it. The ten-minute short was released in mid-1932 after Archie had already appeared in at least three full-length motion pictures.

Having worked steadily for over three years, Archie was in need of a vacation. He decided to drive to California in a Packard Phaeton touring sedan which he had bought in 1928, even before he knew how to drive the thing. Before taking off, Archie and a music-composer acquaintance who was to make the trip with him, drove first to the Palace Theatre on Broadway to say goodbye to their friends. The Shuberts gave Archie a promise of employment whenever he wished to return, and Bill Grady, an agent with the William Morris office, provided him with the Hollywood office address of a friend, Walter Herzbrun, for the purpose of receiving mail.

Once in Hollywood, and after a few days devoted to gazing at the lush scenery, Archie contacted Grady's friend, Herzbrun. It was December 1931. Through him he met Marion Gering, a former Broadway stage director who had also transplanted himself to California.

Gering had plans for his actress wife to make a screentest at Paramount, and B. P. Schulberg, then the studio's West Coast head, arranged for Archie to make the test with her. As a result, Archie was offered a long-term contract, which, he says, he "accepted with alacrity." Little notice was given of Mrs. Gering.

Archie's beginning salary was stipulated at $450 a week, but the Paramount chieftains insisted that he change his professional name. That evening, when he was joined at dinner by Fay Wray, once a Paramount contractee, and her husband, it was suggested that he adopt the name of Cary Lockwood, the character he had played in their ill-fated Broadway stint. The next day, at a studio meeting that would decide the fate of Archie Leach, he was told that Cary was acceptable as a first name, but since there was once an actor named Lockwood (Harold) in films, the Lockwood name might prove confusing to the public. Furthermore, in keeping with the trend, it was preferred that a shorter name be chosen. From a list of potential last names, one of the studio executives picked Grant and began the murmur that was soon tried on everyone present for rhythmic feeling and tonal quality—Cary Grant. (It was also conveniently close in sound to the studio's then troublesome Gary Cooper, who, upon the hiring of Grant as a backstop, took the hint. Cooper thereafter returned to the studio fold a more amenable performer.) The Cary Grant contract was prepared, signed, and delivered. Cary Grant was thus born in January 1932, a few days before his twenty-eighth birthday.

His screen debut was as Olympic javelin ace, Stephen Mendanich, in *This Is the Night* (Paramount, 1932),‡ based on the Avery Hopwood play of 1925, *Naughty Cinderella*.† In the comedy-set-to-music film version, Grant is in Los Angeles throwing javelins professionally, while his wife (Thelma Todd) is in Paris playing footsie with Roland Young. Cary returns unexpectedly to find the two of them together, but Young becomes frightened at the sight of the weaponlike javelins and invents a wife to disguise his wolfish intentions. He elicits the help of his pal Charles Ruggles to find a girl (Lily Damita) to pose as the mock spouse. The five of them then journey forth to Venice where Grant becomes interested in Damita to the point of proposing to the girl. Grant is eventually reunited with Todd and all ends blissfully.

Of Cary's first feature-film acting job—a lead role, no less—Mordaunt Hall wrote in the *New York Times* that he was "efficient," while the *New*

---

*Millard Mitchell, who was later to become well known on the screen as a character actor, was another of the sailors.
‡Official release date: April 13, 1932.
†*Naughty Cinderella*, starring Henry Kendall and Irene Bordoni, opened at the Lyceum Theatre on November 9, 1925 for a 121-performance run.

York Herald-Tribune critic noted: "As the jealous husband, an undistinguished straight role, Cary Grant, who was Archie Leach on the Broadway stage, plays with amiable assurance." In his own way, Grant had given an auspicious start to his full-fledged silver-screen career.

Cary's second film, *Sinners in the Sun* (Paramount, 1932), provided him with a much smaller part, but many women became enthralled with the handsome cut of his figure in white tie and tails, and duly noticed his dimpled chin and bright smile. In the role of Ridgeway, he is a rich playboy who gambles and travels his way around the world with Rita La Roy. Carole Lombard encounters the deluxe pair while traveling with her temporary love (Walter Byron), but discourages Cary's advances because she is truly in love with Chester Morris, who is back home toiling as chauffeur to Adrienne Ames. When La Roy commits suicide, remorseful Lombard realizes that the glittery cafe society is not for her and she returns home to Morris. The film was just the kind of nifty morality tale that appealed to depression-engulfed movie audiences.

In *Merrily We Go to Hell* (Paramount, 1932), Cary's part was not much more than a glorified walk-on. The film, based on the Cleo Lucas play, *I, Jerry, Take Thee, Joan,* dealt with a newsman (Fredric March) who drinks too much and continues to play around with the leading lady (Adrianne Allen) in the show he has somehow managed to write. Cary, as Miss Allen's onstage leading man, Charlie Exeter, appears in only one minor scene.

Marion Gering, Cary's "discoverer" for movies, directed his fourth film, *The Devil and the Deep* (Paramount, 1932), which also served as Charles Laughton's debut in American-made features.* Gering managed to have Grant's role enlarged, but, in Harry Hervey's story as scripted by Benn Levy, there was not a great deal that could be done with the character. Commander Sturm (Laughton), in charge of a submarine based on the African coast, is wildly jealous of his wife, Pauline (Tallulah Bankhead), and suspects her of having affairs with his junior officers, specifically, Lieutenant Jacques (Grant). Although Bankhead is infatuated with the handsome officer, he is too loyal to his commander to take advantage of her amorous feelings. On arriving home from a party, Laughton slaps her face and tells her he is transferring Grant for inefficiency. She pleads with him to spare the lieutenant, and Laughton devises

a plan for testing her fidelity. He has her invite Grant to their home that same night, and he (Laughton) listens from the veranda. When nothing unusual happens, Laughton accuses Bankhead of having somehow warned the lieutenant. He transfers the young man. Laughton's problems are far from over, however, because Bankhead then falls for Grant's replacement, Gary Cooper. The climactic scenes, which have become a camp favorite of nostalgia devotees, take place aboard the sub when Laughton, in a jealous rage, rams the vessel into a freighter and puts the blame on Cooper. Tallulah produces a pistol and holds off her mad husband while the crew escapes. She and Cooper get out just in time, and Laughton drowns within his disintegrating submarine.

Although Cary had not yet learned how to relax before the camera, this role was his largest in some time and marked the beginning of the end of his supporting status as a lesser competitor to Gary Cooper, George Raft, Fredric March, Phillips Holmes, or Gene Raymond. Cary's next assignment was as affluent playboy Nick Townsend in *Blonde Venus* (Paramount, 1932), directed by Josef von Sternberg, Marlene Dietrich's mentor. On the first morning of shooting, von Sternberg suddenly halted production and called for a hair comb. Without explanation, he took the comb and switched the part in Grant's hair from the left to the right side of his head. Cary must have agreed with von Sternberg that the change gave him a more suave appearance, because his hair has remained with its right-side parting ever since.

In *Blonde Venus,* based on a story by von Sternberg, former German nightclub singer Helen Faraday (Dietrich) returns to the New York stage in an effort to earn $1,500 for the European medical treatments necessary to cure her chemist husband (Herbert Marshall) of radium poisoning. Man-about-town Grant takes a shine to her and gives her a check for $300, which she turns over to Marshall. Cary then stations her and her son (Dickie Moore) in a swank apartment, while she serves as his mistress in exchange for his continuing financial assistance. When Marshall returns, cured, from his European treatments, he learns of Marlene's faithlessness and threatens to take Moore from her. She runs away with the child—in the best Constance Bennett woman-of-the-pavement cinema tradition—but returns the boy to his father when she discovers that she is unable to provide him with an adequate home life. Shortly

*Laughton was billed as "The Eminent English Character Actor."

136

thereafter she becomes the toast of Paris, clad in top hat and tuxedo with Grant breathing heavily by her side. When they come to New York with her stage revue she simply cannot resist caressing her boy again, and Cary gallantly turns her over to Marshall, who is overwhelmed at learning of her loyalty to him.

Mordaunt Hall's observation in the *New York Times* was that "Cary Grant is worthy of a much better role." Cary later gave full thanks to Dietrich," who smilingly accepted my immaturity and inexperience with comforting patience."

Cary received top billing for *Hot Saturday* (Paramount, 1932), playing opposite the studio's once popular Nancy Carroll. In this picture he is Homer Sheffield, a wealthy small-town rake whose Saturdays are spent dancing, making love, and consuming booze. On such a reckless day, he is joined by Carroll, who has just quarrelled with her beau (Randolph Scott). She loses her job as a bank typist because of her meeting with the libertine and once more is spurned by Scott. Cary, however, comes to her timely defense with a plausible explanation to the town that theirs was nothing more than a youthful, fun-loving, frolicsome Saturday. They are exonerated, and Carroll regains her reputation. As the British *Picturegoer* magazine attested, Cary played "the dour he-man lover somewhat woodenly."

Cary's busy year concluded with *Madame Butterfly* (Paramount), his seventh release of 1932. Guided once again by Marion Gering, he is *the* Lieutenant Pinkerton of the John Luther Long story and the David Belasco play.* He is in love for a time with a Japanese woman, Cho-Cho San (Sylvia Sidney), who was preparing to become a Geisha before meeting the American naval officer. The film is basically straight drama, with periodic laugh lines provided by Charles Ruggles as a fellow Navy lieutenant. Giacomo Puccini's melodic opera score was used only as background music. Within the eighty-six-minute feature, Grant weds the Oriental girl but leaves their house of love when his fleet is sent back to the States. In the three years he is gone, she has his son and maintains their home, convinced he will return to her. When he does come back, it is with an American wife (Sheila Terry), whose attitude toward the bereft Sidney is one of compassion. Unable to bear the humiliation of having waited three years

for a man who does not love her, Sidney sends her son away with a servant while she commits suicide. Of his early moviemaking period, Grant's *Madame Butterfly* role remains most closely associated with the actor as an illustration of the charming, callous character of his film roles.

A glorified but untrue legend has it that Mae West "discovered" Cary Grant. According to the popular tale, he was walking across the Paramount lot from the set of *Madame Butterfly* wearing his crisp Navy whites. She supposedly stopped her studio limousine, extended a limp, bejeweled arm in his direction, and drawled: "Hmmmm, if he can talk, I'll take him" (as the leading man in her second motion picture, that is).‡ The truth is that forty-year-old Mae, generally unknown to movie audiences at large, was more a sensational personality than a conventional beauty. Paramount was convinced they required a handsome young man to play opposite her since no one was quite sure that her highly sexual brand of humor would be welcome to the majority of film audiences. Cary was simply one of the studio contractees who was interviewed by Mae's managers, and he was later informed that he had been selected for screen breeding, "Westian" style.

She Done Him Wrong (Paramount, 1933) was effectively toned down for the screen by Harvey Theu and John Bright from Miss West's raucous stage play, *Diamond Lil.*† The main character's name was changed to Lady Lou. Dripping with gems, feather boas, and withering double-entendres, West runs an 1890s Bowery saloon next door to a mission, while her boyfriend (Owen Moore) is serving time in jail. The head of the mission is Captain Cummings (Grant), who is actually "The Hawk," a U.S. government agent in search of a notorious gang of counterfeiters. West falls for Grant after their initial meeting when she greets him with "Hello, there, warm, dark and handsome." She then issues her famous invitation: "Why don't you come up sometime and see me?" When he reacts with charming aloofness, she says: "Aw, you can be had."

Later in *She Done Him Wrong*, West and Grant have their boudoir rendezvous. Each is anxious to reappraise the other, and their conversational exchanges are a testing of the other person's moral fiber.

*The Belasco play opened at the Herald Square Theatre on March 5, 1900, and ran for 24 performances, Puccini saw the later 1900 London version and turned it into the opera, which debuted at La Scala in Milan in February 1904 with Rosina Storchio and Giovanni Zenatello. The first New York performance was at the Metropolitan Opera (February 11, 1907) with Geraldine Farrar and Enrico Caruso starring.
‡She had made her motion-picture debut in a featured role in George Raft's *Night after Night* (Paramount, 1932).
†Opened on Broadway on April 9, 1928, at the Royale Theatre for a 323-performance run, with Curtis Cooksey as Captain Cummings. In the 1949 Broadway revival (Coronet Theatre: February 5, 1949, 29 performances), Richard Coogan was Captain Cummings.

With Mae West in SHE DONE HIM WRONG (Par '33)

West: Cigarette?
Grant: No thanks. I don't smoke.
West: Yes, I guess smoking is going to make a man look effeminate before long.

A short time later, Grant confesses: "I'm sorry you think more about your diamonds than you do about your soul."

West: I'm sorry that you think more about my soul than you do about my diamonds.

Then Grant asks: "Haven't you ever met a man who could make you happy?"

West: Sure. Lots of times.

Underneath her hardboiled exterior, West's character is that of a sentimentalist who buys the mission for Cary when he is unable to pay the rent, helps her boyfriend escape capture when he breaks jail to see her, attempts to befriend Russian Rosie (Rafaela Ottiano), the head of a group involved in white slavery, and saves a feckless young girl (Rochelle Hudson) from killing herself. West accidentally kills Ottiano, who is laden

with counterfeit money, and is apprehended by Grant, who by then has revealed his true identity. As the gang is hauled away, Cary puts Mae into the back seat of a horse-drawn carriage next to him. She thinks she is going to be jailed too, but he tells her that she is going to be sentenced, instead, to becoming his wife. He calls her a "bad girl," to which she languidly replies: "Hmmmmh. You'll find out!"

The far-out film went on to become a solid box-office hit, made Mae West even more of a household word than before, and was instrumental in establishing Grant as a romantic lead because of what *Motion Picture Herald* aptly termed his "personal attractiveness."

Woman Accused (Paramount, 1933) first appeared as a ten-chapter serial, with each installment written by a well-known author* in *Liberty* magazine. In the film version, Cary, as Jeffrey Baxter, is reunited with sparkling-eyed Nancy Carroll, she as Glenda O'Brien. Just as Grant and Carroll are about to indulge in a passionate on-screen romance, her former beau (Louis Calhern) returns and decides to have Grant killed. On learning of his homicidal plan, Carroll bashes in Calhern's head. Then she and Grant escape on a pleasure cruise but are joined by a suspicious police detective (John Halliday) who conducts a mock trial aboard ship. Carroll confesses her deed, whereupon she is arrested and arraigned before the district attorney (Irving Pichel). When Cary forces a gunman (Jack La Rue) to reverse his previous testimony, Carroll is freed and rushes into Grant's waiting arms. It was the kind of run-of-the-mill film guaranteed not to further anyone's career, but Grant collected good notices for his efforts: " . . . continues to be one of the most pleasant of the screen juveniles" (Richard Watts, Jr., *New York Herald-Tribune*); "Cary Grant is better than usual. In fact, he gives his best performance. . ." (John S. Cohen, Jr., *New York Sun*); " . . . Cary Grant, as a shadowy hero, is straightforward, as usual" (Norbert Lusk, *Picture Play*).

The Eagle and the Hawk (Paramount, 1933) was based on a story by John Monk Saunders and was Mitchell Leisen's second job as a feature-film director. It was also a motion picture in which an established star (Carole Lombard) appeared in a significant but small role. Such circumstances were highly unusual in 1933, and Paramount's competitors complained that she was cast merely

*Vicki Baum, Zane Grey, Rupert Hughes, Vina Delmar, Irwin S. Cobb, Gertrude Atherton, Ursula Parrott, Polen Banks, J. P. McEvoy, and Sophie Kerr.

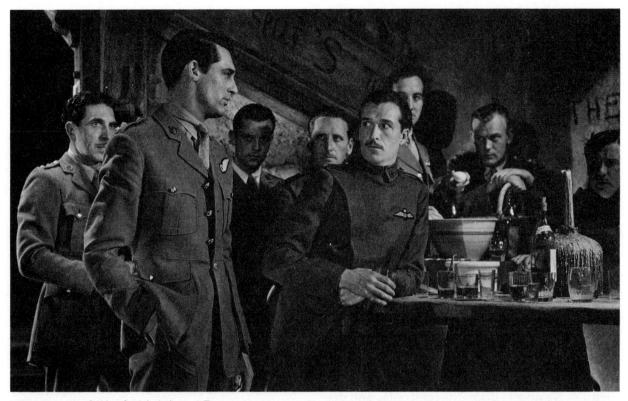

With Dennis O'Keefe (right) and Forrester Harvey (far right) in THE EAGLE AND THE HAWK (Par '33)

for box-office enticement. Actually Miss Lombard did it as a personal favor to Leisen.

The tale* centers around two flyers with the British Flying Corps of World War I. Young (Fredric March) is cynical about the war after having seen so many of his friends die needlessly in combat. Crocker (Grant) seeks adventure but is unable to obtain his wings and believes March is responsible. Cary is March's aerial observer. They dislike one another, but are a good team in the air. When March becomes progressively more disturbed, he is given a ten-day leave in London, where he meets a beautiful lady (Lombard) with whom he has a brief affair. Back on duty, he shoots down a hated German ace, but learns that his victim was only a boy. March then makes a dramatic speech in which he denounces war. While his buddies celebrate his victory over the enemy flyer, March retreats to his quarters, where he kills himself. In a moving sequence, Grant discovers the body and, rather than divulge the truth about his rival's death, he takes the body up in a plane and fires bullets into it to make it appear that March died while in action. In the final scene, Grant stands over March's grave until a policeman tells him to move along.

According to Mitchell Leisen in *Hollywood Director* (1973) by David Chierichetti, Cary, during the shooting of *The Eagle and the Hawk*, was much more concerned with tap dancing when not in front of the camera than with listening to directions. One scene called for a bomb to strike the roof of a building, causing wooden beams and splinters to fall everywhere. Leisen carefully instructed everyone where his or her safe spot was to be when the action took place, but Cary "wasn't paying much attention." When the special-effects people touched off the explosives, prematurely, everyone leaped to safety except Cary. "He just stood there looking up and got hit right in the face so badly they had to send him to the hospital."

In 1933 Elias Leach died in Bristol, England, of what was called "extreme toxicity." Cary, always reluctant to talk about him, only occasionally referred to the death, with such veiled remarks as "[it] was more probably the inevitable result of a slow-breaking heart, brought about by an inability to alter the circumstances of his life." Forbidden by law to divorce his mentally disturbed wife, Elias had entered into a common-law relationship in which he had fathered a son.

*The 1950 Paramount picture of the same title has no relationship to the March-Lombard-Grant entry.

Cary got top billing for *Gambling Ship* (Paramount, 1933) after Carole Lombard dropped out of the femme lead in favor of what she considered to be a more interesting story (*Brief Moment*, Columbia, 1933). Benita Hume inherited the role of Eleanor LaVelle, the mistress of the operator (Arthur Vinton) of a gambling ship in the Atlantic. As Ace Corbin, Grant is a semiretired big-time gambler. He meets Hume on a train but hides his identity from her, thinking she is too virtuous for the likes of him. The ship, which is badly in debt, is offered to Grant, but he wants nothing to do with it until he learns that his competitor is an old rival (Jack La Rue). He then buys the vessel builds up its popularity and steals most of the trade away from La Rue. In an attempt to blow up Grant's ship, La Rue is killed for his efforts, while Cary and Hume have exchanged true confessions and find solace in each other's arms. Grant's gambling ship sinks, but he and Hume make it safely to shore.

Paramount was prompt to reunite Cary with the hour-glass-figured Mae West in a contemporary romp situated, for the most part, in a circus. Entitled *I'm No Angel* (1933), the screenplay and dialog were the distinctive handiwork of Miss West. She is "The Incomparable Tira," a sideshow vamp, when New York socialite Jack Clayton (Grant) appears and tries to dissuade her from dating his besmitten cousin (Kent Taylor). It is not long before Taylor has exited from the arena of amour and West is concentrating on Grant, whom she had preferred to his cousin from the start. Grant, however, is unable to be affirmative, and Mae sues him for breach of promise. The headlined case goes to trial, where she cross-examines him and wins the verdict because Cary realizes that she is really in love with him. In the end, of course, she wins him too, and feels his arm muscles, which is a little habit of hers with men who temporarily enter her life. One senses that one day, Grant's Jack Clayton, too, will be replaced.

With its double-level, provocative dialog, *I'm No Angel* was well liked, earning a gross of $2.25 million in U.S.-Canadian rentals, and over a million dollars more worldwide. *Variety* recorded: "Cary Grant does nice work as the sweetheart but is at all times overshadowed by Miss West." Miss West probably would not have allowed it to be any other way. Of Miss West, Cary has said: "I learned everything from her. Well, not—not quite everything, but almost everything. She knows so

On the set of I'M NO ANGEL (Par '33) with Noël Coward and Mae West

much. Her instinct is so true, her timing so perfect, her grasp of the situation so right."

In *Alice in Wonderland* (Paramount, 1933), Cary, as the Mock Turtle, was recognizable to his fans when he spoke and to his friends when he danced. Based on Lewis Carroll's classic of 1865 and his sequel of 1871 (*Alice through the Looking Glass*), the studio thrust about everyone who crossed their lot into oddball costumes for this one. In the very familiar story, young Alice (Charlotte Henry)* eats and drinks magic food and shrinks small enough to tumble through a rabbit hole which leads her to Wonderland. The sad-faced turtle who sings of "Beautiful, Beautiful Soup" is but one of the humanistic animals she encounters before she awakens from her wonder sleep.

Cary was Paramount's third choice for the role, and he obtained it only after negotiations failed to materialize with crooners Bing Crosby and Russ Columbo. However, certain critics thought that Grant, too, should have made himself unavailable. Howard Barnes stated in the *New York Herald-Tribune:* "The most unfortunate aspect of the screen version is in its generous but ill-advised

*A role originally intended for Ida Lupino, whom Paramount had imported from England.

assembling of film notables." The public felt robbed because their screen favorites (among them, W. C. Fields, Jack Oakie, Jackie Searl, Richard Arlen, et al.) were too well concealed behind the elaborate animal costumes.

Cary, thus far, seemed to be treading water. "There were a lot of leading men with dark hair and teeth like mine," he has said, "and the studio couldn't be buying stories for each of us. Besides, I seemed to be getting all the roles Gary Cooper didn't want. I saw no reason why Gary and Cary should be confused." Since he had no viable alternative but to serve out his cinema apprenticeship, he made the most of it by earning money and banking a good portion of it. At the age of thirty, he gave little thought to anyone else and, he admits: "I was conceited and impossible. I was so conscious of my clothes and the way they looked that I never knew there was another actor on the set."

Late in 1933, Cary fancied himself in love with blonde Virginia Cherrill,* whom he had met earlier that year and thought was in love with him. They sailed to England in January 1934, and were married in London on February 9, 1934, with the groom in the recuperative stages of a severe case of influenza. Immediately following the ceremony, they sailed for the United States aboard the S. S. *Paris.* On their arrival in Hollywood they announced that they intended to "live a simple, quiet life."

His next screen assignment was in *Thirty-Day Princess* (Paramount, 1934) with Sylvia Sidney in a dual role and the direction handled by Marion Gering. This was to have been Grant's first chic drawing-room screen comedy, but very often throughout its seventy-three minutes it falls flat. He is Porter Madison, a swank newspaper publisher whose specialty is baiting big bankers. When Princess Catterina of Taronia (Sidney) comes to New York on a goodwill visit, with the incidental intention of promoting a bond loan for her Balkan country, Grant's course is obvious. Unknown to him, the real princess has contracted a case of mumps and an actress named Nancy Lee (also Miss Sidney) is paid to impersonate her. He finds himself liking the girl he thinks to be the princess and although he is peeved when he learns the truth, he is also relieved because it means he can marry her without a rash of red tape. Most of the charm that surrounds this Ruritanian romantic comedy was credited to Sidney.

Born to Be Bad (United Artists, 1934) was made on loan-out to Darryl F. Zanuck's new Twentieth Century company, but Cary would have been better off remaining on the home lot. Said Joe Bigelow in *Variety:* "This story is so bad in completed form, it's hard to see how it was thought to contain enough merit to warrant production in the first place." Loretta Young, out of her element, is seen in a most uncharacteristic role as Letty Strong, a girl who schemes to seduce the man (Grant) who has adopted her illegitimate son (Jackie Kelk). Her plan is to later blackmail Cary. She almost succeeds in alienating him from his wife (Marion Burns), but she abandons her dishonorable tactics when the son is saved from drowning by his adopted mother. (Parts of the film had to be reshot before the Hays Office would grant its approval.) *Variety's* critique of Grant was that "he gives a colorless, meaningless performance."

In 1934 Cary Grant was chosen by *Vanity Fair* magazine as one destined for future stardom. This prediction was based mainly on his screen work in *Blonde Venus* and *She Done Him Wrong.*

Kiss and Make Up (1934) returned Cary to Paramount as Dr. Maurice Lamar, who creates beautiful women in his Parisian beauty salon. The *New York American* applauded the film as "one of the most rare of the Hollywood products, a good farce comedy . . ." Within the Harlan Thompson–directed feature, Grant is loved by his secretary (Helen Mack), but he bypasses this girl of plain good looks when he falls for Eve Caron (Genevieve Tobin), a lady who has been made extra lovely through the devout application of the doctor's prescribed treatments. They marry, but on the honeymoon he finds that not only is he bound to a cosmetic worshipper, but that she has developed an insatiable appetite for flirtation with all men. In short time, he becomes disgusted with the egotistical dame. He destroys his salon and turns to his loyal secretary, much to her delight. In this film, Grant's voice is heard singing "Love Divided by Two." One of the promotional gimmicks used for this film was the casting of recent Wampas Baby Star winners in minor distaff roles.

Ladies Should Listen (Paramount, 1934) came next, in which, in the opinion of *Script* magazine, "Cary surprises everyone with his delightful flair for light comedy." On the other hand, *Variety* found him "brutally miscast," and said, "He plays the part for comedy, miscuing several

---

*Born April 12, 1908, in Carthage, Illinois, she gained cinema fame for her portrayal of the poverty-stricken flower girl opposite Charles Chaplin in *City Lights* (United Artists, 1931). She had been previously wed to Irving Adler and in 1932 to William Rinelander Stewart.

times." Guided by director Frank Tuttle, Grant is a financier worried about the expiration of his option on a Chilean nitrate concession. Frances Drake, the pert switchboard operator at his hotel, listens in to all his conversations and, by so doing, knows as much about his affairs as he. She saves him from scheming women, and eventually salvages his nitrate dealings. Naturally, he falls in love with the handy-to-have-around telephone girl.

By September 1934, the "simple, quiet" Grant-Cherrill marriage had developed into one of the stormiest in the movie colony. Virginia had admitted her love for another man (the British Earl of Jersey) and left Cary. The following month, some newspapers headlined that Cary had attempted suicide over the marital breakup and had consequently been admitted to a sanitarium. The truth was that he had become drunk with a group of friends and, when he had gotten home and collapsed into bed, he had telephoned Virginia with gibberish about not being able to live without her. She rushed to his home with police and found him unconscious with a bottle of sleeping tablets nearby. He was taken to a hospital for observation, and was released a short time later. A few weeks passed, and the couple's separation was formally announced. They were divorced on March 26, 1935.

Before his marriage to Cherrill, Cary had shared a beach house with Paramount's thirty-two-year-old Randolph Scott. Their bachelor digs had been the subject of several fan-magazine layouts. After his divorce from the actress, Cary and Scott again shared a residence, this time occupying a house on West Live Oak Drive which became known as "Bachelor Hall." Columnists, with some prompting from the Paramount publicity department, had a field day trying to guess which of Cary's girlfriends (Mary Brian, Ginger Rogers, Mary Carlisle, Phyllis Brooks) would become the next Mrs. Grant. "There'll be no marriages for me," Cary answered. "It will be five years before I'm ready for that." His friend and roommate Scott said: "Cary will never know peace as long as his name spells news. I've seen him actually lose sleep and weight after reading certain items that touched upon his personal life."

Young Elliott Nugent directed Cary's entry into the field of screen opera in *Enter Madame* (1934), based on the prior Broadway show (Garrick Theatre; August 16, 1920, 366 performances).[*] Paramount decided to leap onto the operatic bandwagon after Columbia's surprising success with Metropolitan diva Grace Moore in her cinematic comeback, *One Night of Love* (1934). Although Elissa Landi was the celebrated prima donna of *Enter Madame,*[†] Cary was allowed to sing (with three other men) the Anvil Chorus from *Il Trovatore*. The film contained a number of near-slapstick sequences, a specialty of director Nugent.

Variety concluded that Cary "tops all his past work" in *Wings in the Dark* (Paramount, 1935), his next film, as a flier involved with perfecting instrument-flying in fog or darkness. His work is halted when a gas explosion blinds him, and he retreats to a country hideaway with a seeing-eye dog. Sheila Mason (Myrna Loy) is a sky-writing flier who loves him, but he discourages her devotion. When she is later lost in the fog on a dangerous promotional flight from Moscow to New York, Grant rushes to an airfield, takes off in a plane, and guides her to safety by radio, all the while pouring out his stored-up love for her. In this meaty dramatic assignment, Grant eschewed the glib charm that had become his celluloid trademark. As *Variety* reported: "The part gave him dimension to play with and he took it headlong."

The Last Outpost (Paramount, 1935) came on the heels of the studio's previous, more expansive look at British-Indian conflicts, *The Lives of a Bengal Lancer* (1935), which had proved successful. In *The Last Outpost,* Grant, as trim-mustached British officer Captain Michael Andrews, is captured by the Kurds, who, with the Turks, are hitting hard at British defenses in India. Grant's captor is incognito British Intelligence officer Claude Rains, who allows him to escape. At a Cairo base hospital where he is recuperating, Grant falls in love with his nurse (Gertrude Michael), who, unknown to him, is Rains's wife. Thereafter a romantic triangle forms, leading to Rain's demoniac pursuit of Grant to the battlefields of the Sahara. However, when Rains is wounded and near death, he commends the care of his wife to Grant. In this adventurous, he-man role, more readily suitable to the likes of Gary Cooper, Grant revealed that his acting credibility extended beyond the boudoir, and that he was just as appealing in military fatigues as in dress suit, top hat, silk scarf, and walking stick.

---

[*]The 1922 Metro version had starred Clara Kimball Young and Elliott Dexter.
[†]Her voice was dubbed by soprana Nina Koshetz.

With Myrna Loy in a publicity pose for WINGS IN THE DARK (Par '35)

Director George Cukor arranged to borrow Cary on behalf of RKO for the part of Jimmy Monkley, a Cockney thief of petty notions in *Sylvia Scarlett* (1935). Cukor has said (in *On Cukor* [1972] by Gavin Lambert): "Up to then Cary had been a conventional leading man. This part was extremely well written,* and he knew this kind of raffish life, he'd been a stilt-walker in a circus. And he'd had experience by this time to know what he was up to, and suddenly this part hit him, and he felt the ground under his feet."

In the ninety-four-minute story, when Henry Scarlett (Edmund Gwenn) commits larceny, his daughter (Katharine Hepburn) cuts her hair and dons boys' clothing to aid and accompany his flight from France. In London they encounter a glib Soho native (Grant) who influences their swindling habits. To escape detection by the authorities, they join a Harlequin-type caravan circus revue and take to the English roads.† Hepburn eventually reveals her feminity when she meets pretty-boy artist Brian Aherne and really turns on the girlish allure when a Russian adventuress (Natalie Paley) also makes a romantic play for the artist.

Most everyone—critics and audiences—panned *Sylvia Scarlett,* with one critic, Eileen Creelman of the *New York Sun* boldly stating: "The picture is a tragic waste of time and screen talent . . ." But all the critics liked Grant. Thornton Delehany observed in the *New York Post:* "Cary Grant comes near to stealing the picture with his bitingly humorous portrait of a Cockney ne'er-do-well"; *Time* magazine found that the picture was made somewhat memorable by the actor's "superb depiction of the Cockney"; and *Variety* reiterated the *Post's* observation that he "steals the picture." Of his different kind of screen role, Grant said, "For once they didn't see me as a nice young man with regular features and a heart of gold."

It was inevitable, in the era of the suave screen detective, personified by William Powell's *Thin Man* series, that Cary Grant, too, should portray such a role. In *Big Brown Eyes* (Paramount, 1936), he is Danny Barr investigating the theft of a priceless gem. His wisecracking girlfriend (Joan Bennett) helps him find clues through her job as a newspaper columnist and sob sister. In her attempts, she is fired for writing a false story on behalf of Grant, who is later taken captive by the

---

*Gladys Unger, John Collins, and Mortimer Offner were responsible for the screenplay, adapted from Compton MacKenzie's novel, *The Early Life and Adventures of Sylvia Scarlett.*
†Filmed entirely in California.

With Edmund Gwenn, Katharine Hepburn, Dennie Moore, and Brian Aherne in SYLVIA SCARLETT (RKO '35)

With Jean Harlow in SUZY (MGM '36)

jewel thieves' leader (Walter Pidgeon). Grant escapes and points the finger of guilt on the wily gang.

Then, on loan to MGM, Cary gained a more interesting movie role than those his home studio was providing him. It was a part Metro's Robert Montgomery or even Robert Young might have handled had their schedules or interests permitted. In *Suzy* (1936) Grant is a philandering French air ace of 1914 who marries a knockout American showgirl named Suzy (Jean Harlow), who is already wed to an Irish inventor, Franchot Tone, whom she believes to have been killed by a German spy (Benita Hume). (Complicated? Yes, but no more so than many a 1930s movie plot!) Tone turns up in Paris to have his new plane tested by Grant but does not reveal his relationship to Harlow. Tone *is* killed by the ubiquitous lady spy with whom he had been keeping company behind Harlow's back. When Hume escapes in a car with her henchman, Grant follows in a plane. He machine-guns the car and kills the passengers. On his return to safety, he encounters German planes, but successfully flies to freedom. He and Harlow then place Tone's body in the plane to

With Joan Bennett, Charles Middleton, Conrad Nagel, Charles McAvoy, and Jack Cheatham in WEDDING PRESENT (Par '36)

make it appear that he was killed in action, and he is posthumously honored as a national hero. (This plot device is similar to the one used in *The Eagle and the Hawk*.) At the end, Cary and Harlow resume their delayed marital relationship. The *Hollywood Spectator* declared that Grant "is something more than just a leading man. Since his outstanding performance in *Sylvia Scarlett*, his talents for varied characterizations have been recognized." Scenes from *Suzy* would be incorporated into the MGM compilation feature, *Big Parade of Comedy* (1964) and *That's Entertainment* (1974).

Unfortunately, Paramount seemed unmindful of the growing elasticity of Cary Grant's acting acumen and continued typecasting him in trivia like *Wedding Present* (1936). Again opposite blonde Joan Bennett, he is a newspaper editor (another ever-recurring role of the era) named Charlie who is somewhat scatterbrained. Because of his nutty antics, his girlfriend (Bennett) breaks off their romance and later becomes engaged to staid Conrad Nagel. Grant's main preoccupation then, or so the screwball comedy would have us believe, is trying to decide what to buy Bennett as

a fitting wedding present. On the day of her scheduled nuptials, knowing her fondness for excitement, he sends fire engines, police cars, and a hearse to the scene. Nothing was missing from these proceedings but the Three Stooges and Alice Brady. When Grant shows up in a hospital's psychopathic-ward pickup wagon, Bennett succumbs to his wild charms. Finis!

With the expiration of Cary's contract in 1936, Paramount unilaterally went ahead and rewrote it with his salary increaed to $3,500 weekly, but he refused to sign. He insisted upon script approval, which the studio would not permit. Cary then announced that he would select his own scripts and his own studios by selling his talents to the highest-bidding producer. Paramount executives found this egocentric plan difficult to fathom and impossible to accept. Cary has said: "I was the very first freelance actor in Hollywood. It was a big step to take, I can tell you, but I was fed up with what I was doing." Carole Lombard was another Paramount star who would soon follow his example.

His initial freelance commitment was an unfortunate one, but he thought it best to leave Holly-

145

wood for a few months and the E. Phillips Oppenheim story of *The Amazing Quest of Ernest Bliss** appealed to him. He sailed to England and starred in the Garrett Klement production. In the title role he inherits two million pounds, and his lethargy is diagnosed as underwork. He then makes a wager that he can live for a year without benefit of his inheritance and cheerfully obtains employment as an oven salesman, a greengrocer, and a chauffeur. On the sales job he meets a secretary named Frances (Mary Brian). Out of love for her he quickly breaks his wager and proposes to her. The *London Times* credited Cary with a "smooth and tactful performance."

Back in Hollywood he entered into nonexclusive agreements with both Columbia Pictures and RKO Radio, explaining that "working for more than one company has its advantages. You are able to get staple assignments and often a studio will buy a story with you in mind."

At Columbia he played second-fiddle support to Grace Moore in *When You're in Love* (1937), and one wonders why. Although the movie was a success in cosmopolitan areas where opera buffs enjoyed it, it was a bit too arch for the average moviegoer. The film is Miss Moore's all the way. Grant is a vagabond American artist of wealth who marries Australian singer Louise Fuller (Moore) so she can enter the United States from Mexico to sing at her uncle's musical festival. Along the way she sings "Minnie the Moocher," "Our Gang," "In the Gloaming," "Schubert's Serenade," "Siboney," a Mexican song, and arias from *Tosca* and *Madama Butterfly*. With all the focus so clearly on the Metropolitan Opera star, it was amazing that Grant, nevertheless, attracted so much critical and audience attention: ". . . an ideal foil for the beautiful blonde. . . . He plays his part with so much ease and casualness that he takes the starch out of the star's performance and she, therefore, impresses one as more of a screen personality and less of a prima donna than ever before" (Kate Cameron, *New York Daily News*). It would be a consistent feature of any Cary Grant movie over the years that he would always make his co-stars look and act much better than they usually did. Many attribute this asset to his

unique ability to put his vis-à-vis so totally at ease in front of the camera.

In the spring of 1937, comedy director Hal Roach, most noted for his Laurel and Hardy and Our Gang comedies productions, and once a frequent visitor at the Grant-Scott beach house, asked Cary to play the ghostly husband in his production for MGM of the Thorne Smith story, "The Jovial Ghosts." Cary was at first reluctant to take the assignment, because of the uncertainty of audience reactions to ghosts, but Roach convinced him that the property had the makings of a screwball hit with its proposed comedic sequences and with Jean Harlow and W. C. Fields slated as his co-stars. The end result was that Cary agreed to portray George Kerby at a fee of $50,000. The title was changed to *Topper* and Grant took second billing to Constance Bennett (as Marion Kerby), who was signed after Harlow became unattainable. Irascible Roland Young became Cosmo Topper when negotiations failed with W. C. Fields and his agents.

George and Marion Kerby are the handsome, empty-headed,‡ rich, partying chief stockholders of a bank headed by austere Roland Young. When the Kerbys' speeding roadster crashes into a tree, its owner-occupants are killed. However, they materialize as ghosts and discover that they must accomplish one good deed before they can be forwarded to a final resting place. They set as their goal the transforming of henpecked banker Young into a life-loving man. Through the means of photographic double exposure they appear and disappear at will throughout the film, causing bedlam through their invisible mischief. Because of them, Young gets drunk, is arrested, and goes through zany moments, but comes through a much happier man to whom his wife (Billie Burke) promises to be more kind and loving. With their "last chance to do a good deed" done, Cary and Constance, viewing Young from his rooftop, bid him farewell and drift out of sight.† *Topper* did much to restore Bennett's sagging screen career, and it served as a reminder that, as a farceur, Grant ranked in the same league with William Powell, Robert Montgomery, and Melvyn Douglas.

*Released in England in 1936 and in the United States on March 2, 1937, under the title *Romance and Riches*. It had been previously filmed in England as *The Amazing Quest of Mr. Ernest Bliss* (Imperial, 1921) and was released as both a five-part serial and a five-reel feature. Henry Edwards and Chrissie White had the leads.

‡At a stockholders' meeting, Grant, while doodling, says aloud: "It can't be done." When someone asks what, he answers: "Writing your name upside down and backwards without stopping."

†In *Topper Takes a Trip* (United Artists, 1939), Constance Bennett repeated her Marion Kerby role, but because of a salary dispute, Grant did not join her in the new entry. A few minutes of his footage from *Topper* was utilized in this followup picture. *Topper Returns* (United Artists, 1941) found Joan Blondell as a buxom ghostly apparition, with Roland Young and Billie Burke for a third time playing the Toppers. In the 1953 video series (79 episodes), Robert Sterling and Anne Jeffreys were the Kerbys, with Leo G. Carroll and Lee Patrick as the Toppers.

On set of TOAST OF NEW YORK (RKO '37) with Frances Farmer

Toast of New York (1937) was next released by RKO with Cary in the fictitious characterization of a partner (Jay Gould) to Jim Fisk (Edward Arnold), the nineteenth-century financier who rose from medicine-showman to one of Wall Street's shrewdest figures. On the climb to his fortune, Arnold takes actress Josie Mansfield (Frances Farmer) as his mistress, although she loves Nick Boyd (Grant). Arnold, in his attempts to corner the gold market, is responsible for America's "Black Friday" of 1869, and is murdered when a frenzied mob attempts to impose law and order.

For $50,000 Cary was asked by Columbia's Harry Cohn to co-star with Irene Dunne (who was receiving $40,000 salary) under Leo McCarey's* direction in the comedy *The Awful Truth* (1937).† After studying those portions of the script that were completed, Grant, Miss Dunne, and the third star, Ralph Bellamy, all asked to be released from their obligations because no one could make proper sense of its continuity. However, Cohn forced them into the production, with Grant as Jerry Warriner and Irene Dunne as his wife, Lu-

cy. When differences of opinion enter their facile lives, he pretends to be taking a Florida trip while she goes to a party with her music teacher (Alexander D'Arcy). Neither believes the other's story and they decide on a divorce, although it is obvious that they still love each other.

In the divorce court, Dunne gets custody of their pet white terrier, Mr. Smith (actually the *Thin Man* pooch Asta, borrowed from MGM), with Grant receiving visitation rights twice a month. With twenty-four hours remaining before their divorce becomes final, Dunne becomes engaged to hickish Bellamy and Grant strikes up a warm acquaintanceship with a nightclub entertainer (Joyce Compton). At the eleventh hour, Dunne determines to win Grant back and concocts various madcap ways of doing so. Ultimately, they are reunited.

Although McCarey's methods of direction (presenting the cast with each day's script on the very day of shooting) were unfamiliar to any of the players, they soon got into the swing of things, which resulted in *the* top comedy of 1937. Both Grant and Dunne were classified as masters of comedy after its release, and McCarey won an Oscar as Best Director of the year. (In 1953 Columbia would remake *The Awful Truth* as the musical *Let's Do It Again,* starring Ray Milland and Jane Wyman. By that point in time both the story and its stars had lost their kick.)

When producer-director Howard Hawks asked Ray Milland, Robert Montgomery, and Ronald Colman to play the role of David Huxley in *Bringing up Baby* (RKO, 1938), he was refused in turn. Grant was Hawks's fourth choice, but he was happy with the way things turned out, and later cited Cary as "the finest comedian of American motion pictures."

Bringing up Baby emerged as 102 minutes of uninhibited fun with Grant and Katharine Hepburn, in their second motion picture together, leading an assemblage of very adept supporting players. In this, Miss Hepburn's first screen comedy—and a madcap one at that—Grant is an archeologist in frenzied search of the bones of a Brontosaurian skeleton he is recreating. On a golf course he meets Hepburn, a wacky heiress who insists that everything he has is hers, from his golf balls to his car. She disrupts his pursuit of archaeology by involving him in several nutty situations, and he tells her: "Our relationship has been

*Cohn's choice to replace ace director Frank Capra, who had defected from the Columbia fold.
†Based on the play (Henry Miller Theatre: September 18, 1922, 144 performances) starring Ina Claire and Bruce McRae. The 1925 Producers Distributing Corp. silent-film version starred Agnes Ayres and Warner Baxter. In the 1929 Pathé rendition, Claire repeated her stage role with Henry Daniel (*sic*) as her leading man.

With Irene Dunne in a publicity pose for THE AWFUL TRUTH (Col '37)

With Katharine Hepburn in BRINGING UP BABY (RKO '38)

a series of misadventures." It's not until he meets her friend, "Baby," a huge, sweet-hearted leopard, that chaos really develops. She talks him into driving "Baby" to the farmhouse of her aunt (May Robson) in Connecticut when his car hits a wagon filled with poultry. He discovers that "Baby" can be placated by the song "I Can't Give You Anything But Love," and, arriving at the farmhouse, he removes his clothing, which has become rather soiled by one thing and another during the wild trip. The only garment he can find is Hepburn's robe, which he tells the aunt he is wearing "because I just went gay all of a sudden." The dog (Asta) steals one of the precious Brontosaurian bones and "Baby" escapes. Grant and Hepburn search the fields and woods of Connecticut singing and whistling "I can't give you anything but love—BABY!" until the leopard finally returns to their care. Riotous episode followed riotous episode, with little let-up of the hilarity.

Otis Ferguson in the *New Republic* said that Cary "does a nice job of underlining the situation," while *Life's* comment was that he handled the role "with usual comic skill." *Time* magazine found that the film "comes off second only to last year's whimsical high spot, *The Awful Truth.*"

By March 1938, clearly recognized as a star after two solid screen hits in a row, Cary was invited to take lunch regularly with the Columbia executives in the studio dining room, which had been built by Harry Cohn in anger at his not being permitted to dine at the nearby Brown Derby Restaurant on Vine Street without a jacket or suitcoat. After a few of the luncheons, however, Cary asked that he be excluded from the group because of the daily discussions of football, a sport he clearly did not fancy.

His third film with Katharine Hepburn was *Holiday* (Columbia, 1938),* a bit of serious frivolity concerned with Johnny Case (Grant), who takes a vacation from work to see how the rest of the world lives. He becomes engaged to Julia Seton (Doris Nolan), a rich snob whose older sister (Hepburn) is a rebellious, liberated woman of the 1930s, much more in line with the type of girl he truly wants. On New Year's Eve, while Nolan celebrates with her society pals, Hepburn and Grant find it more fun to be in another room of the Seton mansion with people they understand. It is then

that their true feelings for each other are expressed.†

On the heels of three successful comedy roles, agile Cary Grant then turned to adventure in *Gunga Din* (RKO, 1939). Inspired by the Rudyard Kipling poem, George Stevens directed Ben Hecht and Charles MacArthur's story into an exciting motion picture about a trio of mischievous British sergeants (Grant, Victor McLaglen, Douglas Fairbanks, Jr.‡), who are sent to an outstation in India to learn why communications have been cut off between the command posts. With their water boy, Gunga Din (Sam Jaffe), they encounter a hidden mountain temple where the Guru (Eduardo Ciannelli) and his fiendish, fanatical followers plot the destruction of the British troops. The inseparable sergeants and Gunga Din are taken prisoners and are tortured, but escape to the temple's dome where the wounded water boy sounds a clarion bugle call to warn the advancing Empire troops. Although bloody by 1939 standards, the movie inspired a desire in many a youngster to join some form of military life where, supposedly, adventure and camaraderie reigned. Cary demonstrated that he was nearly as adept in this swashbuckling genre as Fairbanks.

Meanwhile, at Columbia, Cary was stubborn Jeff Carter, owner of an airline delivering mail over the Andes Mountains, in *Only Angels Have Wings* (1939). Produced, directed, and written by Howard Hawks, the setting is a banana town in Ecuador where the fliers experience calamitous situations each time one of their planes lifts into the sky. On top of all these problems, women appear on the scene. Showgirl Jean Arthur is waiting for a ship that will return her to American civilization, while Rita Hayworth, Grant's former fiancée, arrives with her flier husband, Richard Barthelmess, with whom she is bored. Film devotees noticed a "refreshing" cynicism about Cary's performance as the woman-toughened pilot who has a hard time renewing his faith in life. At long last, dapper Cary Grant was cinematically coming of age.

Cary returned to RKO for his final 1939 film, his thirty-fourth feature-picture appearance of the decade. *In Name Only* was a melodramatic woman's picture of the type of genre that Cary had left behind when his skill for comedy was allowed to come to the fore. In the Richard Sherman screen-

---

*Irene Dunne had wanted the role very much.
†*Holiday,* based on the Philip Barry play (Plymouth Theatre: November 26, 1928, 230 performances), had previously been filmed by RKO-Pathé in 1930 with Ann Harding, Robert Ames, and Mary Astor in the lead roles.
‡United Artists would remake the theme in 1962 as *Sergeants Three* with Frank Sinatra, Dean Martin, and Peter Lawford, with an American Western setting. Sammy Davis, Jr. was their faithful follower—in this instance, an ex-slave.

With John Carroll and Jean Arthur in ONLY ANGELS HAVE WINGS (Col '39)

Advertisement for IN NAME ONLY (RKO '39)

play, he is very wealthy Alec Walker, lovelessly wed to socialite Kay Francis. One fine day, he meets Julie Eden (Carole Lombard), a widow, and falls in love with her. Francis sweetly tells him that she will, of course, give him a divorce, but then she departs on a European jaunt with his parents, who consider her of noble character. While they are away, Grant, Lombard, and her daughter (Peggy Ann Garner) prepare for their new domestic bliss and count the days. When Francis does return, she tells Grant she has no intention of giving him a divorce. He goes out, becomes drunk, and develops a case of pneumonia. At the hospital, Lombard confronts Kay and the latter tells her that what she wants is the Grant family money. For that reason, she is going to hold on until the father is dead. Cary's parents overhear this confession and thus learn of her true, base nature. Presumably the way is now clear for Cary and Carole to obtain their long-awaited happiness. While the decorum of John Cromwell's direction was to be applauded and the controlled performance of Kay Francis to be admired, there was little substance to Grant's impersonation of Alec Walker. He seemed particularly indifferent to the demands of the precise genre when he undertook his fever scenes, seemingly content that his unshaven, blurry-eyed look could suffice for dramatic intensity.

Cary's private life, in 1940, consisted of effervescent parties at which he was not known to turn away a drink, nor could he resist passing a piano without sitting down to enchant the other guests with his bawdy-versed renditions of popular songs. His own New Year's Eve gatherings were among Hollywood's best, with people vying for invitations. All of his off-duty daylight hours were devoted to lying on a beach getting a tan, which became something of an obsession with him.

While those who knew Cary only from his screen work assumed he was the personification of masculine charm, industry workers were aware of another dimension to the man. He was known as a chronic worrier, a man of so many indecisions and fluctuating moods that he allegedly sent more than one director to the hospital with shattered nerves. There were those who called him stingy, aloof, moody, shy, undependable, vacillating, and even resentful.

But at the same time there was the Countess Barbara Hutton Haugwitz-Reventlow,* who thought that Cary Grant was just divine, a movie star with the perfect profile, from his low hairline to the jut of his dimpled chin. She was reputed to be the world's richest girl,† being the heiress granddaughter of the founder of the Woolworth store chain. Having been reintroduced by Countess Dorothy DiFrasso (they met for the first time in 1938 on board the *Normandie* bound for New York from England), she and Cary became one of Hollywood's most famous couples during their courtship.

Howard Hawks produced and directed Grant's next excursion into cinematic comedy, *His Girl Friday* (Columbia, 1940), based on the hit play *The Front Page*, by Ben Hecht and Charles MacArthur.‡ Harry Cohn's choice for the role of the city editor was Walter Winchell, with Grant as the reporter, Hildy Johnson, but Hawks had the bright idea of a slight rewrite with the part of Hildy being switched to a female's, thereby making a romantic story out of it. Columbia found the idea acceptable, and Grant was set to play Walter Barnes, the editor. The list of feminine possibilities for the role of Hildy encompassed Irene Dunne and Claudette Colbert, but narrowed down to Rosalind Russell. Charles Lederer's script established that Burns and Hildy were a divorced couple, along with being employer and employee. Lederer inserted the role of Bruce Baldwin (Ralph Bellamy) as Hildy's fiancé, who is never quite with it.

In the film, Russell is about to resign her job in order to marry Bellamy, but Cary goads her into covering one last story, that of escaped convict-murderer John Qualen. While Bellamy, a rather simple-minded insurance man from Albany, receives merciless insults from Grant, Russell finds the convict and hides him until she can turn in an exclusive front-page story. Although the couple had divorced because there never seemed to be time in their lives for romance, Russell decides that Grant is more her type, after all, and that she would probably be miserable in Albany as the wife of an insurance man.

His Girl Friday has been credited with having the fastest-paced dialog in motion-picture history, and the *Nation's* critique included the following pithy comment: "Rosalind Russell and Cary

*Born November 14, 1912, in New York, she was wed from 1932 to 1935 to Prince Alexis Mdivani of Russia. Husband number two was Danish Count Haugwitz-Reventlow (son Lance by him died in a plane crash in 1972).
†There was constant conjecture as to who had the most money, Barbara Hutton or Doris Duke.
‡First produced on Broadway in 1928 (Times Square Theatre: August 14, 1928, 276 performances), it was to be revived in 1969 with Robert Ryan and Bert Convy. It was also a United Artists–released film in 1931 with Adolphe Menjou and Pat O'Brien. In 1974, Billy Wilder filmed yet another remake (for Universal release in 1975) with Walter Matthau and Jack Lemmon.

Grant give such entertaining performances that nobody in the roaring audience seems to notice the tastelessness, to say the least, of playing hide-and-seek with a man condemned to death."

Cary's fee was $100,000 for his next film, *My Favorite Wife* (RKO, 1940), a look at the loony side of matrimony, produced by Leo McCarey and directed by Garson Kanin. Nick Arden (Grant) has his wife declared legally dead after an absence of seven years, and marries Gail Patrick. That same morning, the first wife (Irene Dunne) returns, stating that she had been stranded on a desert island. Grant, who does not want to explain the situation to Patrick, takes her to a mountain lodge for their honeymoon, but they are followed by determined Dunne. The desk clerk (Donald MacBride) questions his checking in with two women, to which Grant says with pride: "My reputation for respectability is just as high as your hotel," but attempts an explanation with: "Now, I came up here with my wife—my bride really. Now, my wife—not my bride, my wife—well, why should I bore you with the details?" During the lodge episode, Grant is forced to dash between his wives' rooms. Patrick asks: "Do you love me?" Grant replies with firmness: "Bianca, you are one of the most attractive girls I know." She cries: "I'm your wife!" When it develops that Dunne was not alone on that island for seven long years, but in the company of tall, muscular Randolph Scott, Grant suddenly becomes jealous, and eventually returns full time to Dunne.°

Time magazine stated that the film "tends to get bedroomatic and limp, but it pulls itself together in scenes like those in which Cary Grant scampers between his wives' hotel rooms." When compared to *My Favorite Husband* (Columbia, 1940), starring Jean Arthur, Melvyn Douglas, and Fred MacMurray, a picture with a similar premise, *My Favorite Husband* seems an even richer cinematic dish than when judged alone.

In keeping with his self-made policy of making a dramatic film for every two comedies, Cary chose *The Howards of Virginia* (Columbia, 1940) as his next film. From Elizabeth Page's novel, *The Tree of Liberty*, the script relates with great pageantry the story of Thomas Jefferson's backwoods friend Matt Howard (Grant), who obtains

---

°The film was to be remade in 1963 by Twentieth Century–Fox as *Move Over, Darling*, with James Garner, Doris Day, and Polly Bergen in the principal roles.

With Alan Marshal (second left), Pat Somerset, and Richard Carlson in THE HOWARDS OF VIRGINIA (Col '40)

With Virginia Weidler, Mary Nash, and Katharine Hepburn in THE PHILADELPHIA STORY (MGM '40)

a job as surveyor for the very British Fleetwood Peyton (Sir Cedric Hardwicke). Grant falls in love with Peyton's daughter (Martha Scott) and marries her. As the years pass, he enters colonial politics and sides with the colonists at the advent of the fight for independence. Against Scott's wishes, he joins the revolutionary army. For the sake of authenticity and to save on reconstructing actual sites, Columbia filmed much of the picture against the backdrop of newly restored Colonial Williamsburg, Virginia.

Katharine Hepburn, who, among others, had been labeled Hollywood "Box-Office Poison" in 1939, acted on Broadway in Philip Barry's play, *The Philadelphia Story* (Shubert Theatre: March 28, 1939, 417 performances), which brought her renewed glory. When MGM bought the screen rights, Hepburn went along with the package deal, but the film had to be completed within eight weeks since she was scheduled to take the comedy on a national tour.

Directed by George Cukor, with virtually no retakes, *The Philadelphia Story* (1940) has Cary in top billing as C. K. Dexter Haven,* the former husband of Tracy Lord (Hepburn),† whom he calls a "virgin goddess." She is of the Philadelphia Main Line Lords, high on the social register and low in democratic spirit. The pattern for what follows is set in the opening scene when Hepburn kicks Grant out of the Lord mansion, throws his golf clubs after him, and cracks one of the clubs over her knee and flings it to the ground. Grant stalks up to her and punches her on the chin. In preparing for her upcoming wedding to John Howard, newsman James Stewart and photographer Ruth Hussey are invited to record the moment for posterity. The haughty, faultless Hepburn learns a sense of compassion and understanding from Stewart, whom she tries not to love. When Howard leaves after being humiliated by his prospective bride, both Stewart and Grant volunteer to fill in as her groom. Until the last minute, an aura of suspense hovers over the ceremony as to which man will marry her, but Cary, of course, is the one to recapture the beauty.‡

When the film premiered at Radio City Music

*Robert Montgomery had rejected the bid to play Joseph Cotten's stage role onscreen.
†This was to be Grant's fourth and final film with Hepburn.
‡The story was to be redone in 1956 as a musical, entitled *High Society* (MGM), with Bing Crosby as Dexter and Grace Kelly as Tracy Lord.

Hall on December 26, 1940, Eileen Creelman of the *New York Sun* wrote: "Cary Grant plays the ex-husband with dignity and a sharp humor."[**]

In 1941 Grant was heard on radio with Rosalind Russell in a repeat of their *His Girl Friday* roles in the "Gulf Screen Guild's" version of the film. He was also a panelist on NBC radio's ill-fated "The Circle," which was the forerunner of the television discussion show. With Ronald Colman as Master of Ceremonies, "The Circle" was short-lived even with such notables as Madeleine Carroll, Carole Lombard, and Groucho Marx carrying on conversations and telling jokes among themselves.

Penny Serenade (Columbia, 1941) earned Cary his first Academy Award nomination as Roger Adams (again, a newsman).[*] The plotline concerns Julie Adams (Irene Dunne), who is preparing to walk out of her marriage, which has grown stale. She stops to play phonograph records that bring back memories of her marriage in flashback sequences. The couple meet, marry, and go to Japan where she becomes pregnant. An earthquake ruins their home and causes her to have a miscarriage. Saddened and empty, they return to the United States, take on the ownership of a coastal California town newspaper, and adopt a baby which brightens their lives. Because of their poor financial situation, however, a judge (Wallis Clark) threatens to remove the baby from their home. Grant's appeal is one of the most poignant scenes ever recorded on celluloid. His plea stays the judge's decision and the child is returned to them, but dies at age six. Dunne's phonograph records have brought us up to date, but then comes word that a second baby they had hoped to adopt is waiting for them. This brings the couple back together.

To a certain extent Grant had George Steven's well-modulated direction to thank for his imaginative acting job, of which Otis Ferguson wrote in *The New Republic:* "Cary Grant is thoroughly good, in some ways to the point of surprise, for there is not only that easy swing and hit of the devil in him, but faith and passion expressed, the character held together where it might so easily have fallen into the component parts of the too good, the silly, etc."

Suspicion (RKO, 1941) was adapted for the screen by Samson Raphaelson, Joan Harrison, and Alma Reville from *Before the Fact*, a novel by Francis Iles. The book's ending, which had Johnnie Aysgarth (Grant) as a villain who mails a letter by which he unknowingly accuses himself of a murder, was altered by RKO because it was inadvisable, they felt, for Grant ever to appear villainous. Instead the movie concludes on an upbeat note when he has a plausible explanation to offer his shy, inhibited, rich wife (Joan Fontaine) for his strange behavior.[‡] Although he had always been a liar and a cheat, he becomes sincere when he weds her, but she constantly imagines that he is trying to kill her for her money. According to the reconstructed scenario, all those fears are only in her fertile mind. This was the first of Grant's several excursions into the directorial world of Alfred Hitchcock. Largely because his characterization lacked proper definition—was he or was he not a homicidal bounder?—Cary's performance merged as too tenuous: at one moment charming, at another duplicitous, at still another uncomfortably ambiguous. Then too, the action is focused on the heroine's interactions with, and thoughts about, Cary, leaving him very much of a tinsel figure, too nebulous for any sort of positive audience identification.

David O. Selznick wanted Cary for the leading role in his screen version of *Claudia*, but was turned down for personal reasons.[†] Cary was planning to be married again.

On June 26, 1942, after waiting almost five years after filing his application, Cary was given American citizenship. At the same time, he legally changed his name to Cary Grant. A few days later, on July 8, 1942, he and Barbara Hutton were quietly married at the home of his business manager at Lake Arrowhead, California (east of Los Angeles). Cary was thirty-eight and his sullen-faced bride was thirty. With a staff of eleven servants and with her son by her second marriage, bride and groom moved into a large home in Pacific Palisades rented from Douglas Fairbanks, Jr. Hedda Hopper would later write in her *The Whole Truth and Nothing But* (1963): "Cary had by far the biggest bedroom, complete with wood-burning fireplace, beautiful antiques, private entrance, and a private bathroom approximately the size of Marineland." Privately, at the time of their marriage, Cary signed a waiver relinquishing all claims to the Hutton maxi-fortune. Publicly, he said: "If she wants to buy diamond overshoes, that is her privilege. But all routine household

[**]The $125,000 salary Grant received for *The Philadelphia Story* was donated to the British War Relief.
[*]He lost to his former Paramount rival Gary Cooper, who won for *Sergeant York* (Warner Bros., 1941).
[‡]Miss Fontaine won an Oscar for her portrayal.
[†]In the 1943 Twentieth Century–Fox version of *Claudia*, Robert Young played David to Dorothy McGuire's title role.

With Irene Dunne in PENNY SERENADE

Advertisement for PENNY SERENADE (Col '41)

items, as rent and groceries will be strictly on me"*

The Talk of the Town (Columbia, 1942) came next, again under the direction of George Stevens. As Leopold Dilg, Grant is charged with arson in connection with a factory fire in which his foreman is believed to have been killed. He escapes from prison and hides in the home of a schoolteacher (Jean Arthur), which she has rented to a famed law professor (Ronald Colman). She tells Colman that Cary is the gardener, and goes to great lengths to protect him. Colman, by discussing legal ethics with Grant, soon finds that the town officials are corrupt and, furthermore, that the allegedly dead foreman is still very much alive and is responsible for the blaze. When Grant is recaptured by the police, a lynch mob is ready to render instant punishment, but the professor presents the "dead" foreman to clear the innocent businessman. Some called the matching of Colman and Grant a tie, but in this talky photoplay, Colman emerged as the more urbane and measured soul, capable of gaining tremendous effect through the nuances of his well-modulated voice.

Once upon a Honeymoon (RKO, 1942) remains one of the most enjoyable screen ventures in which either Grant or Ginger Rogers singly or jointly have participated. Its breezy 116-minute account takes place in 1938 with radio newsman Pat O'Toole (Grant) covering the political scene in Austria. There he happens onto Katie O'Hara (Rogers), an ex-burlesque stripper from Brooklyn who feigns a pedigree and manages to marry Baron von Luber (Walter Slezak). It takes forever for her to perceive what Grant knows from the start, that Slezak is an Austrian Nazi agent, fomenting Continental trouble as per direct orders from the Führer. While the nations of Europe fall to the Germans, one by one, Cary and Ginger fall in love. They escape the Nazis, drown the pursuing baron, and get married. Under Leo McCary's direction, the two stars keep the film from getting too serious by their deft light touches.

"If it hadn't been for *Mr. Lucky* [RKO, 1943]," Grant once said, "I don't know how much longer I'd have held the public's interest." Just what the star meant is dubious, since the film, called a "disgusting story" by Manny Farber of the *New Republic,* casts him as a draft-dodging gambler who assumes the identity of a dead gangster in order to evade the draft. He continues his gam-

With Frank Mills in MR. LUCKY (RKO '43)

bling ways, unaffected by his local draft board. He later becomes involved with a war relief agency and its bankroll, but heiress Laraine Day leads him onto the path of righteousness.

Philip T. Hartung in the *Commonweal* wrote: "*Mr. Lucky* is what is known as a vehicle picture. If it weren't for Cary Grant's persuasive personality the whole thing would melt away to nothing at all. Its story is preposterous."‡

In real life, Grant did not dodge the draft. He tried to gain admission to the Army Air Corps but was rejected for being overage (he was thirtynine). But in February 1944 he toured the so-called back-water service camps where he talked with servicemen on whatever subject they wished. He had asked Barbara to accompany him because he thought the boys "would have gotten a kick out of just looking at her," but she would have none of it.

A big bolster to Cary's screen career was his trek to Warner Bros. for *Destination Tokyo* (1943) in which he is the commander of the submarine *Copperfin,* ordered from San Francisco on Christ-

---

*Cary's 1941 income had been closely tabulated at $351,562.
‡"Mr. Lucky," a teleseries (CBS-TV: October 24, 1959, 34 episodes) derived from the theatrical feature, starred John Vivyan, as a hard-hitting, honest professional gambler who becomes involved in turbulent adventures aboard his gambling ship. RKO's *Gambling House* (1950) was also a reworking of *Mr. Lucky,* with Victor Mature and Terry Moore in the pivotal roles.

With Warner Anderson in DESTINATION TOKYO (WB '43)

mas Eve to pick up a meteorologist in the Aleutians. The sub is then to proceed to Tokyo Bay where the specialist will go ashore to provide weather information for General Doolittle's air raid. Except for Faye Emerson, seen briefly as Grant's wife, it had an all-male cast, and was deftly directed by Delmer Daves. *Newsweek* magazine commented that "the newest tribute to the Armed Forces rates very near the top of the list" and "Cary Grant gives one of the soundest performances of his career."

Once upon a Time (Columbia, 1944) was as successful as any film in making movie audiences forget the war. Cary is seen as theatre producer Jerry Flynn, who admits he is "resting between miracles" after three successive stage flops. He tosses a nickel over his shoulder for luck and quickly finds two kids (Ted Donaldson and Mickey McGuire) with a caterpillar named "Curly" who dances to "Yes, Sir, That's My Baby" played by Pinky (Donaldson) on his harmonica. Opportunist Grant soon latches onto the kid and his boxed "Curly," whom he calls the "Fred Astaire of the insect world" and says: "By the time I get through with it, I think we can make a fortune."

Further into *Once upon a Time*, Grant takes the box to his office, where his stooge The Moke

(James Gleason) inquires: "What's going on here?" Grant glibly replies: "A miracle. I'm going to hold onto my theatre." He runs into opposition, however, in the form of Donaldson's sister (Janet Blair), who does not think the publicity is good for her nine-year-old brother, but Cary charms her into going along with it—ostensibly for Donaldson's sake. No one, though, believes that the insect can dance until national news commentator Gabriel Heatter takes an interest and talks about it on his evening radio broadcast. Grant next plans to sell the mystical "Curly" to Walt Disney for $100,000, but Donaldson loses faith and "Curly" disappears. One afternoon, while Cary plays the caterpillar's favorite song on the piano, a butterfly comes into the room, dances about, and while Grant, Blair, and Donaldson watch, flies out a window. Some people carped at the film's pseudomorality or the overcuteness of the plotline as derived from Norman Corwin's popular radio play, *My Client Curly*. Still others thought it significant that Cary had been reduced to playing support to a jumping insect.

Cary returned to a strongly dramatic role in *None But the Lonely Heart* (RKO, 1944), in which, as in *Sylvia Scarlett,* he again played a Cockney type far removed from his typical screen

With Ted Donaldson and Alex Melesh in ONCE UPON A TIME (Col '44)

persona. Because the Clifford Odets–directed/ scripted picture is so filled with sleek camera tricks, clean faces, philosophical phrases,° lighting effects, etc., the true picture of lower-class British life is soon obliterated. Nevertheless, the film leaves the sensitive viewer with an insight into a strong mother-son relationship, thanks mainly to the acting of Grant and Ethel Barrymore.

At a salary of $150,000, plus ten percent of the film's gross over $1,500,000, Grant's name appeared above the title. He is Ernie Mott, a bitter young rake of an Englishman who turns crooked because he is sick of seeing his mother (Barrymore) work so hard at running a second-hand shop in order to support them both. Grant's Ernie would not know how to maintain an honest job. Through his petty thievery he discovers that his mother has become a "fence" in an effort to earn fast money, which she intends to pass on to him soon, since she is dying from cancer. He returns home one day to find her gone. She has been taken to a hospital where she dies, and he then de-cides to find a better life within, or outside, the London slums.

James Agee of the *Nation* stated that Grant "plays its far from Cary Grantish hero so attentively and sympathetically that I all but overlooked the fact that he is not well constituted for the role." *Theatre Arts* magazine championed that the star "has a rare chance to burrow inside of a character and come out with something more than his usual charm and skillfully turned comic touches." Grant received his second Academy Award nomination for *None But the Lonely Heart,* but lost to Bing Crosby for *Going My Way* (Paramount).†

Arsenic and Old Lace (Warner Bros., 1944), filmed in Hollywood in 1941, was temporarily shelved in agreement with the stage producers' demand that it not be released until the Broadway commitment had been fulfilled.‡

As Mortimer Brewster, seemingly the only sane member of the family, Grant was accused by some critics of overacting.† Said Leo Mishkin (*New York Morning Telegraph*) in the star's de-

° "When is the world coming out of its midnight? When is the human race going to get off its knees?"
† Miss Barrymore won a Best Supporting Actress Oscar for her *None But the Lonely Heart* performance.
‡ The play (Fulton Theatre: January 10, 1941, 1,444 performances) featured Allyn Joslyn in the role assumed in the movie by Cary.
† Bob Hope was among those who rejected the screen lead.

With Leo White and Priscilla Lane in ARSENIC AND OLD LACE (WB '44)

fense: "Not in years has Brother Grant had such a chance to show off his mugging. Not in years has he mugged with such wonderful effect. There are some who may object to even Cary Grant mugging a movie—but just wait'll they see what can be done with the right material and under the proper circumstances."

The film opens with the words: "This is a Halloween tale of Brooklyn where anything can happen and it usually does." Grant is a New York drama critic, a symbol of bachelorhood who has written a book entitled *Marriage, a Fraud and a Failure,* and says: "Marriage is a superstition, it's old fashioned." Nevertheless, he is about to marry Priscilla Lane, a vicar's daughter. He goes home after slyly obtaining a wedding license and finds his two dear old aunts (Josephine Hull, Jean Adair) up to their favorite tricks. They "help lonely, old men find peace" by feeding them poisoned elderberry wine and then having their brother (John Alexander), who thinks he is *the* "Rough Rider" Teddy Roosevelt, dig graves in the cellar ("the Panama Canal") for these "yellow fever victims." The sisters cannot see that there is anything wrong with their acts of "kindness" and fail to appreciate Cary's horrified attitude. Grant is further distressed by his discovery that the

twelfth victim has yet to be buried and is in the living-room window seat awaiting completion of a new canal lock. Into this stage melee comes another Brewster, Grant's older brother Jonathan (Raymond Massey), an escaped criminal. With him is his slimy colleague Dr. Einstein (Peter Lorre). They, too, have a body in tow, which complicates the burial system. "Insanity runs in my family," Grant cries, "It practically gallops." He manages to contact Mr. Witherspoon (Edward Everett Horton) of Happydale Sanitarium to take away the uncle, and the aunts accompany him. The police (led by Jack Carson) apprehend Massey and deranged Lorre. As the aunts leave, they give Grant the best gift possible. They reveal that he is not really a Brewster since he was an adopted child.

While the play version of *Arsenic and Old Lace* is constantly revived for stage presentation and newly structured television specials, the motion picture remains a cinematic oddity, suffering from its vastly "overstated and strained" qualities. Most jarring to the picture's well-being are the inserted romantic interludes between Grant and Lane, completely out of keeping with the buoyant mayhem breaking loose about them. This is one of the few times oncamera where Cary

Grant's presence was a detraction and hindrance to the picture's well-being. There was more than sufficient goofiness and gore to sustain audience interest without having to be content with Cary's enlarged straight-man part and oversized star presence. Unfortunately, the film continually vacillated between the poles of make-believe and reality, a dangerous situation for any self-respecting fantasy.

Cary made one other screen appearance for 1944 release. He was in a ten-minute film made by Warner Bros. on behalf of the Fifth War Bond Drive. The short subject, *Road to Victory,* opened in an American home in 1951 and flashbacked to 1944. Also in the short were Bing Crosby, Dennis Morgan, Frank Sinatra, Jack Carson, Irene Manning, Charles Ruggles, Jimmy Lydon, and Olive Blakeney.

In January 1945, Cary received another accolade, one of which most female filmgoers had been aware for many years. A Boston sculptress, Katharine Ward Lane, named him one of the ten most handsome American men. The spinster admitted that there were few men that she would care to look at for more than five seconds.

If Grant's movie career was progressing at a steady clip, his domestic relationship was not.

During the course of the Grant-Hutton marriage, there were two trial separations due to their vastly different life styles. Although she reportedly spent evenings knitting his socks, she claimed to be bored, yet she disliked going out for fear of being photographed or attacked by autograph seekers. Her friends disliked his friends and *vice versa.* In Hollywood, on July 10, 1945, she filed a suit for divorce which was granted on August 30, 1945. It was one of the simplest divorce proceedings to be heard in court. The following dialogue between Judge Thursmond Clarke and Miss Hutton was heard:

Hutton: Well, Mr. Grant and myself did not have the same friends. On more than one occasion when I gave dinner parties, he would not come downstairs, but would have dinner in bed. When he did come down, he was obviously not amused, and naturally it was embarrassing.
Judge: How did that affect you?
Hutton: It made me rather nervous.
Judge: Did you require the services of a doctor?
Hutton: Yes I did.
Judge: That's enough. Decree granted.

With Louella Parsons, Bebe Daniels, and Darryl Zanuck participating in an ABC radio World War II Victory broadcast, August 15, 1945

Cary and Barbara had been married three years and fifty-two days. Miss Hutton later said: "Cary never took me out when we were married. I hardly saw him. At night, he was always busy with his clippings or the radio." She added: "Since our divorce, we've become very good friends. He's really very sweet and kind." Grant's gallant public statement was: "The trouble wasn't with her. People just can't disassociate her from her money and they act like idiots around her. She seldom gets to know people as they really are. I ask you to have a little patience and tolerance for Barbara, whom I know is a very dear woman."

Cary then took a smaller house in Brentwood, which he never really found time to enjoy. The carefree star of the 1930s, who had romped around town with his pal Randolph Scott, was now a serious, brooding man in his early forties. The image of his screen personality as the glib, facile bon vivant who could charm a smile from a dyspeptic, was in marked contrast to a severely introspective offcamera figure, who was solemnly trying to piece together the segments of his well-appointed but unfulfilling existence.

His next film was the career biography of his elite friend, witty society composer Cole Porter (1891–1964). It was called *Night and Day* (Warner Bros., 1946) and executed on a grand 132-minute Technicolor scale by producer Arthur Schwartz and director Michael Curtiz. Cary portrayed the songwriter as the film explored and distorted Porter's career from his days at Yale of 1914, where he received the encouragement and friendship of his professor Monty Woolley (played by Woolley) up through his composition of "Miss Otis Regrets." Mask-faced and wooden, Alexis Smith played his wife Linda, just as she had played George Gershwin's girlfriend the previous year in *Rhapsody in Blue* (Warner Bros.) In this hardly serious fantasy biography of one of America's great songwriters, there was the *de rigueur* scene in which Grant's Porter sits struggling at the piano for day after day, trying to translate his creative idea into a workable song. Suddenly his patient wife (Smith) appears at the door. Grant looks up, and with divine inspiration the song comes to him. "Night and day . . . you are the one!" Thus an enduring song was born.

While most of the delight to be found in *Night and Day* was delivered by vivacious Ginny Simms ("Do I Love You," "I Get a Kick out of You," "You're the Top," "I've Got You under My Skin," etc.) and Mary Martin ("My Heart Belongs to Daddy"), Cary instilled the fake biography

In NIGHT AND DAY (WB '46)

with an élan that was ironically all of *his* own and has little resemblance to Porter's. Evidently Cary was so in awe of his occasional friend Porter, and played down the characterization so greatly, that what emerged oncamera was pure Cary Grant. From that time on people forever insisted that the real-life composer was not whom he claimed to be, for they had seen the movie, and Porter was *not* Grant. This pandering screen biography earned over $4 million in U.S. and Canadian rentals, which proved that the Warner Bros. clan knew how to fool a great many people a good deal of the time.

Cary was next seen briefly in an unbilled "guest" shot in RKO's *Without Reservations* (1946), starring Claudette Colbert and John Wayne. Playing himself, a big movie star, he dances with authoress Colbert in a Hollywood nightclub sequence.

In April 1946, Grant, ever anxious to break away from the confining ties of studio supervision, formed a producing company in partnership with British-based Alexander Korda. He flew to London to investigate the possibility of putting together a film version of Daphne Du Maurier's novel *The King's General,* with himself in the lead. When nothing came of the idea, Grant returned to Hollywood aboard the luxury liner *Queen Mary.* On board ship he spotted a girl he wanted to meet and asked Merle Oberon (the ex-Mrs. Korda) to intercede on his behalf. Miss Oberon approached the girl and invited her to have lunch with them. The girl, Betsy Drake,* was homeward bound after an eight-month run in the London stage production of *Deep Are the Roots.*

Cary went to work for Alfred Hitchcock again, this time in *Notorious* (RKO, 1946), which dealt with Germans in South America plotting the restoration of world Nazism. As Devlin, an American intelligence agent, he meets anti-Nazi Alicia Huberman (Ingrid Bergman), whose father has been convicted as a German spy. They fall in love and Grant persuades her to accompany him to Rio de Janiero to undertake a secret mission. Her special task is to contact one of her father's friends (Claude Rains) to obtain vital facts concerning a suspicious project which Rains and his Nazi cohorts are developing undercover. Soon Rains asks her to marry him, and she accepts, partly to further her patriotic mission and somewhat to attain masochistic revenge on Grant for having put her in the immoral and dangerous situation in which she finds herself.

Once wed to the mother-dominated Rains, she has the run of her husband's house, where she pieces together bits of information and concludes that the secret is in the wine cellar. Sure enough she and Grant find that some special wine bottles contain uranium ore samples which obviously can be used for only one purpose, the construction of an atom bomb. Later, only by the chanciest method, Grant manages to bluff his way back into Rain's home to rescue Bergman who is being slowly poisoned by her desperate husband.

If critics and moviegoers had stood in amazement at the torrid romancing of Ingrid Bergman and Humphrey Bogart in *Casablanca* (Warner Bros., 1942), they were enthralled by the screen teaming of Bergman and Grant. Their steamy love scenes stick in the viewer's mind long after the details of the women's-magazine espionage tale have faded from recollection. Moviegoers and fan magazines alike were eager for more Grant-Bergman screen-teaming, but such an event was not to be for some time to come.

Cary's salary for 1946, as reported by the U.S. Treasury Department, was $278,125. He outgrossed such top-salaried men as Bob Hope and William Randolph Hearst.

While many of the leading debonair stars of the 1930s (William Powell, Herbert Marshall, Ronald Colman, Robert Montgomery, Melvyn Douglas, David Niven, Adolphe Menjou, et al.) were slipping into marked career declines due to advancing age and the changing tastes of audiences in the post–World War II era, Grant remained very much the same as before. He was still plowing ahead with roles in quality productions that ensured a continuation of his top box-office position. It was not just that he seemed to show his age less than his contemporaries, or that he was more enterprising than his confreres in snagging career-saving assignments. It was becoming much more than that—he had become a symbol of dapper charm to American womanhood, a person whom women fantasized about and men used as a standard of comparison. America needed and wanted a Cary Grant; no one of similar substance had come upon the scene to replace him, and he was perfectly willing to carry on in the previous manner, updating his oncamera attack, if not his style, in accomplishing this demand.

His initial film of 1947 was *The Bachelor and the Bobby Soxer* (RKO). Cary plays an artist who gets arrested when the nightclub in which he is a patron is raided. The stern judge (Myrna Loy)

---

*Born September 11, 1923, in Paris, France, she had been a Harry Conover model before embarking on a stage career.

With Kay Christopher, Marilyn Mercer, and Shirley Temple in THE BACHELOR AND THE BOBBY SOXER (RKO '47)

reprimands but acquits him. The next day, after delivering a lecture to a high school art class, he is followed by Shirley Temple, a student who has become infatuated with him. Temple later gains admittance to his apartment and is found there with him by the judge, who is her sister, and by an assistant district attorney (Rudy Vallee). Although the judge can lock Grant up on several unattractive counts, she lets him off, but only if he will be attentive to Temple until the infatuation has run its course. He reluctantly agrees, in lieu of going to jail. By the finale, Grant and barrister Loy are in love. As Bosley Crowther noted in the *New York Times,* "The performance of Cary Grant . . . is one of the brightest and sharpest of his many light-comedy jobs." After fifteen years in the movies, Cary had not lost one bit of his deft touch.

For release by RKO, Samuel Goldwyn produced what Philip T. Hartung (*Commonweal*) called "a sophisticated Christmas Carol." The picture was *The Bishop's Wife.* The script has Cary as an angel sent from heaven to help stuffy bishop David Niven in his efforts to finance the building of a cathedral which will satisfy his rich flock. Grant cannot give Niven proof of his "angelship," but he assures the bishop and his wife

(Loretta Young) that he will help their cause. In the end, Niven learns that a wealthy congregation has put him no nearer to God than the poor people he previously served. Dorothy Kilgallen in *Modern Screen* said of Grant and *The Bishop's Wife:* "As a normal member of the female population, I always have considered Cary Grant 'divine' in the colloquial sense of the word, but I must confess it never occurred to me that he would make a splendid angel." Miss Kilgallen went on to say: "He is not only more attractive-looking than ever before, if possible, but he is guilty of some of the most brilliant acting of the year."

Early in 1948, Betsy Drake came to Hollywood. Cary soon took her under his protective wing because "anybody needs a helping hand in Hollywood." After introducing her to RKO's production chief, Dore Schary, he placed her in an apartment and became her constant about-town escort.

Mr. Blandings Builds His Dream House (RKO, 1948) was true to life, in comedy form, for anyone who has ever gone through the frustrations of constructing his own "castle." For that reason, together with a delightful screenplay by Norman Panama and Melvin Frank and the well-honed

With Monty Woolley and Loretta Young in THE BISHOP'S WIFE (RKO '48)

With Betsy Drake in EVERY GIRL SHOULD BE MARRIED (RKO '48)

light touch of Grant, Myrna Loy, and Melvyn Douglas, the film was one of the funniest of the decade. In the story, the Blandings family (Grant, Loy, Sharyn Moffett, Connie Marshall) acquire a 170-year-old house in Connecticut. They buy it for much more than its worth (on the 1948 market) and find, after taking possession, that it is slowly falling apart. Whereupon, Jim Blandings (Grant) decides to tear down the relic and build a modern structure that will be a "dream house." Through countless problems, including a triangle of sorts with the family lawyer (Douglas) as the apex, the house is completed. (Grant and Betsy Drake would later be heard in a radio series based on this popular movie.)

Every Girl Should Be Married (RKO, 1948) introduced Betsy Drake to the motion-picture screen. She sells children's wear in a department store owned by Franchot Tone. In search of a husband, she methodically sets her sights on a baby doctor (Grant) whom she follows all over town. The good physician finally submits to her ensnarement. It is obvious that Cary arranged for Miss Drake to take center-ring attention for her debut film, and his deliberate underplaying is noticeable, even in a story that is rather short on comedy. Miss Drake's tousle-haired naturalness is fresh at first, but soon becomes irritating even to the extent of the viewer's wishing her to marry anyone, just to put an end to the proceedings. Diana Lynn and Franchot Tone were wasted in supporting feed-line parts.

Howard Hawks directed *I Was a Male War Bride* (Twentieth Century–Fox, 1948) on location in occupied Germany, and made it a very funny motion picture which has endured the test of time. Grant is Captain Henri Rochard, the French commanding officer of American WAC Ann Sheridan. They work closely together but hate each other, a feeling that eventually turns to love and leads to matrimony. However, marriage is not all that easy for them. They endure so much red tape (they must be married four times) that Grant is a civilian by the time he is ready to kiss the bride. But this action, too, is handicapped by Sheridan's orders to report to her unit for debarkation to the States. When Grant cannot spend the night with her, Sheridan the next day devises a means of getting him to America via the War Brides Act, which governs "alien spouses of military personnel." He fills in the requisite forms containing questions as to his possible pregnancy, female disorders, etc., but he still cannot stay with her. To the remark that the American Army is "very careful" he replies: "They're so careful they're not going to have any American children if they don't watch out." He almost gets onto the ship that will carry Sheridan home, but he has a fight with the tough soldier in charge and is kicked off the vessel. Eventually Sheridan hits on the idea of dressing him as a WAC named "Florence" using a horse's tail for a wig. *Newsweek* magazine approved of the picture by saying: "Although some of the proceedings may try the Legion of Decency's patience, they are handled too delightfully by both Grant and Miss Sheridan to offend any but the most squeamish."

On Christmas Day, 1949, Grant and Betsy Drake were flown by RKO studio boss Howard Hughes to a ranch twenty miles from Phoenix, Arizona, where they were married. Cary was forty-five and she was twenty-six. "I never did know how many people were present at the ceremony," Betsy said later. "I couldn't see because I didn't have my glasses on. What girl wants to be married wearing glasses?" Cary gave his bride a matched string of graduated pearls with a marquise diamond clasp and a miniature poodle named Suzy. After moving into Grant's newly acquired Beverly Hills home, she commented: "Cary is too successful, too well established ever to worry about me becoming the star in the family. And we'll never act together again. People would tend to think that I was put into a film just because my husband is a success."

Cary's single 1950 release was *Crisis* (MGM), a slow-moving, talky, suspense drama directed by Richard Brooks, in which brain surgeon Cary is ordered to operate on the tumored cranium of the evil dictator (Jose Ferrer) of a South American country. The picture was banned in Italy because its presentation of a dictator was too similar to their own Mussolini.

Now in the price-salary bracket of $300,000 per film, Cary made a comedy for Twentieth Century–Fox called *People Will Talk* (1951). Directed by Joseph L. Mankiewicz, the story is an updating of the German play *Dr. Praetorious*, in which a nonconforming, freethinking medical man engenders both favorable and unfavorable gossip because of his strong beliefs. He treats unmarried Jeanne Crain for a rather common disorder—pregnancy out of wedlock—and then marries her. His reason is one of pity, initially, but he soon finds that he loves her.

David O. Selznick, in 1951, negotiated with Grant to star in a movie version of F. Scott Fitzgerald's *Tender Is the Night*, with Jennifer Jones slated as the co-star. The efforts were dropped when Selznick refused to meet Cary's stiff salary demands. (Eleven years later the project was fitfully realized with Jones playing opposite Jason Robards, Jr. in the Twentieth Century–Fox, CinemaScope color release.)

In spite of Miss Drake's earlier pronouncement that she and her husband would not act together again, they came along together in *Room for One More* (Warner Bros., 1952). In the Rose household live Poppy (Cary), Anna (Betsy), their three children (Gay Gordon, Malcolm Cassell, George "Foghorn" Winslow), and several pets. Betsy is a real softy for strays, and soon branches out from homeless animals to humans. Little Iris Mann joins the family and in time is convinced that she is wanted for herself. Then comes Jimmy-John (Clifford Tatum, Jr.), a mean kid with braces on his legs and a chip on his shoulder. He is almost given up as a lost cause but finally breaks down and cries, showing that his outer shell has been penetrated by the Rose family's kindness. The Venice Film Festival of 1952 cited this movie with a special-mention award for its "positive treatment of social problems regarding childhood and adolescence." However, there were viewers who thought this low-keyed, folksy comedy-drama was a downward step for the once elegant superstar that was Cary Grant.

Cary sported a crew-cut hair style for the Howard Hawks–directed comedy *Monkey Business* (Twentieth Century–Fox, 1952). As in *Bringing up Baby*, he is a dedicated scientist (in thick-lensed horn-rimmed glasses), but this time he is in search of a formula that will restore youthful vigor to those in the middle years or beyond. One of the chimpanzees used for experimental purposes meddles with the ingredients one day, and concocts a mixture that winds up in the water cooler. Professor Grant is the first to drink from the cooler, and the brew causes him to act like a college boy. He takes a secretary (Marilyn Monroe) skating, swimming, and for a fast spin in a new car. His wife (Ginger Rogers) then has a cup of water and acts like an overaged adolescent. The third time around, they both drink—still not knowing that the water contains the formula—and they revert to unruly childhood.

About Cary's next film, the *Los Angeles Times* critic said it was "a rather fantastic comedy contrived to allow Cary Grant a field day with his typical facial and vocal tricks." The picture, *Dream Wife* (MGM, 1953), has him as a businessman who wants to be married immediately. By means of a cablegram, he proposes to the Princess Tarji (Betta St. John) of Bukistan, whom he met while on a trip to that country. But by the film's end he returns to his old love, Effie (Deborah

With Robert Cornthwaite, Ginger Rogers and Marilyn Monroe in MONKEY BUSINESS (20th '52)

Kerr), who has learned that her State Department post is not everything.

In the early 1950s, Cary stopped smoking. He credited this achievement to the work of Betsy, who put him into a hypnotic state and prompted his decision. He also gave up drinking. "Now I can devote my energy to the only vice I've got left —lovemaking," he said. Cary has also credited Betsy with teaching him how to relax. He has said: "I believe that sixty is the prime of life—it will be for me. Everyone shapes himself like a sculptor. If you decide that you are going to be handsome, youthful and fit for the rest of your life, you will be. It's as simple as that."

Despite the fact that the Grants financially supported a foster child in Italy, Cary got the Hollywood reputation of being a miser. The Grants seldom entertained, and he was said to derive his chief enjoyment from reading, yoga, astrology, and a daily steam bath with massage. Like Robert Montgomery and Adolphe Menjou, among others, he carried nothing in his pockets that might make a bulge in his clothing. His pockets contained only keys and a folded $50 bill for emergencies. One of his theories was that men were self-centered idiots until they were thirty-five. As he has admitted: "I know I was impossible before that age. I'm barely possible now. I may be more of a bore, but I feel I'm less of a boor." Mental health became of prime interest to him, and through a psychiatrist he began a series of controlled sessions with a hallucinogenic drug known as LSD 25. He has described it since in the following manner: "The feeling is that of an unmarshaling of the thoughts as you've customarily associated them. The lessening of conscious control, similar to the mental process which takes place when we dream."

Late in 1953, columnist Sheilah Graham wrote: "I guess Cary Grant doesn't realize the good old bad days of huge salaries will never come back." She referred to his demands of $300,000 to co-star at Warner Bros. with Judy Garland in the musicalized *A Star Is Born* (1954). Since the studio could not afford him in this George Cukor–directed picture, James Mason got the assignment. About the same time, Grant turned down the role of Linus Larrabee in Paramount's *Sabrina* (1954) and Humphrey Bogart was substituted.

The Grants acquired a home in Palm Springs, where they spent much of their time, as well as two Rolls Royces, one for use in California (costing $13,000) and one kept in London (costing $18,000). While filmland commentators speculated on his possible screen retirement, Grant accepted Alfred Hitchcock's offer of $300,000, or ten percent of the gross, to star in a mystery melodrama. For the filming he and Betsy went to France in September 1954. They stopped over in Bristol, England, where they visited Elsie Leach. Grant claimed to have derived a deeper understanding of both parents through his "acid" treatments, and longed to be friends with the mother he had not seen in more than twenty years.

Grant's third film with Hitchcock, *To Catch a Thief* (Paramount, 1955) was opulent in the manner of a later Ross Hunter film production, and was photographed in VistaVision and color by Robert Burks against the splendor of Cannes. John Robie (Grant), a notorious jewel thief known in his heyday as "The Cat," is retired and reformed, and lives peaceably on the Riviera. His complacency is shattered when a series of thefts are committed in his style. He is immediately suspected by the police, but the representative (John Williams) of the insurance company hit hardest by the robberies believes he is innocent and helps him find the emulator. Next on the probable list of victims is Mrs. Stevens (Jessie Royce Landis), a very rich, very outspoken widow with a beautiful daughter (Grace Kelly), for whom she hopes to snare a proper husband. Grant falls in love with Kelly and she finds him exciting because he had been a thief, although he has no intention of re-

With Grace Kelly in TO CATCH A THIEF (Par '55)

turning to his past vocation. "Why should I steal?" he says, "I'm rich." She asks: "How did you become rich?" and he replies: "By stealing." With everyone aiding Grant, the thief is apprehended after a rooftop chase. And, of course, Grace catches her own thief (Grant) for a spouse.

Said *Variety:* "Grant once again demonstrates he is a master of timing, getting laughs where a lesser talent would draw a blank." Filmgoers were particularly enthusiastic about the romantic scenes between Cary and blonde Kelly, reminiscent of the best moments from *Notorious.* In addition, *To Catch a Thief** contains the famous *double-entendre* sequence in which picnicking Kelly asks Grant whether he would prefer a leg or a breast (of chicken, naturally).

In the mid-1950s, Italian sexpot actress Sophia Loren made several badly produced Hollywood-financed features. There were *Boy on a Dolphin* (Twentieth Century–Fox, 1957) with Alan Ladd, and *Legend of the Lost* (United Artists, 1957) with John Wayne. Then there was Stanley Kramer's production of C. S. Forester's novel *The Gun,* entitled *The Pride and the Passion* (United Artists, 1957). Filmed in Spain, the story revolves around the rescue of a giant cannon from the Spanish which is to be delivered to a British warship. The time is during the Napoleonic wars of the early 1800s when the French armies occupied much of Spain. Grant, as the English sea captain (he is the "Pride") who has a knowledge of ordnance, is in charge of the project. Frank Sinatra (he is the "Passion") is the Spanish guerrilla leader, who wants and gets the cannon in order to blast the French out of his occupied village. The terrorists then help the British lug the monumental cast-iron firearm across Spain. Loren is the lovely, large-chested patriot who is loved by both men. The picture was an artistic bust. "Plainly, there are more logistics than logic in this film. Without passion and without logic, it merely rambles in the realm of massive display. This is what often happens when producers try to be Cecil B. DeMille" (Bosley Crowther, *New York Times*). *The Pride and the Passion* was to be Grant's third and final foray into historical period pieces. He was too contemporary by temperament to emote properly in such visual set pieces.

According to the consensus of reports at the time, Grant fell in love with twenty-three-year-

* *To Catch a Thief* grossed $4.5 million in distributor's domestic rentals, $300,000 less than *Notorious.* The video series, "It Takes a Thief" (ABC-TV: January 9, 1968, 65 episodes), starring Robert Wagner, was based on the Grant-Kelly-Hitchcock feature film.

With Sophia Loren in THE PRIDE AND THE PASSION (UA '57)

old Sophia, but was discouraged in his romantic pursuit by her devotion to producer Carlo Ponti. Betsy Drake had paid a short visit to Spain during the six months her husband was there, but reportedly left in good humor and with friendly words, later for her husband.* Cary took a protective interest in Miss Loren and attempted to lure her to Hollywood to star in a film with him there. He thought she would do better in American films than in those of Italy. However, she decided to return home, for the time being, where she married Ponti in 1957.

Grant's next outing was *An Affair to Remember* (Twentieth Century–Fox, 1957) in which he is Nickie Ferrante, a polished, mature artist who is enroute from Europe to New York to meet his fiancée (Neva Patterson). On board the transatlantic liner is Deborah Kerr, a former nightclub singer with her own past to hide. They fall in love, but endure a long separation before they are eventually reunited, each having proven to the other's satisfaction in the meantime, that he or she is a sound human being, he as a painter, she as a children's tutor. Moviegoers who had been around in 1939 recalled this story as having been the basis of *Love Affair* (RKO) with Charles Boyer and Irene Dunne. The new version, also directed by Leo McCarey, suffered from overexpansion, the utilization of saccharin musical interludes, and too much dependence on the virtues of the CinemaScope film process rather than the essential ingredients of romantic film fare. In the years since *Dream Wife,* Kerr had developed into a far more freer performer, capable of not only complementing but revitalizing Cary's brand of screen elan. It was unfortunate that this new film did not present them in the best light.

When Sam Spiegel asked Cary if he would be interested in playing the role of Shears in his Columbia production of *The Bridge on the River Kwai* (1957), the actor's immediate response was affirmative. By the time Cary received the script, though, he had just returned to Hollywood from Europe and was tired of traveling. Since the picture was to be shot largely on location in Ceylon, Grant told Spiegel that he would "think it over." In the meantime, William Holden had been contacted and he postponed a year's vacation from moviemaking to accept the stellar assignment. "By then, of course, I realized what a great part I had lost," said Cary.

While in San Francisco in the spring of 1957

With Deborah Kerr in AN AFFAIR TO REMEMBER (20th '57)

for the lensing of *Kiss Them for Me* (Twentieth Century–Fox, 1957) Grant talked with the want-ad staff of the *San Francisco Examiner.* During his address he described the "slice of life" type of actor: "He tries not to stay still because he feels so vulnerable before the all-seeing camera. It's really most difficult to be yourself, serene, relaxed. But, alas, the critics, knowing what we do, give prizes for the easiest type of parts to play." When a member of the staff asked if it was easy to turn on emotion before getting into a scene, he replied: "Really no emotion is involved. It's a matter of almost hypnosis. You stand off and watch yourself act—like a child throwing a tantrum in front of a mirror." Responding with the famous flashing smile when questioned as to his favorite screen role, he said: "I haven't got one. I love them all— even the flops. I love my business."

Director Stanley Donen turned back the clock for San Francisco's Nob Hill in order to create the atmosphere of 1944 for *Kiss Them for Me,* based on the Luther Davis play (Belasco Theatre: March 20, 1945, 110 performances)‡ and the novel *Shore Leave* by Frederic Wakeman. The story is of three Navy fliers (Grant, Ray Walston, Larry Blyden) in

With Ingrid Bergman in INDISCREET (WB '58)

na Kalman (Bergman). Everyone was so busy being overly polite in this symmetrical vehicle that an antiseptic air hung over the movie like a cloak of death. Sadder to note was the obvious fact that time had withered the romantic sparks that once had jumped so passionately between Cary and Ingrid.

For *Houseboat* (Paramount, 1958) Cary's co-star was Sophia Loren, whose beauty and acting ability Carlo Ponti had sold to that studio for four features. As Cinzia Zaccardi, Sophia, as the daughter of musician Eduardo Ciannelli, is accompanying her father on a tour of America. She finds herself becoming the houseboat babysitter to Grant's three children (Charles Herbert, Mimi Gibson, Paul Peterson) and a competitor with wealthy Martha Hyer for Grant's romantic attentions. Hyer may have lost Grant in the film, but she became another convert to his gracious on-the-set manner. "Cary is wonderful to work with —he is fun as well as always professionally perfect." *Houseboat,* no worldbeater at setting new artistic standards, was just the type of inoffensive screen entertainment that continued to make money in distribution. In U.S. and Canadian playdates alone it grossed over $3.5 million in rentals, proving that Cary Grant's name still meant a great deal at the box office.

But on the home front, the Grant charisma was not so attractive. Betsy Drake moved out of the Grant house in September 1958. She said: "I left Cary, but physically, he'd left me long ago. I was still in love with him, and I'm not ashamed to say so. But he's going through a tremendous change. Who knows? He may come back to me, or not marry at all, or marry somebody quite different from me. He's dizzy! Enormously stimulating! Younger than many men I know." Cary composed the following announcement to the press on both their behalfs: "We have had, and shall always have, a deep love and respect for each other, but, alas, our marriage has not brought us the happiness we fully expected and mutually desired. So, since there are no children needful of our affection, it is consequently best that we separate for a while."

Once again, Grant became an open target for the romance rumor mills. In Europe, at the Cannes Film Festival of May 1959, he was photographed dancing all night with Kim Novak, and in London he was coupled with young Yugoslav actress Luba Otasevic. The latter had been Sophia Loren's double for *The Key* (Columbia, 1958).

San Francisco on a four-day leave. They acquire a suite at the Fairmount Hotel where they go to a wild party and meet Jayne Mansfield, a dramatically shapely blonde, who is doing all she can for the war effort. Said *Motion Picture Herald:* "Grant, even though a bit old as a dashing pilot, is wonderful, be he romantic, comic, bitter or sad."

In March 1957, Grant accepted for Ingrid Bergman the Academy Award as Best Actress for her performance in *Anastasia* (Twentieth Century–Fox, 1956). He had remained friendly with her throughout the long early 1950s period when her offscreen romance-marriage to Italian director Roberto Rosellini had made her *persona non grata* in the Hollywood community.

Indiscreet (Warner Bros., 1958) came next on Cary's agenda, being his second film opposite Ingrid Bergman and his second with director Stanley Donen. Described by *Catholic World* as "an attempt to revive the kind of urbane romantic comedy that was popular some twenty years ago," it was adapted by Norman Krasna from his play *Kind Sir.** Although the film's action takes place in London, it was actually shot in Hollywood, with Cary playing a financial wizard who becomes besmitten with West End stage actress An-

*On Broadway (Alvin Theatre: November 4, 1953, 165 performances) the comedy starred Mary Martin and Charles Boyer.

Alfred Hitchcock, who once called Cary his favorite actor, starred him in his 1959 production, *North by Northwest* (MGM). Sophia Loren was to have played the feminine lead, but Eva Marie Saint took over that role when Hitchcock and Ponti were unable to come to terms. It is one of the brightest shaggy-dog spy capers to have ever appeared on screen, an adroit mixture of sophisticated dialog, visual splendor, and a steady pacing that prevents the viewer from grasping too quickly all the plot absurdities. Before the action winds to a finish, the perplexed hero (Grant) has embarked on a cross-country chase which concludes in and about the massive stone faces that adorn Mount Rushmore. He discovers that James Mason and his spy ring have mistaken him for a nonexistent spy named Kaplan who was manufactured by a U.S. Government agent known as the Professor (Leo G. Carroll). Blonde, icy Saint is Mason's accomplice, who transfers her attention and affections to the beguiling, bemused, aggressive Grant.

Critics were unable to believe much of the action, but the public liked the film to the comfortable tune of providing $6.31 million in MGM domestic rentals.

Operation Petticoat (Universal, 1959) was produced by Grant's own company, Granart.* In the role of Sherman, the skipper of a submarine badly damaged in the Philippines by the Japanese, he uses his facial expressions (at which he had become a master) in place of a lot of talk in order to convey his oversized reactions to the subsequent comic happenings. The sub is nearly junked by the U.S. Navy as irreparable, but Grant and his crew are determined to see it in operation again. In drydock at Port Darwin they take on an admiral's aide (Tony Curtis) who is most adept at procuring the necessities that help get the sub in working order. He also provides, as passengers, a bevy of nurses headed by Joan O'Brien (for himself) and Dina Merrill (for Grant). This Blake Edwards–directed silliness grossed $9.5 million in distributors domestic rentals.

Cary bought the London stage comedy *The Grass Is Greener*† as a property for his company. The film went before the cameras in England in January 1960, and was released through Universal on November 29, 1960. Directed by Stanley Donen, it boasted a cast of four big names: Grant, Deborah Kerr, Robert Mitchum, and Jean Sim-

In NORTH BY NORTHWEST (MGM '59)

mons.‡ The comedy of impolite manners is set into motion when Victor, the earl of Rhyall (Grant), and Countess Hilary (Kerr) open the major portion of their elegant estate to weekly tourists. A paid sightseer, Texas oilman Mitchum, happens into the owners' private room where he makes a play for Kerr. When she does not discourage his advances, Cary becomes jealous and enlists the aid of family friend Simmons to make a pass, in turn, at the pushy American.

That Touch of Mink (Universal, 1962) was another feature financed by Cary's company. This time he chose the "Miss Clean" of the American motion-picture screen, Doris Day, as his co-star. She had entered a very successful phase of her movie career with a series of well-mounted sex comedies with Rock Hudson. For all its derivative inventiveness, this new Grant film could have been *Pillow Talk* (Universal, 1959) or *Lover, Come Back* (Universal, 1962). Under Delbert Mann's direction, the premise (will wealthy bachelor Grant get Manhattan newcomer Day to bed or the altar?) extended for ninety-nine profitable minutes. The film grossed $8.5 million in the

*Grant originated his own producing company in 1958. Known by various names at assorted times (Granart, Granox, Grandon, Granley), the firm's offices were at Universal Studios until Grant moved out when the studio's commercial tours interfered with his serenity.
†Based on the London stage hit (St. Martin's Theatre: December 2, 1958, 493 performances) that starred Hugh Williams, Celia Johnson, Joan Greenwood, and Edward Underdown in the roles played oncamera by Cary, Kerr, Simmons, and Mitchum.
‡One of the few times in her career onscreen that Miss Simmons has played it for laughs.

With Moray Watson and Robert Mitchum in THE GRASS IS GREENER (Univ '61)

With Doris Day in THAT TOUCH OF MINK (Univ '62)

United States and Canada alone. Grant was now showing all of his fifty-six years.

On August 14, 1962, almost four years after their separation, Grant and Betsy Drake were divorced. Although they remained friends, Betsy said: "He preferred watching TV to talking to me. He appeared to be bored with me. He once told me he didn't want to be married. He showed no interest in my friends." On the subject of the failure of his three marriages, Grant said: "I thought too much about my career and not enough about my wives. I was emotionally immature and persisted in my stupidities." At the same time, he was in pursuit of a young (twenty-two-year-old) actress named Dyan Cannon.*

Warner Bros. seemed intent on transforming Cary into a movie musical star by offering him, first, the Professor Hill role in the screen version of *The Music Man* (1962). "Not only will I not do it," he told them, "but if you don't use Robert Preston, I won't go to see it." Secondly, the studio came to him with a lucrative deal to talk-sing his way through a screen portrayal of Henry Higgins in *My Fair Lady* (1964). He turned it down, explaining: "I just didn't think anyone could do better than Rex Harrison." Pertaining to both screen roles, he added: "I just think that once something

*Born Camille Firesen in Tacoma, Washington. She had appeared in several video shows under the name Diane Cannon.

172

has been done to perfection, why interfere with success?"*

Some may have thought that Cary was so firmly entrenched as a movie-industry-establishment symbol that he had no awareness of changing tastes and interests in the filmmaking business. But he was fully cognizant of his capabilities in front of a camera and how to best showcase them for contemporary public approval. "There is no doubt that I am aging," he admitted in the early 1960s. "My format of comedy is still the same as ever. I gravitate toward scripts that put me in an untenable position. Then the rest of the picture is spent in trying to squirm out of it. I always get the girl in the end."

Charade (Universal, 1963), produced and directed by Stanley Donen, was the same Grant formula, but with a few twists. For one thing it greatly benefited from the presence of his leading lady number fifty, Audrey Hepburn, as the woman whose husband is murdered before she can divorce him. Grant's Peter Joshua† agrees to help the Parisian miss out of her plight when she is threatened by three of her late spouse's former colleagues (James Coburn, George Kennedy, Ned Glass). Grant comes to the rescue. Another upbeat diversion to this thriller, shot largely on location in the French capital, was Donen's decision to give the picture a very mod look, from its Charles Lang cinematography, to Miss Hepburn's Givenchy wardrobe, to the Henry Mancini score. In addition, Grant went through athletic paces in his confrontations with the terrible three and with alleged CIA agent Hamilton Bartholomew (Walter Matthau) that were exhausting enough to tire a much younger screen hero.

Father Goose (Universal, 1964) was Cary's twenty-eighth film to play at New York's Radio City Music Hall during Christmas week, the prime showplace and the prize showtime. His record tops all others, with Katharine Hepburn's twenty-two films next in line.

For the first time in his screen career, Cary played a true bum—unshaven (which hid his age), unkempt, and, for the most part, drunk. He is Walter Eckland, who has withdrawn from civilization to an uninhabited Pacific isle. It is wartime and he is tricked by Australian naval officer Trevor Howard into watching and reporting from his launch the movement of Japanese planes and ships. His radio code designation is "Mother Goose." In attempting to rescue a fellow watcher on a neighboring island, he finds the man dead

With Audrey Hepburn in CHARADE (Univ '63)

and a French woman (Leslie Caron) with seven little girls hiding from the Japs. Despite, or perhaps because of, its conventional plotting and execution, *Father Goose* grossed over $6 million in distributors domestic rentals.

On June 22, 1965, David O. Selznick died of a coronary occlusion. At the funeral service, a few days later, at Forest Lawn Cemetery, Grant read a tribute written by William Paley, the head of CBS Television and a good friend of Selznick's. Paley had intended to read it himself, but was too overcome with grief. Grant read: "I cannot help but think that our world will never be the same—nor will heaven. And, if we are lucky enough to get there, too, David will see that all arrangements are made."

One month later, on July 22, 1965, Grant and Dyan Cannon were married in secrecy at Las Vegas, Nevada. Grant was sixty-one, while she was twenty-six. For their honeymoon, they visited his eighty-seven-year-old mother in Bristol, England, who habitually called her son's new bride by the name of Betsy. Before she married him, Dyan was aware that Grant was a stay-at-home. "Then it didn't bother me, because I was working," she had said. "But later it became quite a difficult

---

*Rex Harrison, in repeating the Henry Higgins role onscreen, won the Academy Award as Best Actor of 1964.
†The public, for the first time, saw Cary with silver streaks (real ones) throughout his hair.

With Leslie Caron in FATHER GOOSE (Univ '65)

thing to stay at home all day and watch TV at night." Soon after their marriage, Dyan suspected that she was pregnant. When this was medically confirmed, the couple celebrated by going to a night baseball game to watch Grant's favorite team, the Los Angeles Dodgers.

Grant hurried to Tokyo to fulfill an obligation on behalf of his Granley Company and Sol C. Siegel. In *Walk, Don't Run* (Columbia, 1966),* Grant is William Rutland, a titled British industrialist in Tokyo during the 1964 Olympics. Unable to find lodgings, he talks Samantha Eggar into letting him share half of her apartment. Then, after meeting an American long-distance runner (Jim Hutton), Grant subleases half of his half to him. A highlight of this less than ebullient comedy was a sequence in which Grant, dressed only in his underwear, jauntily joins a cross-city Olympic marathon race. Said Arthur Knight (*Saturday Review*) of "the unflawed elegance of Mr. Grant," "With a light, bright touch and a debonair smile, he gives the film the happy sheen of a charade that must never be taken seriously. It almost works." Other critics were too concerned that Grant, for the first time in his movie career,

did not win the girl, and let the chance go by to appraise the Cary Grant touch. A shame, for it was to be his final motion picture.

On February 26, 1966, Jennifer Grant was born two months prematurely at St. Joseph's Hospital in Burbank, California. She weighed four pounds, eight ounces. A father for the first time (at sixty-two), Cary enthusiastically took part in Jennifer's daily care. "She's the most winsome, captivating girl I've ever known," he said, "and I've known quite a few girls." Jennifer was not given a middle name because "if she wants one, she can choose it later," he said. "Every child should have this privilege. I used to cringe at my name."

In July 1966, Cary and Dyan took Jennifer to Bristol to meet the infant's grandmother, but by then the marriage had turned sour. In 1967 the Grants separated, although they continued to live together, for the baby's sake. On November 6, 1967, Dyan made her return to Broadway as the star of a sex comedy, *Ninety Day Mistress*, which featured Martin Milner, Ruth Ford, and Walter Abel in the cast.‡ It folded after twenty-four performances.

On March 12, 1968, the rented limousine in

*A remake of *The More the Merrier* (Columbia, 1943), in which Charles Coburn originated the role played in 1966 by Grant. Coburn's performance got him the 1943 Oscar as Best Supporting Actor.
‡She had previously had a minor part in the Jane Fonda–Bradford Dillman "comedy" *The Fun Couple* then trying for a run in London (Lyceum Theatre: October 26, 1962, 3 performances).

With Jim Hutton in WALK, DON'T RUN (Col '66)

which Grant was being driven on the Long Island Expressway toward Kennedy Airport was hit by a truck. The chauffeur, Grant's passenger, Baroness Gratia von Furstenberg, and the star wound up in St. John's Queens Hospital. Cary suffered chest pains, and because his lips and nose were swollen, he had to be fed intravenously. During his seventeen-day hospitalization, he received some 650 get-well letters from women around the country, and a friend remarked that the flowers in his room outnumbered those found at state funerals. Cary remarked, "I feel like I'm in a B picture." In a damage suit against the trucking company, he was awarded $70,000, which he split with the baroness. The rental car company was awarded an additional $2,500.

On April 1, 1968, Cary and Dyan Cannon were granted a divorce during a turbulent courtroom hearing in which she accused him of abusing her in front of servants and spanking her while he was on an LSD trip. Dyan's former agent confirmed her contention that Cary had tried to "break" her and transform her in accordance with his special concept of what a wife should be. Dyan received custody of Jennifer, as well as $50,000 annually in alimony and child support. There were several restrictive clauses written into the agreement. It was ordained that Jennifer would spend ninety days a year with her father.

With then wife Dyan Cannon and their daughter Jennifer, 1966

(It now seemed *so* long ago that Grant, in jubilation over the birth of his child and his happy marriage had made his recording debut with a 45 RPM for Columbia Records called "Christmas Lullaby," with lyrics by his good friend Peggy Lee.) At Cary's further insistence, the court also decreed that Jennifer's face should never be photographed because of his fear of kidnappers.

Later in 1968, Grant sued Twentieth Century–Fox for using scenes in which he appeared with Marilyn Monroe in *Monkey Business* for their *Marilyn* compilation feature. Cary claimed that the scenes were utilized without his express permission. He further stated that he had received no payment and that the action hurt him professionally. His $1 million lawsuit was settled out of court for ten dollars.

Over the years since *Walk, Don't Run* there had been rumors that Cary would make his screen return in this or that film, but nothing materialized, not even a part in his good friend Mervyn LeRoy's projected feature *Cowboys and Indians*. Cary repeatedly refused all sorts of beguiling offers to appear on various television shows, although he did relent in 1969 to being a guest on a planned Mae West video special, which was filmed in part, but was never aired. When Cary was appointed to the board of directors of Faberge, Inc., in May 1968, the dye seemed cast that he was abandoning the show-business world in his capacity as entertainer. He was asked how it felt to be a big businessman. He replied, "What makes you think I wasn't always a big businessman? Do you know of any other business where a man can earn a million dollars in ten weeks?" Later he became an executive of Western Airlines, but devoted most of his activities to being a goodwill ambassador for Faberge, especially after their Brut Productions division entered into motion-picture and television activities.

At the forty-second annual award ceremony of the Academy of Motion Picture Arts and Sciences, held April 7, 1970, at the Dorothy Chandler Pavilion of the Los Angeles County Music Center, Cary Grant was honored with a special Oscar. The accolade, voted by the directors of the academy weeks before and publicized, was to have been presented to him by Grace Kelly. A few weeks prior to the event, a false allegation had been published stating that Cary was the father of the daughter of a Los Angeles woman, Mrs. Cynthia Bouron.* When Mrs. Bouron filed a paternity

suit, Cary counter-sued and announced his intention of not appearing at the Award ceremony. When the suit was dismissed because Mrs. Bouron refused to take a blood test, Cary agreed to be present for the April 7 telecast.

Princess Grace then cabled regrets that she was not able to appear because one of her children was ill. Frank Sinatra was substituted for Miss Kelly in presenting the award for "sheer brilliance; no actor had ever made acting seem easier." Clips were shown of some of Grant's films. He thanked the Academy directors and predicted: "There's an even more glorious era around the corner." He brushed away tears from his eyes and avowed that he would cherish the award "Until I die, for no honor is greater than the respect of one's colleagues."

In 1972 Cary became a U.S. advisor to a development company involved with the building of a $10 million, seven-hundred-room resort near Shannon, Ireland. Cary reserved a three-acre plot for himself because "I just thought that Jennifer is growing up. When she is a teenager, she will want somewhere to take her friends."

Cary Grant of the 1970s

---

*Mrs. Bouron, a friend of Gardner McKay, and ex-wife of actor Milos Milos, former stuntman to Alain Delon, was murdered in November 1973. Her bludgeoned body was found stuffed into the trunk of a car parked at a Studio City, California, supermarket.

Also in 1972, Cary sued *Esquire* magazine for $3 million for its unauthorized use of his photographs (taken from a 1946 authorized *Esquire* fashion ad) shown promoting Forum Sportswear.

Although he turned down a major role in *Sleuth* (Twentieth Century–Fox, 1972) with "I decided it would be too much work," he continued his court actions against Dyan whenever he thought she was not complying with the law or his demands with regards to Jennifer. Dyan was unable to take a role in *Night Watch* (Avco Embassy, 1973), one of Faberge's Brut Productions, because she was prevented from going to London with the child. Next, she was forbidden to take Jennifer to Europe while she filmed *The Last of Sheila* (Warner Bros., 1973), but Cary later took their daughter to see Dyan at her French Riviera location, claiming that the girl was lonesome for her mother.

New charges were registered by Dyan in 1973 when Cary bought a beach house at Malibu, a few houses away from her. She complained that he was spying on her and claimed that he made Jennifer change her clothing whenever she visited him because he did not approve of Dyan's choice of wardrobe. In November 1973, they went to court over custody of Jennifer's passport. The judge ruled that they would have alternate custody, with Grant taking charge of the document during even-numbered years.

On January 18, 1974, Cary noted his seventieth birthday, but he declined to participate in the plans of friends to exploit the event. He said that he was not really certain that it was his seventieth birthday because his birth records had been destroyed in Bristol during the war. While some news sources were insisting he was dating twenty-seven-year-old Maureen Donaldson, a Hollywood gossip-magazine writer, others insisted that young Victoria Morgan was *the* woman in his life. Cary, meantime, seemed to be interested in the welfare of only one young lady, his daughter Jennifer.

Meanwhile, in July, 1975, Cary was elected to the board of Metro-Goldwyn-Mayer, Inc. According to the film company, the decision was due to the star's "credits as an actor and as an astute businessman."

Since he refuses to settle down into any sort of standard retirement, there can be no living postscript to the career of Cary Grant. Perhaps the thrust of his life to date is best summed up by his remark of a few years ago: "I know I'm sticking my neck out in saying this, and the ill-fortuned won't agree with me. But I do believe people can do practically anything they set out to do—if they apply themselves diligently and learn. Few people recognize opportunity because it comes disguised as hard work and application.

"Too often people are afraid of disappointment. But how can you learn without disappointment—or without making the mistakes that lead to disappointment? How else can you grow?"

Cary Grant

THIS IS THE NIGHT (PAR, 1932) 65 M.

Director, Frank Tuttle; based on the play Pouche *by Rene Peter, Henri Falk; screenplay, Avery Hopwood; dialog-lyrics, George Marion, Jr.; music, Ralph Rainger; camera, Victor Milner.*

Lily Damita (Germaine); Charles Ruggles (Bunny West); Roland Young (Gerald Grey); Thelma Todd (Claire); Cary Grant (Stephen); Irving Bacon (Jacques); Claire Dodd (Chou-Chou); Davison Clark (Studio Official).

SINNERS IN THE SUN (PAR, 1932) 70 M.

Director, Alexander Hall; based on the story, "Beach-Comber" by Mildred Cram; screenplay, Waldemar Young, Samuel Hoffenstein; camera, Ray June.

Carole Lombard (Doris Blake); Chester Morris (Jimmie Martin); Adrienne Ames (Claire Kinkaid); Alison Skipworth (Mrs. Blake); Walter Byron (Eric Nelson); Reginald Barlow (Mr. Blake); Zita Moulton (Mrs. Florence Nelson); Cary Grant (Ridgeway); Luke Cosgrave (Grandfather Blake); Ida Lewis (Grandmother Blake); Russ Clark (Fred Blake); Frances Moffett (Mrs. Fred Blake); Pierre De Ramey (Louis); Veda Buckland (Emma); Rita La Roy (Lil); Maude Turner Gordon (Wife); Anderson Lawler (Gigolo).

MERRILY WE GO TO HELL (PAR, 1932) 88 M.

Director, Dorothy Arzner; based on the play I, Jerry, Take Thee, Joan *by Cleo Lucas; screenplay, Edwin Justus Mayer; camera, David Abel.*

Sylvia Sidney (Joan Prentice); Fredric March (Jerry Corbett); Adrianne Allen (Claire Hempstead); Skeets Gallagher (Buck); Florence Britton (Charlie); Esther Howard (Vi); George Irving (Mr. Prentice); Kent Taylor (Dick Taylor); Charles Coleman (Damery); Leonard Carey (Butler); Milla Davenport (Housekeeper); Robert Greig (Baritone); Reverend Neal Dodd (Minister); Mildred Boyd (June); Cary Grant (Charlie Exeter, the Stage Leading Man); Edwin Maxwell (Agent).

THE DEVIL AND THE DEEP (PAR, 1932) 70 M.

Director, Marion Gering; story, Harry Hervey; screenplay, Benn Levy; costumes, Travis Banton; art director, Bernard Herzbrun; sound, J. A. Goodrich; camera, Charles Lang; editor, Otho Lovering.

Tallulah Bankhead (Pauline Sturm); Gary Cooper (Lieutenant Sempter); Charles Laughton (Commander Sturm); Cary Grant (Lieutenant Jaeckel); Paul Porcasi (Hassan); Juliette Compton (Mrs. Planet); Henry Kolker (Hutton); Dorothy

Christy (Mrs. Crimp); Arthur Hoyt (Mr. Planet); Gordon Westcott (Lieutenant Toll); Jimmie Dugan (Condover); Kent Taylor (A Friend); Lucien Littlefield (Shopkeeper); Peter Brocco (Wireless Operator); Wilfred Lucas (Court Martial Judge); Henry Guttman, George Magrill, Dave O'Brien (Submarine Crewmen).

BLONDE VENUS (PAR, 1932) 85 M.

Director-story, Josef von Sternberg; screenplay, Jules Furthman, S. K. Lauren; art director, Wiard Ihnen; songs, Sam Coslow and Ralph Rainger; Leo Robin and Dick Whiting; music, Oscar Potoker; camera, Bert Glennon.

Marlene Dietrich (Helen Faraday); Herbert Marshall [Edward (Ned) Faraday]; Cary Grant (Nick Townsend); Dickie Moore (Johnny Faraday); Francis Sayles (Charlie Blaine); Robert Emmet O'Connor (Dan O'Connor); Gene Morgan (Ben Smith); Rita La Roy (Taxi Belle Hooper); Sidney Toler (Detective Wilson); Morgan Wallace (Dr. Pierce); Evelyn Preer (Lola); Mildred Washington (Black Girl); Gertrude Short (Receptionist); Harold Berquist (Big Fellow); Dewey Robinson (Greek Proprietor); Davison Clark (Judge Night Court/Bartender); Brady Kline (New Orleans Officer); Clifford Dempsey (Judge at Nightclub); Bessie Lyle (Grace); Sterling Holloway (Hitchhiker); Al Bridge (Bouncer); Mary Gordon (Landlady); Cecil Cunningham (Cabaret Owner); Hattie McDaniel (Cora, the Maid); Marcelle Corday (French Maid); Pat Somerset (Companion); Kent Taylor (Extra).

HOT SATURDAY (PAR, 1932) 73 M.

Director, William A. Seiter; based on the novel by Harvey Ferguson; adaptors, Josephine Lovett, Joseph Moncure March; screenplay, Seton I. Miller; camera, Arthur L. Todd.

Nancy Carroll (Ruth Brock); Cary Grant (Romer Sheffield); Randolph Scott (Bill Fadden); Edward Woods (Conny Billop); Lilian Bond (Eva Randolph); William Collier, Sr. (Harry Brock); Jane Darwell (Mrs. Brock); Rita La Roy (Camille); Rose Coughlan (Annie Brock); Oscar Apfel (Ed W. Randolph); Jessie Arnold (Aunt Minnie); Grady Sutton (Archie).

MADAME BUTTERFLY (PAR, 1932) 86 M.

Director, Marion Gering; based on the story by John Luther Long, and the play by David Belasco; screenplay, Josephine Lovett, Joseph Moncure March; music from the opera by Giacomo Puccini; music, W. Franke Harling; camera, David Abel.

Sylvia Sidney (Cho-Cho San); Cary Grant (Lieutenant B. F. Pinkerton); Charlie Ruggles (Lieutenant Barton); Sandor Kallay (Goro); Irving Pichel (Yomadori); Helen Jerome Eddy (Cho-Cho's Mother); Edmund Breese (Cho-Cho's Grandfather); Judith Vosselli (Madame Goro); Louise Carter (Suzuki); Dorothy Libaire (Peach Blossom); Sheila Terry (Mrs. Pinkerton); Wallis Clark (Commander Anderson); Berton Churchill (American Consul); Philip Horomato (Trouble).

SHE DONE HIM WRONG (PAR, 1933) 66 M.

Producer, William LeBaron; director, Lowell Sherman; based on the play Diamond Lil by Mae West; screenplay, Harve Thew, John Bright; songs, Ralph Rainger; art director, Bob Usher; costumes, Edith Head; choreography, Harold Hecht; assistant director, James Dugan; sound, Harry M. Lindgren; camera, Charles Lang; editor, Alexander Hall.

Mae West (Lady Lou); Cary Grant [Captain Cummings (The Hawk)]; Owen Moore (Chick Clark); Gilbert Roland (Serge Staneoff); Noah Beery, Sr. (Gus Jordan); David Landau (Dan Flynn); Rafaela Ottiano (Russian Rita); Dewey Robinson (Spider Kane); Rochelle Hudson (Sally); Tammany Young (Connors); Fuzzy Knight (Ragtime Kelly); Grace LaRue (Frances); Robert E. Homans (Doheney); Louise Beavers (Pearl); Wade Boteler (Pat); Aggie Herring (Mrs. Flaherty); Tom Kennedy (Big Billy); James C. Eagles (Pete); Tom McGuire (Mike); Al Hill, Arthur Housman (Bar Flies); Mary Gordon (Cleaning Lady); Michael Mark (Janitor); Mike Donlin (Tout); Harry Wallace (Steak McGarry); Lee Kohlmar (Jacob-

son); Frank Moran (Framed Convict); Heinie Conklin (Street Cleaner); Jack Carr (Patron); Ernie Adams (Man in Audience).

WOMAN ACCUSED (PAR, 1933) 73 M.

Director, Paul Sloane; based on the magazine serial authored by Rupert Hughes, Vicki Baum, Zane Grey, Vina Delmar, Irvin S. Cobb, Gertrude Atherton, J. P. McEvoy, Ursula Parrott, Polen Banks, Sophie Kerr; screenplay, Bayard Veiller; camera, Karl Struss.

Nancy Carroll (Glenda O'Brien); Cary Grant (Jeffrey Baxter); John Halliday (Stephen Bessemer); Irving Pichel (District Attorney Clarke); Louis Calhern (Leo Young); Norma Mitchell (Martha); Jack La Rue (Little Maxie); Frank Sheridan (Inspector Swope); John Lodge (Dr. Simpson); William J. Kelly (Captain of Boat); Harry Holman (Judge Osgood); Jay Belasco (Tony Graham); Gertrude Messinger (Evelyn Craig); Lona Andre (Cora Matthews); Donald Stuart (The Steward); Gregory Golubeff (Band Leader); Robert Quirk (Cheer Leader); Amo Ingraham (Third Girl); Dennis Beaufort, Gaylord (Steve) Pendleton (Boys).

THE EAGLE AND THE HAWK (Par, 1933) 72 M.

Director, Stuart Walker; story, John Monk Saunders; screenplay, Bogart Rogers, Seton I. Miller; associate director, Mitchell Leisen; camera, Harry Fischbeck.

Fredric March (Jerry Young); Cary Grant (Henry Crocker); Jack Oakie (Mike Richards); Carole Lombard (The Beautiful Lady); Sir Guy Standing (Major Dunham); Forrester Harvey (Hogan); Kenneth Howell (John Stevens); Leyland Hodgson (Kinsford); Virginia Hammond (Lady Erskine); Craufurd Kent (General); Douglas Scott (Tommy Erskine); Robert Manning (Voss); Adrienne D'Ambricourt (Fifi); Jacques Jou-Jerville (French General's Aide); Russell Scott (Flight Sergeant); Paul Cremonesi (French General); Yorke Sherwood (Taxi Driver); Lane Chandler, Dennis O'Keefe (Fliers); Olaf Hytten (Story-Telling Officer).

GAMBLING SHIP (PAR, 1933) 72 M.

Directors, Louis Gasnier, Max Marcin; based on stories by Peter Ruric; adaptor, Claude Binyon; screenplay, Marcin, Seton I. Miller; camera, Charles Lang.

Cary Grant (Ace Corbin); Benita Hume (Eleanor La Velle); Roscoe Karns (Blooey); Glenda Farrell (Jeanne Sands); Jack La Rue (Pete Manning); Arthur Vinton (Joe Burke); Charles Williams (Baby Face); Edwin Maxwell (District Attorney); Harry Shutan, Frank Moran (Gunmen); Spencer Charters, Otho Wright (Detectives); Evelyn Selbie (Indian Woman); Kate Campbell (Woman Detective); Edward Gargan, Jack Grey (Deputies); William Welsh (Conductor); Sid Saylor (Sailor); Hooper Atchley (Doctor); Larry Alexander (Telephone Operator); Louis Natheaux (Croupier); Gum Chung (Cook).

I'M NO ANGEL (PAR, 1933) 87 M.

Producer, William LeBaron; director, Wesley Ruggles; based on the scenario The Lady and the Lions by Lowell Brentano; continuity, Harlan Thompson; screenplay-dialog, Mae West; songs, Harvey Brooks, Gladys du Boise, and Ben Ellison; sound, F. E. Dine; camera, Leo Tover; editor, Otho Lovering.

Mae West (Tira); Cary Grant (Jack Clayton); Gregory Ratoff (Benny Pinkowitz); Ralf Harolde (Slick Wiley); Edward Arnold (Big Bill Barton); Kent Taylor (Kirk Lawrence); Gertrude Michael (Alicia Hatton); Russell Hopton (Flea Madigan, the Barker); Dorothy Peterson (Thelma); Libby Taylor, Hattie McDaniel (Maids); Gertrude Howard (Beulah); Irving Pichel (Bob, the Attorney); Nigel de Brulier (Rajah); Tom London (Spectator); William B. Davidson (Ernest Brown, the Chump); Monte Collins, Ray Cooke (Sailors); George Bruggeman (Omnes); Walter Walker (Judge); Morrie Cohan (Chauffeur); Edward Hearn (Courtroom Spectator); Dennis O'Keefe (Reporter).

ALICE IN WONDERLAND (PAR, 1933) 90 M.

Director, Norman McLeod; based on the books by Lewis Carroll; screenplay, Joseph L. Mankiewicz, William Cameron Menzies; music director, Nathaniel Finkstein; music, Dmitri Tiomkin; art director, Robert Odell; costumes-masks, Wally Westmore, Newt Jones; sound, Eugene Merritt; special effects, Gordon Jennings, Farciot Edouart; camera, Henry Sharp, Bert Glennon; editor, Edward Hoagland.

Charlotte Henry (Alice); Richard Arlen (Cheshire Cat); Roscoe Ates (Fish); William Austin (Gryphon); Gary Cooper (White Knight); Jack Duffy (Leg of Mutton); Leon Errol (Uncle Gilbert); Louise Fazenda (White Queen); W. C. Fields (Humpty Dumpty); Alec B. Francis (King of Hearts); Skeets Gallagher (White Rabbit); Cary Grant (Mock Turtle); Lillian Harmer (Cook); Raymond Hatton (Mouse); Sterling Holloway (Frog); Edward Everett Horton (Mad Hatter); Roscoe Karns (Tweedledee); Baby LeRoy (Joker); Lucien Littlefield (Father William's Son); Mae Marsh (Sheep); Polly Moran (Dodo Bird); Jack Oakie (Tweedledum); Edna May Oliver (Red Queen); George Ovey (Plum Pudding); May Robson (Queen of Hearts); Charlie Ruggles (March Hare); Jackie Searle (Dormouse); Alison Skipworth (Duchess); Ned Sparks (Caterpillar); Billy Barty (White Pawn); Billy Bevan (Two of Spades); Charles McNaughton (Five of Spades); Patsy O'Byrne (Aunt); Colin Campbell (Garden Frog); Harry Ekezian, Meyer Grace, Joe Torillo (Executioners); Julie Bishop (Alice's Sister); Will Stanton (Seven of Spades).

THIRTY-DAY PRINCESS (PAR, 1934) 73 M.

Producer, B. P. Schulberg; director, Marion Gering; based on the story by Clarence Budington Kelland; adaptors, Sam Hellman, Edwin Justus Mayer; screenplay, Preston Sturges, Frank Partos; camera, Leon Shamroy.

Sylvia Sidney [Nancy Lane/Princess Catterina Theodora Margerita (Zizzi)]; Cary Grant (Porter Madison III); Edward Arnold (Richard Gresham); Henry Stephenson (King Anatole XII); Vincent Barnett (Count Nicholaus); Edgar Norton (Baron Passeria); Ray Walker (Dan Kirk); Lucien Littlefield (Parker); Robert McWade (Managing Editor); George Baxter (Donald Spottswood); Eleanor Wesselhoeft (Mrs. Schmidt, the Landlady); Frederic Sullivan, William Augustin (Detectives); Ed Dearing (Tim, the Policeman at Mrs. Schmidt's); Bruce Warren (Spottswood's Friend); William Arnold (City Editor); J. Merrill Holmes (Radio Man at Boat); Dick Rush (Sergeant of Police); Jean Chatburn (Blonde); Major Sam Harris (Court Officer); Skippy (The Wire-Haired Terrier Dog).

BORN TO BE BAD (UA, 1934) 61 M.

Associate producers, William Goetz, Raymond Griffith; director, Lowell Sherman; story-adaptor, dialog, Ralph Graves; continuity, Harrison Jacobs; art directors, Richard Day, Joseph Wright; music director, Alfred Newman; camera, Barney McGill; editor, Maurice Wright.

Loretta Young (Letty Strong); Jackie Kelk (Mickey Strong); Cary Grant (Malcolm Trevor); Henry Travers (Fuzzy); Russell Hopton (Steve Karns); Andrew Tombes (Max Lieber); Howard Lang (Dr. Dropsy); Harry Green (Adolph); Marion Burns (Alice Trevor); Paul Harvey (Lawyer); Charles Coleman (Butler); Matt Briggs (Truant Officer); Geneva Mitchell (Miss Crawford); Eddie Kane (Headwaiter); George Irving, Mary Forbes, Edward Keane (Admirers at Club); Etienne Girardot (J. K. Brown); Guy Usher (Judge McAffee); Wade Boteler (Detective); John Marston (Doctor).

KISS AND MAKE UP (PAR, 1934) 80 M.

Producer, B. P. Schulberg; director, Harlan Thompson; based on the play by Stephen Bekeffi; adaptor, Jane Hinton; screenplay, Thompson, George Marion, Jr.; associate director, Jean Negulesco; art directors, Hans Dreier, Ernst Fegte; songs, Ralph Rainger and Leo Robin; sound, Jack Goodrich; camera, Leon Shamroy.

Cary Grant (Dr. Maurice Lamar); Helen Mack (Anne); Genevieve Tobin (Eve Caron); Edward Everett Horton (Marcel Caron); Lucien Littlefield (Max Pascal); Mona Maris (Countess Rita); Kay Williams (Vilma); Lucille Lund (Magda); Rafael Storm (Rolando); Mme. Bonita (Mme. Severac); Doris Lloyd (Mme. Durand); Milton Wallace (Maharajah of Baroona); Sam Ashe (Plumber); Helena Phillips (Landlady); Toby Wing (Consuelo of Claghorne); Henry Armetta (Chairman of Banquet); George Andre Beranger (Jean, the Valet); Judith Arlen, Jean Gale, Hazel Hayes, Lee Ann Meredith (Beauty Clinic Nurses); Betty Bryson, Julie Bishop (Beauty Clinic Patients); Ann Sheridan (Beauty Operator); Dorothy Christy (Greta); Rita Gould (Mme. Dupont); Ann Hovey (Lady Rummond-Dray); Gigi Parrish (Radio Listener); Helen Cohan (Radio Announcer); Jean Carmen (Maharajah's Wife).

LADIES SHOULD LISTEN (PAR, 1934) 63 M.

Producer, Douglas MacLean; director, Frank Tuttle; story, Alfred Savoir, Guy Bolton; adaptor, Guy Bolton; screenplay, Claude Binyon, Frank Butler; art directors, Hans Dreier, Ernst Fegte; sound, Earl Hayman; camera, Harry Sharp.

Cary Grant (Julian de Lussac); Frances Drake (Anna Mirelle); Edward Everett Horton (Paul Vernet); Rosita Morena (Marguerite Cintos); George Barbier (Joseph Flamberg); Nydia Westman (Susie Flamberg); Charles Ray (Henri, the Porter); Charles Arnt (Albert, the Manservant); Rafael Corio (Ramon Cintos); Ann Sheridan (Blanche, the Telephone Operator); Joe North (Butler).

ENTER MADAM (PAR, 1935) 83 M.

Producer, A. Benjamin Gilbert; director, Elliott Nugent; based on the play Enter Madame by Gilda Varesi Archibald, Dorothea Donn-Byrne; screenplay, Charles Brackett, Gladys Lehman; art directors, Hans Dreier, Ernst Fegte; costumes, Travis Banton; sound, M. M. Paggi; camera, Theodor Sparkuhl, William Mellor.

Elissa Landi (Lisa Della Robbia); Cary Grant (Gerald Fitzgerald); Lynne Overman (Mr. Farnum); Sharon Lynne (Flora Preston); Michelette Burani (Bice); Paul Porcasi (Archimede); Adrian Rosley (The Doctor); Cecelia Parker (Aline Chalmers); Frank Albertson (John Fitzgerald); Wilfred Hari (Tamamoto); Torben Meyer (Carlson); Harold Berquist (Bjorgenson); Diana Lewis (Operator); Richard Bonelli (Scorpia on Stage).

WINGS IN THE DARK (PAR, 1935) 75 M.

Producer, Arthur Hornblow, Jr.; director, James Flood; story, Nell Shipman, Philip D. Hurn; adaptors, Dale Van Every, E. H. Robinson; screenplay, Jack Kirkland, Frank Partos; art directors, Hans Dreier, Earl Hedrick; aeronautics chief, Captain Earl H. Robinson; sound, Earl S. Hayman; aerial camera, Dewey Wright; camera, William C. Mellor.

Myrna Loy (Sheila Mason); Cary Grant (Ken Gordon); Roscoe Karns (Nick Williams); Hobart Cavanaugh (Mac); Dean Jagger (Tops Harmon); Bert Hanlon (Yipp Morgan); James Burtis (Joy Burns); Russell Hopton (Jake Brashear); Samuel S. Hinds (Kennel Club Secretary); Arnold Korff (The Doctor); Matt McHugh (Sheila's First Mechanic); Graham McNamee (Radio Announcer); Alfred Delcambre (Cameraman); Lee Phelps (Ken's Mechanic); Henry Roquemore (Air Show Chief); Sam Flint (George Rockwell); Stanley Andrews (Jack, an Official); Phil Tead (Reporter); Perry Ivins (Radioman); Virgil Simons (Boy at Coney Island); Esther Michelson (Boy's Mother); Tola Nesmith (Housekeeper); Allen Fox, Ben Sharpe, Charley Hines (Reporters in Ken's Hanger); Peter Hancock, Antrim Short (Radio Announcers at Field); Phil Teed, Gene Morgan (Reporters); Hyman Fink, J. B. Scott, Herb Watson (Photographers at Last Flight); Charley Hines, Duke York, Allen Fox (Reporters at Last Flight); Arthur S. Byron (Guard).

THE LAST OUTPOST (PAR, 1935) 75 M.

Producer, E. Lloyd Sheldon; directors, Charles Barton, Louis Gasnier; based on the story "The Drum" by F. Britton Austin; adaptors, Frank Partos, Charles Brackett; screenplay, Philip MacDonald; assistant director, Edgar Anderson; art di-

rectors, Hans Dreier, Earl Hedrick; sound, A. W. Singley; camera, Theodor Sparkuhl; editor, Jack Dennis.

Cary Grant (Michael Andrews); Claude Rains (John Stevenson); Gertrude Michael (Rosemary Haydon); Kathleen Burke (Ilya); Colin Tapley (Lieutenant Prescott); Akim Tamiroff (Mirov); Billy Bevan (Corporal Foster); Georges Renavent (Turkish Major); Margaret Swope (Nurse Rowland); Jameson Thomas (Cullen); Nick Shaid (Haidor); Harry Semels (Amrak); Meyer Ouhayoun (Armenian Patriarch); Frazier Acosta (Armenian Officer); Malay Clu (Armenian Guard); Elspeth Dudgeon (Head Nurse); Beulah McDonald (Nurse); Robert Adair (Sergeant in General's Office); William Brown (Sergeant Bates); Claude King (General); Olaf Hytten (Doctor); Frank Elliott, Ward Lane (Colonels); Frank Dawson (Surgeon); Ramsey Hill (Captain); Mark Strong, Carey Harrison (Officers).

SYLVIA SCARLETT (RKO, 1935) 94 M.

Producer, Pandro S. Berman; director, George Cukor; based on the novel by Compton Mackenzie; screenplay, Gladys Unger, John Collier, Mortimer Affner; art directors, Van Nest Polglase, Sturges Carne; costumes for Miss Hepburn, Muriel King; costumes for Miss Paley, Bernard Newman; music director, Roy Webb; sound, George D. Ellis; camera, Joseph August; editor, Jane Loring.

Katharine Hepburn (Sylvia Scarlett); Cary Grant (Jimmy Monkley); Brian Aherne (Michael Fane); Edmund Gwenn (Henry Scarlett); Natalie Paley (Lily); Dennie Moore (Maudie Tilt); Lennox Pawle (Drunk); Daisy Belmore, Nola Luxford, Daisy Goodill, Harold Entwistle, Elsa Buchanan, Lilyan Irene, Kay Deslys, May Beatty, Thomas A. Braidon, Elspeth Dudgeon, Ellis McKenzie, Roger Roughton, Ethel Rawson, Alec Harford, Frank Moran, Colin Campbell, Connie Lamont, Lorimer Johnston, Gwendolyn Logan, Montague Shaw, Elsie Mackay, Patricia Caron, Robert Hale, Madame Borget, Carmen Beretta, Harrington Reynolds, Violet Seaton, Pat Somerset (Bits); George Nardelli (Frenchman); Dina Smirnova (Russian); Jack Vanaire (Steward); E. E. Clive, Edward Cooper, Olaf Hytten (Customs Inspectors); Bunny Beatty (Maid); Peter Hobbes, Leonard Mudie (Stewards); Adrienne D'Ambricourt (Stewardess); Gaston Glass, Michael S. Visaroff (Pursers); Harold Entwistle (Conductor); Lionel Pape (Sergeant Major); Robert (Bob) Adair (Turnkey); Harold Cheevers (Bobby).

BIG BROWN EYES (PAR, 1936) 76 M.

Producer, Walter Wanger; director, Raoul Walsh; story, James Edward Grant; screenplay, Walsh, Bert Hanlon; art director, Alexander Toluboff; set decorator, Howard Bristol; music director, Boris Morros; costumes, Helen Taylor; sound, Hugo Grenzbach; camera, George Clemens; editor, Robert Simpson.

Cary Grant (Danny Barr); Joan Bennett (Eve Fallon); Walter Pidgeon (Richard Morey); Lloyd Nolan (Russ Cortig); Alan Baxter (Cary Butler); Marjorie Gateson (Mrs. Cole); Isabel Jewell (Bessie Blair); Douglas Fowley (Benny Bottle); Henry Brandon (Don Butler); Joseph Sawyer (Jack Sully); Dolores Casey (Cashier); Doris Canfield (Myrtle); Edwin Maxwell (Editor); Helen Brown (Mother); Sam Flint (Martin); John Picorri (Defense Attorney); Charlie Wilson (Prosecuting Attorney); Charles Martin (Red); Francis McDonald (Malley); Eddy Conrad (Joe); Ed Jones (Chauffeur); Guy Usher (Judge Davis); Bert Hanlon (Farrell); Frances Morris, Mary Bovard, Betty Van Auken, Dorothy Thompson, Kay Gordon, Betty Gordon, Eleanor Huntley, Janette Warren, Roberta Theiss, Gale Goodson, Helaine Moler, Beulah McDonald, Jinx Falkenburg, Ethel Sykes (Manicurists); Phil Dunham, Francis Sayles, Mal Merrihugh, George Warren, Lloyd Taylor, Bill McGeery, Curly Wright, Jack Dillon, Bill Sullivan (Barbers); Fred "Snowflake" Toones, Eddie Hines (Shoe Shiners); Rex Moore, Hal Greene (Pages); Ray Cordell, Fred Anderson (Elevator Boys); Geraldine Leslie, Ethel Mantell (Maids); Jack Daley (Mooney); Jack Kennedy (Mahoney); Lee Phelps

(Jailer); Charles Hamilton (Clerk); Steve Strilich, John Reese (Prisoners); Allen Connor (Husband); Charles Wilson (Prosecuting Attorney); George MacQuarrie (Chief Attorney); Homer Dickinson (Police Clerk); Don Brodie (Man); Bud Geary (Gangster); Ed Jones (Chauffeur); Billy Arnold (Customer).

SUZY (MGM, 1936) 95 M.

Producer, Maurice Revnes; director, George Fitzmaurice; based on the novel by Herbert Gorman; screenplay, Dorothy Parker, Alan Campbell, Horace Jackson, Lenore Coffee; art directors, Cedric Gibbons, Gabriel Scognamillo, Edwin B. Willis; costumes, Dolly Tree; music, Dr. William Axt; song, Walter Donaldson and Harold Adamson; assistant director, Sandy Roth; sound, Douglas Shearer; camera, Ray June; editor, George Boemler.

Jean Harlow (Suzy Trent); Franchot Tone (Terry Moore); Cary Grant (Andre Charville); Benita Hume (Madame Diane Eyrelle); Lewis Stone (Baron Charville); Reginald Mason (Captain Barsanges); Inez Courtney (Maisie); Greta Meyer (Mrs. Schmidt); David Clyde (Knobby McPherson); Elspeth Dudgeon (Mrs. Boggs); Tyler Brooke (Raoul, the Airman); Robert Livingston (Pierre, an Officer); Dennis Morgan (Lieutenant Charbret); Christian Rub (Pop Gaspard, the Pianist); George Spelvin (Gaston); Juan De La Cruz (Clubfoot); Luana Walters (Check Room Girl); Drew Demorest (Aviator); George Davis (Bartender); Frank Dawson (Albert, the Butler); Charles McNaughton (Peter); Theodor von Eltz (Suave Producer of Revue); Una O'Connor (Mrs. Bradley, the Landlady); Tempe Pigott (Old Woman); Forrester Harvey, John Rogers (Counter Men); Harry Cording (Chauffeur); Adrienne d'Ambricourt (Cab Driver); Joseph R. Tozer (Colonel); Hugh Huntley (Adjutant); Robert A'dair (Landon).

WEDDING PRESENT (PAR, 1936) 81 M.

Producer, B. P. Schulberg; director, Richard Wallace; screenplay, Paul Gallico; assistant director, Ray Lissner; art directors, Hans Dreier, Earl Hedrick; sound, Jack Goodrich; camera, Leon Shamroy; editor, Robert Bischoff.

Joan Bennett [Rusty (Monica Fleming)]; Cary Grant (Charlie Mason); George Bancroft (Stagg); Conrad Nagel (Dodacker); Gene Lockhart (Archduke); William Demarest ("Smiles" Benson); Inez Courtney (Mary Lawson); Edward Brophy (Squinty); Purnell Pratt (Van Dorn); Douglas Wood (Willett); George Meeker (Blaker); Lois Wilson (Laura Dodacker); John Henry Allen (Jonathan); George Offerman, Jr. (Sammy Smith); Damon Ford (Haley); Heinie Conklin, Billy Engel, Ray Hanson (German Band); Jack Mulhall, Cy Ring, Charles Williams, Marshall Ruth, Eddie Phillips, Eddie Borden, Ted Thompson, Charles Sherlock, Eddie Fetherston, Dagmar Oakland, Allen Fox (Reporters); Bradley Page (Givens); Torben Meyer (Winternitz); Charles Middleton (Turnbull); Clarence H. Wilson (Simmons); Katherine Perry Moore (Miss Chandler); Harry C. Bradley (Ticket Seller); Frank Darien (Cashier); Otto Hoffman (Printer); Hal K. Dawson (Furniture Salesman); Harry Tyler (Marriage License Clerk); Richard Powell (Hotel Room Waiter); George Davis (Cafe Waiter); Russ Powell (Beer Wagon Driver); Edd Russell (Telegraph Editor); Lee Shumway (Motorcycle Cop); Charles Meakin (Pompous Man); Ralph McCullough (Timid Man); Ernie Shields (Man with Key); Walter Long, Jimmy Dundee, Charles Sullivan (Gangsters); Milton Kahn, Rex Moore (Office Boys); Estelle Eterre, Frances Morris (Switchboard Operators); Charles McAvoy (Fire Chief); Jack Cheatham (Ambulance Attendant).

THE AMAZING QUEST OF ERNEST BLISS (UA, 1936) 80 M.

Producer-director, Alfred Zeisler; based on the novel by E. Phillips Oppenheim; adaptor, John L. Balderston; art director, David Rawnsley; dialog director, Charles Lincoln; sound, A. J. Bronker; camera, Otto Heller.

Cary Grant (Ernest Bliss); Mary Brian (Frances Clayton); Peter Gawthorne (Sir James Aldroyd); Henry Kendall (Lord

Ronnie Honiton); Leon M. Lion (Dorrington); John Turnbull (Masters); Arthur Hardy (Crawley); Iris Ashley (Clare Winters); Garry Marsh (The Buyer); Andrea Malandrinos (Giuseppe); Alfred Wellesley (Montague); Marie Wright (Mrs. Heath); Buena Bent (Mrs. Mott); Charles Farrell (Scales); Hal Gordon (Bill Bronson); Quinton MacPherson (Clowes); Ralph Richardson (Waiter).

U.S. release title: ROMANCE AND RICHES (Grand National, 1937) 70 M.

Television title: AMAZING ADVENTURE.

WHEN YOU'RE IN LOVE (COL, 1937) 110 M.

Associate producer, Everett Riskin; director, Robert Riskin; idea, Ethel Hill, Cedric Worth; screenplay, Robert Riskin; assistant director, Arthur S. Black; music director, Alfred Newman; songs, Jerome Kern and Dorothy Fields; Cab Calloway, Irving Mills, Clarence Glaskill, Al Siegel; choreography, Leon Leonidoff; costumes, Bernard Newman; art director, Stephen Goosson; camera, Joseph Walker; editor, Gene Milford.

Grace Moore (Louise Fuller); Cary Grant (Jimmy Hudson); Aline MacMahon (Marianne Woods); Henry Stephenson (Walter Mitchell); Thomas Mitchell (Hank Miller); Catherine Doucet (Jane Summers); Luis Alberni (Luis Perugini); Gerald Oliver Smith (Gerald Meeker); Emma Dunn (Mrs. Hamilton); George Pearce (Mr. Hamilton); Frank Puglia (Carlos); Barnett Parker (Butler); Marcelle Corday (Marie, Louise's Maid); Enrique de Rosas (Hotel Manager); William Pawley, Don Rowan (Bruisers); Billy Gilbert (Jose, the Bartender); Romaine Callender (Waiter); Arthur Hoyt, Otto Fries, Harvey Leach (Men); Dewey Robinson (Reporter); Pat West, Harry Holman (Babbitt Brothers); Edward Keane (Stage Manager); Peggy Stratford, Ruth Williard, May Wallace, Isabelle LaMal, Georgia Cooper, Helen Dickson (Women); Robert Emmet O'Connor, George Cooper (Assistant Immigration Officers); Emery D'Arcy (Scarpia); Herbert Ashley (Immigration Chief); Hector V. Sarno (Jail Guard); Antonio Vidal (Justice of Peace); Soledad Jimenez (Wife of Justice of Peace); Carmen Samaniego, Nena Sandoval, Robert Linden, Dave O'Brien, Jose Fernandez, Gene Morgan (Dancers); Fletcher Norton (Teacher); Lucille Ward (Music Teacher); Robert McKenzie (Charlie Perkins); Scotty Beckett (Boy); Henry Roquemore (Ticket Clerk); Arthur Stuart Hull (Business Man); Jean De Briac (Headwaiter); Ann Doran (Secretary); J. P. Lockney (Doorman); Bruce Sidney (Stage Manager); Frank Leyva, Raoul Lechuga (Mexican Policemen); Dick Botiller, Joe Dominguez (Mexicans); Wilson Millar (Italian); Joe Forte (Waiter's Assistant); Manuel Paris (Hotel Clerk); Gus Reid (Fat Waiter); Bess Flowers, Leyland Hodgson (Couple in Dressing Room); Cyril Ring, Olive Morgan, Catherine Wallace, Carlos Montalban (Bits); Louise Brooks (Chorus Girl); Bud Geary (Reporter); Chris-Pin Martin (Servant); C. Montague Shaw (Attorney); Alphonse Martel (Announcer); Chuck Hamilton (Tony, the Assistant Stage Manager).

TOPPER (MGM, 1937) 98 M.

Producer, Hal Roach; associate producer, Milton H. Bren; director, Norman Z. McLeod; based on the story by Thorne Smith; screenplay, Jack Jerne, Eric Hatch, Eddie Moran; music, Edward Powell, Hugo Friedhofer; music supervisor, Marvin Hatley; music arranger, Arthur Morton; song, Hoagy Carmichael; art director, Arthur Rouce; camera effects, Roy Seawright; camera, Norbert Brodine; editor, William Terhune.

Constance Bennett (Marion Kerby); Cary Grant (George Kerby); Roland Young (Cosmo Topper); Billie Burke (Henrietta Topper); Alan Mowbray (Wilkins); Eugene Pallette (Casey); Arthur Lake (Elevator Boy); Hedda Hopper (Mrs. Stuyvesant); Virginia Sale (Miss Johnson); Theodor Von Eltz (Hotel Manager); J. Farrell MacDonald (Policeman); Elaine Shepard (Secretary); Doddles Weaver, Si Jenks (Rustics); Three Hits and a Miss (Themselves); Donna Dax (Hat Check-girl at Rainbow Nightclub); Hoagy Carmichael (Bill, the Pianoplayer); Claire Windsor, Betty Blythe (Ladies).

TOAST OF NEW YORK (RKO, 1937) 109 M.

Producer, Edward Small; director, Rowland V. Lee; based on The Book of Daniel Drew by Bouck White and Robber Barons by Matthew Josephson; screenplay, Dudley Nichols, John Twist, Joel Sayre, Van Nest Polglase; music director, Nathaniel Shilkret; songs, Shilkret, Allie Wrubel, and L. Wolfe Gilbert; special camera, Vernon L. Walker; camera, Peverell Marley; editor, George Hively.

Edward Arnold (Jim Fisk); Cary Grant (Nick Boyd); Frances Farmer (Josie Mansfield); Jack Oakie (Luke); Donald Meek (Daniel Drew); Thelma Leeds (Fleurigue); Clarence Kolb (Vanderbilt); Robert McClung (Bellhop); Dudley Clements (Collins); Marie Marks (Check Room Girl); Ginger Connolly (Call Boy); Joseph De Stefani (Headwaiter); George Offerman, Jr. (Usher); Lloyd Ingraham, Ted Thompson, Jack Luden, Reed Howes, Wally Dean, Jay Eaton (Men in New York Restaurant); Fred Lee (Bostonian in Restaurant); Craufurd Kent, Otto Hoffman, Winter Hall, Frank Darien, Earl Dwire (Board of Directors); George Cleveland (Secretary); Ben Hall, James Finlayson, Frank Swales, Foy Van Dolsen (Inventors); Lon Poff, Frank Hammond (Mountaineers); Nelson McDowell, Clem Bevans (Panhandlers); Maxine Hicks (Mother); Daisy Bufford (Maid); Stanley Blystone (Sheriff); Jack Kenny, Chris Frank (Deputy Sheriffs); Frank Rasmussen (Clerk); Robert Dudley (Janitor); Mary Gordan (Charwoman); Dewey Robinson (Beefy Dolan); Reginald Barlow (Hotel Proprietor); Stanley Fields (Top Sergeant); Jack Egan, Charles Doherty, Mike Jeffries, Lynton Brent, Max Wagner, Jack Carson, Eddie Hart, Bentley Hewlett (Reporters); Homer Dickinson (Toastmaster); Margaret Morris, Isabel La Mal (Women); Pete Gerrard, Ed Heim (Painters); Sidney Bracy (Waiter); William Gould, Don Brodie, Tom Brewer (Bits); Francis Tilton (Artist); Oscar Apfel (Wallack); Geoge Irving, James Barnes, William Jeffrey, Walter Murray, Robert Brister, Tom O'Grady, Jack Mulhall, Hal Craig, William Lemuels, Billy Arnold, James Carlyle (Brokers); Gavin Gordon (Southern Major); Edward Peil, Sr., Malcolm Graham, Gladden James (Gentlemen); Allan Cavan, Clarence Harvey, Lionel Belmore, Tom Ricketts (Board of Directors); Edward Le Saint (President of Board); Harvey Clark, Frank Hall Crane (Tailors); Russell Hicks (Lawyer); Nick Thompson (Italian Driver); Frank Mills, Russ Powell, Ethan Laidlaw (Mugs); Joyce Compton, Virginia Carroll (Southern Girls); Al Greer, Tyrone Brereton (Southern Crackers); Frank Hemphill (Stage Hand); Tom Chatterton, John Marshall (Fisk Brokers); Emile Durelle, Larry Steers, J. C. "Jack" Fowler, Cameron Smith (Buyers); Ernest Shield (Clerk); Jerry Storm (Little Broker); William Worthington (Judge); John Maurice Sullivan (President of Exchange); James Quinn (News Butcher); Tom Coleman (Sergeant); Dick Kipling (Southerner).

THE AWFUL TRUTH (COL, 1937) 89 M.

Associate producer, Everett Riskin; director, Leo McCarey; story, Arthur Richmond; screenplay, Vina Delmar; assistant director, William Mull; costumes, Kalloch; music director, Morris Stoloff; art directors, Stephen Goosson, Lionel Banks; interior decorator, Babs Johnstone; songs, Ben Oakland and Milton Drake; sound, Edward Bernds; camera, Joseph Walker; editor, Al Clark.

Irene Dunne (Lucy Warriner); Cary Grant (Jerry Warriner); Ralph Bellamy (Daniel Leeson); Alexander D'Arcy (Armand Duvelle); Cecil Cunningham (Aunt Patsy); Molly Lamont (Barbara Vance); Esther Dale (Mrs. Leeson); Joyce Compton [Dixie Belle Lee (Toots Binswanger)]; Robert Allen (Frank Randall); Robert Warwick (Mr. Vance); Mary Forbes (Mrs. Vance); Claud Allister (Lord Fabian); Zita Moulton (Lady Fabian); Scott Colton (Mr. Barnsley); Wyn Cahoon (Mrs. Barnsley); Paul Stanton (Judge); Mitchell Harris (Jerry's Attorney); Alan Bridge, Edgar Dearing (Motor Cops); Leonard Carey (Butler); Miki Morita (Japanese Servant); Frank Wilson (M.C.); Vernon Dent (Police Sergeant); George C. Pearce (Caretaker); Bobby Watson (Hotel Clerk); Byron Foulger (Secretary); Kathryn Curry (Celeste); Edward Peil, Sr. (Bailiff); Bess Flowers (Viola Heath); John Tyrrell (Hank); Edward Mortimer (Lucy's Attorney).

BRINGING UP BABY (RKO, 1938) 102 M.

Producer, Howard Hawks; associate producer, Cliff Reid; director, Hawks; based on the story by Hagar Wilde; screenplay, Dudley Nichols, Wilde; music director, Roy Webb; art directors, Van Nest Polglase, Perry Ferguson; costumes, Howard Greer; assistant director, Edward Donahue; special effects, Vernon L. Walker; camera, Russell Metty; editor, George Hively.

Katharine Hepburn (Susan Vance); Cary Grant (David Huxley); Charles Ruggles (Major Horace Applegate); May Robson [Aunt Elizabeth (Mrs. Carlton Random)]; Barry Fitzgerald (Mr. Gogarty); Walter Catlett (Slocum, the Constable); Fritz Feld (Dr. Fritz Lehman); Leona Roberts (Hannah Gogarty); George Irving (Alexander Peabody); Virginia Walker (Alice Swallow); Tala Birell (Mrs. Lehman); John Kelly (Elmer); Nissa (Baby, the Leopard); Asta (George, the Dog); Edward Gargan, Buck Mack (Zoo Officials); Geraldine Hall (Maid); Stanley Blystone (Doorman); William Benedict (David's Caddy); Buster Slaven (Caddy); Jack Gardner (Bit); Frank Marlowe (Joe); Pat West (Mac); Jack Carson (Roustabout); Richard Lane (Circus Manager); Frank M. Thomas (Barker); Ruth Alder (Dancer); Pat O'Malley (Deputy); Ward Bond (Motor Cop); Adalyn Asbury (Mrs. Peabody); Jeanne Martel, Judith Ford (Cigarette Girls); George Humbert (Louis, the Headwaiter); Billy Bevan (Bartender); D'Arcy Corrigan (Professor La Touche).

HOLIDAY (COL, 1938) 94 M.

Associate producer, Everett Riskin; director, George Cukor; based on the play by Philip Barry; screenplay, Donald Ogden Stewart; art directors, Stephen Goosson, Lionel Banks; set decorator, Babs Johnstone; music, Sidney Cutner; music director, Morris Stoloff; assistant director, Clifford Broughton; costumes, Kalloch; sound, Lodge Cunningham; camera, Franz Planer; editors, Otto Meyer, Al Clark.

Katharine Hepburn (Linda Seton); Cary Grant (Johnny Case); Doris Nolan (Julia Seton); Lew Ayres (Ned Seton); Edward Everett Horton (Nick Potter); Henry Kolker (Edward Seton); Binnie Barnes (Laura Cram); Jean Dixon (Susan Potter); Henry Daniell (Seton Cram); Charles Trowbridge (Banker); George Pauncefort (Henry); Charles Richman (Thayer); Mitchell Harris (Jennings); Neil Fitzgerald (Edgar); Marion Ballou (Grandmother); Howard Hickman (Man in Church); Hilda Plowright (Woman in Church); Harry Allen, Edward Cooper (Scotchmen); Margaret McWade (Farmer's Wife); Frank Shannon (Farmer); Aileen Carlyle (Farm Girl); Matt McHugh (Taxi Driver); Maurice Brierre (Steward); Esther Peck (Mrs. Jennings); Lillian West (Mrs. Thayer); Luke Cosgrave (Grandfather); Bess Flowers (Countess); George Hickman (Telegraph Boy); Maude Hume (Maid).

GUNGA DIN (RKO, 1939) 117 M.

Producer, Pandro S. Berman; director, George Stevens; inspired by Rudyard Kipling's poem; story, Ben Hecht, Charles MacArthur; screenplay, Joel Sayre, Fred Guiol; art directors, Van Nest Polglase, Perry Ferguson; set decorator, Darrell Silvera; technical advisors, Sir Robert Erskine Holland, Captain Clive Morgan, Sergeant-Major William Briers; assistant directors, Edward Killy, Dewey Starkey; music, Alfred Newman; sound, John E. Tribby, James Stewart; special effects, Vernon L. Walker; camera, John H. August; editors, Henry Berman, John Lockert.

Cary Grant (Cutter); Victor McLaglen (MacChesney); Douglas Fairbanks, Jr. (Ballantine); Sam Jaffe (Gunga Din); Eduardo Ciannelli (Guru); Joan Fontaine (Emmy); Montagu Love (Colonel Weed); Robert Coote (Higginbottam); Abner Biberman (Chota); Lumsden Hare (Major Mitchell); Cecil Kellaway (Mr. Stebbins); Reginald Sheffield (Journalist); Ann Evers, Audrey Manners, Fay McKenzie (Girls at Party);

Charles Bennett (Telegraph Operator); Les Sketchley (Corporal); Frank Levya (Merchant); George Ducount, Jamiel Hasson, George Regas (Thug Chieftains); Bryant Fryer (Scotch Sergeant); Lal Chand Mehra (Jadoo); Roland Varno (Lieutenant Markham); Clive Morgan (Lancer Captain).

ONLY ANGELS HAVE WINGS (COL, 1939) 121 M.

Producer-director-story, Howard Hawks; screenplay, Jules Furthman; music director, Morris W. Stoloff; music, Dmitri Tiomkin; art director, Lionel Banks; costumes, Kalloch; technical advisor-chief pilot, Paul Mantz; special effects, Roy Davidson, Edwin C. Hallor; aerial camera, Elmer Dyer; camera, Joseph Walker; editor, Viola Lawrence.

Cary Grant (Geoff Carter); Jean Arthur (Bonnie Lee); Richard Barthelmess (Bat McPherson); Rita Hayworth (Judith); Thomas Mitchell (Kid Dabb); Sig Ruman (Dutchman); Victor Kilian (Sparks); John Carroll (Gent Shelton); Allyn Joslyn (Les Peters); Donald Barry (Tex Gordon); Noah Beery, Jr. (Joe Souther); Melissa Sierra (Lily); Lucio Villegas (Dr. Logario); Forbes Murray (Hartwood); Cecilia Callejo (Felice); Pat Flaherty (Mike); Pedro Regas (Pancho); Pat West (Baldy); Manuel Maciste (Balladeer); Sammee Tong (Native); Candy Candido (Musician); Charles Moore (Servant); Inez Palange (Lily's Aunt); Rafael Corio (Purser); Lew Davis, Jim Millican, Al Rhein, Curley Dresden, Ed Randolph, Ky Robinson, Bud Wolfe, Eddie Foster (Mechanics); Stanley Brown (Hartwood, Jr.); Cecilia Callejo (Felice, a Spanish Blonde Girl); Francisco Maran (Planter Overseer); Wilson Benge (Assistant Purser); Vernon Dent (Boat Captain); Elana Duran (Spanish Blonde Girl); Budd Fine (First Mate); Victor Travers (Planter Overseer); Jack Lowe, Tex Higginson (Banana Foremen); Enrique Acosta, Raoul Lechuga, Dick Botiller, Harry Batley, Amore Navarro, Tessie Murray (Tourists).

IN NAME ONLY (RKO, 1939) 94 M.

Executive producer, Pandro S. Berman; producer, George Haight; director, John Cromwell; based on the novel Memory of Love by Bessie Brewer; screenplay, Richard Sherman; music, Roy Webb; art directors, Van Nest Polglase, Perry Ferguson; set decorator, Darrell Silvera; Miss Lombard's gowns by Irene; other gowns, Edward Stevenson; assistant director, Dewey Starkey; sound, Hugh McDowell, Jr.; special effects, Vernon L. Walker; camera, J. Roy Hunt; editor, William Hamilton.

Carole Lombard (Julie Eden); Cary Grant (Alec Walker); Kay Francis (Maida Walker); Charles Coburn (Mr. Walker); Katharine Alexander (Laura); Jonathan Hale (Dr. Gateson); Maurice Moscovich (Dr. Muller); Nella Walker (Mrs. Walker); Peggy Ann Garner (Ellen); Spencer Charters (Gardener); Alan Baxter (Charley); Harriet Mathews, Sandra Morgan (Women on Boat); Harold Miller (Man on Boat); John Dilson, Doug Gordon (Stewards); James Adamson, Tony Merlo (Waiters); Frank Puglia (Manager); Alan Pollard (Butler); Charles Coleman (Archie Duress); Florence Wix, Clive Morgan, Major Sam Harris, Kathryn Wilson (Party Guests); Grady Sutton (Escort); Bert Moorhouse (College Man); Byron Foulger (Owen); Arthur Aylsworth (Farmer on Truck); Lloyd Ingraham (Elevator Operator); Gus Glassmire (Hospital Attendant); Mary MacLaren (Nurse); Robert Strange (Hotel Manager); Jack Chapin, Allan Wood, Harold Hoff (Bellhops); George Rosener (Hotel Doctor); Edward Fligle (Night Clerk); John Laing (Chauffeur); Frank Mills (Bartender).

HIS GIRL FRIDAY (COL, 1940) 92 M.

Producer-director, Howard Hawks; based on the play The Front Page by Ben Hecht, Charles MacArthur; screenplay, Charles Lederer; music director, Morris W. Stoloff; camera, Joseph Walker; editor, Gene Havlick.

Cary Grant (Walter Burns); Rosalind Russell (Hildy Johnson); Ralph Bellamy (Bruce Baldwin); Gene Lockhart (Sheriff Hartwell); Helen Mack (Mollie Malloy); Porter Hall (Murphy); Ernest Treux (Roy Bensinger); Cliff Edwards (Endicott); Clarence Kolb (Mayor); Roscoe Karns (McCue); Frank Jenks (Wilson); Regis Toomey (Sanders); Abner Biberman (Diamond Louie); Frank Orth (Duffy); John Qualen (Earl Williams); Alma Kruger (Mrs. Baldwin); Billy Gilbert (Joe Pettibone); Pat West (Warden Cooley); Edwin Maxwell (Dr. Egelhoffer); Irving Bacon (Gus); Earl Dwire (Mr. Davis); Ralph Dunn (Guard); Pat Flaherty, Edmund Cobb (Cops).

MY FAVORITE WIFE (COL, 1940) 88 M.

Producer, Leo McCarey; director, Garson Kanin; story, Sam and Bella Spewack, McCarey; screenplay, the Spewacks; art directors, Van Nest Polglase, Mark-Lee Kirk; set decorator, Darrell Silvera; costumes, Howard Greer; music, Roy Webb; assistant directors, Ruby Rosenberg, James H. Anderson; sound, John E. Tribby; camera, Rudolph Mate; editor, Robert Wise.

Irene Dunne (Ellen Arden); Cary Grant (Nick Arden); Randolph Scott (Stephen Burkett); Gail Patrick (Bianca); Ann Shoemaker (Ma); Scotty Beckett (Tim Arden); Mary Lou Harrington (Chinch Arden); Donald MacBride (Hotel Clerk); Hugh O'Connell (Johnson); Granville Bates (Judge); Pedro de Cordoba (Dr. Rohlmar); Brandon Tynan (Dr. Manning); Leon Belasco (Henri); Harold Gerald (Assistant Clerk); Murray Alper (Bartender); Earle Hodgins (Court Clerk); Cyril Ring (Contestant); Clive Morgan, Bert Moorhouse (Lawyers); Florence Dudley, Jean Acker (Witnesses); Joe Cabrillas (Phillip); Frank Marlowe (Photographer); Thelma Joel (Miss Rosenthal); Horace McMahon (Truck Driver); Chester Clute (Little Man); Eli Schmudkler (Janitor); Franco Corsaro (Waiter); Cy Kendall (Detective); Pat West (Caretaker).

THE HOWARDS OF VIRGINIA (COL, 1940) 117 M.

Producer, Frank Lloyd; associate producer, Jack H. Skirball; director, Lloyd; based on the novel The Tree of Liberty by Elizabeth Page; screenplay, Sidney Bochman; art director, John Goodman; set decorator, Howard Bristol; music, Richard Hageman; costumes for Miss Scott, Irene Saltern; technical advisor, Waldo Twitchell; assistant director, William Tummel; sound, William H. Wilmarth; montage effect, Slavko Vorkapich; camera, Bert Glennon; editor, Paul Weatherwax.

Cary Grant (Matt Howard); Martha Scott (Jane Peyton Howard); Sir Cedric Hardwicke (Fleetwood Peyton); Alan Marshal (Roger Peyton); Richard Carlson (Thomas Jefferson); Paul Kelly (Captain Jabez Allen); Irving Bacon (Tom Norton); Elisabeth Risdon (Aunt Clarissa); Anne Revere (Mrs. Betsy Norton); Tom Drake (James Howard at Age Sixteen); Phil Taylor (Peyton Howard at Age Eighteen); Rita Quigley (Mary Howard at Age Seventeen); Libby Taylor (Dicey); Richard Gaines (Patrick Henry); George Houston (George Washington); Sam McDaniel (Uncle Robert, the Butler); Virginia Sale (Neighbor); Ralph Byrd (James Howard); Dickie Jones (Matt Howard at Age Twelve); Buster Phelps (Thomas Jefferson at Age Eleven); Wade Boteler (Uncle Reuben); Mary Field (Susan Howard); R. Wells Gordon (Colonel Jefferson); Charles Francis (Mr. Douglas); Olaf Hytten (Gentleman); Emmett Vogan (Representative); J. Anthony Hughes (Tidewater Representative); Lane Chandler (Major); Brandon Hurst (Wilton); Alan Ladd (Neighbor); Pat Somerset, James Westerfield (Friends).

THE PHILADELPHIA STORY (MGM, 1940) 112 M.

Producer, Joseph L. Mankiewicz; director, George Cukor; based on the play by Philip Barry; screenplay, Donald Ogden Stewart; art directors, Cedric Gibbons, Wade B. Rubottom; set decorator, Edwin B. Willis; costumes, Adrian; music, Franz Waxman; hair styles, Sydney Guilaroff; sound, Douglas Shearer; camera, Joseph Ruttenberg; editor, Frank Sullivan.

Cary Grant (C. K. Dexter Haven); Katharine Hepburn (Tracy Lord); James Stewart (Macauley Connor); Ruth Hussey (Elizabeth Imbrie); John Howard (George Kittredge); Roland Young (Uncle Willie); John Halliday (Seth Lord); Mary Nash (Margaret Lord); Virginia Weidler (Dinah Lord); Henry Daniell (Sidney Kidd); Lionel Pape (Edward); Rex Evans

(Thomas); Russ Clark (John); Hilda Plowright (Librarian); Lita Chevret (Manicurist); Lee Phelps (Bartender); David Clyde (Mac); Claude King (Willie's Butler); Robert De Bruce (Dr. Parsons); Veda Buckland (Elsie); Dorothy Fay, Florine McKinney, Helen Whitney, Hillary Brooke (Main Liners).

PENNY SERENADE (COL, 1941) 120 M.

Producer, George Stevens; associate producer, Fred Guiol; director, Stevens; based on the story by Martha Cheavens; screenplay, Morrie Ryskind; music director, Morris Stoloff; music, W. Franke Harling; art director, Lionel Banks; sound, John Goodrich; camera, Joseph Walker; editor, Otto Meyer.

Irene Dunne (Julie Gardiner); Cary Grant (Roger Adams); Beulah Bondi (Miss Oliver); Edgar Buchanan (Applejack); Ann Doran (Dotty); Eva Lee Kuney (Trina at Age Six); Leonard Wiley (Dr. Hartley); Wallis Clark (Judge); Walter Soderling (Billings); Baby Biffle (Trina at Age One); Edmund Elton (Minister); Billy Bevan (McDougal); Nee Wong, Jr. (Sung Chong); Michael Adrian Morris (Bill Collector); Grady Sutton, Stanley Brown (Men); Beryl Vaughn (Flower Girl); John Tyrrell (Press Operator); Iris Han (O-Hanna-San); Otto Han (Sam, the Cook); Ben Taggart (Policeman); Frank Moran (Taxi Driver); Lynton Brent (Reporter); Al Seymour (Bootlegger); Dick Wessel (Joe); Charles Flynn (Bob); Arline Jackson, Mary Bovard, Georgia Hawkins (Girls); Fred "Snowflake" Toones (Train Porter); Ed Peil, Sr. (Train Conductor); Eddie Laughton (Cab Driver); Doris Herbert (Minister's Wife); Bess Flowers (Mother); John Ferguson (Father); Lani Lee (Chinese Waitress); Rollin Moriyama, Ben Kumagai (Rickshaw Boys); Lillian West (Nurse); Henry Dixon (Old Printer); Dorothy Adams (Mother); Albert Butterfield (Boy).

SUSPICION (RKO, 1941) 99 M.

Director, Alfred Hitchcock; based on the novel Before the Fact by Francis Iles; screenplay, Samson Raphaelson, Joan Harrison, Alma Neville; art directors, Van Nest Polglase, Carroll Clark; set decorator, Darrell Silvera; costumes, Edward Stevenson; music, Franz Waxman; sound, John E. Tribby; special effects, Vernon L. Walker; camera, Harry Stradling; editor, William Hamilton.

Cary Grant (Johnnie Aysgarth); Joan Fontaine (Lina McLaidlaw); Sir Cedric Hardwicke (General McLaidlaw); Nigel Bruce (Beaky); Dame May Whitty (Mrs. McLaidlaw); Isabel Jeans (Mrs. Newsham); Heather Angel (Ethel, the Maid); Auriol Lee (Isobel Sedbusk); Reginald Sheffield (Reggie Wetherby); Leo G. Carroll (Captain Melbeck); Maureen Roden-Ryan (Winnie, the Maid); Carol Curtis-Brown (Jessie Barham); Constance Worth (Mrs. Fitzpatrick); Violet Shelton (Alice Barham); Pax Walker (Phoebe, the Maid); Leonard Carey (Jenner, the Butler); Gertrude Hoffman (Mrs. Wetherby); Kenneth Hunter (Sir Gerald); Clyde Cook (Photographer); Faith Brook (Alice Barham); Dorothy Lloyd (Miss Wetherby); Elsie Weller (Miss Wetherby); Aubrey Mather (Mr. Webster); Rex Evans (Mr. Bailey); Edward Fielding (Antique Shop Proprietor); Hilda Plowright (Postmistress); Ben Webster (Registrar); Gavin Gordon (Bertram Sedbusk); Nondas Metcalf (Phyllis Swinghurst); Lumsden Hare (Inspector Hodgson); Clara Reid (Mrs. Craddock); Vernon Downing (Benson); Billy Bevan (Ticket Taker); Alec Craig (Hogart Club Bit).

THE TALK OF THE TOWN (COL, 1942) 118 M.

Producer, George Stevens; associate producer, Fred Guiol; director, Stevens; based on a story by Sidney Harmon; adaptor, Dale Van Every; screenplay, Irwin Shaw, Sidney Buchman; assistant director, Norman Deming; art directors, Lionel Banks, Rudolph Sternad; gowns for Miss Arthur, Irene; music, Frederick Hollander; music director, Morris Stoloff; montage effects, Donald Starling; sound, Lodge Cunningham; camera, Ted Tetzlaff; editor, Otto Meyer.

Cary Grant (Leopold Dilg); Jean Arthur (Nora Shelley); Ronald Colman (Michael Lightcap); Edgar Buchanan (Sam Yates); Glenda Farrell (Regina Bush); Charles Dingle (Andrew Holmes); Emma Dunn (Mrs. Shelley); Rex Ingram (Til-ney); Leonid Kinskey (Jan Pulaski); Tom Tyler (Clyde Bracken); Don Beddoe (Chief of Police); George Watts (Judge Grunstadt); Clyde Fillmore (Senator James Boyd); Frank M. Thomas (District Attorney); Lloyd Bridges (Forrester); Ralph Peters, Max Wagner (Moving Men); Pat McVey (Cop); Eddie Laughton (Henry); Billy Benedict (Western Union Boy); Harold "Stubby" Kruger (Ball Player); John Tyrrell, George Hickman, Frank Mills, Bud Geary, Holger Bendixen, Joe Garcia, Jay Guedalia, Oscar Hendrian, Dave Harper, Dick Jensen, Robert Keats, Herman Marks, Charles Perry, Al Rhein, Al Seymour, Charles St. George, Victor Travers, Ralph Volkie (Men); Maynard Holmes (Vendor); Jack Carr (Usher); Ralph Dunn, Bill Lally, Edward Hearn (Sergeants); Roberta Smith, Dorothy Babb (School Girls); Lee Phelps, Al Ferguson (Detectives); Edward Coke, Jack Shay, Eddie Bruce (Reporters); Ferike Boros (Mrs. Pulaski); Jack Gardner (Cameraman); William Gould (Sheriff); Lee "Lasses" White (Hound Keeper); Joe McGuinn (Jailer); Dewey Robinson (Jake); Georgia Backus, Lelah Tyler (Women); Lew Davis, Gino Corrado (Waiters); Frank Sully (Road Cop); Dan Seymour (Headwaiter); Mabel Todd (Operator); Lee Prather (Sergeant at Arms); Clarence Muse (Doorkeeper); Leslie Brooks (Secretary); Alan Bridge (Desk Sergeant); Joe Cunningham (McGuire); Jack Lowe (Workman); Robert Walker (Deputy Sheriff).

ONCE UPON A HONEYMOON (RKO, 1942) 116 M.

Producer-director-story, Leo McCarey; screenplay, Sheridan Gibney; art directors, Albert S. D'Agostino, Al Herman; music, Robert Emmett Dolan; camera, George Barnes; editor, Theron Warth.

Ginger Rogers (Katie O'Hara); Cary Grant (Pat O'Toole); Walter Slezak (Baron Von Luber); Albert Dekker (Le Blanc); Albert Bassermann (Borelski); Ferike Boros (Elsa); Harry Shannon (Cumberland); John Banner (Kleinoch); Hans Conried (French Fitter); Natasha Lytess (Anna, the Hotel Maid); Peter Seal (Polish Orderly); John Peters (Kleinoch's Driver); Hans Wollenberger (Waiter); Joseph Kamaryt, Rudolph Myzet (Czech Officials); Walter Stahl, Russell Gaige, Gohr Van Vleck (Baron's Guests); Alex Melesh (Hotel Clerk in Warsaw/Bar Waiter); Dina Smirnova, Alex Davidoff, Major Nichols, Ted Nicova (Warsaw Travelers); Felix Basch (Herr Kelman); Eugene Marum (Anna's Son); Bob O'Connor (Polish Operator); Ace Bragunier (Plane Pilot); Joe Diskay (Warsaw Desk Clerk); Emil Ostlin (German Captain); Fred Giermann, Ernst Hausman (Germans); George Irving (America Consul); William Vaughn (German Colonel); Otto Reichow (German Private); Hans Schumm, Hans Furberg, Bob Stevenson, Henry Victor, Fred Aldrich, Henry Guttman (German Storm Troopers); Hans Von Twardowski, Walter Bonn, Gordon Clark, Jack Martin, Manart Kippen, George Sorel, Bill Martin, Arno Frey (German Officers); Jacques Vanaire (French Radio Announcer); Lionel Royce (Marshall Mocha); Dell Henderson (American Attache); Frank Alten (Spontaneity); Carl Ekberg (Hitler); Fred Niblo (Ship Captain); Oscar Lorraine (Ship Steward); Bert Roach (Bartender); Emory Parnell (Quisling); Boyd Davis (Chamberlain); Claudine De Luc (Hotel Proprietor); Brandon Beach (Civilian); Edgar Licho, Albert Petit (French Waiters).

MR. LUCKY (RKO, 1943) 100 M.

Producer, David Hempstead; director, H. C. Potter; based on the story "Bundles for Freedom" by Milton Holmes; screenplay, Holmes, Adrian Scott; music, Roy Webb; music director, C. Bakaleinikoff; production designer, William Cameron Menzies; art directors, Albert S. D'Agostino, Mark-Lee Kirk; set decorators, Darrell Silvera, Claude Carpenter; assistant director, Harry Scott; sound, Richard Van Hessen, James G. Stewart; special effects, Vernon L. Walker; camera, George Barnes; editor, Theron Warth.

Cary Grant (Joe Adams); Laraine Day (Dorothy Bryant); Charles Bickford (Hard Swede); Gladys Cooper (Captain Steadman); Alan Carney (Crunk); Henry Stephenson (Mr. Bryant); Paul Stewart (Zepp); Kay Johnson (Mrs. Ostrander);

Erford Gage (The Gaffer); Walter Kingsford (Commissioner Hargraves); J. M. Kerrigan (McDougal); Edward Fielding (Foster); Vladimir Sokoloff (Greek Priest); Florence Bates (Mrs. Van Every); Al Rhein, Sammy Finn, Al Murphy, Fred Rapport (Gamblers); John Bleifer (Siga); Juan Varro (Bascopolus); Frank Mills (Workman at Slot Machine); Mary Forbes (Dowager); Mary Stuart, Rita Corday, Ariel Heath (Bits); Don Brodie (Dealer); Joe Crehan, Kernan Cripps (Plainclothesmen); Art Yeoman, Jack Gargan (Reporters); Major Sam Harris (Gambling Extra); Isabel Withers, Daphne Moore (Nurses); Emory Parnell (Dock Watchman); Lloyd Ingraham (Taxi Driver); Hilda Plowright (Maid); Ray Flynn (Cop); Budd Fine (Stevedore); Charles Lane (Comstock); Frank Henry (Reporter on Street); Robert Strange (Captain Costello); Hal Dawson (Draft Board Director).

DESTINATION TOKYO (WB, 1944) 135 M.

Producer, Jerry Wald; director, Delmer Daves; story, Steve Fisher; screenplay, Daves, Albert Maltz; art director, Leo K. Kuter; set decorator, Walter Tilford; technical advisor, Lieutenant Commander Phillip Compton; music, Franz Waxman; music director, Leo F. Forbstein; orchestrator, Leon Raab; assistant director, Art Lueker; sound, Robert B. Lee; special effects, Lawrence Butler, Willard Van Enger; camera, Bert Glennon; editor, Christian Nyby.

Cary Grant (Captain Cassidy); John Garfield (Wolf); Alan Hale (Cookie); John Ridgely (Reserve Officer Raymond); Dane Clark (Tin Can); Warner Anderson (Executive Officer Andy); William Prince (Pills); Robert Hutton (Tommy); Tom Tully (Mike); Faye Emerson (Mrs. Cassidy); Peter Whitney (Dakota); Warren Douglas (Larry, a Diving Officer); John Forsythe (Sparks); John Alvin (Sound Man); Bill Kennedy (Pete, the Gunnery Officer); William Challee (Quartermaster); Whit Bissell (Yo Yo); John Whitney (Communications Officer); George Lloyd (Chief of Boat); Maurice Murphy (Toscanini); John Hudson (Radio Man); Jimmy Evans, George W. Robotham, Dan Borzage, Bernie Sell, Paul Parry, "Sailor" Vincent, Charles Sherlock, Warren Cross, Wally Walker, William Hudson, Charles Sullivan, Cy Malis, Bob Creasman, John Sylvester, Duke York, Ted Jacques, Harry Bartell, Jay Ward, John Forrest, Alan Wilson (Crew Members); Paul Langton (Barber); Joy Barlowe (Wolf's Girl); Bill Hunter (Market Street "Commando"); Hugh Prosser (Pilot); Frank Tang (Jap Pilot); Angel Cruz (Jap Bombardier); Pierre Watkin (Admiral); Mark Stevens, Jack Mower (Admiral's Aides); Cliff Clark (Admiral on *Hornet*); Charles Thompson (Rear Admiral); Russ Whiteman (First Class Yeoman); Tony Hughes (Navy Air Officer); Deborah Daves (Debby Cassidy); Michael Daves (Michael Cassidy); Bob Lowell (Radio Operator); George Anderson (Officer); Eddie Lee, Wing Foo (Japs at Listening Post); Ya Sing Sung (Jap on Beach); Benson Fong, James B. Leong (Japs); Bruce Wong (Jap Antenna Man); Roland Got (Jap Officer); Mary Landa (Tin Can's Girl); Carlyle Blackwell (Man on Phone); Dorothy Schoemer (Saleslady); Kirby Grant (Captain at Briefing); Herbert Gunn (Lieutenant); Warren Ashe (Major); Lane Chandler (C.P.O.); Lou Marcelle (Narrator).

ONCE UPON A TIME (COL, 1944) 89 M.

Producer, Lewis F. Edelman; director, Alexander Hall; based on the radio play My Client Curly by Norman Corwin, Lucille F. Herrmann; adaptor, Irving Fineman; screenplay, Lewis Meltzer, Oscar Saul; art directors, Lionel Banks, Edward Jewell; set decorator, Robert Priestley; music, Frederick Hollander; music director, Morris Stoloff; sound, John Goodrich; camera, Franz F. Planer; editor, Gene Havlick.

Cary Grant (Jerry Flynn); Janet Blair (Jeannie Thompson); James Gleason (The Moke); Ted Donaldson (Pinky Thompson); Howard Freeman (McKenzie); William Demarest (Brandt); Art Baker (Gabriel Heatter); Paul Stanton (Dunhill); Mickey McGuire (Fatso); Ed Gargan, Harry Strang, Billy Bevan (Cops); Cliff Clark, Emory Parnell (Radio Cops); Torben Meyer (Hotel Manager); William Austin (Assistant Hotel Manager); Isabel Withers, Almeda Fowler, Nell Keller (Women); Lane Chandler (Doorman); Esther Howard, Eddie Bruce (Clerks); Nolan Leary (Elevator Man); John Abbott, Ian Wolfe, Jack Lee, Charles Arnt (Reporters); Don Barclay, Fred Howard (Photographers); Alex Melesh, George Davis (Waiters); William Gould (Editor); George Eldredge, Dick Gordon, Lewis Wilson, Freeman Wood, Cy Ring (Men); Pedro de Cordoba, Vaughan Glaser, Erwin Kaiser (Scientists); Lucille Brown (Miss Flemmin); Anne Loos, Mary Currier (Secretaries); Charles Bates, Hugh McGuire, Tom Brown, Gary Gray, Cecil Weston (Bits); Garry Owen (Mug); Harrison Greene, George Anderson, John Dilson, James Flavin, Emmett Vogan, Vernon Dent (Business Men); Nelroy Ashley (Business Woman); Christian Rub (Janitor); Robert Williams (Stage Manager); Vi Athens, Marilyn Johnson, Sybil Merritt, June Millarde, Thelma Joel (Chorus Girls); Ronnie Rondell, Robert Tafur (Gauchos); Lionel Braham (Weight Lifter); Joseph Greene (Rajah Pirate); Murray Alper (Soldier); Iris Adrian (Girl); Tom Kennedy, John Kelly (Truckmen); Spec O'Donnell, John Tyrrell (Ushers); Pierre Watkin (Radio Stage Manager); Alan Stone (Radio Technician); Phyllis Kennedy, Sandra Coles, Eula Guy, Grace Lenard, Pauline Drake (Telephone Operators); Syd Saylor (Ship Yard Worker); Tom Dugan (Police Announcer); Buddy Yarus (Jitterbug); Jeff Donnell (Brooklyn Girl); Fern Emmett (Teacher Type); Ida Moore (Gossipy Woman); Mary Field, Barbara Pepper (Taxi Girls); William Yip, Jung Lim (Chinamen); Ruth Warren (Fatso's Mother); Ray Teal, Eddie Acuff (Shipyard Workers); Charles Coleman, Leonard Carey (English Bobbies); Norval Mitchell (Masseur); Charles Waldron (Preacher); Walter Pietila, George Bruggeman (Trapeze Artists); Eddie Hall (Bike Rider); Frank Hagney (Assistant Cyclist); Clyde Fillmore (F.B.I. Executive); Kirk Alyn (Attendant); Walter Fenner (Walt Disney Double); Bill Chaney, Lawrence Lathrop (Call Boys); Henry Armetta (Barber); Jack Norton (Customer); Lloyd Bridges (Captain); George Neise, Robert Lowell (Lieutenants); Gary Bruce (Technical Sergeant).

NONE BUT THE LONELY HEART (RKO, 1944) 113 M.

Producer, David Hempstead; associate producer, Sherman Todd; director, Clifford Odets; based on the novel by Richard Llewellyn; screenplay, Odets; production designer, Mordecai Gorelik; art directors, Albert D'Agostino, Jack Okey; set decorators, Darrell Silvera, Harley Miller; music, Hanns Eisler; music director, C. Bakaleinikoff; assistant director, Ruby Rosenberg; costumes, Renie; sound, Richard Van Hessen; special effects, Vernon L. Walker; camera, George Barnes; editor, Roland Gross.

Cary Grant (Ernie Mott); Ethel Barrymore (Ma Mott); Barry Fitzgerald (Twite); June Duprez (Ada); Jane Wyatt (Aggie Hunter); George Coulouris (Jim Mordiney); Dan Duryea (Lew Tate); Konstantin Shayne (Ike Weber); Eva Leonard Boyne (Ma Chalmers); Morton Lowry (Taz); Helene Thimig (Sister Nurse); William Challee (Knocker); Joseph Vitale (Cash); Roman Bohnen (Dad Pettyjohn); Renie Riano (Flo); Marcel Dill (Percy); David Clyde (Policeman with Stripes); Roy Thomas (Rookie Policeman); Amelia Romano (Lame Girl); Queenie Vassar (Ma Snowden); Art Smith (Marjoriebanks); Rosalind Ivan (Mrs. Tate); Claire Verdera (Barmaid); Elsie Prescott (Old Lady); Katherine Allen (Millie Wilson); Diedra Vale (Miss Tate); Herbert Heywood (Dad Fitchitt); Helena Grant (Old Woman in Shop); Virginia Farmer (Ma Segwiss); Walter Soderling (Pa Floom); Polly Bailey (Ma Floom); Bill Wolfe (Blind Man); George Atkinson (Man with Gramaphone); Barry Regan, Rosemary Blong, Jack Jackson, Rosemary La Planche (Dancers); Ted Billings (Cockney Bum); Milton Wallace (Ike Lesser); Eric Wilton, David Thursby (Prison Guards); Sammy Blum, Alec Harford (Drunks); Skelton Knaggs (Slush); Forrester Harvey (Bloke); Al Rhein, Al Murphy (Henchmen); Yorke Sherwood (Call Block Cop); Matthew Boulton, Herbert Evans (Police Sergeants); Joe North (Old Man); Ida Shoemaker (Old Lady); Chef Milani (Rossi); Keith Hitchcock (Roly Poly Man); Lita Gordon, Nancy Russell,

Marina Bohnen (Girls); Robin Sanders Clark, Sayre Dearing, Ernie Shield (Men); William Ambler (Bus Driver); Marie De Becker (Madame La Vaka); Bill O'Leary (Cab Driver); Leyland Hodgson, John Meredith (Cops); Diane Dyer (Baby); Charles Irwin (Cop at Crash); Tiny Jones (Woman); Colin Kenny (Cop Outside).

ARSENIC AND OLD LACE (WB, 1944) 118 M.

Producer-director, Frank Capra; based on the play by Joseph Kesselring; screenplay, Julius J. Epstein, Philip G. Epstein; assistant director, Russ Saunders; music, Max Steiner; music director, Leo F. Forbstein; orchestrator, Hugo Friedhofer; art director, Max Parker; sound, C. A. Riggs; special effects, Byron Haskin, Robert Burks; camera, Sol Polito; editor, Danny Mandell.

Cary Grant (Mortimer Brewster); Raymond Massey (Jonathan Brewster); Priscilla Lane (Elaine Harper); Josephine Hull (Abby Brewster); Jean Adair (Martha Brewster); Jack Carson (O'Hara); Edward Everett Horton (Mr. Witherspoon); Peter Lorre (Dr. Einstein); James Gleason (Lieutenant Rooney); John Alexander (Teddy "Roosevelt" Brewster); Grant Mitchell (Reverend Harper); Edward McNamara (Brophy); Garry Owen (Taxi Driver); John Ridgely (Saunders); Vaughan Glaser (Judge Cullman); Chester Clute (Doctor Gilchrist); Charles Lane (Reporter); Edward McWade (Gibbs); Leo White (Man in Phone Booth); Spencer Charters (Marriage License Clerk); Hank Mann (Photographer); Lee Phelps (Umpire).

NIGHT AND DAY (WB, 1946) C—132 M.

Producer, Arthur Schwartz; director, Michael Curtiz; based on the career of Cole Porter; adaptor, Jack Moffitt; screenplay, Charles Hoffman, Leo Townsend, William Bowers; assistant directors, Frank Heath, Robert Vreeland; montages, James Leicester; art director, John Hughes; set decorator, Armor Marlowe; costumes, Milo Anderson; makeup, Perc Westmore; dance number created-choreographed, LeRoy Prinz; dialog director, Herschel Dougherty; dance costumes, Travilla; songs, Cole Porter; additional music-music adaptor, Max Steiner; vocal arranger, Dudley Chambers; production numbers orchestrated-conducted by Ray Heindorf; music director, Leo F. Forbstein; sound, Everett A. Brown, David Forrest; special effects, Robert Burks; camera, Peverell Marley, William Skall; editor, David Weisbart.

Cary Grant (Cole Porter); Alexis Smith (Linda Lee Porter); Monty Woolley (Himself); Ginny Simms (Carole Hill); Jane Wyman (Gracie Harris); Eve Arden (Gabrielle); Victor Francen (Anatole Giron); Alan Hale (Leon Dowling); Dorothy Malone (Nancy); Tom D'Andrea (Bernie); Selena Royle (Kate Porter); Donald Woods (Ward Blackburn); Henry Stephenson (Omar Porter); Paul Cavanagh (Bart McClelland); Sig Ruman (Willowsky); Carlos Ramirez, Milada Mladova, Estelle Sloan, George Zoritch (Specialty Dancers); Adam and Jayne DiGalano (Specialty Team); Mary Martin (Herself); James Dobbs, John Compton, John Miles, Art Kassel, Paul Garkie, Laddie Rucker (Students); Frank Dae, Boyd Irwin, Sam Flint, Charles Miller (Professors); John Alvin (Petey); Harlan Briggs (Doorman); Harry Seymour (Clarence, the Piano Player); Clarence Muse (Caleb); JoAnn Marlowe (Tina); Regina Wallace, Frank Ferguson (Tina's Parents); George Meader (Minister); Virginia Sale (Minister's Wife); Bertha Woolford, Armba Dandridge (Servants); Gregory Muradian (Small Caroler); Lisa Golm, Ernest Golm (Foreign Couple); John Goldsworthy (Yale Gentleman); Gary Owen (Bartender); Crane Whitley (Commercial Artist); Lynne Baggett (Sexboat); Rebel Randall, Arlyne Roberts (Chorus Girls); Paula Drew, Patricia Clark, Jane Harker (Specialty Trio); Creighton Hale, Paul Gustine (Men in Theatre); Bob McKenzie (Hansom Cab Driver); Alan Shute, Bill Hind, Eric Wilton (English Officers); Edgar Caldwell, George Volk, Allen Marston (American Officers); Leon Lenoir, Michael Panaieff, Pierre Duval (French Officers); James Dodd (Red); Emile Hilb (Orchestra Leader); Bernard

Deroux (Assistant to Giron); George Suzanne, Henry DeSoto (Waiters); Marie Melesch (Scrub Woman); Adrian Doeshou, Rene Mimieux (Men at Bar); Fred Dash, Maurice Brierre, Albert Petit (French Waiters); Frank Marlowe (Army Driver); Rune Hultman (American Lieutenant); Peter Camlin (French Lieutenant); George Riley (O'Halloran); Fern Emmett (Secretary); Ruth Matthews, Betty Blair, Valerie Ardis, Edna Harris, Ellen Lowe, Joan Winfield (Nurses); Frank Marlowe (Army Driver); Dick Erdman, Robert Arthur, Caren Harsh, Patsy Harmon, Dorothy Reisner (Young Customers); Claire Meade, Charles Williams (Customers); Mayo Newhall (Bearded Man); George Nokes (Wayne Blackburn—Child); Gordon Richards (Coachman); Laura Treadwell (Woman in Theatre); Frank Miliott (Man in Theatre); Howard Freeman (Producer); Bobby Watson (Director); Philip Van Zandt (Librettist); Harry Crocker (Newspaperman); John "Red" Pierson, Herman Bing ("Peaches"); Chester Clute (Music Publisher); Joyce Compton, Helen O'Hara, Suzanne Rosser (Chorines); Dick Bartell (Photographer); Eddie Kane (Headwaiter); Louis Quince, Marion Gray, Willis Claire, Leota Lorraine (Couples); Rudy Friml (Orchestra Leader); John Vosper (Man); Helen Pender (Pretty Nurse); Eddie Kelly (Callboy); Bill Hardsway, Jack Richardson, Tom McGuire, Ed Biby (Surgeons); Laurie Shermain (Interne) Hobart Cavanaugh, Almira Sessions (Couple in Hospital Corridor); Gene Garrick (Soldier); Jacqueline Milo (French Girl); George Kirby (Cab Driver); Wally Scott (Chauffeur); Colin Kenny (Doorman); Herbert Evans (Bobby); Gladden James, Mike Lally, Dick Earle, J. W. Johnstone (Doctors); Buddy Gorman (English Page Boy); Harold DeBecker (English Workman); Jack Mower (Livery Chauffeur); Elizabeth Valentine (Matron in Hospital); Cyril Ring, Vivien Oakland (Married Couple); Pat Gleason (Dance Director); Don Roy (Band Leader); Hans Herbert (Headwaiter); Ruth and Dorothy Costello (Twins—Dance Team); George Boyce (Stage Manager); Fred Deming (Guest); Bert Moorhouse, Marshall Ruth, Fred Santley (Yale Alumni—Class of 1916); Joe Kirkwood, Jr., Gene Stanley (Classmates of Cole Porter); Henry Hasting (Black Bartender); Nicodemus "Nick" Stewart (Black Waiter).

WITHOUT RESERVATIONS (RKO, 1946) 107 M.

Producer, Jesse L. Lasky; director, Mervyn LeRoy; based on the novel by Jane Allen, Mae Livingston; screenplay, Andrew Solt; assistant director, Lloyd Richards; art directors, Albert S. D'Agostino, Ralph Berger; set decorators, Darrell Silvera, James Altwies; music, Roy Webb; music director, C. Bakaleinikoff; sound, Clem Portman, Francis M. Sarver; special effects, Vernon L. Walker; camera, Milton Krasner; editors, Harold Stine, Jack Ruggiero.

Claudette Colbert (Kit); John Wayne (Rusty); Don DeFore (Dink); Anne Triola (Gennie); Phil Brown (Soldier); Frank Puglia (Oraga); Thurston Hall (Baldwin); Dona Drake (Dolores); Fernando Alvarado, Michael Economides, Jose Alvarado, Miguel Tapia, Rosemary Lopez, Henry Mirelez, Hebert Espinosa (Mexican Youths); Charles Arnt (Salesman); Louella Parson, Jack Benny, Cary Grant (Themselves); Charles Evans (Jerome); Harry Hayden (Mr. Harry Randall); Lela Bliss (Mrs. Randall); Houseley Stevenson (Turnkey); Junius Matthews (Porter); Griff Barnett (Train Conductor); Will Wright (Pullman Conductor); Thelma Gyrath (WAC); J. Louis Johnson (Car Porter); Frank Dae (Man with Book); Ian Wolfe (Charlie Gibbs); Grace Hampton (Lois); Minerva Urecal (Sue); Esther Howard (Sarah); Dick Dickerson (Young Sailor); Joel Fluellen (Waiter in Club Car); Jack Parker, John Crawford, Henry Vroom, Lee Bennett (Soldiers); Oscar O'Shea (Conductor); Ruth Roman (Girl in Negligee); William Challee (Corporal); Sam McDaniel (Freddy); Henry Hastings (Waiter); Ralph Hubbard, Russ Whiteman (Sailors); Tay Dunn (Navy Ensign); Harold Davis, Tom Hubbard, Bob Wallace, Sid Davies, Charles Elmergreen, Fleet White, Bill Shannon, Roger Creed, Peter Michael, Joe Haworth (Marines); Brock Hunt, Bruce Brewster (Army Lieutenants); John Gilbreath, Bill Udell (Navy N.C.s); Bill O'Leary (Candy Butcher); Chef Milani

(Diner Captain); Ernest Anderson (Waiter); Harry Evans, Paul Gustine (Travelers); Art Miles (Truck Driver); Charles Hall (Window Washer); John Bleifer (Coal Heaver); Jan Wiley (Manicurist); June Glory (Girl); Bob Pepper (Man); Wallace Scott, Harry Holman (Gas Station Attendants); Warren Smith, Eric Alden (Chauffeurs); Leona Maricle (Baldwin's Secretary); Jean Koehler (Western Union Operator); William Benedict (Western Union Boy); Lorin Raker (Mr. Klotch); Tom Chatterton (Pullman Conductor); Charlie Moore (Redcap); Lois Austin (Congresswoman); Blanca Vischer (Mexican Beauty); Lisa Golm (Alma); Marvin Miller (Announcer); John Kellogg, Robin Short, Nanette Vallon, Jean Wong (Reporters); Harry Strang (Policeman); Tom Chatterton (Pullman Conductor); Cy Kendall (Bail Bondsman); Jesse Graves (Porter); Al Rosen (Train Mechanic); Raymond Burr (Paul Gill); Fred Coby (French Officer); Verne Richards (Brakeman); George Economides (Mexican Boy); Marilyn Buford (WAC).

NOTORIOUS (RKO, 1946) 103 M.

Producer, Alfred Hitchcock; associate producer, Barbara Keon; director-original subject, Hitchcock; screenplay, Ben Hecht; assistant director, William Dorfman; music, Roy Webb; music director, C. Bakaleinikoff; art directors, Albert S. D'Agostino, Carroll Clark; set decorators, Darrell Silvera, Claude Carpenter; costumes, Edith Head; sound, John E. Tribby, Terry Kellum; special effects, Vernon L. Walker, Paul Eagler; camera, Ted Tetzlaff; editor, Theron Warth.

Cary Grant (Devlin); Ingrid Bergman (Alicia Huberman); Claude Rains (Alexander Sebastian); Louis Calhern (Paul Prescott); Madame Konstantin (Mme. Sebastian); Reinhold Schunzel ("Dr. Anderson"); Moroni Olsen (Walter Beardsley); Ivan Triesault (Eric Mathis); Alex Minotis (Joseph); Wally Brown (Mr. Hopkins); Gavin Gordon (Ernest Weylin); Sir Charles Mendl (Commodore); Ricardo Costa (Dr. Barbosa); Eberhard Krumschmidt (Hupka); Fay Baker (Ethel); Antonio Moreno (Señor Ortiza); Frederick Ledebur (Knerr); Luis Serrano (Dr. Silva); William Gordon (Adams); Charles D. Brown (Judge); Ramon Nomar (Dr. Silva); Peter Von Zerneck (Rossner); Fred Nurney (Huberman); Herbert Wyndham (Mr. Cook); Aileen Carlyle (Woman at Party); Harry Hayden (Defense Council); Dink Trout (Clerk at Court); Howard Negley, Frank Marlowe, George Lynn (Photographers); Warren Jackson (District Attorney); Howard Mitchell (Bailiff); Sandra Morgan, Lillian West, Beulah Christian, Leota Lorraine, Almeda Fowler (Women); Garry Owen, Lester Dorr (Motor Cops); Patricia Smart (Mrs. Jackson); Tina Menard (Maid); Richard Clark, Frank McDonald (Men); Frank Wilcox (F.B.I. Man); John Vosper, Eddie Bruce, Don Kerr, Ben Erway Emmett Vogan, Paul Bryan, Alan Ward, James Logan (Reporters); Bea Benaderet, Virginia Gregg, Bernice Barrett (File Clerks); Ted Kelly (Waiter); Alfredo De Sa (Ribero).

THE BACHELOR AND THE BOBBY SOXER (RKO, 1947) 95 M.

Producer, Dore Schary; assistant to producer, Edgar Peterson; director, Irving Reis; story-screenplay, Sidney Sheldon; art directors, Albert S. D'Agostino, Carroll Clark; set decorators, Darrell Silvera, James Altwies; costumes, Edward Stevenson; music, Leigh Harline; music director, C. Bakaleinikoff; assistant director, Nate Levinson; sound, John L. Cass, Clem Portman; special effects, Russell A. Cully; camera, Robert de Grasse, Nicholas Musuraca; editor, Frederic Knudtson.

Cary Grant (Dick Nugent); Myrna Loy (Judge Margaret Turner); Shirley Temple (Susan Turner); Rudy Vallee (Tommy); Ray Collins (Beemish); Harry Davenport (Thaddeus); Johnny Sands (Jerry); Don Beddoe (Tony); Lillian Randolph (Bessie); Veda Ann Borg (Agnes Prescott); Dan Tobin (Walters); Ransom Sherman (Judge Treadwell); William Bakewell (Winters); Irving Bacon (Melvin); Ian Bernard (Perry); Carol Hughes (Florence); William Hall (Anthony Herman); Gregory Gay (Maitre d'Hotel); Richard Flato (Waiter at Tick Tock Club);

Kay Christopher, Marilyn Mercer, Priscilla Gates, Lydia Ann McKim, Ann Duncan, Bebe Allen (Girls); Charles Halton (Mr. Mittwick); Myra Marsh (Miss Weels); Charles Marsh (Mr. Roberts); Stephen Wayne, Richard Townsend, Howard Keiser (Boys); Harold Hutchinson (Tall Boy); Bonnie Jean Hartley (Waitress); J. Farrell MacDonald (Mac, the Bailiff); Ellen Corby (Woman); Mickey Simpson, Jack Gargan (Cops in Courtroom); Elena Warren, William Forrest (Mr. & Mrs. Baldwin); Carlotta Jelm (Doris Baldwin); Ned Roberts (Cab Driver); Norman Thomson (Bailiff); Bob Pepper, Garry Owen (Cops at Airport); Robert Bray (Man at Gate); Carl Kent (Ticket Taker); William Davidson (Anniversary Man at Club); Buzz King (Bit in Nightclub).

THE BISHOP'S WIFE (RKO, 1947) 105 M.

Producer, Samuel Goldwyn; director, Henry Koster; based on the novel by Robert Nathan; screenplay, Robert Sherwood, Leonardo Bercovici; music, Hugo Friedhofer; orchestrator, Jerome Moross; vocal director, Charles Henderson; music director, Emil Newman; art directors, George Jenkins, Perry Ferguson; set director, Julie Heron; costumes, Irene Sharaff; makeup, Robert Stephanoff; sound, Fred Lou; special camera effects, John Fulton; camera, Gregg Toland; editor, Monica Collingwood.

Cary Grant (Dudley); Loretta Young (Julia Broughton); David Niven (Henry Brougham); Monty Woolley (Professor Wutheridge); James Gleason (Sylvester); Gladys Cooper (Mrs. Hamilton); Elsa Lanchester (Matilda); Sara Haden (Mildred Cassaway); Karolyn Grimes (Debby Brougham); Tito Vuolo (Maggenti); Regis Toomey (Mr. Miller); Sarah Edwards (Mrs. Duffy); Margaret McWade (Miss Trumbull); Anne O'Neal (Mrs. Ward); Ben Erway (Mr. Perry); Erville Alderson (Stevens); Bobby Anderson (Defense Captain); Teddy Infuhr (Attack Captain); Eugene Borden (Michel); Almira Sessions, Claire DuBrey, Florence Auer (Ladies in Michel's); Margaret Wells (Hat Shop Proprietress); Kitty O'Neill (Hat Shop Customer); Isabel Jewell (Hysterical Mother); David Leonard (Blind Man); Dorothy Vaughn (Delia); Edgar Dearing (Cop); Edythe Elliott (Saleslady); Joseph J. Greene (Santa Claus); Shirley O'Hara (Girl at Table).

MR. BLANDINGS BUILDS HIS DREAM HOUSE (RKO, 1948) 94 M.

Executive producer, Dore Schary; producers, Norman Panama, Melvin Frank; director, H. C. Potter; based on the novel by Eric Hodgins; screenplay, Panama, Frank; assistant director, James Lane; music, Leigh Harline; music director, C. Bakaleinikoff; art directors, Albert S. D'Agostino, Carroll Clark; set decorators, Darrell Silvera, Harley Miller; costumes, Robert Kalloch; makeup, Gordon Bau; technical advisor, John Swope; sound, Francis M. Sarrer, Clem Portman; special effects, Russell A. Cully; camera, James Wong Howe; editor, Harry Marker.

Cary Grant (Jim Blandings); Myrna Loy (Muriel Blandings); Melvyn Douglas (Bill Cole); Reginald Denny (Simms); Sharyn Moffett (Joan Blandings); Connie Marshall (Betsy Blandings); Louise Beavers (Gussie); Harry Shannon (Tesander); Ian Wolfe (Smith); Tito Vuolo (Mr. Zucca); Nestor Paiva (Joe Appollonio); Jason Robards, Sr. (John Retch); Lurene Tuttle (Mary); Lex Barker (Carpenter Foreman); Emory Parnell (Mr. P'Delford); Will Wright (Eph); Frank Darien (Judge Quarles); Stanley Andrews (Murphy); Cliff Clark (Jones); Franklin Parker (Simpson); Charles Middleton (Wrecker); Cy Slocum (Man); Jack Jahries (Elevator Operator); Robert Bray, Frederich Ledebur (Workmen); Don Brodie (Charlie); Hal K. Dawson (Mr. Selby); Kernan Cripps (Cop); Ralph Stein (Proprietor); Mike Lally, Bud Wiser (Customers); Gene Leslie (Taxi Driver).

EVERY GIRL SHOULD BE MARRIED (RKO, 1948) 84 M.

Executive producer, Dore Schary; producer-director, Don Hartman; based on the short story by Eleanor Harris; screen-

play, Stephen Morehouse Avery, Hartman; art directors, Albert S. D'Agostino, Carroll Clark; set decorators, Darrell Silvera, William Stevens; costumes, Irene Sharaff; makeup, Gordon Bau; music, Leigh Harline; music director, C. Bakaleinikoff; sound, Francis Sarver, Clem Portman; special effects, Russell A. Cully; camera, George E. Diskant; editor, Harry Marker.

Cary Grant (Dr. Madison Brown); Franchot Tone (Roger Sanford); Diana Lynn (Julie Hudson); Betsy Drake (Anabel Sims); Alan Mowbray (Mr. Spitzer); Elizabeth Risdon (Mary Nolan); Richard Gaines (Sam McNutt); Harry Hayden (Gogarty); Chick Chandler (Soda Clerk); Leon Belasco (Violinist); Fred Essler (Pierre); Anna Q. Nilsson (Saleslady); Charmienne Harker (Miss King); Marjorie Walker, Alvina Temin, Rosalie Coughenour, Joan Lybrook (Models); Louise Franklin (Elevator Girl); Dan Foster (Cigar Store Clerk); Gwyn Shipmen (Mother); Arnolda Brown, Jean Andren (Customers); Elaine Riley (Young Lady); Lois Hall, Pat Hall (Girls); Carol Hughes (Girl at Counter); Claire Du Brey (Mrs. Willoughby); Helen Brown (Dignified Woman); Kate Lawson (Large Woman); Anne Nagel (Woman); James Griffith (Insurance Salesman); Al Rhein (Photographer); Joe Granby (Louis, the Barber); Selmer Jackson (Clergyman).

I WAS A MALE WAR BRIDE (20th, 1949) 105 M.

Producer, Sol. C. Siegel; director, Howard Hawks; based on the novel by Henri Rochard; screenplay, Charles Lederer, Leonard Spigelgass, Hagar Wilde; art directors, Lyle Wheeler, Albert Hogsett; set decorators, Thomas Little, Walter M. Scott; music director, Lionel Newman; music, Cyril Mockridge; orchestrator, Herbert Spencer; sound, George Leverett, Roger Heman; special camera effects, Fred Sersen; camera, Norbert Brodine, O. H. Borradaile; editor, James B. Clark.

Cary Grant (Captain Henri Rochard); Ann Sheridan (Lieutenant Catherine Gates); William Neff (Captain Jack Rumsey); Marion Marshall, Randy Stuart (WACS); Eugene Gericke (Tony Jowitt); Ruben Wendorf (Innkeeper's Assistant); John Whitney (Trumble); Ken Tobey (Seaman); Joe Haworth, John Zilly (Shore Patrol); William Pullen, William Self, Bill Murphy (Sergeants); Robert Stevenson, Harry Lauter (Lieutenants); Barbara Perry (Tall WAC); Otto Reichow, William Yetter (German Policemen); David McMahon (Chaplain); Alfred Linder (Bartender); Andre Charlot (French Minister); Lester Sharpe, Alex Gerry (Waiters); Gil Herman (Naval Officer); Ben Pollock (Officer); William McLean (Expectant G.I.); Russ Conway (Commander Willis); Mike Mahoney (Sailor); Kay Young (Major Prendergast); Lillie Kann (Innkeeper's Wife); Carl Jaffe (Jail Officer); Martin Miller (Schindler); Paul Hardmuth (Burgermeister); John Serret (French Notary); Patricia Curts (Girl in Door).

CRISIS (MGM, 1950) 95 M.

Producer, Arthur Freed; director, Richard Brooks; based on the short story "The Doubters" by George Tabori; screenplay, Brooks; art directors, Cedric Gibbons, Preston Ames; set decorators, Edwin B. Willis, Hugh Hurd; makeup, Jack Dawn; assistant director, Howard Koch; guitar solo, Vincente Gomez; music, Miklos Rozsa; sound, Douglas Shearer; special effects, A. Arnold Gillespie, Warren Newcombe; camera, Ray June; editor, Robert J. Kern.

Cary Grant (Dr. Eugene Ferguson); Jose Ferrer (Raoul Farrago); Paula Raymond (Helen Ferguson); Signe Hasso (Señora Isabel Farrago); Ramon Novarro (Colonel Adragon); Gilbert Roland (Gonzales); Leon Ames (Sam Proctor); Antonio Moreno (Dr. Emilio Nierra); Teresa Celli (Rosa Aldana); Vincente Gomez (Cariago); Martin Garralaga (Señor Magano); Pedro de Cordoba (Father Del Puento); Soledad Jimenez (Senora Farrago); Jose Dominguez (Rubio); Robert Tafur (Marco Aldana); Maurice Jara (Luis); Rodolfo Hoyos, Jr. (Chauffeur); Rita Conde (Pretty Girl); Roque Ybarra (Man in Car); Felipe Turich (Man with Valise); Charles Rivero, Mickey Contreras (Ad Libs); Captain Garcia (Muguel Farrago); Carlos Condi (Man); George Lewis (Desk Clerk); Carlo Tricoli (Nervous Man in

Lobby); Kenneth Garcia, Harry Vejar, Trina Varela, Bridget Carr (Guests); Audrey Betz (Servant); Robert Lugo, Myron Marks (Soldiers); Alex Montoya (Robust Indian); Margaret Martin (Indian Woman); Juan Duval (Proud Little Man); Al Haskell, Rafael Gomez, Z. Yacconelli (Soldiers); Fernando Del Valle (Bull Routine Man); A. Carrillo, Robert Polo, Jerry Riggio (Men at Table); Melba Meredith (Woman in Cafe); Lillian Israel, Carlotta Monti, Connie Montoya (Nurses); George Novarro (Dr. Gracian); Orlando Beltran, Eddie Gomez (Doctor's Assistants); Pepe Hern, David Cota, George Brady, Joaquin Garay, Neyle Morrow, Larry Crane (Students); Felipe Turich (Voice on Loudspeaker); Danilo Valenti (Eduardo); Sam Herrera (Man at Door); William M. McCormack (Man with Scar); Carlos Figueroa (Old Man); Robert Cabal (Very Young Man); Manuel Paris (Julio) Carlos Barbee, Amapola Del Vando (Farrago's Friends).

PEOPLE WILL TALK (20th, 1951) 109 M.

Producer, Darryl F. Zanuck; director, Joseph L. Mankiewicz; based on the play Dr. Praetorius by Curt Goetz; screenplay, Mankiewicz; music from Brahms and Wagner; orchestrator, Edward Powell; music director, Alfred Newman; assistant director, Hal Klein; art directors, Lyle Wheeler, George W. Davis; set decorators, Thomas Little, Walter M. Scott; costumes, Charles LeMaire; makeup, Ben Nye; sound, W. D. Flick, Roger Heman; special effects, Fred Sersen; camera, Milton Krasner; editor, Barbara McLean.

Cary Grant (Dr. Noah Praetorius); Jeanne Crain (Annabel Higgins); Finlay Currie (Shunderson); Hume Cronyn (Professor Elwell); Walter Slezak (Professor Barker); Sidney Blackmer (Arthur Higgins); Basil Ruysdael (Dean Lyman Brockwell); Katherine Locke (Miss James); Will Wright (John Higgins); Margaret Hamilton (Miss Pickett); Esther Somers (Mrs. Pegwhistle); Carleton Young (Technician); Larry Dobkin (Business Manager); Jo Gilbert (Nurse); Ann Morrison (Dietician); Julia Dean (Old Lady); Gail Bonney (Secretary); William Klein (Student Manager); George Offerman (Haskins); Adele Longmire (Mabel); Billy House (Coonan); Al Murphy (Photographer); Irene Seidner (Cook); Farley Baer (Toy Salesman); Joyce MacKenzie (Gussie); Maude Wallace (Night Matron); Kay Lavelle (Bella); Jack Kelly, Paul Lees, William Mauch, Leon Taylor (Students); Stuart Holmes (Board Member).

ROOM FOR ONE MORE (WB, 1952) 97 M.

Executive producer, Jack L. Warner; producer, Henry Blanke; director, Norman Taurog; based on the book by Anna Perrott Rose; screenplay, Jack Rose, Melville Shavelson; assistant director, Sherry Shourds; music, Max Steiner; orchestrator, Murray Cutter; art director, Douglas Bacon; set decorator, William L. Kuehl; costumes, Leah Rhodes, Marjorie Best; makeup, Gordon Bau; sound, Charles Lang; camera, Robert Burks; editor, Alan Crosland, Jr.

Cary Grant ("Pappy" Rose); Betsy Drake (Anna Rose); Lurene Tuttle (Miss Kenyon); Randy Stuart (Mrs. Foreman); John Ridgely (Harry Foreman); Irving Bacon (The Mayor); Mary Lou Treen (Mrs. Roberts); Hayden Rorke (The Doctor); Iris Mann (Jane); George "Foghorn" Winslow (Teensie); Clifford Tatum, Jr. (Jimmy-John); Gay Gordon (Trot); Malcolm Cassell (Tim); Larry Olson (Ben); Mary Newton, Ezelle Poule, Dorothy Kennedy, Marcorita Hellman, Karen Hale, Doris Kemper, Mary Alan Hokanson, Felice Richmond (Women); Ray Page (Gas Station Attendant); Charles Meredith (Mr. Thatcher); Oliver Blake (Mr. Doran); Frank Ferguson (Steve); Don Beddoe (School Principal); Lillian Bronson (Teacher); William Bakewell (Milkman); Douglas Fowley (Ice Man); John McGovern (Senior Patrol Leader); Gretchen Hartman (Chairwoman); Tony Taylor (Joey); Dabbs Greer (Scoutmaster); Stevie Wooten (Little Brother).

MONKEY BUSINESS (20th, 1952) 97 M.

Producer, Sol C. Siegel; director, Howard Hawks; based on an unpublished story by Harry Segall; screenplay, Ben Hecht,

I. A. L. Diamond, Charles Lederer; art directors, Lyle Wheeler, George Patrick; set decorators, Thomas Little, Walter M. Scott; costumes, Travilla; wardrobe director, Charles LeMaire; makeup, Ben Nye; music, Leigh Harline; music director, Lionel Newman; orchestrator, Earle Hagen; sound, W. D. Flick, Roger Heman; special camera effects, Ray Kellogg; camera, Milton Krasner; editor, William B. Murphy.

Cary Grant (Professor Barnaby Fulton); Ginger Rogers (Edwina Fulton); Charles Coburn (Mr. Oliver Oxly); Marilyn Monroe (Lois Laurel); Hugh Marlowe (Hank Entwhistle); Henri Letondal (Dr. Siegfried Kitzel); Robert Cornthwaite (Dr. Zoldeck); Larry Keating (Mr. G. J. Culverly); Douglas Spencer (Dr. Bruner); Esther Dale (Mrs. Rhinelander); George "Foghorn" Winslow (Little Indian); Emmett Lynn (Jimmy); Gil Stratton, Jr. (Yale Man); Faire Binney (Dowager); Harry Carey, Jr. (Reporter); and: Jerry Sheldon, Joseph Mell, George Eldredge, Heinie Conklin, Kathleen Freeman, Olan Soule, John McKee, Billy McLean, Paul Maxey, Mack Williams, Forbes Murray, Marjorie Halliday, Harry Carter, Harry Seymour, Harry Bartell, Jerry Paris, Roger Moore, Ruth Warren, Isabel Withers, Olive Carey, Dabbs Greer, Russ Clark, Ray Montgomery, Melinda Plowman, Terry Goodman, Jimmy Roebuck, Louis Lettiere, Robert Nichols, Ronnie Clark, Rudy Lee.

DREAM WIFE (MGM, 1953) 98 M.

Producer, Dore Schary; director, Sidney Sheldon; based on an unpublished story by Alfred Lewis Levitt; screenplay, Sheldon, Herbert Baker, Levitt; assistant director, Arvid Griffin; music, Conrad Salinger; songs, Charles Wolcott, Jamshid Shelbani; art directors, Cedric Gibbons, Daniel B. Cathcart; set decorators, Edwin B. Willis, Alfred E. Spencer; women's costumes, Helen Rose; men's costumes, Herschel McCoy; makeup, William Tuttle; sound, Douglas Shearer; special effects, A. Arnold Gillespie, Warren Newcombe; camera, Milton Krasner; editor, George White.

Cary Grant (Clemson Reade); Deborah Kerr (Effie); Walter Pidgeon (Walter McBride); Betta St. John (Tarji); Eduard Franz (Khan); Buddy Baer (Vizier); Les Tremayne (Ken Landwell); Bruce Bennett (Charlie Elkwood); Richard Anderson (Henry Malvine); Dan Tobin (Mr. Brown); Movita (Rima); Gloria Holden (Mrs. Landwell); June Clayworth (Mrs. Elkwood); Dean Miller (George); Steve Forrest (Louis); Jonathan Cott (Sailor); Patricia Tiernan (Pat); Mary Lawrence (Mrs. Malvine); Faire Binney (Mrs. Parker); Dan Barton (Marine); Kay Riehl (Woman); Edward Cassidy (Customs Official); Jean Andren (Bit); Perry Sheehan (Evelyn, the Receptionist); Harry Stanton, Steve Carruthers, James Farrar (Men); Virginia Mullen (Annie); Marie Brown (Miss Temple); Dick Rich (Delivery Man); Bert Moorhouse (Attlow); Jimmy Moss (Small Boy); Gail Bonney ("Mommy"); Lillian Culver (Woman at Airport); Forbes Murray, Donald Dillaway, Gayne Whitman (Men at Airport); John Alvin, Dorothy Kennedy, William Hamel (Reporters); Allen O'Locklin (Clerk); Andre d'Arcy, William McCormick, Bernie Gozier, Mohamed Ilbagi (Bukistanians); Jim Cronin, Paul F. Smith (Bellhops); Alphonse Martel (Headwaiter); Jack Chefe (Captain); Margie Liszt (Woman Cab Driver); Charles Sullivan (Truck Driver); William Vedder (Old Man); Vernon Rich (McBride's Assistant); Robert E. Nichols (Elevator Boy); Kathleen Freeman (Chambermaid); Aram Katcher (Bukistanian/Messenger); Rudy Rama (Servant); Bob Lugo (Guard); Dabbs Greer (Elevator Boy); Hassan Khyyam (Bukistanian Priest); Gordon Richards (Sir Cecil); Jack George (Clarence); Beryl McCutcheon, Margaret Hedin, Inez Gorman (Secretaries).

TO CATCH A THIEF (PAR, 1955) C—103 M.

Producer-director, Alfred Hitchcock; based on the novel by David Dodge; screenplay, John Michael Hayes; assistant director, Daniel McCauley; art directors, Hal Pereira, Joseph MacMillan Johnson; gowns for Miss Kelly, Edith Head; music, Lynn Murray; sound, Harold Lewis, John Cope; second unit camera, Wallace Kelley; camera, Robert Burks; editor, George Tomasini.

Cary Grant (John Robie); Grace Kelly (Frances Stevens); Jessie Royce Landis (Mrs. Stevens); John Williams (H. H. Hughson); Charles Vanel (Bertani); Brigitte Auber (Danielle); Jean Martinelli (Foussard); Georgette Anys (Germaine); Roland Lessaffre (Claude); Jean Hebey (Mercier); Rene Blancard (Lepic); Wee Willie Davis (Big Man in Kitchen); Dominique Davray (Antoinette); Edward Manouk (Kitchen Help); Russell Gaige (Mr. Sanford); Marie Stoddard (Mrs. Sanford); Paul "Tiny" Newlan (Vegetable Man in Kitchen); Lewis Charles (Man with Milk in Kitchen); Aimee Torriani (Woman in Kitchen); John Alderson, Frank Chelland (Chefs); Don Megowan, John Alderson, Bela Kovacs, Guy De Vestel, George Adrian, Alberto Morin (Detectives); Leonard Penn, Michael Hadlow (Monaco Policemen); Margaret Brewster (Cold Cream Woman); Adele St. Maur (Woman with Bird Cage); Eugene Borden (French Waiter); Philip Van Zandt (Jewelry Clerk); Steven Geray (Desk Clerk); Albert Pollet, George Paris, George A. Nardelli, Manuel Paris, Louis Mercier (Croupiers); Gladys Holland (Elegant French Woman); Ed Le Baron, Barry Norton (Frenchmen); Jeanne Lafayette, Loulette Sablon, Nina Borget (Frenchwomen); Alfred Hitchcock (Solemn Bus Passenger).

THE PRIDE AND THE PASSION (UA, 1957) C—130 M.

Producer-director, Stanley Kramer; based on the novel The Gun *by C. S. Forester; screenplay, Edna and Edward Anhalt; assistant directors, Alfonso Acebal, Jose Ma Ochoa, Isidoro Ferry; music, Georges Antheil; music conductor, Ernest Gold; art directors, Fernando Carrere, Gil Parrondo; costumes, Joe King; makeup, Bernard Ponedel, John O'Gorman, Jose Ma Sanchez; title designer, Saul Bass; sound, Joseph de Bretagne; sound effects, Walter Elliott, Bates Mason; military adviser, Lieutenant Colonel Luis Cano; special effects, Willis Cook, Maurice Ayers; camera, Franz Planer; editors, Frederic Knudtson, Ellsworth Hoagland.*

Cary Grant (Anthony); Frank Sinatra (Miguel); Sophia Loren (Juana); Theodore Bikel (General Jouvet); John Wengraf (Sermaine); Jay Novello (Ballinger); Jose Nieto (Carlos); Carlos Larranaga (Jose); Philip Van Zandt (Vidal); Paco El Laberinto (Manolo); Julian Ugarte (Enrique); Felix De Pomes (Bishop); Carlos Casaravilla (Léonardo); Juan Olaguivel (Ramon); Nana De Herrera (Maria); Carlos De Mendoza (Francisco); Luis Guedes (French Soldier).

AN AFFAIR TO REMEMBER (20th, 1957) C—114 M.

Producer, Jerry Wald; director, Leo McCarey; based on the unpublished story by McCarey and Mildred Cram; screenplay, Delmer Daves, McCarey; music, Hugo Friedhofer; music conductor, Lionel Newman; orchestrators, Edward B. Powell, Pete King; songs, Harry Warren, Harold Adamson, McCarey; art directors, Lyle R. Wheeler, Jack Martin Smith; set decorators, Walter M. Scott, Paul S. Fox; executive wardrobe designer, Charles LeMaire; makeup, Ben Nye; vocal supervisor, Ken Darby; sound, Charles Peck, Harry M. Leonard; special camera effects, L. B. Abbott; camera, Milton Krasner; editor, James B. Clark.

Cary Grant (Nickie Ferrante); Deborah Kerr (Terry McKay); Richard Denning (Kenneth); Neva Patterson (Lois Clarke); Cathleen Nesbitt (Grandmother); Robert Q. Lewis (Announcer); Charles Watts (Hathaway); Fortunio Bonanova (Courbet); Matt Moore (Father McGrath); Louis Mercier (Mario); Geraldine Wall (Miss Webb); Sarah Selby (Miss Lane); Nora Marlowe (Gladys); Alberto Morin (Bartender); Genevieve Aumont (Gabrielle); Jesslyn Fax (Landlady); Butch Bernard, Theresa Emerson, Richard Allen, Tina Thompson, Scotty Morrow, Kathleen Charney, Terry Ross Kelman, Norman Champion III (Orphans); Mary Carroll, Suzanne Ellers, Juney Ellis (Teachers); Don Pietro (Page Boy); Paul Bradley (Man); Tony De Mario (Waiter); Bert Stevens (Maitre D'); Brian Corcoran (Boy at Age Five); Priscilla Garcia (French Child); Marc Snow (Ship's Photographer); Anthony Mazzola (Page Boy);

Helen Mayon (Nurse); Walter Woolf King, Robert Lynn (Doctors); Roger Til (French Commentator); Jack Raine (English TV Commentator); Dino Bolognese (Italian Commentator); Jack Lomas (Painter); Dorothy Adams (Settlement Worker); Al Bain (Ex-Fighter); Danny Scott (Boy); Ken Kane (Elevator Operator); Patricia Powell (Blonde); Alena Murray (Airline Stewardess).

KISS THEM FOR ME (20th, 1957) C—103 M.

Producer, Jerry Wald; director, Stanley Donen; based on the play Kiss Them for Me *by Luther Davis and the novel* Shore Leave *by Frederic Wakeman; screenplay, Julius Epstein; assistant director, David Hall; music, Lionel Newman; orchestrators, Pete King, Skip Martin; song, Carroll Coates and Newman; art directors, Lyle R. Wheeler and Maurice Ransford; set decorators, Walter M. Scott and Stuart A. Reiss; executive wardrobe designer, Charles LeMaire; makeup, Ben Nye; sound, Charles Peck, Frank Moran; special camera effects, L. B. Abbott; camera, Milton Krasner; editor, Robert Simpson.*

Cary Grant (Crewson); Jayne Mansfield (Alice); Suzy Parker (Gwenneth); Leif Erickson (Eddie Trunbill); Ray Walston [Mac (Lieutenant McCann)]; Larry Blyden (Mississip); Nathaniel Frey (C.P.O. Ruddle); Werner Klemperer (Commander Wallace); Jack Mullaney (Ensign Lewis); Ben Wright (R.A.F. Pilot); Michael Ross (Gunner); Harry Carey, Jr. (Roundtree); Frank Nelson (Neilson); Ann McCrea (Lucille); Caprice Yordan (Debbie); John Doucette (Shore Patrol Lieutenant); Kip King (Small Marine); B. Suiter (Bit); James Stone (Bellhop); Bob St. Angelo (Hotel Porter); Barbara Gould (WAC Corporal); Mike Mahoney (Marine); Sue Collier (Girl at Party); Jan Reeves (Blonde); Jack Mather (Man); Peter Leeds (Reporter); Jonathan Hale (Nightclub Manager); Hal Baylor (Big Marine); Jane Burgess (Girl); William Phipps (Lieutenant Hendricks); Ray Montgomery (Lieutenant J. G.); Larry Lo Verde (C.P.O., Submarine); Michael Fox, Robert Sherman, Harry Carter, Richard Shannon (War Correspondents); Kathleen Freeman (Nurse Wilinksi); Nancy Kulp (Wave at Switchboard); Richard Deacon (Hotchkiss); Maudie Prickett (Chief Nurse); Linc Foster (Co-Pilot); Rachel Stephens (Wave).

INDISCREET (WB, 1958) C—100 M.

Producer, Stanley Donen; associate producer, Sydney Street; director, Donen; based on the play Kind Sir *by Norman Krasna; screenplay, Krasna; assistant director, Tom Pevsner; music, Richard Bennett, Ken Jones; song, Sammy Cahn and James Van Heusen; music conductor, Muir Mathieson; art director, Don Ashton; Mr. Grant's clothes by Quintino; makeup, John O'Gorman; sound, Richard Bird, Len Shilton; camera, Frederick A. Young; editor, Jack Harris.*

Cary Grant (Philip Adams); Ingrid Bergman (Anna Kalman); Cecil Parker (Alfred Munson); Phyllis Calvert (Margaret Munson); David Kossoff (Carl Banks); Megs Jenkins (Doris Banks); Oliver Johnston (Finleigh); Middleton Woods (Finleigh's Clerk).

HOUSEBOAT (PAR, 1958) C—112 M.

Producer, Jack Rose; director, Melville Shavelson; screenplay, Shavelson, Rose; assistant director, Michael D. Moore; music, George Duning; songs, Jay Livingston and Ray Evans; art directors, Hal Pereira, John Goodman; set decorators, Sam Comner, Grace Gregory; costumes, Edith Head; makeup, Wally Westmore; sound, Hugo and Charles Grezbach; process camera, Farciot Edouart; special effects, John P. Fulton; camera, Ray June; editor, Frank Fracht.

Cary Grant (Tom Winston); Sophia Loren (Cinzia Zaccardi); Martha Hyer (Caroline Gibson); Harry Guardino (Angelo); Eduardo Ciannelli (Arturo Zaccardi); Murray Hamilton (Alan Wilson); Mimi Gibson (Elizabeth Winston); Paul Petersen (David Winston); Charles Herbert (Robert Winston); Madge Kennedy (Mrs. Fransworth); John Litel (Mr. Farnsworth); Werner Klemperer (Harold Messner); Peggy Connelly (Elizabeth Wilson); Kathleen Freeman, Helen Brown (Women in Laundromat); Julian Rivero (Spanish Diplomat); Mary

Forbes (British Society Woman); Wally Walker, Brooks Benedict, Joe McTurk (Pitchmen); Marc Wilder (Specialty Dancer); Pat Moran (Clown); Bill Hickman (Handsome Man); Gilda Oliva (Pitch Saleswoman).

NORTH BY NORTHWEST (MGM, 1959) C—136 M.

Producer, Alfred Hitchcock; associate producer, Herbert Coleman; director, Hitchcock; screenplay, Ernest Lehman; production designer, Robert Boyle; art directors, William A. Horning, Russell Pye; assistant director, Robert Saunders; makeup, William Tuttle; sound, Franklin Milton; special effects, A. Arnold Gillespie, Lee LeBlanc; music, Bernard Herrmann; camera, Robert Burks; editor, George Tomasini.

Cary Grant (Roger Thornhill); Eva Marie Saint (Eve Kendall); James Mason (Phillip Vandamm); Jessie Royce Landis (Clara Thornhill); Leo G. Carroll (The Professor); Philip Ober (Lester Townsend); Josephine Hutchinson (Handsome Woman); Martin Landau (Leonard); Adam Williams (Valerian); Edward C. Platt (Victor Larabee); Robert Ellenstein (Licht); Les Tremayne (Auctioneer); Philip Coolidge (Dr. Cross); Patrick McVey, Ken Lynch (Chicago Policemen); Edward Binns (Captain Junket); Doreen Lang (Maggie); John Beradino (Sergeant Emile Klinger); Nora Marlowe (Anna, the Housekeeper); Doreen Lang (Maggie); Alexander Lockwood (Judge Anson B. Flynn); Stanley Adams (Lieutenant Harding); Lawrence Dobkin (Cartoonist); Harvey Stephens (Stockbroker); Walter Coy (Reporter); Madge Kennedy (Housewife); Baynes Barron, Jimmy Cross (Taxi Drivers); Tommy Farrell (Elevator Starter); Harry Seymour (Captain of Waiters); Frank Wilcox (Waiter); Robert Shayne (Larry Wade); Carleton Young (Fanning Nelson); Ralph Reed (Bellboy); Paul Genge (Lieutenant Hagerman); Robert B. Williams (Patrolman Waggonner—at Glen Cove); Maudie Prickett (Elise, the Maid); James McCallion (Valet); Doris Singh (Indian Girl); Sally Fraser (Girl on Loudspeaker); Mara McGiveney, Susan Whitney (Girl Attendants); Ned Glass (Ticket Agent); Howard Negley (Conductor); Jesslyn Fax, Lucille Curtis, Anne Anderson (Women); Jack Daly (Steward); Tol Avery, Tom Greenway (Detectives); Ernest Anderson (Porter); Malcolm Atterbury (Man on Road); Andy Albin (Farmer); Carl Milletaire (Clerk); Olan Soule (Assistant Auctioneer); Helen Spring (Woman at Auction); John Damler, Len Hendry (Police Lieutenants); Patricia Cutts, Hugh Pryor, Charles Postal (Bits); Taggart Casey (Man with Razor); Bobby Johnson (Waiter); Wilson Wood (Photographer); Bill Catching (Attendant); Dale Van Sickel (Ranger); Frank Marlowe (Dakota Cab Driver); Harry Strang (Assistant Conductor); Alfred Hitchcock (Man Who Misses Bus).

OPERATION PETTICOAT (UNIV, 1959) C—124 M.

Producer, Robert Arthur; director, Blake Edwards; suggested by a story by Paul King, Joseph Stone; screenplay, Stanley Shapiro, Maurice Richlin; art directors, Alexander Golitzen, Robert E. Smith; set decorators, Russell A. Gausman, Oliver Emert; music, David Rose; assistant director, Frank Shaw; makeup, Bud Westmore; gowns, Bill Thomas; sound, Leslie I. Carey, Vernon W. Cramer; special camera, Clifford Stine; camera, Russell Harlan; editors, Ted J. Kent, Frank Gross.

Cary Grant (Commodore Matt Sherman); Tony Curtis (Lieutenant Nick Holden); Joan O'Brien (Dolores Crandall); Dina Merrill (Barbara Duran); Arthur O'Connell (Tostin); Gene Evans (Molumphrey); Richard Sargent (Stovall); Virginia Gregg (Major Edna Howard); Robert F. Simon (Captain J. B. Henderson); Robert Gist (Watson); Gavin MacLeod (Hunkle); George Dunn (Prophet); Dick Crockett (Harmon); Madlyn Rhue (Lieutenant Claire Reid); Marion Ross (Lieutenant Ruth Colfax); Clarence E. Lung (Ramon); Frankie Darro (Dooley); Tony Pastor, Jr. (Fox); Robert Hoy (Reiner); Nicky Blair (Kraus); John W. Morley (Williams); William Bryant, Nino Tempo (Crewmen); Bert Beyers (Gowman); Tony Corrado (Fireman Lye); Glenn Jacobson (Control Talker); Robert Keys, Dale Cummings (M.P.s); Joseph Kim (Filipino); Leon Lontoc (Filipino Farmer); James F. Lanphier (Lieutenant Commander Daly); Alan Dexter (Navy Chief); Nelson Leigh

(Admiral Koenig); Francis De Sales (Captain Kress); Preston Hanson (Lieutenant Colonel Simpson); Hal Baylor (M.P. Sergeant); Bob Stratton (Marine Lieutenant); Malcolm Cassell, Larry Gilliland, Fred Harlfinger II (Sailors); Harry Harvey, Jr., Haile Chace, Howard Venezia (Soldiers); Vi Ingraham (Pregnant Filipino Woman); Vince Deadrick, William Kinney (Ad Libs); Alan Scott (Chief of Demolition Crew); Francis L. Ward (Third Class Petty Officer); William R. Callihan (Lieutenant Morrison); Gordon Casell (Colonel Higginson); Robert C. Youmans (Lieutenant); Robert Gibson (Seaman); Tusi Paiivae (Witch Doctor).

THE GRASS IS GREENER (UNIV, 1961) C—105 M.

Producer, Stanley Donen; associate producer, James Ware; director, Donen; based on the play by Hugh and Margaret Williams; screenplay, Hugh and Margaret Williams; music, Noel Coward; music conductor, Muir Mathieson; art director, Paul Sheriff; set decorator, Vernon Dixon; Miss Simmons' clothes, Christian Dior; Miss Kerr's clothes, Hardy Amies; makeup, John O'Gorman, Eric Allwright; assistant director, Roy Stevens; main titles designer, Maurice Binder; sound, John Cox, John W. Mitchell; camera, Christopher Challis; editor, James Clarke.

Cary Grant (Victor Rhyall); Deborah Kerr (Hilary Rhyall); Robert Mitchum (Charles Delacro); Jean Simmons (Hattie Durrant); Moray Watson (Sellers).

THAT TOUCH OF MINK (UNIV, 1962) C—99 M.

Executive producer, Robert Arthur; producers, Stanley Shapiro, Martin Melcher; director, Delbert Mann; screenplay, Shapiro, Nate Monaster; music, George Duning; art director, Alexander Golitzen, Robert Clatworthy; set decorators, George Milo; gowns, Rosemary Odell; makeup, Bud Westmore; assistant directors, Phil Bowles, Carl Beringer; sound, Waldon O. Watson, Corson Jowett; camera, Russell Metty; editor, Ted J. Kent.

Cary Grant (Philip Shayne); Doris Day (Cathy Timberlake); Gig Young (Roger); Audrey Meadows (Connie); Alan Hewitt (Dr. Gruber); John Astin (Beasley); Richard Sargent (Young Man); Joey Faye (Short Man); Laurie Mitchell (Showgirl); John Fiedler (Mr. Smith); Willard Sage (Hodges); Jack Livesey (Dr. Richardson); John McKee (Collins); Jan Burrell (Miss Jones); June Ericson (Millie); Russ Bender (Williams); Roger Maris, Mickey Mantle, Yogi Berra (Themselves); Art Passarella (Umpire); Ralph Manza (Taxi Driver); William Lanteau (Leonard); Kathryn Givney (Mrs. Haskell); Alice Backes (Miriam); Richard Deacon (Mr. Miller); Fred Essler (Mr. Golden); Helen Brown (Mrs. Farnum); Nelson Olmsted (Mr. Hackett); Clegg Hoyt (Truck Driver); Isabella Albonico (Lisa); Billy Greene (Al); Melora Conway (Miss Farrell); Yvonne Peattie (Fashion Consultant); Jon Silo (Mario); Tyler McVey (Doorman); Louise Arthur (Woman); John Morley (Man); Edna Bennett (Mrs. Wilson); Sally Hughes (Secretary) William Gleason (Hotel Manager); Rosalind Roberts, Dorothy Abbott (Stewardesses); Cathie Merchant (Irene); Barbara Collentine (Mrs. Smith); Jan Burrell (Miss Jones); Jack Rice (Customer in Automat); Suzanne Barton, Bette Woods, Doris Lynn (Models); George Simmons (Bellboy).

CHARADE (UNIV, 1963) C—113 M.

Producer, Stanley Donen; associate producer, James Ware; director, Donen; based on the story "The Unsuspecting Wife" by Peter Stone, Marc Behm; screenplay, Stone; assistant director, Marc Maurette; music, Henry Mancini; song, Mancini and Johnny Mercer; art director, Jean D'Eaubonne; Miss Hepburn's clothes, Givenchy; makeup, Alberto de Rossi, John O'-Gorman; main title designer, Maurice Binder; animator, Robert Ellis; sound, Jacques Carrere, Bob Jones; camera, Charles Lang; editor, James Clarke.

Cary Grant (Peter Joshua); Audrey Hepburn (Regina "Reggie" Lampert); Walter Matthau (Hamilton Bartholomew); James Coburn (Tex Penthollow); George Kennedy (Herman Scobie); Ned Glass (Leopold Gideon); Jacques Marin (Inspector Edouard Grandpierre); Paul Bonifas (Felix); Dominique Minot (Sylvie Gaudet); Thomas Chelimsky (Jean-Louis Gaudet).

FATHER GOOSE (UNIV, 1964) C—116 M.

Producer, Robert Arthur; director, Ralph Nelson; based on the unpublished story "A Place of Dragons" by S. H. Barnett; screenplay, Peter Stone, Frank Tarloff; assistant directors, Tom Shaw, James Welch; music, Cy Coleman; music supervisor, Joseph Gershenson; art directors, Alexander Golitzen, Henry Bumstead; set decorators, John McCarthy, George Milo; costumes, Aghayan; makeup, Bud Westmore; song, Coleman and Caroline Leigh; sound, Waldon O. Watson, William Russell; camera, Charles Lang, Jr.; editor, Ted J. Kent.

Cary Grant (Walter Eckland); Leslie Caron (Catherine Freneau); Trevor Howard (Commodore Frank Houghton); Jack Good (Lieutenant Stebbins); Verina Greenlaw (Christine); Pip Sparke (Anne); Jennifer Berrington (Harriet); Stephanie Berrington (Elizabeth); Lourelle Felsette (Angelique); Nicole Felsette (Dominique); Sharyl Locke (Jenny); Simon Scott (Submarine Captain); John Napier (Submarine Executive); Richard Lupino (Radioman); Alex Finlayson (Doctor); Peter Forster (Chaplain); Don Spruance (Navigator); Ken Swofford (Helmsman).

WALK, DON'T RUN (COL, 1966) C—114 M.

Producer, Sol C. Siegel; director, Charles Walters; story, Robert Russell, Frank Ross; screenplay, Sol Saks; assistant director, Jim Myers; music, Quincy Jones; production designer, Joe Wright; set decorators, George R. Nelson, Robert Priestley; costumes, Morton Haack; makeup, Ben Lane; sound, James Z. Flaster, Jack Haynes; camera, Harry Stradling; editors, Walter Thompson, James Wells.

Cary Grant (William Rutland); Samantha Eggar (Christine Easton); Jim Hutton (Steve Davis); John Standing (Julius P. Haversack); Miiko Taka (Aiko Kurawa); Ted Hartley (Yuri Andreyovitch); Ben Astar (Dimitri); George Takei (Police Captain); Teru Shimada (Mr. Kurawa); Lois Kiuchi (Mrs. Kurawa); James Yagi (Rutland's Driver); Craig Matsunaga (Boy); Patty Siu (Girl); Miyoshi Jingu (Woman); Ishimoto, Frank Kumagai (Plain Clothesmen); William Saito (Japanese Athlete); C. K. Yang (Nationalist Chinese Athlete); Bert Santos (Mexican Athlete); Sonya Harrison, Kenneth Parker, Gail Peters, Mel Profit (American Athletes); Bert Santos, Isabel Boniface (Mexican Athletes); Holger Abro, Alex Rodine, David Draper, Sonja Haney (Swedish Athletes); Peggy Rea (Russian Shot Putter); Ilona Wilson, Andre Hemmers (German Athletes); Wendee Tochihara, Jodee Tochihara (Japanese Twins); Jane Tochihara (Japanese Mother); Noriko, Mori Moto, Anna Shin, Irene Mizushima, Yuki Tani (Bath Attendants); Susan Ikeda, June Kawai, Miko Mayama (Japanese Waitresses); Randy Okazaki (Cab Driver); George Matsui, Roy Taguchi (Desk Clerks); Kay Shimatsu, Bob Kino (Assistant Managers); Rollin Moriyama (Manager); Sheri Yamasaki (Hostess); Vickey Cason (Contortionist); Alan Chee, Lei Kim, Lukas Shimatsu, Roy Ogat, Yangi Kitadani, Monty O'Grady (Ad Libs).

In MY FAIR LADY (WB '64)

Chapter Four

Rex Harrison

6'1"
170 pounds
Brown hair
Brown eyes
Pisces

Can such different types as Henry Higgins, the King of Siam, Julius Caesar, and Doctor Dolittle really be one and the same person? Yes, when the actor portraying these stage and screen figures is none other than Rex Harrison, the very versatile, methodical, and articulate British performer.

Like fellow Britisher Cary Grant, Rex has been tied into a public image as a sex symbol, although it's a more refined type than Grant's. Indeed, long ago, Harrison was tagged "Sexy Rexy," an approbation given him perhaps for his having courted and married five women to date. Three of his spouses,—Lilli Palmer, Kay Kendall and Rachel Roberts—have been his very delightful stage and screen co-stars. All of his love mates have been necessary to provide the star with the emotional stability he so badly requires to function at his witty, facile, lightning-quick best.

Some of those who know Harrison well claim he can be exceedingly waspish and arbitrary in his relentless quest for perfection in himself and in others, and that he is often childishly selfish on both a professional and a personal level. This may well be true, but for the public at large, it matters little, especially when the subject in question has provided the pivotal force of such entertainment projects as *Anna and the King of Siam* (Twentieth Century–Fox, 1946), *The Fourposter* (Columbia, 1952), and *My Fair Lady* (Warner Bros., 1964), in which, by repeating his long-running stage characterization, he earned a well-deserved Academy Award.

England nurtured Rex, Hollywood made him an international movie star, and the Continent now beckons him for its social hunting grounds. Whereas other actors have rushed back to the stage to regain their composure after unhappy motion-picture escapades, Rex apparently gravitates back to the footlights to gain new sustenance from live audiences and they re-establish his elan and sparkle for further cinema excursions.

If he was dark, thin, and suave in the 1930s when onscreen he toyed with Vivien Leigh in *Storm in a Teacup* (United Artists–British, 1937) or Merle Oberon in *Over the Moon* (United Artists–British, 1937), by the 1970s he was the wiry silver fox who, over the years, had lost little of his vitality or appeal. He has honed his package of talents into an even more irresistible entertainment attraction. The irony is that he is now the peer of high comedy in a world that little relishes stage-screen high comedies, and Rex the actor always has been reluctant to let anyone, even audiences, observe his flair for heavier fare.

Reginald Carey Harrison was born on Thursday, March 5, 1908, in the small village of Huyton, Lancashire, England, which is now a part of the northwestern coastal city of Liverpool. The third of three children (preceded in birth by two girls),* he was the blue-eyed, dark-haired son of Edith Carey Harrison and William Reginald Harrison. His father had trained to be an engineer, but, his son was to relate years later, "I can't remember what he ultimately did, but whatever he did, he did it on the Liverpool-Manchester stock exchange."

Reginald's mother was reputedly related to Edmund Kean, the great nineteenth century Shakespearean actor, as well as being descended from a line of clergymen. His father's ancestors were said to have been men of substantial wealth, with a family crest bearing the motto "Courage Sans Peur" (Courage without Fear) and an estate called Belle Vale, which later was transformed into a jam factory. By 1908 all that remained of the legacy was the Harrison motto, and Reginald grew up in a middle-class environment.

He was a sickly boy whose early recollections incuded constantly boiling kettles. He has said: "Nobody could guess what was the matter with me. But it passed. Some years ago [prior to 1956], a calcified gland was found in my intestines. Apparently, I had had tuberculosis of the intestines which cured itself." A severe bout of measles left him with a bad eye, which interfered with his ability to learn to read at a time when most other children his age had accomplished this. Despite these illnesses, he was a cheerful child who developed a comfortable relationship with his mother, who doubled as his constant nurse. He was never close to his father, whose Victorian attitudes persistently estranged him from his son throughout his life.

In his eighth year, Rex's parents took him to the theatre for the first time, which led the enthralled youth to transform his bed into a stage, with an old blanket as a curtain. From behind the blanket, he would repeatedly step forth and bow to his mother and sisters, who applauded the feat. It was, thus far, the only thing that appeared to interest him. In school he was a loner and a comparatively poor student who found it difficult to grasp the knack of learning, partially due to his inability to clearly see the blackboard. His mother was forced to provide him with spectacles. "I still can't see an elephant right beside me without my glasses," he has said.

At the age of ten Reginald was enrolled at Birkdale Preparatory School in Derbyshire, where, he claims, he was "unbright, dull and good at nothing except a bit of cricket." He had, by now, earned the nickname of Rex, and his young life took on an new dimension through his participation in school plays. For the part of Thisbe in *A Midsummer Night's Dream,* his mother made him a blond wig and for the role of the cat in *The Bluebird,* she fashioned a tail and attached it to his scrawny backside. He was astonished, but happy on hearing his stage efforts applauded.

One of Rex's schoolmasters remembered him as "what we called a posh boy, always neat and well groomed. Pretty unusual in a schoolboy. But he was likable." However, he was still agonizingly slow at his studies. At the age of sixteen he quit Liverpool College, which he had attended for two years. His father expected him to take a job as a clerk in a Liverpool steel firm, but he received instead an offer from the Liverpool Repertory Theatre, considered to be the best in the country. It was the theatre's practice to hire local youngsters with stage aspirations to act as understudies and to take walk-on parts.

Accepting the stage bid without question, Rex earned thirty shillings a week, lived at home, and, through the period of three years with the group, performed in fifty roles in Liverpool theatres and in touring repertory. One of his first parts, at the age of sixteen, was as the husband in a one-act play, *Thirty Minutes in a Street,* in which his initial line was: "Baby! Fetch a doctor." He rehearsed the line for days, and on opening night, due to his nervousness, the line poured forth as: "Doctor! Fetch a baby." The theatre reverberated with audience laughter. "I stood onstage," he recalled, "asking myself, 'What the hell have I said?'" It required several days before the memory of that humiliating debut was partially dimmed.

By the time he was nineteen, and ready to take the next step in his career, he had altered from a backward boy to a somewhat forward young man, inclined to charm attractive girls with the minimum of effort. He acquired the habits of carrying a long cigarette-holder and wearing a monocle in his bad eye, and he developed a fondness for Scotch whiskey and jazz music. He was popular with both men and women and became an expert at the Charleston and the Black Bottom. "At that time," he once said, "I didn't have a bean. I lived on rehearsal money. I admired the great farceurs

---

*One sister would marry David Maxwell Fyfe, Britian's onetime Lord Chancellor, while the other remained unmarried.

of the period—Seymour Hicks, Ralph Lynn, Charles Hawtrey, Ronnie Squire, and above all, Gerald du Maurier, all of whom were light comedians." He decided to try his luck on the London stage and so informed William Armstrong, the Liverpool Repertory's director, who suggested that it might be wiser if he gave up acting altogether. "I thought to myself," Harrison remembers, " 'what a rotten thing to say. What a rotten thing to say.' "

Once established in London show-business circles, he earned the part of Jack in *Charley's Aunt,* with a company that toured the English provinces. This led to other jobs in such productions as *Potiphar's Wife, Alibi, The Chinese Bungalow,* and *A Cup of Kindness.* Of these experiences, he allowed: "I was able to play a different part each week during the formative stage of my career by going from one group to another. It's hard training, but it's acting and constant acting can mean constant progress." The touring companies usually took night trains from town to town where the actors cajoled landlords into allowing them to have good rooms for small rent and where they often subsisted on sandwiches and tea. "I hardly remember being obsessed with either failure or success," he told Jon Bradshaw of *Esquire* magazine in July 1972. "I was learning my job. The provincial touring companies were very successful. I began to earn five pounds a week and lived in boarding-houses which cost me thirty shillings a week, all in all, I enjoyed myself immensely." He was quoted by *Newsweek* magazine in a 1956 article as saying, "It's unfortunate that more American actors don't get that kind of experience. It's a marvelous backlog for you to learn the hard way."

In 1930 Rex made his film debut in *The School for Scandal* (Paramount-British), a new version of the famed comedy starring Madeleine Carroll. Later that year Harrison had the tiny role of George in *The Great Game* (Gaumont). Neither part gave any indication that Harrison had a future in the cinema.

Much more fortuitous was his West End stage bow, which occurred at the Everyman Theatre (November 26, 1930) in *Getting George Married.* He had the role of the Honorable Freddy Thrippleton. The most powerful London theatre critic at the time was James Agate. A mention in his reviews, no matter how slight, was considered a triumph. Rex stayed up on opening night to await Agate's column, and in the last paragraph of the great man's review, he read: "Last night's play was a scratch affair, but it had one redeeming feature. A young man in it, whose name escapes me, seems to have a real talent for comedy." Harrison was chagrined by the omission of his name, but there was no doubt as to the actor's identity.

In February 1932, he was at the Prince of Wales Theatre in *The Ninth Man,* and during the year played in repertory at Cardiff, followed by a tour in *After All.* In 1933 he toured in *Other Men's Wives* and *For the Love of Mike,* before returning to London for a short run at the Lyric Theatre in *Another Language.* On tour again, he was in *Road House* and *Mother of Pearl,* and back in London he played the Whitehall Theatre in *No Way Back.* Because of the audience reception of his work he preferred comedy to drama. With a touring group, the Aldwych Farces, he played in *Charity Begins, Not Quite a Lady,* and *The Wicked Flee.* His roommate at a flat in Mayfair was actor Thomas Macaulay, who once recalled: "Rex was always very smart. Beautifully groomed in lounge suits, very suave, an elegant walker. He had tremendous ambition and sacrificed everything to his acting. Except girls. He was a great one for living secondhand. If he didn't have a car, he knew girls who did. He was always considered dangerously attractive."

Rex was rarely out of work; in 1934 he was with the Piccadilly Theatre Company in *Our Mutual Father* as John Murdoch, and he appeared at the Fulham Theatre as Anthony Fair in *Anthony and Anna.* By this point he had amassed a tremendous reservoir of acting experience in a wide variety of entertainments.

In 1934 the very eligible bachelor about town wed a pretty Cornish blonde named Noel Marjorie Collette Thomas, who preferred to be known as Collette. The daughter of a retired British Army major, she was a French teacher and an accomplished skier. "I remember the first time I saw Rex on stage," she once said, "I thought . . . that he was a contributor, a contributor to all our enjoyment. He may have put on or acted up as a man, but never as an actor. I don't think he grew in himself, but his acting did." Immediately upon meeting him in 1933 and after their marriage, she took trains to the suburbs to watch him perform, but she was made happy when, in February, 1935, he settled in at London's St. Martin's Theatre for a comparatively long run of *Man of Yesterday.* This gave him a good opportunity, she felt, to become better acquainted with their son, Noel, who was born on January 29, 1935.

Meanwhile, Rex had made three more film appearances. In a comedy, *Get Your Man* (Paramount-British, 1934), his was the bit part of Tom

With Sebastian Shaw (left) in GET YOUR MAN (Paramount-British '34)

Jakes. In *Leave It to Blanche* (First National–British 1934), starring Henry Kendall and Olive Blakeney, he was fifth-billed as Ronnie. In *All at Sea* (Fox-British, 1935), a romantic comedy, he was the Honorable Aubrey Bellingham on board the cruise ship S.S. *Levantic,* where he was the chief rival of the film's star, Tyrrell Davis, for the affections of Googie Withers. *Kinematograph Weekly* said he "overacts" in that part.

In November 1935, Rex appeared at the Queens Theatre in Robert Morley's play *Short Story,* starring A. E. Matthews, Sybil Thorndike, and Margaret Rutherford. However, the real start of his success came in the United States on March 2, 1936, when he was Tubbs Barrow in *Sweet Aloes,* a tearjerker written by Joyce Carey and starring Evelyn Laye. Although the play, which had been an enormous success in London, ran only twenty-four performances at the Booth Theatre, Rex left a favorable impression on New York theatregoers.[*] He next returned to London for the June 1936 opening of *Heroes Don't Care* at the St. Martin's Theatre.

Perspicacious film producer Alexander Korda

then offered Harrison a film contract at the impressive sum of £2,500 a year, and he accepted because of the money, not because he was eager to work again in motion pictures.

In November 1936, he acquired the lead role in Terence Rattigan's play *French without Tears,*[†] which played the Criterion Theatre for two years with Kay Hammond his co-star. During this period, he acted in Korda films by day, while performing nocturnally on stage.

Men Are Not Gods (1936)[‡] was his first film under the Korda–London films contract and counts as his *first* screen credit so far as Rex is concerned, for he prefers to forget his "quickie quotas" of past years. Hollywood's Samuel Goldwyn, who was also releasing his products through United Artists, made a loan to Korda of Miriam Hopkins as star of the film, which was written and directed by Walter Reisch. Also starring Gertrude Lawrence and Sebastian Shaw, the film provided Harrison with the role of Tommy Stapleton, the second male lead. Called an "out and out woman's picture" by *Kinematograph Weekly,* it revolves around the eternal-triangle

[*]In the film version, called *Give Me Your Heart* (Warner Bros., 1936), Roland Young had Harrison's role.
[†]With Frank Lawton in the less than successful Broadway showing that same year. On screen, in the Paramount release of 1940, Ray Milland inherited Rex's part.
[‡]Released in the United States through United Artists on January 18, 1937.

theme. The secretary (Hopkins) of a drama critic (A. E. Matthews) is asked by a stage actress (Lawrence) to intercept and soft-pedal the review of her husband's (Shaw) inept rendition of Othello. In doing so, the secretary is fired from her job, meets the actor, and soon sets up housekeeping with him. When Lawrence reveals she is pregnant by Shaw, he plans to kill her while she performs Desdemona to his Othello in the last act, but the secretary senses what is being plotted and prevents the murder at the risk of her own life. Rex was the secretary's newspaper pal who write obituary columns.

As the plot of *Men Are Not Gods* would indicate, the movie switches from the lighthearted to the overly dramatic, not giving the puzzled viewer much emotional stability with which to appreciate the proceedings. In retrospect, the picture would have been far more engaging if more of the plot and camera time had focused on lithesome Lawrence and Harrison, each of whom was far more deft than the major figures at projecting entertaining characterizations.

For his second Korda film, Harrison was co-starred with Vivien Leigh in *Storm in a Teacup* (United Artists, 1937), the screen adaptation of Bruno Frank's play *Sturm in Wasserglass.** Produced and co-directed by Victor Saville (with Ian Dalrymple), the film was described by Frank S. Nugent (*New York Times*) as a "splendid comic brew." In the story, Mrs. Hegarty (Sara Allgood), a heavily brogued Scotswoman, has a dog named Patsy for whom she has neglected to purchase a license. When the dog is impounded, Allgood is fined £5 by the mean old Provost (Cecil Parker), a sum that she refuses to pay. Harrison, a crusading newspaper reporter, takes up her cause on the front page of his paper, thereby humiliating Parliament-bound Parker into relenting. Coincidentally, Parker has a daughter (Leigh), who succumbs to the reporter's charms. Basil Wright in the *Spectator* said that "the Chief Laurels go to Rex Harrison, a comparative newcomer, Vivien Leigh and Cecil Parker." When shown in New York in March 1938 at the Little Carnegie Playhouse, the film proved to be popular with American audiences. Slowly but surely, U.S. filmgoers were becoming aware of the charming, angular Britisher.

Harrison continued with his hard-paced working schedule, indubitably one of the causes of the continual separations and reunions between him

With Sebastian Shaw in MEN ARE NOT GODS (United Artists-British '36)

and Collette. Korda then loaned him to the J. H. Hoffberg Company for the bedroom farce *School for Husbands* (General Film Distributors, 1937)‡ in the lead role of Leonard Drummond, a novelist knowledgeable in the romance department. Two bored, married ladies (Diana Churchill and June Clyde) flirt with him over sips of champagne while their husbands (Henry Kendall and Romney Brent) simmer. Because of the sophisticate's reputation, the husbands seek Rex's advice regarding matrimonially bored wives, and he stresses the importance of gifts and an occasional compliment. "I call it 'wife insurance'" he says, and cautions them to remember that all women possess the "siren instinct." In the meantime, he has arranged to elope with one (Clyde) of the wives, but this plan fizzles through a device of his own making which enables the husbands to recapture their wives. Called an "elegant presentation" by *Kinematograph Weekly*, it was pointed out that Harrison's performance was "polished." In alerting its readers to this picture, it said: "If the censors don't wield the scissors too freely, there is enough spice, dual meaning chit-chat and

---

*Roger Livesey starred in the English stage version, called *Storm in a Teacup* (1936), and also in the Broadway version, entitled *Storm over Patsy* (Theatre Guild Theatre: March 8, 1937, 48 performances).
‡Released in the United States in January 1939.

With June Clyde and Diana Churchill in SCHOOL FOR HUSBANDS (General Film Distributors '37)

undraped femininity . . ." *Variety* went on to mention that "Rex Harrison plays the novelist with distinction. Hollywood sleuths might do much worse than give him the o.o. [once over]." On a level aimed more at the layman, Frank S. Nugent (*New York Times*) reported that Rex, as the "devil with ladies," "seems to have tried to keep it clean and clever, but what is a man to do when his script compels him to invite a matron to see his etchings?"

Korda put him to work in a property that London Films had been holding for a while. Originally titled *Playboy* and scheduled for Jack Hulbert as star, it was retagged *Over the Moon* (United Artists–British, 1937) and boasted a screenplay from a story by Robert Sherwood. With Merle Oberon, Korda's favorite,* as co-star, Rex is a doctor who is attracted to her. His infatuation leads him to withdraw his savings from the bank in order to finance a trip to Monte Carlo, a fashion spot she has always wished to enjoy. As they are about to marry, she learns that an estate amounting to $90 million has been left her by an uncle previously believed to be impoverished. The doctor then backs down from marrying her because of his

pride, and she travels throughout the Continent from Monte Carlo to Switzerland to Italy with a conglomerate of parasitic worshippers. (This jaunt allows for a variety of landmark settings for the Technicolor cameras.) After having been absent from the storyline for some time, Rex reappears toward the end and renews his relationship with her when it becomes evident to him that she has gained a solid new, set of values and a more reasonable life style. The "comedy" was not very successful in Europe, nor did it fare well in the U.S. release, commencing in December 1940.

Collette Harrison left home for good in the summer of 1938, taking young Noel with her. It hardly seems probable that Rex had much opportunity to miss either of them for he was then put on loan to Mayflower Productions, newly formed by Charles Laughton in partnership with Erich Pommer (famed for the Geman film, *The Cabinet of Dr. Caligari* [1919]). Harrison was in support of Laughton and Vivien Leigh in *St. Martin's Lane* (Associated British Producers, 1938)‡ in the role of Harley Prentiss, a society man who is also a songwriter. He is one of a group entertained at a sidewalk coffee stall by Libby (Leigh), a quick-

*Miss Oberon was later to become Korda's wife.
‡Released in the United States as *Sidewalks of London* (Paramount, 1940) solely on the strength of Miss Leigh's Oscar-winning performance in *Gone with the Wind* (MGM, 1939).

With Merle Oberon in OVER THE MOON (United Artists-British '37)

witted waif who sings on the streets for coins.†
She steals Harrison's gold cigarette case and is
followed by Laughton, chief of all the street en-
tertainers (called "buskers"), from whom she has
lifted parts of her act. She is talked into sharing
Laughton's living quarters, but laughs at his marriage proposal because by now she has become
infatuated with Harrison. Ambitious Leigh
knows that Harrison can help her achieve her goal
—the legitimate stage. Later Laughton is sent to
prison. When he is released he finds that Leigh
has accomplished her professional aim.

MGM borrowed Rex in 1938 for that studio's
second film to be shot at its British studios, *The
Citadel* (1938). King Vidor directed the adaptation of A. J. Cronin's well-received novel, with
internationally famous Robert Donat in the lead
role. Rosalind Russell, the only American in the
cast, was Christine, the sensible, sympathetic,
schoolteacher wife of Donat. The latter, a young
doctor whose ambition is to medically assist the
poor people of a Welsh mining town, changes his
goal when he perceives there is easy and plentiful
money to be earned as a West End society specialist. In London, he encounters the cynical Dr.
Lawford (Harrison), a suave, fashionable doctor

With Robert Donat in THE CITADEL (MGM-British '38)

†Tyrone Guthrie was also in the group of society men.

whose exclusive Blue Book patients have only minor ailments. Donat follows the unprincipled society doctor's example for a time, but then realizes, with the help of his wife, that he is not doing humanity much good. Therefore, he returns to Wales, where he finds fulfillment through the resumption of his original plan, that of aiding the poor.

Although *The Citadel* was nominated for four Academy Awards (Best Actor—Donat, Best Picture, Best Direction, Best Written Screenplay), it failed to achieve a victory in any category. It was, however, accoladed with the *Look* magazine Achievement Award as Best Motion Picture, and the National Board of Review named it one of the year's ten best.

MGM thought Harrison good enough to offer him a seven-year contract, *if* he would agree to move to Hollywood, but he declined. He had no intention of leaving England then, especially with his career on the upswing. The thought of travailing in America for seven long years seemed horrendous.

With the final curtain of *French without Tears* (1,039 performances), Rex next played the boards at the Haymarket Theatre (January 25, 1939) as Leo in Noël Coward's *Design for Living*,* and was joined by Anton Walbrook and Diana Wynyard.

Harrison was next assigned to starring with Valerie Hobson in British Paramount's *The Silent Battle* (1939),† which the *New York Times's* Bosley Crowther called "another of those British spy thrillers." Like *The Lady Vanishes*, (MGM-British), the Alfred Hitchcock masterpiece of 1938, most of the action takes place on a train, this time on the Simplon-Orient Express out of Paris. Harrison is the mysterious passenger named Jacques Sauvin who turns out to be a secret service agent working for the Balkan country of Brosnia. Also on the fast-moving train is Draguisha Montescu (Hobson), who has been persuaded by Bartoff (Kaye Seely), a dastardly armaments king, to throw a bomb at the Brosnian prime minister. Harrison prevents her from tossing the explosive, thus stopping an event that could have triggered the next world war. Had a more astute director than Herbert Mason helmed this picture, it would not be the forgotten screen item it is today. But as the *Kinematograph Weekly* dutifully pointed out,

"Rex Harrison is both convincing and interesting. . ." If only he could find a picture to match his talents.

Also in 1939, Harrison appeared in *Ten Days in Paris* (1939),‡ produced in England for Columbia Pictures. The movie employed the theme of amnesia, a reliable source for film mystique which probably caused thousands of moviegoing kids to secretly half-wish it would happen to them as an escape valve from reality. Harrison's Robert Stevens awakens in a Paris nursing home with a gunshot wound, but insists that an airplane accident had been responsible for his incapacitation. In retracing his fuzzily recalled activities, it is revealed that he had survived the plane crash ten days earlier, but he has no recollection of the time between the crash and the moment he opened his eyes in the nursing home. When he is fully recovered, he sets out to piece together the missing span of days. In unraveling the confounded mystery, he learns that he was deeply involved with espionage agents who used him as a tool in the establishing of military fortifications that could have been injurious to the security of Britain. He eventually sets things right, dispatches the unfriendly agents, and finds romance with Kaaren Verne in the process. The ever-observant *Kinematograph Weekly* reported that Rex "has an easy, nonchalant way with him, and his talent and attractive personality do much to keep the fantastic yet intriguing story in sane perspective." It was further written that he "injects considerable feminine appeal into the role," and he has a "polished and [a] natural sense of humour."

The film contract with Korda, by this time, had expired. Korda's future plans in Hollywood did not particularly include Rex, a situation which was satisfactory to the actor. Therefore, in 1940 he was at liberty, and had it not been for the British wartime shortages of time and personnel, he would have made many more pictures than the one in which he co-starred. This was Carol Reed's *Gestapo* (MGM-British, 1940), a.k.a. *Night Train to Munich*.‡ It was yet another espionage yarn conceived in the heady tradition of *The Lady Vanishes* and the less resilient *The Silent Battle*, with much of the action taking place aboard a train.

In *Gestapo* (*Night Train to Munich*) Rex is a British government agent posing as a song-plug-

---

*Produced on Broadway (Ethel Barrymore Theatre: January 24, 1933, 135 performances) with Noel Coward in Rex's role; and filmed by Paramount in 1933 with Gary Cooper in the parallel assignment.
†Released as *Continental Express* in the United States through Monogram Pictures in 1942.
‡Columbia distributed the film in America as *Missing Ten Days* (1941).
‡ Released in the United States as *Night Train* (Twentieth Century–Fox, 1940).

ger.† For the first time in his career, he "sang." The song was a simple thing containing the words, "For only love can lead the way, as time rolls on and on."

Within the tensely plotted film, an elderly inventor (James Harcourt) is captured by the English and taken from Prague to England. His daughter (Margaret Lockwood) is then imprisoned by the Germans in retaliation. She escapes with a fellow prisoner (Paul von Henreid),° who is actually a conniving SS officer. Lockwood naively leads von Henreid to her father in London and then both are abducted by the Nazis. A British agent (Harrison) masquerades as a Gestapo officer, Ulrich Hertzell, and joins the group by boarding the train back to Germany where he plans to rescue Harcourt and Lockwood. When Rex is revealed to be an Englishman, Lockwood is amazed that he does not attempt to fight his way out of it. Slim, angular Rex asks her: "What do you take me for, Bulldog Drummond?" In the exciting final scenes (later much copied by Hollywood filmmakers), they use dangling mountain cable cars to escape into Switzerland amid rifle fire and serial-type background music that would have made Tom Tyler proud. Theodore Strauss (*New York Times*) credited Harrison with being "not only dashing, but expert as the British spy." It was becoming obviously clear on both sides of the Atlantic that Rex Harrison, even more than the well-established Robert Donat, was the emerging sex symbol of the British cinema.

In the summer of 1940, during the Battle of Britain, Gabriel Pascal produced and directed, under enemy fire, George Bernard Shaw's *Major Barbara* (General Film Distributors, 1941),‡ with scenario and dialogue contributed by the venerable Shaw. The theme of the film centers around the Salvation Army's Major Barbara Undershaft (Wendy Hiller). She begins to doubt her devotion to the duty of saving souls when she learns that the Army will take money even from her sardonic father (Robert Morley). Eventually she comes to terms with herself in the realization that money,

†In *St. Martin's Lane*, Rex's character had been a popular song composer.
°Later to become known in American films as Paul Henreid.
‡First on the London stage in 1905 and on Broadway in 1915 with Ernest Lawford in Rex's screen role; revived in 1928 with Eliot Case in the role and again in 1956 with Burgess Meredith.

With Walter Hudd, David Tree, Penelope Dudley-Ward, Marie Lohr, and Wendy Hiller in MAJOR BARBARA (General Film Distributions '41)

regardless of the source, acts as a conditioner of the soul. Rex plays the role of Adolphus Cusins, her wealthy suitor, who dons the Salvation Army uniform while claiming to be an agnostic.

During the filming Shaw was often on the set, which gave the players ample opportunity to become acquainted with him, and Rex once stated that the last scene was "difficult for all of us. He sat down with us and read the five-page scene aloud. When he finished, he said 'Ah, what a terrible scene!' That was it. No help. Nothing."

For most American filmgoers who have seen *Major Barbara* on original release or through revivals and video showings, its continued esteem remains something of a mystery. It is, in essence, a total transcript of the stage play, which in itself might have been better as a dinner-table discussion than as a theatre piece. For instance, Otis Ferguson (*New Republic*) opined: "As something aimed at the kind of life and power we have come to expect of a good movie, it just isn't there, it dies on its own clubfeet." As for the performers, Morley as the unmindful, outspoken father is clearly most at home in the environs, settling into this scene or that, much like a garrulous, proud-minded neighbor come for a solid chat. Even in 1940, Miss Hiller was a bit thick in the waist and perhaps a bit too sensible to be portraying the evangelistic heroine, but her adeptness with the Shavian lines redeems her presence. There is little to be said for Harrison's drum-beating scholar: he is lanky, languid, pleasant, but unmemorable in his overenthusiastic presence. It would be several more years before he did Shaw justice on the stage and screen, with *My Fair Lady*.

Not to let time slip through his fingers, Harrison agreed to star with Diana Wynyard in the West End edition of S. N. Behrman's comedy, *No Time for Comedy* (Haymarket Theatre: March 27, 1941, 348 performances).* In the supporting cast was a lovely twenty-six-year-old brunette actress of Austrian birth, Lilli Palmer.† Their paths had crossed a year earlier when they performed on tour in different plays, but working together gave them the opportunity to get to know each other better. By the time the play was judged a hit, they were seldom apart. Some years later, Miss Palmer was to recall: "He was very self-conscious, as all Englishmen are when they're attracted to a woman." She also revealed a nervous habit of his. "We went for a drive. He was wearing big fur gloves, and he was continually taking off one of his gloves to pull his nose. I watched him for a while and then said, 'Let me pull your nose for you. It'll be easier—and safer.' "

In mid-1941, thirty-three-year-old Rex Harrison left the cast of *No Time for Comedy* to join the Royal Air Force. Because of his poor eyesight, he was not permitted to be a pilot, but was instead assigned to the radar section and later became a radar instructor.

The following year, Collette Harrison divorced him, naming Lilli Palmer as co-respondent. The court gave Collette custody of their seven-year-old son.

On January 25, 1943, Rex and Lilli were married during one of his rare, brief leaves from active duty. He was thirty-four, she was twenty-eight. They took up residence in a house near Denham, which, soon after, was partially destroyed when a German bomb exploded some fifty feet away. They were in the house at the time of the bombing, and, although neither was seriously hurt when portions of the ceiling fell on them, Harrison received a gash across his forehead.

The Harrisons' son, Carey, was born February 19, 1944, in Denham at another house to which they had moved.

Later in 1944, the RAF Film Unit was given facilities at Pinewood Studios for the production of an air force documentary film, *Journey Together* (RKO, 1945), written by Terence Rattigan. With the exception of Edward G. Robinson and Bessie Love, everyone connected with the film was a member of the Royal Air Force or an Allied unit, including Flight Lieutenant John Boulting, its able director. Those who helped in detailing the progress of student pilots in the picture were Richard Attenborough, Jack Watling, John Justin, and Sebastian Shaw. Rex's small part was scarcely visible by the time the film reached the United States in March 1946.

It seemed that the war was always literally at the Harrisons' front door steps. Early in 1945, a German V-2 rocket exploded in the front yard of the actor's home, resulting in only minor damage. The baby's perambulator was sprinkled with fragments of glass, but Carey was not injured.

After his discharge from the RAF, when the Axis forces in Europe were on the run and the need for aerial radar teams was minimized, Harrison appeared in support of Anna Neagle and Dean

---

*Produced on Broadway (Ethel Barrymore Theatre: April 17, 1939, 185 performances) with Laurence Olivier and Katharine Cornell; Warner Bros. did the film version with James Stewart.
†Born Maria Lilli Peiser in Posen, Germany, on May 24, 1914. She made her stage debut in Berlin in *Die eiserne Jungfrau* (1934). Her feature film debut is regarded as *Crime Unlimited* (British First National, 1934).

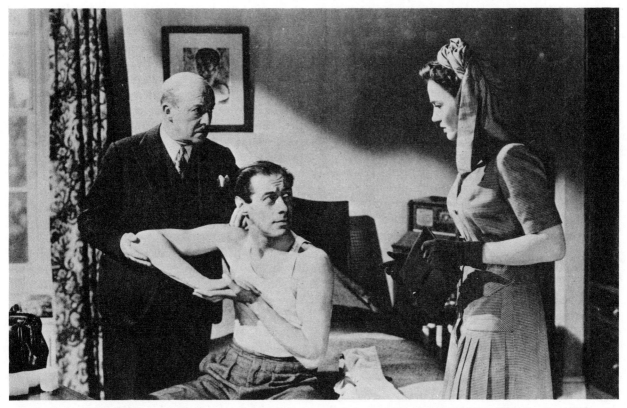

With Hugh Wakefield and Constance Cummings in BLITHE SPIRIT (General Film Distributors '45)

Jagger in *I Live in Grosvenor Square* (Pathe, 1945).* Directed by her husband Herbert Wilcox for Wilcox–Associated British Productions as a tribute to Anglo-American cooperation, it relates the story of a WAAF (Neagle) of noble birth who falls in love in London with an American Air Force sergeant (Dean Jagger). Harrison is David Bruce, a British officer who not only loses his girl to the American, but is also defeated in his bid for Parliament. Of Rex's performance, *Variety* offered: "[he] is sure to impress American femmes in the service, even though the heroine jilts him."

Following his success at writing, producing, co-directing, and appearing in the film *In Which We Serve* (British Lion, 1942), Noël Coward had formed his own producing company called Cineguild. The second film turned out by the film was *This Happy Breed* (Eagle Lion, 1944) from Coward's play. *Blithe Spirit* (General Film Distributors, 1945) was chosen as its third venture. Adapted from the Coward comedy‡ by David Lean, Ronald Neame, and Anthony Havelock-Al-

lan, the Technicolor film version was directed by Lean. In this somewhat watered down translation from stage to screen, Rex is Charles Condomine, a popular novelist who plans to write a book exposing a fake medium. As a way of doing research he invites the local supernaturalist (Margaret Rutherford) to his home to try out her special powers on his wife of five years (Constance Cummings) and a couple of his friends (Joyce Carey and Hugh Wakefield). The medium manages to bring the novelist's first wife (Kay Hammond) from the netherworld, but her presence is only seen by the husband. When it is considered high time for the spirit to depart, Rutherford, unfortunately, cannot recall the vanishing formula, so the ghost stays throughout the remainder of the ninety-six-minute film. The wife, jealous because her husband talks about and to his dead wife, has a hell of a time understanding it all.

Of his performance in the celluloid *Blithe Spirit,* Noël Coward told Rex, "After me, you're the best light comedian in the world," while *Variety*

*Known as *A Yank in London* (Twentieth Century–Fox, 1946) when shown in the United States.

‡First presented at the Piccadilly Theatre in London on July 2, 1941, with Cecil Parker (Charles), Fay Compton (Ruth), Kay Hammond (Elvira), and Margaret Rutherford (Mme. Arcati). Before the run was through, it had transferred to two other theatres and chalked up a record of 1,997 performances. On Broadway (Morosco Theatre: November 5, 1941, 657 performances), the cast was headed by Clifton Webb, Peggy Wood, Leonora Corbett, and Mildred Natwick. On television's "Ford Star Jubilee" (CBS, January 14, 1956), Coward, Claudette Colbert, Lauren Bacall, and Mildred Natwick had the main parts. In the Broadway musicalization, entitled *High Spirits* (Alvin Theatre: April 7, 1964, 63 performances), the cast was Edward Woodward, Louise Troy, Tammy Grimes, and Beatrice Lillie.

indicated that Harrison's playing of "a Noël Coward lead would seem to be just about the tops." Alton Cook of the *New York World-Telegram* found Rex's performance to be "full of debonair, carefree glitter" and the *New York Herald-Tribune's* Otis L. Guernsey, Jr. described his delivery with "He shapes his lines with a fluid, cultured English drawl, colors them with a smile that is both knowing and ingratiating, and tosses them off with deceptive carelessness."

In May and June of 1945, Rex toured English and American armed forces camps in Europe, including those in Germany, in a revival of his successful 1936 play, *French without Tears*.

Next on the Harrison film agenda was *The Rake's Progress* (Eagle Lion, 1945),* produced by Frank Launder at the Gainsborough Studios for Individual Productions. Written by Launder and Sidney Gilliat,† and directed by the latter, it tells the adult life story of Vivian Kenway (Harrison), an utterly charming, egotistical scoundrel. It begins with his expulsion from Oxford University, where he has climbed to the highest steeple on campus and placed a chamber pot for all the world to see.‡ From this boyish prank, he goes to Brazil for a job with a coffee company, arranged by his father (Godfrey Tearle). There he has an affair with the wife (Marie Lohr) of the company's owner (Garry Marsh) and is fired for his amatory pursuits. He then marries an Austrian Jewess (Lilli Palmer) on the pretense of rescuing her from Nazism, but swindles her out of everything she has, including her emotions. He is also loved by his father's secretary (Margaret Johnston), but jilts her and is then responsible for the death of his father in an auto accident. Finally, with World War II in full swing and his past having caught up with his recalcitrant conscience, he joins up and dies, of all things, a hero's death.

Evidently there is nothing so fascinating as a rogue, for moviegoers were entranced by Harrison's latest screen characterization. Said Bosley Crowther (*New York Times*): "for those who enjoy a characterization done with polish and subtlety, Mr. Harrison's portrait of this scoundrel will be a strange but intriguing display. . . ."

At this point, and thanks to the focus given Har-

rison by *The Rake's Progress,* Rex was dubbed "Sexy Rexy." There are several ideas of just how he acquired the label. Some sources credit Walter Winchell, others say that Rex himself started it as a publicity gag, but the question of originator seemed to have been settled by Harrison himself in a 1972 interview with Esquire's Jon Bradshaw. Rex claimed that an English actress, whom he preferred not to name, was responsible for the tag because of his refusal to make love to her.† He told Bradshaw: "It annoys me because I'm a more serious person than that vaudevillian label suggests."

Rex had received Hollywood offers as early as 1936 when he appeared in Broadway's ill-fated *Sweet Aloes*, but he had ignored them. However, the accumulated interest in Harrison's stage and screen careers built to a crescendo with *I Live in Grosvenor Square* and *The Rake's Progress*. As *Variety* phrased its reaction to Rex in the latter picture: "To see Harrison's technique with glamorous girl after glamorous girl is to make one wonder where he's been all these years." Rex decided to answer that question in person. In the autumn of 1945, he accepted a seven-year contract with Darryl F. Zanuck of Twentieth Century–Fox while Lilli Palmer was signed to a short-term deal by Warner Bros.

At this stage of the acting game, Rex was willing to forget some gentlemen's-handshake deals in order to hasten his sailing to America. In his autobiography, *Twenty-Five Thousand Sunsets* (1967), producer-director-autobiographer Herbert Wilcox recalls that when he returned from America, where he had sold *I Live in Grosvenor Square* to Fox, he came back to London to be told by Rex that he was negating their arrangement for him to buy Wilcox's farmhouse in Chalfont as a gift for Lillie Palmer. "This is my first Hollywood nibble, Herbert, "and I must take it. You can easily get rid of your farm." Harrison's leaving also axed forthcoming projects that he and Wilcox planned to work on together. ‡

After signing with Zanuck for a salary of $4,000 a week, Rex explained: "My contract specifies I may have six months in Hollywood and the rest of the year at home [England]. It also specifies that

---

*Released in the United States as *Notorious Gentleman* (Universal, 1946).
†Lauder's and Gilliat's writing credits include *The Lady Vanishes* (1936) and *Gestapo* (1940).
‡For the American release print, a new scene was shot, in which, instead of a chamber pot, a top hat is placed on the steeple.
†English stage actress Coral Browne, recently linked with Vincent Price, claimed at one point that she originated the name.
‡It was Wilcox who so ably described the Rex Harrison manner of this period: "Rex's repose is second to none. With a glance he can convey more than most actors applying every trick in the book. He has figure and clothes sense, and an effortless technique which hides technique but which can blaze into anger and fury at the drop of a hat, coupled with the most engaging smile."

my leave from the studio here must coincide with that of my wife whose contract also carries that provision, since we don't believe in married couples being separated."

Harrison once remembered that Hollywood of 1945 was "very exciting. Everyone was coming back from the war and the major studios were going full blast." Lilli recalled the parties, "I remember going to a party at the Rathbones' where all the walls of the main room were carpeted with gardenias. Parties where everybody seemed to be —Hoagy Carmichael on the piano, Judy Garland singing, Gable and Bogart drinking in the corner. After the war, everyone was only too keen to be lavish."

Rex's first American film was *Anna and the King of Siam* (Twentieth Century–Fox, 1946) as King Mongkut (Rama IV).* Adapted from Margaret Landon's and Anna H. Leonowens's books by Talbot Jennings and Sally Benson and directed by John Cromwell, it was a lavishly expensive production, although executed in black-and-white photography. Sixty-seven exteriors and thirty-four interiors, all decorated in rococo Oriental at a cost of $300,000, were constructed on Twentieth's back lot. Bonnie Cashin's costumes cost $26,000; $10,000 was spent to duplicate the king's royal state barge, and the cost of lensing King Chulalongkon's lavish coronation was $80,000.

Rex researched everything pertinent he could find on Siam and its potentates and later said: "I saw the amazing possibilities of creating a character I had never played before. I could try to leave Rex Harrison in England and become a Siamese King—It was the kind of challenge that actors like."

Although Irene Dunne received top billing in the picture portraying Anna Leonowens, the gentle British governess who becomes the king's secretary as well as teacher to his wives and tribe of children, Harrison's king role emerged as the pivotal, memorable one. The plot is set in Siam of 1862, where the ruler is a bit eccentric and overly proud, although eager to learn new ways while still remaining steadfast to his feudal customs. His "native" costumes of droopy bloomers and ornate, spiked head-pieces were, alone, comical, and Rex's humane interpretation of the enigmatic monarch supplied the film's poignant humor. Through Dunne he learns humility and how to

With Lilli Palmer in THE RAKE'S PROGRESS (a.k.a. NOTORIOUS GENTLEMAN) (Eagle Lion '45)

handle platonic love, both lessons being depicted with complete subtlety by director Cromwell.

The critics were unanimous in praising Rex: "Here is a new type of movie hero, who demonstrates that the flexing of wits is more fascinating than the flexing of muscles" (*Esquire* magazine); "Harrison's death enactment is probably as splendid as anything pictures have offered in years" (*Los Angeles Times*); "Beautifully acted" (*Life* magazine); "Nothing short of perfect" (*New York Herald-Tribune*); "Harrison has a field day as the naive, intelligent tyrant" (*Newsweek* magazine); "Positively perfect" (*New York Post*).

The film won Oscars for art directors Lyle Wheeler and William Darling and cinematographer Arthur Miller. *Photoplay* magazine gave it a citation as one of the eight best films of 1946, and the National Board of Review chose it as one of the year's ten best. Ironically Harrison was not even nominated for a Best Actor Award in the year that Fredric March won in the category for *The Best Years of Our Lives* (RKO).†

---

*Zanuck's first choices for the role were James Mason and Robert Montgomery.

†On Broadway (St. James Theatre: March 29, 1951, 1246 performances), Yul Brynner enacted the king in the musical version called *The King and I.* Rex cabled him: "The king is dead, long live the King." Brynner was also to appear in Twentieth Century–Fox's 1956 screen version of *The King and I,* for which he won the Oscar. In 1972 Brynner starred in a short-lived ABC-TV "The King and I" series.

With Deanna Durbin and Lilli Palmer in Hollywood, November, 1946

With Irene Dunne in ANNA AND THE KING OF SIAM (20th '46)

While Harrison was gaining new legions of film fans, he was alienating the Hollywood press. One columnist stated that "he is Boyer with an Oxford accent. Suave; Sophisticated. Old world sex appeal," terminology and comparisons which Rex found appalling. Hedda Hopper and Louella Parsons were ignored when they requested interviews because he simply did not care to enter into the publicity game, which he mockingly referred to as "Calling everyone Darling." He was known as a snob by the press, and the *Hollywood Reporter* lashed out at him with: "We don't remember an actor, foreign or domestic, who breached so many rules of good taste in his conduct among fellow workers. The wonder of the whole thing is that Harrison didn't have his face bashed in."

Compounding his problems was the fact that Twentieth Century–Fox was in a dilemma about what to do with Rex after *Anna and the King of Siam*. His being so patently English was one limiting factor, and they did not want to typecast him as a mysterious Oriental. He rejected several scripts, one of which was *13 Rue Madeleine* (1946),† but settled for *The Ghost and Mrs. Muir* (Twentieth Century–Fox, 1947), based on R. A. Dick's novel. Shooting commenced on August 5, 1946, at Twentieth's studios with Joseph Mankiewicz directing Philip Dunne's scenario.

Sea captain Daniel Gregg (Harrison) has been dead four years; committed suicide, they say, "to save someone the trouble of assassinating him," but it is further said that he haunts Gull Cottage at White Cliff where he lived. Lucy Muir (Gene Tierney), a widow with a child (Natalie Wood), rents the cottage despite the legend. On her first night, in the dark kitchen, she is startled by a man's laugh and the words, "Light the candle . . . go ahead, light it." She does and we see the captain's beaver-bearded ghost. "Why do you haunt?" she questions when her initial fright has dissipated. "I have plans for me house and they don't include a pack of strangers." His plans to turn the house into a home for retired seamen were thwarted by his death, which, he explains, was accidental, since he fell asleep in a chair and his foot hit the gas valve.

Later in the film, Tierney becomes impoverished when her husband's gold mine fails, and, in order to maintain the roof over her head, the captain, who has come to like her, offers to put his salty sea experiences ("I've led a man's life and

I'm not ashamed of it") into book form with her as its "ghost" author. "It's my experience," he advises her, "that women will do anything for money." The book becomes a success. When she falls in love with a fellow writer (George Sanders), a ne'er do-well with a wife (Anna Lee), Harrison decides to cease his haunting and allow the widow to lead her own life. He bids her farewell while telling her she will not remember him. After his exit, the picture suddenly becomes slow and plodding. Tierney grows old with her housekeeper (Edna Best) after the grown daughter (Vanessa Brown) marries, and the movie's end finds the captain returning to claim the widow's spirit when she dies in her sleep.*

Aside from *Cue* magazine, which insisted that Rex was "miscast," the critics were enamored of him. "Rex Harrison is the spirit and that makes everything all right" (*Los Angeles Herald-Examiner*); "[he] presents a gusty and delightful characterization" (*Variety*); "Approaches perfection" (*Hollywood Reporter*); "He makes a robust ghost, complete with beard and fiendish laugh. When he goes, audience interest goes with him" (*New York Sun*).

Following these somewhat ethereal roles in his first two American-made features, Harrison announced: "I had to convince audiences that I was in love with Irene Dunne without making love to her, and as the Ghost in *Mrs. Muir* I had to make passes at Gene Tierney without touching her. I'm going back to playing flesh-and-blood parts. Spiritual lovemaking is not exactly my cup of tea."

While waiting for a suitable, more corporeal film role, he filled in his professional time with radio, a medium perfectly suited to his well-modulated voice with its catchy "foreign" accent. He was heard on "The Theatre Guild on the Air," "Screen Guild Players," "This Is Hollywood," and "The Academy Award Theatre." On July 24, 1947, he quit his scheduled appearance on NBC's "Eve Arden Show," because he considered the script to be in bad taste. Cast as "Bugsie," a gangster with an English accent, he was to remark about King George: "Oh yes, he's the English answer to Atwater Kent."‡ He was replaced by personality Vera Vague as that show's guest-of-the-week, with the script rewritten to accomodate her different talents.

Just as Continental Lilli Palmer was having difficulties on the Warner Bros. lot obtaining proper

†James Cagney played the role offered to Rex.
*NBC-TV and later ABC-TV serialized the story (September 21, 1968, 50 episodes) with Edward Mulhare as the Captain and Hope Lang as the attractive widow.
‡Kent was then one of Hollywood's most lavish hosts.

screen roles,† so Harrison was stagnating at Twentieth Century–Fox. The studio had under contract such male players as Tyrone Power, Victor Mature, Richard Widmark, John Payne, Cornel Wilde, George Montgomery, Dana Andrews, Dan Dailey, Lon McCallister, Clifton Webb, and Mark Stevens, which immediately suggests the thrust of Zanuck's filmmaking program: *Americana*. Rex, under this setup, could only be a cultural oddity whose talents were very tangential to the studio's product output. At best he could only hope to take the leftovers of the star roster, as with *The Foxes of Harrow* (Twentieth Century–Fox, 1947), a property which had been turned down by Twentieth's pet male lead, Tyrone Power. Adapted by Wanda Tuchock from Frank Yerby's fat novel, the 117-minute film, directed by John Stahl, had predictable plots and subplots concerning dashing Stephen Fox (Harrison), an illegitimate Irishman who woos a New Orleans lovely (Maureen O'Hara), weds her, and quarrels with her on their wedding night when he vows to never again enter her boudoir. It is the era (1800s) of duels and grace when fortunes were made and quickly lost. When Harrison's money nearly runs out and the son, conceived before the wedding-night quarrel, is killed, he takes measure of his life and returns to his waiting wife's arms.

Although the *New York World-Telegram* suggested that Rex brought the film to life "merely by his walking into a scene," the *New York Time's* Bosley Crowther thought that he "plays the top Fox with a grim and somewhat testy air which is mildly sardonic and intriguing but doesn't reveal anything." More importantly, *The Foxes of Harrow* was not greeted with public enthusiasm. Filmed in black and white rather than color (with Power out of the project why waste the extra money? reasoned Zanuck), and containing an unhealthy brew of native voodooism, soap opera, and strong-willed creatures (Harrison and O'Hara), the story was neither one thing nor another, fitting into no particular genre with ease.

In November 1947, Rex joined British and American film stars in London in a stage presentation for the benefit of the Cinematograph Trade Benevolent Fund, with the King and Queen in attendance. Interviewed by an American newspaperman after the show, Harrison said, with reference to American-British films, "The more exchanging back and forth we do between the two countries, the better for all of us concerned." He

†Palmer had a featured, but inconsequential part in *Cloak and Dagger* (Warner Bros., 1946). She was far more effective in *Body and Soul* (United Artists, 1947) than in the later *My Girl Tisa* (Warner Bros., 1948).

With Richard Haydn in THE FOXES OF HARROW (20th '47)

praised Hollywood's facilities as "unbelievably wonderful." From a personal standpoint, he acknowledged that his enjoyments were golf, tennis, riding, fishing, gardening, and trumpeting. He revealed that his collection of swing-music recordings greatly outnumbered Lilli's recordings of opera.

Escape (1948), an updating of the British Radio film of 1930,[*] was directed in England by Joseph Mankiewicz, from the play by John Galsworthy.[†] Photographed against a rural English setting, it relates the story of Matt Denant (Harrison), who accidentally kills a detective during the policeman's attempts to arrest a tart (Betty Ann Davies) with whom Harrison had been casually talking. His past exemplary war record notwithstanding, ex-RAF pilot Harrison is sentenced on circumstantial evidence to three years at Dartmoor Prison. Angered by the court's injustice, he escapes from confinement and encounters Dora Winton (Peggy Cummins), who aids him. Since they share such unconventional thoughts, they quickly fall in love, and, finally, when cornered in a village church, he gives himself up rather than jeopardize the reputation of the vicar (Norman Wooland), who would lie to protect him. *Escape* made very little impact on the American movie market.

While in London, Harrison met Carole Landis,[†] the twenty-nine-year-old, four-time married, former Twentieth Century–Fox contractee whose beauty had earned her the Hollywood tag of "Cinemablonde." Emotional and sentimental, she wore all four of her wedding rings on one finger and had a reputation among her friends for having a bent toward suicide.[‡] Rex openly dated her after Lilli went to New York, and after she completed *The Noose* (Pathe-British, 1948) and *The Brass Monkey* (United Artists–British, 1948) they returned to Hollywood together, in March 1948, when Miss Landis filed for divorce from husband number four, W. Horace Schmidlapp, a millionaire Broadway producer.

In June 1948, Rex went to work as the star of

[*]Starring Sir Gerald du Maurier and Edna Best.
[†]Produced on Broadway (Booth Theatre: October 26, 1927, 176 performances) with Leslie Howard in the key role.
[†]There to prepare for her Broadway appearance as Cleopatra in *Caesar and Cleopatra*, opposite Sir Cedric Hardwicke.
[‡]Born Frances Lillian Mary Ridste on January 1, 1919, in Fairchild, Wisconsin. She reached Hollywood in 1936 and had bits in *A Star Is Born* (United Artists, 1937), *The King and the Chorus Girl* (Warner Bros., 1937), etc., before making her "name" in *One Million B.C.* (United Artists–Hal Roach, 1940). Her first Twentieth Century-Fox picture was *Moon Over Miami* (1941) with Betty Grable. Her last at the studio was *It Shouldn't Happen to a Dog* (1946) with Allyn Joslyn.
  Her husbands included: Irving Wheeler (1934–38), a fellow student at San Bernardino High School; Willis Hunt, Jr. (1940–40) a yachtsman; Thomas Wallace (1943–45), an ex-Eagle Squadron captain; and W. Horace Schmidlapp (1945–48).

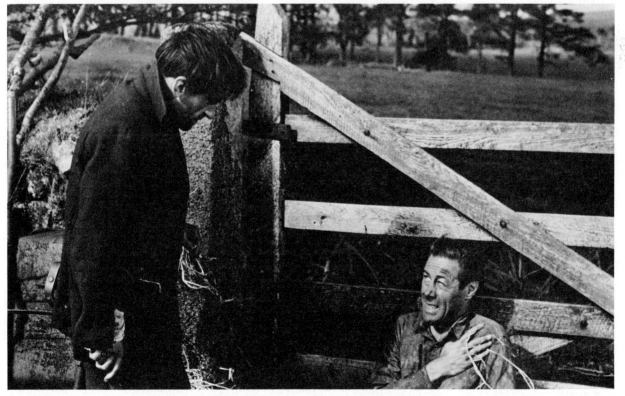

With George Woodbridge in ESCAPE (20th Century-Fox-British '48)

With Linda Darnell in UNFAITHFULLY YOURS
(20th '48)

Unfaithfully Yours (Twentieth Century–Fox, 1948) from an original story by Preston Sturges and directed and produced by Sturges, who, the year before, had signed a lucrative agreement with the studio after his debacle with Howard Hughes's filmmaking enterprises. Of Sturges, Rex would later admit that he was "a most extraordinary and ingenious creature. The whole thing was like a party. He directed in a red fez. He would have a Doberman Pinscher on the set with him. Before he would start, he would stuff a handkerchief in his mouth to stop from laughing."

Although Sturges found his work worthy of such mirth, the critics of 1948 were not in tune, and the film died at the box office. Not until years later was it appreciated when Pauline Kael, for one, called it "one of the best comedies ever made in this country." She went on to state that "Harrison gives perhaps his most amusing screen performance since Carol Reed's 1940 thriller, *Night Train.*"

In Sturges's black-and-white film, Sir Alfred de Carter (Harrison),* is a mustached symphony-orchestra conductor who becomes convinced that

his wife (Linda Darnell), whom he deeply loves, has been unfaithful. He devises ways of retribution against the wife and the man (Rudy Vallee) whom he suspects her of sleeping with. His revenge methods are acted out in Walter Mitty style while conducting in concert before a filled house of upper-class patrons. During Rossini's *Semiramide Overture,* he concocts a smooth scheme of disposing of his wife through a murder for which the "lover" is to be found guilty. While conducting Wagner's *Venusberg Music* from *Tannhauser,* he envisions himself surrendering the wife, without question, to the other man and sealing the bargain with a healthy bit of money in the form of a check. The third solution, dreamed up while leading the orchestra in Tchaikovsky's *Francesca da Rimini,* is a suicide gamble between the two men with the wife as the winner's prize.

In the latter vision sequence, Harrison displayed his accustomed agility with the dialog and tempo of drawing-room comedy.

Harrison: You're not laughing quite so hard now.
Darnell: What are you going to do with that [gun]?
Harrison: Have you ever heard of Russian roulette?
Darnell: Certainly . . . I used to play it all the time with my father.
Harrison: I doubt that you played Russian roulette all the time with your father.
Darnell: Yes, I certainly did. You play it with two packs of cards. . .
Harrison: [Acidly] That is Russian bank. Russian roulette is a very different amusement which I can wish your father had played continually before he had you.

Bosley Crowther (*New York Times*), one of the few critics who exonerated the film at the time of its release, wrote that Rex "makes a most pleasantly diverting personality in a Sturges farce." Harrison was quick to admit that this role, which found him in front of the cameras in almost every scene, was "a better part than Hamlet." As James Ursini observed in *Preston Sturges: An American Dreamer* (1973): "The rapid pace of the dialogue and the frequent variations in mood required a professionalism few actors could supply.† Whether enunciating 'What happy updraft wafts you hither?' or ripping the clothes off a nosy August [Vallee] (both, incidentally, within the same

*Rex's character is drawn on a real-life figure, flamboyant Sir Thomas Beecham, whose family wealth derived from liver pills. In America the comparable product is Carter's Little Liver Pills, thus Sturges's "in" joke is to name conductor Sir Alfred de Carter.
† Robert Montgomery, Melvyn Douglas, and William Powell are some others.

scene), Harrison supplies the energy and ability prerequisite to the part."

On July 4, 1948, while still at work on *Unfaithfully Yours*, Rex had dinner with Miss Landis and left her home early because of the next morning's shooting schedule. Upon being telephoned by her maid the following afternoon he returned there and dashed up the stairs to her bedroom. A short time later he came down to tell the anxious maid that Miss Landis was dead. He telephoned the police, without giving his name, and drove away. One note was found by the actress's body, addressed to her mother, which gave no indication of why she had taken an overdose of seconal capsules. This unpleasant episode provided just the fuel Hollywood columnists needed to revenge themselves on the aloof Britisher. It was suggested by some reporters that a second note, addressed to Rex, had been left by Miss Landis, but if such a letter existed, it never was publicly discovered. Louella Parsons, no friend of Harrison, broadly suggested in her syndicated column that Miss Landis "had been deeply in love with a man who was forced to tell her that nothing could come of their romance."

Lilli flew to Hollywood and attended the Landis funeral with her husband. The Los Angeles Deputy Coroner ordered Rex not to leave the city because he was wanted for further questioning, and Rex told reporters: "Her death is something to be deeply deplored and should not be the subject of sensational innuendos." Later, he was to admit: "I felt no guilt complex—no, none at all, but I did spend months afterwards, going to psychiatrists, discussing the suicide with them, seeking the reasons for it. The plain fact is that Carole had a death wish!"

Legally cleared of all implications concerned with the Landis suicide, the Harrisons prepared to leave Hollywood. By "mutual" agreement, his contract with Twentieth was abrogated and the furnishings in the couple's Mandeville Canyon home were put up for auction. Prior to his departure, the exiled star had these words to say: "Hollywood is done for. Hollywood and I have no future in common and I don't know if Hollywood has any future at all. It's top heavy in its internal and financial economy. It is so egocentric it doesn't know the rest of the world exists, and its social life is one of simply incredible, preposterous boredom. Hollywood is seriously ill. It is run by a coterie of moronic gossips and it would hard-

ly be going too far to say that Hollywood is in their power." In retaliation, Hedda Hopper, who would soon be having a journalistic field day with another movieland *persona non grata,* Ingrid Bergman, smoothed her ruffled locks by flatly predicting: "Rex Harrison's career is as dead as a mackerel."

The Harrisons flew to New York, where he contracted to do a new play. Late in 1948, the U.S. Treasury Department reported that Rex's 1947 income amounted to $219,750, and in December 1948 the British court ordered him to pay his first wife $24,000 a year maintenance along with $28,000 owing on back alimony.

While rehearsing for Maxwell Anderson's *Anne of the Thousand Days,* Rex was hospitalized for a few days with what x-rays revealed to be a stomach ulcer. He was put on a bland diet, and soon was sufficiently fit to open as England's King Henry VIII (1491–1547) in the Anderson verse drama on December 8, 1948, at the Shubert Theatre.* In the title role, which refers to Queen Anne Boleyn's short reign as Henry's wife, was Joyce Redman. The reviewers had high praise for Harrison's articulate peformance. "His Henry is regal, and commanding—brusque, vain, lusty, humorful, a ruler given to anguish, self-analysis, to strutting and to roaring, but a man who is capable and likable for all his bestiality" (Ward Morehouse, *New York Sun*); "[he] gives another penetrating performance that conveys the good humor, the boyish charm as well as the coarseness and cruelty of this perplexing monarch." The tributes for Miss Redman were equally effusive. The play ran 286 performances, closing on October 8, 1949.

Among those invited to the ceremonies honoring the Antoinette Perry Awards for best Broadway stage achievement of 1948–49 was Hedda Hopper of Hollywood. She was requested to present the award to the best dramatic actor, and stood on the dais holding the sealed envelope containing the winner's name. As she slit open the envelope, she read, undoubtedly to her consternation, the name of the winning actor, her "dead mackerel," Rex Harrison. She managed a gracious smile—for the cameras—as she handed him the award. Lilli Palmer remembers the occasion as "a marvelous moment."

After an absence of five years from the London stage, Rex returned in 1950 as Harcourt Reilly in T. S. Eliot's verse play, *The Cocktail Party.*†

*The play would be picturized in 1969 by Universal, with Richard Burton as Henry VIII and Genevieve Bujold as Anne.
†Also produced on Broadway that year with Alec Guinness.

With Brenda de Banzie in THE LONG DARK HALL (British Lion '51)

of 233 performances. In the play, Rex is a publisher surrounded by witches, one of whom (Lilli) he loves, but leaves when he learns of her eccentricities. She then discovers that she is, after all, a woman with real emotions, and they reconcile. *Time* magazine noted: "Even in the fast company of demons, Rex Harrison provides a mere human being with dash."

Author Van Druten, obviously taken with Rex's charm, said: "I think he is probably the most brilliant actor I've ever worked with. He is fantastically meticulous. He will pause to think out every suggestion, and then try it over and over again until he's satisfied." Also appearing on Broadway at that time was Jose Ferrer,* who admitted seeing six matinees in a row of *Bell, Book and Candle* because "I've been in this business a long time, and Rex Harrison is the only actor doing comedy that I can learn from."

The Long Dark Hall (British Lion, 1951) scripted by Nunnally Johnson from an Edgar Lustgarten novel, was made with the Harrisons while they were in England in 1950. The *New York Times* judged it "a very tidy murder drama." As Arthur Groome, Rex is a man who strays from his matrimonial vows once too often and becomes involved with a pretty chorus girl (Patricia Wayne) who is later murdered. He is put on trial for the murder, based on circumstantial evidence, while his wife (Lilli) nobly stands beside him. She is very much aware of his weakness for the ladies and lends him strength and wisdom (a role that was perhaps not unlike hers in private life). The denouement relies on a twist of fate when the maniacal killer sends a letter of confession to the police, thinking that Harrison's execution has already taken place. Of his performance in this courtroom drama, the *Times* said he "is completely natural and convincing."

The summer of 1951 saw the finishing touches applied to a hideaway villa the Harrisons had built at the fishing village of Portofino, on the Italian Riviera.† They announced their plans to spend as many of their free weeks there as possible.

In August 1951, producer Stanley Kramer signed the Harrisons for Columbia's screen version of Jan de Hartog's play *The Fourposter.*‡ On the couple's return to the despised Hollywood, a studio spokesman made it clear that "all is forgiv-

While in England, he contributed to an article in *Picturegoer* magazine, in which he took a further jab at the world known as Hollywood. "A big Hollywood studio is a factory," he wrote, "an efficient, rather terrifying piece of machinery, bound by its own structure, to turn out a set number of productions each year. In Hollywood I played parts that I feel weren't right for me—I did the best I could, but I was often unhappy about the results. A deadly feeling of hopelessness and helplessness would overcome me." He concluded the piece with remarks aimed to alienate even that city's Chamber of Commerce. "I found the climate monotonous and unstimulating; the luxury is ruinous, and the shop talk is worst of all. It's not just films in the wide sense, it's studio gossip, scandal, and trivia. On and on and on."

In November 1950, the Harrisons were back on Broadway jointly appearing at the Barrymore Theatre in Irene Mayer Selznick's staging of John Van Druten's play, *Bell, Book and Candle.*† They opened on November 14, 1950, and enjoyed a run

---

†Columbia produced the screen version in 1958 with James Stewart and Kim Novak. It is said that Harrison rejected the male lead in the movie edition when he learned that Novak had been cast for the production.

*Ferrer was then starring in *The Silver Whistle.*

†Years later, Palmer would quip: "We own homes in Munich, Zurich and Portofino, and to maintain all these homes, we have to live out of a suitcase."

‡Opened on London's West End on October 12, 1950, at the Ambassador with Michael Denison and Dulce Gray in the starring roles.

en. All we care about is that Harrison is boxoffice."

As a film, the two-character vehicle, which spans forty-five years of marriage, had everything going for it: direction by Irving Reis, gowns by Jean Louis, music by Dmitri Tiomkin, and UPA‡ animated cartoons to bridge the episodes. All the action occurs in John's (Harrison) and Abby's (Palmer) Sutton Place bedroom, beginning with their wedding night when he reveals his bridegroom's gift—a four-poster bed which he jiggles playfully, and saying, "The springs. The greatest invention of the nineteenth century. Would you care to try it?" He has the devil of a time cajoling her to go to bed, though, and at one point they quarrel because she is scared and desperately wants to return home to her family. He tells her that he understands "because you're married, your youth is over," which does not help matters. He assures her that he loves her and she sighs, "I hope you mean it." He, at the point of nervous exasperation, tells her, "I do, I do, I do, I do, with all my heart."

Through the animation effects we see the man lose his teaching job, and back in the bedroom a few years later, we learn that his book of poems has been rejected by every publisher in New York and Boston. "I'm a washout," he decides, but she helps him find success. Another sequence presents him as a famous novelist with a large female following, and as the years pass, the couple lose their son in World War I, they spat and break up, they reconcile, they grow old, and she dies of cancer. Her spirit then returns, in youthful form, to coerce him into joining her in the great beyond.

By the time the film was finished, the New York stage presentation of *The Fourposter*° was in progress with Hume Cronyn and Jessica Tandy, which prevented Columbia from releasing their picture. The Cronyns opened on October 24, 1951 and closed, after 632 performances on May 2, 1953. The movie was released in October 1952.

Newsweek magazine critiqued the movie version with "the obviously svelte and sophisticated team of Harrison and Palmer do not seem to be exactly at home among the drama's homely domestic tribulations." Bosley Crowther (*New York Times*) defended them as "fluid and charming performers but they are stuck with a difficult job." *Variety* observed: "Harrison has captured much

‡Creators of the popular cartoon, *Gerald McBoing-Boing.*
°Revived as a musical, *I Do, I Do,* (Forty-Sixth Street Theatre: December 5, 1966, 561 performances) with Mary Martin and Robert Preston.

With Lilli Palmer in THE FOURPOSTER (Col '52)

of the boyish quality inherent in the husband's character, though the final scene, in which the deceased wife returns in his imagination, becomes rather trite theatrics." Because of its talky nature, small-town America was disappointed that the film with the suggestive title did not present a sexier view of a bedroom marriage. In explaining the effects of the Motion Picture Production Code on the film's staging, Rex offered: "Both of us can not be in the bed at the same time. I believe the ruling is that if one party is in the bed, the other must at least keep his foot on the floor. The same as in billiards."

At this juncture, Rex participated in a movie project which, for him, became a lost cause. Gabriel Pascal was producing a picturization of George Bernard Shaw's *Androcles and the Lion* for release by Howard Hughes's RKO. Rex was hired to play Caesar, with Jean Simmons as Lavinia, Dana Andrews as the Captain, Robert Newton as Ferrovius, and, in a bit of offbeat casting, Harpo Marx as Androcles. Under Chester Erskine's direction, the black-and-white feature shot for about five weeks at the RKO studios. Then Hughes happened to see Alan Young performing his comedy routines on television and thought he would be better as the little tailor than the already employed Harpo. The production was halted, and by the time the picture resumed shooting with Young as Androcles, Rex was no longer available. He was replaced by Maurice Evans, in a cast which now included: Victor Mature (Captain), Jean Simmons (Lavinia), Robert Newton (Ferrovius), and Elsa Lanchester (Megaera). When the movie was finally released in late 1952, it won no plaudits with the public.

On February 13, 1952, Rex and Lilli returned to Broadway, this time in *Venus Observed,* Christopher Fry's comedy about the middle-aged Duke of Atair (Rex was then forty-four) who goes about the business of choosing a new wife. Directed by Laurence Olivier,* the play at the Century Theatre received the Drama Critics Award as best foreign play of the year on April 8, 1952. It closed eighteen days later, on April 26.

The Harrisons then summered at Portofino, where they fished, swam, and in their speedboats cut the Riviera waves. Rex remained on friendly terms with Collette, who lived nearby in a hotel with Noel. The wives—ex and present—and their two sons got along well enough, with Rex more or less serving as the head of both households. For

some reason, he was not comfortable at Portofino, though, and excused his ambivalent feelings with "I'm not really a country man in the hearty sense."

The Harrisons were back on Broadway at the Shubert Theatre on January 15, 1953, in Peter Ustinov's play, *The Love of Four Colonels.*† Rex played all four officers (British, American, French, and Russian) in Allied-occupied Germany who woo the same lady (Lilli). Some adjudged the comedy "the most aggressively whimsical piece of literature since Peter Rabbit" (John Chapman, *New York Daily News*). As both director and co-star, Harrison won generally favorable comments. "[He] has a good bit of fun with his impersonations of a battered jailbird, a gouty Parisian cuckold, and a tongue-twisting Elizabethan fool. His more casual moments are perhaps unduly mannered—there is a heavy dose of artifice in his lolling all over a conference table —but in the evening's later moments he pops his head through a theatre curtain with rakish cajolery and brightens many a faltering line." After 141 performances, the play closed on May 16, 1953.

The Harrisons, at the same time, made a cameo appearance along with other theatre celebrities in *Main Street to Broadway* (MGM, 1953). In a dull film which should have been a stimulating look at the behind-the-scenes workings of Broadway, Rex and Lilli are found walking along Forty-Fourth Street discussing the prospect of eating a three-decker sandwich. The flimsy plot showed how a small-town playwright (Tom Morton) manages to have his play produced, with the help, among others, of Tallulah Bankhead.

Because of an increasing number of quarrels with her husband, Mrs. Harrison then took a trial separation from marriage. She once said: "Let's face it, Englishmen don't like women, at least not in the way that Italians or Frenchmen like women. The greatest compliment Rex can pay me is to say that being with me is as good as being with a pal. He's a man's man, an Englishman."

While she rested in Italy, Harrison went to Hollywood, where he smeared his face with dark makeup, donned Arabic robes designed by Marjorie Best, and cavorted as Saladin in Warner Bros.' *King Richard and the Crusaders* (1954). Very loosely adapted by John Twist from Sir Walter Scott's *The Talisman,* the widescreen, color venture was directed by David Butler and un-

---

*Olivier had earlier enacted the role of the duke on the London stage.

†Presented in London at the Wyndham's Theatre on May 23, 1951, with Moira Lister as the sleeping princess, and Alan Gifford, Colin Gordon, Eugene Decker, and Theodore Bikel as the colonels.

With Virginia Mayo in KING RICHARD AND THE CRUSADERS (WB '54)

reeled one step this side of sheer boredom. King Richard I (George Sanders) is in the thick of Crusade Number Three, with a Scottish Knight (Laurence Harvey) pledged to protect him for the man he is, not because he is the English king. The white-skinned villain, Sir Giles (Robert Douglas), makes an attempt on the king's life and frames the knight. Harvey rides into the desert, where he is chased and captured by the Saracen chief (Harrison). Next thing we know, the king's cousin(!) (Virginia Mayo) is captured by the combined desert armies of Italy, France, and Austria, who oppose Richard of England. The Saracens join the English to rescue Virginia. As for Harrison's participation in this child's play, the *New York Times* summed it all up with: "As for Mr. Harrison astride a horse—gad, sir!"

The Harrisons again reconciled and in 1954 contracted to perform *Bell, Book and Candle* in London.

Thereafter, Sir Alexander Korda, who had had various well-touted plans for Harrison, which always seemed to fail to materialize (e.g., new versions of *The Scarlet Pimpernel* and *The Admirable Crichton*), persuaded him for a goodly sum to star in the comedy *The Constant Husband*

(British Lion, 1955).* Sidney Gilliat and Val Valentine wrote the screenplay with the former directing and co-producing with Frank Launder. It all begins one Fifth of September when the man (Harrison) awakens in a Welsh bedroom and muses: "I wonder what I'm doing in Wales." Furthermore, he does not know who he is or where he properly belongs.

In this latest adventure of an amnesiac, he further muses; "Am I good or am I bad? . . . Am I anything or anybody? . . . I might be anything from an arch deacon to a confidence man." He locates a psychiatrist (Cecil Parker), who helps him find his home through a car-rental agency and also discovers that he is known as Charles Hathaway. At his home he is warmly welcomed by his wife, Monica (Kay Kendall), a lovely, chic fashion photographer whom he does not remember, but he decides to be nice to her anyway. He is next abducted in Soho by a couple of characters who whisk him off to his "wife" (Nicole Maurey), an Italian circus performer who insists his name is Pietro. Amid tears he escapes from her and is then arrested on the charge of bigamy. It developes that he has a total of "seven wives, pending a re-count." To his psychiatrist friend, he gasps:

*Released theatrically in the United States in July 1957.

215

"At last I know what I was—a professional biga-mist." He goes on trial at Old Bailey with a lady lawyer (Margaret Leighton) defending him. She enters a plea of not guilty, but he changes that to a guilty plea after seeing and hearing his many wives testify in court. He decides he would prefer the "solitude and peace" of prison to living with any of them. All seven are waiting at the prison's front gates when he is released, so he asks a guard to show him to the side exit. There, waiting in her car, is his attorney, who coaxes him into the vehicle and presumably yet another venture into matrimony.

Korda must have had a notion that *The Constant Husband* was a dud, for he entered into special arrangements with America's National Broadcasting Corporation, whereby for the sum of $250,000 the network would have the right to screen the picture (ahead of U.S. theatrical release) on a onetime showing. Midst great hoop-lah, the film premiered—in America, that is—on NBC, on Saturday, November 6, 1955. It proved a disappointing venture to all concerned. Said Jack Gould (*New York Times*): ". . . very routine fare, a far cry from even the general run of English films currently available on the home screen. . . . In Mr. Harrison's hands a farce need have only a wisp of plausibility to survive, but *The Constant Husband* was more than even he could be expected to sustain." When the film had its delayed theatrical distribution, the twenty-eight minutes shorn from the video print were restored.

Thereafter, Harrison became very interested in Kay Kendall,* to the extent that some Londoners referred to Rex and Lilli's play as "Bell, Book and Kendall." Kay was a vivacious redhead of whom a friend once remarked: "She was marvel-ously fey. She had neither malice nor guile."

According to show-business legend, on a win-tery Sunday in 1955, Alan Jay Lerner and Freder-ick Loewe took a walk with Rex through Hyde Park. Their purpose was to try to persuade him to star in a stage musical version of Shaw's *Pygma-lion†* to be called *Lady Lisa.* They had earlier considered other possible actors (Ray Milland, for one), but had settled on Rex. After two hours of walking and talking, Rex agreed to take on the job. Messrs. Lerner and Loewe, through the aus-pices of their producer, Herman Levin, bought

out Harrison's *Bell, Book and Candle* contract and signed him to a year's deal with *Lady Lisa* at a salary of $5,000 weekly, with New York rehears-als to begin at once.

On February 6, 1956, Lilli obtained a divorce in Cuidad, Mexico, on the grounds of "incom-patibility of character." She asked for no alimony, but did take title to the villa at Portofino, which had been christened Villa San Genesio. She also received custody of twelve-year-old Carey. A few months later she married actor Carlos Thompson.

Back in New York, twenty-year-old Julie An-drews‡ was selected to portray Eliza Doolittle and Moss Hart was called upon to stage the musi-cal. Cecil Beaton designed the costumes, Oliver Smith created the sets, and Hanya Holm devised the dances. Lerner and Loewe worked arduously in writing songs for Rex to coincide with his speech-song tonal range of only two or three notes. In the first week of rehearsal, Loewe con-ceived "Why Can't a Woman Be More Like a Man" while recovering from an appendix opera-tion. A perfectionist in interpreting Shavian char-acters, Rex carried a copy of *Pygmalion* in his pocket throughout rehearsal to insure that the text was being followed. "The key to Rex," Moss Hart once revealed, "is that he's not a frivolous actor. What he achieves, he gets from digging, digging. Once I discovered this, I could forgive him a great deal. There were tremendous rages and stalkings-off during rehearsals." Loewe said: "No one who is a perfectionist is easy to work with. He did everything over and over again—relentless-ly."

The musical underwent a name change and emerged at the New Haven tryout in February 1956 as *My Fair Lady.* Alan Jay Lerner was to write for *TV Guide* of November 1973: "I remem-ber: The howling blizzard that February night. The booming reception the show received, even though the first act was twenty minutes too long."

Rex made his initial Broadway appearance as Professor Henry Higgins, the professional bache-lor and phonetics expert, on March 15, 1956, at the Mark Hellinger Theatre. Within weeks, tick-ets were almost impossible to obtain; scalpers were demanding $50 or more a seat. Producer Levin predicted that they would gross $5 million on the $401,000 production, with another gross of

*Born Kay Justine Kendall McCarthy, of Irish ancestry, in 1927, she became an international film celebrity as the trumpet-blowing madcap in *Genevieve* (1953) while under contract to J. Arthur Rank. MGM had tried several times to purchase her contract, but Rank was always unamenable.
†Initially performed on stage at the Hofburgtheater in Vienna on October 16, 1913, and then at the Lessingtheater in Berlin on November 1, 1913. Its first London showing was at His Majesty's Theatre (April 11, 1914) with Herbert Beerbohm Tree as Higgins and Mrs. Patrick Campbell as Eliza. Philip Merivale played Pickering. Later that fall (October 12, 1914) Mrs. Campbell appeared in the show on Broadway at the Park Theatre.
‡Born Julia Vernon, she had performed in British musical-hall revues since early childhood. Up to 1955, she was best remembered as Polly Brown in *The Boy Friend,* Sandy Wilson's parody of the 1920s, which ran successfully in London and New York.

With Robert Coote in THE CONSTANT HUSBAND (British Lion '55)

$3 million from the Columbia LP original-cast recording. Audiences were delighted with Harrison's insults to the awkward Cockney girl as he wins a bet by turning her into the belle of London society. When she had a mouthful of marbles during her elocution session, and she swallowed one, he said happily: "Don't worry, I have plenty more."

Humorist James Thurber called the show "the finest union of comedy and music." Charles Laughton was quoted as saying: "In all my theatre experience, I've seen only a handful of performances to match Rex's. He makes every man in the audience laugh at himself, and every woman laugh at the man beside her." Brooks Atkinson of the *New York Times* said it was "one of the best musicals of the century," while Orson Welles defined Rex's brilliance as "Chic—style without pressure." *Time* magazine recapped the show as "Broadway's biggest hit, and its forty-eight-year-old star is Broadway's most unexpected new bright light." Rex admitted: "I always find it less difficult than some actors to be irascible without being unpleasant. I've taken over some of Higgins and he's taken over some of me."

On April 21, 1956, Rex was presented with his second Tony Award, this one for Best Actor in a

With Julie Andrews on Broadway in MY FAIR LADY (1956)

217

Musical (Judy Holliday won the distaff award for *Bells Are Ringing*).

During vacation from *My Fair Lady* in February 1957, Rex accompanied Kay Kendall to Hollywood, where she discussed making *Les Girls* (1957) at MGM. At a film colony party, it was rumored that Rex had twice slapped Frank Sinatra on the face because of the latter's pointed interest in Miss Kendall. She later explained that she had simply admired Sinatra's shirt and he had thanked her with a kiss.

Back in New York, Rex gobbled up pills prescribed by "my doctors" because "there always has to be this nervous tension. After the show I wonder why my stomach muscles haven't gone 'whoop' during the day. Then I can take a drink and relax for a bit. It's the only time I do relax, late at night, when most respectable people are in bed." His offstage relaxation was done in luxury on a rented estate in Westbury, Long Island. Despite the adulation he received onstage as Henry Higgins, Rex was a lonely man. Son Carey was at an expensive British prep school; son Noel had gone from Olympic skiing to playing a guitar in European nightclubs; Lilli was in Portofino with her new husband. His salvation came in the person of Kay Kendall, whom he married in New York City in the chapel of the Universalist Church of Divine Paternity at midnight on June 23, 1957. At thirty-one it was her first marriage, while at forty-nine, it was his third.

Like his past wives, Kay was efficient, beautiful, and exuberant. But she was a victim of leukemia. Her doctors confided to Harrison that she had three to five years to live, a prognosis that was concealed from her. Lilli said later: "Loving her, he accepted it. It must have been a terrible secret to live with, but he kept it."

After almost two years and 1,000 performances as Henry Higgins in New York, Rex left the show in 1958 when he contracted to recreate his stellar part for the London stage.[*]

First, however, he made the Technicolor comedy, *The Reluctant Debutante* (MGM, 1958), in Paris with Kay. Adapted for the screen by William Douglas Home from his own play, the story centers around Lord and Lady Broadbent (Harrison and Kendall) and their attempts to find a suitable husband for the lord's daughter (Sandra Dee), an offspring from a former marriage.[†] Dee arrives in London from America, but is reluctant to be launched into society via dinners, dances, and dates with eligible young Englishmen. She takes a liking to an American jazz drummer (John Saxon), an association her parents find revolting as they attempt to force her into the arms of a dull lieutenant (Peter Myers) in the Royal Horse Guards. Also on the prowl for the stuffy, but promising lieutenant is Mrs. Claremont (Angela Lansbury) on behalf of her daughter (Diana Clare). When Harrison discovers that Saxon is in reality the Italian Duke of Positano, Dee is allowed to pursue her feelings and eventually, by wedding him, she marries well after all.

In the estimation of *Saturday Review*'s Hollis Alpert, "[the] screenplay is almost a bore to describe but half the time it's hilarious . . . mainly because Rex Harrison and Kay Kendall bring to bear exquisite senses of timing on everything they do." More importantly, *Time* magazine had to admit, "Actor Harrison still reigns as king of his wacky parlor empire, but an enormously talented queen has moved in close to his side." In fact, many people thought Kendall (not to mention acerbic Lansbury) stole the show from Harrison, a situation so alien for the star that, in retrospect, it seems likely that it was achieved out of love for the talented, beautiful, but ailing Mrs. Harrison. It was to no one's surprise, except perhaps the players in question, that bland Dee and Saxon, ostensibly the focal point of the story, were relegated to the sidelines, mere pawns in this elaborate drawing-room comedy. When all was said and done, one remembered the "very British badinage" saturating the proceedings and the lush drawing-room settings.[†]

When *My Fair Lady* opened in London (April 30, 1958), the management of the Drury Lane Theatre was forced to limit the number of curtain calls to ten "lest enthusiasm get out of hand." The *London Daily Herald's* front-page banner headline cried: "It isn't Fair—It's Fabulous." Rex's contractual salary agreement, at ten percent of the box-office receipts, amounted to some $3,360 a week. He and Kay had received $280,000 from MGM for *The Reluctant Debutante,* and they celebrated their financial good fortune by purchasing a $16,800 Rolls Royce.

[*]His immediate successor was Edward Mulhare. The musical closed in September 1962 after 2,717 performances, then the longest-running show in Broadway's history.

[†]First staged in London at the Cambridge Theatre (May 24, 1955) with Wilfrid Hyde White and Celia Johnson as the anxious parents, and Anna Massey in the title role. On Broadway, White and Adrianne Allen were the parents, with Miss Massey again the daughter. It had a 154-performance run at the Henry Miller Theatre (October 10, 1956).

[†]Ironically, the film was shot in Paris, because there was no available soundstage space in London and Harrison was on a tight schedule to prepare for the West End opening of *My Fair lady.*

As a sideline, and especially to distract his fading wife, Harrison directed Kay in a play, *Bright One,* which opened on December 10, 1958, at the Winter Garden Theatre in London's West End. To their disappointment, the play flopped after only twelve performances.

He gave his last London appearance as Henry Higgins in April 1959, when he stated that his favorite song from the musical was "I've Grown Accustomed to Her Face" and told pressmen: "It's too long to play one part, much too long. I originally signed for only one year, from the date of opening out-of-town. I loathe long runs. As a matter of fact, the way I feel now I think this is the only musical I'll ever do. After all, musicals are not my job, I'm an actor." Asked if he would miss playing Higgins, he replied: "I doubt it. Actors are not made that way. I don't miss what I'm not doing." When questioned if he would ever play it again, he said: "Yes, if I could take all the receipts home after the performance." Kay said she hated the show because "I haven't had a dinner with my husband in years." When pressed as to her favorite song from the show, she quipped: "'God Save the Queen.' It's played in London right after the final curtain goes down."

In MY FAIR LADY

Queen Elizabeth II and Prince Philip talking with Rex Harrison and Julie Andrews backstage after a London performance of MY FAIR LADY, May 5, 1958

On March 22, 1959, Noel Harrison married Canadian model Mrs. Sara Tufnell in London.

In the summer of 1959, while at work on *Once More with Feeling* (Columbia, 1960), Kay collapsed and was taken to a London clinic, where she was proffered a fabricated story that she was merely suffering from complicated bronchitis-anemia. She was back on her feet in a few days and was able to rejoin co-star Yul Brynner in finishing shooting the comedy.* She died in Rex's arms on September 6, 1959, and was buried in Hampstead Churchyard. According to Rex's agent, Larry Evans, "When she died, he donated a large sum of money to the cancer research fund—anonymously. I think the rot set in only after her death, and his departure from *Fair Lady.* He was never the same after that."

Due to a persistent case of the flu, Rex was unable to attend the christening in London, on September 27, 1959, of his first grandchild, Cathryn Mary Lee Harrison, born to Noel and Sara. It was as hard to believe that "Sexy Rexy" was a grandfather as it had been a decade earlier to conceive of Marlene Dietrich as a *grand-mère.*

Three months after Kay's death, on December 9, 1959, Rex opened at New York's Anta Theatre in Lucienne Hill's adaptation of Jean Anouilh's Paris stage success, *L'Hurliberlu.* Originally translated to *Time's Fool,* it debuted at the Anta as *The Fighting Cock,* the story of a retired French general who dreams of restoring the glory of France. After eighty-seven performances, the overly-talky, philosophizing play closed on February 20, 1960, although Associated Press drama critic William Glover had observed that "Rex Harrison is in peak form." During the Philadelphia tryout of the Anouilh play there were rumors of great difficulties with the production, with Harrison demanding both a new leading lady and a new, special onstage writing desk.

A more fortuitous appearance for Harrison was his guest-starring role on *The Fabulous Fifties.* This was CBS-TV's $425,000 live and taped tribute to the decade, telecast on January 31, 1960. The two-hour special, produced by Leland Hayward and directed by Norman Jewison, featured Rex, Julie Andrews, Jackie Gleason, Henry Fonda, Shelley Berman, Betty Comden, and Adolph Green in separate song-dance-comedy routines. Rex's contribution was a scene depicting his fumbling and nervous attempts to sing in front of the *My Fair Lady* orchestra. "This is a juiced-up re-construction, of course, but I *was* really pretty frightened by having to sing in front of an orchestra." By this time, Harrison was wearing a hair piece on the front portion of his scalp, and he warned photographers against taking his picture unless his head was covered either by a hat or by his false hair.

In August 1960, it was rumored that Rex and Tammy Grimes (who bore a resemblance to Kay Kendall) were a romantic item,† but Miss Grimes insisted: "Mr. Harrison and I are good friends, but more than that I can not say."

Harrison then accepted a bid to return to Hollywood for a film. Upon arrival in the town he had sworn he would never again visit for play or work, he was quoted as saying: "Yes, the place has really changed since I was under contract here. That was just after the war, when the boys were coming back. . . . Hollywood seems much quieter now. There seems to be no big parties anymore, no real colony at all. But I like it here. I have pleasant memories of Hollywood on the whole."

The picture in question was Ross Hunter's *Midnight Lace* (Universal, 1960), a sumptuously produced thriller starring Doris "Pillow Talk" Day. It was directed by David Miller, who had done such wonders with Joan Crawford in *Sudden Fear* (RKO, 1952). Hunter had hired Harrison and two of his *Fighting Cock* teammates (Roddy McDowall and Natasha Parry), so it seemed, to give the proceedings some elan. The film's title is derived from a negligee that Kit Preston (Day) purchases to take on a delayed honeymoon trip to Venice with her husband (Harrison). At the last minute, however, the suave financier finds that he cannot leave town due to unexpected business problems. Day then begins receiving threatening phone calls and hears voices as she walks through the London fog. She is told that she will die. John Gavin as a building contractor is a suspect, as is McDowall, her housekeeper's son, and, likewise, Herbert Marshall, the financially embarrassed business associate of Harrison. Myrna Loy, as Day's fluffy aunt, makes brief appearances for the sake of nostalgia and comedy relief, but to little avail. *Midnight Lace* emerged as synthetic as the film's pseudo-English ambiance, and Harrison, in a smooth but implausible characterization, is eminently forgettable in the subordinate role.

Rex returned to the London stage in 1960, at the Royal Court in the title role in the Chekhov play

---

*The picturization of Harry Kurnitz's play (National Theatre: October 21, 1958, 272 performances) was a crashing bore, redeemed only slightly by the piquant presence of smashing Miss Kendall, who posthumously received fine reviews.

† They worked together on NBC-TVs' "Great Mysteries" in the episode *The Datchet Diamonds,* televised on September 20, 1960.

With Myrna Loy in MIDNIGHT LACE (Univ '60)

Platonov. Also in the cast was Rachel Roberts. The following year, at the Edinburgh Film Festival, he starred in the Nigel Dennis play *August for the People.* Again, Miss Roberts was included in the cast, this time as the love mistress of the character portrayed by Rex. He later withdrew from the play because he was forced by the dialog to denounce democracy as "disgusting" and he was apparently a strong candidate for knighthood in the Honours List of 1962. "I don't want to be in anything subversive," he said of his withdrawal. The actor has yet to become Sir Rex Harrison.

He then went to Madrid for *The Happy Thieves* (United Artists, 1962), a would-be comedy directed by George Marshall from John Gay's screenplay based on Richard Condon's novel, *The Oldest Profession.* Produced by James Hill for Hillworth Productions, Rex's co-star was Hill's wife at that time, Rita Hayworth. Unfortunately Rita was no longer *Gilda* and Rex was no longer the *Notorious Gentleman.*

Within the lackadaisical screenplay, Harrison and Hayworth are a duo engaged in stealing art masterpieces. He is photographed stealing a Velasquez from the Duchess Blanca (Alida Valli),

and when Rita's plans to smuggle it into Paris are outwitted by the fanatical Dr. Munoz (Gregoire Aslan), she wants to run away and become honest. Rex marries her and persuades her to help in duplicating Goya's *Second of May,* which will keep Aslan from exposing him as a thief by means of the telltale photograph. The duplicate Goya is substituted for the original, but all ends "well" when the painting is returned, and Rex goes to jail knowing that Rita will wait for him.

Of this fiasco, *Time* magazine cruelly but accurately stated: "Rita Hayworth, forty-two when this picture was made [April 1961], and Rex Harrison, fifty-three, are both old enough to know better...."

In September 1961, Harrison quite innocently contracted with Twentieth Century–Fox to portray Julius Caesar in *Cleopatra* (1963),* the spectacle to end all spectacles (which later proved instrumental in the studio's economic decline). He was guaranteed $10,000 a week salary, plus expenses and a chauffeured limousine. He was also to receive billing over Richard Burton *if* his knighthood were ordained.

The traumatic production saga of *Cleopatra* is

*Laurence Olivier, the first choice, turned the part down, as did Rex when the film's announced (and first) director was Rouben Mamoulian. Peter Finch filmed some scenes, which were later discarded, and Trevor Howard was next considered. Harrison finally agreed to joining the problem-plagued epic when Mamoulian was replaced by director-scriptor Joseph Mankiewicz.

With Joseph Wiseman in THE HAPPY THIEVES (UA '62)

On the set of CLEOPATRA (20th '63) with Richard Burton and director Joseph Mankiewicz

In CLEOPATRA

now well known, with its incredibly expensive delays, squabbles, shows of temperament, script problems, shifts of locations, etc., etc. Rex had been involved with the Rome-based situation for almost a year when he said facetiously: "My co-stars [Burton, Elizabeth Taylor] were giving each other black eyes, so there were long stops in the filming. Otherwise, it went swimmingly."

On March 21, 1962, during one of the film's frequent shut-downs, Rex and Rachel Roberts arrived at the city hall in Genoa, Italy, where they were to be married. Surrounded by photographers and noisy spectators, Rex grabbed a camera and smashed it against a wall. His demands for a quiet room were granted and they were married in an Italian ceremony with a lawyer translating the words in English. Rex was then fifty-four, Rachel, the daughter of a Baptist minister, was thirty-four (she had divorced Alan Russell in July 1961). Lilli Palmer graciously agreed to temporarily vacate the Portofino villa to give the newlyweds honeymoon space.

The multimillion-dollar *Cleopatra* was officially unleashed on June 13, 1963, as a roadshow attraction. Two months prior to that date, Harrison brought a much-publicized suit against Twentieth Century–Fox demanding that he be given "equal billing" with Burton.* He asserted that the studio was "attempting to capitalize on the world-wide publicity Burton and Elizabeth Taylor have received." Rex lost his case, and was given third billing. However, his face was painted into the huge billboard advertisement for the picture, which graced Time Square, and focused on Burton and Taylor (in a romantic embrace on a couch) as *the* stars of the film.

According to the *New York Times's* Bosley Crowther, Rex's "faceted performance is the best in the film." As Julius Caesar (100 B.C.–44 B.C.),† the Roman general and would-be emperor, who is captivated by the charms of Cleopatra and places her on the throne as queen of Egypt, he all but steals every scene in which he appears, till midway through the picture when he is assassinated oncamera. As written by Mankiewicz, Harrison's imperial figure becomes human despite his position as ruler of the Roman world. He professes love for Cleopatra, but is aware that she is after his regal position, hoping to unite Rome with Egypt. Said *Variety:* "Rex Harrison is superb as Caesar. His are the film's most brilliant lines, and something is lost with his assassination." The *New Republic* offered: "Harrison's Caesar is authoritative, dexterous, thoroughly believable." On the other hand, Rex admitted: "I found Caesar's oratory scenes the most difficult. Here, an actor has to become a sort of superb after-dinner speaker, and actors are notoriously bad at that."

Harrison was honored with an Oscar nomination as Best Actor of 1963, but lost to Sidney Poitier for *Lillies of the Field* (United Artists). Rachel Roberts was nominated as Best Actress for her performance in *This Sporting Life* (Continental Distributing), but lost out to Patricia Neal for *Hud* (Paramount). It was one of the few times on record that a husband and wife were nominated for Academy Awards in the same year. In the Best Picture category, *Cleopatra* lost to *Tom Jones* (United Artists), but it did take the honors for color cinematography, color art, and set direction, color costuming, and for special visual effects.

With the ardors of the intense problems both on and off the set of *Cleopatra* behind him, Rex spent a lengthy recuperative period at Portofino with Rachel, who described their marriage as a "volatile peace." He commented: "I can say without a second's pause that because of her, this is the happiest time of my life."

When Warner Bros. purchased the screen rights to *My Fair Lady* for an unprecedented $5.5 million, the role of Henry Higgins was offered to Cary Grant, who turned it down saying that no one, but no one, could play it like Rex Harrison. Peter O'Toole, Jack Warner's second choice, also refused it, and the screen part then became Rex's. After accepting a contract, he said: "I've been away from the part, you see, for more than two years and by the time we start filming next July [1963], it should all be fresh and new again." Rachel, enthusiastic at the prospect of a long stay in California, said: "Imagine seeing all the interesting things in America as Mrs. Rex Harrison."

Shooting began at the Burbank studio in mid-August with George Cukor directing Rex in his 1,007th appearance as Higgins. Warners sent the movie industry into further shock by casting Audrey Hepburn as Eliza rather than taking a "chance" with the comparatively unknown Julie Andrews. The production cost of $17 million included $500,000 for Cecil Beaton's costumes, and $1 million for the sets, all of which were constructed on the Warner soundstages.

When the film was released at roadshow prices on October 21, 1964, audiences were again treated to Harrison's speech-singing of "Men are so decent, such regular chaps. . . . Why can't a woman be a chum?" as he asks his comrade in the science of phonetics, Colonel Pickering (Wilfrid Hyde White), "Why Can't a Woman Be More Like a Man?" Thus Henry Higgins establishes his film-long inability to understand his all-time prize pupil, Eliza Doolittle. "I'll make a queen of that barbarous wretch," he proclaims after the Cockney flower-girl enters his household, and he does just that, and nearly loses her in the process.

Along with influencing the interior-design trend of the use of wallpaper in American homes, *My Fair Lady* had collected $32 million in box-office receipts by early 1973, making it the number ten all-time Hollywood moneymaker.†

After *My Fair Lady*, which many consider the "apex" of his screen career, Rex went to Britain for MGM's *The Yellow Rolls Royce* (1965). It was presented by the same trio (producer Andre de Grunwald, director Anthony Asquith, writer Terence Rattigan) who had made *The V.I.P.'s* (MGM,

* He had not received his knighthood.

† Most notably played in the past by Warren William in Paramount's 1934 epic, produced and directed by Cecil B. DeMille.

† The film was sold to NBC-TV for two airings for $3 million and was shown for the first time on the small screen on Thanksgiving Night, 1973. Much to the network's consternation, the picture received a far smaller audience-share rating than anyone could have anticipated.

At the 37th Annual Academy Awards, with producer Jack L. Warner, Audrey Hepburn, and director George Cukor

1963). Composed of three episodes involving three individual owners of an elegant Rolls Royce in which assignations are regularly committed, the film's glittery star is the elegant automobile itself. While in production, Rex said: "One of the interesting qualities [of the film] is that there are three distinct styles of acting, each of the three episodes is quite different from the others. Not any one of the characters runs through the film."

As the Marquess of Frinton, Rex appears in the first tale. He buys the Rolls, brand new, as a gift for his wife (Jeanne Moreau). Their chauffeur drives them to the Ascot races on a golden, summer day in 1930, where the Marquess's horse, June the Tenth, is the favorite to win the Gold Cup. Before the race, his wife informs him that she is not feeling well and returns to the car. He then listens to a bit of gossip from his lady friend (Moira Lister) that the marchioness is having an affair with his young business aide (Edmund Purdom). With the race in full progress off camera, he summarily returns to the car and finds therein, on the back seat, his wife with Purdom. Without a word, he solemnly walks to the track, where he bows his head against his winning horse's neck and moans: "My boy, my boy." On the way home, he asks his wife: "What are we to do?" She calmly replies: "Go, on, I suppose, what else is there to

do?" He looks straight ahead and says: "Oh, God, I'm going to hate living from now on." When they are deposited at the front entrance to their estate, he turns back to the chauffeur and firmly orders: "Have the motor car returned to Hoopers . . . it displeases me."

The second episode takes place in Italy with George C. Scott, a Mafia gangster, owning the Rolls, and in the final segment, Ingrid Bergman has it in Trieste, where she is persuaded by Omar Sharif to aid the Yugoslavians in the war against the Nazis.

From England, Rex went to Rome, where he co-starred with Charlton Heston in Philip Dunne's overlong screenplay of the monumental Irving Stone novel *The Agony and the Ecstasy* (Twentieth Century–Fox, 1965). Admitting to having read "scores of books" in preparation for his role as Pope Julius II (1443–1513), he also said: "Now, there's a part! A part! A Renaissance bull of a man, an unpopelike pope, fighting duels, siring illegitimate children." Released in Todd-AO widescreen process, it is a wordy, tedious (140 minutes!), but ornately colorful film, largely enhanced by Harrison's appearance as the imperious, impatient papal leader who commissions Michelangelo (Heston), a sculptor, to paint frescoes on the ceiling of his private Sistine Chapel.

With Jeanne Moreau in THE YELLOW ROLLS ROYCE (MGM '65)

"You will speak only when I give permission, and then not of money," he informs the humble artistic genius. The initial fee offered is two thousand coins "plus a house I will provide for you," but when Heston lays out a more elaborate design for the Pope's consideration during a battle scene, the artist asks for more. Harrison says haughtily: "You dare to dicker with your Pontiff?" but he agrees to paying him six thousand ducats, "plus the rent of your house, of course." As the task commences, the Pope says reverently: "I planned a ceiling; he planned a miracle." But the work drags on and on and on (to the poor viewer's discomfort) with Harrison periodically shouting to the scaffolding above his altar: "When will you make an end?" and Heston shouting down his reply: "When I am finished." Although many historians have placed the two men on the suspect list, only a hint of homosexual arrangement is touched upon in this family-audience film. For romantic purposes Diane Cilento as the Contessa de' Medici, obviously in love with the artist, is occasionally on hand to minister to his wounds when he falls from the scaffolding, and to confess her devotion to him.

Bosley Crowther (*New York Times*) described Rex's performance as "interesting" and "quizzical" in the production, which was "not a strong

In THE AGONY AND THE ECSTASY (20th '65)

and soaring drama but an illustrated lecture on a slow artist at work."

With the unpopular *The Agony and the Ecstasy* behind him, Rex then took Rachel to Portofino for vacation where he was notified that he and Tony Franciosa had been honored in Hollywood by the California's Men's Apparel Club as the Best Dressed Man in Films and Television, respectively. They were cited for "their salutary influence on the dressing habits of American men." Greer Garson accepted the award on Rex's behalf.

Whereas Rex had encouraged his previous actress wives to work, he now preferred that Rachel leave the family employment to him. (It was a decision she did not find very salutary.) In February 1965, the couple announced their plans to adopt a baby, which, they said, was scheduled to be born that September. In March 1965, Rex was given the Ninth Annual Humanitarian Award of the March of Dimes.

When the 1964 Oscar nominations were announced, Rex was among those selected for the playoff round of Best Actor of the year.* In accordance with this latest prestige, Harrison underwent a new battery of interviews. Among the more intriguing reflections to come from this period was the report of Melton S. Davis, who interviewed the star in Portofino for the *New York Times*. "There is little likelihood that winning an Oscar would change much of Rex Harrison's life. For too long he has accepted only roles that pleased him, seen only chosen friends, dressed as he liked, gone where it suited him, in general followed a pattern of living expected of a 'Distinguished British actor,' that dwindling breed of screen gentlemen most of whom came to Hollywood from London's West End."

On April 5, 1965, the Oscar winners were announced and *My Fair Lady* did extremely well in the sweepstakes. It received an award as Best Picture, George Cukor was named Best Director, and Rex was presented the Best Actor Oscar by Audrey Hepburn,‡ a previous Best Actress winner (in 1953, for Paramount's *Roman Holiday*). Awards also went to *My Fair Lady* for color cinematography, art-set decoration, sound, music scoring, and color costume design. Rex was also named Best Actor by the New York Film Critics.

After leaving Hollywood, following the award ceremony, the Harrisons stopped off in New York for a few days while he talked with Joseph Man-

kiewicz about a new film project, and with Alan Lerner about doing another musical film. Then the couple, with Homer, their Bassett, sailed on the *Queen Mary* to Europe, where Rex kept a date to act as a judge at the 1965 Cannes Film Festival in May.

Discord in the Harrison household flourished in the next months, resulting in break-ups and reconciliations. Their plans for adopting a baby were abandoned, and in October 1965, Rex was in Venice† once more working for his great friend, Joseph Mankiewicz. Mankiewicz wrote and directed *The Honey Pot* (United Artists, 1967)‡, based on Frederick Knott's play, *Mr. Fox in Venice*, which was based on Thomas Sterling's novel *The Evil of the Day*, which, in turn, was adapted from Ben Jonson's play *Volpone*.

As in *Volpone* (updated, of course), Cecil Fox (Harrison) invites three of his former and wealthy mistresses to his palazzo in Venice, on the pretense that he is a dying man. They do not actually see the "millionaire" Mr. Fox, who communicates with them through an accomplice (Cliff Robertson). He requests that they remain as his guests after his death and until his will is read. There is Merle McGill (Edie Adams), a former silver-screen sex symbol, Princess Dominique (Capucine), and Lone-Star Crockett Sheridan (Susan Hayward), the latter being the richest of the trio, and also an incurable hypochondriac. It is she who insists the loudest that Harrison's inheritance should be hers since she was once his common-law wife. When Hayward is found dead from an overdose of sleeping pills, all are suspected of her murder, including Sarah (Maggie Smith), her nurse companion. However, it is Smith who takes a ride on a dumbwaiter and ends up in Harrison's chambers, where she finds the "dying" man pirouetting about the room. He explains that he had always wanted to dance ballet. It develops that Harrison, who is stone broke, is Hayward's killer and had hoped to get his hands on her money. When he is exposed, he dances into a canal and Smith inherits Hayward's wealth, as well as Robertson.

Maggie Smith tagged most of the acting honors for *The Honey Pot*, but of Harrison, *Time* magazine noted, "The . . . sweetest moments come when Harrison is trading double entendres with his ex-mistresses or pirouetting around his mansion like Nureyev on LSD." Judith Crist on the

---

*The nominees were Richard Burton (*Becket*), Peter O'Toole (*Becket*), Anthony Quinn (*Zorba the Greek*), Peter Sellers (*Dr. Strangelove*), and Harrison.

‡Miss Hepburn was not a nominee for her enactment of Eliza Doolittle; the Best Actress award for 1964, ironically, was bestowed on Julie Andrews for *Mary Poppins* (Buena Vista).

†Where he was honored with the Italian Silver Mace Award (Oscar equivalent) for an ensemble of his "outstanding past performances."

‡Released in Europe in 1966 as *Anyone for Venice?*

NBC-TV "Today" show, commented: "Certainly, any movie that has Rex Harrison and Maggie Smith is, in large part, pure gold, and both, thank goodness, have large parts." *The Honey Pot,* however, was not a commercial success.

In July 1966, Rex received Genoa's Golden Caravel Award as "the outstanding figure of the year in the motion picture, television or theatrical world." The following year he was named honorable national chairman of the American Humane Association and headed the organization's Fifty-Third Annual "Be Kind to Animals" Campaign in Los Angeles.

The latter distinction was bestowed on Rex while he was in Hollywood filming interiors for the $15 million production of *Doctor Dolittle* (Twentieth Century–Fox, 1967). Alan Lerner's initial plans to put Hugh Lofting's children stories* onto film was taken over by Leslie Bricusse, who wrote the screenplay, lyrics, and music after the Lofting family finally consented to sell the material for motion-picture use.

Prior to completing the Hollywood-based portions of the film and embarking for England and the British West Indies, where director Richard Fleischer and his crew would shoot the remainder of the picture, Rex and Rachel attended a Bel Air party hosted by the Irish actor Richard Harris and his very attractive wife, Elizabeth. There, as the party swung into the morning hours, Rex jumped into the swimming pool wearing only his undershorts while Rachel dived into the water wearing black panties and bra. Pamela Mason, in her *Photoplay* magazine gossip column, described Elizabeth Harris as "good-natured, sweet and charming and apparently unperturbed by all that goes on around her, which is plenty."

The cast of *Doctor Dolittle,* including 1,500 various breeds of animals, was then transported abroad. The cost of training, housing, and moving the animals amounted to $1.5 million, with an additional cost per week of $750 to maintain each featured animal. Since the quarantine laws of Britain stated that an imported animal could not remain in the country for longer than six months, the entire production was placed on a tight schedule.

Within the fantasy tale, Doctor Dolittle (Harrison) of Puddleby-on-the-Marsh in 1842 England quits the medical practice of ministering to grumpy humans in favor of attending to the needs of his animal friends. His first patients are Sheila, a nervous fox whose children have flat feet, So-

With Susan Hayward in THE HONEY POT (UA '67)

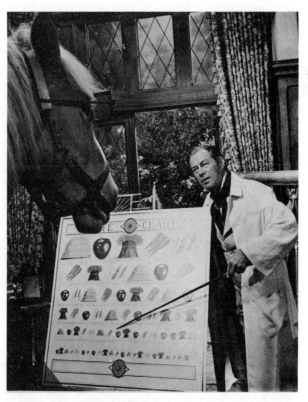

In DOCTOR DOLITTLE (20th '67)

*Published in 1920, the stories originated in letters that Lofting wrote home to his children in England while he was serving in France during World War I.

phie, a husband-lonesome seal, and Pushmi-Pull-yu, a two-headed llama. With the help of a parrot named Polynesia, he learns two hundred animal languages which had taken her one hundred years to learn. He concedes "There are times when the English are rather tiresome" and gets rid of his housekeeping sister (Portia Nelson). He has a full-time job with the animals because he suddenly has "six hundred mouths to feed including the mice." Since Harrison's John Dolittle is a devoted vegetarian whose "highly nutritious" diet is meatless, he does not covet any of the animals for anything other than comradeship, and "It is a matter of principle—one should always try to avoid hitting one's friends." Later Harrison goes on trial for murder because a human accuses him of having shoved a woman off a cliff (it was actually Sophie the seal whom he sent off to the North Pole to unite her with her husband). He is then committed to an asylum, but escapes his fate and boards the ship *Flounder* in search of the Great Pink Sea Snail. The ship wrecks and the crew (including Anthony Newley and Samantha Eggar) land on a floating island. The elusive sea snail is found, and when word filters back that the

doctor has been reprieved because all the animals in England have gone on strike, he returns home aboard the Great Lunar Moth.

Judith Crist liked the 152-minute film, calling it "the most appealing 'family' film around" and stated that Rex "is again Professor Higgins. Well, I like Professor Higgins." According to *Variety:* "Rex Harrison, physically, is not at all like the rotund original, but histrionically, he's perfect."*

At Portofino in December 1967, Rex admitted to making six hundred bottles of wine a year. "I've been making wine for about twelve years and have my own presses. It's delicious, a white wine and very delicate. We label it 'San Genosio.'"

"A castastrophe! An absolute bust everywhere," is what Darryl F. Zanuck said of Rex's next film, also for Twentieth Century–Fox. Rachel was one of his co-stars in *A Flea in Her Ear* (1968).* "Rachel does not enjoy herself when she is not acting. It's nicer to be acting together than separately."

Based on Georges Feydeau's nineteenth-century farce, Rex has the dual role of an elegant Parisian lawyer and a bordello porter. The latter, who drinks a good deal too much, becomes innocently

*Fox, hoping to duplicate its blockbuster *The Sound of Music* (1965), found itself saddled with a vast box-office disappointment in *Doctor Dolittle*.
‡Produced in 1966 at the National Theatre in London with Albert Finney.

In A FLEA IN HER EAR (20th '68)

embroiled in a case of infidelity when the barrister's wife (Rosemary Harris) mistakes one for the other with Suzanne (Rachel Roberts) in a compromising situation. Audiences of the 1960s were not attuned to such artificial farcical situations, in which the most exaggerated violence oncamera was the slamming of bedroom doors.

A special Tony Award was presented to Harrison on April 20, 1969, for no apparent reason other than to insure his presence at the ceremony. Others who received the special honor were Sir Laurence Olivier, Leonard Bernstein, and the Negro Ensemble Company.

A number of marital separations had occurred between the Harrisons and at one time they reconciled their feelings by taking a Mediterranean cruise with Richard and Elizabeth Harris among other people. However, in December 1969, Rachel left her husband for the last time.

Rex received $1 million to star as Charlie in Charles Dyer's screenplay of his own play, *Staircase* (Twentieth Century–Fox, 1969).* Richard Burton was chosen to depict Harry, the sober half of a middle-aged homosexual couple. In Paris, $200,000 worth of sets were constructed depict-

ing the rundown Brixton suburb of London in which the couple lived, off and on together, for thirty years. They are barbers: Harrison with a full head of thick, wonderful hair, and Burton with a constant turban to hide his baldness. They fight, they bed, they coo to each other. Harrison, during one of their many bitchy arguments, bellows: "You picked me up! You matriculated me to the glory of a two-bit blasted barber. Well, you can take your bloody striped pole, dear, and stuff it." When Harrison's presence is requested at a law court on a charge of disturbing the peace while in drag, Burton offers to go with him, but Harrison yells: "God, no. . . . They'd give me ninety years." At the streetcorner, on his way to court, he loses his courage, however, and screams for Burton, who runs down and accompanies him to the hearing, proving that they need each other in spite of their many differences.

Of the offbeat roles, Rex has said: "It was a challenge to both of us, since for heterosexuals to play homosexuals without making a comment on the subject is far from easy. We were both terrified of over-playing, or looking as though we were being camp or rampant queers. It was damned

*Produced onstage at London's Aldwych Theatre in the autumn of 1967 with Paul Scofield (Charlie) and Patrick Magee (Harry). On Broadway (Biltmore Theatre: January 10, 1968, 61 performances), Eli Wallach was Charlie and Milo O'Shea was Harry.

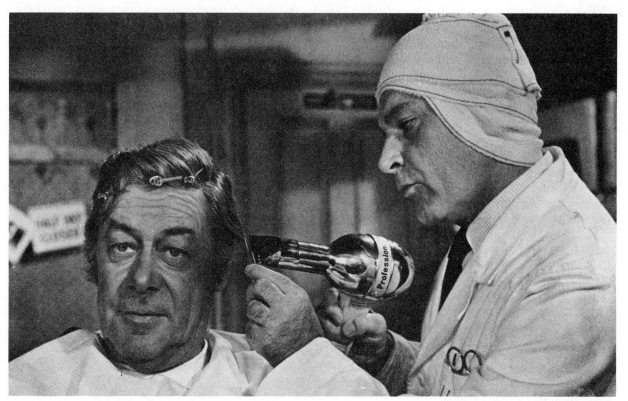

With Richard Burton in STAIRCASE (20th '69)

With wife Rachel Roberts and talk show host David Frost at a London party, November, 1969

difficult to keep my part within the realm of total reality."

The *Los Angeles Herald-Examiner* said: "The sight of Harrison and Burton camping it up is too big a joke. The very idea of it dominates the film. These stars have images and the shows of their private lives fall over the film and deaden its effect." Of the "R" rated movie, *Variety's* comment was: "Harrison's and Burton's scenes are *tours de force* with each man building his character through revealing confrontations," and of Rex, the *New Yorker* opined: "One is watching a brilliant hi-comedy actor doing something that seems to scare him stiff, and the inevitable result is a turn." Once again a costly Rex Harrison vehicle did not live up to commercial expectations.

Harrison then agreed to appear on the London stage in *Sleuth*° as well as playing the title role in the musical version of *Scrooge* (National General, 1970) when originally-intended Richard Harris withdrew.† Instead, he chose to star in George Hulme's play *The Lionel Touch*, which opened at London's Lyric Theatre on November 5, 1969. The play folded three weeks later. With Vanessa Redgrave, he was then announced to make *Nicholas and Alexandra* (Columbia, 1971), but he was eventually replaced in the film by a younger man (Michael Jayston) and Miss Redgrave was replaced by Janet Suzman.

During this period, Rex and Elizabeth Harris, who was in the process of divorcing Richard Harris, were constantly in each other's company.

Rachel Roberts Harrison filed suit for divorce in Los Angeles on September 21, 1970, in which she asked for a $1 million settlement. She expressed to the *Los Angeles Times:* "Rex and I were deeply in love—perhaps too much so. We may have burned each other out. The separation between us is very painful to me." She went on to say: "I am an actress; Rex is a star. There is a big difference, you know." The divorce was granted on March 1, 1971, with Rex getting custody of Homer, the Bassett hound.‡

Rex and Elizabeth Harris, the mother of three sons, were married at Alan Lerner's estate at Oyster Bay, New York, on August 26, 1971. Rex's fifth wife, the daughter of Lord and Lady Ogmore, was called a "lush blonde." He was sixty-three and

°Anthony Quayle was later signed for the part.
†Albert Finney ultimately played *Scrooge.*
‡Miss Roberts said after her divorce: "Oh, Rex will marry again. He's a glutton for marriage."

she was thirty years his junior. When Elizabeth was asked, "What is the real Rex Harrison like?" she answered, "Impossible and adorable." One writer quipped about her good fortune at not having to redo her monogrammed possessions.

In July 1972, Rachel appealed to a high court for unpaid alimony payments, and in September, Elizabeth announced that she would open a boutique in the heart of London because she was tired of being just a housewife. In October, it was rumored along Madison Avenue that Rex's name had suddenly become available for television commercials.

Rex left his fashionable townhouse in London's Belgravia section in late 1972, to star in Toronto in Luigi Pirandello's play of 1922, *Emperor Henry IV*, about an Italian who goes mad and impersonates the twelfth-century German monarch. After three weeks in Canada, the show moved to the new Shubert Theatre in Los Angeles, where it played from January 30, 1973, through February 17. Los Angeles critics and friends were vastly enthusiastic about Rex's reappearance in California and on the stage at that. To further welcome him back into the fold of filmland's good graces, the Hamburger Hamlet, a chain of restaurants in and around the Los Angeles area, added the Emperor Henry IV to its menu of exotic-style hamburgers.

Rex was a Tony Award presenter on March 25, 1973, at New York's Imperial Theatre, along with Celeste Holm, Sandy Duncan, and Jerry Orbach. On March 28, he opened as *Emperor Henry IV* at the Ethel Barrymore Theatre for a limited month's run. The New York critics, with theatre patrons following suit, were somewhat cool to the show and to Rex's portrayal. Richard Watts's *New York Post* review was typical: " . . . although, despite Rex Harrison's characteristically brilliant performance in the title role, I think it is lacking in the warmth of humanity. It is a dramatized intellectual puzzle."

Also in March 1973, Rex was immortalized in Hollywood's Movieland Wax Museum in a scene from *My Fair Lady*.

Next, he was seen in the title role of CBS-TV's April 23, 1973, two-hour-long, $500,000 presentation of *Don Quixote,* sponsored by IBM Corporation.* Filmed in Spain, where Rex sweltered in his suit of simulated armor on the Spanish desert, and at Ealing Studios, London, the drama was

With Rosemary Leach in THE ADVENTURES OF DON QUIXOTE (CBS-TV, April 23, 1973)

directed by Alvin Rafkoff, from Cervante's classic of the sixteenth century. During production, Harrison informed the press: "It's the best thing that's ever happened to me. How many parts are there in an actor's life which he really wants and actually gets to play? Not many, let me tell you." Of the televised show, Alan Howard said in the *Hollywood Reporter* that Rex's Don Quixote "ranks with his best work, including *My Fair Lady.*"

In October 1973, the Harrisons acquired a villa at Cap Ferrat on the French Riviera, where their neighbors were David Niven, Gregory Peck, and Otto Preminger, with their respective families. The Harrisons also continued to maintain their Belgravia home.

Rex was awarded an honorary doctorate degree by Boston University's School of Fine and Applied Arts on November 9, 1973. A month later, his granddaughter Cathy (age fourteen) stated that she wished to make a career of drama. Rex declared: "I am delighted." Cathy had then already appeared in two features, the German-British *The Pied Piper* (Paramount, 1972) and *Images* (Columbia, 1972).

Meanwhile, Rex's younger son, Carey, had turned his back on show business to become a

*It was shown earlier over BBC-TV in January 1973.

$6,000-a-year teacher at a tiny British university. "I could've capitalized on my father's name and made it big in show business," he said. "But the glitter and glamour just don't interest me. I want to teach." At one time, after his graduation from Cambridge University, it had seemed that Carey would follow in his dad's footsteps, for he worked as a director with the Leicester Repertory Theatre, wrote his first play (*Dante Kaput*) there, and later spent a year as a director with London's National Theatre and then as a writer for a Manchester TV company. Now, in his spare time from teaching literature at Essex University in Colchester, Carey and his blonde wife, Mary (who teaches college also), raise goats. Says Carey: "I don't need fancy hotel suites, big sleek cars and expensive foods—goat milk suits me fine. . . . Living my own way makes me happier than I've ever been."

Rex announced that he was "retiring" from acting for the time being to write his memoirs for Macmillan publication in England. "This memoir," he said, "is going to deal principally with

Receiving an honorary doctorate of humanities from Boston University, November 9, 1973

reminiscences about my career on stage and screen, and the many important and exciting people I have worked with. If my publishers don't like the finished result, it is mutually agreed that it won't be published. But I must say, I'm enjoying working on it more than I had anticipated."

A few months later, Rex changed his mind and agreed to take *Emperor Henry IV* to the London stage, and director Alvin Rakoff and producer Frederick Brogger said they had begged Rex to star as the blind lawyer in their film version of John Mortimer's *Voyage around My Father.*

Emperor Henry IV had its splashy opening at Her Majesty's Theatre on February 20, 1974, with Yvonne Mitchell in the co-starring spot that Eileen Herlie had undertaken on the American stage. The British were kinder in their reception to Rex's showcase, with the London critics more perceptive about the intrinsic values displayed by their noted countryman. Said the *Observer*: ". . . his perennial vigour is amazing. Mr. Harrison is almost a great actor—who fits, by a truly Pirandellian irony, into hardly any of the great parts—and his wit, authority and vocal resources are to be treasured."

Americans were not being denied Rex's presence while he was busy on the London stage. On May 1, 1974, on NBC-TV's special *Short Stories of Love,* derived from tales by Daphne Du Maurier, Somerset Maugham, and Kurt Vonnegut, Jr., and starring Bill Bixby, Leonard Nimoy, Agnes Moorehead, and Lorne Greene, Rex served as the agile host who introduced this trio of romantic stories.

When Terence Rattigan's *In Praise of Love* appeared on the London West End with Donald Sinden and Joan Greenwood, many assumed its story of a famed man whose wife was dying of a dread disease, was a direct borrow from the Harrison-Kay Kendall episode. This conclusion was further substantiated when Rex agreed to star on Broadway in the drama, with Julie Harris his co-star. The play, featuring Martin Gabel as the friend-confessor, opened at the Morosco Theatre on December 10, 1974, to polite but not rave reviews. The critics lauded Miss Harris' Greta Garbo-like performance of the former Estonian freedom fighter, but reserved most of their enthusiasm for Harrison. *Newsweek* magazine which judged the show "a flimsy and sentimental work," thought Rex ". . . a rare master, the Olivier of light comedy, and he gives a masterly performance as the charmingly selfish literary critic who after 28 years of marriage finally falls in love with his wife when he learns of her illness."

However, by early 1975, there were distinct rumbles along Broadway that all was not well with the cast of *In Praise of Love*. There were constant complaints by theatre patrons that Rex was mumbling and forgetting his lines; diverting attention from Julie Harris' entrances and curtain calls, and just plain acting "non-professional." Such behavior led many playgoers to lose their faith in the critics who had said of Harrison in this show, ". . . [he] is letter perfect. . . . His nasal drawl, his lounge-lizard posture, his Swiss-clock comic timing are on superb display" (*Time* magazine). Suddenly, stories about Rex's missed performances and alleged temperament during the *My Fair Lady* Broadway run began to surface again. Evidently there was, is, and always will be, a marked duality to the superstar, a dichotomy not at all clear to even the actor himself.

This was made evident when his autobiography *Rex* was published in early 1975 by William Morrow & Company. In the brief preface, the subject says of himself: "I have been in the theatre for fifty years and, although I make no pretense of having enjoyed every one of them, it has been and is being a good life for me. . . . One of my hopes . . . in deciding to write an autobiography was to find out more about the subject, and that is why I preferred to do it myself rather than give the job to a professional. The subject cannot be said to be totally thrilled with his discoveries, but at least he cannot blame anybody else for distorting the truth."

As show business (auto)biographies go, *Rex* is a rather shallow book, giving the reader little insight into the famed subject. There is much more emphasis on glibness than stark honesty. As *Variety's* reviewer said, "his prose style will never give literary critics gasp, . . ." The polite scribe for that journal admits of the tome, ". . . though he [Harrison] does not dig very deeply into his emotional life, he makes a good companion for the couple of hours it takes to while away his book."

One reader who did NOT enjoy the autobiography was ex-wife Lilli Palmer, whose own memoirs is a bestseller in West Germany and will be published in an English language edition. She told the press, "He said [in the book] I didn't have a sense of humor. Remember that we spent fifteen years together. He must have been long-suffering." On another occasion, sparked by Harrison's evaluation of her, she announced of Rex, "One woman wasn't enough for Rex—he just couldn't be faithful. . . . He'd see some woman and believe he'd fallen head over heels in love with her. It was just his personality, I suppose."

On Broadway in 1974 with Julie Harris.

Recalling their union, Lilli synopsized, "I lived with Rex before our marriage—from 1940 to 1943. It may not have been very fashionable in those days, but we were so in love we didn't care. Then, in 1943, we got married. It was a marriage that broke up in 1954, although we didn't get our divorce until three years later. . . . I suppose it's symptomatic of my love for him that we stayed together until 1954. I loved him through all those years, but when we split up I guess it had all withered away . . . There was nothing left—I felt no regrets."

After the closing of *In Praise of Love* at the end of May, 1975, Rex told Broadway observer Earl Wilson, "I shall be coming back next year to 'old Broadway.' I love Broadway. I've *been* on Broadway more—*echtually*—more than I've *been* to London. They don't treat me as a stranger here."

When Wilson asked if he was typical of any school of acting, Rex responded, "The school of naturalism. You attempt to behave exactly as you would in life. I sprang from a long line of drawing room actors. I may be the only one left."

As for his immediate plans, Rex returned to his wife (scotching the rumors of a divorce), basset hound Homer and his house and boat at Cap Ferrat, France. He had thoughts of attending the

Moscow Film Festival, and planned to be busy considering the possibilities of which new play to try out, or what teleseries had the most potential.

One thing is certain. He will not give up show business. "Retire? Never! Why should I? I'm going to stick to acting for at least another 50 years. . . . I've never been happier or felt younger in my life." '

"Life has been good to me, but never better than in these past two-and-a-half years since I've been married to Elizabeth. Being with her all the time keeps me young as well.

"God knows what I would do if I weren't married to Elizabeth and weren't still working."*

On the subject of his much-publicized romantic life, Rex explains: "I've never been a woman-izer. I'm strictly the marrying kind, totally uninterested in casual relationships. . . . The fact that one can attract a beautiful woman late in one's own life is marvelous. It may annoy some people—I can't help that."

On another occasion, he had words to say on politics: "I have always believed that actors should keep out of politics and should not participate in political rallies. With things . . . so extraordinary, it might be argued that today we should participate. However, I still believe that it is not our place to interfere in world affairs. We are here to entertain."

Although now in his late sixties, Harrison shows no signs of slowing down his active professional-social pace. Simply and shortly he confesses: "I'm feeling at the peak of my form."

*Elizabeth filed a divorce petition in August, 1975, in London.

Rex Harrison

THE SCHOOL FOR SCANDAL (Paramount-British, 1930) 76 M.
Producer-director, Maurice Elvey; based on the play by Richard Brinsley Sheridan; screenplay, Jean Jay.
Basil Gill (Sir Peter Teazle); Madeleine Carroll (Lady Teazle); Ian Fleming (Joseph Surface); Henry Hewitt (Charles Surface); Edgar K. Bruce (Sir Oliver Surface); Hayden Coffin (Sir Harry Bumper); Hector Abbas (Moses); Dodo Watts (Maria); Anne Grey (Lady Sneerwell); John Charlton (Benjamin Backbite); Stanley Lathbury (Crabtree); Henry Vibart (Squire Hunter); May Agate (Mrs. Candour); Maurice Braddell (Careless); Gibb McLaughlin (William); Wallace Bosco (Rawley); Rex Harrison (Bit).

THE GREAT GAME (Gaumont, 1930) 79 M.
Producer, L'Estrange Fawcett; director, Jack Raymond; story, William Hunter, John Lees; screenplay, W. P. Lipscomb, Ralph Gilbert Bettinson.
John Batten (Dicky Brown); Renee Clama (Peggy Jackson); Jack Cock (Jim Blake); Randie Ayrton (Henderson); Neil Kenyon (Jackson); Kenneth Kove (Bultitude); A. G. Poulton (Banks); Billy Blyth (Billy); Lew Lake (Tubby); Wally Patch (Joe Miller); Rex Harrison (George).

GET YOUR MAN (Paramount-British, 1934) 67 M.
Director, George King; based on the play Tu M'Espouseras *by Louis Verneuil; screenplay, George Dewhurst.*
Dorothy Boyd (Nancy McAlpine); Sebastian Shaw (Robert Halbeam); Clifford Heatherley (Parker Halbeam); Hugh E. Wright (Reverend John Vivien); Kay Walsh (Mary Vivien); Helen Ferrers (Agatha McAlpine); Rex Harrison (Tom Jakes).

LEAVE IT TO BLANCHE (First National-British, 1934) 51 M.
Producer, Irving Asher; director, Harold Young; story, Roland Brown; screenplay, Brock Williams.
Henry Kendall (Peter Manners); Olive Blakeney (Blanche Wetherby); Miki Hood (Doris Manners); Griffith Jones (Philip Amesbury); Rex Harrison (Ronnie); Hamilton Keene (Brewster); Julian Royce (Patteridge); Elizabeth Jenns (Blossom); Harold Warrender (Guardee); Phyllis Stanley (Singer).

ALL AT SEA (Fox-British, 1935) 60 M.
Director, Anthony Kimmins; based on the play by Ian Hay.
Tyrell Davis (Joe Finch); Googie Withers (Daphne Tomkins); James Carew (Julius Mablethorpe); Cecily Byrne (Mary Maggs); Rex Harrison (Aubrey Bellingham); Dorothy Vernon (Mrs. Humphrey); James Harcourt (Mr. Humphrey); Colin Lesslie (Tony Lambert).

MEN ARE NOT GODS (United Artists-British, 1936) 82 M.
Producer, Alexander Korda; director, Walter Reisch; story by G. B. Stern, Iris Wright; adaptor, Reisch; camera, Charles Rosher; editor, Henry Cornelius.
Miriam Hopkins (Ann Williams); Gertrude Lawrence (Barbara Halford); Sebastian Shaw (Edmund Davey); Rex Harrison (Tommy Stapleton); A. E. Matthews (Skeates); Val Gielgud (Producer); Laura Smithson (Katherine); Lawrence Grossmith (Stanley); Sybil Grove (Painter); Winifred Willard (Mrs. Williams); Wally Patch (Gallery Attendant); James Harcourt (Porter); Noel Howlett (Cashier); Rosamund Greenwood (Piano Player); Paddy Morgan (Kelly); Nicholas Nadyin (Iago); Michael Hogarth (Cassio).
U.S. release: UA (1937).

STORM IN A TEACUP (United Artists-British, 1937) 87 M.
Producer, Victor Saville; directors, Saville, Ian Dalrymple; based on the play Sturm in Wasserglass *by Bruno Frank; screenplay, Dalrymple, Donald Bull; camera, M. Greenbaum; editors, Hugh Stewart, Cyril Randell.*
Vivien Leigh (Victoria Gow); Rex Harrison (Frank Burdon); Sara Allgood (Mrs. Hegarty); Cecil Parker (Provost Gow); Ursula Jeans (Lisbet Skirving); Gus McNaughton (Horace Skirving); Arthur Wontner (Fiscal); Edgar K. Bruce (McKellar); Robert Hale (Lord Skerryvore); Quinton McPherson (Baillie Callender); Eliot Makeham (Sheriff); Ivor Barnard (Watkins); W. G. Fay (Cassidy).

SCHOOL FOR HUSBANDS (General Film Distributors, 1937) 71 M.

Producer, Richard Wainwright; director, Andrew Marton; based on the play by Frederick Jackson; screenplay, Frederick Jackson, Austin Melford, Gordon Sherry; camera, Phil Tannura.

Diana Churchill (Marion Carter); June Clyde (Diana Cheswick); Rex Harrison (Leonard Drummond); Romney Brent (Morgan Cheswick); Henry Kendall (Geoffrey Carter); Roxie Russell (Kate); Richard Golden (Whittaker); Judith Glick (Joan); Joan Kemp-Welsh (Maid).

U.S. release: (1939).

OVER THE MOON (United Artists-British, 1937) C—78 M.

Producer, Alexander Korda; directors, Thornton Freeland, William K. Howard; story, Robert E. Sherwood, Lajos Biro; screenplay, Anthony Pelissier, Arthur Wimperis, Alec Coppel; music, Mischa Spoliansky; songs, Spoliansky and Desmond Carter; camera, Harry Stradling.

Merle Oberon (June Benson); Rex Harrison (Dr. Freddie Jarvis); Ursula Jeans (Lady Millie Parsmill); Robert Douglas (John Flight); Louis Borell (Count Pietro d'Altamura); Zena Dare (Julie Deethorpe); Peter Haddon (Lord Petcliffe); David Tree (Journalist); Mackenzie Ward (Lord Guy Carstairs); Carl Jaffe (Michel); Elisabeth Welch (Singer); Herbert Lomas (Ladbrooke); Wilfred Shane (Frude); Gerald Nodin (Cartwright).

U.S. release: (1940).

ST. MARTIN'S LANE (Associated British Producers, 1938) 85 M.

Producer, Erich Pommer; director, Tim Whelan; screenplay, Clemence Dane; music, Arthur Johnson; songs, Johnson and Eddie Pola; choreography, Philip Buchel; music director, Muir Mathieson; camera, Jules Kruger; editors, Hugh Stewart, Robert Hamer.

Charles Laughton (Charles Saggers); Vivien Leigh (Libby); Rex Harrison (Harley Prentiss); Larry Adler (Constantine); Tyrone Guthrie (Gentry); Gus McNaughton (Arthur Smith); Basil Gill (Magistrate); David Burns (Hackett); Edward Lexy (Mr. Such); Alf Goddard (Doggie); Romilly Lunge (Duchesi); Marie O'Neill (Mrs. Such); Polly Ward (Frankie); Helen Haye (Lady Selena); Phyllis Stanley (Delia Fordingbridge); Carroll Gibbons and His Orchestra, The Luna Boys (Themselves).

U.S. release title: SIDEWALKS OF LONDON (PAR, 1940).

THE CITADEL (MGM, 1938) 110 M.

Producer, Victor Saville; director, King Vidor; based on the novel by A. J. Cronin; screenplay, Ian Dalrymple, Frank Wead, Elizabeth Hill, Emlyn Williams; art directors, Lazare Meerson, Alfred Junge; music, Louis Levy; assistant director, Pen Tennyson; sound, C. C. Stevens, A. W. Watkins; camera, Harry Stradling; editor, Charles Frend.

Robert Donat (Andrew Manson); Rosalind Russell (Christine Manson); Ralph Richardson (Denny); Rex Harrison (Dr. Lawford); Emlyn Williams (Owen); Penelope Dudley Ward (Toppy Leroy); Francis L. Sullivan (Ben Chenkin); Mary Clare (Mrs. Orlando); Cecil Parker (Charles Every); Nora Swinburne (Mrs. Thornton); Edward Chapman (Joe Morgan); Athene Seyler (Lady Raebank); Felix Aylmer (Mr. Boon); Joyce Bland (Nurse Sharp); Percy Parsons (Mr. Stillman); Dilys Davis (Mrs. Page); Basil Gill (Dr. Page); Joss Ambler (Dr. A. H. Llewellyn).

THE SILENT BATTLE (Paramount-British, 1939) 84 M.

Producer, Anthony Havelock-Allan; director, Herbert Mason; based on the novel Le Poisson Chinois by Jean Brommart; screenplay, Wolfgang Wilhelm, Rodney Ackland; music director, Francis Chagrin; sound, A. W. Watkins; camera, Bernard Browne; editor, Philip Charlot.

Rex Harrison (Jacques Sauvin); Valerie Hobson (Draguisha

Montescu); John Loder (Rene Bordier); Muriel Aked (Madame Duvivier); George Devine (Sonneman); John Salem (Ernest); Kaye Seeley (Bartoff); Carl Jaffe (Rykoff); Megs Jenkins (Louise); Arthur Maude (Editor).

U.S. release title: CONTINENTAL EXPRESS (MON, 1942).

TEN DAYS IN PARIS (Columbia-British, 1939) 82 M.

Associate producer, Jerome J. Jackson; director, Tim Whelan; based on the novel The Disappearance of Roger Tremayne by Bruce Graeme; screenplay, John Meehan, Jr., James Curtis; camera, Otto Kanturek; editor, Hugh Stewart.

Rex Harrison (Bob Stevens); Kaaren Verne (Diane de Guermantes); Leo Genn (Lanson); Joan Marion (Denise); Anthony Holles (Francois); John Abbott (Andre); Robert Rendel (Sir James Stevens); Mavis Clair (Marie); Andre Morell (Victor); Hay Petrie (Benoit); Frank Atkinson (Pierre).

U.S. release title: MISSING TEN DAYS (COL, 1941).

GESTAPO (NIGHT TRAIN TO MUNICH) MGM-British, 1940) 95 M.

Producer, Edward Black; director, Carl Reed; story, Gordon Wellesley; screenplay, Sydney Gilliat, Frank Launder; art director, Vetchinsky; music director, Louis Levy; camera, Otto Kanturek; editor, R. E. Dearing.

Margaret Lockwood (Anna Bomasch); Rex Harrison (Gus Bennett); Paul von Henreid (Karl Marsen); Basil Radford (Charters); Naunton Wayne (Caldicott); James Harcourt (Axel Bomasch); Felix Aylmer (Dr. Fredericks); Wyndham Goldie (Dryton); Roland Culver (Roberts); Eliot Makeham (Schwab); Raymond Huntley (Kampenfeldt); Austin Trevor (Captain Prada); Keneth Kent (Controller); C. V. France (Admiral Hassinger); Frederick Valk (Gestapo Officer); Morland Graham (Attendant).

U.S. release title: NIGHT TRAIN (20th, 1940) 93 M.

MAJOR BARBARA (General Film Distributors, 1941) 121 M.

Producer, Gabriel Pascal; directors, Pascal, Harold French, David Lean; based on the play by George Bernard Shaw; screenplay, Anatole de Grunwald, Shaw; music, William Walton; camera, Ronald Neame.

Wendy Hiller (Major Barbara Undershaft); Rex Harrison (Adolphus Cusins); Robert Morley (Mr. Undershaft); Emlyn Williams (Snobby Price); Robert Newton (Bill Walker); Sybil Thorndike (The General); Deborah Kerr (Jenny Hill); David Tree (Charles Lomax); Penelope Dudley-Ward (Sarah Undershaft); Marie Lohr (Lady Brittomart); Walter Hudd (Stephen Undershaft); Marie Ault (Rummy Mitchens); Donald Calthrop (Peter Shirley); Felix Aylmer (James); Stanley Holloway (P.C.).

U.S. release: (UA, 1941) 115 M.

I LIVE IN GROSVENOR SQUARE (Pathe, 1945) 113 M.

Producer-director, Herbert Wilcox; story, Maurice Cowan; screenplay, Nicholas Phipps, William D. Bayles.

Anna Neagle (Lady Pat Fairfax); Rex Harrison (Major David Bruce); Dean Jagger (Sergeant John Patterson); Robert Morley (Duke of Exmoor); Jane Darwell (Mrs. Patterson); Nancy Price (Mrs. Wilson); Irene Vanbrugh (Mrs. Catchpole); Edward Rigby (Innkeeper); Walter Hudd (Vicar); Elliott Arluck (Benjie Greenburg); Francis Pierlot (Postman); Aubrey Mallalieu (Bates); Michael Shepley (Lieutenant Lutyens); Charles Victor (Taxi Driver); Ronald Shiner (Paratrooper); and: Irene Manning, Alvah Liddell, Gerry Wilmot, Carroll Gibbons and his Orchestra.

U.S. release title: A YANK IN LONDON (20th, 1946) 109 M.

BLITHE SPIRIT (General Film Distributors, 1945) C—96 M.

Producer, Noel Coward; associate producer, Anthony Havelock-Allan; director, David Lean; based on the play by Noel

Coward; screenplay, Lean, Havelock-Allan; music, Richard Addinsell; art director, C. P. Norman; music director, Muir Mathieson; camera, Ronald Neame; editor, Jack Harris.

Rex Harrison (Charles Condomine); Constance Cummings (Ruth Condomine); Kay Hammond (Elvira Condomine); Margaret Rutherford (Mme. Arcati); Hugh Wakefield (George Bradman); Joyce Carey (Violet Bradman); Jacqueline Clark (Edith).

JOURNEY TOGETHER (RKO-British, 1945) 95 M.

Producer, Royal Air Force Film Unit; director, John Boulting; story, Terence Rattigan; screenplay, Boulting; music, Gordon Jacob; production designer, John Howell; special effects, Ray Morse; camera, Harry Waxman.

Sergeant Richard Attenborough (David Wilton); Aircraftsman Jack Walting (John Aynesworth); Flying Officer David Tomlinson (Smith); Warrant Office Sid Rider (A Fitter); Squadron Leader Stuart Latham (A Flight Sergeant Fitter); Squadron Leader Hugh Wakefield (An Acting Lieutenant); Leading Aircraftsman Bromley Challenor (A.D.2 Jay); Flying Officer Z. Peromowski (An Anson Pilot); Edward G. Robinson (Dean McWilliams); Patrick Waddington (Flight Lieutenant Mander); Flight Lieutenant Sebastian Shaw (Squadron Leader Marshall); Wing Commander Ronald Adam (The Commanding Officer); Bessie Love (Mary McWilliams); Sergeant Norvell Crutcher (A Driver); Rex Harrison (Bit); and Personnel of the Royal Air Force, Royal Canadian Air Force, and United States Army.

U.S. release: (English Films, 1946) 95 M.

THE RAKE'S PROGRESS (Eagle Lion, 1945) 123 M.

Producers, Frank Launder, Sidney Gilliat; director, Gilliat; story, Val Valentine; screenplay, Launder, Gilliat; art director, Norman Arnold; music, William Alwyn; camera, Wilkie Cooper; editor, Thelma Myers.

Rex Harrison (Vivian Kenway); Lilli Palmer (Rikki Krausner); Godfrey Tearle (Colonel Kenway); Griffith Jones (Sandy Duncan); Margaret Johnston (Jennifer Calthrop); Guy Middleton (Fogroy); Jean Kent (Jill Duncan); Marie Lohr (Lady Parks); Garry Marsh (Sir Hubert Parks); David Horne (Sir John Brockley); Alan Wheatley (Edwards); Brefni O'Rorke (Bromhead); Charles Victor (Old Sweet); Joan Maude (Alice); Patricia Laffan (Miss Fernandez); Howard Marion Crawford (Guardsman); Emrys Jones (Bateson).

U.S. release title: NOTORIOUS GENTLEMAN (UNIV, 1946) 108 M.

ANNA AND THE KING OF SIAM (20th, 1946) 128 M.

Producer, Louis D. Lighton; director, John Cromwell; based upon the book by Margaret Landon and the books by Anna H. Leonowens; screenplay, Talbot Jennings, Sally Benson; art directors, Lyle Wheeler, William Darling; set decorators, Thomas Little, Frank E. Hughes; music, Bernard Herrmann; assistant director, Sol Wurtzel; sound, Bernard Freericks, Roger Heman; special camera effects, Fred Sersen; camera, Arthur Miller; editor, Harmon Jones.

Irene Dunne (Anna Owens); Rex Harrison (King Mongkut); Linda Darnell (Tuptim); Lee J. Cobb (Kralahome); Gale Sondergaard (Lady Thiang); Mikhail Rasumny (Alak); Dennis Hoey (Sir Edward); Tito Renaldo (Prince—Grown up); William Edmunds (Moonshee); Richard Lyon (Louis Owens); John Abbott (Phya Phrom); Leonard Strong (Interpreter); Mickey Roth (Prince); Connie Leon (Beebe); Diana Van Der Ecker (Princess Fa-Ying); Si-lan Chen (Dancer); Marjorie Eaton (Miss MacFarlane); Helena Grant (Mrs. Cortwright); Stanely Mann (Mr. Cortwright); Addison Richards (Captain Orton); Neyle Morrow (Phra Palat); Yvonne Rob (Lady Sno Kim); Julian Rivero (Government Clerk); Laurette Luez, Chabing, Marianne Quon, Lillian Molieri, Buff Cobb, Sydney Logan (Wives of King); Hazel Shon (Slave); Pedro Regas (Guide); Ted Hecht, Ben Welden (Judges).

THE GHOST AND MRS. MUIR (20th, 1947) 104 M.

Producer, Fred Kohlmar; director, Joseph L. Mankiewicz; based on the novel by R. A. Dick; screenplay, Philip Dunne; music, Bernard Herrmann; art directors, Richard Day, George Davis; set decorators, Thomas Little, Stuart Reiss; assistant director, Johnny Johnston; sound, Bernard Freericks, Roger Heman; special effects, Fred Sersen; camera, Charles Lang; editor, Dorothy Spencer.

Gene Tierney (Lucy Muir); Rex Harrison (The Ghost of Captain Daniel Gregg); George Sanders (Miles Fairley); Edna Best (Martha); Vanessa Brown (Anna—Grown up); Anna Lee (Mrs. Miles Fairley); Robert Coote (Coombe); Natalie Wood (Anna as a Child); Isobel Elsom (Angelica); Victoria Horne (Eva); Whitford Kane (Sproule); Brad Slaven (Enquiries); Helen Freeman (Authoress); William Stelling (Bill); David Thursby (Sproggins); Stuart Holmes (Man on Train); Heather Wilde (English Maid).

THE FOXES OF HARROW (20th, 1947) 117 M.

Producer, William A. Bacher; director, John M. Stah; based on the novel by Frank Yerby; screenplay, Wanda Tuchock; assistant director, Joseph Behm; music, David Buttolph; music arranger, Maurice de Packh; music director, Alfred Newman; art directors, Lyle Wheeler, Maurice Ransford; set decorators, Thomas Little, Paul S. Fox; sound, George Leverett, Roger Heman; camera, Joseph LaShelle; editor, James B. Clark.

Rex Harrison (Stephen Fox); Maureen O'Hara (Odalie D'Arceneaux); Richard Haydn (Andre LeBlanc); Victor McLaglen (Captain Mike Farrell); Vanessa Brown (Aurore D'Arceneaux), Patricia Medina (Desiree); Gene Lockhart (The Vicomte); Charles Irwin (Sean Fox); Hugo Hass (Hugo Ludenbach); Roy Roberts (Tom Warren); Dennis Hoey (Master of Harrow); Marcel Journet (St. Ange); Helen Crozier (Zerline); Sam McDaniel (Josh); Libby Taylor (Angelina); Renee Beard (Little Inch); Suzette Marbin (Belle); Perry William Ward (Etienne Fox at Age Six); Clear Nelson, Jr. (Little Inch at Age Three); James Lagano (Etienne at Age Three); Dorothy Adams (Mrs. Fox); Celia Lovsky (Minna Ludenbach); Eugene Borden (French Auctioneer); Gordon Clark (Fop); Robert Emmett Keane (Auctioneer); Bernard DeRoux (Creole Waiter); Frederick Burton (Creole Gentleman); Wee Willie Davis (Sailor); Randy Stuart (Mother of Stephen Fox).

ESCAPE (Twentieth Century-Fox-British, 1948) 78 M.

Producer, William Perlberg; director, Joseph L. Mankiewicz; based on the play by John Galsworthy; screenplay, Philip Dunne; art director, Vetchinsky; music, William Alwyn; music director, Muir Mathieson; assistant director, Ray Parkinson; sound, W. H. Lindop; camera, Frederick A. Young; editors, Alan L. Jaggs, K. Heeley-Ray.

Rex Harrison (Matt Denant); Peggy Cummins (Dora Winton); William Hartnell (Inspector Harris); Felix Aylmer (Old Gentleman); Norman Wooland (Parson); Jill Esmond (Grace Winton); Frederick Piper (Brownie); Marjorie Rhodes (Mrs. Pinkes); Betty Ann Davies (Girl in Park); Cyril Cusack (Rodgers); John Slater (Car Salesman); Frank Pettingell (Village Constable); Michael Golden (Plainclothesman); Frederick Leister (Judge); Walter Hudd (Defense Counsel); Maurice Denham (Crown Counsel); Jacqueline Clarke (Phyllis); Frank Tickle (Mr. Pinkem); Cyril Smith (Policeman); Patrick Troughton, Cameron Mackinlay (Shepherds); Molly Lumsley (Old Lady); Ian Russel (Car Driver); Stuart Lindsell (Sir James).

UNFAITHFULLY YOURS (20th, 1948) 105 M.

Producer-director-screenplay, Preston Sturges; art directors, Lyle Wheeler, Joseph C. Wright; set decorators, Thomas Little, Paul S. Fox; music, Gioacchino Rossini, Richard Wagner, Peter Tchaikowsky; music director, Alfred Newman; assistant director, Gaston Glass; makeup, Ben Nye, Henry Vilardo, Frank Prehoda; costumes, Bonnie Cashin; sound, Arthur L.

Kirbach, Roger Heman; special effects, Fred Sersen; camera, Victor Milner; editor, Robert Fritch.

Rex Harrison (Sir Alfred de Carter); Linda Darnell (Daphne de Carter); Barbara Lawrence (Barbara); Rudy Vallee (August); Kurt Kreuger (Anthony); Lionel Stander (Hugo); Edgar Kennedy (Sweeney); Al Bridge (House Detective); Julius Tannen (Tailor); Torben Meyer (Dr. Schultz); Robert Greig (Jules); Evelyn Beresford (Mme. Pompadour); Georgia Caine (Dowager); Isabel Jewell, Marion Marshall (Telephone Operators); Frank Moran (Fire Chief); Ruth Clifford (Saleslady); Charles Tannen (Information Man); Dave Morris, Franz Roehm, George Matthews (Musicians); Major Sam Harris (Man).

THE LONG DARK HALL (British Lion, 1951) 86 M.
Producer, Peter Cusick; directors, Anthony Bushell, Reginald Beckl; screenplay, Nunnally Johnson, William Fairchild; art director, George Paterson; set decorator, Ronald Kinnoch; music, Benjamin Frankel; sound, Fred Tuttle; camera, Wilkie Cooper; editor, Tom Simpson.

Rex Harrison (Arthur Groome); Lilli Palmer (Mary Groome); Denis O'Dea (Sir Charles Morton); Raymond Huntley (Inspector Sullivan); Patricia Wayne (Cutts) (Rose Mallory); Anthony Dawson (The Man); Anthony Bushell (Clive Bedford); Meriel Forbes (Marjorie); Brenda de Banzie (Mrs. Rogers); William Squires (Sergeant Cochran); Michael Medwin (Leslie Scott); Colin Gordon (Pound); Eric Pohlmann (Polaris).

U.S. release: (Eagle Lion, 1951) 86 M.

THE FOURPOSTER (COL, 1952) 103 M.
Producer, Stanley Kramer; director, Irving Reis; based on the play by Jan de Hartog; screenplay, Allan Scott; music-music conductor, Dmitri Tiomkin; production designer, Rudolph Sternad; art director, Carl Anderson; set decorators, William Kiernan, Louis Diage; sound, Russell Malmgren; camera, Hal Mohr; interscenes, John Hubley; editor, Henry Batista.

Rex Harrison (John); Lilli Palmer (Abby).

MAIN STREET TO BROADWAY (MGM, 1953) 102 M.
Producer, Lester Cowan; director, Tay Garnett; story, Robert E. Sherwood; screenplay, Samson Raphaelson; art director, Perry Ferguson; camera, James Wong Howe; editor, Gene Fowler, Jr.

Tom Morton (Tony Monaco); Mary Murphy (Mary Craig); Agnes Moorehead (Mildred Waterbury); Herb Shriner (Frank Johnson); Rosemary De Camp (Mrs. Craig); Clinton Sundberg (Mr. Craig); Gertrude Berg (Landlady); and: Tallulah Bankhead, Ethel Barrymore, Lionel Barrymore, Shirley Booth, Louis Calhern, Leo Durocher, Faye Emerson, Richard Rodgers, Oscar Hammerstein II, Rex Harrison, Helen Hayes, Joshua Logan, Mary Martin, Lilli Palmer, John van Druten, Cornel Wilde (Themselves).

KING RICHARD AND THE CRUSADERS (WB, 1954) C—114 M.
Producer, Henry Blanke; director, David Butler; based on the novel The Talisman by Sir Walter Scott; screenplay, John Twist; assistant director, Oren Haglund; music, Max Steiner; art director, Bertram Tuttle; camera, J. Peverell Marley; editor, Edith Morra.

Rex Harrison (Emir Ilderim); Virginia Mayo (Lady Edith); George Sanders (King Richard III); Laurence Harvey (Sir Kenneth); Robert Douglas (Sir Giles Amaury); Michael Pate (Montferrat); Paula Raymond (Queen Berengaria); Lester Matthews (Archbishop of Tyre); Antony Eustrel (Baron De Vaux); Henry Corden (King Philip of France); Wilton Graff (Duke Leopold of Austria); Nick Cravat (Nectobanus); Leslie Bradley (Castelain Captain); Nejla Ates (Moorish Dancing Girl); Larry Chance (Castelain Bowman); Robin Hughes (King's

Guard); Leonard Penn, Lumsden Hare, Leonard Mudie (Physicians); Erik Blythe (Drill Master); John Alderson (Mob Leader); Harry Cording (Castelain Spokesman); Paul Marion (Arab Falconer); Abdullah Abbas (Arab); Mark Hanna (Courier); John Epper (Wounded Castelain).

THE CONSTANT HUSBAND (British Lion, 1955) C—88 M.
Producer, Frank Launder, Sidney Gilliat; director, Gilliat; screenplay, Gilliat, Val Valentine.

Rex Harrison (Charles Hathaway); Margaret Leighton (Miss Chesterman); Kay Kendall (Monica); Cecil Parker (Llewellyn); Nicole Maurey (Lola); George Cole (Luigi Sopranelli); Raymond Huntley (J P Hassett); Michael Hordern (Judge); Robert Coote (Jack Carter); Eric Pohlmann (Papa Sopranelli); Marie Burke (Mama Sopranelli); Valerie French (Bridget); Jill Adams (Miss Brent); Muriel Young (Clara); John Robinson (Secretary).

U.S. release: (Stratford Pictures, 1957).

THE RELUCTANT DEBUTANTE (MGM, 1958) C—96 M.
Producer, Pandro S. Berman; director, Vincente Minnelli; based on the play by William Douglas Home; screenplay, Home; art director, A. J. d'Eaubonne; set director, Robert Christides; assistant director, William McGarry; makeup, Jean-Paul Ulysse; wardrobe for Miss Dee, Helen Rose; wardrobe for Miss Kendall, Miss Lansbury, and Miss Clare, Pierre Balmain; dance music-arranger, Eddie Warner and Orchestra; sound, Guy Rophe; camera, Joseph Ruttenburg; editor, Adrienne Fazan.

Rex Harrison (Jimmy Broadbent); Kay Kendall (Sheila Broadbent); John Saxon (David Parkson); Sandra Dee (Jane Broadbent); Angela Lansbury (Mabel Claremont); Peter Myers (David Fenner); Diane Clare (Clarissa Claremont); Sheila Raynor (Maid); Ambrosine Phillpotts (Secretary); Charles Cullum (English Colonel).

MIDNIGHT LACE (UNIV, 1960) C—108 M.
Producers, Ross Hunter, Martin Melcher; director, David Miller; based on the play Matilda Shouted Fire by Janet Green; screenplay, Ivan Goff, Ben Roberts; art directors, Alexander Golitzen, Robert Clatworthy; set decorator, Oliver Emert; Miss Day's gowns, Irene; makeup, Bud Westmore; assistant directors, Phil Bowles, Carl Beringer, Doug Green; music, Frank Skinner; songs, Joe Lubin and Jerome Howard; Allie Wrubel and Maxwell Anderson; music supervisor, Joseph Gershenson; sound, Waldon O. Watson, Joe Lapis; camera, Russell Metty; editors, Leon Barsha, Russell F. Schoengarth.

Doris Day (Kit Preston); Rex Harrison (Tony Preston); John Gavin (Brian Younger); Myrna Loy (Aunt Bea); Roddy McDowall (Malcolm); Herbert Marshall (Charles Manning); Natasha Parry (Peggy Thompson); John Williams (Inspector Byrnes); Hermione Baddeley (Dora); Richard Ney (Daniel Graham); Rhys Williams (Victor Elliott); Doris Lloyd (Nora); Richard Lupino (Simon Foster); Anthony Dawson (Ash); Anna Cheselka, Vladimir Oukhtomsky (Ballet Dancers); Rex Evans (Basil Stafford); Jim Hyland (Policeman); Mary Flynn (Nurse); Tom Toner, Donald Journeau (Porters); Paul Collins (Kevin); Jimmy Fairfax (Bus Driver); John Sheffield (Attendant); Joan Staley (Blonde); Peter Fontaine (Workman); Leon Charles (Man).

THE HAPPY THIEVES (UA, 1962) 88 M.
Director, George Marshall; based on the novel The Oldest Profession by Richard Condon; screenplay, John Gay; art director, Ramiro Gomes; music, Mario Nascimbene; Miss Hayworth's wardrobe, Pierre Balmain, Pedro Rodrigues; camera, Paul Beeson; editor, Oswald Hafenrichter.

Rex Harrison (Jim Bourne); Rita Hayworth (Eve Lewis); Joseph Wiseman (Jean Marie Calbert); Gregoire Aslan (Dr. Munoz); Alida Valli (Duchess Blanca); Virgilio Texeira (Cayetano); Peter Illing (Mr. Pickett); Brita Ekman (Mrs. Pickett);

Julio Pena (Señor Elek); Gerard Tichy (Antonio); Lou Weber, Antonio Fuentes (Guards); George Rigaud (Inspector); Barta Barri (Chern); Karl-Heinz Schwerdtfeger (Police Official).

CLEOPATRA (20th, 1963) C—243 M.

Producer, Walter Wanger; director, Joseph L. Mankiewicz; based upon Histories by Plutarch, Suetonius, Appian, and The Life and Times of Cleopatra by C. M. Franzero; screenplay, Mankiewicz, Ranald MacDougall, Sidney Buchman; music-music conductor, Alex North; associate conductor, Lionel Newman; production designer, John De Cuir; art directors, Jack Martin Smith, Hilyard Brown, Herman Blumenthal, Elven Webb, Maurice Pelling, Boris Juraga; set decorators, Walter M. Scott, Paul S. Fox, Ray Moyer; choreography, Hermes Pan; Miss Taylor's costumes, Irene Sharaff; additional costumes, Vittorio Nino Novarese, Renie; makeup, Alberto De Rossi; assistant director, Fred R. Simpson; sound, Fred Hynes, James Corcoran, Bernard Freericks, Murray Spivack; special camera effects, L. B. Abbott, Emil Kosa, Jr.; camera, Leon Shamroy; second unit camera, Claude Renoir, Pietro Portalupi; editor, Dorothy Spencer.

Elizabeth Taylor (Cleopatra); Richard Burton (Mark Antony); Rex Harrison (Julius Caesar); Pamela Brown (High Priestess); George Cole (Flavius); Hume Cronyn (Sosigenes); Cesare Danova (Apollidorus); Kenneth Haigh (Brutus); Roddy McDowall (Octavian); Martin Landau (Rufio); Andrew Keir (Agrippa); Robert Stephens (Germanicus); Francesca Annis (Eiras); Gregoire Aslan (Pothinos); Martin Benson (Ramos); John Cairney (Phoebus); Jacqui Chan (Lotos); Isabelle Cooley (Charmian); John Doucette (Achillas); Andrew Faulds (Canidius); Michael Gwynn (Cimber); Michael Hordern (Cicero); John Hoyt (Cassius); Marne Maitland (Euphranor); Carroll O'Connor (Casca); Richard O'Sullivan (Ptolemy); Gwen Watford (Calpurnia); Douglas Wilmer (Decimus); Marina Berti (Queen at Tarsus); John Karlsen (High Priest); Loris Loddi (Caesar at Age Four); Jean Marsh (Octavia); Gin Mart (Marcellus); Furio Marcellus (Mithridates); Kenneth Nash (Caesarion at Age Twelve); Del Russell (Caesarion at Age Seven); John Valva (Valvus).

MY FAIR LADY (WB, 1964) C—170 M.

Producer, Jack L. Warner; director, George Cukor; based upon the play Pygmalion by George Bernard Shaw and the musical play, book and lyrics by Alan Jay Lerner, Frederick Loewe; screenplay, Lerner; costumes, scenery, production designer, Cecil Beaton; art director, Gene Allen; music supervisor-music conductor, Andre Previn; additional music, Loewe; vocal arranger, Robert Tucker; orchestrators, Alexander Courage, Robert Franklyn, Al Woodbury; choreography, Hermes Pan; set decorator, George James Hopkins; makeup, Gordon Bau; assistant director, David Hall; sound, Francis J. Scheid, Murray Spivak; camera, Harry Stradling; editor, William Ziegler.

Audrey Hepburn (Eliza Doolittle); Rex Harrison (Henry Higgins); Stanley Holloway (Alfred Doolittle); Wilfrid Hyde-White (Colonel Pickering); Gladys Cooper (Mrs. Higgins); Jeremy Brett (Freddie); Theodore Bikel (Zoltan Karpathy); Mona Washbourne (Mrs. Pearce); Isobel Elsom (Mrs. Eynsford-Hill); John Holland (Butler); Singing Voice of Marni Nixon (Eliza); Singing Voice of Bill Shirley (Freddie); Owen McGiveney (Man at Coffee Stand); Laurie Main (Hoxton Man); Lois Battle, Jacqueline Squire (Maids); John Holland (Butler); Iris Bristol (Flower Girl); Moyna MacGill (Lady Boxington); Ben Wright (Footman at the Ball); Alan Napier (Ambassador); Geoffrey Steele (Taxi Driver); Buddy Bryan (Prince); Nick Navarro (Dancer); Barbara Pepper (Ad Lib at Church); Major Sam Harris (Guest at Ball); Henry Daniell (Prince Gregor of Transylvania).

THE YELLOW ROLLS-ROYCE (MGM, 1965) C—122 M.

Producer, Anatole de Grunwald; associate producer, Roy Parkinson; director, Anthony Asquith; screenplay, Terence Rattigan; music, Riz Ortolani; assistant director, Kip Gowans; clothes, Castillo of Paris, Edith Head, Pierre Cardin; camera, Jack Hildyard; editor, Frank Clarke.

Rex Harrison (Marquess of Frinton); Jeanne Moreau (Marchioness of Frinton); Edmund Purdom (John Fane); Moira Lister (Lady St. Simeon); Isa Miranda (Duchess d'Angouleme); Roland Culver (Norwood); Michael Hordern (Harmsworth); Lance Percival (His Assistant); Harold Scott (Taylor); Shirley MacLaine (Mae Jenkins); George C. Scott (Paolo Maltese); Alain Delon (Stefano); Art Carney (Joey); Riccardo Garrone (Bomba); Ingrid Bergman (Mrs. Gerda Millett); Omar Sharif (Davich); Joyce Grenfell (Miss Hortense Astor); Wally Cox (Ferguson); Guy Deghy (Mayor); Carlo Groccolo (Mrs. Millett's Chauffeur).

THE AGONY AND THE ECSTASY (20th, 1965) C—140 M.

Producer-director, Carol Reed; based on the novel by Irving Stone; screenplay, Philip Dunne; art director, Jack Martin Smith; music-music conductor, Alex North; orchestrator, Alexander Courage; assistant director, Gus Agostini; costumes, Vittorio Nino Novarese; special camera effects, L. B. Abbott, Emil Kosa, Jr.; camera, Leon Shamroy; editor, Samuel E. Beetley.

Charlton Heston (Michelangelo); Rex Harrison (Pope Julius II); Diane Cilento (Contessina de 'Medici); Harry Andres (Bramante); Alberto Lupo (Duke of Urbino); Adolfo Celi (Giovanni de'Medici); Venantino Venantini (Paris DeGrassis); John Stacy (Sangallo); Fausto Tozzi (Foreman); Maxine Audley (Woman); Tomas Milian (Raphael).

THE HONEY POT (UA, 1967) C—150 M.

Producers, Charles K. Feldman, Joseph L. Mankiewicz; director, Mankiewicz; based on the play Mr. Fox of Venice by Frederick Knott; adapted from the novel The Evil of the Day by Thomas Sterling; based on play Volpone by Ben Jonson; screenplay, Mankiewicz; music, John Addison; assistant director, Gus Agosti; production designer, John De Cuir; art director, Boris Juraga; choreography, Lee Theodore; sound, David Hildyard; camera, Gianna Di Venanzo; editor, David Bretherton.

Rex Harrison (Cecil Fox); Susan Hayward (Mrs. Lone-Star Crockett Sheridan); Cliff Robertson (William McFly); Capucine (Princess Dominique); Edie Adams (Merle McGill); Maggie Smith (Sarah Watkins); Adolfo Celi (Inspector Rizzi); Herschel Bernardi (Oscar Ludwig); Cy Grant, Frank Latimore (Revenue Agents); Luigi Scavran (Massimo); Mimmo Poli (Cook); Antonio Corevi (Tailor); Carlos Valles (Assistant Tailor); Players in a Performance of Volpone: Hugh Manning (Volpone); David Dodimead (Mosca).

A.k.a.: IT COMES UP MURDER. ANYONE FOR VENICE?

DOCTOR DOLITTLE (20th, 1967) C—152 M.

Producer, Arthur P. Jacobs; associate producer, Mort Abrahams; director, Richard Fleischer; based on stories by Hugh Lofting; screenplay, Leslie Bricusse; art directors, Jack Martin Smith, Ed Graves; set decorators, Walter M. Scott, Stuart A. Reiss; assistant director, Richard Lang; songs, Bricusse; music scorers-music conductors, Lionel Newman, Alexander Courage; choreography, Herbert Ross; music editor, Robert Mayer; vocal supervisor, Ian Fraser; makeup, Ben Nye; costumes, Ray Aghayan; sound, James Corcoran, Murray Spivack, Douglas Williams, John Myers, Bernard Freericks; titles designer, Don Record; special camera effects, L. B. Abbott, Art Cruickshank, Emil Kosa, Jr., Howard Lydecker; camera, Robert Surtees; editors, Samuel E. Beetley, Marjorie Fowler.

Rex Harrison (Dr. John Dolittle); Anthony Newley (Matthew Mugg); Peter Bull (General Bellowes); William Dix (Tommy Stubbins); Portia Nelson (Sarah Dolittle); Samantha Eggar (Emma Fairfax); Richard Attenborough (Albert Blossom); Muriel Landers (Mrs. Blossom); Geoffrey Holder (Willie Shakespeare); Norma Varden (Lady Petherington).

A FLEA IN HER EAR (20th, 1968) C—94 M.

Producer, Fred Kohlmar; director, Jacques Charon; based on the play La Puce a L'Oreille *by Georges Feydeau and English language adaptation by John Mortimer; screenplay, Mortimer; production designer, Alexandre Trauner; art director, August Capelier; set decorators, Maurice Barnathan, Pierre Charon; music, Bronislau Kaper; music conductor, Lionel Newman; title song, Kaper and Sammy Cahn; orchestrator, Bert Spencer; costumes, Andre Levasseur; makeup, Marvin Westmore, Alberto De Rossi; assistant director, Paul Feyder; sound, Joseph De Bretagne, David Dockendorf; camera, Charles Lang; second unit camera, Walter Wottitz; editor, Walter Thompson.*

Rex Harrison (Victor Chandebisse/Poche); Rosemary Harris (Gabrille Chandebisse); Louis Jourdan (Henri Tournel); Rachel Roberts (Suzanne de Castilian); John Williams (Dr. Finache); Gregoire Aslan (Monsieur Max); Edward Hardwicke (Pierre); Georges Descrieres (Don Carlos); Isla Blair (Antoinette); Frank Thornton (Charles); Victor Sen Yung (Oke Saki); Laurence Badie (Eugenie); Dominique Davray (Olympe); Olivier Hussenot (Uncle Louis); Estella Blain (Defendant); Moustache (Fat Man); David Horne (Prosecutor); Roger Carel (Taxi Driver).

STAIRCASE (20th, 1969) C—96 M.

Producer-director, Stanley Donen; based on the play by Charles Dyer; screenplay, Dyer; music, Dudley Moore; art director, Willy Holt; assistant directors, Marc Grunebaum, Pierre Roubaud; wardrobe, Clare Rendlesham; makeup, Alberto De Rossi, Ron Berkeley; sound, Kenout Peltier, Alex Front, Jean-Louis Ducarme; camera, Christopher Challis; editor, Richard Marden.

Rex Harrison (Charlie Dyer); Richard Burton (Harry Leeds); Cathleen Nesbitt (Harry's Mother); Beatrix Lehmann (Charlie's Mother); Stephen Lewis (Jack); Neil Wilson (Policeman); Gordon Heath (Postman); Avril Angers (Miss Ricard); Shelagh Fraser (Cub Mistress); Gwen Nelson (Matron); Patty Heywood (Nurse); Dermot Kelly (Gravedigger); Rogers and Starr (Drag Singers).

With Jane Wyman in LET'S DO IT AGAIN (Col '53)

Chapter Five

Ray Milland

6′1½″
175 pounds
Dark brown hair
Blue eyes
Capricorn

Playboy-about-London Ray Milland entered the movies in the late 1920s as a lark. Throughout most of the 1930s Hollywood regarded Ray, if they thought about him at all, as a slick piece of merchandise, but still just another expendable leading-man type. However, *The Jungle Princess* (Paramount, 1936), which introduced saronged Dorothy Lamour to the cinema, proved that if her native girl could regard co-star Milland as the most delectable dish to fall from the skies since coconuts, so could moviegoers.

Parmount quickly groomed Ray to continue in the footsteps of Cary Grant, and Milland soon proved that he could be polished, relaxed, fatuous, slick, and charming in front of the cameras. His success was guaranteed with *Arise, My Love* (1941) in which, as Claudette Colbert's vis-à-vis, he demonstrated just how far he had traveled since they were last teamed (*The Gilded Lily,* Paramount, 1935).

Milland was one of Paramount's (and Hollywood's) top drawing cards in the 1940s. He could make Paulette Goddard and a minor farce, *The Lady Has Plans* (1942), palatable to movie audiences. He gave life to Ginger Rogers's comic talents in *The Major and the Minor* (1942). Just when everyone was convinced he was World War II's second-best choice (there was *still* Cary Grant) for Mr. Cosmopolitan Charm, Milland added a new dimension to his acting array. In *The Uninvited* (1944) and *Ministry of Fear* (1945) he was the agile, convincing hero of two well-groomed screen thrillers. He could register terror oncamera as well as a gracious, but devilish, smile. Hollywood perspicaciously took notice of his new status. Moviegoers everywhere applauded when he emerged as the red-eyed, unshaven, alcoholic mess in *The Lost Weekend* (1945), and the industry complimented him with an Oscar. Milland had finally paid back the hand that had fed him so luxuriously over the years; he had offered a consummate performance that is still a landmark of American cinema.

Like other debonair leading men who had gone dramatic onscreen, Milland soon was shoved back into his "proper" niche, making charming love in a succession of forgettable screen comedies. Occasionally there would be another meaty role, as in the murder mystery *The Big Clock* (1948) or the unsuccessful fantasy-allegory *Alias Nick Beal* (1949), but generally it was the bland fare of Rosalind Russell's *A Woman of Distinction* (Columbia, 1950).

By 1953, Milland and Paramount had parted company and in 1955 he proved that the likes of his TV series "Meet Mr. McNutley" (a.k.a. "The Ray Milland Show") could not be totally dismissed, for he showed directorial adeptness by helming the Western *A Man Alone* (Republic) in which he starred.

As he proceeded into his fifties in the 1960s, he took on the guise of a less acerbic George Sanders type in the likes of *The Premature Burial* (American International, 1962). *Love Story* (Paramount, 1970) earned a box-office mint and coined the gooey phrase "Being in love means you never have to say you're sorry," but it also revealed a bald-headed Ray Milland. Moviegoers asked whether it was possible. The immediate answer was yes, and Ray did not give a damn about the change in his image. He was very tired of dressing up for the camera, and wanted to put his toupee into mothballs along with his prior leading-man status. After all, he was a working man, more famous than most, who just wanted to earn his high-stationed keep. Obviously, in the progression of career changes over the decades, he had kept his ego and his view of himself and his career in perspective.

It was on Thursday, January 3, 1907, that a blue-eyed son was born to Alfred Jones, a construction engineer, and his wife, Elizabeth Truscott-Jones, the daughter of the owner of a steamship company. The event occurred at Neath, a busy seaport town near the center of the world's tin-plate industry on the Bristol Channel of Glamorganshire, Wales. Christened Reginald, he was the only boy in the family. Soon after their fourth baby was born, his parents divorced. The mother then wed a fellow Welshman named Mullane, a steel-mill superintendent, who adopted Reginald and gave him his name.

Welsh was the sole language spoken in both the Jones and Mullane households. It was not until Reginald entered primary school that he learned to speak English. His early education was relatively spotty because the family was not given a chance to root for very long in any one place due to Mullane's job, which required him to transfer from place to place. The boy's summers, for the most part, were spent at an uncle's horse-breeding farm in Wales where he was the pet of various aunts who clannishly resided with the uncle. When old enough to ride, Reginald was given his own pony and became an adept young horseman.

In his early teens he developed a monumental inferiority complex because of his height. By his sixteenth birthday, he was a gangling six-footer, seemingly composed of nothing but arms and legs. He acquired summer work, first on a potato boat operating in Bristol Channel, then as a worker in a steel mill, and finally as a cabin boy on a steamship owned by yet another uncle. Reginald was an avid reader and studiously devoured every type of literature he could find.

His family decided that Reginald should pursue a career in architecture, and although the young man was not convinced of the fitness of this vocation for himself, he attended Monks Preparatory School, and then Kings College, University of Wales (at Cardiff). However, schooling bored him, and after two years at Kings College, he departed for London, convinced an education based on experience would be far more useful than one gained from textbooks.

He was eighteen, restless, and quite adventurous. He took an apartment in London and found a modest job to provide rent money. Then a friend with the Household Cavalry, an exclusive regiment whose duties were to guard the Royal Family, visited him wearing his glamorous uniform of tight breeches, breastplate, epaulettes, and jackboots. "I thought it was the most beautiful thing I had ever seen," Reginald recalled some years later, "and he told me all he had to do was ride four hours a day and that they were the most sought-after young men in London. I joined up, and we were out every night and sometimes would show up at six a.m. for stable muster still dressed in white tie and tails."

Included in the aristocratic training of guardsmen recruits were fencing, boxing, shooting, and nine months of strenuous instruction in horsemanship. Only after the applicant could qualify as an expert in all these categories was he fully accepted into the elite ranks. Reginald passed the tests and, as well, went on to win the British Army championship in both handgun and rifle marksmanship, thus gaining nationwide fame. For the next three years, by day, he was an "equestrian statue" wearing the colorful uniform with its pocketless, form-fitting breeches, which, in his words, caused him to be "continually numb from toe to belt." The nocturnal social aspects of being a guardsman were greatly to his liking. "Life was all that it was supposed to be for a dashing young cavalryman. There was fencing, horsemanship, wooing lovely young ladies, drinking—all things I was good at, I must say. And nothing a man could make a living at, more's the pity." At the end of the three-year period, "my father couldn't afford to support me. To be employed in the Household Cavalry required an independent income." Lieutenant Mullane resigned his commission and repaired to London civilian life.

At a party he met American actress Estelle Brody, who took an immediate liking to the personable, handsome, twenty-two-year-old and invited him to take lunch with her at the Wardour Studio the following day. As he drove up to the studio gates in a borrowed touring sedan, a producer saw him and asked if he would like to be in a movie. "What for?" Reginald asked. The producer, nonplussed by this cheeky retort, told him that *most* people *wanted* to be in movies. Since he had nothing to lose, Reginald agreed to doing a small part in *The Plaything* (Wardour, 1929) for two guineas a day.* "So I showed up the next day in my white tie and tails for a party scene," he recalled to Gail Rock of the *New York Times* in June 1972, "but before I got on camera, someone else saw me and wanted me for a different picture and that afternoon I was on the 2:30 train for Scotland. But when I got there, it rained for nine days and they couldn't shoot."

A few days after returning to London, he received a phone call from Wardour Films. They required a sharpshooter to replace the Dutchman they had imported for their needs but who had been killed in an accident with a double-decker bus. The job consisted of shooting a mirror out of the hands of star Lya de Putti in a scene for *The Informer* (Wardour, 1929), the second of four versions of Liam O'Flaherty's drama. This version was produced with synchronized musical effects and some dialog. Reginald also filled in as an extra. For his audition for the task, he said later, "I drew a circle the size of a half-crown on the wall, stepped back sixty paces and put fourteen successive shots into the same hole. They hired me."

Concurrently, on a neighboring cinema-making stage, was a film in production called *The Flying Scotsman* (Warner Bros.–British, 1929). One of the actors, Cyril McLaglen (brother of Victor), had broken a leg, and the producer requested Reginald to test for the role. "I didn't even know what the hell a 'test' was. I thought you had to urinate in a bottle or something. They said, 'take your tie off.' They smeared my face with dirt and said, 'stand there and swear.' Well, I had been in the cavalry, so I could swear pretty good, and I got the part. But the producer of *The Informer* wouldn't let me out of my sharpshooting contract, so while I did my first film, I went next door and did the sharpshooting on my lunch hour. I didn't eat lunch for ten weeks."

The Flying Scotsman, released prior to *The Plaything* and *The Informer,* contained sound effects and dialog added in the last reel. Billed as Raymond Milland, he is a novice train stoker who has an affair with the veteran engineer's daughter (Pauline Johnson). When the old engineer (Moore Marriott) learns of what he considers an illicit relationship, he knocks the stoker off the cab of the moving train with a shovel. The British *Bioscope* singled out the novice performer for comment with, "Raymond Milland makes a pleasing lover."

In *The Lady from the Sea* (Paramount–British, 1929), he is again billed as Raymond Milland, one of two sons of a fisherman (Moore Marriott). He rescues Anita Graham, the sole survivor of a ship wrecked on the Goodwin Sands. She is an unprincipled flirt who charms first one brother and then the other (Bruce Gordon). The British *Bioscope* complained that "the two young fishermen speak like Oxford undergraduates."

Milland's photogenic face was spotted by Robert Rubin, an MGM producer, who recommended that he try his luck in Hollywood. He suggested that Milland might work himself into the on-screen playboy mold of Metro's contract player Robert Montgomery. A short-term contract was assured, at a $150 weekly salary, plus a first-class steamer ticket for New York aboard the S.S. *Majestic.* Because Milland enjoyed making films, and since he had not trained for any other practical profession, he accepted the offer.

After a stay in New York, he headed for California. His initial chores at Metro were unbilled parts in two currently shooting features. In *Way for a Sailor* (MGM, 1930), which nominally starred the fast-declining John Gilbert, Milland wore a moustache in his role as a Canadian ship's officer. In *Passion Flower* (MGM, 1930), directed by William De Mille and starring Kay Francis, Milland was in front of the camera only very briefly. The studio suggested that he adopt a shorter first name for his next billing, as C. Aubrey Smith's son in *The Bachelor Father* (MGM, 1930), and he simply abbreviated it to Ray. He was then alternately billed as Ray or Raymond, and the last name was occasionally spelled as Millande. Marion Davies, the star of *The Bachelor Father,* played his sprite of a sister. Milland was nervous during much of his early acting career, and director Robert Z. Leonard's impatience made him even more self-conscious. Miss Davies gave the fledgling a few helpful hints, one of

*Milland's four 1929 British films were not released in the order of production.

In THE LADY FROM THE SEA (Paramount-British '29)

which was "to pretend that the director isn't there."

William Haines and Irene Purcell were the selling points of *Just a Gigolo* (MGM, 1931), based on the Broadway production, *Dancing Partner.†* As Freddie, Milland had little more than a walk-on. But then his services were sold to Warner Bros. for *Bought* (1931), a typical Constance Bennett weeper, which provided him with his meatiest role up to that time. In fifth billing as Charles Carter, he was the snob playboy who discards Miss Bennett as a paramour when he learns that she is the illegitimate daughter of an elderly philanderer (Richard Bennett). It was the type of cavalier role that Milland could handle very efficiently, so much so that he soon became typecast in this type of one-dimensional part.

Two more loan-outs followed. At Fox, he wore a moustache as a native son of Sylvania, the mythical nation where Will Rogers as *Ambassador Bill* (1931) finds time to twirl his famous lariat between moments of royal intrigue. Then in Warner Bros.' *Blonde Crazy* (1931), featuring James Cagney and Joan Blondell, Ray was the non-crook in Blondell's racy life, stockbroker Reynolds, whom

she marries but leaves when she realizes it is con artist Cagney whom she truly loves.

Obviously, Ray's career was not building any momentum in Hollywood. His Metro studio bosses merely considered him a fancy dress extra. He decided to return home. "MGM kindly paid my fare back to England," Milland admits, but in London he soon discovered that he missed acting. He won a role in the third company of an American play, *The Woman in Room 13,* but when the show was playing its tryout engagement in Southport, Milland was fired on opening night for general incompetence. But now he was convinced he wanted to be an actor, and that he really did like the tinsel of Hollywood. He obtained a job in an advertising film to earn money for the return passage to California, and in six weeks he was set financially. "I came back the cheapest possible way. On a passenger freighter through the Panama Canal. The company let me keep the modern wardrobe I'd used in their commercials, and I arrived back with $150 in my pocket. It was in the depths of the Depression and for months I made a living playing bridge and practically starved."

In January 1932, at a Beverly Hills garden par-

†Debuted at the Belasco Theatre (August 5, 1930) for a 119-performance engagement, with Irene Purcell and Lynne Overman.

ty, he met brunette, nineteen-year-old Malvina Muriel Webber, a University of Southern California student who had aspirations of becoming an elementary-school teacher. Many years later she remembered their meeting: "A friend introduced me to this very polite, quiet Englishman. He was mannerly and very soft-spoken—not at all like the boys I'd been going out with. I remember how impressed I was by the fact that he actually listened to what I had to say. And I was really impressed by the wealth of knowledge he had stored in his head." A few months later, on September 30, 1932, they were married.

Meanwhile, Ray's screen career had not been flourishing. He was at Warner Bros. again for a bit part in George Arliss's *The Man Who Played God,* and then in Marion Davies's *Polly of the Circus* (MGM, 1932), in which rising Clark Gable was a clergyman (!), Milland was tossed into the proceedings as a rich young man. The crowning blow to his career was his brief appearance in *Payment Deferred* (MGM, 1932), based on the Broadway production* and starring Charles Laughton. Milland was cast as the star's Australian nephew with "a well-stuffed wallet." The uncle, desperate for money, poisons the nephew's

With Charles Bickford and Kay Francis in PASSION FLOWER (MGM '30)

*Opened September 30, 1931, at the Lyceum Theatre for a 70-performance run with Charles Laughton recreating the role he had created originally on the London stage in May 1931.

With Ralph Forbes, Halliwell Hobbes, C. Aubrey Smith (seated), Edgar Norton, Marion Davies, and Nena Quartaro in THE BACHELOR FATHER (MGM '31)

scotch and soda and buries the body in the yard of his home. Director Lothar Mendes became so impatient with Ray's nervous interpretation in *Payment Deferred* that the studio front-office decided to terminate Milland's contract.

Milland again returned to England, leaving his wife behind. At Gaumont-British he obtained a secondary role as a soldier in *Orders Is Orders* (Ideal, 1933), a spoof on moviemaking starring Americans James Gleason and Charlotte Greenwood. In *This Is the Life* (British Lion, 1933), Ray was cast as a non-wealthy artist.

Between the two films, he supplemented his income by riding in steeplechases two days a week. It was at the Sandown Park course of thirty-two jumps that he made film history of a different sort. At the three-and-a-quarter-mile jump, his horse stopped dead in its track while seven other horses and riders crashed into him. Newsreel cameras captured for posterity one of the most spectacular equestrian entanglements in the history of the steeplechase.

When he recovered, Milland returned to Hollywood in the early autumn of 1933, but did not live with his wife. Instead, he rented a furnished room at the Orange Grove Apartments on Sunset Boulevard. There had been a severe earthquake in the Long Beach area a few days before Ray took up residency on the top floor of the apartment house, and repeated after-shocks had been felt in the entire Los Angeles area. It had always been the actor's habit to sleep in the nude with a pair of pajamas tucked under his pillow for use in emergency situations. One night, when a quake rocked his building, he leaped out of bed and grabbed for his pajamas. He hurried into the top garment and raced down five flights to the street. He made headlines the next morning because he had jumped into a water fountain on discovering that he was bare from the waist down.

In his search for work, Ray claims to have "worn out carpets and chair pads at every studio in town" without luck. Eventually, when his finances ran out, friends loaned him money for food and rent. Then, one morning, so the story goes, he was en route to an eight A.M. appointment for a job interview at a gasoline station near Paramount Studios. As he disembarked from the bus, which had stopped in front of the studio gates, he was spotted by a casting director Joe Egli. Egli claimed to have been looking all over for him for the role of an English lord in the new

Wesley Ruggles film, *Bolero* (Paramount, 1934), and rushed him into the director's office. Milland won the job at $300 a week, with a two-week guarantee. The film starred George Raft and Carole Lombard, and Ray played a stiff, mustached member of the British peerage, who weds Lombard during World War I. Because of the shallowness of the script, movie audiences were never quite sure whether Lombard, as Raft's dancing partner, had wed Milland for his title and wealth, or for his character's gentility. Largely on the basis of exploiting Raft's gigolo lover–underworld's-pal image, *Bolero* made a nice financial return at the box office. The exploitation and choreographed interpretation of Maurice Ravel's composition "Bolero," however, left a great deal to be desired artistically.

Milland was the first to admit that "I knew nothing about acting at all. I used to talk to people like Sir Guy Standing. He taught me a lot. Frank Lloyd was [in later years] a marvelous friend to me. So was Sam Wood." Ray used to attend movies frequently to study the actors' techniques, being particularly fond of the screen work of Walter Huston, Edward G. Robinson, and Fredric March. Of the latter, he said: "I admired the frank theatricalism of March, and still do. His overacting is admirable. To overact as he does requires skill."

Nevertheless, Paramount was satisfied with Ray's *Bolero* performance, and Carole Lombard suggested him for a part in her comedy-musical, *We're Not Dressing* (1934). Far removed from Sir James Barrie's play original, *The Admirable Crichton*,* the new edition was designed purely as an audience escapism from the depression doldrums. The film boasted Bing Crosby and Ethel Merman crooning and belting, respectively, while George Burns, Gracie Allen, and Leon Errol offered comedy relief. Ray appeared as the effete Prince Michael Stofani with a yen for Lombard's wealth. He is a passenger aboard her yacht when it is wrecked on an almost-deserted island. Ray's name was listed in eighth billing, but on the strength of this and his previous performance in *Bolero,* he was signed to a seven-year Paramount contract at $300 weekly. The pact was concluded on February 14, 1934.

Obviously, his poverty days had ended. He repaid his friends, reconciled with his wife, and moved into a large, modern apartment in Hollywood.

---

*The Sir James Barrie play opened at the Duke of York's Theatre, London, on November 4, 1902, where it ran until August 28, 1903. On Broadway, William Gillette starred in H. B. Irving's role of the resourceful butler, when the show played the Lyceum Theatre (November 17, 1903, 144 performances). A more notable film version of the show was *Male and Female* (Paramount, 1919) with Gloria Swanson and Thomas Meigham.

Then followed a succession of roles in "B" movies which gave little impetus in establishing Ray in any particular screen mold. There was *Many Happy Returns* (Paramount, 1934), another Burns and Allen romp, this time to the accompaniment of Guy Lombardo's sweet music. The *London Daily Telegraph* reported of this celluloid potpourri: "It is all very bravely and conscientiously done, but no amount of bravery and conscientiousness can turn what is essentially a music-hall act into a full-sized film." He next went to Fox where he portrayed, of course, a Britisher, and a prime murder suspect in *Charlie Chan in London* (1934), while in *Menace* (Paramount, 1934) he is a mining engineer in British East Africa who, early in the spooky tale, commits suicide for having neglected his duties. His irresponsible actions caused a dam to burst, which killed his sisters. Gertrude Michael was the hysterical heroine of the piece with John Lodge as the mysterious visitor who proves to have some connection with Milland. Next, Ray was demoted to another of Paramount's low-budget offerings. He had eleventh billing for *One Hour Late* (1934).

His second feature for Wesley Ruggles, *The Gilded Lily* (Paramount, 1935), was his first with Claudette Colbert. In what was labeled a "merry" comedy, Milland, as Charles Gray, meets stenographer Colbert in a crowded New York subway and a lukewarm romance ensues. However, when he fails to reveal his true identity as an English peer, newspaperman Fred MacMurray snitches on him. Colbert feels wronged and decides, in the end, that jaunty MacMurray is more her style. Andre Sennwald of the *New York Times* called Milland "handsome and personable." Although Milland and Colbert seemed to work well together, offscreen they scarcely spoke to each other because he felt insecure in her lustrous presence.

In the dramatic *Four Hours to Kill* (Paramount, 1935)* he is the kept lover of Gertrude Michael. Ray had not yet gained professional confidence in embracing properly a leading lady and this deficiency caught up with him on this production. In one scene requiring him to kiss Miss Michael, he pecked her lightly on the mouth. Director Mitchell Leisen called for a retake. After a quick conversation between Leisen and Michael, the troublesome scene was redone. This time, the ac-

*Derived from the play *Small Miracle* (John Golden Theatre: September 26, 1934, 118 performances) and starring Joseph Spurin-Calleia, who soon thereafter went to Hollywood where he appeared under the name Joseph Calleia.

With Richard Barthelmess, Helen Mack, Joe Morrison, Gertrude Michael, and Noel Madison (on couch) in FOUR HOURS TO KILL (Par '35)

tress took the initiative and French-kissed Milland. "I thought my collar button would rip off. I was terribly shocked." Nevertheless, the scene played to everyone's satisfaction, and Milland and Leisen, who would work together frequently in subsequent years, became good friends.

The Glass Key (Paramount, 1935), adapted from Dashiell Hammett's mystery novel of the same title, came next. The vehicle was geared to George Raft's measurements, with the star portraying a taciturn, but loyal bodyguard to political maneuverer Edward Arnold. Ray was assigned the part of Taylor Henry, brother to Janet (Claire Dodd) and son of Senator Henry (Charles Richman).† The son is murdered and the crime is blamed on Arnold, who, with the senator, had closed down an underworld czar's gambling salon. The film was rated "crisply exciting" (*New York Times*). However, Ray was burdened with a characterization that had no backbone, a typical mid-1930s role for him that led the studios and the public alike to assume that his screen potential was severely limited.

Ironically, when Ray had a professional opportunity to break out of his career rut, he rejected it. Mitchell Leisen asked him to play the lead in what was assumed to be another modest comedy, *Hands Across the Table* (Paramount, 1935), but Milland pleaded: "Please don't ask me to do it because I know I can't play comedy." As a result, the part went to Fred MacMurray, and with that picture MacMurray consolidated his position in Hollywood as a light comedy star.

Instead, Milland went on loan to Universal for two pictures. *Alias Mary Dow* (1935) is a tearjerker in which Sally Eilers poses as the long-missing daughter of Henry O'Neill and Katharine Alexander. Ray is the man of her dreams whom she weds. His role in *Next Time We Love* (Universal, 1936) was a bizarre bit of Hollywood convention. He was the continual presence who lends courage to Margaret Sullavan whenever her foreign-correspondent husband (James Stewart) is off news-hunting throughout the world. Then, back at Paramount, it was Ray's turn to be cast as an American foreign correspondent. He is involved with jewel thieves (reformed Gertrude Michael, and unrecalcitrant Sir Guy Standing) in *The Return of Sophie Lang* (1936). Despite Milland's slick portrayal of the handsome good guy, it was Standing who claimed most audience and critical attention.

The Big Broadcast of 1937 (Paramount, 1936) was one in a series that gave moviegoers a chance to see their favorite radio performers onscreen. Jack Benny, George Burns, Gracie Allen, Bob Burns, and Martha Raye are there, with Milland and studio newcomer Shirley Ross providing the incidental romance. Mitchell Leisen was again at the directing helm.

Milland's next film, *Jungle Princess* (Paramount, 1936), is the one that caused the first major increase in his fan mail, possibly because he bared his chest. It is also the film in which screen beginner Dorothy Lamour introduces the sarong, originally called "shift." She is the native Malayan beauty set upon a group of explorers who believe they can civilize her, but Milland, as Christopher Powell, realizes that she has the right idea and joins her in the simple life. Between Lamour's animated display of her curvaceous charm, her singing of "Moonlight and Shadows," the caperings of Liamu the Tiger and Bogo the Chimpanzee, there was little opportunity for Milland to steal the limelight, but he does have his moments as he attempts to introduce the jungle girl to Western customs.

Universal again borrowed him for two more films, beginning with Deanna Durbin's debut feature, *Three Smart Girls* (1936). He was polite and respectable as the dapper English lord involved with the Lyons sisters (Durbin, Nan Grey, and Barbara Read), and a far more likable alternative than bland John King or conniving Mischa Auer, the latter as a bogus count. Universal was so pleased by Ray's affability that they asked him to remain on the lot for *Wings over Honolulu* (1937), which cost him a role in Claudette Colbert's *I Met Him in Paris* (Paramount, 1937), the part going to Metro's Robert Young. *Wings over Honolulu* offered viewers a prewar look at the U.S. Navy's peacetime facilities at Pearl Harbor, with Milland piloting a bomber plane across the tropical sky, while casual Wendy Barrie is his neglected, bored wife.

Mitchell Leisen finally convinced Ray to tackle screen comedy in *Easy Living* (Paramount, 1937). In his study of movie comedies, *Lunatics and Lovers* (1973), Ted Sennett judges this $625,000 production "one of the most enjoyable and representative Cinderella comedies of the thirties." Within its rapidly twisting plot, Jean Arthur, an impoverished employee of *Boy's Constant Companion*, finds herself becoming the pet charity of portly millionaire Edward Arnold, and the romantic object of Arnold's handsome son, Milland.

---

†Richard Denning assumed the role in the 1942 Paramount remake.

With Edward Arnold and Jean Arthur in EASY LIVING (Par '37)

The latter, working as an Automat busboy (to prove he can be self-sufficient), instigates the film's wildest scene. He tries to sneak food to Arthur, but is nearly caught by an observant cafeteria policeman. In the ensuing skirmish, a switch is yanked which throws open all the dispensing slots at one time, discharging food all over the place. A horde of avaricious people rush to grab the free goodies, creating a fantastic melee. Balancing such sequences of mayhem are calm interludes in which Arthur and Milland realize the extent of their mutual affection for one another. In this film assignment, Milland demonstrated that he was fast mastering the requisite finesse that had made Robert Montgomery, Melvyn Douglas, and Cary Grant such popular movie farceurs.

By this point in his Paramount career, Milland was considered a studio leading man. But on that bustling lot, with the constant turnover of executive regimes, this status carried very little practical weight. The company was over-rich with talent. The male-player stable included stars Gary Cooper, George Raft, Fred MacMurray, and declining Warren William; comedians Jack Benny, W. C. Fields, Harold Lloyd, George Burns, Ben Blue, Charles Butterworth, and Roscoe Karns; sometime Western leads William Boyd and Randolph Scott; vocalist Bing Crosby; and character

lead Edward Arnold. More problematical as far as Ray's studio fate was concerned was the plethora of youngish utility actors, all eager to graduate from the ranks of programmer leading men, "A" feature "other men," or sometimes villains. They ranged from Lew Ayres, trying to reestablish his cinema following, to such contractees as Lee Bowman, Robert Cummings, James Ellison, Leif Erickson, John Howard, John Payne, Anthony Quinn, and John Trent.

In *Ebb Tide* (Paramount, 1937), based on the Robert Louis Stevenson short story, and filmed in the three-strip Technicolor process, Ray was the romantic male lead (with character performers Oscar Homolka and Barry Fitzgerald as fellow beachcombers). The trio happen onto an island ruled by treacherous Lloyd Nolan and inhabited by, among others, strikingly beautiful Frances Farmer. Is it necessary to say Ray and Frances fall madly in love?

Feeling reassured about Ray's abilities to handle himself on camera, Paramount tested Milland in a role that had been a great boost to suave, swashbuckling Ronald Colman, that of the British detective Bulldog Drummond. Only an unforgettable impression could be gained from comparing the two superior United Artists–Colman–*Bulldog Drummond* entries (1929, 1934) and Milland's *Bulldog Drummond Escapes* (Paramount, 1937). The latter, although claiming its origin from H. C. (Sapper) McNeile's play *Bulldog Drummond Again*, more closely paralleled the Colman pictures. In the rather carefully structured new entry, Milland's gentleman sleuth was required to protect heroine Heather Angel from the assorted dangers lying in wait for her at Graystone Manor. Milland manages to clean up the mysteries involved, albeit ineptly, and even appears to be on the verge of wedding the grateful Angel. However, the actor lacked the necessary devil-may-care approach that would have distinguished his characterization. Thereafter Paramount continued the detective series, on a programmer basis, with John Howard as Drummond.

Ray then was loaned to RKO for *Wise Girl* (1937) in which an unkittenish Miriam Hopkins endeavors to lead him out of the Bohemian artist's way of life into a successful existence as an accomplished painter. He was slick, facile, but uninvolved, features which also exemplified this imitation screwball comedy. Thereafter, Paramount reunited Ray with Dorothy Lamour for another lush tropical outing. *Her Jungle Love* (Paramount, 1938), may not have had much originality to its screenplay, but it could label itself as the first color jungle picture, it did have such pleasing songs as "Coffee and Kisses" (Milland reprises a bit of this Lamour number), "Jungle Love," and "Lovelight in the Starlight." Gaga the Chimpanzee, Meewa the lion cub, and most of all exotic Lamour cavorting in her tropical garb, delighted most male filmgoers. While Milland and Lamour seemed to be taking the nonsense seriously, Lynne Overman, as one of the aviators who crashes on the island, steals the film with his dry delivery of the script's best lines, such as, "Those *Esquire* cartoons must be right; there's always just one girl on a desert island."

In 1938, the Millands purchased their first home, a nine-room Georgian farmhouse-style abode on Elm Avenue in Beverly Hills, across the street from Mitchell Leisen. Ray became a naturalized American citizen in 1938. That also was the year of the "Big Quest" by David O. Selznick for the exact casting of *Gone with the Wind* (MGM, 1939). Milland was among the actors, including Melvyn Douglas, considered for the role of Ashley Wilkes. In *Memo from David O. Selznick* (1972), Rudy Behlmer reveals a note written by Selznick to an associate: "I am aware of the deficiencies of Milland's accent, which are almost as great as those of Clark Gable! I think Mr. Milland very definitely is a sensitive actor, possessing the enormous attractiveness and at the same time the weakness that are the requirements of Ashley."*

Dorothy Lamour's sarong, along with the Ozark antics of Bob Burns and the wide-mouthed mugging of Martha Raye, in *Tropic Holiday* (Paramount, 1938), were featured in a Mexican setting. Frank S. Nugent observed in the *New York Times* that when sarong-clad Lamour sings of love, "Mr. Milland just melts gracefully." Then, Ray took to the skies for *Men with Wings* (Paramount, 1938), a William A. Wellman production, in which he again loses the girl (here Louise Campbell) to Fred MacMurray. For the quasi-comic *Say It in French* (Paramount, 1938) Milland received top billing as the young golf champion who returning home with a poor wife (Olympe Bradna) from France, discovers that his bankrupt parents (Janet Beecher and Holmes Herbert) intend that he should wed skittish, wealthy Irene Hervey. Milland was working against a lumbering script and heavy pacing by director Andrew L. Stone, which led *Variety* to judge: ". . . Milland is bumptious without imbuing the part with either wit or wits."

Back in January 1936, Paramount had begun filming a remake of its *Hotel Imperial* (1926)‡ under the title of *I Loved a Soldier*. Marlene Dietrich and Charles Boyer were the stars. Dietrich walked off the trouble-plagued film, and Margaret Sullavan replaced her. But the latter was injured on the set, and the production was shelved. Some two years later it was resurrected as a vehicle for the studio's new Italian import, Isa Miranda, in many ways similar to Dietrich in looks. Milland now inherited the role of the Hungarian officer who in 1916 is suspected by Polish dancer Miranda of being the cause of her sister's death. With J. Carrol Naish cast in the film as a Russian loyalist, that assumption was rather naive, as was the film.

Milland was at his handsomest as John in Paramount's 1939 remake of *Beau Geste*.† *Newsweek* magazine claimed that Robert Carson's new adaptation of the Percival Christopher Wren novel "parallels the action of the old version almost sequence for sequence." It is the story of three orphaned brothers who are the wards of an aunt possessing the "Blue Water" sapphire valued at £30,000. The older brother, Beau (Gary Cooper),

---

*Leslie Howard was the final choice to play Ashley Wilkes.
‡Pola Negri and James Hall were the stars of the silent version.
†Enacted by Ralph Forbes in the 1926 silent film. Later, in 1966, Universal was to remake it with Doug McClure as John.

is thought to have snatched the gem to prevent the aunt from selling it, and joins the French Foreign Legion. His brothers Digby (Robert Preston) and John follow into the ranks where they encounter a sadistic sergeant (Brian Donlevy). Ray is the sole survivor after an Arab attack on Fort Zinderneuf, and he returns to England with the jewel and a message from Cooper vindicating himself. As a change of pace in his cinema career, Milland actually won the heroine, in this case Susan Hayward.

Twentieth Century–Fox borrowed Milland to help decorate the snowy outdoors with male pulchritude in *Everything Happens at Night* (1939), the sixth and weakest of Scandinavian Sonja Henie's nine Fox musicals. Milland and Robert Cummings are lighthearted rival newsmen in search of a Nobel Peace Prize winner reported dead, but presumed to be hiding in Switzerland with his daughter. Henie's "Blue Danube Waltz" on ice and her conga skating routines were the salvation of this hapless feature.

By now Ray was such a firm fixture in Hollywood's working and nightlife circles that he could pontificate on most any subject and be assured of an avid following, especially in the fan magazines. One subject close to his heart in 1939 was the area of "friends." He explained: "When my friends begin to bore me—when I can stand off and watch someone I know well in the centre of a group, watch his reactions, listen to him pull the same lines I have heard him pull many times before and know exactly what's going on in his mind—exactly why he's doing what he is and exactly how he's trying to impress his listeners, I know it's time to make a change.

"Don't misunderstand me. I'm not conceited. Just as many people tire of me as I do of them. Just as many people have dropped me as I have ever dropped. I seldom have an open break with anyone. We just sense that we have nothing left to give each other and drift apart. Sometimes, after six months or a year, we are drawn together again."

Ray was considered for the film version of Rudyard Kipling's *The Light that Failed* (Paramount, 1939), but that movie became a Ronald Colman–Walter Huston vehicle. Instead, Ray with his pregnant wife and accompanied by Ellen Drew, his next co-star, sailed to England on the *Aquitania*. Paramount's publicity department made a big thing out of his going to wartime England as the American male lead in a predominantly all-British cast of *French without Tears* (Paramount,

With Andy Devine in MEN WITH WINGS (Par '38)

251

With Olympe Bradna and Irene Hervey in a publicity pose for SAY IT IN FRENCH (Par '38)

With Susan Hayward in BEAU GESTE (Par '39)

1939).* The trip seemed hardly worth it, for the picture emerged "superlatively heavy" (*New York Times*). Drew was miscast as the innocent flirt who disrupts a French school for English gentlemen, with Milland barely being able to stay above water as the humorous Britisher.

The actor returned to Hollywood to join with another expatriate British performer, Anna Neagle, in the movie version of *Irene* (RKO, 1940).† Neagle won plaudits for her impersonation of the Irish-accented shopgirl who is suddenly elevated from a poor New York shopgirl to the envy of the Long Island social set. Among her suitors are Milland and Alan Marshall, with May Robson as her "Granny," Roland Young as the proprietor of the Fifth Avenue dress shop, and fluttery Billie Burke as a blue-blooded suburban matron. The highlight of the feature was the Technicolor sequence in which Neagle sang and danced to "Alice Blue Gown." *Irene's* mothball-scented screen rendition would later have a bigger commercial impact in the nostalgia-crazed marketplace of the 1970s.

On March 6, 1940, Milland was skiing at Sun Valley, Idaho, when word reached him that he was the father of a baby boy. He anxiously returned to Los Angeles on a chartered plane to see his heir, who had arrived two weeks ahead of medical schedule. The six-pound boy was named Daniel David. Kay Proctor wrote in *Photoplay* magazine: "Never have I seen so proud a father as Ray, nor a home where a baby was wanted with such desperate longing." In the midst of his joy, Milland became philosophical when he told Miss Proctor: "How could I help but have faith in the future? We ourselves can give our son everything of love and comforts. We have insured his financial security insofar as it is humanly possible by planning and saving for the tomorrow in which we live."

Then came the feature that established Ray as an important actor of comedy roles. Columbia borrowed him to work as a novice brain surgeon opposite Loretta Young's professional bachelor girl in *The Doctor Takes a Wife* (1940). Ray was

---

*Opened at London's Criterion Theatre (November 6, 1936) with Rex Harrison in the lead and ran for 1,039 performances. On Broadway, with Frank Lawton starred, it played at the Henry Miller Theatre (September 28, 1937, 128 performances). Paramount had purchased the screen rights as a vehicle for Marlene Dietrich.

†Opened on Broadway at the Vanderbilt Theatre (November 1, 1919, 675 performances). It was revived to great success at the Minskoff Theatre (March 13, 1973) in New York with Debbie Reynolds (later Jane Powell) in the title role. In the 1926 First National Pictures' film version, Colleen Moore was Irene, and Lloyd Hughes was Don Marshall.

cast as Tim Sterling, a prominent young physician who believes marriage is the answer to a girl's prayer, just the opposite of the philosophy of professional single girl Loretta, who has gained fame with her book *Spinsters Aren't Spinach.* In the best manner of nutty Hollywood scenarios, the two opposite types are forced by circumstances to pretend they are blissfully wed and to even share the same apartment. Their repartee, as could be expected, is first vicious, then merely vitriolic, and finally romantic; all this despite the aggravating presence of Ray's domineering fiancée, Gail Patrick. Milland even goes through the paces of the classic situation in which he must hustle back and forth between two apartments, entertaining both Loretta and Patrick, hoping neither will discover he is involved with the other. For Ray's relaxed, unassuming manner, the critics acclaimed him: "Thanks to Mr. Milland's genteel clowning . . . the comic pace is generally maintained" (Bosley Crowther, *New York Times*).

His next film, *Untamed* (Paramount, 1940),* however, was definitely not a comedy. He is discovered in the frozen north as a doctor beset by bears, blizzards, and an epidemic of strep throat.

Ray Milland in 1939.

*A remake of *Mantrap* (Paramount, 1926), featuring Clara Bow, Percy Marmont, and Ernest Torrence.

With Reginald Gardiner in THE DOCTOR TAKES A WIFE (Col '40)

All the while he is flirting with outcast Patricia Morison, the wife of growling guide Akim Tamiroff. No one but a six-year-old would have thought the story "untamed," but Milland's ardent supporter Wanda Hale (*New York Daily News*) noted that he "is more handsome in color than in black and white." Milland fared much better for "Lux Radio Theatre" on June 3, 1940, in the Tyrone Power role of *Alexander's Ragtime Band,* with Alice Faye and Robert Preston.

Arise My Love (Paramount, 1940) was originally scheduled to star Claudette Colbert with Joel McCrea, but when producer Walter Wanger refused the loan of contractee McCrea, Ray got the job at Colbert's request. They became great friends during the filming, which began on June 29, 1940. Directed by Mitchell Leisen, with a screenplay by Charles Brackett and Billy Wilder, *Arise My Love* is the story of a brash female news reporter (Colbert) who rescues an American flyer-of-fortune (Milland) from a Spanish firing squad by posing as his wife. Her intent is to obtain the inside story of the Spanish Civil War. He thinks of her as a newsman rather than a woman capable of emotions and tells her: "You're all cast iron and all fish." Nevertheless, predictably, love blossoms. What gives the picture dimension is the scenario's underlying message. Colbert and Milland are sailing back to America when their ship, the *Athenia,* is torpedoed by the Germans. They suddenly realize that for them and America isolationism has become outmoded; everyone must participate in saving democracy on the European battleground. If the 113-minute feature revolves around Colbert, Ray for a change was not just a stereotyped leading man. His particular screen qualities were in full evidence and audiences appreciated his individuality, which could so pleasingly blend jocularity, pensiveness, resourcefulness, and modest deep commitment within a framework of smooth British-accented charm.

Milland began taking flying lessons months before he went to Randolph Field, Texas, for location filming of Mitchell Leisen's *I Wanted Wings* (Paramount, 1941). During a lunch-hour break from emoting as a rich Long Island playboy training to become an Army Air Corps pilot, he decided to get in an hour of flying instruction on his own. He hopped into the plane after his instructor and adjusted his parachute. About seven thousand feet up, the motor unexpectedly died. The instructor yelled back that they were out of gas.

The actor unhooked his safety belt and lifted one leg out of the cockpit preparatory to jumping, but the instructor waved him back. "Emergency tank," he yelled. When they were back on the airstrip, Ray joined the cast and crew in the cafeteria and told of his experience. Overhearing the monolog, the head property man gulped a few times and said: "Mr. Milland, that parachute pack you were wearing—it's just a prop."

I Wanted Wings, a cinematic salute to the Army's aerial division, was the studio's most popular film of 1941, undoubtedly because most young male Americans were anxious to join in the battle against Nazism, and the Army Air Corps seemed the most glamorous means of doing so. William Holden (the garage mechanic) and Wayne Morris (the college athlete) were two other cadets, while Brian Donlevy was their all-knowing instructor pilot. Constance Moore as a photographer and Veronica Lake (with that famed peek-a-boo hairdo) as a siren were inserted into the scenario for oncamera romantic pleasantries. No one was quite prepared for the spectacular public endorsement of Lake. This was the blonde's first big movie role and the publicity surrounding her trendsetting coiffure certainly obscured the presence of the trio of lead actors, even to the extent of making some moviegoers call out in theatres for more of Veronica and less of the aerial action footage.

I Wanted Wings was Ray's first picture under his revised favored-son's Paramount contract. His next role was in *Skylark* (Paramount, 1941), replacing the originally scheduled Melvyn Douglas as Claudette Colbert's husband, an aristocratic advertising man. The film was originally a 1939 Broadway stage vehicle for Gertrude Lawrence, Donald Cook, and featured player Vivian Vance.* The studio purchased the screen rights for $60,000 and assigned Allen Scott to adapt it from Samson Raphaelson's play. The movie's three principals, including Brian Aherne as Colbert's extramarital diversion, are put through a variety of pratfalls which advances (?) the production from the sophisticated to the semi-slapstick. *Variety* pointed out what most female filmgoers already knew, that "Ray Milland is top notch." The three stars repeated their roles for "Lux Radio Theatre" on February 2, 1942.

The Lady Has Plans (Paramount, 1942) ("and they're on her back," the ads read provocatively) had Paulette Goddard as a radio commentator's leg woman in Lisbon who is mistaken for a tatooed spy (Margaret Hayes). When Goddard's

*Opened at the Morosco Theatre (October 11, 1939) for a 256-performance run.

With Paulette Goddard in THE LADY HAS PLANS (Par '42)

boss (Milland) winds up in the same Nazi jail, the film's general tone turns to one of drama. The laughs in this one are too few for the film's own good.

Reap the Wild Wind (Paramount, 1942), budgeted at $1,650,000 and with a 222-day shooting schedule, was set to begin with background camera work in June 1940. At that time, director Cecil B. DeMille did not want Ray Milland as one of the color spectacle's stars. It was felt that Milland was not a good enough actor to take on something so far removed from comedy, nor did DeMille consider him to be box-office worthy. Paramount's vice-president, Y. Frank Freeman, disagreed and persuaded DeMille to take a poll of distributors to rate the box-office draw of Milland as compared to other leading men on the studio payroll. The results showed that he was Number One. The poll convinced DeMille, and Milland won the role of Stephen Tolliver, a Charleston sea lawyer who "drips lace and leads the Georgia quadrille." In top billing and in tight pants and frilled shirts of the 1840s, designed by costumer

Natalie Visart, he permitted his hair to be curled* and foppishly sported a pet terrier named "Romulus," which talked via "ventriloquism" with Milland's voice.†

In the epic story, based on a *Saturday Evening Post* serial by Thelma Strabel, the shipwreck-salvage business of Floridian beauty Loxi Claiborne (Paulette Goddard) is threatened by competitor King Cutler (Raymond Massey), whose boats are always too conveniently the first at the scene of any wreck. Massey is suspected of being responsible for wrecking many of the vessels. Goddard recruits the help of Captain Jack Stuart (John Wayne) with whom she is in love. She talks him into marrying her aboard ship, but Milland who is as much a male as anyone else beneath those frills and curls, interrupts the ceremony by throwing Goddard overboard. Wayne and he fight it out with Milland eventually being knocked out by his strong opponent. Milland regains consciousness with Goddard attentively ministering to his wounds. "You make a lovely good samaritan," he tells her.

*Years later, Ray revealed; "I had black, wiry hair and always worried every morning before going on location how to damp it down. The role [in *Reap the Wild Wind*] demanded curly hair. They gave me women's permanents with the electric curlers and all that. After seven weeks of shooting, I found my hair coming out by the handfuls. Ever since . . . I used a hairpiece."

†"Speaks good English, don't you think?" Milland says when he notes Goddard's initial reaction to a talking dog, "considering her mother spoke nothing but Gaelic."

A goodly portion of the second half of the feature is devoted to the two rivals, in divers' suits, battling a giant squad on the ocean floor in the wreck of a ship they have gone down to investigate and in which Goddard's cousin (Susan Hayward) was killed. Wayne is killed by the squid and Milland survives to win Goddard as his.

For the lengthy underwater shots, DeMille ordered 800,000 gallons of the Pacific Ocean pumped into a tank measuring one hundred feet long by fifty feet wide by twenty feet deep, constructed of heavy plate glass and steel at Santa Monica's Pan Pacific Marine Museum. Into the tank, equipped with an electrical heating apparatus to keep the water at exactly seventy degrees, the museum placed several hundred brilliantly hued tropical fish. The special marine life was joined by a forty-five-foot squid of deep, red-colored sponge rubber with a twenty-four-button electric keyboard that caused the beast's tentacles to curl and twine. The spectacular job of underwater photography was accomplished by Dewey Rigley, A.S.C.

In an unsympathetic role, Wayne's acting is surpassed by that of Ray in all the scenes in which they are together. Goddard's characterization is reminiscent of Scarlett O'Hara, the plum role she lost in 1939. Included in the large cast of 153 speaking parts was Cyril McLaglen, whom

Milland had replaced in 1929's *The Flying Scotsman*.

To celebrate the new film, in conjunction with the observance of DeMille's thirtieth year of filmmaking, a lavish world premiere was held on March 18, 1942, at the new Hollywood Paramount Theatre, across the street from Grauman's. It was the first wartime gala in Hollywood, complete with kleig lights, Cadillac convertibles and furs and tuxedos in abundance.

Milland went on record with the assertion that DeMille did not know a thing about acting. "He couldn't tell you the first word about how to play a scene. He set it up, camerawise, you see, and there is nothing you can do but repeat the lines and go to the spots he tells you to. You're on your own from then on. He had coaches on the set, drama coaches, who would tell him what to tell us." Unhappy in the tight pants, Milland called *Reap the Wild Wind* a "horrible" ordeal, but the critics responded favorably to him. *Variety* said that he "manages very ably"; the *Hollywood Reporter* noted that "both actresses [Goddard and Hayward] are overshadowed by the vigor of Milland and Wayne"; the *New York Herald-Tribune* found Milland to be "particularly good." *Reap the Wild Wind* went on to gross $4 million in distributors domestic rentals.

Offscreen, it was said that Ray looked "fuller

With Monte Blue (rear, left), Martha O'Driscoll, Susan Hayward, Paulette Goddard, and Janet Beecher in REAP THE WILD WIND (Par '42)

and taller" than oncamera, and in 1942 his hair was rapidly graying along the temple lines. He looked more like an ambassador than an actor. He was one of Hollywood's better-read residents, and he was a veritable storehouse of factual information on a wide variety of subjects. He had an encyclopedic knowledge of astronomical physics and his contemporary-art collection was second only to that of Edward G. Robinson. The Millands' closest friends were the Fred MacMurrays, Claudette Colbert, and Mitchell Leisen, whom they entertained in their new ten-room English Tudor stone house in the exclusive Coldwater Canyon section of Beverly Hills. The actor's hobbies were skiing (his favorite slopes were at Alta, Utah), hunting, and riding horses. In addition, he was a victim of migraine headaches.

Ray's next film was *Are Husbands Necessary?* (Paramount, 1942), a tepid comedy with infrequent laughs. Betty Field was his scatterbrained wife. Then he was sent to Wisconsin for the location filming of *The Major and the Minor* (Paramount, 1942), a superlative comedy with Ginger Rogers at her coyest best. Milland is Major Philip Kirby of the U.S. Army, an instructor at the Wallace Military Academy.* On a train he encounters Rogers posing as a twelve-year-old in order to travel home to Stevenson, Iowa, for half-fare. She spends the night in the lower bunk in his drawing room and he then takes her with him to the academy. As he introduces her to the student body of three hundred curious, anxious boys, he tells her: "This is a treat that doesn't come to one girl in a million." He houses her with his snooty fiancée (Rita Johnson) "until Sunday," but it stretches into a three-day visit during which time the school all but comes apart. At the picture's end, Rogers reveals her true oncamera age, and back in Iowa, she captures Milland when he pays her a visit. The delightful script was by Charles Brackett and Billy Wilder and the film was directed by Wilder, his first.[†]

The year 1942 wound down to a finish with *Star Spangled Rhythm* (Paramount), one of those all-star variety films with more celebrities than taste or plotline. The climax is a show staged for members of the U.S. Navy. This is the skit-filled celluloid potpourri in which Dorothy Lamour, Paulette Goddard, and Veronica Lake sang of their cinema virtues with "The Sweater, the Sa-

rong and the Peek-a-Boo Bob." Milland's contribution was a sketch in which he played bridge, distaff style, with Fred MacMurray, Lynne Overman, and Franchot Tone.

Unlike other actors in their thirties or older, Ray did not go into military service during World War II. (He was eligible but never called into duty by the British Army.) However, he did devote a great deal of time to entertaining American troops overseas at USO camp shows. On one such early outing, a belligerent G.I. shouted out: "Why aren't you in the Army?" Instantaneously, Ray shot back, in a tongue-in-cheek manner: "What, with a war going on? Think I'm crazy?" This jocular yet thought-provoking reply made the rounds of military camps in the months ahead, and earned Ray a special popularity with the troops.

Scenarist Virginia Van Upp, whose previous credits included such outstanding scripts as *Cafe Society* (Paramount, 1939) and *Virginia* (Paramount, 1940), should have been ashamed at turning out something as nonsensical as *The Crystal Ball* (1943). The Elliott Nugent–directed feature had been assembled on the Paramount lot but then sold in a package for United Artists distribution. Paulette Goddard was the unconvincing fake fortuneteller who eventually steals Milland away from possessive Virginia Field.

In March 1943, almost two years after the idea was conceived and put into initial execution, RKO released *Forever and a Day*, a film produced, written, and acted by 107 British nationals in Hollywood as a tribute to their home country's courage during World War II. All the artists involved worked without pay, and the proceeds realized in the United States went to the National Foundation for Infantile Paralysis. The chronicle story was a huge slice of nostalgia about the inhabitants of a London house, beginning with the year of its construction in 1804 by Sir C. Aubrey Smith, whose son, Milland, is killed in naval action against the French.

In early October 1943, Milland was a guest on Gertrude Lawrence's weekly variety radio show, "Revlon Revue." For a flat $3,000 he acted and "sang" selections from his forthcoming Paramount film, *Lady in the Dark*,[‡] including a duet with Miss Lawrence, "The Saga of Jenny."

Variety reported at the end of 1943 that Milland's annual salary was $169,000, and his next

*Filmed at St. John's Military Academy, Delafield, Wisconsin.
†When Paramount remade the picture as *You're Never Too Young* (1955), Jerry Lewis had the revamped Ginger Rogers role, and Dean Martin was the Ray Milland cast parallel.
‡Gertrude Lawrence starred in the Broadway presentation (Alvin Theatre: January 23, 1941, 162 performances; reopened September 1, 1941, for 305 additional performances). Macdonald Carey was Charley Johnson in the original production.

With C. Aubrey Smith in FOREVER AND A DAY (RKO '43)

With Mischa Auer, Mary Philips, and Ginger Rogers in LADY IN THE DARK (Par '44)

film in release was *The Uninvited* (Paramount, 1944). Dodie Smith and Jack Partos adapted Dorothy Macardle's popular novel, *Uneasy Freehold,* about two very real ghosts who haunt a villa on the Cornish coast of England. It is a credit to the creative talent involved in the film that the story was not rewritten (and possibly ruined) for realistic-oriented moviegoers by devising an earthly explanation for the ghosts' existence. Ray is a Londoner who, with his sister (Ruth Hussey), moves into Windward House. The hauntings do not come to the fore until the daughter (Gail Russell) of the house's previous owner comes for a visit. Then, doors unexpectedly swing open, curtains billow wildly, weeping sounds are heard, and the scent of mimosa fills the air. *Newsweek* magazine judged it "a superior and satisfying shocker."

After sitting on a Paramount shelf for a year after its completion, *Lady in the Dark* was released in mid-February 1944. The delay, according to director Mitchell Leisen (who also adapted the Moss Hart–Kurt Weill show for the film) was caused by the backlog of unreleased films during the war. Regardless, the 100-minute color film is spectacular for its sets and costumes designed by Raoul Pene du Bois, Edith Head, Leisen, and Babs Wilomez,* but as a total package, it is disappointing and, in many vital areas, just plain dull.

Milland is seen as the sarcastic and insolent Charley Johnson, advertising manager to Liza Elliott (Ginger Rogers), a fashion-magazine tycoon who finds that she can no longer make decisions. She undergoes psychoanalysis and is told that her problem is psychosomatic. Through three dreams —one in blue, one in gold, and the third in circus motif—her dilemma is solved and she discovers that she does not love either of her two suitors (Warner Baxter and Jon Hall), but that good old Milland is the man for her.

Midway through the shooting of the elaborate feature, Ginger Rogers took off for two weeks to wed husband number three, Jack Briggs. Ray, the essence of professionalism, had the following to say of his co-star: "Can you imagine anything more inappropriate than Ginger Rogers playing a Moss Hart script? She was physically competent and she had been wonderful for *The Major and the Minor* but this was way beyond her. And disappearing in the middle of shooting was the last straw."

In the circus dream segment of *Lady in the Dark,* Milland, dressed in "a tailcoat of paillettes of magenta and blue, white twill cavalry britches and boots up to the knee," is the prosecuting attorney when Rogers is brought to "trial" because she cannot make up her mind. He sings the proclamation that begins the trial, and "of course I couldn't sing, although I'd been a good singer when I was a child." One of the major disappointments of the cinema's *Lady in the Dark* was the omission, at producer B. G. De Sylva's insistence, of the show's most beautiful song, "My Ship," certainly one of Kurt Weill's more memorable American-written numbers.

During the remaining war years, Milland continued with his USO touring and made regular appearances at the Hollywood Canteen, and, because he spoke Spanish fluently, he was often the commentator on government-sponsored radio broadcasts to the Latin American countries.

Till We Meet Again (Paramount, 1944), directed and produced by Frank Borzage, is perhaps noteworthy only for the cinematography by German-born Theodor Sparkuhl. The film, about a French nun (Barbara Britton) who helps an American aviator (Milland) escape from the Nazis via the French underground, is slow-paced and often meanders into unnecessary areas of sentiment and psychology.

Another noncomedic role for Ray was in *Ministry of Fear* (Paramount, 1945), taken from the novel by the master of adventure fiction, Graham Greene. Milland is an Englishman recently released from an insane asylum for mercy-killing his desperately ill wife. He becomes the accidental owner of a layer cake containing a copy of the Allies' plans for the invasion of Nazi-held Europe. When the cake is stolen by a blind man the plot thickens considerably, and Milland plays amateur sleuth, aided by two Viennese, Marjorie Reynolds and Carl Esmond. For an actor who, a scant few years before, was known best for his clipped British accent and his way of wearing a dinner jacket, Milland had matured into a polished dramatic performer. Through wonderfully expressive eyes he fully conveys the haunting anxieties that are permeating his being in this film as he grapples with this life-and-death patriotic situation, wondering all the time whether he is losing grip of his reason.

Ray told Lloyd Shearer of *Liberty* magazine that the possible reason he won the part of Don Birnam in *Lost Weekend* (Paramount, 1945) was because there was no other actor on the Paramount lot who could do it. He explained: "All the

*Especially astonishing were Rogers's mink evening dress and the pink wedding dress embroidered in pearls.

With Carl Esmond and Marjorie Reynolds in MINISTRY OF FEAR (Par '44)

studio had was Alan Ladd, Eddie Bracken, Sonny Tufts and myself, although they could have borrowed practically anybody else they wanted." *Newsweek* magazine further observed that "it took a lot of courage for Paramount to bring Charles Jackson's terrifying case study of an alcoholic to an escapist-minded audience." Jackson's novel was translated to the screen by the writer-director-producer team of Billy Wilder and Charles Brackett.

Several weeks before shooting began on *Lost Weekend,* Ray recalled: "I studied drunks in dozens of bars. It got so that I could tell an alcoholic from a drunk, a dipso from a sot. I watched the way alcoholics walked and talked, the way they screwed up their faces, hunched their shoulders, bent their heads. At the library I boned up on alcohol and its effects on the human body. I asked doctors why men were driven to drink, how many different types of hangovers there were. I tried to get the feel of an alcoholic's life." After the intense filming got underway, he lived and thought like an alcholic offscreen, too. "I had a hold on the characterization," he said, "and I was determined not to lose it." He further admitted: "I knew that I had the best part I would ever get. I gave it everything I had." He gave it so much that his wife publicly stated that he was difficult to live with. They separated on March 31, 1945, af-ter fourteen years of marriage. They agreed that it was to be just a "trial separation" due to "differences in temperament." Hollywood wondered.

At Paramount's Marathon Street studio, the interior shots were made of Don Birnam's apartment, an exact duplication of a New York brownstone flat, of the dypsomaniac ward at Bellevue Hospital, of barroom locales, and of a staircase down which the stupored character eventually plunges. For three weeks, however, the company went on location to New York's then dingy Third Avenue (with its elevated train) where Milland's Don Birnam, failed writer, attempts to peddle his typewriter for the money needed to purchase drink. Unshaven, and generally disreputable looking, the actor scuffed along Third Avenue while cameras and their operators, hidden in trash cans, milk trucks, and large crates, picked up his movements as he went, unrecognized, past and around native pedestrians.

Back in Hollywood, the Millands reconciled on June 28, 1945, after three months' separation (during which time he was romantically linked with Margaret Banks, a soloist with the [American] Ballet Theatre).

The Lost Weekend, the harrowing account of a five-day bender, was released on August 14, 1945. Ray's Don Birnam uses alcohol as a means of escaping from the realization that he is a failure. He suddenly comprehends: "I'm not just a drunkard —I'm a drunk!" He maneuvers his brother (Phillip Terry) and his girlfriend (Jane Wyman) out of his way for the stupification period so that he can wallow in his drunken state. Terry removes visible liquor supplies and money from the apartment, but does not count on the large booze stock that is cleverly hidden. Milland drinks, has D.T.'s, spills his story to a sympathetic barkeep (Howard da Silva), is kicked out of a bar for attempted theft of a woman's handbag, fails to pawn his typewriter because it is a holiday, and winds up in an alcoholic ward. The script ends on an upbeat note, with the writer finally sitting down to start that elusive novel, now bent on describing what it is like to be a full-fledged drunk. Throughout the film, Milland's engaging dramatics are effectively aided by the music score of Miklos Rozsa, which was performed for the soundtrack on an electronic theremin.

The critics all applauded. "Ray Milland is convincing and often disturbing in his hangovers, his delirium tremens, his melancholy" (Newsweek magazine). "Milland gives far and away the best performance of his career" (Time magazine). "Ray Milland's performance . . . is debatable at first, but so absorbed and persuasive as the picture moves along that he all but wins the picture and the doubters over" (James Agee, the Nation). In addition, the film's cinematographer, John F. Seitz, stated that "six months ago, I considered him just the handsome leading-man type. But, in this picture, Ray has proved himself to be perhaps the most interesting subject I have ever photographed." Although Milland actually drank about sixteen gallons of cold tea during the filming (in place of alcohol), his absorption with the D.T.'s affected him so greatly that afterward he claimed: "I even lost my taste for a cocktail before dinner."

The viewing public got quite carried away with Ray's performance. In his fan mail came one, two, and three single dollar bills asking for hideous poses of himself as the drunken Don Birnam. Alcoholics wrote for advice, relatives of drunks wrote bawling him out for showing new places for hiding bottles. One woman, whose husband was an unsober soul, wrote: "Now, everyday we have to feel the bag of the vacuum cleaner." Jokes were devised about the film. An invitation for a drink came out as: "Let's lose a weekend." Another popular quip was: "So-and-so has invented a new type of home bar. When you want a drink you push a button and Ray Milland pops out and breathes in your face."

After fifteen years of bouncing about in films in Hollywood and London as the charming and vir-

ile young lover, Ray was finally taken seriously as a performer. Paramount, fearful of losing its now-prized property, rewrote his contract, providing for a $200,000 yearly salary. Offers of radio work poured in and he made appearances on such shows as "Information Please," "Theatre Guild on the Air," "The Family Theatre," and was a guest with Milton Berle, Hedda Hopper, Louella Parsons, Fred Allen, Edgar Bergen, Jack Benny, et al. on their respective shows. These shows earned him an additional $60,000 annually.

The awards stacked up—at last. At Grauman's Chinese Theatre, on March 7, 1946, Ray was handed an Oscar by the previous year's Best Actress, Ingrid Bergman. Master of ceremonies Bob Hope quipped: "I'm surprised they just handed it to him. I thought they'd hide it in the chandelier." Oscars for The Lost Weekend also went to Wilder as Best Director, Wilder and Brackett for Best Screenplay, and the film itself was named Best of 1945. Furthermore, the National Board of Review of Motion Pictures named Milland 1945's best actor, as did the New York Film Critics, Look magazine, Redbook magazine, and the Foreign Language Press Film Critics of New York. Ray was honored at the International Film Festival at Cannes. A different type of tribute came from the House of Seagram in full-age ads complimenting Milland and urging the public to see the film because of "our own long held and published belief that some men should not drink." Ray was further awarded the Brazilian equivalent of the Oscar by the Association of Brazilian Cinema Critics and received a gold statuette from the Motion Picture and Theatrical Critics of Cuba.

(For those who speculated how another performer might have interpreted the staggering role of The Lost Weekend's Don Birnam, Robert Montgomery provided the comparison on his "Robert Montgomery Presents" anthology video show on February 14, 1955. In an equally refined but more glib manner, he went through the histrionic wringer displaying "the tortures and cravings of a chronic alcoholic.")

Ray's first post-Weekend film release was Kitty (Paramount, 1945), actually completed late in 1944. With Mitchell Leisen as director, the film was based on Rosamund Marshall's novel and shared similarities with Forever Amber, Pygmalion, and The Amorous Adventures of Moll Flanders, all of which works received cinema versions at one time or another. Milland's role of Sir Hugh March was very secondary to that of Paulette Goddard in the flashy title role. He is a degenerate nobleman in eighteenth-century England who grooms a guttersnipe (Goddard) so that she might

With Jane Wyman in THE LOST WEEKEND (Par '45)

With Paulette Goddard in KITTY (Par '45)

marry into wealth and be able to support her one-time instructor. Milland's character, described by his old oncamera friend (Patric Knowles) as "the most obnoxious boy at school," is foppishly reminiscent of his role in *Reap the Wild Wind*. With its rich, colorful production values, *Kitty* is a pictorial delight, dramatically bolstered by the exaggerated playing of such supporting performers as Constance Collier, Reginald Owen, and Sara Allgood.

Ray was still basking in the glow of his Oscar victory, and his association with the award-winning picture. On March 10, 1946, he was invited to appear on CBS radio on the Jack Benny program. He and Benny did a satire on *The Lost Weekend*. However, Ray was rather unhappy with his life style, believing that his existence should encompass more than just moviemaking. He later remembered: "When I used to get burned up and disgusted with pictures, I used to take a small plane up as far as I could go, cut the engine and just circle down. It was so quiet and peaceful, so perfect, you could finally get back to yourself."

Professionally, Ray could not gain much solace from his studio assignments. "Right after that [*The Lost Weekend*] I made three of my worst

pictures, one after another, because they shove you into everything they can after a hit."

He was seen as a U.S. Navy officer in search of a magnum of champagne with which to launch a ship. In finding one, he also finds Olivia de Havilland. The film was a disappointing comedy named *The Well-Groomed Bride* (Paramount, 1946).

In 1946, Ray's earnings were revealed by the U.S. Treasury Department to have been $234,000, and that same year his name appeared on the list of America's best-dressed men. In November, he was presented in Command Performance before the King of England. Then he and Mrs. Milland visited adoption agencies in England in hopes of locating a companion for their son. Adoption of an English child was blocked because the actor was no longer a British subject, so they went to France, but that country's laws prohibited a child from leaving its native soil.

California (Paramount, 1946) had Ray as a rugged gent of 1848 who wins Barbara Stanwyck, and it was a Technicolor stinker. "If *California* had been made as a B picture, it mightn't have been so bad. Claiming as it does to be the 'first of Paramount's postwar outdoor epics' and trying as it does to out-Western every other Western, it

With Olivia de Havilland and William Edmunds in THE WELL-GROOMED BRIDE (Par '46)

With Albert Dekker and Gavin Muir in CALIFORNIA (Par '46)

quickly loses its stirrups and ends up caught by its chaps in a clump of cactus" (*Newsweek* magazine). Morever, its soundstage-conceived outdoor sets gave most perceptive viewers claustrophobia. Next came *The Imperfect Lady* (Paramount, 1947), in which Teresa Wright, dressed in a Victorian wardrobe of 1892, tries to marry Milland, a candidate for Parliament. She is also a woman with a past. It was unfortunate that so soon on the heels of *The Imperfect Lady, The Trouble with Women* (Paramount, 1947) should be released. It also co-starred the talented but undynamic Teresa Wright. The picture had been completed in July 1945, but remained on the shelf for two years. In this Sidney Lansfield–directed feature, she is smitten with Milland, a psychology professor whose definition of love is "a feeling which is essentially chemical."

At least behind the camera Ray had much better results with *Golden Earrings* (Paramount, 1947), an oddly premised feature that grossed a million dollars in a few short months at the box office. Marlene Dietrich, of all actresses, is a grubby, messy gypsy smeared with dark, greasy ointment who makes frantic passes at Milland, a British intelligence officer whom she hides from the Nazis during World War II. He resists her at first, but relents and even goes back later to claim her. In

In GOLDEN EARRINGS (Par '47)

Hollywood Director (1973), director Mitchell Leisen informed writer David Chierichetti that Ray did not want to make the film because he felt unsympathetic towards Dietrich and thought he was too young (thirty-nine) for the role. The director added: "He calmed down a little by the end, but he and Marlene fought the whole time."

Milland's annual income continued to climb, and his earnings for 1947 were reported by the U.S. Treasury Department to be $253,333.

For public consumption, in March 1948, Ray authoritatively commented on the effects of alcohol with regards to women, which was published by *Newsweek* magazine on April 5, 1948. "Let a woman take one drink—a hairpin falls out—She takes another drink—down comes a lock of hair—As she keeps on drinking, there is a gradual disintegration. Lipstick under the nose or on the teeth. She forgets to sit down gracefully. Finally, she looks a downright mess."

On June 7, 1948, Hedda Hopper scooped all other gossip columnists by reporting the news that the Millands were expecting a baby in December. However, Mrs. Milland suffered a miscarriage.

Milland was oncamera very briefly in *Variety Girl* (Paramount, 1947), but in *The Big Clock* (Paramount, 1948) he was the focal character. The picture co-starred him with Charles Laughton. Unlike the earlier film in which they worked together (*Payment Deferred*), Milland now received billing over Laughton. This new thriller had publishing tycoon Laughton murder his bitchy mistress (Rita Johnson) with a sun-dial clock which had been procured for her in a bar by Milland. A witness had seen Laughton enter the girl's apartment and the tycoon dispatches his *Crimeways* magazine editor, George Stroud (Milland), to track down that witness. Milland had become an expert at locating missing persons while on a West Virginia newspaper through his "system of irrelevant clues." Actually Milland is the witness, but he was drunk at the time, and George Macready, Laughton's deputy, had altered the time on a broken clock in the girl's apartment, which confused the time of the murder. The film's title refers to a two-story clock in Laughton's building which shows the time in many parts of the world by means of twenty-five dials. The role of George Stroud was Milland's meatiest offering since *The Lost Weekend.*

On April 12, 1948, Ray was heard over radio in the "Lux Radio Theatre" version of *The Perfect Marriage.* His audio co-star, Lizabeth Scott, remembers him as "amiable and charming." Also in

April 1948, Milland was guest of honor at the Lima, Peru, opening of the new 145-seat Paramount Tacna Theatre, where he delighted luminaries by displaying both his sense of humor and his knowledge of Spanish.

So Evil My Love (Paramount, 1948), originally titled *For Her to See,* had been lensed in England in May of 1947. In this obviously costly period film, Milland is a caddish artist who entices a missionary's widow (Ann Todd) into a life of sexual and ethical amorality, including the pinning of a murder charge on her old schoolmate, Geraldine Fitzgerald. While James Agee of the *Nation* could say it was "good enough work by Ray Milland," the film was stagnant, and the emotional scenes were thin and phony. As *Cue* magazine properly exclaimed, it was "actually a case of murder without movement, of crime without excitement."

In August 1948, Paramount assigned Ray the role of the Duke of Ferrara, opposite Paulette Goddard as Lucretia Borgia, in Mitchell Leisen's *A Mask for Lucretia.* It would have been Milland's seventh picture with Goddard and his ninth with Leisen. However, Milland refused the part, saying that it was not suitable for his talents.* He was placed on suspension for ten weeks. John Lund replaced him in the film, which was eventually released as *Bride of Vengeance* (Paramount, 1949) and proved to be one of the less frequently seen, bigger bombs of the cinema season.

Meanwhile, both Milland and director Mitchell Leisen offered walk-on cameos in *Miss Tatlock's Millions* (Paramount, 1948), a light comedy starring John Lund and Wanda Hendrix. Thereafter, Milland was seen in *Sealed Verdict* (Paramount, 1948) as an American major in occupied Germany who falls in love with the ex-girlfriend of a Nazi criminal. This film is forgettable, as was the Czech discovery, Florence Marley, who played the distaff lead.

Alias Nick Beal (Paramount, 1949) was Ray's last film under his standing Paramount contract. He is suave and sinister as the devil in human form. The script was inspired obviously by Goethe's *Faust.* Milland as the devil is after the soul of the district attorney (Thomas Mitchell) and almost succeeds in totally corrupting the honest politician. Ray's sterling performance proved once again that, when given a role with solid potential, he could elaborate on the part with a sophisticated sense of intuition.

*According to the Hollywood *Citizen-News,* Ray "walked out on this one because of the effeminate nature of the wardrobe designed for him to wear."

With Ann Todd in SO EVIL MY LOVE (Par '48)

With Audrey Totter in ALIAS NICK BEAL (Par '49)

Once Ray and Paramount had made up their differences over *Bride of Vengeance,* they announced that he would work with musical-comedy performer Betty Hutton in *The Broadway Story,* but again he refused. (Victor Mature inherited the role intended for Milland in the project retitled, *Red, Hot and Blue* [Paramount, 1949].) With nothing on the studio lineup for Milland, it was decided to loan him to MGM for *The Conspirator* (1950), to be shot in England, but eventually Robert Taylor took the part. Instead, Ray went over to Twentieth Century–Fox for *It Happens Every Spring* (1949), a mild comedy about a chemistry teacher (Milland) who accidentally compounds a recipe that makes a baseball repulsive to wood. Leaving his laboratory, he becomes a pitcher, baffles Paul Douglas at bat any number of times, and wins pretty Jean Peters.

On November 18, 1949, the Millands officially adopted a six-year old American girl who had been living with them for almost a year. Milland told the press: "We are very fond of the little girl. We have been very happy with her." He disclosed that they had named her Victoria Francesca and had entered into an understanding with the people from whom she was adopted. "The agreement was that she is not to be photographed until she is twelve years old and that her real identity will be guarded forever with the utmost secrecy."

Again on loan-out, Ray went to Columbia for a slapstick bout called *A Woman of Distinction* (1950) opposite zany Rosalind Russell. He is a British astronomer, she is the dean of a New England girls' school. Together they do their best to obtain laughs through Keystone-type pratfalls.

Paramount had hopes of putting Ray back to work* in a project called *Jack of Diamonds.* The script, focusing on the Manhattan gem center, was based on a Berne Giler story as adapted by Jonathan Latimer. Nothing developed from this concept, and, instead, Ray went to MGM for *A Life of Her Own* (1950), a picture more suited to the 1935s days of Kay Francis and George Brent. Milland portrayed a rich Montana mine owner with a crippled wife back home (Margaret Phillips) and a beautiful mistress in New York (Lana Turner). When the latter learns of the former, she bravely leaves the plush penthouse where she has been kept to face the world alone. One of the few joys of the synthetic proceedings was Anna Dvorak's performance as a used-up model who can no longer tolerate life.

Ray did return to Paramount for a cliché-ridden outing called *Copper Canyon* (1950). It was in

*The star and the studio agreed to a new nonexclusive pact, calling for one picture a year. In the deflated studio production years of the 1950s, it was a compliment to Milland's standing that he received even this token bid for career stability.

With Paul Douglas in IT HAPPENS EVERY SPRING (20th '49)

color and had Hedy Lamarr as co-star. John Farrow directed Milland as a displaced southerner in the post–Civil War West who becomes a trick-shot artist with an itinerant carnival. Lamarr is the woman who catches his eyes. The actor once confessed in a later interview that he "hated working with Hedy Lemarr."

Ray turned in his best performance of the early 1950s in *Night into Morning* (MGM, 1951) as a college professor whose life is suddenly altered with the accidental death of his wife and son. Jean Hagen was the tart who offers him solace, as does his understanding friend Nancy Davis. However, the picture was a box-office loser. "The effort to dramatize a message of hopeful solace seems even more hopeless, leaves the picture tediously uneventful, as sincere and futile as a note of condolence" (*Time* magazine). At least Ray earned a trip abroad for *Circle of Danger* (Eagle Lion, 1951), filmed in England, Wales, and Scotland. It offered the star as an American in quest of the truth concerning his brother's mysterious death during a World War II commando raid.

In *Rhubarb* (Paramount, 1951) Milland was back in the baseball business, with a cat as his boss and owner of the team. It was a zany little comedy from the novel by H. Allen Smith. His next film, *Close to My Heart* (Warner Bros., 1951), demonstrated the chaotic conditions so prevalent in television-scared Hollywood. The project had first been selected as a vehicle for Dennis Morgan and Betsy Drake. When they proved unavailable, it went to Ray and Gene Tierney. It was a low-budget entry in which he yearns to adopt a child from Fay Bainter's orphanage, but insists on first checking into the baby's background.

Warner Bros. called him into action a second time for a Western entitled *Bugles in the Afternoon* (1952). He is seen as a cavalry sergeant who has an old score to settle with Captain Hugh Marlowe, whom he reencounters in the Dakota Territory. Helena Carter is the girl. At the time (mid-1950), it seemed a lovely merchandizing idea to cast Oscar winners Ray, Joan Fontaine, and Teresa Wright in a story of a member (Milland) of Alcoholics Anonymous who takes a large interest in a drinking-prone actress (Fontaine) while his wife (Wright) patiently waits in the wings. However, when *Something To Live For,* directed by George Stevens, was completed in July 1950, studio executives were so unimpressed by the venture that its distribution was delayed until after

Stevens's more prestigious *A Place in the Sun* (Paramount, 1951). The results were more traumatic than Fontaine's alcoholic tremors. "But, oh! that script by Dwight Taylor! It is a fearsomely rigged and foolish thing, planted with fatuous situations that even Mr. Stevens can't disguise. And how that long arm of coincidence keeps batting you in the face! At first it is simply embarrassing. Then it is vexingly absurd" (Bosley Crowther, *New York Times*).

The Thief (United Artists, 1952) was a film with a gimmick that still almost holds up today. Its soundtrack contained recorded background noises and an atmospheric musical score by Herschel Gilbert, but no dialog. The entire story is put across by action. Milland is a nuclear physicist, the winner of an international award, who is persuaded to sell out to foreign agents, leading to homicide. This is the movie in which Rita Gam made her debut, after a widespread publicity campaign search for the "sex-without-words girl." Of Milland's work, *Newsweek* magazine found that he gave an "intelligently modulated performance in a role that otherwise might have called for a few purple patches of overacting." *The Thief* is an excellent showcase of the actor's ability to pantomime with his expressive face and his very telling eyes.

In December 1952, producers Samuel Colt and Anthony Z. Landi announced that Milland had made a commitment with them to direct and star in *Stranger in Munich,* to begin shooting in Germany in the spring of 1953. However, due to inability to reach a proper monetary agreement, the deal collapsed.

Two inconsequential 1953 features came next. In *Jamaica Run,* done in color for Paramount's low-budget William Pine–William Thomas production unit, Milland was a schooner's skipper who straightens out Arlene Dahl's bizarre family with its closet full of skeletons. *Let's Do It Again* at Columbia was a weak musical remake of the studio's classic *The Awful Truth* (1937)[*] with Jane Wyman as the wife conniving to win back her husband's affections by flirting with various other men, including Aldo Ray. As the husband, Ray did not seem to care one way or another, and neither player was up to the sophisticated standards set by Irene Dunne and Cary Grant in the 1930s original.

Still another remake was proposed for Milland in 1953, but it did not get off the ground, at least

[*] *The Awful Truth* on Broadway opened at the Henry Miller Theatre (September 12, 1911) for a 144-performance run. It was filmed in 1925 by Producers Distributing Corp. with Agnes Ayres; Ina Claire recreated her stage role for the 1929 Pathé picture.

In COPPER CANYON (Par '50)

With Hugh Sinclair and Marjorie Fielding in CIRCLE OF DANGER (Coronado-Eagle Lion '51)

With Gene Tierney in CLOSE TO MY HEART (WB '51)

With Forrest Tucker and William ''Bill'' Phillips in BUGLES IN THE AFTERNOON (WB '52)

In THE THIEF (UA '52)

not then, and not with him. It was to have been *My Man Godfrey* with Milland as butler Godfrey and Paulette Goddard as the rich girl who brings him home from a scavenger hunt.†

On September 17, 1953, Ray debuted on CBS-TV as an absent-minded professor married to Phyllis Avery, in the comedy series "Meet Mr. McNutley."‡ The show was seen on Thursday at 8:00 P.M. E.S.T. and was heard on CBS radio an hour later. "I went into television because my agent talked me into it," he said. "Anyway, I was tired of making a lot of bad movies." During the first six months of the "McNutley" series, the character was a silly man who created his own situations, thus leaving himself open to viewer ridicule. In April 1954, the format was altered to make the professor an innocent victim of the comic happenings, thereby making him more appealing. The star's character name was changed, too, from McNutley to McNulty. When Ben Gross of the *New York Daily News* inquired whether it wasn't unusual to change a comedy series after launching, Milland replied: "Why should it be? Consider a Broadway play. It is tinkered with in rehearsal, also during the out-of-town tryouts and sometimes even after the first night."

†The original 1936 Universal feature starred William Powell and Carole Lombard, and it was not remade until 1957, with David Niven and June Allyson in the pivotal roles.
‡Ray called it "a pratfall name."

With Patric Knowles and Wendell Corey in JAMAICA RUN (Par '53)

270

The mercurial Millands separated again on October 20, 1953, and august journalist Louella Parsons deemed it necessary to write in her syndicated column: "There is very serious trouble between the Ray Millands, and their friends are hoping that this marriage, which was thought to be so happy, will not suffer because of a big misunderstanding. . . . I am sorry to have to print this, but the whole town is discussing it . . . and Mal [his wife] does not deny that there is trouble." Rumor had it that Milland's "nervous tension" was a result of his personal interest in his latest film co-star, Grace Kelly, in *Dial M for Murder* (Warner Bros., 1954). At any rate, the Millands were reunited as of November 17.

Dial M for Murder was Ray's sole release in 1954. Alfred Hitchcock directed from Frederick Knott's screenplay, based on his popular play of the same title. Milland was Tony,* the suave husband of rich, unfaithful Kelly, whom he arranges to have murdered in their London flat by serpentine Anthony Dawson. The scheme backfires when the wife stabs her would-be attacker. Milland then switches plans to make it look like premeditated murder with blackmail as the reason. The superclue is a missing key to the flat, which Milland attempts to retrieve, in so doing revealing himself as the culprit. Robert Cummings is ineffectually on hand as the wife's lover, while John Williams as the detective quietly steals every scene in which he appears. The color feature was shot in the 3-D process, but was released in the standard film format.

On September 16, 1954, after the summer respite, Ray's CBS-TV series returned for another season with yet another change—this time in the title, which was renamed "The Ray Milland Show." In addition, Ray's role as Professor Ray McNulty, a college drama professor, was described as "a sensible, rather sophisticated guy."

The Girl in the Red Velvet Swing (Twentieth Century–Fox, 1955), the partially true story of showgirl Evelyn Nesbit, starred Milland as socialite architect Stanford White. Milland's White, a mature married man, is murdered by another of the woman's suitors, Harry Thaw, played by firmfaced, wild-eyed Farley Granger. British Joan Collins was the Evelyn of Walter Reisch and Charles Brackett's screenplay. Bosley Crowther (*New York Times*) wrote that Milland's performance "models precisely the masculine elegance and nobility" of the older, melancholy lover. The

In DIAL M FOR MURDER (WB '54)

color, CinemaScope process allowed for lush period settings that were definitely the highlight of the picture.

Long-aching to direct a film, Ray made a deal with Republic Pictures in 1954 for two to four directorial jobs, but at the studio's insistence, he also was to star in the pictures. The first was *A Man Alone* (1956),‡ a Western with Milland as a loner on the range who is mistakenly accused of massacring the passengers of a stagecoach. He hides out from a lynch mob in the home of the sheriff's daughter (Mary Murphy).† Of his directing, *Variety* reported, "he acquits himself fairly well in the new chore. He's a mite too deliberate with his pacing, particularly in handling the character he plays, but shows plenty of promise in his guidance of other players and in an ability to develop dramatics beyond the level of the usual outdoor feature."

As his second directorial job, Milland selected an original story by Martin Rackin, a property that Paramount had purchased earlier for Joan Crawford, but was then unable to adapt for her special talents. Ray bought the story for $25,000 and hired William Bowers to rewrite it. *Lisbon* (Republic, 1956) was filmed on location in the Portuguese capital. Along with the city's beauty in Trucolor, the movie contained the presence of the redhaired Maureen O'Hara and brunette

*On Broadway (Plymouth Theatre: October 29, 1952, 552 performances), Maurice Evans played the male lead.
‡Originally titled *The Gunman*.
†Joan Evans, Milland's first choice for the role, had to back out due to pregnancy.

With Joan Collins in THE GIRL IN THE RED VELVET SWING (20th '55)

French actress Yvonne Furneaux. Claude Rains easily stole the show as a callous international smuggler who hires Milland, an expatriate American with a boat, to rescue O'Hara's husband (Percy Marmont) from behind the Iron Curtain. The credits list Raymond Milland as producer, R. Milland as director, and Ray Milland as star. On its completion, he said: "We shot the whole thing in thirty days and I believe we got a darned good picture in Cinemascope and color. Exteriors are out of this world." The *New York Times* called it "a workmanlike melodrama," but there is not much suspense to it. Best remembered about the film is its title song, "Lisbon Antiqua," and the sequence in which cool Rains smashes birds on his windowsill for his pet cat's breakfast.

On television, in 1956, Ray starred on NBC's "Screen Directors Playhouse" and the "Ford Theatre," as well as in an episode of the CBS offering, "General Electric Theatre."

In 1957, Milland worked at Twentieth Century-Fox in two films, the first of which was *Three Brave Men,* taken from a series of Pulitzer Prize-winning newspaper articles by Anthony Lewis concerning the true case of a Navy Department civil servant suspended from his job as a security risk. Ernest Borgnine played the wronged man while Milland was his defense lawyer in the hearings that finally vindicated the accused. Secondly, in *The River's Edge,* an Allan Dwan–directed, in-color programmer, Milland was the nasty ex-boyfriend of Debra Paget, who returns to her with a suitcase of ill-gotten dollars. She is married to farmer, Anthony Quinn, so Milland forces them to accompany him toward the Mexican border. The bad man receives his just reward by falling off a cliff above the Rio Grande.

Bored and nervous when not at work, the fifty-year-old Milland scrambled for movie jobs in a diminishing market which offered little opportunity even to far younger actors. To his credit, he did come up with some fitfully intriguing screen projects. In England, he directed and starred with an all-British cast in *The Safecracker* (MGM, 1958). In the title role, he is an honest locksmith turned to crime. He later becomes known as one of the country's five best safecrackers and when he is caught, he is transferred from a prison to a World War II commando job in Belgium. There, he cracks a difficult safe in a German Gestapo headquarters. It was a far more low-key presentation of a theme used to ostentatious advantage in *The Dirty Dozen* (MGM, 1967) and others. *The Safecracker* played on the bottom portion of double bills in the United States. Also, in England, he starred, again with a British cast, in *High Flight* (Columbia, 1958) as a wing commander of young recruits at the Royal Air Force College (shades of *I Wanted Wings*). In relegating the tedious film to the dustbin, the *New York Daily News* casually remarked: "[it] has two saleable assets—it stars Ray Milland and has some fine sequences of the Royal Air Force in action . . ."

Throughout 1957 and 1958, Ray appeared in

several guest shots on established television "theatre" shows.* Then, on May 2, 1959, CBS-TV premiered a new half-hour series titled "Markham," with Milland in the title role as Roy Markham, a wealthy lawyer-investigator who lives on New York's exclusive Sutton Place. He was one of the show's three producers† and directed many of the segments. His friend, Mitchell Leisen, was called in to direct fourteen programs during 1960 when other directors ran into problems in confining their segments to the allotted time.

It had been made well-known by Milland that he had "asked" his way out of his last video series. "Why am I doing another half-hour TV series when I was dissatisfied with 'Meet McNulty' . . . The reason is simple. Mainly I guess, because I want to keep busy. I was thinking of retiring and did, for six months. All my wife could think of was how to get me back to work. I'm a nervous guy and I've got to keep myself occupied." "Markham" lasted for sixty episodes before it died in the rating game. It had been planned to do a great deal of the series' filming on location in Europe, but too much of the time the segments were shot on backlot sets at Revue Studios on the Universal City lot.

With the demise of "Markham," the Millands

*"G. E. Theatre," "Goodyear Theatre," etc.
†The other two producers were Joseph Sistrom and Warren Duff.

With Mrs. Milland and son Daniel in 1957

vacationed in Europe, where, in September 1960, the actor announced from his Nice base that he now intended giving up acting "to concentrate on production. My time is past." He stressed that he did not intend to desert the United States for good. The next year Hedda Hopper revealed that another generation of the Milland family was en-

With Victor Maddern (rear) and Percy Herbert (right) in THE SAFECRACKER (MGM '58)

273

tering the acting field. She reported that Danny Milland, "a handsome lad, six feet four and one-half inches tall, twenty-one years old, two weeks out of the Army and a natural-born actor," had signed a long-term contract with the APA Production Company, an organization newly formed by Jack Lemmon, Richard Quine, Blake Edwards, and Max Arnow. Not much came of the son's acting career, and a few years later he enrolled at UCLA with a major in geology.

If actresses like Bette Davis and Joan Crawford might revive their film careers via the macabre genre (e.g., *What Ever Happened to Baby Jane?* [Warner Bros., 1962]), why not the likes of Ray Milland? It was a far cry from the ambiance of *Skylark* or the artistry of *The Lost Weekend* to amble about in the cheaply concocted cinema world of Edgar Allan Poe adaptations, but the actor gave it a whirl in *The Premature Burial* (American International, 1962). The picture was shot in England by producer-director Roger Corman, and the film's derivation from authentic Poe was distant, but slight enough for the movie company to capitalize on the author's popularity with horror-film fans. Vincent Price, the logical successor to celluloid spook king Boris Karloff, had had good luck with Corman–American International–Poe, much more so than Milland did in *The Premature Burial*. For in this eighty-one-minute col-

or feature, Milland was strangely stiff in his portrayal of a man with a psychotic fear of being buried alive. The *New York Herald-Tribune* labeled his performance as filled with "dogged solemnity," which was not what this type of movie required. One unintentionally funny sequence occurs when stolid Milland escorts his wife (Heather Angel) and the family doctor (Alan Napier) on a deluxe tour of an escape-geared mausoleum. The colorful Gothic settings and Ronald Stein's effective musical score were the film's highlights.

Whatever critical-artistic reservations there might have been about Ray's dabbling in horror films, American International felt there was sufficient residue in the Milland name to allow him to direct *and* star in a science fiction entry, *Panic in Year Zero* (American International, 1962). He and his family are on a camping trip in the Southern California mountains when an atomic bomb is dropped near Los Angeles. They are not the sole survivors, but appear to be the only ones left who are reasonably compassionate, although Milland, as head of the family, is forced to rob and shoot a man for provisions. Milland later complained that the film company rushed him to completion a week ahead of schedule. *Variety* commented: "[he] manages capably in the dual role of director and star, but it's safe to observe that he'd prob-

With Hazel Court in THE PREMATURE BURIAL (AIP '62)

With Frankie Avalon in PANIC IN YEAR ZERO (AIP '62)

ably have done twice as well by halving his assignment, one way or the other." Jean Hagen was his wife, with Frankie Avalon and Joan Freeman as their teenage children.

In 1963, Milland narrated the hour-long television program, "Hollywood, Come Home," a documentary plea to filmmakers to return to Los Angeles County. The show included scenes of barren soundstages, auctions of studio props, and interviews with the unemployed of Hollywood. It was a sad, but very true, picture.

X–The Man with the X-Ray Eyes (1963) was Ray's third film for American International, a novelty-shock feature in the science fiction genre concerning a scientist (Milland) who concocts an eye-drop formula that produces x-ray vision. When warned that things supernatural are best left to the gods, he snarls: "Well, I'm closing in on the gods." The gimmicky picture has developed its own coterie of fans over the years.

Ginger Rogers and her husband, William Marshall, turned producers with *The Confession*, completed in 1964 at their studio facilities in Jamaica. With Rogers as an unusual madame, Milland as a master thief, and Barbara Eden as an unwed mother, the picture had obvious novelty appeal. Golden Eagle gave it brief distribution in 1965, then it remained shelved until the early 1970s when, during the peak of Elliott Gould's popularity, it was decided to reissue this film in which he had a small role as a mute. It was retitled *Quick, Let's Get Married* (a.k.a. *Seven Differ-*

ent Ways). It fared no better the second time around, and was branded an embarrassing, amateurish mishmash best relegated to the curiosity shelf. With his unbecoming beret accenting his jowled countenance, Milland looked every bit his age.

In 1965, Ray was offered a road-company version of *My Fair Lady*, but he declined. This was his second invitation to play Professor Henry Higgins onstage. He explained to Gail Rock of the *New York Times*: "In the early '50s, four men came around telling me about a musical version of *Pygmalion* that they thought I would be right for. I told them I hadn't the time and didn't want to and that it was the most asinine thing I ever heard of. Rex Harrison got the part." Soon after turning down the 1965 offer, however, "Fonda, Stewart and MacMurray were over for dinner— you know how it is, guys get together in the kitchen at two a.m. and get loaded." The next morning Mrs. Milland told her husband that she was pleased he had agreed to do *My Fair Lady*. He had no idea to what she was referring. "You were all four on the phone last night and you agreed to do it," she reminded him. Milland found himself replacing Brian Aherne, who had begun the tour, and "I was shooting a film and never even had a chance to read the script until eight days before we opened. I had never even seen the damned play. But we got good notices, even from Claudia Cassidy, the toughest critic in Chicago. Some of my friends called and accused me of sleeping with her." Milland toured the United States as Henry Higgins for twenty weeks in the Midwest and on the East Coast.

In September 1964, Milland's son Danny had wed Cleo Janet in Los Angeles. In December of 1966, they were sent to a California state institution for treatment as drug addicts after their arrest for the possession of heroine. They also pleaded guilty to forging prescriptions in order to obtain drugs.*

Having shunned stage work for years, Ray was theatre-bitten after his *My Fair Lady* tour, and accepted the offer to star in New York in *Hostile Witness* (Music Box Theatre: February 17, 1966, 157 performances), which had enjoyed success on the London stage with Michael Denison starred. The courtroom drama by Jack Roffey was directed by Reginald Denham. Thanks to the professionalism of Milland, Melville Cooper, Edgar Daniels, and others, the potentially static show proved an engrossing evening of theatre. Associated Press critic William Glover reported: "Milland gives an urbane, sharply etched portrayal that avoids those pitfalls of stereotype frequent in such parts. And

for a man who's spent most of his life in front of cameras, Milland is remarkably free of that in-person edginess which haunts film refugees." Said Whitney Bolton (*New York Morning Telegraph*) of Milland's interpretation of a falsely accused and much badgered lawyer: "He handles the quieter moments with a spirit of the impatience expected of a successful man when confronted with a mockery of fate, he assumes total and commanding power when driving, at the trial toward the denouement. Welcome to our theatre, Mr. Milland."

Milland may have been a relative novice at theatre work, but having quickly grasped the refinements of the medium, he displayed a cool, superior professionalism on the stage as he had before the camera for so many years. In fact, he admitted: "There's a 22 minute segment in the play where I'm sitting onstage, not saying anything. But I don't waste it. I'm making up budgets for places I'd like to live. Right now I'm budgeting a flat in London on Grosvenor Square. Simple house, three bedrooms and three baths. Lovely. A possible."

*Danny Milland, age thirty-four, was in the news again in October, 1974. He had been divorced from Cleo Janet and was now engaged to socialite Jacqueline May. But the forty-one-year-old lady cancelled her plans to wed him. She explained, "Being a movie star's son does have its problems, believe it or not, and it does make it difficult for him to lead a normal life." She went on to describe Milland's life as a fledgling actor who cannot be accepted as his own person. Danny according to Miss May receives a $100 per week allowance from his father. "He lives in a terrible place in West Hollywood where they play cards all day long. He eats in hamburger joints. It's sad. After the opulence he grew up with, it's hard for him to keep his head straight in depressing surroundings."

With Joan Fontaine, Joan Bennett, and Gloria Swanson backstage after a performance of Ray Milland's Broadway show, HOSTILE WITNESS (February, 1966)

The star was not so enthusiastic about the environs of New York City: "[it] is a dreadful place to live. Not only is the city filthy with dirt, it is filthy other-wise. When I first came to New York in the 30s, I expected it to be like London and Paris, where a single man expected to be accosted in the streets by prostitutes. I thought New York would be the same or more so, since it was such a lively city. But there were no prostitutes on the streets of New York. Now you see them everywhere."

Milland agreed to tour with *Hostile Witness*, the road company opening on September 6, 1966, at the Auditorium in Denver, Colorado, from there to the Huntington Hartford in Los Angeles for one month and closing at the Coconut Grove Playhouse in Miami on February 27, 1967. From there, it was taken to Australia, and later in 1967, Ray directed and starred in the black-and-white film version at London's Shepperton Studios. It was completed in five weeks for a total cost of $700,000. Scheduled for United Artists release, the film was shelved and was not distributed until well into 1970, and then on a very limited basis. Reviewers from Ray's homeland were not kind to the cinema version. "Coming after the somewhat off-beat films Ray Milland has been associated with in recent years, this present piece seems an entirely conventional and unprofitable choice. . . . Milland's own performance consists mainly of worried close-ups, and the few moments of tension at the end when the murderer is revealed are hardly worth the wait" (British *Monthly Film Bulletin*).

While he was in London with the filming of *Hostile Witness* it was rumored that Ray would star in the musical stage version of Oscar Wilde's *The Picture of Dorian Gray*, adapted by Constance Cox, with songs by Christopher Matthew and Jerry Wayne. The venture never materialized.

In 1968, he was one of the stars of an NBC telefeature, *The Protectors*, filmed in Denver. His role was that of a desperate businessman who resorts to hiring a hit man from a Murder, Inc. to eliminate troublesome competition. Diana Lynn was his wife and Van Johnson was an efficient cop. Because of its too adult nature, the feature was released to theatres by Universal in September 1970, and did not reach television until 1972. Along the way, it received a title change to *Company of Killers*.

Also in 1968, Milland was seen in a cameo role in *Red Roses for the Fuehrer* (Dino Films), but most of his talents were devoted to television, which he claimed to prefer. "Making a picture is a bore," he said.

On December 9, 1969, he starred with Gene Tierney and Don Murray in the ABC telefeature, *Daughter of the Mind*, a mixture of espionage, ESP, and soap opera about parents who will not accept their daughter's death.

Ray's vacant hours—it is difficult to believe there were many—were filled with his hobby of writing stories and articles. Using various pen names, a number of them were published in national magazines and one piece won the Southern California Press Club Award. He also found time to star in a summer tour of the musical *Take Me Along*.

Then in 1970, after not being seen in anything resembling a major motion-picture production for seven years, he took off his toupee and allowed the hair dye to vanish. He shocked audiences ("But Ray Milland can't be bald? Why he's only . . My God!") by appearing older than they cared to see him in his role as Oliver Barrett III, Ryan O'Neal's straight-laced, Brahmin father who does not know how to narrow the generation gap in *Love Story* (Paramount). In fourth billing, he is a Harvard-educated lawyer-banker, dripping in snobbery and determined that his son shall become a similar "success." "Tell me, Oliver," he says sour-facedly to his son: "have you heard from law school?" which means: "If you haven't I'll see to it that you do." When the son informs him in a staid gentleman's-club dining room that he intends to marry a girl who lacks the proper background (Ali MacGraw), papa threatens: "If you marry her now, I'll not give you the time of day." Oliver IV replies: "Father, you don't *know* the time of day."

At the conclusion of *Love Story* Milland was back oncamera for a brief but telling scene. It revealed his consummate artistry as clearly as any of the best moments of fellow-acting-veteran Melvyn Douglas in the same year's *I Never Sang for My Father*. MacGraw has died, and a teary-eyed O'Neal is leaving the Fifth Avenue hospital. At the front entrance he encounters an emotionally embarrassed Milland, a man so proud that he finds it difficult to display any degree of sympathetic vulnerability. Milland mumbles, "I didn't know . . . why didn't you tell me?" When he learns his daughter-in-law is dead, he responds with a bewildered "I'm sorry," a little bit amazed that the reply came more from his heart than from politeness. Weepy O'Neal repeats the film's immortal catch line: "When you're in love, you don't have to say you're sorry." Finis.

Called "one of the greatest tear-jerkers in Hollywood history" by *TV Guide, Love Story* was from Erich Segal's scenario, which was published in novella form after the film's release and

With Ryan O'Neal in LOVE STORY (Par '70)

was itself a bestseller for a year. The film did fantastic business, thanks to a cagey promotional campaign, and by 1973, the motion picture had grossed over $50 million, making it the then fourth-highest winner of all time.*

Ray jaunted to Acapulco with Suzanne Pleschette, Dack Rambo, Roger Davis, and Melissa Newman for the "ABC Movie of the Week," *River of Gold* (March 9, 1971). He was scheduled to appear with Joan Fontaine at California's New Arlington Park Theatre in *Relatively Speaking,* but he backed out a few days before the June 29, 1971, opening. He was replaced by Ian Martin. Reportedly, he had conflicts with Fontaine on billing and script changes.

After lensing *The Big Game* (Comet, 1972) in South Africa, a succession of horror films followed. *Frogs* (American International, 1972) established the pattern with reptiles crawling over his crippled body. It was filmed at Florida's Eden Park Historical Museum. "I just did that film in a hurry so I could get out of town for Thanksgiving," he explained. "I thought it was so awful that it would never be released—now it's making a lot of dough." The Gothic ecology film did receive the expected critical roasting, with *Films in Re-*

view blasting: " . . . most of the cast, beginning with Ray Milland, deserve annihilation."

With ex-football player Rosie Grier, Milland provided the extra pasty-faced head in *The Thing with Two Heads* (American International, 1972). The picture's questionable premise found Milland as the crochety head of the Kirshner Hospital and Transplant Foundation who, because of his advanced arthritis, is wheelchair-ridden. Unknown to his co-workers he is dying of cancer. The irony of the tale finds racial bigot Milland with his head fused to the neck of convicted (but innocent) black killer Grier. To columnist Dorothy Manners, Milland admitted in October, 1972: "I saw old 'Two Heads' with an audience the other night, and you know something—the damned thing's entertaining! The audience was eating it up. Even I was going along for the ride."

Milland's screen career glided along, at a low but steady ebb. He was stern to rubber-faced Frankie Howerd in the British-made *The House in Nightmare Park* (MGM, 1973), and the *London Observer* allowed that "[he] is excellent as the blandly lethal head of the household . . . " Ray skulked as a man devoted to the care of a deaf-mute hunchback in the sluggish *Terror in the Wax*

*Surpassed by *The Godfather* ($82 million), *Gone with the Wind* ($77 million), and *The Sound of Music* ($73 million).

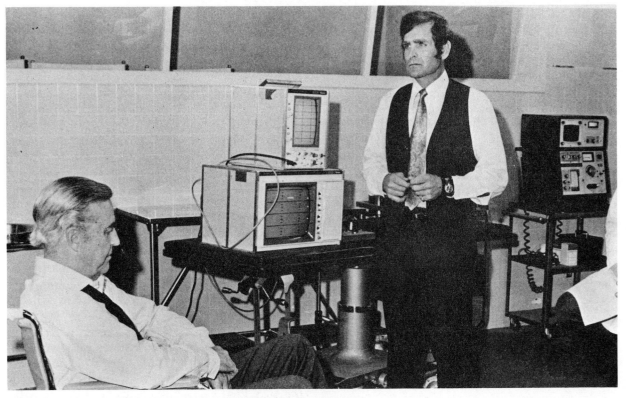

With John Bliss in THE THING WITH TWO HEADS (AIP '72)

Museum (Cinerama, 1973). He told Gail Rock of the *New York Times:* "I've done these shockers because I've got to work. I can't stand doing the same junk over and over again, and if anything has any originality to it at all, I'll do it."

He appeared several times as a guest on "Hollywood Squares," the television guessing-game show, and during one broadcast shocked everyone with an impromptu discourse against "dirty movies." Later, when he reappeared as a guest on the program, he was noticeably subdued.

In October 1973, Milland was signed to work on the Michael Klinger production of *Gold* with Peter Hunt directing, based on Wilbur Smith's novel *Goldmine.* Filmed in Johannesburg, South Africa, the cast included Roger Moore, Susannah York, and Bradford Dillman. Milland portrayed York's grandfather. An interesting sidelight of *Gold* was that three of its players were writers with published, or soon-to-be released, books: Milland was awaiting his autobiography, Miss York had written *In Search of Unicorns,* and Moore had *The James Bond Diary* to his credit.

While on location, Milland received trade-paper attention when he was misquoted as saying he was retiring, but he clarified that he meant he was

retiring from playing the debonair roles as of old.* From his new French base (he had recently sold his California home), he planned to continue plying his craft. Recently he said: "Funny thing, I never liked acting. . . . It always embarrassed me. But I like working. I've retired twice, and always had to come back because I got so darn bored. So now I pick the parts I figure I can get some enjoyment out of."

As to the richness of his past: "Sure I've lived the good life. I've been very lucky, both in my career and my private life.

"Life was just a bowl of cherries in the early days: I was a handsome kid, a bit of a playboy, with all my suits made free by the best tailors. I had a ball.

"But it all happened by luck, and I was just in there at the right place and at the right time."

Regarding his acting: "I never think of what I've done in my career. All I want is to be thought of as a tolerant and gentle person. I don't care too much whether I've made a success of things or not.

"Looking back, strangely enough, *Lost Weekend* doesn't stick out as my favorite.

"I prefer *Alias Nick Beal* in which I played the

*In Walt Disney's *Escape to Witch Mountain* (Buena Vista, 1975), he plays a multi-millionaire obsessed with the idea of employing clairvoyants to augment his power and wealth.

evil, old Nicholas Beelzebub. And *The Big Clock,* a thriller in which I played a publisher. I liked both those.

"I added my films up the other day, and they've got to be nearly 200. I've done six in the past 20 months. This [*Gold*] is the kind of part I like, a good easy role without too much hard work in it. A little character to it. I'm not after any more Oscars, hell no!

"No, I've had a good life, and I'm grateful. I married an absolute jewel—Mal and I have been together 42 years, would you believe that? Yet I could have married some bums. If you're successful in this business and young, you can't help getting a bit spoiled and a bit intolerant.

"I went through the night club routine. I've danced with Mistinguette—Christ! I've even danced with Zsa Zsa Gabor. What the hell is there left?"

With the publication of *Wide-Eyed in Babylon* (William Morrow & Company), in the fall of 1974, the erudite star skyrocketed into the front and center of multi-media attention. Unlike some other current autobiographies, Ray's book displayed both wit, clarity, perception, and a facility to see beyond his filmmaking perimeters. As *Variety* reviewed the book, "Milland has the virtue of humor. A nice irony runs through his narrative. As often happens in memoirs, youth and young manhood are featured and the later years telescoped." The reviewer did have one query, wondering "at the preoccupation of so many Hollywood familiars when they wax autobiographical to dwell unduly upon their own personal plumbing....Milland is a bladder man."

Appearing on a host of television talk shows and making the rounds of major cities to be interviewed, Milland discussed a variety of topics. Of contemporary films, he says, "I have a particular opinion about them and it's not very high, but I find some of the actors interesting. Charles Bronson, for instance."

The star admitted, "I much prefer being interviewed as an author than as an actor. I never concerned myself with Hollywood and movies. I just stayed home, and I never really got over the feeling that I was psychologically and emotionally not cut out to be an actor. I think your own emotions should be private."

Milland admits that when he sold his California home, he put his Oscar into storage, but he regards the trophy with distinct pride. "It assured me that I could now call myself an actor. When your colleagues accept you as one of their own it's a pretty wonderful thing."

As to his future, there are always acting roles for someone of Ray's caliber, even if they are quickie guest-starring cameos of which he has little regard (i.e., the NBC-TV video film *The Dead Don't Die,* January 14, 1975 *Ellery Queen,* NBC-TV, March 23, 1975, or the upcoming 12-hour ABC telefeature, *Rich Man, Poor Man,* based on the Irwin Shaw novel). But insists the veteran performer, "I have a whole new career ahead of me as a writer. The book's not about Hollywood and it's totally fiction. It's all here [pointing to his head]. Now all I've got to do is figure out where to start." He and Mrs. Milland are returning to France. for just such contemplation. ("We're gypsies again," insists the star).

As if anticipating the usual reportage query, Milland flatly admits and repeats, "The day you start to retire is the time you start to die." Thus whether it is acting, directing, or writing, Ray Milland intends to remain active on the entertainment scene for years to come.

In GOLD (AA '74)

Ray Milland

THE FLYING SCOTSMAN (WB-British, 1929) 5,502′

Director, Castleton Knight; story, Joe Grossman; screenplay, Victor Kendall, Garnett Weston.

Moore Marriott (Bob White); Pauline Johnson (Joan White); Raymond Milland (Jim Edwards); Alec Hurley (Crow); Dino Galvani (Headwaiter); Billy Shine (Barman).

THE LADY FROM THE SEA (Paramount-British, 1929) 5,540′

Director, Castleton Knight; story, Joe Grossman; screenplay, Garnett Weston, Victor Kendall.

Moore Marriott (Old Roberts); Mona Goya (Claire le Grange); Raymond Milland (Tom Roberts); Bruce Gordon (Dick Roberts); Eugenie Amami (Rose); Anita Graham (Mrs. Roberts); Wilfred Shine (Doctor).

THE PLAYTHING (Wardour, 1929) 78 M.

Director, Castleton Knight; based on the play Life Is Pretty Much the Same *by Arthur Black; screenplay, Violet Powell.*

Estelle Brody (Joyce Bennett); Heather Thatcher (Martyn Bennett); Nigel Barrie (Wallace McKinnel); Marguerite Allan (Madeleine McKinnel); John St. John (Claud); Raymond Milland (Ian).

THE INFORMER (Wardour, 1929) 83 M.

Director, Arthur Robinson; based on the play by Liam O'Flaherty; screenplay, Benn W. Levy, Rolfe E. Vanio.

Lya de Putti (Katie Fox); Lars Hansen (Gypo Nolan); Warwick Ward (Dan Gallagher); Carl Harbord (Francis McPhillip); Dennis Wyndham (Murphy); Janice Adair (Bessie); Daisy Campbell (Mrs. McPhillip); Craighall Sherry (Mulholland); Ellen Pollock (Prostitute); Johnny Butt (Publican); Raymond Milland (Bit).

WAY FOR A SAILOR (MGM, 1930) 83 M.

Director, Sam Wood; based on the novel by Albert Richard Wetjen; screenplay, Laurence Stallings, W. L. River; additional dialog, Charles MacArthur, Al Boasberg; art director, Cedric Gibbons; wardrobe, Vivian Beer; sound, Robert Shirley, Douglas Shearer; camera, Percy Hilburn; editor, Frank Sullivan.

John Gilbert (Jack Berley); Wallace Beery (Tripod McMasters); Leila Hyams (Joan Jones); Jim Tully (Ginger); Polly Moran (Mamie); Doris Lloyd (Flossy); Lena Malena, Desmond Roberts (Bits); Pat Moriarity (Mate); Sojin (Proprietor of Shanghai House); John George (Dwarf); Leo White (Sailor); Raymond Milland (Canadian Ship's Officer).

PASSION FLOWER (MGM, 1930) 79 M.

Director, William De Mille; based on the story by Kathleen Norris; adaptor-dialog, Martin Flavin; additional dialog, Laurence G. Johnson, Edith Fitzgerald; art director, Cedric Gibbons; gowns, Adrian; sound, J. K. Brock, Douglas Shearer; camera, Hal Rosson; editor, Conrad A. Nervig.

Kay Francis (Dulce Morado); Kay Johnson (Katherine Pringle Wallace); Charles Bickford (Dan Wallace); Winter Hall (Leroy Pringle); Lewis Stone (Antonio Morado); ZaSu Pitts (Mrs. Harney); Dickie Moore (Tommy); Raymond Milland (Bit).

THE BACHELOR FATHER (MGM, 1931) 90 M.

Director, Robert Z. Leonard; based on the play by Edward Childs Carpenter; screenplay, Laurence E. Johnson; sound, Karl Zint; camera, Oliver T. Marsh; editor, Harry Reynolds.

Marion Davies (Tony); C. Aubrey Smith (Sir Basil Winter-ton); Ralph Forbes (Ashley); Halliwell Hobbes (Butler); Raymond Milland (Geoffrey Trent); Guinn Williams (Dick Berney); David Torrence (Dr. MacDonald); Edgar Norton (Bolton); Doris Lloyd (Mrs. Webb); Nena Quartaro (Marie Credaro); Elizabeth Murray (Mrs. Berney); James Gordon (Mr. Creswell).

JUST A GIGOLO (MGM, 1931) 66 M.

Director, Jack Conway; based on the play Dancing Partner *by Alexander Engel, Alfred Grunwald; English adaptation, Frederic and Fanny Hatton; screenplay, Richard Schayer, Claudine West, Hans Kraly; sound, Jack Jordan; camera, Oliver T. Marsh; editor, Frank Sullivan.*

William Haines (Lord Robert Brummell); Irene Purcell (Roxana Hartley); C. Aubrey Smith (Lord George Hampton); Charlotte Granville (Lady Jane Hartley); Lilian Bond (Lady Agatha Carol); Maria Alba (Claudette, a French Wife); Albert Conti (A French Husband); Raymond Milland (Freddie); Lenore Bushman (Gwenny); Gerald Fielding (Tony); Yola d'Avril (Maid); George Davis (Waiter); Henry Armetta (Hotel Manager); Rolfe Sedan (Headwaiter); Ann Dvorak (Dance Extra).

BOUGHT (WB, 1931) 70 M.

Director, Archie Mayo; based on the novel Jackdaw's Strut *by Harriet Henry; screenplay, Charles Kenyon, Raymond Griffith; camera, Ray June; editor, George Marks.*

Constance Bennett (Stephany Dale); Ben Lyon (Nicky Amory); Richard Bennett (Dave Meyer); Dorothy Peterson (Mrs. Dale); Raymond Milland (Charles Carter); Doris Lloyd (Mrs. Barry); Maude Eburne (Mrs. Chauncy); Mae Madison (Natalie Ransome); Clara Blandick (Miss Sprigg); Arthur Stuart Hull (Carter, Sr.); Edward J. Nugent (Jimmy Graham); Paul Porcasi (Rapello).

AMBASSADOR BILL (FOX, 1931) 70 M.

Director, Sam Taylor; suggested by the story "Ambassador from the United States" by Vincent Sheean; screenplay, Guy Bolton; art director, Duncan Cramer; camera, John Mescall; editor, Harold Schuster.

Will Rogers (Bill Harper); Marguerite 'Churchill (The Queen); Greta Nissen (Countess Ilka); Tad Alexander (King Paul); Raymond Milland (Lothar); Gustav von Seyffertitz (Prince De Polikoff); Arnold Korff (The General); Ferdinand Munier (Senator Pillsbury); Edwin Maxwell (Monte); Ernest Wood (Northfield Slater); Tom Ricketts (Littleton); Theodore Lodi (French Ambassador); Herbert Bunston (British Ambassador); Russ Powell (Drunk).

BLONDE CRAZY (WB, 1931) 73 M.

Director, Roy Del Ruth; story-screenplay, Kubec Glasmon, John Bright; music director, Leo F. Forbstein; songs, E. A. Swan; Gerald Marks and Buddy Fields; Roy Turk and Fred Ahlert; Sidney Mitchell, Archie Gottler, and George W. Meyer; makeup, Perc Westmore; camera, Sid Hickox; editor, Ralph Dawson.

James Cagney (Bert Harris); Joan Blondell (Ann Roberts); Louis Calhern (Dapper Dan Barker); Noel Francis (Helen Wilson); Guy Kibbee (A. Rupert Johnson, Jr.); Raymond Milland (Joe Reynolds); Polly Walters (Peggy); Charles Lane (Four Eyes, the Desk Clerk); William Burress (Colonel Bellock); Peter Erkelenz (Dutch); Maude Eburne (Mrs. Snyder); Walter Percival (Lee); Nat Pendleton (Hank); Russell Hopton (Jerry); Dick Cramer (Cab Driver); Wade Boteler (Detective); Ray Cooke, Edward Morgan (Bellhops); Phil Sleman (Conman).

THE MAN WHO PLAYED GOD (WB, 1932) 81 M.

Producer, Jack L. Warner; director, John G. Adolfi; based on a short story by Gouverneur Morris and the play The Silent Voice by Jules Eckert Goodman; screenplay, Julian Josephson, Maude Howell; camera, James Van Trees; editor, William Holmes.

George Arliss (Montgomery Royle); Violet Heming (Mildred Miller); Ivan Simpson (Battle); Louise Closser Hale (Florence Royle); Bette Davis (Grace Blair); Andre Luguet (The King); Donald Cook (Harold Van Adam); Charles Evans (The Doctor); Oscar Apfel (The Lip Reader); Paul Porcasi (The Concert Manager); Raymond Milland (Eddie); Dorothy LeBaire (Jenny); William Janney (Boy); Grace Durkin (Girl); Russell Hopton (Reporter); Murray Kinnell (The King's Aide); Harry Stubbs (Chittendon); Hedda Hopper (Alice Chittendon); Wade Boteler (Detective); Alexander Ikonikoff, Michael Visaroff (Russian Officers); Fred Howard (Man).

POLLY OF THE CIRCUS (MGM, 1932) 72 M.

Director, Alfred Santell; based on the play by Margaret Mayo; screenplay, Carey Wilson; dialog, Laurence Johnson; sound, J. K. Brock; camera, George Barnes; editor, George Hively.

Marion Davies (Mme. Polly); Clark Gable (Reverend John Hartley); C. Aubrey Smith (Bishop James Northcott); Raymond Hatton (Downey); David Landau (Beef); Ruth Selwyn (Mitzi); Maude Eburne (Mrs. Jennings); Little Billy (Half-Pint); Clark Marshall (Don); Lillian Elliott (Mrs. McNamara); Raymond Milland(e) (Rich Young Man).

PAYMENT DEFERRED (MGM, 1932) 75 M.

Director, Lothar Mendes; based on the play by Jeffrey Dell; screenplay, Ernest Vajda, Claudine West; camera, M. B. Gerstad; editor, Frank Sullivan.

Charles Laughton (William Marble); Maureen O'Sullivan (Winnie Marble); Dorothy Peterson (Annie Marble); Verree Teasdale (Mme. Collins); Raymond Milland (James Medland); Billy Bevan (Hammond); Halliwell Hobbs (Prospective Tenant); William Stack (A Doctor).

ORDERS IS ORDERS (Ideal, 1933) 88 M.

Producer, Michael Balcon; director, Walter Forde; based on the play by Ian Hay, Anthony Armstrong; screenplay, Leslie Arliss, Sidney Gilliat, James Gleason.

James Gleason (Ed Waggenmeyer); Charlotte Greenwood (Wanda); Cyril Maude (Col. Bellamy); Cedric Hardwicke (Brigadier); Ian Hunter (Captain Harper); Raymond Milland (Dashwood); Jane Carr (Patricia Bellamy); Donald Calthrop (Pavey); Eliot Makeham (Private Slee); Hay Plumb (Private Goffin); Wally Patch (R.S.M.); Finlay Currie (Dave); Edwin Lawrence (Quartermaster); Jane Cornell (Starlet).

THIS IS THE LIFE (British Lion, 1933) 78 M.

Producer, Herbert Smith; director, Albert de Courville; story, Clifford Grey; screenplay, Grey, R. P. Weston, Bert Lee.

Gordon Harker (Albert Tuttle); Binnie Hale (Sarah Tuttle); Betty Astell (Edna Wynne); Raymond Milland (Bob Travers); Jack Barty (Bert Scroggins); Charles Heslop (Mr. Diggs); Percy Parsons (Lefty Finn); Ben Welden (Two Gun Mullins); Norma Whalley (Miss Vavasour); Julian Royce (Bronson); Percival Mackey and His Band (Themselves).

BOLERO (PAR, 1934) 71 M.

Director, Wesley Ruggles°; story, Carey Wilson, Kubec Glasmon, based on an idea by Ruth Ridenour; screenplay, Horace Jackson; music, Ralph Rainger; composition "Bolero" by Maurice Ravel; sound, Earl Hayman; camera, Leo Tover; editor, Hugh Bennett.

George Raft (Raoul DeBaere); Carole Lombard (Helen Hathaway); Sally Rand (Arnette); Frances Drake (Leona); William Frawley (Mike DeBaere); Raymond Milland (Lord Coray); Gloria Shea (Lucy); Gertrude Michael (Lady D'Argon); Del Henderson (Theatre Manager); Frank G. Dunn (Hotel Manager); Martha Bamattre (Belgian Landlady); Paul Panzer (Bailiff); Adolph Milar (German Beer Garden Manager); Annie Shaw (Young Matron); Phillips Smalley (Leona's Angel); John Irwin (Porter); Gregory Golubeff (Orchestra Leader).

WE'RE NOT DRESSING (PAR, 1934) 74 M.

Associate producer, Benjamin Glazer; director, Norman Taurog; based on the play The Admirable Crichton by Sir James Barrie; adaptor, Glazer; screenplay, Horace Jackson, Francis Martin, George Marion, Jr.; songs, Harry Revel and Mack Gordon; art directors, Hans Dreier, Ernst Fegte; camera, Charles Lang; editor, Stuart Heisler.

Bing Crosby (Stephen Jones); Carole Lombard (Doris Worthington); George Burns (George); Gracie Allen (Gracie); Ethel Merman (Edith); Leon Errol (Hubert); Jay Henry (Prince Alexander Stofani); Raymond Milland (Prince Michael Stofani); John Irwin (Old Sailor); Charles Morris (Captain); Ben F. Hendricks, Ted Oliver (Ship's Officers); Ernie Adams (Sailor); Stanley Blystone (Doris's Officer).

MANY HAPPY RETURNS (PAR, 1934) 66 M.

Director, Norman McLeod; story, Lady Mary Cameron; screenplay, J. P. McEvoy, Claude Binyon, Keene Thompson, Ray Harris; camera, Henry Sharpe; editor, Richard Currier.

Guy Lombardo (Himself); Gracie Allen (Gracie); George Burns (George); Joan Marsh (Florence Allen); George Barbier (Horatio Allen); Raymond Milland (Ted Mabert); William Demarest (Brinker); Johnny Arthur (Davies); Stanley Fields (Joe); John Kelly (Mike); Egon Brecher (Dr. Otto von Strudel); Franklin Pangborn (Horatio's Secretary); Morgan Wallace (Nathan Silas); Kenneth Thomson (Motion Picture Director); Yolanda Veloz, Frank Veloz (Dance Team); Larry Adler (Harmonica Player); John Taylor, Clark Rutledge (Tap Dancers); Kent Taylor (Actor).

CHARLIE-CHAN IN LONDON (FOX, 1934) 79 M.

Producer, John Stone; director, Eugene Forde; screenplay, Philip MacDonald; music director, Samuel Kaylin; gowns, Royer; sets, Duncan Cramer; camera, L. W. O'Connell.

Warner Oland (Charlie Chan); Drue Leyton (Pamela Gray); Douglas Walton (Paul Gray); Alan Mowbray (Geoffrey Richmond); Mona Barrie (Lady Mary Bristol); Raymond Milland (Neil Howard); George Barraud (Major Jardine); Paul England (Bunny Fothergill); Madge Bellamy (Becky Fothergill); Walter Johnson (Jerry Garton); Murray Kinnell (Phillips); E. E. Clive (Detective Sergeant Thacker); Elsa Buchanan (Alice Perkins); David Torrence (Sir Lionel Bashford, the Home Secretary); Claude King (R.A.F. Commandant); Reginald Sheffield (Flight Commander King); Perry Ivins (Kemp); John Rogers (Lake); Helena Grant (Miss Johnson, the Secretary); Montague Shaw (Doctor); Phyllis Cochlan (Nurse); Margaret Mann (Housemaid); Carli Taylor, Doris Stone (Guests); Arthur Clayton (Warden); Ann Doran (Stand-In).

MENACE (PAR, 1934) 58 M.

Director, Ralph Murphy; story, Philip MacDonald; screenplay, Anthony Veiller, Chandler Sprague; camera, Benjamin Reynold.

Gertrude Michael (Helen Chalmers); Paul Cavanagh (Colonel Leonard Crecy); Henrietta Crosman (Sybil Thornton); John Lodge (Ronald Cavendish); Raymond Milland (Freddie Bastion); Berton Churchill (Norman Bellamy); Halliwell Hobbes (Skinner); Robert Allen (Andrew Forsythe); Forrester Harvey (Wilcox); Montagu Love (Police Inspector); Arletta Duncan (Gloria Chalmers); Gwenllian Gill (Alison Bastion); Doris Llewellyn (Cynthia Bastion); Desmond Roberts (Underwood); Arthur Clayton (Police Officer); Rita Carlyle (English Landlady); A. S. Byron (English Police Sergeant).

°Final dance scene reshot by director Mitchell Leisen.

ONE HOUR LATE (PAR, 1934) 75 M.

Producer, Albert Lewis; director, Ralph Murphy; story, Libbie Block; screenplay, Kathryn Scola, Paul Gerard Smith; songs, Sam Coslow, Lewis Gensler, and Leo Robin; camera, Ben Reynolds.

Joe Morrison (Eddie Blake); Helen Twelvetrees (Bessie Dunn); Conrad Nagel (Stephen Barclay); Arline Judge (Hazel); Ray Walker (Cliff Miller); Edward Craven (Maxie); Toby Wing (Maizie); Gail Patrick (Mrs. Eileen Barclay); Charles Sellon (Simpson); Edward Clark (Mr. Meller); Raymond Milland (Tony St. John); George E. Stone (Benny); Bradley Page (Jim); Sidney Miller (Orrville); Gladys Hulette (Gertrude); Jed Prouty (Mr. Finch); Billy Bletcher (Smith); Betty Farrington (Miss Jones); Arthur Hoyt (Barlow); Matty Fain (The Crook); Hallen Hill (Sick Woman); Diana Lewis (Her Daughter); Frank Mayo (Kearney); Eddie Phillips (Elevator Starter); Phil Tead (Wally); James P. Burtis (Art); Maxine Elliot Hicks (Elsie Kelsey); Frank Losee, Jr., Alfred Delcambre (Friends); Jack Norton (Manager); Sam Ash (Phil Romaine); William Norton Bailey (Clayton); Jack Mulhall (Whittaker); William H. Strauss (Man Who Is Robbed); Carol Holloway (Nurse); George Lloyd (Collier); Monte Vandegrift, Lee Shumway (Detectives); Frank Rice (Engineer); Robert Kent (Soda Clerk); Harry Depp (Fiddle Player); Billy Dooley (Attendant in Radio Station); Rhea Mitchell (Stage Mother); Shirley Jeanne Rickert (Child); Charles Morris (Man outside Radio Room); William Jeffrey (Master of Ceremonies); Francis Sayles, Duke York (Mixers); Genevieve Phillips (Information Girls); Buck Mack (Property Man); Jack Raymond (Musician); Robert Littlefield (Orchestra Leader); Ann Sheridan (Bit).

THE GILDED LILY (PAR, 1935) 80 M.

Producer, Albert Lewis; director, Wesley Ruggles; story, Melville Baker, Jack Kirkland; screenplay, Claude Binyon; song, Sam Coslow and Arthur Johnston; camera, Victor Milner; editor, Otho Lovering.

Claudette Colbert (Lillian David); Fred MacMurray (Peter Dawes); Raymond Milland [Charles Gray (Granville)]; C. Aubrey Smith (Lloyd Granville); Eddie Craven (Eddie); Luis Alberni (Nate); Donald Meek (Hankerson); Michelette Burani (Lily's Maid); Claude King (Boat Captain); Charles Irwin (Oscar); Ferdinand Munier (Otto Bushe); Rita Carlyle (Proprietor's Wife); Forrester Harvey (Proprietor of English Inn); Edward Gargan, James T. Quinn (Guards); Leonid Kinskey (Vocal Teacher); Jimmie Aubrey (Purser); Robert Dudley (Store Clerk); Phil Tead (Rollercoaster Attendant); Eddie Borden (Photographer); Charles Wilson (Pete's Editor); Walter Shumway (Assistant Editor); Reginald Barlow (Managing Editor); Rollo Lloyd (City Editor); Cameron Smith (Assistant City Editor); Esther Muir (Divorcee); Patsy O'Bryne, Dixie Loftin, Monte Vandergrift, Mark Strong (Neighbors); Hayden Stevenson, Perry Ivins, Cherry Campbell, Samuel E. Hines (Reporters-Cameramen at New York Apartment); Eddie Dunn (Reporter); Grace Bradley (Daisy); Pat Somerset (Man in London Club); Clive Morgan (Englishman in London Cafe); Jerry Fletcher (Barney); Ambrose Barker, David Thursby (English Reporters); Stanley Mann (Steward with Telegram); Mel Ruick (English Band Leader); Neil Fitzgerald (English Waiter); Tom Dugan (The Bum); Bob Thom (Customs Inspector); Warren Hymer (Taxi Driver); George Humbert (Pop Corn Man); George Billings (Guard's Son); Jerry Mandy (Waiter at Nate's Cafe); William Begg, Dick French, Ronald Rondell, Rebecca Wassem, Adele Corliss, Gale Ronn (Patrons at Nate's Cafe); Albert Pollet, Cyril Ring (Headwaiters); Rudy Cameron, Jack Egan, Jack Norton (Photographers); Jay Eaton, Jay Belasco, Major Francis (Cafe Patrons in London).

FOUR HOURS TO KILL (PAR, 1935) 74 M.

Producer, Arthur Hornblow, Jr.; director, Mitchell Leisen; based on the play Small Miracle by Norman Krasna; screenplay, Krasna; camera, Theodor Sparkuhl; editor, John D. Harrison.

Richard Barthelmess (Tony); Joe Morrison (Eddie); Helen

Mack (Helen); Gertrude Michael (Sylvia); Dorothy Tree (Mae Danish); Roscoe Karns (Johnson); Ray Milland (Carl); Charles C. Wilson (Taft); Henry Travers (Mac Mason); Paul Harvey (Captain Seavers); Noel Madison (Anderson); Christian Rub [Pa (Herman)]; Greta Meyer (Ma); Lois Kent (Little Girl); Bruce Mitchell (Healy); Olive Tell (Mrs. Madison); John Huettner (Stanley); Alfred Delcambre (Donald); Sam Ash (Harris); Frank Losee, Jr. (Assistant House Manager); Robert Kent (George Nelson); Paul Gerrits (Phone Repairman); Hugh Enfield (Craig Reynolds) (Frank); John Howard (Assistant Repairman); Gertrude Astor (Little Girl's Mother).

THE GLASS KEY (PAR, 1935) 80 M.

Producer, E. Lloyd Sheldon; director, Frank Tuttle; based on the novel by Dashiell Hammett; screenplay, Kathryn Scola, Kubec Glasmon, Harry Ruskin; camera, Henry Sharp; editor, Hugh Bennett.

George Raft (Ed Beaumont); Edward Arnold (Paul Madvig); Claire Dodd (Janet Henry); Rosalind Keith (Opal Madvig); Charles Richman (Senator Henry); Robert Gleckler (Shad O'Rory); Guinn Williams (Jeff); Ray Milland (Taylor Henry); Tammany Young (Clarkie); Harry Tyler (Henry Sloss); Charles C. Wilson (Farr); Emma Dunn ("Mom"); Matt McHugh (Puggy); Patrick Moriarity (Mulrooney); Mack Gray (Duke); Frank Marlowe (Walter Ivans); Herbert Evans (Senator's Butler); George H. Reed (Serving Man); Percy Morris (Bartender); Irving Bacon (Waiter); Ann Sheridan (Nurse); Henry Roquemore (Hinkle); Frank O'Connor (McLaughlin); Michael Mark (Swartz); Del Cambre (Reporter); Veda Buckland (Landlady); George Ernest (Boy).

ALIAS MARY DOW (UNIV, 1935) 65 M.

Producer, Lou Ostrow; director, Kurt Neumann; story, William Johnston, Forrest Halsey; screenplay, Gladys Unger, Rose Franken; camera, Joseph Valentine.

Sally Eilers (Sally); Ray Milland (Peter Marshall); Henry O'Neill (Mr. Dow); Chick Chandler (Jimmy); Katharine Alexander (Mrs. Dow); Clarence Muse (Rufe); Lola Lane (Minna); Maude Turner Gordon (Aunt Helena); Addison Richards (Martin); Corbet Morris (Valet); Phyllis Crane (Maid); Nam Didot (Devil Waiter); Harry Lipman (Angel Waiter); Alphonse Martell (Hotel Clerk); Sammy Blum (Tourist); Nell Craig (Tourist's Wife); Arthur Stuart Hull, Leah Winslow (Elderly Couple); Alan Bridge, Monte Montague (Ditch Diggers); Frank Adams, Earl Eby, Hal Cook, Frank Holliday, William Newell (Reporters); Pat Gleason (Boy Friend); Eddy Chandler (Bouncer); Ray Cooke (Ticket Taker); Andy Rice, Jr. (Master of Ceremonies); John Carradine (Griffe); Stanley Andrews, Emmett Vogan (Detectives); Anne Darling, Bill Roberts, Marina Passerowa, Mary Wallace, Bernadene Hayes, Robert Dalton, Vera Lewis, Jane Meredith (Party Guests); Alice Ardell (Maid); Charles Fallon (Cab Driver); Gene Perry (Gendarme); Major Farrell (Porter); Lois Verner (Fat Girl); Lillian Elliott (Matron); Jane Barnes (Councilor); Arnold Korff (Doctor); Lillian West, Frances Morris, Lillian Irene, Mary MacLaren, Marion Lessing, Alena Carroll, Grace Cunard, Marie Quillan, Winifred Drew (Nurses).

NEXT TIME WE LOVE (UNIV, 1936) 87 M.

Producer, Paul Kohner; director, Edward H. Griffith; based on the story "Say Goodbye Again" and the novel Next Time We Live by Ursula Parrott; screenplay, Melville Baker; camera, Joseph Valentine; editor, Ted Kent.

Margaret Sullavan (Cicely Tyler); James Stewart (Christopher Tyler); Ray Milland (Tommy Abbott); Grant Mitchell (Michael Jennings); Anna Demetrio (Madame Donato); Robert McWade (Frank Carteret); Ronnie Cosbey (Kit Tyler); Florence Roberts (Mrs. Talbot); Christian Rub (Otto); Charles Fallon (Professor Dindet); Nat Carr (Assistant Stage Manager); Gottlieb Huber (Porter); Harry C. Bradley (Desk Clerk); Jack Daley, Broderick O'Farrell (Conductors); Buddy Williams (Porter); Dutch Hendrian, Philip Morris, Al Hill, Jack Cheatham (Taxi Drivers); Hattie McDaniel (Hanna); Emmett Vogan (Bartender); Harry Bowen, Jack Mower, George Davis, Ludwig Lowey (Waiters); Donna Mae Roberts (Cigarette Girl); Albert Conti (Charles); Tyler Brooke (Author); Leonid Kinskey (Designer); Eddie Phillips (Ticket Taker); John Dilson (Stage Manager); Nat Carr (Assistant); Clark Williams (Leading Man); John King (Juvenile); Nan Grey (Ingenue); Tom Manning, King Baggott (Character Men); Clive Morgan (Leading Man); Daisy Bufford (Maid); Alfred P. James (Aquarium Attendant); Billy Gratton (Kit at Age Three); Jacqueline Smylle (Susan); Paddy O'Flynn (Reporter); Jane Keckley (Nurse); Teru Shimada (Steward); Otto Fries (Conductor); Julie Carter (Sob Sister); Arthur Aylesworth (Secretary); Don Roberts (City Editor); Harry Tracy (Valet); Miki Morita (Dr. Ito); Selmer Jackson (Dr. Campbell).

THE RETURN OF SOPHIE LANG (PAR, 1936) 65 M.

Producer, A. M. Botsford; director, George Archainbaud; story, Fredrick Irving Anderson; screenplay, Brian Marlow, Paterson McNutt; camera, George Clemens.

Gertrude Michael (Sophie Lang); Sir Guy Standing (Max Bernard); Ray Milland (Jimmy Lawson); Elizabeth Patterson (Araminta Sedley); Colin Tapley (Purser); Paul Harvey (Inspector Parr); Garry Owen (Nosey Schwartz); Don Rowan (Buttons McDermott); Purnell Pratt (Mr. Chadwick); Ted Oliver, James Blaine (Detectives); Charles Coleman (Dining Steward); David Thursby (Deck Steward); Keith Daniels, Don Roberts, Jack Chapin, Jay Owens, Ralph McCullough, Eddie Fetherston, Arthur Rowland, Frank MacCready (Reporters); Jack Raymond (Cameraman); Anderson Lawler (Jennings); Forrester Harvey (Deck Steward); Guy Usher (Dr. Dutton); Herbert Evans (Butler); Monte Vandergrift, Budd Fine, Hal Price (Cops); Paddy O'Flynn (Man); Oscar Rudolph (Bellboy); Edward Earle (Hotel Clerk); Arthur S. (Pop) Byron (Porter); Tom Kennedy (Cop on Switchboard); Joseph R. Tozer (Ship's Captain); Frank Benson (Taxi Driver); Harry Allen (Caretaker at Graveyard); James Aubrey (Steward); Lee Phelps (Police Announcer); Harry Owen (McOwen).

THE BIG BROADCAST OF 1937 (PAR, 1936) 100 M.

Producer, Lewis Gensler; director, Mitchell Leisen; screenplay, Edwin Gelsey, Arthur Kober, Barry Travers, Walter deLeon, Francis Martin; art directors, Hans Dreier, Robert Usher; music, Boris Morros; songs, Leo Robin and Ralph Rainger; camera, Theodor Sparkuhl; editor, Stuart Heisler.

Jack Benny (Jack Carson); George Burns and Gracie Allen (Mr. and Mrs. Platt); Bob Burns (Bob Black); Martha Raye (Patsy); Shirley Ross (Gwen Holmes); Ray Milland (Bob Miller); Frank Forest (Frank Rossman); Benny Field (Himself); Sam Hearn (Schlepperman); Stan Kavanaugh (Kavvy); Benny Goodman and His Orchestra, Leopold Stokowski and His Symphony Orchestra (Themselves); Virginia Weidler (Flower Girl); David Holt, Billy Lee (Train Bearers); Louis Da Pron, Eleanore Whitney, Larry Adler (Specialties); Irving Bacon (Property Man); Ernest Cossart (The Uncle); Billie Bellport (Mrs. Peters); Billy Bletcher (Property Man); Harry Depp (Assistant Stage Manager); Pat West (Stage Manager); Cupid Ainsworth (Penelope); Don Hulbert (Page Boy); Frank Hagney (Cowboy); Frank Jenks (Trombone Player); Avril Cameron (Woman Singer); Hal Greene (Elevator Boy); Nora Cecil (Home Economics Woman); Harrison Greene (Violinsky); Leonid Kinskey (Russian); John Marlowe (Anemic Character); Gino Corrado (Violinist); Rosemary Glosz (Fat Lady); Henry Arthur (Tap Dancer); Ann Evers (Information Clerk); Alex Schonberg (Scientist); Maurice Cass (Announcer); Edward J. LeSaint (Minister); Gail Sheridan, Irene Bennett, Priscilla Lawson (Bridesmaids); Jack Mulhall (Clerk); Ted Thompson (Hotel Clerk); Ellen Drew (Telephone Girl/Member of Bridal Party); Florence Dudley (Telephone Operator); Murray Alper (Taxi Driver); Paddy O'Flynn (Attendant); Billy Arnold (Jones); Robert Cochrane (Newsboy); Bob Littlefield (Starter); Eddie Dunn (Clerk); Nell Craig, Jeanne Hart, Peggy Leon, John Tyrrell, Louis Natheaux, Matt McHugh, Art Rowlands

(Bits); Paul Gustin (Headwaiter); Jeanne Perkins, Nick Lukats, William Hopper, Marten Lamont, John Morley (Members of Bridal Party).

THE JUNGLE PRINCESS (PAR, 1936) 84 M.

Producer, E. Lloyd Sheldon; director, William Thiele; story, Max Marcin; screenplay, Cyril Hume, Gerald Geraghty, Gouverneur Morris; music director, Boris Morros, song, Frederick Hollander and Leo Robin; camera, Harry Fischbeck; editor, Ellsworth Hoagland.

Dorothy Lamour (Ulah); Ray Milland (Christopher Powell); Akim Tamiroff (Karen Neg); Lynne Overman (Frank); Molly Lamont (Ava); Ray Mala (Melan); Hugh Buckler (Colonel Nelville Lane); Sally Martin (Ulah as a Child); Roberta Law (Lin); Limau (The Tiger); Bogo (The Chimpanzee); Erville Alderson (Priest); Bernard Siegel (Ulah's Grandfather); Richard Terry (Malay Hunter); Nick Shaid (Headman of Tribe); Dan Crimmins (Head Tribesman); Bernard Siegel, John George, Shogwan Singh, Eddie Sturgis, James F. Spencer, Al Kikume, Kim Maki, Mickey Phillips, Inez Gomez, Mural Sharada, Emilia Diaz, Ray Roubert (Natives).

THREE SMART GIRLS (UNIV, 1936) 86 M.

Executive producer, Charles R. Rogers; associate producer, Joseph Pasternak; director, Henry Koster; story, Adele Comandini; screenplay, Comandini, Austin Parker; songs, Gus Kahn, Bronislau Kaper, and Walter Jurmann; music director, Charles Previn; camera, Joseph Valentine; editor, Ted J. Kent.

Deanna Durbin (Penny Craig); Binnie Barnes (Donna Lyons); Alice Brady (Mrs. Lyons); Ray Milland (Lord Michael Stuart); Charles Winninger (Judson Craig); Mischa Auer (Count Arisztid); Nan Grey (Joan Craig); Barbara Read (Kay Craig); Ernest Cossart (Binns); Hobart Cavanaugh (Wilbur Lamb); John King (Bill Evans); Lucile Watson (Trudel); Nella Walker (Dorothy Craig); Dennis O'Keefe (Club Extra); Gladden James (Waiter); Wade Boteler (Sergeant); Lane Chandler (Cop); Charles Coleman (Butler); Franklin Pangborn (Jeweler); Albert Conti (Count's Friend).

WINGS OVER HONOLULU (UNIV, 1937) 78 M.

Executive producer, Charles R. Rogers; associate producer, E. M. Asher; director, H. C. Potter; story, Mildred Cram; screenplay, Isabel Dawn, Boyce DeGaw; camera, Joseph Valentine; editor, Maurice Wright.

Wendy Barrie (Lauralee Curtis); Ray Milland (Lieutenant Stony Gilchrist); Kent Taylor (Greg Chandler); William Gargan (Lieutenant Jack Furness); Polly Rowles (Rosalind Furness); Samuel S. Hinds (Admiral Furness); Mary Philips (Hattie Penletter); Margaret McWade (Nellie Curtis); Clara Blandick (Evie Curtis); Louise Beavers (Mammie); Jonathan Hale (Judge Advocate); Granville Bates (Grocery Clerk); Robert Gleckler (Lieutenant Commander of Squadron); Joyce Compton (Caroline, the Blonde on Telephone); Charles Irwin (Al's Friend, the Drunk); Maude Turner Gordon (Mrs. MacEwen); Maynard Holmes (Tommy); Ivan Miller (Officer); Ruth Robinson (Mrs. MacEwen's Friend); Franklyn Ardell (Al, the Drunk); Milburn Stone (Telephone Operator); Frank Melton (Budge); Mildred Gover (Cook); George H. Reed (Fauntleroy); Jack Mulhall (Officer); Max Wagner, Frank Marlowe, Sherry Hall, Jack Egan, Arthur Singley (Marines); Virginia Rogan (Hawaiian Dancer); Billy Wayne (Orderly); Eddie Fetherston (Radio Enlisted Man); Michael Loring, Robert Andersen (Naval Officers); Phillip Hurlic (Robert Lee); Mabelle Palmer (Woman in Beauty Shop); Louise Latimer (Woman); Grace Cunard (Mrs. Strange); Isabel La Mal (Woman Shopper); Edith Penn (Woman at Car); Al Kikume (Hawaiian); Martin Turner (Porter); Ray Turner (Waiter); George Offerman, Jr., John Bruce, Buddy Messinger (Boys); Rudolph Chavers (Pickaninny); Bernard Kikume (Hawaiian Policeman); Loretta Sayers (Woman with Baby); Lucia Lusca (Woman Washing Dishes); Hazel Langton (Woman in Beauty Shop).

EASY LIVING (PAR, 1937) 88 M.

Producer, Arthur Hornblow, Jr.; director, Mitchell Leisen; based on an unpublished story by Vera Caspary; screenplay, Preston Sturges; art directors, Hans Dreier, Ernst Fegte; costumes, Travis Banton; music, Boris Morros; camera, Ted Tetzlaff; editor, Doane Harrison.

Jean Arthur (Mary Smith); Edward Arnold (J. B. Ball); Ray Milland (John Ball, Jr.); Luis Alberni (Mr. Louis Louis); Mary Nash (Mrs. Ball); Franklin Pangborn (Van Buren); Barlowe Borland (Mr. Gurney); William Demarest (Wallace Whistling); Andrew Tombes (E. F. Hulgar); Esther Dale (Lillian); Harlan Briggs (Office Manager); William B. Davidson (Mr. Hyde); Nora Cecil (Miss Swerf); Robert Greig (Butler); Vernon Dent, Edwin Stanley, Richard Barbee (Partners); Marsha Hunt, Lee Bowman, Elisa Connor, Ethel Clayton, Gloria Williams, Nick Lukats (Bits); Bennie Bartlett (Newsboy); Jack Raymond, Adia Kuznetzoff (Bums); Florence Dudley (Cashier); Bob Murphy (Automat Detective); Bernard Suss (Man in Automat); Rex Moore (Elevator Boy); John Marshall (Osric); Dora Clement (Saleslady); Hayden Stevenson (Chauffeur); Arthur Hoyt, Hal Dawson (Jewelers); Hector V. Sarno (Armenian Rug Salesman); Gertrude Astor (Saleswoman); Lee Phelps (Hotel Detective); Hal Greene (Bellhop); Jesse Graves (Porter); Frances Morris (Assistant Secretary); Sidney Bracy (Chauffeur); Lois Clinton (Brunette); Laura Treadwell (Wife); Virginia Dabney (Blonde); John Dilson (Nervous Man); Forbes Murray (Husband); John Picorri (Oinest); Kathleen Hope Lewis, Helen Huntington (Stenographers); Harold Entwistle (Elevator Man); Dennis O'Keefe (Office Manager); Robert Homans (Private Guard); Stanley Andrews (Captain); Leonid Snegoff (Chef); Wilson Benge (Butler); Harry Worth (Hindu); George Cowl (Bank President); Kate Price (Laundress); Lu Miller, Amelia Falleur (Housemaids); Don Brodie (Auto Salesman); Florence Wix (Woman in Hat Shop); Olaf Hytten, Frances Sayles (Housemen); William Wagner (Valet).

EBB TIDE (PAR, 1937) C—94 M.

Producer, Lucien Hubbard; director, James Hogan; based on the story by Robert Louis Stevenson; adaptor, Lloyd Osbourne; screenplay, Bertram Milhauser, costumes, Edith Head; special effects, Gordon Jennings; camera, Ray Rennahan, Leo Tover; editor, LeRoy Stone.

Oscar Homolka (Captain Therbecke); Frances Farmer (Faith Wishart); Ray Milland (Robert Herrick); Lloyd Nolan (Attwater); Barry Fitzgerald (Huish); Charles Judels (Port Doctor); David Torrence (Tapena Tom); Lina Basquette (Attwater's Servant); Harry Field (Tahiera); George Piltz (Sally Day); Manuella Kalili (Fiji Islander); Jim Spencer (Cook); Arthur Allen, Joe Molina (Native Sailors); Sonny Chorre (Attwater's Guard); David Hope (Sailor); Leonard Sues (Native Boy); Inez Palange (Native Woman); Gloria Williams, Nancy Chaplin (Women); Jacques Vanaire (Assistant Port Doctor); Antrim Short, Don Wayson, Bob Haines (Men); Bernard Siegal (Waiter); Al Kikume (Native Policeman); Stella Francis (Woman Tourist); Olaf Hytten (English Tourist); Eugene Beday (Port Officer); Jack George (Band Leader); Jack Clark, Elizabeth Hartman (Tourists).

BULLDOG DRUMMOND ESCAPES (PAR, 1937) 65 M.

Director, James Hogan; based on the play Bulldog Drummond Again *by H. C. (Sapper) McNeile, Gerard Fairlie; screenplay, Edward T. Lowe; camera, Victor Milner; editor, William Shea.*

Ray Milland (Captain Hugh "Bulldog" Drummond); Sir Guy Standing (Inspector Nielson); Heather Angel (Phyllis Clavering); Reginald Denny (Algy Longworth); Porter Hall (Norman Merridew); Fay Holden (Natalie Selden); E. E. Clive (Tenny); Walter Kingsford (Professor Stanton); Patrick Kelly (Stiles, the Butler); Charles McNaughton (Constable Higgins); Clyde Cook (Alf, the Constable); Frank Elliott (Bailey); David Clyde (Gower); Doris Lloyd (Nurse); Colin Tapley (Dixon); Zeffie Tilbury (Drunk); Barry Macollum (Blodgson); Ernie Stanton, Pat Somerset (Reporters); Robert Adair (Wool-

sey); Henry Mowbray (Bobby); John Power (Custom Officer); Bobbie Hale, Gunnis Davis (Attendants).

WISE GIRL (RKO, 1937) 70 M.

Producer, Edward Kaufman; director, Leigh Jason; story, Allan Scott, Charles Norman; screenplay, Scott; camera, Peverell Marley; editor, Jack Hively.

Miriam Hopkins (Susan Fletcher); Ray Milland (John O'Halloran); Walter Abel (Karl); Henry Stephenson (Mr. Fletcher); Alec Craig (Dermont O'Neil); Guinn Williams (Mike); Betty Philson (Joan); Marianna Strelby (Katie); Margaret Dumont (Mrs. Bell-Rivington); Jean de Briac (George); Ivan Lebedeff (Prince Michael); Rafael Storm (Prince Ivan); Gregory Gaye (Prince Leopold); Richard Lane, Tom Kennedy (Detectives); James Finlayson (Jailer).

HER JUNGLE LOVE (PAR, 1938) C—81 M.

Producer, George M. Arthur; director, George Archainbaud; story, Gerald Geraghty, Kurt Siodmak; screenplay, Joseph Moncure March, Lillie Hayward, Eddie Welch; costumes, Edith Head; songs, Frederick Hollander and Ralph Freed, Leo Robin and Ralph Rainger; camera, Ray Rennahan; editor, Hugh Bennett.

Dorothy Lamour (Tura); Ray Milland (Bob Mitchell); Lynne Overman (Jimmy Wallace); J. Carrol Naish (Kuasa); Virginia Vale (Eleanor Martin); Jonathan Hale (J. C. Martin); Archie Twitchell (Roy Atkins); Edward Earle (Captain Avery); Jiggs (Gaga, the Chimpanzee); Meewa (The Lion Cub); Sonny Chorre, Tony Urchel (Guards); Richard Denning (Pilot); Phillip Warren (Co-Pilot); Bill Caldwell (Bit).

TROPIC HOLIDAY (PAR, 1938) 75 M.

Producer, Arthur Hornblow, Jr.; director, Theodore Reed; story, Don Hartman, Frank Butler; screenplay, Hartman, Butler, John C. Moffett, Duke Atteberry; songs, Ned Washington and Augustin Lara, Leo Robin and Ralph Rainger; camera, Ted Tetzlaff; editor, Archie Marshek.

Bob Burns (Breck Jones); Dorothy Lamour (Manuela); Ray Milland (Ken Warren); Martha Raye (Midge Miller); Binne Barnes (Marilyn Joyce); Tito Guizar (Ramon); Elvira Rios (Rosa); Roberto Soto (Roberto); Michael Visaroff (Felipe); Bobby Moya (Pepito); Fortunio Bonanova (Barrera); Pepito (Chico); Matt McHugh (Joe); Ofelia Ascencio, Sara Ascencio, Emmy Del Rio (Ascencio del Rio Trio); Chris Pin Martin (Pancho); Frank Puglia (Co-Pilot); Jesus Topete (Pedro); Jesus Castillon, Mario Santos, Jose Mendoza (Ensenada Singers); Carlos Villarias (Commandante); Anna Demetrio (Shopkeeper); Blanca Vischer (French Maid); Paul Lopez (Young Man); Pedro Regas, Charles Stevens (Peons); Robert O'Conor (Enrique, the Big Peon); Victor Romito, Manuel Valencia (Henchmen); Duncan Renaldo (Young Blood); Eduardo, Castro, Maria and Teresa Olguin (Bullfighters).

MEN WITH WINGS (PAR, 1938) C—105 M.

Producer-director, William A. Wellman; screenplay, Robert Carson; aerial camera, Charles Marshall; camera, W. Howard Greene; editor, Tommy Scott.

Fred MacMurray (Pat Falconer); Ray Milland (Scott Barnes); Louise Campbell (Peggy Ranson); Andy Devine (Joe Gibbs); Lynne Overman (Hank Rinebow); Walter Abel (Nick Ranson); Porter Hall (Hiram F. Jenkins); Kitty Kelly (Martha Ranson); Virginia Weidler (Peggy Ranson at Age Eight); Donald O'Connor (Pat Falconer at Age Ten); Billy Cook (Scott Barnes at Age Ten); James Burke (J. A. Nolan); Willard Robertson (Colonel Hadley); Dennis Morgan (Galton); Charles Trowbridge (Alcott); Jonathan Hale (Long); Juanita Quigley (Patricia Falconer at Age Six); Joan Leslie (Patricia Falconer at Age Eleven); Mary Brodel (Patricia Falconer at Age Seventeen); Archie Twitchell (Nelson); Dorothy Tennant (Mrs. Hill); Helen Dickson, Lillian West, Ethel Clayton (Women); Kitty McHugh (Nurse); Grace Goodall (Matron); Charles William (Telegraph Operator); Harry Woods (Baker); Jack Chapin (Sentry); Pat West, Lee Phelps, David Newell, Charles Hamilton (Photographers); Ronnie Rondell, Frank Mills (Mechanics); Art Rowlands, Garry Owen, Bobby Tracy, James Burtis, Paul Kruger, Jerry Storm (Reporters); Norah Gale, Dorothy White, Dolores Casey, Evelyn Keyes, Sheila Darcy, Cheryl Walker, Jane Dewey, Jean Fenwick, Kitty McHugh (Nurses); George Chandler (Cody); Al Hill (Mail Driver); Syd Saylor (Jimmy); Billy Bletcher (Red Cross Man); Franklin Parker (Mail Truck Driver); Sherry Hall (Field Official); Frank Clarke (Burke); Robert E. Perry (Waiter); Russell Hicks (General Marlin); Ruth Rogers (Girl); Jack Hubbard (Attendant); Dell Henderson (Chairman); Edward Earle (Officer); Paul Mantz (Pilot).

SAY IT IN FRENCH (PAR, 1938) 70 M.

Producer-director, Andrew L. Stone; based on the play by Jacques Deval; screenplay, Frederick Jackson; music director, Boris Morros; song, Hoagy Carmichael and Helen Meinardi; process camera, Farciot Edouart; camera, Victor Milner, editor, LeRoy Stone.

Ray Milland (Richard Carrington, Jr.); Olympe Bradna (Julie); Irene Hervey (Auriol Marsden); Janet Beecher (Mrs. Carrington); Mary Carlisle (Phyllis Carrington); Holmes Herbert (Richard Carrington, Sr.); William Collier, Sr. (Howland); Walter Kingsford (Hopkins); Erik Rhodes (Irving); Mona Barrie (Lady Westover); George P. Huntley (Lady Westover); Gertrude Sutton (Daisy); Forbes Murray (Dr. Van Gulden); Billy Daniels (Messenger Boy); Billy Lee (Boy with Lollypop); Jean Fenwick (Nursemaid); Joseph Swickard (Old Man); Grace Goodall (Miss Briggs); Gus Glassmire (Mr. Nolan); George Hickman (Messenger); Walter Soderling (Commodore Simms); Major Sam Harris (Commodore Chapman); Billy Benedict (Red-Haired Boy); George Magrill, George Cooper (Taxi Drivers); Marek Windheim (Headwaiter); Archie Twitchell (Elevator Operator); Richard Denning, Ruth Rogers (Elevator Passengers); Bert Roach, Max Barwyn (Waiters); Byron Foulger (Swedish Janitor); Bernice Pilot (Washerwoman); Clara Mackin Blore (Dowager); Edward Earle, Hooper Atchley (Men); Paul Newlan (Customs Inspector); George Davis (Steward); Ed Cecil (Lift Boy); Hayden Stevenson (Elevator Boy); Luana Walters (Hat Check Girl); Gwen Kenyon, Joyce Matthews, Harriette Haddon, Dolores Casey, Marie Burton, Sheila Darcy, Paula de Cardo, Norah Gale, Helaine Moler, Dorothy White, Judith King (Girls); Ethel Clayton (Woman).

HOTEL IMPERIAL (PAR, 1939) 67 M.

Director, Robert Florey; based on the play by Lajos Biro; screenplay, Gilbert Gabriel, Robert Thoeren; camera, William Mellor; editor, Chandler House.

Isa Miranda (Anna); Ray Milland (Lieutenant Nemassy); Reginald Owen (General Videnko); Gene Lockhart (Elias); J. Carrol Naish (Krupin); Curt Bois (Anton); Henry Victor (Sultancy); Albert Dekker (Sergeant); Don Cossack Chorus (Themselves); Ernst Verebes (Ivan); Robert Middlemass (General Von Schwartzberg); Michel Werboff (Russian Sergeant); Spencer Charters (Visoff); Betty Compson (Soubrette); Bodil Rosing (Ratty Old Woman); Wolfgang Zilzer (Limping Tenor); Bert Roach (Fat Comic); Agostino Borgato (Old Actor); Paul Everton (Troupe Manager); George Magrill (Austrian Sentry); Lee Shumway (Russian Officer); Davison Clark (Irate Officer); Harry Tenbrook, Paul Kruger, Ethan Laidlaw (Sentries); William Bakewell (Cadet); Norman Phillips (Butcher Boy); Robert Frazer (Austrian Courier); Russell Hicks (Austrian Officer); George MacQuarrie (Frightened Old Man); Arthur Cernitz, General Savitsky, Joseph Marievsky, Andre Marsaudon (Staff Officers); Bull Anderson (Videnko Sentry); Marek Windheim (Feinberger); Gustav Von Seyffertitz (Priest); Sheila Darcy, Norah Gale, Paula de Cardo, Judith King, Luana Walters (Nurses); Robert Kortman (Austrian Sergeant); Jack Knoche (Cossack Soldier); Stanley Andrews (Colonel Paloff); Harry Holman (Burgomaster).

BEAU GESTE (PAR, 1939) 114 M.

Producer-director, William A. Wellman; based on the novel by Percival Christopher Wren; screenplay, Robert Carson; art directors, Hans Dreier, Robert Odell; technical adviser, Louis Van Der Ecker; music, Alfred Newman; orchestrator, Edward Powell; sound, Hugo Grenzbach, Walter Oberst; camera, Theodor Sparkuhl, Archie Stout; editor, Thomas Scott.

Gary Cooper (Beau Geste); Ray Milland (John Geste); Robert Preston (Digby Geste); Brian Donlevy (Sergeant Markoff); Susan Hayward (Isobel Rivers); J. Carrol Naish (Rasinoff); Albert Dekker (Schwartz); Broderick Crawford (Hank Miller); Charles Barton (Buddy McMonigal); James Stephenson (Major Henri de Beaujolais); George F. Huntley (Augustus Brandon); Heather Thatcher (Lady Patricia Brandon); Harold Huber (Voisin); Donald O'Connor (Beau Geste as a Child); Billy Cook (John Geste as a Child); Martin Spellman (Digby Geste as a Child); Ann Gillis (Isobel Rivers as a Child); David Holt (Augustus Brandon as a Child); Harvey Stephens (Lieutenant Martin); Harry Woods (Renoir); Stanley Andrews (Maris); Arthur Aylesworth (Renault, a Deserter); Henry Brandon (Renour, Another Deserter); Barry Macollum (Krenke); Ronnie Rondell (A Burgler); Frank Dawson (Burdon, the Butler); George Chandler (Cordier); Duke Green (Glock); Thomas Jackson (Colonel in Recruiting Office); Jerome Storm (Sergeant-Major); Joseph Whitehead (Sergeant); Harry Worth (Corporal); Nestor Paiva (Corporal Golas); George Regas, Francis McDonald (Arab Scouts); Carl Voss (Legionaire S. Roberts); Joe Bernard (Legionaire W. Williams); Robert Perry (Legionaire L. Paul); Larry Lawson (Legionaire N. Fenton); Henry Sylvester (Legionaire T. Clements); Joseph William Cody (Legionaire A. Virginia); Joe Colling (Trumpeter O. Leo); Gladys Jeans (Girl in Port Said Cafe).

EVERYTHING HAPPENS AT NIGHT (20th, 1939) 77 M.

Producer, Darryl F. Zanuck; associate producer, Harry Joe Brown; director, Irving Cummings; screenplay, Art Arthur, Robert Harari; skating numbers staged by Nick Castle; camera, Edward Cronjager; editor, Walter Thompson.

Sonja Henie [Louise Favers (Norden)]; Ray Milland (Geoff Thompson); Robert Cummings (Ken Morgan); Maurice Moscovich (Fr. Hugo Norden); Leonid Kinskey (Groder); Alan Dinehart (Fred Sherwood) Fritz Feld (Gendarme); Jody Gilbert (Hilda); Victor Varconia (Cavas); William Edmunds (Hotel Clerk); Michael Visaroff (Otto, the Woodcutter); Christian Rub (Telegrapher); Frank Reicher (Becher, the Pharmacist); John Bleifer, Adolph Milar (Sled Drivers); Lester Mathews (Philip); Russ Powell (Hilda's Papa); George Davis (Bellhop); Paul Porcasi (Bartender); Eleanor Weselhoeft (Woodcutter's Wife); Ferdinand Munier (Conductor); Rolfe Sedan (Felicien, the Waiter); Louis Mercier (Taxi Driver); Eugene Borden (Waiter); Jeanne Lafayette (Brunette); Nick Kobliansky (Doorman); Albert Conti (Maitre d'Hotel); Martha Bamattre (Pharmacist's Wife); Glen Cavender (Guide); Torben Meyer (Station Master); Joseph De Stefani (Norden Servant); Georges Renavent (Gendarme on Dock); Jean Del Van (Gendarme); Holmes Herbert (Featherstonebaugh); Roger Imhof (Judge); Wolfgang Zilgzer (Dock Lounger).

FRENCH WITHOUT TEARS (Paramount-British, 1939) 85 M.

Producer, Mario Zampi; director, Anthony Asquith; based on the play by Terence Rattigan; screenplay, Rattigan, Ian Dalrymple, Anatole de Grunwald; camera, Bernard Knowles; supervising editor, David Lean.

Ray Milland (Alan Howard); Ellen Drew (Diana Lake); Janine Darcey (Jacqueline Maingot); Roland Culver (Commander Rogers); David Tree (Chris Neilan); Jim Gerald (Maingot); Guy Middleton (Brian Curtis); Kenneth Morgan (Kenneth Lake); Margaret Yarde (Marianne); Toni Gable (Chi-Chi).

U.S. release: PAR (1940) 67 M.

IRENE (RKO, 1940) 101 M.°

Producer-director, Herbert Wilcox; based on the play by James H. Montgomery; screenplay, Alice Duer Miller; music director, Anthony Collins; orchestrator, Collins, Gene Rose; songs, Harry Tierney and Joseph McCarthy; art director, L. P. Williams; special effects, Vernon Walker; montage, Douglas Travers; camera, Russell Metty; editor, Elmo Williams.

Anna Neagle (Irene O'Dare); Ray Milland (Don Marshall); Roland Young (Mr. Smith); Alan Marshal (Bob Vincent); May Robson (Granny O'Dare); Billie Burke (Mrs. Herman Vincent); Arthur Treacher (Betherton); Marsha Hunt (Eleanor Worth); Isabel Jewell (Jane McGee); Doris Nolan (Lillian); Stuart Robertson (Freddie); Ethel Griffies (Princess Minetti); Tommy Kelly (Michael O'Dare); Juliette Compton (Emily Newlands Grey); Roxanne Barkley (Helen); Johnny Long and His Orchestra (Themselves); Martha Tilton (Susie Smith); The Dandridge Sisters (Singers); Hattie Noel (Mama); Louis Jean Heydt (Biffy Webster, the Columnist); Rod Bacon (Usher); Cyril Ring, Tom Quinn, Rosemary La Planche (Dance Extras); Larry Steers, Major Sam Harris (Guests); Nella Walker (Mrs. Marshall); Alex D'Arcy (Dumont, the Couturier); Sid Saylor (Gardener).

THE DOCTOR TAKES A WIFE (COL, 1940) 89 M.

Producer, William Perlberg; director, Alexander Hall; story, Aleen Leslie; screenplay, George Seaton, Ken Englund; camera, Sid Hickox; editor, Viola Lawrence.

Loretta Young (June Cameron); Ray Milland (Dr. Timothy Sterling); Reginald Gardiner (John Pierce); Gail Patrick (Marilyn Thomas); Edmund Gwenn (Dr. Lionel Sterling); Frank Sully (Slapcovitch); Gordon Jones (O'Brien); Georges Metaxa (Jean Rovere); Charles Halton (Dr. Streeter); Joseph Eggenton (Dr. Nielson); Paul McAllister (Dean Lawton); Chester Clute (Johnson); Hal K. Dawson (Charlie); Edward Van Sloan (Burkhardt); John Wray (Farmer); Edgar Dearing (Motor Cop); Irving Bacon (Gas Station Attendant); Spencer Charters (Mr. Quinn); Edward Gargan (Doorman); Don Beddoe, Charles Lane (Reporters); Olin Howland (Hotel Clerk); Frank Darien (Greenwich Editor); Frank Orth (New York Editor); William Austin (Hotel Manager); Ian Maclaren (Professor); Jane Goude (Mrs. Nielson); Erville Alderson (Harrison); Virginia Sale (School Teacher); Helen Ainsworth (Amazon); Myra Marsh (Lydia Johnson); Mary Gordon (Scrub Woman); Edward Earle, Vernon Dent, Sumner Getchell (Men); Gertrude Sutton (Mabel); Edgar Buchanan (Doorman); Ann Lee (Maid); Jane Keckley (Mrs. Quinn); Wesley Giraud (Western Union Boy); Renie Riano (Telegraph Operator); Dorothy Ann Seese, Catherine Courtney, Charlotte Treadway, Helen Davis, Dorothy Appleby (Women).

UNTAMED (PAR, 1940) C—83 M.

Producer, Paul Jones; director, George Archainbaud; based on the novel Mantrap *by Sinclair Lewis; screenplay, Frederick Hazlitt Brennan, Frank Butler; art directors, Hans Dreier, William Flannery; music, Victor Young; camera, Leo Tover, W. Howard Greene; editor, Stuart Gilmore.*

Ray Milland (Dr. William Crawford); Patricia Morison (Alverna Easter); Akim Tamiroff (Joe Easter); William Frawley (Les Woodbury); Jane Darwell (Mrs. Maggie Moriarty); Esther Dale (Mrs. Smith); J. M. Kerrigan (Angus McGavity); Eily Malyon (Mrs. Sarah McGavity); Fay Helm (Miss Olcott); Clem Bevans (Smokey Moseby); Sibyl Harris (Mrs. Dillon); Roscoe Ates (Bert Dillon); J. Farrell MacDonald (Dr. Billar); Gertrude W. Hoffman (Miss Rhine); Charles Waldron (Dr. Hughes); Darryl Hickman (Mickey Moriarty); Charlene Wyatt (Milly Dee); Bahe Denetdeel (Skoodum); Donna Jean Lester (Judy); Byron Foulger (Nels); Helen Brown (Mrs. Jarvis); Guy Wilkerson (Sim Jarvis); Susan Paley, Marion Martin (Girls); Charles Stevens (Indian Trapper); Brenda Fowler (Chief Nurse); Hazel Keener (Nurse in Apartment); Ann Doran, Pau-

line Haddon, Dorothy Adams (Nurses); Betty Ross Clarke (Mother); Wilfred Roberts (Interne).

ARISE MY LOVE (PAR, 1940) 113 M.

Producer, Arthur Hornblow, Jr.; director, Mitchell Leisen; based on an unpublished story by Benjamin Glazer, John S. Toldy; adaptor, Jacques Thery; art directors, Hans Dreier, Robert Usher; music, Victor Young; Miss Colbert's gowns, Irene; camera, Charles Lang, Jr.; editor, Doane Harrison.

Claudette Colbert (Augusta Nash); Ray Milland (Tom Martin); Dennis O'Keefe (Shep); Walter Abel (Phillips); Dick Purcell (Pink); George Zucco (Prison Governor); Frank Puglia (Father Jacinto); Esther Dale (Susie); Paul Leyssac (Bresson); Ann Codee (Mme. Bresson); Stanley Logan (Colonel Tubbs-Brown); Lionel Pape (Lord Kettlebrock); Aubrey Mather (Achille); Cliff Nazarro (Botzelberg); Michael Mark (Botzelberg's Assistant); Jesus Topete (Guard); Nestor Paiva (Uniformed Clerk); Fred Malatesta (Mechanic); Juan Duval (Spanish Driver); Paul Bryar (Desk Clerk); George Davis (Porter); Alan Davis (Cameraman); Jean Del Val (Conductor); Jon Easton (Waiter at Cafe Magenta); Eugene Borden, Jean De Briac (Waiters at Maxim's); Sarah Edwards, Fern Emmett (Spinsters); Jacques Vanaire, Olaf Hytten, Louis Mercier, Guy Repp (Employees); Paul Everton (Husband); Mrs. Wilfrid North (Wife); Maurice Marsac, Marcel de la Brosse, Francois Richier (French Newsboys); Douglas Kennedy (College Boy); Charles de Ravenne (Bellboy); Charles Bastin (Elevator Boy); Nadia Petrova (Girl at Maxim's); Major Fred Farrell (Cab Driver); Reginald Sheffield (Steward); Tempe Pigott (Woman in Irish Pub); Alphonse Martell (Uniformed French Correspondent); Hans Fuerberg (German Sentry); Sherry Hall (American Correspondent); Rafael Storm (French Uniformed Correspondent); Leyland Hodgson (Uniformed English Correspondent).

I WANTED WINGS (PAR, 1941) 130 M.

Producer, Arthur Hornblow, Jr.; director, Mitchell Leisen; story by Eleanore Griffin, Commander Frank Wead from the book by Beirne Lay, Jr.; screenplay, Richard Maibaum, Lay, Jr., Sid Herzig; art directors, Hans Dreier, Robert Usher; music, Victor Young; songs, Young and Ned Washington, William J. Clinch; aerial camera, Elmer Dyer; process camera, Farciot Edouart; special effects, Gordon Jennings; camera, Leo Tover; editor, Hugh Bennett.

Ray Milland (Jeff Young); William Holden (Al Ludlow); Wayne Morris (Tom Cassidy); Brian Donlevy (Captain Hunter); Constance Moore (Carolyn Bartlett); Veronica Lake (Sally Vaughn); Harry Davenport (Sandbags Hiley); Phil Brown (Jimmy Masters); Edward Fielding (President of the Court); Willard Robertson (Judge Advocate); Richard Lane (Flight Commander); Addison Richards (Flight Surgeon); Hobart Cavanaugh (Mickey); Douglas Aylesworth (Lieutenant Hopkins); John Trent (Lieutenant Ronson); Archie Twitchell (Lieutenant Clankton); Richard Webb (Cadet Captain); John Hiestand (Radio Announcer); Harlan Warde (Montgomery, the Co-Pilot); Lane Chandler (Ranger); Jack Chapin, Charles Drake, Alan Hale, Jr., Renny McEvoy (Cadets); Arthur Gardner (Mechanic); Lane Allan (Corporal Mechanic); Jack Shea (Crew Chief); Ed Peil, Sr., Frank O'Connor (Detectives); Michael Gale, James Millican (Corporals); Emory Johnson (Sergeant); Russ Clark (Supply Sergeant); George Turner, Hal Brazeale (Privates); Warren Ashe (Cadet Adjutant); Charles A. Hughes (Meteorology Instructor); George Lollier (Buzzer Class Instructor); Hedda Hopper (Mrs. Young); Herbert Rawlinson (Mr. Young); Rod Cameron (Voice on Loud Speaker); Jack Luden (Captain at Court Martial); Lee Shumway (Policeman in Car); Phillip Terry (Radio Operator).

SKYLARK (PAR, 1941) 92 M.

Producer-director, Mark Sandrich; based on the novel and play by Samson Raphaelson; adaptor, Z. Myers; screenplay, Allan Scott; assistant director, Mel Epstein; art directors,

Hans Dreier, Roland Anderson; camera, Charles Lang; editor, LeRoy Stone.

Claudette Colbert (Lydia Kenyon); Ray Milland (Tony Kenyon); Brian Aherne (Jim Blake); Binnie Barnes (Myrtle Vantine); Walter Abel (George Gore); Grant Mitchell (Frederick Vantine); Mona Barrie (Charlotte Gorell); Ernest Cossart (Theodore); James Rennie (Ned Franklin); Fritz Feld (Maitre d'Hotel); Warren Hymer (Beefy Individual in Subway Car); Hobart Cavanaugh (Little Individual in Subway Car); Leon Belasco (Long-Haired Individual in Subway Car); Edward Fielding (Scholarly Individual in Subway Car); Irving Bacon (Ferryman); Leonard Mudie (Jewelry Clerk); Armand Kaliz (Jeweler); Patricia Farr (Lil, the Waitress at Hamburger Stand); William Newell (Hamburger Stand Counterman); Margaret Hayes (Receptionist); Robert Dudley (Pedestrian); James Flavin (Subway Guard); Howard Mitchell (Man in Front of Tony); Edward Peil, Sr. (Man behind Tony); Frank Orth (Subway Cashier); May Boley (Fat Woman in Subway Car); Minerva Urecal, Virginia Sale (Middle-Aged Women in Subway Car); Ella Neal (Usherette); Henry Roquemore (Bartender); Keith Richards (Counterman at Second Hamburger Stand); Francisco Maran (Mr. Harrison, the Travel Agency Man).

THE LADY HAS PLANS (PAR, 1942) 77 M.

Associate producer, Fred Kohlmar; director, Sidney Lanfield; story, Leo Birinski; screenplay, Harry Tugend; camera, Charles Lang; editor, William Shea.

Ray Milland (Kenneth Harper); Paulette Goddard (Sidney Royce); Roland Young (Ronald Dean); Albert Dekker (Baron Von Kemp); Margaret Hayes (Rita Lenox); Cecil Kellaway (Peter Milen); Addison Richards (Paul Baker); Edward Norris (Frank Richards); Charles Arnt (Pooly); Hans Schumm, Hans von Morhart (Germans); Genia Nikola (German Maid); Gerald Mohr (Joe Scalsi); Lionel Royce (Guard); Thomas W. Ross (Abner Spencer); Arthur Loft (Mr. Weston); Paul Phillips, Warren Ashe (G-Men); Lee Shumway (Cop); Terry Ray (Taxi Driver); Mel Ruick (Announcer); Keith Richards, George Dobbs (Hotel Clerks); Yola d'Avril (Hotel Maid); Richard Webb (Hotel Information Clerk); Nestor Paiva (Portuguese Porter); Sigfrid Tor (German Guard).

REAP THE WILD WIND (PAR, 1942) C—123 M.

Producer, Cecil B. DeMille; associate producer, William Pine; director, DeMille; story, Thelma Strabel; screenplay, Alan LeMay, Charles Bennett, Jesse Lasky, Jr.; music, Victor Young; art directors, Hans Dreier, Roland Anderson; process camera, Farciot Edouart; special effects, Gordon Jennings; camera, Victor Milner; editor, Anne Bauchens.

Ray Milland (Stephen Tolliver); John Wayne (Captain Jack Stuart); Paulette Goddard (Loxi Claiborne); Raymond Massey (King Cutler); Robert Preston (Dan Cutler); Lynne Overman (Captain Phillip Philpott); Susan Hayward (Drusilla Alston); Charles Bickford (Mate of the "Tyfib"); Walter Hampden (Commodore Devereaux); Louise Beavers (Maum Maria); Martha O'Driscoll (Ivy Devereaux); Elisabeth Risdon (Mrs. Claiborne); Hedda Hopper (Aunt Henrietta); Victor Kilian (Widgeon); Oscar Polk (Salt Meat); Janet Beecher (Mrs. Mottram); Ben Carter (Chinkapin); Wee Willie Davis (The Lamb); Lane Chandler (Sam); Davison Clark (Judge Marvin); Frank M. Thomas (Dr. Jepson); Keith Richards (Captain Carruthers); J. Farrell Macdonald (Port Captain); Victor Varconi (Lubbock); Harry Woods (Mace); Raymond Hatton (Master Shipwright); Milburn Stone (Lieutenant Farragut); Barbara Britton, Julia Faye (Charleston Ladies); Constantine Romanoff (Pete on the Sponge Boat); Nestor Paiva (Man with Suspenders); James Flavin (Father of Girl); Frank Lackteen, Alan Bridge, Al Ferguson (Cutler Men in Barrel Room); Dick Alexander (Stoker Boss); Byron Foulger (Devereaux Courier); Dorothy Sebastian (Woman in Ballroom); Jack Luden (Southern Gentleman at Tea); Monte Blue (Officer at Tea); Dale Van Sickel (Member of Falcon Crew); Leo Sulky, Cap Anderson, Sam Appel, Harry Dean, Billy Elmer (Jurymen).

ARE HUSBANDS NECESSARY? (PAR, 1942) 79 M.

Director, Norman Taurog; based on the novel Mr. and Mrs. Cugat by Isabel Scott Rorick; screenplay, Tess Slesinger, Frank Davis; camera, Charles Lang.

Ray Milland (George Cugat); Betty Field (Mary Elizabeth Cugat); Patricia Morison (Myra Ponsonby); Eugene Pallette (Bunker); Charles Dingle (Duncan Atterbury); Leif Erickson (Bill Stone); Elisabeth Risdon (Mrs. Westwood); Richard Haydn (Chuck); Kathleen Lockhart (Laura Atterbury); Phillip Terry (Cory Cartwright); Cecil Kellaway (Dr. Buell); Anne Revere (Anna); Charles Lane (Mr. Brooks); Charlotte Wynters (Mrs. Finley); Clinton Rosemond (Enos); Olive Blakeney (Miss Bumstead); Cecil Cunningham (Miss Jenkins); Edmund Mortimer, John W. Johnston, Catherine Price, William Marion (Guests at Atterbury Home); Mikhail Rasumny (Pierre); Edward McWade (Mr. Greenfield); Eleanor Durkin (Woman Accompanist); Catherine Wallace, Leota Lorraine (Women); Jack Roberts (Headwaiter); Ed Peil, Sr. (Mailman); James Burke (Tough Mug); Paul McVey (Head Potentate); Joe Whitehead (Waiter); George Chandler, Eddie Dunn, Jimmy Conlin, Pat West (Piano Movers); Francine Bordeaux (Yvonne); Marta Downes (Saleslady).

THE MAJOR AND THE MINOR (PAR, 1942) 100 M.

Producer, Arthur Hornblow, Jr.; director, Billy Wilder; suggested by the play Connie Goes Home by Edward Childs Carpenter and the story "Sunny Goes Home" by Fannie Kilbourne; screenplay, Charles Brackett, Wilder; art director, Hans Dreier, Roland Anderson; costumes, Edith Head; music, Robert Emmett Dolan; assistant director, C. C. Coleman, Jr.; sound, Harold Lewis, Don Johnson; camera, Leo Tover; editor, Doane Harrison.

Ginger Rogers (Susan Applegate); Ray Milland (Major Kirby); Rita Johnson (Pamela Hill); Robert Benchley (Mr. Osborne); Diana Lynn (Lucy Hill); Edward Fielding (Colonel Hill); Frankie Thomas (Cadet Osborne); Raymond Roe (Cadet Wigton); Charles Smith (Cadet Korner); Larry Nunn (Cadet Babcock); Billy Dawson (Cadet Miller); Lela Rogers (Mrs. Applegate); Aldrich Bowker (Reverend Doyle); Boyd Irwin (Major Griscom); Byron Shores (Captain Durand); Richard Fiske (Will Duffy); Norma Varden (Mrs. Osborne); Gretl Dupont (Mrs. Shackleford); Stanley Desmond (Shumaker); Dell Henderson (Doorman); Ed Peil, Sr. (Station Master); Ken Lundy (Elevator Boy); Ethel Clayton, Gloria Williams (Women); Marie Blake (Bertha); Mary Field (Mother in Railway Station); Will Wright, William Howell (Ticket Agents); Tom Dugan (Dead Beat); Carlotta Jelm (Little Girl in Train Station); George Anderson (Man with Esquire); Stanley Andrews, Emory Parnell (Conductors); Guy Wilkerson (Farmer/Truck Driver); Milton Kibbee (Station Agent); Archie Twitchell (Sergeant); Alice Keating (Nurse); Billy Ray (Cadet Summerville); Don Wilmot, Jack Lindquist, Billy Clauson, John Borgden, Bradley Hail (Cadets).

STAR SPANGLED RHYTHM (PAR, 1942) 99 M.

Associate producer, Joseph Sistrom; director, George Marshall; screenplay, Harry Tugend; music, Robert Emmett Dolan; songs, Johnny Mercer and Harold Arlen; art director, Hans Dreier; camera, Leo Tover, Theodor Sparkuhl; editor, Paul Weatherwax.

Betty Hutton (Polly Judson); Eddie Bracken (Jimmy Webster); Victor Moore (Pop Webster); Anne Revere (Sarah); Walter Abel (Frisbee); Cass Daley (Mimi); Macdonald Carey (Louie, the Lug); Gil Lamb (Hi-Pockets); William Haade (Duffy); Bob Hope (Master of Ceremonies); Fred MacMurray, Franchot Tone, Ray Milland, Lynne Overman (Men Playing Cards Skit); Dorothy Lamour, Veronica Lake, Paulette Goddard, Arthur Treacher, Walter Catlett, Sterling Holloway (Sweater, Sarong, and Peekaboo Bang Number); Tom Dugan (Hitler); Paul Porcasi (Mussolini); Richard Loo (Hirohito); Alan Ladd (Scarface); Mary Martin, Dick Powell, Golden Gate Quartette (Dreamland Number); William Bendix, Jerry Colonna, Maxine Ardell, Marjorie Deanne, Lorraine Miller, Marion Martin,

Chester Clute (Bob Hope Skit); Vera Zorina, Johnnie Johnston, Frank Faylen (Black Magic Number); Eddie "Rochester" Anderson, Katherine Dunham, Slim and Sam, Woodrow W. Strode (Smart as a Tack Number); Susan Hayward (Genevieve—Priorities Number); Ernest Truex (Murgatroyd—Priorities Number); Marjorie Reynolds, Betty Rhodes, Dona Drake, Louise La Planche, Lorraine Miller, Donivee Lee, Don Castle, Frederic Henry, Sherman Sanders (Swing Shift Number); Bing Crosby (Old Glory Number); Virginia Brissac (Lady from Iowa—Old Glory Number); Irving Bacon (New Hampshire Farmer—Old Glory Number); Matt McHugh (Man from Brooklyn—Old Glory Number); Peter Potter (Georgia Boy—Old Glory Number); Edward M. Marr (Heavy—Old Glory Number); Gary Crosby (Himself); Albert Dekker, Cecil Kellaway, Ellen Drew, Jimmy Lydon, Charles Smith, Frances Gifford, Susanna Foster, Robert Preston, Christopher King, Alice Kirby, Marcella Phillips (Finale); Walter Dare Wahl and Company (Specialty Act); Cecil B. DeMille, Preston Sturges, Ralph Murphy (Themselves); Maynard Holmes, James Millican (Sailors); Eddie Johnson (Tommy); Arthur Loft (Casey); Dorothy Granger, Barbara Pepper, Jean Phillips, Lynda Grey (Girls); Boyd Davis (Captain Kingsley); Frank Moran (Bit Man with Preston Sturges); Eddie Dew, Rod Cameron (Petty Officers); Barney Dean, Jack Hope (Themselves); John Shay (Sentry); Keith Richards (Officer); Jack Roberts (Assistant Director); Karin Booth (Kate); Gladys Blake (Liz).

THE CRYSTAL BALL (UA, 1943) 81 M.

Producer, Richard Blumenthal; director, Elliott Nugent; story, Steven Vas; adaptor, Virginia Van Upp; music, Victor Young; art directors, Hans Dreier, Roland Anderson; camera, Leo Tover; editor, Doane Harrison.

Ray Milland (Brad Cavanaugh); Paulette Goddard (Toni Gerard); Gladys George (Madame Zenobia); Virginia Field (Jo Ainsley); Cecil Kellaway (Pop Tibbets); William Bendix (Biff Carter); Mary Field (Foster); Frank Conlan (Dusty); Ernest Truex (Mr. Martin); Mabel Paige (Lady with Pekinese); Regina Wallace (Mrs. Smythe); Peter Jamieson (Brad's Secretary); Donald Douglas (Mr. Bowman); Nestor Paiva (Stukov); Sig Arno (Waiter at Stukov's); Hillary Brooke (Friend of Jo's); Tom Dugan (Plumber); Iris Adrian (Mrs. Martin); Babe London, June Evans (Tandem Riders); Reginald Sheffield (Dad in Shooting Gallery); Maude Eburne ("Apple Annie" Character); Yvonne De Carlo, Maxine Ardell (Secretaries).

FOREVER AND A DAY (RKO, 1943) 105 M.

Producer-directors, Rene Clair, Edmund Goulding, Cedric Hardwicke, Frank Lloyd, Victor Saville, Robert Stevenson, Herbert Wilcox; screenplay, Charles Bennett, C. S. Forrester, Lawrence Hazard, Michael Hogan, W. O. Lipscomb, Alice Duer Miller, John Van Druten, Alan Campbell, Peter Godfrey, S. M. Herzig, Christopher Isherwood, Gene Lockhart, H. C. Sheriff, Claudine West, Norman Corwin, Jack Hartfield, James Hilton, Emmett Lavery, Frederick Lonsdale, Donald Ogden Stewart, Keith Winters; art directors, Albert S. D'Agostino, Lawrence P. Williams, Al Herman; music director, Anthony Collins; special effects, Vernon L. Walker; camera, Robert De Grasse, Lee Garmes, Russell Metty, Nicholas Musuraca; editors, Elmo J. Williams, George Crone.

Anna Neagle [Miriam (Susan)]; Ray Milland (Bill Trimble); Claude Rains (Pomfret); C. Aubrey Smith (Admiral Trimble); Dame May Whitty (Mrs. Trimble); Gene Lockhart (Cobblewick); Ray Bolger (Sentry); Edmund Gwenn (Stubbs); Lumsden Hare (Fitts); Stuart Robertson (Lawyer); Claud Allister (Barstow); Ben Webster (Vicar); Alan Edmiston (Tripp); Patric Knowles (Courier); Bernie Sell (Naval Officer); Halliwell Hobbes (Doctor); Helene Pickard (Maid); Doris Lloyd, Lionel Belmore (Bits); Louis Bissiner (Baby); Clifford Severn (Nelson Trimble); Charles Coburn (Sir William); Alec Craig (Butler); Ian Hunter (Dexter); Jessie Matthews (Mildred); Charles Laughton (Bellamy); Montagu Love (Sir John Bunn); Reginald Owen (Mr. Simpson); Cedric Hardwicke (Dabb); Noel Madison (Mr. Dunkinfield); Ernest Cossart (Mr. Blinkinsep);

Peter Godfrey (Mr. Pepperdish); Buster Keaton (Dabb's Assistant); Wendy Barrie (Edith); Ida Lupino (Jenny); Brian Aherne (Jim Trimble); Edward Everett Horton (Sir Anthony); Isobel Elsom (Lady Trimble-Pomfret); Wendell Hulott (Augustus); Eric Blore (Selsby); June Duprez (Julia); Mickey Martin (Boy); Queenie Leonard (Housemaid); May Beatty (Cook); Merle Oberon (Marjorie); Una O'Connor (Mrs. Ismay); Nigel Bruce (Major Garrow); Anita Bolster (Mrs. Garrow); Marta Gale (Miss Garrow); Roland Young (Mr. Barringer); Gladys Cooper (Mrs. Barringer); Robert Cummings (Ned Trimble); Herbert Evans (Bobby); Kay Deslys, Vangie Beilby (Woman Drunks); Richard Haydn (Mr. Fulcher); Emily Fitzroy (Mrs. Fulcher); Odette Myrtil (Mrs. Dallas); Elsa Lanchester (Mamie); Sara Allgood (Cook in 1917); Clyde Cook (Taxi Driver); Dorothy Bell (W.A.A.C. Girl); Jean Prescott (A.T.S. Girl); Robert Coote (Blind Officer); Art Mulliner, Ivan Simpson (Elderly Bachelors); Pax Walker, Lola Vanti (Housemaids in 1917); Bill Cartledge (Telegraph Boy); Charles Hall, Percy Snowden (Men); Donald Crisp (Captain Martin); Ruth Warrick (Leslie); Kent Smith (Gates Pomfret); June Lockhart (Daughter); Lydia Bilbrook (Mother); Billy Bevan (Cabby); Stuart Robertson (Air Raid Warden); Herbert Marshall (Curate); Victor McLaglen (Spavin); Harry Allen (Cockney Watcher); Ethel Griffies (Wife); Gabriel Canzona (Man with Monkey); Joy Harrington (Bus Conductress); Reginald Gardiner (Man); Walter Kingsford (Man); Mary Gordon, Evelyn Beresford, Moyna MacGill, Arthur Treacher, Anna Lee, Cecil Kellaway (Bits); Stuart Hall, Barry Heenan, Barry Norton, Philip Ahlin (Card Players); Daphne Moore (Nurse); Dorothy Bell (Flower Girl).

THE UNINVITED (PAR, 1944) 98 M.

Producer, Charles Brackett; director, Lewis Allen; based on the novel by Dorothy Macardie; screenplay, Dodie Smith; art directors, Hans Dreier, Ernst Fegte; set decorator, Stephen Seymour; assistant director, C. C. Coleman; music, Victor Young; sound, Hugo Grenzbach, John Cope; process camera, Farciot Edouart; camera, Charles Lang; editor, Doane Harrison.

Ray Milland (Roderick Fitzgerald); Ruth Hussey (Pamela Fitzgerald); Donald Crisp (Commander Bench); Cornelia Otis Skinner (Miss Holloway); Dorothy Stickney (Miss Hird); Barbara Everest (Lizzie Flynn); Alan Napier (Dr. Scott); Gail Russell (Stella Meredith); Jessica Newcombe (Miss Ellis); John Kieran (Foreword Narrator); Rita Page (Annie, a Maid); David Clyde (Boot Owner); Norman Ainsley (Chauffeur); Evan Thomas (Colonel Carlton); Ottola Nesmith (Mrs. Carlton); Evan P. Simpson (Will Hardy, Tobacconist); Moyna Macgill (Mrs. Coatsworthy); Queenie Leonard (Mrs. Taylor); Betty Farrington (Voice of Mary Meredith); Leyland Hodgson (Taxi Driver); Holmes Herbert (Charlie Jessup); Helena Grant (Servant); George Kirby (Gas Station Attendant); Elizabeth Russell (Portrait of Mary Meredith); Lynda Grey (Ghost of Mary Meredith/Body for Portrait).

LADY IN THE DARK (PAR, 1944) C—100 M.

Executive producer, B. G. DeSylva; producer, Dick Blumenthal; director, Mitchell Leisen; based on the play by Moss Hart, Kurt Weill, and Ira Gershwin; screenplay, Frances Goodrich, Albert Hackett; art director, Hans Dreier; set decorator-costumes, Raoul Pene du Bois; modern costumes, Edith Head, Leisen, Babs Wilomez; songs, Gershwin and Weill; Johnny Burke and Jimmy Van Heusen; Robert E. Dolan; Clifford Grey and Victor Schertzinger; orchestrator, Robert Russell Bennett; choreography, Billy Daniel, Don Loper; technical effects, Paul Lerpae; process camera, Farciot Edouart; special effects, Gordon Jennings; camera, Ray Rennahan; editor, Alma Macrorie.

Ginger Rogers (Liza Elliott); Ray Milland (Charley Johnson); Jon Hall (Randy Curtis); Warner Baxter (Kendall Nesbitt); Barry Sullivan (Dr. Brooks); Mischa Auer (Russell Paxton); Mary Phillips (Maggy Grant); Phyllis Brooks (Allison DuBois); Edward Fielding (Dr. Carlton); Don Loper (Adams); Mary Parker (Miss Parker); Catherine Craig (Miss Foster);

Marietta Canty (Martha); Virginia Farmer (Miss Edwards); Fay Helm (Miss Bowers); Gail Russell (Barbara at Age Seventeen); Kay Linaker (Liza's Mother); Harvey Stephens (Liza's Father); Rand Brooks (Ben); Pepito Perez (Clown); Charles Smith (Barbara's Boy Friend); Audrey Young, Eleanor DeVan, Jeanne Straser, Arlyne Varden, Angela Wilson, Dorothy O'Kelly, Betty Hall, Fran Shore, Lynda Grey, Christopher King, Maxine Ardell, Alice Kirby, Louise LaPlanche (Office Girls); Paul Pierce, George Mayon, James Notaro, Jacques Karre, Byron Poindexter, Kit Carson (Specialty Dancers); Bunny Waters, Susan Paley, Dorothy Ford, Mary MacLaren (Models); Paul McVey (Librarian); Jack Mulhall (Photographer); Grandon Rhodes, Lester Dorr, Emmett Vogan (Reporters); Phyllis M. Brooks (Barbara at Age Seven); Marjean Neville (Liza at Age Five and Seven); Buz Buckley (Freckle-Faced Boy).

TILL WE MEET AGAIN (PAR, 1944) 88 M.

Associate producer, David Lewis; director, Frank Borzage; based on a play by Alfred Maury; screenplay, Lenore Coffee; art directors, Hans Dreier, Robert Usher; set decorator, Ray Moyer; assistant director, Lou Borzage; music, David Buttolph; sound, Max Hutchinson, John Cope; process camera, Farciot Edouart; special camera effects, Gordon Jennings; camera, Theodor Sparkuhl; editor, Elmo Veron.

Ray Milland (John); Barbara Britton (Sister Clothilde); Walter Slezak (Vitrey, the Mayor); Lucille Watson (Mother Superior); Konstantin Shayne (Major Krupp); Vladimir Sokoloff (Cabeau); Marguerite D'Alvarez (Madame Sarroux); Mona Freeman (Elise); William Edmunds (Henri Maret); George Davis (Gaston, the Waiter); Peter Helmers (Examiner); John Wengraf (Gestapo Chief); Mira McKinney (Portress); Tala Birell (Mme. Bouchard); Buddy Gorman (Messenger); Dawn Bender (Francoise); Eilene Janssen (Yvonne); Henry Sharp (Andre); Alfred Paix, Eugene Borden (Refugees); Muni Seroff (Jacques); Philip Van Zandt (Lieutenant); Georges Renavent (Gabriel); Diane Dubois, Janet Gallow, Nils Rich, Sharon McManus, Mary Thomas, Diana Martin, Yvette Duguay (Orphans); Byron Nelson, Don Cadell, Hans Furberg, Robert Stevenson (German Soldiers); Frances Sandford, Iris Lancaster (Girls in Restaurant); Nina Borget (Jeannette); George Sorel (Gendarme); Marcelle Corday (Elderly Waitress); Francis McDonald (Driver of the Cart); Crane Whitley (Man with Silver).

MINISTRY OF FEAR (PAR, 1944) 85 M.

Producer, Seton I. Miller; director, Fritz Lang; based on the novel by Graham Greene; screenplay, Miller; art directors, Hans Dreier, Hal Pereira; set decorator, Bert Granger; assistant director, George Templeton; music, Victor Young; sound, W. C. Smith; camera, Henry Sharp; editor, Archie Marshek.

Ray Milland (Stephen Neale); Marjorie Reynolds (Carla Hilfe); Carl Esmond (Willi Hilfe); Hillary Brooke (Mrs. Bellaire #2); Percy Waram (Prentice); Dan Duryea [Cost (Travers)]; Alan Napier (Dr. Forrester); Erskine Sanford (Mr. Rennit); Thomas Louden (Mr. Newland); Aminta Dyne (Mrs. Bellaire #1); Eustace Wyatt (Blind Man); Mary Field (Miss Penteel); Byron Fougler (Mr. Newby); Lester Matthews (Dr. Morton); Helena Grant (Mrs. Merrick); Connie Leon (Lady Purchaser of Cake); Evelyn Beresford (Fat Lady); Frank Dawson (Vicar); Eric Wilton, Boyd Irwin, Frank Baker (Scotland Yard Men); Wilson Benge (Air Raid Warden); Leonard Carey (Porter); Olaf Hytten (Clerk in Tailor Shop).

THE LOST WEEKEND (PAR, 1945) 101 M.

Producer, Charles Brackett; director, Billy Wilder; based on the novel by Charles R. Jackson; screenplay, Brackett, Wilder; art directors, Hans Dreier, Earl Hedrick; set decorator, Bertram Granger; assistant director, C. C. Coleman; music, Miklos Rozsa; sound, Stanley Cooley; special camera effects, Gordon Jennings; process camera, Farciot Edouart; camera, John F. Seitz; editor, Doane Harrison.

Ray Milland (Don Birnam); Jane Wyman (Helen St. James); Phillip Terry (Nick Birnam); Howard da Silva (Nat, the Bar-

tender); Doris Dowling (Gloria); Frank Faylen (Bim); Mary Young (Mrs. Deveridge); Anita Bolster (Mrs. Foley); Lilian Fontaine (Mrs. St. James); Lewis L. Russell (Charles St. James); Frank Orth (Opera Attendant); Gisela Werbiseck (Mrs. Wertheim); Eddie Laughton (Mr. Brophy); Harry Barris (Piano Player); Craig Reynold (M. M.'s Escort); Jayne Hazard (M. M.); Walter Baldwin (Albany); Fred "Snowflake" Toones, Clarence Muse (Washroom Attendants); Gene Ashley, Jerry James, William Meader (Male Nurses); Emmett Vogan (Doctor); Milton Wallace (Pawnbroker); Pat Moriarty, William O'Leary (Irishmen); Lester Sharpe, Bertram Warburgh (Jewish Men); Theodora Lynch, John Garris (Opera Singers); Byron Foulger (Shopkeeper).

KITTY (PAR, 1945) C—103 M.

Producer, Karl Tunberg; director, Mitchell Leisen; based on the novel by Rosamund Marshall; screenplay, Darrel Ware, Tunberg; art directors, Hans Dreier, Walter Tyler; set decorator-costumes, Raoul Pene Du Bois; music, Victor Young; choreography, Billy Daniel; assistant director, John Coonan; sound, Don McKay, Don Johnson; special effects, Gordon Jennings; process camera, Farciot Edouart; camera, Daniel L. Fapp; editor, Alan Macrorie.

Paulette Goddard (Kitty); Ray Milland (Sir Hugh Marcy); Patric Knowles (Brett Hardwood, the Earl of Carstairs); Reginald Owen (Duke of Malmunster); Cecil Kellaway (Thomas Gainsborough); Constance Collier (Lady Susan Dewitt); Dennis Hoey (Jonathan Selby); Sara Allgood (Old Meg); Eric Blore (Dobson); Gordon Richards (Sir Joshua Reynolds); Michael Dyne (The Prince of Wales); Edgar Norton (Earl of Campton); Patricia Cameron (Elaine Carlisle); Mary Gordon (Nancy); Anita Bolster (Mullens); Heather Wilde (Lil); Charles Coleman (Major Domo); Mae Clarke (Molly); Ann Codee (Madame Aurelia); Douglas Watson (Philip); Alec Craig (McNab); Edward Cooper (Sir Herbert Harbord); Anne Curson (Duchess of Gloucester); Tempe Pigott (Woman in Window); John Rice (Cockney Cart Driver); Doris Lloyd (Woman Fish Hawker); Sybil Burton (Magic Lantern Woman); Snub Pollard (Hugh's Rental Coachman); Ruth St. Denis (Duchess); Mary McLeod (Mrs. Sheridan); Dodo Bernard (Taffy Tarts Peddler); Gibson Gowland (Prison Guard); Cyril Delevanti ("All Hot" Hawker); Byron Poindexter (Colonel St. Leger).

THE WELL-GROOMED BRIDE (PAR, 1946) 75 M.

Producer, Fred Kohlmar; director, Sidney Lanfield; story, Robert Russell; screenplay, Claude Binyon, Russell; art directors, Hans Dreier, Earl Hedrick; set decorator, Kenneth Swartz; music, Roy Webb; assistant director, Oscar Rudolph; sound, Wallace Nogle, Joel Moss; process camera, Farciot Edouart; special camera effects, Gordon Jennings; camera, John F. Seitz; editor, William Shea.

Olivia de Havilland (Margie); Ray Milland (Lieutenant Briggs); Sonny Tufts (Torchy); James Gleason (Captain Hornby); Constance Dowling (Rita Sloane); Percy Kilbride (Mr. Dawson); Jean Heather (Wickley); Jay Norris (Mitch); Jack Reilly (Buck); George Turner (Goose); Tom Fadden (Justice); Donald Beddoe (Hotel Clerk); William Forrest (Major James Smith); Dale Van Sickel, James Millican (S.P.s); Frank Faylen (Taxi Driver); Noel Neill, Roberta Jonay (Waves); Jean Carlin (Elevator Girl); Eddie Laughton (Waiter); Tom Dillon (Mr. Bennett); William L. Haade, Roger Creed, Charles Mayon, Clark Eggleston, Stan Johnson, Walter Wilson (M.P.s); Larry Thompson (Lieutenant Cutler); Luke Chan (Chinaman).

CALIFORNIA (PAR, 1946) C—97 M.

Producer, Seton I. Miller; director, John Farrow; story, Boris Ingster; screenplay, Frank Butler, Theodore Strauss; art directors, Hans Dreier, Roland Anderson; set decorators, Sam Comer, Ray Moyer; music, Victor Young; songs, E. Y. Harburg and Earl Robinson; assistant director, Herbert Coleman; sound,

Stanley Cooley, John Cope; special effects, Gordon Jennings; camera, Ray Rennahan; editor, Eda Warren.

Ray Milland (Jonathan Trumbo); Barbara Stanwyck (Lily Bishop); Barry Fitzgerald (Michael Fabian); George Coulouris (Pharaoh Coffin); Albert Dekker (Mr. Pike); Anthony Quinn (Don Luis Rivera); Frank Faylen (Whitey); Gavin Muir (Booth Pennery); James Burke (Pokey); Eduardo Ciannelli (Padre); Roman Bohnen (Colonel Stuart); Argentina Brunetti (Elvira); Howard Freeman (Senator Creel); Julia Faye (Wagon Woman).

THE IMPERFECT LADY (PAR, 1947) 97 M.

Producer, Karl Tunberg; director, Lewis Allen; based on a story by Ladislaus Fodor; screenplay, Karl Tunberg; art directors, Hans Dreier, Franz Bachelin; set decorators, Sam Comer, James M. Walters; music, Victor Young; choreography, Billy Daniel, Josephine Earl; technical consultant, Hilda Grenler; assistant director, William Forsythe; sound, Harry Lindgren; process camera, Farciot Edouart; camera, John F. Seitz; editor, Duncan Mansfield.

Ray Milland (Clive Loring); Teresa Wright (Millicent Hopkins); Sir Cedric Hardwicke (Lord Belmont); Virginia Field (Rose Bridges); Anthony Quinn (Jose Martinez); Reginald Owen (Mr. Hopkins); Melville Cooper (Lord Montglyn); Rhys Williams (Inspector Carston); George Zucco (Mr. Mallam); Charles Coleman (Sam Travers); Miles Mander (Mr. Hogan); Gordon Richards (Gladstone); Edmond Breon (Lord Chief Justice); Frederick Worlock (Henderson); Michael Dyne (Malcolm Gadby); Joan Winfield (Lucy); Lilian Fontaine (Mrs. Gunner); Leyland Hodgson (Bobby); Olaf Hytten (Butler); Jack H. Lee, Major Sam Harris (Barristers); Doris Lloyd (Woman in Balcony of Theatre); Gavin Muir (Kelvin); Craufurd Kent (Headwaiter); Hilda Plowright (Woman Customer); Montague Shaw, Boyd Irwin, Stanley Mann (Men); Roberta Daniel (Suzanne, Rose's Maid); Lumsden Hare (Hardy); Winifred Harris, Gwendolyn Logan (Dowagers); Colin Hunter (Jury Foreman).

THE TROUBLE WITH WOMEN (PAR, 1947) 77 M.

Producer, Harry Tugend; director, Sidney Lanfield; story, Ruth McKenney; screenplay, Arthur Sheekman; art directors, Hans Dreier, Earl Hedrick; set decorators, Sam Comer, George McKinnon; music, Victor Young, Robert Emmett Dolan; assistant director, Dick McWhorter; sound, Harold Lewis, Philip Wisdom; special camera effects, Gordon Jennings; process camera, Farciot Edouart; camera, Lloyd Lindon; editor, William Shea.

Ray Milland (Professor Gilbert Sedley); Teresa Wright (Kate Farrell); Brian Donlevy (Joe McBride); Rose Hobart (Dean Agnes Meeler); Charles Smith (Ulysses S. Jones); Lewis Russell (Dr. Wilmer Dawson); Iris Adrian (Rita La May); Frank Faylen (Geeger); Rhys Williams (Judge); Lloyd Bridges (Avery Wilson); Norma Varden (Mrs. Wilmer Dawson); James Millican (Keefe); Matt McHugh (Herman); Jimmie Smith (Peanuts); Minor Watson (Mr. Carver); Norman Rainey (Professor Lovell); Nestor Paiva (Tony, the Waiter); Mary Field (Della); Will Wright (Commissioner); Conrad Binyon (Newsboy); Dorothy Adams (Henry's Mother); Byron Foulger (Little Thin Man); Albert Ruiz (Globe Man); Byron Poindexter, Eddie Carnegie, Stan Johnson, Charles Mayon, Jerry James (Reporters); William Haade (Cap); John Hamilton (Judge); Kristine Miller (Coquette); Chester Conklin, Eddie Borden (Comedians); Esther Howard, Edward Gargan (Mr. & Mrs. Fogarty); George Sorel (Romain).

GOLDEN EARRINGS (PAR, 1947) 95 M.

Producer, Harry Tugend; director, Mitchell Leisen; based on the novel by Yolanda Foldes; screenplay, Abraham Polonsky, Frank Butler; art directors, Hans Dreier, John Meehan; set decorators, Sam Comer, Grace Gregory; music, Victor Young; music director, Phil Boutelje; choreography, Billy Daniel; songs, Young, Jay Livingston, Ray Evans; assistant director, Johnny Coonan; sound, Dan McKay, Walter Oberst; special

camera effects, Gordon Jennings; process camera, Farciot Edouart; camera, Daniel L. Fapp; editor, Alma Macrorie.

Ray Milland (Colonel Ralph Denistoun); Marlene Dietrich (Lydia); Murvyn Vye (Zoltan); Bruce Lester (Byrd); Dennis Hoey (Hoff); Quentin Reynolds (Himself); Reinhold Schunzel (Professor Korsigk); Ivan Triesault (Major Reimann); Hermine Sterler (Greta Korsigk); Eric Feldary (Zweig); Gisela Werbiserk (Dowager); Larry Simms (Page Boy); Hans von Morhart (S.S. Trooper); Mme. Louise Colombet (Flower Woman); Robert Val, Gordon Arnold (Gypsy Boys); Martha Bamattre (Wise Old Woman); Antonia Morales (Gypsy Dancer); Jack Wilson (Hitler Youth Leader); Stuart Holmes (Club Member).

VARIETY GIRL (PAR, 1947) 83 M.°

Producer, Daniel Dare; director, George Marshall; screenplay, Edmund Hartmann, Frank Tashlin, Robert Welch, Monte Brice; art directors, Hans Dreier, Robert Clatworthy; set decorators, Sam Comer, Ross Dowd; Puppetoon sequence, George Pal; music director, Joseph J. Lilley; music associate, Troy Sanders; orchestrator, N. Van Cleave; music for Puppetoon sequence, Edward Plumb; songs, Frank Loesser; assistant director, George Templeton; sound, Gene Merritt, John Cope; process camera, Farciot Edouart; special effects, Gordon Jennings; camera, Lionel Lindon, Stuart Thompson; editor, LeRoy Stone.

Mary Hatcher (Catherine Brown); Olga San Juan (Amber LaVonne); DeForest Kelley (Bob Kirby); William Demarest (Barker); Frank Faylen (Stage Manager); Frank Ferguson (J. R. O'Connell); Russell Hicks, Crane Whitley, Charles Coleman, Hal K. Dawson, Eddie Fetherston (Men at Steambath); Catherine Craig (Secretary); Bing Crosby, Bob Hope, Gary Cooper, Ray Milland, Alan Ladd, Barbara Stanwyck, Paulette Goddard, Dorothy Lamour, Veronica Lake, Sonny Tufts, Joan Caulfield, William Holden, Lizabeth Scott, Burt Lancaster, Gail Russell, Diana Lynn, Sterling Hayden, Robert Preston, John Lund, William Bendix, Barry Fitzgerald, Cass Daley, Howard da Silva, Billy De Wolfe, Macdonald Carey, Arleen Whelan, Patric Knowles, Mona Freeman, Cecil Kellaway, Johnny Coy, Virginia Field, Richard Webb, Stanley Clements, Cecil B. DeMille, Mitchell Leisen, Frank Butler, George Marshall, Roger Dann, Pearl Bailey, The Mulcay's, Spike Jones and His City Slickers, Mikhail Rasumny, Rae Patterson, George Reeves, Patricia Barry, June Harris, Wanda Hendrix, Sally Rawlinson, Andra Verne, Nanette Parks (Themselves); Ann Doran (Hairdresser); Glenn Tryon (Bill Farris); Nella Walker (Mrs. Webster); Harry Hayden (Grauman's Chinese Theatre Stage Manager); Janet Thomas, Roberta Jonay (Girls); Eric Alden (Makeup Man); Alma Macrorie (Proprietress); Willa Pearl Curtis (Sister Jenkins); Raymond Largay (Director of Variety Club); Mildred Boyd (Sister Jenkins' Daughter).

°Color sequence.

THE BIG CLOCK (PAR, 1948) 95 M.

Producer, Richard Maibaum; director, John Farrow; based on the novel by Kenneth Fearling; screenplay, Jonathan Latimer; art directors, Hans Dreier, Roland Anderson, Albert Nozaki; set decorators, Sam Comer, Ross Dowd; music, Victor Young; assistant director, William H. Coleman; makeup, Wally Westmore; costumes, Edith Head; sound, Hugo Granzbach, Gene Garvin; special effects, Gordon Jennings; process camera, Farciot Edouart; camera, John Seitz; editor, Eda Warren.

Ray Milland (George Stroud); Charles Laughton (Earl Janoth); Maureen O'Sullivan (Georgette Stroud); George Macready (Steven Hagen); Rita Johnson (Pauline York); Elsa Lanchester (Louise Patterson); Harold Vermilyea (Don Klausmeyer); Dan Tobin (Ray Cordette); Henry Morgan (Bill Womack); Richard Webb (Nat Sperling); Tad Van Brunt (Tony Watson); Elaine Riley (Lily Gold); Luis Van Rooten (Edwin Orlin); Lloyd Corrigan (McKinley); Margaret Field (Secretary); Philip Van Zandt (Sidney Kislav); Henri Letandal (Antique Dealer); Douglas Spencer (Bert Finch); Frank Orth (Burt, the Bartender); Bobby Watson (Milton Spaulding); Frances

291

Morris (Grace Adams); B. G. Norman (George, Jr.); Theresa Harris (Daisy); James Burke (Building Cop); Erno Verebes (Bartender); Noel Neill (Elevator Operator); Earle Hodgins (Guide); Edna Holland (Staff Member); Lane Chandler (Doorman); Lester Dorr (Cabby); Bert Moorhouse (Editor); Bess Flowers (Stylist in Conference Room); Napoleon Whiting (Bootblack); Diane Stewart (Girl); Eric Alden, Ralph Dunn, Harry Anderson (Guards).

SO EVIL MY LOVE (PAR, 1948) 109 M.

Producer, Hal B. Wallis; director, Lewis Allen; based on the novel by Joseph Shearing; screenplay, Leonard Spigelgass, Ronald Millar; art director, Thomas H. Morahan; assistant director, Mark Evans; costumes, Edith Head; music, Victor Young, William Alwyn; music director, Muir Mathieson; sound, W. H. Lindon; camera, Max Greene; editor, Vera Campbell, Leonard Trumm.

Ray Milland (Mark Bellis); Ann Todd (Olivia Harwood); Geraldine Fitzgerald (Susan Courtney); Leo G. Carroll (Jarvis); Raymond Huntley (Henry Courtney); Martita Hunt (Mrs. Courtney); Moira Lister (Kitty Feathers); Raymond Lovell (Edgar); Roderick Lovell (Sir John Curle); Muriel Aked (Miss Shoebridge); Finlay Currie (Dr. Krylie); Ivor Barnard (Mr. Watson); Hugh Griffith (Coroner); Gus Le Fuevre (Dr. Pound); Clarence Bigge (Dr. Cunningham); Leonie Lamartine (Proprietress).

MISS TATLOCK'S MILLIONS (PAR, 1948) 101 M.

Producer, Charles Brackett; director, Richard Haydn; suggested by the play Oh! Brother by Jacques Deval; screenplay, Brackett, Richard L. Breen; art directors, Hans Dreier, Franz Bachelin; set decorators, Sam Comer, Ross Dowd; music, Victor Young; assistant director, Harry Caplan; makeup, Wally Westmore; Costumes, Edith Head; sound, Gene Merritt, John Cope; special effects, Gordon Jennings; process camera, Farciot Edouart; camera, Charles B. Lang, Jr.; editor, Everett Douglas.

John Lund (Burke); Wanda Hendrix (Man Tatlock); Barry Fitzgerald (Denno Noonan); Monty Woolley (Miles Tatlock); Ilka Chase (Cassie Van Alen); Robert Stack (Nickey Van Alen); Dorothy Stickney (Emily Tatlock); Elizabeth Patterson (Cora); Leif Erickson (Dr. Mason); Dan Tobin (Clifford Tatlock); Hilo Hattie (Kamamamaluas); Richard Haydn (Fergel); Clifford Brooke (Pete); Howard Joslin (Assistant Director); Bill Neff (The Real Schuyler); Ray Milland (Himself); Mitchell Leisen (Director); Hugh Allen (Bartender); Beulah Christian (Upstairs Maid).

SEALED VERDICT (PAR, 1948) 83 M.

Producer, Robert Fellows; director, Lewis Allen; based on the novel by Lionel Shapiro; screenplay, Jonathan Latimer; art directors, Hans Dreier, John Meehan; set decorators, Sam Comer, Ray Moyer; music, Hugo Friedhofer; assistant director, Alvin Ganzer; makeup, Wally Westmore; costumes, Mary Kay Dodson; sound, Harry Lindgren, Gene Garvin; special effects, Gordon Jennings; process camera, Farciot Edouart; camera, Leo Tover; editor, Alma Macrorie.

Ray Milland (Major Robert Lawson); Florence Marley (Themis DeLisle); Broderick Crawford (Captain Kinsella); John Hoyt (General Otto Steigmann); John Ridgely (Captain Lance Nissen); Ludwig Donath (Jacob Meyersohn); Paul Lees (Private Clay Hockland); Olive Blakeney (Camilla Cameron); Marcel Journet (Captain Gribemont); Celia Lovsky (Emma Steigmann); Dan Tobin (Lieutenant Parker); James Bell (Elmer Hockland); Elisabeth Risdon (Cora Hockland); Frank Conroy (Colonel Pike); Charles Evans (General Kirkwood); June Jeffery (Erika Wagner); Patricia Miller (Maria Romanek); Selmer Jackson (Dr. Bossin); Ann Doran (Ellie Blaine); Dorothy Granger (Edna Brown); John Eldredge (Colonel Macklin); Eric Alden (Man/M.P. in Corridor); Archie Twitchell (Medical Captain); Otto Reichow (German Soldier); Carole Mathews (Nurse); Edward Van Sloan (Priest); Torben Meyer (Interpreter).

ALIAS NICK BEAL (PAR, 1949) 93 M.

Producer, Endre Bohem; director, John Farrow; story, Mindret Lord; screenplay, Jonathan Latimer; art directors, Hans Dreier, Franz Bachelin; set decorators, Sam Comer, Ross Dowd; music, Franz Waxman; makeup, Wally Westmore, Delven Armstrong, Ted Larson; costumes, Mary Kay Dodson; assistant director, Francisco Day; sound, Philip Wisdom, Gene Garvin; camera, Lionel Lindon; editor, Eda Warren.

Ray Milland (Nick Beal); Audrey Totter (Donna Allen); Thomas Mitchell (Joseph Foster); George Macready (Reverend Thomas Garfield); Fred Clark (Frankie Faulkner); Darryl Hickman (Larry Price); Henry O'Neill (Judge Hobson); Geraldine Wall (Martha Foster); Nestor Paiva (Karl); King Donovan (Peter Wolfe); Charles Evans (Paul Norton); Arlene Jenkins (Aileen); Pepito Perez (Poster Man); James Davies (Gym Instructor); John Shay (Assistant District Attorney); Maxine Gates (Josie); Stuart Holmes, Joe Whitehead (Ministers); Donya Dean (Information Girl); Charles Flickinger (Page Boy); Erno Verebes (Mr. Cox, the Tailor); Tom Dugan (Man); Steve Pendleton (Sergeant Hill, the Detective); Stuart Holmes (Civil Service Man); Philip Van Zandt (Watchman).

IT HAPPENS EVERY SPRING (20th, 1949) 80 M.

Producer, William Perlberg; director, Lloyd Bacon; story, Shirley W. Smith, Valentine Davies; screenplay, Davies; art directors, Lyle Wheeler, J. Russell Spencer; set decorators, Thomas Little, Stuart Reiss; music, Leigh Harline; music director, Lionel Newman; assistant director, Jasper Blystone; makeup, Ben Nye; costumes, Bonnie Cashin; sound, Eugene Grossman, Harry M. Leonard; camera, Joe MacDonald; editor, Bruce Pierce.

Ray Milland (Vernon Simpson); Jean Peters (Deborah Greenleaf); Paul Douglas (Monk Lanigan); Ed Begley (Stone); Ted de Corsia (Dolan); Ray Collins (Professor Greenleaf); Jessie Royce Landis (Mrs. Greenleaf); Alan Hale, Jr. (Schmidt); Bill Murphy (Isbell); William E. Green (Professor Forsythe); Edward Keane (Bell); Gene Evans (Mueller); Al Eben (Parker); Ruth Lee (Miss Collins); John Butler (Fan); Jane Van Duser (Miss Mengalstein); Ray Teal (Mac); Don Hicks (Assistant to Announcer); Mickey Simpson (Policeman); Johnny Calkins (Boy); Harry Cheshire (Doctor); Ward Brant, John McKee (Baseball Players); Debra Paget (Alice); Mae Marsh (Maid); Tom Hanlon (St. Louis Broadcaster); Sam Hayes (New York Announcer); Douglas Spencer (Conductor); Pat Combs (Messenger Boy); Robert Patten (Cab Driver).

A WOMAN OF DISTINCTION (COL, 1950) 85 M.

Producer, Buddy Adler; director, Edward Buzzell; story, Hugo Butler, Ian McLellan Hunter; screenplay, Charles Hoffman; additional dialog, Frank Tashlin; art director, Robert Peterson; music director, Morris Stoloff; camera, Joseph Walker; editor, Charles Nelson.

Rosalind Russell (Susan Middlecott); Ray Milland (Alec Stevenson); Edmund Gwenn (Mark Middlecott); Janis Carter (Teddy Evans); Mary Jane Saunders (Louisa); Francis Lederer (Paul Simons); Jerome Courtland (Jerome); Alex Gerry (Herman Pomeroy); Charles Evans (Dr. McFall); Charlotte Wynters (Miss Withers); Clifton Young (Chet); Gale Gordon (Station Clerk); Jean Willes (Pearl); Wanda McKay (Merle); Elizabeth Flourney (Laura); Harry Tyler (Charlie); Robert Malcolm, William E. Green (Conductors); Harry Cheshire (Stewart); Dudley Dickerson (Waiter); Gail Bonney (Woman); Charles Trowbridge (Jewelry Salesman); John Smith (Boy); Billy Newell (Bartender); Myron Healey (Cameraman); Harry Strang, Donald Kerr, Ted Jordan (Reporters); Lucille Ball (Guest); Harry Harvey, Jr. (Joe); Maxine Gates (Goldie); Lucille Brown (Manicurist).

A LIFE OF HER OWN (MGM, 1950) 108 M.

Producer, Voledemar Vetluguin; director, George Cukor; story-screenplay, Isobel Lennart; art directors, Cedric Gibbons, Arthur Lonergan; camera, George Folsey; editor, George White.

Lana Turner (Lily Brannel James); Ray Milland (Steve Harleigh); Tom Ewell (Tom Caraway); Louis Calhern (Jim Leversoe); Ann Dvorak (Mary Ashlon); Barry Sullivan (Lee Gorrance); Margaret Phillips (Nora Harleigh); Jean Hagen (Maggie Collins); Phyllis Kirk (Jerry); Sara Haden (Smitty); Hermes Pan (Lily's Dance Partner); Carol Brannan, Bethe Douglas, Roberta Johnson, Alice Wallace, Bunny Waters, Pat Davies, Dorothy Abbott, Bridget Carr, Charlene Hardey, Marlene Hoyt (Models); Tom Seidel (Bob Collins); Hilda Plowright (Desk Clerk); Elizabeth Flournoy (Caraway Receptionist); Dorothy Tree (Caraway Secretary); Robert Emmett Keane, Richard Anderson (Hosiery Men); Wilson Wood (Cab Driver); Harry Barris (Piano Player); Beverly Garland (Girl at Party); Whit Bissell (Rental Agent); Kathleen Freeman (Peg); Gertrude Graner (Woman Photographer); Major Sam Harris (Man Model); Frankie Darro (Bellboy); Queenie Leonard (Hotel Matron); Paul Kramer (Airport Gateman); Kenny Garcia, Arthur Loew, Jr., Peter Thompson, Walter McGrail, Joan Valeries, Kerry O'Day, Carol Brewster, Beverly Thompson, Lee Lynn, Meredith Leeds (People at Party).

COPPER CANYON (PAR, 1950) C—83 M.

Producer, Mel Epstein; director, John Farrow; story, Richard English; screenplay, Jonathan Latimer; art directors, Hans Dreier, Franz Bachelin; camera, Charles B. Lang, Jr.; editor, Eda Warren.

Ray Milland (Johnny Carter); Hedy Lamarr (Lisa Roselle); Macdonald Carey (Lane Travis); Mona Freeman (Caroline Desmond); Harry Carey, Jr. (Lieutenant Ord); Frank Faylen (Mullins); Hope Emerson (Ma Tarbet); Taylor Holmes (Theodosius Roberts); Peggy Knudsen (Cora); James Burke (Jeb Bassett); Percy Helton (Scamper); Philip Van Zandt (Sheriff Wattling); Francis Pierlot (Moss Balfour); Erno Verebes (Professor); Paul Lees (Bat Laverne); Robert Watson (Bixby); Georgia Backus (Martha Bassett); Ian Wolfe (Mr. Henderson); Bob Kortman (Bill Newton); Nina Mae McKinney (Theresa); Len Hendry (Bartender); Earl Hodgins, Robert Stephenson (Miners); Buddy Roosevelt (Lew Partridge); Julia Faye (Proprietor's Wife); Joe Whitehead (Proprietor); Hank Bell (Man); Ethan Laidlaw, Russell Kaplan (Deputies); Alan Dinehart III (Youngest Bassett Boy); Rex Lease (Southerner); Stanley Andrews (Bartender); Kit Guard (Storekeeper/Miner); Stuart Holmes (Barber/Townsman).

NIGHT INTO MORNING (MGM, 1951) 86 M.

Producer, Edwin H. Knopf; director, Fletcher Markle; story-screenplay, Karl Tunberg, Leonard Spigelgass; music, Carmen Dragon; art directors, Cedric Gibbons, James Basevi; camera, George J. Folsey; editors, George White, Robert Watts.

Ray Milland (Phillip Ainley); John Hodiak (Tom Lawry); Nancy Davis (Katherine Mead); Lewis Stone (Dr. Horace Snyder); Jean Hagen (Girl Next Door); Rosemary De Camp (Anne Ainley); Dawn Addams (Dotty Phelps); Jonathan Cott (Chuck Holderson); Celia Lovsky (Mrs. Niemoller); Gordon Gebert (Russ Kirby); Katharine Warren (Mrs. Anderson); Harry Antrim (Mr. Anderson); Mary Lawrence (Waitress); Herb Vigran (Bartender); Wheaton Chambers (Conductor); John Eldredge, Matt Moore (Instructors); Whit Bissell (Stone Yard Proprietor); Percy Helton, John "Skins" Miller (Drunks).

CIRCLE OF DANGER (Coronada-Eagle Lion, 1951) 86 M.

Producer, David E. Rose, Joan Harrison; director, Jacques Tourneur; based on the novel White Heather by Philip MacDonald; screenplay, MacDonald.

Ray Milland (Clay Douglas); Patricia Roc (Elspeth Graham); Marius Goring (Sholto Lewis); Hugh Sinclair (Hamish McArran); Naunton Wayne (Reggie Sinclair); Marjorie Fielding (Mrs. McArran); Edward Rigby (Idwal Llewellyn); John Bailey (Pape Llewellyn); Colin Gordon (Colonel Fairbairn); Dora Bryan (Bubbles); Michael Brennan (Bert Oakshott); Reginald Beckwith (Oliver); David Hutcheson (Tony Wrexham).

RHUBARB (PAR, 1951) 95 M.

Producers, William Perlberg, George Seaton; director, Arthur Lubin; based on the novel by H. Allen Smith; screenplay, Dorothy Reid, Francis Cockrell; additional dialog, David Stern; art directors, Hal Pereira, Henry Bumstead; music, Van Cleave; camera, Lionel Lindon; editor, Alma Macrorie.

Ray Milland (Eric Yeager); Jan Sterling (Polly Sickles); Gene Lockhart (Thaddeus J. Banner); William Frawley (Len Sickles); Elsie Holmes (Myra Banner); Taylor Holmes (P. Duncan Munk); Willard Waterman (Orlando Dill); Henry Slate (Dud Logan); James J. Griffith (Oggie Meadows); Jim Hayward (Doom); Donald MacBride (Phenny); Hal K. Dawson (Mr. Fisher); Strother Martin (Shortly McGirk); Hilda Plowright (Katie); Adda Gleason (Maid); Richard Karlan (Pencil Louie); Edwin Max (Fish Eye); Anthony Radecki, Leonard Nimoy, Bill Thrope, Frank Fiumara, Lee Miller (Ball Players); Roy Gordon, Stuart Holmes, Eric Wilton, Wilbur Mack (Golfers); Harry Cheshire (Mr. Seegle); John Breen (Western Union Boy); Tristram Coffin (Dr. Stillman); Donald Kerr (Taxi Driver); Mack Gray (Detective); Oliver Blake (Cadaver Jones); Paul Douglas (Man in Park); Stanley Orr (Newspaper Reporter).

CLOSE TO MY HEART (WB, 1951) 90 M.

Producer, William Jacobs; director, William Keighley; based on the story "A Baby for Midge" by James R. Webb; screenplay, Webb; art director, Leo K. Kuter; music, Max Steiner; camera, Robert Burks; editor, Clarence Kolster.

Ray Milland (Brad Sheridan); Gene Tierney (Midge Sheridan); Fay Bainter (Mrs. Morrow); Howard St. John (B. O. Frost); Mary Beth Hughes (Arlene); Ann Morrison (Mrs. Barker); James Seay (Heilner); Baby John Winslow (The Baby); Nan Boardman (Woman Patient); Elizabeth Flournoy (Receptionist); John Alvin (Haggard Man); Louis Jean Heydt (Mr. Duncan); Ralph Byrd (Charlie); Kathleen Stendal (Woman Doctor); Lois Hall, Rodney Bell (Young Parents); George LaMond (Hotel Clerk); Fred Graham (Guard); Lee Prather (Farmer.)

BUGLES IN THE AFTERNOON (WB, 1952) C—85 M.

Producer, William Cagney; director, Roy Rowland; based on the story by Ernest Haycox; screenplay, Geoffry Homes, Harry Brown; art director, Edward Carrere; music director, Ray Heindorf; camera, Wilfrid M. Cline; editor, Thomas Reilly.

Ray Milland (Kern Shafter); Helena Carter (Josephine Russel); Hugh Marlowe (Garnett); Forrest Tucker (Donovan); Barton MacLane (Moylan); George Reeves (Lieutenant Smith); James Millican (Sergeant Hines); Gertrude Michael (May); Stuart Randall (Bannack Bill); William "Bill" Phillips (Tinney); Dick Rich (Bierss); John Pickard (McDermott); John War Eagle (Red Owl); Sheb Wooley (General Custer); Charles Evans (General Terry); Nelson Leigh (Major Reno); Ray Montgomery (Osborne); Virginia Brissac (Mrs. Carson); John Doucette (Bill); Bud Osborne (Teamster); Hugh Beaumont (Lieutenant Cooke); Harry Lauter (Corporal Jackson); Bob Steele (Horseman); Mary Adams, Lucille Shamburger (Women).

SOMETHING TO LIVE FOR (PAR, 1952) 89 M.

Producer-director, George Stevens; screenplay, Dwight Taylor; music, Victor Young; art directors, Hal Pereira, Walter Tyler; camera, George Barnes; editor, William Hornbeck.

Ray Milland (Alan Miller); Joan Fontaine (Jenny Carey); Teresa Wright (Edna Miller); Richard Derr (Tony Collins); Douglas Dick (Baker); Herbert Heyes (Crawley); Harry Bellaver (Billy); Paul Valentine (Albert); Frank Orth (Waiter); Bob Cornthwaite (Young Man); Helen Spring (Mrs. Crawley); Rudy Lee (Chris); Patric Mitchell (Johnny); Richard Barron (Headwaiter); Paul Newlan (Bartender); John Indirseno (Party Guest); Jessie Proctor, Lillian Clayes, Genevieve Bell, Patsy O'Byrne, Helen Dickson, Cora Shannon (Old Ladies); Mari Blanchard (Hat Check Girl); Mary Field, Judith Allen

(Women); Kerry Vaughn (Cocktail Waitress); Sherry Jackson (Little Girl); Rolfe Sedan (Frenchman); Jean Acker Valentino (Wife); Sue Carlton (Intellectual); Alex Akimoff (Waiter); King Donovan (Stage Manager); Eric Alden (Pharoah); Ida Moore (Woman); Jody Gilbert (Woman in Telephone Booth); Norman Field (Man); Maurice Cass (Critic).

THE THIEF (UA, 1952) 85 M.

Producer, Harry M. Popkin; associate producer, Clarence Greene; director, Russell Rouse; screenplay, Greene, Rouse; music, Herschel Gilbert; production designer, Joseph St. Amend; camera, Sam Leavitt.

Ray Milland (Allan Fields); Martin Gabel (Mr. Bleek); Rita Gam (The Girl); Harry Bronson (Harris); John McKutcheon (Dr. Linstrum); Rita Vale (Miss Philips); Rex O'Malley (Beal); Joe Conlin (Walters).

JAMAICA RUN (PAR, 1953) C—92 M.

Producers, William H. Pine, William C. Thomas; director, Lewis R. Foster; based on the novel The Neat Little Corpse *by Max Murray; screenplay, Foster; art directors, Hal Pereira, Earl Hedrick; camera, Lionel Lindon; editor, Howard Smith.*

Ray Milland (Patrick Fairlie); Arlene Dahl (Ena Dacey); Wendell Corey (Todd Dacey); Patric Knowles (William Montague); Laura Elliot (Janice Clayton); Carroll McComas (Mrs. Dacey); William Walker (Human); Murray Matheson (Inspector Mole); Clarence Muse (Mose); Michael Moore (Robert Clayton); Rex Evans (Judge Henry); Robert Warwick (Court Judge); Lester Mathews (Judge); Robert A. Davis (Rob).

LET'S DO IT AGAIN (COL, 1953) C—95 M.

Producer, Oscar Saul; director, Alexander Hall; based on the play The Awful Truth *by Arthur Richman; screenplay, Mary Loos, Richard Sale; songs, Lester Lee and Ned Washington; choreography, Lee Scott, Valerie Bettis; music director, Morris Stoloff; additional music, George Duning; assistant director, Earl Bellamy; gowns, Jean Louis; art director, Walter Holscher; set decorator, William Kiernan; camera, Charles Lawton, Jr.; editor, Charles Nelson.*

Jane Wyman (Constance Stuart); Ray Milland (Gary Stuart); Aldo Ray (Frank McGraw); Leon Ames (Chet Stuart); Valerie Bettis (Lilly Adair); Tom Helmore (Courtney Craig); Karin Booth (Deborah Randolph); Mary Treen (Nelly); Richard Wessel (Mover); Kathryn Givney (Mrs. Randolph); Herbert Heyes (Mr. Randolph); Maurice Stein (Willie); Frank Remley (Pete); Don Gibson (Gas Station Attendant); Bob Hopkins (Mover); Anthony De Mario (Wine Steward); Herb Vigran (Charlie, the Theatre Manager); Walter Clinton (Attendant); Frank Connor (Man); Major Sam Harris, Leoda Richards (Bits); Howard Negley (Charlie, the Cop); Douglas Evans (Black Cat Club Manager); Joey Ray (Chauffeur).

DIAL M FOR MURDER (WB, 1954) C—88 M.

Producer-director, Alfred Hitchcock; based on the play by Frederick Knott; screenplay, Knott; art directors, Edward Carrere, George James Hopkins; music-music conductor, Dmitri Tiomkin; costumes, Moss Mabry; sound, Oliver S. Garretson; camera, Robert Burks; editor, Rudi Fehr.

Ray Milland (Tom Wendice); Grace Kelly (Margot Wendice); Robert Cummings (Mark Halliday); John Williams (Chief Inspector Hubbard); Anthony Dawson (Captain Swan Lesgate); Leo Britt (The Narrator); Patrick Allen (Pearson); George Leigh (William); George Alderson (The Detective); Robin Hughes (A Police Sergeant); Alfred Hitchcock (Man in Club Photo).

THE GIRL IN THE RED VELVET SWING (20th, 1955) C—109 M.

Producer, Charles Brackett; director, Richard Fleischer; screenplay, Walter Reisch, Brackett; art directors, Lyle R. Wheeler, Maurice Ransford; music, Leigh Harline; orchestrator, Edward B. Powell; music director, Lionel Newman; wardrobe, Charles LeMaire; choreography, David Robel; assistant director, Ben Kadish; camera, Milton Krasner; editor, William Mace.

Ray Milland (Stanford White); Joan Collins (Evelyn Nesbit Thaw); Farley Granger (Harry K. Thaw); Luther Adler (Delphin Delmas); Cornelia Otis Skinner (Mrs. Thaw); Glenda Farrell (Mrs. Nesbit); Frances Fuller (Mrs. White); Philip Reed (Robert Collier); Gale Robbins (Gwen Arden); James Lorimer (McCaleb); John Hoyt (William Travers Jerome); Harvey Stephens (Dr. Hollingshead); Emile Meyer (Greenbacher); Richard Travis (Charles Dana Gibson); Harry Seymour (Arthur); Ainslie Pryor (Sport Donnally); Kay Hammond (Nellie); Betty Caulfield (Alice); Karolee Kelly (Margaret); Jack Raine (Mr. Finley); Leslie Parrish, Diane DuBois, Suzanne Alexander, Peggy Connelly, Rosemary Ace, Jean McCallen (Flora Dora Girls); Edmund Cobb (Jury Foreman); James Conaty (Reverend McEven); Oliver Cross (Head Steward); Max Wagner, Steve Darrell, Henry Kulky (Wardens); Edith Evanson (Josie); William Forrest (Simpson); Stuart Holmes (Old Man at Restaurant); Major Sam Harris (Old Man at Show);

A MAN ALONE (REP, 1955) C—96 M.

Producer, Herbert J. Yates; director, Ray Milland; story, Mort Briskin; screenplay, John Tucker Battle; art director, Walter Keller; music director, Victor Young; assistant director, Ivan Volkman; costumes, Adele Palmer; camera, Lionel Lindon; editor, Richard I. Van Enger.

Ray Milland (Wes Steele); Mary Murphy (Nadine Corrigan); Ward Bond (Gil Corrigan); Raymond Burr (Stanley); Arthur Space (Dr. Mason); Lee Van Cleef (Clantin); Alan Hale (Anderson); Douglas Spencer (Henry Slocum); Thomas B. Henry (Maybanks); Grandon Rhodes (Luke Joiner); Martin Garralaga (Ortega); Kim Spalding (Sam Hall); Howard J. Negley (Wilson); Julian Rivero (Tio Rubio); Lee Roberts (Higgs); Minerva Urecal (Mrs. Maule); Thorpe Whiteman (Boy); Dick Rich (Kincaid); Frank Hagney (Dorfman).

LISBON (REP, 1956) C—90 M.

Producer-director, Ray Milland; story, Martin Rackin; screenplay, John Humberto Madeira; music, Nelson Riddle; camera, Jack Marta; editor, Richard L. Van Enger.

Ray Milland (Captain Robert John Evans); Maureen O'Hara (Sylvia Merrill); Claude Rains (Aristides Mavros); Yvonne Furneaux (Maria Maddalena Masanet); Francis Lederer (Serafim); Percy Marmont (Lloyd Merrill); Jay Novello (Joao Casimiro Fonseca); Edward Chapman (Edgar Selwyn); Harold Jamieson (Phillip Norworth); Humberto Madeira (Tio Rabio).

THREE BRAVE MEN (20th, 1957) 88 M.

Producer, Herbert B. Swope, Jr.; director, Phillip Dunne; based on articles by Anthony Lewis; screenplay, Dunne; art directors, Lyle R. Wheeler, Mark-Lee Kirk; music, Hans Salter; special camera effects, Ray Kellogg; camera, Charles G. Clarke; editor, David Brotherton.

Ray Milland (Joe di Marco); Ernest Borgnine (Bernie Goldsmith); Frank Lovejoy (Captain Winfield); Nina Foch (Lieutenant McCoy); Dean Jagger (Rogers); Virginia Christine (Helen Goldsmith); Edward Andrews (Major Jensen); Frank Faylen (Enos Warren); Diane Jergens (Shirley Goldsmith); Warren Berlinger (Harry); Andrew Duggan (Browning); Joseph Wiseman (Jim Barron); James Westerfield (O'Reilly); Richard Anderson (Lieutenant Horton); Olive Blakeney (Miss Scott); Robert Burton (Dietz); Jason Wingreen (Perry); Ray Montgomery (Sanford); Sandy Descher (Alice); Patty Ann Gerrity (Ruthie); Jonathan Hole (Gibbons); Barbara Gould (Susie); Fern Barry (Miss Howell); Lee Roberts (Investigator); Selmer Jackson (Retired Admiral); John Close (Photographer); Keith Vincent (East); Tom Daly (Sherrod); Juanita Close (Bernie's Secretary); Edith Claire (Dietz's Secretary); Walter Woolf (Admiral Mason); Gene O'Donnell (Washington Correspondent); Carleton Young (Board Chairman).

THE RIVER'S EDGE (20th, 1957) C—87 M.

Producer, Benedict Bogeaus; director, Allan Dwan; based on the novel The Highest Mountain *by Harold Jacob Smith; screenplay, Smith, James Leicester; music, Louis Forbes; songs, Forbes and Bobby Troup; camera, Harold Lipstein; editor, Leicester.*

Ray Milland (Nardo Denning); Anthony Quinn (Ben Cameron); Debra Paget (Meg Cameron); Harry Carey, Jr. (Chet); Chubby Johnson (Whiskers); Byron Foulger (Barry); Tom McKee (U.S. Border Patrol Captain); Frank Gerstle (U.S. Border Patrolman)

THE SAFECRACKER (MGM, 1958) 96 M.

Producer, John R. Sloan; director, Ray Milland; based on the story "The Willie Gordon Story" by Lieutenant Colonel Rhys Davies, Bruce Thomas; screenplay, Paul Monash; art director, Elliot Scott; assistant director, David Middlemas; makeup, Bill Lodge; music, Richard Rodney Bennett; music conductor, Muir Mathieson; technical advisor, Captain J. I. H. Owen; sound, Jerry Turner, J. B. Smith; camera, Gerald Gibbs; editor, Ernest Walter.

Ray Milland (Colley Dawson); Barry Jones (Bennett Carfield); Jeannette Sterke (Irene); Ernest Clark (Major Adbury); Melissa Stribling (Vi); Victor Maddern (Morris); Cyril Raymond (Inspector Frankham); Barbara Everest (Mrs. Dawson); Bernard Fox (Shafter); Richard Shaw (Bailey); Ian MacNaughton (Thomson); Henry Vidon (Guerin); David Horne (Fenwright); Jackie Collins (Fenwright's Secretary); Colin Tapley (Colonel Charles Mercer); Ferdy Mayne (Greek Ship Owner); John Robinson (Assistant Chief of Staff); David Lodge (Parachute Instructor); Wolf Frees (German Commandant); Ernest Walder (German Security Policeman).

HIGH FLIGHT (COL, 1958) 102 M.

Producers, Irving Allen, Albert R. Broccoli; associate producer, Phil C. Samuel; director, John Gilling; story, Jack Davies; screenplay, Joseph Landon, Kenneth Hughes; assistant director, Bluey Hill; music, Kenneth V. Jones, Douglas Gamley; music conductor, Muir Mathieson; choreography, Tutte Lemkow; tunes, Eric Coates; Anthony Newley; art director, John Box; technical advisor, Group Captain John Pringle; second unit directors, Max Varnel, Anthony Squire, Bernard Mainwaring; makeup, Freddie Williamson; sound, Don Saunders, David Elliott; special effects, Cliff Richardson; camera, Ted Moore; editor, Jack Slade.

Ray Milland (Wing Commander David Rudge); Bernard Lee (Flight Sergeant Harris); Kenneth Haigh (Tony Winchester, Jr.); Anthony Newley (Rodger Endicott); Kenneth Fortescue (John Fletcher); Sean Kelly (Cadet Day); Helen Cherry (Louise); Leslie Phillips (Squadron Leader Blake); Kynaston Reeves (Air Minister); John LeMesurier (Commandant); Jan Holden (Jackie); Richard Wattis (Chauffeur); Andrew Keir (Valetta Instructor); Noel Hood (Tweedy Lady); Ian Fleming (Bishop); Grace Arnold (Commandant's Wife); Douglas Gibbon (Cadet Seymour); Bernard Horsfall (Radar Operator).

THE PREMATURE BURIAL (AIP, 1962) C—81 M.

Producer-director, Roger Corman; based on the story by Edgar Allan Poe; screenplay, Charles Beaumont, Ray Russell; art director, Daniel Haller; costumes, Marjorie Corso; music, Ronald Stein; camera, Floyd Crosby; editor, Ronald Sinclair.

Ray Milland (Guy Carrell); Hazel Court (Emily Gault); Richard Ney (Miles Archer); Heather Angel (Kate Carrell); Alan Napier (Dr. Gideon Gault); John Dierkes (Sweeney); Richard Miller (Mole); Brendan Dillon (Minister).

PANIC IN YEAR ZERO (AIP, 1962)) 92 M.

Executive producer, James H. Nicholson, Samuel Z. Arkoff; producers, Arnold Houghland, Lou Rusoff; director, Ray Milland; story, Jay Simms; screenplay, Simms, John Morton; music, Les Baxter; art director-set decorator, Daniel Haller; makeup, Ted Cooley; titles, Ray Mercer; assistant director, Jim Engle; sound, Steve Bass, Al Bird; special effects, Pat Dinga, Larry Butler; camera, Gil Warrenton; editor, William Austin.

Ray Milland (Harry Baldwin); Jean Hagen (Ann Baldwin); Frankie Avalon (Rick Baldwin); Mary Mitchel (Karen Baldwin); Joan Freeman (Marilyn Hayes); Richard Garland (Mr. Johnson); Richard Bakalyan (Carl); Rex Holman (Mickey); Neil Nephew (Andy); Willis Bouchey (Dr. Strong); O. Z. Whitehead (Hogan); Byron Morrow (Haenel); Shary Marshall (Mrs. Johnson); Russ Bender (Harkness); Hugh Sanders (Becker).

THE MAN WITH THE X-RAY EYES (AIP, 1963) C—80 M.

Executive producers, James H. Nicholson, Samuel Z. Arkoff; producer-director, Roger Corman; story, Ray Russell; screenplay, Robert Dillon, Ray Russell; art director, Daniel Haller; costumes, Marjorie Corso; makeup, Ted Cooley; assistant director, Jack Bohrer; music, Les Baxter; camera, Floyd Crosby; editor, Anthony Carras.

Ray Milland (Dr. James Xavier); Diana Van Der Vlis (Dr. Diane Fairfax); Harold J. Stone (Dr. Sam Brant); John Hoyt (Dr. Willard Benson); Don Rickles (Crane); John Dierkes (Preacher); Lorie Summers (Party Dancer); Vicki Lee (Young Girl Patient); Kathryn Hart (Mrs. Mart); Carol Irey (Woman Patient); Morris Ankrum (Foundation Head); Richard Meller (John Trask/Hickler).

THE CONFESSION (Golden Eagle, 1965) C—100 M.

Producer, William Marshall; director, William Dieterle; screenplay, Allen Scott; art directors, Jim Sullivan, Willis Connor; production supervisor, Lee Lukather; music, Michael Colicchio; title designs, Sal Maimone; camera, Robert Bronner; editor, Carl Lerner.

Ginger Rogers (Mme. Ranaldi); Ray Milland (Mario Forni); Barbara Eden (Pia Pacelli); Carl Schell (Beppo); Michael Ansara (Mayor Pablo); Walter Abel (The Thief); Vinton Haworth (Aguesta); David Hurst (Gustave); Pippa Scott (Gina); Cecil Kellaway (The Bishop); Elliott Gould (The Mute); and: Julian Upton, Mara Lynn, Carol Ann Daniels, Leonard Cimino, Michael Youngman.

A.k.a.: QUICK, LET'S GET MARRIED; SEVEN DIFFERENT WAYS.

HOSTILE WITNESS (UA, 1968) 101 M.

Producer, David E. Rose; associate producer, Pat Green; director, Ray Milland; based on the play by Jack Roffey; screenplay, Roffey; assistant director, Ray Frift; art director, George Provis; sound, Brian Marshall; camera, Gerry Gibbs; editor, Bernard Gribble.

Ray Milland (Simon Crawford, Q.C.); Sylvia Sims (Sheila Larkin); Felix Aylmer (Mr. Justice Osborne); Raymond Huntley (John Naylor); Geoffrey Lumsden (Major Hugh Maitland); Norman Barrs (Charles Milburn); Percy Marmont (Sir Matthew Gregory); Dulcie Bowman (Lady Gregory); Ewan Roberts (Hamish Gillespie); Richard Hurndall (Inspector Elsy); Ronald Leigh-Hunt (Dr. Wimborne); Sandra Fehr (Joanna Crawford); Edward Waddy (Usher); Maggie McGrath (Julia Kelly); Ballard Berkeley (Court Clerk).

RED ROSES FOR THE FUEHRER (Dino Films, 1968) C—100 M.

Director, Fernando Di Leo; screenplay, Luigi Petrini; music, Gino Pegreri; sets, Elio Baletti; camera, Franco Villan.

With: James Daly, Anna-Maria Pierangeli, Peter Van Eyck, Ray Milland, Nino Castelnuovo, Mia Gemberg, Gianni Garko.

DAUGHTER OF THE MIND (ABC-TV, 1969) C—90 M.

Producer-director, Walter Grauman; based on the novel The Hand of Mary Constable *by Paul Gallico; teleplay, Luther Davis.*

Don Murray (Lauder); Ray Milland (Professor Constable); Gene Tierney (Lenore); Barbara Dana (Tina); Edward Asner (Wiener); Pamelyn Ferdin (Mary); Ivor Barry (Cryden);

George Macready (Ferguson); William Beckley (Bessmer); John Carradine (Bosch); Cecile Ozorio (Devi); Frank Maxwell (General Augstadt); Bill Hickman (Enemy Agent); Hal Frederick (Technician); Virginia Christine (Helga).

COMPANY OF KILLERS (UNIV, 1970) C—90 M.

Producers, E. Jack Neuman, Jerry Thorpe; associate producer, Lloyd Richards; director, Thorpe; screenplay, Neuman; music, Richard Hazard; assistant director, Paul Cameron; art directors, Alexander Golitzen, Joseph Alves; camera, Jack Marta; editor, John Elias.

Van Johnson (Sam Cahill); Ray Milland (Georges DeSalles); John Saxon (Dave Poohler); Clu Gulager (Frank Quinn); Brian Kelly (Nick Andros); Fritz Weaver (John Shankalien); Susan Oliver (Thelma Dwyer); Diana Lynn (Edwina De-Salles); Robert Middleton (Owen Brady); Terry Carter (Max Jaffie); Ahna Capri (Maryjane Smythe); Anthony James (Jimmy Konic); Marian Collier (Sylvia Xavier); Nate Esformes (Peterson); Mercer Harris (Luke); Joyce Jameson (Marnie); Gerald Hiken (Chick); Vince Howard (Dale Christian); Larry Thor (Clarington); Donna Michelle (Gloria); Jeanne Bal (Patricia Cahill).

LOVE STORY (PAR, 1970) C—100 M.

Executive producer, David Golden; producer, Howard G. Minsky; director, Arthur Hiller; screenplay, Erich Segal; music, Francis Lai; art director, Robert Gundlach; set decorator, Phil Smith; assistant director, Peter Scoppa; costumes, Alice Manougian Martin, Pearl Somner; makeup, Martin Bell; sound, Jack Jacobson; camera, Dick Kratina; editor, Robert C. Jones.

Ali MacGraw (Jenny Cavilleri); Ryan O'Neal (Oliver Barrett IV); Ray Milland (Oliver Barrett III); Katherine Balfour (Mrs. Oliver Barrett III); John Marley (Phil Cavilleri); Russell Nype (Dean Thompson); Sydney Walker (Dr. Shapely); Robert Modica (Dr. Addison); Walker Daniels (Ray); Tom Lee Jones (Hank); John Merensky (Steve); Andrew Duncan (Reverend Blauvelt); Bob O'Connell (Tommy, the Doorman); and: Sudie Bond, Milo Boulton, Julie Garfield, Charlotte Ford.

RIVER OF GOLD (ABC-TV, 1971) C—90 M.

Producers, David Friedkin, Mort Fine; director, Friedkin; teleplay, Salvatore C. Puedes; music, Fred Steiner.

Ray Milland (Evelyn Rose); Suzanne Pleshette (Anna); Dack Rambo (Riley Briggs); Roger Davis (Marcus McAllister); Melissa Newman (Julie); Jorge Luke (Tomas); Pedro Armendariz, Jr. (Angel); Jose Chavez (Rodrigo); Eduardo Lopez Rojas (Cepeda); Teddy Stauffer (Jay Marston); Barbara Angeli (Tina Marston); Francisco Cordova (Priest).

THE BIG GAME (Comet, 1972) C—90 M.

Producer, Stanley Norman; director, Robert Day; screenplay, Norman, Day; camera, Mario Fioretti.

With: Stephen Boyd, France Nuyen, Ray Milland, Cameron Mitchell, Brendon Boone, Michael Kirner, John Stacy, George Wang, John Van Dreelan.

FROGS (AIP, 1972) C—91 M.

Executive producer, Norman T. Herman; producers, George Edwards, Peter Thomas; director, George McCowan; story, Robert Hutchison; screenplay, Hutchison, Robert Blees; music, Les Baxter; music supervisor, Al Simms; wardrobe, Phyllis Garr; makeup, Tom Burman; electronics effects, Joe Sidore; camera, Mario Tosi; editor, Fred R. Feitshans, Jr.

Ray Milland (Jason Crockett); Sam Elliott (Pickett Smith); Joan Van Ark (Karen Crockett); Adam Roarke (Clint Crockett); Judy Pace (Bella Berenson); Lynn Borden (Jenny Crockett); Mae Mercer (Maybelle); David Gilliam (Michael Martindale); Nicholas Cortland (Kenneth Martindale); George Skaff (Stuart Martindale); Lance Taylor, Sr. (Charles); Holly Irving (Iris Martindale); Dale Willingham (Tina Crockett); Hal Hodges (Jay Crockett); Carolyn Fitzsimmons (Lady in Car); Robert Sanders (Bobby, the Young Boy in Car).

THE THING WITH TWO HEADS (AIP, 1972) C—93 M.

Executive producer, John Lawrence; producer, Wes Bishop; director, Lee Frost; story, Frost, Bishop; screenplay, Bishop, Frost, James Gordon White; songs, Porter Jordan; Mike Curb Congregation.

Ray Milland (Dr. Max Kirshner); Rosey Grier (Jack Moss); Don Marshall (Dr. Fred Williams); Roger Perry (Dr. Philip Desmond); Kathy Baumann (Nurse Patricia); Chelsea Brown (Lila); John Dullaghan (Thomas); John Bliss (Dr. Donald Smith); Rick Baker (Gorilla); Lee Frost (Sergeant Hacker); Dick Whittington (TV Newscaster); William Smith (Hysterical Condemned Man); Tommy Cook (Chaplain); Jerry Butler, George E. Carey, Albert Zugsmith (Guest Performers); and: Britt Nilson, Phil Hoover, Michael Viner.

EMBASSY (Hemdale, 1972) C—90 M.

Producer, Mel Ferrer; director, Gordon Hessler; based on the novel by Stephen Coulter; screenplay, William Fairchild; additional material, John Bird; assistant director, Frank Ernst; production designer, John Howell; art director, Maurice Labbaye Fenykovy; set decorator, Klary Confalonieri; music, Jonathan Hodge; song, Biddu; sound, Joe Christo; camera, Raoul Coutart; editor, Willy Kemplen.

Richard Roundtree (Shannon); Chuck Connors (Kesten); Marie-Jose Nat (Laure); Ray Milland (Ambassador); Broderick Crawford (Dunninger); Max von Sydow (Gorenko); David Bauer (Kadish); Larry Cross (Gamble); David Healy (Phelan); Karl Held (Rylands); Sarah Marshall (Miss Harding); Dee Pollack (Stacey); Afif Boulos (Foreign Minister); Leila Buheiry (Leila); Gail Clymer (Switchboard Operator); Edmond Rannania (First Man in Black); Mounir Massari (Michel el Fahdi); Saladin Nader (Roger); David Parker (Tuler); Dean Turner (Clem Gelber); Peter Smith (Cypher Clerk).

THE HOUSE IN NIGHTMARE PARK (MGM-British, 1973) C—95 M.

Executive producer, Beryl Verture; producers, Clive Exton, Terry Nation; director, Peter Sykes; screenplay, Exton, Nation; assistant director, Michael Dryhurst; art director, Maurice Carter; set decorator, Andrew Campbell; music, Harry Robinson; costumes, Judy Moorcroft; sound, Rene Borisewitz, Ken Barker; camera, Ian Wilson; editor, Bill Blunden.

Frankie Howerd (Foster Twelvetrees); Ray Milland (Stewart Henderson); Hugh Burden (Major Reginald Henderson); Kenneth Griffith (Ernest Henderson); John Bennett (Patel); Rosalie Crutchley (Jessica Henderson); Ruth Dunning (Agnes Henderson); Elizabeth MacLennan (Verity); Aimee Delamain (Mother); Peter Munt (Cabbie).

TERROR IN THE WAX MUSEUM (CIN, 1973) C—93 M.

Executive producer, Charles A. Pratt; producer, Andrew J. Fenady; director, Georg Fenady; story, Andrew J. Fenady; screenplay, Jameson Brewer; music, George Duning; production designer, Stan Jolley; set decorator, Carl Biddiscombe; assistant director, Floyd Joyer; sound, David Ronne, David Dockendorf; camera, William Jurgensen; editor, Melvin Shapiro.

Ray Milland (Harry Flexner); Broderick Crawford (Amos Burns); Elsa Lanchester (Julia Hawthorn); Maurice Evans (Inspector Daniels); Shani Wallis (Laurie Mell); John Carradine (Claude Dupree); Louis Hayward (Tim Fowley); Patric Knowles (Southcott); Mary K. Edwards (Sergeant Michael Hawks); Lisa Lu (Madame Yang); Steven Marlo (Karkov); Nicole Shelby (Meg); Ben Wright (Constable); Matilda Calman, Peggy Stewart (Charwomen); Don Herbert (Jack the Ripper); Judy Wetmore (Lizzie Borden); George Farinia (Bluebeard); Rosa Huerta (Lucretia Borgia); Rickie Weir (Marie Antoinette); Ben Brown (Attila the Hun); Paul Wilson (Ivan the Terrible).

GOLD (AA, 1974) C—118 M.

Producer, Michael Klinger; director, Peter Hunt; based on

the novel Goldmine *by Wilbur Smith; screenplay, Smith, Stanley Price; production designer, Alec Vetchinsky, Syd Cain; music, Elmer Bernstein; assistant director, Peter Price; sound, John Mitchell; camera, Ousama Rawi; editor, John Glen.*

Roger Moore (Rod Slater); Susannah York (Terry Steyner); Ray Milland (Hurry Hirschfeld); Bradford Dillman (Manfred Steyner); John Gielgud (Farrell); Simon Sabela (Big King); Tony Beckley (Stephen Marais); Marc Smith (Tex Kiernan); John Hussey (Plummer); Bernard Horsfall (Kowalski); Norman Coombes (Lemmer); George Jackson (Mine Doctor); Ken Hare (Jackson); Paul Mafela (Jimmy); Ralph Norvel (Girl in Bar); Garth Tuckett, Albert Raphael, Lloyd Lilford, Alan Craig, John Kingley (Miners); Karl Duering, Paul Hansard, Andre Maranne, Nadim Sawalha, Gideon Kolb, John Bay (Syndicate Members).

THE DEAD DON'T DIE (NBC-TV, 1975) C—90 M.

Executive producers, Douglas S. Cramer, Wilford Lloyd Baumes; producer, Henry Colman; director, Curtis Harrington; teleplay, Robert Bloch; costumes, Oscar Rodriquez, Betsy Cox; music, Robert Prince; camera, James Crabe; editor, Ronald Fagan.

George Hamilton (Don Drake); Ray Milland (Jim Moss); Linda Cristal (Vera La Valle); Joan Blondell (Levenia); James McEachin (Frankie Specht); Ralph Meeker (Lieutenant Reardon); Reggie Nalder (Perdido); Jerry Douglas (Ralph Drake); Milton Parsons (Undertaker); William O'Connell (Priest).

ESCAPE TO WITCH MOUNTAIN (BV, 1975) C—97½ M.

Executive producer, Ron Miller; producer, Jerome Courtland; director, John Hough; based on the book by Alexander Key; screenplay, Robert Malcolm Young; music, Johnny Mandell; art directors, John Mansbridge, Al Roelofs; set decorator, Hal Gausman; costumes, Chuck Keehne, Emily Sundby; makeup, Robert Schiffer; sound, Herb Taylor; special effects, Art Cruickshank, Danny Lee; camera, Frank Phillips; editor, Robert Stafford.

Eddie Albert (Jason); Ray Milland (Aristotle Bolt); Donald Pleasence (Deranian); Kim Richards (Tia); Ike Eisenmann (Tony); Walter Barnes (Sheriff Purdy); Reta Shaw (Mrs. Grindley); Denver Pyle (Uncle Bene); Alfred Ryder (Astrologer); Lawrence Montaige (Ubermann); Terry Wilson (Biff Jenkins); George Chandler (Grocer); Dermott Downs (Truck); Shepherd Sanders (Guru); Don Brodie (Gasoline Attendant); Paul Sorensen (Sergeant Foss); Tony Giorgio, Rex Holman (Hunters); Harry Holcombe (Captain Malone); Dan Seymour (Psychic); Eugene Daniels (Cort); Sam Edwards (Mate); Tiger Joe Marsh (Lorko); Al Dunlap (Deputy).

THE SWISS CONSPIRACY (WB, 1976)

Executive producer, Raymond R. Homer; producer, Maurice "Red" Silverstein; director, Jack Arnold; based on the novel by Michael Stanley; screenplay, Stanley.

David Janssen, Senta Berger, John Ireland, John Saxon, Ray Milland, Elke Sommer.

With Norma Shearer in RIPTIDE (MGM '34)

Chapter Six

Robert Montgomery

6'
160 pounds
Brown hair
Blue eyes
Gemini

What is a Robert Montgomery? It seemed that Hollywood and MGM in particular, hardly waited, let alone cared, to actually find out. Rather early (1929) in his moviemaking career, he was pegged by the studio as the perfect flippant-society-playboy type and in that sophisticated but vapid capacity he ambled through most of the 1930s from one drawing-room drama or comedy to another. *Soignée* Norma Shearer, the Queen of the Metro lot, found his combination of handsome smirk, upper-class cockiness, and a pleasing look in white tie and tails, to her liking, and decreed that he be cast prominently in five of her studio features: *Their Own Desire* (1929), *The Divorcee* (1930), *Strangers May Kiss* (1931), *Private Lives* (1931), and *Riptide* (1934). Particularly in *Private Lives* he rose to his stereotype mettle, offering his penultimate petulant-rich-guy characterization, a man who loathed working at a job or at romance, but was quite capable of spending money and energy on the good life. Few other actors could be so callow or shallow oncamera and win audience approval. With a casually expressed drollery or an arched eyebrow. Robert agilely conveyed the essence of depression-style beautiful people. His "Damned if I'll try" ambiance summed up the whole species perfectly.

But offcamera, Montgomery felt damned for not trying to alter his professional and private image. He constantly fought with his studio-mogul boss, Louis B. Mayer, insisting that he was indeed capable histrionically of moving outside the pale of backlot Park Avenue–Bermuda–Mayfair. In *Night Must Fall* (MGM, 1937) as the Cockney psychopath, he gave an Oscar-nominated performance as fully etched as one could wish, demonstrating that he had certainly been correct in his own assessment of his acting talents. But from the grim solidarity of that picture he was whisked back to the likes of *Live, Love and Learn* (1937) and *Three Loves Has Nancy* (1938), two more eminently forgettable Metro pictures and Montgomery performances.

While he was fighting with his studio bosses for roles such as *The Earl of Chicago* (1940) and *Rage in Heaven* (1941), he was displaying an unexpected social conscience offscreen by helping to organize and promulgate the Screen Actors Guild on one hand, and on the other, substantiating his political and patriotic beliefs by enlisting in the Navy during World War II.

The global war changed the world and its life style, but the now mature Robert was not to be left in its wake, for he returned to Hollywood with new notions of extending his show-business career in directions far removed from his old debonair, facile mold. Having directed and starred in the stark, innovative *Lady in the Lake* (1946) at his old studio, he made a few more features, and then switched coasts of operations and media of expression. In the field of television with his "Robert Montgomery Presents," he hosted and starred in one of video's finest anthology series. On radio as a news analyzer and commentator, he displayed an initiative and resourcefulness that more than compensated for his occasional political naivete, or his later well-meaning but patsy role as television advisor to President Dwight D. Eisenhower.

By birth, inclination, and exposition, Robert has always been a gilt-edged patrician. This life style has alienated him from many segments of his professional and private associates, who felt he was just too high-toned—in fact, downright snobbish—for his own good. His allegedly undemocratic way of life made it all the more easy for leery observers to carp at his occasional acting excesses (as in *Rage in Heaven*) or to assess his light-comedy style not as acting finesse but as just "being" himself. And when the scenario called for him to be exceedingly vain, selfish, and cowardly, as in Metro's *The Divorceé* and *Forsaking All Others* (1934), it provided ample ammunition for his detractors to suggest that the "real" Robert Montgomery was now emerging oncamera.

The joys of Robert Montgomery's screen years remain in his crisp acting performances; the sorrows are the unrealized acting and directing projects that would have made his long, productive show-business career even more memorable and certainly more versatile.

Henry Montgomery, Jr, was born on Saturday, May 21, 1904, in Fishkill Landing, Dutchess County, on the Hudson River in New York. He was the first of two sons born to Henry and Mary Weed Bernard Montgomery. As MGM publicity releases would insistently maintain and the facts seem to indicate, Henry Sr., a vice president of the New York Rubber Company, was affluent for a long stretch of his business career. His family enjoyed the very best in clothing, housing, and

Robert Montgomery at the age of ten

education and undertook European vacations that often lasted for months. If true, this background would make it most natural for the future cinema star to play Park Avenue gay blades with the greatest of ease and familiarity.

The countryside around the Montgomery home provided numerous varieties of wild game, while the nearby Hudson River was abundant with fish. When not involved with childhood studies doled out in leisurely fashion by a private tutor, Henry Jr. became a master sharpshooter, an expert fisherman, and an able equestrian. When he was fifteen, he was enrolled at the austere, but plush, Pawling School for Boys, a first-rate preparatory institution at Pawling, New York. Many years later, for a MGM studio-biography profile, he was to (agree to) say: "When I was in school I was one of those unfortunates who never seemed to belong. I used to envy with all my heart the other boys who displayed no trace of inner trepidation, who laughed and talked easily among themselves and to strangers. At night I would think of all the smart, wise-cracking things I would say the next day. Then, when the opportunity came, my tongue seemed to be tied. I actually suffered when I had to meet strangers."

At Pawling School, he fostered an interest in writing and was one of the school-newspaper editors. In 1920, when Henry Jr. was just sixteen, his father died suddenly. The estate was quickly audited, and, after payment was made to Montgomery's creditors, the widow and her sons were informed that they were no longer well-heeled, but were, indeed, very close to being penniless.

Mary Montgomery, with her younger son, Donald, accepted the hospitality/charity of relatives. Henry was forced to quit school and find employment, suitable or otherwise. With no previous training or educational degree toward a specific vocation, he accepted the first paying post available, that of a mechanic tapping railway wheels for overheated journal boxes with the New York, New Haven and Hartford Railroad. Relatives volunteered to support his way through Princeton University *if* he would pursue a career in law or in business. However, he uncompromisingly informed them that his interest lay in the field of writing. The avuncular souls had no desire to subsidize his college education in a field as unstable as journalism.

Instead, he plodded along in his railroad job and managed to save a few hundred dollars with which he moved to New York City in 1922. He rented a tiny room in Greenwich Village, bought an inexpensive typewriter, and began cranking out fiction pieces, mostly devoted to the sea. He worked diligently and submitted several short stories to magazine and book publishers, but met with consistent rejections. As the "no thanks" slips piled up, his money dwindled. Often his daily diet consisted only of milk. Fortunately, he was fanatically devoted to the liquid.

Within a year, he was flat broke and took a job on the *Caddo*, a Standard Oil tanker. He intended to write of his sea experiences, but found life so dull on the oil tanker that, instead, he slept during his off-duty hours. After one around-the-world voyage, he returned to Greenwich Village to again try his hand at writing. This time, however, rather than devoting his full efforts to it, he took short-term jobs in order to support himself.

One of Montgomery's Village friends was actor-playwright Sam Janney, who had just won a job as the assistant stage manager for a production called *The Mask and the Face* (Bijou Theatre: September 10, 1924), starring William Faversham. Janney believed Henry had the makings of an actor and persuaded his new employers to give him a chance at walk-ons in the production. Henry was not overly excited about trying the stage, but it was a job and he still had not sold any of his stories. After a few days of rehearsal he became intrigued with the ways of the theatre, but told himself that he was there chiefly to learn the techniques of drama so that he might write a play one day. "Of course, I was kidding myself," he said in a *Collier's* magazine interview in 1939. "From the time I stepped on that stage, I wanted to act. I didn't know myself for a long while, but finally I caught on. After that, nothing counted but the stage."

The Mask and the Face was Chester Bailey Fer-

nald's adaptation of the Italian play *La Maschera e il Volto* by Luigi Chiarelli, which had first been produced in London at the Everyman Theatre, Hampstead, on February 5, 1924, and then transferred to the Criterion Theatre (in Piccadilly) on May 27, 1924. Many thought the plot of this much-touted show quite trite: an Italian nobleman pretends to have thrown his wife into Lake Como and then is placed on trial for her murder. Despite the critical disappointment with the show's substance ("Some of the persons responsible for *The Mask and the Face* have marred it with awkward, old fashioned stage-directing and prosy and formless adaptation," said the *New York Herald*), Henry was jubilant at his good fortune. In the show he had five walk-on parts at $5 a day each, plus two sets of offstage voices at $10 a day. However, after a scant nine performances Faversham had him fired. The star insisted that the young man was unsuited for the stage and imperiously told him: "The march of trade is yearning for young men like you and my advice to you is to get out and stay out of the theatre." Ironically, *The Mask and the Face* closed after only thirteen performances.

But the acting 'bug," having bitten hard, left its indelible mark. Henry Montgomery had become enamored of the theatre and the potential monetary rewards therefrom. Because his name bore too many "y's" with "e" sounds, he promptly changed his first name to Robert, after one of the characters he played in *The Mask and the Face*. He then acquired the small role of Louis Rhodes in *Dawn* (Harris Theatre: November 24, 1924). The Tom Barry drama focused on forty-eight hours in the life of a jazz baby (Zita Johann) who, despite her Puritanical father, manages to be a zesty flapper. The *New York World* reported of the show: "Its second act brings to Broadway as free and furious a jazz party as the younger generation has staged all season long, and still . . . this production bears a stern-faced message for humanity." Despite a sterling performance by Emma Dunn as Johann's mother, the trite show failed after forty-eight public showings. Nevertheless, one boon to Montgomery was to meet Elizabeth-Bryan Allen, a southern girl who had a part in *Dawn*.

The following spring, Robert was Blink in Louis E. Busch's *The Complex* (Booth Theatre: March 3, 1925), an "almost incredibly wordy" (*New York Times*) play dealing with the then still novel subject of psychoanalysis. It was a subjective drama in which a good deal of the action took place in the mind of the central character (Miss

Percy Haswell, who also directed the show). Of his performance, *Billboard* magazine said Montgomery was "satisfactory," a judgment which was encouraging to him, even if the drama did collapse after forty-seven airings.

He was then accepted by a Rochester, New York, stock company after begging the manager to add him to the group. For Montgomery had come to realize that, "I started out wrong with the idea that all I had to do to become an actor was to appear in plays in New York. It was a silly idea, going at the thing backwards." In the Rochester ensemble, Robert appeared in approximately fifty different plays, usually playing an old man. He would later recall: "Every time an old man role was offered, the manager remembered my plea for work. I got the role." Among the guest actors who worked with the Rochester company were Billie Burke, Ralph Morgan, Wallace Ford, and Miriam Hopkins.

One of Montgomery's weaknesses in front of audiences was simple stage fright, which sent his voice up several registers to a falsetto. A veteran actor advised him to overcome this by taking a good look at the audience when he first went onstage at every performance. Montgomery followed the tip and was amazed to discover that it worked for him. One habit he could not correct, despite the persistent nagging of stage managers, was the constant wringing of his hands. This fault was not eliminated until he went into motion-picture work and saw the rushes. The embarrassment at witnessing his distracting behavior made him realize how foolish it looked.

He was back in New York in *The Carolinian* (Harris Theatre: November 2, 1925). The Rafael Sabatini–J. Harold Terry play was a combination swashbuckling costume thriller and domestic drama, in which a too plump Sidney Blackmer was miscast as the hero of 1774 Charleston. Martha-Bryan Allen functioned as the heroine with Reginald Owen as the British spy. Montgomery had the minute role of Captain Shenstone, a messenger who must run onstage all out of breath. To accurately achieve this condition, he would run up and down a flight of stairs, offstage, just before making his entrance. The lethargic production expired after twenty-four viewings.

Otto H. Kahn was a philanthropist banker along Broadway who extended loans to actors whom he thought talented. He considered staking Robert Montgomery to a sizable amount of money, but after a few conferences, Kahn was of the opinion that the young player would do quite nicely on his own, without help. Rumors started, however, that Kahn was backing Montgomery's career. At about this time, a destitute playwright-actor named Perry Ivins had put together a revue called *Bad Habits of 1926* (Greenwich Village Theatre: April 30, 1926) and required financial assistance. He sent for Montgomery, believing he was Kahn's newest protégé. They became friends after each discovered that the other was flat broke, and began a partnership search for a rich godfather to back the show. Finally, they heard of Irving Strouse, who was interested in investing in a show, and they went to see him. Strouse supplied the money and rehearsals began. Montgomery lived at the rehearsal hall and slept on a rolled-up quilted piano cover. His safety razor and toothbrush were carried in his pockets and a cleaning woman took pity on him by supplying the diligent player with a pot of fresh coffee every morning. In spite of these trying circumstances, Robert managed to be well-groomed, even down to wearing lemon-tinted gloves borrowed from the show's art director, Joe Mullen. Mullen once said: "Bob was the glummest man in the world when he was completely broke. But, if he had one dollar, he was the gayest youngster in town. I never met anybody else that could get so effervescent on one buck." It was said that Montgomery could make a $15 suit look like one worth ten times that much.

The two-act revue, *Bad Habits of 1926*, opened to unpleasant critical reaction. "It was noisy. It was rough in spots and smooth none of the time" (*New York Sun*). As to the cast, which included Flora Borden, Hume Derr, Florence Selwyn, and Montgomery, Alan Dale of the *New York American* chided: "The misguided young people who appeared in this sorry and almost gruesome affair are probably nice, well-groomed boys and girls, just mistaken as to their mission in life." One other New York aisle-sitter reported: ". . . the actors enjoyed themselves while audiences slept."

But on the whole, Robert was quite pleased with his contributions to the tattered revue show. One of the production's many sketches, entitled "The Creaking Gorilla," a satire on the successful 1925 Broadway production *The Gorilla*, was written by Montgomery. As for his stage presence, Richard W. Watts, Jr. of the *New York Herald-Tribune* said of Montgomery that he was "a promising juvenile." It was the same opinion the actor held of himself.

Strouse withdrew his backing from *Bad Habits of 1926* after a few performances and the company limped along on a percentage basis for another week before closing. Montgomery's share of the take per week was $3.41. The show ended its run on May 15, 1926.

An undaunted Montgomery returned to Rochester, where he resumed stock work, specializing, again, in old men's roles. From there, he spent a few weeks with the resident company at the Cape Playhouse in Dennis, Massachusetts (where years later his daughter Elizabeth would be an actress). Then he went on a brief tour in a small part in *One of the Family,* followed by a second tour in another past Broadway show, *The Garden of Eden.*

Early in 1928, Robert returned to the Broadway scene a self-confident and somewhat haughty young man. He and Elizabeth-Bryan Allen, whom he had continued to court in the years following *Dawn,* were married on April 14, 1928.

Renowned newspaper columnist Louis Sobol authored the play *The High Hatters* (Klaw Theatre: May 10, 1928) and chose Montgomery for a prominent role in the three-act farce. The show opened to generally unfavorable reviews, but even before its debut, Sobol had become totally disenchanted with Montgomery, whom he came to consider as even too high hat for a play bearing that label. "I'm not high hat," Montgomery retorted. "I'm too good for this putrid play of yours and I know that, too, but I need the money." An enraged Sobol incorrectly predicted: "You'll be playing for coffee and cake money the rest of your life." The curtain fell for the last time on *The High Hatters* on May 16, 1928. Montgomery's notices were as unfruitful as those for the play. "Robert Montgomery, as the juvenile, was hardly a knockout, but he was at least so much better than his companions as to be spared something of the condemnation his fellow thespians could hardly escape" (Richard Watts, Jr., *New York Herald-Tribune*).

That summer, Robert appeared in a stock-company production of *The Bad Man* at the Auditorium in Baltimore, and then was selected to appear in Edgar Selwyn's comedy *Possession* (Booth Theatre: October 2, 1928), which was being staged by the playwright. It was another one of those studies of a bungling paterfamilias (here Walter Connolly) who is dragged back to the family hearthside he has flown. Montgomery was seen as the son, Edward Whiteman, and was singled out for his "verve and bounce," his "zest and abandon," and for contributing "a capital performance." Arthur Pollock (*Brooklyn Daily Ea-*

gle) offered an interesting point when he reported: "The son is done by Robert Montgomery, a popular member of the cast last night. I think some girl must at some time have called him bright eyes and he took it to heart."

A talent scout representing Samuel Goldwyn was among the audiences at one of the thirty-seven performances of *Possession.* He thought Montgomery had screen potential and arranged for the actor and his then pregnant wife to go Hollywood, where Montgomery was to test opposite Vilma Banky for *This Is Heaven* (United Artists, 1929). The twenty-five-year-old Hungarian actress had enjoyed great American cinema popularity when cast opposite Ronald Colman in a series of silent romances, but Goldwyn had split the team apart, hoping for each to make box-office records on their own. Banky's trial run in *The Awakening* (United Artists, 1928), with Walter Byron as her new leading man, was less than monumental, and now for her (part) talking film debut, Goldwyn determined that yet another vis-à-vis should be used to stimulate the white-blonde beauty into recapturing her once ardent public following.

Robert made the test with the heavily accented Banky, and the results were shown to iconoclastic Goldwyn. The movie mogul quickly decided that Montgomery was too skinny and, moreover, that next to Banky, the year-younger Montgomery photographed young enough to have been her son. Means of making the cinema fledgling appear more mature oncamera were considered, such as having him grow a moustache. However, Goldwyn, by this time convinced that the talkies were perhaps nothing more than a fad, decided to make *This Is Heaven* as a silent film with talking sequences, music score, and sound effects. This being the case, there was no longer a special need for an articulate leading man, and Montgomery was temporarily forgotten. The role opposite Banky went to James Hall.

Fortunately for Robert, Edgar Selwyn, the author-director of Broadway's *Possession,* persuaded his brother-in-law, Joseph M. Schenck, a United Artists producer-executive, that Montgomery might be suitable for that company's talking version of the comedy-melodrama, *Three Live Ghosts* (1929).* Montgomery was assigned the role of William Foster, a fast-talking American who is wanted by the authorities for embezzling from his father's business. He joins the

---

*Earlier, it was a 1922 Paramount silent release with Norman Kerry as Foster, and it was to be made a third time in 1936 by MGM with Richard Arlen in the role. All three film versions were based on the Frederic Stewart Isham–Max Marcin Broadway play (Greenwich Village Theatre: September 29, 1920), which had a 250-performance run.

With Joan Bennett in THREE LIVE GHOSTS (UA '29)

Allied army to escape the law, but is later captured by the Germans. With two unsavory English buddies (Charles McNaughton, Claud Allister), he escapes from the German prison camp and goes to London, where all three are listed as dead. Playing Rose Gordon, the girl whom he had met on the transatlantic crossing, was Joan Bennett. Although *Three Live Ghosts* was Montgomery's first feature appearance, it would be his fourth-released screen performance.

Meanwhile, Joseph Schenck's brother, Nicholas, then a power at Metro-Goldwyn-Mayer, after seeing Montgomery's screentest, convinced Louis B. Mayer and the other studio executives to sign the boyish-faced, well-spoken actor to a five-year contract at $350 a week. For his contract debut, Robert received second billing as Biff, a good-looking, energetic society playboy who becomes a campus footballer, in the musical melodrama *So This Is College* (MGM, 1929). He wore shoulder and arm padding to make him seem convincingly muscular. With Elliott Nugent in top billing as Eddie, he forms a gridiron friendship that, according to the script, they vow will not be jeopardized by anyone, especially by some girl (in particular, campus cutie Sally Starr). It was the start of a comradeship offscreen as well. The picture received above-par notices: "Well, of all the surprises! Here's a college picture that acts and looks like college!" (*Chicago Herald Examiner*). A highlight of this film, released in both sound and silent versions, was the football game between the University of Southern California and Stanford.

In 1929, just as professional recognition was slowly coming to Robert, he and his wife had an added joy. A daughter was born to them. However, because of subsequent tragic events, to be detailed later on, the name and birthdate of the little girl have never been made available to the public.

One aspect of Montgomery's career, as of the careers of many other screen celebrities, has received scant mention: the difficult adjustment period he endured at MGM. Not only was he busy manipulating his career so that the proper executives and creative talent would consider him for key screen assignments, but he was forced to contend with a rather unfriendly united front among his fellow players. He was one of those New York stage actors with nice-sounding voices who were jeopardizing the future well-being of already established silent-screen favorites. Montgomery's perfect enunciation and his evenly pitched voice, albeit boyish, were envied by many of the onetime stars whose careers were being swept down the drain by the advent of sound. The fact that he was intellectually and culturally superior to many of his co-workers, or, in particular, to most of his company bosses, did not sit well with the studio's bureaucracy. It would be an important deficit that would haunt and distort his entire screen stay at MGM's Culver City lot.

Despite the repercussions of the above circumstantial and personality factors, which made Montgomery such a difficult offcamera commodity at MGM, studio chief Louis B. Mayer, and especially his astute, very civilized young production head, Irving G. Thalberg, recognized that Montgomery was a potential general-utility player. And the studio badly needed versatile new, leading men. With the advent of sound, the star roster at MGM was forced to undergo traumatic changes. Lon Chaney, Sr., the great character star, would make one talkie picture before cancer ended his career too soon. Romantic leads John Gilbert and to a lesser extent, Ramon Novarro and Nils Asther were at sea in the new talking medium, as was comic genius Buster Keaton (in contrast to the studio's funnymen Stan Laurel and Oliver Hardy, who thrived in the new format). The expense and ramifications of turning out sound Western movies caused Tim McCoy to move to other studio berths. Smart-alecky William Haines, for whom newcomer Montgomery seemed a likely backstop substitute, had made the silent-to-sound transition well, but a rash of inferior, stereotyped roles, plus some hard-to-hush off-the-lot behavior would soon end his studio tenure. Singer Charles King and musical comedian Cliff Edwards would be lost in the shuffle following the end of the all-talking, all-singing, all-dancing musical-film craze of the late 1920s, and imported vaudevillian Jack Benny at this juncture in his career just did not have sufficient screen presence to pass himself off as an engaging leading man. In addition there were the team or single performances of Karl Dane and George K. Arthur, but neither they nor the utilization of waning Conrad Nagel, William Bakewell, or John Mack Brown (at least as a non-Western screen lead) were sufficient to stock properly the output of MGM features.

Little wonder then that Metro was practical enough to overlook Robert's personality "deficiencies" and cast him in a series of substantial *nonshowcasing* roles opposite the studio's prize leading ladies. Montgomery rose to the challenge with a characteristic nonchalance, using the same glib attitude that he so effortlessly displayed on-screen. He would give the backup role all that was demanded of him, and perhaps a little more, but never strained to grab the limelight with his facile playboy characterizations. That his impersonations of rich men became so adept, as did his comedy timing, was a rewarding result which probably neither MGM nor even the self-appreciative Montgomery fully expected.

Montgomery was given a very big chance as Joan Crawford's leading man in her first all-talking picture, *Untamed* (MGM, 1929). It laid the ground work for the type of role he would generally enact in the years to follow. He is a sophisticated, charming, well-dressed, but poor fellow named Andy, the love target of Bingo (Crawford),* an uncivilized, jungle-flower oil heiress from the wilds of South America, who is in New York to learn the social graces. *Photoplay* magazine observed: "Robert Montgomery, the hero, is in for a load of fan mail."

Nepotism-watchers always claimed Norma Shearer owed her screen success and longevity to her perspicacious husband, Irving Thalberg. However, more generous and subtle souls rightly

*This is still the nickname by which she is called by her San Francisco friends who knew her then.

With Sally Starr and Cliff Edwards (rear) in SO THIS IS COLLEGE (MGM '29)

305

have reckoned that the ambitious, talented, imperious Miss Shearer would have continued to capture the public eye, even if she had not married Louis B. Mayer's fair-haired executive partner. Shearer was then in the midst of a series of society screen dramas, which her husband insisted was the proper backdrop to display her charms. *Their Own Desire* (MGM, 1929) was one of many such pseudosophisticated ventures. Here the screen time was divided between well-to-do Shearer's resort romance with a pleasant fellow (Montgomery) and the repercussions from the clandestine affair that her father (Lewis Stone) is conducting with none other than Montgomery's mother (Belle Bennett). While the elders decide it is wiser for each of them to return to their legal spouses, the members of the younger generation continue their romantic union. Montgomery's ability to complement in his usual offhanded way Shearer's *soignée* presence made him an ideal teammate for the Queen of the Metro lot, a fact she kept well in mind when supervising the casting of her future motion pictures.

While Robert's screen stock was soaring, his personal life suffered a calamitous turn. In January 1930, the eleven-month-old Montgomery baby died suddenly. Montgomery refused to discuss the child's death, repressing the grief deep within himself. Soon after the infant's death, he met James Cagney, who instinctively understood his grief and subtly shared it. The two men became close friends, a companionship that many Hollywood people found incongruous since they were so outwardly different. It has been said that their idea of a good time was to read poetry aloud.

Montgomery chose to dissipate his unhappiness in hard work, and, therefore returned to his film career with greater determination. In a mild musical, *Free and Easy* (MGM, 1930), he is Larry, a movie name, loved by a beauty-contest winner from Kansas, played by Anita Page. The film's star, Buster Keaton, ambled his way through the proceedings as Page's manager. One potentially brighter sequence found him leading a comic chase through a Hollywood studio where he disrupts the soundstage work of Lionel Barrymore, Jackie Coogan, Cecil B. DeMille, and Dorothy Sebastian. *Photoplay* magazine listed the picture as one of the six best of the month. When Norma Shearer decided that it was time for her to stop portraying the perfect lady onscreen, she persuaded Thalberg to acquire the screen rights to Ursula Parrott's novel *Ex-Wife* as the basis for *The Divorcee* (MGM, 1930). The scenario was smartly doctored to make the picture a seemingly daring

expose of the time-honored double-standard, but never allowing the action to become overly vulgar or shocking to the average filmgoer. Metro went to a great deal of expense to alert potential moviegoers to the treat in store for them when they viewed *The Divorcee*. The ads enticingly stated: "Her sin was no greater than his but she was a woman." The billboard posters then went on to rhetorically inquire: "If the world permits the husband to philander—why not the wife? Here is a frank, outspoken and daring drama that exposes the hypocrisy of modern marriage. Norma Shearer again proves her genius in the most dazzling performance of her career."

The plot of *The Divorcee* would sustain any television soap opera for a good two months of storyline. When socialite Shearer weds newsman Ted (Chester Morris), they both agree to maintain a liberal attitude toward their legalized union. However, when on their third wedding anniversary, Shearer learns that Morris has been having an affair with another woman, she turns to her husband's best friend (Robert Montgomery) for more than just comfort. Morris, on learning that she has been adulterous (although not knowing it was Montgomery), refuses to accept her having affairs with men, and the couple divorce, going their separate ways. After numerous romantic encounters, Shearer encounters Paul (Conrad Nagel), whom she thought she had loved before her marriage. He promises to divorce his wife (Florence Eldridge), who had been disfigured in a car accident one night when Nagel was driving while drunk. However, Shearer concludes that honor demands he stay with Eldridge, and besides, her heart still belongs to Morris. In Paris, on New Year's Eve, the ex-marrieds reconcile.

The most sophisticated critics agreed that *The Divorcee* was only a pale shadow of Parrott's spicy novel and that the film is "virtually a suspenseless affair, particularly as it is garnished with the inevitable embrace in the final fade-out" (Mordaunt Hall, *New York Times*). As for Norma, called by some "the American beauty rose of the Metro-Goldwyn-Mayer nurseries," she was credited with lending an air of dignity to some rather specious doings. In fact, so impressed were members of the Academy of Motion Pictures Arts and Sciences that she was given an Oscar for Best Actress of the Year for her work in both *The Divorcee* and *Their Own Desire*.

Montgomery had a rather thankless assignment in *The Divorcee*. Playing the roguish seducer of the moderne heroine, he was billed below up-and-coming Morris and established Nagel. Being

With Norma Shearer in a publicity pose for THEIR OWN DESIRE (MGM '29)

With Norma Shearer in THEIR OWN DESIRE

the wisecracking, smirking dandy who sneaked behind his friend's back to make love to a married woman was hardly a sympathetic part.

There is one particularly condemning sequence in which Robert's Don encounters Morris at a restaurant. Montgomery is fearful that his pal may suspect he is the culprit in the marital situation and gingerly tries to avoid the very subject which is devastating, embittered Morris. Having angled out of this close call, Montgomery slinks off to Europe to forget his guilt among the rich set. This is not to say that Montgomery did not handle his work with felicity, for few others who were so new to the cinema could have given equal credibility to a skunky gent as adept at imitating a trained monkey as he is at fawning on married Shearer. *Variety* complimented: ". . . unusually fine work is contributed by Robert Montgomery, the husband's friend, who helps himself to the wife as he would to an extended cocktail."

For Metro's big June 1930 release, *The Big House,* Robert stepped out of the fun-loving character mold for that of the unsavory Kent Marlowe. He is the dandy who is guilty of drunken driving on New·Year's Eve and is sentenced to ten years in prison for manslaughter. As prisoner #48642 he is informed by the warden: "Prison does not give a man a yellow streak, but if he has one it brings it out." He is paired with cellmates Wallace Beery and Chester Morris, Beery being the most incorrigible prisoner of all. Conniving Robert does not succumb to the camaraderie of prison life, but remains aloof, only joining the other prisoners in order to use them for his own ends. One of his stunts causes Morris to be put in solitary confinement, the latter vowing revenge. Morris later escapes, and then encounters Montgomery's sister (Leila Hyams)* with whom he falls in love. However, Morris is recaptured and sent back to prison, just in time to learn about and participate in the Thanksgiving Day prison escape being planned by Beery. True to form, devious Montgomery squeaks to the law-enforcers, hoping that his own sentence will be shortened. In the massacre that occurs during the stymied prison break, both Beery and Montgomery are killed, but Morris lives to be eventually paroled.

With its sociological import and graphic prison-action byplay, *The Big House* proved to be vital screen entertainment, helping to usher in the

*Frances Marion's scenario had originally called for Hyams's character to be Montgomery's wife.

With Joan Crawford in OUR BLUSHING BRIDES (MGM '30)

cycle of gangster films. Beery's position as an MGM character star was ensured,* and Robert in another bit of contracasting proved that his acting range went far beyond portraying tuxedoed dandies with the souls of callow juveniles.

But MGM's casting department, still finding it convenient to cast Montgomery as the darling of the spoiled rich, refused to allow him to escape this pigeon-hole métier. In *Sins of the Children* (MGM, 1930),† he is the rich, spoiled son of the most powerful man in the community (Robert McWade) and refuses to wed the daughter (Leila Hyams) of the town barber after he "compromises" her. He feels that she is not at his social level. In this undistinguished screenfare, he was given second billing, just ahead of Elliott Nugent, who was also credited with having written the dialog.

Robert was reunited with Joan Crawford in *Our Blushing Brides* (MGM, 1930), in which he plays the dapper, older son of the department-store owner who employs Crawford as a mannequin. She thwarts his attempts to romance her, but he eventually realizes that she is far and away more

*The part had originally been planned for the ailing Lon Chaney, Sr.
†A.k.a. *Father's Day* and *The Richest Man in the World*.

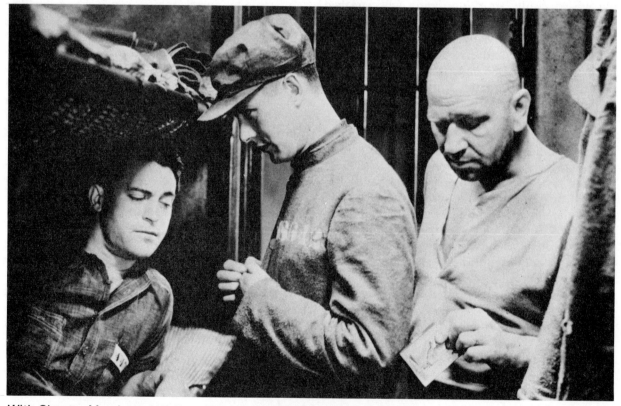

With Chester Morris and Wallace Beery in THE BIG HOUSE (MGM '30)

than the customary working girl and he falls in love with her.

Montgomery rounded out 1930 in, first, another musical comedy, *Love in the Rough* (MGM),* set in chic country clubs, and finally in a war drama, *War Nurse* (MGM). As an American aviator with the French Army of World War I, he becomes enamored of the head nurse (June Walker) of a volunteer group in France. Montgomery, now an established part of the MGM stock company, received top billing in both these assembly-line films.

When he was not oncamera, impeccably dressed amid penthouse or country-club surroundings, briskly shaking cocktails while giving out with urbane chitchat, Montgomery was either at his home in the Hollywood hills with his collection of fine etchings or on a tennis court. He also had a preference for fast motor cars and owned one of the first Bentleys in Hollywood. On Sundays he played polo, a popular sport with the aristocratic Hollywood colony, and one at which he was an expert.

On learning that his next assignment was opposite Greta Garbo, the usually voluble Montgomery felt at a professional disadvantage being in tandem with this awesome *artiste* of the cinema. He reported for work in a new blue suit, a white shirt with a striped tie, and with a monogrammed handkerchief carefully arranged in his breast pocket. Studio hands were accustomed to his immaculate appearance, but when one of them chose to taunt him for wearing the natty handkerchief for Garbo, he was too embarrassed to flash back a smart reply. Instead he blurted out: "This is because I have a cold."

Inspiration (MGM, 1931) was one of six films that the Swedish actress completed within rapid succession during a twenty four-month period, little of which did much to enhance her overall craft status.† The Clarence Brown–directed *Inspiration*, with story and screenplay by Gene Markey, is a mawkish tale of a Parisienne artist's model (Garbo) whose checkered past is uncomfortably littered with castaway lovers, including her latest, wealthy, suitor, middle-aged Lewis Stone. It is because of this that Andre Martel

(Montgomery), her present beloved, leaves her and returns to his fiancée; he then changes his simple mind and returns to inform Garbo that he is giving up everything for love of her. When he falls asleep, she writes a tearful farewell note and departs because she refuses to ruin his life. *Motion Picture* magazine, in a later evaluation of Garbo's career, noted that "the ending is *Camille* [MGM, 1937] without the cough."

Inspiration was an unfortunate title for this Garbo drama, a forlorn piece of fluff not up to snuff by any reasonable person's standards.† The actress had long since run the proper gamut of world-weary ladies onscreen, and her portrayal here of the jaded belle of Paris (within the film she says of herself that she is "not too nice and not too young") is stolid rather than solid, uninvigorating rather than enriching in its screenfare. One might blame both the screenplay and the direction for Garbo's Sapho-like creature emerging without proper bite. However, Robert's impersonation was so much out of joint that it was evident to all that the actor was not up to handling a badly conceived role with any degree of conviction. Whether staring raptuously into his leading lady's thick-lashed eyes, carrying her up the third flight of stairs to her humble apartment, or riding about the Parisian streets (backlot MGM) in a victoria coach, he was a sour note in this one-dimensional but demanding part as the youthful French consular-service apprentice. As Mordaunt Hall (*New York Times*) observed of his acting: "Virtually all Mr. Montgomery succeeds in impressing upon the audience is his embarrassment."

Regardless of the critical (or even public) reception to Robert's emoting in *Inspiration*, it was a status symbol to have played opposite MGM's most illustrious leading lady. The press was naturally eager to obtain the newcomer's impression of the Swedish butterfly, since obviously as her celluloid vis-à-vis, he most certainly must have had ample opportunity to study her renowned elusive nature at close range. Montgomery's seemingly fatuous reply ("Being Garbo's leading man is not necessarily an introduction to the woman") in retrospect makes a good deal of sense.

---

*A remake of the MGM's 1927 silent film *Spring Fever*, with William Haines, Joan Crawford; both screen works derived from Vincent Lawrence's play *Spring Fever* (Maxine Elliott Theatre: August 3, 1925, 56 performances).
†*Romance* (MGM, 1930), *Inspiration, Susan Lenox: Her Fall and Rise* (MGM, 1931), *Mata Hari* (MGM, 1931), *Grand Hotel* (MGM, 1932), *As You Desire Me* (MGM, 1932).
†Actually a modern-dress version of Clyde Fitch's 1900 play *Sapho*, which was based on a novel by Alphonse Daudet and a French play by Mme. Daudet and a collaborator. It was first produced in the United States at Wallack's Theatre on February 5, 1900 with Olga Nethersole and Hamilton Revelle in the leading roles. It received a good deal of publicity when it was temporarily closed for being "immoral." *Sapho* also appeared as a Massenet opera, first performed at the Opera Comique on November 27, 1897, with Emma Calve in the leading role. On November 7, 1909, the opera debuted at the Manhattan Opera with Mary Garden in the "Garbo role."

MGM next cast slick Montgomery as the leading man of top box-office attraction Constance Bennett, then at the peak of her screen popularity. *The Easiest Way* (MGM, 1931)* was billed as "the frank, fearless drama of a woman who sinned." It was yet another of the series of honest-girl-turned-prostitute dramas that Bennett then so often essayed in the cinema. Having fallen prey to debonair Adolphe Menjou, Bennett is amazed to find herself the object of the affections of wholesome, wealthy Argentine rancher Montgomery. Should she, or, really, can she, give up Menjou and find happiness with gentle-natured Montgomery? Fate answers the question, for when, during Montgomery's absence, she returns to Menjou, she arouses the rancher's distrust, and in the long run loses Menjou as well. All that is left for her to become is a full-fledged streetwalker. *Film Daily* trade paper summarized: "It fails to hold conviction with the artificial plot." Bennett returned to RKO-Pathé, Montgomery accepted his unflattering reviews ("again is out of his element" said the *New York Times*), and virtual screen newcomer Clark Gable, cast as Bennett's truck-driving brother-in-law stole what few notices there were, indicating that his virile presence would be a stellar attraction in forthcoming Metro releases.

For *Strangers May Kiss* (MGM, 1931) Montgomery was back with Norma Shearer in another muddled exercise on the double-standard devised by expedient novelist Ursula Parrott. In the last Shearer-Parrott effort, *The Divorcee*, Shearer's journalist vis-à-vis who believed in the "single" standard only in theory was Chester Morris. Here the more dapper Neil Hamilton had a similar assignment, while Montgomery was in proper form as the "fashionable young inebriate" who supplies the *deus ex machina* for her globe-trotting indiscretions, that is, until unyielding Hamilton can find it in his heart to forgive "erring" Shearer. As in most quality MGM pictures, and especially in most any Shearer-MGM film, the production values were superior. The affable cast, surroundings, and direction allowed for "a brisk and good-looking entertainment which goes on its way so gracefully that it leaves little time for examining structural weaknesses in the story and characterizations" (Andre Sennwald, *New York Times*).

In *Shipmates* (MGM, 1931) Montgomery is a sailor who falls in love with the admiral's daugh-

*Eugene Walter's stage drama premiered at the Belasco Theatre (January 19, 1909, 157 performances) starring Frances Starr. On September 26, 1921, it was revived at the Lyceum Theatre for a 21-performance run, with Miss Starr again playing the lead.

With Neil Hamilton, Norma Shearer, and Irene Rich in STRANGERS MAY KISS (MGM '31)

With Hobart Bosworth and Dorothy Jordan in SHIPMATES (MGM '31)

ter (Dorothy Jordan). The *New York Times* said: "In this, the picture which elevates him, as the saying goes, to stardom, he is still a friendly, personable young man of no particular distinction." Sam Wood's *The Man in Possession* (MGM, 1931*) finds him as a sheriff's assistant, of all things, who poses as a butler. Irene Purcell was his leading lady. (The film would be remade by Metro in 1936, with Robert Taylor and Jean Harlow as the stars, as *Personal Property*.)

Robert was rightfully chafing at the rash of undistinguished roles in unworthy films being tossed in his direction. Then too, it did not require much perspicacity on Montgomery's part to observe the deterrent effects for him of the meteoric rise of MGM's Clark Gable, who was rushing back and forth between prestige pictures with Norma Shearer, Marion Davies, Joan Crawford, and another promising personality, Jean Harlow.

Undoubtedly, Montgomery was aware that he could not satisfactorily handle the Gable type of he-man roles, but still he felt that he was histrionically equipped to assume more energetic parts than the stable of celluloid leisure-life dandies MGM insisted he play.

Just when it seemed the cocksure performer would brook no more front-office guff, Norma Shearer, for very selfish reasons, came to Montgomery's rescue, in this case requesting him as her vis-à-vis in the "daring" screen adaptation of Noël Coward's *Private Lives* (MGM, 1931).† She smartly realized that of all her confreres encamped on the Metro lot, Robert was most readily the perfect leading man for a showcase drawing-room comedy, and in particular, this acerbic divertissement on the subject of matrimony.

The screen rendition of Coward's clever three-act comedy retained most of the chic dialog and

---

*Based on the H. M. Harwood play, which opened at the Booth Theatre on November 3, 1930, for 97 performances with Leslie Banks and Isabel Jeans starred.

†Author Coward and Gertrude Lawrence originated the lead roles at London's Phoenix Theatre on September 24, 1930, for a limited engagement, and later opened at the Times Square Theatre in New York (January 27, 1931, 248 performances). Coward and Lawrence left the cast after three months with their parts assumed by Otto Kruger and Madge Kennedy. On July 27, 1947, Tallulah Bankhead and Donald Cook opened a touring version of the play in Chicago, which concluded its engagements on June 1, 1948, in San Francisco. They brought the show to New York in October 1948, and then continued to tour with the comedy until June 3, 1950. On December 4, 1969, Tammy Grimes and Brian Bedford opened at the Billy Rose Theatre in a 204-performance revival. In 1944 a London revival starring John Clements and Kay Hammond enjoyed a 716-performance run, and in 1972 Maggie Smith and Robert Stephens brought the play back to the West End for a very long run. In the film *Star!* (Twentieth Century–Fox, 1968), Julie Andrews as Gertrude Lawrence and Daniel Massey as Noel Coward enact a scene from *Private Lives*. By a long shot, this couple, Andrews in particular, were the least engaging Amanda and Elyot.

With Norma Shearer in PRIVATE LIVES (MGM '31)

hectic incidents, providing ample occasions for the two screen leads to match talents: Montgomery's alacrity versus Shearer's vivacity. In the course of the well-known plot (in the movie the ending takes place at a cozy Alpine chalet rather than in Paris), the two principals had been wed for two years but are now divorced and have just married others (he to demanding, whiny Una Merkel, she to patronizing, stuffy Reginald Denny). Montgomery and Shearer find themselves with their new spouses in adjacent suites of the Riviera hotel where they had once honeymooned in their more innocent youth. The quick shifts from surprise to anger to wistfulness to new-blooming romance to jealousy to courtship are admirably handled by Shearer (at times aping Gertrude Lawrence's elegant manner) and Montgomery under Sidney Franklin's civilized direction, which made a good deal of Coward's brisk words.

The terrace sequence, played directly to the audience as in the play, finds Shearer and Robert both anxious to preserve their propriety, pride, and self-fantasies, but incapable of repressing their merrier instincts.

Montgomery: What are you doing here?
Shearer: I'm on my honeymoon.

Montgomery: How interesting. So am I.
Shearer: I hope you're enjoying it.
Montgomery: It hasn't started yet.
Shearer: Neither has mine.

Very soon, the two leads, who have been exchanging their barbs from their respective patios, cross through the barrier of potted trees to spark a new romance.

Shearer: What have you been doing lately.
Montgomery: Traveling about. . . . I went around the world you know, after.
Shearer: Yes I know—how was it? China must be very interesting.
Montgomery: Very big, China.
Shearer: And Japan?
Montgomery: Very small—Darling. I love you so.
Shearer: I never loved anyone else for an instant.

By part two of the film, devil-may-care Montgomery and Shearer have left their bewildered spouses, and traipsed off to a Swiss chalet where they settle down for a hopefully blissful affair. Each is fully aware of the other's impertinent selfishness, and they promise each other that rather than fight they will merely use the code words "Solomon Isaacs" (later shortened to "Sollochs") as a signal to avoid the obvious cycle of battling, brooding, and making up. However, when dazzling Shearer, stretches out cozily on the sofa after dinner, rejects Montgomery's bid for a bit of sexual adventuring on the spot, he utters that famous insult—she has no sense of glamour. Self-possessed, witty Shearer responds appropriately, inquiring how can she have a sense of glamour when she has a crick in the neck. Immediately the two drawing-room lovers launch into a battle royale with her cracking a phonograph record over his head. Before long the ski-lodge interior is a shambles of broken furniture. Next morning the two lovers patch up their quarrel, sit in amazement as the less imaginative Denny and Merkel arrive to commence their own less inspired domestic spat, allowing for the amused Shearer-Montgomery team to skip out on a fresh lark. As John Baxter would review in his *Hollywood in the Thirties* (1968): "For polish, few comedies of the Thirties can equal this early alliance of cinema and stage." Shearer, as could be expected, was given every advantage in the staging of this four-sided conversational comedy and emerged the glittering conquerer of audience interest. Montgomery fared a little less well, largely because too many critics and filmgoers at large were remembering (or aware of) the brilliant interpretation of Elyot Chase by the play's author who knew exactly how to expose every nuance of the maliciously witty drawing-room exercise. (When this major picture opened in London in Coward's homeland, the *London Times* reported: "Mr. Robert Montgomery seems rather taken aback to discover that his lines, usually so amiable, have, in this instance, taken on a catty and quite ungentlemanly venom").*

His first 1932 release was *Lovers Courageous* (MGM) with top billing as Willie Smith, a poor Londoner with a yen for still another admiral's daughter (Madge Evans). It is a preposterous story (even considering it was the first screenplay by the eminent playwright Frederick Lonsdale) in which the couple marry in the face of all possible adversities and he becomes a playwright who turns out a masterpiece of drama. *But the Flesh Is Weak* (MGM, 1932),† his next picture, has him penniless, but managing to be clad in fancy evening finery as he woos Nora Gregor, an actress fresh from Max Reinhardt's Vienna Theatre. Mordaunt Hall (*New York Times*) tossed Robert a meaningless critical bouquet, labeling his performance "irrepressible and good-natured."

In another Joan Crawford film, *Letty Lynton* (MGM, 1932), Montgomery was purely a supporting actor as suave Hale Darrow, who meets Crawford aboard a South America–to–New York luxury ship, proposes marriage, and is accepted before the ship docks. The wedding almost does not occur, however, because Crawford determines the only way to eliminate past lover-roué Nils Asther is to drop poison into his wine glass. Understanding Montgomery and Crawford's suddenly thoughtful dowager mother (May Robson) unite to supply the necessary alibi to effect the young lady's release from police custody.

The public greeted *Letty Lynton* as another glamorous exercise in MGM's efficient manner in which the Montevideo and shipboard settings and Crawford's Adrian wardrobe were given more artistic attention than the screen dialog of John Meehan and Wanda Tuchock. Observant filmgoers noted that Crawford now affected Marlene Dietrich–like penciled, arched eyebrows and that in yet another thankless straight-man role, Montgomery did "capital work."

However, a few people were far more interested

With Nora Gregor in BUT THE FLESH IS WEAK (MGM '32)

in the similarity of the film's plotline to the stage play *Dishonored Lady* (Empire Theatre: February 4, 1930), which had starred Katharine Cornell and had run for 127 performances. That play's authors, Edward Sheldon and Margaret Ayer Barnes, like novelist Marie Belloc Lowndes (upon whose work *Letty Lynton* was "based"), had relied upon the transcripts of *Notable British Trials*, published in 1927, which detailed the events in the case of Madeleine Smith, who was placed on trial for her life in 1857 Scotland for allegedly having poisoned her lover. Sheldon and Barnes initiated a copyright infringement suit against Loew, Inc., which caused *Letty Lynton* to be yanked from its successful distribution. By the time (1939) the final accountings had been made after elaborate court appeals and retrials, the determined plaintiffs were awarded $150,000, estimated to be one-fifth of the picture's profits. To this day, this picture, *Letty Lynton,* is unavailable to television or home-rental film users, a forbidden fruit which this book's authors yearn to sample.

---

*At one point in *Private Lives,* Montgomery blurts out to Shearer: "You're a mean, evil-minded vampire. I hope I never set eyes on you again as long as I live."

†Based on Ivor Novello's paly *The Truth Game,* which had its American debut at the Ethel Barrymore Theatre (December 29, 1930) for a 105-performance run.

Meantime, Robert, believing that he was now a thoroughly established box-office draw,* presented himself one afternoon at Louis B. Mayer's offices. He fully realized that in the debonair-leading-man sweepstakes, he was MGM's chief contender for the Hollywood throne. Samuel Goldwyn at United Artists had Ronald Colman, Fox had Warner Baxter, Warner Bros. enjoyed the services of William Powell, George Brent, and the more genteel Leslie Howard, Paramount fostered the careers of Britishers Herbert Marshall and Cary Grant, RKO sometimes pampered Lowell Sherman, and Adolphe Menjou made the profitable rounds of the lots. As nearly as Montgomery or anyone else at the time could reckon, Robert Young, a pleasant but weak fish, and New York stage recruit Franchot Tone were Montgomery's sole competitors at Metro for any debonair boudoir roles of a major sort. Such status gave Montgomery the impetus to request politely a salary raise, which the naturally avaricious Mayer firmly, but also politely, refused. Whereupon Montgomery glared at the pint-sized scion and snarled: "If you were a younger man, Mr. Mayer, I'd give you a beating." To the best of anyone's knowledge the threat was never carried out, but the somewhat cowed Mayer did concede to permit the actor to have a barber's chair placed in his dressing room for the purpose of comfort while being made up for the day's soundstage filming. A small enough victory but in the California mecca of the infantile and tangible, movie people (copying New York corporate practice) judged status and respect by the uniqueness of one's studio dressing-room accommodations.

While Robert continued to fret over his dour artistic fate at MGM and melodramatic Mayer bemoaned aloud his bad luck in having such an ungrateful wretch on his high-priced payroll, both parties knew each benefited from the special rewards the other had to offer. More importantly, thanks to an iron-clad employee contract, each knew the other *would* deliver the goods. Thus Mayer, goaded on by Irving Thalberg, continued to cast Montgomery opposite the great ladies of the cinema who graced MGM's many soundstages. Quite frequently it was the women themselves who requested Montgomery's services, accepting the reality that he was admirable box-office insurance for showcasing their own talents to better advantage.

Rounding out his 1932 film chores, Montgomery joined with two of the most engaging stars in the business, Marion Davies and Tallulah Bankhead. Ironically, both women were extremely talented performers who, for very different reasons, were rarely able to communicate properly their entertainment skills to filmgoers. As luck would have it, and Montgomery seemed to have very little by Hollywood standards (not by those of the average man in the depression breadline), both these movie releases were commercial disappointments.

Miss Davies, the very expensive paramour of newspaper czar William Randolph Hearst, had earlier in the year romped—reservedly—through *Polly of the Circus* (MGM, 1932) as a trapeze artist enamored of minister (!) Clark Gable. Far more felicitous, but almost equally lacking the necessary elements of a career-promoting vehicle, was *Blondie of the Follies* (MGM, 1932). Hearst's favorite screenwriter, Frances Marion, contributed the story-continuity of two New York girls who graduate from tenements to luxury via show business, and Anita Loos supplied the "salty" dialog of the chorus girls. Andre Sennwald (*New York Times*) observed: "The assumption in *Blondie of the Follies,* which was jamming the auditorium of the Capitol yesterday, is that there is still something to record about the life of a Follies girl. Whether one accepts this premise or not, the film does offer a number of good features." Among the plus factors which the reviewer listed were the presence of comedian Jimmy Durante (who along with Davies did a catchy impersonation of Greta Garbo and John Barrymore from *Grand Hotel* [MGM, 1932]), Billie Dove as Davies's slum-building buddy, James Gleason as Davies's plebeian dad, and Montgomery as the game playboy who decides that Davies's gold-digging Blondie McClune is the woman for him.

Blondie of the Follies made commercial inroads even if it set no new levels of screen entertainment. However, *Faithless* (MGM, 1932) was a box-office turkey. Dixie-ite Tallulah Bankhead, who had to encamp to London's West End to find her metier on the stage, returned to America in early 1931 to undertake a new plunge at filmmaking. Her sponsor was Paramount Pictures, who reasoned that if they could mold Marlene Dietrich into a sophisticated box-office attraction, they could just as easily reassemble Bankhead's charms for the edification of middle America. This proved to be a forlorn hope. They tried, but *Tarnished Lady* (1931), *My Sin* (1931), *The Cheat* (1931), *Thunder Below* (1932), a guest appearance

* *Vanity Fair* magazine reported his fan mail to be 1,500 letters per week.

in *Make Me a Star* (1932), and *The Devil and the Deep* (1932) were no boon to the studio, to the public, or to Bankhead. Paramount loaned her to MGM for *Faithless,* hoping that a new set of creative talents might show them where they had failed with the actress. *Faithless* should have been retitled *Faithful,* for it adhered strictly to the formula so overused in Hollywood since Constance Bennett had proved its resounding marketability in *Common Clay* (Fox, 1930) and *The Common Law* (RKO, 1931). In these distaff pilgrim's progresses, the leading lady (albeit Bennett, Dietrich, Garbo, or as here, Bankhead) uses and then is abused by the idle rich, usually ending up as a tart of the streets who plies her trade to earn money for an ailing husband or to support her fatherless baby.

With Marion Davies in BLONDIE OF THE FOL-LIES (MGM '32)

Faithless ran the full gamut of gaunt emotions as Bankhead's Carol Morgan shifts her moods, whims, and social scales, all amounting to a fatuous array of nothingness. She tosses away her millions, becomes a parasite of the wealthy, and then is rescued by Montgomery's Larry Belmont, whom she had rejected when he was a $20,000-a-year advertising executive because he insisted she live only on his salary. Now a man of the people, Montgomery has lost his job as a truck-driver, and his new bride (Bankhead) determines to become a

With Louise Closser Hale and Tallulah Bankhead in FAITHLESS (MGM '32)

315

streetwalker to earn money to pay for his medical bills (he has some undescribed ailment). An Irish cop, filled with sentiment and a brogue, prevents Bankhead from making this fatal immoral error.

The flop of *Faithless* could not be blamed on a lack of publicity, for prior to its release, Bankhead had been the subject of a sensational interview in *Motion Picture* magazine in which she told interviewer Gladys Hall her "I Want a Man" story, being overly candid in her explanation of her moral and emotional code of ethics. More prudent and prurience-conscious readers were aghast at Bankhead's unabridged (so it seemed) unorthodox interview. The motion-picture industry's Hays Office demanded some action be taken against this emancipated woman, and the ready weapon at hand was to demand far-reaching cuts in Bankhead's movie of the moment, which happened to be *Faithless*. The required editing left the picture in a shambles, and the resultant seventy-six-minute feature emerged as a chronicle "of misery without benefit of drama" (*New York Times*). While most of the critics were busy lambasting the picture as trashy and pitying Bankhead's treatment at the hands of crass Hollywood, one reviewer, Richard Watts, Jr. (*New York Herald-Tribune*) took occasion to lament the treatment being given Bankhead's very accommodating leading man, Montgomery. Watts editorialized: ". . . this is merely another of the series of unhappy roles recently awarded him. Now that the leading man of the new picture has developed from a pleasant juvenile to a comedian of guile and charm, it would seem that his customarily resourceful studio would provide him with parts of some importance. . . . [Instead] he is saddled [here] with a role that is vapid and passive in a film that is soggy in its dramatic and less than exhilarating in its comedy."

Robert, who had, and would, survive worse years of filmmaking, would later recall of *Faithless* and Bankhead: "I got appendicitis just as the picture was starting. The studio offered to find her a new leading man, but she said she'd be glad to wait for me. That was nice of her, because I was a comparatively new [!!] boy."

In the early 1930s most of Hollywood's higher-priced stars were members of the Academy of Motion Picture Arts and Sciences, a mild version of a company union which offered no security protection to the bit players and extras. In 1933, it was estimated that between 22,000 and 24,000 actors lived in Hollywood, all in heated quest of the easy money allegedly to be made in the movies. Extras stood in long lines at the Central Casting

Agency for days, sometimes, in the vain hope of obtaining a few hours' work. On an average, six hundred extras were placed per day. Chorus girls often worked as much as twenty-two hours without a real break, in spite of a California law which stated that a woman could work only sixteen hours per day.

Robert, who would become an authority on the subject, later revealed to *Collier's* magazine writer Alva Johnston: "Top pay for an extra was ten dollars a day, and an extra was lucky to get three days' worth a month. Most of these extras were not actors, had no ambition to be actors. Barbers and cab drivers and waiters were all registered with Central Casting. If they were called, they'd just take a day off from their regular jobs to pick up some extra money. Real actors and actresses, people who had been trained for years in their profession, were registered, too, but it seemed as if the amateurs were called more often."

In 1933, the Screen Actors Guild was formed in conjunction with the American Federation of Labor as a means of protecting the professional actor. Among the organizers of SAG were Alan Mowbray, Boris Karloff, C. Aubrey Smith, Ralph Morgan, and Lucille and Jimmy Gleason. Soon, the bigger names in the industry, such as Eddie Cantor, Joan Crawford, James Cagney, Chester Morris, Fredric March, Franchot Tone, and Robert Young, also joined the guild. Cagney explained the labor situation to Montgomery, who up until then, was apparently content to live a quiet life with no major interests other than polo, clothing, and automobiles. "It's all right for us," Cagney told him, "hell, we're overpaid anyhow, but those poor devils can't do anything about it. If they squawk, they get fired." He told Montgomery to look around at the extras who were obliged to work fifteen hours without adequate rest. And Montgomery did start to look around and he began to ask questions. He found Cagney to be right and withdrew from the academy to join SAG. The conservatives in Hollywood were amazed when so many top actors joined up with the "troublemakers" of SAG, but Montgomery was adamant about his decision and soon became an articulate, outspoken champion for the cause of the underdog motion-picture actor/extra.

In the midst of his labor-union revelation and organizing, Robert and his wife, on April 14, 1933, became the parents of a second daughter, Elizabeth.

Hell Below (MGM, 1933) was Montgomery's gutsiest picture since *The Big House* back in 1930. Jack Conway directed this seafaring ac-

With Walter Huston and Robert Young in HELL BELOW (MGM '33)

count, set at an Allied naval base in the Mediterranean off the Italian coast in the crucial war years of 1917–18. As Lieutenant Knowlton, Montgomery disobeys his commanding officer (Walter Huston) and is dishonorably discharged. He dies heroically after sneaking back on the submarine. The film contained several jarring elements, ranging from the obtrusive comedy of Jimmy Durante and Eugene Pallette (respectively the cook and chief torpedo mate of the vessel *Al-14*) to the bizarre love interest between Montgomery and Madge Evans, she the daughter of Huston and married to a crippled aviator veteran. On the whole, "however, there are scenes in the undersea craft that are extremely well pictured and so are others depicting what happens on the surface of the water" (Mordaunt Hall, *New York Times*). Audiences were far more impressed with the gruesome sight of eight crew members dying from inhalation of chlorine gas than by the camaraderie of fellow officers Montgomery and Robert Young in tandem with strict disciplinarian Huston. Montgomery received his fair share of good reviews. The *New York Evening Post* alerted

readers that the actor here was "more mature and virile than this reviewer ever remembers him, handles the feature role, giving an uncommonly restrained and authentic portrayal." During the making of *Hell Below,* Montgomery had his share of mishaps. At one point the craft took an unscheduled dive while he was still on deck. He ran to the conning tower and clung to the periscope. The sub was raised just in time to save him. Later, during the same film, he was slightly burned by acid used in making a smoke screen.

As Jimmie Lee* in *When Ladies Meet* (MGM, 1933) he is a newspaperman given to little work and light chatter. He loves novelist Myrna Loy, who is infatuated with Ann Harding's publisher husband, Frank Morgan. Harding and Loy had functioned well in RKO's chic rendition of *The Animal Kingdom* (1932) and here displayed greater acting acumen as they exchanged views on the propriety of marriage and adultery. When Harding, the gold-and-white-china beauty, and almond-eyed, beauteous Loy were not dominating the screen, Alice Brady in her sound-film debut was holding forth as the gabby hostess who must

*Enacted by Walter Abel on Broadway in the stage version of Rachel Crowther's play (Royale Theatre: October 6, 1932, 173 performances), and by Robert Taylor in the 1941 MGM remake.

With Myrna Loy and Ann Harding in WHEN LA-
DIES MEET (MGM '33)

referee the four-sided romantic contest between
Harding, Loy, Morgan, and Robert. If there is any
legitimate complaint about any facet of
Montgomery's subordinate role as the patient,
well-heeled lover, it would be in line with Philip
K. Scheuer (*London Times*), who noted that the actor's performance "verges closer to the farcical
than seems always needful, although this slight
exaggeration is effective in relieving the various
tensions as they occur." MGM executives obviously decided that director Harry Beaumont
had overdone his delineation of the sophisticated
fare, for the picture was cut from eighty-seven to
seventy-three minutes before actual release.

In *Made on Broadway* (MGM, 1933), the film-
makers blended bits of *Pygmalion* and *Chicago*
into a yarn of a dashing Broadwayite (Montgomery) who molds a starving, illiterate girl (Sally Eilers) into his conception of a dream woman, only
to later find that she is a homicidal double-cros-
ser. He finally realizes that his patient ex-wife
(Madge Evans) is the one true woman for him.
This role of Jeff Bidwell, the glib public-relations
man who heads a high-powered business, might

have been better suited to the special talents of
Lee Tracy, but Montgomery offered a craftsman-
like account, allowing moviegoers to enjoy his
full bag of acting tricks.

Robert then made two successive films with
Helen Hayes, who, he has admitted, was his favorite screen actress. Miss Hayes had captured an
Oscar for her Madame X–type performance in
The Sin of Madelon Claudet (MGM, 1931), but
since then had had great difficulty in obtaining
proper showcasing roles at Metro or on loan-out.
Like Alfred Lunt and Lynn Fontanne, who fled
back to the New York theatre after *The Guardsman* (MGM, 1931), she did not appreciate the mechanics and politicking involved in moviemaking.
Had it not been for Irving Thalberg and Norma
Shearer, who were close friends of Miss Hayes
and her playwright husband Charles MacArthur,
she would have undoubtedly maneuvered her
way out of her MGM contract at a very early stage
of its execution.

First, in Rose Franken's *Another Language*
(MGM, 1933) as Miss Hayes's husband,* Montgomery is oblivious to the love his nephew (John
Beal) has for his wife. The role of Victor Hallam
required Robert to enact a prig fanatically devoted to his family and fully ignorant of the discomfiture of his wife, who does not fit into the new
environs and discovers that her mother-in-law
(Louise Closser Hale) and her disciplined brood
speak "another language." During the first week's
run of this film at Capitol Theatre in New York
City, Montgomery, with Irene Purcell, performed
onstage in a scene from the second act of *Private
Lives*. Of the featured stage presentation, Bosley
Crowther wrote in the *New York Times:* "By the
way Mr. Montgomery and Miss Purcell have at
each other one would assume that they mean to
emulate Mr. Coward and Miss Gertrude Lawrence in physical violence if not in histrionic accomplishment. Patrons who saw the picture
version of the play are probably satisfied."

Night Flight (MGM, 1933) was next, adapted
for the screen by Oliver H. P. Garrett from the
novel by the French aviator Antoine de Saint-Ex-
upéry. The film boasted a stellar star line-up similar to that of *Grand Hotel* (MGM, 1932) but,
unlike the latter, the stars of *Night Flight* had
small parts. Aviation was the true star. ("It is
probably the most authentic flying story that has
come to the screen. The glimpses of the pilots in
the planes sending messages to the radio control

*Performed on Broadway in 1932 by Glenn Anders (Booth Theatre: April 25, 1932, 348 performances; Waldorf Theatre: May 8, 1933, 80
performances).

318

room on an aviation field and then the reception of the messages, are most effective" [Mordaunt Hall, *New York Times*]). In fifth billing, following John Barrymore, Miss Hayes, Clark Gable, and Lionel Barrymore, Montgomery is a light-hearted air-express pilot who dashes to the field in evening clothes, throws his flying outfit on over them, and hops into the air on schedule. One of his perilous missions is to fly a cache of serum from Santiago, Chile, to Buenos Aires across the stormy Andes. Gable fared little better, spending most of his screen time (before his oncamera demise) in the cockpit of a plane. It was John Barrymore who stole the show as the airline director who subjects his pilots to iron discipline, all in order to maneuver his pilots to fly their cargo planes through the treacherous darkness and arrive at their destinations on time. *Variety* thought "Montgomery lends little more than color."

In February 1934 Robert, along with four others, was elected by his fellow actors to represent them on the Actor-Producer Five-Five Committee under the National Recovery Administration. The function of the committee was to negotiate with film producers for improved working conditions, equitable pay scales, etc. In June 1934, Montgomery endorsed writer-reformer Upton Sinclair, the Democratic Party's nominee in California's gubernatorial contest. (Louis B. Mayer and other MGM executives were pro-Republican.) Sinclair's platform, EPIC ("End Poverty in California"), was a complicated economic solution to the Depression. He was the unsuccessful candidate. Later, in 1934, Montgomery was voted vice-president of the Screen Actors Guild.

His career continued in the vein of lighthearted comedy. As an innocent escapee from prison, he is in romantic pursuit of Madge Evans in *Fugitive Lovers* (MGM, 1934) in which Ted Healy and the Three Stooges were the comedy focal point. Viewers used to seeing Montgomery at his well-appointed best were dismayed to find him "gaunt, harrassed, worried, and unshaven" (*Variety*) throughout most of the helter-skelter picture, which largely transpired on a California-bound trip aboard a Greyhound bus.

Edgar Selwyn, who had been so instrumental in engineering Montgomery's entry into motion pictures, directed *The Mystery of Mr. X* (MGM, 1934), loosely based on Philip MacDonald's Crime Club novel, *Mystery of the Dead Police*. The setting was foggy London, where a rash of homicides have claimed the lives of five bobbies, each stabbed by a sword cane with an eighteen-inch blade. The sixth such murder occurs outside the mansion where Nicholas Revel (Montgomery) is stealing the Drayton diamond. When he is suspected by Scotland Yard Inspector Connor (Lewis Stone), Montgomery and his accomplices, cabby Forrester Harvey and diamond clerk Ivan Simpson, set out to apprehend the real killer. Along the way blithe Robert—reputed to be the most dashing cracksman since Raffles—romances Elizabeth Allan,* who fortuitously happens to be the comely daughter of Henry Stephenson, the head of Scotland Yard. Montgomery's silk-hatted jewel thief displays a keen sense of humor, which does much to make the unraveling of his predicament tenable to filmgoers, who might have carped at the unorthodox ploy of pulling a killer out of the drawer.

Norma Shearer had been offscreen since *Smilin' Through* (MGM, 1932), devoting her energies to caring for ailing Irving Thalberg. *Riptide* (MGM, 1934) was devised as a glorious return vehicle for the great star, to be personally supervised by Thalberg as his initial independent production under his revised MGM pact. The stellar cast included not only Robert (in his fifth and final outing with Shearer), but Herbert Marshall, Mrs. Patrick Campbell (in her film debut), and a host of high-caliber feature players. Director Edmund Goulding was instructed to concoct a screenplay that would be a grandiloquent exercise in drawing-room romance, and, of course, as such, would be set among the titled British crowd in England and on the Continent. Apparently, all creative forces involved forgot that in the five years since Miss Shearer's award-winning *The Divorcee* (largely U.S. set) the depression had hit, changing American moviegoers' entertainment interests and values. It was too late in the game to be aping that former successful film. *Riptide* met with embarrassing indifference from the majority of moviegoers, and encountered severe resistance from many critical quarters.

Perhaps the most engaging episode in *Riptide* occurs in the opening sequences of the film in which Marshall is seen dressed in the horns and antennae of a water beetle, and Shearer is costumed as a June bug. He is a nobleman and a very important member of the League of Nations Commission while she is a footloose Manhattan chorine with a spicy past. They soon wed and return

*The British-born (April 9, 1910: Skegness, England) actress crossed the Atlantic to fulfill an MGM contract in 1933, and is not to be confused with Montgomery's wife, Elizabeth-Bryan Allen.

to the majestic beauty of England. Five years pass. When he embarks on one of his endless diplomatic treks abroad, she is persuaded by her madcap aunt (Mrs. Patrick Campbell) to travel herself to Cannes. Once there she reencounters Tommy Trent (Montgomery), a reckless flame from her New York City days. He is immediately attracted to the fun-seeking Lady Mary and informs her: "Wither thou goest, beautiful lady, so will I follow on . . ." There follows a riptide of jollity, as the pleasure-bent couple go swimming in their evening clothes, and, while wrapped in blankets, kiss each other and drink cocktails in the moonlight. Drunken Montgomery cannot be persuaded that enough is enough, and when he attempts to climb to Shearer's hotel room by scaling the balcony, he falls to an awning below. The sensational event is fully reported in the tabloid newspapers and read with great horror, albeit properly restrained, by Marshall. When he accuses his wife of being guilty of a bigger indiscretion with Montgomery than she actually committed, she decides to leave him and actually have an affair with her alleged lover. However, the thought of breaking up the household permanently and not seeing her child again causes a last-minute reconciliation between her and Marshall.

In actuality, this plotline is no worse than a good many other similarly styled features, but there was such a self-conscious attempt to have Shearer immersed in a sea of British accents and wallowing in noble titles that movie patrons could not accept the outdated story with any degree of graciousness. As for Montgomery, his pencil-thin role was such old hat that he could play it with his eyes closed, which he frequently did within the film. His drunk scene was merely an extended repeat of many past inebriated oncamera moments. However, he received a few plaudits for the general excellence of his self-created stereotype. "Some of the comedy allotted to him verges on the inane, but he is successful in lifting it up, and gains the reward of abundant laughter" (Edwin Schallert, *Los Angeles Times*). The disappointing results of *Riptide* were met with childish glee by Mayer and his followers on the MGM lot, who had come to regard Thalberg as a too-powerful, demanding presence in the studio set-up.

Hide-Out (MGM, 1934) was filmed partially on location at Santa Cruz, California, and had the benefit of efficient W. S. Van Dyke II to guide it through the eighty-two-minute storyline. However, the director was unable to instill the imagination and verve in this yarn that he had in *Manhattan Melodrama* and *The Thin Man* (both

1934 MGM releases and both starring William Powell, who had moved over to Metro from Warner Bros., and already was receiving the prime roles that once might have gone to Montgomery). In *Hide-Out*, Robert played an elegantly attired mobster who insinuates his way into the management of several swank New York nightclubs but then has to take it on the lam to New England, where he seeks refuge at the Connecticut chicken farm of Whitford Kane, Elizabeth Patterson, and their pert daughter (Maureen O'Sullivan). The rather touching finale finds Montgomery being led off to prison clutching two rabbits presented him by the farmer's son (Mickey Rooney).

It was at this juncture that Robert's MGM contract was up for renegotiation. The studio moguls made an offer. The actor added an additional $25,000 to the annual figure for a total of $200,000 and Louis B. Mayer approved it! With the signing of the new agreement, Montgomery pressured more than ever for better, more versatile roles. His parts "were a little difficult to tell apart," he justifiably complained.

David O. Selznick, who had been the executive producer of *Night Flight*, proposed to Arthur Loew, in 1934, that MGM consider a remake of Warner Bros.' John Barrymore film of 1924, *Beau Brummel*, with Montgomery in the title role. Nothing came of this engaging idea, however.

Montgomery was one of nine actors whose facial features were superimposed, one on another, to form a photograph of the "Ideal Male Star" in 1934 by the editors of *Vanity Fair*. The other eight actors were Gary Cooper, Fredric March, George Brent, Richard Arlen, Franchot Tone, Johnny Weissmuller, Dick Powell, and George Raft.

"Overland Bus," a short story by Samuel Hopkins Adams, first appeared in *Cosmopolitan* magazine. MGM purchased the screen rights and prepared to shoot the film on a cross-country trip, utilizing two buses. Montgomery was chosen to star, with Richard Boleslavsky directing. The plans were abandoned in the autumn of 1933, however, because MGM officials did not like the manner in which the heroine's father was depicted. Columbia Studios bought the property for $5,000 but had no one in mind to star.

Previously, MGM had borrowed director Frank Capra from Columbia on the basis of loaning Robert Montgomery in exchange whenever Harry Cohn, Columbia's chief, asked for his services. Cohn now asked, but Montgomery refused since he had already starred in one unappreciated bus tale (*Fugitive Lovers*), and believed it would be humiliating to be exiled to a smaller studio, one fresh from Poverty Row. Clark Gable, who was not then an actual star of Montgomery's stature, was chosen as the goat, much to his displeasure. "Overland Bus," translated into *It Happened One Night* (Columbia, 1934), made Gable MGM's hottest star and won him the Best Actor Oscar for that year. The film was named Best, as were Claudette Colbert (of Paramount Pictures) and director Capra. Columbia was thereby elevated forever above the stigma of Poverty Row.

Montgomery was then offered the role of Roger Ryam, who sails on his first cruise as a midshipman in *Mutiny on the Bounty* (MGM, 1935), but he turned it down because it was of a supporting nature. Franchot Tone, then wed to Joan Crawford, played the part and won an Oscar nomination as Best Actor.[*]

Instead, Robert took the comedy part of Dill Todd[†] in *Forsaking All Others* (MGM, 1935), in third billing as a selfish hedonist who deserts Joan Crawford on the eve of their marriage in order to wed another woman (Frances Drake). Later he returns to Crawford, who then, on the brink of marrying him, realizes it is Clark Gable whom she truly loves. The assorted dalliances of the Park Avenue–Long Island set was handled in silky fashion by director W. S. Van Dyke II, who decided to enliven the star-triangle interplay with heavy doses of slapstick. Thus, viewers see Crawford falling off a masseuse's table, plunking down in the mud after a bicycle accident, emerging battered from a car accident, and, most coy of all, tinkering in the kitchen with unfamiliar culinary tools. As the sybarite with the morals of a tomcat, Montgomery's playboy had his share of broad comedy moments, but they seemed vastly unamusing, perhaps because of the selfish tone to his character. It proved difficult for anyone to muster any chuckles at his pseudo-pneumonia wheezing or his backside-burning attempts to warm himself at the fireside. Gable, on the other hand, in a role filled with virile, sardonic humor, wisely refrained from engaging in any of the broader on-screen shenanigans.

This film was followed by the unworthy *Biography of a Bachelor Girl* (MGM, 1935) in which Montgomery is the venom-packed magazine editor in support of miscast Ann Harding (could anyone really believe she was *supposed* to be a gay,

---

[*]Three stars were nominated from the cast of *Mutiny on the Bounty* (Gable, Charles Laughton, Tone), but all lost out to Victor McLaglen of RKO's *The Informer*.

[†]Played by Andrew Lawlor in the March 1, 1933, Times Square Theatre production of the Edward Barry Roberts–Frank Morgan Cavett play, which was produced by and starred Tallulah Bankhead and lasted for 101 performances.

With Joan Crawford and Frances Drake in FORSAKING ALL OTHERS (MGM '35)

high-hearted woman with a disastrous gift of tolerance who had knocked European nobility for a loop?). Montgomery's part* required him to be in continual conflict with himself. Outwardly he wants painter Harding to make her tell-all autobiography a best seller, but inwardly he views her work as an indictment of the corrupt society he so detests. Much of the time he was oncamera, Montgomery had to rant and rave, which he accomplished with unconvincing fierceness. The contrived saccharine ending has him agree that publishing the book would be a bad trick on those exposed within, and then wedding Harding (in the play Harding leaves the editor, throws away the manuscript and rushes off to Hollywood with a composer who is writing for the movies).

Robert then permitted MGM to place him as Helen Hayes's roommate after her husband (Otto Kruger) is committed to a mental institution in *Vanessa, Her Love Story* (MGM, 1935). Miss Hayes disliked the screenplay, which was adapted by Hugh Walpole and Lenore Coffee from Walpole's novel. She performed in the period picture on threat of a law suit for nonfullfillment of her contract. The film was unbelievable because of its implication that the Hayes-Montgomery relationship did not extend into the bedroom. It marked the end of her career as a cinema leading lady. As for Montgomery, Eileen Creelman (*New York Sun*) analyzed: "There is something a little too modern about Mr. Montgomery for this part. Even when struggling with those long, heavily romantic speeches, he seemed on the verge of a wisecrack—or even of leaping upon the handlebars of a bicycle and performing gymnastics."

In 1935, Robert succeeded Eddie Cantor as president of the Screen Actors Guild. His immediate action was to unleash a campaign for higher wages for the bit players. The Association of Motion Picture Producers labeled him and his rebels "bolshevistic," a charge which he made ridiculous by introducing arch-conservative George Arliss as main speaker at a SAG meeting, as "Commissar George Arliss."

His final screen appearance of 1935 was in MGM's *No More Ladies,* again with Joan Crawford. In the role of Sherry Warren,† he is a rake who loves, changes, and leaves women. Crawford weds him in spite of his past philandering and, finally, aided by her modern grandmother (Edna May Oliver), she evens the score by tossing a

shindig attended by all his former girlfriends and their current mates. She then pretends to run off for a fling with *in*eligible Franchot Tone. The ruse works. Like so many films which followed in the wake of *The Thin Man, No More Ladies* attempted to focus on a sophisticated marital situation, but strained in the attempt. The film did provide a good illustration of how devious a filmmaker could be in getting his way around the Production Code in having the lead character, a husband, confess his marital straying.

On January 6, 1936, a son was born to the Montgomerys. He was named Robert Jr., although the onetime Henry Montgomery, Jr. had never legally switched his name to Robert. In addition, the baby received the nickname of "Skip."

From the time Robert's own father had died and the family was forced to relinquish the expensive home in the New York countryside, he had yearned to have a mansion of his own in the same area. In 1936 he purchased just such a place at Towners, New York, where his family resided during the summer months. Montgomery raised ponies, erected game preserves, grew apples, and was an ardent hunter of pheasants. He confided to interviewers that his secret passion was to write and direct films as well as to act in them. He admitted his envy for multitalented men like Noël Coward.

Frank Curran of Brooks Brothers clothiers, whose clientele included the Duke of Windsor, publicly said that he considered Montgomery the best-dressed man he had ever seen. It was revealed that Montgomery purchased his garments from Brooks and McDonald-Heaths and his shoes came from Maxwell's of London. Although he was an incessant cigarette smoker, he never carried them in his pockets lest the package destroy the drape of his jacket or suit coat. He either carried his cigarettes in his hand or borrowed them from friends. He was an exponent of the daily "cat nap," and once said: "Sleep is the big thing, of course. I'd have folded up long ago if it hadn't been for the cat naps. But, I've depended on other things too. Reading, for example. If I can pick up a book and read, the whole world can blow up around me and I won't be aware of it."

Professionally, Robert swept into 1936 with MGM's *Petticoat Fever,* as Dascom Dinsmore, a wireless operator in isolated Labrador. ‡ For two years he has not seen a white woman. Then Myr-

---

*Played by Earle Larimore in the S. N. Berhman Broadway offering called *Biography* (Guild Theatre: December 12, 1932, 210 performances).

† Melvyn Douglas had the job in the Broadway rendition of the A. E. Thomas play (Booth Theatre: January 23, 1934, 162 performances).

‡ The Max Reed play appeared on Broadway at the Ritz Theatre on March 4, 1935 for a 137-performance engagement. Dennis King undertook the part of Dascom.

With Reginald Owen and Myrna Loy in PETTICOAT FEVER (MGM '36)

na Loy, with her titled fiancé (Reginald Owen) appear at his front stoop, victims of a plane crash. The inevitable happens when a love-hungry man discovers an attractive woman. For added complications, Montgomery's former sweetheart, Winifred Shotter, appears on the scene, arousing Loy to some amusing jealousy. More perceptive filmgoers were quick to note that even in such a far-off place (obvious MGM soundstage sets), Montgomery had boiled shirts and Loy performed in Parisian gowns. The expected finale found Montgomery and fur parka-clad Loy eloping on a dog sled.

Robert had hoped to be included in the cast of Norma Shearer's *Romeo and Juliet* (MGM, 1936) as her onscreen lover, but the part went to Leslie Howard after both Robert Donat and Fredric March rejected it. Instead, Montgomery undertook *Trouble for Two* (MGM, 1936), slightly based on Robert Louis Stevenson's *Suicide Club* stories in *New Arabian Nights*. The ludicrous tale had moustached Montgomery as Prince Florizel of a mythical Balkan kingdom who sets out in search of excitement before he is forced to enter into a political marriage with Princess Brenda of Irania

(Rosalind Russell), whom he has not seen in twenty years. In London he enters the Suicide Club, formed by those persons in society who have tired of life, and he has a great deal of trouble escaping. As could be easily fathomed, the snooty Miss Vandeleur turns out to be none other than the princess. Said Regina Crewe (*New York American*): "This odd melange of half-jelled romance, comedy melodrama and mystery clucks rather than clicks."

Metro's *Piccadilly Jim* was the Montgomery comedy offering of the summer of 1936, and it provided more than its share of hilarious moments, aided by supporting characters Frank Morgan, Billie Burke, Eric Blore, and Robert Benchley. Taken from a P. G. Wodehouse novel of 1916, Robert is Jim Crocker, whose souse of a father (Morgan) is unable to wed Burke due to her rich family's objections. Jim, a caricaturist, draws a comic strip with Burke's family as the subjects, which soon makes them the laughing stock of London. Madge Evans is the fly in the ointment.* The cartoonist loves her but does not realize that she, too, is related to Burke's household. Then the fun begins with the locale moving to New York

*This was Miss Evans's fifth and final feature with Montgomery. She would request the opportunity to play opposite him in *Night Must Fall* (MGM, 1937), but the studio was more interested in showcasing Rosalind Russell.

City. The *New York Evening Journal* announced: "Give Bob Montgomery an impudent role and he goes to town." Sadly, MGM refused to promote the picture and word-of-mouth was insufficient to insure its proper box-office reception. ("Picture isn't the kind that sticks with its audience, creating any lasting impressions or leaving any wonderful illusions. Its function is to entertain in a snappy yet simple and innocuous manner, with interesting people as the characters," *Variety*.)

Three times during 1936 Montgomery was heard in abridged dramatizations of screenplays over "Lux Radio Theatre," affording listeners some indications of how he might have handled varied assignments onscreen. On July 5 he played *Beau Brummel* with Madge Evans; on September 13 he was Norman Maine to Janet Gaynor's Esther Blodgett in *A Star Is Born*; on December 7 he took on the 1926 Adolphe Menjou role in *The Grand Duchess and the Waiter*, with Elissa Landi as his radio co-star.

By 1937, Robert's status on the Metro lot had both declined and stabilized itself on its new level. Since Irving Thalberg's death (September 14, 1936), there was no one to intercede on Montgomery's behalf with dictatorial Louis B. Mayer. The MGM chief not only disliked Montgomery for his inbred arrogance and his unheard-of (or so he pretended) salary demands, but also for his continued stand on the expensive Screen Actors Guild situation. More importantly, he had a full and varied male-actor roster. Besides virile Clark Gable and Spencer Tracy as box-office attractions, the studio had the antic-prone Marx Brothers, operatic Nelson Eddy, and jungle-clad Johnny Weissmuller. In addition, MGM enjoyed a full complement of players in the debonair category. William Powell had been entrenched at the studio since 1934 and proved that both in and out of *Thin Man* films with popular Myrna Loy, he was a top marquee drawer in sophisticated filmfare. Melvyn Douglas had proved to be such an excellent farceur in *Theodora Goes Wild* (Columbia, 1936) that Metro gladly agreed to share his contract with that studio. On a lesser scale there were general utility players Robert Young, Franchot Tone, James Stewart, and handsome newcomer Robert Taylor to consider, along with veteran Edmund Lowe, and more sinisterly inclined Henry Daniell and Douglass Dumbrille. In short, the company could function quite nicely without Montgomery's services, but as long as he could be

With Ralph Forbes, Frank Morgan, Joan Crawford, and Nigel Bruce in THE LAST OF MRS. CHEYNEY (MGM '37)

exploited and controlled, his star quality was worth the price, for the public continued to desire his celluloid presence.

The Last of Mrs. Cheyney (MGM, 1937), adapted from Frederick Lonsdale's play,* is an excellent example of the treatment MGM was giving Robert. The property was translated into a vehicle for Joan Crawford at the very least, and, hopefully, at best into a showcase for Crawford and dapper William Powell. They represent a pair of charming jewel swindlers who mingle with, and filch from, British aristocrats. She is the American who, because of her glib, charming persuasiveness, is taken in by London's trusting upper class, while Powell is the droll con artist who poses as her butler. Montgomery is imperious Lord Arthur Dilling, who dallies with Crawford as a refreshing distraction from the women of his own social set. In his actions he often reveals himself to be as caddish and undesirable as his high-toned titled friends. Director Richard Boleslawski, who died after completing this film, focused the lion's share of the screen time on Crawford, Powell (who gave added strength to his actually lesser role), and the bevy of subordinate players, leaving less assured Montgomery to filter in and out of the action with his customary cute and winsome flippancy. But his uneasiness with the role was quite evident. Irene Thirer (*New York Evening Post*) reckoned: he "is quite without his customary twinkle. He plays straight." This film represented the sixth and final time that Montgomery acted oncamera with Crawford.

During a visit to New York City in the autumn of 1936, Robert had become fascinated with a play, then on Broadway, called *Night Must Fall,*† It was written by and starred Emlyn Williams as a homicidal maniac who carries the head of his latest victim in a hatbox. Long fed-up with his typecast roles as the bright-eyed, pretty-faced, cocktail-shaking, brittle-tongued playboy of high society. Thirty-two-year-old Montgomery returned to the West Coast where he badgered studio executives into purchasing the screen rights to the play as a starring vehicle for him. They thought he was balmy, and threatened to suspend him, then suddenly changed their minds. Montgomery explained the capitulation with: "They

okayed my playing in it because they thought the fan reaction to me, in such a role, would humiliate me." Since Montgomery had agreed to subsidize part of the cost of the production, it was the consensus of opinion that the studio had decided it would not mind the anticipated moderate financial loss *if* it meant humbling the actor and making it easier to withstand his aggressive battles on behalf of the Screen Actors Guild.

The *Night Must Fall* camera started rolling in January 1937, with Dame May Whitty repeating her stage role of the elderly hypochrondriac who befriends the former hotel page-boy and is murdered by him. Rosalind Russell, hoping to expand her celluloid repertoire by playing a part of greater substance than she was receiving, played the cardigan-sweatered spinster niece of the old lady who, because she is physically attracted to the young man, ignores her initial suspicions that he has less than honorable intentions. Hunt Stromberg produced, with Richard Thorpe directing.

The English cottage set, the street, and cricket field were duplicated on Metro's back lot from over five hundred photographs taken in England of the real things. Whereas Williams had a Welsh accent onstage, Montgomery affected an Irish one, which for him was easier to adopt. A black cat was not part of the stage action, but Thorpe had the part included in his film because he believed such a feline creature in the movie would bring good luck.

When the film opened at Grauman's Chinese Theatre in Hollywood on the evening of May 4, 1937 (some five days after the New York premiere), MGM distributed handbills to ticket buyers disclaiming all responsibility for what they were about to see. Additionally, a trailer preceded the film's unreeling which further absolved the studio's obligations. Both were discontinued within a few days when the glowing reviews arrived. *Time* magazine printed: "Any picture in which Robert Montgomery, whose previous contribution to the screen has been a seven-year marathon of ingenuous charm, gives a first-rate performance in a different role, rates as at least a major surprise . . ." Otis Ferguson in the *New Republic* found that it "is one of the most vivid and powerful effects the films have managed."

*The original London production (St. James Theatre: September 22, 1925, 514 performances) starred Gladys Cooper (Fay), Gerald du Maurier (Arthur), and Ronald Squire (Charles). The American rendition (Fulton Theatre: November 9, 1925, 283 performances) featured Ina Claire, Roland Young, and A. E. Matthews. Basil Rathbone played the role in MGM's previous 1929 version starring Norma Shearer, and in the later Greer Garson edition, retitled *The Law and the Lady* (MGM, 1951), Fernando Lamas had the rejuggled part. There was also a 1962 German-made version of the high comedy.

†The drama premiered on London's West End at the Duchess Theatre (May 31, 1935) for a 435-performance run; the Broadway version opened at the Ethel Barrymore Theatre on September 28, 1936 for a 64-performance run. Dame May Whitty played the old lady in both the London and New York versions and was brought to Hollywood to recreate her original role in the film.

Ferguson accoladed Montgomery for his determination to rise above his prior screen status: "Although subject to correction as being far from the scene, let's say that I am near enough to it in hope and faith to cheer for Mr. Robert Montgomery of the Screen Actors' Guild, and for what he stands for in the movies." *Cue* magazine observed: "The movie version, seems to us to be more powerful than the original. It reveals, incidently, Robert Montgomery as an actor with an extraordinary talent for melodrama, hitherto unsuspected." The *Los Angeles Times* critic bitterly found the film "too long and not box office" and predicted that "such fan support as Montgomery has gained is likely to be missing." That Southern California reviewer undoubtedly lived to regret his critique.

The film, along with the picturization of *Love from a Stranger* (United Artists, 1937), was one of the first in the "psychological chiller" category, and remains Robert's favorite. Of his psychopathic role as a killer who enjoyed eliminating his human prey, Montgomery has said: "The part of the murderer was a challenge to any actor. You see, no one on the screen knows that the man is the murderer. The audience knows it, though, and the hard part is to make the audience like the character." James Cagney told him, after seeing the film, "You've given the rest of us something to shoot at. Boy, you're an actor!" Montgomery was nominated for an Academy Award as Best Actor, but lost to Spencer Tracy, also on MGM's payroll for *Captains Courageous* (1937). It has often been hinted that studio bigwigs instructed their Academy members to vote against Montgomery. (MGM would produce a weak remake of *Night Must Fall* in 1964 with Albert Finney and Susan Hampshire featured.)

Whatever were the results of the publicity-oriented contest MGM instituted in New York, which asked movie patrons to write a brief essay on whether or not they wished Robert to continue in such dramatic roles (top prize was $250), the studio chose to ignore his newly achieved thespian fame and assigned him to play yet another vapid, romantic, rich-boy role in *The Bride Wore Red* (MGM, 1937) opposite Joan Crawford. He rebelled against such casting, however, and the part became Robert Young's. As punishment, Montgomery went on loan to Warners for *Ever Since Eve* (1937).

The star of that feckless comedy was none other than Marion Davies, who, to avoid further competition with Norma Shearer and additional altercations between William Randolph Hearst and Louis B. Mayer's coterie, had encamped at Warner Bros. in Burbank. Jack Warner's studio had gotten the better of the deal, for in exchange for the Hearst newspapers highly touting the Warners' film product, that motion-picture company starred Davies in a series of unthoughtful, not *too* expensive productions which somehow managed to make some box-office coin. The quality of Davies's features had deteriorated in rapid procession, and it is hard to decide which is more tattered, *Page Miss Glory* (Warner Bros, 1935), *Hearts Divided* (Warner Bros., 1936), *Cain and Mable* (Warner Bros., 1936), or *Ever Since Eve.*

Like *Page Miss Glory,* in which Dick Powell was Davies's on and offcamera romance, *Ever Since Eve* cast the comedienne as a beautiful girl who masquerades as a plain Jane. However, by the time of this latest picture, directed by Lloyd Bacon and wardrobed by Orry-Kelly, Davies was fast approaching forty years of age, and had too early succumbed to the dehabilitations of middle age. More devastating to the *leitmotif* of the comedy was Robert's performance as Freddy Mathews. He was cast as an irresponsible novelist whom publisher Louise Fazenda bulldozes into hopefully completing a contracted-for novel. He is the one who falls in love with the pretty Marge Winton (Davies), not knowing she is one and the same as his new secretary (Davies), the girl with the horn-rimmed glasses and unflattering wig. In his biography, *Marion Davies* (1972), Fred Lawrence Guiles reassesses, and most fairly at that: " . . . Robert Montgomery had walked through his roles of novelist with an annoyingly patronizing manner, as though he were simply fulfilling a contractual obligation." *Ever Since Eve,* which opened at Radio City Music Hall, had one lasting distinction, it was the final film of the unfairly maligned Miss Davies.

In May 1937, when six thousand painters, makeup men, scenic artists, and members of eight other crafts went on strike against the studios for union recognition and closed shops, sympathetic SAG members debated going on a strike which would shut down every film studio. SAG's president, Montgomery, feverishly negotiated with producers' representatives for higher wages, steadier work, and improved working conditions for the thousands of technicians and bit players. At an eleventh-hour strike meeting, Robert took to the podium at Hollywood's American Legion Stadium to coolly announce that an agreement had been reached which included the granting of a guild shop, the increase of extras' pay by ten percent with a $5.50 per day minimum, and overtime

With Marion Davies in EVER SINCE EVE (WB '37)

pay for players in the lower salary brackets. The agreement also included a revision of the "Call Bureau," which, theretofore, had permitted a producer to obtain a twenty-four-day option on the services of any actor, thus tying up that actor indefinitely if such options were renewed. Exhausted from the strenuous negotiations, Montgomery was loudly cheered for his concrete achievement.

His next two movies were cute, dull programmers. *Live, Love and Learn* (MGM, 1937) was a comedy that takes a turn for the serious (" . . . points a moral, and nearly chokes with laughter while so doing," said the *New York Sun*) as Greenwich Village landscape painter Montgomery is captured into marriage by Rosalind Russell and learns humility. In *The First 100 Years* (MGM, 1938) he is the facile designer of yachts for the rich. With Virginia Bruce, a badly misused star with Metro, as his radiant wife, he sang "Put on Your Old Gray Bonnet," which did not launch a full-fledged singing career for either of them.

But in *Yellow Jack* (MGM, 1938), *Newsweek* magazine found that "Robert Montgomery again gives a fine performance in a dramatic role."

Again with a thick Irish brogue, he is a Marine volunteer, O'Hara*, who, along with four others, offers himself as a guinea pig for the cure of yellow fever in 1899 Cuba. As a distraction from this earnest study of the endeavor to conquer one of man's worst diseases, there is a conventional love interest between dashing Robert and brave, lovely nurse Frances Blake (Virginia Bruce). Unlike *Men in White* (MGM, 1934), *The Story of Louis Pasteur* (Warner Bros., 1935), and others, Metro did not give this humanitarian drama the proper box-office push, and it passed too quickly into undeserved obscurity. Next, in support of Janet Gaynor in a fluff called *Three Loves Has Nancy* (MGM, 1938), Robert and the ex-Fox star were required to go through the paces of a labored madcap comedy. Said Bosley Crowther (*New York Times*), "in spite of its sneaking resemblance, in plot and character, to a host of dubious ancestors—one has to give the devilish its due. It's good, clean fun." Montgomery was the glib fiction writer to Franchot Tone's playboy publisher. Why it took four well-known Hollywood screenwriters to concoct this slender tale remains a mystery.

*Played by James Stewart on Broadway at the Martin Beck Theatre (March 6, 1934, 79 performances) and by Alfred Ryder in a revival staged by the American Repertory Theatre (International Theatre: February 27, 1947, 21 performances).

With Rosalind Russell and Helen Vinson in LIVE, LOVE AND LEARN (MGM '37)

With Virginia Bruce in YELLOW JACK (MGM '38)

With Janet Gaynor in THREE LOVES HAD NANCY (MGM '38)

On June 27, 1938, at the invitation of host Cecil B. DeMille, Robert was heard on "Lux Radio Theatre" as Mr. Rochester in *Jane Eyre* opposite his favorite actress, Helen Hayes. And, on February 2, 1939, he enacted *The Count of Monte Cristo,* a role suitable for his resonant voice, but one in which he most likely would never have been believable onscreen. His co-star was Josephine Hutchinson. Also in 1939, he was a guest star for the first time on "Nobody's Children," a radio show emanating from Station KHJ in Los Angeles. Orphans, accompanied by each week's guest celebrity, were heard in unrehearsed conversation. Often such children were adopted as a result of the broadcasts.

Louis B. Mayer's Santa Monica beach house provided the scene on May 9, 1939, for a meeting between studio spokesmen and Robert, accompanied by SAG's executive secretary, Kenneth Thomson. Also on hand were Willie Bioff and George Browne "representing" another union, the International Alliance of Theatrical Stage Employees, covering technicians, carpenters, electricians, makeup personnel, and cameramen. When the SAG men announced that the entire membership would go on strike unless the producers recognized their union as a bargaining agent, Bioff and Browne left the room with Mayer but

returned minutes later with the word that studios would recognize the guild.

From all appearances, Bioff and Browne were in direct sympathy with the actors, but Montgomery informed his associate: "Behind that friend-of-labor routine I sniffed the rank stench of crook." Three weeks later, Bioff telephoned the guild office and ordered that a girl who had been suspended from SAG for doing two jobs—acting and makeup—be reinstated immediately. When the message was relayed to Montgomery, he called Bioff and said: "The only way I can explain the stupidity of your message is that some oaf in your office got the wrong number."

That started the union war. Bioff obtained trade-paper ad space announcing that his union was going to fully represent the actors. Robert was urged by friends to acquire bodyguard protection. The next day he found the tires and upholstery of his car slashed and a few days later a bomb was uncovered beneath the back seat of a guild car. Montgomery then persuaded the guild to give him $5,000 to spend for an undisclosed purpose and he turned the money over to two former FBI agents to probe deeply into Bioff's unsavory background. They unearthed evidence which directly linked Bioff and Browne with the Al Capone syndicate, plus further information

Robert Montgomery returning to the U.S. after a short stay at the battle front in France, June, 1940

that Bioff, earlier convicted in Chicago of pandering, had drawn a six-month sentence but had served less than week of it. To save time, Robert turned over the complete dossier to national columnist Westbrook Pegler, who then wrote a series of highly explosive articles. As a result of the crusade, Bioff and Browne were eventually tried, convicted, and sentenced to a federal penitentiary, while Pegler was awarded a Pulitzer Prize for his journalism efforts. Film producer Joseph M. Schenck received a jail sentence for payoffs to Bioff and Browne.

Montgomery still found time, in 1939, to make a comedy-mystery in the *Thin Man* tradition, *Fast and Loose,* a sequel to MGM's 1938 feature, *Fast Company,* which had starred Melvyn Douglas and Florence Rice. Montgomery and Rosalind Russell took on the roles of the married sleuths who make a living buying and selling rare books, and become involved with solving a case of a missing Shakespeare manuscript worth $500,000.°
Variety reported of Montgomery: "... in standard happy-go-lucky and self-assured manner, plays

his role rather broadly in the unwinding of the murder mysteries dropped in his lap."

With Maureen O'Sullivan, Montgomery went to MGM's studio at Denham, England, near London in September 1939 for the filming of the Dorothy L. Sayers novel and play *Busman's Honeymoon,*† which underwent a screen title change to *Haunted Honeymoon* (MGM, 1940). When the British Prime Minister, Neville Chamberlain, declared war against Germany on September 3, Miss O'Sullivan scurried back to New York. She was replaced in the picture by Constance Cummings. Three days after filming started, the studio was threatened with Nazi bombing by German radio's Lord Haw Haw in retaliation for a strong anti-German film, *The Lion Has Wings,* made at Denham by Alexander Korda. It took months to complete Montgomery's film assignment because of air alerts and shortages of supplies and personnel. The director, Arthur Woods, an RAF pilot, was available only at such intervals as were permitted by the RAF. Elizabeth Allan Montgomery, who had gone to Denham with her husband, returned to the States via the liner *President Roosevelt* in the spring of 1940 to be with her children in Hollywood.

While *Haunted Honeymoon* was undergoing the travails of being completed for release, Robert made *The Earl of Chicago* (MGM, 1940). Director Richard Thorpe, who had helmed *Night Must Fall,* had agreed originally with Montgomery that the film should be lensed in England, but because of the precarious conditions there, it was shot in Hollywood, with rear-projection photography utilized to give the impression of a London locale. It was another piece of decidedly offbeat casting, with Montgomery projecting a winning performance as a charming bootlegger of the Prohibition era, who inherits a British title. A superlative supporting cast included Edward Arnold as the conniving lawyer who double-crosses Montgomery and Edmund Gwenn as a loyal valet. Despite the presence of too many moronic grimaces and an unsettling cackle, Montgomery's interpretation of the twelfth Earl of Gorley, who goes to the gallows (he eventually kills Arnold) with dignity and nobility, was sterling, proving "that his brilliant performance in *Night Must Fall* was not just an accident" (P. T. Hartung, *Commonweal* magazine). B. R. Crisler in the *New York Times* was even more enthusiastic about this contracasting assignment: "... the Earl as played to the

°Also in 1939 MGM put Franchot Tone and Ann Sothern into yet another sequel called *Fast and Furious.*
†Opened at the Comedy Theatre in London on December 16, 1936, for a 413-performance run.

proverbial hilt by Robert Montgomery is probably the most amusing peer you ever met on a motion-picture screen, a fantastic, overgrown Fauntleroy, or rather, a cross between the heir of Dorincourt and Little Caesar." With all due respect to Montgomery, his performance owes something to Edward G. Robinson's way of life in *Thunder in the City* (Columbia, 1937). George Raft, who had made a less successful similar foray into the metier by playing a slangy American law-enforcer who becomes involved with British-gentry crooks in *Midnight Club* (Paramount, 1933), would long harbor the desire to remake, as star and director, Robert's *The Earl of Chicago*.

On May 30, 1940, Montgomery arrived in Paris to begin an estimated six months' volunteer duty as an ambulance driver with the American Field Services in France. The AFS was equipped with thirty-eight men, six three-quarter-ton Chevrolet trucks, and twenty field ambulances. Less than a month later, on June 20, Montgomery landed in New York aboard the Clipper, where, as *Time* magazine sarcastically put it, "he became Hollywood's foremost authority on World War II."

"An Open Letter to a German Hero," written by agitated Montgomery, appeared in *Collier's* magazine of July 27, 1940. In the letter, he explained to "Otto, Fritz or even Adolf" how it was with the AFS, Section One, on "the road between Corbeil-Cerf and Marines" after the German bombing of a French ambulance. "There were big Red Crosses painted on both sides and on top of the ambulances," he wrote, "so you had a good target. The driver was the only one saved. He had been carried off, wounded, just a few minutes before we got there. The Captain seemed to have been killed by the bomb in front. The stretcher cases were killed by the machine-gun bullets. We could see that for ourselves." A paragraph at the end of the two-page magazine piece read: "Payment for this 'letter' has been made, at Mr. Montgomery's request, to the American Field Service."

The United States Treasury Department revealed in 1941 that Robert's income for 1940 had been a whopping $211,416.

Back in Hollywood, he furthered his unpopularity with industry leaders by stating at a Forum on Current Problems in October 1940: "I am convinced that the weakness of leadership under which, to my knowledge, this industry has been struggling is directly responsible for the poor quality of its average product in the past and will make it impossible for the industry to perform its function in national defense in the present crisis with any appreciable degree of success." He added that "any resemblance between the motion-

With Reginald Owen, Matthew Boulton, and Colin Kenny in THE EARL OF CHICAGO (MGM '40)

picture industry and creative art is purely coincidental."

Haunted Honeymoon had its delayed release in October 1940 at Loew's Criterion Theatre, New York City. It was a leisurely, bookish detective fable in which detective Lord Peter Wimsey (Montgomery) and his mystery novelist bride (Constance Cummings) uncover a dead body in the basement of their quiet honeymoon cottage in Devonshire, England. Among the suspects are Joan Kemp-Welch, the squeaking niece of the deceased (Roy Emerton), Robert Newton, the glum and suspicious handyman, Louise Hampton, the inebriated housemaid, constable James Carney, who paid an unexplained visit to the cottage on the night of the murder, and Reverend Aubrey Mallalieu, who turned up the morning after the crime with a gun and a dead weasel in his hand. Sadly, this pleasant picture never received its proper due.* Part of the blame was placed on the fact that it was "little more than a minor relic of days gone by" (*New York Morning Telegraph*), that the two American leads were struggling with British accents, and that in essence the picture was "not so much haunted as halted" (*Christian Science Monitor*).

Robert switched political affiliations in the 1940 Presidential campaign, declaring himself in favor of Wendell Willkie. He was then appointed chairman of Hollywood's Republican Committee to elect Willkie, while the candidate, during a swing into Madison, Wisconsin, mentioned that Democrats had charged him with splitting infinitives and had bragged about Katharine Hepburn's support of Franklin D. Roosevelt. "All I can say," Willkie announced, "is that I admit I split my infinitives and that Robert Montgomery and Mary Pickford are for me."

Jimmy Fidler, the powerful Hollywood columnist and radio broadcaster, sent Montgomery a wristwatch during this period, which was immediately returned by the star. Said Montgomery: "Fidler has the effrontery to appoint himself the giver of what he called, 'The Jimmy Fidler Award for Americanism.' He had the further gall to award it to me. Before I could send it back with a rude suggestion as to how he could best dispose of it, a number of my friends had called me on the phone to rib me as 'you great big wonderful American, you!' "

After applying for a commission in the U.S. Navy and while awaiting disposition from Washington, thirty-six-year-old Robert made four features for 1941 release, three of them on loan-out. At RKO he starred with Carole Lombard in Alfred Hitchcock's first and only American comedy farce, *Mr. and Mrs. Smith,* a labored film devoted to the age-old marital question, "If you had it to do over again, would you marry me?"† When this rhetorical idea becomes actuality in the early part of the Norman Krasna screenplay, attorney Montgomery must court and repropose to his silly, beautiful, strong-willed wife (Lombard). Making a third side to the triangle is Montgomery's law partner, Gene Raymond, who, with dyed hair, sun-bronzed face, and a self-satirical stolidness, competes for Lombard's affection. Two well-publicized gimmicks in the film were the inclusion of the Parachute Jump amusement ride from the World's Fair at Flushing Meadows, New York, and the unusual step of letting Lombard supervise director Hitchcock in his standard walk-on bit in the picture.

Hitchcock, who did the picture as a favor to beguiling Lombard (the ex-wife of MGM farceur William Powell and the then spouse of MGM king Clark Gable), relied on traditional madcap comedy ploys to push along his ninety-five-minute yarn. With Lombard and Robert in the forefront, the picture had a lot going for it, as they battle in their bedroom, quarrel in front of a department-store window to the edification of a gathering crowd, and exchange unpleasantries during the Lake Placid cabin sequences wherein Montgomery and Raymond vie in hot pursuit of the antic, frivolous blonde Lombard. Montgomery broadened his farcical repertoire with such stunts as punching himself in the nose to cause a nose bleed and win Lombard's sympathy, or near the climax where he feigns frostbite and inanimation as he allows her to shave him.

MGM put him to work with Ingrid Bergman (on loan from David O. Selznick) in *Rage in Heaven* (1941). (Some say Robert's assignment was MGM's way of punishing him for his outspoken comments about Hollywood.) Christopher Isherwood and Robert Thoeren adapted the screenplay from the James Hilton novel in which Robert, as Philip Monrell, is the unstable heir to a British industrial fortune. His mother (Lucile

---

*In *The Detective in Film* (1972), author William K. Everson states: "Montgomery, an expert light comedian, has been almost forgotten today by critics who extol the comedic performances of Cary Grant in the thirties but forget that Montgomery had been doing it—as a star—since 1930. His breezy detectives were few but always memorable (as witness also his Lord Peter Wimsey in *Haunted Honeymoon* and make an interesting comparison with his later much more serious work as star and director in the Philip Marlowe mystery *Lady in the Lake*."

† *This Thing Called Love* (Columbia, 1941), *Come Live with Me* (MGM, 1941), and *We're Not Married* (Twentieth Century–Fox, 1952) would also employ offshoots of this plot gimmick.

With Carole Lombard in MR. AND MRS. SMITH (RKO '41)

Watson) is unaware that he is an escapee from a French mental hospital, and blithely allows him to court and wed her companion-secretary (Bergman). Quickly his mental instability and possessive jealousy become evident, as he persists in accusing her of having an affair with Ward Andrews (George Sanders), his onetime engineer friend and business associate. In an act of final desperation and cunning, Montgomery's character stabs himself, having previously set the stage so that Sanders will be blamed. Bergman finds evidence of her husband's psychotic condition and saves Sanders at the final moment before his prison execution. The potentially promising picture suffered from its overstatement of the psychiatric condition, a subject already becoming familiar to Americans through the Broadway musical *Lady in the Dark* and, with its lagging moments, "never [becomes] quite as macabre or full of ghoulish terror as it could and should be" (William Boehnel, *New York World-Telegram*).

Knowing Robert's penchant for offbeat assignments, the critics verbalized what the more discerning public must have felt about *Rage in Heaven,* if they gave the celluloid thriller that much close thought. One New York critic penned: "The whole thing is another of the trick parts that Mr. Montgomery has taken such a fancy

to. . . . If, however, Mr. Montgomery were a better actor, a more sincere actor, an actor with more depth and persuasion than he actually commands, the trick might come off better. But all these trick parts of Mr. Montgomery's are surface parts—it's as if Mr. Montgomery were imitating the character he is playing, rather than actually playing it. As if Mr. Montgomery were standing there in front of you on the screen, and every once in a while saying, 'Look, watch this expression now. Isn't that good?' Or again, 'Notice how I suffer here, notice how I crinkle up my eyes. Doesn't that impress you?' " This criticism is an overstatement perhaps, but it contains a heavy element of truth.

At Columbia, which seven years earlier he considered a second-rate studio, Robert was Joe Pendleton, a happy-go-lucky prizefighter whose soul enters heaven fifty years too soon in *Here Comes Mr. Jordan* (Columbia, 1941). To remedy matters, the heavenly arbiter, Mr. Jordan (Claude Rains), with the bungling assistance of celestial messenger #7013 (Edward Everett Horton), returns Montgomery to earth in the body of a dishonest financier who has just been killed by his wife (Rita Johnson) and her lover (John Emery). The film's gimmick, a variation of the *Topper* premise, has Montgomery "being" the new person to the

With Ingrid Bergman and George Sanders in RAGE IN HEAVEN (MGM '41)

With James Gleason in HERE COMES MR. JORDAN (Col '41)

characters within the film, but photographing as himself to filmgoers. For the role, Montgomery affected a Bronx accent, and *Newsweek* magazine declared that he "turns in another of his better-than-most characterizations." This was perhaps an understatement for the jaunty personage Robert created, who plays a "mean" saxophone, romances Evelyn Keyes, exasperates his fight manager (James Gleason), and, when his soul is disembodied again, returns in the body of a boxer who has just been murdered, and goes on to win the championship bout. Montgomery won his second Academy Award nomination for *Here Comes Mr. Jordan,* but lost to Gary Cooper for *Sergeant York* (Warner Bros., 1941). (When Columbia filmed a musical sequel to the *Jordan* film, called *Down to Earth* [1947], with Rita Hayworth and Larry Parks starred, both Claude Rains and Edward Everett Horton repeated their popular roles.)

Finally, in 1941, at Universal, he was back to his rich-playboy mold, this time with premiere farceuse Irene Dunne in *Unfinished Business.* The thrust of the Gregory La Cava–directed feature was that in every woman's life there is a bit of unconcluded romantic interplay. Dunne was too mature and sophisticated to be playing the Messina, Ohio, choir singer who, having married off her younger sister, takes a fling in New York, only to fall passionately in love with irresponsible, wealthy Preston Foster on the Manhattan-bound train. Before she has reached Grand Central Station she has lost her heart to him, but he regards her as only a passing fancy. Not so to Foster's brother (Montgomery), who is quickly smitten with would-be opera singer Dunne. On a drunken lark (of whizz booms) they elope to Gretna Green, South Carolina, and live to regret their hasty decision. Dunne still carries a torch for Foster, which she insists upon playing out, causing Robert to enlist in the Army. A year later he reencounters her when attending the Metropolitan opera (she is in the chorus line of *Martha*). They eventually reconcile. The picture was not up to snuff, but John Rosenfield (*Dallas Morning News*) could report of the screen exercise: "It recognized his post-juvenility without depriving him of flipness and suavity. At that Mr. Montgomery has a range you seldom notice. Who else could have recalled his dear old grandmother or sobbed so unabashedly at his wife's desertion without ruining the picture?"

On August 1, 1941, commissioned a lieutenant in the U.S. Naval Reserve, Robert began duty as an assistant naval attaché at the U.S. Embassy in London. After receiving a fourteen-week leave of

With Irene Dunne and Walter Catlett in UNFINISHED BUSINESS (Univ '41)

absence from his contract, he boarded a plane and quipped to newsmen: "I'm washed up with Hollywood for the duration." His duties as an intelligence officer included running the Naval Operations Room wherein were charted the locations of all British ships. He cabled MGM to extend his leave for an indefinite period and in November 1941 was ordered to the White House in Washington. There, he set up the same kind of operations room for his commander-in-chief, the man he did *not* vote for in 1940, Franklin D. Roosevelt. Soon after, Montgomery requested sea duty and trained at the Torpedo Boat School in Connecticut.

He took a formidable step toward maintaining his interests in show business by co-producing in partnership with Elliott Nugent a play called *All in Favor* at the Hudson Theatre in New York on January 21, 1942. This play was the first to be staged by the Montgomery-Nugent partnership known as Neptune Productions, but it unfortunately lasted only seven performances.

This Is War! was a half-hour radio broadcast on Saturday, February 21, 1942, over the four major U.S. networks encompassing seven hundred affiliate stations. Sponsored by the office of Facts and Figures, the program was the first in a series of thirteen designed to make Americans conscious of the war. Authored by Norman Corwin, the program started with a message by President Roosevelt which was read by poet Archibald MacLeish. The remainder of the thirty minutes was narrated by Montgomery, and at the end he addressed the people of the United Nations: "Take heart! Resist much! Fight how you can! We are building for you, we are on the move." The program was also transcribed in Spanish and Portuguese and broadcast by short wave to South America. A week later, recorded in other languages, it went to European listeners.

On finishing the Newport course, Robert first commanded PT-boats in the Panama Canal area and later saw action at Guadalcanal and the Marshall Islands in the Pacific, where he was upgraded to the rank of lieutenant commander. In April 1943, he returned to Hollywood, a malaria convalescent and twenty-two pounds lighter than when he had left his family two years prior. After a month's rest, he was dispatched to a naval school in New England for further sea training. He was then assigned as operations officer aboard a destroyer and was one of the first to enter Cherbourg harbour in the D-Day invasion. For "meritorious achievement" during the invasion he was awarded the Bronze Star.

Robert returned to America in the autumn of 1944, still classified on the active-duty rosters. On December 4, he made a foray into show business by acting with Laraine Day on "Lux Radio Theatre" in *The Unguarded Hour,* based on the 1936 MGM feature which had starred Loretta Young and Franchot Tone.

A few months later, the forty-year-old Montgomery rejoined Metro as Navy Lieutenant John Brickley in *They Were Expendable* (MGM, 1945), a piece of casting that was close to real life. As a PT-boat commander, he and co-star John Wayne become expendable when their vessels are assigned the task of evacuating officers and their families from Bataan under fire. Director John Ford suffered a fractured leg three weeks before the film was completed, and Robert took over the directorial tasks. After viewing the finished product, Ford said he could not tell where he had left off and Montgomery had begun directing. The *Saturday Evening Post* called the 135-minute picture "the closest thing to a perfect movie this year." The upper-crust *New Yorker* magazine reviewer might snidely judge that it "has the freshness and simplicity of a well-told adventure story for juveniles." Nevertheless, the public took a fancy to the well-mounted production and it grossed over $3.256 million in distributors' domestic grosses. During the making of this film, which cast Donna Reed as Wayne's Army nurse love interest, Montgomery received a Navy Department promotion to full commander.

The second Broadway endeavor of Neptune Productions opened at the Royale Theatre on April 2, 1945. Called *A Place of Our Own,* written by Elliott Nugent, and featuring Mercedes McCambridge, Jeanne Cagney, J. C. Nugent, and Robert Keith, it closed after eight performances.

For some years, Robert had pleaded with his Metro bosses to allow him to direct a film. He also insisted that he had a revolutionary idea in which the camera would be the leading actor and the action would be seen through the camera lens, which would serve as the actor's eyes. Because of his efforts in *They Were Expendable* the studio hierarchy allowed him to proceed with his ideas on Steve Fisher's fast-paced screen adaptation of Raymond Chandler's novel, *Lady in the Lake* (MGM, 1946).

In the meantime, Montgomery had been discharged from the Navy and resumed his activities with the Screen Actors Guild. In 1946, he was elected president of the guild for a fourth term. In October 1946, another strike hit Hollywood in a dispute over union job designations. The task of

With Ward Bond and Donald Curtis in THEY WERE EXPENDABLE (MGM '45)

With Audrey Totter in LADY IN THE LAKE (MGM '46)

constructing sets, for example, was given to the carpenters' union, but some of the jobs were interpreted as set erection rather than carpentry. In *Life* magazine of October 14, 1946, Montgomery authored a half-page explanation of the strike, in which he stated that "the Guild rigorously opposes any fascist or communist influence in the industry or the ranks of labor."

Lady in the Lake, filmed on a closed MGM soundstage, was generally acclaimed as unique. *Newsweek* said: ". . . as a brilliant tour de force [it] indicates that Hollywood isn't beyond exploring the uncharted boundaries of its medium." The camera and Robert are detective Philip Marlowe, who finds the body of Leon Ames's wife lying a full five fathoms at the bottom of a lake.* Several more murders occur before the culprit is unveiled. Montgomery is seen only twice on-screen, in an introductory sequence and again when he (or the camera) crosses in front of a mirror. When he lights a cigarette, his hands are visible but the smoke is seemingly exhaled from the camera. When he is supposedly slugged it is the camera that falls to the floor, and when Audrey Totter, as the sultry publishers' editor, kisses him, the camera lens blurs. As *Collier's* magazine describes it: "Everyone working on the film had to adopt a new point of view. They had constantly to regard the camera as a living, breathing person. That they were able to do so is a tribute to director Montgomery."

The year 1947 was one of diversification for Robert. First, he was made a Chevalier in the French Legion of Honor for his efforts at the start of World War II. On January 8, 1947, *The Big Two* opened at Broadway's Booth Theatre featuring Claire Trevor, Philip Dorn, and Felix Bressart. The play was the third by Neptune Productions, with Montgomery directing the action revolving around the relationship between a Soviet officer and a feminine American correspondent. After twenty-one performances, the play closed on January 25.

In March 1947, Robert resigned as SAG president because he shared profits from *Lady in the Lake,* and thus was disqualified from heading the organization.

MGM, which was soon to undergo its own corporate changes, was doing its utmost to cope with the wavering lineup of male box-office attractions under the studio banner. Clark Gable, Robert Taylor, Melvyn Douglas, and, to a far lesser degree, Mickey Rooney returned from the war with their screen reputations intact, joining Spencer Tracy, William Powell, Walter Pidgeon, and Van Johnson as the leading male players on the Culver City lot. As with many others, Montgomery had aged noticeably during the absence, and he no longer could play the bouncy young man. Besides, in post–World War II Hollywood, that type of aristocratic-loafer part was an anachronism. Montgomery had followed the suit of cinema crooner Dick Powell, who changed his image 1940s style by adopting a tough-guy screen guise. *Lady in the Lake,* despite its rare shots of a full-bodied Montgomery, gave moviegoers a satisfying impression of a mature, solid performer who could easily have continued in this new mold. However, the studio attempted to make him revert to the formula of old by casting him opposite Greer Garson in a sticky love story which began filming under George Cukor's direction. However, the project as lensed was largely scrapped when Montgomery balked at the course the production was taking. A new director was brought in, with Richard Hart replacing Montgomery as the slick, smooth-talker, and the picture, *Desire Me* (MGM, 1947), was eventually released, a credit to no one involved. (The film lists no director.)

Robert headed the Hollywood Republican Committee to elect Thomas E. Dewey as the nation's President, in opposition to Harry Truman, and in June 1947, he trekked over to Universal-International to direct and star in *Ride the Pink Horse* (1947)‡ with a Ben Hecht–Charles Lederer screenplay, and handsome photography by Russell Metty. In the caper, Montgomery is an ex-gangster who travels to New Mexico to avenge a pal's death and deals in blackmail with his old boss (Fred Clark). He is assisted by an Indian girl (Wanda Hendrix) and the proprietor of a carousel (Thomas Gomez). *Newsweek* magazine found that "Montgomery, who directed the picture with excellent effect, is properly tough and determined in the lead." In the *Nation,* James Agee said that the story "is so carefully vague you can hardly follow it."

For the preliminary October 1947 hearings held in the House Caucus Room in Washington, D.C., which launched the infamous Hollywood Communist purge, Montgomery was summoned

---

*The character of Marlowe had previously been played onscreen by Dick Powell in *Murder, My Sweet* (RKO, 1944), and later would be played by Humphrey Bogart in *The Big Sleep* (Warner Bros., 1946), George Montgomery in *The Brasher Dubloon* (Twentieth Century–Fox, 1947), James Garner in *Marlowe* (MGM, 1969), and Elliot Gould in *The Long Goodbye* (United Artists, 1973).

‡Remade as the Don Siegel–directed NBC telefeature *The Hanged Man* (1964) starring Robert Culp.

With Art Smith in RIDE THE PINK HORSE (Univ '47)

to testify. He expressed his belief that the matter of Communism within the film industry could best be dealt with by the industry itself rather than by the government.

"The Theatre Guild on the Air" (a.k.a. "The United States Steel Hour") presented him as Alan Squire in an ABC radio adaptation of Robert Sherwood's *The Petrified Forest* on November 2, 1947. Montgomery provided the characterization of the fatalistic idealist with a tone that was in complete contrast to the performance by Leslie Howard on stage or in the (1936) Warner Bros. film.

In February 1948, Robert introduced Harold E. Stassen, former governor of Minnesota, who was seeking the nomination as the Republican Presidential candidate, at a rally held at the Shrine Auditorium in Los Angeles. George Murphy (of MGM) was master of ceremonies for the event.

Montgomery was heard as Philip Marlowe in the "Lux Radio Theatre" version of *Lady in the Lake* on February 2, 1948. Audrey Totter also repeated her screen role. On June 4, 1948, he again did *Jane Eyre* on the "Lux" show, this time with Ingrid Bergman as his co-star.

What proved to be his final chore at MGM was one of three (with Van Heflin and Robert Taylor) narrators of *The Secret Land,* a U.S. Naval docu-

mentary based on 300,000 feet of film lensed during the 1946–47 Admiral Byrd expeditions to Antarctica. It was released simultaneously in eighty American cities, with *Cue* magazine lauding it as a "marvelous example of Polar photography and Naval Adventure." With this task, Robert departed the Metro lot, glad to bring to a close an association that had proved so artistically frustrating for so many years. He saw the approaching new Dore Schary regime as little indication that the future would hold better projects in which he could participate, and he realized he must strike out in new directions on his own.

The Saxon Charm (Universal, 1948), directed by ex-scripter Claude Binyon, was an incisive account of a megalomaniac Broadway producer who thrives on manipulating and crushing the creative-romantic talent about him. Although the public reception to this film verged on the indifferent, despite the presence of Susan Hayward as playwright John Payne's understanding wife, the picture offered Montgomery full occasion to display a range of ruthless, insulting, domineering, tyrannical behavior. "The smallest nuances of [Matt] Saxon's complex nature are perfectly clear in Montgomery's excellent performance" (Otis L. Guernsey, Jr., *New York Herald-Tribune*). Some astute filmgoers wondered just how a man of such

Advertisment for THE SECRET LAND (MGM '48)

impeccably crass actions as Robert's Saxon could have produced stage shows as widely acclaimed and tasteful as is constantly claimed throughout the film.

In her autobiography, *The Lonely Life* (1962), Bette Davis admits that she "loathed" working with Montgomery in *June Bride* (Warner Bros., 1948), which had been her first screen comedy in seven years.* Montgomery appears as Cary Jackson, a smart-aleck foreign correspondent returned home to assist Linda Gilman (Davis), the slick, frosty editor of *Home Life* magazine, on the coverage of a typically American wedding in Crestville, Indiana. Davis's Linda has never forgiven him for standing her up on a date three years previously. She tells him: "You're not really a heel, you just give that impression." He replies: "I'm gay, I'm lovable, and I've got nice teeth." Later he

calls himself: "Fun-loving Cary Jackson, schmoo of the week." He has a very funny scene when he becomes drunk on homemade apple cider which the prospective bride's father (Tom Tully) keeps hidden in a jug tied outside a pantry window. Compared to today's sparse output of entertaining comedy screen fare, *June Bride* seems a jewel. But in 1948, the high-toned *New Yorker* magazine could complain: "Mr. Montgomery's contributions consist of wearing his hat turned up all around and of snapping off electric lights in an attempt to put Miss Davis in a loving mood. In one scene, he puts out so many lights that I got to thinking that I was just a boorish intruder. I suggest that you forget all about it."

Thomas E. Dewey was defeated in the Presidential race of November 1948, thus killing the candidate's plans, if elected, to appoint Robert as

*She complained that he cheated on the close-ups by diverting an unproportionate amount of attention to himself.

340

With Harry Morgan, John Payne, Susan Hayward, and Audrey Totter in THE SAXON CHARM (Univ '48)

With Bette Davis in JUNE BRIDE (WB '48)

Assistant Secretary of the Navy. It was unanimously agreed in Republican Party circles that he would have been ideal in the job because of his maritime knowledge. Instead, on December 13, 1948, Montgomery went on radio one more time for "Lux" in the role created on film by James Mason in *The Seventh Veil* (J. Arthur Rank, 1946). Again, Ingrid Bergman was his broadcasting co-star.

On behalf of Neptune Productions, Montgomery directed and starred in *Once More, My Darling* (Universal, 1949). Originally entitled *Come Be My Love,* and written by Robert Carson, the film was the tale of a young girl (Ann Blyth) infatuated with a middle-aged movie idol (Montgomery), who is also an attorney. Despite some favorable reviews ("Montgomery's performance is his glib best") the public was not particularly impressed with the black-and-white proceedings. It was Montgomery who persuaded the distinguished stage actress Jane Cowl to make her sound-film debut as his onscreen mother.

In 1949, Robert moved to New York City, leaving his wife and children in California. It was known only to the Montgomerys' closest friends that the marriage had grown sour. He negotiated a deal with Britain's Eagle-Lion Films to direct and star in a screenplay by Hugo Butler and Ian Hunter called *Your Witness* (known as *Eye Witness* when released in the States in 1950).

As he prepared to fly to London, however, the Lee Hat Company offered him a "splendid" salary to replace Drew Pearson as commentator over ABC radio network in a weekly fifteen-minute broadcast. He grabbed at the opportunity to speak his mind every Thursday between 10:10 and 10:25 P.M. Appropriately enough, the program was tagged, "Robert Montgomery Speaking." (Later it was changed to "A Citizen Views the News.") A spokesman for Lee Hats stated that Montgomery was "provocative enough to attract the attention of American listeners" while the ex-Hollywood star admitted being a "completely inexpert" news expert. His first program originated from London on September 22, 1949, when he gave a discourse on Britain's socialist state and insisted that he thoroughly distrusted that country's economics. "Where do we, the American people, come into all this?" he asked. "We come in to the extent of seven billion dollars."* The Lee Hat Company then took out a $200,000 libel insurance policy with North American Insurance

*The amount of the U.S. World War II loan to Britain.

With Roland Winters and Jane Cowl in ONCE MORE, MY DARLING (Univ '49)

342

With Patricia Wayne (Cutts) in YOUR WITNESS (a.k.a. EYE WITNESS) (Warner Bros-British '50)

Company, plus an additional $300,000 policy with Lloyds of London. It all made for good publicity copy on the program.

Eye Witness (Eagle-Lion, 1950) is Robert's last screen performance to date. The film's main purpose is to show the differences between American and British manners, colloquialisms, and judicial procedures. Montgomery is brash American lawyer Adam Heywood, who journeys to England to defend a war buddy on a murder charge of which he is innocent. "... it has little suspense or terror, but it has flavor and amusing by-play" (Howard Barnes, *New York Herald-Tribune*). Once again Montgomery's screen direction was ranked as resourceful.

On his return to New York in January 1950, he was named an executive-producer-advisor to NBC Television and in the same month became producer-director-host, and sometime star of a bi-weekly dramatic video show, "Robert Montgomery Presents Your Lucky Strike Theatre." The program with the unwieldy title premiered on Monday, January 30, from 9:30 to 10:30 P.M. E.S.T. with Madeleine Carroll starring in *The Letter*. Of the new airwaves venture, Saul Carson wrote in the *New Republic:* "Montgomery is in his proper slot and television gains another good dramatic program."

Meanwhile, Robert's radio show received a change in time to 9:45–10:10 P.M. E.S.T., and he launched successive crusades (1) against open gambling in Woonsocket, Rhode Island, (2) to separate underworld chieftain Frank Costello from his fraudulent American citizenship, (3) to rid Chicago of its forty-second-ward boss, William J. Connors, "a political mobster—a hoodlum masquerading as a state senator." These were but three of Montgomery's many radio campaigns to effect a clean-up of America. He also utilized the radio time-slot to tell stories of human interest, such as bringing an eleven-year-old refugee from a European displaced person's camp into the studio to relate her story to the listening audience.

On December 5, 1950, Elizabeth Allan Montgomery quietly obtained a divorce through residence in Las Vegas, Nevada. After twenty-two years of marriage, the divorce was granted on grounds of mental cruelty, and Mrs. Montgomery received custody of the children. Four days later, on December 9, 1950, Montgomery was wed to Mrs. Elizabeth Grant Harkness (nicknamed "Buffy"), the divorced wife of Standard Oil magnate William Harkness. Montgomery was forty-six and his very wealthy, socially prominent bride gave her age as "late forties." They were married at Sag Harbor, Long Island, New York, at the home of the Alexander Brookses, the only guests being Mr. and Mrs. N. L. Griggs of New York (Buffy's sister).

Robert continued to build show-business prestige through his television work. He was nominated as Best Actor in the fourth annual Emmy Awards in 1951 but lost to comedian Sid Caesar of "Your Show of Shows." "Robert Montgomery Presents" also received a nomination in the Best Dramatic Show (anthology) category, but lost out to "Studio One."

The actor-personality was much in the news in 1952. In March of that year, John J. Dickerson, chairman of the New Jersey state committee, mayor of Palisades Park, New Jersey, and a member of the Bergen City Board of Freeholders, filed a million-dollar law suit against Montgomery and NBC radio network for statements made by commentator Montgomery on "A Citizen Views the News" during mid-February 1952, in which he dealt with the investigation of gambling in Bergen County and allegedly attacked the plaintiff's reputation. NBC settled the case out of court. Jack I. Straus, president of R. H. Macy and Company, was obliged to defend the election of Robert to the department store's board of directors at the annual Manhattan meeting of stockholders in November 1952. Montgomery explained: "I've been in the business and professional field for thirty years. Whatever my talents are, they are at Macy's service." A lady stockholder replied from the floor: "Thank you, Mr. Montgomery. I see you still have the gift of gab."

In 1952, the Montgomerys purchased a four-hundred-acre farm at Millbrook, New York. As often as possible, they closed their fashionable Manhattan townhouse and drove to Millbrook, which was his preference to big-city dwelling. Rounding out the year, a Sylvania TV trophy for the best dramatic series of 1952 was awarded to "Robert Montgomery Presents" on December 11, 1952.

One morning in January 1953, the newly elected Republican President of the United States, Dwight D. Eisenhower, invited Robert to the White House for brunch. As the result of the auspicious meeting, Montgomery was added to the White House staff as instructor-advisor to the President in the techniques of television delivery. Ike's previous video speeches had been awkward at best, and the audience invariably saw long moments of just the top of his bald head as he bent over his extensive notes. Montgomery raised the lectern, cut down the lights, and encouraged the President to be as natural as possible while oncamera. Montgomery held the job, without financial remuneration throughout Ike's administration, ending in 1960. Asked why he worked without pay, Montgomery responded: "This man, to me, is an incredibly great person. I've become overburdened because of enthusiasm for him—but the fact is, I've never met anybody remotely like him. Working with him, I have a distinct sense of service to my country—and, well, that's reward enough in itself."[*]

On January 4, 1953, Robert inadvertently pulled a Sheridan Whiteside (*The Man Who Came to Dinner*) act when, on leaving the home of friends in Millbrook, he fell on the ice and broke his left arm. In his case, however, he was not returned to the house, but was whisked to St. Francis Hospital in Poughkeepsie for treatment.

The editors of Radio-TV Daily Poll, on January 7, 1953, chose "Robert Montgomery Presents" as the best dramatic show on television. A month later, the series was handed a belated Emmy. On February 22, 1953, at Valley Forge, Pennsylvania, Vice President Nixon presented a Freedom Foundation Award to Montgomery's radio program for its contributions to U.S. liberty during 1952. (The radio show went off the air in December 1952.) The Sylvania TV Awards for 1953 were announced in New York City on December 1. The Award for Best TV adaptation went to Irving Gaynor Nieman for his version of John O'Hara's *Appointment in Samara,* an offering during the TV season on "Robert Montgomery Presents."

Elizabeth Montgomery, Robert's daughter, who had been performing in summer stock and later on such television programs as "Robert Montgomery Presents" and "Studio One," was wed on March 27, 1954, to Frederic Cammann of Neptune Productions. They were divorced, however, on August 9, 1955.

A hankering to return to stage directing led Robert to supervise the stage version of Joseph Hayes's adaptation of his own novel, *The Desperate Hours,* which opened at the Ethel Barrymore Theatre on Broadway on February 10, 1955. Montgomery directed a cast which included Karl Malden and Nancy Coleman as heads of an Indianapolis family held prisoners in their home by a trio of fugitives (Paul Newman, George Grizzard, George Mathews). John Chapman (*New York Daily News*) noted: "Robert Montgomery has di-

---

[*] It was estimated that Robert's annual income in 1954 was $500,000.

344

rected the play to perfection." William Hawkins (*New York World-Telegram*) observed: "[he] has staged the show to a sprint." To *Women's Home Companion* writer, Michael Drury, actress Nancy Coleman had this to say of her director: "You never know quite what he's thinking and women find that provocative."

At the Antoinette Perry Award ceremony in New York on March 27, 1955, *The Desperate Hours* was named Best Drama during the current season. Robert received a Tony as Best Director.* The play closed on August 16, 1955, after 212 performances.

In the summer of 1956, Montgomery formed a permanent acting company, which included his daughter, Elizabeth, in a season of repertory to perform his television series' weekly plays.†

At the conclusion of his 326th television pres-entation on June 24, 1957, he quietly told his audience: "Sometimes we have been terribly proud of the programs we have brought you. Other times we haven't been quite so proud and sometimes we've not been proud at all. But you have always been extremely grateful to work for. So again, as I say sadly, I'm going to have to sign off the program tonight for the last time by saying, 'thank you for still being with us and good night.' " Thus ended the seven-year run of "Robert Montgomery Presents," because NBC was unable to find a new sponsor to finance the relatively expensive program.

In that same year Cagney-Montgomery Productions was formed,‡ and work began on a wartime biographic film of Fleet Admiral William F. Halsey, Jr. Beirne Lay, Jr. and Frank D. Gilroy wrote the screenplay, called *The Gallant Hours*. The

---

*In November 1955, the VistaVision film version from Paramount was released. It was directed by William Wyler and starred Humphrey Bogart as the top fugitive and Fredric March and Martha Scott as the innocent captives.

†Elizabeth was wed to actor Gig Young on December 28, 1956. A few years later she was to become a television favorite in the weekly ABC series "Bewitched" as a devilish spirit who loves and marries a mortal (Dick York, later Dick Sargent), with Agnes Moorehead as her mother-witch. While the series (1964–1972) became a solid hit, Miss Montgomery's marriage grew stale and she divorced Young in January 1963. Ten months later, she married her TV director, William Asher, by whom she had two sons, William and Robert. Recently she has become a popular lead in offbeat telefeatures.

‡Cagney made a rare TV appearance, starring in the *Soldier from the Wars Returning* episode (September 10, 1956) of "Robert Montgomery Presents."

With James Cagney and Admiral William F. Halsey, Jr. on the set of THE GALLANT HOURS (UA '60)

United Artists picture took almost three years to prepare and complete; it was released on June 22, 1960, some months after Halsey's death. Robert told columnist Hedda Hopper: "I wanted to make the Halsey picture because I have tremendous admiration for the man and the things he stood for." When Hopper inquired why he had returned to movie-making after his television work, he replied: "I'm finished with television until such time as television is finished with the networks. I hope the networks will be broken up and we will have pay TV. It may take three to five years for pay TV to be working soundly; there are many problems in talking of free and pay TV, take a look at advertising budgets of any big sponsor and you'll see what they're paying and you are paying through purchases of their products. Who said it's free? What does your TV set cost? And every time you go to the grocery and drug store you're paying."

Robert directed Cagney as Admiral Halsey in the story of naval events at the bloody battle of Guadalcanal in 1942. Howard Thompson in his *New York Times Guide to Movies on TV* argues that because of Montgomery's direction, it is "one of the quietest, most reflective and subtlest jobs that James Cagney has ever done." At the time, the picture met with a poor box-office reception, largely because of its studio-bound ambiance in which there is much talk, thinking, and recapitulating, but very little action. "The film aim—to show the loneliness of and strain of command—is a matchstick in a sea of irrevelance" (London *Evening Standard*). Like James Cagney, Jr., Robert Montgomery, Jr. had a small part in the film. Montgomery Sr. declared: "I had the choice of giving him the part and being accused of nepotism—or turning him down and being a bum. I chose nepotism."

In 1960, when his post ended as advisor to President Eisenhower, Montgomery became communications consultant to John D. Rockefeller. He was also appointed to the board of directors of the Milwaukee Telephone Company.

His last Broadway directorial assignment to date is *Calculated Risk,* also authored by Joseph Hayes. Starring the husband-wife team of Joseph Cotten and Patricia Medina, it told the story of a shrewd businessman's determination to assume control of a New England mill. The play opened at the Ambassador Theatre on October 31, 1962, for a 222-performance run. Said John McClain (*New York Journal American*): "Mr. Montgomery has a lot of people and a lot of words to account for and he sorts them out with authority and unpretentious good taste. His characters are dimensional and plausible, none without reasonable facilities."

Robert narrated a syndicated thirty-minute video-documentary tour of the Metropolitan Museum of Art entitled *Art Heritage* in 1961. He was largely out of the news until July 1, 1966, when he was stricken with chest pains while on his yacht at the Hyannis, Massachusetts, marina.

An Open Letter from a Television Viewer was a book written by Montgomery in 1968. In his foreword, he states: "This is an ill-tempered book. But not one, I hope, the reader will think merely polemic." It was, in actuality, a "scathing indictment of the industry for its monopolistic tactics," in which the author charged the television networks of double-talk with regard to educational television. "If we go down as the age of violence," he wrote, "television can be blamed for it. If acting standards are low it's because television has been a sort of giant brainwashing machine for too many people in front of and behind the camera." One of the more penetrating reviews of the book was by *Variety's* Carroll Carroll, who analyzed: "While it's crystal clear what he hates, it's hard to isolate exactly what he wants. The feeling is that he should have taken a little more time and thought the whole thing out more thoroughly." Montgomery, the author, was quite energetic in promoting the book, and made the rounds of the major video talk shows.

In 1969, after resigning his post with Rockefeller, Robert was named president, on January 22, 1969, of the Lincoln Center Repertory Theatre in New York City. His chore was primarily that of fund-raising. He resigned this prestigious post, however, on April 6, 1970, due to untenable problems encountered in fulfilling his duties.

Never one to be creatively or administratively idle for long, Montgomery wrote a stage adaptation of Dostoyevsky's novel *The Idiot,* called *Subject to Fits: A Response to Dostoyevsky's The Idiot,* which was presented February 14, 1971, by the New York Shakespeare Festival at the Public Theatre (The Other Stage).

Robert's daughter, Elizabeth, continues to carry on the family's name in show business. In 1953, when she first entered the acting profession on a full basis, his advice was: "If you are lucky enough to be a success, by all means enjoy the applause and the adulation of the public, but never, never believe it."

The ubiquitous Mr. Montgomery, however, also once said: "I am convinced of just one thing. A picture may fail and a play may fail, but an audience has never failed."

Robert is a country gentleman these days, residing in retirement with his second wife in Canaan, Connecticut. About four years ago he had major surgery, which required the removal of his bladder, but since then has been in fairly good health. He can view his past, assuredly content in knowing that he has accomplished most of what his sights were set on, with the exception of holding a political office. "I'd love to be in Congress," he admitted in 1958, "But nobody's asked me to run."

In December 1973, columnist Ed Sullivan revealed that Robert had nixed $100,000 to do a TV coffee commercial. Obviously, the actor is still very much his own man. He will exert himself still for charity efforts devoted to the arts, but as of yet has failed to find any new acting-directing project to challenge him out of semi-retirement.

Robert Montgomery

SO THIS IS COLLEGE (MGM, 1929) 110 M.

Director, Sam Wood; screenplay, Al Boasberg, Delmer Daves; dialog, Joe Farnham, Al Boasberg; titles, Joe Farnham; art director, Cedric Gibbons; music, Martin Broones; songs, Jesse Greer, Broones, Fred Fisher and Broones; music conductor, Arthur Lange; interpolations, Fisher, Jesse Greer, Raymond Klages, Charlotte Greenwood, Al Boasberg; wardrobe, Henrietta Frazer; sound, Douglas Shearer; camera, Leonard Smith; editors, Frank Sullivan, Leslie F. Wilder.

Elliott Nugent (Eddie); Robert Montgomery (Biff); Cliff Edwards (Windy); Sally Starr (Babs); Phyllis Crane (Betty); Dorothy Dehn (Jane); Max Davidson (Moe); Ann Brody (Momma); Oscar Rudolph (Freshie); Gene Stone (Stupid); Polly Moran (Polly); Lee Shumway (Coach).

UNTAMED (MGM, 1929) 88 M.

Director, Jack Conway; based on the story by Charles E. Scoggins; adaptor-continuity, Sylvia Thalberg, Frank Butler; dialog, Willard Mack; titles, Lucille Newmark; art directors, Cedric Gibbons, Van Nest Polglase; gowns, Adrian; songs, Joe Goodwin and Louis Alter, Nacio Herb Brown and Arthur Freed; sound, Fred R. Morgan, Douglas Shearer; camera, Oliver Marsh; editors, William S. Gray, Charles Hockberg.

Joan Crawford (Alice "Bingo"); Robert Montgomery (Andy McAllister); Ernest Torrence (Ben Murchison); Holmes Herbert (Howard Presley); John Miljan (Bennock); Gwen Lee (Marjory); Edward Nugent (Paul); Don Terry (Gregg); Gertrude Astor (Mrs. Mason); Milton Fahrney (Jollop); Lloyd Ingraham (Dowling); Grace Cunard (Billie); Wilson Benge (Billcombe).

THEIR OWN DESIRE (MGM, 1929) 66 M.

Director, E. Mason Hopper; based on the novel by Sarita Fuller; screenplay, Frances Marion; additional dialog, James Grant Forbes; music, Fred Fisher, Reggie Montgomery, George Ward; song, Fisher; gowns, Adrian; art director, Cedric Gibbons; sound, Douglas Shearer; camera, William Daniels; editor, Harry Reynolds.

Norma Shearer (Lally); Belle Bennett (Harriet); Lewis Stone (Marlett); Robert Montgomery (Jack); Helene Millard (Beth); Cecil Cunningham (Aunt Caroline); Henry Herbert (Uncle Nate); Mary Doran (Susan); June Nash (Mildred).

THREE LIVE GHOSTS (UA, 1929) 83 M.

Producer, Max Marcin; director, Thornton Freeland; story, Sally Winters; based on the play by Frederic Stewart Isham, Marcin; adaptor-dialog, Marcin; screenplay, Helen Hallett; camera, Robert H. Planck; editor, Robert Kern.

Beryl Mercer (Mrs. Gubbins); Hilda Vaughn (Peggy Woofers); Harry Stubbs (Bolton); Joan Bennett (Rose Gordon); Nancy Price (Alice); Charles McNaughton (Jimmie Gubbins); Robert Montgomery (William Foster); Claud Allister (Spoofy); Arthur Clayton (Paymaster); Tenen Holtz (Crockery Man); Shayle Gardner (Briggs); Jack Cooper (Benson); Jocelyn Lee (Lady Leicester).

FREE AND EASY (MGM, 1930) 75 M.

Director, Edward Sedgwick; screenplay, Richard Schayer; dialog, Al Boasberg; adaptor, Paul Dickey; art director, Cedric Gibbons; songs, Fred E. Ahlert, William Kernell; choreography, Sammy Lee; wardrobe, David Cox; sound, Karl E. Zint, Douglas Shearer; camera, Leonard Smith; editors, William Levanway, George Todd.

Buster Keaton (Elmer Butts); Anita Page (Elvira); Trixie Friganza (Ma); Robert Montgomery (Larry); Fred Niblo (Director); Edgar Dearing (Officer); Gwen Lee, John Miljan, Lionel Barrymore (Bedroom Scene—Themselves); William Haines (Guest); William Collier, Sr. (Master of Ceremonies); Dorothy Sebastian, Karl Dane (Cave Scene—Themselves); David Burton (Director); Cecil B. DeMille, Jackie Coogan, Joe Farnham, Arthur Lange (Themselves).

THE DIVORCEE (MGM, 1930) 84 M.

Director, Robert Z. Leonard; based on the novel Ex-Wife by Ursula Parrott; treatment, Nick Grinde, Zelda Sears; continuity-dialog, John Meehan; art director, Cedric Gibbons; gowns, Adrian; sound, J. K. Brock, Douglas Shearer; camera, Norbert Brodine; editors, Hugh Wynn, Truman K. Wood.

Norma Shearer (Jerry); Chester Morris (Ted); Conrad Nagel (Paul); Robert Montgomery (Don); Florence Eldridge (Helen); Helene Millard (Mary); Robert Elliott (Bill); Mary Doran (Janice); Tyler Brooke (Hank); Zelda Sears (Hannah); George Irving (Dr. Bernard); Judith Wood (Dorothy).

THE BIG HOUSE (MGM, 1930) 88 M.

Director, George Hill; story-screenplay-dialog, Frances Marion; additional dialog, Joe Farnham, Martin Flavin; art director, Cedric Gibbons; sound, Robert Shirley, Douglas Shearer; camera, Harold Wenstrom; editor, Blanche Sewell.

Chester Morris (John Morgan); Wallace Beery (Butch Schmidt); Lewis Stone (Warden James Adams); Robert Montgomery (Kent Marlowe); Leila Hyams (Anne Marlowe); George F. Marion (Pop Riker); J. C. Nugent (Mr. Marlowe); Karl Dane (Olsen); De Witt Jennings (Captain Wallace); Mathew Betz (Gopher); Claire McDowell (Mrs. Marlowe); Robert Emmet O'Connor (Donlin); Tom Wilson (Sandy, the Guard);

Eddie Foyer (Dopey); Rosco Ates (Putnam); Fletcher Norton (Oliver); Adolph Seidel (Prison Barber); Eddie Lambert, Michael Vavitch (Bits).

SINS OF THE CHILDREN (MGM, 1930) 86 M.
Director, Sam Wood; based on the novel Father's Day *by J. C. Nugent, Elliott Nugent; dialog, Elliott Nugent, Clara Lipman; adaptor, Samuel Ornitz; titles, Leslie F. Wilder; art director, Cedric Gibbons; wardrobe, David Cox; sound, Douglas Shearer; camera, Henry Sharp; editors, Frank Sullivan, Leslie F. Wilder.*

Louis Mann (Adolf); Robert Montgomery (Nick Higginson); Elliott Nugent (Johnnie); Leila Hyams (Alma); Clara Blandick (Martha Wagenkampf); Mary Doran (Laura); Francis X. Bushman, Jr. (Ludwig); Robert McWade (Joe Higginson); Dell Henderson (Ted Baldwin); Henry Armetta (Tony); Jane Reid (Katherine); James Donlan (Bide Taylor); Jeane Wood (Muriel Stokes); Lee Kohlmar (Dr. Heinrich Schmidt).

A.k.a.: FATHER'S DAY; THE RICHEST MAN IN THE WORLD.

OUR BLUSHING BRIDES (MGM, 1930) 79 M.
Director, Harry Beaumont; story, Bess Meredyth; continuity-dialog, Meredyth, John Howard Lawson; titles, Helen Mainardi; gowns, Adrian; ballet stager, Albertina Rasch; art director, Cedric Gibbons; sound, Russell Franks, Douglas Shearer; camera, Merritt B. Gerstad; editors, George Hively, Harold Palmer.

Joan Crawford (Jerry); Anita Page (Connie); Dorothy Sebastian (Franky); Robert Montgomery (Tony); Raymond Hackett (David); John Miljan (Martin); Hedda Hopper (Mrs. Weaver); Albert Conti (Monsieur Pantoise); Edward Brophy (Joe Munsey); Robert E. O'Connor (The Detective); Martha Sleeper (Evelyn Woodforth); Mary Doran, Norma Drew, Wilda Mansfield, Gwen Lee, Catherine Moylan, Claire Dodd (Mannequins).

LOVE IN THE ROUGH (MGM, 1930) 85 M.
Director, Charles F. Reisner; based on the play Spring Fever *by Vincent Lawrence; adaptor, Sarah Y. Mason; dialog, Joe Farnham, Robert E. Hopkins; songs, Dorothy Fields and Jimmy McHugh; choreography, Sammy Lee; wardrobe, David Cox; art director, Cedric Gibbons; sound, Ralph Sugart, Douglas Shearer; camera, Henry Sharp; editor, Basil Wrangell.*

Robert Montgomery (Kelly); Dorothy Jordan (Marilyn); Benny Rubin (Benny); J. C. Nugent (Waters); Dorothy McNulty [later Penny Singleton] (Virgie); Tyrrell Davis (Tewksbury); Harry Burns (Gardener); Allan Lane (Johnson); Catherine Moylan (Martha); Edward Davis (Williams); Roscoe Ates (Proprietor); Clarence H. Wilson (Brown).

WAR NURSE (MGM, 1930) 80 M.
Director, Edgar Selwyn; screenplay, Becky Gardiner; additional dialog, Joe Farnham; art director, Cedric Gibbons; wardrobe, René Hubert; sound, Douglas Shearer; camera, Charles Rosher; editor, William Levanway.

Robert Montgomery (Wally); Anita Page (Joy); June Walker (Babs); Robert Ames (Robin); ZaSu Pitts (Cushie); Marie Prevost (Rosalie); Helen Jerome Eddy (Kansas); Hedda Hopper (Matron); Edward Nugent (Frank); Martha Sleeper (Helen); Michael Vavitch (Doctor).

INSPIRATION (MGM, 1931) 74 M.
Director, Clarence Brown; story-screenplay, Gene Markey; sound, J. K. Brock; camera, William Daniels; editor, Conrad A. Nervig.

Greta Garbo (Yvonne); Robert Montgomery (Andre Martel); Lewis Stone (Delval); Marjorie Rambeau (Lulu); Judith Vosselle (Odette); Beryl Mercer (Marthe); John Miljan (Contant); Edwin Maxwell (Julien Montell); Oscar Apfel (Vignaud); Joan Marsh (Madeleine); Zelda Sears (Pauline); Karen Morley (Liane); Gwen Lee (Gaby); Paul McAllister (Jouvet); Arthur Hoyt (Gavarni); Richard Tucker (Garland).

THE EASIEST WAY (MGM, 1931) 78 M.
Director, Jack Conway; based on the play by Eugene Walter; screenplay, Edith Ellis; sound, J. Russell Franks; camera, John Mescall; editor, Frank Sullivan.

Constance Bennett (Laura Murdock); Adolphe Menjou (William Brockton); Robert Montgomery (Johnny Madison); Anita Page (Peg Murdock); Marjorie Rambeau (Elfie St. Clair); J. Farrell MacDonald (Ben Murdock); Clara Blandick (Agnes Murdock); Clark Gable (Nick); Francis Palmer Tilton (Artist); Charles Judels (Gensler); John Harron (Chris).

STRANGERS MAY KISS (MGM, 1931) 82 M.
Director, George Fitzmaurice; based on the novel by Ursula Parrott; adaptor-dialog, John Meehan; gowns, Adrian; camera, William Daniels; editor, Hugh Wynn.

Norma Shearer (Lisbeth Corbin); Robert Montgomery (Steve); Neil Hamilton (Alan); Marjorie Rambeau (Geneva); Irene Rich (Celia); Hale Hamilton (Andrew); Conchita Montenegro (Spanish Dancer); Jed Prouty (Harry); Albert Conti (Count De Bazan); Henry Armetta, George Davis (Waiters); Bess Flowers (Dining Extra); Karen Morley, Wilbur Mack (Dining Companions); Kane Richmond (Bit); Raymond Milland (Admirer).

SHIPMATES (MGM, 1931) 73 M.
Director, Harry Pollard; based on the story "Maskee" by Ernest Paynter; screenplay, Lou Edelman, Delmer Daves, Raymond L. Schrock, Lt. Commander Frank Wead; dialog, Malcolm Stuart Boylan, Daves; sound, J. K Brock; camera, Clyde DeVinna; editor, William Levanway.

Robert Montgomery (Jonsey); Ernest Torrence (Scotty); Dorothy Jordan (Kit); Hobart Bosworth (Admiral Corbin); Cliff Edwards (Bilge); Gavin Gordon (Mike); Joan Marsh (Mary Lou); Edward Nugent (What-Ho); E. Allyn Warren (Wong); George Irving (Captain Beatty); Hedda Hopper (Auntie); William Worthington (Admiral Schuyler).

THE MAN IN POSSESSION (MGM, 1931) 79 M.
Director, Sam Wood; based on the play by H. M. Harwood; screenplay, Sarah Y. Mason, P. G. Wodehouse; sound, Carl Zint; camera, Oliver T. Marsh; editor, Ben Lewis.

Robert Montgomery (Raymond Dabney); Charlotte Greenwood (Clara); Irene Purcell (Crystal Wetherby); C. Aubrey Smith (Mr. Dabney); Beryl Mercer (Mrs. Dabney); Reginald Owen (Claude Dabney); Alan Mowbray (Sir Charles Cartwright); Maude Eburne (Esther); Forrester Harvey (Sheriff); Yorke Sherwood (Butcher).

PRIVATE LIVES (MGM, 1931) 92 ½ M.
Director, Sidney Franklin; based on the play by Noël Coward; screenplay, Hans Kraly, Richard Schayer; continuity, Claudine West; camera, Ray Binger; editor, Conrad A. Nervig.

Norma Shearer (Amanda Chase Paynne); Robert Montgomery (Elyot Chase); Reginald Denny (Victor Paynne); Una Merkel (Sibyl Chase); Jean Hersholt (Oscar); George Davis (Bellboy).

LOVERS COURAGEOUS (MGM, 1932) 78 M.
Director, Robert Z. Leonard; story-screenplay, Frederick Lonsdale; camera, William Daniels; editor, Margaret Booth.

Robert Montgomery (Willie Smith); Madge Evans (Mary); Roland Young (Jeffrey); Frederick Kerr (Admiral); Reginald Owen (Jimmy); Beryl Mercer (Mrs. Smith); Evelyn Hall (Lady Blayne); Halliwell Hobbes (Mr. Smith); Jackie Searl (Willie as a Child); Norman Phillips, Jr. (Walter as a Child); Alan Mowbray (Lamone).

BUT THE FLESH IS WEAK (MGM, 1932) 77 M.
Director, Jack Conway; based on the play The Truth Game *by Ivor Novello; screenplay, Novello; camera, Oliver T. Marsh; editor, Tom Held.*

Robert Montgomery (Max Clement); Nora Gregor (Rosine Brown); Heather Thatcher (Lady Joan Culver); Edward Everett Horton (Sir George Kelvin); C. Aubrey Smith (Florian Clement); Nils Asther (Prince Paul); Frederick Kerr (Duke of Hampshire); Eva Moore (Lady Ridgway); Forrester Harvey (Gooch); Desmond Roberts (Findley).

LETTY LYNTON (MGM, 1932) 62 M.
Director, Clarence Brown; based on the novel by Marie Belloc Lowndes; screenplay, John Meehan, Wanda Tuchock; dialog, Meehan; costumes, Adrian; camera, Oliver T. Marsh; editor, Conrad A. Nervig.
Joan Crawford (Letty Lynton); Robert Montgomery (Hale Darrow); Nils Asther (Emile Renaud); Lewis Stone (Mr. Haney); May Robson (Mrs. Lynton); Louise Closser Hale (Miranda); Emma Dunn (Mrs. Darrow); Walter Walker (Mr. Darrow); William Pawley (Hennessey).

BLONDIE OF THE FOLLIES (MGM, 1932) 97 M.
Producer, Marion Davies; director, Edmund Goulding; story-continuity, Frances Marion; dialog, Anita Loos; art director, Cedric Gibbons; gowns, Adrian; music, Dr. William Axt; songs, Harry Tobias, Gus Arnheim, and Jules Lemare; Harry Link and Nick Kenny; Goulding; Ray Egan and Ted Fiorito; Walter Samuels and Leonard Whitcup; Arthur Freed and Harry Barris; Dave Snell; camera, George Barnes; editor, George Hively.
Marion Davies (Blondie McClune); Robert Montgomery (Larry Belmont); Billie Dove (Lottie Callahan); Jimmy Durante (Jimmy); James Gleason (Pa McClune); ZaSu Pitts (Gertie); Sidney Toler (Pete); Douglass Dumbrille (Murchenson); Sarah Padden (Ma McClune); Louise Carter (Ma Callahan); Clyde Cook (Dancer); The Rocky Twins (Themselves); Dorothy and Harry Dixon (Acrobatic Party Dancers).

FAITHLESS (MGM, 1932) 76 M.
Director, Harry Beaumont; based on the story "Tinfoil" by Mildred Cram; screenplay, Carey Wilson; camera, Oliver T. Marsh; editor, Hugh Wynn.
Tallulah Bankhead (Carol Morgan); Robert Montgomery (William Wade); Hugh Herbert (Mr. Blainey); Maurice Murphy (Anthony Wade); Louise Closser Hale (Landlady); Anna Appel (Another Landlady); Lawrence Grant (Mr. Ledyard); Henry Kolker (Mr. Carter); Sterling Holloway (Photographer); Phil Tead (Reporter); Jack Clifford (Truck Driver); Ben Taggart (Officer Clancy).

HELL BELOW (MGM, 1933) 105 M.
Director, Jack Conway; based on the novel Pigboats *by Commander Edward Ellsberg; adaptors, Laird Doyle, Raymond Schrock; dialog, John Lee Mahin, John Meehan; camera, Harold Rosson; editor, Hal C. Kern.*
Robert Montgomery (Lieutenant Thomas Knowlton); Walter Huston (Lieutenant-Commander Toler); Madge Evans (Joan); Jimmy Durante (Ptomaine); Eugene Pallette (MacDougal); Robert Young (Lieutenant Brick Walters); Edwin Styles (Herbert Standish); John Lee Mahin (Lieutenant Nelson); David Newell (Lieutenant Radford); Sterling Holloway (Seaman Jenks); Charles Irwin (Buck Teeth Sergeant); Henry Kolker (Admiral); Sid Saylor (Chief Engineer Hendrickson); Maude Eburne (Admiral's Wife); Paul Porcasi (Italian).

WHEN LADIES MEET (MGM, 1933) 73 M.
Associate producer, Lawrence Weingarten; director, Harry Beaumont; based on the play by Rachel Crothers; adaptors, John Meehan, Leon Gordon; camera, Ray June; editor, Basil Wrangell.
Ann Harding (Claire Woodruf); Robert Montgomery (Jimmie Lee); Myrna Loy (Mary Howard); Alice Brady (Bridget Drake); Frank Morgan (Roger Woodruf); Martin Burton (Walter); Luis Alberni (Pierre).
Television title: TRUTH IS STRANGER.

MADE ON BROADWAY (MGM, 1933) 68 M.
Director, Harry Beaumont; based on the story "Public Rela-

tions" by Courtenay Terrett; adaptor, Terrett; camera, Norbert Brodine; editor, William S. Gray.*
Robert Montgomery (Jeff Bidwell); Sally Eilers (Mona Martine); Madge Evans (Claire Bidwell); Eugene Pallette (Terwilliger); C. Henry Gordon (Mayor Starling); Jean Parker (Adele); Ivan Lebedeff (Ramon); David Newell (Mayor's Secretary); Vince Barnett (Mr. Lepedis); Joseph Cawthorn (Schultz).

ANOTHER LANGUAGE (MGM, 1933) 75 M.
Associate producer, Walter Wanger; director, Edward H. Griffith; based on the play by Rose Franken; adaptors, Herman J. Mankiewicz, Gertrude Purcell; dialog, Mankiewicz, Purcell, Donald Ogden Stewart; camera, Ray June; editor, Hugh Wynn.
Helen Hayes (Stella Hallam); Robert Montgomery (Victor Hallam); Louise Closser Hale (Mom Hallam); John Beal (Jerry Hallam); Henry Travers (Pop Hallam); Margaret Hamilton (Helen Hallam); Willard Robertson (Harry Hallam); Irene Cattell (Grace Hallam); Minor K. Watson (Paul Hallam); Hal Dawson (Walter Hallam); Maidel Turner (Etta Hallam); William Farnum (Sculpting Instructor); Sherry Hall (Purser).

NIGHT FLIGHT (MGM, 1933) 84 M.
Director, Clarence Brown; based on the novel by Antoine de Saint-Exupery; adaptor, Oliver H. P. Garrett; camera, Oliver T. Marsh, Elmer Dyer, Charles Marshall; editor.
John Barrymore (Riviere); Helen Hayes (Madame Fabian); Clark Gable (Jules Fabian); Lionel Barrymore (Robineau); Robert Montgomery (Auguste Pellerin); Myrna Loy (Brazilian Pilot's Wife); William Gargan (Brazilian Pilot); C. Henry Gordon (Daudet); Leslie Fenton, Frank Conroy (Radio Operators); Harry Beresford (Roblet); Ralf Harolde (Pilot No. 5).

FUGITIVE LOVERS (MGM, 1933) 84 M.
Director, Richard Boleslawsky; story, Ferdinand Reyher, Frank Wead; screenplay, Albert Hackett, Frances Goodrich, George B. Seitz; camera, Ted Tetzlaff; editor, William S. Gray.
Robert Montgomery (Paul Porter); Madge Evans (Letty Morris); Ted Healy (Hector Withington, Jr.); Nat Pendleton (Legs Coffee); C. Henry Gordon (Daly); Ruth Selwyn (Babe Callahan); Larry Fine, Moe Howard, Jerry Howard (Three Julians); Mary Emmons (News Vendor); Earl of Chicester (Extra); George Gorman (Bus Driver); "Dad" Mills (Blind Man); Akim Tamiroff (Bus Passenger).

THE MYSTERY OF MR. X (MGM, 1934) 84 M.
Director, Edgar Selwyn; based on the novel Mystery of the Dead Police *by Philip MacDonald; screenplay, Howard Emmett Rogers, Philip MacDonald, Monckton Hoffe; camera, Oliver T. Marsh; editor, Hugh Wynn.*
Robert Montgomery (Nicholas Revel); Elizabeth Allan (Jane Frensham); Lewis Stone (Inspector Connor); Ralph Forbes (Sir Christopher Marche); Henry Stephenson (Sir Herbert Frensham); Forrester Harvey (Palmer); Ivan Simpson (Hutchinson); Leonard Mudie (Mr. X); Alec B. Francis (Judge Malpas); Charles Irwin (Willis); Colin Kenny (Constable); Pearl Varvell (Barmaid); Henry Mowbray (Detective); Barlowe Borland (Headwaiter); Alfred Cross, Olaf Hytten, Norman Ainslie, Terry Spencer, Victor Gammon, Captain Francis (Reporters); Eric Wilton (Butler); Richard Lancaster, Robert A'Dair, Pat Moriarity (Policemen); Harrington Reynolds (Motor Cop); Milton Royce (London Bobby); William Stack (Travers Gordon); Claude King (Cummings); Douglas Gordon (Court Clerk); Raymond Milland (Forbes); Clive Morgan (Blanchard); Pat Somerset (Bit); Montague Shaw (Doctor); John Power (Bobbie); Raymond Lawrence (Padgot).

RIPTIDE (MGM, 1934) 90 M.
Producer, Irving Thalberg; director-story-screenplay, Edmund Goulding; camera, Ray June; editor, Margaret Booth.
Norma Shearer (Lady Mary Rexford); Robert Montgomery

(Tommy Trent); Herbert Marshall (Lord Philip Rexford); Mrs. Patrick Campbell (Lady Hetty Riversleigh); Richard Skeets Gallagher (Erskine); Ralph Forbes (David Fenwick); Lilyan Tashman (Sylvia); Arthur Jarrett (Percy); Earl Oxford (Freddie); Helen Jerome Eddy (Celeste); George K. Arthur (Bertie Davis); Halliwell Hobbes (Bollard); Cora Sue Collins (Child); Arthur Treacher, George Cowl, Victor Gammon, Donald Stuart (Reporters); Robert A'Dair (Bartender); Charles Requa (Major Mills); E. E. Clive (Sleigh Driver); Conrad Seidemann (German Porter); Otto H. Fries (Doorman); Nola Luxford (English Girl); Anderson Lawler (Henry); Walter Brennan, Stanley Mann (Chauffeurs); Adrian Rosely (Hotel Manager); Andre Cheron (Surete Officer); Paul Porcasi (House Detective); Leo White (Assistant Manager); Fred W. Malatesta (Headwaiter); Lillian Rich (Girl); Yvonne Parker, Erin La Bissoniere (French Women); Louis Mercier (Concierge); Barlowe Borland (Nightingale, the Butler); Horace Cooper (General); Harry Allen (Fire Chief); Constant Franke (Waiter); Desmond Roberts (Hotel Manager); Ferdinand Gottschalk (Orchestra Leader); T. Roy Barnes (Clogg); Emile Chautard (Doctor); Herbert Bunston (Major Bagdall); Clarissa Selwynne (Mrs. Bagdall); Elsa Buchanan (Daphne); Bruce Bennett (Brix); Francisco Maran (French Butler); Montague Shaw (Tring); Ramsey Hill (Sir Geoffrey Mapel); Bobbie Bolder, Herbert Evans, Cosmo Kyrle Bellew (Bits at Aunt Hetty's); Lawrence Grant (Farrington).

HIDE-OUT (MGM, 1934) 82 M.

Director, W. S. Van Dyke II; story, Mauri Grashin; screenplay, Frances Goodrich, Albert Hackett; camera, Ray June, Sidney Wagner; editor, Basil Wrangell.

Robert Montgomery (Lucky Wilson); Maureen O'Sullivan (Pauline); Edward Arnold (MacCarthy); Elizabeth Patterson (Mrs. Miller); Whitford Kane (Mr. Miller); Mickey Rooney (Willie); C. Henry Gordon (Tony Berrelli); Muriel Evans (Babe); Edward Brophy (Britt); Henry Armetta (Louis Shuman); Herman Bing (Jake Lillie); Louise Henry (Millie); Harold Huber (Dr. Warner); Roberta Gale (Hat Check Girl); Arthur Belasco, Billy Arnold, Louis Natheaux (Henchmen); Dick Kipling (Clerk); Frank Leighton (Headwaiter); Lucille Browne, Jeanette Loff, Herta Lind (Girls); Frank Marlowe (Laundry Driver); Bobby Watson (Master of Ceremonies); Frank O'Connor (Policeman); Douglass Dumbrille (Nightclub Owner).

FORSAKING ALL OTHERS (MGM, 1934) 84 M.

Producer, Bernard H. Hyman; director, W. S. Van Dyke II; based on the play by Edward Barry Roberts, Frank Morgan Cavett; adaptor, Joseph L. Mankiewicz; song, Gus Kahn and Walter Donaldson; costumes, Adrian; music, William Axt; camera, Gregg Toland, George Folsey; editor, Tom Held.

Joan Crawford (Mary Clay); Clark Gable (Jeff Williams); Robert Montgomery (Dill Todd); Charles Butterworth (Dillon Todd); Billie Burke (Aunt Paula); Frances Drake (Connie Barnes); Rosalind Russell (Eleanor); Tom Ricketts (Wiffens); Arthur Treacher (Johnson); Greta Meyer (Bella);

BIOGRAPHY OF A BACHELOR GIRL (MGM, 1935) 84 M.

Producer, Irving Thalberg; director, Edward H. Griffith; based on the play Biography *by S. N. Behrman; screenplay, Anita Loos; additional dialog, Horace Jackson; costumes, Adrian; art director, Cedric Gibbons; camera, James Wong Howe; editor, William S. Gray.*

Ann Harding (Marion); Robert Montgomery (Kurt); Edward Everett Horton (Nolan); Edward Arnold (Feydak); Una Merkel (Slade); Charles Richman (Kinnicot); Greta Meyer (Minnie); Willard Robertson (Process Server); Donald Meek (Mr. Irish).

VANESSA: HER LOVE STORY (MGM, 1935) 74 M.

Producer, David O. Selznick; director, William K. Howard; based on the novel Vanessa *by Hugh Walpole; adaptor, Lenore*

Coffee; *screenplay, Walpole, Coffee; camera, Ray June; editor, Frank Hull.*

Helen Hayes (Vanessa); Robert Montgomery (Benjie); Otto Kruger (Ellis); May Robson (Judith); Lewis Stone (Adam); Henry Stephenson (Barney); Violet Kemble-Cooper (Lady Herries); Donald Crisp (George); Jessie Ralph (Lady Mullion); Agnes Anderson (Marion); Lionel Belmore (Leathwaite); Lawrence Grant (Amery); Craufurd Kent (Jamie); Ethel Griffies (Winifred Trent); Elspeth Dudgeon (Vera Trent); Mary Gordon (Mrs. Leathwaite); George K. Arthur (Porter).

NO MORE LADIES (MGM, 1935) 81 M.

Producer, Irving Thalberg; director, Edward H. Griffith; based on the play by A. E. Thomas; screenplay, Donald Ogden Stewart, Horace Jackson; music, Edward Ward; costumes, Adrian; art director, Cedric Gibbons; camera, Oliver T. Marsh; editor, Frank E. Hull.

Joan Crawford (Marcia Townsend); Robert Montgomery (Sherry Warren); Charlie Ruggles (Edgar Holmes); Franchot Tone (Jim Salston); Edna May Oliver (Fanny Townsend); Gail Patrick (Theresa Germaine); Reginald Denny (Oliver Allen); Vivienne Osborne (Lady Diana Moulton); Joan Burfield (Fontaine); Arthur Treacher (Lord Moulton); David Horsley (Duffy); Jean Chatburn (Sally French); Frank Mayo, Jean Acker, Gertrude Astor (Nightclub Extras); Donald Ogden Stewart (Drunk); Charles Coleman (Stafford, the Butler); Dave O'Brien (Party Guest); Brooks Benedict (Joe Williams, the Bar Owner); Isabelle La More (Jacquette); Frank Dawson (Dickens); Walter Walker (Bit); E. J. Babiel (Desk Clerk); Ed Hart (Taxi Driver); Charles O'Malley (Bell Boy); Lew Harvey, David Thursby (Bartenders); Tommy Tomlinson (Dick); Sherry Hall (Captain); Clem Beauchamp (Drunk); Veda Buckland (Maid); Mabel Colcord (Cook).

PETTICOAT FEVER (MGM, 1936) 80 M.

Producer, Frank Davis; director, George Fitzmaurice; based on the play by Mark Reed; screenplay, Harold Goldman; assistant director, Sandy Roth; camera, Ernest Haller; editor, Frederick Y. Smith.

Robert Montgomery (Dascom Dinsmore); Myrna Loy (Irene Campion); Reginald Owen (Sir James Felton); Winifred Shotter (Clara Wilson); Otto Yamaoka (Kimo); George Hassell (Captain Landry); Forrester Harvey (Scotty); Irving Bacon (Carl); Bo Ching (Big Seal); Iris Yamaoka (Little Seal).

TROUBLE FOR TWO (MGM, 1936) 75 M.

Producer, Louis D. Lighton; director, J. Walter Rubin; suggested by the story "Suicide Club" by Robert Louis Stevenson; screenplay, Manuel Seff, Edward E. Paramore, Jr; music, Franz Waxman; art director, Cedric Gibbons; camera, Charles Clarke; editor, Robert J. Kern.

Robert Montgomery (Prince Florizel); Rosalind Russell [Miss Vandeleur (Princess Brenda)]; Frank Morgan (Colonel Geraldine); Reginald Owen (Dr. Franz Noel, President of Club); Louis Hayward (Young Man with Cream Tarts); E. E. Clive (The King); Walter Kingsford (Malthus); Ivan Simpson (Collins); Tom Moore (Major O'Rock); Robert Greig (Fat Man); Guy Bates Post (Ambassador); Pedro de Cordoba (Sergei); Leyland Hodgson (Captain Rich); Pat Flaherty (Ship Captain); Frank Darien (King's Aide); Tom Ricketts (Excited Club Member); Pat O'Malley (Purser); Leonard Carey (Valet); Bill O'Brien (Club Waiter); Paul Porcasi (Cafe Proprietor); Sidney Bracy (Henchman); Frank McGlynn, Jr. (Club Member); Larry Steers (Officer); Olaf Hytten (Butler); Edgar Norton (Herald); Fred Graham (Club Guard).

PICCADILLY JIM (MGM, 1936) 100 M.

Producer, Harry Rapf; director, Robert Z. Leonard; based on the novel by P. G. Wodehouse; screenplay, Charles Brackett, Edwin Knopf; music, William Axt; assistant director, Sandy Roth; camera, Joseph Ruttenberg; editor, William S. Gray.

Robert Montgomery (Jim Crocker); Frank Morgan (Mr.

Crocker); Madge Evans (Ann Chester); Eric Blore (Bayliss); Billie Burke (Eugenia); Robert Benchley (Macon); Ralph Forbes (Lord Charles); Cora Witherspoon (Nesta Pett); Tommy Bupp (Ogden Pett); Aileen Pringle (Paducah); Grant Mitchell (Herbert Pett); E. E. Clive (Editor); Billy Bevan (Taxi Driver); Grayce Hampton (Mrs. Brede); Torben Meyer (Butler); Sidney Miller (Messenger Boy); Dennis Morgan (Bit).

THE LAST OF MRS. CHEYNEY (MGM, 1937) 98 M.

Associate producer, Lawrence Weingarten; director, Richard Boleslawski; based on the play by Frederick Lonsdale; screenplay, Leon Gordon, Samson Raphaelson, Monckton Hoffe; art director, Cedric Gibbons; music, William Axt; gowns, Adrian; camera, George Folsey; editor, Frank Sullivan.

Joan Crawford (Fay Cheyney); William Powell (Charles); Robert Montgomery (Lord Arthur); Frank Morgan (Lord Kelton); Jessie Ralph (Duchess); Nigel Bruce (Willie); Colleen Clare (Joan); Benita Hume (Kitty); Ralph Forbes (Cousin John); Aileen Pringle (Maria); Melville Cooper (William); Leonard Carey (Ames); Sara Haden (Anna); Lumsden Hare (Inspector Witherspoon); Wallis Clark (George); Barnett Parker (Purser); Bob Cory (Deck Hand); Thomas A. Braidon (Head Steward); Vesey O'Davoren (Steward); Wilson Benge (Butler).

NIGHT MUST FALL (MGM, 1937) 117 M.

Producer, Hunt Stromberg; director, Richard Thorpe; based on the play by Emlyn Williams; screenplay, John Van Druten; art director, Cedric Gibbons; music, Edward Ward; camera, Ray June; editor, Robert J. Kern.

Robert Montgomery (Danny); Rosalind Russell (Olivia); Dame May Whitty (Mrs. Bransom); Alan Marshal (Justin); Merle Tottenham (Dora); Kathleen Harrison (Mrs. Terrence); Matthew Boulton (Belsize); Eily Malyon (Nurse); E. E. Clive (Guide); Beryl Mercer (Saleslady); Winifred Harris (Mrs. Laurie).

EVER SINCE EVE (WB, 1937) 80 M.

Producer, Hal B. Wallis; associate producer, Earl Baldwin; director, Lloyd Bacon; story, Gene Baker, Margaret Lee; screenplay, Lawrence Riley, Earl Baldwin, Lillie Hayward; art director, Robert Haas; songs, M. K. Jerome and Jack Scholl; music director, Leo F. Forbstein; camera, George Barnes; editor, William Holmes.

Marion Davies (Marge Winton); Robert Montgomery (Freddy Matthews); Frank McHugh [Mabel De Craven (Mike McGillicuddy)]; Patsy Kelly (Sadie Day); Louise Fazenda (Abigail Belldon); Barton MacLane (Al McCoy); Marcia Ralston (Camille Lansing); Carol Hughes (Manicurist); Frederick Clark (Alonzo); Mary Treen (Employment Clerk); Anderson Lawler (Hotel Clerk); Charles Foy (Bellboy); Arthur Hoyt (Hotel Manager); Spencer Charter (Mike, the Hotel Porter); Charles Trowbridge (Doctor); Frank Faylen (Bandit Leader); Jack Mower (Policeman); Claudia Simmons, Fern Barry, Perc Teeple, Sam Rice, Jack Wise (Pedestrians); Harry Hayden (Mason, the League President); Harry C. Bradley (League Manager); Robert Homans (Sergeant); Don Downen (Office Boy); John T. Murray (Lowell); Pierre Watkin (Barton); William B. Davidson (Henderson); Florence Gill (Annie, the Cleaning Lady); Dorothy Thompson (Hula Dancer); Frank Orth (Waiter); Gertrude Sutton (Homely Girl); Minerva Urecal (Reception Clerk); Don Barclay, Hal Neiman (Neighbors); Pat West (Neighbor with Water); Huey White, Al Herman (Taxi Drivers); Don Turner, Allen Cavens, (Doormen); Jerry Mandy (Italian Barber); Frank Otto (Another Barber); Dudley Dickerson (Bootblack); Ferris Taylor (Elderly Gentleman); Rebecca Wassem (Maid); Joseph Romantini (Maitre D'Hotel); Etta McDaniel (Black Maid); Henry Otho (Bandit); Jerry Fletcher (Bellboy); Frank Shannon (Desk Sergeant); Pat O'-Malley (Officer); Edward Price (Reporter); Wendell Niles (Police Announcer); Spec O'Donnell (Newsboy); The Theodores (Dance Team); Bess Flowers (Dance Extra).

LIVE, LOVE, AND LEARN (MGM, 1937) 78 M.

Producer, Harry Rapf; director, George Fitzmaurice; story, Marion Parsonnet, suggested by a story by Helen Grace Carlisle; screenplay, Charles Brackett, Cyril Hume, Richard Maibaum; camera, Ray June; editor, Conrad A. Nervig.

Robert Montgomery (Bob Graham); Rosalind Russell (Julie Stoddard); Robert Benchley (Oscar); Helen Vinson (Lily Chalmers); Mickey Rooney (Jerry Crump); Monty Woolley (Mr. Bawltitude); E. E. Clive (Mr. Palmiston); Charles Judels (Pedro Filipe); Maude Eburne (Mrs. Crump); Harlan Briggs (Justice of the Peace); June Clayworth (Post); Al Shean (Fraum); George Cooper (Bus Driver); Billy Gilbert (Newsboy); Dorothy Appleby (Lou); Ena Gregory (Bessie); Kate Price (Wilma); Heinie Conklin (Elmer); Billy Dooley (Fritz); John Kelly, Joe Caits, Philip Tully, John Quillan, Frank Marlowe (Sailors); James Flavin, Jack Perrin, Frank Sully, Jerry Miley, Russ Clark (Marines); June Clayworth (Annabella Post); Don Barclay, Harry Lash, Milton Kibbee, Ralph McCullough (Reporters); Chester Clute (Jess, a Reporter); Edith Kingdon, Mariska Aldrich (Dowagers); Ramsey Hill, Edward Earle, Carl Leviness (Salesmen); Arthur Stuart Hull (Marsden); Adrienne d'Ambricourt (The Duchess); John Davidson (Wingate); Robert Emmett Keane (Apartment House Manager); William Austin (Butler); Winifred Harris (Mrs. Colfax-Baxter); E. E. Clive (Mr. Palmiston); Ann Rutherford (Class President); Billy Engle (Dittenfuss); Zeffie Tilbury (Mrs. Venable); Wilbur Mack (Yacht Salesman); Minerva Urecal, Virginia Sale, Maxine Elliott Hicks (Sisters); Tenen Holtz (Socialist); Margaret Lynar (Movie Star); Leila McIntyre (Miss Cross); Rollo Lloyd (Agent); Charles Irwin (Magazine Salesman); Eddie Gribbon (Masseur); Robert Spindola (Italian Boy); Soledad Jimenez (Spanish Woman);.

THE FIRST 100 YEARS (MGM, 1938) 75 M.

Producer, Norman Krasna; director, Richard Thorpe; story, Krasna; screenplay, Melville Baker; song, Bob Wright and Chet Forrest; music, William Axt; art director, Cedric Gibbons; camera, Joseph Ruttenberg; editor, Conrad A. Nervig.

Robert Montgomery (David Conway); Virginia Bruce (Lynn Conway/Lynn Claymore); Warren William (Harry Borden); Binnie Barnes (Claudia Weston); Alan Dinehart (Samuel Z. Walker); Harry Davenport (Uncle Dawson); Nydia Westman (Midge); E. E. Clive (Chester Blascomb); Torben Meyer (Karl); Bodil Rosing (Martha); Irving Bacon (Wilkins); Priscilla Lawson (Mary Brown); Rex Evans (Reggie); Jonathan Hale (Judge Parker); Donald Briggs (Mr. Regan); Lee Bowman (George Wallace); Edgar Dearing (Policeman); Eleanor Lynn (Receptionist); Jean Fenwick (Miss Moffat); Wally Maher, Harry Strang, Monte Vandergrift (Workmen); Roger Converse (Young Actor); Barbara Bedford (Sadie); Frederick Clark (Ito); Roger Moore (Ship's Steward); Lane Chandler (Doorman).

YELLOW JACK (MGM, 1938) 83 M.

Producer, Jack Cummings; director, George B. Seitz; based on the play by Sidney Howard, Paul de Kruif; screenplay, Edward Chodorov; music, William Axt; camera, Lester White; editor, Blanche Sewell.

Robert Montgomery (John O'Hara); Virginia Bruce (Frances Blake); Lewis Stone (Major Reed); Andy Devine (Charlie Spill); Henry Hull (Dr. Jesse Lazear); Charles Coburn (Dr. Finlay); Buddy Ebsen (Jellybeans); Henry O'Neill (Gorgas); Janet Beecher (Miss MacDade); William Henry (Breen); Alan Curtis (Brinkerhof); Sam Levene (Busch); Stanley Ridges (Dr. James Carroll); Phillip Terry (Ferguson); Jonathan Hale (Major General Leonard Wood); C. Henry Gordon (Colonel Wiggins); Phillip Terry (Ferguson); Frank O'Connor, Billy Arnold, Larry Steers (Officers); Harry Strang (Aide); Roger Converse (Lieutenant); Dutch Schlickenmeyer (Corporal);

Francisco Maran (Interpreter); Brick Sullivan (Sergeant); Hudson Shotwell, Brent Sargent, Dick Wessel, Ted Oliver, John Patterson, Charlie Sullivan, George Magrill (Cavalrymen); Rosina Galli (Spanish Woman); Lucio Villegas (Old Man in Bed); Inez Palange (Dr. Finlay's Housekeeper); Joseph Dominguez (Interpreter); Harry Semels (Cuban Carriage Driver); William Newell (Soldier); Douglas McPhail (Joey).

THREE LOVES HAS NANCY (MGM, 1938) 69 M.

Producer, Norman Krasna; director, Richard Thorpe; story, Lee Loeb, Mort Braus; screenplay, Bella and Sam Spewack, George Oppenheimer, David Hertz; camera, William Daniels; editor, Fred Y. Smith.

Janet Gaynor (Nancy Briggs); Robert Montgomery (Malcolm Niles); Franchot Tone (Robert Hansen); Guy Kibbee (Pa Briggs); Claire Dodd (Vivian Herford); Reginald Owen (William); Cora Witherspoon (Mrs. Herford); Emma Dunn (Mrs. Briggs); Charley Grapewin (Grandpa Briggs); Lester Mathews (Dr. Alonzo Stewart); Edgar Dearing (Conductor); Charles Lane (Manager of Cleaning Establishment); Greta Meyer (Mrs. Swanson); Priscilla Lawson (Gertie); Sarah Edwards (Chairwoman); Grace Hayle, Marie Blake, Elise Cavanna, Carol Tevis (Woman); Etta McDaniel (Black Mammy); Eddie Kane (Steward); Sam McDaniel (Black Waiter); Lester Dorr (Newsstand Man); James B. Carson (Waiter); George Chandler (Baggage Master); Tom O'Grady (Bartender); Harold Miller, David Newell, David Alison Horsley, Cyril Ring, Jack Donaldson (Men at Party); Cecille Thurlow, Barbara Salisbury, Jenifer Gray, Bonnie Bannon (Girls at Party); Louis Natheaux (Promoter); Grant Withers (Jack); Kane Richmond, James Flavin (Jack's Friends); Matt McHugh (Traveling Salesman).

FAST AND LOOSE (MGM, 1939) 80 M.

Producer, Frederick Stephani; director, Edwin L. Marin; story-screenplay, Harry Kurnitz; camera, George Folsey; editor, Elmo Vernon.

Robert Montgomery (Joel Sloane); Rosalind Russell (Garda Sloane); Reginald Owen (Vincent Charlton); Ralph Morgan (Nicholas Torrent); Etienne Girardot (Christopher Oates); Alan Dinehart (Dave Hillard); Jo Ann Sayers (Christina Torrent); Joan Marsh (Bobby Neville); Anthony Allan (later John Hubbard) (Phil Sergeant); Tom Collins (Gerald Torrent); Sidney Blackmer (Lucky Nolan); Ian Wolfe (Wilkes).

THE EARL OF CHICAGO (MGM, 1940) 85 M.

Producer, Victor Saville; director, Richard Thorpe; story, Brock Williams, Charles de Grandcourt, Gene Fowler; screenplay, Lester Samuels; art director, Cedric Gibbons; music, Werner R. Heymann; camera, Ray June; editor, Fred Sullivan.

Robert Montgomery (Silky Kilmount); Edward Arnold (Doc Ramsey); Reginald Owen (Gervase Gonwell); Edmund Gwenn (Munsey); E. E. Clive (Redwood); Ronald Sinclair (Gerald Kilmount); Norma Varden (Maureen Kilmount); Halliwell Hobbes (Lord Chancellor); Ian Wolfe (Reading Clerk); Peter Godfrey (Judson); Billy Bevan (Guide); Rex Evans (Vicar); Charles Coleman (Bishop); Kenneth Hunter (Lord Tyrmanell); William Stack (Coroner); Miles Mander (Attorney General); Frederic Worlock (Lord Elfie); John Burton (Clerk); Art Berry, Sr. (Seedman); David Dunbar (Plowman); Harold Howard, Bob Corey (Fishermen); Henry Flynn (Villager); Vangie Beilby (Old Maid); Radford Allen (Boy); Craufurd Kent (Specialist); Montague Shaw (Doctor); Ben Welden (Driver); Olaf Hytten (Hodges); Pierre Watkin (Warden); George Anderson (Guard); Nora Perry (Receptionist); William Haade (Crapshooter); Eddie Marr (Offender); Anthony Warde (Salesman); John Butler (Slim); Gladys Blake (Silken Legs); Lowden Adams (Floor Waiter); Alec Harford (Mr. Dell); Arthur Mulliner (Mr. Brackton); Barlowe Borland (Fingal); Alec Craig (Son); Billy Bevan (Guide); John Power (Tourist); Ivan Simpson (Hargraves); Barbara Bedford (Doc's Secretary); Tempe Pigott (Mrs. Oades); Ben Webster (Gaffer); Ellis Irving

(Russell); Colin Kenny (Sergeant); Matthew Boulton (Ickerton); Paul England (Chief Constable); Boyd Irwin (Presiding Magistrate); Leonard Mudie (Allington); Halliwell Hobbes (Lord High Chancellor); David Clyde, B. J. Kelly (Hangerson); Holmes Herbert (Sergeant-at-Arms); Ralph Stock (Constable); Leyton Lee (Adjutant); Gladden James (Silky's Secretary); Yvonne Severn (Village Girl); Harry Allen (Mayer); Colonel Ford (Villager); Frank Benson (Sexton); Jimmy Aubrey (Cockney); Frank Baker (Policeman); Forbes Murray (Diplomat); Robert Warwick (Clerk at Parliament); Zeffie Tilbury (Old Lady).

HAUNTED HONEYMOON (MGM, 1940) 83 M.

Associate producer, Harold Huth; director, Arthur B. Woods; based on the play Busman's Holiday by Dorothy L. Sayers and the play by Sayers and Muriel St. Claire Byrne; camera, Freddie Young; editor, Al Barnes.

Robert Montgomery (Lord Peter Wimsey); Constance Cummings (Harriet Vane); Leslie Banks (Inspector Kirk); Sir Seymour Hicks (Bunter); Robert Newton (Frank Crutchley); Googie Withers (Polly); Frank Pettingell (Puffett); Joan Kemp-Welch (Aggie Twitterton); Aubrey Mallalieu (Reverend Simon Goodacre); James Carney (Constable Sellon); Roy Emerton (Noakes); Louise Hampton (Mrs. Ruddle); Eliot Makeham (Simpson); Reginald Purdell (MacBride).

MR. AND MRS. SMITH (RKO, 1941) 95 M.

Executive producer, Harry E. Edington; director, Alfred Hitchcock; story-screenplay, Norman Krasna; art directors, Van Nest Polglase, L. P. Williams; music, Roy Webb; special effects, Vernon L. Walker; camera, Harry Stradling; editor, William Hamilton.

Carole Lombard (Ann Smith/Ann Kransheimer); Robert Montgomery (David Smith); Gene Raymond (Jeff Custer); Jack Carson (Chuck Benson); Philip Merivale (Mr. Custer); Lucile Watson (Mrs. Custer); William Tracy (Sammy); Charles Halton (Mr. Deever); Esther Dale (Mrs. Krausheimer); Emma Dunn (Martha); William Edmunds (Proprietor of Lucy's); Betty Compson (Gertie); Patricia Farr (Gloria); Adele Pearce (later Pamela Blake) (Lily); Frank Mills (Taxi Driver); Alec Craig (Thomas, the Clerk); Robert E. Keane (Section Manager); Jack Gardner (Elevator Boy); Ralph Sanford (Store Checker); Murray Alper (Harold, the Driver); Georgia Carroll (Pretty Girl); Ralph Dunn (Clerk); James Flavin (Escort); Ralph Brooks (Waiter Captain); Ronnie Rondell (Waiter); Jim Pierce (Doorman); Barbara Wooddell (Secretary to David); Beatrice Maude (Secretary to Jeff); Allen Wood, Ernie Alexander (Bellhops); Emory Parnell (Conway); Stan Taylor (Clerk).

RAGE IN HEAVEN (MGM, 1941) 82 M.

Producer, Gottfried Reinhardt; director, W. S. Van Dyke II; based on the novel by James Hilton; screenplay, Christopher Isherwood, Robert Thoeren; music, Bronislau Kaper; camera, Oliver T. Marsh; editor, Harold Kress.

Robert Montgomery (Philip Monrell); Ingrid Bergman (Stella Bergen); George Sanders (Ward Andrews); Lucile Watson (Mrs. Monrell); Oscar Homolka (Dr. Rameau); Philip Merivale (Mr. Higgins); Matthew Boulton (Ramsbotham); Aubrey Mather (Clark); Frederic Worlock (Solicitor-General); Francis Compton (Bardsley); Gilbert Emery (Mr. Black); Ludwig Hart (Durand); Lawrence Grant (British Consul); Art Dupuis (Taxi Driver); Victor Kendall (Dr. Boudin); Eldon Gorst (Page Boy); Guy Kingsford (Clerk); Olaf Hytten (Hotel Clerk); Pat Moriarity, Frank Shannon, Harry Cording, David Clyde (Workers' Delegates); Bobby Hale, Leyland Hodgson, Damian O'Flynn, Eric Lonsdale, Dave Thursby, Pat O'Malley (Workers); Lilian Kemble-Cooper (Nurse); Leonard Carey (Eric, the Chauffeur); Major McBride (Bank Clerk); Stuart Hall, Clive Morgan (Traveling Salesmen); Wyndham Standing (Dr. McTernan); Arthur Stuart Hull (Major Bedford); Holmes Herbert (Judge); John Burton (Court Clerk); Harry Allen (Jury Foreman); Colin Kenny (Warden); Jean Del Val (Porter).

HERE COMES MR. JORDAN (COL, 1941) 93 M.

Producer, Everett Riskin; director, Alexander Hall; based on the play Heaven Can Wait *by Harry Segall; screenplay, Sidney Buchman, Seton I. Miller; art director, Lionel Banks; music, Morris W. Stoloff; camera, Joseph Walker; editor, Viola Lawrence.*

Robert Montgomery (Joe Pendleton); Evelyn Keyes (Bette Logan); Claude Rains (Mr. Jordan); Rita Johnson (Julia Farnsworth); Edward Everett Horton (Messenger #7013); James Gleason (Max Gorkle); John Emery (Tony Abbott); Donald MacBride (Inspector Williams); Don Costello (Lefty); Halliwell Hobbes (Sisk); Benny Rubin (Bugs); Bert Young (Taxi Driver); Ken Christy (Plainclothesman); Joseph Crehan (Doctor); Billy Newell (Handler); Abe Roth (Referee); Tom Hanlon (Announcer); Joe Hickey (Gilbert); Warren Ashe (Charlie); Billy Dawson (Johnny); Bobby Larson (Chips); John Kerns (Sparring Partner); Mary Currier (Secretary); William Forrest, Ed Bruce (Reporters); Douglas Wood, Selmer Jackson (Board Members); Joe Conti, Chester Conklin, Gerald Pierce (Newsboys); John Rogers (Escort); Lloyd Bridges (Co-Pilot); Edmund Elton (Elderly Man); Maurice Costello (Ringsider at Fight); John Ince (Bill Collector).

UNFINISHED BUSINESS (UNIV, 1941) 96 M.

Producer-director, Gregory LaCava; screenplay, Eugene Thackrey; art director, Jack Otterson; music director, Franz Waxman; camera, Joseph Valentine.

Irene Dunne (Nancy Adams); Robert Montgomery (Tom Duncan); Eugene Pallette (Elmer); Preston Foster (Steve Duncan); June Clyde (Clarissa); Phyllis Barry (Steve's Wife); Thomas W. Ross (Lawyer); Richard Davies (Jimmy); Esther Dale (Aunt Mathilda); Walter Catlett (Billy Ross); Samuel S. Hinds (Uncle); Dick Foran (Best Man); Kathryn Adams (Bride); Chester Clute, Paul Everton, Reed Hadley, Boyd Irwin, John Sheehan, Matt McHugh, Larry Kent, Fred Santley (Men); Helen Lynd, Phyllis Kennedy, Dorothy Granger, Dora Clement, Norma Drury, Hillary Brooke, Carol Tevis, Sheila Darcy, Flo Wix, Gwen Seager, Isabelle LaMal, Dorothy Haas, Ruth Dwyer (Women); Renie Riano (Secretary); Pierre Watkin (Lawyer); Josephine Whittell (Wardrobe Woman); Virginia Brissac (Aunt); Mary Gordon (Charwoman); Harry Rosenthal (Pianist); Bob Perry, George Davis (Waiters); Helene Millard (Helen); Fortunio Bonanova (Impresario); Reverend Neal Dodd (Minister); Hope Landin (Groom's Mother); Monte Collins, Eddie Fetherston, Jack Voglin (Reporters); Frank Coghlan, Jr. (Page Boy); Jacques Vanaire (Headwaiter); Yolande Mollot (Manicurist); Frank Shannon (Groom's Father); Hugh Beaumont (Groom); Eugene Jackson (Bootblack); Lester Dorr (Yes Man); Amanda McFarland (Baby); Mary Jo Ellis (Bridesmaid).

THEY WERE EXPENDABLE (MGM, 1945) 135 M.

Producer, John Ford; associate producer, Cliff Reid; directors, Ford, (uncredited) Robert Montgomery; based on the book by William L. White; screenplay, Frank Wead; music, Herbert Stothart; art directors, Cedric Gibbons, Malcolm Brown; set decorators, Edwin B. Willis, Ralph S. Hurst; assistant director, Edward O'Fearna; second unit director, James Havens; sound, Douglas Shearer; special effects, A. Arnold Gillespie; camera, Joseph H. August; editors, Frank E. Hull, Douglass Biggs.

Robert Montgomery (Lieutenant John Brickley); John Wayne (Lieutenant (J.G.) "Rusty" Ryan); Donna Reed (Second Lieutenant Sandy Davyss); Jack Holt (General Martin); Ward Bond ("Boots" Mulcahey, C.B.M.); Marshall Thompson (Ensign Snake Gardner); Paul Langton (Ensign Andy Andrews); Leon Ames (Major James Morton); Arthur Walsh (Seaman Jones 1c); Donald Curtis (Lieutenant (J.G.) "Shorty" Long); Cameron Mitchell (Ensign George Cross); Jeff York (Ensign "Lefty" Tony Aiken); Murray Alper ("Slug" Mahan, T.M. 1c); Harry Tenbrook ("Cookie" Squarehead Larsen, SC2c); Jack Pennick ("Doc," the Storekeeper); Alex Havier

(Benny Lacoco, Steward 3c); Charles Trowbridge (Admiral Blackwell); Bruce Kellogg (Lieutenant Elder Tompkins, M.M. 2c); Louis Jean Heydt (Captain Ohio Carter); Russell Simpson (Dad Knowland); Vernon Steele (Army Doctor at Corregidor); Trina Lowe (Gardner's Girl Friend); Robert Shelby Randall, Art Foster, Larry Dods, Jack Stoney, Duke Green, Stubby Kruger, Phil Schumacher, Major Frank Pershing, Joey Ray, Dan Borzage, William Neff, Del Hill, Bill Barnum, Ted Lundigan, Michael Kirby, William McKeever Riley (Boat Crew Members); Frank McGrath (Slim); Sammy Stein (Sammy); Blake Edwards (Gunner); Ernest Seftig, Stephen Barclay, Franklin Parker (Navy Officers); Robert Emmet O'Connor (Bartender at Silver Dollar); Leslie Sketchley (Marine Orderly); Phillip Ahn (Army Orderly); Pacita Tod-Tod (Filipino Girl Singer); Robert Homans (Bartender at Manila Hotel); William B. Davidson (Hotel Manager); Jack Cheatham (Commander); Forbes Murray (Navy Captain); Emmett Vogan (Captain—Navy Doctor); Sherry Hall (Marine Major); Alan Bridge (Lieutenant Colonel); Jack Luden (Naval Air Captain); Jon Gilbreath (Sub Commander); Marjorie Davies, Eve March (Nurses); Karl Miller, Len Stanford, George Bruggeman, Reginald Simpson, James Carlisle, Dutch Schlickenmeyer, Tony Carson, Jack Lorenz, Brad Towne, Charles Calhoun, Leonard Mellin, Frank Donahue, Dan Quigg, Clifford Rathjen, Dick Karl, Jack Lee, Wedgewood Nowell, Dick Thorne, Leonard Fisher, John Roy, Michael Kostrick, Jimmy Magrill, George Magrill, Sam Simone, Paul Kruger, Bruce Carruthers, Jack Semple, Roy Thomas, Bob Thom, Larry Steers, Gary Delmar (Personnel in Admiral's Office); Eleanor Vogel, Leota Lorraine, Almeda Fowler, Betty Blythe, Jane Crowley (Officers' Wives); Charles Murray, Jr. (Jeep Driver); Margaret Morton (Bartender's Wife); George Economides, Michael Economides, Roque Yberra, Jr., Nino Pipitone, Jr. (Bartender's Children); Ralph Soncuya (Filipino Orderly); Vincent Isla (Filipino Schoolteacher); Max Ong (Mayor of Cebu); William Neff (Sub Skipper); Jim Farley (Mate); Ernest Dominguez, Henry Mirelez (Filipino Boys); Lee Tung Foo (Bartender); Max Ong (Filipino); Tom Tyler (Captain of Airport); Bill Wilkerson (Sergeant Smith); John Carlyle (Lieutenant James); Mary Jane French (Lost Nurse); Patrick Davis (Pilot); Roger Cole, Fred Beckner, Jack Ross, Brent Shugar, Kermit Maynard, Bill Donahue, Frank Eldridge, Jack Carrington, Hansel Warner, Charles Ferguson, Jack Trent, Robert Strong, Jon Eppers, Bill Nind, Don Lewis (Officers at Airport); William (Merrill) McCormick (Wounded Officer at Airport); Jack Mower (Officer).

LADY IN THE LAKE (MGM, 1946) 105 M.

Producer, George Haight; director, Robert Montgomery; based on the novel by Raymond Chandler; screenplay, Steve Fisher; art directors, Cedric Gibbons, Preston Ames; set decorators, Edwin B. Willis, Thomas Theuerkauf, music, David Snell; assistant director, Dolph Zimmer; sound, Douglas Shearer; camera, Paul C. Vogel; editor, Gene Ruggiero.

Robert Montgomery (Philip Marlowe); Lloyd Nolan (Lieutenant DeGarmot); Audrey Totter (Adrienne Fromsett); Tom Tully (Captain Kane); Leon Ames (Derace Kingsby); Jayne Meadows (Mildred Haveland); Morris Ankrum (Eugene Grayson); Lila Leeds (Receptionist); Richard Simmons (Chris Lavery); Ellen Ross (Elevator Girl); William Roberts (Artist); Kathleen Lockhart (Mrs. Grayson); Cy Kendall (Jaibi); Ralph Dunn (Sergeant); Wheaton Chambers (Property Clerk); Frank Orth (Greer); William McKeever Riley (Bunny); Robert Williams (Detective); Fred E. Sherman (Reporter); Jack Davis, John Gallaudet, Tom Murray, George Magrill, Budd Fine, John Webb Dillon (Policemen); Robert Spencer (Marlowe's Double); Billy Newell (Drunk); Eddie Acuff (Coroner); Nina Ross, Charles Bradstreet, George Travell, William O'Leary, Bert Moorhouse, Florence Stephens, Sandra Morgan, Fred Santley, Laura Treadwell, Kay Wiley, Frank Dae, David Cavendish, James Nolan, Sherry Hall, Ann Lawrence, Roger Cole (Christmas Party Guests).

YOUR WITNESS (WB-British, 1950) 100 M.

Producers, David E. Rose, Joan Harrison; director, Robert Montgomery; story, Hugo Butler; screenplay, Butler, Ian Hunter; additional dialog, William Douglas Home; music, Malcolm Arnold; music director, John Hollingsworth; art director, Ralph Printon; Miss Wayne's dresses, David Kidd; makeup, Jerry Fletcher; sound, W. Sweeney; camera, Gerald Young; editor, Leo Carruthers.

Robert Montgomery (Adam Heywood); Leslie Banks (Colonel Summerfield); Felix Aylmer (Judge); Andrew Cruickshank (Sir Adrian North K.C.); Patricia Wayne (Cutts) (Alex Summerfield); Harcourt Williams (Beamish); Jenny Laird (Mary Baxter); Michael Ripper (Sam Baxter); Ann Stephens (Susan Stephens) (Sandy Summerfield); Wylie Watson (Widgery); Noel Howlett (Martin Foxglove K.C.); James Hayter (Prouty); John Sharp (P. C. Hawkins); Shelagh Fraser (Ellen Foster); Philip Dale (Jim Foster); Hal Osmond (Taxi Driver); Lyonel Watts (Vicar); Derick Penley (Clerk of Assize); Erik Chitty (Judge's Clerk); Ruth Lee (Miss Hubert); Stanley Baker (Sergeant Bannoch).

U.S. release title: EYE WITNESS (Eagle Lion, 1950).

THE GALLANT HOURS (UA, 1960) 115 M.

Producer-director, Robert Montgomery; screenplay, Beime Lay, Jr., Frank D. Gilroy; music-music conductor, Roger Wagner; art director, Wiard Ihman; set decorator, Frank McKelvy; technical supervisor, Captain Idris B. Monahan, U.S.N. (Ret.); Japanese Naval Technical advisor, James T. Goto; assistant director, Joseph C. Behm; makeup, Loran Cosand; wardrobe, Jack Martell; camera, Joe MacDonald; editor, Frederick Y. Smith.

Robert Montgomery,° Art Gilmore (Narrators); James Cagney (Admiral William F. Halsey, Jr.); Dennis Weaver (Lieutenant Commander Andy Lowe); Ward Costello (Captain Henry Black); Richard Jaeckel (Lieutenant Commandor Roy Webb); Les Tremayne (Captain Frank Enright); Robert Burton (Major General Roy Geiger); Raymond Bailey (Major General Vandergrift); Carl Benton Reid (Admiral Ghormley); Walter Sande (Captain Horace Keys); Karl Swenson (Captain Bill Bailey); Vaughn Taylor (Commandor Mike Pulaski); Harry Landers (Captain Joe Foss); Leon Lontoe (Manuel); Richard Carlyle (Father Gehring); James T. Goto (Admiral Isoroku Hamamoto); James Yagi (Rear Admiral Jiro Kobe); John McKee (Lieutenant Harrison Ludlum); John Zaremba (Major General Harmon); Carleton Young (Colonel Evans Carlson); William Schallert (Captain Tom Lanphier); Nelson Leigh (Admiral Callaghani); Sydney Smith (Admiral Scott); Herbert Lytton (Admiral Murray); Selmar Jackson (Admiral Chester Nimitz); Tyler McVey (Admiral Ernest J. King); Maggie Magennis (Red Cross Girl); Robert Montgomery, Jr., James Cagney, Jr. (Marines).

RIDE THE PINK HORSE (UNIV, 1947) 101 M.

Producer, Joan Harrison; director, Robert Montgomery; based on the novel by Dorothy B. Hughes; screenplay, Ben Hecht, Charles Lederer; art directors, Bernard Herzbrun, Robert Boyle; set decorators, Russell A. Gausman, Oliver Emert; music, Frank Skinner; orchestrator, David Tamkin; sound, Leslie I. Carey, Jack Bolger, Jr.; assistant director, John F. Sherwood; camera, Russell Metty; editor, Ralph Dawson.

Robert Montgomery (Gagin); Thomas Gomez (Pancho); Rita Conde (Carla); Iris Flores (Maria); Wanda Hendrix (Pila); Grandon Rhodes (Mr. Edison); Tito Renaldo (Bellboy); Richard Gaines (Jonathan); Andrea King (Marjorie); Art Smith (Bill Retz); Martin Garralaga (Barkeeper); Edward Earle (Locke); Harold Goodwin (Red); Maria Cortez (Elevator Girl); Fred Clark (Hugo); Paul Maxey (Portly Man); Howard Negley, Jimmy Ames, John Doucette, Jack Worth (Thugs); Leon Lenoir (Mexican Workman); Beatrice Roberts (Manageress);

Julian Rivero (Mexican Man); Paul Bryar, Lyle Latell (State Troopers); Harry J. Vejar (Barber); Charles Stevens (Drunken Mexican); William Ruhl (Mr. Blane); Ernest Hilliard (Elderly Man); Jerry De Castro (Mexican Man); Virginia Wave (Waitress); Ralph Montgomery (Waiter); Amadita Garcia, Connie Asins, Rose Marie Lopez, Martha Brenes, Olga Perez, Carmen Pallais (Mexican Girls); Miguel Tapia, Roque Ybarra, Jr., Jose Alvarado, Harry Garcia (Mexican Boys); Robert Espinosa (Mexican Boy Crying); Enrique Valades, Robert Cabal (Muchachos); Donald Kerr (Headwaiter); Kenneth Ross MacKenzie (Man).

THE SAXON CHARM (UNIV, 1948) 88 M.

Producer, Joseph Sistrom; director, Claude Binyon; based on the novel by Frederic Wakeman; screenplay, Binyon; art director, Alexander Golitzen; set decorators, Russell A. Gausman, Ted Offenbacker; music, Walter Scharf; orchestrator, David Tamkin; assistant director, Frank Shaw; makeup, Bud Westmore; choreography, Nick Castle; costumes, Mary K. Dodson; sound, Leslie I. Carey, Glenn E. Anderson; special effects, David S. Horsley; camera, Milton Krasner; editor, Paul Weatherwax.

Robert Montgomery (Matt Saxon); Susan Hayward (Janet Busch); John Payne (Eric Busch); Audrey Totter (Alma); Henry "Harry" Morgan (Hermy); Harry Von Zell (Zack Humber); Cara Williams (Dolly Humber); Chill Wills (Captain Chatham); Heather Angel (Vivian Saxon); John Baragrey (Peter Stanhope); Addison Richards (Abel Richman); Barbara Challis (Ingenue); Curt Conway (Jack Bernard); Fay Baker (Mrs. Noble); Philip Van Zandt (Chris); Martin Garralaga (Manager); Max Willenz (Proprietor); Fred Nurney (Headwaiter); Archie Twitchell (Mr. Maddox); Barbara Billingsley (Mrs. Maddox); Eula Guy (Harassed Secretary); Al Murphy (Bald Man); Clarence Straight (Mr. McCarthy); Bert Davidson (Mr. Noble); Maris Wrixon (Mrs. McCarthy); Peter Brocco (Cyril Leatham); Donna Martell (Flower Girl); Mauritz Hugo (Designer); Anthony Jochim (Agent); Kathleen Freeman (Nurse); Blanche Obronska (Soubrette); Laura Kasley Brooks (Buxom Nurse); Vivian Mason (Blonde); Basil Tellou (Character Man); Robert Spencer (Leading Man); Paul Rochin (Waiter); Lomax Study (Headwaiter); Robert Cabal (Bus Boy).

THE SECRET LAND (MGM, 1948) C—71 M.

Producer, Orville O. Dull; commentary, Captain Harvey S. Haislip, U.S.N. (Ret.); Commodore William C. Park, U.S.N.R.; music, Bronislau Kaper; sound, Douglas Shearer; camera, Navy Marine Corp, Coast Guard, and Army cameramen; editor, Commodore Frederick Y. Smith, U.S.N.R.

Commentary: Commodore Robert Montgomery, U.S.N.R., Lieutenant Robert Taylor, U.S.N.R., Lieutenant Van Heflin, A.A.F. (Ret.).

JUNE BRIDE (WB, 1948) 97 M.

Producer, Henry Blanke; director, Bretaigne Windust; based on the play Feature for June by Eileen Tishe, Graeme Lorimer; screenplay, Ranald MacDougall; art director, Anton Grot; set decorator, William Wallace; music, David Buttolph; assistant director, Sherry Shourds; makeup, Perc Westmore, Eddie Voight; costumes, Edith Head; sound, Robert B. Lee; special effects, William McGann, H. D. Koenekamp; camera, Ted McCord; editor, Owen Marks.

Bette Davis (Linda Gilman); Robert Montgomery (Carey Jackson); Fay Bainter (Paula Winthrop); Betty Lynn (Boo Brinker); Tom Tully (Mr. Brinker); Barbara Bates (Jeanne Brinker); Jerome Cowan (Carleton Towne); Mary Wickes (Rosemary McNally); James Burke (Luke Potter); Raymond Roe (Bud Mitchell); Marjorie Bennett (Mrs. Brinker); Ray Montgomery (Jim Mitchell); George O'Hanlon (Scott Davis);

°There is unverified evidence that Montgomery plays an extra within the film.

Sandra Gould (Miss Rubens); Esther Howard (Mrs. Mitchell); Jessie Adams (Mrs. Lace); John Vosper (Stafford); Jack Mower (Varga); Lottie Williams (Woody); Mary Stuart (Plane Hostess); Ann Kimbell, Barbara Wittlinger (Girls on Sleigh Ride); Raymond Bond (Minister); Patricia Northrop, Alice Kelly, Debbie Reynolds (Boo's Girl Friends).

ONCE MORE, MY DARLING (UNIV, 1949) 94 M.

Producer, Joan Harrison; director, Robert Montgomery; based on the story "Come Be My Love" by Robert Carson; screenplay, Carson; additional dialog, Oscar Saul; art directors, Bernard Herzbrun, Bert Clatworthy; set decorators, Russell A. Gausman, Ruby R. Levitt; music, Elizabeth Firestone; music director, Frank Skinner; second unit director, Jack Hively; assistant director, John F. Sherwood; makeup, Bud Westmore, John Holden; costumes, Orry Kelly; sound, Leslie I. Carey, Corson Jowett; special effects, David S. Horsley; camera, Frank Planer; editor, Ralph Dawson.

In Order of Appearance: Lillian Randolph (Mamie); Robert Montgomery (Collier Laing); Jane Cowl (Mrs. Laing); Steven Geray (Kalzac); John Ridgely (Burke); Roland Winters (Colonel Head); Maurice Cass (Dr. Grasser); Ann Blyth (Marita Connell); Taylor Holmes (Jed Connell); Charles McGraw (Herman Schmelz); Don Beddoe (Judge Fraser); Louise Lorimer (Mrs. Fraser); Wilton Graff (Mr. Frobisher); Sally Corner (Mrs. Frobisher); D. J. Thompson (Mary Frobisher); George Carleton (Mr. Grant); Edna M. Holland (Mrs. Grant); Ray Teal (Truck Driver); Bert Hicks (Peter Vellon); Ann Pearce (Receptionist); Barbara Payton (Girl Photographer); John Harmon (Georgie); George Chandler (Motel Proprietor); Jack Overman (Grip); Bert Conway (Assistant Director); Maurice Marsac (Henri); Dell Henderson (Hotel Clerk); William Vedder (Alfred); Michael Cisney (Alfred); Phyllis Kennedy (Waitress); Isabel Withers (Woman); Jim Toney (Fruit Dealer); John Pickard (Inspector); Jack Gargan (Mixer); James Linn (Gaffer); Donald Gordon (Kid); Betty Roche (Script Clerk); Robert Coudy (Parking Attendant).

With Gregory Peck in THE GUNS OF NAVARONE

Chapter Seven

David Niven

6'1"
175 pounds
Brown hair
Blue eyes
Pisces

On the April 1974 Academy Award telecast, presenter Burt Reynolds suggested to the viewing audience: "If you want sophistication, go have lunch with David Niven."

For the general public, superstar David Niven has long been synonymous with elite, gentlemanly behavior, not quite in the same league with Cary Grant, but certainly a cut above Brian Aherne and several rungs above an actor like Michael Wilding. This persistent Niven image is rather ironic considering that his greatest box-office success oncamera was as the adventurous, globe-trotting Phileas Fogg in *Around the World in Eighty Days* (United Artists, 1956), that he won an Academy Award for playing the aging reprobate "major" in *Separate Tables* (United Artists, 1958), and that on several occasions he has graced rather tasteless sex farces: *The Moon Is Blue* (United Artists, 1953); *The Little Hut* (MGM, 1957); and *The Statue* (Cinerama, 1971).

Even more strange (and the actor would be the first to admit it), if one studies Niven's forty-year screen career, there are few authentic highlights over the decades. Even from the mid-1930s to the late 1940s, which was his Samuel Goldwyn period, David's most famous picture was *Wuthering Heights* (United Artists, 1939), and in that film, as prim, stuffy Edgar Linton, he took a cinematic back seat to the heavy, romantic brush-strokes of Merle Oberon's Cathy and Laurence Olivier's Heathcliffe. Moreover, in *Raffles* (United Artists, 1939), David was touted as the new Ronald Colman, but it was Colman's splendid performance as the gentleman thief a decade earlier that remained more memorable.

Perhaps if any single quality explains Niven's enduring professional popularity, it is his air of being the persistent good sport. Whether plucking the comic notes of *Bachelor Father* (RKO, 1939) with Ginger Rogers, ministering as the physician-beau to ailing Barbara Stanwyck in *The Other Love* (United Artists, 1947), abiding the sappy domesticity of Doris Day in *Please Don't Eat the Daisies* (MGM, 1960), or seeing it through as a makeshift James Bond in *Casino Royale* (Columbia, 1967), he remains unruffled in front of the camera. His engaging equanimity has made him and keeps him a box-office attraction. Offscreen David is just as imperturbable, as is demonstrated in his well-executed autobiography, *The Moon's a Balloon* (1972), a fabulous best-seller composed in a modest, unassuming manner, guaranteed to woo the most skeptical reader into the Niven camp and to titillate readers with his anecdotes, both funny and racy.

If David of the 1930s was an impish young man full of practical jokes and a blatant disregard for the Establishment, the Niven of today has aged gracefully into veteran celebrity status. His every action still seems to indicate that for him life is a lark and nothing must be taken too seriously, especially anything stemming from one witty, genteel soul named David Niven.

James David Graham Niven was born in London on Tuesday, March 1, 1910*—St. David's Day. He was the fourth child of William E. G. Niven and his French wife, Henriette Etta Degacher Niven. Presumably a very wealthy man, William Niven provided his growing family with an expansive country home at Kirriemuir, Scotland, staffed with all the requisites of gracious living, including butlers, footmen, gamekeepers, and a nanny for the children.

David never really got to know his father, who volunteered for combat duty as a second lieutenant in 1914 and was killed in action at the Dardanelles the following year. It was then discovered that the dead man's debts exceeded his assets and his widow was forced to sell the estate. After several moves she and the family finally settled in London, where in 1917 she remarried. Her new spouse, Sir Thomas Comyn-Platt, took over as head of the household, determining the children's fate as he saw fit. Max, the eldest, already a cadet at the Royal Navy College, Dartmouth, was allowed to remain as such, but Grizel was sent off to a boarding school at Norfolk, and David was dispatched to an Elstree boarding school. Only Joyce was permitted to live at home as her mother's helper.

The stepfather took an intense dislike to six-year-old David. The disenchantment began at Comyn-Platt's wedding to Mrs. Niven. The young Niven disrupted the marriage ceremony by spectacularly picking his nose and then screaming in the church filled to overflowing capacity with British nobility. Deprived of the parental love he sought, David was to spend the next few years as a lonely, insecure child. After two years at Elstree, he was transferred to Heatherdown, a more expensive school situated in Ascot, where his growing pains involved acts of mischief for which he was regularly given a sound caning by the headmaster.

The final blow to his stay at Heatherdown came when he climbed over the school's wall to the next-door girls' dormitory where he promptly stole a cauliflower from their vegetable garden. For this he was expelled at the age of ten and one-half. As an additional punishment, his stepfather

*Some sources state 1909 or 1911.

had him sent for a month's reforming at an institution for "difficult" boys at Southsea on the English coast, a short distance from the Isle of Wight where his mother was then domiciled.

From there, he was enrolled with a vicar who was also famed for preparing boys for the entrance examination to the naval college at Dartmouth. Since David's only chance of earning entrance into Eton had been ended with his expulsion from Heatherdown, it was thought that the Navy was the next best thing. At the age of twelve and one-half he went before the Navy's examining board for verbal questioning and written tests. Mathematics, a subject of the utmost incomprehensibility to him, was the one lack that eliminated all possibilities of his ever leading a sailor's life.

The stepfather, who still did not want his wife's youngest living under the same roof, then arranged for his enrollment at Stowe School in Buckinghamshire. It was there that David obtained his first experience at acting, and he was soon placed in charge of the school's stage activities. He also played a trombone and beat a drum in the Stowe band. By this time he had set his goal on entering the Royal Military College, Sandhurst, the West Point of England, but he was caught cheating in the initial written examination. A short time later, however, he was permitted a second chance and passed. Eighteen months later, commissioned a second lieutenant at the age of eighteen, he was assigned to serve with the Highland Light Infantry, the one regiment with which he least wanted to be affiliated.

In January 1928, he boarded the *Kaisar-i-Hind* (Hindi for Emperor of India) for duty in Malta. "I am ashamed to say," he once said, "that my stay at Malta was one small calamity after another." He and a fellow officer named Trubshawe procured papier-mâché helmets by mail-order from London which they wore in place of the heavy army-issue headgear. A rainstorm, while they were at dress parade, put an end to the substitution when the fake helmets "dropped down over our eyes like uncooked pizza pies." He was again confined to quarters when he displayed his officer's sword, which he had earlier broken off by jabbing a dummy used for bayonet practice. He was the only officer whose weapon emerged from its scabbard

358

as a six-inch dagger. Another confinement resulted when Niven and Trubshawe attended a costumed fancy-dress ball at the local opera house, dressed as goats and sporting rubber udders. After consuming a fair amount of gin, they passed several times in front of the judges. Their costumes were at first suspected of being designed to mock the island's traditional ball, and the suspicions turned to firm belief when David squatted in the middle of the floor while Trubshawe sprinkled black olives behind him.

After three long, prank-filled years at Malta, Niven and his regiment were transferred to Dover, England. Soon after, David met American heiress Barbara Hutton, who "had the smallest feet I have ever seen." He had bought a second-hand automobile with which to drive the short distance from Dover to London on off-duty hours and, as he relates in his autobiography, *The Moon's a Balloon* (1972): "I found myself on the Mayfair hostesses' lists—as usual they were desperately short of available young men." Having met the famous Miss Hutton at a dance, they formed a friendship during her London visit, and she invited him to visit her in New York the following Christmas.

In November 1932, Niven's mother died of cancer. Unable to concentrate on his Army duties, and since he was then entitled to four weeks' leave, he decided to spend them in New York as Miss Hutton's guest. He sold his car, borrowed money from his sister Grizel, who had become a sculptress, and embarked on the S.S. *Georgic* to New York. The ship arrived in New York harbor on Christmas Eve, 1932, where the Britisher was greeted by Miss Hutton, her cousin Woolworth Donahue, and several friends. "I was a bit of a freak in the United States in those days," he has written, "as the vast majority of people had still never met a Briton nor heard an 'English accent.' Nobody went to English movies because he couldn't understand them."

Miss Hutton arranged for his proper lodgings at the plush Hotel Pierre and hostessed a Christmas Eve party at the Central Park Casino where George Murphy and his wife, Julie, ballroom-danced to the music of Eddy Duchin's piano and orchestra. Thereafter, David embarked on a complete socialite's tour of upper-crust New York parties, speakeasys, stage musicals, boxing matches, and his first American football game. He became well acquainted with the ritzy Long Island set, one of whom invited him to drive to St. Augustine, Florida. They eventually wound up at Palm Beach when he "missed the last train that would carry me north to catch my ship home." He wired his commanding officer back in England: "Dear Colonel: Magnificent opportunity big game hunting whale fishing Florida. Request one week extended leave." The colonel's comprehensive reply was: ". . . no whales or big game within a thousand miles Stop Take two." When the extended holiday neared its end, David missed yet another train and as a going-away gift, Woolworth Donahue provided him with a ticket aboard an unsoundproofed plane, which landed at New York after a rocky fourteen-hour flight.

Niven then returned to England. Back in Dover, he went about the serious business of being a competent Army officer, but always insuring that he took full advantage of his proximity to London by driving there in a second-hand Bentley car he had acquired. He became a friend to Ann Todd, Laurence Olivier, and Douglas Fairbanks, Sr. He also made his first screen appearance, as an extra, in *All the Winners*, a racing film made at Sound City.

Next on his military agenda was machine-gun school, which he loathed, mostly because it interfered with his nocturnal social life in London. After arriving at outdoor class one morning, still clad in his evening garb, a major general asked, at the end of a lengthy dissertation, for questions, Niven raised his arm, and, upon receiving recognition, inquired: "Could you tell me the time, sir? I have to catch a train." Once more he was tossed into the brig, but this time his guard was a buddy with a bottle of whiskey. When they had consumed the contents, the guard announced that he had to visit the lavatory and suggested to David that he depart during his absence. Niven escaped. That same evening, from London, he cabled his ranking colonel with "Request Permission Resign Commission." Then, with funds obtained through the quick sale of his Bentley, he sailed with a friend, on a return-trip ticket to Quebec, Canada, in May 1933.

After spending some time on an island in the Rideau Lake region, near Quebec, he decided to cash in his return ticket and head to New York, where he had some lively social contacts. Before he could do this, however, he wound up in an Ottawa hospital with infected tonsils, which had to be removed. While convalescing, he read a book entitled *Fox Hunting in Canada*, and "I am afraid I indulged in a little gentle plagiarism." He copied some of the material and sold four articles, entitled "Hunting of the Canadian Fox," to a newspaper. "It paid the doctor's bills," he admits. He was then invited by friends of friends to rest at their home, where severe postoperative complications set in. He was whisked back to the hospital for blood transfusions.

By October, he felt well enough to travel by train to New York. He rented an inexpensive room at Manhattan's Montclair Hotel and rested in bed for a week before looking up the pals he had met on his previous New York jaunt. "Although they went through the motions of being pleased to see me, I soon realized that there was a big difference between an irresponsible young man over for a short holiday and an anxious young man badly in need of a job." He registered with employment agencies through which he obtained a few jobs, mostly with catering firms handling cocktail parties. Jobs were scarce due to the depression, and most Americans were certainly not inclined to hiring a foreigner for work that a fellow American might do just as well, or, in Niven's case, better.

But the typical Niven *joie de vivre* was not undermined so easily. David had many methods of perking himself up each day. For example, the front door of the Montclair Hotel opened onto the back door of the luxurious Waldorf Astoria. Every morning, Niven left his hotel, entered the Waldorf, and exited through the front door of the prestigious Waldorf. He reversed the route in returning to the Montclair in the evenings. "Very good for the morale," he later explained.

His next venture was selling liquor on a $40-a-week base salary against ten percent of his orders for the "21" Brands, formed by the owners of the plush 21 Club. At a party he met the professional hostess (with the mostest) Elsa Maxwell, who took an immediate liking to him and exclaimed: "Selling liquor—that's no good, no good at all—get you nowhere—you should go to Hollywood. Nobody out there knows how to speak except Ronald Colman." The following week she gave one of her world-famous parties, one in honor of Ernst Lubitsch. She invited Niven with the promise of introducing him to the sophisticated film director. When nothing developed out of their brief meeting, Miss Maxwell suggested that Niven find a rich girl to marry, but that idea got nowhere either. His employers, having discovered what he already knew, that he was an uninspired salesman, discharged him. He then fell in with Douglas Hertz and Lefty Flynn with whom he formed the American Pony Express Racing Association. The idea of the organization was to have teams of polo ponies racing indoors on small tracks. Damon Runyon, one of the early financial backers, warned them not to open their operations in Atlantic City, as planned, because of the mob-

sters who controlled the ocean-front city. They chose not to listen, and their first night was a success. They were visited by gangland representatives who advised them to leave town, but they ignored this cogent advice and were forced to close before the week was out.

Niven returned to New York, nearly flat broke, to find a letter from his sister, Grizel, informing him that his mother had left each of her children a legacy. He collected $800 and went with his ex-partner Lefty Flynn to Bermuda, where they basked for several weeks. Then, having talked with friends who told of the glories of California, and remembering Elsa Maxwell's words about his belonging in the movies, he took a boat to Havana, where he was to connect with the *President Pierce,* a Los Angeles–bound ship of the American President Line fleet. The one-week lay-over in Havana allowed him to become acquainted with many Cuban residents, most of whom hung out at a bar called Sloppy Joe's. One such man was Irish. He explained the aura of unrest that penetrated the city and asked Niven, because of his military background and knowledge of machine-gunnery, to join the people's army. A representative of the British Embassy got to him before he joined any such revolutionary movement, and politely suggested he leave Cuba.

Dennis Bingham was at the Los Angeles dock to meet the *President Pierce* when it docked. With Bingham was a beautiful female companion, Sally Blane, then popular in films. Dockside newsmen encircled Miss Blane in the hope that she was there for a reason meriting headlines. The next day, Niven's picture appeared in the *Los Angeles Examiner,* captioned: "British Sportsman Arrives, Plans to Bring over a Hundred Head of Polo Ponies." Niven has said: "Sally could not have been more gracious to a stranger in this strange new world of California, and she asked where I had planned to stay. With my thin pocketbook in mind, I said it would have to be something quiet and simple." Sally insisted that he go home with her to meet her family. "We may not be quiet and simple," she said, "but we've got lots of room." At a colonial house on outer Sunset Boulevard, he met Sally's mother, Mrs. George Belzer, and the rest of the acting family, who went by the name of Loretta Young, Polly Ann Young, and Georgianna Young. They made him feel so much at home that what began as a weekend visit stretched into months.

The next day, after learning that he hoped to get into movies, Loretta gleefully smuggled him into the Fox Studios where she was at work in *The*

White Parade (1934) with John Boles. "What a strange, wonderful secret world!" he has written. "It pulled me like a magnet." So, he bought a used car and registered with Central Casting, where he was not dissuaded by the large posted sign which warned: "Don't try to become an actor. For every one we employ, we turn away a thousand." He was turned away, however, because he did not then know about the necessity of having an all-important foreigner's work permit.

A few days later he telephoned a girl he had met in New York. She was Lydia Macy, who lived at Montecito, California, a suburb of Santa Barbara. She invited him for the weekend, and he arrived in a fruit truck that had stopped in response to his hitchhiking thumb. Together they attended a Saturday night party aboard the H.M.S. *Norfolk,* a cruiser that had often anchored at Malta. David knew the crew well. He resumed acquaintances that night and remained aboard ship after Miss Macy had departed. "Next morning, about ten-thirty, I woke with a mouth like the inside of a chauffeur's glove." Before he fully knew what was happening, he was shuttled off the *Norfolk* onto the H.M.S. *Bounty,* a complete replica of the eighteenth-century warship built for the MGM production of *Mutiny on the Bounty* (1935).

On board the *Bounty* were Robert Montgomery (then considering a part in the picture) and Frank Lloyd, the film's director, along with various newsmen covering the publicity junket. They sailed to San Pedro, California, where Montgomery gave Niven a lift north to the MGM studios. There, he was introduced to director Edmund Goulding, who asked him to make a test the following day for the part of a drunken young man in *The Flame Within* (1935).* For the hurried screentest, Niven recited an off-color limerick which made a big impression on Goulding, but not on Louis B. Mayer. Goulding passed the test over to director Alexander Hall, who was then preparing a Mae West picture, *Goin' to Town* (Paramount, 1935). Hall, with Miss West, interviewed Niven and liked him but advised the newcomer to find an agent. But, before he could move in any direction, he was visited by a United States Immigration Service man who pointed out that his visitors' visa had expired some four months previously and he had exactly twenty-four hours to leave the country. Further advice was given him that if he were to return to the States, he should first be armed with the proper papers.

Niven hopped a freight train to Mexicali, Mexico, where he spent some five months as a bartender at the Owl Bar while waiting for Grizel to send his birth certificate from England. "This Mexican interlude was one of the dark periods of my life I would rather forget," he later declared. On his return to Hollywood, in January 1935, he was dismayed to discover that the Mae West picture was already in production with Paul Cavanagh in the role for which he had been considered, and that Edmund Goulding was then in New York. After obtaining the necessary work permit, David signed with Central Casting, which categorized him in their files as "Anglo-Saxon Type 2008," but his first "extra" assignment at $2.50 a day was as a Mexican bandit in a "B" western at Universal.† He was handed a sombrero, a blanket, and a black moustache and instructed not to speak. He informed Dean Jennings of the *Saturday Evening Post* in 1958: "My first twenty-seven pictures were bang-bang westerns in which I played a variety of nonspeaking barflies, coach passengers or poker players. I even got into some of the early Hopalong Cassidy pictures [at Paramount]."

Unable to survive on an extra's pay, he supplemented his income with a job on a charter fishing boat out of Balboa, California, catering to Long Beach businessmen in quest of marlin. By then, Goulding had returned to Hollywood. "You must stop being an extra and have a good agent," he said, and got hold of Bill Hawks, who agreed to represent David. Then came a request to test opposite Claudette Colbert for a part in *The Gilded Lily* (Paramount, 1935). Director Wesley Ruggles and two others (Fred MacMurray and Ray Milland) tested for the part. Both of them got Paramount contracts, but Niven got nothing. Goulding then spoke to Irving Thalberg, the lofty MGM executive, and as a result Niven was hired as an extra in *Mutiny on the Bounty,* because, so the story goes, of his earlier connection with the ship at Santa Barbara. As the news mysteriously crept through Hollywood's exclusive circles that Thalberg was planning to sign Niven to a contract, Goulding and Hawks put their creative talent together and convinced Samuel Goldwyn that he should study Niven's screentest. The next day, Goldwyn ordered the Britisher to appear at his office. He told the fledgling: "I'm going to give you a seven-year contract. I'll pay you very little ‡ and I won't put you into a Goldwyn picture till

*The film eventually starred Ann Harding, with Louis Hayward in the part for which Niven had been tested.
†Unfortunately, no verification of Niven's precise moviemaking schedule in this period has been compiled.
‡$100 a week.

you've learned your job. Now you have a base. Go out and tell the studios you're under contract to Goldwyn, do anything they offer you, get experience, work hard, and in a year or so, if you're any good, I'll give you a role!" Niven was then ushered from the mogul's office to the publicity department, where his life story was duly recorded, but glorified (they promoted his father to general), and from there to a production manager's assistant, who showed him to his cubbyhole dressing room. The first thing he did, after strolling around the tradition-bound United Artists studio, was to buy a new car.

His first *speaking* part was in Paramount's *Without Regret* (1935), starring Elissa Landi. Niven's one-liner in that picture, which co-starred Paul Cavanagh, was "Goodbye, my dear," spoken at a railroad-station set. This was followed a few days later with *Barbary Coast* (1935) at United Artists. As a Cockney sailor in San Francisco, he

said, "Orl rite, I'll go," and was summarily thrown out of a soundstage saloon window. At Columbia, he played a fun-loving poet in *A Feather in Her Hat* (1935), a mother-love story starring Pauline Lord. In *The Moon's a Balloon,* Niven tells of his nervousness at playing this one lengthy scene in the film and how director Alfred Santell had him enact the scene of arriving at a party and spreading good humor among the guests, after alerting the entire crew to applaud, no matter how bad he was. The novice stumbled into the action, bumped into people, knocked over drinks, and mixed up dialog. Santell commended him, the crew applauded, and he was asked to try it once more—this time with film in the camera. Then, Niven relaxed.

Goldwyn put him to work in his production of Rachel Crothers's *Splendor* (United Artists, 1935) as the useless son of a once-wealthy family that has lost its finances. The oldest son (Joel McCrea)

Advertisement for SPLENDOR (UA '35)

is supposed to marry into wealth and save his destitute family, but instead he marries for love (Miriam Hopkins). The family's matriarch (Helen Westley) then plots to have her son's wife respond to the advances of a broker (Paul Cavanagh) in the hope that McCrea, in turn, will be handed a posh job. Miss Hopkins rebels, however, and finds her own job. One scene called for Niven to chat with Hopkins while he casually puffed on a cigarette. When director Elliott Nugent saw the rushes, he accused Niven of trying to steal the scene with his odd handling of the cigarette. Niven explained that since he had never smoked before, he did not know what he was doing wrong. At an additional cost of $2,000, a coach was assigned to teach Niven how to hold a cigarette (although he has never taken up the habit of inhaling). Then the sequence was reshot to everyone's satisfaction.

Most filmgoers recall *Rose Marie* (MGM, 1936) as the second outing of Jeanette MacDonald and Nelson Eddy. Some may even recall that in this reconstructed operetta,* James Stewart played the role of Miss MacDonald's fugitive brother, who is hiding in the Canadian woods, only to be captured by Sergeant Bruce (Eddy) of the Canadian Northwest Mounties. If one watches attentively, however, David is also present, as Teddy, one of the many suitors cast aside by the prima donna.

In June 1936, he was seen briefly in Paramount's *Palm Springs*, a modest musical aimed at both furthering the career of Frances Langford and introducing Smith Ballew to filmgoers. It missed its target on both shots. Niven was cast as the wealthy other man who is quickly forgotten by the heroine. Then, still in search of acting experience, David signed for a play at the Pasadena Playhouse. In *Wedding*, his part was not much more than a walk-on with a few lines of dialog in the third act. But after touting his participation as much more than it actually was to his Hollywood friends at various parties, the opening-night audience included Herbert Marshall and Charles Laughton in the front row. Niven was completely flustered by their presence and flubbed his lines after downing several generous portions of Scotch. He was dismissed from the cast.

Goldwyn then placed David into his production of *Dodsworth* (United Artists, 1936) as British Army Major Clyde Lockert, one of those enraptured by Fran Dodsworth (Ruth Chatterton) in her pur-

---

*Opened on Broadway at the Imperial Theatre (September 2, 1934, 581 performances) with Dennis King and Mary Ellis starred.

With Spring Byington in PALM SPRINGS (Par '36)

suit of eternal youth. Her husband (Walter Huston) tries to understand, but eventually gives her up as hopeless. The film version of the 1934 Broadway play (Shubert Theatre: February 24, 1934, 315 performances), which had starred Walter Huston and Fay Bainter, was adapted from the Sinclair Lewis novel by Sidney Howard and directed by William Wyler. The only review about his appearance in the film that Niven kept was from the *Detroit Free Press*. It stated: "In this picture we're privileged to see the great Samuel Goldwyn's latest discovery—All we can say about this actor (?) is that he is tall, dark and not the slightest bit handsome." David admits to a "wooden performance," accountable, in part, to his dislike for Wyler.

He was loaned to Twentieth Century–Fox for a "B" picture, *Thank You, Jeeves* (1936), based on a P. G. Wodehouse story. As Bertie Wooster, Niven, with his valet, Jeeves (Arthur Treacher), becomes involved with a young woman (Virginia Field) in a crisis stemming from gun-running. It was Niven's first leading role. In New York, the film opened at the Palace Theatre on a double-bill with *Two in a Crowd* (Universal, 1936) starring Joan Bennett and Joel McCrea, the latter performer being one of Goldwyn's chief acting props in the mid-1930s.

Warner Bros. then sent for Niven to test for the supporting role of Captain Randall in their screen adaptation of a story by Michel Jacoby to be called *The Charge of the Light Brigade* (1936). The test, under the supervision of an ex-Hungarian cavalry officer, director Michael Curtiz, was with Olivia de Havilland, who was also the feminine star of the swashbuckling picture. Six actors had been tested, and when David's turn came, Curtiz asked where his script was. He replied that it was in the makeup tent at the far end of the studio. "Run and get it," Curtiz demanded. Niven, hot and sweaty in his wool costume, was angry at himself because he figured he would flop the test. He replied curtly: "You can damn well run and get it yourself." While onlookers froze in astonishment, Curtiz thundered: "Dismiss the others, and give him the part." Curtiz built up the role of Captain Randall and thereafter referred to David as "that goddamned Sandhurst man."

At a cost of $1.2 million, *The Charge of the Light Brigade,* loosely based on authoritative British history,* was photographed by Sol Polito at various California sites. A complete fort was

*The 1968 United Artists version attempted to portray correctly the British officers who bungled the military operation. Their roles in the 1936 film were reduced to bit parts as having little to do with the charge. The part of Captain Randall was omitted altogether from the 1968 edition.

With Merle Oberon at a Los Angeles play opening, August, 1936

On the set of THE CHARGE OF THE LIGHT BRIGADE (WB '36) with assistant director Jack Sullivan, Errol Flynn, and director Michael Curtiz

constructed west of the San Fernando Valley, and much of the actual charge was lensed at Chatsworth. The screen accounting was spectacular in depicting the charge of the British Twenty-Seventh Lancers led by Major Geoffrey Vickers (Errol Flynn) against twenty-five thousand Russian infantry, artillery, and cavalry soldiers in the Crimea. Within the lusty adventure film, more than two-thirds of the seven hundred "British" soldiers hired for the film were "killed" in the ride, including Niven's Captain Randall, the second in command.

Niven and Errol Flynn struck up a solid friendship on the Warners' set, and with Flynn's separation from his actress wife, Lili Damita, they became roommates in a house rented by Rosalind Russell. In what Niven describes as "a fairly ostentatious bachelor existence," alcohol was freely consumed, girls were regularly entertained, and they practiced the habit of smoking or chewing what they called "Kef," or marijuana.

On his home lot, David was next cast as Gerald Preston, an English Army officer in love with

Merle Oberon in *Beloved Enemy* (United Artists, 1936).† With the 1921 Irish rebellion as a background, Oberon loves the Irish leader (Brian Aherne), patterned on the real rebel Michael Collins, who is killed by his own people when he votes for a truce with England. In its time, the film received rather more praise than it deserved. Frank S. Nugent (*New York Times*) wrote: "A fine and mature and dignified drama . . . it has the stamp of quality on each of its departments . . ."

Early in 1937, Goldwyn sold Niven's work-a-day time to Universal for a subordinate role in *We Have Our Moments,* which reunited the once popular love team of Sally Eilers and James Dunn. It was not much of a picture, but "the strain of lunacy which weaves its shy, nervous course through the proceedings makes them seem fresh . . ." (William Boehnel, *New York World Telegram*). David was cast as Gilling, a classy English crook in league with the con-artist team of Thurston Hall and Marjorie Gateson. In the course of the shipboard proceedings, Niven is knocked out cold by dillettante detective Dunn.

†Many film historians are convinced that the "GBS" (Great Big Star) with whom Niven had an affair in 1936, and who occupies space in *The Moon's a Balloon* was Merle Oberon, herself under contract to Goldwyn. In fact, during October 1936, Miss Oberon publicly confirmed reports that she and Niven would wed, substantiating the rumors that they had been "that way" as far back as 1935. In *A State of Heat* (1972), Sheilah Graham has many words to say about a famous movie actress with almond-shaped eyes and her amors of the mid-1930s. The linkage is there for anyone who cares to make the possible connection.

The hit of the minor movie was Mischa Auer as a French secret service man.

Later that year, Niven was loaned to David O. Selznick for *The Prisoner of Zenda* (United Artists, 1937), which had some sequences filmed in sepia color. Niven and the film's star, Ronald Colman, were both part of the British colony in Hollywood, and David was convinced that it was because of his friend Colman that he won the role of Fritz von Tarlenheim, the officer in charge of King Rudolf's (Colman) horses.* Told by director John Cromwell to play the role straight, Niven did it that way until he felt certain that "the result was dim." He then asked if he could do it once his way—for comedy—and was permitted to do so. Thus the character appears in the completed movie as the only source of relief from the Ruritanian dramatics. During the long filming schedule of four months, Niven was given his own stand-in (a status symbol) for the first time. But there was still something prankish about Niven, for it was he who gin-spiked the harmless contents of a punch bowl used on the set, which caused the extras in a banquet scene to be more than politely enthusiastic.

Niven was again on loan-out for his next picture, *Dinner at the Ritz* (1937). Filmed at Twentieth Century–Fox's New World studios near London, he is Paul de Brack, a detective disguised as a flippant man-of-the-world who is determined to stamp out financial racketeers. Along with Romney Brent, an American detective, he comes to the aid of Annabella, who is equal in her determination to clear her late father's name. The three of them must combat notorious gunman Paul Lukas. *Variety* yawned about this import: "The pace is so slow on the whole that patience is sorely tried, and nowhere along the line does the story, director or performance take on any sparkle." Frank S. Nugent (*New York Times*) was so uninvolved with the intricacies of the overthick plot that he had time to notice: "There was actually one scene where we thought we detected a crumpet crumb on Mr. Niven's collar."

On his return from England, David found that he was now without living quarters since Errol Flynn had temporarily reconciled with his wife and had taken over the house as a second-honeymoon cottage. Niven rented a beach house at Santa Monica from Marion Davies and acquired two roommates, fellow English actor Robert Coote, and Australian-born Walter Kerry Davis. "It was a very happy combination," Niven recalls, "and we entertained twenty-four hours a day." Carole Lombard, Alice Faye, Ida Lupino, and Cary Grant were among those who gave the house its name of "Cirrhosis-by-the-Sea."

Professionally, Niven had to content himself with further loan-out assignments as Goldwyn shuffled his stock company on and off the lot depending on his production schedules.‡ David got to work with Elsa Maxwell's friend, Ernst Lubitsch, after all, in the remake (1938) of Paramount's *Bluebeard's Eighth Wife*, with screenplay by Charles Brackett and Billy Wilder, based on the English-language version (Ritz Theatre: September 19, 1921, 155 performances) of Alfred Savoir's French farce. "Working with Lubitsch in the company of such professional experts and such privately wonderful human beings as Gary Cooper and Claudette Colbert was a joy that lasted for about three months," Niven later admitted. His role, as a man hopeful of capturing Colbert before she becomes Cooper's wife number eight, however, was undistinguished.† Charles Chaplin's advice to Niven after viewing the film was: "Don't be like the great majority of actors—don't just stand around waiting your turn to speak. Learn to listen!"

Niven went over to Twentieth Century–Fox as one of four brothers who clear their father's name in *Four Men and a Prayer* (1938). The father (C. Aubrey Smith), after a court-martial and dishonorable discharge from His Majesty's Service, is murdered as he is about to turn over proof of a munitions conspiracy to his sons (Richard Greene, George Sanders, Niven, and William Henry). Niven's offcamera friend, Loretta Young, was the heroine of this John Ford–directed picture. She played the daughter of the munitions king who is responsible for Smith's demise.

Niven remained at Fox for *Three Blind Mice* (1938), again with Loretta Young, who, through her mentor, studio boss Darryl F. Zanuck, had a great deal of influence over the casting decisions on her pictures. In this comedy of three Kansas girls (Young, Pauline Moore, and Marjorie Weaver) in search of rich husbands, Joel McCrea is one of those snagged, along with Niven and Stuart Erwin.

---

*In the 1922 Metro film version starring Lewis Stone and Alice Terry, the Fritz role is missing; in the 1952 MGM version with Stewart Granger, Deborah Kerr, and Jane Greer, Robert Coote appeared as Fritz Von Tarlenheim.

‡In 1937–38, the Samuel Goldwyn "family" consisted of Walter Brennan, Gary Cooper, Jerome Cowan, Joel McCrea, Niven, John Payne, Frank Shields, Frances Gifford, Sigrid Gurie, Miriam Hopkins, Helen Jepson, Andrea Leeds, Ella Logan, Merle Oberon, Barbara O'Neil, Evelyn Terry, and Virginia Verrill.

†In the 1923 Paramount version starring Gloria Swanson, Robert Agnew had the Niven role.

With C. Aubrey Smith, George Sanders, Richard Greene, and William Henry in FOUR MEN AND A PRAYER (20th '38)

Although his romance with Merle Oberon had long since dimmed (she would finally wed producer Alexander Korda in 1939), he was assigned to work with her and Gary Cooper in *The Cowboy and the Lady* (United Artists, 1938) as one of her disappointed suitors. Because he impersonated a British diplomat in the picture, the diplomatic corps objected to one of its number receiving the bad end of the stick romantically, and an obliging Goldwyn had his footage excised from the release print.

The Dawn Patrol (Warner Bros., 1938)* was "the picture that graduated me into the major leagues." Requested for the film by his mentor Edmund Goulding, twenty-eight-year-old Niven was teamed with Errol Flynn, Basil Rathbone, and Donald Crisp. When the command of the 59th Squadron of the British Royal Flying Corps in France during World War I is turned over to Major Courtney (Flynn), he is grounded because of the promotion. Forced to make the same kind of decisions for which he called his predecessor (Rathbone) a butcher, Flynn sends the brother (Morton Lowry) of his best friend (Niven) on a bombing flight from which he does not return.

Niven then refused to associate with Flynn, who undertakes the suicidal mission of bombing German ammunition dumps, an assignment for which Niven had volunteered, knowing it meant certain death. When Flynn is shot down, Niven takes over as commander of the squadron. It was a strongly dramatic role guaranteed to bring Niven's screen presence to the fore. For a change he had a part with some depth to it, and in his delineation of Scotty he gave clear indications that the character was a very complex individual.

Odd as it may seem in retrospect, Niven initially turned down the role of Edgar in *Wuthering Heights* (United Artists, 1939) when he learned that William Wyler was the director. Goldwyn put the actor on suspension. Wyler himself persuaded Niven to do it with the promise, "Don't worry, you'll have fun. I'm no son of a bitch anymore," although Niven refers to the role as an "actor's nightmare." ‡ Edgar Linton is a weak, wealthy nobleman who marries Cathy (Merle Oberon) after Heathcliff (Laurence Olivier), her true love, is run off the Yorkshire moors. Niven is later unable to prevent his kindly sister (Geraldine Fitzgerald) from ruining her life by marrying the

*Previously filmed in 1930 by Warner Bros. with Douglas Fairbanks, Jr. in Niven's role.
‡The role would be acted by Ian Ogilvy in the 1971 American-International remake.

With Errol Flynn in THE DAWN PATROL (WB '38)

With Flora Robson and Merle Oberon in WUTHERING HEIGHTS (UA '39)

brooding Olivier, who has returned to the moor country a rich but love-starved man. In his passive role, Niven's Edgar Linton is not on the scene when his beloved wife dies in Olivier's arms. He enters the bedroom with the doctor (Donald Crisp) and finds her dead in bed, where Olivier has placed her after a melodramatic demise.

The emotional scene called for Niven to sob at the foot of the bed, but he was unable to evoke a viable tear. Menthol was puffed into his open eyes, but this method failed. "Instead of tears coming out of my eyes, green slime came out of my nose," he admits, which sent the corpse [Merle Oberon] to her dressing room. The sequence was finally shot from behind Niven as he went through the motions of sobbing over his bereavement.

Despite the calamities of completing his acting chores in *Wuthering Heights,* and despite the lion's share of critical and public attention going to Oberon and Olivier, Niven received his critical due. Otis Ferguson, writing in the *New Republic,* reported: "David Niven triumphs over a weak and unhappy part as he always does, by a controlling sensitivity and intelligence that go beyond simple trouping." Mr. Niven, as a performer, was definitely coming of age.

Ginger Rogers gleefully tossed aside her dancing slippers for *Bachelor Mother* (RKO, 1939) and Niven was loaned to director Garson Kanin as her co-star.* The superlative comedy deals with a salesgirl named Polly (Rogers) who finds a baby on a foundling home's doorstep and is immediately adjudged its mother. She is unable to convince anyone that she is innocent, including her employer (Charles Coburn), who assumes that his playboy son (Niven) is the father. Niven is mortified by her persistent denials of motherhood, but falls in love with her and accepts the status of fatherhood imposed upon him by his elder. In one especially pungent scene, he misreads to Rogers from a baby-care book that has its pages stuck together. He insists the instructions say to "place oatmeal on a piece of gauze and rub it into the baby's navel."

David was back into military uniform in the Goldwyn production *The Real Glory* (United Artists, 1939) as Lieutenant McCool, a soldier of fortune assigned to help quell the guerilla uprising in the Philippines shortly after the Spanish-American War. Gary Cooper and Andrea Leeds were

*In the remake, *Bundle of Joy* (RKO, 1956), starring Debbie Reynolds, Eddie Fisher had the Niven role. Both American versions were derived from *Kleine Mutti* (1935), directed in Germany by Henry Koster.

In BACHELOR MOTHER (RKO '39)

the stars supplying romance between bouts of cholera, native attacks, and friction between Leeds and Kay Johnson, the latter as the commanding officer's wife. Niven and Broderick Crawford were mostly in the story for laughs, the former waggish, the latter burly. Offscreen, Crawford became one of Niven's cohorts and close drinking buddies.

In the summer of 1939, King George VI and his Queen visited President Franklin D. Roosevelt in Washington, D.C. To honor the occasion the British colony in Hollywood devised a radio show to be heard at the time the royal couple were picnicking at Hyde Park. The variety program consisted of songs, recitations, imitations, etc., and employed the talents of Laurence Olivier, Brian Aherne, Reginald Gardiner, Vivien Leigh, Errol Flynn, Ronald Colman, Cary Grant, Niven, et al. It was later discovered that their efforts had been in vain because President Roosevelt's battery-operated radio ran down just before the stellar show was to go on the air.

Loretta Young boosted Niven's career yet again when she requested him for her leading man in *Eternally Yours* (1939), a Walter Wanger production for United Artists. He played the magician known alternately as Tony or the Great Arturo, who marries Young and makes her part of his disappearing act, not counting on her becoming bored with their show-business existence and hankering for a nice home in Connecticut. She leaves him and becomes romantically embroiled with Broderick Crawford, whom she likes but, of course, does not love. Niven pursues her around the world,* but does not win her back until he performs his parachute escape act over the Lagoon of Nations at the New York World's Fair. (Yes, Young is there to cushion his fall.) Despite the promotional gimmick of *Eternally Yours* being the first major feature to tie-in with the 1939 World's Fair, the comedy was slim going. Said *Variety:* "Since the ornateness of tinsel and foil inevitably wears off, it's quite natural that *Eternally Yours* should find itself tottering after 99 minutes."

At this point, carefree Niven awakened to a fact of life that he had heretofore chosen to ignore—

that Goldwyn was receiving huge sums of money each time he loaned him out, while only paying him his contract salary.† His agent, Bill Hawks, was not inclined to make strong demands of Goldwyn, so Niven elicited the help of one of filmdom's top agents, Leland Hayward. Hayward went to see Goldwyn, who, after a two-minute hearing, barred him from the lot. Niven was then suspended when he rejected a "really awful script," and for a time Goldwyn refused to speak to him. Nevertheless, he continued to accept half of Niven's paychecks for the actor's performances on "Lux Radio Theatre" and other radio programs.

Finally, with the help of Fred Astaire and his wife, a "cease-fire" was arranged between Goldwyn and Niven. The film executive offered his protégé a new contract with a new salary, and a film role that Niven was anxious to do, *Raffles* (United Artists, 1939).† It was a tangible verification that Goldwyn *did* actually consider Niven the new Ronald Colman and intended to give him the same big career push he had given Colman a decade or more previous. Before a deal could be worked out between Goldwyn and agent Leland Hayward, however, Niven got himself into boiling water with yet another mogul, Harry Cohn of Columbia. He was sailing with Errol Flynn in the latter's yacht *Sirocco*, when they sighted Cohn's *Jobella* in trouble and towed her into Balboa. When Cohn failed to register proper gratitude for their friendly endeavors, Niven had an attorney draw up an official notification quoting the Salvage Act of 1912 and claimed half-ownership of the *Jobella*. This playful gesture resulted in Niven being barred from Columbia for the rest of Cohn's life (1891–1958).

The new Goldwyn contract was duly signed and then Niven was escorted personally by his employer to a dressing room befitting a star's status. Orders were given to redecorate the room to Niven's liking. He was back home, and all was forgiven.

Raffles, based on E. W. Hornung's novel of 1899, *The Amateur Cracksman,* tells the tale of debonair thief A. J. Raffles, who literally walks away with gems from London society matrons. At

---

*Director Tay Garnett had left-over footage he had shot on a round-the-world cruise, some of which had already been used in *Trade Winds* (United Artists, 1938).

†In his book *Light Your Torches and Pull Up Your Tights* (Arlington House, 1973), Garnett recalls that during the making of *Eternally Yours,* Niven was performing weekly chores on the Sunday night "Kraft Music Hall" radio show, with half of his radio pay going to Goldwyn. Once, the Kraft sponsors sent Niven a basket of delicacies. The actor cut all the contents in half, including the basket, and sent the half-package to Goldwyn.

†Filmed three times previously in the United States: in 1917 (Hiller and Wilk) with John Barrymore, in 1925 (Universal) with House Peters, in 1930 (United Artists) with Ronald Colman. In 1960, a Mexican version would appear with Rafael Bertrand. The play version of *Raffles* had opened in London in May 1906 with Gerald Du Maurier and was revived on the West End with Du Maurier in 1914. It was first presented in New York (Princess Theatre: October 27, 1903, 168 performances) with Kyrle Bellew in the title role. Bellew revived it in New York in 1910 for 24 performances at the Gaiety Theatre.

With Leyland Hodgson and Olivia de Havilland in RAFFLES (UA '39)

the scene of each crime, he frustrates Scotland Yard detective Dudley Digges by leaving a note, such as "Sorry, but I have a better use for this," signed "The Amateur Cracksman." He loves Olivia de Havilland, whose brother (Douglas Watson) owes £1,000 in gambling debts. He offers to help and steals the necklace of Dame May Whitty, who refers to him as "a really charming man." Petty thief Peter Godfrey is accused of the crime and allowed to escape from jail because Digges knows he will lead the police to the real culprit. He does. Whitty's spouse (Lionel Pape) has placed a £1,000 reward on the stolen necklace, which is duly handed over to Niven, who gives it to Watson, and then back again to Pape. Niven escapes, but only long enough to leave a last note for Digges requesting him to meet him at seven o'clock for his "last performance." He climbs through de Havilland's window to bid her goodbye, saying: "I hate to keep anyone waiting but sometimes you have to." She understands and knows he will return to her after he has paid his debt to Scotland Yard by turning himself in to Digges.

Under Sam Wood's direction, the characterizations emerged as real people and Niven appeared very dapper and at ease as the Amateur Cracksman. *Time* magazine found that he "plays the part with crookish cunning" and said that the film was "entertainment as pleasant as pointless." The *New York Times*'s Frank S. Nugent stated that Niven "makes the game worth playing and the film worth seeing." But neither in 1940 nor today does Niven's loosely-limbered performance match the earlier performance of Colman, who gave the crook role that extra dash of civility and gentlemanly recklessness that verged so politely on rakishness.

Twice the production of *Raffles* was reportedly shut down, with the Goldwyn studio announcing that Niven was rejoining the Highland Light Infantry, but the actor did not leave Hollywood until September 1939, soon after the British declared war on the Nazis. Goldwyn had to shelve plans to make both a follow-up to *Raffles* and a London-filmed biography of Colowan Rowan of Scotland Yard, each to star Niven. These proposed pictures might have launched him into major stardom.

Goldwyn's parting words to him were "Don't worry, David, I'll tell Hitler to shoot around you."* In mid-January 1940, *Time* magazine re-

*Supposedly Niven the wag told Goldwyn, in order to convince him to let him have military leave, "Visualize me, Sam, going over the top and yelling, 'Come on, Lads, for God, King, and Sam Goldwyn!'"

ported that Niven was engaged to war nurse Ursula Kenyon-Slaney and "then cinema actor Niven joined the British army." What *Time* did not record was Niven's being turned down by the RAF because "we don't encourage actors to join this service."

Commissioned a second lieutenant in the Rifle Brigade, he was stationed near London when he met a WAAF, Primula Rollo, the daughter of RAF officer William Rollo. "There was never a shadow of doubt in my mind that this was the one," he said, and they were married in the village of Huish near Marlborough, England, in a small Norman church on September 21, 1940. She was twenty-one and he was thirty. Trubshawe, Niven's old buddy from the reckless days of Malta, and his wife were their witnesses. Primmie, as Niven's wife was called, resigned from the service when she married, and spent the remainder of the war at defense plants building Hurricane fighter planes, moving from one bombed-out cottage to another. She had her first baby, David Jr., who was born during an air raid, in December 1942, while Niven was in England as commander of a Phantom squadron, a type of intelligence outfit.

In 1942, the army loaned Niven to British Aviation to co-star with Leslie Howard in *The First of the Few* (General Film Distributors).* One of the clauses of the film contract stipulated: "Work on any picture will be suspended while any invasion attempt is being made, so that David Niven may return to his regiment. Work will be resumed immediately after the invasion attempt has failed." The picture was a biographical study of Reginald Mitchell, the man who designed the Spitfire plane. Howard, who produced and directed the film, played Mitchell, whose story is told in flashback by Niven as a fighter-station commander in the early days of the war. As former test-pilot Geoffrey Crisp, Niven's character knows Mitchell well and recalls that the designer hurried to build a plane "faster than anything on earth—tougher than any other fighter and able to turn on a sixpence." The film's title was derived from Winston Churchill's famous statement: "Never in the field of human conflict was so much owed by so many to so few." In the United States the picture was released as *Spitfire* (RKO, 1943). In reviewing the picture, Thomas M. Pryor (*New York Times*) had some harsh words about Niven's acting style, reporting: "[he] depends chiefly on facial squirming to develop the character."

In 1944 the Army again loaned Niven (by then a major) to Two Cities for a film based on experiments made in psychological training for the Department of Army Psychiatry of the War Office. *The Way Ahead* (Eagle Lion), written by Eric Ambler and Peter Ustinov, told of seven civilian recruits in the British Army and of their adjustment to an infantry platoon. Niven was cast as their commanding officer. Directed by Carol Reed, the film was detailed by *Variety* as: "No soft-pedalling here, no understatement of British guts, but unashamed glorying in a nation's girding up its loins to go and conquer its enemies." The movie was first shown to the British press on D-Day, which inspired even more enthusiasm for the production. C. A. Lejeune (*London Observer*) penned: "But what about the actors, you will ask. Bless their hearts, I had forgotten they were actors. I was thinking they were real." After the public saw *The Way Ahead*, it became a training vehicle at Niven's former school, Sandhurst.

Shortly after Niven's Army enlistment, Winston Churchill told him: "You did a fine thing to give up a most promising career to fight for your country," and added: "Mark you, had you not done so, it would have been despicable." Up until 1944, Niven had not seen actual battlefield action, but when he was assigned, as a lieutenant colonel, to the American First Army division, he was among the first to land at Normandy in June 1944. Before departing, the Nivens were joined in a belated christening celebration for David Jr. by godmother Vivien Leigh and her husband, Laurence Olivier. Godfather Noël Coward was also on hand.

In the spring of 1945, Niven was with a British unit in Western Germany and was about to cross the Rhine. With death everywhere around, he suddenly felt: "I was sure I was running out of borrowed time, and would get it." As the men made last-minute checks of their gear and weapons, a mail sergeant appeared and handed the actor-soldier an envelope which he opened without glancing at the return address. The contents read: "Dear Sir: This is to inform you that we have absorbed the Leland Hayward Agency of which you were a client. Therefore, we are now handling your business. Sincerely, Music Corporation of America." Niven remembers that he "was cheered up considerably. The thought of death no longer chilled my heart. I was in safe hands. MCA had never lost a man, and they weren't going to lose one now." Six months later, after receiving the American Legion of Merit, he was discharged.

*This was Leslie Howard's last film. He was killed in 1943 on a flight from Lisbon to England.

With General Sir Bernard C. T. Paget (right) somewhere in England in November, 1942

With Marius Goring in A MATTER OF LIFE AND DEATH (a.k.a. STAIRWAY TO HEAVEN) (General Film Distributors '46)

Back in London, he immediately sent a cable to Goldwyn, who responded with the news that he was signing him to a new five-year contract. It was a reassuring gesture to a man who had been out of the Hollywood cinema limelight for so long. His first postwar assignment was to be on loan to Michael Powell and Emeric Pressburger for their J. Arthur Rank production of *A Matter of Life and Death* (General Film Distributors, 1946).* "This was a huge relief," Niven has admitted, "because although I had been disguising it from Primmie, I was extremely nervous about my future. Six months is too long for an actor to be out of business; six years is almost certain disaster."

Jack Cardiff photographed Niven's re-entry into the world of film. The film fantasy's earthly scenes were in vivid Technicolor, while the "time" spent in heaven was done in tones of sepia. Niven appears as RAF squadron leader Peter Carter, whose mortal days are scheduled to end when he leaps, without benefit of parachute, from a burning bomber plane over the English Channel in the final days of the war. He is given a

reprieve, however, when the messenger (Marius Goring) sent from heaven to escort him to the regions above is lost in the dense fog. Niven, for that reason, survives his dive, and manages to fall in love with an American WAC (Kim Hunter). The messenger finds him and tries to persuade him to die and go to heaven as scheduled, but Niven refuses. A celestial trial is conducted with Raymond Massey, as the opposing attorney representing the Court of Records, versus Roger Livesey, as the lawyer in favor of giving the pilot another chance at life. As a result of the trial, Niven is spared from being forced to enter the heavenly regions.

With its celestial setting, *A Matter of Life and Death* was bound to be compared with Robert Montgomery's *Here Comes Mr. Jordan* (Columbia, 1941) or Cary Grant's humor-bent *Topper* (MGM, 1937). The more somber-toned British entry did not find many champions in this country. *Redbook* magazine labeled it "a labored fantasy, rather than the delightful whimsy it might have been," while *Time* magazine more generously judged: " . . . it is adult as well as light-hearted

*Released in the United States on December 18, 1946, as *Stairway to Heaven* (Universal).

and has the admirable quality of taking itself seriously only to kid itself." Bosley Crowther (*New York Times*) graciously considered Niven's performance as "sensitive and real." More astute members of John Q. Public noted that the World War II duration had done much more than age the once fractious David Niven; he now had adopted a distracted, detached look that would become an important facet of his screen persona. It was an ambiance that *seemed* to suggest: "Look old boy, I find this moviemaking a bit embarrassing. Do you mind looking the other way, while I go through my paces. Thanks, old chap."

The English took *A Matter of Life and Death* far more seriously than the Americans. The picture was selected as the first of Britain's Royal Film Performances.

Meanwhile, the Nivens' second son, James Graham, was born in November 1945, and almost immediately earned the nickname of "Jamie," which has accompanied him through life to date.

Because of a scarcity of transportation at the war's end, it was decided that Niven should go on ahead to Hollywood to renew his studio obligations and to locate a suitable house for his family. It was agreed that Mrs. Niven and the two boys would follow within a few months.

After a welcoming party in New York at his former place of employment, the 21 Club, he took a train to Los Angeles. Also on board was David O. Selznick, who forebodingly told him: "It's going to be tough for you. It's a whole new ball game now. A lot of new stars and new directors have come up while you've been away. You're lucky to have Goldwyn behind you." A rather concerned Niven was greeted at the Sam Goldwyn lot with a party and was about to attend a bachelor shindig at Romanoff's in his honor when he became suddenly ill with bronchial pneumonia and was placed under hospitalization for several days.

When he was well enough, Goldwyn informed him that he was again going on loan, this time to Universal where he would join his *Bachelor Mother* co-star, Ginger Rogers, in a historical romance, *Magnificent Doll* (1946). Niven was well aware that Miss Rogers was slipping into a career slump and that this picture was not going to change her faltering status. After all, he had read Irving Stone's less-than-factual screenplay based on the adult life of Dolly Madison, wife of the fourth U.S. President. Niven thought the scenario "gibberish" and did not want to make the film, but he could neither afford a suspension nor postpone his reintroduction to Hollywood filmmaking. The old California studio system was already

With Ginger Rogers in THE MAGNIFICENT DOLL (Univ '46)

crumbling, and Niven realized he must reestablish himself somehow with the public—and fast! Staying off the screen would not be one of those ways.

In *The Magnificent Doll*, directed by the once-so-adept Frank Borzage, Niven is, of all people, Aaron Burr, the clever and enigmatic politician who becomes a thorn in the side of American nationalism of the early 1800s. Miss Rogers floundered about not so daintily as a debutante version of the first lady, with Burgess Meredith rather grumpy as dull old James Madison. The consensus of critical opinion and film fans was that Niven was badly miscast.

Back at Samuel Goldwyn Productions, the colorful executive was too concerned in promoting his big picture, *The Best Years of Our Lives* (RKO, 1946), and shepherding the careers of Danny Kaye, Dana Andrews, and Farley Granger, to devote much time to Niven's well-being. Thus the Britisher was shipped over to Paramount where he would join Loretta Young for the fourth time in *The Perfect Marriage* (1946), which Hal B. Wallis was producing. The advertisements for the film proclaimed that Niven and Miss Young "Fight a little . . . Play a little . . . Love a lot." In the story they are a sedentary couple who decide, on their tenth wedding anniversary, that they are no longer in love. After several bickering sessions they conclude that divorce is the only solution, but jealousy creeps into the tale when Eddie Albert appears as Young's suitor and Virginia Field (conveniently) turns up as Niven's old flame raring to renew the acquaintanceship. The divorce plans slow down because of the couple's child (Nona Griffith), and distractingly the action switches from light comedy to serious drama. Needless to say, the couple reconciles and presumably lives happily thereafter. *Newsweek* magazine accoladed Niven's efforts in this hogwash as "gallant," and *Redbook* magazine said that he was "less boyish but as adept as ever in light or emotional scenes."

By the time *The Perfect Marriage* was completed, David had bought a house in Pacific Palisades, next door to the junior Douglas Fairbanks domicile. Built in the early 1900s and once owned by Vicki Baum (*Grand Hotel*'s authoress), Niven's new house had a spectacular view of the Pacific Ocean and the Santa Monica Mountains. The house was painted pink, a favorite exterior treatment in California in those days. (One can only wonder what Senator Joseph McCarthy thought of this fad.)

In May 1946, six weeks after his family had arrived in America, Niven and Primmie left their boys with a nurse-companion and embarked on a week's fishing and golfing sojourn to Monterey, California, with Clark Gable, Rex Harrison, Ida Lupino, and Nigel Bruce. They returned to Hollywood on Sunday, May 19, to attend a party in Primmie's honor at the home of Tyrone Power and his actress wife, Annabella. After an early poolside barbecue, the group, which now included Harrison's celebrity wife, Lilli Palmer, moved indoors where someone suggested playing "sardines," a game of adult hide-and-seek, accomplished in the dark. While David found a hiding place under an upstairs bed, Primmie opened a door, thinking it led to a closet. In the darkness, she plunged down a flight of stairs leading to the cellar. She was rushed to St. John's Hospital in Santa Monica, but died on May 21, 1946, of a fractured skull and brain contusions. The twenty-five-year-old girl never regained consciousness.

Desolate, Niven stayed with the Ronald Colmans for a few weeks while Joan Crawford supervised the care of the Niven children. Later, he moved into the Pink House, where each weekend was party time, in a conscious effort to forget his grief. He buried himself, further, in work on *The Other Love* (United Artists, 1947).

Produced by David Lewis for Enterprises Pictures, the screenplay was from Erich Maria Remarque's gentle story. In its film presentation it became unadulterated soap opera with a beautiful thin pianist (Barbara Stanwyck) slowly dying of consumption and broken career plans midst the serenity of a sanitarium in the Swiss Alps.* Her attending physician is Anthony Stanton (Niven), who has all the "do's" and "don't's" for her convalescence at his fingertips. Quite naturally, she falls in love with him, but is angered when she believes that he cares for her out of pity, and she runs off to Monte Carlo for a brief fling with an international playboy (Richard Conte). The doctor follows her, convinces her of his sincerity, takes her back to the clinic, and marries her. Her final days are spent in tranquil acceptance of her fate.

Stanwyck managed to inject some action into the passive proceedings, whether rising up in frustration at her shattered concert career† and breaking a classical record to which she is listen-

---

*The Swiss Alps "location" scenes were partially shot on Mount Wilson and blended together with soundstage scenery.
†Ania Dorfman provided the offcamera piano playing for Miss Stanwyck.

ing, or careening along a road in a horse-driven carriage. But Niven seemed bemused by the story, his role, and the bristling authority of his co-star, the latter certainly the most dynamic of his vis-à-vis to that date onscreen. Said the *New Yorker* in a rather jocular frame of mind: "In the role of the doctor, David Niven, usually costumed in one of those dust jackets affected by United Cigar Store clerks, has a rather mortuary air, which is not too inappropriate in view of the fact that his patients tend to pop off quite abruptly."

Samuel Goldwyn brought together three of Hollywood's more genteel players for *The Bishop's Wife* (RKO, 1947). The screenplay by Robert Sherwood and Leonardo Bercovici, from Robert Nathan's novel, concerns Bishop Henry Brougham (Niven), who is harassed, curt, and unhappy because of his difficulties in raising money to build a new cathedral. When Gladys Cooper, as an imperious, rich parishioner, instructs him: "You will build that cathedral as I want it or you will not build it at all," he secretly calls her a "ghastly woman" and confides to his wife, Julia (Loretta Young): "I have a good mind to take those blueprints and give her a good whack across the mink coat." Alone in his library, Niven pleadingly prays aloud: "Can't you help me? Can't you tell me? O God, please help me." A choir of heavenly voices is heard, a door slams, and the Angel Dudley (Cary Grant) appears beside the fireplace: "What can I do for you? You asked for help."

Niven cannot believe Grant when he says he was sent in answer to his prayers and asks for proof. "Move the desk—fly around the room or something," he urges. But Grant is very much present, although he disappears and reappears without warning. He takes Niven back to the humble church of his beginnings where he is taught a lesson. Niven is also made to realize that his wife, who has been taken on shopping tours, to a skating rink, and to lunch by Grant, deserves more than he has given her since he became overly preoccupied with his cathedral construction. He emerges from the heavenly encounter a wiser and more peaceful individual.

Bosley Crowther loved *The Bishop's Wife* so much that he wrote in the *New York Times* of December 10, 1947: "We can not recommend you to a more delightful and appropriate Christmas show." Crowther added that Niven gave "a deli-ciously dexterous and droll characterization of a sorely pressed young bishop." Niven's clergyman role did not do for him what the Oscar-winning man-of-the-cloth part did for Bing Crosby in *Going My Way* (Paramount, 1944) and *The Bells of St. Mary* (RKO, 1945), but it was a welcome change of pace from his persistent portrayal of celluloid military men.

Just as David was becoming accustomed to his Pink House, along with bobbing around in the pool with his sons and watching his plantings grow, Goldwyn announced that he had been loaned to Alexander Korda for *Bonnie Prince Charlie* (British Lion, 1947).* He begged off for reasons related to British Inland Revenue and because he did not wish to disrupt the tranquil life of his young children. But Goldwyn knew how to manipulate his contractees. Niven was placed on suspension and was soon forced to give in to his boss's demands. With an entourage that included a nurse for his children, Niven and family were transplanted to headquarters in the outskirts of London, preparatory to the commencement of the costume picture.

In 1956, the star told Dean Jennings of the *Saturday Evening Post* that *Bonnie Prince Charlie* was "a story I loved, and had lived and relived as a boy in Scotland," but in *The Moon's a Balloon*, he calls it "one of those huge florid extravaganzas that reeked of disaster from the start."

With a yellow wig pinned to his dark hair, Niven is the "Young Pretender" to the English and Scots thrones, Charles Edward Stuart (1720–1788). He crosses the English Channel from France in 1745, organizes a troop of followers, and attempts to overthrow the Hanovers, with the help of influential Lord George Murray (Jack Hawkins) and Flora MacDonald (Margaret Leighton). The film "clanked toward its close" after nine working months filled with long hours, always just a day's jump ahead of the scriptwriter. It had been a rather messy experience for all concerned,† costing some $4 million.

On the last evening of shooting of *Bonnie Prince Charlie*, Niven drove toward the studio gates, thinking he would at last have proper time to see his children, but the gateman informed him that a call had just come down requesting his immediate return for additional shots. With great reluctance, he put on the wig, makeup, and costume

---

*Released in the United States on January 6, 1952.

†Niven is fond of retelling the incident that occurred during one of the staged battle scenes. He was crossing a field oncamera, tripped, and his dress sword went through the leg of an extra. Niven became sick to his stomach, but managed to pull out the sword, before he again vomited. The injured man limped off, with Niven running after him: "I say, I'm terribly sorry. Does it hurt too badly?" The extra asked: "Does what hurt?" Niven pointed to the man's leg and became ill yet again. Winding up the story, Niven explains: "Do you know, the man actually had an aluminum leg and my sword had gone right through one of its joints. Six hundred extras in that scene and I happened on the one man who had an aluminum leg."

With Gladys Cooper and Loretta Young in THE BISHOP' WIFE (RKO '47)

and returned to the set. "Where the hell's my chair?" he demanded of the propman, who timidly replied that a lady was now occupying it. "Then get her out of it," he barked. The lady was Sweden's number one model, Hjordis Tersmeden, on her first visit to a movie studio—and she had never before heard of David Niven.

As for *Bonnie Prince Charlie,* the critics were unanimous, almost to the man, in knocking it. Bosley Crowther of the *New York Times* called it "tedious" and said that it "is not a drama, it is a register of events and names." *Newsweek* magazine gave it enough review space to record that it was "one of the most turgid and boring films on record." Even charitable London critics found it "boring and lifeless."

Ten days after their meeting, Niven and Hjordis (whose marriage to Carl Gustaf Tersmeden had been dissolved in May 1947) were married on January 14, 1948, at South Kensington's Registry. The next day, the newly enlarged Niven family boarded the *Queen Elizabeth* bound for America. Some time later, Niven was to say of his second marriage: "I feel like getting down on my knees every morning and thanking God for the second chance I was given to find a new love."

For Christmas, 1948, Goldwyn presented to the

With Finlay Currie (center) in BONNIE PRINCE CHARLIE (British Lion '47)

world John Patrick's screenplay of Rumer God-den's serialized novel *A Fugue in Time* (a.k.a. *Take Three Tenses*). Heralded by the Goldwyn publicity department as entertainment compara-ble to his Oscar-winning *The Best Years of Our Lives,* it was touted as "just about the most won-derful love story ever filmed." *Enchantment* (RKO, 1948), as the story is known onscreen, tells of an old London townhouse and its two genera-tions of lovers. One pair (Niven and Teresa Wright) loved and lost their pursuit of happiness in the era of Queen Victoria. The second pair (Farley Granger and Evelyn Keyes) are the mod-ern (1948) lovers. In his pivotal role, Niven was required to age from a dashing, young guardsman to a man of eighty-seven. Beforehand, he ob-served old men and discerned the obvious, that they did everything slower. "So I had thirty-two pounds of lead distributed about my person. My sleeves were so weighted down I could scarcely raise a glass to my lips; my shoes were so heavy that getting my feet off the ground was a chore; and the lead in the seat of my pants made rising from chairs almost impossible. By ten a.m., I was cooked." To make his hair appear gray onscreen, he was forced to have it bleached eight times. "It hurts like the devil," he said.

Niven's discomfiture paid dividends, for when Bosley Crowther (*New York Times*) reviewed the picture, he pronounced: "David Niven is full of bounce as the young guardsman of the Victorian romance, in studied contrast to his maundering melancholia as the same fellow in his old, nos-talgic days." The Gregg Toland–directed feature never became the lachrymose classic that Gold-wyn and his crew had envisioned, but in the days of the post–World War II realism movement, it was as refreshing to a segment of moviegoers as the later *Love Story* (Paramount, 1970) would be to another generation. The screen exercise also demonstrated that David did not have to be type-cast as the jovial young dapper forever; he was capable of sensitive interpretation within contra-casting roles. However, this capacity was some-thing both David and his future movie employers would be slow in realizing. It was so easy to stick him in the safe marquee niche of the dapper, jovi-al bachelor about town.

For his next assignment, Goldwyn informed David that he was again being loaned to Korda and would be sent to England for six months to work on a most ambitious joint venture. David rebelled again, but the powerful Goldwyn was

supported by the contract and the actor's almost nonexistent bank account. The Nivens, at David's delay-tactic insistence, rode a train to New York, where they took a ship to Liverpool. From Lon-don he wired Goldwyn demanding a six-week va-cation, as specified in his contract. The mogul was forced to return him to California. From there the Nivens flew to Bermuda. At the end of six weeks, he reported to work, without seeing Goldwyn, and was then flown back to England.

The Korda film in question was *The Elusive Pimpernel* in which Niven was to portray Sir Per-cy Blakeney, the disguised Britisher who aids the impoverished and the vanquished in late-eight-eenth-century Revolutionary France during the Reign of Terror.* The film, as directed by Emeric Pressburger and Michael Powell, was one of those projects that never jelled. Despite the pres-ence of Margaret Leighton as Niven's oncamera wife, Jack Hawkins as the dandified Prince of Wales, and Cyril Cusack as Chauvelin, the de-vious ambassador of Robespierre, the classic Bar-oness Orczy tale emerged as a cinematic dud. There were many expensive retakes to bolster the color production into a viable commodity, but nothing seemed to help. The picture was not re-leased in England until 1950. Goldwyn would not accept it for American distribution because it was patently bad. Korda sued Goldwyn, and Goldwyn countersued, with the result that this much-kicked-about picture did not find U.S. re-lease till 1954. Reported *Variety:* "It is brash, noisy and dull. It does little credit to British film production. . . . David Niven . . . is smooth, smil-ing and suave, but all his efforts to lift the picture on to a higher plane are unavailing."

Because of David's recent shenanigans and contretemps with Goldwyn, he was palmed off to Warner Bros. to play opposite Jane Wyman in *A Kiss in the Dark* (1949). She had yet to win her Academy Award for *Johnny Belinda* (Warner Bros., 1948), and it was obvious that by casting the actress in this distinctly unfunny comedy, her studio was evincing as little interest in her as Goldwyn was in Niven. The script concerned a concert pianist (Niven) whose playing annoys his tenant (Broderick Crawford) and who falls in love with Wyman. In discussing his keyboard tinkling in this Delmer Daves–directed trivia, Niven has stated: "During my big concert scene an expert played the piano with his arms through my tail-coat while I rolled my eyes and looked soulful."

He next played second-on-the-marquee to Shir-

*The most memorable oncamera Blakeney was created by Leslie Howard for Korda's *The Scarlet Pimpernel* (1935).

ley Temple in *A Kiss for Corliss* (United Artists, 1949), as a middle-aged rogue on whom teenager Corliss (Temple) gets a divine crush. Much like Cary Grant in *The Bachelor and the Bobby-Soxer* (RKO, 1947), who also had to talk Miss Temple out of her gushy infatuation, Niven worms his way out of the ticklish situation by appearing stuffy and less bright than boys of her own age. Unlike *Kiss and Tell* (United Artists, 1945), from which the Corliss Archer and Temple characterization derived, *A Kiss for Corliss* met with limp box-office response. It was even retitled *Almost a Bride* in the hopes of building a fresh publicity response for the film, but nothing seemed to engender interest for the tame outing.

It was obvious by this point that neither Niven nor Goldwyn was happy with their contractual arrangement. There was talk that the actor would join Ann Blyth, Farley Granger, and Joan Evans in *Our Very Own* (RKO, 1950), but by the time the production went before the cameras, Donald Cook had been substituted in the shortened role. At this juncture, encouraged by others in the industry, Niven cornered the mighty Goldwyn in his office and suggested a release from the contract unless better roles could be promised. Unconcernedly, Goldwyn buzzed for an assistant, saying: "Give Niven his release form as from today. He's through."* Thus ended an odd fourteen-year arrangement wherein, of thirty-three motion pictures in which he appeared, only seven were personally produced by Goldwyn's filmmaking unit.

Ten months were to pass before Niven was seen in a new release. His self-ordained freelance arrangement proved unlucky, even when he was offered the third-billed supporting role of the opera manager in *The Toast of New Orleans* (MGM, 1950). As Jacques Riboudeaux, he discovers the tenor singing talents of a robust young fisherman (Mario Lanza), places him in the star rank, but loses his paramour, la prima donna (Kathryn Grayson), to the shiny-faced youth. It was a sad comedown for the once-so-promising David Niven, heir apparent to the crown of premier screen debonair.

With creditors ready to pounce upon the Pink House, David next took a supporting role in *Soldiers Three* (1951), again at MGM. He has called this film "an appalling travesty of a costume

With Evelyn Keyes in ENCHANTMENT (RKO '48)

thriller. The result was so bad that the audience thought it was a comedy and as such it became faintly successful." Based on the short stories of Rudyard Kipling, whose work had provided the basis of Metro's *Kim* (1950), it tells the tale of three nonconforming British soldiers (Stewart Granger, Robert Newton, Cyril Cusack) who bestow on their commanding officers (Niven and Walter Pidgeon) embarrassment and gray hairs. Bosley Crowther (*New York Times*) complained: "How such a silly, unimaginative and flavorless picture could have been made from Kipling's wonderful stories is beyond this corner's baffled ken."

David's friend and advisor, Humphrey Bogart, told him: "Get outta town, kid, they gotta have time to forget that one." So the Nivens rented the Pink House and moved to England. Soon after they took up residence in London suburbia, David was contracted to star in an RKO-financed film boasting a so-called "international cast" (British, American, and Cesar Romero).

Happy Go Lovely (1951) has a basic Scottish

---

*In his more mature period (1958), Niven could look back on his actions and relate: "Actually the worse slump I've had came about because I began to believe my own publicity. After six and a half years in the war I came back to Hollywood and my contract with Sam Goldwyn. His press agent planted stories that I was God's gift to the movies and it was a miracle that I had returned to save films, and all that.

"After two and a half years of reading that sort of stuff about myself, I couldn't get my hat on. One day I went in to see Mr. Goldwyn, who wanted to use me in a picture, and told him he didn't know his business. I repeated everything the press agent said about myself. Within minutes I was out on the street jobless. What I had forgotten was it was Mr. Goldwyn who was paying for publicity."

setting, although the Technicolored semimusical could have taken place anywhere. Niven is a Scottish lord whose name is used with romantic connotations by an American chorus girl (Vera-Ellen) to further her show-business career. When forced into a showdown, she asks a pleasant-looking man whom she takes to be a newspaperman (Niven) to pose as "her" Lord. When the man turns out to be authentic nobility, she dances and somersaults a course to wedded happiness. The plot was predictable and the musical numbers were routine.

Niven was next found on an island in the English Channel in *Appointment with Venus* (General Film Distributors, 1951), produced by Betty Box for the British Film Makers. This one, a comedy of sorts, had Niven back in uniform as a Scottish major who is dispatched to the island during the Nazi occupation. His mission is to escort a prize heifer cow to the English mainland aboard a destroyer. His guide on the island is Glynis Johns, with whom he falls in love while the cow gives birth to a calf. Despite this last miscalculated and unforeseen situation, the party manages to escape the Germans in the nick of time. When released in the United States, this modest offering was retagged *Island Rescue* (Universal, 1952).

In the summer of 1951, a very ill-at-ease David tried a gambit undertaken before, and since, by many other cinema celebrities: launching an assault on Broadway. Through the help of Noël Coward, he was offered the male lead in John C. Wilson's stage presentation of *Nina*. Translated from the French sex farce of Andre Soussin, the show almost never reached New York. During the Philadelphia engagement, star Gloria Swanson insisted that the vehicle was not to her liking and she wanted her release. She was convinced otherwise (a pity) and the sex comedy struggled on to Broadway, debuting at the Royale Theatre on December 5, 1951. There had been several rewrites of the show, but neither director Gregory Ratoff nor the cast (Swanson as the wife, Niven as the lover, and Alan Webb as her husband) could spark life into the Samuel Taylor English adaptation. Swanson, the eternal ingenue, was mostly reviewed on her self-designed costumes, while the bulk of the plaudits went to Webb as the cuckolded spouse. As for Niven, Walter Kerr (*New York Herald-Tribune*) reported: "He is a pleasing and precise performer, and in another part I am sure Broadway will be glad to have him around. Here he is wasted on interminable telephone calls to his various mistresses and long, windy speech-

With J. Carroll Naish, Mario Lanza, and George Meader in THE TOAST OF NEW ORLEANS (MGM '50)

With his wife Hjordis Tersmedes and their children, David, Jr. and Jamie in Southampton, England, March, 1951

With Walter Pidgeon in SOLDIERS THREE (MGM '51)

es in which he attempts to free himself of the tarantula-like Nina." The show folded after forty-five performances.

He did not have much better luck with *The Lady Says No* (United Artists, 1951), a middling comedy produced and directed for ex-Paramount star(let) Joan Caulfield by her husband, Frank Ross. She is a novelist with a best-selling book warning women of the evil of men, and Niven is a photographer sent by his magazine to do a photo essay on her. They become involved in a few minor screwball situations which culminate in his convincing her that men are not as rotten as she would believe. A. H. Weiler of the *New York Times* aptly labeled it "a limp comedy hardly worth writing [about]."

Unlike many Hollywood actors, when television gave him the come-on Niven responded. With few distinguished film roles to his credit since he had returned from the war, and with a bad stage experience behind him, television represented the necessary boost to his floundering career. His initial appearance on the fast-growing video medium that threatened the security of most movie people was on CBS's "Schlitz Play-house of Stars" on October 5, 1951. His co-star was Helen Hayes. This was followed by a live

David Niven of the early 1950s

With Vera-Ellen and Diane Hart in HAPPY GO LOVELY (RKO '51)

With Peggy Maley (blonde) in THE LADY SAYS NO (UA '51)

presentation with Kim Hunter and Art Carney in New York of *The Petrified Forest* for the "Celanese Theatre" (ABC, February 20, 1952).

In the autumn of 1951, Prentice-Hall became the publishers of Niven's first novel, *Once Over Lightly,* a farcical piece of fiction about a playboy Englishman who becomes a Hollywood star. Of the $2.75 book, the *New York Herald-Tribune* accorded: "The plot is inconsequential, the dialogue crisp, the ladies alluring. The target is diversion, and it is well hit. Not a work of autobiography, the English actor assures you."

Otto Preminger, who had seen Niven perform in *Nina* during one of the tryouts, approached him in the spring of 1952 for, as the actor calls it, "one of the best parts" in an upcoming film, *The Moon Is Blue* (United Artists, 1953).* Preminger stipulated as a condition of their agreement that David first do the play onstage in San Francisco with Diana Lynn and Scott Brady. Niven accepted the offer with its inbuilt challenge, which was the best to come his way in months.

The Moon Is Blue, strange as it may seem to mid-1970s late-show television viewers, was banned by the Catholic Church in the United States and failed to receive an okay from the Motion Picture Production Code because of its candid dialog related to sex. Made curious by the label of "indecent," and the controversial nature of most Otto Preminger–engineered projects, the American public stood in lines to see it and the film grossed $4 million in U.S.-Canadian domestic rentals.[†]

For a picture that created such a tremendous stir, the plotline is amazingly innocent. David Slater (Niven) is an Englishman living in the apartment above that of Donald Gresham (William Holden). Both are incurable skirt-chasers. Holden picks up an outspoken young thing named Patty O'Neill (Maggie McNamara), who gives him permission to go as far as he wants with her so long as her virginity is preserved for the man she marries. Holden leaves the girl alone in his apartment while he attends to grocery shopping, and the middle-aged, martini-drinking gent from upstairs pays a timely call. When Niven gets nowhere with her, physically, she suggests that they turn on the television. He asks: "Is it in color?" Her reply: "Oh, it won't be in color for years." He says: "Let's wait 'til then," turns his

---

*Staged on Broadway (Henry Miller Theatre: March 8, 1951, 924 performances); Donald Cook had the role taken by Niven oncamera.
[†]A German film version, *Die Jungfrau Auf Dem Dach,* was produced with the same technical crew. Johannes Heesters assumed the Niven role.

With William Holden and Maggie McNamara in THE MOON IS BLUE (UA '53)

back on the TV set, and mixes a fresh batch of martinis for himself. Eventually Holden wins the girl, *but* strictly on her established terms.

The film is a talkfest, often to the point of tedium, in spite of its appealing, diverting dialog. The fact that it was translated, almost word from word, from F. Hugh Herbert's stage production, did not give the requisite cinematic touch. *Variety* was quick to describe, rate, and report on Niven's newest screen image: "[his] middleaged playboy is mighty fancy laugh acting." Niven was awarded a Golden Globes prize by members of the Hollywood Foreign Press as having given the best comedy performance of 1953.

The financial tide also turned in Niven's direction when he teamed with Dick Powell and Charles Boyer, in 1952, in the formation of "Four Star Playhouse" for CBS-TV network. They were never able to obtain a permanent fourth star because of the current Hollywood viewpoint on television, but actor friends like Ida Lupino, Ronald Colman, and Merle Oberon assisted them with guest appearances. One of their first filmed half-hour shows cost $10,000, which they thought was excessively expensive, but this proved to be a mere drop in the production budget compared to later episodes.* In the show's format, the three actors alternated appearances in a variety of presentations which included mysteries, dramas, and comedies.

On March 25, 1953, Niven's oldest brother, Max, age fifty-five, died on his farm at Curries Post, Natal, South Africa. It was just another indication to the actor how much the world about him was changing and that, at age forty-three, he was very middle-aged.

In England, Niven worked next in *The Love Lottery* (General Film Distributors) as an internationally famed movie star who is raffled in a global lottery to garner publicity. The film's satirical look at Hollywood did not get past the so-so stage, even with the added inducement of Humphrey Bogart in a surprise guest shot at the film's finale.

Happy Ever After (Associated British Pictures, 1954),† also filmed in England, was directed and produced by Mario Zampi. In this mild diversion Niven is an Irishman who returns home to South Ireland to claim an inheritance, the Great House

of Rathbarney. His avaricious desire to obtain as much as he can get from the land worked by those who live on it is dimly viewed by the local inhabitants, and several slapstick attempts are made to murder him. He decides, finally, that he prefers the arms of Yvonne De Carlo to the monetary rewards of being a land baron and gives up his inheritance in favor of her.

His third successive British-made film was *Carrington, VC* (Independent Film Distributors, 1954),† which again placed him in military uniform. As a British Army officer on trial for embezzling battalion funds, for being AWOL for one day, and for entertaining a lady in the forbidden area of the men's barracks, he is brought to trial in an atmosphere of emotional suspense. His guilt, for the most part, is derived from being wed to a vicious woman (Margaret Leighton) and having a vitriolic commanding officer (Allan Cuthbertson).

"One of the most thorough banalities of the year" was the description applied by Bosley Crowther (*New York Times*) to Niven's next film, made in Hollywood. *The King's Thief* (MGM, 1955) boasted CinemaScope and color, but that was about all. Edmund Purdom had the title role of the thief who steals a black book from the Duke of Brampton (Niven), charging certain nobles around King Charles II (George Sanders) with treason. David's duke, a treacherous fellow, is exposed to the king only after Purdom has run the usual gamut of plumed swashbucklery. Niven appeared very uncomfortable in the role of the prize heel.

The Birds and the Bees (Paramount, 1956), a remake of the studio's near-classic farce *The Lady Eve* (1941), found David in the role originally played by Charles Coburn (!)‡ David is father to a gold-digging lady (Mitzi Gaynor) whose sights are focused on the vegetarian head of a meat-packing firm (George Gobel). The updated script by Sidney Sheldon and Preston Sturges was centered upon the limited sustaining talents of Gobel (his big screen debut) and provided Niven (in third billing) with little more to do than appear connivingly debonair as he plots his daughter's romance with the meat-packer. One critic found Niven a "mite youthful" as Miss Gaynor's father.

Mike Todd, often called the "master show-

---

*Four Star Productions, Inc., later branched out to include such video series as "The Zane Grey Theatre," "The Rifleman," "Wanted, Dead Or Alive," etc.

†Released as *Tonight's the Night* (Allied Artists) in the United States on November 19, 1954.

†Changed to *Court Martial* for its U.S. release (1955) because it was assumed that most Americans would not know that "VC" meant "Victoria Cross." The property had been a play on the London stage (Westminster Theatre: July 28, 1953) with Alec Clunes in the role Niven played oncamera.

‡Cary Grant met a similar superannuation fate when in *Walk, Don't Run* (Columbia, 1966), he inherited Charles Coburn's role from *The More the Merrier* (Columbia, 1943).

man," telephoned Niven one Sunday afternoon and brusquely requested his presence at the home of veteran producer, Joseph Schenck. David responded, and, after a brief meeting with Todd alongside Schenck's pool, went home with the best screen offer of his career, the part of Phileas Fogg, Jules Verne's fictional character in his *Around the World in Eighty Days* (United Artists, 1956).* Known as "Todd's Folly," the film was shot in Todd-AO widescreen process in Spain, London, Paris, Colorado, Oklahoma, and on lots rented by Todd at every Hollywood studio. Costing somewhere in the vicinity of $1 million, Todd's major gimmick was the placement of international screen stars in small parts, for which he coined the word "cameo" rather than refer to them as "bits." As Todd told Martha Weinman of *Collier's* magazine: "Sure, there have been other pictures with a lot of big names. But the stories have always been built around stars. This time we fitted the stars right into the story."

Fogg (Niven) begins the adventure by making a wager with members of the Reform Club of Victorian London that he can girdle the globe in precisely eighty days.† With his newly hired manservant (Cantinflas), he embarks on a global trek that will include several unique forms of transportation—from balloon, to ostrich, to elephant, to train, to sailing yacht. Along the way, they pick up an Indian princess (Shirley MacLaine) and a Scotland Yard detective (Robert Newton) who mistakes Niven for a wanted bank robber.

When the film was officially released on October 18, 1959, the viewer had to be especially alert in order to catch the many personalities in their cameo parts. Beatrice Lillie was a street-corner revivalist in London; Martine Carol was a parasol-twirling pedestrian in France; Frank Sinatra was a piano player in San Francisco; Ronald Colman was a railroad official in India; Charles Boyer owned the balloon that takes Niven to Spain on the first lap of his journey; Cesar Romero and Gilbert Roland were Arab leaders, etc., etc. A total of thirty-seven cameos outfitted the extravaganza, which won the Academy Award for Best Picture of 1956 and has since garnered some $23 million in domestic rentals.

Of David's crucial performance, Archer Winsten in the *New York Post* said: "[he] is letter-

With Shirley MacLaine in AROUND THE WORLD IN 80 DAYS (UA '56)

perfect as 'the most punctual man alive' . . . " Herbert Kupferberg of the *New York Herald-Tribune* said he was "serenely imperturbable" and "the epitome of a Frenchman's conception of a Britisher."

It was hard to follow such a colossal act, and his next film assignment was a comedown. He played the pivotal role of psychiatrist Dr. Alan Coles in *Oh, Men! Oh, Women!* (Twentieth Century–Fox, 1957).† In the adaptation by Nunnally Johnson (writer, producer, director), Niven is first seen analyzing Natalie Schaefer as the credits roll down the screen. After she bids him farewell in a lovesick fashion, he discovers from "listening" that his second patient (Tony Randall) is in love with his own fiancée (Barbara Rush). Before he can attempt to straighten out his personal affairs, however, he is forced to persuade another patient (Ginger Rogers) that she ought to remain with her movie-star husband (Dan Dailey). The final scene, in Miss Rush's apartment, proves to be a highlight of low-comedy playing by all principals

*The multiscened *Around the World in 80 Days* (Adelphi Theatre: May 31, 1946, 74 performances), with music by Cole Porter, had been a stage fiasco. It was presented by Orson Welles, who appeared as villain Dick Fix; Arthur Margetson was Phileas Fogg.
†The members are played by Robert Morley, Trevor Howard, Finlay Currie, Basil Sydney, and Ronald Squire.
†On the Broadway stage (Henry Miller Theatre: December 17, 1953, 382 performances), Franchot Tone played the doctor. Other cast roles were played by Gig Young, Anne Jackson, and Betsy von Furstenberg.

With Tony Randall and John Wengraf in OH, MEN! OH, WOMEN! (20th '57)

when everyone is properly paired off for the fade-out. Niven was quite adept at playing the professional man whose physician's composure is shattered by his personal vulnerability. Whereas some performers might have played the part for all its smutty potential, David garnished his characterization with a meaningful layer of inhibition. He emphasized the contrast of the doctor who preaches to his patients about the ramifications of love but finds his own knowledge on the matter is purely theoretical.

Niven then spent three refreshing months in Rome and London filming *The Little Hut* (MGM, 1957). He played the man who onscreen almost becomes Ava Gardner's lover.* The two, with the latter's husband (Stewart Granger), are castaways on a desert island. Thanks to F. Hugh Herbert's heavy-handed screenplay, the seventy-eight minutes were all talk and very little action. This color film, did, however, expose the fact that Niven had rather spindly legs, certainly no competition for the far more virile Granger.

Back in Hollywood, Niven coasted on his *Around the World* status by accepting the title role in Universal's simpering remake of *My Man Godfrey* (1957).† This time around, Godfrey is a displaced Austrian refugee whom Irene Bullock (June Allyson) takes home as her very own possession. He takes on the job as butler to the madcap household where, time and again, he displays better judgment and more intelligence than those who pay his salary. He teaches a lesson in humility to Allison's stuffy sister (Martha Hyer), saves papa (Robert Keith) from financial ruin, and is captured in wedlock by Allyson. But two decades had passed since this depression-chaser screwball story had been first concocted, and it no longer held pertinent values for 1950s filmgoers. In a cooperative deal, Niven posed for American Airlines magazine advertisements to push both the airline and *My Man Godfrey*. He was listed in the layouts as "The Impeccable Mr. Niven," demonstrating again that to an increasingly larger segment of the public he was becoming synonymous with discreet tastefulness and gentlemanly charms, areas once strictly the provinces of

---

* *The Little Hut* was first presented on the London stage (Lyric Theatre: August 23, 1950) where it has a two-year-plus run, with Robert Morley as the husband, Joan Tetzel as the wife, and David Tomlinson as the lover. On Broadway (Coronet Theatre: October 7, 1953, 29 performances), the respective roles were played by Roland Culver, Anne Vernon, and Colin Gordon. The wild-man was played in London by Geoffrey Toone, in New York by John Granger. In the film the wild-man was portrayed by Walter Chiari.
† Enacted by William Powell in the original Universal film of 1936.

386

Adolphe Menjou, Herbert Marshall, Robert Montgomery, Melvyn Douglas, and, especially, William Powell. Time was indeed marching on; the once reckless Niven was now considered Establishment Old Guard.

Niven returned to England for *The Silken Affair* (RKO, 1956), co-produced by his old friend, Douglas Fairbanks, Jr. The picture added nothing to cinematic legend. The script had David as an accountant who alters the books of a near-bankrupt hosiery firm to make it appear prosperous. William K. Zinsser (*New York Herald-Tribune*) smartly assessed Niven's contributions to this mild screenfare: "Niven, of course, is ideal for this kind of farce, achieving his humor through understatement and a subtle sense of timing."

Then, on the French Riviera, Niven found a new leading lady in Deborah Kerr in Otto Preminger's production *Bonjour Tristesse* (Columbia, 1958), taken from Françoise Sagan's best-selling novel of the same name. Cecile (Jean Seberg), the seventeen-year-old daughter of Niven, a shallow playboy, is insistent in her plans to prevent him from marrying her chic Parisian godmother (Kerr). She brings forth daddy's former mistress (Mylene Demongeot), who was earlier discarded,

In THE LITTLE HUT (MGM '57)

With June Allyson, Jay Robinson, Jessie Royce Landis, Robert Keith, and Martha Hyer in MY MAN GODFREY (Univ '57)

but whom Seberg, in this moment of crisis, feels is better suited. When Kerr overhears Niven speaking ill of her to Demongeot, she becomes hysterical, hops into a car, and drives off to her death. Niven and Seberg suddenly discover the unimportance of their pettiness.

During the course of the on-location filming of *Bonjour Tristesse*, Niven and his *The Moon Is Blue* benefactor, Preminger, came to bitter words. One well-publicized incident found the producer-director snidely inquiring of his star: "Mr. Niven, you are so charming off screen, why can't you be charming on it?" Nevertheless, in his role of a middle-aged hedonist, Niven gave dimension to an essentially paper-thin characterization. Even usually cynical *Time* magazine approved of his work—in a backhanded way, of course: "David Niven is remarkable as the sort of rake that accumulates his life in his face, like a pile of dead leaves."

"My role in *Separate Tables* was the best acting part—and the most difficult—I ever had." Niven told this to *Newsweek* magazine a few weeks after the film's release in December 1958. "*Separate Tables* proves, I think, that I oughtn't be limited just to so-called 'David Niven parts,' " he went on, "an unfortunate identification from more than twenty years in the movies in which I had a cup of tea in one hand and a duchess in the other."

On the Broadway stage of the Music Box Theatre (October 25, 1956, 382 performances), Terence Rattigan's play was divided into two parts, with Margaret Leighton and Eric Portman playing both sets of leads. In the Hecht, Hill, and Lancaster screen version, it becomes one continuous story, with Niven in third billing (following Rita Hayworth and Deborah Kerr) as the aging Major Pollock.* The other male lead is taken by Burt Lancaster. The action takes place at the Beauregard Hotel, run by Wendy Hiller, on the south coast of England. It is winter, when few guests remain. Sybil Railton-Bell (Deborah Kerr), a mousey little thing dominated by her mother (Gladys Cooper), has fainting "states" because she is afraid of people and life. She is secretly in love with the major. One of the major's favorite pastimes is reminiscing about the African campaigns in which he claims to have had an important function. However, shortly after the opening scenes, he is exposed in an article in the *West*

*Laurence Olivier, having originally signed to direct and co-star with his wife, Vivien Leigh, withdrew when he learned that the two playlets would be combined and that four actors would be used rather than two, as it was done on Broadway or on the London stage (St. James Theatre: September 22, 1954) with Portman and Leighton.

With Genevieve Page in THE SILKEN AFFAIR (RKO - British '56)

Hampshire Weekly News as a complete fraud having pleaded guilty to a "charge of insulting behavior in a cinema." It seems he "took other liberties" and changed his seat five times, "always near a female person." The court had placed him on a twelve-month probation period after disclosing that he had served during the war as a second lieutenant in an Army supply depot.

Thus the stage is set for a major confrontation. Dowager Cooper, with her crony Cathleen Nesbitt, calls a meeting of the hotel guests in which she insists that the "common little man" be asked to leave the premises. The guests reluctantly vote in accord with her, and when Miss Cooper gives him the verdict he admits: "I'm far too much a coward to stay on here now." The next morning, after calling a taxi, he enters the dining room for breakfast. From their separate tables, the guests— hesitantly at first—greet him, all save Cooper. When Kerr openly defies her mother for the first time in her life, with a smile and a greeting, too, Niven sends the taxi away. "Very well, then," says Hiller, "lunch at the usual time." Niven's reply, the final line spoken in the film, is "Lunch at the usual time."

Certainly unassuming Niven never quite imagined that the critical reaction would be so favorable to his screen interpretation. *Newsweek* magazine credited him with being "the greatest surprise in the cast," and added that he "handles this sorry figure of a broken man with great skill." *Variety* credited him with giving "one of the best performances of his career"; *Time* called him "excellent"; and the *New York Herald-Tribune* found that he extended "a delicate and touching performance in a difficult role."

He won the New York Film Critics Award as the Best Actor of 1958, and received a nomination for an Academy Award. In the ten weeks between the Academy announcement and the night at Grauman's Chinese Theatre when the awards were handed out, he collected several good-luck charms, although there was always a doubt in his mind that he would win because of its being awarded to an Englishman the previous year (Alec Guinness for *The Bridge on the River Kwai*).

On the evening of April 6, 1959, Niven was one of the three presentation hosts.* After completing his master-of-ceremonies chores, he took a seat in the audience next to his wife. Finally the moment came for the announcement of the Best Actor of 1958.† Irene Dunne came onstage to read the

nominations and winner. She sliced open the Price-Waterhouse envelope and "after an interminable pause, read out my name." Niven ran to the stage, but tripped in mounting the steps. "The reason I just fell down was," he had intended to tell the audience, "because I was so loaded with good-luck charms that I was top heavy." However, he paused after the word "loaded," which sent the gathering into a knowing roar. He did not finish the statement. Later, he said: "Dammit. I must say I wanted to win and I'm happy I did." One of his well-wishers was Samuel Goldwyn, whom Niven had not seen in eight years. "I don't give a goddamn about your award," Goldwyn told him, "I've seen the picture and I want you to know I'm proud of you." On a still later occasion, David admitted: "I won the Oscar that night because two young ladies, Deborah Kerr and Wendy Hiller, cried so well."

Other events in 1958 were not so illustrious for him. A projected video series, "The Man in the Panama Hat," based on the Henri de Gacher novel and adapted for television by Eric Ambler, never left the drawing boards. On the home front, Mrs. Niven suffered her second miscarriage, after which she and her husband went on a long vacation to Jamaica.

Niven was ostensibly the star of *Ask Any Girl* (MGM, 1959), a jubilant slapstick comedy which deftly described the pandemonium that could happen to a "typical" young lady (Shirley MacLaine) who comes to New York seeking a career and husband. But before the ninety-eight-minute color feature had run its course, it was clear that MacLaine as the trouble-prone small-towner was the picture's star, that Gig Young as her aging-playboy boss was the major foil of the story, and that Niven, as Young's older, more conservative brother, was merely an animated *deus ex machina*. Niven's Miles Doughton is the starched bachelor who takes longer than a refrigerator to defrost, and is totally perplexed when MacLaine tosses away her preference for Young to latch on to him as her intended spouse. For one of the increasingly fewer times in the latter part of his reviewing career, Bosley Crowther (*New York Times*) hit the mark when he reported: "Mr. Niven is no bountiful bargain himself. He plays the punctilious researcher as though he were mentally holding his nose. And his humorous and emotional responses appear equally restrained. *Separate Tables* didn't help Mr. Niven if it has

*With Jack Lemmon and Bob Hope.

†The other nominees were Tony Curtis (*The Defiant Ones*), Paul Newman (*Cat on a Hot Tin Roof*), Sidney Poitier (*The Defiant Ones*), and Spencer Tracy (*The Old Man and the Sea*).

With Deborah Kerr in SEPARATE TABLES (UA '58)

made this sort of coxcomb of him." In fairness to Niven, it must be added that moviegoers of the day were more likely drawn into the theatre by his name on the marquee than by word-of-mouth of the film's humorous tale in which Shirley Mac-Laine had a tailor-made role.

Ask Any Girl had its own bounce of spontaneity, despite the contrived comic situations. In contrast, *Happy Anniversary* (United Artists, 1959) wangled its humorous moments *because* of its predictable domestic mishaps. Based on a Broadway success,* director David Miller led Niven and Mitzi Gaynor (this time as his wife) through their paces of double-takes, shouting, and affectionate reconciliations. On his fourteenth wedding anniversary, Chris Walters (Niven) thinks it is rather amusing to disclose that he and the missus had lived together before they were married.† The recipients of this ghastly confession are her parents (Loring Smith and Phyllis Povah), whose reactions are just what might be expected in the moralistic 1950s. Enough filmgoers existed who thought a movie based on the premise that pre-

marital sex relations are indeed quite funny, so that the picture had a healthy reception at the boxoffice.

After the release of the vulgar, banal *Happy Anniversary,* it became problematical what actual acting progress David had made since the day of *The Moon Is Blue.* Could *Separate Tables* have been an aberration in his (or his agents') seemingly well plotted drive to make him the dirty "old" man of the cinema.

In the summer of 1959, the Nivens separated, with Hjordis taking a small house of her own, not far from their home. They issued the typical Hollywood statements about trial separations, and then Niven took the boys on a six-week jaunt to Honolulu. There, while riding the surf, he collided with a rock, which created blood and headlines, but it was a minor calamity and he was in full repair when he reported to MGM for *Please Don't Eat the Daisies* (1960), to be directed by Charles Walters, who had guided *Ask Any Girl* to completion.

A semi-autobiography, *Please Don't Eat the*

*The Broadway play original opened at the Broadhurst Theatre (April 7, 1954) for a 615-performance run, with Kitty Carlisle and MacDonald Carey in the leads.
†The Motion Picture Production Code refused to pass *Happy Anniversary* with a seal of approval until three lines of dialog, spoken by Niven, were added to the soundtrack. Niven thus says: "I was wrong. I never should have taken Alice [Gaynor] to that hotel room before we were married. What could I have been thinking of?"

Daisies was written by Jean Kerr, the wife of Walter Kerr, drama critic for the *New York Herald-Tribune*. The story loosely revolves around drama critic Larry Mackay (Niven), his wife (Doris Day), her mother (Spring Byington), their four children (Charles Herbert, Stanley Livingston, Flip Mark, and Baby Gellert), their rotund maid (Patsy Kelly), and a large white dog named Hobo who loves to eat daisies. Niven writes an honest review panning the musical of a friend (Richard Haydn), which incurs the wrath of the show's star (Janis Paige). Day's desire to move out of the city is fulfilled when she finds a dilapidated country home, but Niven cannot work in such an atmosphere and moves to a Manhattan hotel. From there he writes very clever reviews and becomes very impressed with his own importance. When he is the constant companion of Paige, Day counterattacks by joining the local drama group and staging a play which had been written by Niven in his early days. Not realizing it as his very own, he blasts it in a review. However, the group turns it into a successful comedy and he realizes how wrong and unfair he has been. If the premise sounds overly familiar, it should, as it was used in a similar variation for the stage play *Critic's Choice,* starring Henry Fonda, and for the picturi-

With fellow Oscar winner Susan Hayward after receiving their Academy Awards, April 6, 1959

With Carl Reiner and Mitzi Gaynor in HAPPY ANNIVERSARY (UA '59)

zation (Warner Bros., 1963), featuring Lucille Ball and Bob Hope. Then too, "Please Don't Eat the Daisies" was a video series (NBC-TV, September 14, 1965, 58 episodes), starring Pat Crowley and Mark Miller.

It is inconceivable that when Niven signed for *Please Don't Eat the Daisies* (complete with title song sung by Doris), he did not know that rosy, wholesome Doris Day would be the entire show, and that he would be merely a polite patsy for her apple-pie brand of sly comedy. As Penelope Clark wrote in *Films in Review:* "There isn't much for David Niven to do, and he does it in the amiably bumbling way he has played every role except the one in *Separate Tables.*"

The Nivens reconciled during the filming of *Daisies* and later traveled to Brazil as guests of the government there. He received the key to the city of Rio de Janeiro and was tossed a surprise birthday party at a brothel by some of his Hollywood English friends (Laurence Olivier and Peter Ustinov, among others).

With the increasing problems of air pollution and acts of violence in Los Angeles, David sold the Pink House in 1960. Against the advice of agent and business manager, he resigned from the directorial board of Four Star Productions and

took his family to Europe. They nestled in Switzerland near the Peter Viertels (the distaff side of whom is better known as Deborah Kerr) while Niven worked in *The Guns of Navarone* (Columbia, 1961).

Filmed in Greece and England by director J. Lee Thompson, the title refers to a Nazi emplacement of two huge guns buried in the rocks of the island of Navarone in the Aegean Sea. The weapons dominate a small channel through which the Allies in 1943 hope to evacuate a force trapped on the isle of Kheros. Since the guns cannot be destroyed by sea or air bombardment, a team of six specialists is sent to wipe out the weapons. Niven is the expert in explosives chosen as a member of the group. For the first time in his movie military career, he is not an officer. As Corporal Miller, he is commanded by Major Franklin (Anthony Quayle) until the latter breaks a leg while scaling the face of a sheer cliff which is the only unguarded approach to Navarone. Major Mallory (Gregory Peck) then assumes command. The guns are demolished, at the expense of several lives, and after members of the team are taken prisoner, but escape.

To say that *The Guns of Navarone* was "an exciting piece of entertainment" (*Variety*) was an

With his wife Hjordis, and sons Jamie and David, Jr. in Rhodes, Greece, May, 1960, while on location for THE GUNS OF NAVARONE Col '61)

understatement, for the blockbuster picture was an "experience" which grossed over $13 million in U.S. and Canadian rentals alone. To single out any one of the lead players (Peck, Niven, Anthony Quinn, James Darren, Stanley Baker) as the *raison d'être* for the movie's success would be misleading, for in this type of "mission" picture group action is everything, with the hazardous accomplishment of the task the sole important goal. The *New York Herald-Tribune* could state that Niven, as the cynical humanist, "is, of course, superb," but most of the credit for conveying the suspense and action to its viewers goes to cinematographers Oswald Morris and John Wilcox for their CinemaScope, Eastman Color lensing.

In 1962, Niven and Hjordis adopted Christine, a Swedish girl, and the following year they adopted a second girl, Fiona. "They told me that when you adopt children," David said to Sheilah Graham, "you never know the difference from your own children. It's absolutely true. I simply adore them." A bit later, after scouring the northern Mediterranean area for a place to call home, Hjordis found "an old monstrosity perched in an olive grove" at Cap Ferrat on the French Riviera. Among their first guests were Grace Kelly and her husband, Prince Ranier of Monaco.

I Due Enemici (1961) was filmed in Italy and Israel by Dino De Laurentiis. Niven is back in British military uniform as Major Richardson, whose plane crashes in the Abyssinian desert. He is taken prisoner by Captain Blasi (Alberto Sordi), who allows him to escape because of the Italians' lack of rations. Later Niven captures Sordi and his men, but becomes lost in the desert and the patrol is ambushed by a hostile tribe, who takes their rifles and shoes. Through the blunders committed by both officers, they develop a mutual friendship. It was a quiet little film, which as *The Best of Enemies* (Columbia, 1962), received scant U.S. playdates.

While in Rome, Niven joined with such celebrities as Walter Pidgeon, Annie Girardot, Jean Paul Belmondo, Susan Strasberg, Steve Reeves, Stewart Granger, and many, many others, for cameo spots in *The Shortest Day* (1962), a satire on Twentieth Century–Fox's *The Longest Day* (1962). Niven's chief purpose for being in Rome was to make *La Citta Prigioniera* (1962), which cast him as a British major in a Second World War tale. It was not released until 1964 in the United States, and then under the title *Conquered City* (American International). Niven was so enthusiastic about Italian filmmaking that he announced in August of 1962 that he planned to participate

in the creation of a new $7 million film studio in Rome. "It would be a tremendous gamble," he explained, "but there is a crying need for up-to-date studios." The project, along with Niven's participation, came to naught.

In *The Road to Hong Kong* (United Artists, 1962), Niven did an unbilled guest appearance as a Tibetan monk when Bing Crosby and Bob Hope visit the Grand Lama (Peter Madden), who cures Hope of amnesia. *Variety* noted that Niven "appears for no good reason," while other equally superfluous guest artists, Frank Sinatra, Dean Martin, and Peter Sellers, received favorable attention.

Poorly edited and photographed, *Guns of Darkness* (Warner Bros., 1962) was David's next screen foray, and at best, it could only be labeled a supporting-bill entry. Set in a nonexistent South American nation, but filmed in Spain, the film relates the story of an immature man (Niven) who is unable to hold any one job for very long. His wife (Leslie Caron) is about to leave him when he finds the country's president (David Opatoshu) wounded when his government is overthrown by revolutionary military men. Niven volunteers to help the president reach the border some eighty miles away, and Caron agrees to assist. They make it to the border after several harrowing experiences, but Opatoshu dies. Having become a wiser man, Niven affects a reconciliation with his wife. It was a pity that this low-keyed production was not viewed by more people, for it would have offered an entirely different picture of the so-called Niven touch.

Niven also played a civilian in *55 Days at Peking* (Allied Artists, 1963). A lavish Samuel Bronston production of epic proportions, it was lensed in Madrid and is best remembered for its visual magnificence and stubbornly poor box-office reception. Bronston erected a replica of the ancient city of Peking on the plains of Spain at a reported cost of some $7 million, only to blow up the entire setting for the film's fiery finale, as spectacularly photographed by Jack Hildyard. Set during the Chinese Boxer Rebellion, Niven was Sir Arthur Robertson, an envoy from Britain who remains with American Major Matt Lewis (Charlton Heston) to lead the resistance group numbering five hundred against the Chinese hordes. Few people had good words for this stagnant celluloid bore, although A. H. Weiler (*New York Times*) managed a compliment of sorts when he accoladed David for giving "the outstandingly realistic acting stint in the film."

After his years away from sex farce, *The Pink*

With Leslie Caron in GUNS OF DARKNESS (WB '62)

Panther (United Artists, 1964) returned David to the formula in which most viewers seemed to like him. His role in this Blake Edwards–directed feature was Sir Charles Lytton, alias the Phantom, the famous jewel thief (shades of *Raffles*). The pink panther of the title is a priceless jewel owned by the Princess Dala (Claudia Cardinale), which becomes the objective of the Phantom and his American nephew (Robert Wagner), partners in thievery. They rob Cardinale's safe during a costume party when they are dressed as gorillas, but find it empty except for a white glove (the Phantom's calling card). Inspector Jacques Clouseau (Peter Sellers),* in hot pursuit of the Phantom, becomes the logical suspect when the jewel is found in his pocket, planted there by his wife (Capucine), who happens to be the Phantom's mistress. The princess is also in on the plot. At the finale, the Phantom, his nephew, and Clouseau's wife take off for South America with the promise that they will send a letter to the Italian government clearing Clouseau. It was all absurd, with the humor ranging from slapstick to sophisticat-

ed, but always spiced with naughtiness. Niven played the pivotal role with the requisite smirk. The picture grossed $6 million in U.S.-Canadian rentals, which helped to restore Niven's once-again-fading box-office standing.

The Nivens were back in Hollywood where he filmed *Bedtime Story* (Universal, 1964). This time he was another crook, but one of a far less appealing nature. He poses as a fake prince in order to rob unsuspecting European women of their virtue and their jewels. With his American counterpart (Marlon Brando), Niven sets out to fleece Shirley Jones, whom, they believe, is heiress to a soap family of immense wealth. Brando poses as a psychosomatically ill paraplegic veteran confined to a wheelchair (the ultimate in tasteless black humor), while Niven poses as his merciless psychiatrist. However, when it is learned that Jones is no more than the winner of the title of "Soap Queen" in a beauty contest and is penniless, it is too late because Brando has fallen for her. Unperturbed, Niven goes after a redhead, presumably intent on pursuing his less-than-honest ways. As Rene Jordan said of this picture in his book *Marlon Brando* (1973): "The film is Billy Wilder without the German rigor or Ernst Lubitsch without the Berliner charm. As directed by Ralph Levy, it is as American as apple pie—with a worm in every bite."

In September 1964, Four Star Productions' "The Rogues" debuted on NBC. It was an hour adventure-comedy series starring Niven, Gig Young, Charles Boyer, Niven's former roommate Robert Coote, and Gladys Cooper. They played members of two related families of dapper international forgers and con men. Although the show was well received as a superior piece of adult entertainment, it only lasted for twenty-nine episodes.

Where the Spies Are (MGM, 1965) was yet another imitation James Bond caper, with Niven as a mild-mannered doctor who is pressed into espionage work. He is sent to the Middle East after a British agent is murdered by Communists, but gets sidetracked when he meets a gorgeous model (Françoise Dorleac). When the plane he has missed blows up, he realizes that, after all, his mission is a really serious affair. He eventually winds up in Canada after thwarting an assassination attempt on the life of a pro-British diplomat, but when asked to embark on another spy trip, his

---

*The Clouseau character would reappear in *A Shot in the Dark* (United Artists, 1964) with Sellers again in the role, and in *Inspector Clouseau* (United Artists, 1968), where Alan Arkin would inherit the part. For *The Return of the Pink Panther* (United Artists, 1975) Sellers again played Clouseau.

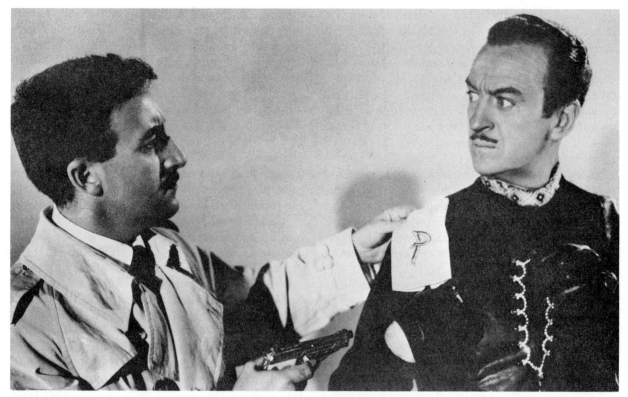
With Peter Sellers in a publicity pose for THE PINK PANTHER (UA '64)

With Leo McKern in BEDTIME STORY (Univ '64)

reply is emphatically in the negative, as it was to requests for whatever sequels MGM might have had in mind.

While filming *Where the Spies Are,* Niven was simultaneously shooting *Lady L* (MGM, 1965). Of his dual efforts, Niven quipped: "It's terribly easy and very refreshing. You just put on a different moustache and a different hat." MGM, however, was not so glib about *Lady L.* Having acquired the screen rights to Romain Gary's novel in 1958, the project had gone through several expensive pre-production drafts and cast restructurings. Finally it was ready to shoot in the fall of 1964, with Julius Blaustein producing, George Cukor directing, and Tony Curtis and Gina Lollobrigida starring. But then the stars refused to act with the Robert Anderson script on tap. At this point, some $2.7 million had been spent on a picture not yet filmed. Peter Ustinov was hired to direct, rescript, and co-star in the movie, on condition that he could ignore all past efforts in translating the Gary work to the screen. ("I didn't want to know where the others got stuck," he explained. "That sort of thing is contagious.")

Ustinov started clean with the project, bringing in his friend Niven to join new stars Paul Newman and Sophia Loren, the latter being the wife of the film's new producer, Carlo Ponti. The film, as such, was completed in April 1965, premiered in London in November 1965, but did not have a New York opening until May 1966. Metro and everyone involved knew all too well that Ustinov had not been able to salvage the persistent fiasco. It was a near total financial disaster.*

The story of *Lady L* is told through flashback, as eighty-year-old Lady Lendale (Loren), an English aristocrat, recalls her early days in Corsica as a laundress named Louisa. When she went to work in a Parisian brothel, she met and fell in love with Newman, an anarchist who plots to assassinate Prince Otto (Ustinov) of Bavaria. In the meanwhile, she has become pregnant and, while posing as a widowed countess, she plans to rob Lord Dicky Lendale (Niven). He wants a wife, however, and offers to save Newman from the police in exchange for her marrying him. She, thereafter reveals to her biographer (Cecil Parker) that, although she was Lady Lendale, she had also married Newman and that the generous lord had hired him as chauffeur so that his lady could be near her lover. As Tony Thomas explains in *Ustinov in Focus* (1971): "*Lady L* has the odd

distinction of being a film laudable for its frivolities rather than its entirety . . ." Ironically, Niven seemed to give more earnestness to his portrayal in this nonsensical outing than he had in many past performances. *Variety* found him to be "immaculately debonair and wittily amusing" while the *Saturday Review* observed he was "believable as a duke but unfortunately is given few believable lines as well as an unbelievable character." For whatever it was worth, the *New Yorker* magazine offered: "In appearance, manners, elocution, and world-weariness, Mr. Niven is a model aristocrat . . ."

"James Bond is back with his morals, his vows and his celebrated image." The line from *Casino Royale* (Columbia, 1967) establishes that Sir James Bond (Niven) has come out of retirement when the international crime organization SMERSH threatens to dominate the world. "You're joke-shop spies," he tells the quartet (John Huston, William Holden, Charles Boyer, and Kurt Kasznar) who appeal to him for help, and stammers that he is "the true one and only original James Bond." He employs a half-dozen 007's along the way to help smash SMERSH, headed by his fiendish nephew Jimmy Bond (Woody Allen), whose front is the Casino Royale. He calls for the French Foreign Legion, American Indians, the U.S. Cavalry, United Nations paratroopers, and the Keystone Kops, who invade the Casino to oust the enemy forces. But Allen has digested a bomb capsule which soon explodes, sending fragments of the casino and its inhabitants into the stratosphere.

Completed at the absurd cost of $12 million, *Casino Royale* was owned and headed by Charles K. Feldman.* Feldman had been unable to negotiate a pact with Harry Saltzman and Albert Broccoli, who owned all the other James Bond stories. His mammoth satirical entry proved unflamboyant at the box office at a time when audiences would accept no one but Sean Connery as the sexy, handsome, ingenious Bond. In the rush to condemn the picture, few cared to remember how appealing a portrayal Niven had offered, considering the circumstances. His notices are worth recalling. "David Niven comes off best because his stylish acting floats far above the script's witless, single-entendre standard . . ." (*Time* magazine); "The concept of Bond as an aging but ultra-agile Edwardian type, embodied to perfection by David Niven . . ." (Judith Crist, *New York World*

---

*Ustinov would later quip: "It did very well in Vienna, which is exactly the kind of town in which I expected it to be successful."

With Joanna Pettet, Terence Cooper, and Barbara Bouchet in CASINO ROYALE (Col '67)

Journal Tribune); "Although David Niven seems justifiably bewildered by the proceedings, he has a neat delivery of throwaway lines and enters into the exuberant physical action with a pleasant blandness" (*Variety*).

Niven seemed to have the 1960s curse of being involved in troubled productions. In the midst of filming *Eye of the Devil* (MGM, 1967), co-star Kim Novak suffered an alleged back injury and left the production, to be hastily replaced by David's frequent co-lead, Deborah Kerr. The film might better have been abandoned altogether, for it was a dreary "haunted chateau picture" in which Niven as the Marquis de Bellac believes that he must follow tradition and sacrifice his life to the barren earth in order that his vineyards will again flourish. The Black Mass rituals which haunt the picture seem to be as confusing to the cast members as to the audience. MGM was so embarrassed by this European-lensed production that it was tossed away on a double-bill entry. Although Arthur Hiller, Michael Anderson, and Sidney J. Furie were at one time or another in-

volved with the picture's direction, J. Lee Thompson took billing (and blame) on the credits as the guide of these "dreary doings" (*Variety*).

"When in doubt return Niven to bedroom comedy," seemed to be the order of the day, with the actor starring in *Prudence and the Pill* (Twentieth Century–Fox, 1968), a sort of twentieth-century Restoration comedy with the focal point being birth-control pills. Niven appears as the very wealthy Gerald Hardcastle, wed to the very rich Prudence (Deborah Kerr), who takes the pill and loves Dr. Alan Hewitt (Keith Mitchel). Niven's mistress - is Elizabeth Brest (Irina Demick). A great deal of genteel and bawdy mate-swapping occurs until Niven and Kerr divorce and each marries the one of his and her choice. Then the babies arrive. Of his child Niven says, it is "the most beautiful child I have ever seen in the whole of my fairly long life." While there was a general lack of subtlety and taste to the script, the cast, particularly Niven, Kerr, and Dame Edith Evans, helped boost the antics onto a more refined level. The picture grossed an amazing $4.5 million,

---

°On CBS's "Climax" video series, a version of *Casino Royale* was performed (October 21, 1954) with Barry Nelson as James Bond. Niven, long a good friend of Ian Fleming, had been the author's original choice for the screen superhero when the books were first bought for filming.

making it all the more strange that *Prudence and the Pill* remains the fifth and final (to date) Niven-Kerr screen venture.

On Broadway Alan King (and later Sam Levene) had had a field day in the play *The Impossible Years* (Playhouse Theatre: October 13, 1965, 670 performances). When MGM acquired the screen rights, the studio was in desperate financial straits, and hoped that this antic comedy, in the tradition of the play-movie *Take Her, She's Mine* (Twentieth Century–Fox, 1963), might salvage the situation. It was directed at a frantic pace, but seemed a futile exercise as diluted for the silver screen. In the 1968 Metro release, David was cast as a square papa, a psychiatrist no less, married to a square mama (Lola Albright). Both of them are horrified by their teenage daughter (Christina Ferrare) and her constant trouble at school or with the police for protest picketing. When the daughter mends her ways and becomes just the opposite, it is revealed that she is secretly married but has been afraid to tell her parents because of their rather stodgy opinions. This regressive filmfare was more "Ozzie and Harriet" than *Happy Anniversary*. Said *New York* magazine: "It's all smuttied-up Andy Hardy stuff, complete with student protest, hippie and nudie gags plete with student protest, hippie and nudie gags that the meanest television series would consider old hat, and the sight of Niven prat-falling and guzzling and throwing hysterics around provides the ultimate comment on what the movies, let alone the image of psychiatrists, have descended to."

Another misfire in which Niven participated was *The Extraordinary Seaman,* intended by MGM for 1967 release, but not generally thrown to the winds until 1969. One reason given for its delayed public exposure was that the film contained a great many excerpts from vintage 1940s newsreels and the studio was afraid to distribute the movie until proper clearances had been obtained. Its slender thread of a story concerned Lieutenant Commander Finchhaven, a British naval officer condemned to eternally sail the seas in his dilapidated World War I warship until he can vindicate the honor of his family, which he blackened by falling overboard and drowning during the heat of a battle. Niven looked rather dapper with his beard and dressed in his officer's whites. To save on money, the film was lensed in Mexico. To date, it remains director John Frankenheimer's only attempt at screen comedy, although he prefers to label it an "anti-war film," which he thinks is "very funny."

With Deborah Kerr in PRUDENCE AND THE PILL (20th '68)

Obviously, when a leading man is approaching sixty, he cannot be too fussy about the type of movie roles he accepts. In 1969, unable to settle back into any particular screen niche, David again went military oncamera. In *Before Winter Comes* (Columbia, 1969), filmed in Austria, he is again a British major. This time he has a gimpy leg suffered when his disregard for orders resulted in the loss of two hundred of his men as well as the infliction of his wound. He is now (1945) assigned to a displaced-persons' camp on the Austrian border where it is his duty to determine whether refugees should be sent to the American or Russian zones. His interpreter (Topol), a refugee, turns out to be an escaped Russian soldier who romances the same girl (Anna Karina) as the major. When the interpreter, who had made most of the camp decisions, is revealed as an escapee, he is returned via truck to Russia. The major then receives word that he is being reassigned to yet another refugee camp for having done such a satisfactory job at the present one. The few words of praise this J. Lee Thompson–directed film received were for the English-language film debut of Topol. Any compliments for Niven were by way of indirection. Judith Crist (*New York*) reported: "[he] reveals that the fine actor within has

not been slaughtered by all the inane roles he's filled in recent years." In a more positive tone, Miss Crist added: "He creates the Army Mind in all its manifestations in an unforgettable manner."

His other release of the year, *The Brain* (Paramount, 1969), did not emerge as a profit-making venture for its company. Niven was cast as a British colonel with NATO who is the mastermind of an elaborate plan to rob that international organization of an enormous amount of money. The results added up to very little, despite the presence of Jean-Paul Belmondo, Bourvil, and Eli Wallach in the cast. It was "another of those multi-nation comedies in which national characteristics (English cool, Italian hysteria, etc.) are presumed to be screamingly funny and where the ill-assorted cast is therefore encouraged to overplay *ad lib*" (British *Monthly Film Bulletin*).

With Peter Finch, Liv Ullmann, and Max Von Sydow, Niven then went into rehearsal for *Man's Fate,* a Carlo Ponti–Fred Zinnemann production of Andre Malraux's complex novel. After the expenditure of close to $5 million, and just prior to the actual start of principal photography, the project was halted in November 1969, when MGM underwent another changeover of executives and

With Faye Dunaway and Alan Alda in THE EXTRAORDINARY SEAMAN (MGM '69)

With Topol in BEFORE WINTER COMES (Col '69)

a severe cutback was ordered by the new regime. Suits and countersuits were filed, but the net results were still that *Man's Fate* was permanently shelved by the Metro hierarchy.

Niven was then off the screen (big and little) for two years, devoting most of his energies to his family, to writing, and to his constant pursuit of recreation. As was his custom, he would concentrate his full attention on the Continental ski slopes during *the* season, refusing to allow any show-business work to interfere with this athletic occupation. It was his major contentment, his escape, and his means of remaining "young" and trim.

While most of his fellow debonair actors had either died (Adolphe Menjou, Herbert Marshall), retired (William Powell, George Brent, Robert Montgomery, Cary Grant), or graduated to atypical character work (Melvyn Douglas, Ray Milland, Brian Aherne), Niven refused to surrender to the demanding inroads of time. Like another Britisher, Rex Harrison, he was blessed with the luck still to be able to conjure up the proper on-screen look, that of the aging but very capable

genteel rake. This ability allowed Niven to retain the professional image that neither he nor film-makers wanted him to shed. The public remained a passive onlooker.

Perhaps the nadir of David's screen career was *The Statue* (Cinerama, 1971), a film of unquestionably poor taste. It had a one-joke premise, and it was strictly phallic at that. Niven was Alex Bolt, who has had time to see his wife (Virna Lisi) only eighteen days during the past three years because he is so preoccupied with developing a universal language. U.S. Ambassador Robert Vaughn commissions Lisi to sculpt a statue of her Nobel Prize –winning husband to be displayed in the American Embassy in London. Her labor results in an eighteen-foot, 750-pound nude likeness which she privately unveils for her hubby. Niven is aghast to find that the statue resembles him in all areas but that of the genitalia. Convinced that she has a lover, he makes a list of all the men who have visited her in the past months, and sets out to find the man whose privates match those of the statue. Puerile! Smutty! Amateurish! The ending was even a pathetic cop-out. It seems that Lisi had used Michelangelo's David for her inspiration in carving out the vital area. A sure sign that Niven regarded this crude excursion as a low-point of his oncamera energies was his constant tweaking of his ear, one of his nervous habits that has increased over the years. Anitra Earle (*San Francisco Chronicle*) summed up the film best, labeling it "a sniggering comedy carried to such extremes that it becomes difficult to tell which is more offensive: its prissy hypocrisy, its blatant banality, or the clumsily-fashioned 'double entendres' that sit in the script like flies in the soup."[*]

If David's cinema standing had dwindled to his being labeled a British Gig Young, he redeemed his reputation as a person, when in 1972 G. P. Putnam's Sons published his autobiography, *The Moon's a Balloon.* This 150,000-word essay had sold, by mid-December 1973, over three million copies (in hardback and paperback) worldwide, and reportedly earned its author some $600,000 in royalties. In penning this best-seller, Niven stated in his preface: "My offering is a period piece. I hope you may enjoy looking back over my shoulder." Not only book buyers but literary critics as well were responsive to this celebrity excursion, which, like Mary Astor's *My Story* (1959) and Shirley MacLaine's *Don't Fall off the Mountain*

[*]Niven was awarded the Best Actor prize for *The Statue* at the First International Comic Film Festival held at the resort town of Cauterets, France, in August 1973.

400

In THE STATUE (Cin '71)

(1970), ranks among the best show-business-oriented biographies of the twentieth century. "A juicy, all-day lollipop of a book!" said the *New York Times.* "There are successes, heartbreaks, comedies, glamorous names, inside Hollywood stories, plenty of out-loud laughs, and many of the best anecdotes can't be printed here. What David Niven is telling us, what his life demonstrates—there are more ways to get high than one can shake a stick at!" One of the most astute perceptions on this book came from political observer William F. Buckley, Jr., yet another friend of Niven. He stated: "David Niven is known among his friends as, quite simply, an incomparable companion. Always, when asked why, they were never able to communicate his particular magic. Now all we have to do is say: read his book. It's all here." The ever-modest Niven would say of his tome, which when published in England became the number-one seller there, "I often found the book was badly balanced because I found when I got lucky and 'successful,' I became frightfully dull."

Between completing another book and pursuing his sports activities, Niven accepted a role in *King, Queen, Knave,* a joint German-U.S. venture filmed in Munich in 1971, and taken from the novel by Vladimir Nabokov. As directed by Jerzy Skolimowski, it is a black comedy of a husband (Niven), his sexually starved wife (Gina Lollobrigida), and his recently orphaned nephew (John Moulder-Brown). To give this love triangle a gimmick, there is introduced an inventor who has devised a way of making life-like mannequins. Lo and behold, when Lollobrigida, who has plotted Niven's death, is drowned, what mannequin is first produced by the inventor? None other than a replica of the late woman. Because the picture was tucked away in a distributor's warehouse until late 1973 when it had some showings in England, American moviegoers have to take the word of the British *Monthly Film Bulletin,* which judged it "beautifully acted, extremely funny, and entirely delightful."

Considering the thrust of Niven's latter-day screen career, it was no big shock to learn that he had signed in 1973 to star in *Vampira,* to be filmed in London for Columbia Pictures by Clive Donner. With mock seriousness, David portrayed the infamous Count Dracula,* who, thirsting for

*Previously enacted oncamera, in order, by Max Schreck, Bela Lugosi, Lon Chaney, Jr., John Carradine, Francis Lederer, Noel Williams, Christopher Lee, and William Marshall.

their blood, lures beauty-contest winners to his castle. Their blood is then transferred to his countess (black actress Teresa Graves), who has been dead some fifty years. Niven took the venture jocularly, refusing to acknowledge what a comedown this movie was for the man once touted as being the "new" Ronald Colman. (The film has yet to "sneak" into U.S. release; it was panned when distributed abroad.)

More in keeping with his sophisticated image was Niven's agreement to narrate three CBS-TV network travel-adventure specials. The first, *The Forbidden Desert of the Danakil*, aired on April 25, 1973. Howard Thompson commended "the excellent narration spoken by David Niven." Another in the series, *We Live with Elephants,* was telecast on March 13, 1974, with Niven again supplying the "leisurely narrative" (*Variety*). In 1974, David was also seen and heard in Pan American Airways video commercials, and was signed to appear with Toshiro Mifune in *Paper Tiger* (1975), shot on location in Southeast Asia and Bavaria. "The third TV special, with Niven narrating, *Gorilla* was telecast on February 28, 1975.

In addition to owning a chalet in Switzerland and the "monstrosity" at Cap Ferrat, the Nivens were reported to have purchased land on the island of Bora Bora, where he completed his next book, *Bring on the Empty Horses*. Published by G. P. Putnam's Sons in the fall of 1975, the tome is "bursting with riotous inside stories of Hollywood in its heyday!" Among the subjects dealt with by raconteur David are Clark Gable, Greta Garbo, Samuel Goldwyn, and William Randolph Hearst. Of his pal Errol Flynn, Niven writes, "With Errol, you knew exactly where you were. He always let you down." In reviewing this potential best-seller, *Publishers Weekly* noted, "With a good deal of shrewdness and warmth of feeling peeping through that air of bewildered detachment that seems to be his trademark as an actor, a writer and a man, he brings us Hollywood as he knows it in its golden prime, from the early 30s to the age of TV. Above all he brings us *them*— the outstanding stars, producers, directors, writers, tycoons and oddballs, many of whom were his friends."

In mid-1975 David made his first feature for Walt Disney when he was signed to star in *Double Trouble*. It seems nothing is beyond the work-conscious Niven.

With Gina Lollobrigida and John Moulder-Brown in HERZBUBE (a.k.a. KING, QUEEN, KNAVE) (MMG '72)

For a globe-trotting playboy, David managed to do quite well in rearing his children. Once, when asked to speak on the subject, he confided his philosophy: "It's really unfair to the kids to be in the movie business. I remember when my two boys were going to school in California—there were two sorts of reactions from their schoolmates: there were those who were impressed by the fact that father was in the movies, and then there was the kind who jeered, 'I saw your Dad last night and does he stink.'

"I had a way of getting around this and I think it's the only wise thing I've ever done. I used to rehearse them before they went to school in the morning with their little buckets of milk. I stood them up and said, 'Now I'm a horrible, spotty child in your school and I'm going to ask you a question: what does your father do?' Then I gave them their line: 'One, two, three. He's a very, very bad actor but he absolutely loves doing it.' "

As for these sons, David Niven, Jr., in 1974, owned a restaurant in London called "Drones" and was European chief of Paramount Pictures. His brother, Jamie, a London banker, has no interest in any form of show business. Both speak fluent French and Italian, besides English.

David was one of the masters of ceremonies on the April 9, 1974, Academy Award telecasts. As if he were the straight man in one of his own films, he informed the auditorium and home-viewing audiences that what the prize-giving event needed was Mae West streaking across the stage. No sooner said, than almost done, for later on in his segment of the ceremonies, a male streaker did zoom across the stage. With his most typical oncamera look, one of mixed embarrassment, amusement, seriousness, and conspiracy, Niven tweaked his ear and carried on with his hosting duties, ever in command of the situation, as one would expect of a dapper gentleman.

David made an appearance as host of *The Bluffers* (NBC-TV, May 28, 1974), a rather embarrassing sixty minutes of television non-entertainment, branded by the *Hollywood Reporter* as "the worst rip-off of 'Laugh-In' ever done." It was certainly not the guide to instant erudition as advertised. A little more felicitous was David's portrayal on "Bell System Family Theatre" in *The Canterville Ghost* (NBC-TV, March 10, 1975). He recreated the role played by Charles Laughton in the 1944 MGM feature in which Margaret O'Brien stole the limelight from the rotund spook.

As for the future, Niven insists he will keep his primary home base in the tiny village in the south of France. "I am really a very private person. I want privacy to enjoy myself with my family. I want to spend time with my daughters, because in a few years their childhood will be over."

In 1974, at the age of sixty-four, David Niven stated that he wished his epitaph to read: "He tried it all." Dry-witted entertainment columnist and commentator Rona Barrett added: "Believe me, kids, he *has!*" As for his profession, Niven insists: "Actors should get down on their knees each morning and thank God for the opportunity given them to still play games like children—and for a fortune, too."

David Niven

MUTINY ON THE BOUNTY (MGM, 1935) 132 M.

Producer, Irving Thalberg; director, Frank Lloyd; based on the novel by Charles Nordhoff, James Norman Hall; screenplay, Talbot Jennings, Jules Furthman, Carey Wilson; music, Herbert Stothart; song, Gus Kahn, Bronislau Kaper, and Walter Jurmann; camera, Arthur Edeson; editor, Margaret Booth.

Clark Gable (Fletcher Christian); Charles Laughton (Captain Bligh); Franchot Tone (Roger Byam); Dudley Digges (Bachus); Henry Stephenson (Sir Joseph Banks); Herbert Mundin (Smith); Donald Crisp (Burkitt); Eddie Quillan (Ellison); Francis Lister (Captain Nelson); Spring Byington (Mrs. Byam); Movita (Tehani); Mamo Clark (Maimiti); Byron Russell (Quintal); Percy Waram (Coleman); David Torrence (Lord Hood); John Harrington (Mr. Purcell); Robert Livingston (Young); Douglas Walton (Stewart); Ian Wolfe (Samuel Maggs); De Witt C. Jennings (Fryer); Ivan Simpson (Morgan); Vernon Downing (Hayward); Wallis Clark (Morrison); Alec Craig (McCoy); Dick Winslow (Tinkler); Doris Lloyd (Cockney Moll); Eric Wilton (Captain of Board); Lionel Belmore (Innkeeper); Nadine Beresford (Ellison's Mother); Marion Clayton (Mary Ellison); Mary Gordon (Pedlar); Winter Hall (Chaplain); James Cagney, David Niven (Extras); Charles Mauu, Sam Wallace Driscoll (Bits).

WITHOUT REGRET (PAR, 1935) 74 M.

Producer, B. P. Fineman; director, Harold Young; story, Roland Pertwee, Harold Dearden; screenplay, Doris Anderson, Charles Brackett; camera, William C. Mellor.

Elissa Landi (Jennifer Gage); Paul Cavanagh (Sir Robert Godfrey); Frances Drake (Mona Gould); Kent Taylor (Steven Paradine); Gilbert Emery (Inspector Hayes); David Niven (Bill Gage); Betty Holt (Godfrey's Baby); Marina Schubert (Given); Joseph North (Jessup); Colin Tapley (Cleaver); Mrs. Wong Wing (Fat Chinese Woman); Virginia Bassett (Sour-Faced Old Dame); Eddie Lee (Chinese Officer); Victor Wong (Soldier); Henry Roquemore (Stout Man); Tom Gubbins, Gino Corrado (Men); Tetsu Komai (General Wu Chen); Luke Chan (Wing); Peter Hobbes (Fred); Doris Stone (Girl); Clive Morgan (Boy); Stuart Hall (Drunk); Reginald Sheffield (Reporter); Forrester Harvey (Doctor); Alex Pollard (Waiter).

BARBARY COAST (UA, 1935) 97 M.

Producer, Samuel Goldwyn; director, Howard Hawks; screenplay, Charles MacArthur, Ben Hecht; music director, Alfred Newman; camera, Ray June; editor, Edward Curtis.

Miriam Hopkins [Swan (Mary Rutledge)]; Edward G. Robinson (Louis Chamalis); Joel McCrea (Jim Carmichael); Walter Brennan (Old Atrocity); Frank Craven (Colonel Marcus Aurelius Cobb); Brian Donlevy (Knuckles Jacoby); Otto Hoffman (Peebles); Rollo Lloyd (Wigham); Donald Meek (Sawbuck McTavish); Roger Gray (Sandy Ferguson); Clyde Cook (Oakie); Harry Carey (Jed Slocum); J. M. Kerrigan (Judge Harper); Matt McHugh (Broncho); Wong Chung (Ah Wing); Russ Powell (Sheriff); Fredrik Vogeding (Ship's Captain); Dave Wengren (First Mate); Anders Van Haden (McCready, the Second Mate); Jules Cowles (Pilot); Cyril Thornton (Steward); Clarence Wertz (Drunk); Harry Semels (Lookout); Bert Sprotte, Claude Payton, Frank Benson, Bob Stevenson (Passengers); David Niven (Sailor Thrown Out of Saloon); Constantine Romanoff (Bouncer); Victor Potel (Wilkins); Patricia Farley (Dance Hall Girl); Hank Mann, Doc Wilson (Waiters); Harry Holman (Mayor); Ethel Wales (Mayor's Wife); Herman Bing (Fish Peddler); Kit Guard (Kibitzer); Jim Thorpe (Indian); Tom London (Ringsider).

A FEATHER IN HER HAT (COL, 1935) 70 M.

Producer, Everett Riskin; director, Alfred Santell; story, I. A. R. Wylie; screenplay, Lawrence Hazard; camera, Joseph Walker; editor, Viola Lawrence.

Pauline Lord (Clarissa Phipps); Basil Rathbone (Captain Courtney); Louis Hayward (Richard Orland); Billie Burke (Julia Trent Anders); Wendy Barrie (Pauline Anders); Nydia Westman (Emily Judson); Victor Varconi (Paul Anders); Thurston Hall (Sir Elroyd Joyce); Nana Bryant (Lady Drake); J. M. Kerrigan (Pobjoy); Lawrence Grant (Dr. Phillips); Doris Lloyd (Liz Vining); David Niven (Leo Cartwright); John Rogers (Henry Vining); E. E. Clive (Higgins, the Pub Proprietor); Leonard Mudie (Orator); Harry Allen (Alf); Ottola Nesmith (Susan); Tempe Pigott (Katy); Lois Lindsey (Woman); Leyland Hodgson (Leading Man); Olaf Hytten (Taxi Driver); Major Sam Harris, Lorimer Johnston (Men); Doreen Munroe (Mrs. Pobjoy); Wilson Benge, James May (Butchers); Gil Perkins (Ticket Taker); Vivien Patterson (Nurse).

SPLENDOR (UA, 1935) 77 M.

Producer, Samuel Goldwyn; director, Elliott Nugent; story-screenplay, Rachel Crothers; music director, Alfred Newman; camera, Gregg Toland; editor, Margaret Clancey.

Miriam Hopkins (Phyllis); Joel McCrea (Brighton); Helen Westley (Mrs. Lorrimore); Katharine Alexander (Martha); David Niven (Clancey); Ruth Weston (Edith); Paul Cavanagh (Deering); Billie Burke (Clarissa); Ivan F. Simpson (Fletcher); Arthur Treacher (Captain Ballinger); Torben Meyer (Von Hoffstatter); Reginald Sheffield (Billy Grimes); William R. (Billy) Arnold (Jake); Maidel Turner (Mrs. Hicks); Clarence H. Wilson (Process Server); Frederick Lee (Track Attendant); Violet Axelle (Brighton Maid); Nina Penn (Woman Opera Attendant); Eddie Craven (Elevator Man); Connie Howard, Cosmo Kyrle Bellew (Guests at Dinner); William O'Brien (Theatre Ushers); Bob Heasley (Western Union Messenger); Jeanie Roberts (Gertie); Clinton Lyle (Chauffeur).

ROSE MARIE (MGM, 1936) 113 M.

Producer, Hunt Stromberg; director, W. S. Van Dyke II, based on the operetta by Otto A. Harbach, Oscar Hammerstein II, Rudolf Friml, Herbert Stohart; screenplay, Frances Goodrich, Albert Hackett, Alice Duer Miller; music director, Stothart; songs, Harbach, Hammerstein II, and Friml, Kahn and Stothart, Sam Lewis, Joe Young, and Harry Akst, Shelton Brooks; totem pole dance staged by Chester Hale; operatic episodes staged by William von Wymetal; art director, Cedric Gibbons, Joseph Wright, Edwin B. Willis; gowns, Adrian; sound, Douglas Shearer; camera, William Daniels; editor, Blanche Sewell.

Jeanette MacDonald (Marie de Flor); Nelson Eddy (Sergeant Bruce); James Stewart (John Flower); Reginald Owen (Meyerson); Allan Jones (Romeo); Gilda Gray (Bella); George Regas (Boniface); Robert Greig (Cafe Manager); Una O'Connor (Anna); Lucien Littlefield (Storekeeper); Alan Mowbray (Premier); David Niven (Teddy); Herman Bing (Mr. Daniels); James Conlin (Joe); Dorothy Gray (Edith); Mary Anita Loos (Corn Queen); Aileen Carlyle (Susan); Halliwell Hobbes (Mrs. Gordon); Paul Porcasi (Emil); Ed Dearing (Mounted Policeman); Pat West (Traveling Salesman); Milton Owen (Stage Manager); David Clyde (Doorman); Russell Hicks (Commandant); Rolfe Sedan, Jack Pennick (Men); David Robel, Rinaldo Alacorn (Dancers); Leonard Carey (Louis); Bert Lindley (Trapper).

PALM SPRINGS (PAR, 1936) 72 M.

Producer, Walter Wanger; director, Aubrey Scotto; story, Myles Connolly; screenplay, Joseph Fields; music director, Boris Morros; songs, Leo Robin and Ralph Rainger, Mack Gordon and Harry Revel; camera, James Van Trees.

Frances Langford (Joan Smith); Sir Guy Standing (Captain Smith); Ernest Cossart (Starkey); Smith Ballew (Slim); David Niven (George Brittel); E. E. Clive (Morgan); Spring Byington (Aunt Letty); Sterling Holloway (Oscar); Grady Sutton (Bud); Sarah Edwards (Miss Pinchon); Ed Moose (Motorcycle Cop); Mary Jane Temple (Nurse); June Horn, Ann Doran, Ella McKenzie (School Girls); Fred "Snowflake" Toonnes (Porter); Frances Morris (Maid); David Worth (Leonard); Annabelle & Marianne Brudie (Twins); Lee Phelps (Bartender); Maidel Turner (Mrs. Baxter); Bert Gale (Caterer); Cyril Ring (Reception Clerk).

DODSWORTH (UA, 1936) 90 M.

Producer, Samuel Goldwyn; associate producer, Merritt Hulburd; director, William Wyler; based on the novel by Sinclair Lewis; screenplay, Sidney Howard; art director, Richard Day; costumes, Omar Kiam; assistant director, Eddie Beroudy; music, Alfred Newman; sound, Oscar Lagerstrom; special effects, Ray Binger; camera, Rudolph Mate; editor, Daniel Mandell.

Walter Huston (Sam Dodsworth); Ruth Chatterton (Fran Dodsworth); Paul Lukas (Arnold Iselin); Mary Astor (Edith Cortright); David Niven (Lockert); Gregory Gaye (Kurt von Obersdorf); Maria Ouspenskaya (Baroness von Obersdorf); Odette Myrtil (Madame de Penable); Kathryn Marlowe (Emily); John Payne (Harry); Spring Byington (Matey Pearson); Harlan Briggs (Tubby Pearson).

THANK YOU, JEEVES (20th, 1936) 57 M.

Producer, Sol M. Wurtzel; director, Arthur Greville Collins; based on the story by P. G. Wodehouse; screenplay, Joseph Hoffman, Stephen Gross; camera, Barney McGill; editor, Nick DeMaggio.

Arthur Treacher (Jeeves); Virginia Field (Marjorie Lowman); David Niven (Bertie Wooster); Lester Matthews (Elliott Manville); Colin Tapley (Tom Brock); John Spacey (Jack Stone); Ernie Stanton (Mr. Snelling); Gene Reynolds (Bobby Smith); Douglas Walton (Edward McDermott); Willie Best (Drowsy); Paul McVey (Mr. Brown); Colin Kenny (Crook); Jimmie Aubrey (Cab Driver); Joe North (Butler); Dorothy Phillips (Mrs. Brown); Ed Dearing (Motor Cop).

THE CHARGE OF THE LIGHT BRIGADE (WB, 1936) 116 M.

Producer, Hal B. Wallis; associate producer, Sam Bischoff; director, Michael Curtiz; suggested by the poem by Alfred Tennyson; story, Michel Jacoby; screenplay, Jacoby, Rowland Leigh; music, Max Steiner; music director, Leo F. Forbstein; art director, Jack Hughes; technical adviser, Captain E. Rochfort-John; tactical and military drills, Major Sam Harris; camera effects, Fred Jackman; camera, Sol Polito; editor, George Amy.

Errol Flynn (Captain Geoffrey Vickers); Olivia de Havilland (Elsa Campbell); Patric Knowles (Captain Perry Vickers); Donald Crisp (Colonel Campbell); Henry Stephenson (Sir Charles Macefield); Nigel Bruce (Sir Benjamin Warrenton); David Niven (Captain James Randall); G. P. Huntley, Jr. (Major Jewett); Spring Byington (Lady Octavia Warrenton); C. Henry Gordon (Surat Khan); E. E. Clive (Sir Humphrey Harcourt); Lumsden Hare (Colonel Woodward); Robert Barrat (Count Igor Voloneff); Walter Holbrook (Cornet Barclay); Charles Sedgwick (Cornet Pearson); J. Carrol Naish (Subahdar Major Puran Singh); Scotty Beckett (Prema Singh); Princess Gaigum (Prema's Mother); George Regas (Wazir); Helen Sanborn (Mrs. Jowett); George Sorel (Surwan); Dick Botiller (Native); Phillis Coghlan (Woman at Ball); Arthur Thalasso, Stephen Moritz (Sepoys); Georges Renavent (General Canrobert); Charles Croker King (Lord Cardigan); Brandon Hurst (Lord Raglan); Craufurd Kent (Captain Brown).

BELOVED ENEMY (UA, 1936) 90 M.

Producer, Samuel Goldwyn; associate producer, George Haight; director, H. C. Potter; story, John Balderston; screenplay, Balderston, Rose Franken, William Brown Meloney, David Hart; camera, Gregg Toland; editor, Sherman Todd.

Merle Oberon (Helen Drummond); Brian Aherne (Dennis Riordan); Karen Morley (Cathleen); Jerome Cowan (O'Rourke); David Niven (Gerald Preston); Henry Stephenson (Lord Athleigh); Donald Crisp (Burke); Ra Hould (Jerry); Granville Bates (Ryan); P. J. Kelly (Rooney); Leo McCabe (Connor); Pat O'Malley (Callahan); Jack Mulhall (Casey); Claude King (Colonel Loder); Wyndham Standing (Thornton); Robert Strange (Perrins); Lionel Pape (Crump); John Burton (Hall); Leyland Hodgson (Hawkins); David Torrence (Alroyd); Theodore Von Eltz (O'Brien); Donald Barry (Bit).

WE HAVE OUR MOMENTS (UNIV, 1937) 67 M.

Associate producer, Edmund Grainger; director, Alfred L. Werker; story, Charles F. Belden, Frederick Stephani; screenplay, Bruce Manning, Charles Grayson; art director, Jack Otterson; music director, Charles Previn; camera, Milton Krasner; editor, Frank Gross.

Sally Eilers (Roselyn); James Dunn (Wade); Thurston Hall (Rutherford); Marjorie Gateson (Mrs. Rutherford); Warren Hymer (Smacksey); David Niven (Gilling); Mischa Auer (Enrico); Franklin Pangborn (Bartender); George Davis, Gunnis Davis (Waiters); Margaret McWade (Woman in State Room); Olaf Hytten (Steward); Alice Ardell (Stewardess); Alphonse Martell (Headwaiter); Jerry Larkin (Assistant Purser); Adrienne d'Ambricourt (Maid); Jack Chefe (Croupier); Joyce Compton (School Teacher); John Maurice Sullivan (Bank Manager).

THE PRISONER OF ZENDA (UA, 1937) 101 M.°

Producer, David O. Selznick; director, John Cromwell, W. S. Van Dyke II; based on the novel by Anthony Hope; screenplay, John Balderston, Wells Root, Donald Ogden Stewart; art director, Lyle Wheeler; music, Alfred Newman; special effects, Jack Cosgrove; camera, James Wong Howe; editor, Hal C. Kern.

Ronald Colman (King Rudolf V/Rudolf Rassendyl); Madeleine Carroll (Princess Flavia); Douglas Fairbanks, Jr. (Rupert of Hentzau); Mary Astor (Antoinette De Mauban); C. Aubrey Smith (Colonel Zapt); Raymond Massey (Black Michael); David Niven (Captain Fritz von Tarlenheim); Eleanor Wesselhoeft (Cook); Byron Foulger (Johann); Montagu Love (Detchard); William Von Brincken (Kraftstein); Phillip Sleeman (Lauengram); Ralph Faulkner (Bersonin); Alexander D'Arcy (De Gautet); Torben Meyer (Michael's Butler); Ian MacLaren (Cardinal); Lawrence Grant (Marshal Strakencz); Howard Lang (Josef); Ben Webster (British Ambassador); Evelyn Beresford (British Ambassador's Wife); Emmett King (Lord High Chamberlain); Al Shean (Orchestra Leader); Florence

°Some sepia sequences.

Roberts (Duenna); Francis Ford (Man); Russ Powell, D'Arcy Corrigan (Travelers).

DINNER AT THE RITZ (20th, 1937) 82 M.

Producer, Robert T. Kane; director, Harold D. Schuster; story, Roland Pertwee, Romney Brent; screenplay, Pertwee; music-songs, Lee Sims; costumes, Rene Hubert; camera, Philip Tannura; editor, James B. Clark.

Annabella (Ranie Racine); Paul Lukas (Philip de Beaufort); David Niven (Count Paul de Brack); Romeny Brent (Jimmy Raine); Francis L. Sullivan (Brogard); Stewart Rome (Henri Racine); Nora Swinburne (Lady Railton); Tyrrell Davis (Duval); Frederick Leister (Tarade); William Dewhurst (J. R. Devine); Vivienne Chatterton (Marthe, the Maid); Ronald Shiner (Sydney, the Porter); Raymond Huntley (Gibont); Ralph Truman (Auctioneer).

BLUEBEARD'S EIGHTH WIFE (PAR, 1938) 80 M.

Producer-director, Ernst Lubitsch; based on the play by Alfred Savoir; English play adaptor, Charlton Andrews; screenplay, Charles Brackett, Billy Wilder; art directors, Hans Dreier, Robert Usher; music, Frederick Hollander, Werner R. Heymann; orchestrator, John Leipold; sound, Harry D. Mills; camera, Leo Tover; editor, William Shea.

Claudette Colbert (Nicole De Leiselle); Gary Cooper (Michael Brandon); Edward Everett Horton (Marquis de Loiselle); David Niven (Albert De Regnier); Elizabeth Patterson (Aunt Hedwige); Herman Bing (Monsieur Pepinard); Warren Hymer (Kid Mulligan); Franklin Pangborn, Armand Cortes (Assistant Hotel Managers); Rolfe Sedan (Floorwalker); Lawrence Grant (Professor Urganzeff); Lionel Pape (Monsieur Potin); Tyler Brooke (Clerk); Tom Ricketts (Uncle Andre); Barlowe Borland (Uncle Fernandel); Charles Halton (Monsieur de la Coste—President); Pauline Garon (Customer); Sheila Darcy (Maid); Alphonse Martell (Hotel Employee); Alex Woloshin, George Davis (Porters); Ellen Drew (Secretary); Leon Ames (Ex-Chauffeur); Henry Roquemore (Fat Man); Olaf Hytten (Valet); Jacques Vanaire (Manager); Michael Visaroff (Vice President); Paul Bryar (Radio Announcer).

FOUR MEN AND A PRAYER (20th, 1938) 85 M.

Producer, Darryl F. Zanuck; associate producer, Kenneth Macgowan; director, John Ford; based a play by David Garth; screenplay, Richard Sherman, Sonya Levien, Walter Ferris; music director, Louis Silvers; art directors, Bernard Herzbrun, Rudolph Sternad; camera, Ernest Palmer; editor, Louis Loeffler.

Loretta Young (Lynn); Richard Greene (Goeff); George Sanders (Wyatt); David Niven (Chris); C. Aubrey Smith (Leigh); J. Edward Bromberg (Torres); William Henry (Rod); John Carradine (General Sebastian); Alan Hale (Furnoy); Reginald Denny (Loveland); Berton Churchill (Cherrington); Cecil Cunningham (Piper); Barry Fitzgerald (Mulcahey); Frank Dawson (Mullins); John Sutton (Drake); Lina Basquette (Ah-Nee); Will Stanton (Cockney); Paul McVey (Sanders, the Secretary); Manuel Paris (Captain); Robert Lowery (Sailor); C. Montague Shaw, Winter Hall, John Spacey (Barristers); Chris Pin Martin (Soldier); Selmer Jackson (Yacht Captain); Barbara Denny, Ruth Clifford (Telephone Operators); Helen Ericson (Joan).

THREE BLIND MICE (20th, 1938) 75 M.

Producer, Raymond Griffith; director, William A. Seiter; based upon the play by Stephen Powys; screenplay, Brown Holmes, Lynn Starling; camera, Ernest Palmer; editor, James B. Morley.

Loretta Young (Pam); Joel McCrea (Van Smith); David Niven (Steve Harrington); Stuart Erwin (Mike); Marjorie Weaver (Moira); Pauline Moore (Elizabeth); Binnie Barnes (Miriam); Jane Darwell (Mrs. Killian); Leonid Kinskey (Young Man); Spencer Charters (Hendricks); Franklin Pangborn (Clerk); Herbert Heywood (Workman); Ben Hendricks (Bartender);

Elisha Cook, Jr. (Boy); Lillian Porter (Girl); Antonio Filauri (Maitre d'Hotel); Alex Pollard (Butler).

THE DAWN PATROL (WB, 1938) 103 M.

Executive producer, Hal B. Wallis; associate producer, Robert Lord; director, Edmund Goulding; based on the story "Flight Commander" by John Monk Saunders; original screenplay, Saunders, Howard Hawks; new screenplay, Seton I. Miller, Dan Totheroh; music, Max Steiner; orchestrator, Hugo Friedhofer; art director, John Hughes; technical adviser, Captain L. G. S. Scott; assistant director, Frank Heath; sound, C. A. Riggs; special effects, Edwin A. DuPar; camera, Tony Gaudio; editor, Ralph Dawson.

Errol Flynn (Courtney); David Niven (Scott); Basil Rathbone (Major Brand); Donald Crisp (Phills); Melville Cooper (Watkins); Barry Fitzgerald (Bott); Carl Esmond (Von Mueller); Peter Willes (Hollister); Morton Lowater (Ronny Scott); Michael Brooke (Squires); James Burke (Flaherty, the Motorcycle Driver); Stuart Hall (Bentham, the Singer); Herbert Evans (Scott's Mechanic); Sidney Bracy (Ransom, Brand's Orderly); John Sutton (Adjutant); George Kirby (Kirby, the Orderly); Tyrone Brereton, Tim Henning, Douglas Gordon (Orderlies); Rodion Rathbone (Russell, the Replacement); Norman Willis (German Aviator); Anthony Marsh (Moorehead); Gordon Thorpe (Smythe).

WUTHERING HEIGHTS (UA, 1939) 103 M.

Producer, Samuel Goldwyn; director, William Wyler; based on the novel by Emily Bronte; screenplay, Ben Hecht, Charles MacArthur; music director, Alfred Newman; art director, James Basevi; assistant director, Walter Mayo; set decorator, Julie Heron; costumes, Omar Kiam; makeup, Blagoe Stephanoff; sound, Paul Neal; camera, Gregg Toland; editor, Daniel Mandell.

Merle Oberon (Cathy Linton); Laurence Olivier (Heathcliff); David Niven (Edgar Linton); Donald Crisp (Dr. Kenneth); Flora Robson (Ellen Dean); Hugh Williams (Hindley); Geraldine Fitzgerald (Isabella Linton); Leo G. Carroll (Joseph); Cecil Humphreys (Judge Linton); Miles Mander (Lockwood); Sarita Wooton (Cathy as a Child); Rex Downing (Heathcliff as a Child); Douglas Scott (Hindley as a Child); Romaine Callender (Robert, the Butler); Helena Grant (Miss Hudkins); Susanne Leach (Guest); Tommy Martin, Schuyler Standish (Little Boys); William Stelling (Dancer); Mme. Alice Ahlers (Frau Johann, the Harpsichordist); Vernon Downing (Giles); Eric Wilton (Linton Servant); Major Sam Harris (Wedding Guest).

BACHELOR MOTHER (RKO, 1939) 81 M.

Executive producer, Pandro S. Berman; producer, B. G. DeSylva; director, Garson Kanin; story, Felix Jackson; screenplay, Norman Krasna; assistant director, Edward Killy; special effects, Vernon Walker; camera, Robert de Grasse; editors, Henry Berman, Robert Wise.

Ginger Rogers (Polly Parrish); David Niven (David Merlin); Charles Coburn (J. B. Merlin); Frank Albertson (Freddie Miller); E. E. Clive (Butler); Elbert Coplen, Jr. (Johnnie); Ferike Boros (Mrs. Weiss); Ernest Truex (Investigator); Leonard Penn (Jerome Weiss); Paul Stanton (Hargraves); Frank M. Thomas (Doctor); Edna Holland (Matron); Dennis Moore (Mary); June Wilkins (Louise King); Donald Duck (Himself); Horace MacMahon, Murray Alper (Bouncers).

THE REAL GLORY (UA, 1939) 96 M.

Producer, Samuel Goldwyn; director, Henry Hathaway; based on the novel by Charles L. Clifford; screenplay, Robert Presnell, Jo Swerling; art director, James Basevi; set decorator, Julia Heron; assistant director, Eddie Bernoudy; associate director, Richard Talmadge; technical adviser, Colonel William H. Shutan; costumes, Jeanne Beakhurst; music director, Alfred Newman; sound, Jack Noyes; special camera effects, R. O. Binger, Paul Eagler; camera, Rudolph Mate; editor, Daniel Mandell.

Gary Cooper (Dr. Bill Canavan); Andrea Leeds (Linda Hartley); David Niven (Lieutenant McCool); Reginald Owen (Captain Hartley); Broderick Crawford (Lieutenant Larson); Kay Johnson (Mabel Manning); Charles Waldron (Padre Rafael); Russell Hicks (Captain George Manning); Roy Gordon (Colonel Hatch); Benny Inocencio (Miguel); Vladimir Sokoloff (Datu); Rudy Robles (Lieutenant Yabo); Henry Kolker (General); Tetsu Komai (Alipang); Elvira Rios (Mrs. Yabo); Luke Chan (Top Sergeant); Elmo Lincoln (U.S. Captain); John Villasin (Moro Priest); Kam Tong (Filipino Soldier).

ETERNALLY YOURS (UA, 1939) 95 M.

Producer, Walter Wanger; director, Tay Garnett; story-screenplay, Gene Towne, Graham Baker; art director, Alexander Golitzen; assistant director, Charles Kerr; music, Werner Janssen; song, L. Wolfe Gilbert, Janssen; sound, Fred Lau; camera, Merritt Gerstad; editor, Dorothy Spencer.

Loretta Young (Anita Halstead); David Niven [Tony Halstead (The Great Arturo)]; Hugh Herbert (Benton); Billie Burke (Aunt Abbey); C. Aubrey Smith [Gramps (Bishop Hubert Peabody)]; Raymond Walburn (Harley Bingham); ZaSu Pitts (Carrie Bingham); Broderick Crawford (Don Barnes); Virginia Field (Lola De Vere); Eve Arden (Gloria); Ralph Graves (Mr. Morrissey); Lionel Pape (Mr. Howard); Walter Sande (Ralph); Leyland Hodgson (Captain Vickers); Fred Keating (Master of Ceremonies); The Kettering Triplets (Gloria's Baby); Eleanor Stewart, Evelyn Woodbury, Patricia Stillman, Doreen McKay, Luana Walters (Girls at Shower); Hillary Brooke (Blonde on Stage); Mary Field (Isabell, the Maid); Jack Perrin, Broderick O'Farrell (Ship's Officers); Herman the Rabbit (Himself); Frank Jaquet (Doctor); Paul Le Paul (Butler).

RAFFLES (UA, 1939) 71 M.

Producer, Samuel Goldwyn; director, Sam Wood; based on the novel The Amateur Cracksman by E. W. Hornung; screenplay, John Van Druten, Sidney Howard; set decorator, Julie Heron; music, Victor Young; costumes, Travis Banton; camera, Gregg Toland; editor, Sherman Todd.

David Niven (Raffles); Olivia de Havilland (Gwen); Dame May Whitty (Lady Melrose); Dudley Digges (Bunny); Lionel Pape (Lord Melrose); E. E. Clive (Barraclough); Peter Godfrey (Crawshay); Margaret Seddon (Maud Holden); Gilbert Emery (Bingham); Hilda Plowright (Wilson); Vesey O'Davoren (The Butler); George Cathrey (The Footman); Keith Hitchcock (Morton); Forrester Harvey (Umpire); James Finlayson (Cabby); George Atkinson (Attendant); Gibson Gowland, George Kirby, Herbert Clifton (Villagers); Wilfred Lucas, Larry Dodds, John Power, Colin Kenny, Charles Coleman (Bobbies).

THE FIRST OF THE FEW (General Film Distributors, 1942) 117 M.

Producers, Leslie Howard, George King, John Stafford, Adrian Brunel; director, Howard; story, Henry C. James, Katherine Strueby; screenplay, Anatole de Grunwald, Miles Malleson; music, William Walton; music director, Muir Mathieson; camera, Jack Hildyard.

Leslie Howard (R. J. Mitchell); David Niven (Geoffrey Crisp); Rosamund John (Diana Mitchell); Roland Culver (Commander Bride); Annie Firth (Miss Harper); David Horne (Higgins); John H. Roberts (Sir Robert Maclean); Derrick de Marney (S/L Jefferson); Rosalyn Boulter (Mable Livesey); Tonie Edgar Bruce (Lady Houston); Gordon McLeod (Major Buchan); Erik Freund (Messerschmidt); Filippo del Guidice (Bertorelli); Brefni O'Rourke (Specialist); Gerry Wilmott (Announcer).

U.S. release title: SPITFIRE (RKO, 1943).

THE WAY AHEAD (Eagle Lion, 1944) 115 M.

Producers, John Sutro, Norman Walker; director, Carol Reed; story, Eric Ambler; screenplay, Ambler, Peter Ustinov; camera, Guy Green.

David Niven (Lieutenant Jim Perry); Raymond Huntley (Davenport); Billy Hartnell (Sergeant Fletcher); Stanley Holloway (Brewer); James Donald (Lloyd); John Laurie (Luke); Leslie Dwyer (Beck); Hugh Burden (Parsons); Jimmy Hanley (Stainer); Renee Asherson (Marjorie Gillingham); Penelope Dudley Ward (Mrs. Perry); Reginald Tate (C.O.); Leo Genn (Commander); Mary Jerrold (Mrs. Gillingham); Raymond Lovell (Garage Proprietor); Alf Goddard (Instructor); A. E. Matthews (Colonel Walmsley); Peter Ustinov (Rispoli); Tessie O'Shea (Herself); Jack Watling (Marjorie's Boy Friend.)

U.S. release: 20th (1945).

A MATTER OF LIFE AND DEATH (General Film Distributors, 1946) C—104 M.

Producers-directors-script, Michael Powell, Emeric Pressburger; production designer, Alfred Junge; music, Allan Gray; art director, Arthur Lawson; special effects, Douglas Woolsey, Henry Harris; camera, Jack Cardiff.

David Niven (S/L Peter Carter); Roger Livesey (Dr. Reeves); Raymond Massey (Abraham Farian); Kim Hunter (June); Marius Goring (Conductor 71); Robert Coote (Bob); Robert Atkins (Vicar); Edwin Max (Dr. McEwen); Abraham Sofaer (Judge); Kathleen Byron (Angel); Richard Attenborough, Bonar Colleano, Jr. (Pilots); Joan Maude (Recorder).

U.S. release title: STAIRWAY TO HEAVEN (UNIV, 1946).

THE MAGNIFICENT DOLL (UNIV, 1946) 95 M.

Producers, Jack H. Skirball, Bruce Manning; director, Frank Borzage; story-screenplay, Irving Stone; assistant director, John F. Sherwood; art director, Alexander Golitzen; set decorators, Russell A. Gausman, Ted Offenbecker; music, Harry J. Salter; sound, Charles Felstead; camera, Joseph Valentine; editor, Ted J. Kent.

Ginger Rogers (Dolly Payne); David Niven (Aaron Burr); Burgess Meredith (James Madison); Horace McNally (John Tedd); Peggy Wood (Mrs. Payne); Frances Williams (Amy); Robert H. Barrat (Mr. Payne); Grandon Rhodes (Thomas Jefferson); Henri Letondal (Count D'Arignon); Joe Forte (Senator Ainsworth); Erville Alderson (Darcy); George Barrows (Jedson); Francis McDonald (Barber Jenks); Emmett Vogan (Mr. Gallentine); Arthur Space (Alexander Hamilton); Byron Foulger (Servant); Joseph Crehan (Williams); Larry Blake (Charles); Pierre Watkin (Harper); Jack Ingram (Lane, the Courier); Lee Phelps (Hatch, a Bettor); Vera Lewis (Mrs. Brown); Cliff Clark (Fire Chief); George Chandler (Man); Anna Q. Nillson (Saleslady).

THE PERFECT MARRIAGE (PAR, 1946) 87 M.

Producer, Hal B. Wallis; director, Lewis Allen; based on the play by Samson Raphaelson; screenplay, Leonard Spigelgass; art director, Lionel Banks; set decorators, Sam Comer, Grace Gregory; music, Frederick Hollander; assistant director, Chico Alonso; sound, Harry Lindgren, Joel Moss; process camera, Farciot Edouart; camera, Russell Metty; editor, Ellsworth Hoagland.

Loretta Young (Jenny Williams); David Niven (Dale Williams); Eddie Albert (Gil Cummins); Charlie Ruggles (Dale Williams, Sr.); Virginia Field (Gloria); Rita Johnson (Mabel); ZaSu Pitts (Rosa); Nona Griffith (Cookie Williams); Jerome Cowan (Addison Manning); Luella Gear (Dolly Haggerty); Howard Freeman (Peter Haggerty); Catherine Craig (Julie Camberwell); John Vosper (Jack Camberwell); Ann Doran (Secretary); Carol Coombs (Lola); Lyle Latell (Bulaski); Boyd Davis (Doctor); Walter Baldwin (Horse Ring Attendant); Frank Ferguson (Gentleman); Georges Renavent (Waiter Captain).

THE OTHER LOVE (UA, 1947) 96 M.

Producer, David Lewis; director, Andre de Toth; based on the novel by Erich Maria Remarque; screenplay, Ladislas Fodor, Harry Brown; music, Miklos Rozsa; music director, Mort Glickman; assistant director, Joe Kramer; sound, William E.

Clark; special effects, Howard & Theodore Lydecker; camera, Alfred Keller; editor, Walter Thompson.

Barbara Stanwyck (Karen Duncan); David Niven (Dr. Anthony Stanton); Maria Palmer (Roberta); Joan Lorring (Celestine); Richard Conte (Paul Clermont); Richard Hale (Professor Linnaker); Edward Ashley (Richard Shelton); Natalie Schafer (Dora Shelton); Lenore Aubert (Yvonne); Jimmy Horne (Pete); Mary Forbes (Mme. Gruen); Ann Codee (The Florist); Kathleen Williams (Florist's Assistant); Gilbert Roland (Croupier).

THE BISHOP'S WIFE (RKO, 1947) 109 M.

Producer, Samuel Goldwyn; director, Henry Koster; based on the novel by Robert Nathan; screenplay, Robert Sherwood, Leonardo Bercovici; music, Hugo Friedhofer; orchestrator, Jerome Moross; vocal director, Charles Henderson; music director, Emil Newman; song, Edgar DeLange, Newman, and Herbert Spencer; art directors, George Jenkins, Perry Ferguson; set decorator, Julie Heron; costumes, Irene Sharaff; makeup, Robert Stephanoff; sound, Fred Lau; special camera effects, John Fulton; camera, Gregg Toland; editor, Monica Collingwood.

Cary Grant (Dudley); Loretta Young (Julia Brougham); David Niven (Henry Brougham); Monty Woolley (Professor Wutheridge); James Gleason (Sylvester); Gladys Cooper (Mrs. Hamilton); Elsa Lanchester (Matilda); Sara Haden (Mildred Cassaway); Karolyn Grimes (Debby Brougham); Tito Vuolo (Maggenti); Regis Toomey (Mr. Miller); Sarah Edwards (Mrs. Duffy); Margaret McWade (Miss Trumbull); Anne O'Neal (Mrs. Ward); Almira Sessions, Claire DuBrey, Florence Auer (Ladies in Michel's); Margaret Wells (Hat Shop Proprietress); Isabell Jewell (Hysterical Mother); Joseph J. Greene (Santa Claus).

BONNIE PRINCE CHARLIE (British Lion, 1947) C—135 M.

Producer, Sir Alexander Korda; director, Anthony Kimmins; screenplay, Clemence Dane; music, Ian Whyte; camera, Robert Krasker, Osmond Borrodaile; editor, Grace Garland.

David Niven (Prince Charles Edward Stuart); Margaret Leighton (Flora Macdonald); Morland Graham (Donald); John Laurie (Blind Jamie); Judy Campbell (Clementina Walkinshaw); Henry Oscar (King James III); Finlay Currie (Marquis of Tullibardine); Jack Hawkins (Lord George Murray); Guy Lefeuvre (Cameron of Lochiel); Franklin Dyall (Macdonald of Keppoch); Herbert Lomas (Kinloch Moidart); Ronald Adam (Maclead of Maclead); Stuart Lindsell (Macdonald of Armadale); John Longden (Colonel O'Sullivan); Hector Ross (Glenaladale); Martin Miller (King George II); Elwyn Brook-Jones (Duke of Cumberland); G. H. Mulcaster (Duke of Newcastle); James Hayter (Kingsburgh); Torin Thatcher (Colonel Ker); Nell Ballantyne (Mrs. Kingsburgh); Patricia Fox (Annie Kingsburgh).

U.S. release: BONNIE PRINCE CHARLES (Snader, 1952) C—100 M.

ENCHANTMENT (RKO, 1948) 102 M.

Producer, Samuel Goldwyn; director Gregg Toland; based on the novel Take Three Tenses originally published as the serial A Fugue in Time by Rumer Godden; screenplay, John Patrick; art director, George Jenkins; set decorator, Julia Heron; music, Hugo Friedhofer; music director, Emil Newman; assistant director, Joe Boyle; choreography, Billy Daniels; costumes, Mary Wills; makeup, Robert Stephanoff; sound, Fred Lau; camera, Toland; editor, Daniel Mandell.

David Niven (General Sir Roland Dane); Theresa Wright (Lark Ingoldsby); Evelyn Keyes (Grizel Dane); Farley Granger (Pilot Officer Pax Masterson); Jayne Meadows (Selina Dane); Leo G. Carroll (Proutie); Philip Friend (Pelham Dane); Shepperd Strudwick (Marchese Del Laudi); Colin Keith-Johnston (Mr. Dane); Gigi Perreau (Lark as a Child); Peter Miles (Rollo as a Child); Sherlee Collier (Selina as a Child); Warwick Gregson (Pelham as a Child); Marjorie Rhodes (Mrs. Sampson); Henry Stephenson (General Fitzgerald); Edmund

Breon (Uncle Bunny); Melville Cooper (Jeweler); William Johnstohne (Narrator).

A KISS IN THE DARK (WB, 1949) 87 M.

Producer, Harry Kurnitz; director, Delmer Daves; story, Everett Devery Freeman; screenplay, Harry Kurnitz; art director, Stanley Fleischer; music, Max Steiner; camera, Robert Burke; editor, David Weisbart.

David Niven (Eric Phillips); Jane Wyman (Polly Haines); Victor Moore (Horace Willoughby); Wayne Morris (Bruce Arnold); Broderick Crawford (Mr. Botts); Joseph Buloff (Peter Danilo); Maria Ouspenskaya (Madame Karina); Curt Bois (Schloss); Percival Vivian (Benton); Raymond Greenleaf (Martin Soames); Parker Eggleston (Willie); Norman Ollestad (Freddie); Frank Dae (Hiram Knabe); Joe Devlin (Electrician); Grayce Hampton (Mrs. Stuybedan); Claire Meade (Anna, the Cook); Betty Hill (Mrs. Beal); Jack Mower (Chris, the Chauffeur); Creighton Hale (Tenant); Phyllis Coates (Mrs. Hale); Jimmy Dodd (Stuffy Nelson); Stuart Holmes (Stage Manager); Larry Rio (Cab Driver).

A KISS FOR CORLISS (UA, 1949) 88 M.

Executive producer, James Nasser; producer, Colin Miller; director, Richard Wallace; based on characters created by F. Hugh Herbert; story-screenplay, Howard Dimsdale; art director, Rudolph Sternad; set decorator, Edward G. Boyle; music, Werner R. Heymann; music director, Rudolph Polk; assistant directors, Robert Aldrich, Frank Bauer; makeup, Karl Herlinger, Jr.; costumes, Eloise Jenssen; sound, Frank Webster; camera, Robert de Grasse; editor, Frank Doyle.

Shirley Temple (Corliss Archer); David Niven (Kenneth Marquis); Tom Tully (Harry Archer); Darryl Hickman (Dexter); Virginia Welles (Mildred); Robert Ellis (Raymond); Richard Gaines (Taylor); Kathryn Card (Louise); Gloria Holden (Mrs. Archer); Roy Roberts (George).

A.k.a.: ALMOST A BRIDE.

THE ELUSIVE PIMPERNEL (British Lion, 1950) C—109 M.

Producers, Samuel Goldwyn, Alexander Korda; directors, Michael Powell, Emeric Pressburger; based on the novel The Scarlet Pimpernel by Baroness Orczy; screenplay, Powell, Pressburger; camera, Christopher Challis; editor, Reginald Mills.

David Niven (Sir Percy Blakeney); Margaret Leighton (Marguerite Blakeney); Jack Hawkins (Prince of Wales); Cyril Cusack (Chauvelin); Robert Coote (Sir Andrew Foulkes); Edmond Audran (Armand St. Juste); Danielle Godet (Suzanne de Tournai); Arlette Marchal (Comtesse de Tournai); Gerard Nery (Philippe de Tournai); Charles Victor (Colonel Winterbottom); David Hutcheson (Lord Anthony Dewhurst); Eugene Deckers (Captain Merieres); John Longden (Abbot); Arthur Wontner (Lord Grenville).

U.S. release title: THE FIGHTING PIMPERNEL (Carroll, 1954).

THE TOAST OF NEW ORLEANS (MGM, 1950) C—97 M.

Producer, Joe Pasternak; director, Norman Taurog; story-screenplay, Sy Gomberg, George Welles; art directors, Cedric Gibbons, Daniel B. Cathcart; music director, Georgie Stoll; songs, Sammy Cahn and Nicholas Brodszky; camera, William Snyder; editor, Gene Ruggiero.

Kathryn Grayson (Suzette Micheline); Mario Lanza (Pepe Abellard Duvalle); David Niven (Jacques Riboudeaux); J. Carroll Naish (Nicky Duvalle); James Mitchell (Pierre); Richard Hageman (Maestro P. Trellini); Clinton Sundberg (Oscar); Sig Arno (Mayor); Rita Moreno (Tina); Romo Vincent (Manuelo); George Davis (Stooge); Marietta Canty (Angelique); Alex Gerry (Headwaiter); Wallis Clark (Mr. O'Neill); Paul Frees (Narrator); Henry Corden, Nick Thompson (Fishermen); Mary Benoit (Woman); Betty Daniels, Louise Bates (Dowagers); Leon Belasco (Orchestra Leader); Fred Essler (Emile); Nino Pipitone (Store Keeper); Eduard Moreno, Dino Bolognese, Guy DeVestal (Waiters).

SOLDIERS THREE (MGM, 1951) 87 M.

Producer, Pandro S. Berman; director, Tay Garnett; based on the novel by Rudyard Kipling; screenplay, Marguerite Roberts, Tom Reed, Malcolm Stuart Boylan; music, Adolph Deutsch; art directors, Cedric Gibbons, Malcolm Brown; camera, William Mellor; editor, Robert J. Kern.

Stewart Granger (Private Archibald Ackroyd); Walter Pidgeon (Colonel Brunswick); David Niven (Captain Pindenny); Robert Newton (Private Jock Sykes); Cyril Cusack (Private Dennis Malloy); Greta Gynt (Crenshaw); Frank Allenby (Colonel Groat); Robert Coote (Major Mercer); Daniel O'Herlihy (Sergeant Murphy); Michael Ansara (Manik Rao); Richard Hale (Govind-Lal); Walter Kingsford (Fairfax); Charles Cane (Boggs); Patrick Whyte (Major Harrow); Movita Castenada (Proprietress); Charles Lang (Merchant); Cyril McLaglen (Scot); Stuart Hall (Lieutenant); John Sheehan (Drunk).

HAPPY GO LOVELY (RKO, 1951) C—87½ M.

Producer, Marcel Hellman; director, Bruce Humberstone; story, F. Dammann, H. Rosenfeld; screenplay, Val Guest; art director, John Howell; music, Mischa Spoliansky; music director, Louis Levy; song, Jack Fishman and Spoliansky; choreography, Jack Billings; sound, Harold V. King, Cecil V. Thornton; camera, Erwin Hillier; editor, Bert Bates.

David Niven (B. G. Bruno); Vera-Ellen (Janet Jones); Cesar Romero (Jack Frost); Bobby Howes (Charlie); Diane Hart (Mae); Gordon Jackson (Paul Tracy); Barbara Couper (Madame Amanda); Henry Hewitt (Dodds); Gladys Henson (Mrs. Urguhart); Hugh Dempster (Bates); Sandra Dorne (Betty); Joyce Carey (Bruno's Secretary); John Laurie (Jonskill); Wylie Watson (Stage Doorkeeper).

APPOINTMENT WITH VENUS (General Film Distributors, 1951) 89 M.

Producer, Betty E. Box; director, Ralph Thomas; based on the novel Transit of Venus by Jerrard Tickell; art director, George Provis; music, Benjamin Frankel; sound, John W. Mitchell, Gordon McCallum; camera, Ernest Steward; editor, Gerald Thomas.

David Niven (Major Valentine Moreland); Glynis Johns (Nicole Fallaize); George Coulouris (Captain Weiss); Barry Jones (Provost); Kenneth More (Lionel Fallaize); Noel Purcell (Trawler Langley); Bernard Lee (Brigadier); Martin Boddey (Sergeant Vogel); Richard Wattis (Executive); David Horne (Magistrate); Geoffrey Sumner (Major); Anton Diffring (German); Patric Doonan (Sergeant Forbes).

U.S. release title: ISLAND RESCUE (UNIV, 1952).

THE LADY SAYS NO (UA, 1951) 80 M.

Producers, Frank Ross, John Stettman, Jr.; director, Ross; story-screenplay, Robert Russell; art director, Perry Ferguson; music director, Emil Newman; camera, James Wong Howe; editor, George Amy.

Joan Caulfield (Dorinda); David Niven (Bill); James Robertson Justice (Uncle Matt); Lenore Lonergan (Goldie); Frances Bavier (Aunt Alice); Peggy Maley (Midge); Henry Jones (Potsy); Jeff York (Goose); George Davis (Bartender); Robert Williams (General); Mary Laurence (Mary).

THE MOON IS BLUE (UA, 1953) 99 M.

Producer-director, Otto Preminger; based on the play by F. Hugh Herbert; screenplay, Herbert; camera, Ernest Laszlo; editor, Otto Ludwig.

William Holden (Donald Gresham); David Niven (David Slater); Maggie McNamara (Patty O'Neill); Tom Tully (Michael O'Neill); Dawn Addams (Cynthia Slater); Fortunio Bonanova (TV Announcer); Gregory Ratoff (Taxi Driver).

THE LOVE LOTTERY (General Film Distributors, 1954) C—89 M.

Producer, Monja Danischewsky; director, Charles Crichton; story, Charles Neilson-Terry, Zelma Bramley-Moore; screenplay, Harry Kurnitz.

David Niven (Rex Allerton); Peggy Cummins (Sally); Anne Vernon (Jane); Herbert Lom (Amico); Charles Victor (Jennings); Gordon Jackson (Ralph); Felix Aylmer (Winant); Hugh McDermott (Rodney Wheeler); Stanley Maxted (Stanton); June Clyde (Viola); John Chandos (Gulliver Kee); Theodore Bikel (Parsimonious); Sebastian Cabot (Suarez); Eugene Deckers (Vernet); Hattie Jacques (Chambermaid); Humphrey Bogart (Bit); John Glyn-Jones (Prince Borris); Nellie Arno (Russian Woman); Gabrielle Blunt (Doreen); Mark Baker (Maxie); Marcel Poncin (Priest); Andrea Malandrinos (Fodor); Nicholas Stuart (American Radio Announcer).

HAPPILY EVER AFTER (Associated British Producers, 1954) C—88 M.
Producer, Mario Zampi; associate producer, Giulio Zampi; director, Mario Zampi; story-screenplay, Jack Davies, Michael Pertwee; art director, Ivan King; assistant director, Gus Agosti; music, Stanley Black; song, Michael Carr and Black; cameras, Stanley Pavey, Robert Walker.
David Niven (Jasper O'Leary); Yvonne De Carlo (Serena McGlusky); Barry Fitzgerald (Thady O'Heggarty); George Cole (Terence); Robert Urquhart (Dr. Flynn); Eddie Byrne (Lannigan); A. E. Matthews (General O'Leary); Noelle Middleton (Kathy McGlusky); Anthony Nicholis (Solicitor); Liam Redmond (Regan); Michael Shepley (Major McGlusky); Joseph Tomelty (Dooley).
U.S. release title: TONIGHT'S THE NIGHT (AA, 1954).

CARRINGTON VC (Independent Film Distributors, 1954) 106 M.
Producer, Teddy Baird; director, Anthony Asquith; based on the play by Dorothy and Campbell Christie; screenplay, John Hunter; camera, Desmond Dickinson.
David Niven (Major Carrington); Margaret Leighton (Valerie Carrington); Noelle Middleton (Captain Alison Graham); Maurice Denham (Lieutenant Colonel B. R. Reeve); Geoffrey Keen (President); Laurence Naismith (Major R. E. Panton); Clive Morton (Lieutenant Colonel T. B. Huxford); Mark Dignam (Prosecutor); Allan Cuthbertson (Lieutenant Colonel Henniker); Victor Maddern (Sergeant Owen); John Glyn-Jones (Evans); Newton Blick (Mr. Tester-Terry); Raymond Francis (Major Mitchell); R.S.M. Brittain (Sergeant Major).
U.S. release title: COURT MARTIAL (Kingsley International, 1955).

THE KING'S THIEF (MGM, 1955) C—78 M.
Producer, Edwin H. Knopf; director, Robert Z. Leonard; story, Robert Hardy Andrews; screenplay, Christopher Knopf; music, Miklos Rozsa; costumes, Walter Plunkett; assistant director, Robert Saunders; art directors, Cedric Gibbons, Malcolm Brown; camera, Robert Planck; editor, John McSweeney, Jr.
Ann Blyth (Lady Mary); Edmund Purdom (Michael Dermott); David Niven (Duke of Brampton); George Sanders (Charles II); Roger Moore (Jack); John Dehner (Captain Herrick); Sean McClory (Sheldon); Tudor Owen (Simon); Melville Cooper (Henry Wynch); Alan Mowbray (Sir Gilbert Albot); Rhys Williams (Turnkey); Joan Elan (Charity Fell); Ashley Cowan (Skene); Ian Wolfe (Fell); Paul Cavanagh (Sir Edward Scott); Lillian Kemble Cooper (Mrs. Fell); Isobel Elsom (Mrs. Bennett); Milton Parsons (Adam Urich); Lord Layton (Jacob Hall); Queenie Leonard (Apothecary's Wife); Owen McGiveney (Hoskins); Bob Dix, Michael Dugan (Huskies); James Logan (Guard); Matt Moore (Gentleman).

THE BIRDS AND THE BEES (PAR, 1956) C—94 M.
Producer, Paul Jones; director, Norman Taurog; based on the story "The Lady Eve" by Monckton Hoffe; screenplay, Sidney Sheldon, Preston Sturges; art directors, Hal Pereira, Roland Anderson; music-music conductor, Walter Scharf; songs, Harry Warren and Mack David; choreography, Nick

Castle; assistant director, John Coonan; costumes, Edith Head; camera, Daniel L. Fapp; editor, Archie Marshek.
George Gobel (George Hamilton); Mitzi Gaynor (Joan Harris); David Niven (Colonel Harris); Reginald Gardiner (Gerald); Fred Clark (Mr. Hamilton); Harry Bellaver (Marty Kennedy); Hans Conried (Duc Jacques de Montaigne); Clinton Sundberg (Purser); Milton Frome (Assistant Butler in Hamilton Home); Rex Evans (Burrows—the Butler in Hamilton Home); King Donovan (Waiter); Mary Treen (Mrs. Burnside); Charles Lane (Jenkins—the Bartender in Hamilton Home); Barlett Robinson, Douglas Evans, Harry Bernard, Kathryn Card, Harold A. Miller, Mary Benoit, Richard H. Gordon, Stuart Holmes (Guests); Kevin Corcoran (Hans); Steven Geray (Bartender); Charles Evans (Father); Roscoe Ates (Vendor); Rolfe Sedan (Cabin Steward); Marion Gray, Evelyn Ceder (Mothers).

AROUND THE WORLD IN 80 DAYS (UA, 1956) C—168 M.
Producer, Michael Todd; assistant producer, William Cameron Menzies; director, Michael Anderson; based on the novel by Jules Verne; screenplay, S. J. Perelman; music, Victor Young; costumes, Miles White; choreography, Paul Godkin; art directors, James Sullivan, Ken Adams; set decorator, Ross Dowd; assistant directors, Ivan Volkman, Lew Borzage, Dennis Bertena, Farley James; second unit director, Kevin O'-Donovan McClory; sound, Joseph Kane; special effects, Lee Zavitz; camera, Lionel Lindon; editors, Paul Weatherwax, Gene Ruggiero.
David Niven (Phileas Fogg); Cantinflas (Passepartout); Shirley MacLaine (Princess Aouda); Robert Newton (Inspector Fix); Charles Boyer (Monsieur Casse); Joe E. Brown (Station Master); Martine Carol (Tourist); John Carradine (Colonel Proctor Stamp); Charles Coburn (Clerk); Ronald Colman (Railway Official); Melville Cooper (Steward); Noël Coward (Hesketh-Baggott); Finlay Currie (Whist Partner); Reginald Denny (Police Chief); Andy Devine (First Mate); Marlene Dietrich (Hostess); Luis Miguel Dominguin (Bullfighter); Fernandel (Coachman); Hermione Gingold (Sportin' Lady); Jose Greco (Dancer); Sir John Gielgud (Foster); Sir Cedric Hardwicke (Sir Francis Gromarty); Trevor Howard (Falletin); Glynis Johns (Companion); Buster Keaton (Conductor); Evelyn Keyes (Flirt); Beatrice Lillie (Revivalist); Peter Lorre (Steward); Edmund Lowe (Engineer); Victor McLaglen (Helmsman); Colonel Tim McCoy (Commander); Mike Mazurki (Character); John Mills (Cabby); Alan Mowbray (Consul); Robert Morley (Ralph); Edward R. Murrow (Narrator); Jack Oakie (Captain of "S.S. Henrietta"); George Raft (Bouncer at Barbary Coast Saloon); Gilbert Roland (Achmed Abdullah); Cesar Romero (Henchman); Frank Sinatra (Saloon Pianist); Red Skelton (Drunk); Ronald Squire, A. E. Mathews, Basil Sydney (Club Members); Ava Gardner (Spectator); Harcourt Williams (Hinshaw).

THE SILKEN AFFAIR (RKO-British, 1956) 96 M.
Producers, Douglas Fairbanks, Jr., Fred Feldkamp; director, Roy Kellino; based on an idea by John McCarten; story-screenplay, Robert Lewis Taylor; music, Peggy Stuart.
David Niven (Roger Tweakham); Genevieve Page (Genevieve Gerard); Ronald Squire (Marberry); Beatrice Straight (Theora); Wilfrid Hyde White (Sir H. Hogg); Dorothy Alison (Mrs. Tweakham); Richard Wattis (Worthington); Miles Malleson (Mr. Blucher); Joan Sims (Lady Barber); Irene Handl (Receptionist); Charles Carson (Judge).
U.S. release: DCA (1957).

OH, MEN! OH, WOMEN! (20th, 1957) C—90 M.
Producer-director, Nunnally Johnson; based on the play by Edward Chodorov; screenplay, Johnson; assistant director, Hal Herman; wardrobe, Charles LeMaire; music, Cyril J. Mockridge; art directors, Lyle R. Wheeler, Maurice Ransford; special camera effects, Ray Kellogg; camera, Charles G. Clarke; editor, Marjorie Fowler.
Dan Dailey (Arthur Turner); Ginger Rogers (Mildred Tur-

ner); David Niven (Dr. Alan Coles); Barbara Rush (Myra Hagerman); Tony Randall (Cobbler); Natalie Schafer (Mrs. Day); Rachel Stephens (Miss Tacher); John Wengraf (Dr. Krauss); Cheryll Clarke (Melba); Franklin Pangborn (Steamship Clerk); Franklyn Farnum (Steamship Clerk); Charles Davis (Steward); Joel Fluellen (Cab Driver); Clancy Cooper (Mounted Policeman).

THE LITTLE HUT (MGM, 1957) C—78 M.

Producers, F. Hugh Herbert, Mark Robson; director, Robson; based on the play by Andre Roussin and English stage adaptation by Nancy Mitford; screenplay, Herbert; art director, Elliott Scott; music, Robert Farnon; song, Eric Maschwitz, Marcel Stellman, and Peggy Cochrane; costumes, Christian Dior; assistant director, David Middlemas; camera, Freddie Young; editor, Ernest Waller.

Ava Gardner (Lady Susan Ashlow); Stewart Granger (Sir Philip Ashlow); David Niven (Henry Brittingham-Brett); Walter Chiari (Mario); Finlay Currie (Reverend Brittingham-Brett); Jean Cadell (Mrs. Brittingham-Brett); Jack Lambert (Captain MacWade); Henry Oscar (Mr. Trollope); Viola Lyel (Miss Edwards); Jaron Yaltan (Indian Gentleman).

MY MAN GODFREY (UNIV, 1957) C—92 M.

Producer, Ross Hunter; director, Henry Koster; based on the novel by Eric Hatch and the screenplay by Morris Ryskind, Hatch; new screenplay, Everett Freeman, Peter Berneis, William Bowers; art directors, Alexander Golitzen, Richard H. Riedel; music director, Joseph Gershenson; music, Frank Skinner; assistant director, Frank Shaw; gowns, Bill Thomas; camera, William Daniels; editor, Milton Carruth.

June Allyson (Irene Bullock); David Niven (Godfrey); Jessie Royce Landis (Angelica Bullock); Robert Keith (Mr. Bullock); Eva Gabor (Francesca); Jay Robinson (Vincent); Martha Hyer (Cordelia Bullock); Jeff Donnell (Molly); Herbert Anderson (Hubert); Eric Sinclair (Brent); Dabbs Greer (Lieutenant O'Connor); Fred Essler (Captain); Harry Cheshire (Elliott); Robert Clarke (George); William Hudson (Howard); Richard Deacon (Farnsworth); Thomas B. Henry (Henderson); Robert Foulk (Motor Cop); Fred Coby (Investigator); Robert Brubaker (Man with Monkey); Jack Mather (Detective); Paul Levitt (Young Man at Bar); Voltaire Perkins (Man at Bar).

BONJOUR TRISTESSE (COL, 1958) C—93 M.

Producer, Otto Preminger; associate producer, John Palmer; director, Preminger; based on the novel by Françoise Sagan; screenplay, Arthur Laurents; art director, Raymond Simm; set director, Georges Petitot; assistant directors, Adrian Pryce-Jones, Serge Friedman; music, Georges Auric; music conductor, Lambert Williamson; choreography, Tutte Lemkow; costume co-ordinator, Hope Bryce; makeup, George Frost; titles, Saul Bass; sound, David Hildyard, Red Law; camera, Georges Perinal; editor, Helga Cranston.

Deborah Kerr (Anne Larsen); David Niven (Raymond); Jean Seberg (Cecile); Mylene Demongeot (Elsa Mackenbourg); Geoffrey Horne (Philippe); Juliette Greco (Nightclub Singer); Walter Chiari (Pablo); Martita Hunt (Philippe's Mother); Roland Culver (Mr. Lombard); Jean Kent (Mrs. Lombard); David Oxley (Jacques); Elga Anderson (Denise); Jeremy Burnham (Hubert Duclos); Eveline Eyfel (Maid); Tutte Lemkow (Pierre Schube).

SEPARATE TABLES (UA, 1958) 98 M.

Producer, Harold Hecht; director, Delbert Mann; based on the play by Terence Rattigan; screenplay, Rattigan, John Gay; music, David Roskin; songs, Harry Warren and Harold Adamson; assistant director, Thomas F. Shaw; gowns for Miss Hayworth by Edith Head; costumes, Mary Grant; production designer, Harry Horner; art director, Edward Carrere; set decorator, Edward G. Boyle; makeup. Harry Maut, Frank Prehoda; camera, Charles Lang, Jr.; editors, Marjorie Fowler, Charles Ennis.

Rita Hayworth (Ann Shankland); Deborah Kerr (Sibyl Rail-

ton-Bell); David Niven (Major Pollock); Wendy Hiller (Miss Cooper); Burt Lancaster (John Malcolm); Gladys Cooper (Mrs. Railton-Bell); Cathleen Nesbitt (Lady Matheson); Felix Aylmer (Mr. Fowler); Rod Taylor (Charles); Audrey Dalton (Jean); May Hallatt (Miss Meacham); Priscilla Morgan (Doreen); Hilda Plowright (Mabel).

ASK ANY GIRL (MGM, 1959) C—98 M.

Producer, Joe Pasternak; director, Charles Walters; based on the novel by Winifred Wolfe; screenplay, George Wells; music-music conductor, Jeff Alexander; song, Jimmy McHugh and Dorothy Fields; art directors, William A. Horning, Henry Grace; costumes, Helen Rose; assistant director, Al Jennings; makeup, William Tuttle; sound, Franklin Milton; special effects, Robert R. Hoag; camera, Robert Bronner; editor, John McSweeney, Jr.

David Niven (Miles Doughton); Shirley MacLaine (Meg Wheeler); Gig Young (Evan Doughton); Rod Taylor (Ross Taford); Jim Backus (Mr. Maxwell); Claire Kelly (Lisa); Elisabeth Fraser (Jeannie Boyden); Dody Heath (Terri Richards); Read Morgan (Bert); Mickey Shaughnessy (Cigarette Sampler); Carmen Phillips (Refined Young Lady); Helen Wallace (Hotel Manager); Myrna Hansen, Kasey Rogers, Carrol Byron, Norma French, Kathy Reed (Girls); Mae Clarke (Woman on Train).

HAPPY ANNIVERSARY (UA, 1959) 83 M.

Producer, Ralph Fields; associate producer, George Justin; director, David Miller; based on the play Anniversary Waltz by Joseph Fields, Jerome Chodorov; screenplay, Fields, Chodorov; songs, Robert Allen and Al Stillman; music-music conductor, Allen; production designer, Paul Heller; assistant director, Tony La Marca; makeup, Herman Buchman; sound, James Gleason; sound effects, Don Hall; camera, Lee Garmes; editor, Richard Meyer.

David Niven (Chris Walters); Mitzi Gaynor (Alice Walters); Carl Reiner (Bud); Loring Smith (Mr. Gans); Monique Van Vooren (Jeanette); Phyllis Povah (Mrs. Gans); Elizabeth Wilson (Millie); Patty Duke (Debbie Walters); Kevin Coughlin (Okkie Walters).

PLEASE DON'T EAT THE DAISIES (MGM, 1960) C—111 M.

Producer, Joe Pasternak; associate producer, Martin Melcher; director, Charles Walters; based on the book by Jean Kerr; screenplay, Isobel Lennart; art directors, George W. Davis, Hans Peters; set decorators, Henry Grace, Jerry Wunderlich; costumes, Morton Haack; assistant director, Al Jennings; makeup, William Tuttle; music, David Rose; songs, Marilyn Hooven, Joe Hooven, and By Dunham; Jay Lubin; Jay Livingston and Ray Evans; sound, Franklin Milton; camera, Robert Bronner; editor, John McSweeney, Jr.

Doris Day (Kate Mackay); David Niven [Lawrence (Larry) Mackay]; Janis Paige (Deborah Vaughn); Spring Byington (Mrs. Suzie Robinson); Richard Haydn (Alfred North); Patsy Kelly (Maggie); Jack Weston (Joe Positano); John Harding (Reverend Dr. McQuarry); Margaret Lindsay (Mona James); Carmen Phillips (Mary Smith); Mary Patton (Mrs. Hunter); Charles Herbert (David Mackay); Stanley Livingston (Gabriel Mackay); Flip Mark (George Mackay); Baby Gellert (Adam Mackay); Hobo (Himself).

THE GUNS OF NAVARONE (COL, 1961) C—157 M.

Producer, Carl Foreman; associate producers, Cecil F. Ford, Leon Becker; director, J. Lee Thompson; based on the novel by Alistair MacLean; screenplay, Foreman; music-music conductor, Dmitri Tiomkin; art director, Geoffrey Drake; assistant director, Peter Yates; costumes, Monty Berman, Olga Lehman; makeup, Wally Schneiderman, Pamela Davies; sound, John Cox, George Stephenson, Vivian C. Greenham; special effects, Bill Warrington, Wally Veevers; camera, Oswald Morris; additional camera, John Wilcox; editors, Alan

Osbiston, Raymond Poulton, John Smith, Oswald Hafenrichter.

Gregory Peck (Captain Mallory); David Niven (Corporal Miller); Anthony Quinn (Andrea Stavros); Stanley Baker (C.P.O. Brown); James Darren (Spyros Pappadimos); Anthony Quayle (Major Franklin); Irene Papas (Maria Pappadimos); Gia Scala (Anna); James Robertson Justice (Jenson/Narrator); Richard Harris (Barnsby); Bryan Forbes (Cohn); Allan Cuthbertson (Baker); Michael Trubshawe (Weaver); Percy Herbert (Grogan); George Mikell (Sessler); Walter Gotell (Mussel); Norman Wooland (Group Captain); Albert Lieven (Commandant); Tutte Lemkow (Nicholai); Cleo Scouloudi (Bride); Nicholas Papakonstantinou (Patrol Boat Captain); Christopher Rhodes (German Gunnery Officer).

I DUE NEMICI (THE TWO ENEMIES) (COL, 1961) C—104 M.

Producer, Dino De Laurentiis; associate producer, Luigi Luraschi; director, Guy Hamilton; story, Luciano Vincenzoni; adaptors, Age Scarpelli, Suso Cecchi D'Amico; screenplay, Jack Pulman; art director, Mario Garbuglia; set decorator, Giorgio Herrmann; costumes, Ezio Frigerio, Dario Cecchi; assistant directors, Mario Maffei, Yoel Silberg; sound, Piero Cavazzuti, Bruno Brunacci; camera, Giuseppe Rotunno; editor, Bert Bates.

David Niven (Major Richardson); Alberto Sordi (Captain Blasi); Michael Wilding (Lieutenant Burke); Amedeo Nazzari (Major Fornari); Harry Andrews (Captain Rootes); David Opatoshu (Captain Bernasconi); Aldo Giuffre (Sergeant Todini); Tiberio Mitri (Corporal Moccia); Kenneth Fortescue (Lieutenant Thomlinson); Duncan Macrae (Sergeant Trevethan); Noël Harrison (Lieutenant Hilary); Bernard Cribbins (Private Tanner); Ronald Fraser (Corporal Prefect); Robert Desmond (Private Singer).

U.S. release title: THE BEST OF ENEMIES (COL, 1962).

IL GIORNO PIU CORTO (THE SHORTEST DAY) (Titanus, 1962) 89 M.

Director, Sergio Corbucci.

With: Franco Franchi, Ciccio Ingrassia, Walter Pidgeon, Annie Giradot, Gino Cervi, Virna Lisi, Folco Lulli, Simone Signoret, Jacques Sernas, Daniel Mele, Toto, Sylva Koscina, Steve Reeves, Yvone Sanson, Walter Chiari, Umberto Orsini, Eleanora Rossi Drago, Stewart Granger, Tomas Miliam, Susan Strasberg, Renato Rascel, Philipe Leroy, Ettore Manni, Massimo Serato, Paulo de Filippo, Scilia Gabel, F. Citti, Aldo Fabrizi, Eduardo de Filippo, Marcello Mastroianni, Ugo Tognazzi, Vittorio Gassman, Sandra Milo, David Niven, Gordon Scott, Massimo Girotti, Ric Battaglia, Gino Ferzetti, Francisco Mule.

LA CITTA PRIGIONIERA (THE CAPTIVE CITY) (Italian, 1962) 91 M.

Director, Joseph Anthony

With: David Niven, Ben Gazzara, Michael Craig, Martin Balsam, Lea Massari.

U.S. release: American International (1969).

THE ROAD TO HONG KONG (UA, 1962) 91 M.

Producer, Melvin Frank; director, Norman Panama; screenplay, Panama, Frank; production designer, Roger Furse; art directors, Sydney Cain, Bill Hutchinson; set decorator, Maurice Fowler; main titles designed by Maurice Binder; costumes, Anthony Mendleson; assistant director, Bluey Hill; makeup, Dave Aylott; music-music conductor, Robert Farnon; music associates, Douglas Gamley, Bill Meyers; songs, Sammy Cahn and Jimmy Van Heusen; choreography, Jack Baker, Sheila Meyers; sound, A. G. Bambler, Red Law, Chris Greeham; special effects, Wally Veevers, Ted Samuels; camera, Jack Hildyard; editors, Alan Osbiston, John Smith.

Bing Crosby (Harry Turner); Bob Hope (Chester Babcock); Joan Collins (Diane); Dorothy Lamour (Herself); Robert Mor-

ley (The Leader); Walter Gotell (Dr. Zorbb); Roger Delgado (Jhinnah); Felix Aylmer (Grand Lama); Peter Madden (Lama); Julian Sherrier (Doctor); Frank Sinatra, Peter Sellers, Dean Martin, David Niven, Jerry Colonna (Guest Performers); Bill Nagy (Agent); Allan Gifford, Robert Ayres, Robin Hughes (American Officials); Mei Ling (Chinese Girl); Guy Standeven (Photographer).

GUNS OF DARKNESS (WB, 1962) 103 M.

Executive producer, Ben Kadish; producer, Thomas Clyde; director, Anthony Asquith; based on the novel Act of Mercy *by Francis Clifford; screenplay, John Mortimer; music-music conductor, Benjamin Frankel; art director, John Howell; wardrobe, Anthony Mendleson; makeup, Jim Hydes; assistant director, David Tomblin; sound, Norman Coggs, Len Shilton, Charles Crafford, A. W. Lumkin; camera, Robert Krasker; editor, Frederick Wilson.*

Leslie Caron (Claire Jordan); David Niven (Tom Jordan); David Opatoshu (President Rivera); James Robertson Justice (Hugo Bryant); Eleanor Summerfield (Mrs. Bastian); Ian Hunter (Dr. Swann); Derek Godfrey (Hernandez); Richard Pearson (Mr. Bastian); Sandor Eles (Lieutenant Gomez); Steven Scott (Gabriel); Tutte Lemkow (Gabriel's Cousin); Dorita Sensier (Nightclub Singer); John Carson (First Officer); Ali Nagi (Indian Boy); Barry Shawzin (General Zoreno); Peter Allenby (Sergeant).

55 DAYS AT PEKING (AA, 1963) C—154 M.

Producer, Samuel Bronston; executive associate producer, Michael Waszynski; associate producer, Alan Brown; director, Nicholas Ray; screenplay, Philip Yordan, Bernard Gordon; additional dialog, Robert Hamer; music-music conductor, Dmitri Tiomkin; song, Tiomkin and Paul Francis Webster; art directors-costumes, Veniero Colasanti, John Moore; title paintings, Dong Kingman; wardrobe, Gloria Mussetta; assistant directors, Jose Lopez Rodero, Jose Maria Ochoa; second unit directors, Andrew Marton, Noel Howard; makeup, Mario Van Riel; sound, David Hildyard, Gordon K. McCallum; camera, Jack Hildyard; second unit camera, Manuel Berenguer; editors, Robert Lawrence, Magdalena Paradell.

Charlton Heston (Major Matt Lewis); Ava Gardner (Baroness Natalie Ivanoff); David Niven (Sir Arthur Robertson); Flora Robson (Dowager Empress Tzu Hsi); John Ireland (Sergeant Harry); Harry Andrews (Father de Beam); Leo Genn (General Jung-Lu); Robert Helpmann (Prince Tuan); Ichizo Itami (Colonel Shiba); Kurt Kasznar (Baron Sergei Ivanoff); Phillipe Leroy (Julliard); Paul Lukas (Dr. Steinfeldt); Lynne Sue Moon (Teresa); Elizabeth Sellars (Lady Sarah Robertson); Jacques Sernas (Major Bobrinski); Joseph Furst (Captain Hanselman); Alfred Lynch (Gerald); Alfredo Mayo (Spanish Minister); Nicholas Ray (American Minister); Mervyn Jones (Clergyman); and: Kenji Takako, Dong Kingman, Soong Ling, Stephen Young, Andy Ho, John A. Tinn, John Moulder-Brown.

THE PINK PANTHER (UA, 1964) C—113 M.

Producer, Martin Jurow; associate producer, Dick Crockett; director, Blake Edwards; screenplay, Maurice Richlin, Edwards; music, Henry Mancini; song, Mancini, (Italian lyrics) Fran Migliacci, and (English lyrics) Johnny Mercer; art director, Fernando Carrere; set decorators, Reginald Allen, Jack Stevens, Arrigo Breschi; wardrobe for Miss Cardinale and Capucine principally by Yves St. Laurent; main titles, De Patie-Freleng Enterprises; assistant director, Ottavio Oppo; sound, Alexander Fisher; special effects, Lee Zavitz; camera, Philip Lathrop; editors, Marshall M. Borden, David Zinnemann.

David Niven (Sir Charles Lytton); Peter Sellers (Inspector Jacques Clouseau); Robert Wagner (George Lytton); Capucine (Simone Clouseau); Claudia Cardinale (Princess Dala); Brenda De Banzie (Angela Dunning); Fran Jeffries (Greek "Cousin"); Colin Gordon (Tucker); John Le Mesurier (Defense Attorney); James Lanphier (Saloud); Guy Thomajan

(Artoff); Michael Trubshawe (Novelist); Riccardo Billi (Greek Shipowner); Meri Wells (Hollywood Starlet); Martin Miller (Photographer).

BEDTIME STORY (UNIV, 1964) C—99 M.

Executive producer, Robert Arthur; producer, Stanley Shapiro; director, Ralph Levy; screenplay, Shapiro, Paul Henning; music, Hans J. Salter; assistant director, Joseph E. Kenny; art directors, Alexander Golitzen, Robert Clatworthy; Miss Jones' wardrobe by Jean Louis; titles, Pacific Title; camera, Clifford Stine; editor, Milton Carruth.

Marlon Brando (Freddy); David Niven (Lawrence); Shirley Jones (Janet); Dody Goodman (Fanny Eubank); Aram Stephan (Andre); Parley Baer (Colonel Williams); Marie Windsor (Mrs. Sutton); Rebecca Sand (Miss Trumble); Frances Robinson (Miss Harrington); Henry Slate (Sattler); Norman Alden (Dubin); Susanne Cramer (Anna); Cynthia Lynn (Frieda); Ilse Taurins (Hilda); Francine York (Gina).

WHERE THE SPIES ARE (MGM, 1965) C—113 M.

Producers, Val Guest, Steven Pallos; associate producer, Frank Sherwin Green; director, Guest; based on the novel Passport to Oblivion *by James Leasor; screenplay, Wolf Mankowitz, Guest; additional scenes, Leasor; art director, John Howell; music, Mario Nascimbene; music director, Alfredo Antonini; sound, A. W. Watkins; camera, Arthur Grant; editor, Bill Lenny.*

David Niven (Dr. Love); Françoise Dorleac (Vikki); Nigel Davenport (Parkington); John Le Mesurier (Macgillivray); Ronald Radd (Stanislaus); Cyril Cusack (Rosser); Eric Pohlmann (Farouk); Paul Stassino (Simmias); Geoffrey Bayldon (Lecturer); George Pravda, Gabor Baraker (Agents); Noël Harrison (Jackson); Derek Patridge (Duty Officer); Robert Raglan (Sir Robert); Riyad Ghomieh, Muhsen Samrani (Taxi Drivers); George Mikell (Assassin); Richard Marner (Josef); Basil Dignam (Major Harding); Gordon Tanner (Inspector); Bill Nagy (Aeradio); Alan Gifford (Security Man).

LADY L (MGM, 1965) C—124 M.

Producer, Carlo Ponti; director, Peter Ustinov; based on the novel by Romain Gary; screenplay, Ustinov; art directors, Jean D'Eaubonne, Auguste Capelier; set decorator, Maurice Barnathan; special makeup, William Tuttle; makeup, Michel Deruelle, Guiseppe Annunziata; assistant director, Paul Feyder; costumes, Marcel Escoffier, Jacqueline Guyot; sound, William Sivel; special effects, Karl Baumgartner; camera, Henri Alekan; editor, Roger Dwyre.

Sophia Loren (Louise); Paul Newman (Armand); David Niven [Lord Lendale (Dicky)]; Cecil Parker (Sir Percy); Claude Dauphin (Inspector Mercier); Marcel Dalio (Sapper); Phillipe Noiret (Amboise Gerome); Michel Piccoli (Lecoeur); Jean Wiener (Krajewski); Daniel Emilfork (Kobeleff); Eugene Deckers (Koenigstein); Jacques Dufilho (Beale); Tanya Lopert (Agneau); Catherine Allegret (Pantoufle); Hella Petri (Madam); Peter Ustinov (Prince Otto).

CASINO ROYALE (COL, 1967) C—131 M.

Producers, Charles K. Feldman, Jerry Bresler; associate producer, John Dark; directors, John Huston, Ken Hughes, Val Guest, Robert Parrish, Joe McGrath; additional sequences, Guest; suggested by the novel by Ian Fleming; screenplay, Wolf Mankowitz, John Law; assistant directors, Roy Baird, John Stoneman, Carl Mannin; second unit directors, Richard Talmadge, Anthony Squire; production designer, Michael Stringer; art directors, John Howell, Ivor Beddoes, Lionel Couch; set decorator, Terence Morgan; music-music director, Burt Bacharach; song, Bacharach and Hal David; choreography, Tutte Lemkow; titles-montage effects, Richard Williams; sound, John W. Mitchell, Sash Fisher, Bob Jones, Dick Langford; camera, Jack Hildyard; additional camera, John Wilcox, Nicholas Roeg; editor, Bill Lenny.

David Niven (Sir James Bond); Peter Sellers (Evelyn Tremble); Ursula Andress (Vesper Lynd); Orson Welles (Le Chiffre); Joanna Pettet (Mata Bond); Daliah Lavi (The Detainer); Deborah Kerr (Agent Mimi); Woody Allen (Jimmy Bond); William Holden (Ransome); Charles Boyer (Le Grand); John Huston (M); Kurt Kasznar (Smernov); Terence Cooper (Cooper); Barbara Bouchet (Moneypenny); Angela Scoular (Buttercup); Tracey Crisp (Heather); Elaine Taylor (Peg); Gabriella Licudi (Eliza); Jacqueline Bisset (Miss Goodthighs); Alexandra Bastedo (Meg); Anna Quayle (Frau Hoffner); Derek Nimmo (Hadley); George Raft (Himself); Jean-Paul Belmondo (French Legionnaire); Peter O'Toole (Piper); Stirling Moss (Driver); Ronnie Corbett (Polo); Colin Gordon (Casino Director); Bernard Cribbins (Taxi Driver); Tracy Reed (Fang Leader); John Bluthal (Casino Doorman/M.I. 5 Man); Geoffrey Bayldon (Q); John Wells (Q's Assistant); Duncan Macrae (Inspector Mathis); Graham Stark (Cashier); Chic Murray (Chic); Jonathan Routh (John); Richard Wattis (British Army Officer); Vladek Sheybal (Le Chiffre's Representative); Percy Herbert (First Piper); Penny Riley (Control Girl); Jeanne Roland (Captain of Guards); Greta Van Rantywck (Painted Girl); Dannie Sheridan, Gina Warwick, Jean Stewart, Fiona Lewis (Fang Girls); Dolly Read (Orgy Girl); Antonia Ellis (Oriental Dancer); Susan and Jennifer Baker (Blonde Twins).

EYE OF THE DEVIL (MGM, 1967) 90 M.

Producer, Martin Ransohoff, John Calley; director, J. Lee Thompson; based on the novel Day of the Arrow by Philip Loraine; screenplay, Robin Estridge, Dennis Murphy; art director, Elliot Scott; music, Gary McFarland; costumes, Julie Harris, John Furness; titles, Maurice Binder; sound, A. W. Watkins; camera, Erwin Hillier; editor, Ernest Walter.

Deborah Kerr (Catherine); David Niven (Philippe de Montfaucon); Donald Pleasence (Pere Dominic); Edward Mulhare (Jean-Claude Ibert); Flora Robson (Countess Estelle); Emlyn Williams (Alain de Montfaucon); Sharon Tate (Odile); David Hemmings (Christian de Caray); John Le Mesurier (Dr. Monnet); Suky Appleby (Antoinette); Donald Bisset (Rennard); Robert Duncan (Jacques); Michael Miller (Grandee).

PRUDENCE AND THE PILL (20th, 1968) C—92 M.

Producers, Kenneth Harper, Ronald Kahn; director, Fielder Cook; based on the novel by Hugh Mills; screenplay, Mills; assistant director, Ted Sturgis; production designer, Wilfrid Shingleton; art director, Fred Carter; set decorator, John Jarvis; music-music director, Bernard Ebbinghouse; titles, Richard Williams; animator, Errol Le Cain; sound, Albert Ross; camera, Ted Moore; editor, Norman Savage.

Deborah Kerr (Prudence Hardcastle); David Niven (Gerald Hardcastle); Robert Coote (Henry Hardcastle); Irina Demick (Elizabeth); Joyce Redman (Grace Hardcastle); Judy Geeson (Geraldine Hardcastle); Keith Michell (Dr. Alan Hewitt); Dame Edith Evans (Lady Roberta Bates); David Dundas (Tony Bates); Vickery Turner (Rose); Hugh Armstrong (Ted); Peter Butterworth (Chemist); Moyra Fraser (Woman in Tea Shop); Annette Kerr (Gerald's Secretary); Harry Towb (Race Track Official); Jonathan Lynn (Chemist's Assistant).

THE IMPOSSIBLE YEARS (MGM, 1968) C—97 M.

Producer, Lawrence Weingarten; director, Michael Gordon; based on the play by Bob Fisher, Arthur Marx; screenplay, George Wells; art directors, George W. Davis, Preston Ames; set decorators, Henry Grace, Hugh Hunt; makeup, William Tuttle; assistant director, Arthur Jacobsen; music, Don Costa; title song, The Tokens; sound, Franklin Milton; camera, William H. Daniels; editor, James E. Newcom.

David Niven (Jonathan Kingsley); Lola Albright (Alice Kingsley); Chad Everett (Richard Merrick); Ozzie Nelson (Dr. Herbert Fleischer); Cristina Ferrare (Linda Kingsley); Jeff Cooper (Bartholomew Smuts); John Harding (Dean Harvey Rockwell); Rich Chalet (Freddie Fleischer); Mike McGreevey (Andy McClaine); Don Beddoe (Dr. Elliot Fish); Darleen Carr (Abbey Kingsley); Louise Lorimer (Mrs. Celia Fish); Karen Norris (Mrs. Rockwell); Susan French (Miss Hammer); Trudi Ames (Francine).

THE EXTRAORDINARY SEAMAN (MGM, 1969) C—79 M.

Producer, Edward Lewis; associate producer, Hal Dresner; co-producer, John Cushingham; director, John Frankenheimer; story-screenplay, Philip Rock; assistant directors, Enrico Isacco, Michael Glick; music, Maurice Jarre; makeup, William Tuttle; art directors, George W. Davis, Edward Carfagno; set decorator, Henry Milton Rice; sound, Franklin Milton; special camera effects, J. McMillan Johnson, Milton Rice; camera, Lionel Lindon; editor, Fredric Steinkamp.

David Niven (Lieutenant Commander Finchhaven, R.N.); Faye Dunaway (Jennifer Winslow); Alan Alda (Lieutenant (J.G.) Morton Krim); Mickey Rooney (Cockswain 3c W. W. J. Oglethorpe); Jack Carter (Gunner's Mate Orville Toole); Juano Hernandez (Ali Shar); Manu Tupou (Seaman 1C Lightfoot Star); Barry Kelley (Admiral Barnwell); Leonard O. Smith, Richard Guizon, John Cochran (Dyaks); Jerry Fujikawa (Admiral Shimagoshi).

BEFORE WINTER COMES (COL, 1969) 108 M.

Producer, Robert Emmett Ginna; director, J. Lee Thompson; based on the short story "The Interpreter" by Frederick L. Keefe; screenplay, Andrew Sinclair; music-music conductor, Ron Grainer; art director, John Blezard; wardrobe, Eddie Joyce; makeup, Constance Reeve; assistant director, Jake Wright; sound, Cyril Collick, Winston Ryder; editor, Willy Kemplen.

David Niven (Major Giles Burnside); Topol (Janovic); Anna Karina (Maria Holz); John Hurt (Lieutenant Francis Pilkington); Anthony Quayle (Brigadier-General Bewley); Ori Levy (Captain Kamenev); John Collin (Sergeant Woody); Karel Stepanek (Count Derassy); Guy Deghy (Kovacs); Mark Malicz (Komenski); Gertan Klauber (Russian Major); Anna-Maria Pravda (Beata); George Innes (Bill); Tony Selby (Ted); Christopher Sandford (Johnny); Jerry Tarrant, John Savident (British Corporals); Britt Bern (Marta); Gisela Fritsch (Anna); Harry Kalenberg (Policeman); Karin Schroeder (Pregnant Girl); Peter Mathes (Malik).

THE BRAIN (LE CERVEAU) (PAR, 1969) C—115 M.

Producer, Alain Poire; director, Gerard Oury; screenplay, Oury, Marcel Jullian, Daniele Thompson; assistant director, Gerard Guerin; technical advisor for camera, Armand Thirard; second unit director, Claude Clement; art director, Jean Andre; music, Georges Delerue; title song, Eddie Snyder and Larry Kulck; costumes, Tanine Autre; sound, Jean Rieul, Louis Hochet; camera, Vladimir Ivanov; editor, Albert Jurgenson.

David Niven (The Brain); Jean-Paul Belmondo (Arthur); Bourvil (Anatole); Eli Wallach (Scannapieco); Silvia Monti (Sofia); Fernand Valois (Bruno); Raymond Gerome (Commissioner); Jacques Balutin (Pochet); Jacques Ciron (Duboeuf); Fernand Guiot (Mazurel); Henri Genes (Chief Warder); Tommy Duggan (Superintendent).

THE STATUE (CIN, 1971) C—92 M.

Executive producer, Josef Shaftel; producer, Anis Nohra; director, Rod Amateau; based on the play Chip Chip Chip by Alec Coppel; screenplay, Coppel, Denis Norden; music-music conductor, Riz Ortolani; songs, Ortolani and Norman Newell; Luis Enriquez Bacalov and Audrey Nohra; choreography, Gino Landi; art director, Bruno Avesani; set decorator, Franco Fumagalli; second unit director, Maurizio Lucidi; titles, National Screen Service; makeup, Amato Garbini; costumes, Orietta Nasalli Rocca; assistant director, Rae Mottola; sound,

David Hawkins, Amelio Verona, Doug Turner; camera, Piero Portalupi; second unit camera, Carlo Lastricati; editors, Ernest Hosler, Fergus McDonell.

David Niven (Alex Bolt); Virna Lisi (Rhonda Bolt); Robert Vaughn (Ray Whitely); Ann Bell (Pat Demarest); Mircha Carven (Joachim); John Clees (Harry); Bettine Milne (Dunhill); Derek Francis (Sanders); Tim Brooke-Taylor (Hillcrest); Desmond Walter-Ellis (Mr. Southwick); Susan Travers (Mrs. Southwick); Zoe Sallis (Mrs. Euston); David Mills (Mr. Euston); Maureen Lane (Mrs. Westbury); David Allister (Mr. Westbury); Tony Gardner (Hunter); Granville Van Dusen (Chuck); Sergio Silverio, Antonino D'Acquisto (Marines); Lorenzo Fineschi (Mike); John Frederick (Military Adviser); Bill Vanders (Lawyer); Ann Ferguson (Miss Page); Marco Gobbi (Hank Wills); Luigi Scavran (Senior Meteroa Monk); Christopher Cruize (Interviewer); Roberto Lande (Young Italian).

HERZBUBE (KING, QUEEN, KNAVE) (LMG, 1972) C—92 M.

Producer, Lutz Hengst; associate producers, David L. Wolper, Horst Jaedicke; director, Jerzy Skolimowski; based on the novel Korol, Dama, Valet by Vladimir Nabokov; screenplay, David Shaw, David Selzter; assistant director, Wolfgang Glattes; art director, Rolf Zehetbauer; music, Stanley Myers; electronic music, Francis Monkman; music adviser-songs, Tom Winter, Jr.; sound, Kersten Ullrich, Hans-Joachim Richter; camera, Charly Steinberger; editor, Melvin Shapiro.

Gina Lollobrigida (Martha Dreyer); David Niven (Charles Dreyer); John Moulder-Brown (Frank Dreyer); Mario Adorf (Professor Ritter); Carl Fox-Duering (Enricht); Barbara Valentin (Optician); Sonia Hofmann (Sonia); and: Erica Beer, Christine Schubert, Felicitas Peters, Christopher Sandford, Elma Karlowa, Mogens von Gadow.

VAMPIRA (COL, 1974) C—88 M.

Producer, Jack H. Wiener; director, Clive Donner; screenplay, Jeremy Lloyd; assistant director, Bert Batt; music-music director, David Whitaker; songs, Anthony Newley; costumes, Vanie Harrison; makeup, Phil Leakey; art director, Philip Harrison; sound editor, Charles Crafford; camera, Tony Richmond; editor, Bill Butler.

David Niven (Count Dracula); Teresa Graves (Countess Vampira); Peter Bayliss (Maltravers); Jennie Linden (Angela); Nicky Henson (Marc); Linda Hayden (Helga); Bernard Bresslaw (Pottinger); Cathie Shirriff (Nancy); Andrea Allan (Eve); Veronica Carlson (Ritva); Minah Bird (Rose); Christopher Sandford (Milton); Freddie Jones (Gilmore); Frank Thornton (Mr. King); Aimi MacDonald, Patrick Newell (Couple in Hotel Room); Kenneth Cranham (Paddy, the Delinquent); Carol Cleveland (Jane—His Victim); Nicola Austine, Penny Irving (Playboy Bunnies).

PAPER TIGER

Producer, Euan Lloyd; director, Ken Annakin; screenplay, Jack Davies; art director, Herbert Smith; sound, George Peterson; camera, John Cabrera; editor, Alan Pattilo.

With: David Niven, Toshiro Mifune, Hardy Kruger, Ando Kazuhito, Irene Tsu, Milko Taka, Jeff Corey, Patricia Donahue.

DOUBLE TROUBLE (BV, 1976)

Executive producer, Ron Miller, director, Norman Tokar; story, Joe McEveety; screenplay, Arthur Alsberg, Don Nelson, With: David Niven.

In a publicity pose with Myrna Loy from EVELYN PRENTICE (MGM '34)

Chapter Eight

William Powell

6'
160 pounds
Brown hair
Brown eyes
Leo

Long before *Mame*, he was "huskin' the charm off of corn," although he began his stage and film career specializing in hissable villains. At Paramount his Boldini in *Beau Geste* (1926) was typical of his silent-screen bad guy, the oily, unredeemable scoundrel.

But then with the magic of sound pictures, William Powell's movie career—which was in danger of stagnation or possible extinction—took on new dimensions. Paramount cast him in *The Canary Murder Case* (1929) in which he capered about as S. S. Van Dine's resourceful gentleman detective, Philo Vance. He quickly established himself with Hollywood and moviegoers as having as much, or even more, displayable charm and dapperness as anything Adolphe Menjou or Lowell Sherman could provide.

Although Bill stood six feet tall, his frame gave the appearance of being on the dumpy side, but it scarcely mattered to women filmgoers, who soon regarded him as the epitome of gentle virility. Interestingly enough, because of the amazing aura of his civilized manner, he could tread on any side of the law in a film and still retain audience sympathy. *Man of the World* and *Ladies' Man*, both Paramount 1931 releases and each co-starring his wife-to-be, Carole Lombard, were excellent examples of Powell at his cosmopolitan best; the blasé con artist who masks a sense of kindness and fair play beneath his glib, trickster exterior.

In 1931, along with Kay Francis and Ruth Chatterton, he switched from Paramount to Warner Bros., where with Miss Francis, he performed in *One Way Passage* (1932), an unforgettable tearjerker which demonstrated how compelling a hero figure Powell could be. Warners tried him out as Philo Vance again in *The Kennel Murder Case* (1933) and allowed him a free, sharp tongue in the Busby Berkeley–choreographed *Fashions of 1934* (1934), but the studio was too engrossed with promulgating its tough-guy trio (James Cagney, Edward G. Robinson, Paul Muni) to foster Powell into the proper showcasing.

If Kay Francis had meshed well with Bill oncamera, chic, chipper Myrna Loy worked even better, and from *Manhattan Melodrama* (1934), his first feature at his new studio, MGM, it was evident that a terrific screen team had emerged. Clark Gable was the very important third part of the triangular love tale in *Manhattan Melodrama*, but in *The Thin Man* (1934), Powell and Loy as a husband-and-wife amateur sleuthing team set the movie industry back on its heels. The two performers were so enticing as the loving, quipping, drinking, socializing Nick and

Nora Charles that they started a terrific vogue for sophisticated yet madcap detective-film entries. But no one could equal the elan of Powell and Loy.

Sometimes Bill, in tandem with Loy, moved into other screen environs, as when he was *The Great Ziegfeld* (1936) to her Billie Burke in that musical extravaganza, or occasionally the screen duo threw all caution to the wind as in the outrageously slapstick *Love Crazy* (1941). But Powell was equally adept at spellbinding other leading ladies, as with his ex-wife, Carole Lombard, in *My Man Godfrey* (Universal, 1936) or his offscreen lady fair, Jean Harlow, in *Reckless* (1935) and *Libeled Lady* (1936).

Post–World War II found Hollywood running out of worldly roles suitable for perennially popular Bill, but not before the fifty-five-year-old actor tackled the best role of his career: Clarence Day, Sr., in *Life with Father* (Warner Bros., 1947). He was Oscar-nominated for this, his most sought-after screen role. Thereafter his screen career petered out, with an occasional flurry of the "old Powell charm" as in *How to Marry a Millionaire* (Twentieth Century–Fox. 1953) and *Mister Roberts* (Warner Bros., 1955).

Watching a vintage William Powell film today may be a trip into nostalgia, but there is hardly a viewer who does not agree that his polished sophistication is unimpeachable, a testament to his meticulous sense of oncamera timing and a feel for everything that is debonair about man in life.

William Horatio Powell was born in Pittsburgh, Pennsylvania, on Friday, July 29, 1892. His mother, Nettie Brady Powell, and his father, Horatio Warren Powell, a public accountant, planned from the start that their son should be a lawyer. He seemed to them an exceptionally intelligent child, and his mother once remarked proudly that young William made speeches from the time he was able to talk.

A love for all sorts of dogs was his early obsession until he was old enough to discover the wondrous offerings of the Bijou Theatre in Pittsburgh. Then he became a regular patron in the gallery and fell in love with the musical comedies and the players who frolicked across the Bijou's stage. With money coaxed from his wary parents he spent as many afternoons as were financially possible in the theatre, where he studied the performers and tried to memorize bits of their impressive dialog. At home, behind closed doors and in front of a mirror, he recited lines and imitated the action he had witnessed onstage.

In 1907, when William was fifteen, the family moved to Kansas City, Missouri. There, at Central Union High School, he was a cheerleader. It was suggested that he study elocution when one of his teachers learned that he was intended for a future in law. He joined the class in public speaking and was pleased to observe that during his first delivery the other students were really listening to him. "At that moment," he recalled years later, "a ham was born. You know there's plenty of ham in all of us. It just needs to be brought out. I hadn't spoken twenty words in that class before I knew that the law was not for me. I was going to be an actor." Speech class became his favorite, and it

was not unusual for him to quote complete passages from the classics from memory. This impressed his classmates even further, although some were to describe him as having "an almost visible mantle of aloofness."

In a school Christmas production of Richard Brinsley Sheridan's comedy *The Rivals*, he had the supporting role of Captain Absolute, but his mature performance made the balance of the cast appear no more than amateurs. During his free time in his junior and senior years, Powell was an usher at the Kansas City Opera House. At his high school graduation ceremonies, he delivered the class oration, "A Plea for Benedict Arnold." The praise he received for the polished performance further convinced him that his proper future lay in acting.

Nevertheless, in September 1911, he matriculated at the University of Kansas, the first step toward four years of college, to be followed, presumably, by three additional years of law courses. Within a week he was back home. He explained to his annoyed parents that the field of law was overcrowded, and he revealed his preference for becoming an actor. "They didn't seem a bit surprised. I thought I had kept my acting ambitions to myself, but I guess I hadn't." He expressed a desire to study at the American Academy of Dramatic Arts in New York City, but his father was adamant that there would be no funds forthcoming for an education of that type.

The annual tuition at the American Academy was then $400. Bill estimated that he would also need almost that much for living expenses during a year, so he went to work as a clerk for the Kansas City telephone company at the salary of $50 a month. "At the end of ten months I didn't save a cent and I owed my father twenty dollars. I was desperate." He disliked his job and longed to be on his own. There seemed but one possible source of revenue left to him; a fairly wealthy great aunt, Mrs. Elizabeth Heywood, back in Mercer, Pennsylvania. He had not seen her in several years, but nevertheless, he composed a twenty-three-page letter telling her how wonderful she was and pointing out that, because of his lack of money, the American stage was being deprived of a great actor. He requested the loan of $1,400, promising to pay it back with six percent interest as soon as he had proved himself in the theatre.

William waited and waited for a response to his letter. Finally, when he had decided to get to New York as best he could on his own and attempt to work his way through the academy, a letter came from Aunt Elizabeth stating that she was instructing her attorney to write him a check for $700. The check arrived in due time, and Powell went to New York.

Among his classmates at the academy were Edward G. Robinson and Joseph Schildkraut. "Even then they both stood out," he later said. After six months, Bill's money was depleted. His only alternative was to tread the path, already well beaten by hundreds of his predecessors, from theatrical agency to theatrical agency. Too proud to give in to defeat by going home, he stuck doggedly to a rigid daily routine of inquiring at each agency. When he was penniless, hungry, without permanent lodgings, and despondent, the thought of suicide via the East River grew dramatically in his mind. But then he met another young hopeful from Kansas City, Ralph Barton, a cartoonist. Barton talked him out of suicide and remained to share his poverty and dreams. They pawned everything they could in order to rent a dingy room wherein they found hidden a small rifle and several boxes of bullets. Some of their frustrations were unleashed by shooting at the cockroaches that lived with them. This earned their ejection by a furious landlord, but they managed to pawn the rifle for $2.50. Three days later, Barton sold a drawing for $35.* The pair's financial future was insured for the time being.

In August 1912 Bill landed the job of playing three small parts in a pre-Broadway presentation of Charles Klein's four-act play *The Ne'er-Do-Well* at the salary of $40 weekly. He played a young man, a middle-aged person, and in the last

act wore white whiskers. The play opened in Cleveland but only lasted two weeks.† His only salaried jobs during the winter of 1912 were two weeks as a monologist around New York City and two weeks in vaudeville as an "Irish villain." In the spring of 1913, he joined one of the road companies of Bayard Veillers' *Within the Law* (Eltinge Theatre: September 12, 1912, 541 performances). Powell was cast in the featured part of an Englishman named Eddie Griggs, the hissable villain. He was with the show on the road for almost two years, but, as he said later, "I suddenly realized that I wasn't learning much playing the same part night after night, month after month, so I broke away." The break, however, was not made alone. During the course of the engagement he had fallen in love with Eileen Wilson, also in the cast, and they were wed in April 1915.

In the years that followed, Bill earned while he learned, either in stock and vaudeville, or in forty weeks of one-night stands from Portland, Oregon, to Detroit, Michigan, and then to Buffalo, New York. As he recalled: "I played more than 200 different parts in two years." In most productions he played two or more roles. "I remember one company," he later told Jim Marshall of *Collier's* magazine, "that possessed only one silk hat, though several members of the cast appeared in toppers. As the hero of the piece, I always bowed off at the left stage, stuck the silk hat behind the vision of the audience and stood there, stalling for time. In the meantime, the hat had been taken out of my hidden hand by a stage hand who went backstage to the opposite side just in time to put it into the villain's hand. The villain then came into the scene in the same silk hat that I had worn a minute before."

In 1917, Bill was back in New York, where he had a minor role in *The King* (George M. Cohan Theatre: November 20, 1917, 127 performances), starring Leo Ditrichstein, followed by a small part out of town in *The Judge of Zalamea*, also starring Ditrichstein. Neither play was a really big commercial hit, but Powell later admitted: "I learned more from him [Ditrichstein] than I ever learned, either before or after that time."

On Christmas Day, 1917, *Going Up* (Liberty Theatre), a musical comedy, opened on Broadway, with Frank Craven and Edith Day in the leads and Bill in support.‡ Of this play, which lasted a year in New York, Powell has said: "I sang, but never alone, always with three or four

---

*Barton would become a noted caricaturist, and, ironically, would commit suicide at the peak of his career.
†Opened at the Lyric Theatre on Broadway on September 2, 1912, for a 40-performance run. Hale Hamilton was the star.
‡Powell is not listed in the cast for the show's opening; most likely he assumed a role later in the run.

417

others. But, it did me a lot of good. I learned a lot from that grand trouper [Frank Craven]."

When *Going Up* finally closed, Powell took another trip into stock, this time performing in the Boston area. Then, in 1920, he won the role of Javier, the villain who is redeemed through death in the last scene of *Spanish Love* (Maxine Elliott Theatre: August 17, 1920, 307 performances). The play, translated from the Spanish by Avery Hopwood and Mary Roberts Rinehart, starred James Rennie. It caused much excitement along the Broadway circuit, primarily for its novel staging in which the cast would frequently enter onstage from the rear of the audience or the platformed areas over the theatre boxes. The show enjoyed forty weeks of success, with Powell receiving some stimulating critical notices. The *Variety* reporter enthused: "[he] easily annexed the histrionic honors of the evening. The sympathy was entirely with him, and his sibilant, passionate hissing through clenched teeth in times of impending physical combat with his former assailant . . . was a thing to marvel at. Crouching, pitiable in his physical slightness compared to the burly Pancho, [Rennie] simply 'brought down the house.' It was a personal triumph that does not fall to the lot of the average performer." Casting agents in the years immediately ahead would not easily forget how adept Powell was at essaying hasty villains who possessed a depth of recognizable humanity beneath their dastardly pose. It would become a working stereotype from which the actor would only escape with the coming of sound pictures.

One evening in the fall of 1921, Bill dropped by the Lambs' Club, popular with New York actors, for a drink. John Barrymore, flush from his recent stage success as *Richard III,* was there with Al Parker, a producer-director of motion pictures. Barrymore introduced the two men and imperiously instructed Parker to hire the former villain of *Spanish Love* to portray a similar role in the film they had been discussing, called *Sherlock Holmes* (Goldwyn, 1922). Believing that the idea might be nothing more than a drink-induced whim of Barrymore's, Parker casually suggested that Powell drop by his office for a reading. Parker forgot about it, but Powell *did* drop by and *did* get the job.

Sherlock Holmes, adapted from the William Gillette stage version of the stories of Sir Arthur Conan Doyle's sleuth, was shot in New York. A still youthful, exuberant Barrymore had the flashy title role with wry Roland Young as the intrepid Dr. Watson. Powell had the small part of Forman Wells, a nefarious agent of Holmes's archenemy, the evil Professor Moriarty. The entire production was aimed at grand dramatics, counterpoised by atmospheric shots of backwater London.*

Bill quickly grasped the techniques of filmmaking (he claims to have learned a great deal from observing Barrymore on the set), and he soon found himself fairly busy at movie work in and around New York City. William Randolph Hearst hired him as a replacement for Jose Ruben who, due to an eye injury incurred on the set, was forced to drop out of his assigned part of Francis I, the King of France, in *When Knighthood Was in Flower* (Paramount, 1922). This film was a Hearst's paean to his mistress, Marion Davies. Bill was rushed to the uptown Manhattan studio where he unsuccessfully struggled to slip into the costume designed for his predecessor. A quickie outfit was rigged up for him and he went oncamera, again as the heavy.† In this case, he schemes to wed English King Henry VIII's (Lyn Harding) sister, Mary Tudor (Davies) but loses her to commoner Charles Brandon (Forrest Stanley). The picture, which was in production for some 160 working days and cost over $1.2 million, proved to be one of Davies' most successful celluloid vehicles.

Theatrically, however, it was a bad-luck period for Bill. Several shows for which he rehearsed folded before reaching Broadway. Two other productions which did open in New York closed rather quickly. *Bavu* (Earl Carroll Theatre: February 25, 1922, 25 performances) was more noteworthy for being the debut of a new theatre than for sound dramatics. Producer Carroll wrote the romantic drama of a Bolshevist involved with a Russian princess (Carlotta Monterey) and a half-breed Turk. Bill was the hero! In *The Woman Who Laughed* (Longacre Theatre: August 16, 1922, 13 performances) Powell was embroiled in a romantic triangle between Gilda Leary and Martha Hedman.

Instead, because of his dark hair, sinister style, mustache, and a long narrow scar at the point of his nose (the origin of which he frankly admitted was the result of a brawl in an upstate New York roadhouse), Bill entered into a succession of vil-

---

*In *The Detective in Film* (1972), pp. 8–10, author William K. Everson describes a recent attempt to reconstruct the release print from surviving negative footage.
†*The Whole Truth and Nothing But* (1962), Hedda Hopper has Marion Davies reminiscing: "Remember those symmetricals he [Bill] wore to make his legs look pretty? When we ran that [film] at San Simeon, Carole Lombard was with him. She never got over his symmetricals. He was a real villain in that picture."

lainous film roles. He was the heavy in *The Out-cast* (Paramount, 1922) starring Elsie Ferguson and David Powell (no relation), as well as in *The Bright Shawl* (Associated First National, 1923). The latter, produced by Richard Barthelmess's company, Inspiration Pictures, was filmed in Cuba. At the Lambs' Club, Bill and star Barthelmess had previously avoided each other, taking a mutual dislike to each other. On the deck of the ship taking the company to Havana, however, the two men one day found themselves face to face. They exchanged glances equivalent to the winters at Valley Force and then Barthelmess suddenly suggested a drink in his stateroom. They drank and drank and talked and talked. By the time the ship docked in Cuba, they were good friends. Theirs was a friendship that endured the rest of their lives.*

Bill was a Frenchman again in *Under the Red Robe* (Goldwyn-Cosmopolitan, 1923), another film for the William Randolph Hearst outfit. In this production, based on Stanley Wigmon's classic novel, Powell as the dastardly Duke of Orleans persuades his easily influenced brother, King Louis XIII of France (Ian MacLaren), to dismiss the prime minister, Cardinal Richelieu (Robert Mantell), from court. This corrupt scheme eventually leads to the duke's own ousting. (In Twentieth Century–Fox's 1937 version, Powell's character is not present in the plot.) In *Dangerous Money* (Paramount, 1924), Bill's nationality was changed to Italian. As the fortune-hunting Prince Arnolfo da Pescia, he weds Bebe Daniels because of her attractive legacy.

In 1924, some thirteen years after borrowing the $700 from his Aunt Elizabeth, Powell repaid the loan with the six percent interest as promised. This deed made her his number one supporter until her death some years later.

Metro-Goldwyn distributed *Romola* (1924), a production by Inspiration Pictures, filmed in and around Florence, Italy, with the Gish sisters and Ronald Colman in the leads. Bill was cast as the villain, Tito Melema, an ingrate Greek who weds Lillian and drowns Dorothy in the Arno River. He later plunges to his own watery death when an angry mob assails him. Because of the city's tell-tale signposts of modern times (trolley tracks, power poles, etc.), a replica of fifteenth-century Renaissance Florence had to be constructed outside the city. The *Chicago Daily Tribune* labeled Powell's performance as "smooth and crafty."

On the completion of the heavily budgeted

*Barthelmess died on August 17, 1963.

With Lillian Gish in ROMOLA (Metro-Goldwyn '24)

Romola, Bill took advantage of his geographical position and toured Europe for the first time. When he returned to New York some months later, a call came from Famous Player–Lasky Studios. Richard Dix had requested him for the part of Julio, another villain, in Dix's new feature, *Too Many Kisses* (Paramount, 1925), a contemporary romantic comedy set in Spain. Since it was to be filmed in California, Powell packed his belongings and, with his newly pregnant wife, took a train west.

In *Too Many Kisses*, the character of Julio is a captain in the Basque civil guard who loves Yvonne Hurja (Frances Howard), but when American Richard Gaylor, Jr. (Dix) enters the scene and also makes claim to Howard, Powell challenges him to a duel. When the girl talks Dix out of dueling, Powell has his bandit gang kidnap Dix. The whimsical yarn ends with Dix beating Powell in a fight, thereby winning Howard. Famous Player–Lasky Studio, on the strength of his performance in *Too Many Kisses*, then signed Powell to a contract.

Meanwhile, Eileen Wilson Powell gave birth to a male heir early in 1925, in Los Angeles. The child was named William David Powell.

Before Bill's Paramount contract went into effect, he made several other California-shot features. Two were shot under the aegis of producer B. P. Schulberg, who was soon to join Famous Player–Lasky's Paramount Pictures and become West Coast production head. In *Faint Perfume* (B. P. Schulberg, 1925) Powell is Barnaby Powers, who divorces his wife (Seena Owen) after six years of marriage and falls in love with his ex-wife's sister (Alyce Mills). In *My Lady's Lips* (B. P. Schulberg, 1925) Powell was again with Alyce Mills. In this script he is a star reporter out to get a scoop on a gang of gamblers by posing as an ex-con.

On the request of his friend Richard Barthelmess, Powell returned to New York for *The Beautiful City* (First National, 1925), which starred Barthelmess and Dorothy Gish. Bill, as Nick Di Silva, was, of course, the culprit of the piece, playing a gangster operating a Chinese theatre as a front.

Bill had two films released on March 7, 1926. *White Mice* (Associated Exhibitors)—the title refers to a club dedicated to aiding people in distress—found Powell as Roddy Forrester, a charter member of this club. He travels to a Latin American republic, falls in love with the president's daughter (Jacqueline Logan), and succeeds in freeing the president (Lucius Henderson) from a prison cell. It was Powell's first real screen lead. In *Sea Horses* (Paramount), Powell was heinous and drunken as Lorenzo Salvia in an East African port where he has gone into hiding after deserting his wife (Florence Vidor). Jack Holt, as a ship's captain, was the film's hero.

Powell was next seen as a murderous outlaw in *Desert Gold* (Paramount, 1926), a Western filmed in the Arizona desert. One of that film's supervisors was again B. P. Schulberg, the enterprising film producer who had brought Clara Bow to Paramount as part of a package deal. Miss Bow was the heroine of Powell's next film, *The Runaway* (Paramount, 1926), which featured Warner Baxter as a Kentucky mountaineer. Powell had a sympathetic role as a movie producer on location in Tennessee. He is used by Bow, an actress who seeks rapid advancement. When Powell is accidentally shot by a wild pistol discharge, the actress flees the film set, suspecting she will be blamed for the deed. Her way of life is changed when she encounters Baxter.

Bill's next film, *Aloma of the South Seas* (Par-amount, 1926), was shot in Puerto Rico, and was based on the rather popular Broadway play.[*] He appeared as dapper Van Templeton, married to Julanne Johnston. Despite his marital status, he proposes marriage to the beautiful dancer of Paradise Island, Aloma (Gilda Gray). When Powell is lost in a canoe during a storm, his widow finds love with Percy Marmont, while Gray is reunited with her original love (Warner Baxter). The most exciting aspect of this photoplay was Harry Fischbeck's camerawork, supervised by director Maurice Tourneur.

In his next film, Bill played Boldini, an Italian thief despised by the entire French Foreign Legion garrison of forty brave men guarding a remote fort in the arid African desert. He is a stool pigeon for the feared but respected Sergeant Lejaune (Noah Beery). In addition, he is no friend of *Beau Geste* (Paramount, 1926), played by Ronald Colman, and Beau's brothers (Neil Hamilton, Ralph Forbes). Beery, who also hates him for the cringing man that he is, sends Powell into the fort's tower during the attack by four thousand Arabs. Death by rifle fire is a certainty, and Powell dies still not fully believing that Beery could have sacrificed him.[†] Powell could not have appeared more cowardly or darkly conniving as the despicable Boldini. When *Beau Geste* opened as a road-show attraction at the Criterion Theatre in New York on August 25, 1926, it was hailed as a rousing adventure tale, much more of a man's picture than even *The Big Parade* (MGM, 1925); " . . . it is a motion picture without a heroine and without a love story, which in itself constitutes a novelty" (*Boston Herald*). Powell received excellent notices for the type of role he did so well and seemingly so easily. Richard Watts, Jr. (*New York Herald-Tribune*) wrote: "Powell is so tremendously vivid in his few appearances—particularly toward the end of the picture when he cows from the death that he knows is facing him—that, were not Beery's portrayal so fine, the picture would be his."

Powell's film performances for the year of 1926 culminated, first, with *Tin Gods* (Paramount, 1926), recounted in flashback form, in which he is the third portion of a temporary romantic triangle involving Thomas Meighan and Aileen Pringle. Then, his final picture of the year was *The Great Gatsby* from F. Scott Fitzgerald's novel (1925) and from the play by Owen Davis.[‡] While *The*

[*]Opened at the Lyric Theatre on April 20, 1925, for a 163-performance run with Vivienne Osborne as Aloma.
[†]In the 1939 Paramount remake, the character of Boldini underwent a name change to Rasinoff and was played by J. Carrol Naish. In 1966, the coward renamed Boldini, was played by David Mauro in Universal's uncostly version of the Percival Wren novel.
[‡]Opened at the Ambassador Theatre in New York on February 2, 1926, for a 113-performance run with James Rennie (Gatsby) and Florence Eldridge (Daisy).

With Warner Baxter and Clara Bow in THE RUNAWAY (Par '26)

Great Gatsby was considered a prestigious production in its day, neither Fitzgerald's literary/social reputation nor the economics of the film industry demanded that it become *the* picture of the year, as occurred with the 1974 Paramount debacle starring Robert Redford and Mia Farrow. The 1926 edition proved to be a reunion for several *Beau Geste* talents. Herbert Brenon was again directing, while Neil Hamilton was once more the second male lead. Likewise, Powell again was representing an unpleasant type of humanity, herein with more justification. As George Wilson, a garage-keeper,† he was dour-faced throughout the proceedings because his wife (Georgia Hale) is having an affair with upper-crust Tom Buchanan (Hale Hamilton). Powell forces a showdown with Hale. The latter dashes into the street and is run down by Daisy Buchanan (Lois Wilson) who is driving Jay Gatsby's (Warner Baxter) roadster. The garage-keeper then vengefully shoots Baxter. Said Mordaunt Hall (*New York Times*) of Bill, " . . . while not quite in his element, [he] gives an unerring portrayal of the chauffeur."

Bill began the new year on film as he had ended the previous one, as a murderer. In *New York*

In BEAU GESTE (Par '26)

†Later to be enacted by Howard Da Silva in Paramount's 1949 remake, and by Scott Wilson in the studio's 1974 version.

(Paramount, 1927), filmed in Manhattan, he is one of four old buddies who rendezvous at a Bowery cabaret, but of the quartet he is the only one who is outside the law. *Love's Greatest Mistake* (Paramount, 1927) found Powell blackmailing Evelyn Brent, who did not seem to mind since she ultimately elopes with him. He was much more despicable in *Señorita* (Paramount, 1927) as a scheming South American bandit who leads an attack against the ranch of his lifelong enemy (Bebe Daniels). Following these films, he was the con artist who menaces the life of blundering mail-carrier Eddie Cantor in *Special Delivery* (Paramount, 1927), and in the farce, *Time to Love* (Paramount, 1927), he was a French nobleman who loses his intended bride (Vera Veronina) at the altar when Raymond Griffith carries her off in a giant balloon.

In his first film on a loan-out basis, Bill was a Balkan prince—complete with large moustache, white jacket, and dangling monocle—in *Paid to Love* (Fox, 1927). Virginia Valli was the leading lady and Howard Hawks the director. Bill was back at Paramount for *Nevada* (1927), a Zane Grey Western brought to silent action by scenarists John Stove and L. G. Rigby. As Clan Dillon, the trusted ranch foreman and suitor of Thelma Todd, Powell was eventually unmasked as the leader of a gang of rustlers. Gary Cooper had the title role. Powell's final screen appearance of 1927 was in a production, described as a "burlesque," entitled *She's a Sheik* (Paramount). Bebe Daniels, the effervescent granddaughter of an Arabian sheik (Paul McAllister), is sought by Powell, the desert renegade. However, she insists on having a Christian husband and abducts an American for this pleasurable task (Richard Arlen).

By 1928 Bill had settled into a comfortable, if not entirely artistically satisfying, career routine, perpetually cast as the polished villain (when the part did not call for the more dastardly oncamera evilness of Noah Beery). With the likes of Gary Cooper, Neil Hamilton, Charles "Buddy" Rogers, Richard Arlen, and Clive Brook on the Paramount payroll, there was little likelihood that Bill would ever be tapped to play the good guy in a studio release. On the social scene, the Powells, with a very pleasant income, and the proper status of a tie to an important film company, were regarded as the "right type" of Hollywood young marrieds.

During 1928, before Paramount fully accepted the microphone as a tool of moviemaking, Bill appeared in eight productions, a few of which have become landmarks of the silent cinema. *The Last Command* (Paramount, 1928), not generally publicly seen for many years, was heralded in its

In a publicity pose with James Hall for SEÑORITA (Par '27)

422

day as a masterpiece of moviemaking. The *London Daily Sketch* lavishly praised: "It is the greatest film in the world. There is no qualifying sentence to that praise of *The Last Command*." The film was directed by Josef von Sternberg, from his own scenario based upon an idea advanced to him verbally by Ernst Lubitsch. Powell was cast as a former Russian revolutionary agitator turned movie director who puts his decrepit old adversary, czarist General Dolgorucki (Emil Jannings), through the paces as a movie extra. Despite the scene-stealing presence of character star Jannings, Powell reaped his own critical rewards. Mordaunt Hall (*New York Times*) was among those who complimented him for a "sterling portrait."

The same day (January 22, 1928) that *The Last Command* opened at New York's Rialto Theatre, *Beau Sabreur* (Paramount) debuted across the street at the Paramount Theatre. The latter was based on another novel by Percival Christopher Wren, and was intended by the studio as an appropriate sequel to the earlier *Beau Geste*. The picture did little to showcase popular Evelyn Brent or the fast-rising star of Gary Cooper, and critics and public alike agreed that the new production merely rehashed the past success (even to using leftover desert footage lensed for *Beau Geste*). Powell as the French traitor Becque was "a great heavy" (*Film Daily*) but unable to carry the load of an unworthy adventure yarn.

Feel My Pulse (Paramount, 1928), a comedy from director Gregory La Cava, had Powell in the minor role of a hijacker of rum cached at an island sanitarium recently inherited by hypochondriac Bebe Daniels. *Partners in Crime* (Paramount, 1928) starred Wallace Beery and Raymond Hatton, a late arrival in the silent comedy teams, who never quite gained sufficient popularity. Hatton portrayed dual roles, one good and one bad, while Powell was the henchman to the sinister Hatton.

The Dragnet (Paramount, 1928), another Josef von Sternberg feature, found Powell as Dapper Frank Trent, the leader of a gang of hijackers who is eliminated by gallant, ex-alcoholic, Two-Gun Nolan (George Bancroft). While not of the same high caliber as von Sternberg's previous *Underworld* (Paramount, 1927), *The Dragnet* had its own group of film champions, who found deep meaning in the emotion-charged encounters between lawless Evelyn Brent and gangster Bancroft. In the book *Hollywood in the Twenties* (1968), Dav-

With Richard Arlen in FEEL MY PULSE (Par '28)

id Robinson appraises: "Sternberg's pictorialism proved an entirely dynamic and in no way static element; the story and its characters are developed through well-observed visual details." Once again, Powell rose to the occasion, and performed to the mark as the natty, duplicitous scoundrel.

The Vanishing Pioneer (Paramount, 1928), a Zane Grey Western of the Jack Holt school of melodrama, had Bill as corrupt politician John Murdock, who is shot by Holt after confessing to the killing of a rancher. *Forgotten Faces* (Paramount, 1928)* was pure soap opera, concerned with Clive Brook's wife (Olga Baclanova), who has been cheating with Powell. Brook murders Bill early in the tale, which continues onward to include an abandoned child, prison, and final retribution when Baclanova goes to jail for killing Brook.

Interference (1929) was Paramount's initial all-talking feature film. It debuted in Los Angeles on November 18, 1928, two days after the New York premiere, but was then immediately taken out of circulation for further revisions and was issued for general viewing on January 5, 1929. Based on the play by Roland Pertwee and Harold Dearden, Powell was Philip Voaze,‡ an Englishman report-

*The film was first made as *Heliotrope* (Paramount, 1920) and later remade as *Forgotten Faces* (Paramount, 1926) and *Gentleman after Dark* (United Artists, 1942).

‡Played by A. E. Matthews in the Broadway stage original (Empire Theatre: October 18, 1927, 226 performances).

With Evelyn Brent and Francis McDonald in THE DRAGNET (Par '28)

With Clive Brook in FORGOTTEN FACES (Par '28)

edly killed in World War I combat. Instead, he lives in London under an assumed name, but is discovered by a former love (Evelyn Brent), who attempts to blackmail his wife (Doris Kenyon). She, in turn, has remarried, this time to a nobleman (Clive Brook). Learning that he has a fatal heart ailment and has nothing to lose, Powell kills his former love and then turns himself over to the authorities. The *Boston Herald* critic, Elinor Hughes, wrote of Powell: "His cultivated and expressive voice, his smooth, polished manner and easy assumption of emotion masked under flippant cynicism, made him the outstanding person in the cast."

Sound was indeed the savior of Bill's motion-picture career. In silent films, he had been overly typecast as the villain or social roué to the point where he just was repeating his pantomimed actions in each successive oncamera appearance. By the end of 1928, in silents, he had dropped from the lead and second male lead to a supporting player's status. From William Powell's standpoint, Paramount found its "voice" just at the right moment. After so many years of acting without voiced dialog, Bill now found that he learned his lines best through the arduous task of writing his scripts in longhand and then speaking them into a dictaphone machine, which he played back until he felt that he had the words down pat.

Paramount executives took wise advantage of their contractee with the mellow voice and starred him next as Philo Vance in *The Canary Murder Case* (1929), adapted from S. S. Van Dine's detective novel by Florence Ryerson and Albert S. Le Vino. Ironically, the picture started out as a silent, but during the course of production (September–December 1928) it was decided to make it a full talking film. The studio was forced to dub in Margaret Livingston's voice for actress Louise Brooks, since the latter was on film assignment in Germany and could not return for the additional work.

Philo Vance, a fanciful society gent and amateur detective, unwittingly opened a new career door for Bill, just as Samuel Goldwyn proved that his contractee Ronald Colman was admirably suited for the sound medium by starring him in the detective caper *Bulldog Drummond* (United Artists, 1929). The "Canary" of the picturized case is actually a musical-comedy dancer (Brooks)

who is murdered in her apartment. Four men are under suspicion, three of whom were blackmail subjects of the deceased. Powell is called in on the caper by an old friend (Charles Lane) who turns out to be a major suspect. The "100 percent talk" film was well received by audiences and critics. One New York trade paper analyzed: "It is a relief to see a good, honest murder built with the precision of a mathematical problem." Those who saw the sound version of the film (for it was also released in a silent edition for theatres not yet equipped for sound) were impressed by the denouement, which involved the hearing of a phonograph-recorded voice behind a locked door.

As for Bill's performance as the dapper Manhattan sleuth who provides District Attorney Markham (E. H. Calvert) with several lessons in the art of detecting, the reviewers were enthusiastic. *Variety* reported: "Another personal smash for Powell, right now a number one name in the talker field and perhaps the best straight dramatic player on the sound screen so far. . . . The women will go for William Powell as an actor if not a romantic figure."

Before the full impact of Bill's new and sudden appeal was actually felt at the all-important box office, however, he was seen in supporting parts in two dramas. In *The Four Feathers* (Paramount, 1929),* with some filming in Africa and boasting a musical score and sound effects only, he was Captain Trench, one of the three companions who each send a white feather signifying cowardice to Harry Faversham (Richard Arlen). In *Charming Sinners* (Paramount, 1929) he was used by Ruth Chatterton to regain the love and attention of her erring husband (Clive Brook). The story was adapted for the screen by Doris Anderson from W. Somerset Maugham's play, *The Constant Wife.*†

On August 11, 1929, Paramount brought Philo Vance back to movie screens in *The Greene Murder Case.* Powell, again cast as the gentleman investigator, is requested to dislodge the killer of three members of Manhattan's wealthy, unpopular Greene family, once presided over by the bedridden Mrs. Greene (Gertrude Norman). With Powell in seemingly casual pursuit, as attentive to good manners as to spotting clues, the killer eventually plunges to her death into the wintry waters of the Hudson River. For broad comedy relief,

---

*This was the only American film version of Edward E. W. Mason's novel of 1902. The story was filmed three times by the British: 1921, 1939, and in 1956 (*Storm over the Nile*).
†Produced on Broadway with Ethel Barrymore at the Maxine Elliott Theatre (November 29, 1926, 295 performances), and revived by Katharine Cornell at the National Theatre (December 8, 1951, 139 performances). Fay Compton starred in the London premiere (1927), with Ruth Chatterton as the heroine in a 1937 West End version, and Ingrid Bergman the star in a 1973 version on the London stage.

Eugene Pallette was introduced into the series as the rotund, dense Sergeant Heath, a woeful soul better at double-takes than rounding up the culprits.‡

As a change of pace, Bill was seen next as a rich, powerful theatrical producer in *Pointed Heels* (Paramount, 1929). He is smitten with musical-comedy star Fay Wray, but loses her, romantically, to novice songwriter Phillips Holmes. When the composer is later disinherited by his conventional family, Powell hopes to entice the star back into his life, but these hopes are shattered when Holmes's first song becomes a show hit.

Bill adopted an Italian accent for his role as Gardoni, the glib stage entertainer in *Behind the Make-up* (Paramount, 1930). Again, Fay Wray was his co-star, with Kay Francis in support as an adventuress in this, her sixth film credit. The *New York Times* found that "the voices are well recorded" and that Powell "utters whole sentences in Italian, and his performance throughout is excellent." By today's standards, the Robert Milton–directed feature seems exceedingly obvious and its show-business plot quite unsophisticated. However, in its time the picture was considered quite credible, aided to a great extent by vaudevillian Hal Skelly, *soignée* Francis of the New York stage, Continental Paul Lukas, and the presence of such screen reliables as demure Wray, smooth Powell, and dependable E. H. Calvert.

Street of Chance (Paramount, 1930) was based by Howard Estabrook on Oliver H. P. Garrett's expansive "story" of the notorious New York City gambler, Arnold Rothstein.* David O. Selznick, then a Paramount executive producer, encouraged Garrett to write the story and then cast Powell as the Broadway gambler whose name was fictionalized to "Natural" Davis. Powell's Davis is the big man with the cards in New York and sends his younger brother (Regis Toomey) in California $10,000 as a wedding gift. Toomey increases the stake to $50,000 in West Coast gambling spas and is then ready, he feels, to face the number-one man in New York, not knowing that it is his brother. When the kid brother wipes him out at cards, Bill is dispatched by gunshot, according to the gamblers' code. Definitely a man's picture, Kay Francis and Jean Arthur were in support as, respectively, the New York gambler's wife and the younger brother's wife.

‡When Paramount remade *The Greene Murder Case* as *Night of Mystery* (1937), with Grant Richards as Vance, Roscoe Karns's role as the slow-witted Sergeant Heath was expanded to even greater prominence.
*Estabrook was nominated for an Oscar for his writing achievement, but lost to Frances Marion of *The Big House* (MGM, 1930).

With Kay Francis and John Risso in STREET OF CHANCE (Par '30)

In PARAMOUNT ON PARADE (1930)

With Marion Shilling in a publicity pose from SHADOW OF THE LAW (Par '30)

Before Paramount could produce its next Philo Vance installment, MGM acquired the screen rights to *The Bishop Murder Case* and released a film version of the S. S. Van Dyne tale in January 1930 with Basil Rathbone cast as Vance. Three months later, Paramount premiered its *The Benson Murder Case*, with Bill for the third time enacting the role of Vance.* This time the murder and its solution occur at an isolated hunting lodge. Likewise, it is ultracivilized Bill, not District Attorney John F. X. Markham (E. H. Calvert) or Sergeant Heath (Eugene Pallette), who detects the actual killer midst the gathering of suspects, each of whom has a logical motive for the slaying. Frank Tuttle, who replaced both Lothar Mendes and Louis Gasnier as director of the film, speeded up the film's pacing, but still turned out the weakest of the Powell–Paramount–Philo Vance feature trilogy. Later, in April 1930, Bill was to be seen again as Philo Vance in the studio's all-star revue, *Paramount on Parade* (1930). In a skit with Clive Brook as Sherlock Holmes, Powell's Vance pursues the Oriental fox, Fu Manchu (Warner Oland).

For *Shadow of the Law* (Paramount, 1930), the studio put Powell on the wrong side of prison bars as an engineer who accidentally kills an inebriated, wealthy broker in his bedroom and is sentenced to jail. When Paramount had previously translated the plot to the screen as *City of Silent Men* (1921), Thomas Meighan originated the Powell screen role of the unjustly accused individual who is eventually cleared of his conviction.

Since the changeover to talkies, Paramount, like the other studios, had been sorting through its roster of established players, eliminating those veterans who could not make the transition to sound films, and filling in the gaps from a variety of sources. Some of these replacements came up from the ranks of filmmaking, like Jean Arthur and Frances Dee; others were imported from the European cinema, like Marlene Dietrich. Most of the studio's new blood came, quite naturally, from the Broadway stage, and included Fredric March, Helen Kane, Claudette Colbert, Sylvia Sidney, Phillips Holmes, Skeets Gallagher, Miriam Hopkins, and Kay Francis. The latter, with her seemingly natural sophisticated aura, an ability to wear the latest fashions in the most chic manner, and a burgeoning sense of high comedy, had already shown in two assignments with Bill

*In the Spanish-language version of *The Benson Murder Case*, *El Cuerpo Del Delito* (Paramount, 1930), Ramon Pereda played Philo Vance.

that together they created a cosmopolitan ambiance that enhanced a picture's box-office worth.

Such was the case with *For the Defense* (Paramount, 1930), which offered Bill as William Foster, a thinly-veiled characterization of the late New York criminal lawyer, William J. Fallon. Oliver H. P. Garrett, who was a master at turning out successful screenplays of New York's smart set, ably plied his craft here. Bill was the gangland mouthpiece and a member of Manhattan's top society who is clever until he falls in love with Irene Manners (Francis). She is troubled by the law, which eventually prompts him to bribe a juror with $2,000. His unprofessional methods are discovered, and Powell receives a five-year jail sentence. As he is being led off in the rain to prison, he bids farewell to Francis, who promises to wait for him. As the *New York Times* reported of Powell's screen impersonation: "Suavity being one of Mr. Powell's film characteristics, it is almost needless to say that William Foster's manner is just that. He remains calm through the bad moments of other people's trials, and through his own—which probably is the test."

Having completed six feature films for 1930 release, Powell decided it was time to enjoy a European vacation. This decision also provided an excellent reason to put more distance between himself and his estranged wife, whom he would divorce the following year. Later, Bill would succinctly analyze the marital discord, "We rubbed each other the wrong way. That was all."

Not even Powell was aware at the time how much this trip would alter his mode of private life. In a 1936 *Photoplay* magazine interview he looked back on those decisive times:

"I was going to be one of these Riviera playboys. And I was for almost four months. I was dripping with irresponsibility. But after a while I began to get bored with loafing. Finally, I went on a tour of the French chateau country.

"I remember going up into a tower room in one of those fine old castles, late one night, where I could look across a lake. It was beautiful up there. So beautiful that my throat got all lumpy. I sat there until daybreak. For the first time in many years, I was really lonely. As a playboy, I was a flop. From that moment I think I began to mature. The age of maturity differs with the individual. Shirley Temple is mature at six. I got mine up there on that turret by the lake. I decided to go home and go to work.

"The day I arrived in Hollywood I met Carole [Lombard]. The first thing I did was to propose to her. . . . I thought she was about as swell a gal as I had ever run into. I still think so. She sat down

With Kane Richmond (left) and Kay Francis in FOR THE DEFENSE (Par '30)

and we talked for five hours. I made a date with her for that night, and we talked for hours more. She said 'No' to my proposal of marriage, and kept on saying 'No'...."

Whether Powell was recalling those 1930s days through a mist of accuracy or romanticism, it is true that upon his return to California and to Paramount he was introduced to twenty-two-year-old Carole Lombard,* who had been selected to appear opposite him in his new feature. The unpretentious, lively manner of this five-foot, two-inch blonde immediately appealed to Powell, who was admittedly quiet and somewhat shy with strangers. They soon proved to be inseparable. Her pet name for him was "Philo."

Bill and his wife were divorced in early 1931, with Eileen Wilson Powell acquiring custody of their son, but the decree provided that Powell might visit his son whenever he wished. That year, also, the senior Powells moved to Los Angeles at the actor's request.

The first Powell-Lombard film, *Man of the World* (Paramount, 1931), presented him in a type of role he so adeptly handled: the well-bred, but shady, character who is so charming that one scarcely minds his underhanded dealings. Here he portrayed an American writer in Paris who soon discovers that blackmailing rich Americans is far more lucrative than honest work. His accomplice is tough, but caring, Wynne Gibson, who remains loyal to Powell despite his intense love affair with debutante Lombard. Lombard's rascally uncle (Guy Kibbee) is blackmailed by the con artists, but Powell, en route to South America with Gibson, tears up the payment check, thus making him something of an honorable crook. *Photoplay* magazine summed it up best: "A good picture; not much action but plenty of drama and a great performance by William Powell."

At Bill's request, he and Lombard were teamed again, two months later, in *Ladies Man* (Paramount, 1931), also written in a smart style that hid its formula plotline by Herman J. Mankiewicz. Again the title refers to Bill, whose debonair qualities cause women of all ages to bestow expensive gifts upon him, which he graciously accepts. He then exchanges the booty for cash, which pays for his plush way of life. One of his benefactors, Mrs.

With Carole Lombard in MAN OF THE WORLD (Par '31)

Fendley (Olive Tell), has a daughter (Lombard) who quickly falls in love with him. Mr. Fendley (Gilbert Emery), determined to put an end to the romantic inclinations of the female members of his family, visits the lothario and, in the ensuing argument, pushes him through a window to his death fifteen stories below. Kay Francis, as Powell's true love who has seen the sensitive romantic beneath his glib surface, stands near the body and tells a gaping policeman: "He loved me. They can never take that from me." In seventy short minutes, *Ladies Man* presents, dissects, and offers commentary on a way of life that seemed risqué and strangely promising to depression-weary filmgoers. Even by today's "anything goes" standards the film offers a titillating picture of amoral high living interlaced with righteous retribution (Powell's death) and giddy romanticism (Francis's abiding love for the high-priced gigolo).

*She was born Jane Alice Peters on October 6, 1908, in Fort Wayne, Indiana. In 1914, when her parents separated, she and her two older brothers went with the mother to live in Los Angeles. In 1921 she was selected by director Allan Dwan to portray Monte Blue's sister in *A Perfect Crime* (Fox), her first movie role. Not long after completing Virgil Junior High School, Jane was spotted by a Fox Films executive, later screentested, and given the role opposite Edmund Lowe in *Marriage in Transit* (1925). As Carole Lombard she made three more Fox films, then in 1927 she joined Mack Sennett's comedy-film factory where she performed in at least fourteen short subjects. After making *The Divine Sinner* (Rayart, 1928), Carol moved to Pathé, where, except for *Me, Gangster* (Fox, 1928), she remained until *The Arizona Kid* (Fox, 1930). In 1930 she negotiated a $350 weekly contract with Paramount. After her second film there, *Fast and Loose* (Paramount, 1930), the studio officially adopted Carole Lombard as her screen name.

Eight months after they met, Powell and Carole Lombard were married on June 26, 1931, in Los Angeles. Among those present at the ceremony were the actress's mother and her two brothers, Frederick and Stuart. Bill was thirty-eight, and Carole was twenty-two. Thereafter the newlyweds embarked on a honeymoon cruise to Hawaii.

Meanwhile, the shape of Bill's screen career was being altered by one Myron Selznick, son of motion-picture pioneer and onetime tycoon Lewis J. Selznick,* and older brother of David O. Selznick. Myron had unsuccessfully tried to launch a career in the production side of filmmaking and in 1926 had become a talent agent with director Lewis Milestone as his first client. By mid-1931, his client roster included some of Hollywood's top talent, and he added to it William Powell, Kay Francis, and Ruth Chatterton, three of Paramount's brightest stars, whose contracts were up for renewal. Myron was a shrewd ten-percenter and knew that Warner Bros. was anxious to acquire stars with whom to expand their sound-film program. He negotiated contracts with Warners for the three performers, thus depriving Paramount of a trio of top box-office draws. This action was considered a coup in the business of agentry, a business that only a few years before had been looked upon with the greatest degree of disrespect.

Bill signed a lucrative studio contract which provided him with a $6,000 weekly salary, plus story approval on each film in which he appeared. Above and beyond the financial and power considerations of his contract, Warner Bros. seemed the ideal studio for the actor to join. The Warner Bros.–First National payroll had aristocratic George Arliss, tough Edward G. Robinson and James Cagney, wholesome Richard Barthelmess, funnyman Joe E. Brown, and, on a lower-status rung, romantic Douglas Fairbanks, Jr., folksy Chic Sales, youngster Dickie Moore, and dapper Warren William. Only the latter could be considered competition for Powell in the studio's free-and-clear dapper-Dan roles, still such a favorite part with cinema audiences. Besides, it seems that distinguished, articulate William could never broaden his cinema standing sufficiently to be anything more than a gentlemanly leading man. Yet as time and his eight Warner Bros.–First National pictures would prove, this new studio

headquarters was merely a stopgap in the progression of Powell's overall movie career.

His first film under the Warners banner was revealed to the public on October 4, 1931. It was *The Road to Singapore,* directed by Alfred E. Green from the play *Heat Wave* by Roland Pertwee.‡ Powell appeared as a hard-drinking individual of much notoriety in steamy Calcutta. He is pursued by the nurse-wife (Doris Kenyon) of a doctor (Louis Calhern) who has forsaken his wife in favor of his profession. The doctor's attractive sister (Marian Marsh) also makes a play for Powell, but is eventually rejected. The *London Times* offered an interesting commentary on Powell's screen persona as displayed in *The Road to Singapore.* "He is the ideal devil's disciple and has a remarkable gift of making vice appear at once more becoming and more honest than virtue. . . . His self-possession is overwhelming, and we are quite unable to believe that a man so sure of himself could have done anything really wrong."

During 1932 Warners kept Powell reasonably busy in four releases, of which one is distinguished. In January, his first film of the year was *High Pressure* (Warner Bros., 1932), a fast-talking melodrama that zipped through its seventy-four minutes so quickly that viewers scarcely had the opportunity to analyze, let alone comprehend, its confused plot. Powell was typecast as the get-rich-quick Gar Evans, a con artist who forms the Golden Gate Artificial Rubber Company, based on the "discovery" of a crackpot inventor (Harry Beresford). With his partner (George Sidney), Powell prepares to make a mint until it is realized that the inventor (who claims he can make rubber from sewage) is a true mental case. The day is saved, however, by the executives of a real rubber company. Evelyn Brent was Powell's loyal lady friend throughout the Mervyn Le Roy–directed proceedings.

In July, his next film was *Jewel Robbery* (Warner Bros., 1932)†, which provided the logically inevitable step of reuniting Bill and Kay Francis. Powell was as slick, conniving, and irresistible as ever, while Kay, decked out in a lavish wardrobe, was as stylish and appealing as ever. He was the suave, smooth-spoken jewel thief (of course) while she was the bored (of course) frivolous wife of a wealthy manufacturer (Henry Kolker). The backdrop is Vienna, the setting a plush jewelry

*The senior Selznick, whose motto had been "Selznick Pictures Make Happy Hours," went broke in 1923. Several attempts to resurrect his film-producing career were unsuccessful, and he died on January 25, 1933 at the age of sixty-three.
‡Opened at the Fulton Theatre on February 17, 1931, for a 15-performance run on Broadway.
†The Broadway version (Booth Theatre: January 13, 1932, 54 performances) had starred Basil Sydney and Mary Ellis.

shop. The plot provides ample opportunity for the two leads to be as charming as possible in the best Continental manner. The story concerns the plights of a veteran genteel thief (Powell) who magnificently executes a gem robbery while noblewoman Francis succumbs to his charms. At the finish, the two part, but the audience knows she will blithely leave her stolid husband and her would-be-lover (Hardie Albright) to reconvene in Nice with Powell. While delightful on its own level, *Jewel Robbery* hardly equals a later Kay Francis film, *Trouble in Paradise* (Paramount, 1932), in which she matches wits and charms with refined Herbert Marshall under Ernst Lubitch's direction.

The Warners-Powell October offering, *One Way Passage* (Warner Bros., 1932), proved to be the actor's most auspicious film for the studio. Robert Lord wrote the tragic love tale and later won an Academy Award for Best Original Story. Tay Garnett directed on a comparatively small budget with an eye towards subtlety and adroitness in keeping the romance from becoming one more weepy soap opera. Bill is Dan Hardesty,* a polished criminal on his way to San Quentin, handcuffed to a detective (Warren Hymer). Kay

Francis is Joan Evans, a wealthy woman-of-the-world who has an incurable heart ailment. They all board a ship in Hong Kong, bound for San Francisco. On the high seas Powell and Francis fall in love, and although each learns of the other's future, they pretend innocence, promising to keep a date at an Agua Caliente bar on New Year's Eve. "Whatever happens," Kay sighs to Bill during a love scene, "we belong to each other always." He responds, "If only it would never."† (In the richly romantic finale, the spirits of Kay and Bill do meet for that New Year's Eve drink, and their cocktail glasses are shown being lifted for the symbolic toast.)

The Christmas, 1932, Bill Powell film was the comedy-drama *Lawyer Man* (Warner Bros.). Powell ably fulfilled the title's image as an all-knowing barrister whose practice is devoted chiefly to ghetto clients. His talents are soon needed further up the social scale where he becomes involved in a jam with pretty Claire Dodd and is later indicted for blackmail. When a hung jury fails to convict him, the now cynical and worldly attorney seeks underworld clients. His success in that quarter, along with political juggling, eventually earns him the title of assistant prosecutor.

*Played by George Brent in the 1940 Warners remake with Merle Oberon, entitled *Til We Meet Again*.
†Thus ended likewise the co-starring team of Powell and Francis.

With Kay Francis in ONE WAY PASSAGE (WB '32)

Throughout, snappy Joan Blondell is his ever alert secretary.

Private Detective 62 (Warner Bros., 1933) had a plot similar to *Lawyer Man* except that Powell is an ex-spy who has turned detective rather than lawyer and slips from respectability. Powell played his role efficiently, but the characterization of Donald Free lacked conviction. Perhaps John S. Cohen, Jr. (*New York Sun*) described the situation best in his appraisal of this film. "In the old days, he [Powell] played crooks who knew they were crooks and who didn't reform. Or if they did eventually reform through love, there was, in the beginning, none of this superimposing of a set of ethics. This set of ethics which Mr. Powell's screen character now disports and which causes him to shudder a bit at what he is doing, serves merely to inspire disbelief, to cause the crook tales in which he appears to assume the air of third-rate magazine fiction. They are so obviously an effort to sentimentalize completely (for the sake of the bosomed admirers of Mr. Powell) whatever harsh reality his roles used to possess. . . . What has become of the William Powell who played Rothstein so superbly in *Street of Chance?*"

If moviegoers assumed the offscreen Powell was identical to his impersonations, Hollywood columnist James Fidler set them straight in a *Photoplay* magazine article entitled "Bill Powell Exposed." The writer reported: "An evening in his company is as entertaining and rewarding as an evening with O'Henry or de Maupassant. He is as full of information as the encyclopedia; as up-to-date as today's newspaper." Little was stated in the profile about Powell's marriage to Carole Lombard, she pushing her way up the professional rungs at Paramount and engaging in a far more active social life than her basically stay-at-home spouse.

Powell was considered at one time for the lead in *Counsellor-at-Law* (Universal, 1933), but the role went to John Barrymore. Instead Warners loaned Powell to RKO for *Double Harness* (1933) in which his majestic co-star was ash-blonde Ann Harding. The story deals with a society playboy (he owns a steamship line) trapped into marriage by a domesticity-bent, blueblood lady. Not only was the grave, slightly matronly Miss Harding miscast, but the John Cromwell–directed picture "suffers from its grim determination to be smart and witty and sophisticated, when really it is none of these things" (Richard Watts, Jr., *New York Herald-Tribune*). One of the less taxing, if overplayed, moments was the final sequence,

with Harding hostessing an elaborate dinner for the influential postmaster general (Wallis Clark) at which everything goes wrong, including Powell's initial absence from the head of the table.

On August 18, 1933, Powell and Carole Lombard surprised none of their friends by obtaining a divorce. As she told intimates: "The son of a bitch is acting even when he takes his pajamas off." She would frequently describe her spouse's routine of burying himself in the library for hours at a time, hoping to digest impressive new words from the dictionary with which to impress his set of acquaintances as being a cultivated and erudite gentleman offscreen as well as on. She told the press that she was a bit weary of playing detective games at home with her husband and ever-present Dick Barthelmess. She added of her ex-mate: "I must like the man, or I wouldn't have married him in the first place! Now that we're divorced, we're still the best of friends." The divorce decree was granted in Carson City, Nevada, on grounds of cruelty. Lombard's lawyers stated that during the twenty-eight months of marriage, Powell was "a very emotional man, cruel and cross in manner of language." Following the divorce, Powell entered a period of his life which columnists, friends, and relatives termed "hermitage."

Counting on audience acceptance of an established screen character, Warners put together, on a relatively low budget, the S. S. Van Dine novel *The Kennel Murder Case* (Warner Bros., 1933). Bill's fourth time as the patrician Philo Vance was directed by Michael Curtiz. Employing such techniques as the "wipe," a split screen, a moving camera, and other innovative tricks, Curtiz fashioned a whodunit film which is often cited as a classic of the decade. This time, Powell with his "amiable smugness" is on hand to deduce that the first corpse, thought by the police to be a suicide, was actually a murder. When the murdered man's brother (Frank Conroy) is also found dead, there is no doubt but that foul play is in motion. With the aid of a Doberman Pinscher and a Scotty (hence the title), Vance filters out the clues that lead to the identity and arrest of the culprit. As the reviewers and public alike had agreed at the time of Powell's Paramount trilogy of Philo Vance films, his civilized sleuth remains "one of Mr. Powell's best characterizations" (Richard Watts, Jr., *New York Post*).

In September 1933, a month after their divorce, Bill and Carole Lombard were scheduled by Warners to star in *Bedside*, an original story by Manny Seff and Harvey Thew. The studio counted on the starring combination as a box-office draw after

With Monte Vandergrift, Eugene Pallette, and Ralph Morgan in THE KENNEL MURDER CASE (WB '33)

the nationwide publicity splash caused by their divorce. Both stars vetoed the idea, and Warners went ahead and filmed it with Warren William and Jean Muir.

In October 1933, Bill gave his approval to the script of a film tentatively called *King of Fashion,* and began work as Sherwood Nash, "a pirate and a parasite" of the dress-designing industry. The film was released in January 1934 as *Fashions of 1934* (First National), in which the star's name appeared above the title. Powell is at his debonair best as the swindler who bootlegs Paris fashions off the ships as soon as they dock in New York harbor, takes them to his headquarters where Frank McHugh photographs them for duplication and (very blonde) Bette Davis sketches them. Later, in Paris, they are caught red-handed trying to photograph (a camera is hidden in the top of McHugh's cane) creations of a world-renowned couturier (Reginald Owen) who is discouraged from pressing charges through blackmail tactics. They all join forces to stage a legitimate fashion show set to extravagant dance and music. The elaborate "Spin a Little Web of Dreams" number, staged by Busby Berkeley, contained such living tableaus as the Hall of Human Harps (curvaceous girls seemingly clad only in ostrich feathers) and Venus with her Galley Slaves. *Photoplay* maga-zine said of this snappy movie: "Powell, Bette Davis, Frank McHugh and Reginald Owen are letter-perfect."

During the winter of 1933, Bill worked in what was to be his final film under the Warner contract. In *The Key* (Warner Bros., 1934), not released un-til after his first picture away from the studio was shown in public, Powell is a captain in the British Army of 1920 when the Black and Tans were causing a ruckus in Ireland. Captain Tennant, as Powell is known, is "a fighter and a philanderer" who claims to have been decorated "three times, once for valor and twice for indiscretions." He encounters a former love (Edna Best) who is mar-ried to Captain Kerr (Colin Clive) of British intel-ligence. Clive, on finding them together in his apartment, drowns his worries in drink, and then is captured by the Irish and held as a hostage. The finale finds the apparently callous Powell emerg-ing as a likable bounder when he engineers Clive's release at the cost of a three-year jail sen-tence for himself. Despite the imaginative direc-tion of Michael Curtiz and the presence of an excellent supporting cast (Donald Crisp, J. M. Kerrigan, Arthur Treacher, Halliwell Hobbes, Henry O'Neill), the film was not well received. "It would be hard to stray farther from the histori-cal field than is done in *The Key*" (Thornton Dele-

With Frank McHugh and Bette Davis in FASHIONS OF 1934 (FN '34)

hanty, *New York Post*). Regina Crewe (*New York American*) was audacious in her suggestion: "This one, it would seem, might have been a natural for ['Warner Bros.'] George Brent, who not only is of Irish birth, but was actually there [in 1920]." *Variety* pinpointed the problem with Powell's *The Key* part. "It's a role that's as wooden as the central plot itself. . . . Later, when the tale gives way to self-sacrificing, Powell becomes no longer a focal point of attention. From then on he's a puppet moving this way and that to the tug of the strings. To the femme following, the Powell assignment here will likely prove disappointing."

On completion of his task in *The Key,* Bill was notified that his salary, because of studio economic measures in the face of sagging audience attendance at theatres, was being reduced to $4,000 a week. He told the studio that he would not tolerate such an action. He was released from his contract* and stated publicly that it was due to his desire to freelance, but Warners later revealed the truth. Now on the open market, both Columbia

and Universal reportedly vied for his services, but David O. Selznick, despite the protests of several Metro executives, signed him as the second lead in *Manhattan Melodrama* (MGM, 1934).

Clark Gable, an MGM contractee who earned less money than Powell, received top billing in *Manhattan Melodrama*. The feminine lead was assigned to Montana-born Myrna Loy, who, heretofore, had played a variety of screen roles, many of which required her to be either nasty and/or exotically Oriental, Asian, or Eurasian. Directed by W. S. Van Dyke II, the film told the story of three youngsters from New York's East Side who grow up together after their relatives drown in a boating accident. Jim Wade (Powell) matures to become assistant district attorney, while Blackie Gallagher (Gable) becomes a gambling-house operator and Joe Patrick (Leo Carrillo) turns to the priesthood. Gable, who has been connected with several gangland slaughters, has a mistress (Loy) who wants him to go straight, but he refuses to believe that honesty pays. Powell and Loy meet and fall in love. She asks Gable to help dissuade a

*Powell had been scheduled to appear in the next Warner Bros.–Philo Vance entry, *The Dragon Murder Case,* but the role went to Warran William. Thereafter the detective was played by Paul Lukas in *The Casino Murder Case* (MGM, 1935), Edmund Lowe in *The Garden Murder Case* (MGM, 1936), Grant Richards in *A Night of Mystery* (Paramount, 1937), Wilfred Hyde-White in *The Scarab Murder Case* (British Paramount, 1937), Warren William in *The Gracie Allen Murder Case* (Paramount, 1939), James Stephenson in *Calling Philo Vance* (Warner Bros., 1940), Alan Curtis in *Philo Vance's Secret Mission* (Eagle-Lion, 1947) and *Philo Vance's Gamble* (PRC, 1947), and William Wright in *Philo Vance Returns* (PRC, 1947). On radio, Jackson Beck and later Jose Ferrer were heard as Philo Vance.

disgruntled former civil servant (Thomas Jackson) from jeopardizing Powell's chances in the New York gubernatorial election. Gable later kills the man and is sent to prison before Powell, having learned the truth from Loy, can alter the court's sentence. Gable dies in the electric chair with his childhood friend, the priest, standing beside him.*

Of the film, which by Selznick's own admission "cost very low, indeed" and was an "enormous moneymaker," the *Hollywood Reporter* said: ". . . story, direction and performance unite to give distinction to the clash of love, ambition and politics." The *Film Daily* subscribers were told that "Powell, Gable and Miss Loy will get critical raves for their superb playing. Powell unquestionably topping his best past offerings." The *London Film Weekly* found that "William Powell steals the picture from Clark Gable and, by clever acting, saves it from lapsing into sentimentality."

Now convinced that Selznick had brought them a brilliant actor rather than a has-been Warners refugee, MGM signed Bill to a long-term contract.

W. S. Van Dyke II liked the Powell-Loy combination and asked his boss, Louis Burt Mayer, to team them in a screen version of Dashiell Hammett's comic detective novel *The Thin Man*, which he, Van Dyke, wanted to direct. Mayer thought the idea was insane, insisting that both named players were essentially "heavies." Van Dyke argued that the feature could be assembled on a very low budget, in the short time of sixteen days, and in such a way as to not interfere with whatever other scripts the studio might have in mind for them. Mayer relented.

Known in the industry as "One-Take" Van Dyke, the director kept his word by bringing *The Thin Man* (MGM, 1934) to completion within his allotted sixteen days. ". . . and that sweet smell of success was in every frame" he later said. In this now-revered film, Nick Charles (Powell), a retired detective, goes with his socialite wife, Nora (Loy), to New York for the Christmas holidays. They love liquor, especially martinis. In a speakeasy, Bill informs the bartender: "The important thing is the rhythm. The dry martini you always shake to waltz time." Their drinking is temporarily interrupted by Dorothy Wynant (Maureen O'Sullivan), who calls to ask Powell to help locate her father (Edward Ellis), a slim, eccentric inventor

*Since both producer David O. Selznick and scripter Oliver H. P. Garrett were involved in *For the Defense* (Paramount, 1930) and *Manhattan Melodrama,* it is no coincidence that Powell's William Foster and Gable's Blackie Gallagher have so many similarities in character.

who had disappeared months earlier.* Later, two people are killed, and with the help of Loy and Asta (their wirehair white Terrier), Powell locates the decomposing body of "the thin man," unrecognizable except for a war wound in one of his legs. The killer is named when the Charleses invite all the suspects to dinner. "The killer is right in this room," Powell begins, and then proceeds to analyze each guest.

The dialog between Bill and Loy, thanks to the scenario by Albert Hackett and Frances Goodrich, was witty, urbane, and often insolent, a wide departure from the usual stereotyped conversations presented by oncamera spouses. But throughout *The Thin Man*, the viewer always knew that the couple were devotedly in love. Example:

Powell: How'd you like Grant's tomb?
Loy: It's lovely. . . . I'm having a coffin made for you.

He considers her scatterbrained, and therefore, does all the thinking for the two. However, she is the realistic one (not to mention the financial mainstay of the household through her family funds), who often has to bring his fancies down to earth. And, through it all, they drink martinis. A new brand of cinema love was presented by *The Thin Man*. On Christmas morning, after a night that was alcohol-oriented, Loy presents him with an air pistol. Still clad in pajamas and robe, he stretches out on the sofa, bends his knees, and props the pistol between his feet. "This is the best Christmas present you ever gave me," he says, as he shoots several balls off the Yule tree.

Time magazine reported: "To the incredulous delight of U.S. cinemillions, two people could be in love though married." The *Motion Picture Herald* printed: "It offers William Powell in the type of role in which he has enjoyed his best success—the detective." *Variety* championed: "For its leads the studio couldn't have done better than to pick Powell and Miss Loy, both of whom shade their semi-comic roles beautifully." Otis Ferguson in the *New Republic* opined: "William Powell seems to need watching, lest he be too gay. But on the whole it was thoroughly well conceived and carried out—a strange mixture of excitement, quips, and hard-boiled (but clear and touching)

sentiment. It is a good movie and should not be missed."

In the 1934 Academy Award sweepstakes, *The Thin Man*, nominated as one of the best films, was an odds-on-favorite to win, but another sleeper, *It Happened One Night* (Columbia), took the honor. Powell received his first Oscar nomination as Best Actor, as did Frank Morgan (*Affairs of Cellini*) and Clark Gable (*It Happened One Night*). Gable won. *The Thin Man* was selected by 424 critics through *Film Daily* as one of the ten best of 1934. It was voted into sixth place, between *Little Women* (RKO) and *Viva, Villa!* (MGM). Asta put wirehair Terriers into demand and became the most famous dog of the 1930s, second only to Fala, the Scotty pet of Franklin D. and Eleanor Roosevelt. Louis B. Mayer happily reported that the film grossed $2 million.‡

The Key was released by Warners a week after *The Thin Man*. Thus (with *Manhattan Melodrama*) Powell had three pictures running simultaneously in larger cities in May 1934.

Later in 1934, Powell was seen opposite Myrna Loy in a film different from *The Thin Man* in that it lacked the latter's crisp dialog and *joie de vivre*. In *Evelyn Prentice* (MGM) Loy retaliates for the indiscretion of her criminal-lawyer husband (Powell) by having an affair with a young poet (Harry Stephens) who turns out to be a contemptible blackmailer. Loy kills him, or so she thinks, when he threatens to reveal certain letters of affection. The remainder of the picture is courtroom melodrama which Andre Sennwald (*New York Times*) described as "agreeable rather than stimulating," but "still Mr. Powell and Miss Loy are surely the most winning of the screen's fictional couples."

RKO borrowed Bill for *Star of Midnight* (1935), taken from a novel by Arthur Somers Roche. It was undoubtedly intentional that the character of Clay Dalzell was an almost duplication of Nick Charles: debonair, cocktail-loving, witty—except that in place of a Nora there was Ginger Rogers as a tenacious young lady who wants to wed him. In *Star of Midnight*, Powell is a New York attorney by profession, an amateur criminologist by avocation. The caper in question concerned the mysterious disappearance of the leading lady of a Broadway musical called *Midnight*. She never makes an oncamera appearance in the picture (we

---

*The character Clyde Wynant, as portrayed by Ellis, was the actual *The Thin Man*, although it was popularly assumed that the title referred to detective Charles, an assumption fostered by the MGM sequels.

‡In 1941, NBC radio was to cash in on the popularity of *The Thin Man* with a weekly series beginning with Lester Damon as Nick and Claudia Morgan as Nora. Later, in 1957, a 72-episode NBC video series was run with Peter Lawford and Phyllis Kirk as the witty couple. In 1974, MGM-TV hired Robert Wagner to be "The Thin Man" in a new teleseries pilot.

do hear her voice on a recording), and scripters Howard J. Green, Anthony Veiller, and Edward Kaufman forgot one important structural detail of *The Thin Man* formula: the gathering of the suspects and the final sorting out of clues. Here only the guilty person turns up at the ending, robbing the finale of a good climax.

On April 17, 1935, Powell appeared in his first movie with Jean Harlow,* she divorced from her third husband, cinematographer Harold Rosson. After the making of *Reckless*, originally intended for Joan Crawford, Bill began dating the well-liked (by audiences and co-workers) platinum blonde, who abhorred the confinement of brassieres.

Reckless was a melodrama with music, produced by David O. Selznick, directed by Victor Fleming, and with words and music by such songsmiths as Jerome Kern, Oscar Hammerstein II, Con Conrad, Herbert Magdison, Jack King, Edwin Knof, and Harold Adamson.‡ Powell's role, that of theatrical agent Ned Riley, was a change of pace for him. (*Variety* thought it an unfortunate switch: "His is a tongue-in-cheek role and no amount of yeoman application can make the hapless part hold up.") He loves musical star Mona Leslie (Harlow) whom he represents, although he has never made his feelings known to her. He is unhappy when she weds richboy Franchot Tone, and even unhappier when the scion of millions commits suicide while in a drunken state, thus creating unfavorable newspaper publicity for Harlow and Bill. She gives birth to Tone's child, which the deceased's family allows her to keep when she relinquishes the rights to the family inheritance. At the outset of a new Broadway musical which Powell has staged for her, she is ridiculed by the audience, but her sincere replies to their insults gain applause and she goes on to delight them musically.† She and Powell then wed. Because of its lavish production values, *Reckless* won favor at the boxoffice, but critically it was quickly dismissed as inferior goods. "The title is appropriate enough, for throughout this film the actions and emotions of the principal characters are completely unrestrained" (*London Times*).

Powell was scheduled to be reunited with Myrna Loy in his next vehicle, but instead Metro starred him with Viennese actress Luise Rainer (pronounced Rye-ner) in her Hollywood-debut film, *Escapade* (MGM, 1935). Based on a German movie, *Maskerade* (1934), scripted by Walter Reisch, *Escapade* proved to be a tedious affair with Powell as an accomplished Viennese artist named Fritz Heideneck who breaks the hearts of all the local ladies. What began as a comedy turned into a laborious, lugubrious tragedy under the direction of Robert Z. Leonard. As an epilogue to the feature, Powell introduced Miss Rainer to moviegoers and stated that he believed she would be a big American favorite.

Rosalind Russell, called "Metro-Goldwyn-Mayer's second-string Myrna Loy" by the *New York Times*'s Andre Sennwald, was Bill's co-star in *Rendezvous* (MGM, 1935), his fourth and final film of the year. The spy film was based on the book *American Black Chamber* by Herbert O. Yardley, who had been in the U.S. War Department's Intelligence Division during World War I. Contrary to other studios, when Metro made a thriller it tried to disguise the taut atmosphere with a mixture of nonchalance and tongue-in-cheek. *Rendezvous* was such a case. Bill is seen as an expert at decoding German messages who would rather be fighting on the front lines during the First World War. However, through his association with Russell, the niece of the assistant secretary of state, he is ordered to break a new enemy code. In the course of the ninety-six minutes (the picture was originally 106 minutes), there is a suicide, two or three murders, encounters with Russian spy Binnie Barnes and her associate (Cesar Romero), and the Gracie Allen–like stunts of Russell. In typical MGM style, this espionage picture ends on a humorous note. Powell and Russell are in a tight spot. To protect her from flying bullets, he knocks her out. By the time she revives, the opponents have been subdued, and she is convinced her loss of consciousness was merely due to Bill's caveman romantic tactics. The success of *Rendezvous* in 1935, and even for today's audience, was and is due to the caliber of Bill's performance. "Mr. William Powell can submerge

*Born Harlean Carpenter on March 3, 1911, in Kansas City, Missouri. She began her education at Miss Barstow's School for Girls in Kansas City, but when she was ten her parents divorced, and she moved to Los Angeles with her mother. Three years later Mrs. Carpenter and her daughter returned to Kansas City, where, in 1927, she wed businessman Charles F. McGrew. The newlyweds moved to Los Angeles. She soon gravitated to movie extra work, and, in 1928, had featured bits in two Laurel and Hardy two-reel silent comedies made for Hal Roach. Her big screen break occurred when producer-director Howard Hughes hired her to star with Ben Lyon and James Hall in *Hell's Angels* (United Artists, 1930), a sound-screen revamping of Hughes's partially scrapped silent version of the aerial epic. She shuttled back and forth between the major studios for roles in *The Public Enemy* (Warner Bros., 1931) and *Platinum Blonde* (Columbia, 1931) before signing on at Metro where she began her contract with *The Beast of the City* (MGM, 1932). Not long after her marriage to Paul Bern in July 1932, the Metro production executive committed suicide.
‡The film is based on the life of Libby Holman, a select Broadway stage star, and her husband, Zachary Smith Reynolds, heir to the Reynolds Tobacco fortune.
†Harlow's singing voice was dubbed by Virginia Verrell.

With Frank O'Connor, Lionel Atwill, and Samuel S. Hinds in RENDEZVOUS (MGM '35)

sentimentality in a witty and amatory line; he can slide with ease and assurance through the most dramatic situation; he can suggest thought where there is little in the script; he can foreshadow action, however far off it may be; and he can be as effectively idle in love as he can be vigorous in war" (*London Daily Telegraph*).

Late in 1935, Bill supervised the building of a "dream house" for himself in Beverly Hills. He told a *Picturegoer* reporter a few years later: "I thought I knew everything about home-building. I built a house of dreams that turned out to be a house of devilish gadgets. The secret panels and disappearing doors never worked right. I'd push one button to go into the parlour and I'd find myself in the kitchen or the garden. There were thirty-two rooms in that house and in every one something unanticipated was always happening. I've been haunted by weird, nightmarish memories ever since."

Nevertheless, the house became a showplace of Southern California. All the doors were operated by electric foot switches, alarm bells foretold the arrival of a visitor, and a salon was convertible to either a motion-picture theatre or a guest bedroom. Each of the major rooms had a bar, one of which, by pushing a button, turned into a grill room with a spit rising out of the floor and char-

coal burners appearing out of a closet. Jean Harlow helped in the interior decoration as did William Haines, an actor turned designer, who did the master bedroom in red, the color of wine.

"I didn't build that house for myself," Bill told another reporter. "Heaven forfend! I couldn't have used all those rooms in fifty years. The real reason I built it was because I didn't know what else to do with my money." Columnists and friends speculated about the possibility of Powell's marrying Miss Harlow. While he would not comment specifically on his future relationship with the star, he did say: "When a film actor marries a film actress, they talk about the movie industry until both have to scream." A mutual friend of the two celebrities did state to the press that "they're very fond of each other. Very. There probably isn't a more companionable couple in Hollywood today. They're both lonely people who have discovered that, together, they aren't lonely; they have a million laughs together."

Bill lived alone in the big house until he could no longer tolerate the situation. He then sold it and took another, far less elaborate home in partial payment. This house, too, proved to be a headache and, forced to sell it as well, he leased a small house in Bel Air, saying: "My worries as a man of property are over." When a fan-magazine

438

interviewer asked why he did not live with his son, the reply was: "Every weekend I spend with Bill Jr. My father and mother are usually along. It's a regular family reunion. He's a great boy—and all boy. He goes to a private school here on the coast and spends his summers at camp and rates high with the other fellows for what he is, not for what his father may be. I want to keep things that way. I'd like to have him with me, but I can't do that and expect him to have a normal life. The spotlight would be on him. And the spotlight isn't good for any growing boy, no matter whose son he is."

The following year—1936—was to be one of Bill's most successful in motion pictures. Since his shift to MGM he had consolidated his position as the cinema's prime debonair leading man. It seemed that no one could be more charming or wry in films. Metro had Robert Montgomery and, on a lower rung, Franchot Tone and Robert Young to play handsome playboy types. However, no one on the lot, including newly acquired Melvyn Douglas (whose services were to be shared with Columbia), could top Bill in the art of elegant suavity. Confident of his status on the home field and in the industry, Bill told the press of his career plans when his present MGM contract expired. "A few years ago, I used to think seriously of retirement. I realize now, however, that I have worked too long to be content as a man of full-time leisure. It requires plenty of practice to loaf successfully and I haven't had it. But two movies a year will make an ideal schedule."

Powell's most glorious and productive cinema season began with the April 1936 release of *The Great Ziegfeld* (MGM). With his hair parted on the left, and with graying temples, Powell portrayed Florenz Ziegfeld, Jr. (1867–1932), the Chicago-born son of a musician who, at the age of twenty-four, began his career as a barker on the midway at Chicago's Columbia Exposition of 1893. He later became Broadway's master showman. Flo, as he was called by some, introduced the revue to the American musical stage. His *Follies* were famous for statuesque girls, dazzling costumes, and extravagant sets. He promoted many of his finds to first-rank stardom (W. C. Fields, Fanny Brice, Nora Bayes, Ed Wynn, Mae Murray, Sophie Tucker, Will Rogers, Marilyn Miller, and on and on). He became a millionaire, went broke, made another fortune, and died a poor man at the age of sixty-three.

The Great Ziegfeld, produced by Hunt Stromberg and directed by Robert Z. Leonard, was the epitome of screen musical biographies. In keep-

With Myrna Loy on the set of THE GREAT ZIEGFELD (MGM '36)

ing with the tradition established by the egomaniacal "Zieggy," the film contained numerous extravagantly mounted musical numbers, such as "A Pretty Girl Is Like a Melody." Luise Rainer, in her second screen role, was Anna Held, the beautiful French actress whom Ziegfeld met in Paris in 1897 and introduced to New York audiences. Miss Rainer was definitely miscast as Broadway's hot sex kitten who had a very naughty way of singing a song (but on the strength of a teary telephone sequence she won the Academy Award as the Best Actress of the Year). Myrna Loy played the role of Billie Burke, displaying only a few of the more charming mannerisms of that performer with whom Powell's Flo falls in love. Fanny Brice, with the unlikely face of a star who made it to the show-business top with talent and personality, portrayed herself. Virginia Bruce, a onetime Broadway starlet, was Audrey Lane (really Lillian Lorraine), temperamental and, later, alcoholic showgirl.

Previewed in San Francisco in March 1936, with top studio chiefs in attendance, *The Great Ziegfeld* ran close to four hours. Hunt Stromberg reluctantly but realistically agreed to several footage cuts. When released the next month, Otis Ferguson (the *New Republic*) reported: "The story has nice fun and sentiment, but its setting and numbers are even more important to its effect." Ferguson found that Luise Rainer did the best acting job and "William Powell is a plausible Ziegfeld, dressy, flashy, mostly surface." In the Oscar race, besides Rainer's victory, *The Great Ziegfeld* won as Best Picture of 1936, while in a lesser category, Seymour Felix won a Dance Direction citation for the "A Pretty Girl Is Like a Melody" number.

Frank S. Nugent (*New York Times*) labeled *The Ex-Mrs. Bradford* (RKO, 1936) "one of the year's top-flight comedies." Bill is seen as a doctor with a divorced wife (Jean Arthur) who writes mystery stories. The film's title is really misleading in that it might be deduced that this picture is knee-deep in soap suds concerning a heroine who is either very bad or extremely noble. Quite the contrary. Arthur's Mrs. Bradford is an overimaginative creature whose vocation has caused her to be suspicious of everyone and everything. She assumes a murder has been committed after reading a newspaper story and promptly enlists her surgeon-friend/ex-husband (Powell) to help. Before "The End" appears onscreen, three people are killed and the doctor, as suspect number one, is forced to solve the mystery.

On June 8, 1936, with Myrna Loy, Bill recreated his *The Thin Man* on "Lux Radio Theatre."

Proving that friendship and professional wisdom outlive matrimony, Carole Lombard asked that Bill star with her in *My Man Godfrey* (Universal, 1936). MGM agreed to loan him to Universal, and the film became the smash comedy hit of the year, if not *the* funniest (screwball) movie of the thirties.* Although dated, it still ranks as top comedy. Directed by Gregory La Cava and adapted for the screen by Morrie Ryskin and Eric Hatch from the latter's novel, the dialog is sparkling, pinpointing not only the comic situations but the sharp jibes at American social strata and mores.

The plot is simplicity itself, if hectic in its outcome. While on a scavenger hunt emanating from New York's high-class "Waldorf Ritz" Hotel, debutante Irene Bullock (Lombard) is in search of a "forgotten man." She locates Godfrey Parke (Powell) in the city dump, at 32 East River, Sutton Place, smoking his pipe. Asked why he lives in such surroundings, he smoothly replies:

*Universal was to remake the film with dismal results in 1957, with David Niven as Godfrey and June Allyson as Irene.

With Carole Lombard in MY MAN GODFREY (Univ '36)

"Because my real estate agent thought the altitude would be good for my asthma." Because he is someone whom nobody wants ("Nobody wants me at all"), Irene claims him ahead of her imperious and totally disagreeable sister (Gail Patrick), but not before Powell forces Patrick into an ash pile. "That's something I've wanted to do since I was six," Lombard jibes in merriment.

As *My Man Godfrey* progresses, Lombard takes Powell home to 1011 Fifth Avenue and informs her parents (Alice Brady and Eugene Pallette) and her mother's "Protégé" (Mischa Auer) that he is the new butler. "May I be frank?" Powell asks the maid (Jean Dixon), who asks in return; "Is that your name?" It is later revealed through Tommy Gray (Alan Mowbray) that Bill, actually from a wealthy family, was his Harvard classmate. Powell explains that a doomed love affair brought him to the verge of suicide at the dump, but that his will to live has been revived through the optimism of his dump-mates as well as by madcap Lombard who is spoiled and lonely. Powell ultimately expels Auer from the household, solves Pallette's financial crisis, makes Patrick eat humble pie, and is caught in marriage by Lombard.

Said *Variety:* "It's Powell's job to be normal and breezily comic in the madcap house, and that doesn't require stretching for him." *Time* magazine cheered it: "Made out of material as old as show business and as tricky as cobwebs—emerges with that evasive quality that is not skillful playing, or direction, but something that mysteriously adds itself to these things, and makes a tip-top picture."

The cast of *My Man Godfrey* was represented in all four acting categories in the 1936 Oscar field. Bill was a nominee but lost to Paul Muni of *The Good Earth* (MGM); Carole Lombard lost to Luise Rainer (*The Good Earth*) as Best Actress; while in the recognized-for-the-first-time classification of Best Supporting Players, Alice Brady lost to Gale Sondergaard of *Anthony Adverse* (Warner Bros.) and Mischa Auer was defeated by Walter Brennan of *Come and Get It* (United Artists).

Powell had the opportunity to explain the picture's success to Quentin Reynolds of *Collier's* magazine: "Probably no one ever lived who was like Godfrey. But La Cava, who directed it, made the man seem quite plausible. Actually that was La Cava's picture. Every morning he'd give us some dialogue that he'd written during the night, and it was good dialogue. Working with someone like Van Dyke or La Cava is a great help to an actor. You have confidence in them."

Irving Thalberg offered to Powell the role of Mercutio in *Romeo and Juliet* (MGM, 1936) in replacement of John Barrymore, who was then having serious alcohol problems which adversely affected his work. Powell refused, stating that Barrymore was his friend. He could not in all conscious take over for the man who had been helpful to him in the early days and who was responsible for his first screen acting job (*Sherlock Holmes*). Thalberg's final decision was to retain Barrymore in the role.

Libeled Lady (MGM, 1936) was unveiled on October 7 with four of the studio's top box-office attractions in tip-top form. In another of the amiable comedies of the period, Powell, this time, is a newspaperman hired by his former managing editor (Spencer Tracy) to marry the editor's brash fiancée (Jean Harlow), which is to be a matrimonial union in name only. Powell then is to charm aristocratic Connie Allenbury (Myrna Loy) into falling in love with him so that his wife will sue for alienation of affection, thus negating a suit that Loy has instigated against the editor's newspaper for printing a false story about her. The action, complicated and slow-moving, can best be attributed to Jack Conway's direction. The screenplay by Maurice Watkins, Howard Emmett Rogers, and George Oppenheimer was seemingly devised to display the fast-retort talents of shapely Miss Harlow. When Tracy informs her that she is to marry Bill platonically with "Don't worry about him, he's just like my brother," her quick reply is: "Maybe so, but he's not *my* brother."

On October 20, 1936, at the invitation of Sid Grauman, and with a flashbulb fanfare, Bill and his frequent co-star, Myrna Loy, imprinted their feet and hands in individual cement squares in the forecourt of Grauman's Chinese Theatre on Hollywood Boulevard. Bill signed his name above the prints, dated it, and wrote: "Sid, old boy. I am happy to put my foot in it for you."

MGM had quite naturally considered featuring Powell in further adventures of Philo Vance, but after the success of *The Thin Man*, which so closely identified him with that role, the studio decided to reserve his oncamera sleuthing for sequels to that 1934 blockbuster. Thus came about *After the Thin Man* (MGM, 1936), again directed by W. S. Van Dyke II. It was sheer bravado by all concerned to attempt to recapture the magic of the first opus, but the critics and the public loved it almost as much as the original. In this installment of the life of Nick and Nora Charles, the couple is back in California, specifically atop San Francisco's Nob Hill, where Asta has found a female

With Myrna Loy in LIBELED LADY (MGM '36)

companion and where the alcoholic beverages are just as abundantly downed by Powell and Loy. Keeping in the holiday mood, perhaps as a reason for imbibing, the story opens on New Year's Eve when the unpopular husband (Alan Marshal) of Loy's cousin (Elissa Landi) is murdered. The suspects list mounts, as seen in the personages of James Stewart, Paul Fix, and Dorothy McNulty (later to be renamed Penny Singleton and herein the vocalizer of "Smoke Dreams" and "Blow that Horn"). Bill uncovers the murderer, of course, and the final sequence has Loy knitting baby booties, which leaves the viewer in an anticipatory mood. Frank S. Nugent decided in the *New York Times* that "William Powell and Myrna Loy still persuade us that Mr. and Mrs. Nick Charles are exactly the sort of people we should like to have on our calling list on New Year's Day and for all the rest of the year."

Offcamera, Powell continued to lead a private life away from the flashiness of nightclubs or Hollywood parties. He was a loner who preferred not to be interviewed and absolutely refused to discuss his relationship with Jean Harlow. In defense of his life style he said: "Cultivate solitude

and quiet and a few sincere friends,[*] rather than mob merriment, noise and thousands of nodding acquaintances, and you're called a hermit. They suspect you of having a grudge against the world, or going high-hat. So far as I know, I haven't been accused of that yet. That's where Nick Charles and *My Man Godfrey* and some of the other boys have done me a good turn. No one would accuse *them* of being stuck-up. So I'm not accused."

A great number of those who supported movies at the nation's box offices presumed that Bill and Myrna Loy were married for real. To most, they represented the symbol for wholesome, happily wedded bliss. Fan letters poured into MGM requesting the couple's connubial advice or congratulating them on their union. Powell modestly confided to London's *Picturegoer* magazine: "I hear occasional rumors that I am the perfect husband of the screen, even that Myrna Loy and I are the perfect Mr. and Mrs. of the screen, yet she marries another man, and one of my best friends at that."[†]

Bill worked with Joan Crawford in *The Last of Mrs. Cheyney* (MGM, 1937), their only film together. Adapted from Frederick Lonsdale's play,

[*]His best friends were Richard Barthelmess, Ronald Colman, and Warner Baxter.
[†]Miss Loy married her first husband, film producer Arthur Hornblow, Jr., in 1936.

Miss Crawford and Bill are accomplished jewel thieves circulating, undetected, among the ultra-elite of British society. Fay Cheyney (Crawford), rich in elegance and glib in flirtatious conversation, while tagging the prospective gems to be stolen, feels superior to the wealthy matrons who wear them. Posing as a butler,‡ Powell ensconces himself at a countryside mansion where the thieves plan to make a large heist during a weekend gala. Powell said at the time: "Because I played a butler in *My Man Godfrey,* it was conceded by those who know nothing about it that I could again play a butler to perfection. Yet I am no authority on the act of being a butler, and what little I have learned was obtained by observing my man, Theodore, in my own home."

The Emperor's Candlesticks (MGM, 1937), which teamed Bill and Luise Rainer for the third and final time, is an easily forgotten film, except for its sets and lavish costuming. Baroness Orczy wrote the original novel, inspired by a pair of ornate candlesticks, each of which held a secret compartment, and purportedly had been owned by Marie Antoinette. Powell and Rainer are spies on opposite sides of the fence in Russia of the 1910s. Although Powell's characterization designated him as a Polish agent, he performed his assignment "with his usual midwestern charm and gets it over" (*New York Sun*). The film, eighty-nine minutes of "intrigue" and "romance," was basically a bore. (Almost simultaneously, a Continental film version of this same novel was produced, and it has now slid into almost equal obscurity.)

During the shooting of his next film, *Double Wedding* (MGM, 1937), Bill re-enunciated his career plans. "My contract is up after this picture, and I'm hoping to settle for two pictures a year, one here and one, perhaps, in England. Anything I make over two pictures goes to the tax collector, anyway. Also, I've a hunch that, with fewer pictures, the public won't weary of this physiognomy so soon. I still want to be around years hence."

Jean Harlow, suffering from a curable uremic infection, was kept away from medical care by her Christian Scientist mother until it was too late. During the filming of *Saratoga* (MGM, 1937)

‡On Broadway (Fulton Theater: November 9, 1925, 283 performances), the role was played by A. E. Matthews, while in the 1929 MGM film it was played by George Barraud, and in the 1951 version, called *The Law and the Lady,* Michael Wilding had the part.

With Donald Meek, Ernie Alexander (rear), Edgar Kennedy, Florence Rice, Jessie Ralph, and Myrna Loy in DOUBLE WEDDING (MGM '37)

she was rushed to the Good Samaritan Hospital in Los Angeles, where she died on June 7, 1937, at the age of twenty-six.[*] Powell, who was at her side when she died, reportedly cried out: "Oh God, why did this have to be? I loved her, I loved her." He was finally quieted by Jean's mother.

A few days later, in Forest Lawn Cemetery's Sanctuary of Benediction, chosen by grief-stricken Powell, Jeanette MacDonald sang "Indian Love Call," Nelson Eddy sang "Ah, Sweet Mystery of Life," and Mary Baker Eddy recited the Lord's Prayer, together with a forty-eight-word eulogy. Jean's body was then taken to a $25,000 mortuary chamber purchased by Powell which allowed space for three bodies. The lovable blonde actress-comedienne was laid to rest near the Hollywood greats who had preceded her in death: Will Rogers, Marie Dressler, Irving Thalberg, Flo Ziegfeld, Lon Chaney, Rudolph Valentino, Wallace Reid, and Alexander Pantages.

Louella Parsons, in the *Los Angeles Herald-Examiner* of September 16, 1964, was reminded of the Powell-Harlow romance by the advent of two feature films entitled *Harlow*. The columnist reported: "Bill was the only man Jean ever loved. This, she told me herself. She was deeply, deeply in love with the debonair Bill and he was the man in her life at the time of her death."[†]

In *Double Wedding*, released on September 23, 1937, Bill tells Myrna Loy: "I'll be quite frank with you. I suppose I'm what you'd call a cad." In this film, advertised as "farce," those words were the only sane ones in the script. This film was an obvious effort by MGM to capitalize on the success of *My Man Godfrey*. Richard Thorpe directed Bill as a hippie-type artist in the days before the word "hip" applied to people rather than to a portion of the human anatomy. This artist, named Charlie Lodge, lives in a trailer parked in an auto lot next to a bar and makes a play for Florence Rice through whom he hopes to trap her starched sister (Loy). His ploy eventually works, with Rice marrying patient John Beal and Powell pairing off with his seventh-time co-star. In this entry, visual slapstick played a definite major role.

Bill then took a leave of absence and went to Europe on vacation aboard the *Statendam*. He found that he now hated the Riviera, which he had previously considered for retirement and vowed that California had far more to offer him. At a party in Paris, he met the French gamine Annabella, who had recently been signed by Twentieth Century–Fox. Producer Raymond Griffith intended to change her image by starring her in a screen version of Ladislaus Bus-Fekete's play, *The Lady Has a Heart*.[‡] The man-lead role was that of a butler. "Please won't you ask Mr. Powell for the part?" Annabella pleaded of Griffith. "It would be marvelous, making my first American film with him." Griffith asked Mayer, who owed Fox a loan-out, and Powell reluctantly agreed to fulfill the studio's obligation. (His salary was $40,000 per week for five weeks' work.)

The property was retitled *The Baroness and the Butler* (Twentieth Century–Fox, 1938), and Frank S. Nugent (*New York Times*) called it "a feeble exercise for William Powell's drollery, none at all for Annabella's volatile charm." It all takes place in Hungary with Powell as Johann, butler to that nation's prime minister (Henry Stephenson). Although wed to parasitic Baron George Marissey (Joseph Schildkraut), the Baroness Katrina (Annabella) loves the passionate butler, and when the latter is elected to Parliament on a political ticket opposite to that of his employer and is about to relinquish his career of servitude, Annabella confesses her love for him to the parliamentary assemblage. Mr. Nugent of the *Times* correctly reported that Powell "wears a pained and embarrassed expression" throughout.

As early as December 1937, Bill had expressed his desire to play the lead (Max deWinter) in David O. Selznick's proposed film of Daphne du Maurier's fast-selling novel *Rebecca*. The producer rejected the star's bid because it was then thought that Ronald Colman would be Max. When Colman became unavailable, the field was again open, but Selznick turned to Laurence Olivier because the Englishman's salary requirements were $50,000 compared to Powell's $150,000. Interestingly, Ruby Behlmer in *Memo from David O. Selznick* (1972), records a memo from the executive to Lowell V. Calvert, general manager in charge of sales and distribution for Selznick International: "The decision instead should be based solely on whether William Pow-

[*]On June 15, 1937, Louis B. Mayer announced that *Saratoga* would be restructured to suit a "new and entirely different personality." Mayer revealed that an unknown brunette from Worcester, Massachusetts, named Rita Johnson would take on the role. Miss Johnson, however, declined the part, and *Saratoga* was completed, using a double (Mary Dees) for Miss Harlow's few remaining long shots.
[†]Not too long before Harlow's death, Powell stated *re* matrimony: "I believe there is something in my nature which prevents my making a successful marriage. It may be my fault or it may be Hollywood's, but my marriages seem to be fated. . . . I never seem able to catch up with happiness."
[‡]The Broadway version (Longacre Theatre: September 25, 1937, 90 performances) starred Elissa Landi and Vincent Price.

ell is likely to add hundreds of thousands of dollars to the gross." (In the summer of 1939, Olivier was chosen to enact the role.)

It was revealed in January 1938 in an international survey conducted by *Motion Picture Herald* that Shirley Temple was the number-one box-office attraction, followed by Clark Gable and William Powell. Powell was also named one of the world's best-dressed men at an international congress of stylists. "Personally, I do not know one-hundredth of what constitutes style," he remarked. "If I am well-dressed, it is not because I know anything about correct wardrobe. The laurels belong to my tailor, not me, and he should take the bow. He selects the styles I must wear and he makes the clothes for me."

Early in March 1938, Bill was preparing for a pleasure trip to South America when, "I began bleeding from the rectum. The doctor found a cancer, smaller than the nail of your little finger, between three and four inches up inside my rectum. They recommended removal of the rectum. Then I'd have had to have a colostomy and evacuate into a pouch, through an artificial opening, for the rest of my life." Powell decided to risk the medical alternative—a temporary colostomy and radiation treatments. At Cedars of Lebanon Hospital, surgeons removed part of his colon through an incision in his abdomen and after other medical procedures were carried through, the cancer was excised. Fortunately, it had not spread.

None of the above facts were made known publicly until more than twenty-five years later. Instead, at the time, the star's illness was brushed off lightly to the press as a case of "minor abdominal disorders" or "ulcers."

As a further precautionary measure, platinum needles containing tiny radium pellets were implanted in the rectum. "For the next six months we simply waited," Bill has said. "I had a lot of examinations but led a reasonably normal life. The worst thing about the situation was the esthetics of it."

During this critical period, Bill could not work in movies and turned down bids to star in *Intermezzo* (United Artists, 1939) and *Ninotchka* (MGM, 1939), parts played respectively by Leslie Howard and Melvyn Douglas. Powell did accept occasional radio work as a means of diversion and on May 9, 1938 was heard, with original cast members Carole Lombard, Gail Patrick, and Mischa Auer, in the "Lux Radio Theatre" version of *My Man Godfrey.** He was a guest on Bob Hope's

With Annabella in a publicity pose for THE BARONESS AND THE BUTLER (20th '38)

audio show, and acted as host, alternating with Dick Powell, Fred MacMurray, and Herbert Marshall, on Louella Parsons's "Hollywood Hotel" series. On January 9, 1939, he returned to "Lux" for *Mayerling*, with Janet Gaynor.

In August 1938, agent Myron Selznick announced that Powell and Carole Lombard were joining the growing number of Hollywood actors and directors agreeing to work on a share-of-the-profits basis rather than salary.

In November 1938, some six months after surgery, with the cancer apparently eradicated, Bill's surgeon rearranged his intestines in the natural fashion and returned him to normal body functions. Bill said simply: "I was one of the lucky ones."

Becoming anxious about the marquee durability of Powell's name during his many months off-screen, MGM decided to return him to the screen not only with Myrna Loy, but in another *Thin Man* adventure. The title, *Another Thin Man* (MGM, 1939), refers to Nick Charles, Jr., born sometime between *After the Thin Man* and this current sequel, and enacted by eight-month-old William A. Poulsen. Again W. S. Van Dyke II was

*The transcription of this broadcast was recently issued on a LP album, (Pelican #PR-115).

445

With Myrna Loy and William Anthony Poulsen in ANOTHER THIN MAN (MGM '39)

director, and this time famed detective novelist Dashiell Hammett supplied the script. Again, the Charleses are back on the East Coast, at Long Island as the weekend guests of aged Colonel MacFay (C. Aubrey Smith). A greasy fellow named Phil Church (Sheldon Leonard) is also in attendance and predicts death via his dreams. Smith is victim one, but when Leonard dreams that Powell is dead, it is Leonard himself who is soon murder number two. Among the contrasting suspects are Otto Kruger, Virginia Grey, and Ruth Hussey. The *Newsweek* magazine critic declared that "both Myrna Loy and William Powell are as effective as ever in their projection of the Charles family's perspicacity and persiflage," but the *New York Times*'s Frank S. Nugent stated: " . . . a few of the running gags are beginning to show signs of pulling up lame."

At a studio party in October 1939, Powell met a witty, gay, and vivacious MGM starlet named Diana Lewis.* On another occasion she was the cheesecake decoration sent to Powell's poolside to pose for publicity pictures. They ran into each other again at Chasen's Restaurant a few months later. There, they went to an upstairs room where someone was playing nostalgic tunes on a piano. Miss Lewis stood and sang the songs. "I couldn't believe that a youngster like her knew the oldies," Powell said. "I went for her and knew she was for me." He wooed her for three weeks. Then, on Friday, January 5, 1940, after telephoning Jean Harlow's mother to let her in on the secret, Bill drove Diana to the Hidden Well (Dude) Ranch at Warm Springs, Nevada, near Las Vegas. There, in front of an improvised altar, they were wed by Justice of the Peace B. D. Hickman. Bill wore a gray suit with a blue sweater, the bride was clad in a blue-flowered print dress with a matching turban. Among the witnesses were actress Edna Best and movie agent Nat Wolff. Again, as in the

---

*Born on September 18, 1915, in Asbury Park, New Jersey, Diana Dailey's parents were both in show business. She made her acting debut at the age of two in their act. One of her two older sisters, Maxine, won a spot in Earl Carroll's *Vanities* in New York and became a vocalist. When Mr. Dailey took his son John to Los Angeles for a possible film-theatre career, Diana went along, and when her brother did his own show. *Shim-Sham*, Diana begged for an onstage part. Francis Lederer caught the show, and the movie player arranged for her to be screentested at RKO. Instead she won a contract at Paramount, where she had bit-featured roles in *It's a Gift* (1934), *One Hour Late* (1934), *Enter Madame!* (1934), and *All the King's Horses* (1935). She then returned to the stage, appearing at the Pasadena Community Playhouse in *Rhythm Madness* and in *Thumbs West* at the Hollywood Town Theatre. She was then signed to go to New York to sing with Larry Leeds's band at the Casa Manana Club, but a Warner Bros.' contract developed. At that studio she appeared, to good notices, in *He Couldn't Say No* (1938) and *Golddiggers in Paris* (1938). She then transferred her acting services to MGM.

past, the discrepancy in ages was apparent, Powell being forty-seven and Diana twenty-four. They returned to Hollywood after a weekend honeymoon so she could take a featured role in *Forty Little Mothers* (MGM, 1940) starring Eddie Cantor. Mickey Rooney, one of those who previously dated her (and with whom she played in *Andy Hardy Meets Debutante* [MGM, 1940]), admitted ruefully: "Mr. Powell's more suave than I am." Powell gave his bride the nickname of "Mousie" because she reminded him of a cute, fast-moving little brown-haired mouse. In retaliation, she named him "Mr. Poo, the Cat."

Bill's first film after his marriage was *I Love You Again* (MGM, 1940), opposite none other than Myrna Loy, the recently dubbed "Queen of Hollywood" (Clark Gable had been named the industry's "King" in Ed Sullivan's survey). This lively comedy, directed by the stars' long-standing friend, W. S. Van Dyke II, has Bill married to Loy through nine years of boredom, during which he has been a sanctimonious, unlovable, unbearable provider. As the film begins, he is hit on the head during a sea voyage and emerges with a different personality and a new name, and is unable to believe that he supposedly manages a pottery firm and is an officer of all the town's

praiseworthy societies. Loy, who was on the verge of divorcing the original man, finds the change most attractive and decides to remain by the hearthside. It develops that Powell had suffered from amnesia some nine years before and the recent head concussion had brought back the *real* him. "You've turned my head," he tells her after the personality change. "I've often wished I could turn your head," she answers truthfully, "on a spit over a slow fire." Audiences enjoyed the perfect couple's capering in a much freer on-camera manner than would have been possible in their *Thin Man* characterizations.

The U.S. Treasury Department reported Bill's salary, during 1940, at the substantial annual figure of $256,250. However, in comparison to his alleged income of $600,000 for 1937, this was an appreciable decline.

Love Crazy (MGM, 1941) came next, living up to its title completely. Bosley Crowther (*New York Times*) summed it up nicely in his critique: "Of course, there are sometimes slow stretches, and a bit of the fun is forced. But who wants to laugh every minute?" The plot: Powell weds Myrna Loy. On the night of their fourth anniversary, he is discovered in a compromising situation with his old romance, Gail Patrick. Loy plans to

With Nella Walker in I LOVE YOU AGAIN (MGM '40)

With Myrna Loy in a publicity pose for LOVE CRAZY (MGM '41)

sue for divorce. Powell abhors the notion and employs various (outrageous) means of holding his estranged wife. Quite predictably, each scheme lands him in more mirthful scrapes. The Powell mustache, famous through his twenty years of moviemaking, disappears as he adopts the guise of his synthetic, schizophrenic, matronly sister, complete with high collar, ruffled-sleeve dress, and pince-nez. *Newsweek* magazine commended the star: "The burden of the wacky whimsies rests on Powell, who staggers only occasionally under the load."

The Charleses were back on the silver screen in 1941, with Nickie Jr. (Dickie Hall) older and duller, but with Nick and Nora still as clever in their wisecracks and still tossing down the liquor in *Shadow of the Thin Man* (MGM). By this time, the studio's advertising department had given up trying to remind viewers that the *Thin Man* title did not refer to Nick Charles. At any rate, Powell is involved in a racetrack murder, and views the affair with near complacency until a second homicide occurs. Then he opts for complete involvement, which takes him and tagalong Myrna Loy through stables, into a fight arena, and through

run-down hotels, until, by the ninety-seventh minute, the guilty party is found.

The only William Powell film in 1942 was *Crossroads* (MGM) with Hedy Lamarr, who, in Louis B. Mayer's words, was "the hottest actress we have on the lot." In her 1966 alleged autobiography, *Ecstasy and Me*, the actress stated: "*Crossroads* was no big hit." Set in 1935 France, Powell is a French diplomat. After marrying the beautiful Lamarr, he begins to have doubts concerning his past. All recollections of his early life end with a railway accident, but blackmailers Basil Rathbone and Claire Trevor come along to capitalize on this veil of doubt. Despite a fitfully uneven script, which director Jack Conway chose to work with rather than alter, the *New York Times* applauded Powell as "flawlessly urbane and crisp, [he] is an actor whose talent for understatement is perfectly adapted for a melodrama of this genre." Quite rightly, observant filmgoers complained that Metro's movie ads for *Crossroads*, gave away what little plot suspense the film actually held.*

In 1942, Bill made his first request of Louis B. Mayer that the studio purchase the long-running

---

* *Crossroads* in its original Gallic version, with Charles Vanel starred, had already been released in New York in 1939.

Advertisement for CROSSROADS (MGM '42)

Broadway hit, *Life with Father.*† Mayer refused to acquire the screen rights, largely because the asking price of $500,000 seemed excessive. Powell periodically reintroduced the subject, but the movie mogul either could not or would not be swayed from his original decision.

Powell did a guest appearance (before they were called "cameos") in *The Youngest Profession* (MGM, 1943) along with such other studio stars as Lana Turner, Greer Garson, Walter Pidgeon, and Robert Taylor. This vehicle concerning a nosey little lady who thinks she is a Miss Fixit, starred Virginia Weidler.

The Heavenly Body (MGM, 1943) was Bill's second and last film with Hedy Lamarr. Instead of playing the forlorn romantic, as in *Crossroads,* Powell was back to the screwball-comedy genre. Under Alexander Hall's direction, Powell is an

eccentric astronomer, so completely absorbed with charting the course of a new comet that he finds little time to notice his wife (Lamarr). His madcap antics, when he is at home, cause a series of maids to depart. When his wife takes up a diversionary interest in astrology, he informs her: "Astronomy and astrology may sound alike, but that's all. Astronomy's a science. And astrology, my love, stinks!" (An astrological prediction within the plot was that a tall, dark, handsome stranger would enter her life, as he did in the person of James Craig, which complicated Powell's life even more.) Of the disappointing *The Heavenly Body, Newsweek* magazine said: "Powell works like a trouper to save the day. But [it] is strained in the long stretches and spontaneously amusing only in spots."

While Bill was emoting in *The Heavenly Body,*

†The nostalgic comedy opened on November 8, 1939, at the Empire Theatre on Broadway. Written by Howard Lindsay and Russel Crouse, it ran for 3,224 performances with co-author Lindsay and his wife Dorothy Stickney starred in the original production. A less successful sequel, *Life with Mother,* would appear on Broadway in 1948, also with Lindsay and Stickney.

With Hedy Lamarr and James Craig in THE HEAVENLY BODY (MGM '43)

his wife, Diana, was on another MGM soundstage performing in *Cry Havoc* (MGM, 1943), which proved to be her last film appearance to date. Connie Gilchrist, who played one of the maids in *The Heavenly Body,* recently recalled that when she finished her scenes in this film, "Bill kissed me and said, 'Now Connie, you can go and help the other half of the family,' " and the character player hustled over to the *Cry Havoc* set for scenes in that wartime picture.

On March 23, 1944, at age forty-five, Myron Selznick died in Santa Monica Hospital from internal hemorrhages. Among those in attendance for the funeral services at Temple Israel in Beverly Hills were moguls Louis B. Mayer, Samuel Goldwyn, Darryl F. Zanuck, and Jack L. Warner. Services were conducted by Rabbi Max Nussbaum, with Powell reading the eulogy written by Gene Fowler. Over the years. Myron had been instrumental in obtaining Powell's high-figured salary, and his demise was a great personal and professional blow to the star.

While a good many of Hollywood's famous were overseas in military service in World War II, including MGM's Clark Gable, Robert Montgomery, Robert Taylor, Robert Young, and Mickey Rooney, past-fifty-year-old Powell remained on the home front. During the changing 1940's, he

had seen the new screen team of Greer Garson and Walter Pidgeon become the public's favorites, with such movies as *Blossoms in the Dust* (MGM, 1941), *Mrs. Miniver* (MGM, 1942), and *Madame Curie* (MGM, 1943). However, whatever wistfulness Bill may have felt at the change in the type of roles portrayed in films, his box-office standing remained strong, if somewhat impeached by the newer blood in celluloid productions. Unlike Robert Montgomery, who had long been at loggerheads with the studio hierarchy, Powell had always retained an amiable relationship with the MGM executives. Louis B. Mayer, in particular, had remained his ardent supporter, and he suggested that for the sake of both the company and Powell, the star make yet another *Thin Man* film.

Powell agreed, knowing that Myrna Loy, semi-inactive from moviemaking due to a new marriage and her wartime charity work, would keep her promise to return to the Culver City soundstages when, and if, Powell requested her to join in another picture. Thus *The Thin Man Goes Home* (MGM, 1944) came into being and renewed the series after almost four years of inactivity. "Home" in the title refers to Sycamore Springs, where mother (Lucile Watson) and Dr. Charles (Harry Davenport) reside. Nick and Nora

With Irving Bacon and Virginia Sale in THE THIN MAN GOES HOME (MGM '44)

are on the wagon in this one, with nothing more than apple cider to drink. *Newsweek* wondered whether the abstinance was "due to the war or the liquor shortage." Even Sycamore Springs is not safe from murder. When an artist is killed, Powell reluctantly (as always) gets involved in the case. This was the first *Thin Man* episode without W. S. Van Dyke II (who had died) at the helm, being directed instead by Richard Thorpe. The lessening of pacing and production values was quite evident.

In 1945, Bill's father died and was buried in the Powell mausoleum in Forest Lawn Cemetary. Then, in October 1945, Powell went to court in Los Angeles to oppose extra income-tax assessments for the period 1937–38, amounting to $189,860.15. His claim that the income was received by his first wife, Eileen Wilson, and that she had paid the taxes on it, was upheld by the court.

Bill was again Flo Ziegfeld in MGM's long-in-production *Ziegfeld Follies (of 1946)*. This time, on color film, he is in his tastefully decorated penthouse in heaven from whence he observes the Broadway of "today" and wishes for an opportunity to stage another Follies with the currently available MGM talent (Gene Kelly, Fred Astaire, Judy Garland, Fanny Brice, Lucille Bre-

mer, Cyd Charisse, Kathryn Grayson, Red Skelton, Esther Williams, Victor Moore, et al.). The 110-minute revue had no storyline and consisted of production numbers in lush, extravagant, colorful settings. Vincente Minnelli directed, with George Folsey and Charles Rosher behind the cameras. The picture grossed $4 million in distributors domestic rentals.

Powell's only other release of 1946 was *The Hoodlum Saint* (MGM) with Esther Williams performing on dry land. Set in post–World War I days, Powell is a newspaperman in what the *New York Times* judged "a tediously involved plot" and "a somewhat jumbled and tepid drama." He turns from the fourth estate to finance to religion as the proponent of the Good Thief, St. Dismas. Angela Lansbury, as a torch singer,* is the girlfriend who does not wait for him to settle down, so he winds up with Miss Williams.

William David Powell, a brilliant student at Princeton University, graduated *magna cum laude* in June 1946, and returned to Los Angeles, where he obtained a post as story editor at Warner Bros. In the spring of 1947, he married Irene Booth, but it was an unhappy union and they divorced in August 1948.

*Her songs were dubbed by Doreen Tryden.

451

With wife Diana Lewis at the Los Angeles Tennis Club, September, 1946

On July 23, 1947, the sixth and final chapter in the *Thin Man* feature-film saga was released as *Song of the Thin Man* (MGM), directed by Eddie Buzzell. This one opens with the killing of a bandleader on a gambling ship. The Charleses are again imbibing liquor, and when a bottle of Scotch is shot out of Powell's hands, it is just cause for him to become fully involved in the proceedings. In one scene, as well-groomed Bill walks into the kitchen for breakfast, Myrna Loy greets him with: "Good morning, dear. My, you look like something out of *Esquire*." Nickie Jr. (Dean Stockwell), now nine years old, pipes up with: "Not the ones I see." Miss Loy stopped the action because she did not feel that a nine-year-old would say those words. Connie Gilchrist, who played the family maid in the film, stood beside her old friend from Broadway days, director Buzzell. She spoke up, saying she thought the line was original and would get "a nice laugh." Powell agreed, and the line was left in the release print. *Motion Picture* magazine commented: "The Thin Man's song turns out to be jive, on the beat, reet, and ready to fly."

"If you think I'm going to stand there and let Dr. Lloyd [Edmund Gwenn] splash me with water, you're mistaken." These words—and a great

With Charles Trowbridge in THE HOODLUM SAINT (MGM '46)

many more—were spoken with tyrannical finality by a voice that seemed new to the screen soundtracks. In February 1946, Warner Bros. purchased the film rights to *Life with Father* and after testing Louis Calhern (who had portrayed Father for a short time on Broadway and for a long duration on the road, and was Howard Lindsay's first choice as the patriarch Clarence Day), borrowed Powell for the role he had so long coveted. The part of Vinnie (Day's wife) was not as easily cast. Warners tested Mary Pickford and Dorothy Stickney before finally selecting Irene Dunne.° Shirley Temple, director Michael Curtiz's original choice as Mary Skinner,† the girl whose visit to the Day home changes the lives of all four members, was not available due to a full schedule. Elizabeth Taylor, far more suited for the role anyway, was borrowed from MGM to fill that slot.

Since the entire Day family had hair the color of carrots, Powell dyed his hair *and* mustache red.† Miss Dunne and the four boys (Jimmy Lydon, Martin Milner, Derek Scott, and Johnny Calkins) were also required to undergo two hair-dying shampoos each week during the filming. They were all ordered to stay out of their swimming pools because the chlorine would turn their hair green.

Life with Father (Warner Bros., 1947), based on the recollections of Clarence Day, Jr. (played in the film by Lydon), was written for the screen by Donald Ogden Stewart. The scenarist carefully omitted Father's many "damns" from the stage play. However, the movie censors did not frown upon such expletives as "Oh, gads!" or "What in tarnation," even though certain elegant ladies of the story's era (1883) would have considered them as being of an irreverent nature. For the most part, the plot centers on Dunne's insistence that Powell be baptized, an act that had been overlooked somehow in his infancy. Powell is just as insistent that he will not be baptized, but relents when Dunne is forced to take to her sickbed with an ailment that perplexes even Dr. Humphries (Moroni Olsen). The story is interlaced with assorted family occurrences that never fail to upset Powell's plans to run the household as he would a business.

Bill's voice even changed in his Father role. It took on a different tonal quality. He told the *Saturday Evening Post* a year after the film's release: "It probably required a certain flexibility of imag-

ination for movie-goers to accept The Thin Man as Father in the picture. But I found the transition from modern detecting to 1880 paternalism quite easy to make." Powell admitted that it was his favorite screen role, because "[it] was an exceptionally well-written vehicle, and I liked the fact that it was high comedy instead of low comedy or farce. In farce you make mental banjo eyes at the audience; in high comedy you put your tongue in your cheek and pretend it isn't there."

The critics generally approved of the filmed *Life with Father*. "The Warner Brothers can be proud of a job well done and the rest of us thankful that a classical slice of Americana has been preserved intact" (*New York Times*). About Powell, it was said: "The great performance of a highly distinguished career" (Howard Barnes, *New York Herald-Tribune*); "He has summoned up a robust gusto that no other role ever indicated was among his resources" (Alton Cook, *New York World-Telegram*); "His Father is not merely a performance; it is character delineation of a high order and he so utterly dominates the picture that even when he is not on hand, his presence is felt" (Thomas M. Pryor, *New York Times*). However, not everyone was totally impressed. James Agee wrote in the *Nation*: "William Powell acts, rather than is, Father rather well, but it's strictly an impersonation."

The motion picture grossed $6 million and was honored with four Oscar nominations, but failed to win in any category. Bill, in his third nomination as Best Actor, lost to his friend Ronald Colman of *A Double Life* (Universal). But there were some consolation prizes for Powell. The New York Film Critics voted Powell as Best Actor of the year based on his performance in *Life with Father* and *The Senator Was Indiscreet* which was his next film. Mrs. Powell presented her husband with her own specially ordered miniature Oscar, shaped as a man with a golden derby hat, and inscribed with the words: "For your superb triumph, Life with Mousie."

Powell's acting of the suave, sophisticated, debonair (adjectives he always has detested in relation to himself) leading man onscreen ended with *Life with Father*. His screen career had come full cycle, and he was destined again to play character roles, although not of the sinister variety. On loan to Universal for *The Senator Was Indiscreet* (1947), his hair was bushy and white, while his

---

° An elaborate equal-billing status had to be arranged for Miss Dunne and Powell.
† Played on Broadway by newcomer Teresa Wright.
‡ Diana "Mousie" Powell, in a facetious attempt to persuade Bill to retain his *Father* hair coloring after the movie's completion, was met with a disdainful refusal on the grounds that it made him look like a mature Van Johnson.

With Irene Dunne in LIFE WITH FATHER (WB '47)

white mustache was trimmed close to the handle-bar stage. He is the senator—Ashton by name—who is capable of little else but to be President of the United States—a bumbling, naive, windy, inoffensive man. He innocently maintains a diary which, when it is discovered, proves embarrassing to all who have known him. Ella Raines, as an industrious reporter, intends to expose the old fellow as a fraud. However, in the process she finds him to be a genuine person, and, in addition, finds romance with Peter Lind Hayes. Myrna Loy makes a brief, unbilled, and unexpected appearance at the end of the film as the senator's wife. It was to be their thirteenth and final film together.

The critical reaction to *The Senator Was Indiscreet* ranged from "feeble" (the *Nation*) to "we haven't laughed so much in years" (*Motion Picture* magazine). An adverse response came from an unexpected source. Senator Joseph McCarthy, just then beginning his highly publicized Communist witch-hunt, termed *Senator* "Un-American."

Mr. Peabody and the Mermaid, Powell's only 1948 film, again found him on loan to Universal. The film displays the actor as a man from Boston who feels he has not accomplished very much in his fifty years, but who also insists that he is not yet ready for the rocking chair. One day, while fishing in the sunshine on St. Hilda's Island, he hooks a beautiful, dark-tressed mermaid (Ann Blyth), who does not speak a word of any known language. He takes her to his villa and places her in his pool, hoping to hide her existence from his wife (Irene Hervey). He falls in love with her, which revitalizes his life, but eventually he is forced to return her to the deep from whence she came. *Newsweek* magazine proclaimed: "William Powell is perfect as a Bostonian who will never see either fifty or a mermaid again."

Take One False Step (1949) was another Universal film with Bill back in the business of amateur detecting, but *Newsweek* properly observed: "[he] acts more than a little tired of sleuthing." Neither the character he plays, nor the women (Shelley Winters, Marsha Hunt, Dorothy Hart) in the case, nor the script are similar to those previous successes concerning Nick Charles, although the ever-present dumb cop (in this case two of them, James Gleason and Sheldon Leonard) is on hand. What few enjoyable incidents exist in the movie are quickly overshadowed by acts of violence as Powell fights for his life with a brute watchdog and is later forced to stand helpless while a man goes to a grisly death beneath the wheels of a train. "Through it all," wrote Bosley Crowther (*New York Times*), "Mr. Powell meanders in a conspicuously humorless way, broken now and then by bewildering explosions in a vein of shallow farce."

Bill next appeared for Twentieth Century–Fox in *Dancing in the Dark* (1949), based on the revue *The Bandwagon.** As produced by George Jessel and directed by Irving Reis, the color musical concerned a conceited ex-matinee-screen idol named Emery Slide (Powell) who has fallen on lean days as much from egotism as from age. He is hired by Fox Studio boss Grossman (Adolphe Menjou in a take-off on Darryl F. Zanuck) to journey to New York to talk a musical-comedy star into coming west for a screen version of *Bandwagon*. Instead of the star, he returns to Hollywood with an unknown actress (Betsy Drake) whom the studio accepts after additional prodding from a press agent (Mark Stevens). Up to this point, the story is light and frothy, but it becomes turgid when Drake suddenly learns that Powell is actually her father, who had deserted her mother when she was just a kid. At a time when Betty Grable, Doris Day, Betty Hutton, Judy Garland, and June Haver musicals were still the order of

the cinema day, *Dancing in the Dark* made little lasting impact.

It's a Big Country (MGM, 1951) returned Bill to his alma mater in a cameo role. Metro was no longer the same. Louis B. Mayer was on his way to final ouster. Dore Schary and his message-picture philosophy were in control, and most of the old guard box-office names (Robert Montgomery, Myrna Loy, Melvyn Douglas, Robert Young, Johnny Weissmuller, et al.) had moved on to less prestigious studio homes or had drifted into other phases of show business. *It's a Big Country*, boasting eight writers and seven directors, was termed an "American Anthology," and depicted unrelated incidents in the lives of everyday Americans from various walks of life. Done in eight segments, many of which were interminably belabored, it attempted to convince nonbelievers that the United States is not only big, but contains honest, moral, earthy, compassionate people. Bill appeared in the opening segment as the Professor, out for a train ride. He is approached by James Whitmore, a simple soul, whose statement that "this is a great country, all right" sends the Pro-

*The George F. Kaufman show opened on Broadway at the New Amsterdam Theatre (June 3, 1931) and ran for 262 performances. Not to be confused with the Adolph Green–Betty Comden–written *The Band Wagon* (MGM, 1953), a musical starring Fred Astaire and Cyd Charisse, which, like the 1949 Fox film, was a new invention nearly all told.

With Ella Raines and Peter Lind Hayes in THE SENATOR WAS INDISCREET (Univ '47)

With Adolphe Menjou, Betsy Drake, and Mark Stevens in DANCING IN THE DARK (20th '49)

fessor off on a tangent of defining just which portion of the country's life styles Whitmore is discussing. *Cue* magazine found the entire mixture "mostly soapy, sentimental, sugary and as elementary as a comic strip."

The Treasure of Lost Canyon (Universal, 1952) was considered a return to cinema acting for Bill, but it was not much of a showcase. He played an aged prospector involved with buried treasure and the effect it has on the lives of those in search of it, including Charles Drake, Julia Adams, Rosemary De Camp, Henry Hull, and, most of all, a youngster named Tommy Ivo. Those onetime ardent filmgoers who were not home viewing their television sets and caught the double-bill item, *The Treasure of Lost Canyon*, must have sighed at how time had distinguished but also diminished the dapper screen image known as William Powell.

In April 1953, the release of *The Girl Who Had Everything* (MGM) revealed Powell's name third in the billing, below that of Elizabeth Taylor and Fernando Lamas. An updated remake of the memorable *A Free Soul* (MGM, 1931), itself

based on a novel and a Broadway play,* Powell had the diluted role which had won an Oscar for Lionel Barrymore, that of a lawyer who has brought up his motherless daughter (Taylor) to live as she pleases. She falls for an unscrupulous gambler-client (Lamas), which causes Powell great heartache. So that wholesome Taylor would not end up with corrupt but virile Lamas, the script has the latter the victim of a gangland shooting at the climax. The film emerged as a slick, but hollow melodrama.

This disappointing feature completed Powell's contract with MGM. Because of his length of time on the studio's payroll (twenty years), the sexagenarian actor was entitled to a pension.

How to Marry a Millionaire (1953), written for Twentieth Century–Fox by producer Nunnally Johnson and partially derived from a Zöe Akins play,† was aimed at exploiting the innovative CinemaScope and stereophonic processes and the curvaceous presence of Betty Grable, Marilyn Monroe, and Lauren Bacall. The female trio appeared as three gold diggers who pool their resources and rent a lush Manhattan-penthouse

---

*The drama opened at the Playhouse Theatre on January 12, 1928, for a 100-performance run.
†Produced on Broadway (as *The Greeks Had a Word for It*) at the Sam Harris Theatre (September 25, 1930) for 253 performances, it was translated into the film, *The Greeks Had a Word for Them* (United Artists, 1932).

With Charles Drake, Jack Perrin, Henry Hull (seated), Marvin Press, and John Doucette in THE TREASURE OF LOST CANYON (Univ '52)

With Gig Young, Fernando Lamas, and Elizabeth Taylor in THE GIRL WHO HAD EVERYTHING (MGM '53)

apartment in order to better pursue their prey: rich, available males. Bill is J.D. Hanley, a Texas oil tycoon who takes a particular shine to Bacall. He has her altarbound until she makes a last-minute switch in suitors and chooses younger Cameron Mitchell, whom she thinks is poor, but is actually a millionaire. Very definitely in support of the three ladies, as well as Mitchell, Rory Calhoun, and David Wayne, Powell made the most of a small role which only allowed him brief chances to display his polished wit. It was more than midway to the end of his distinguished film career.

The Powells, in addition to a Beverly Hills home, had acquired a rambling bungalow on the north end of Palm Springs, California. This desert resort town was chosen by Bill as his soon-to-be-realized retirement spot, and he became a member of Charles Farrell's Palm Springs Racquet Club. He was then coaxed back to screen work for his last feature to date, *Mister Roberts* (Warner Bros., 1955) because "Mousie had never been to Hawaii. The film was to be on location there and she could get a free ticket over."

The director originally scheduled for the film, John Ford, left the production due to illness and was replaced by Mervyn LeRoy. The screenplay was by Frank Nugent and Joshua Logan, from the play by Thomas Heggen and Logan.* In the color feature, Navy cargo ship *Reluctant*, during World War II, sails between the islands of "Tedium" and "Apathy," with side trips to "Monotony." The crew is made up of seamen who are more civilian than naval, most of whom do not fully comprehend what the war is all about or where it is being fought. Mr. Roberts (Henry Fonda), the chief cargo officer, wants active duty, but the ship's persnickety captain (James Cagney), a tyrannical, dictatorial little man with a pet palm tree, sees Fonda only as a means of acquiring a promotion and turns down each of his transfer requests. In third billing as "Doc," the ship's philosophical medic, Bill calmly takes it all in stride and escapes, when the situations become too wild, in cabin-concocted booze. A. H. Wheiler (*New York Times*) declared that Powell's "polished portrayal of the middle-aged ennui-filled medico is subdued and effective."

Mister Roberts was nominated for an Oscar as Best Picture of 1955, but lost to *Marty* (United Artists). However, Jack Lemmon, for his portrayal of Ensign Pulver, was awarded the Best Support-

*Opened on Broadway at the Alvin Theatre (December 18, 1948) for a 1,157-performance run, with Robert Keith as Doc.

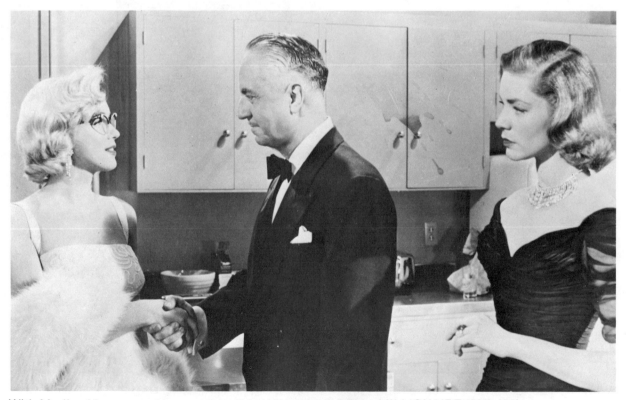

With Marilyn Monroe and Lauren Bacall in HOW TO MARRY A MILLIONAIRE (20th '53)

ing Actor statue. (In the puerile successsor to *Mister Roberts*, entitled *Ensign Pulver* [Warner Bros., 1964], Robert Walker, Jr. was in the title role, Burl Ives was the Captain, with Walter Matthau as Doc.)

The Powells gave up Hollywood and Beverly Hills by moving permanently to Palm Springs. "I take no pride in the fact," Powell has said, "but I was one of the first actors to sense the poison that lurked in the Hollywood air [i.e., smog]. I've been back there only a couple of times and get through and out as fast as I can."

William David Powell, then a television story editor with NBC-TV and an associate producer for Universal and Warner Bros., married Patricia Parsons on December 22, 1956, in a civil ceremony. This marriage, too, was short, and they divorced on September 19, 1957.

On May 27, 1959, at the age of eighty-six, Bill's mother, Nettie, died in Beverly Hills. She is buried in Forest Lawn Cemetery, next to her husband.

In 1964, the Irving Shulman biographical novel *Harlow* was published and became a best-seller. Listed as nonfiction, the book supposedly told the "true" story of Jean Harlow's hectic life. Bill called it "scurrilous" and said: "It's the greatest *fiction* I've ever read." Two films were made of

Miss Harlow's life, one by Joseph E. Levine for Paramount with Carroll Baker, and the second for Magna Distributing Corporation, filmed in the speedy Electrovision, with Carol Lynley. They were both released in 1965, a month apart. Powell refused to be portrayed in either film. Sidney Boehm, who wrote the screenplay for the expensive Levine color version of Harlow, was quoted as saying: "As far as I'm concerned, Bill Powell is not necessary to the story—and so he will be omitted."

On March 13, 1968, William David Powell, age forty-three, committed suicide in his apartment by stabbing himself to death in the upper portion of his body. Because of a chronic kidney illness, he had been forced to stop writing and was reportedly overcome with despondency. He left a rambling four-page note which included: "Things are not good here. I am going where things are better."

In the years that followed, Powell and "Mousie" remained in Palm Springs, with annual summer vacations spent at the Garden of the Gods Club in Colorado Springs. While "Mousie" played tennis or golf (she sponsored an annual one-day pro-amateur golf tournament called the "Mousetrap Open"), Powell, who had grown hard of hearing, rode the golf cart or just sat and

With Henry Fonda and Jack Lemmon in MR. ROBERTS (WB '55)

459

watched. At Palm Springs, Powell admitted: "Television is our major entertainment. We have our dinner in front of the set. Then, if we want to watch different shows, we can retire to our rooms, where each of us have a set." They observed their thirtieth wedding anniversary (he was seventy-seven and she was fifty) in 1970 when he gave her a diamond bracelet and she remembered the event with a diamond tie pin.

Bill, who is sometimes confined to a wheelchair these days, has occasionally been asked to enact one role or another on screen or television during past years. However, he has said: "I ask myself, why would I do it? For the glory? The ham in me has been pretty well burned out with the years. For the money? I'd just be put into a higher tax bracket. So, I just say 'No.' "

William Powell

SHERLOCK HOLMES (Goldwyn, 1922) 8,200'

Producer, F. J. Godsol; director, Albert Parker; based on the play by William Gillette, derived from the stories by Sir Arthur Conan Doyle; screenplay, Marion Fairfax, Earle Browne; camera, J. Roy Hunt.

John Barrymore (Sherlock Holmes); Roland Young (Dr. Watson); Carol Dempster (Alice Faulkner); Gustav von Seyffertitz (Professor Moriarty); Louis Wolheim (Craigin); Percy Knight (Sid Jones); William H. Powell (Forman Wells); Hedda Hopper (Madge Larrabee); Peggy Bayfield (Rose Faulkner); Margaret Kemp (Therese); Anders Randolf (James Larrabee); Robert Schable (Alf Bassick); Reginald Denny (Prince Alexis); David Torrence (Count Von Stalburg); Robert Fischer (Otto); Lumsden Hare (Dr. Leighton); John Willard (Inspector Gregson); Jerry Devine (Billy).

WHEN KNIGHTHOOD WAS IN FLOWER (PAR, 1922) 11,618'

Director, Robert G. Vignola; based on the novel by Charles Major; adaptor, Luther Reed; set designer, Joseph Urban; music, William Frederick Peters; assistant director, Philip Carle; costumes, Gretl Urban Thurlow; armor advisor, Bashford Dean; fencing supervisor, James Murray; camera, Ira Morgan, Harold Wenstrom.

Marion Davies (Princess Mary Tudor); Forrest Stanley (Charles Brandon); Lyn Harding (King Henry VIII); Theresa Maxwell Conover (Queen Catherine); Pedro de Cordoba (Duke of Buckingham); Ruth Shepley (Lady Jane Bolingbroke); Ernest Glendenning (Sir Edwin Caskoden); Arthur Forrestt (Cardinal Wolsey); Johnny Dooley (Will Somers); William Kent (The King's Tailor); Charles Gerrard (Sir Adam Judson); Arthur Donaldson (Sir Henry Brandon); Downing Clarke (Lord Chamberlain); William Norris (Louis XII of France); Macey Harlam (Duc de Longueville); William H. Powell (Francis I); George Nash (Captain Bradhurst); Gustav von Seyffertitz (Grammont); Paul Panzer (Captain of the Guard); Guy Coombes (Follower of Buckingham); Flora Finch (French Countess); Red Wing, Black Diamond (Themselves); Winchester (Horse); Mortimer Snow, George Ogle (Bits).

OUTCAST (PAR, 1922) 7,309'

Director, Chet Withey; based on the play by Hubert Henry Davies; screenplay, Josephine Lovett.

Elsie Ferguson (Miriam); David Powell (Geoffrey Sherwood); William David (Tony Hewlitt); Mary MacLaren (Valentine Moreland); Charles Wellesley (John Moreland); Teddy Sampson (Nellie Essex); William Powell (De Valle).

THE BRIGHT SHAWL (Associated First National, 1923) 7,503'

Presenter, Charles H. Duell; director, John S. Robertson; based on the novel by Joseph Hergesheimer; adaptor, Edmund Goulding; art director, Everett Shinn; camera, George Folsey; editor, William Hamilton.

Richard Barthelmess (Charles Abbott); André Beranger (Andres Escobar); Edward G. Robinson (Domingo Escobar); Margaret Seddon (Carmenita Escobar); Mary Astor (Narcissa Escobar); Luis Alberni (Vincente Escobar); Anders Randolf (Cesar y Santacilla); William Powell (Gaspar de Vaca); Dorothy Gish (La Clavel); Jetta Goudal (La Pilar); George Humbert (Jaime Quintara).

UNDER THE RED ROBE (Goldwyn-Cosmopolitan, 1923) 12,000'

Director, Alan Crosland; based on the novel by Stanley J. Weyman; screenplay, Bayard Veiller; sets, Joseph Urban; music, William Frederick Peters; costumes, Gretl Urban; art titles, Oscar C. Buchheister; camera, Harold Wenstrom.

Robert B. Mantell (Cardinal Richelieu); John Charles Thomas (Gil de Berault); Alma Rubens (Renee de Cocheforet); Otto Kruger (Henri de Cocheforet); William H. Powell (Duke of Orleans); Ian MacLaren (King Louis XIII); Genevieve Hamper (Duchess de Chevreuse); Mary MacLaren (Anne of Austria); Rose Coghlan (Marie de Medici); Gustav von Seyffertitz (Clon); Sidney Herbert (Father Joseph); Arthur Housman (Captain La Rolle); Paul Panzer (Lieutenant in the French Army); Charles Judels (Antoine); George Nash (Jules, the Innkeeper); Evelyn Gosnell (Madame de Cocheforet).

DANGEROUS MONEY (PAR, 1924) 7,234'

Presenters, Adolph Zukor, Jesse L. Lasky; director, Frank Tuttle; based on the play Clark's Field by Robert Herrick; adaptor, John Russell; screenplay, Julie Herne; camera, Roy Hunt.

Bebe Daniels (Adele Clark); Tom Moore (Tim Sullivan); William Powell (Prince Arnolfo da Pescia); Dolores Cassinelli (Signorina Vitale); Mary Foy (Auntie Clark); Edward O'Conner Sheamus Sullivan); Peter Lang (Judge Daniel Orcutt); Charles Slattery (O'Hara); and Diane Kane.

ROMOLA (Metro-Goldwyn, 1924) 12,974'

Director, Henry King; based on the novel by George Eliot; screenplay, Will M. Ritchey; art director, Robert M. Haas; shipbuilder, Tito Neri.

Lillian Gish (Romola); Dorothy Gish (Tessa); William H. Powell (Tito Melema); Ronald Colman (Carlo Buccellini); Charles Lane (Baldassarre Calvo); Herbert Grimwood (Savonarola); Bonaventure Ibanez (Bardo Bardi); Frank Puglia (Adolpo Spini); Amelia Summerville (Brigida); Angelo Scatigna (Bratti); Edulilo Mucci (Nello); Tina Rinaldi (Monna Ghita); and Alfredo Bartone, Alfredo Martinelli, Ugo Ucellini.

TOO MANY KISSES (PAR, 1925) 5,759'

Presenters, Adolph Zukor, Jesse L. Lasky; director, Paul Sloane; based on the story "A Maker of Gestures" by John Monk Saunders; screenplay, Gerald Duffy; camera, Hal Rosson.

Richard Dix (Richard Gaylord, Jr.); Frances Howard (Yvonne Hurja); William Powell (Julio); Frank Currier (Richard Gaylord, Sr.); Joseph Burke (Mr. Simmons); Albert Tavernier (Manuel Hurja); Arthur Ludwig (Miguel); Alyce Mills (Flapper); Paul Panzer (Pedro); Harpo Marx (The Village Peter Pan).

FAINT PERFUME (B. P. Schulberg, 1925) 6,186'
Director, Louis Gasnier; based on the novel by Zona Gale; adaptor, John Goodrich; camera, Allen Siegler.

Seena Owen (Richmiel Crumb); William Powell (Barnaby Powers); Alyce Mills (Ledda Perrin); Mary Alden (Ma Crumb); Russell Simpson (Grandpa Crumb); Betty Francisco (Pearl Crumb); Jacqueline Saunders (Tweet Crumb); Philo McCullough (Richmiel's Lover); Ned Sparks (Orrin Crumb); Dicky Brandon (Oliver Powers); Joan Standing (Hired Girl).

MY LADY'S LIPS (B. P. Schulberg, 1925) 6,609'
Director, James P. Hogan; story-continuity, John Goodrich; camera, Allen Siegler.

Alyce Mills (Dora Blake); William Powell (Scott Seddon); Clara Bow (Lola Lombard); Frank Keenan (Forbes Lombard); Ford Sterling (Smike); John Sainpolis (Inspector); Gertrude Short (Crook Girl); Matthew Betz (Eddie Gault); Sojin (Orienta).

THE BEAUTIFUL CITY (FN, 1925) 6,466'
Director, Kenneth Webb; screenplay-titles, Don Bartlett, C. Graham Baker; adaptor, Violet E. Powell; writer, Edmund Goulding; art titles, H. E. E. Studios; camera, Roy Overbaugh, Stuart Kelson; editor, William Hamilton.

Richard Barthelmess (Tony Gillardi); Dorothy Gish (Mollie); William Powell (Nick Di Silva); Frank Puglia (Carlo Gillardi); Florence Auer (Mamma Gillardi); Lassie Bronte (The Dog).

WHITE MICE (Associated Exhibitors, 1926) 5,412'
Producer, Royal W. Wetherald; director, Edward H. Griffith; based on the novel by Richard Harding Davis; adaptor, Randolph Bartlett; camera, Marcel Le Picard.

Jacqueline Logan (Inez Rojas); William Powell (Roddy Forrester); Ernest Hilliard (Colonel Vega); Bigelow Cooper (R. B. Forrester); Lucius Henderson (General Rojas); Marie Burke (Senora Rojas); Harlan Knight (MacKildrick); Reginald Sheffield (Peter' de Peyster); F. Vaux Wilson (Dr. Vincenti); William Wadsworth (Sylvanus Codman); Richard Lee (Manuel); George De Richelevie (El Commandante); Vivian Vernon (La Borrachita).

SEA HORSES (PAR, 1926) 6,565'
Presenters, Adolph Zukor, Jesse L. Lasky; director, Allan Dwan; based on the novel by Francis Brett Young; adaptor, Becky Gardiner; screenplay, James Shelley Hamilton; camera, James Howe.

Jack Holt (George Glanville); Florence Vidor (Helen Salvia); William Powell (Lorenzo Salvia); George Bancroft (Cochran); Mack Swain (Bimbo-Bomba); Frank Campeau (Senor Cordoza); Allan Simpson (Harvey); George Nichols (Marx); Mary Dow (Cina Salvia); Dick La Reno (Henry); Frank Austin (Cheadle).

DESERT GOLD (PAR, 1926) 6,900'
Presenters, Adolph Zukor, Jesse L. Lasky; supervisors, Hector Turnbull, B. P. Schulberg; director, George B. Seitz; based on the novel by Zane Grey; screenplay, Lucien Hubbard; camera, Edgar Schoenbaum.

Neil Hamilton (George Thorne); Shirley Mason (Mercedes Castanada); Robert Frazer (Dick Gale); William Powell (Landree); Josef Swickard (Sebastian Castanada); George Irving (Richard Stanton Gate); Eddie Gribbon (One Round Kelley); Frank Lackteen (Yaqui); Richard Howard (Sergeant); Bernard Siegel (Goat Herder); George Regas (Verd); Ralph Yearsley (Halfwit); Aline Goodwin (Alarcon's Wife).

Technicolor sequences.

THE RUNAWAY (PAR, 1926) 6,218'
Presenters, Adolph Zukor, Jesse L. Lasky; director, William C. De Mille; based on the novel The Flight to the Hills by Charles Neville Buck; adaptor, Albert Shelby Le Vino; camera, Charles Boyle.

Clara Bow (Cynthia Meade); Warner Baxter (Wade Murrell); William Powell (Jack Harrison); George Bancroft (Lesher Skidmore); Edythe Chapman (Wade's Mother).

ALOMA OF THE SOUTH SEAS (PAR, 1926) 8,514'
Presenters, Adolph Zukor, Jesse L. Lasky; director, Maurice Tourneur; based on the play by John B. Hymer, Leroy Clemens; screenplay, James Ashmore Creelman; art director, Charles M. Kirk; camera, Harry Fischbeck; editor, E. Lloyd Sheldon.

Gilda Gray (Aloma); Percy Marmont (Bob Holden); Warner Baxter (Nuitane); William Powell (Van Templeton); Harry Morey (Red Malloy); Julanne Johnston (Sylvia); Joseph Smiley (Andrew Taylor); Frank Montgomery (Hongi); Madame Burani (Hina); Ernestine Gaines (Taula); Aurelio Coccia (Sailor).

BEAU GESTE (PAR, 1926) 10,600'*
Presenters, Adolph Zukor, Jesse L. Lasky; director, Herbert Brenon; based on the novel by Percival Christopher Wren; adaptors, John Russell, Brenon; screenplay, Paul Schofield; art director, Julian Boone Fleming; music, Hugo Riesenfeld; assistant director, Ray Lissner; camera, J. Roy Hunt.

Ronald Colman (Michael "Beau" Geste); Neil Hamilton (Digby Geste); Ralph Forbes (John Geste); Alice Joyce (Lady Brandon); Mary Brian (Isobel); Noah Beery (Sergeant Lejaune); Norman Trevor (Major de Beaujolais); William Powell (Boldini); George Regas (Maris); Bernard Siegel (Schwartz); Victor McLaglen (Hank); Donald Stuart (Buddy); Paul McAllister (St. Andre); Redmond Finlay (Cordere); Ram Singh (Prince Ram Singh); Maurice Murphy (Beau as a Child); Philippe De Lacey (Digby as a Child); Mickey McBan (John as a Child).

TIN GODS (PAR, 1926) 8,568'
Presenters, Adolph Zukor, Jesse L. Lasky; associate producer, William Le Baron; director, Allan Dwan; based on the play by William Anthony McGuire; adaptors, Paul Dickey, Howard Emmett Rogers; screenplay, James Shelley Hamilton; camera, Alvin Wyckoff.

Thomas Meighan (Roger Drake); Renee Adoree (Carita); Aileen Pringle (Janet Stone); William Powell (Tony Santelli); Hale Hamilton (Dr. McCoy); John Harrington (Dougherty); Joe King, Robert E. O'Connor (Foremen); Delbert Emory Whitten, Jr. (Billy).

THE GREAT GATSBY (PAR, 1926) 7,296'
Presenters, Adolph Zukor, Jesse L. Lasky; director, Herbert Brenon; based on the novel by F. Scott Fitzgerald and the play by Owen Davis; adaptor, Elizabeth Meehan; screenplay, Becky Gardiner; assistant director, Ray Lissner; camera, Leo Tover.

Warner Baxter (Jay Gatsby); Lois Wilson (Daisy Buchanan); Neil Hamilton (Nick Carraway); Georgia Hale (Myrtle Wilson); William Powell (George Wilson); Hale Hamilton (Tom Buchanan); George Nash (Charles Wolf); Carmelita Geraghty (Jordan Baker); Eric Blore (Lord Digby); "Gunboat" Smith (Bert); Claire Whitney (Catherine).

NEW YORK (PAR, 1927) 6,877'
Presenters, Adolph Zukor, Jesse L. Lasky; associate producer, William Le Baron; director, Luther Reed; story, Becky Gardiner, Barbara Chambers; screenplay, Forrest Halsey; camera, J. Roy Hunt.

Ricardo Cortez (Michael Angelo Cassidy); Lois Wilson (Marjorie Church); Estelle Taylor (Angie Miller); William Powell (Trent Regan); Norman Trevor (Randolph Church); Richard "Skeets" Gallagher (Buck); Margaret Quimby (Helena Matthews); Lester Scharff (Sharpe) (Izzy Blumenstein); Charles Byer (Jimmie Wharton).

LOVE'S GREATEST MISTAKE (PAR, 1927) 6,007'

Presenters, Adolph Zukor, Jesse L. Lasky; associate producer, William Le Baron; director, Edward Sutherland; based on the novel by Frederic Arnold Kummer; screenplay, Becky Gardiner; camera, Leo Tover.

Evelyn Brent (Jane); William Powell (Don Kendall); James Hall (Harvey Gibbs); Josephine Dunn (Honey McNeil); Frank Morgan (William Ogden); Iris Gray (Sara Foote); Betty Byrne (Lovely Gibby).

SEÑORITA (PAR, 1927) 6,643'

Presenters, Adolph Zukor, Jesse L. Lasky; associate producer, B. P. Schulberg; director, Clarence Badger; story, John McDermott; screenplay, McDermott, Lloyd Corrigan; titles, Robert Hopkins; camera, H. Kinley Martin, William Marshall.

Bebe Daniels (Señorita Francesca Hernandez); James Hall (Roger Oliveros); William Powell (Ramon Oliveros); Josef Swickard (Don Francisco Hernandez).

SPECIAL DELIVERY (PAR, 1927) 5,524'

Presenters, Adolph Zukor, Jesse L. Lasky; associate producer, B. P. Schulberg; director, William Goodrich; story, Eddie Cantor; continuity, John Goodrich; titles, George Marion, Jr.; camera, Henry Hallenberger.

Eddie Cantor (Eddie); Jobyna Ralston (Madge); William Powell (Harold Jones); Donald Keith (Harrigan); Jack Dougherty (Flannigan); Victor Potel (Nip); Paul Kelly (Tuck); Mary Carr (The Mother).

TIME TO LOVE (PAR, 1927) 4,926'

Presenters, Adolph Zukor, Jesse L. Lasky; associate producer, B. P. Schulberg; director, Frank Tuttle; story, Alfred Savoir; screenplay, Pierre Collings; camera, William Marshall.

Raymond Griffith (Alfred Sava-Golu); William Powell (Prince Alado); Vera Voronina (Countess Elvire); Josef Swickard (Elvire's Father); Mario Carillo, Pierre De Ramey (Duelists); Helene Giere (Elvire's Guardian); Alfred Sabato (Hindu Mystic).

PAID TO LOVE (FOX, 1927) 80 M.

Presenter, William Fox; director, Howard Hawks; story, Harry Carr; adaptor, Benjamin Glazer; screenplay, William M. Conselman, Seton I. Miller; assistant director, James Tinling; camera, L. William O'Connell.

George O'Brien (Crown Prince Michael); Virginia Valli (Gaby); J. Farrell MacDonald (Peter Roberts); Thomas Jefferson (King Leopold); William Powell (Prince Eric); Merta Sterling (Maid); Hank Mann (Servant); Jack Pennick (A Guard); Alphonse Martel (Michael's Valet); Francis McDonald (Pierre); Gino Corrado (Guide); Sally Eilers (Excited Girl Tourist).

NEVADA (PAR, 1927) 6,258'

Presenters, Adolph Zukor, Jesse L. Lasky; director, John Waters; based on the novel by Zane Grey; screenplay, John Stone, L. G. Rigby; titles, Jack Conway; camera, C. Edgar Schoenbaum.

Gary Cooper (Nevada); Thelma Todd (Hettie Ide); William Powell (Clan Dillon); Philip Strange (Ben Ide); Ernie S. Adams (Cash Burridge); Christian J. Frank (Sheriff of Winthrop); Ivan Christy (Cawthorne); Guy Oliver (Sheriff of Lineville).

SHE'S A SHEIK (PAR, 1927) 6,015'

Presenters, Adolph Zukor, Jesse L. Lasky; director, Clarence Badger; story, John McDermott; screenplay, Lloyd Corrigan, Grover Jones; titles, George Marion, Jr.; camera, J. Roy Hunt.

Bebe Daniels (Zaida); Richard Arlen (Captain Colton); William Powell (Kada); Josephine Dunn (Wanda Fowler); James Bradbury, Jr. (Jerry); Billy Franey (Joe); Paul McAllister (Sheik Yusiff ben Hamad); Al Fremont (The Major).

THE LAST COMMAND (PAR, 1928) 90 M.

Presenters, Adolph Zukor, Jesse L. Lasky; supervisor, J. G. Bachmann; associate producer, B. P. Schulberg; director, Josef von Sternberg; story, Lajos Biro; adaptor-screenplay, John P. Goodrich;° titles, Herman J. Mankiewicz; set designer, Hans Dreier; makeup, Fred C. Ryle; technical director, Nicholas Kobyliansky; camera, Bert Glennon; editor, William Shea.

Emil Jannings [General Dolgorucki (Grand Duke Sergius Alexander)]; Evelyn Brent (Natascha Dobrowa); William Powell (Leo Andreiev); Nicholas Soussanin (Adjutant); Michael Visaroff (Serge, the Valet); Jack Raymond (Assistant Director); Viacheslav Savitsky (Private); Fritz Feld (Revolutionist); Harry Semels (Soldier); Alexander Ikonnikov, Nicholas Kobyliansky (Drillmasters).

BEAU SABREUR (PAR, 1928) 6,704'

Presenters, Adolph Zukor, Jesse L. Lasky; director, John Waters; based on the novel by Percival Christopher Wren; adaptor, Tom J. Geraghty; titles, Julian Johnson; camera, C. Edgar Schoenbaum; editor, Rose Lowenger.

Gary Cooper (Major Henri de Beaujolais); Evelyn Brent (Mary Vanbrugh); Noah Beery (Sheikh El Hammel); William Powell (Becque); Roscoe Karns (Buddy); Mitchell Lewis (Suleman the Strong); Arnold Kent (Raoul de Redon); Raoul Paoli (Djfour); Joan Standing (Maudie); Frank Reicher (General de Beaujolais); Oscar Smith (Djikki).

FEEL MY PULSE (PAR, 1928) 5,808'

Presenters, Adolph Zukor, Jesse L. Lasky; director, Gregory La Cava; story, Howard Emmett Rogers; screenplay, Keene Thompson, Nick Barrows; titles, George Marion, Jr.; camera, J. Roy Hunt; editor, E. Lloyd Sheldon.

Bebe Daniels (Barbara Manning); Melbourne MacDowell (Uncle Wilburforce); George Irving (Uncle Edgar); Charles Sellon (Sanitarium Caretaker); Heinie Conklin (Patient); William Powell (Rumrunner); Richard Arlen (Reporter).

PARTNERS IN CRIME (PAR, 1928) 6,600'

Presenters, Adolph Zukor, Jesse L. Lasky; director, Frank Strayer; story-screenplay, Grover Jones, Gilbert Pratt; titles, George Marion, Jr.,; camera, William Marshall; editor, William Shea.

Wallace Beery (Mike Doolan); Raymond Hatton (Scoop McGee/Knife Reagan); Mary Brian (Marie Burke); William Powell (Smith); Jack Luden (Richard Deming); Arthur Housman (Barton); Albert Roccardi (Kanelli); Joseph W. Girard (Chief of Police); George Irving (B. R. Cornwall); Bruce Gordon (Dodo); Jack Richardson (Jake).

THE DRAGNET (PAR, 1928) 7,866'

Director, Josef von Sternberg; based on the story "Night Stick" by Oliver H. P. Garrett; adaptor, Jules Furthman; screenplay, Jules Furthman, Charles Furthman; set designer, Hans Dreier; camera, Harold Rosson; editor, Helen Lewis.

George Bancroft (Two-Gun Nolan); Evelyn Brent (The Magpie); William Powell (Dapper Frank Trent); Fred Kohler (Gabby Steve); Francis McDonald (Sniper Dawson); Leslie Fenton (Shakespeare).

THE VANISHING PIONEER (PAR, 1928) 5,834'

Director, John Waters; story, Zane Grey; adaptor, John Goodrich; screenplay, J. Walter Ruben; titles, Julian Johnson; camera, C. Edgar Schoenbaum; editor, Doris Drought.

Jack Holt (Anthony Ballard/John Ballard); Sally Blane (June Shelby); William Powell (John Murdock); Fred Kohler (Sheriff Murdock); Guy Oliver (Mr. Shelby); Roscoe Karns (Ray

°Von Sternberg later asserted that the scenario was written by himself, based upon an idea orally given him by Ernst Lubitsch.

Hearn); Tim Holt (John Ballard at Age Seven); Marcia Manon (The Apron Woman).

FORGOTTEN FACES (PAR, 1928) 75 M.

Presenters, Adolph Zukor, Jesse L. Lasky; supervisor, David Selznick; director, Victor Schertzinger; based on the story "Whiff of Heliotrope" by Richard Washburn Child; adaptor, Oliver H. P. Garrett; screenplay, Howard Estabrook; titles, Julian Johnson; camera, J. Roy Hunt; editors, Selznick, George Nicholls, Jr.

Clive Brook (Heliotrope Harry Harlow); Mary Brian (Alice Deane); Olga Baclanova (Lilly Harlow); William Powell (Froggy); Fred Kohler (Number 1309); Jack Luden (Tom).

INTERFERENCE (PAR, 1929) 75 M.

Director (Silent version), Lothar Mendes; director (Sound sequences) Roy J. Pomeroy; based on the play by Roland Pertwee, Harold Dearden; adaptor, Hope Loring; continuity, Louise Long; dialog, Ernest Pascal; titles, Julian Johnson; sound, Franklin Hansen; camera, Henry Gerrard; editor, George Nicholls, Jr.

William Powell (Philip Voaze); Evelyn Brent (Deborah Kane); Clive Brook (Sir John Marlay); Doris Kenyon (Faith Marlay); Tom Ricketts (Charles Smith); Brandon Hurst (Inspector Haynes); Louis Payne (Childers); Wilfred Noy (Dr. Gray); Donald Stuart (Freddie); Raymond Lawrence (Reporter).

THE CANARY MURDER CASE (PAR, 1929) 81 M.

Director, Malcolm St. Clair; based on the story by S. S. Van Dine; adaptors, Florence Ryerson, Albert S. Le Vino; dialog, Van Dine; titles, Herman J. Mankiewicz; camera, Harry Fischbeck; editor, William Shea.

William Powell (Philo Vance); James Hall (Jimmy Spotswoode); Louise Brooks° (Margaret O'Dell); Jean Arthur (Alyce La Fosse); Gustav von Seyffertitz (Dr. Ambrose Lindquist); Charles Lane (Charles Spotswoode); Eugene Pallette (Ernest Heath); Lawrence Grant (Charles Cleaver); Ned Sparks (Tony Skeel); Louis John Bartels (Louis Mannix); E. H. Calvert (Markham); Oscar Smith (Stuttering Hallboy); and George Y. Harvey, Tim Adair.

°Dialogue spoken by Margaret Livingston.

THE FOUR FEATHERS (PAR, 1929) 81 M.

Associate producer, David Selznick; directors, Merian C. Cooper, Ernest B. Schoedsack, Lothar Mendes; based on the novel by Alfred Edward Woodley Mason; adaptor, Hope Loring; screenplay, Howard Estabrook; titles, Julian Johnson, John Farrow; assistant director, Ivan Thomas; music, William Frederick Peters; camera, Robert Kurrle, Cooper, Schoedsack; editor, Schoedsack.

Richard Arlen (Harry Faversham); Fay Wray (Ethne Eustace); Clive Brook (Lieutenant Durrance); William Powell (Captain Trench); Theodore von Eltz (Lieutenant Castleton); Noah Beery (Slave Trader); Zack Williams (Idris); Noble Johnson (Ahmed); Harold Hightower (Ali); Philippe De Lacy (Harry at Age Ten); E. J. Radcliffe (Colonel Eustace); George Fawcett (Colonel Faversham); Augustin Symonds (Colonel Sutch).

CHARMING SINNERS (PAR, 1929) 66 M.

Director, Robert Milton; based on the play The Constant Wife by William Somerset Maugham; adaptor-screenplay, Doris Anderson; sound, Earl Hayman; camera, Victor Milner; editor, Verna Willis.

Ruth Chatterton (Kathryn Miles); Clive Brook (Robert Miles); Mary Nolan (Anne-Marie Whitley); William Powell (Karl Kraley); Laura Hope Crews (Mrs. Carr); Florence Eldridge (Helen Carr); Montagu Love (George Whitley); Juliette Crosby (Margaret); Lorraine Eddy (Alice); Claud Allister (Gregson).

THE GREENE MURDER CASE (PAR, 1929) 71 M.

Director, Frank Tuttle; based on the novel by S. S. Van Dine; screenplay, Louise Long; dialog, Bartlett Cormack; titles, Richard H. Diggs, Jr.; camera, Henry Gerrard.

William Powell (Philo Vance); Florence Eldridge (Sibella Greene); Ullrich Haupt (Dr. Von Blon); Jean Arthur (Ada Greene); Eugene Pallette (Sergeant Heath); E. H. Calvert (John F. X. Markham); Gertrude Norman (Mrs. Tobias Greene); Lowell Drew (Chester Greene); Morgan Farley (Rex Greene); Brandon Hurst (Sprott), Augusta Burmeister (Mrs. Mannheim); Marcia Harris (Hemming); Mildred Golden (Barton); Mrs. Wilfred Buckland (Mrs. Greene's Nurse); Helena Phillips (Miss O'Brien, Police Nurse for Mrs. Greene); Shep Camp (Medical Examiner); Charles E. Evans (Lawyer Canon); Harry Strang (Cop).

POINTED HEELS (PAR, 1929) 61 M.†

Director, A. Edward Sutherland; based on the story by Charles William Brackett; adaptors-dialog, Florence Ryerson, John V. A. Weaver; dialog director, Perry Ivins; songs, Richard A. Whiting and Leo Robin; Mack Gordon and Max Rich; sound, Harry M. Lindgren; camera, Rex Wimpy; editor, Jane Loring.

William Powell (Robert Courtland); Fay Wray (Lora Nixon); Helen Kane (Dot Nixon); Richard "Skeets" Gallagher (Dash Nixon); Phillips Holmes (Donald Ogden); Adrienne Dore (Kay Wilcox); Eugene Pallette (Joe Clark).

†Color sequences.

BEHIND THE MAKE-UP (PAR, 1930) 68½ M.

Director, Robert Milton; based on the story "The Feeder" by Mildred Cram; adaptors-dialog, George Manker Watters, Howard Estabrook; songs, Leo Robin, Sam Coslow, and Newell Chase; sound, Harry D. Mills; camera, Charles Lang; editor, Doris Drought.

Hal Skelly (Hap Brown); William Powell (Gardoni); Fay Wray (Marie Gardoni); Kay Francis (Kitty Parker); Paul Lukas (Count Boris); E. H. Calvert (Dawson); Agostino Borgato (Chef Pierre); Jean De Briac (Sculptor); Torben Meyer (Waiter); Bob Perry (Bartender).

STREET OF CHANCE (PAR, 1930) 75 M.

Director, John Cromwell; story, Oliver H. P. Garrett; adaptor, Howard Estabrook; dialog, Lenore J. Coffee; titles, Gerald Geraghty; sound, Harry D. Mills; camera, Charles Lang; editor, Otto Levering.

William Powell [John B. Marsden (Natural Davis)]; Jean Arthur (Judith Marsden); Kay Francis (Alma Marsden); Regis Toomey (Babe Marsden); Stanley Fields (Dorgan); Brooks Benedict (Al Mastick); Betty Francisco (Mrs. Mastick); John Risso (Tony); Joan Standing (Miss Abrams); Maurice Black (Nick); Irving Bacon (Harry); John Cromwell (Imbrie).

THE BENSON MURDER CASE (PAR, 1930) 69 M.

Director, Frank Tuttle; suggested by the novel by S. S. Van Dine; screenplay, Bartlett Cormack; dialog director, Perry Ivins; sound, Harold M. McNiff; camera, A. J. Stout; editor, Doris Drought.

William Powell (Philo Vance), Natalie Moorhead (Fanny Del Roy); Eugene Pallette (Sergeant Heath); Paul Lukas (Adolph Mohler); William (Stage) Boyd (Harry Gray); E. H. Calvert (District Attorney John F. X. Markham); Richard Tucker (Anthony Benson); May Beatty (Mrs. Paula Banning); Mischa Auer (Albert); Otto Yamaoka (Sam); Charles McMurphy (Burke); Dick Rush (Welch); Perry Ivins (Dealer).

PARAMOUNT ON PARADE (PAR, 1930) 128 M.°

Producer, Albert S. Kaufman; production supervisor, Elsie Janis; directors, Dorothy Arzner, Otto Brower, Edmund Goulding, Victor Heerman, Edwin H. Knopf, Rowland V. Lee, Ernst Lubitsch, Lothar Mendes, Victor Schertzinger, A. Edward Sutherland, Frank Tuttle; sound, Harry M. Lindgren;

choreography, David Bennett; songs, Janis and Jack King; Ballard MacDonald and Dave Dreyer; Ernesto De Curtis; L. Wolfe Gilbert and Abel Baer; Richard A. Whiting and Raymond B. Eagan; Whiting and Leo Robin; David Franklin; Sam Coslow; set designer, John Wenger; camera, Harry Fischbeck, Victor Milner.

Iris Adrian, Richard Arlen, Jean Arthur, Mischa Auer, William Austin, George Bancroft, Clara Bow, Evelyn Brent, Mary Brian, Clive Brook, Virginia Bruce, Nancy Carroll, Ruth Chatterton, Maurice Chevalier, Gary Cooper, Cecil Cunningham, Leon Errol, Stuart Erwin, Henry Fink, Kay Francis, Skeets Gallagher, Edmund Goulding, Harry Green, Mitzi Green, Robert Greig, James Hall, Phillips Holmes, Helen Kane, Dennis King, Abe Lyman and His Band, Fredric March, Nino Martini, Mitzi Mayfair, Marion Morgan Dancers, David Newell, Jack Oakie, Warner Oland, Zelma O'Neal, Eugene Pallette, Joan Peers, Jack Pennick, William Powell, Charles "Buddy" Rogers, Lillian Roth, Rolfe Sedan, Stanley Smith, Fay Wray (Guest Performers).

°Color sequences.

SHADOW OF THE LAW (PAR, 1930) 68 M.

Director, Louis Gasner; based on the novel The Quarry by John A. Morosco and the play The Quarry by Max Marcin; screenplay, John Farrow; sound, Harold M. McNiff; camera, Charles Lang; editor, Robert Bassler.

William Powell (John Nelson alias Jim Montgomery); Marion Shilling (Edith Wentworth); Natalie Moorhead (Ethel Barry); Regis Toomey (Tom Owen); Paul Hurst (Pete Shore); George Irving (Colonel Wentworth); Frederic Burt (Detective Lieutenant Mike Kearney); James Durkin (Warden); Richard Tucker·(Lew Durkin); Walter James (Captain of the Guards); Oscar Smith (Elevator Operator); Edward LeSaint (Judge); Allan Cavan (Juror); Harry Strang (Barber); Harry Wilson (Convict); Leo Willis (Engineer); Ed Peil, Sr. (Usher); Frank O'Connor (Doctor).

FOR THE DEFENSE (PAR, 1930) 63 M.

Director, John Cromwell; story, Charles Furthman; screenplay, Oliver H. P. Garrett; sound, Harold M. McNiff; camera, Charles Lang; editor, George Nichols, Jr.

William Powell (William Foster); Kay Francis (Irene Manners); Scott Kolk (Defoe); William B. Davidson (District Attorney Stone); John Elliott (McGann); Thomas Jackson (Daly); Harry Walker (Miller); James Finlayson (Parrott); Charles West (Joe); Charles Sullivan (Charlie); Ernest Adams (Eddie Withers); Bertram Marburgh (Judge Evans); Edward Le Saint (Judge); George Hayes (Ben, the Waiter); Billy Bevan (Drunk); Kane Richmond (Young Man at Speakeasy); Sid Saylor (Evening Sun Reporter); Bob Homans (Lineup Lieutenant).

MAN OF THE WORLD (PAR, 1931) 71 M.

Directors, Richard Wallace, Edward Goodman; story-screenplay, Herman J. Mankiewicz; sound, H. M. Lindgren; camera, Victor Milner.

William Powell (Michael Trevor); Carole Lombard (Mary Kendall); Wynne Gibson (Irene Hoffa); Guy Kibbee (Harold Taylor); Lawrence Gray (Frank Thompson); Tom Ricketts (Mr. Bradkin); Andre Cheron (Victor); George Chandler (Fred); Tom Costello (Spade Henderson); Maud Truax (Mrs. Jowitt).

LADIES' MAN (PAR, 1931) 70 M.

Director, Lothar Mendes; story, Rupert Hughes; screenplay, Herman J. Mankiewicz; sound, H. M. Lindgreen; camera, Victor Milner.

William Powell (James Darricott); Kay Francis (Norma Page); Carole Lombard (Rachel Fendley); Gilbert Emery (Horace Fendley); Olive Tell (Mrs. Fendley); Martin Burton (Anthony Fendley); John Holland (Peyton Weldon); Frank Atkinson (Valet); Maude Turner Gordon (Therese Bianton).

THE ROAD TO SINGAPORE (WB, 1931) 70 M.

Director, Alfred E. Green; based on the play Heat Wave by Roland Pertwee and a story by Denise Robins; screenplay, J. Grubb Alexander; camera, Robert Kurrle; editor, William Holmes.

William Powell (Hugh Dawltry); Doris Kenyon (Philippa Crosby); Marian Marsh (Rene); Alison Skipworth (Mrs. Wey-Smith); Lumsden Hare (Wey-Smith); Louis Calhern (Dr. George March); Ethel Griffies (Mrs. Everard); Arthur Clayton (Mr. Everard); A. E. Anson (Dr. Muir); Douglas Gerrard (Simpson); H. Reynolds (Duckworth); Colin Campbell (Reginald); Amar N. Sharma (Khan); Huspin Ansari (Ali); Tyrell Davis (Nikki); Margaret Martin (Ayah).

HIGH PRESSURE (WB, 1932) 74 M.

Director, Mervyn Le Roy; based on the story "Hot Money" by S. J. Peters; screenplay, Joseph Jackson; camera, Robert Kurrle; editor, Ralph Dawson.

William Powell (Gar Evans); Evelyn Brent (Francine); George Sidney (Colonel Ginsburg); Frank McHugh (Mike Donoghey); Guy Kibbee (Clifford Gray); Evalyn Knapp (Helen); Ben Alexander (Geoffrey); Harry Beresford (Dr. Rudolph); John Wray (Jimmy Moore); Charles Judels (Salvatore); Luis Alberni (Colombo); Lucien Littlefield (Oscar Brown); Charles Middleton (Banks); Alison Skipworth (Mrs. Miller); Harold Waldridge (Vanderbilt); Lilian Bond (Millie); Maurice Black (Poppolus); Bobby Watson (The Baron).

JEWEL ROBBERY (WB, 1932) 68 M.

Director, William Dieterle; based on the play by Ladislaus Fodor: screenplay, Erwin Gelsey; camera, Robert Kurrle; editor, Ralph Dawson.

William Powell (The Robber); Kay Francis (Baroness Teri von Horhenfels); Hardie Albright (Paul); Andre Luguet (Count Andre); Henry Kolker (Baron Franz von Horhenfels); Spencer Charters (Johann Christian Lenz); Alan Mowbray (Fritz); Helen Vinson (Marianne); Lawrence Grant (Johann Christian); Jacques Vanaire (Manager); Harold Minjur (Clark); Ivan Linow (Chauffeur); Charles Coleman (Charles, the Butler); Ruth Donnelly (Berta, the Maid); Clarence Wilson (The Commissionery); Leo White (Assistant Robber); Donald Brodie, Eddie Kane (Robbers); William Elliott (Girl-Chasing Gendarme).

ONE WAY PASSAGE (WB, 1932) 69 M.

Director, Tay Garnett; story, Robert Lord; screenplay, Wilson Mizner, Joseph Jackson; camera, Robert Kurrle; editor, Ralph Dawson.

William Powell (Dan Hardesty); Kay Francis (Joan Ames); Frank McHugh (Skippy); Aline MacMahon [Betty (The Countess)]; Warren Hymer (Steve Burke); Frederick Burton (Doctor); Douglas Gerrard (Sir Harold); Herbert Mundin (Steward); Wilson Mizner (Singing Drunk); Mike Donlin (Hong Kong Bartender); Roscoe Karns (Bartender on Ship); Dewey Robinson (Honolulu Contact); Bill Halligan (Agua Caliente Bartender); Stanley Fields (Captain); Willie Fung (Curio Dealer); Heinie Conklin (Singer); Allan Lane, Ruth Hall (Friends); Harry Seymour (Ship's Officer).

LAWYER MAN (WB, 1932) 68 M.

Director, William Dieterle; associate director, Stanley Logan; based on the novel by Max Trell; screenplay, Rian James, James Seymour; camera, Robert Kurrle.

William Powell (Anton Adam); Joan Blondell (Olga Michaels); Helen Vinson (Barbara Bentley); Alan Dinehart (Granville Bentley); Allen Jenkins (Izzy Levine); David Landau (John Gilmurry); Claire Dodd (Virginia St. Johns); Sheila Terry (Flo); Kenneth Thomson (Dr. Frank Gresham); Jack La-Rue (Spike); Rockcliffe Fellows (Kovaks); Roscoe Karns (Merritt, a Reporter); Dorothy Christy (Chorus Girl); Ann Brody (Mrs. Levine); Curley Wright (Guiseppi); Edward McWade (Moyle); Tom Kennedy (Jake, the Iceman); Sterling

Holloway (Olga's Dining Friend); Vaughn Taylor (Reporter); Wade Boteler (Court Officer); Hooper Atchley (Anton's Aide); Irving Bacon (Court Guard); Frederick Burton (Judge); Henry Hall (Juror); Wilfred Lucas (Jury Foreman); Dewey Robinson (Client).

PRIVATE DETECTIVE 62 (WB, 1933) 67 M.

Director, Michael Curtiz; based on the short story by Raoul Whitfield; screenplay, Rian James; art director, Jack Okey; camera, Tony Gaudio.

William Powell (Donald Free); Margaret Lindsay (Janet Reynolds); Ruth Donnelly (Amy Moran); Gordon Westcott (Tony Bandor); James Bell (Whitey); Arthur Byron (Tracey); Natalie Moorhead (Helen Burns); Sheila Terry (Mrs. Wright); Arthur Hohl (Dan Hogan); Hobart Cavanaugh (Harcourt S. Burns); Theresa Harris (Maid); Renee Whitney (Alice); Ann Hovey (Rose); Irving Bacon (Cab Driver); Georges Renavent (Captain La Farge); Eddie Phillips (Lover); Toby Wing (Girl Friend); Pat Wing (Secretary); Eddie Dunn (Doorman); George Brent (Club Extra); Bill Elliott (Gambling Kibitzer); Rolfe Sedan (Casino Man); Harry Seymour (Gambler); Charles Wilson, Heinie Conklin (Bartenders); Charles Lane (Process Server).

Television title: MAN KILLER.

DOUBLE HARNESS (RKO, 1933) 69 ½ M.

Executive producer, Merian C. Cooper; associate producer, Kenneth Macgowan; director, John Cromwell; based on the play by Edward P. Montgomery; adaptor, Jane Murfin; art directors, Van Nest Polglase, Charles Kerk; music director, Max Steiner; sound, George D. Ellis; camera, J. Roy Hunt; editor, George Nicholls, Jr.

Ann Harding (Joan Colby); William Powell (John Fletcher); Henry Stephenson (Colonel Colby); Lilian Bond (Monica Page); George Meeker (Dennis); Lucile Browne (Valerie Colby); Reginald Owen (Butler); Kay Hammond (Eleanor Weston); Leigh Allen (Leonard Weston); Hugh Huntley (Farley Drake); Wallis Clark (Postmaster General); Fredric Santley (Shop Owner).

THE KENNEL MURDER CASE (WB, 1933) 73 M.

Director, Michael Curtiz; based on the novel by S. S. Van Dine; screenplay, Robert N. Lee, Peter Milner; art director, Jack Okey; camera, William Reese; editor, Harold McLarnin.

William Powell (Philo Vance); Mary Astor (Hilda Lake); Eugene Pallette (Sergeant Heath); Ralph Morgan (Raymond Wrede); Helen Vinson (Doris Delafield); Jack LaRue (Eduardo Grassi); Paul Cavanagh (Sir Bruce MacDonald); Robert Barrat (Archer Coe); Arthur Hohl (Gamble); Henry O'Neill (Dubois); Robert McWade (John F. X. Markham); Frank Conroy (Brisbane Coe); Etienne Girardot (Dr. Doremus); Spencer Charters (Snitkin); Charles Wilson (Hennessey); James Lee (Liang); Harry Allen (Sandy, the Dog Trainer); George, Chandler (Reporter); Milton Kibbee (Charlie Adler, the Reporter); Wade Boteler (Sergeant); Leo White (Desk Clerk); Don Brodie (Photographer); James Burke (Cop); Monte Vandergrift (Detective).

FASHIONS OF 1934 (FN, 1934) 77 M.

Producer, Henry Blanke; director, William Dieterle; story, Harry Collins, Warren Duff; screenplay, F. Hugh Herbert, Gene Markey, Kathryn Scola, Carl Erickson; songs, Sammy Fain and Irving Kahal; music director, Leo F. Forbstein; choreography-dance stager, Busby Berkeley; art directors, Jack Okey, Willy Pogany; gowns, Orry-Kelly; camera, William Rees; editor, Jack Killifer.

William Powell (Sherwood Nash); Bette Davis (Lynn Mason); Frank McHugh (Snap); Verree Teasdale [Grand Duchess Alix (Mable McGuire)]; Reginald Owen (Oscar Baroque); Hobart Cavanaugh (M. Gautier); Henry O'Neill (Duryea); Phillip Reed (Jimmy); Hugh Herbert (Joe Ward); Gordon Westcott (Harry Brent); Dorothy Burgess (Glenda); Etienne Girardot (Glass); William Burress (Feldman); Nella Walker

(Mrs. Van Tyle); Spencer Charters (Telephone Man); George Humbert (Caponelli); Frank Darien (Jules); Harry Beresford (Book Seller); Helen Freeman (Margot); Tibby (Lynn's Scotch Terrier Dog); Sam McDaniel (Cleaning Man); Lee Phelps (Desk Clerk); Arthur Treacher (Butler); Martin Kosleck (Dance Director); Jane Darwell (Dowager); George Renavent (Fashion Salon Owner); Eric Wilton (Duchess' Butler); Laura Treadwell (Woman); Juliet Ware (Girl).

MANHATTAN MELODRAMA (MGM, 1934) 93 M.

Director, W. S. Van Dyke; story, Arthur Caesar; screenplay, Oliver T. Marsh, Oliver H. P. Garrett, Joseph L. Mankiewicz; song, Richard Rodgers and Lorenz Hart; camera, James Wong Howe; editor, Ben Lewis.

Clark Gable (Blackie Gallagher); William Powell (Jim Wade); Myrna Loy (Eleanor Parker); Leo Carrillo (Father Joe); Nat Pendleton (Spud); George Sidney (Pappa Rosen); Isabel Jewell (Annabelle); Muriel Evans (Tootsie); Thomas Jackson (Snow); Claudelle Kaye (Miss Adams); Frank Conroy (Blackie's Attorney); Noel Madison (Mannie Arnold); Mickey Rooney (Blackie at Age Twelve); Jimmy Swenson (Jim at Age Twelve); Vernon Dent (Dancer on Boat); Pat Moriarity (Heckler); Leonid Kinskey (Trotskyite); Edward Van Sloan (Yacht Captain Swenson); George Irving (Politician); Emmett Vogan (Assistant Prosecutor); Lee Phelps (Bailiff); Sam McDaniel (Black Convict); Samuel S. Hinds (Warden); Wade Boteler (Guard); Shirley Ross (Cotton Club Singer); John Marston (Coates); Charles Dunbar (Panhandler); Leslie Preston (Jim's Dance Partner); Harrison Greene (Eleanor's Dance Partner); Jay Eaton (Drunk); Herman Bing (German Proprietor); Stanley Taylor (Police Interne); Jim James (Chemin De Fer Dealer); Lew Harvey (Crap Dealer); Charles R. Moore (Black Boy in Speakeasy); William N. Bailey, King Mojave, W. R. Walsh (Croupiers); Harry Seymour (Piano Player); Landers Stevens (Inspector of Police); Allen Thompson (Spectator on Street); G. Pat Collins (Miller in Prison); James C. Eagles (Boy in Prison); Don Brodie, Ralph McCullough, Eddie Hart (Reporters); Garry Owen (Campaign Manager); Bert Russell (Blind Beggar); Lee Shumway, Carl Stockdale, Jack Kenny (Policemen); Curtis Benton (Announcer); Dixie Lonton (Irish Woman); Pepi Sinoff (Jewish Woman); Bert Sprotte, William Irving (German Note Holders); Donald Haynes (Stud); Alexander Melesh (Master of Ceremonies); Henry Roquemore (Band Leader); Jack Lipson (Uncle Angus); Leo Lance (Trotsky); Stanley Blystone, William Augustin (Detectives); Oscar Pafel (Assembly Speaker).

THE KEY (WB, 1934) 72 M.

Director, Michael Curtiz; based on the play by R. Gore Browne, J. L. Hardy; screenplay, Laird Doyle; art director, Robert Haas; camera, Ernest Haller; editors, William Clemens, Thomas Richards.

William Powell (Captain Tennant); Edna Best (Norah Kerr); Colin Clive (Andre Kerr); Halliwell Hobbes (General); Hobart Cavanaugh (Homer); Henry O'Neill (Dan); J. M. Kerrigan (O'Duffy); Donald Crisp (Conlan); Arthur Treacher (Lieutenant Merriman); Maxine Doyle (Madline O'Connor); Arthur Aylsworth (Kirby); Lew Kelly (Angular Man); Dixie Loftin (Irish Woman); Olaf Hytten, Desmond Roberts, David Thursby (Regulars); Robert Homans, Ralph Remley (Bartenders); Luke Cosgrave (Man); John Elliott (Padre); James May (Driver); Douglas Gordon (Operator); Mary McLaren (Street Walker); Pat Somerset (Lamaeur); Wyndham Standing (Officer); Aggie Herring, Katerin Clare Ward (Flower Women); Anne Shirley (Flower Girl); Gertrude Short (Barmaid); Charles Irwin (Master of Ceremonies); Lewin Cross (Dispatch Rider); Edward Cooper (Lloyd).

THE THIN MAN (MGM, 1934) 91 M.

Producer, Hunt Stromberg; director, W. S. Van Dyke II; based on the novel by Dashiell Hammett; screenplay, Albert Hackett, Frances Goodrich; assistant director, Les Selander; art directors, Cedric Gibbons, David Townsend, Edwin B.

Willis; costumes, Dolly Tree; sound, Douglas Shearer; music director, Dr. William Axt; camera, James Wong Howe; editor, Robert J. Kern.

William Powell (Nick Charles); Myrna Loy (Nora Charles); Maureen O'Sullivan (Dorothy Wynant); Nat Pendleton (Lieutenant John Guild); Minna Gombell (Mimi Wynant); Porter Hall (MacCauley); Henry Wadsworth (Tommy); William Henry (Gilbert Wynant); Harold Huber (Nunheim); Cesar Romero (Chris Jorgenson); Natalie Moorhead (Julia Wolf); Edward Brophy (Joe Morelli); Thomas Jackson, Creighton Hale, Phil Tead, Nick Copeland, Dink Templeton (Reporters); Ruth Channing (Mrs. Jorgenson); Edward Ellis (Clyde Wynant); Gertrude Short (Marion); Clay Clement (Quinn); Cyril Thornton (Tanner); Robert E. Homans (Bill, the Detective); Raymond Brown (Dr. Walton); Douglas Fowley, Sherry Hall (Taxi Drivers); Polly Bailey, Dixie Laughton (Janitresses); Arthur Belasco, Ed Hearn, Garry Owen (Detectives); Fred Malatesta (Headwaiter); Rolfe Sedan, Leo White (Waiters); Walter Long (Stutsy Burke); Kenneth Gibson (Apartment Clerk); Tui Lorraine (Stenographer); Bert Roach (Foster); Huey White (Tefler); Ben Taggart (Police Captain); Charles Williams (Fight Manager); John Larkin (Porter); Harry Tenbrook (Guest); Pat Flaherty (Cop/Fighter).

EVELYN PRENTICE (MGM, 1934) 80 M.

Producer, John W. Considine, Jr.; director, William K. Howard; based on the novel by W. E. Woodward; screenplay, Lenore Coffee; music, Oscar Raclin; art directors, Cedric Gibbons, Arnold Gillespie, Edwin B. Willis; wardrobe, Dolly Tree; camera, Charles G. Clarke; editor, Frank Hull.

Myrna Loy (Evelyn Prentice); William Powell (John Prentice); Una Merkel (Amy Drexel); Harvey Stephens (Lawrence Kennard); Isabel Jewell (Judith Wilson); Rosalind Russell (Nancy Harrison); Henry Wadsworth (Chester Wylie); Edward Brophy (Eddie Delaney); Cora Sue Collins (Dorothy Prentice); Jessie Ralph (Mrs. Blake); Perry Ivins (Dr. Gillette); Sam Flint (Dr. Lyons); Pat O'Malley (Detective Pat Thompson); J. P. McGowan (Detective Mack Clark); Jack Mulhall (Gregory); Clarence Hummel Wilson (Public Defender); Mariska Aldrich (Matron); Herman Bing (Klein, the Antique Dealer); Wilbur Mack, Garry Owen, Phil Tead (Reporters); Francis McDonald (Charles, the Chauffeur); Jack Mack (Albert, the Butler); Milton Owen (Waiter); Samuel S. Hinds (Newton); Georgia Caine (Mrs. Newton); John Hyams (Mr. Humphreys); Howard Hickman (Mr. Whitlock); Richard Tucker (Mr. Dillingham); Sam McDaniel (Porter); Billy Gilbert (Barney, the Cafe Owner); Frank Conroy (District Attorney Farley); Sherry Hall (Court Clerk); Stanley Andrews (Judge); Matty Roubert (Newsboy); Craufurd Kent (Guest); Ruth Warren (Miss Meade, John Prentice's Secretary); Bob Perry (Juryman); Larry Steers (Diner/Extra).

STAR OF MIDNIGHT (RKO, 1935) 90 M.

Producer, Pandro S. Berman; director, Stephen Roberts; based on the novel by Arthur Somers Roche; screenplay, Howard J. Green, Anthony Veiller, Edward Kaufman; music director, Max Steiner; camera, J. Roy Hunt; editor, Arthur Roberts.

William Powell (Clay Dalzell); Ginger Rogers (Donna Mantin); Paul Kelly (Jim Kinland); Gene Lockhart (Horatio Swayne); Ralph Morgan (Roger Classen); Leslie Fenton (Tim Winthrop); J. Farrell MacDonald (Inspector Doremus); Russell Hopton (Tommy Tennant); Vivien Oakland (Gerry Classon); Frank Reicher (Abe Ohlman); Robert Emmet O'Connor (Sergeant Cleary); Francis McDonald (Kinland Gangster); Paul Hurst (Corbett); Spencer Charters (Doorman); George Chandler (Witness); Sid Saylor (Deliveryman); Charles McMurphy (Officer Lewis); John Ince (Doctor); Hooper Atchley (Hotel Manager).

RECKLESS (MGM, 1935) 96 M.

Producer, David O. Selznick; director, Victor Fleming; story, Oliver Jeffries; screenplay, P. J. Wolfson; songs, Jerome Kern and Oscar Hammerstein II; Jack King, Edwin Knopf, and

Harold Adamson; Con Conrad and Herbert Magidson; camera, George Folsey; editor, Margaret Booth.

Jean Harlow (Mona); William Powell (Ned Riley); Franchot Tone (Bob Harrison); May Robson (Granny); Ted Healy (Smiley); Nat Pendleton (Blossom); Robert Light (Paul Mercer); Rosalind Russell (Jo); Henry Stephenson (Harrison); Louise Henry (Louise); James Ellison (Dale Every); Leon Waycoff (Ames) (Ralph Watson); Man Mountain Dean (Himself); Farina (Gold Dust); Allan Jones (Allan); Carl Randall, Nina Mae McKinney (Themselves).

ESCAPADE (MGM, 1935) 87 M.

Producer, Bernard H. Hyman; director, Robert Z. Leonard; based on the screenplay Maskerade by Walter Reisch; screenplay, Herman J. Mankiewicz; music, Bronislaw Kaper, Walter Jurmann; songs, Kaper, Jurmann, Gus Kahn and Harold Adamson; camera, Ernest Haller; editor, Tom Held.

William Powell (Fritz); Luise Rainer (Lepoldine); Virginia Bruce (Gerta); Mady Christians (Anita); Reginald Owen (Paul); Frank Morgan (Karl); Laura Hope Crews (Countess); Henry Travers (Concierge); Mathilde Comont (Carmen); Charles Chrysler (Doorman); Will Stanton, Billy Gilbert (Singers); Bess Flowers, Jean Fenwick, Vessie Farrell, Monya Andre, Lita Chevret (Guests); Mary MacLaren (Nurse); Scott Mattraw (Cab Driver); Lilyan Irene (Maid); Michael S. Visaroff (Doorman); Mahlon Hamilton (Announcer); Tom Ricketts (Old Dandy); Charles Requa (Young Dandy).

RENDEZVOUS (MGM, 1935) 96 M.

Producer, Lawrence Weingarten; director, William K. Howard; based on the book American Black Chamber by Herbert O. Yardley; screenplay, Bella and Samuel Spewack, P. J. Wolfson, George Oppenheimer; music, Dr. William Axt; camera, William Daniels; editor, Hugh Wynn.

William Powell [Lieutenant Bill Gordon (Anson Meridan)]; Rosalind Russell (Joel Carter); Binnie Barnes (Olivia Karloff); Lionel Atwill (Major Charles Brennan); Cesar Romero (Captain Nikki Nikolajeff); Samuel S. Hinds (John Carter, Assistant Secretary of War); Henry Stephenson (Russian Ambassador Gregory); Frank Reicher (Dr. Jackson); Charles Grapewin (Professor Martin); Leonard Mudie (Roberts); Charles Trowbridge (Secretary of War Baker); Margaret Dumont (Mrs. Hendricks); Sid Silvers (Recruiter); Eileen O'Malley (Red Cross Nurse); Murray Kinnell (de Segroff); Bert Moorehouse (Second Lieutenant); Blair Davies (Sentry); Cyril Ring, Rollo Dix (Orderlies); Earl Eby (G—Man); Henry Mowbray (Diplomat); Lowden Adams (Butler); Winter Hall (Chaplain); Sherry Hall (Private Dean, a Decoder); John Arthur (Code Room Clerk); Leonid Snegoff (Kaieneff); Jack Hatfield (Drug Store Clerk); William Stack (Headwaiter); Bob Perry (G—Man); Richard Powell (Taxi Driver); Samuel R. McDaniel (Porter); James P. Burtis (Private); James Flavin, Edgar Dearing (M.P.s); Arno Frey (Army Officer); Al Bridge (Sergeant); John Harmon (Telegrapher); Lee Phelps (Cop); Harry "Zoup" Welsh (Barber); Morgan Wallace (Gardner, Decoding Expert); Monte Vandergrift (Sailor); Rudolph Anders (Radio Operator); Sam Ash (Mexican); Sidney Bracy (Doctor's Assistant); Frank Lackteen (Customs Officer in Mexico); Charles Coleman (Doorman); Wally Maher (Reporter); Harry C. Bradley (Cashier); Lee Kohlmar (Tailor); Tom Dugan (Agent Patrick O'Reilly); Guy Usher (Ship's Captain); Milburn Stone (Carter's Aide); Theodore Von Eltz (Desk Clerk-Assistant); William V. Mong (Desk Clerk); Edward Earle (Man in Code Room); Gino Corrado (Code Room Clerk); Belle Mitchell (Mexican Peasant); Lynton Brent (Decoder); Larry Steers (Extra in Church); David Burns (Bellhop Who Speaks German); Frank O'Connor (Officer).

THE GREAT ZIEGFELD (MGM, 1936) 180 M.

Producer, Hunt Stromberg; director, Robert Z. Leonard; story-screenplay, William Anthony McGuire; art director, Cedric Gibbons; costumes, Adrian; music director, Arthur Lange; or-

chestrator, Frank Skinner; songs, Walter Donaldson and Harold Adamson; Irving Berlin; Harriet Hoctor Ballet: lyrics, Herb Magidson, ballet music, Con Conrad; choreography, Seymour Felix; sound, Douglas Shearer; camera, Oliver T. Marsh, Ray June, George Folsey, Merritt B. Gerstad; editor, William S. Gray.

William Powell (Florenz Ziegfeld); Luise Rainer (Anna Held); Myrna Loy (Billie Burke); Frank Morgan (Billings); Reginald Owen (Sampston); Nat Pendleton (Sandow); Virginia Bruce (Audrey Lane); Ernest Cossart (Sidney); Robert Greig (Joe); Raymond Walburn (Sage); Fannie Brice (Herself); Jean Chatburn (Mary Lou); Ann Pennington (Herself); Ray Bolger (Himself); Harriett Hoctor (Herself); Charles Trowbridge (Julian Mitchell); Gilda Gray (Herself); A. A. Trimble (Will Rogers); Joan Holland (Patricia Ziegfeld); Buddy Doyle (Eddie Cantor); Charles Judels (Pierre); Leon Errol (Himself); Marcelle Corday (Marie); Esther Muir (Prima Donna); Herman Bing (Customer); Paul Irving (Erlanger); William Demarest (Gene Buck); Alfred P. James (Stage Door Man); Miss Morocco (Little Egypt); Suzanne Kaaren (Miss Blair); Sarah Edwards (Wardrobe Woman); James P. Burtis (Bill); Mickey Daniel (Telegraph Boy); William Griffith (Husband); Grace Hayle (Wife); Richard Tucker, Clay Clement, Lawrence Wheat, Selmer Jackson (Customers); Alice Keating (Alice); Rosina Lawrence (Marilyn Miller); Jack Baxley (Detective); Charles Coleman (Carriage Starter); Eric Wilton (Desk Clerk); Mary Howard (Miss Carlisle); Bert Hanlon (Jim); Evelyn Dockson (Fat Woman); Franklyn Ardell (Allen); John Larkin (Sam); David Burns (Clarence); Phil Tead (Press Agent); Susan Fleming (Girl with Sage); Adrienne d'Ambricourt (Wife of French Ambassador); Charles Fallon (French Ambassador); Boothe Howard (Willie Zimmerman); Edwin Maxwell (Charles Froman); Ruth Gillette (Lillian Russell); John Hyams (Dave Stamper); Wallis Clark (Broker); Ray Brown (Inspector Doyle); Pat Nixon (Extra).

THE EX-MRS. BRADFORD (RKO, 1936) 87 M.

Associate producer, Edward Kaufman; director, Stephen Roberts; story, James Edward Grant; screenplay, Anthony Veiller; music director, Roy Webb; camera, J. Roy Hunt; editor, Arthur Roberts.

William Powell (Dr. Lawrence Bradford); Jean Arthur (Paula Bradford); James Gleason (Inspector Corrigan); Eric Blore (Stokes); Robert Armstrong (Nick Martel); Lila Lee (Miss Prentiss); Grant Mitchell (Mr. Summers); Erin O'Brien-Moore (Mrs. Summers); Ralph Morgan (Mr. Hutchins); Lucile Gleason (Mrs. Hutchins); Frank M. Thomas (Salsbury); Frank Reicher (Henry Strand); Charles Richman (Turf Club President); John Sheehan (Murphy); Paul Fix (Lou Pender); Johnny Arthur (Frankenstein Process Server); Spencer Charters (Coroner); James Donlan (Cabby); Dorothy Granger (Receptionist); Stanley Blystone (Police Radio Operator); Sid Saylor (Detective); Rollo Lloyd (Landlord); Charles McMurphy (Cop); Sam Hayes (Race Announcer); Edward McWade (Minister—on Film); John Dilson (Analyst).

MY MAN GODFREY (UNIV, 1936) 93 M.

Producer-director, Gregory La Cava; based on the novel by Eric Hatch; screenplay, Morrie Ryskind, Hatch, La Cava; music Charles Previn; assistant director, Scott R. Beal; art director, Charles D. Hall; camera, Ted Tetzlaff; editor, Ted Kent.

William Powell (Godfrey Parke); Carole Lombard (Irene Bullock); Alice Brady (Angelica Bullock); Gail Patrick (Cornelia Bullock); Jean Dixon (Molly); Eugene Pallette (Alexander Bullock); Alan Mowbray (Tommy Gray); Mischa Auer (Carlo); Robert Light (Faithful George); Pat Flaherty (Mike); Franklin Pangborn (Score Keeper); Robert Perry (Bob, the Hobo); Selmer Jackson (Blake, the Guest); Grace Field, Kathryn Perry, Harley Wood, Elaine Cockrane, David Horsley, Philip Merrick (Socialites); Ernie Adams (Forgotten Man); Phyllis Crane (Party Guest); Grady Sutton (Von Rumple); Jack Chefe (Road Waiter); Eddie Fetherston (Process Server); Edward Gargan, James Flavin (Detectives); Arthur Wanzer (Man); Art

Singley (Chauffeur); Reginald Mason (Mayor); Jane Wyman (Girl at Party); Bess Flowers (Guest).

LIBELED LADY (MGM, 1936) 98 M.

Producer, Lawrence Weingarten; director, Jack Conway; story, Wallace Sullivan; screenplay, Maurine Watkins, Howard Emmett Rogers, George Oppenheimer; art directors, Cedric Gibbons, William A. Hornung, set decorator, Edwin B. Willis; music, Dr. William Axt; wardrobe, Dolly Tree, sound, Douglas Shearer; camera, Norbert Brodine; editor, Frederick Y. Smith.

William Powell (Bill Chandler); Myrna Loy (Connie Allenbury); Jean Harlow (Gladys Benton); Spencer Tracy (Warren Haggerty); Walter Connolly (James B. Allenbury); Charley Grapewin (Hollis Bane); Cora Witherspoon (Mrs. Burns-Norvell); E. E. Clive (Evans, the Fishing Instructor); Bunny Lauri Beatty (Babs Burns-Norvell); Otto Yamaoka (Ching); Charles Trowbridge (Graham); Spencer Charters (Magistrate McCall); George Chandler (Bellhop); Greta Meyer (Connie's Maid); William Benedict (Joe); Hal K. Dawson (Harvey Allen); Fred Graham (Press Man); William Stack (Editor); Selmer Jackson (Adams, editor of Washington *Chronicle*); William Newell (Divorce Detective); Duke York (Taxi Driver); Pat West (Detective); Ed Stanley (Clerk); Wally Maher, Pinky Parker, Harry Lash, Pat Somerset (Photographers); Tom Mahoney (Alex); Richard Tucker (Barker); Libby Taylor (Tiny, Gladys' Maid); Eric Lonsdale, Olaf Hytten (Reporters); Charles Irwin (Steward); Eddie Shubert (Mac, the Circulation Editor); George Davis (Waiter); Thomas Pogue (Minister); Myra Marsh (Secretary); Hattie McDaniel (Maid in Hall); Howard Hickman (Cable Editor); James T. Mack (Pop); Jack Mulhall, Dennis O'Keefe, Charles King (Barkers); Nick Thompson (Hot Dog Stand Man); Ines Palange (Fortune Teller); Harry C. Bradley (Justice of Peace); Bodil Ann Rosing (Wife of Justice of Peace); Barnett Parker (Butler); Robin Adair (Palmer, the English Reporter); Charles Croker King (Charles Archibald, the Lawyer); Sherry Hall (Denver *Courier* Editor); Alphonse Martel (Table Captain); Eric Wilton (Steward on Dock); Jay Eaton, Ralph Brooks (Dance Extras).

AFTER THE THIN MAN (MGM, 1936) 110 M.

Producer, Hunt Stromberg; director, W. S. Van Dyke II; story, Dashiell Hammett; screenplay, Frances Goodrich, Albert Hackett; songs, Arthur Freed and Nacio Herb Brown; Bob Wright, Chet Forrest, and Walter Donaldson; music, Herbert Stothart; art director, Cedric Gibbons; sound, Douglas Shearer; camera, Oliver T. Marsh; editor, Robert J. Kern.

Myrna Loy (Nora Charles); William Powell (Nick Charles); James Stewart (David Graham); Joseph Calleia (Dancer); Elissa Landi (Selma Landis); Jessie Ralph (Aunt Katherine Forrest); Alan Marshal (Robert Landis); Sam Levene (Lieutenant Abrams); Penny Singleton (Polly Byrnes); Dorothy Vaughn (Charlotte); Maude Turner Gordon (Helen); Teddy Hart (Floyd Casper); William Law (Lum Kee); William Burress (General); Thomas Pogue (William); George Zucco (Dr. Adolph Kammer); Tom Ricketts (Henry, the Butler); Paul Fix (Phil Byrnes); Joe Caits (Joe); Joe Phillips (Willie); Edith Kingdon (Hattie); John T. Murray (Jerry); John Kelly (Harold); Clarence Kolb (Lucius); Zeffie Tilbury (Lucy); Donald Briggs, Frederic Santley, Jack Norton (Reporters); Baldwin Cooke, Sherry Hall, Jack E. Raymond (Photographers); Ed Dearing (Bill, the San Francisco Policeman); Dick Rush (San Francisco Detective); Monte Vandergrift, Eddie Allen, Jimmy Lucas (Men); Heinie Conklin (Trainman); Mary Gordon (Rose, the Cook); Ben Hall (Butcher Boy); George H. Reed (Porter); John Butler (Racetrack Tout); Vince Barnett (Wrestler's Manager); Ethel Jackson (Girl with Fireman); Arthur Housman (Man Rehearsing Welcome Speech); Jack Daley (Bartender); Bert Scott (Man at Piano); George Guhl (San Francisco Police Captain); Norman Willis (Fireman); Edith Craig (Girl with Fireman); Kewpie Martin (Boy Friend of Girl Standing on Hands); Bert Lindley (Station Agent); James Blaine (San Francisco Policeman); Guy Usher (Chief of Detectives); Bob Murphy (Arresting Detective); Harry Tyler (Fingers); Bobby Watson (Leader of Late Crowd); Eric Wilton (Peter, the Butler); Henry Roquemore (Actor's Agent); Constantine Romanoff (Wrestler); Sam McDaniel (Pullman Porter); Ernie Alexander (Filing Clerk in Morgue); Louis Natheaux (Racetrack Tout); Jonathan Hale (Night City Editor); Jennie Roberts (Girl Who Works with Jerry); Charlie Arnt (Drunk); Harvey Parry (Man Who Stands on Hands); Jesse Graves (Red Cap); Alice H. Smith (Emily); Richard Powell (Surprised Policeman); Cecil Elliott, Phyllis Coghlan (Servants); Frank Otto (Taxi Driver); Jack Adair (Escort of Dizzy Blonde); Irene Coleman, Claire Rochelle, Jean Barry, Jane Tallant (Chorus Girls); Sue Moore (Sexy Blonde); Edith Trivers (Hat Check Girl); George Taylor (Eddie); Lee Phelps (Flop House Proprietor); Chester Gan (Chinese Waiter); Richard Loo (Chinese Headwaiter); Lew Harvey, Jimmy Brewster (Thugs); Harlan Briggs (Burton Forrest); Billy Benedict (Newsboy); Murray Alper (Kid); Charles Trowbridge (Police Examiner); Eadie Adams (Girl).

THE LAST OF MRS. CHEYNEY (MGM, 1937) 98 M.

Associate producer, Lawrence Weingarten; director, Richard Boleslawski; based on the play by Frederick Lonsdale; screenplay, Leon Gordon, Samson Raphaelson, Monckton Hoffe; art director, Cedric Gibbons; music, Dr. William Axt; sound, Douglas Shearer; camera, George Folsey; editor, Frank Sullivan.

Joan Crawford (Fay Cheyney); William Powell (Charles); Robert Montgomery (Arthur); Frank Morgan (Lord Kelton); Jessie Ralph (Duchess); Nigel Bruce (Willie); Colleen Clare (Joan); Benita Hume (Kitty); Ralph Forbes (Cousin John); Aileen Pringle (Maria); Melville Cooper (William); Leonard Carey (Ames); Sara Haden (Anna); Lumsden Hare (Inspector Witherspoon); Wallis Clark (George); Barnett Parker (Purser).

THE EMPEROR'S CANDLESTICKS (MGM, 1937) 89 M.

Producer, John W. Considine, Jr.; director, George Fitzmaurice; based on the novel by Baroness Orczy; screenplay, Monckton Hoffe, Harold Goldman; montage, Slavko Vorkapich; art director, Cedric Gibbons; music, Franz Waxman; sound, Douglas Shearer; camera, Harold Rosson; editor, Conrad A. Nervig.

William Powell (Wolensky); Luise Rainer (Countess Muranova); Frank Morgan (Colonel Baron Suroff); Maureen O'-Sullivan (Maria); Henry Stephenson (Prince Johann); Robert Young (Grand Duke Peter); Douglass Dumbrille (Korun); Bernadene Hayes (Mitzi); Donald Kirke (Antone); Charles Waldron (Dr. Malcher); Barnett Parker (Rudolph); Frank Reicher (Pavloff); Paul Porcasi (Santuzzi); Bert Roach (Porter); E. E. Clive (Auctioneer); Spencer Charters (Usher); Ian Wolfe (Leon); Theodore von Eltz (Adjutant); Mitchell Lewis (Plainclothesman); Egon Brecher (Chief of Police); Erville Alderson (Conductor); Clarence H. Wilson (Stationmaster); Emma Dunn (Housekeeper); Lionel Pape (Sugar Daddy); Maude Turner Gordon (Concierge); Rollo Lloyd (Jailer); Frank Conroy (Colonel Radoff); William Stack (Czar); Ramsay Hill, Olaf Hytten (Conspirators); Torben Meyer (Train Announcer); Davison Clark, Harvey Clark (Conductors); King Baggott (Customs Official); George Davis (Waiter); Russ Powell (Coachman); Clarice Sherry (Blonde); Frank Lawson (Prince Johann's Butler); Leonard Carey (Valet to Walensky); Mariska Aldrich (Ugly Woman); John Picorri (Italian Ambassador); Roland Varno (Czar's Officer); Cyril Thornton, Vernon Downing, Bruce Mitchell, George Davis, Agostino Borgato, Carole Landis (Bits).

DOUBLE WEDDING (MGM, 1937) 87 M.

Producer, Joseph L. Mankiewicz; director, Richard Thorpe; based on the play Great Love by Ferenc Molnar; screenplay, Jo Swerling; art director, Cedric Gibbons; music, Edward Ward; sound, Douglas Shearer; camera, William Daniels; editor, Frank Sullivan.

William Powell (Charles Lodge); Myrna Loy (Margit Ag-

new); John Beal (Waldo Beaver); Florence Rice (Irene Agnew); Jessie Ralph (Mrs. Kensington-Bly); Edgar Kennedy (Spike); Sidney Toler (Keough); Barnett Parker (Flint); Katharine Alexander (Claire Lodge); Priscilla Lawson (Felice); Mary Gordon (Mrs. Keough); Donald Meek (Reverend Dr. Flynn); Henry Taylor (Angelo); Bert Roach (Shrank); Irving Lipschultz (Violinist); Doodles Weaver (Fiddle Player); Charles Coleman (Mrs. Bly's Butler); Billy Dooley (Saxophonist); Roger Moore (Pianist); Oscar O'Shea (Turnkey); Josephine Whittell (Woman Customer); E. Alyn Warren (Al); Jules Cowles (Gus); Jack Baxley (Bartender); Mitchell Lewis (Orator); Gwen Lee (Woman in Crowd); John "Skins" Miller (Pickpocket); Roger Gray (Mike); George Guhl (Pete); Jack Dougherty (Chauffeur); G. Pat Collins (Mounted Policeman).

THE BARONESS AND THE BUTLER (20th, 1938) 75 M.

Producer, Darryl F. Zanuck; associate producer, Raymond Griffith; director, Walter Lang; based on a play by Ladislaus Bus-Fekete; screenplay, Sam Hellman, Lamar Trotti, Kathryn Scola; art directors, Bernard Herzbrun, Hans Peter, Thomas Little; music director, Louis Silvers; camera, Arthur Miller; editor, Barbara McLean.

William Powell (Johann); Annabella (Katrina); Henry Stephenson (Count); Nigel Bruce (Major Andrea); Helen Westley (Countess); Joseph Schildkraut (Georg); J. Edward Bromberg (Zorda); Lynn Bari (Klari); Alphonz Ethier (President); Paul McVey (Clerk); Ruth Peterson (Theresa); Maurice Cass (Announcer); Margaret Irving (Princess); Ivan Simpson (Dorno); Sidney Bracy, Frank Baker, Wilfred Lucas (Members of Parliament); John Bleifer (Chauffeur); Edward Cooper, Lowden Adams, Denis d'Auburn (Footmen); Burr Caruth (Gardener); Eleanor Wesselhoeft (Housekeeper); Antonio Filauri (Cook); Bert Sprotte, Glen Cavender (Peasants); George Davis (Electrician); Claire Du Brey (Secretary); Tom Ricketts (Old Man); Edward Keane (Guard); Alex Pollard (Butler); William Sabbet, Jack Vlaskin, Esther Brodelet, Lucille Miller (Gypsy Dancers); Doris Lloyd, Charlotte Wynters (Bit Women); Inez Palange (Gypsy Fortune Teller).

ANOTHER THIN MAN (MGM, 1939) 102 M.

Producer, Hunt Stromberg; director, W. S. Van Dyke II; screenplay, Dashiell Hammett; art director, Cedric Gibbons; music, Edward Ward; sound, Douglas Shearer; camera, Oliver T. Marsh, William Daniels; editor, Frederick Y. Smith.

William Powell (Nick Charles); Myrna Loy (Nora Charles); C. Aubrey Smith (Colonel Burr MacFay); Otto Kruger (Van Slack, the Assistant District Attorney); Nat Pendleton (Lieutenant Guild); Virginia Grey (Lois MacFay); Tom Neal (Freddie Coleman); Muriel Hutchinson (Smitty); Ruth Hussey [Dorothy Waters (Linda Mills)]; Sheldon Leonard (Phil Church); Phyllis Gordon (Mrs. Bellam); Don Costello ("Diamond Back" Vogel); Patric Knowles (Dudley Horn); Harry Bellaver ("Creeps" Binder); Abner Biberman (Dum-Dum); Marjorie Main (Mrs. Dolley, the Landlady); Asta (Himself); Horace McMahon (MacFay's Chauffeur); Nell Craig (Maid); William Anthony Poulsen (Nicky, Jr.); Milton Kibbee (Les, the Deputy); Walter Fenner, Thomas Jackson (Detectives); Charles Brokaw, Frank Coletti, Edwin Parker, William Tannen (Troopers); Edward Gargan (Quinn, the Detective); Joseph Dowling, Matty Fain (Thugs); Bert Roach (Cookie, the Drinker); Shemp Howard (Wacky, the Temporary Father); Nellie V. Nichols (Mrs. Wacky); Eddie Gribbon, Ralph Dunn (Baggage Men); George Guhl (Guard at Gate); Claire Rochelle (Telephone Operator); Winstead "Doodles" Weaver, Paul "Tiny" Newlan (Guards); Roy Barcroft (Slim, the Guard); Joe Devlin (Barney, the Bodyguard); Paul E. Burns (Station Agent); Milton Parsons (Medical Examiner); Dick Elliott (Investigator); Jack Gardner (Driver); Nestor Paiva (Cuban Proprietor); Anita Camargo (Hat Check Girl); Gladden James (Fingerprint Man); Charles Sherlock (Police Photographer); John Kelly (Father); Edward Hearn (Detective); Eddie Buzzard (Newsboy); Martin Garralaga (Pedro, the Informant); Alexander D'Arcy (South American); Jack Clifford, Howard Mitchell, William Pagan, Lee C. Shumway (Policemen); Stanley Taylor (Taxi Driver); Frank Sully (Pete); Murray Alper (Louie); Frank Moran (Butch); James Guilfoyle (Jake); Richard Calderon (Wacky's Baby); James G. Blaine (Policeman in Charles' Suite); Rosemary Grimes, Blanca Vischer, Sandra Andreva, Tina Menard, Toni LaRue (Cafe Bits); Guy Rett, Alberto Morin, Alphonse Martel (Waiters).

I LOVE YOU AGAIN (MGM, 1940) 99 M.

Director, W. S. Van Dyke II; based on the novel by Leon Gordon, Maurine Watkins; screenplay, Charles Lederer, George Oppenheimer, Harry Kurnitz; music director, Franz Waxman; art director, Cedric Gibbons; sound, Douglas Shearer; camera, Oliver T. Marsh; editor, Gene Ruggiero.

William Powell (Larry Wilson/George Carey); Myrna Loy (Kay Wilson); Frank McHugh (Doc Ryan); Edmund Lowe (Duke Sheldon); Donald Douglas (Herbert); Nella Walker (Kay's Mother); Pierre Watkin (Mr. Sims); Paul Stanton (Mr. Littlejohn); Morgan Wallace (Mr. Belenson); Charles Arnt (Billings); Harlan Briggs (Mayor Carver); Dix Davis (Corporal Belenson); Carl "Alfalfa" Switzer (Harkspur, Jr.); Bobby Blake (Littlejohn, Jr.); Winifred Harris (Mrs. Watkins); Mary Currier (Mrs. Gordon); Hazel Keener (Mrs. Lederer); Bea Nigro (Mrs. Kurnitz); Leni Lynn (Maurine); Edward Earle (Mr. Watkins); Harry Hayden (Mr. Wayne); Harry Lash (Steward); William Tannen (Clerk); Ray Teal (Watchman); Barbara Bedford (Miss Stingecombe); George Lloyd (Policeman Sergeant); Charles Wagenheim (Fingerprint Man); Jack Mulhall, Jason Robards, Sr., John Dilson, Ted Thomson, Hooper Atchley, Warren Rock, Paul Parry, Hal Cooke, Raymond Bailey (Men); Nell Craig (Maid); Arthur Hoyt (Floorwalker); Joe Bernard (Watchman); Jack Daley (Band Leader); Eric Wilton (Headwaiter); George Lollier (Police Photographer); Howard Mitchell (Ranger Leader); Sally Payne, Claire Rochelle, Gladys Blake (Salesgirls); Edward Hearn (Guard).

LOVE CRAZY (MGM, 1941) 100 M.

Producer, Pandro S. Berman; director, Jack Conway; story, David Hertz, William Ludwig; screenplay, Ludwig, Charles Lederer, Hertz; art director, Cedric Gibbons; music, David Snell; sound, Douglas Shearer; camera, Ray June; editor, Ben Lewis.

William Powell (Steven Ireland); Myrna Loy (Susan Ireland); Gail Patrick (Isobel Grayson); Jack Carson (Ward Willoughby); Florence Bates (Mrs. Cooper); Sidney Blackmer (George Hennie); Vladimir Sokoloff (Dr. Klugle); Kathleen Lockhart (Mrs. Bristol); Sig Rumann (Dr. Wuthering); Donald MacBride ("Pinky" Grayson); Sara Haden (Cecilia Landis); Fern Emmett (Martha); Elisha Cook, Jr. (Elevator Boy); Joseph Crehan (Judge); Jimmy Ames (Taxi Driver); George Meeker (DeWest); Aldrich Bowker (Doorman); George Guhl, Harry Fleischmann (Drivers); Barbara Bedford (Secretary); Clarence Muse (Robert); Jay Eaton, Larry Steers, James H. McNamara, Richard Kipling, Broderick O'Farrell (Guests); Ian Wolfe, Edward Van Sloan, George Irving, Douglas Wood, Byron Shores, Roy Gordon, Emmett Vogan, Selmer Jackson (Doctors); William Tannen (Attendant); Jesse Graves (Butler); Jack Mulhall (Court Clerk); Joan Barclay (Telephone Operator); Ralph Bushman, Lee Phelps, George Magrill, Bill Lally, Ken Christy (Guards); Harry Strang (Sergeant); Wade Boteler (Captain of Detectives); Ed Peil, Sr., Dick Allen, Eddie Hart, Philo McCullough, Kai Robinson, George Lollier, James Millican, Paul Palmer, Charles McMurphy, Pat Gleason, James Pierce, Rudy Steinbock (Detectives).

SHADOW OF THE THIN MAN (MGM, 1941) 97 M.

Producer, Hunt Stromberg; director, W. S. Van Dyke II; story, Harry Kurnitz; screenplay, Irving Brecher, Kurnitz; art director, Cedric Gibbons; sound, Douglas Shearer; camera, William Daniels; editor, Robert J. Kern.

William Powell (Nick Charles); Myrna Loy (Nora Charles); Barry Nelson (Paul Clarke); Donna Reed (Molly Ford); Sam Levene (Lieutenant Abrams); Alan Baxter (Whitey Barrow);

Dickie Hall (Nick Charles, Jr.); Loring Smith (Link Stephens); Joseph Anthony (Fred Macy); Henry O'Neill (Major Jason I. Sculley); Stella Adler (Claire Porter); Lou Lubin ("Rainbow" Benny Loomis); Louise Beavers (Stella); Will Wright (Maguire); Edgar Dearing (Motor Cop); Noel Cravat (Baku); Tito Vuolo (Luis); Oliver Blake (Fenster); John Dilson, Arthur Aylsworth (Coroners); James Flavin, Edward Hearn, Art Belasco, Bob Ireland, Robert Kellard (Cops); Cliff Danielson, J. Louis Smith, Jerry Jerome, Roger Moore, Buddy Roosevelt, Hal Le Sueur (Reporters); Cardiff Giant (Bouncing Tschekov); Richard Frankie Burke (Buddy Burns); Tor Johnson (Jack the Ripper); Johnnie Berkes (Paleface); John Kelly (Meatballs Murphy); Joe Oakie (Spider Webb); Jody Gilbert (Lana); Dan Tobey (Announcer); Tommy Mack (Soft Drink Vendor); Joe Devlin (Mugg); Bill Fisher, Aldrich Bowker (Watchmen); Charles Calvert (Referee); Joey Ray (Stephen's Clerk); Inez Cooper (Girl in Cab); Adeline deWalt Reynolds (Landlady); Duke York (Valentino); Seldon Bennett (Mario); Sidney Melton (Fingers); George Lloyd (Pipey); Patti Moore (Lefty's Wife); Jerry Mandy (Waiter); Hardboiled Haggerty, Eddie Simms, Abe Dinovitch, Wee Willie Davis, Sailor Vincent, Jack Roper, Harry Wilson (Muggs); Ray Teal (Cab Driver); Sam Bernard (Counterman); Ken Christy (Detective); David Dornack (Lefty's Kid); Lyle Latell, Matt Gilman, Fred Graham (Waiters with Steaks); Harry Burns (Greek Janitor); Fred Walburn (Kid on Merry-Go-Round); Arch Hendricks (Photographer); Pat McGee (Handler).

CROSSROADS (MGM, 1942) 84 M.

Producer, Edwin Knopf; director, Jack Conway; story, John Kafka, Howard Emmett Rogers; screenplay, Guy Trosper; art director, Cedric Gibbons; music, Bronislau Kaper; song, Howard Dietz and Arthur Schwartz; camera, Joseph Ruttenberg; editor, George Boemler.

William Powell (David Talbot); Hedy Lamarr (Lucienne Talbot); Claire Trevor (Michelle Allaine); Basil Rathbone (Henri Sarrow); Felix Bressart (Dr. Andre Tessier); Margaret Wycherly (Mme. Pelletier); Reginald Owen (Concierge); Philip Merivale (Commissionaire of Police); Sig Ruman (Dr. Alex Benoit); Vladimir Sokoloff (Le Duc); H. B. Warner (Prosecuting Attorney); Guy Bates Post (President of Court); Fritz Leiber (Deval); John Mylong (Baron de Lorraine); Frank Conroy (Defense Attorney); James Rennie (Martin); Bertram Marburgh (Landers); Harry Fleischmann (Assistant Defense Attorney); Louis Montez, Octavio Giraud, Enrique Acosta, Adolph Faylauer (Associate Judges); Jean Del Val (Court Clerk); Paul Weigel, Torgen Meyer (Old Men); John St. Polis (Professor); Jack Zoller (Student); Francis X. Bushman, Jr. (Giant Policeman); Christian J. Frank (Guard); Alex Davidoff (Detective); Theodore Rand (Orchestra Leader); Anna Q. Nilsson (Mme. Deval); Alphonse Martell (Headwaiter); Hector Sarno (Organ Grinder); William Edmunds (Driver); Armand Cortes (Clerk); Lester Sharpe, George Davis (Clerks); Marek Windheim (Clerk at Airport); John Picorri (Waiter); Billy Roy, Frank Morales, Jo Jo LaSavio, Adrian Kerbrat (Boys); Ferdinand Munier (Fat Man); Guy D'Ennery, Shirley McDonald, Gibson Gowland, Jack Chefe, Louis Natheaux, Edith Penn, Sandra Morgan (Reporters); Irene Shirley (Maid); Alice Ward (Nurse Receptionist); Grace Hayle (Patient); Lester Sharpe, Budd Fine (Paris Policemen).

THE YOUNGEST PROFESSION (MGM, 1943) 81 M.

Producer, B. F. Ziedman; director, Edward Buzzell; based on the book by Lillian Day; screenplay, George Oppenheimer, Charles Lederer, Leonard Spigelgass; art directors, Cedric Gibbons, Edward Carfagno; set decorators, Edwin B. Willis, Helen Conway; assistant director, Julian Silberstein; music, David Snell; sound, Wilhelm W. Brockway; camera, Charles Lawton; editor, Ralph Winters.

Virginia Weidler (Joan Lyons); Edward Arnold (Lawrence Lyons); John Carroll (Hercules); Jean Porter (Patricia Drew); Marta Linden (Edith Lyons); Dick Simmons (Douglas Sutton); Ann Ayars (Susan Thayer); Agnes Moorehead (Miss

Featherstone); Marcia Mae Jones (Vera Bailey); Raymond Roe (Schuyler); Scotty Beckett (Junior Lyons); Jessie Grayson (Lilybud); Greer Garson, William Powell, Lana Turner, Walter Pidgeon, Robert Taylor (Guest Stars); Beverly Tyler (Thyra Winters); Patricia Roe (Polly); Marjorie Gateson (Mrs. Drew); Thurston Hall (Mr. Drew); Aileen Pringle (Miss Farwood); Nora Lane (Hilda); Dorothy Christy (Sally); Mary Vallee (Mary); Gloria Tucker (Gladys); Jane Isbell (Jane); Hazel Dawn (Hazel); Beverly Boyd (Beverly); Randa Allen (Randa); Ann MacLean (Ann); Gloria Mackey (Gloria); Bobby Stebbins (Richard); Shirley Coates, Mary McCarty (Girls); Mark Daniels (Les Peterson); William Tannen (Hotel Clerk); Ann Codee (Sandra's Maid); Eddie Buzzell (Man in Theatre); George Noisom (Delivery Boy); Alice Keating (Governess); Leonard Carey (Valet); Harry Barris (Man); Herberta Williams (Hortense); Sara Haden (Salvation Army Lass); Leigh De Lacey, Vangie Beilby, Ruth Cherrington, Claire McDowell, Sandra Morgan, Leota Lorraine (Montage Bits); Ray Teal (Taxi Driver); Polly Bailey, Margaret Bert, Violet Seton, Hazel Dohlman (Governess); Dorothy Morris (Secretary); Roland Dupree, Robert Winkler (Mail Room Boys).

THE HEAVENLY BODY (MGM, 1943) 93 M.

Producer, Arthur Hornblow, Jr.; director, Alexander Hall; story, Jacques Thery; adaptor, Harry Kurnitz; screenplay, Michael Arlen, Walter Reisch; art directors, Cedric Gibbons, William Ferrari; set decorators, Edwin B. Willis, McLean Nisbet; assistant director, Bill Lewis; music, Bronislau Kaper; sound, Wilhelm W. Brockway; special effects, Arnold Gillespie; camera, Robert Planck; editor, Blanche Sewell.

William Powell (William B. Whitley); Hedy Lamarr (Vickey Whitley); James Craig (Lloyd X. Hunter); Fay Bainter (Margaret Sibyll); Henry O'Neill (Professor Stowe); Spring Byington (Nancy Potter); Robert Sully (Strand); Morris Ankrum (Dr. Green); Franco Corsaro (Sebastian Molas); Connie Gilchrist (Beulah); Max Willenz (Dr. Gurtchakoff); Earl Schenck (Forbes); Arthur Space (Pierson); Helen Freeman (Stella); Phyllis Kennedy (Ethel); Marietta Canty (Pearl Harrison); Nicodemus (Willie); Howard Mitchell (Nicholas); Dan B. Sheffield (Frank); Gertrude W. Hoffman (Mrs. Potter's Mother); Alex Melesh (Vladimir); James Basquette (Black Porter); Jac George (Accompanist); Elspeth Dudgeon (Lady); Bertram Marburgh (Old Man); Wheaton Chambers (Old Gentleman); Evllyn Dockson (Maid); Jacqueline Miller (W. U. Girl); Ralph Sanford, John Sheehan (Cops); Lloyd Ford (Ethel's Husband); Buddy Gorman (Newsboy); Cliff Nazarro (Milkman); William Sabbot (Knife Thrower); Andre Charlot (Dr. Burns); John Elliott (Professor Collier); Howard Hickman, Henry Sylvester, Gus Glassmire (Scientists); Bobby Watson (Hitler—Photo Insert); Rex Evans (Goering—Photo Insert).

THE THIN MAN GOES HOME (MGM, 1944) 100 M.

Producer, Everett Riskin; director, Richard Thorpe; based on characters created by Dashiell Hammett; story, Robert Riskin, Harry Kurnitz; screenplay, Robert Riskin, Dwight Taylor; art directors, Cedric Gibbons, Edward Carfagno; set decorator, Edward B. Willis; assistant director, Al Jennings; sound, James K. Burbridge; music, David Snell; camera, Karl Freund; editor, Ralph E. Winters.

William Powell (Nick Charles); Myrna Loy (Nora Charles); Lucile Watson (Mrs. Charles); Gloria DeHaven (Laura Ronson); Anne Revere (Crazy Mary); Harry Davenport (Dr. Charles); Helen Vinson (Helena Draque); Lloyd Corrigan (Bruce Clayworth); Donald Meek (Willie Crump); Edward Brophy (Brogam); Leon Ames (Edgar Draque); Paul Langton (Tom Clayworth); Donald MacBride (Chief MacGregory); Minor Watson (Sam Ronson); Anita Bolster (Hilda); Charles Halton (Tatum); Morris Ankrum (Willoughby); Nora Cecil (Miss Peavy); Wally Cassell (Bill Burns); Arthur Hohl (Charlie); Anthony Warde (Captain); Bill Smith, Lucille Brown (Skating Act); Mickey Harris (Contortionist); Rex Evans (Fat Man); Harry Hayden (Conductor); Connie Gilchrist (Woman with Baby); Robert Emmet O'Connor (Baggage Man); Dick Botiller

(Big Man's Companion); John Wengraf (Big Man); Ralph Brooks (Tom Burton); Jane Green (Housekeeper); Irving Bacon (Tom, the Proprietor); Virginia Sale (Tom's Wife); Garry Owen (Pool Player); Saul Gorss (Bartender); Bert May (Sailor); Chester Clute (Drunk); Clarence Muse (Porter); Tom Fadden, Joseph Greene, Sarah Edwards, Frank Jaquet (Train Passengers); Oliver Blake (Reporter); Don Wilson (Masseur); Etta McDaniel (Ronson's Maid); Tom Dugan (Slugs); Ed Gargan (Mickey); Thomas Dillon, Bill Hunter (Officers); Marjorie Wood (Montage Shot Mother); Catherine McLeod (Montage Shot Daughter); Clancy Cooper (Butcher); Joe Yule (Barber); Robert Homans (Railroad Clerk); Lee Phelps (Cop); Helyn Eby Rock, Jean Acker (Tarts); Mike Mazurki, Mitchell Lewis, Ray Teal (Men).

ZIEGFELD FOLLIES (MGM, 1946) C—110 M.

Producer, Arthur Freed; director, Vincente Minnelli; art directors, Cedric Gibbons, Merill Pye, Jack Martin Smith; set decorators, Edwin B. Willis, Mac Alper; choreography, Robert Alton; music director, Lennie Hayton; orchestrators, Conrad Salinger, Wally Heglin; music adaptor, Roger Edens; songs; Arthur Freed and Harry Warren; Arthur Freed and Earl Brent; Ralph Blane and Hugh Martin; Philip Braham and Douglas Furber; Brent and Roger Edens; Ralph Freed and Edens; Ira and George Gershwin; assistant director, Jack Greenwood; puppet sequence decors, William Ferrari; sound, Douglas Shearer; camera, George Folsey, Charles Rosher; editor, Albert Akst.

William Powell (The Great Ziegfeld); *Ziegfeld Days:* Fred Astaire, Bunin's Puppets; *Meet the Ladies:* Astaire, Lucille Ball; *Love:* Lena Horne; *This Heart of Mine:* Astaire (The Imposter); Lucille Bremer (The Princess); Count Stefenelli (The Duke); Naomi Childers (The Duchess); Helen Boice (The Countess); Robert Wayne (Retired Dyspeptic); Charles Coleman (The Major); Feodor Chaliapin (The Lieutenant); Sam Flint (The Flunky); *We Will Meet Again:* Esther Williams, James Melton; *The Interview:* Judy Garland (Herself); Rex Evans (The Butler); *When Television Comes:* Red Skelton; *The Babbit and the Bromide:* Fred Astaire, Gene Kelly; *Traviata:* James Melton, Marion Bell; *Liza:* Lena Horne, Avon Long; *The Sweepstakes Ticket:* Fannie Brice (Norma); Hume Cronyn (Monty); William Frawley (Martin); Arthur Walsh (Telegraph Boy); *Limehouse Blues:* Astaire (Tai Long); Bremer (Moy Ling); Captain George Hill, Jack Deery (Men); *Pay the Two Dollars:* Victor Moore, Edward Arnold (Themselves); Ray Teal (Special Officer); Joseph Crehan (Judge); William B. Davidson (Presiding Judge); Harry Hayden (Warden); Eddie Dunn, Garry Owen (Officers); *The Cowboy:* James Melton: *Finale:* There's Beauty Everywhere.

THE HOODLUM SAINT (MGM, 1946) 93 M.

Producer, Cliff Reid; director, Norman Taurog; screenplay, Frank Wead, James Hill; art directors, Cedric Gibbons, Harry McAffee; set decorator, Edwin B. Willis; assistant director, Horace Hough; music, Nathaniel Shilkret; sound, Douglas Shearer; special effect, Warren Newcombe; camera, Ray June; editor, Ferris Webster.

William Powell (Terry Ellerton O'Neill); Esther Williams (May Lorrison); Angela Lansbury (Dusty Millard); James Gleason (Sharp); Lewis Stone (Father Nolan); Rags Ragland (Fishface); Frank McHugh (Three–Fingers); Slim Summerville (Eel); Roman Bohnen (Father O'Doul); Charles Arnt (Cy Nolan); Louis Jean Heydt (Mike Flaherty); Charles Trowbridge (Uncle Joe Lorrison); Henry O'Neill (Lewis J. Malbery); Matt Moore (Father Duffy); Trevor Bardette (Rabbie Meyerberg); Addison Richards (Reverend Miller); Tom Dugan (Buggsy); Emma Dunn (Maggie); Mary Gordon (Trina); Ernest Anderson (Sam); Charles D. Brown (Ed Collner); Paul Langton (Burton Kinston); Al Murphy (Benny); Jack Davis, Garry Owen (Cops); Byron Foulger (J. Cornwall Travers); Will Wright (Allan Smith); Mary Lord (Mary); Sam Finn, William A. Janssen, Harry Tenbrook, Sol Davis, Phil Friedman, John George, Captain Fred Somers, Billy Engle, Al Thompson, Heinie Conklin (Muggs); Aileen Haley, Alice Wallace, Marilyn Kinsley, Beryl McCutcheon, Frances Donelan (Bridesmaids); Jean Thorsen, Lucille Casey, Mary Jane French, Ethel Tobin (Second Group of Bridesmaids); Charles Judel (Waiter Captain); William Newell (Waiter); Connie Weiler, Peggy O'Neill (Cigarette Girls); William B. Davidson (Annoyed Man); Tom Dillon, Chester Conklin (Cops); William Eddritt, Gordon Dumont, Jack Daley, Bob Thom, Charles Griffin, William "Billy" Wayne, James Darrell, Leonard Mellin, Phil Dunham, George Bunny, Jessie Arnold, Lucille Curtis, Rhea Mitchell (Reporters); Nolan Leary, Roger Cole, Hansel Warner, Henry Sylvester, Tom Coleman (Reporters in Utility Offices); George Sherwood (Well-Dressed Pool Player); Stanley Blystone (Cop at Employment Office); Budd Buster (Jitney Driver); Roy Butler, Tom Leffingwell, Walter Bacon (Board Executives); Hope Landin (Mae, the Spinster); Joe Devlin (Bartender); Fred Nurney (Big Jim Banby); Katherine Booth, Tim Murdock (Bridal Couple); Eddie Dunn (Gateman); Miska Egan (Chef); Ruthellen Johnson (Prize Daughter); Robert Emmet O'Connor (Conductor); Fred "Snowflake" Toone (Pullman Porter); George Renavent (Jeweler); John Valentine (Man Servant); Helyn Eby-Rock, Margaret Bert (Secretaries); Jack Cheatham (Jailer); Harry Denny (Elevator Man); Jerry Lascoe, Jr. (Newsboy); George Carleton (Apartment Manager); Sarah Edward, Betty Blythe (Women); Frances McInnerney (Pert Secretary); Russell Hicks (Marty Martindale); Frank Orth (*Chronicle* Editor); Stanley Andrews (*Chronicle* Publisher); Jack Norton (Drunk); Robert Emmett Keane (Doctor); Dwayne Hickman (Johnny Ryan); Leila McIntyre (Mrs. Ryan); Charles Bates (Johnny's Brother); Charles Wagenheim (Mr. Cohn); Ruth Robinson (Mrs. Cohn); Jill Gervon, Adrienne Trazillo, Charles Polizzi (Cohn Children); Paul E. Burns (Mr. Smith); Harry Hayden (Mr. Sameuls); Forbes Murray (Prosperous Man).

LIFE WITH FATHER (WB, 1947) C—118 M.

Producer, Robert Buckner; director, Michael Curtiz; based on the play by Howard Lindsay, Russel Crouse; screenplay, Donald Ogden Stewart; art director, Robert Haas; set decorator, George James Hopkins; wardrobe, Milo Anderson; music, Max Steiner; music director, Leo F. Forbstein; assistant director, Robert Vreeland; dialog director, Herschel Daugherty; technical advisor, Mrs. Clarence Day; makeup, Perc Westmore; sound, C. A. Riggs; montages, James Leicester, special effects, William McGann; special effects director, Ray Foster; camera, Peverell Marley, William V. Skall; editor, George Amy.

William Powell (Clarence Day); Irene Dunne (Vinnie Day); Elizabeth Taylor (Mary); Edmund Gwenn (Reverend Dr. Lloyd); ZaSu Pitts (Cora); Jimmy Lydon (Clarence); Emma Dunn (Margaret); Moroni Olsen (Dr. Humphries); Elisabeth Risdon (Mrs. Whitehead); Derek Scott (Harlan); Johnny Calkins (Whitney); Martin Milner (John); Heather Wilder (Annie); Monte Blue (Policeman); Nancy Duff (Delia); Mary Field (Nora); Queenie Leonard (Maggie); Clara Blandick (Mrs. Wiggins); Frank Elliott (Dr. Somers); Clara Reid (Scrub Woman); Philo McCullough (Milk Man); Loie Bridge (Corsetierre); George Meader (Salesman); Douglas Kennedy (Mr. Morley); Phil Van Zandt (Clerk); Russell Arms (Stock Quotation Operator); Faith Kruger (Hilda); Jean Del Val (Francois); Michael and Ralph Mineo (Twins); Creighton Hale (Father of Twins); Jean Andren (Mother of Twins); Elaine Lange (Ellen); Jack Martin (Chef); Arlene Dahl (Girl in Delmonico's); Gertrude Valerie, David Cavendish, Henry Sylvester, Hallene Hill, Laura Treadwell (Church Goers); John Beck (Perkins, the Clerk); James Metcalf (Customer); Joe Bernard (Cashier); Lucille Shamberger (Nurse Maid).

SONG OF THE THIN MAN (MGM, 1947) 86 M.

Producer, Nat Perrin; director, Edward Buzzell; based on characters created by Dashiell Hammett; story, Stanley Roberts; screenplay, Steve Fisher, Perrin; additional dialog, James

O'Hanlon, Harry Crane; art directors, Cedric Gibbons, Randall Duell; set decorators, Edwin B. Willis, Alfred E. Spencer; music, David Snell; song, Herb Magidson and Ben Oakland; assistant director, Jerry Bergman; sound, Douglas Shearer; camera, Charles Rosher; editor, Gene Ruggiero.*

William Powell (Nick Charles); Myrna Loy (Nora Charles); Keenan Wynn (Clarence "Clinker" Krause); Dean Stockwell (Nick Charles, Jr.); Phillip Reed (Tommy Drake); Patricia Morison (Phyllis Talbin); Gloria Grahame (Fran Page); Jayne Meadows (Janet Thayar); Don Taylor (Buddy Hollis); Leon Ames (Mitchell Talbin); Ralph Morgam (David L. Thayar); Warner Anderson (Dr. Monolaw); William Bishop (Al Amboy); Bruce Cowling (Phil Brant); Bess Flowers (Jessica Thayar); Connie Gilchrist (Bertha); James Burke (Callahan); Tom Trout (Lewie, the Shiv); Henry Nemo (The Neem); Marie Windsor (Helen Amboy); Asta, Jr. (Asta); Tom Dugan (Davis, the Cop); John Sheehan (Manager); Lennie Bremen, Lyle Latell (Mugs); Eddie Simms, Jimmy O'Gatty (Hoods); James Flavin (Reardon, the Cop); Bill Harbach (Whitley); George Anderson (Dunne); Donald Kerr (News Photographer); Alan Bridge (Nagle, the Policeman); Esther Howard (Counterwoman); Harry Burns (Italian); William Roberts (Pete); Clarke Hardwicke (Bert); Henry Sylvester (Butler); Matt McHugh (Taxi Driver); Clinton Sundberg (Desk Clerk); Gregg Barton (Nurse); Earle Hodgins (Baggage Man); Howard Negley (Kramer); George Sorel (Headwaiter); Charles Sullivan (Sergeant); Robert Strickland (Musician); Jeffrey Sayre (Croupier); Morris Ankrum (Inspector); Maria San Marco (Oriental Girl); George Chan (Chinese); Jerry Fragnol (Young Nick at Age Five).

THE SENATOR WAS INDISCREET (UNIV, 1947) 88 M.

Producer, Nunnally Johnson; associate producer, Gene Fowler, Jr.; director, George S. Kaufman; story, Edwin Lanham; screenplay, Charles MacArthur; art directors, Bernard Herzbrun, Boris Levin; set decorators, Russell A. Gausman, Ken Swartz; music, Daniele Amfitheatrof; assistant director, Jack Voglin; sound, Leslie I. Carey, Richard De Weese; special effects, David S. Horsley; camera, William Mellor; editor, Sherman A. Rose.

William Powell (Senator Melvin G. Ashton); Ella Raines (Polly McNaughton); Peter Lind Hayes (Lew Gibson); Arleen Whelan (Valerie Shepherd); Ray Collins (Houlihan); Allen Jenkins (Farrell); Charles D. Brown (Dinty); Hans Conried (Waiter); Whit Bissell (Oakes); Norma Varden (Woman at Banquet); Milton Parsons ("You Know Who"); Francis Pierlot (Frank); Cynthia Corley (Helen); Oliver Blake, Chief Thundercloud, Chief Yowlachie, Iron Eyes Cody (Indians); Boyd Davis, Rodney Bell, Tom Coleman, John Alban (Politicos); Edward Clark (Eddie); William Forrest (U.S. Officer); Douglas Wood (University President); Tom Dugan (Attendant at Stand); George K. Mann (Texas); Claire Carleton (Ingred); William H. Vedder (Book Dealer); Nina Lunn (Girl in Elevator); John R. Wald (Broadcaster); Vincent Pelletier (Quiz Master); Alex Davidoff, Forrest Dickson, Howard Mitchell (Guests); Don Wilson (Commentator); Beatrice Roberts (Woman); Martin Garralaga, John Bagni (Italian Waiters); Leon Lenoir (French Waiter); Billy Newell (Elevator Operator); Billy Bletcher (Newsboy); John A. Butler, John O'Connor, Franklin Parker, Clarence Straight (Reporters); Mervin Williams (Newsreel Man); Eddie Coke (Ticket Buyer); Bruce Riley, Ethan Laidlaw, Richard Gordon, Walton DeCardo, Watson Downs, Cedric Stevens, Rex Dale (Men); Sven Hugo Borg (Swedish Waiter); John Valentine (Desk Clerk); Walter Soderling (Hotel Clerk); Jimmy Clark, Russ Whiteman (Bellboys); Mike Stokey (Night Clerk); Laura R. Parrish (Aunt Abby); Dutch Schlickenmeyer (Man Buying Ticket); Gene Fowler, Sr. (Charlie); Myrna Loy (Mrs. Ashton).

MR. PEABODY AND THE MERMAID (UNIV, 1948) 89 M.

Producer, Nunnally Johnson; associate producer, Gene Fowler, Jr.; director, Irving Pichel; based on the novel by Guy and Constance Jones; screenplay, Johnson; art directors, Ber-

nard Herzbrun, Boris Leven; set decorator, Russell Gausman; music, Robert Emmett Dolan; assistant director, Fred Frank; costumes, Grace Houston; sound, Leslie Carey, Corson Jowett; camera, Russell Metty; editor, Marjorie Fowler.

William Powell (Mr. Peabody); Ann Blyth (Mermaid); Irene Hervey (Mrs. Polly Peabody); Andrea King (Cathy Livingston); Clinton Sundberg (Mike Fitzgerald); Art Smith (Dr. Harvey); Hugh French (Major Hadley); Lumsden Hare (Colonel Mandrake); James Logan (Lieutenant); Frederick N. Clark (Basil); Beatrice Roberts (Mother); Mary Field (Wee Shop Clerk); Cynthia Corley (Nurse); Tom Stevenson, Richard Ryen (Waiters); Mary Somerville (Lady Trebshaw); Bobby Hyatt (Boy); Winifred Harris, Lydia Bilbrook (Voices); Carol Savage (Daphne); Ola Lorraine (Receptionist).

TAKE ONE FALSE STEP (UNIV, 1949) 94 M.

Producer, Chester Erskine; associate producer, Jack Hively; director, Erskine; based on the story "Night Call" by Irwin and David Shaw; screenplay, Shaw, Erskine; art directors, Bernard Herzbrun, Emrich Nicholson; set decorators, Ruby Levitt; music, Walter Scharf; assistant director, John Sherwood; makeup, Bud Westmore, Emile LaVigne; costumes, Orry-Kelly; sound, Leslie I. Carey, Richard De Weese; camera, Franz Planer; editor, Russell Schoengarth.

William Powell (Andrew Gentling); Shelley Winters (Catherine Sykes); Marsha Hunt (Martha Wier); Dorothy Hart (Helen Gentling); James Gleason (Gledhill); Felix Bressart (Professor Morris Avrum); Art Baker (Henry Pritchard); Sheldon Leonard (Pacciano); Howard Freeman (Dr. Markheim); Houseley Stevenson (Thatcher); Paul Harvey (Mr. Arnspiger); Francis Pierlot (Doctor Watson); Jess Barker (Arnold Sykes); Mikel Conrad (Freddie); Enid Markey (Clara); Tony Curtis (Hot Rod Driver); Sandra Gould (Newspaper Girl); Dorothy Vaughan (Leona); Minerva Urecal (Woman Gas Station Attendant); Maurice Marsac (Louis, the Maitre D'); Tommy Ivo (Boy); Ralph Peters (Portly Man); Harland Tucker (Clerk); Lyle Latell (Reporter); George Lynn, Charles J. Flynn, Edmund Cobb, Charles McAvoy (Policemen); Lennie Bremen (Truck Driver); Herbert Heywood (Attendant); Jack Rice (Good Humor Man); Marjorie Bennett (Waitress); Frank Cady, Paul Brinegar (Players); Helen Crozier (Maid); Jim Toney (Bartender); Ethyl May Halls (Woman at Window).

DANCING IN THE DARK (20th, 1949) C—93 M.

Producer, George Jessel; director, Irving Reis; based on the play The Bandwagon *by George S. Kaufman; adaptor, Marion Turk; screenplay, Mary C. McCall; additional dialog, Jay Dratler; art directors, Lyle Wheeler, George W. Davis; set decorators, Thomas Little, Paul S. Fox; vocal director, Ken Darby; orchestrators, Herbert Spencer, Earle Hagen; music director, Alfred Newman; songs, Howard Dietz and Arthur Schwartz; assistant director, Henry Weinberger; makeup, Ben Nye, Thomas Tuttle, Bill Riddle; choreography, Seymour Felix; costumes, William Travilla; sound, Bernard Freericks, Roger Heman; special effects, Fred Sersen; camera, Harry Jackson; editor, Louis Loeffler.*

William Powell (Emery Slide); Mark Stevens (Bill Davis); Betsy Drake (Julie); Adolphe Menjou (Grossman); Randy Stuart (Rosalie); Lloyd Corrigan (Barker); Hope Emerson (Mrs. Schlaghammer); Walter Catlett (Joe Brooks); Don Beddoe (Barney Basset); Jean Hersholt (Himself); Sid Grauman (Himself); Louis Bacigalupi (Rubber); Syd Saylor (Projectionist); Milton Parsons (Butler); Byron Foulger (Makeup Man); Bob Adler (Officer); Ann Corcoran, Phyllis Planchard, Claire Richards (Women); George MacDonald (Boy); Joe Bautista (Filipino); Fred Fisher, Sammy Finn, Cosmo Sardo, Harry Seymour (Men); Elaine Edwards (Girl); Walter Clinton, George Beranger (Waiters); Frank Ferguson (Sharkey); Charles Tannen (Jack); Harry Crocker (Master of Ceremonies); Edward Clark (Costumer); Max Willenz (Sommelier); Gregory Gay (Headwaiter); Helen Brown (Esther); Sherry Hall (Cameraman); Dick Cogan (Wes); Jean "Babe" London (Hulu Girl); Sally Forrest (Secretary); Erville Anderson

(Neighbor); Grandon Rhodes (Producer); Belle Daube, Larry Keating, Claire Whitney, John Davidson, Joseph Crehan (Board Members); George E. Stone (Cutter).

IT'S A BIG COUNTRY (MGM, 1951) 89 M.

Producer, Robert Sisk; directors, Charles Vidor, Richard Thorpe, John Sturges, Don Hartman, Don Weis, Clarence Brown, William Wellman; story, Edgar Brooks, Ray Chordes, Joseph Petracca, Lucille Schlossberg, Dore Schary, Claudia Cranston; screenplay, William Ludwig, Helen Deutsch, George Wells, Allen Rivkin, Dorothy Kingsley, Isobel Lennart; art directors, Cedric Gibbons, Malcolm Brown, William Ferrari, Eddie Imazu, Arthur Lonergan, Gabriel Scognamilo; music supervisors, Bronislau Kaper, Rudolph G. Koff, David Raksin, David Rose; camera, John Alton, Ray June, William Mellor, Joseph Ruttenberg; editors, Ben Lewis, Frederick Y. Smith.

Ethel Barrymore (Mrs. Brian Patrick Riordan); Keefe Brasselle (Sergeant Maxie Klein); Gary Cooper (Texan); Nancy Davis (Miss Coleman); Van Johnson (Adam Burch); Gene Kelly (Icarus Xenophon); Janet Leigh (Rosa Szabo); Marjorie Main (Mrs. Wrenley); Fredric March (Papa Esposito); George Murphy (Mr. Callaghan); William Powell (Professor); S. Z. Sakall (Stefan Szabo); Lewis Stone (Sexton); James Whitmore (Mr. Stacey); Keenan Wynn (Michael Fisher); Leon Ames (Secret Service Man); Angela Clarke (Mama Esposito); Bobby Hyatt (Joseph Esposito); Sharon McManus (Sam Szabo); Elisabeth Risdon (Woman); Bill Baldwin (Austin); Mickey Martin (Copy Boy); William H. Welsh, Sherry Hall, Fred Santley, Roger Moore, Roger Cole, Harry Stanton, Henry Sylvester (Officials); Ned Glass (Receptionist); June Hedin (Kati); Luana Mehlberg (Lenka); Jeralyn Alton (Yolande); Tony Taylor (Baby Sitter); Jacqueline Kenley (Margit); Benny Burt (Soda Jerk); George Economides (Theodore); Hal Hatfield, George Conrad, Richard Grindle, Anthony Lappas, Tom Nickols, David Alpert, Costas Morfis (Greek Athletes); A. Cameron Grant (Proprietor of Inn); Don Fields (George); Jerry Hunter (Frank Grillo); Donald Gordon (Mervin); Lucile Curtis (Miss Bloomburg); Dolly Arriaga (Concetta Esposito); Elena Savanarola (Amelia Esposito); Carol Nugent (Girl); George McDonald, Charles Myers, David Wyatt, Mickey Little (Boys); Tiny Francone (Girl in Classroom); Rhea Mitchell (School Teacher).

THE TREASURE OF LOST CANYON (UNIV, 1952) C—81½ M.

Producer, Leonard Goldstein; director, Ted Tetzlaff; based on the story "The Treasure of Franchard" by Robert Louis Stevenson; screenplay, Brainerd Duffield, Emerson Crocker; art directors, Bernard Herzbrun, Alexander Golitzen; music director, Joseph Gershenson; camera, Russell Metty; editor, Milton Carruth.

William Powell (Doc Homer Brown); Julia Adams (Myra Wade); Rosemary De Camp (Samuella); Charles Drake (Jim Anderson); Henry Hull (Lucius Cooke); Tommy Ivo (David); John Doucette (Gyppo); Marvin Press (Paddy); Chubby Johnson (Dan); Griff Barnett (Judge Wade); Frank Wilcox (The Stranger); Virginia Mullen (Mrs. Crabtree); Paul "Tiny" Newlan (Coach Driver); Jimmy Ogg (Guard); Hugh Prosser (Fire Captain); George Taylor (Clem); Philo McCullough, Ed Hinkle (Miners); Edward Rickard (Bit); Jack Perrin (Sheriff).

THE GIRL WHO HAD EVERYTHING (MGM, 1953) 69 M.

Producer, Armand Deutsch; director, Richard Thorpe; based on the novel A Free Soul *by Adela Rogers St. Johns; screenplay, Art Cohn; art directors, Cedric Gibbons, Randall Duell; camera, Paul Vogel; editor, Ben Lewis.*

Elizabeth Taylor (Jean Latimer); Fernando Lamas (Victor Y. Ramondi); William Powell (Steve Latimer); Gig Young (Vance Court); James Whitmore (Charles "Chico" Menlow); Robert Burton (John Ashmond); William Walker (Julian); Harry Bartell (Joe); Elmer Peterson (Himself); Dan Riss (Counsel); Paul Harvey (Senator Drummond); Dean Miller (Radio Announcer); Wilson Wood (Newsman); Doug Carter (Bellboy); Emory Parnell (Auctioneer); Earle Hodgins (Spotter); Frank Dae (Old Man Kinkaid); Roy Butler (Trainer); John McKee (Male Secretary); Bobby Johnson (Attendant); Anthony Warde, Philip Van Zandt (Colleagues); Jonathan Cott, John Maxwell, Stu Wilson (Newspaper Men); James Horne, Perry Sheehan, Dee Turnell, Sally Musick (Guests in Town House); George Brand, A. Cameron Grant, George Sherwood, Pat O'Malley (Senate Board Members); Jack Sterling (Cab Driver).

HOW TO MARRY A MILLIONAIRE (20th, 1953) C—95 M.

Producer, Nunnally Johnson; director, Jean Negulesco; based on plays by Zoë Akins, Dale Eunson, Katherine Albert; screenplay, Johnson; music directors, Alfred Newman, Cyril Mockridge; art directors, Lyle Wheeler, Leland Fuller; camera, Joe MacDonald; editor, Louis Loeffler.

Betty Grable (Loco); Marilyn Monroe (Pola); Lauren Bacall (Schatze Page); David Wayne (Freddie Denmark); Rory Calhoun (Eben); Cameron Mitchell (Tom Brookman); Alex D'Arcy (J. Stewart Merrill); Fred Clark (Waldo Brewster); William Powell (J. D. Hanley); George Dunn (Mike, the Elevator Man); Harry Carter (Elevator Operator); Robert Adler (Cab Driver); Tudor Owen (Mr. Otis); Maurice Marsac (Antoine); Emmett Vogan (Man at Bridge); Hermone Sterler (Madame); Abney Mott (Secretary); Rankin Mansfield (Bennett); Ralph Reid (Jewelry Salesman); Jan Arvan (Tony); Ivis Goulding (Maid); Dayton Lummis (Justice); Van Des Autels (Best Man); Eric Wilton (Butler); Ivan Triesault (Captain of Waiters); Herbert Deans (Stewart); George Saurel (Emir); Hope Landin (Mrs. Salem); Tom Greenway (Motorcycle Cop); Charlotte Austin, Merry Anders, Ruth Hall, Lida Thomas, Beryl McCutcheon (Models); James Stone, Tom Martin (Doormen);

Eve Finnell (Stewardess); Benny Burt (Reporter); Richard Shackleton (Bellboy).

MISTER ROBERTS (WB, 1955) C—123 M.

Producer, Leland Hayward; directors, John Ford, Mervyn Le Roy; based on the play by Joshua Logan, Thomas Heegen; screenplay, Frank Nugent, Logan; art director, Art Loel; set decorator, William L. Kuehl; music, Franz Waxman; orchestrator, Leonid Raab; makeup, Gordon Bau; assistant director, Wingate Smith; technical advisers, Admiral John Dale Price, U.S.N.; Commander Merle MacBain, U.S.N.; sound, Earl N. Crain; camera, Winton C. Hoch; editor, Jack Murray.

Henry Fonda [Lieutenant (J.G.) Roberts]; James Cagney (Captain); Jack Lemmon (Ensign Frank Thurlowe Pulver); William Powell (Doc); Ward Bond (C.P.O. Dowdy); Betsy Palmer (Lieutenant Ann Girard); Phil Carey (Mannion); Nick Adams (Reber); Harry Carey, Jr. (Stefanowski); Ken Curtis (Dolan); Frank Aletter (Gerhart); Fritz Ford (Lidstrom); Buck Kartalian (Mason); William Henry (Lieutenant Billings); William Hudson (Olson); Stubby Kruger (Schlemmer); Harry Tenbrook (Cookie); Perry Lopez (Rodrigues); Robert Roark (Insignia); Pat Wayne (Bookser); Tige Andrews (Wiley); Jim Moloney (Kennedy); Denny Niles (Gilbert); Francis Conner (Johnson); Shug Fisher (Cochran); Danny Borzage (Jonesy); Jim Murphy (Taylor); Kathleen O'Malley, Maura Murphy, Mimi Doyle, Jeanne Murray-Vanderbilt, Lonnie Pierce (Nurses); Martin Milner (Shore Patrol Officer); Gregory Walcott (Shore Patrolman); James Flavin (M.P.); Jack Pennick (Marine Sergeant); Duke Kahanaomoku (Native Chief); Carolyn Tong (Chinese Girl Who Kisses Bookser); George Brangier (French Colonial Officer); Clarence E. Frank (Naval Officer).

Credits

JAMES ROBERT PARISH, New York–based biographer, was born in Cambridge, Massachusetts, and grew up in Whitman, a town twenty-five miles south of Boston. He attended the University of Pennsylvania and graduated as a Phi Beta Kappa with a degree in English. A graduate of the University of Pennsylvania Law School, he is a member of the New York Bar. As president of Entertainment Copyright Research Co., Inc., he headed a major researching facility for the film and television industries. Later he was a film interviewer-reviewer for *Motion Picture Daily* and *Variety*. He is the author of such books as *The Fox Girls, The Paramount Pretties, The RKO Gals, Hollywood's Great Love Teams,* and *The Great Movie Series.* He is co-author of, among other books, *The Cinema of Edward G. Robinson, The MGM Stock Company, The Glamour Girls,* and *The Great Spy Pictures.*

DON E. STANKE in the past few years has interviewed more than forty personalities of American film and stage and has had career articles published on most of them in various cinema periodicals. Interviewing and writing is avocational, since Stanke is a full-time administrative manager with a medical X-ray firm in San Leandro, California. With Mr. Parish, he is the co-author of *The Glamour Girls* and has contributed to the book *The Real Stars#2.*

T. ALLAN TAYLOR, godson of the late Margaret Mitchell, has long been active in book publishing and is presently the production manager of one of the largest abstracting and technical indexing services in the United States. He was editor of such volumes as *The Fox Girls, The MGM Stock Company, Good Dames, Vincent Price Unmasked, The Great Gangster Pictures,* and *Liza!*

Brooklynite JOHN ROBERT COCCHI has been viewing and collecting data on motion pictures since childhood and is now regarded as one of the most thorough film researchers in the United States. He is the New York editor of *Boxoffice* magazine. He was research associate of *The American Movies Reference Book, The Fox Girls, The Great Spy Pictures, The Glamour Girls,* and many other volumes, and has written cinema-history articles for such journals as *Film Fan Monthly* and *Screen Facts.* He is the co-founder of one of Manhattan's leading film societies.

MICHAEL R. PITTS has been the entertainment editor of the *Anderson* (Indiana) *Daily Bulletin* and holds a B.A. in history and an M.A. in journalism from Ball State University. He has been published in numerous cinema journals and is the co-author of such volumes as *The Great Spy Pictures, Film Director's Guide,* and *The Great Gangster Pictures.*

New York–born FLORENCE SOLOMON attended Hunter College and then joined Ligon Johnson's copyright research office. Later she was director for research at Entertainment Copyright Research Co., Inc., and is presently a reference superviser at ASCAP's Index Division. Ms. Solomon has collaborated on such works as *The American Movies Reference Book, TV Movies, The Slapstick Queens,* and others. She is the niece of the noted sculptor, the late Sir Jacob Epstein.

EARL ANDERSON, a native of San Francisco, was educated at San Francisco State College (B.A.) and the University of Washington (M.A.). Over the years he has contributed career articles on Marion Davies, Wallace Beery, Gladys Cooper, and others to *Films in Review.* Since 1960 he has been the assistant to the director of the California Palace of the Legion of Honor, where he has written museum bulletins devoted to aspects of the collection and has organized film series devoted to Irene Dunne, Mary Pickford, and the Western film.

Index

Index

Numerals in italics indicate pages showing
photographs of the individuals and movies
mentioned

479

486

507